Cultural and Technological Influences on Global Business

Bryan Christiansen
PryMarke, LLC, USA

Ekaterina Turkina
HEC Montreal, Canada

Nigel Williams
Bournemouth University, UK

BUSINESS SCIENCE *Reference*

Managing Director:	Lindsay Johnston
Editorial Director:	Joel Gamon
Book Production Manager:	Jennifer Yoder
Publishing Systems Analyst:	Adrienne Freeland
Development Editor:	Christine Smith
Assistant Acquisitions Editor:	Kayla Wolfe
Typesetter:	Henry Ulrich
Cover Design:	Jason Mull

Published in the United States of America by
Business Science Reference (an imprint of IGI Global)
701 E. Chocolate Avenue
Hershey PA 17033
Tel: 717-533-8845
Fax: 717-533-8661
E-mail: cust@igi-global.com
Web site: http://www.igi-global.com

Library of Congress Cataloging-in-Publication Data

Cultural and technological influences on global business / Bryan Christiansen, Ekaterina Turkina and Nigel Williams, editors.
pages cm
Includes bibliographical references and index.
Summary: "This book emphasizes the importance of deeply exploring developing cultures and technologies and their effects on the business sector"--Provided by publisher.
ISBN 978-1-4666-3966-9 (hardcover) -- ISBN 978-1-4666-3967-6 (ebook) -- ISBN 978-1-4666-3968-3 (print & perpetual access) 1. International business enterprises. 2. Management--Cross-cultural studies. 3. International trade. 4. Information technology--Management. I. Christiansen, Bryan, 1960- II. Turkina, Ekaterina. III. Williams, Nigel.
HD2755.5.C846 2013
658.3008--dc23

2013002772

British Cataloguing in Publication Data
A Cataloguing in Publication record for this book is available from the British Library.

Editorial Advisory Board

Table of Contents

Detailed Table of Contents

due to its specific Apartheid past and its post-Apartheid challenges related to diversity management. Lastly, Norway is ranked among the best and most equal countries in the world. By exploring these different examples, we question the assumption that there can be a one best way to manage diversity in an international context.

Organizations have started to compete in a challenging and competitive environment with the effects of globalization. In today's world, organizations must manage many environmental factors. Technological developments are one of those factors to which organizations must manage and adapt themselves to gain competitive advantage. With increasing data flow, it has become more difficult for organizations to store this data and gain useful knowledge to manage their business operations and functions. This explosive growth in data and databases has generated an urgent need for new techniques and tools that can intelligently and automatically transform the processed data into useful information and knowledge. This situation is especially more difficult for global organizations that have various branches in different countries around the world. Parallel with these developments in information technology for business applications, management information systems and business intelligence solutions have gained more importance. This paper investigates the importance of using business intelligence solutions and techniques for decision making process in the perspective of business functions in global organizations. Business intelligence solutions and techniques will be introduced, followed by explanation of the use of these systems in decision making processes within the context of global organizations.

The purpose of this chapter is to empirically examine firms' internal and external factors that can affect their foreign market mode choice. The model is comprised of internal factors such as control, domestic business experience, and industry type; and external factors in terms of culture of foreign markets and intensity of competition. A mail-out survey to Australian firms involved in international business generated 315 useful responses. The hypotheses were tested using direct logistic regression analysis. Among the five variables, industry type, domestic business experience, and intensity of competition were found statistically significant. While industry type and domestic business experience encourage non-export mode, intensity of competition favours export mode. The major contributions of this study are the discovery of a variable, domestic business experience that is new in the literature; and the reinforcement of the importance of examining both internal and external factors when making a foreign market entry mode choice.

In the advertising research literature, polysemy is defined as different interpretations for the same advertising message. The multiple ad-interpretations can be attributable to complexities and diversities in culture and/or consumers' own demographics, perceptions, attitudes, lifestyles, values, behavior, and psychographics. We provide a bipolar and dichotomous perspective on advertising polysemy as positive and negative polysemy with research and practice examples from the print advertisements for alcoholic beverages and corporate social responsibility to explain the conditions that lead to the emergence of positive and negative polysemic contexts for the same message. Furthermore, the study explores how polysemy leads to better branding. The research investigates the concept of polysemy and the generation of idiosyncratic meanings, and examines the impact of advertising polysemy on consumer-based brand equity. The research proposes and measures the advertising polysemy and consumer-based brand equity conceptual framework supported by accommodation theory, consumer response theory, and theory of hierarchy of effects, leading to stronger ad-evoked feelings, ad and brand attitudes, and consumer-based brand equity.

This study focuses on two Arab developing countries following the view that scope, role, and positioning of management accounting differ across organisations and countries, and, in the same direction, the study draws on the recent literature on localisation of global management control systems. Furthermore, the study embeds the view that certain contextual variables such as country differences and organisational culture possess particular cultural characteristics, which in turn affect individuals to respond distinctively to Management Accounting Systems' (MAS) applications. The main objective of this study is to investigate whether or not there are significant associations between the use and levels of importance of operational non-financial performance indicators (ONFPIs) and the extent of a set of contextual variables including firms' and managers' characteristics and workforce involvement. The study reports and discusses findings of surveying manufacturing firms belonging to various industry sectors in Egypt and Saudi Arabia (SA) in mid-2005. Findings show that levels of importance of ONFPIs in Egyptians firms are higher than those in use at their Saudi peers' firms. In general, findings on significant positive associations between the levels of importance of ONFPIs and the incorporated contextual variables in the Egyptian firms seem to be in line with prior literature findings drawn from global practices. Interestingly, the effect of organisational culture seems to be witnessed in Saudi firms evident by the negative, rather than positive, associations between two variables belonging to managers' characteristics and workforce involvement and levels of importance of ONFPIs.

Two significant trends have been gaining momentum in software development: the utilization of Agile development methodologies, and the continuing trend of companies to outsource development work offshore. These two trends have changed the way companies develop software and business applications. This chapter seeks to evaluate how a company can successfully manage both trends in conjunction with each other on global business. The primary question addressed is whether the benefits derived from Agile development methodologies and the savings from outsourced software development efforts cancel each other out when applied together, or whether they create a synergy greater than the sum of the parts. In order to answer this question, this chapter intends to examine several relevant business practices and industry experiences. From lessons learned, we identify factors which seem to influence a successful combination of Agile methodology and offshoring in global software development projects.

The pace and intensity of social change in modern society is increasing, particularly through advances in modern technology and the remarkable innovations in information and communications technology (ICT), as well as through social movements, especially globalisation (Synott, 2004). This chapter will discuss the concept of globalisation and its impact on the economies, cultures, and international business in developing countries and, in particular, Vietnam. The chapter provides an insight into how national culture and technology affects business operations, including current issues in technological readiness for e-business adoption in Vietnam. By applying theories of globalisation to explain changes and progress in Vietnamese economic development, the chapter also provides a better understanding of the complex mix of culture, technology, and business operations in Vietnam. Recommendations are also made for the development of an appropriate environment for e-business in small to medium enterprises that will further strengthen the country's international business operations.

This chapter portrays a quantitative framework regarding entry mode choice and ownership structures by measuring performance under given ownership structures as the degree of efficiency in technology transfer, and knowledge exchange in the form of a residual productivity growth variable. This method has been shown to be a proxy for or an indirect measure of transaction costs, in that ownership structures are validated by the growth in technology/knowledge-based productivity that they caused. In the process, the chapter discusses hierarchical entry modes and adjustment of ownership structures with respect to minimizing transaction costs incurred in the transfer and internalization of complementary assets, both tangible and intangible. Previous research has dealt with subsidiary performance mainly in terms of financial measures (e.g., profitability, ROA, ROE, ROI), instability, and lifespan. By contrast, this chapter extends existing research by providing a specific quantitative framework for optimizing technology/knowledge-based productivity growth. The second important contribution of the chapter is the linkage of the quantitative results to their applicability and potential for implementation in Japanese equity-based subsidiaries in Latin America over the lifetime of the subsidiaries. Other factors important in the implementation and internalization of new technologies and knowledge have also been analyzed quantitatively and linked to case studies qualitatively. The chapter further analyzes adaptations to regional contexts and parent companies of nationalities other than Japanese. Therefore, the model presented in the chapter addresses IJV ownership structures which are optimal to productivity growth linked to new technologies and knowledge and by adaptation of variables, and discusses results for emerging markets in Latin America, such as Peru, Colombia, and the newly industrialized Brazil. The chapter also highlights advantages and disadvantages of forming IJVs with a local partner of different levels of technological sophistication, and the degree of managerial and equity involvement to allow the local partner.

This chapter presents a preliminary understanding of cross-cultural challenges and synergistic experiences of multicultural students engaged in Global Virtual Teams (GVTs). In this case study, we introduce the GVT structure as a novel learning platform which utilizes Computer Mediated Communication (CMC) tools as part of its virtual-based learning. We administer the case study with 30 students (n=30) in the United of Emirates (UAE) who engage in GVTs across the globe—encompassing 26 universities and 22 countries. Qualitative data is collected in the form of documents—reflective reports of the students' experiential learning over a 10-week period. We content analyse the reports based on the thematic analysis with two distinctive categories—cultural challenges and cultural synergies based on the first seven weeks of the experiential learning process. In this study, we find that students experienced challenges such as managing technical difficulty, language barriers, deteriorating motivations, geographical distance, time differences, and non-committed and unresponsive attitude. However, students also experience synergies from the GVTs such as strong relationships and continued friendships, formation of emergent leadership, learned diverse managerial styles and competencies skills, varied use of varied CMC tools, and international exposure to diverse cultures without the need to travel abroad.

An Industrial and Organizational (I/O) psychologist is commonly referred to as an I/O practitioner and as an I/O consultant. I/O psychology is the branch of psychology concerned with the application of psychological principles in the workplace. To practitioners, I/O psychology is the application or extension of psychological methods and principles to the solution of organizational and workplace problems, both in the domestic and international arenas. Most commonly, I/O psychology is concerned with those problems caused by human performance and those which affect human performance within organizational contexts. As such, I/O psychologists employ psychological measurement and research findings related to human abilities, motivation, perception, and learning in seeking to improve the fit between the needs of the work organization and those of the people who populate it. Thus, an I/O psychologist plays a paramount role in successful global ventures by addressing two key factors—culture and behavior—resulting in positive return-on-investment (ROI).

Many industries have observed the rise of Virtual Teams (VTs) as highly productive team structures taking advantage of members scattered around the globe while being able to accomplish assigned tasks by communicating through internet based technologies. Nonetheless, the looked-for achievable gains of VTs working heavily rest on meeting the requirements prescribed by the antecedents and critical success factors associated with specific idiosyncrasies of VTs such as the multiculturalism dominating their working environment. In this regard, it is widely recognized that when it comes to adopting VTs, the managerial/leadership matters are among the main challenges facing organisations. The major parts of foregoing issues are stemmed from the limitations of mediums of communications exacerbated by cultural diversity and disparity of members. This chapter first aims at critically analysing the different

conflicts. This study attempts to determine the different types and levels of conflicts within a multicultural workforce by considering various factors such as ethnicity and geographic and lingual diversities within the global context. The scope is to find possible solutions to reduce and/or eliminate group related and, to a certain extent, individual conflicts within the work place, which have become a matter of concern for any international organization. The findings reveal systematic conflicts between and within work-groups and suggest that regardless of type, relationship, and process, conflicts are detrimental to the operation and total outcome. Those conflicts have a negative impact on performance in the production, especially when they escalate. Displays of interpersonal hostility (yelling, name-calling, throwing things at people and making derogatory inferences about others' own cultures) prevent productive work in all groups, which are inefficient and do not seem motivated to complete their tasks. Increased bickering and hostile behaviour inhibits talking about and working on the immediate task. To a certain extent, the situation could be described as a "toxic working environment." A key finding reveals through interviews and participative and non-intrusive observations demonstrated that members of these work-groups are psychologically distressed when there are frequent arguments about interpersonal issues. Consequently, the intrinsic problems which escalate over a five year period, together with extrinsic economic problems due to the global economic downturn, cause the company to have high cost of labor and material. With less than expected sales and, operational destruction due to distress about going concern, PTI is put to challenge. Hence, PTI faces a serious test in solving the existing group conflicts. Failure to improve the working relationships could jeopardize the strategic going concern of the company.

Knowledge Management (KM) is an organization-wide, strategic change management initiative dealing with people, processes, and Information Communication Technology (ICT) to achieve a competitive advantage through learning, productivity improvement, and innovation. Based on the current literature review of KM and its challenges in global business, a general framework for KM in terms of leadership, organization, and ICT is proposed. The role of leadership includes developing an international strategy for KM, executing strategic change management, practicing a mix of transformational and transactional leadership style, and developing KM performance metrics. The organizational parameters include learning, processes, culture, and organizational structure. ICT plays a crucial role in the learning and processes to acquire, store, share, and apply knowledge. Some of the KM challenges in global business include global leadership competencies and strategy, project-based flexible global virtual teams, global knowledge integration, and working with ICT gaps across different economies.

With the increasing globalization of the business world, websites have become ever more important tools in international business. After the invention of websites, researchers have begun to analyze the websites as they have for traditional communication channels. Websites, as the communication medium of global firms, are not culturally neutral mediums. Website components should be analyzed very carefully in terms of their interaction with cultural issues to come up with culturally adapted websites. In this chapter, 114 studies on culture and websites are critically reviewed, and selected papers among them from a variety of areas such as marketing, communications, management, information technologies, and others, are analyzed in detail to consolidate the existing knowledge and approaches. This chapter aims

cites research by Gartner that indicated £4bn was wasted on poorly managed contracts by European businesses in the previous year. This highlights the business significance of outsourcing decisions and shows that the impact of major outsourcing decisions is likely to be strategic in that the competitive position of a company is influenced by the outcomes. The argument for use of a systematic decision support system to assist with outsourcing decisions is persuasive. The Holistic Approach Business, Information, Organisation (HABIO) Framework offers a holistic approach which takes account of interrelated strategies and complex considerations that may vary according to the circumstances and priorities of the decision-maker. It also facilitates monitoring decisions over the life of the outsourcing arrangements, thereby supporting timely anticipation and response to significant changes in the economic, political, or social environment. The HABIO model could be used in consideration of intra-national outsourcing decisions to areas such as North Staffordshire where decline in industries traditionally associated with the locality created needs and opportunities for regeneration.

Managerial Communication today is an integral component of many business related disciplines (strategic management, leadership, strategic marketing, business ethics, etc.). However, within the context of global business management, Managerial Communication follows under the broad umbrella of "Business Communication." Communication with internal and external stakeholders demands careful consideration regardless of the industry. Having a managerial communication policy in place allows for strategic information dissemination as well as the protection of transmission of confidential data. This chapter discusses the topic of communication in general with emphasis on managerial communication within the cross-cultural context. The result of a qualitative study used in this chapter confirms that efficient communication strategies and effective communications policy implementation can propel a firm to success. Within this framework and that of managerial leadership effectiveness, managerial communication does not refer to media communication or journalism for that matter; instead, it focuses solely on managerial communication within the context of global business management.

The development of expatriates' social relationships in a local environment is critical given that social ties are considered the key players of a Multinational Corporation's (MNC) network and a prerequisite for knowledge transfer within the organization. By building on the national and organizational culture literature, we develop a conceptual model to better understand how expatriates can effectively build local embeddedness. Our conceptual arguments include how four groups of culture-related factors predict expatriates' local embeddedness, expatriates' cross-cultural experience, expatriates' cultural orientation, local national culture, and MNCs' organizational culture. Finally, we also investigate under what conditions expatriates' social ties within the MNC can influence the expatriates' effectiveness in knowledge transfer.

Foreword

Over the past three decades, terms such as globalization, information, communication, and technology have become not only frequently used, but have also been applied to different aspects of life. These can include the physical sciences such as atmospheric research in terms of global warming; in business and commercial affairs; in education; and in culture. The basis of all these involvements was science and computer applications since 1950, but especially after 1990 with the development and widespread practical use of the Internet. E-mail and all other facilities in the electronic media have rendered daily life into nationally and internationally transparent, multi-cultural, and multi-linguistic forms. Improvements in technological advancement can act as a double-edged sword regarding information and knowledge management where not only crisp engineering rules, but also social, cultural, and expert views play significant roles. In this manner, international business, strategic management, and other business activities gain vital importance with future prospects in almost all societies around the world. Each society, nation, firm, or institution takes its share depending on the cultural background, administrational system (democracy or other modes of rule), liberalization, education, and national specifications.

In general terms, globalization is the name of the process which leads to an increase in social, cultural, political, and economic interdependence with impacts on some changes and impacts on business environment–the main concern of this book. One can see the increasing number of super-, mega- and other business affairs in his/her environment actually or through mass media such as television and internet facilities, where each sector seeks market opportunities and experiences threats as major effects of globalization. Contemporary globalization is expected to make more changes to business in the coming years, and the world has experienced this process via increasing trends on economic, financial, social, cultural, political, market, and environmental issues providing interdependence on these aspects among nations.

For now, globalization has replaced crisp borders with fuzzy alternatives, but in the future, borders will most likely have far more transparent features. During this process, different countries will experience different shares of the market pie, but consequently they will take roughly the same level in the long run. Such effects are very obvious in business transactions today.

Although globalization is a set of processes including increased social and cultural inter-connectedness, political interdependence, economic interchanges, and financial/market integrations, to a great extent it has caused the destruction of local entrepreneurship. The vast subject of this book encompasses significant aspects of economy, society, technology, and culture. It is necessary to provide up-to-date and authentic information on culture and technology to augment efficient administration and management of human resources through timely and effective decision-making procedures. Globalization of the 21st century has changed economic and other realities far beyond the expectations of most individuals; the worldwide financial meltdown of 2008 serves as a particularly pervasive example. Experts in business, education, finance, government, and other fields continue to work on revising these various systems and infrastructures which will operate in a robust manner within the new realities of today. The task at hand is highly important and daunting for all concerned, but humanity will succeed.

It gives me a great pleasure to witness such efforts which have been made by the editors and contributing authors of this book to highlight current issues on culture and technology. I am confident this work will serve as an important reference book for various users, including scholars, business executives, practitioners, and university students who are involved in global business.

Zekâi Şen
Istanbul Technical University, Turkey
January 2013

Zekâi Şen *obtained his B. Sc. and M. Sc Degrees from Technical University of İstanbul, Civil Engineering Faculty, Department of Reinforced Concrete, in 1972. His further post-graduate studies were carried out at the University of London, Imperial College of Science and Technology. He was granted a Diploma of Imperial College (DIC) in 1972, M. Sc. in Engineering Hydrology in 1973, and Ph. D. in Stochastic Hydrology in 1974. He worked in different countries such as England, Norway, Saudi Arabia, and Turkey. He worked in different faculties such as the King Abdulaziz University, Faculty of Earth Sciences, Hydrogeology Department; Istanbul Technical University, Faculty of Astronautics and Aeronautics, Meteorology Department. His main interests are hydrology, water resources, hydrogeology, atmospheric sciences, hydrometeorology, hydraulics, science philosophy and history. He has published about 230 SCI scientific papers in different international top journals. Currently he is at the Technical University of Istanbul, Civil Engineering Faculty.*

Preface

Technology is a key driver behind the effects of contemporary globalization on business and other organizations worldwide. Understanding this phenomena in connection with the impact of cultural variations is key to improving business and product life cycles in an era in which corporate capital and liquidity buffers must be increased for unexpected developments in global markets. In addition, little extant literature exists regarding the processes underlying decision-makers' assessments of performance in contemporary globalism. Therefore, the primary purpose of this book is that of a reference publication for business scholars who need to understand the need for more culturally- and technologically-responsive decision making within a global context. Other readers can include business practitioners and business students who wish to broaden their understanding of the direct relationship between culture and technology in the international business realm.

There is no doubt that 21st century globalization has changed economic realities far beyond anyone's expectations. As the global economy of today continues to develop into an increasingly complex entity, it becomes necessary for companies to access multiple sources of knowledge for organizational effectiveness. Among other things, this entails developing employees who are capable of operating across cultures and continents. To address the most critical issues involved, we will cover a multitude of issues such as the following:

- Advertising Polysemy
- Business Intelligence
- Case Studies
- Communicative Strategies in Transnational Research Teams
- Culture and Market Expansion
- Human Resource Management
- Industrial & Organizational Psychology
- Innovation
- International Diversity Management
- Knowledge Management
- Leading Virtual Teams
- National Culture on International Business Development
- Performance Measurement in Manufacturing Firms
- Qualitative Research Methods
- Websites Interaction

The justification for this book is based largely on the extensive and practical international business experience of the authors as well as their respective academic backgrounds. The desired result is to provide a foundation from which to pursue further applied research in the fields discussed in the book. It is also desired that the same material shall provide thought-provoking material from which business executives can work to develop responsible corporate policies for all concerned.

Organizations of all types and sizes today must constantly navigate high levels of turbulence to remain sustainable and viable over the long-term. Therefore, it is imperative for them to consider a wide variety of questions such as: 1) How can we manage across cultures?; 2) How should we develop effective virtual networks?; 3) How does global interdependency affect us in the long-term?; and 4) How should we contend with rapidly changing employee expectations and diversity? This publication provides a number of examples towards answering these and related questions.

Chapter 1 concerns the foundations of Human Resource Management (HRM) which sets the tone for the remainder of the book. Managing a foreign workforce can differ drastically from managing a domestic one. HRM in the international context requires managing diverse workforces originating from different nationalities with various cultures. Therefore, workforce diversity has become increasingly important for organizations which plan to expand into global markets and target different consumer groups.

Chapter 2 develops earlier work in the field of Diversity Management by Özbilgin and Tatli, and uses examples of three countries–the USA, South Africa, and Norway–to illustrate the complexity of managing diversity across national borders. Key challenges of international diversity management are highlighted. These three cases have been selected using a theoretically driven, maximum variation approach.

Chapter 3 discusses the role of Business Intelligence (BI) in decision-making for global companies. Organizations have started to compete in a challenging and competitive environment with the effects of globalization. In today's world, organizations must manage many environmental factors. Technological developments are one of those factors to which organizations must manage and adapt themselves to gain competitive advantage. With increasing data flow, it has become more difficult for organizations to store this data and gain useful knowledge to manage their business operations and functions. This explosive growth in data and databases has generated an urgent need for new techniques and tools that can intelligently and automatically transform the processed data into useful information and knowledge.

Chapter 4 empirically examines the internal and external factors of companies which can affect their foreign market mode choice. The model is comprised of internal factors such as control, domestic business experience, and industry type; and external factors in terms of culture of foreign markets and intensity of competition. A mail-out survey to Australian firms involved in international business generated 315 useful responses. The hypotheses were tested using direct logistic regression analysis.

Chapter 5 is a study which explores how polysemy leads to better branding. The research investigates the concept of polysemy and the generation of idiosyncratic meanings, and examines the impact of advertising polysemy on consumer-based brand equity. The research proposes and measures the advertising polysemy and consumer-based brand equity conceptual framework supported by accommodation theory, consumer response theory and theory of hierarchy of effects, leading to stronger ad-evoked feelings, ad and brand attitudes, and consumer-based brand equity.

Chapter 6 focuses on two Arab developing countries following the view that scope, role, and positioning of management accounting differ across organisations and countries, and, in the same direction, the study draws on the recent literature on localisation of global management control systems. The study embeds the view that certain contextual variables such as country differences and organizational culture possess particular cultural characteristics, which in turn affect individuals to respond distinctively to Management Accounting Systems' (MAS) applications.

Chapter 7 examines two significant trends which have been gaining momentum in software development: the utilization of Agile development methodologies, and the continuing trend of companies to outsource development work offshore. These two trends have changed the way companies develop software and business applications. This chapter seeks to evaluate how a company can successfully manage both trends in conjunction with each other on global business.

Chapter 8 discusses the concept of globalisation and its impact on the economies, cultures, and international business in developing countries and, in particular, Vietnam. The chapter provides an insight into how national culture and technology affects business operations, including current issues in technological readiness for e-business adoption in Vietnam. By applying theories of globalisation to explain changes and progress in Vietnamese economic development, the chapter also provides a better understanding of the complex mix of culture, technology, and business operations in Vietnam.

Chapter 9 portrays a quantitative framework regarding entry mode choice and ownership structures by measuring performance under given ownership structures as the degree of efficiency in technology transfer, and knowledge exchange in the form of a residual productivity growth variable. This method has been shown to be a proxy for or an indirect measure of transaction costs, in that ownership structures are validated by the growth in technology/knowledge-based productivity that they caused. In the process, the chapter discusses hierarchical entry modes and adjustment of ownership structures with respect to minimizing transaction costs incurred in the transfer and internalization of complementary assets, both tangible and intangible.

Chapter 10 presents a preliminary understanding of cross-cultural challenges and synergistic experiences of multicultural students engaged in Global Virtual Teams (GVTs). In this case study, we introduced the GVT structure as a novel learning platform which utilized Computer Mediated Communication (CMC) tools as part of its virtual-based learning. We administered the case study with thirty students (n=30) in the United of Emirates (UAE) who engaged in GVTs across the globe—encompassing 26 universities and 22 countries.

Chapter 11 discusses the role and purpose of Industrial / Organizational (I/O) Psychologists in global business. Most commonly, I/O psychology is concerned with those problems caused by human performance and those which affect human performance within organizational contexts. As such, I/O psychologists employ psychological measurement and research findings related to human abilities, motivation, perception, and learning in seeking to improve the fit between the needs of the work organization and those of the people who populate it. Thus, I/O psychologists plays a paramount role in successful global ventures, by addressing two key factors—culture and behavior—resulting in positive Return-on-Investment (ROI).

Chapter 12 provides an integrated approach to lead and manage transcultural virtual teams. Many novel team working structures have emerged due to the push from the industry to improve performance. The pressure on organizations to use more effective team working structures has increased due to invasive globalization and decentralization. Researchers have conducted a noticeable number of studies aimed at harnessing the capabilities of technology for satisfying the requirements of different industries in team working. Outcomes of the foregoing publications and the reports of successful cases within various industries have catalyzed the trend of merging technology into team working procedures.

Chapter 13 examines both theoretically and empirically how market orientation as a cultural factor is related to the internationalization processes of Small- and Medium-sized Enterprises (SMEs). This hopefully helps us to understand how SMEs can develop their businesses to a global level. The chapter presents a qualitative study of four Finnish SMEs representing different phases of internationalization. Finally, discussion on the results and future research directions are presented.

Chapter 14 shows how national culture influences people's perceptions of the world, and what actions they subsequently take due to those perceptions. Research has shown this also follows in the actions taken by firms which reside in those national cultures. The authors discuss the two ways a firm can pursue disruption and how culture might affect that pursuit. Additionally, it argues the coexistence of disruptive business models and the opportunities of the bottom of the pyramid markets.

Chapter 15 is a Case Study of work group conflicts at an Italian firm and how these conflicts affect conflict dynamics.

Chapter 16 investigates Knowledge Management (KM) and its challenges in global business. Some of the KM challenges in global business include global leadership competencies and strategy, project-based flexible global virtual teams, global knowledge integration and working with Information Communication Technology (ICT) gaps across different economies.

Chapter 17 discusses issues and perspectives regarding culture and website interaction. This chapter analyzes how scholarly research on the interaction of culture and websites has developed. The studies are categorized according to the framework developed and a selected 40 of them are discussed in details, under some subcategories. A number of conceptual and methodological issues that deserve more attention are discussed to fulfill high potential of websites. A state-of-the-art review of several innovative advances in culture and websites topic is provided to stimulate new streams for future research, thus future research recommendations are proposed at the end of the chapter.

Chapter 18 presents a conceptual discussion about investigating management issues relating to global business operations. Current global business operations provide an opportunity to conduct so-called Ex-Cultura research. This term represents the situation where researchers conduct investigations beyond their own culture. A Grounded Theory approach within a qualitative perspective is proposed so newly emerging themes may be identified.

Chapter 19 highlights the effects of culture on the internationalization of business activities regarding Small- and Medium-size Enterprises (SMEs) in Medellin, Colombia. As an emerging market, global business is of greatest importance in Colombia and several efforts are implemented to keep up with the international competitive environment. However, these efforts should be accompanied with the development of entrepreneurial capabilities in a wide range of ambits, among others, cross-cultural management. This chapter describes cultural influences in internationalisation activities of Medellin's small and medium enterprises based on original research results using descriptive multi-case methods within five companies and documentary review of business publications.

Chapter 20 discusses Business Process Outsourcing (BPO) in the United Kingdom. Outsourcing is a widespread practice in the modern global economy, with decisions motivated by the expectation of various advantages of which cost reduction is often the primary factor. Recent trends have been towards Business Process Outsourcing (BPO) and offshore outsourcing, and more recently Knowledge Process Outsourcing (KPO) has emerged as an established area of the market. Despite the potential attractions, there are a range of risks associated with outsourcing, and these are demonstrated by the substantial number of arrangements which fail to meet expectations.

Chapter 21 examines transcultural managers and transcultural communications. Transcultural Communication today is an integral component of many business related disciplines (strategic management, leadership, strategic marketing, business ethics, etc.). However, within the context of global business management and to a certain extent, Transcultural Communication follows under the broad umbrella of "Managerial Communication." This chapter discusses the topic of communication in general with emphasis on Transcultural communication. The result of a qualitative study used in this chapter confirms that efficient communication strategies and effective communications policy implementation can propel a firm to success.

Chapter 22 inspects local embeddedness and expatriates' effectiveness for knowledge transfer within Multinational Corporations (MNCs). The development of expatriates' social relationships in a local environment is critical given that social ties are considered the key players of an MNC network and a prerequisite for knowledge transfer within the organization. By building on the national and organizational culture literature, we develop a conceptual model to better understand how expatriates can effectively build local embeddedness.

Chapter 23 study concerns networking and Information Communication Technology (ICT)-mediated collaboration in transnational research teams with Russian participation which are affected by cultural differences. The core interest lies in investigation of communicative strategies and effects of visual and interactive techniques, including video-conferencing, participatory social media, podcasting, among others, and, to collaboratively construct, interpret, and theorize participants' accounts of cooperation.

Chapter 24 compares students' cultural influence on global assessment of higher education service quality. In particular, this study surveyed full-time students at the Central Queensland University (CQU) in Australia. CQU has 10 campuses and is one of the largest universities in Australia with more than 14,000 students in which 3,000 students are enrolled as full-time students and 11,000 as part-time students. An online survey was undertaken, and 227 responses from full-time students were returned for data analysis. Exploratory factor analysis and confirmatory factor analysis were performed to determine valid and reliable dimensions of perceived service quality. Tests of differences such as ANOVA and t-test were conducted to examine the differences of perceived service quality in terms of four cultural dimensions; power distance, individualism, uncertainty avoidance, and masculinity.

Chapter 25 addresses the extent to which quality management is "culture-specific." The chapter presents the results of a survey administered across 21 countries which seeks to examine quality priorities and practices by adopting the Global Leadership and Organizational Behaviour Effectiveness (GLOBE) framework. Drawing on previous research, data was collected in 2009 as part of the fifth iteration of the International Manufacturing Strategy Survey (IMSS). This study shows that adopting the GLOBE framework provides an invaluable insight into understanding quality management across countries.

Chapter 26 examines the complex of e-booking and e-purchasing travel behaviors among Slovenes. This is important as no research on Slovene tourists has been previously conducted. In detail, the relationship between e-booking and paying travel accommodation and travel transportation on the Internet during a five year period was investigated.

Chapter 27 explores the internationalization process of Italian Small- and Medium-sized Enterprises (SMEs) in the Chinese market, focusing on entry and distribution choices within the framework of facilitating factors and perceived difficulties. The following main research questions were formulated: how do Italian SMEs enter the Chinese market and distribute their products? Which are the main facilitating factors and difficulties perceived by Italian companies selling in the Chinese market? This exploratory study was conducted in two steps: a quantitative research, based on a structured questionnaire; a qualitative research, with open-ended interviews. The findings could provide marketing executives useful insights in developing entry and distribution strategies for SMEs in the Chinese market.

Chapter 28 is a comparative analysis of functionalities in three Customer Relationship Management (CRM) products; namely, Salesforce.com, mySAP.com, and SiebelCRM. In the era of IT-enabled relationship management, organizations have a host of CRM software products from which they can choose. These products come with different functionalities and support the different functions of a firm, thereby changing the face of global business today. In an era of so-called Cloud computing, support for web-based functionalities is the prime requisite for any CRM software product.

The reader should remember the following material is meant to provoke questions which will develop further research inquiry in the fields covered in this book. We trust this publication will assist in this goal to provide applicable results which are needed more than ever before in an era of hyper-competition and increasingly scarce global resources. As such, we have provided a wide range of topics which address the effects of cultural and technological influences on global business today.

REFERENCES

Bagozzi, R. P. (2007). The Legacy of the Technology Acceptance Model and a Proposal for a Paradigm Shift. *Journal of the Association for Information Systems*, *8*(4).

Black, J. S., Mendenhall, M., & Oddou, G. (1991). Toward a Comprehensive Model of International Adjustment: An Integration of Multiple Theoretical Perspectives. *Academy of Management Review*, *16*, 291–317.

Campbell, B. A., Coff, R., & Kryscynski, D. (2012). Rethinking Sustained Competitive Advantage from Human Capital. *Academy of Management Review*, *37*(3), 376–395. doi:10.5465/amr.2010.0276.

Christiansen, B. (2012). *Cultural Variations and Business Performance: Contemporary Globalism*. Hershey, PA: IGI Global.

Desai, V. M. (2008). Constrained growth: How experience, legitimacy, and age influence risk taking in organizations. *Organization Science*, *19*, 594–608. doi:10.1287/orsc.1070.0335.

Herrera, R. (2008). *A Study of the Relationships Between Attitudes Toward Diversity Management and Cultural Preferences*. Published Doctoral Dissertation, Our Lady of the Lake University, San Antonio, TX.

Hofstede, G. (2001). *Culture's Consequences: Comparing Values, Behaviours, Institutions, and Organizations Across Nations*. London: Sage Publications.

Ireland, R. D. (2012). Management Research and Managerial Practice: A Complex and Controversial Relationship. *Academy of Management Learning & Education*, *11*(2), 263–271. doi:10.5465/amle.2012.0090.

Jordan, A. H., & Audia, P. G. (2012). Self-Enhancement and Learning from Performance Feedback. *Academy of Management Review*, *37*(2), 211–231. doi:10.5465/amr.2010.0108.

Kirkman, B., Lowe, K., & Gibson, C. (2006). A Quarter Century of Culture's Consequences: A Review of Empirical Research Incorporating Hofstede's Cultural Values Framework. *Journal of International Business Studies*, *37*(3), 285–320. doi:10.1057/palgrave.jibs.8400202.

Kirkman, B. L., Chen, G., Farh, J.-L., Chen, Z. X., & Lowe, K. (2009). Individual Power Distance Orientation and Follower Reactions to Transformational Leaders: A Cross-Level, Cross-Cultural Examination. *Academy of Management Journal*, *52*(4), 744–764. doi:10.5465/AMJ.2009.43669971.

Mohrman, S. A., & Lawler, E. E. (2012). Generating Knowledge That Drives Change. *The Academy of Management Perspectives*, *26*(1), 41–51. doi:10.5465/amp.2011.0141.

Ng, K. Y., Van Dyne, L., & Ang, S. (2012). Cultural intelligence: A review, reflections, and recommendations for future research. In Ryan, A. M., Leong, F. T., & Oswald, F. L. (Eds.), *Conducting multinational research: Applying organizational psychology in the workplace* (pp. 29–58). Washington, DC: American Psychological Association. doi:10.1037/13743-002.

Nummela, N., Saarenketo, S., & Puumalainen, K. (2004). A global mindset – A prerequisite for successful internationalization? *Canadian Journal of Administrative Sciences*, *21*(1), 51–64. doi:10.1111/j.1936-4490.2004.tb00322.x.

Özbilgin, M. F. (2008). Global Diversity Management. In Smith, P., Peterson, M. F., & Thomas, D. C. (Eds.), *The Handbook of Cross-Cultural Management Research* (pp. 379–396). London: Sage Press. doi:10.4135/9781412982764.n23.

Özer, M. (2011). A Moderated Mediation Model of the Relationship Between Organizational Citizenship Behaviors and Job Performance. *The Journal of Applied Psychology*. doi:10.1037/a0023644 PMID:21574674.

Porter, M. (1985). *Competitive Advantage: Creating and Sustaining Superior Performance*. New York: Free Press.

Turban, E., Sharda, R., & Delen, D. (2011). *Decision Support and Business Intelligence Systems*. Upper Saddle River, NJ: Pearson. [headings: Subhead1-4].

Chapter 1
Globalization and Human Resources Management:
Managing the Diverse Workforce in Global Organizations

Yasemin Bal
Yildiz Technical University, Turkey

Serdar Bozkurt
Yildiz Technical University, Turkey

ABSTRACT

As a result of globalization, many firms have begun to compete on a worldwide basis. This situation has led Human Resources Management (HRM) to gain more importance in the global arena and "international HRM" field. Over the past few decades, international HRM has gained considerable attention from both academicians and practitioners. The increasing globalization of business has required organizations to manage their workforces effectively. Managing a foreign workforce can differ drastically from managing a domestic one. HRM in the international context requires managing diverse workforces originating from different nationalities with various cultures. Therefore, workforce diversity has become increasingly important for organizations that plan to expand into global markets and target different consumer groups. Organizations can adopt different approaches for managing their workforces and every function of HRM systems should be designed consistent to the workforce diversity of the organization. The purpose of this chapter is to investigate the concept of international HRM and diverse workforce in global organizations. Additionally, the importance of managing diverse workforces effectively in global organizations in the context of HRM functions and the role of HRM in this process will be discussed briefly.

DOI: 10.4018/978-1-4666-3966-9.ch001

INTRODUCTION

The advent of contemporary globalization has compelled even small firms to realize their long-term success depends on marketing and managing effectively abroad. However, this requires establishing management systems to control overseas activities. These systems include managerial controls, planning systems, and human resource management systems for recruiting, selecting, training, appraising and compensating workers abroad (Dessler, 2012). As the term implies, International Human Resources Management (IHRM) covers the worldwide management of human resources. The purpose of IHRM is to enable the Multinational Enterprise (MNE) to be successful globally. This entails being competitive throughout the world—to be efficient, locally responsive, flexible, and adaptable within the shortest time periods and capable of transferring knowledge and learning across their globally dispersed units (Schuler, Budhwar, & Florkowski, 2002). Broadly defined, the field of IHRM is the study and application of all human resource management activities as they impact the process of managing human resources in enterprises in the global environment (Briscoe, Schuler, & Claus, 2009). Over the past few decades, businesses have witnessed from an international context the development of strategic IHRM which is defined as HRM issues, functions, policies, and practices which result from the strategic activities of MNEs and that impact the international concerns and goals of those enterprises (Sparrow & Braun, 2007).

The increased internationalization of business in recent years has made the understanding of IHRM problems more critical for executives in multinational companies (Linehan & Scullion, 2002). Differences in cultures, economic and legal systems influence employer HR practices from country to country (Dessler, 2012). The global HR challenge consists of how to effectively attract, engage, and retain the thousands of MNE employees in many different countries to achieve strategic objectives. This goal not only includes engaging employees in different countries of the MNE, but also the role and importance of globally mobile employees such as expatriates and short-term international assignees. Additionally, aligning core HR processes and activities with the new requirements of competing globally while simultaneously responding to local issues and requirements is another challenge for IHRM (Briscoe, Schuler, & Claus, 2009). One of the key issues facing IHRM today is managing the diversified workforce in the global context consistent with the strategy and mission of the organization. The concept of Diversity Management (DM) is increasingly promoted as a strategic people management technique which will enhance organizational competitiveness (Cooke & Saini, 2010). Today, workforce diversity is a global workplace and marketplace topic. Any successful business must have a borderless view and an unyielding commitment to ensure that workforce diversity is part of its day-to-day business conduct (Childs, 2005).

The impact of cultural diversity varies with the type of environment and firm's overall strategy. As more firms move from domestic, multi-domestic, multinational strategies to operate as a truly global firm, the significance and impact of cultural diversity increases markedly. Diversity includes all groups of people at all levels in a company and requires an organizational culture in which each employee can pursue his or her career aspirations without being inhibited by gender, nationality, race, religion, or other factors which are irrelevant to performance (Kautish, 2012). Diversity not only involves how people perceive themselves, but also how they perceive others. Those perceptions affect their interactions. Successful organizations recognize the need for immediate action and are ready and willing to spend resources on managing diversity in the workplace now (Uma, 2011). In this chapter, the concept of international HRM and workforce diversity will be explained, and then diversity management and the role of HRM on managing diversity will be investigated in the context of HRM functions in global organizations.

INTERNATIONAL HRM AND WORKFORCE DIVERSITY

Diversity has become an increasingly important factor in organizations as the workforce and general population has become more heterogeneous in ethnicity, age, gender, and other factors (Nyambegera, 2009). Additionally, globalization from the organizational perspective builds operations in multiple foreign locations, a fact which inevitably requires an increasingly more diverse multinational workforce. While local employees enable important local market responses to be developed, they also increase the demands on effective inter-unit co-ordination. From this perspective, handling a global workforce becomes an important issue for the modern multinational companies (Peikkari, Welch, & Welch, 1999). The objective of global work force planning is to estimate employment needs of the MNE and to develop plans to meet those needs. One of the characteristics of today's global economy is that added complexity to HRM broadens the scope of enterprises' operations worldwide in dozens locations requiring the use of multiple languages and engaging a wide variety of cultures which are subject to various employment laws (Briscoe, Schuler, & Claus, 2009). Therefore, managers must be aware of and generally adapt their HR policies and practices to the countries in which they are operating (Dessler, 2012).

Critical inter-country differences which influence international HR practices can be listed as cultural, legal, political, labor relations, and economic factors. Employers must adapt their HR practices to the cultures of the countries in which they do business; therefore, differences in economic systems require differences in HRM policies. Additionally, firms operating abroad must be familiar with the labor systems of the countries they are entering and are obliged to ensure their employees overseas are adhering to their firm's ethic codes (Dessler, 2012). Successful organizations of the future will be those which can attract the best global talent then develop and retain it via a compelling work environment and sophisticated succession management strategies (Briscoe, Schuler, & Claus, 2009). This necessitates a global mindset in the management process of MNEs. A manager with a global mindset understands the need for global integration and local responsiveness and works to optimize this duality. The global mindset includes an appreciation for diversity as well as homogeneity and an openness to learn from all possible sources (Pucik, 2007).

Morris, Snell and Wright (2005) argue that since MNEs operate in multiple environments, they possess variations in both their people (reflecting the skill sets created by national business systems) and in their practices (which reflect local requirements, laws, and cultures). They benefit from a global workforce both by capitalizing on the superior skills that can be found by accessing global labor pools and by exploiting the cultural synergies of a diverse workforce. Strategic international HRM practices can contribute to the effective management of a firm's employees by enabling such outcomes (Sparrow & Braun, 2007).

The term Diversity is used to refer to the distribution of personal attributes among the work force in the organization. There are different attributes lying in diversity, one of which can easily be detected while meeting a person (age, gender, racial ethnicity) followed by underlying attributes (personality, values and knowledge) and subsequently attributes which remains in mind after getting to know the person (education, etc.). Diversity refers to the ways in which people are similar or different from each other. It may be defined by any characteristic that varies within a particular work unit such as gender, race, age, education, tenure, or functional background (Bauer & Erdoğan, 2010). The differences in these attributes are diversity (Panaccio & Waxin, 2010).

Anderson and Metcalf (2003) have described workforce diversity using the following dimensions: social category diversity, informational diversity, and value diversity. Social category diversity is explained as differences in demographic characteristics such as age and race. Informational diversity refers to diversity of background such as knowledge, education, experience, tenure and functional background. Value diversity includes differences in personality and attitudes (Ajaya & Pinto, 2011). According to another categorization, diversity is classified as employee differences in terms of three distinctive categories. The categories include demographic diversity, organizational diversity, and socio-cognitive diversity. The first category is demographic diversity such as age, gender, ethnicity, and nationality, whereby Jackson et al. (1995) have commented that these are considered readily detectable attributes which can be easily characterized in particular individuals. The second category is organizational diversity. It is important to note workforce diversity is not limited to the physical or social attributes of the organizational members, as it also involves the organizational context that adds to the diverse perspective of the group dynamism. Organizational diversity may include the occupation, functional or job portfolios of the employees such as marketing. The last category, socio-cognitive diversity, includes cultural and religious values, beliefs, knowledge level, and personality characteristics. It constitutes the underlying attributes of personal characteristics which are not so easily identifiable (Choy, 2007).

There are multiple benefits of diverse workforce in organizations. Diversity increases creativity and innovation which ultimately is beneficial for the organization's outcomes. The advantages of a diverse workforce are numerous. A diverse workforce allows better service to customers who are diverse as well, and it enhances the image and the credibility of the organization. In addition, diverse workforce increases productivity, facilitates innovation, and enables resolution of problems. In any case, understanding and managing diversity is crucial for organizations (Panaccio & Waxin, 2010). The business of workforce diversity is constantly evolving and presents new and different challenges, especially as businesses become more global. Diversity is becoming a key factor helping to define leadership in today's marketplace. Workforce diversity is about effectively reaching customers and markets (Childs, 2005). An important potential benefit of having a diverse workforce is the ability to make higher quality business or managerial decisions. In a diverse work team, people will have different opinions and perspectives. In these teams, individuals are more likely to consider more alternatives and think "outside the box" when making decisions (Bauer & Erdoğan, 2010). HRM and DM specialists argue that equal opportunity practices help organizations capitalize on the benefits of a diverse workforce in terms of reducing turnover and absenteeism, attract the best workers, increasing sales and marketing efforts, enhance creativity and innovation, and improve decision making (Soltani, 2010).

A company with a diverse workforce may create products or services which appeal to a broader customer base. For example, PepsiCo, Inc. recently planned and executed a successful diversification effort. The company was able to increase the percentage of women and ethnic minorities in many levels of the company, including management. Similarly, Harley-Davidson Motor Company is pursuing diversification of employees at all levels because the company realizes it must reach beyond the firm's traditional customer group to stay competitive (Bauer & Erdoğan, 2010).

Diversity initiatives should be internally driven rather than by external factors such as legislative compliance and should focus on maximizing employee's potential rather than raise the issue of discrimination. These initiatives should place emphasis on individuals rather than on specific groups of people, and they should become the responsibility of all employees rather than the concern of only personnel or human resource departments. Additionally, they should place an important emphasis on the nature of the organizational culture and management style rather than on individuals conforming to long-established processes (Soltani, 2010).

DIVERSITY MANAGEMENT

Diversity Management (DM) originated in the USA during the late 1980s supposedly as a new management paradigm focusing on workplace inequality and diversity. In the following decades, the literature on the subject has proliferated and DM became an established field of inquiry in management research (Tatli, 2011). Diversity, workforce diversity, and managing diversity are now frequently used terms in business, and managers have been presented with a plethora of materials in the popular press on how to direct a diverse workforce. The persistent messages regarding the need to address the phenomenon of a changing workforce and consumer base have motivated managers and organizations either to create internal diversity training programs or to hire consultants to sensitize employees to differences in race, gender, culture, religion, age, and abilities (Kirby & Harter, 1992). The basic concept of managing diversity accepts that the workforce consists of a diverse population of people. The diversity consists of visible and non-visible differences mentioned above (Gröschl & Doherty, 1999).

DM is used by Cox (1994) to emphasize the representation of people with distinctive group affiliations such as race, gender, religion, and even personality and political party affiliation (Soltani, 2010). An important corollary is that there should be an appropriate set of HRM policies, built on individual employee differences or employee diversity, to ensure effective recruitment and management of people which are diverse in terms of gender, culture, race, age, religion, language, and nationality. Such a diverse workforce requires an effective DM approach. This management's approach is characterized by capitalizing on the benefits of a diverse workforce (Soltani, 2010). Managers must be cognizant of the importance of diversity and they should articulate objectives for diversity in the organization. They should also communicate with employees about diversity-related goals and motivate them as a compulsory part to accelerate organization performance (Sohail et al., 2011).

DM is not only managing employees under the banner of equal employment opportunity—it also includes ethnic origin, personal work experiences, and personal and corporate background of an individual (Soltani, 2010). When employees feel they are fairly treated, satisfaction increases. However, when employees perceive discrimination, they tend to be less attached to the company, less satisfied with their jobs, and experience more stress at work. Organizations with satisfied employees often experience lower turnover (Bauer & Erdoğan, 2010).

Consistently successful global organizations must maintain a futuristic vision and CEOs, senior line and HR management, and diversity leaders play a key role in that process. Addressing the complex issues of race and gender, the growing concern over child and elder care, and the merging topics of multiculturalism, tolerance of religious practices, and the full inclusion of people with disabilities in the workplace requires diversity professionals to lead these efforts. Workforce diversity cannot be delegated; rather, there must be a partnership (Childs, 2005). DM may be understood as the systematic and planned commitment by organizations to recruit, retain, reward, and promote a heterogeneous mix of employees. It is directed at enabling the diverse workforce to achieve its full potential in a work environment which is equitable with no group possessing any superficial advantages. Additionally, managing diversity is based on the assumption that diverse groups will create new ways of working together which will increase morale, profitability, and productivity. DM attempts to build specific skills and to create policies that derive the best from each employee (Ajaya & Pinto, 2011). In general, DM programs are divided into two categories (Ajaya & Pinto, 2011):

- **Awareness-Based Diversity Training:** A type of diversity management program designed to make people more aware of diversity issue in the workplace and to make them recognize the underlying assumptions they make about people.

- **Skills-Based Diversity Training:** An approach to diversity management that goes beyond awareness based diversity training and is designed to develop people's skills with respect to managing diversity.

Companies also employ work teams, virtual teams, telecommuting, and dual career couples to facilitate effective decision making, improve performance and quality, and increase flexibility with the synergy of diversity management (Uma, 2011). Organizations make every effort to recruit, hire, and promote people and employees who are given a fair chance to succeed without and discrimination based on unrelated job factors such as age, race, gender, language, and nationality. Furthermore, adding value to overall business performance requires diversity initiatives to be embedded into overall organizational strategy (Soltani, 2010). Organizations include flexible working arrangements, work-life balance initiatives, and education and training programs to raise cultural awareness, and equal opportunity policies and practices (Cooke & Saini, 2010).

SHRM has identified outcomes such as the following for effective diversity management: 1) creating a work environment or culture which allows everyone to contribute as much as possible to the organization; 2) leveraging differences and similarities in the workforce for the strategic advantage of the organization; and 3) enhancing the ability of people from different backgrounds to work effectively together. Organizational approaches to managing diversity include a variety of techniques. Some of the most common involve testing, training, mentoring, and programs designed to help personnel effectively balance their work and family lives. Individual approaches to managing diversity typically take two interdependent paths: learning and empathy. The first is based on acquiring real or simulated experience, whereas the second is based on the ability to understand feelings and emotions (Luthans, 2010).

Cox (1994) and Soni (2000) suggest the objective of DM is for organizations to: 1) increase awareness of cultural differences; 2) develop the ability to recognize, accept, and value diversity through organizational intervention to minimize patterns of inequality experienced by those not in the mainstream; and 3) modify organizational culture and leadership practices so that "members of all socio-cultural backgrounds can contribute and achieve their full potential". It has also been argued there are three important reasons for DM: effective people management, market competition, and corporate reputation DM is regarded as a better approach than equal opportunity as it focuses on valuing people as unique individuals rather than on group-related issues covered by legislation (Cooke & Saini, 2010).

THE ROLE OF HRM IN MANAGING A DIVERSE WORKFORCE

Human resource management involves planning, integration, and actions to achieve effective management of all employees. Diversity can be included in the set of human management practices, guaranteeing an alignment between the strategies of human resources and DM goals. Myers (2003) argued HR managers must play decisive roles in DM practices because they can determine the details of practice (Jabbour et al., 2011). Successful DM requires HR managers to possess skills in leadership, organizational development, change management, psychology, communication, measurement, and assessment. Such cross-functional skills might seem broadly useful to the success of any business initiative. For organizations to profit from diversity, the people in those organizations must change how they interact. Diversity's focus on changing human processes requires and defines HR's role in DM (Ajaya & Pinto, 2011). For a wide assortment of employees to function effectively as an organization, HR professionals must contend effectively with issues such as communication, adaptability, and change (Uma, 2011).

According to Agars and Kottke (2004), HR managers should be actively involved in diversity issues by sharing this value with co-workers. These managers should begin with the highest ranking executives because these executives influence many other employees. This process can be accomplished by human resource managers exhibiting exemplary behaviors as an example to other employees. This becomes even more relevant when a DM program requires restructuring (Jabbour et al., 2011). HRM plays an important role in DM for two reasons. First, both HRM and DM are concerned with people management and second there are correlations between HRM and DM. On one hand, workforce diversity affects a firm's HRM policies and practices. However, appropriate HRM helps to achieve DM outcomes such as equality and inclusiveness. A range of HR diversity management programs would enable the firm to effectively management and achieve organizational goals (Shen, Netto, & Tang, 2010). Additionally, both HRM and DM are concerned with the contribution of the human resource function to business strategy and both are also concerned with individual differences, and the development and well-being of each and every individual (Shen etal., 2009).

Many multinational enterprises have not established adequate diversity programs in their overseas operations. Measuring diversity and DM practices is strongly regarded as the initial step of HR diversity management practice (Kossek et al. 2006). Diversity capabilities in organizations could be undermined by the lack of attention to the documented policies and practices and proper record keeping (Shen et al., 2009). The key practices of HRM for DM include recruitment and selection, training and development, performance management, and compensation (Shen et al., 2009). The adoption of a range of HR diversity management programs is regarded as the key to effective diversity management. Providing an equal employment opportunity to candidates in recruitment and selection is compulsory (Shen, Netto, & Tang, 2010). Human resource management involves planning, integration, and actions to achieve effective management of all employees. Diversity can be included in the set of human management practices, guaranteeing an alignment between the strategies of human resources and diversity management goals (Jabbour et al., 2011). To manage diversity in global organizations, HR functions should be designed and managed consistent with the awareness of workforce diversity. We will now examine how the HR functions should be designed in order to manage diversified workforce.

Recruitment and Selection

Managing growth in workforce diversity and increasing the representation of women and minorities is a critical HRM strategy of recruitment and selection for most organizations. Empirical evidence suggests many employees and managers regard DM as being equal to having an equal opportunity for any person entering the organization. Despite several decades of equality legislation and declared commitment to equal opportunities, there still exists a systematic discrimination in the recruitment and selection process. Morrison (1992) proposed that managing diversity can complement affirmative action strategies and new employment policies and practices to address the failure of organizations to promote women and racial and ethnic minorities into higher levels of management (Shen et al., 2009). Companies are investing in projects for diversifying their labor force, based on a gender approach; in other words, they are recruiting more female workers (Fleury, 1999).

In the recruitment process, diversity selection practices might involve developing a job description and selection process which reflects diversity needs criteria specific to individual positions. Such criteria should cover duties, language fluency, qualifications, and experience required, and all should comply with anti-discrimination legislation. Other practices can include attracting applicants by including advertisements in ethnic language press in addition to local daily newspapers, the presence of diverse managers on selection committees, and implementing techniques that allow diverse people to answer questions to the best of their ability and potential. When interviewing, the focus should be on the skills required for the position and not on other factors such as country of origin, skin color, and race (Dagher, D'Netto, & Sohal, 1998).

Training and Development

As organizations embrace diversity, investments are required in training managers and employees to understand diversity. Diversity training should be a part of an overall strategy to develop and value diversity as awareness programs alone will not accomplish diversity objectives (Mathews, 1998). High quality diversity awareness training is one HR function that enhances the effective integration of diverse group members. Awareness training builds a common understanding of the value of diversity, assisting in building social cohesion so that it improves individual and organizational outcomes. According to Maxwell et al. (2001), people normally regard DM as giving a fair chance for all concerned to develop and prosper. Many leading corporations have not been successful in training, retaining, and promoting women and minorities (Goodman et al. 2003). Managers in organizations where there is a lack of effective HR diversity polices are likely to promote or rate highly subordinates who have similar cultural backgrounds and experience (Shen et. al., 2009).

Companies usually send their managers to their head offices for training to achieve greater awareness of cultural differences (Fleury, 1999). Professional development and career planning is another area in which discrimination is visible and needs careful attention while designing DM policies. If the HR practices concerning career progression do not effectively reflect diversity issues, diverse employees develop negative perceptions of the whole process (Richard & Kirby, 1999).

Performance Appraisal

Effective performance appraisal practices in the area of DM should be objective, relevant to the job and to the company, and fair to all employees offering no special treatment (Schuler, Dowling, & DeCieri, 1993). Including non-traditional managers on the appraisal panels can help to create objective criteria and fair performance appraisal practices. When conducting appraisals, the language of appraisal should focus on the individual's performance and not on the personality or race. Hence, the aim should be to make the appraisal as culturally neutral as possible (Shen et al. 2009). Effective performance appraisal practices in the area of DM should also be objective, relevant to the job and the company, and fair to all employees with no special treatment (Schuler, Dowling, & DeCieri, 1993). Effective Performance Appraisal practices in the area of diversity aim to build diversity in decision-making bodies. For instance, minorities can be regularly included on panels that evaluate, select, and promote managers.

The problem of assessing promotion involving candidates who are "different" can be reduced if some of the decision makers are managers from ethnic backgrounds. It can also help to create objective criteria and fair performance appraisal practices. Direct intervention by top-level executives in the promotion process is sometimes necessary to ensure that diversity goals are not overlooked. Candidates must not only be recruited, they must also be adequately prepared to acquire demanding managerial assignments (Dagher, D'Netto, & Sohal, 1998).

Compensation

Pay equality contributes to effective DM and organizational performance. DM management in remuneration requires complete application of the principle of equal pay and a performance-based pay system. At the operational level, a major DM issue arises when an individual tries to balance work and family life. Top management commitment to diversity should be reflected in the organizational vision, mission, and business strategy to remove psychological and operational barriers to managing diversity. Line managers at all levels should play a more important role in DM. Sanglin-Grant and Schneider (2000) found that line managers' iterations of organizational policy on racial equality are sometimes at odds with employees' views of organizational practice. Hence, line management should be involved more in the decision-making process to fully understand and effectively implement DM practices (Shen et al. 2009).

FUTURE RESEARCH DIRECTIONS

One of the main purposes of HRM is to provide equality by managing diversity among employees to obtain the highest efficiency from different qualifications of employees. From this perspective, managing a diversified workforce has become one of the most important functions of HRM today. This issue has also increased the role of HRM in organizations. HRM has gained strategic importance in organizations and it is now viewed as a major factor in sustained competitive advantage. Considering all of these factors, various functions of HRM (performance appraisal, recruitment, training, etc.) has been analyzed theoretically in the context of DM in this chapter. The purpose of this chapter has been to provide insights about the diversified workforce and DM from an HRM perspective consistent with the theme of this book. Empirical research in this field will reveal the theoretical results of this subject in MNEs and will test the outputs of diversity management in organizational context. DM outputs can be investigated by performance measures such as efficiency and profitability so the relationship between DM and organizational outputs can be analyzed. Scales to measure diversity perception and attitudes should be developed in empirical research. To develop these scales, differences between Eastern and Western cultural values should be considered as a key issue. As a result of these future research attempts, the theoretical perspectives in this field will be supported by empirical studies and can be used in organizations for managers.

CONCLUSION

Globalization has created the need for many firms to compete on a worldwide basis. One of the most important issues that global organizations have to manage is workforce diversity. Global organizations have various employees with different gender, age, religion, language, race etc. so they should design all HRM functions and practices consistent with their workforce diversity. In addition, DM programs should be developed in global organizations in order to manage this diverse workforce and increase the perception of diversity among employees. Having a diverse workforce has various advantages for global organizations. Workforce diversity and effective diversity management programs in these organizations increase employee motivation, satisfaction and creativity. Also diverse workforce increases effective decision making process and innovation, and facilitates understanding different customer expectations in the global arena. To develop DM programs in the global context, each country should consider its cultural values and develop programs and procedures to prevent discrimination and prejudgment in the HRM diversity management process. In this manner, the awareness of HRM departments in this field will increase which will lead to greater organizational competitiveness in the global arena.

REFERENCES

Bauer, T., & E. Berrin (2009). Organizational Behavior. *Flat World Knowledge*. 2009.

Briscoe, D. R., Schuler, R. S., & Claus, L. (2009). *International human resource management: Policies and practices for multinational enterprises* (3rd ed.). New York: Routledge.

Childs, J. T. Jr. (2005). Managing workforce diversity at IBM: A global HR topic that has arrived. *Human Resource Management*, *44*(1), 73–77. doi:10.1002/hrm.20042.

Choy, K. W. (2007). Globalization and workforce diversity: HRM implications for multinational corporations in Singapore. *Singapore Management Review.*, *29*(2), 1–19.

Cooke, F. L., & Saini, D. S. (2010). Diversity management in India: A study of organizations in different ownership forms and industrial sectors. *Human Resource Management*, *49*(3), 477–500. doi:10.1002/hrm.20360.

Dagher, J., D'Netto, B., & Sohal, A. S. (1998). Managing workforce diversity in the Australian manufacturing industry. *Human Factors and Ergonomics in Manufacturing*, *8*(2), 177–192. doi:10.1002/(SICI)1520-6564(199821)8:2<177::AID-HFM6>3.0.CO;2-0.

Dessler, G. (2012). *Human resource management* (13th ed.). England: Pearson Education.

Fleury, M. T. L. (1999). The management of culture diversity: Lessons from Brazilian companies. *Industrial Management & Data Systems*, *99*(3), 109–114. doi:10.1108/02635579910252635.

Goodman, J., Fields, D., & Blum, T. (2003). Cracks in the glass ceiling: In what kind of organizations do women make it to the top? *Group & Organization Management*, *28*(4), 475–501. doi:10.1177/1059601103251232.

Gröschl, S., & Doherty, L. (1999). Diversity management in practice. *International Journal of Contemporary Hospitality Management.*, *11*(6), 262–268. doi:10.1108/09596119910281757.

Jabbour, C. J., Gordono, F. S., De-Oliveira, J. H. C., Martinez, J. C., & Battistelle, R. A. G. (2011). Diversity management: Challenges, benefits, and the role of Human Resource Management in Brazilian organizations. *Equality, Diversity and Inclusion. International Journal (Toronto, Ont.)*, *30*(1), 58–74.

Kautish, P. (2012). Paradigm of workforce cultural diversity and Human Resource Management. *The Indian Journal of Management.*, *5*(1), 37–40.

Kirby, E. L., & Harter, L. M. (1992). Speaking the language of the bottom-line: The metaphor of "managing diversity". *Journal of Business Communication*, *40*(1), 28–49. doi:10.1177/002194360304000103.

Kossek, E. E., Lobel, S., & Brown, J. (2006). Human resource strategies to manage work force diversity: Examining "the business case". In Konrad, A. M., Prasad, P., & Pringle, J. K. (Eds.), *Handbook of Workplace Diversity* (pp. 53–74). Thousand Oaks, CA: Sage. doi:10.4135/9781848608092.n3.

Linehan, M., & Scullion, H. (2002). Repatriation of female executives: Empirical evidence from Europe. *Women in Management Review*, *17*(2), 80–88. doi:10.1108/09649420210421781.

Luthans, F. (2010). *Organizational behavior: An evidence-based approach* (12th ed.). New York: McGraw-Hill.

Mathews, A. (1998). Diversity: A principle of Human Resource Management. *Public Personnel Management*, *27*(2), 175–185.

Morris, S. S., Snell, S. A., & Wright, P. M. (2005). A resource-based view of international human resources: Towards a framework of integrative and creative capabilities. In Bjorkman, I., & Stahl, G. (Eds.), *Handbook of Research into International HRM*. London, UK: Edward Elgar.

Nyambegera, S. M. (2009). The ethnic factor in IHRM: A research agenda. In Sparrow, P. (Ed.), *Handbook of International Human Resource Management: Integrating people, process and context*. London, UK: John Wiley & Sons.

Panaccio, A.-J., & Waxin, M.-F. (2010). HRM case study: Diversity management: Facilitating diversity through the recruitment, selection and integration of diverse employees in a Quebec bank. *Journal of the International Academy for Case Studies.*, *16*(4), 53–66.

Piekkari, R. M., Welch, D., & Welch, L. (1999). Adapting a common corporate language: IHRM implications. *The International Journal of International Human Resource Management.*, *10*(3), 377–390. doi:10.1080/095851999340387.

Pinto, A. & P. (2011). Leveraging the power of differences workforce diversity. *SCMS Journal of Indian Management,* 27-39.

Pucik, V. (2007). Reframing global mindset: From thinking to acting. In Schuler, R. S., & Jackson, S. E. (Eds.), *Strategic human resource management* (2nd ed., pp. 200–213). Hoboken, NJ: Blackwell Publishing.

Richard, O., & Kirby, S. (1999). Organizational justice and the justification of work force diversity programs. *Journal of Business and Psychology*, *14*, 109–118. doi:10.1023/A:1022962618674.

Sanglin-Grant, S., & Schneider, R. (2000). *Moving on Up? Racial equality and the corporate agenda*. London, UK: Runnymede Trust.

Schuler, R., Dowling, S. P., & Cieri, H. D. (1993). An integrative framework of strategic international Human Resource Management. *Journal of Management*, *19*(2), 419–459.

Schuler, R. S., Budhwar, P. S., & Florkowski, G. W. (2002). International Human Resource Management: Review and critique. *International Journal of Management Reviews*, *4*(1), 41–70. doi:10.1111/1468-2370.00076.

Shen, J., Chanda, A., D'Netto, B., & Monga, M. (2009). Managing diversity through Human Resource Management: An international perspective and conceptual framework. *International Journal of Human Resource Management*, *20*(2), 235–251. doi:10.1080/09585190802670516.

Shen, J., D'Netto, B., & Tang, J. (2010). Effects of human resource diversity management on organizational citizen behaviour in the Chinese context. *International Journal of Human Resource Management*, *21*(12), 2156–2172. doi:10.1080/09585192.2010.509622.

Sohail, A., & Rehman, K.U., Shams-ul-Haq, I., JaaM, J., Razaq, A., & Sabir, M. S. (2011). The impact of diversity training on commitment, career satisfaction and innovation. *Journal of Economics and Behavioral Studies*, *3*(4), 257–263.

Soltani, E. (2010). The overlooked variable in managing human resources of Iranian organizations: Workforce diversity-some evidence. *International Journal of Human Resource Management*, *21*(1), 84–108. doi:10.1080/09585190903466871.

Sparrow, P. R., & Braun, W. (2007). Human resource strategy in international context. In Schuler, R. S., & Jackson, S. E. (Eds.), *Strategic human resource management* (2nd ed., pp. 162–199). Hoboken, NJ: Blackwell Publishing.

Tatli, A. (2011). Multi-layered exploration of the diversity management field: Diversity discourses, practices and practitioners in the UK. *British Journal of Management, 22*, 238–253. doi:10.1111/j.1467-8551.2010.00730.x.

Uma, S. (2011). Workforce diversity and HR challenges. *Advances in Management., 4*(10), 33–36.

ADDITIONAL READING

Anderson, T., & Metcalf, H. (2003). *Diversity: Stacking up the evidence*. London, UK: Chartered Institute of Personnel and Development.

Cox, T. (1994). *Cultural diversity in organizations*. San Francisco, CA: Berrett-Koehler Publishers, Inc..

Cox, T., & Blake, S. (1991). Managing cultural diversity: Implications for organizational competitiveness. *The Academy of Management Executive, 5*(3), 45–56.

Dahm, M. J., Willems, E. P., Ivancevich, J. M., & Graves, D. E. (2009). Development of an Organizational Diversity Needs Analysis (ODNA) Instrument. *Journal of Applied Social Psychology, 39*(2), 283–318. doi:10.1111/j.1559-1816.2008.00439.x.

Gannon, J., Roper, A., & Doherty, L. (2010). The impact of hotel management contracting on IHRM practices: Understanding the bricks and brains split. *International Journal of Contemporary Hospitality Management, 22*(5), 638–658. doi:10.1108/09596111011053783.

Groeneveld, S. (2011). Diversity and employee turnover in the Dutch public sector: Does diversity management make a difference? *International Journal of Public Sector Management, 24*(6), 594–612. doi:10.1108/09513551111163675.

Gröschl, S. (2011). Diversity management strategies of global hotel groups: A corporate web site based exploration. *International Journal of Contemporary Hospitality Management., 23*(2), 224–240. doi:10.1108/09596111111119347.

Holladay, C. L., & Quinones, M. A. (2008). The influence of training focus and trainer characteristics on diversity training effectiveness. *Academy of Management Learning & Education, 7*(3), 343–354. doi:10.5465/AMLE.2008.34251672.

Ilmakunnas, P., & Ilmakunnas, S. (2011). Diversity at the workplace: Whom does it benefit? *De Economist, 159*, 223–255. doi:10.1007/s10645-011-9161-x.

Jabbour, C. J., & Santos, F. C. A. (2008). The central role of Human Resource Management in the search for sustainable organizations. *International Journal of Human Resource Management, 19*(12), 2133–2154. doi:10.1080/09585190802479389.

Jayne, M. E. A., & Dipboye, R. L. (2004). Leveraging diversity to improve business performance: Research findings and recommendations for organizations. *Human Resource Management, 43*(4), 409–424. doi:10.1002/hrm.20033.

Mark, W. (2010). Managing diversity. *Library leadership and Management, 24*(3).

Ng, E. S., & Sears, G. J. (2012). CEO leadership styles and the implementation of organizational diversity practices: Moderating effects of social values and age. *Journal of Business Ethics, 105*, 41–52. doi:10.1007/s10551-011-0933-7.

Nishii, L., & Özbilgin, M. F. (2007). Global diversity management: Towards a conceptual framework. *International Journal of Human Resource Management, 18*(11), 1883–1894. doi:10.1080/09585190701638077.

Pitts, D. W., Hicklin, A. K., Hawes, D. P., & Melton, E. (2010). What drives the implementation of diversity management programs? Evidence from public organizations. *Journal of Public Administration: Research and Theory*, *20*, 867–886. doi:10.1093/jopart/mup044.

Richard, O. C., Barnett, T., Dwyer, S., & Chadwick, K. (2004). Cultural diversity in management, firm performance, and the moderating role of entrepreneurial orientation dimensions. *Academy of Management Journal*, *47*(2), 255–266. doi:10.2307/20159576.

Soni, V. (2000). A twenty-first-century reception for diversity in the public sector: A case study. *Public Administration Review*, *60*(5), 395–408. doi:10.1111/0033-3352.00103.

Syed, J., & Özbilgin, M. (2009). A relational framework for international transfer of diversity management practices. *International Journal of Human Resource Management*, *20*(12), 2435–2453. doi:10.1080/09585190903363755.

Triana, M. D. C., Garcia, M. F., & Colella, A. (2010). Managing diversity: How organizational efforts to support diversity moderate the effects of perceived racial discrimination on affective commitment. *Personnel Psychology*, *63*, 817–843. doi:10.1111/j.1744-6570.2010.01189.x.

Chapter 2
International Diversity Management:
Examples from the USA, South Africa, and Norway

Joana Vassilopoulou
University of Sussex, UK

Cathrine Seierstad
Brunel University, UK

Jose Pascal Da Rocha
Columbia University, South Africa

Kurt April
University of Cape Town, South Africa

Mustafa Ozbilgin
Brunel University, UK

ABSTRACT

This chapter develops earlier work in the field by Ozbilgin and Tatli (2008) and uses examples of three countries–the USA, South Africa, and Norway–to illustrate the complexity of managing diversity across national borders. Key challenges of international diversity management are highlighted. These three cases have been selected using a theoretically driven, maximum variation approach. The concept of diversity management initially evolved and was developed in the USA. In contrast, South Africa is of interest due to its specific Apartheid past and its post-Apartheid challenges related to diversity management. Lastly, Norway is ranked among the best and most equal countries in the world. By exploring these different examples, we question the assumption that there can be a one best way to manage diversity in an international context.

The term diversity management originated in the USA before it emerged in other regions and countries of the world (Hays-Thomas, 2004; Kaiser & Prange, 2004). The term diversity management often refers to management interventions which seek to recognise and value the contribution of individuals from groups that have been discriminated against or that are different from the

DOI: 10.4018/978-1-4666-3966-9.ch002

dominant and privileged groups (Cox, 2001) and it extends to dealing with individual needs, as well as collective demands of a diverse workforce (Thomas, 1996; 2005). A more nuanced approach will reveal that diversity management is defined as a set of explicit and effective diversity practices, distinct from unmanaged growth in diversity, which tends to reduce corporate performance (Kochan et al., 2003). It is therefore crucial to expand the term of diversity management to its elements, characteristics and dimensions, including guiding paradigms in order to understand how companies reap the benefits of diversity and, at the same time, lessen the cost, so that it does not just become convenient, but rather natural and necessary to embrace diversity through coherent and complementary practices and policies.

Both research and practice provide a rather confusing compilation of best practices which tend to be unorganized, idiosyncratic, unprioritised and often bolted on as an afterthought. Research suggests diverse teams can be more innovative, creative, and thus even more productive (Cox, 2001; Hubbard, 2004), and the reality of Fortune 500 companies seems to reflect these findings. Companies such as IBM (Thomas, 2004) have spent considerable energy and resources to establish the diverse and inclusive company. By the end of the 1990s, three out of four Fortune 500 companies had launched a series of programs, aiming at addressing, enhancing and promoting the diverse workforce (Cauldron, 1998). Today, together with companies and the CEOs, a plethora of consultancy firms and scholarly work has followed suit, in order to help corporate executives and management to identify the milestones and key dimensions for managing diversity.

Using the example of the USA, South Africa and Norway, we illustrate diversity management in different contexts. The first section discusses diversity in the USA and presents the lack of ethnic diversity in senior positions as a key challenge. Next, we outline the different kinds of empowered powerlessness as one of the key challenges of diversity management in South Africa, drawing on interviews with a particular type of under-researched empowered powerlessness, emerging, younger and mainly first-generation, African black executives who are placed in top senior executive positions in private- and non-profit organisations. The last country section elaborates on diversity management and gender equality in Norway and focuses on two key challenges in terms of diversity in that country: the lack of diversity and particular gender diversity in senior positions, and the knowledge gap on how to take advantage of the resources the diverse labour forces in Norway possess. Lastly, we provide concluding remarks.

THE MULTICULTURAL AND DIVERSE ORGANISATION IN THE USA

It is crucial to highlight the role legislation and public policy has played to sustain diverse practices in organisations. This is even more so for the business world, as it typically responds to "what is good for business" (i.e., if corporate executives decide that diversity management no longer benefits the financial goals, then this trend may disappear). This is certainly the case in the USA where the progression of civil rights legislation from the 1960s and later outlawed job discrimination on the basis of sex, race, colour, religion, pregnancy, national origin, age, and disability. Those acts do not provide any protection against discrimination based on political beliefs and membership in organisations, except for a membership in unions. The latest addition to these strong legal acts (in comparison to the EU or other states) is the Lilly Ledbetter Wage Bill, signed by President Barack Obama (AKA Lilly Ledbetter Fair Pay Act of 2009)), aimed at closing a loophole in the US legislation related to equal pay for equal work. In addition to these and other related acts, the strongest measure for companies to accept and allow for diversity management is the matter of compliance with current regulations.

Non-compliance with existing legislation which supports diversity in organisations comes at a high cost for companies since the federal Equal Employment Opportunity and Affirmative Action (EEO/AA) standards sanctions organisations to meet the criteria. This is even the case for multinational corporations, and the EEO Commission has repeatedly disseminated public policy documents based on court based decisions in regards to non-compliance by a foreign employer that is controlled by an American employer in the field of financial control, common ownership, common management, and others (EEO Commission vs. Arabian American Oil Co, 1991). Required by law, EEO/AA programmes tend to be focused on the recruiting policies of companies to attain a certain percentage of minority employees, ensuring that HR policies are not discriminatory in nature and keeping the company out of trouble regarding non-compliance. Yet, the mere creation of conditions which allow for the raw nature of diversity to exist and to subsist are just the beginning of a long story (Harvey & Allard, 2002). Having legally secured and sustained diversity in the company, the creation of long-term mechanisms and strategic initiatives in order to manage diversity are equally important, as they allow for the active development, promotion and inclusion of different skills and perspectives of previously disadvantaged groups. Subsequently, this inclusive politic of diversity will lead to organizational change.

However, a brief overview of available literature on the topic shows an incoherent list of best practices (Schneider, Smith, & Paul, 2001; Kossek, Lobeland, & Brown, 2006; Garcia, Posthuma, & Colella, 2008) or lessons learned (Cox, 1994; 2001), which lack the sophisticated analysis of empirical- and data-driven research. This leads to a distorted understanding and appreciation of beliefs versus facts and the majority of the literature does not allow for evidence for what constitutes an effective strategy and appropriate measures of achievement. Measures of accountability tied to pay and promotion do not necessarily address the actual process of re-designing compensation or performance evaluation systems (Kossek & Lobel, 1996). There is not enough comparative perspective on how various programmes and policies complement one another in an overall diversity strategy. It is also unclear what makes a best practice for an individual firm tick better than for another. It seems overall that best diversity practices were concentrated in certain industries rather than a "one-size-fit-all"-strategy. Therefore, type of industry, company size (smaller companies usually fare better in adaptive strategies), age of a company, location of HQs and affiliates, history with diversity issues, and demographic trends might be various key criteria to look for when attempting to research the linkage between policy and implementation of diversity strategies.

The goal of diversity management is not only about the transformation of organizational culture through the inclusion of a heterogeneous-pluralistic set of values and cultures, it is a form of organizational change. Beyond the mere contingents of leadership and management, the values of diversity need to be viewed as shared responsibility of every single employee in a company (Coleman, 1994). The imposition or implementation of diversity policies will not yield any relevant results if it is not preceded by fundamental changes in the organizational culture (Cox, 2001; Ely & Thomas, 2001). Currently, the trend in the USA is to do the following: 1) embrace diversity as a reality as the workforce is as diversified as pluralistic and companies address the contextual opportunities of demographics (Johnston and Packer, 1987); 2) provide employees with equal opportunities and to promote social justice through company policies and programmes (Kellough, 2006); and 3) to harness the logic of diversity management for companies to gain a global competitive advantage (through such practices as cost reductions due to lower absenteeism and turnover, reduced risks of discrimination lawsuits, effective marketing, improved corporate image, better government contracts, etc.) (Kossek et al., 2006). A growing number of firms in the USA have adopted these three motivations for diversity management into their mission statements, putting great emphasis on the integrative power of a multi-cultural company.

One key challenge in the USA is the lack of ethnic diversity in senior positions. The recession in the country caused a decrease in employment of people of colour, and since demographics in the USA are changing rapidly, most companies are not keeping up with their promises and missions to diversify their workforce. This is especially disconcerting as top-level management in most US companies is not as diverse as some of the slogans may convey. If the diversity programs are not effective in producing a diverse workforce in regards to race, gender, and ethnicity, then most of these programmes are not providing the strategic source for optimizing the values and the profits of the company. This also means that senior management and leadership in an organisation need to understand the benefits of strategic recruitment and knowledge retention.

In fact, many organisations are offering equal opportunity programmes for young graduates. This strategy must be further developed since minorities, and especially African Americans, do not have the same access to higher management as do other ethnic groups. Mentoring and role modelling interventions could be developed and implemented. However, it may be time to re-discuss and re-consider the controversial affirmative action programmes. In many cases, white professionals have entered top positions early on in their careers, while minorities, especially African Americans, tend to reach higher positions much later and only through a dedicated network of mentors and sponsors. The spirit and actions which characterize the commitment and the emphasis on diversity is a leadership decision that continues beyond the policies and programmes of the organisation.

DIVERSITY MANAGEMENT IN SOUTH AFRICA: EMPOWERED POWERLESSNESS

Diversity management remains a pressing issue in a number of on-going and challenging dimensions of South African society and the economy:

- Historical privilege and post-democracy privilege
- Gender-related issues including the gendered nature of work (particularly in the private sector)
- Complex ethnic issues such as the emerging post-Apartheid identity including whiteness
- Exclusion and economic gate-keeping
- Alliances and political gate-keeping
- Diversity issues relating to the changing demographics of the country (including immigrants)
- The worrying effects of economic and social exclusion (such as violent crime and psycho-social unworthiness)
- The challenges relating to the significant poverty gap (two-tiered society, with a marginalised economic poor versus world-class economic minority)
- Current educational and skills development hampered by historical racial practices
- The tensions relating to embracing multiculturalism (dominant mode in democratic South Africa) versus shifting to a more integrated society in which the nation supersedes culture.

During the last 15 years, South Africa has experienced significant and consistent economic growth until the recent global economic crises, and subsequently continued to experience growth. The real GDP growth rate was 4.2% (2005), 5.6% (2006), 5.5% (2007), 3.62% (2008), -1.54% (2009), 2.89% (2010), and 3.12% (2011) (World Bank, 2012). This growth has led to an improved business climate, resulting in increased investment in South Africa, growth of industry and the general expansion of the economy (South Africa Business Forecast Report, 2011). The demand for skilled capacity in South Africa's corporate sector has increased, including the demand for both experienced- and emerging executive leadership. Such demand has brought to light an interesting racial/ethnic dynamic, which we are terming *empowered powerlessness*, particularly among the emerging (black) top executive class.

There are different kinds of *empowered powerlessness* in modern South Africa:

- Skilled foreigners/immigrants (empowered) working in the country in senior jobs (empowered) but finding that they are not fully accepted (powerlessness) and do not enjoy the 'closeness of friendship history' (powerlessness) to be close to the real decisions (powerlessness)
- Identity blurring (powerlessness) for, and non-acceptance (powerlessness) of, South Africans who were educated (empowered) and trained (empowered) in the West and returning to the country
- Senior (empowered), but younger, black executives working in the presence of more junior, but older, black staff (cultural powerlessness)
- The lack of self-esteem (powerlessness) and 'presence credibility' (powerlessness) associated with senior executives (empowered), white and black, who started and run very successful companies (empowered) but never reached high levels of tertiary education (powerlessness)
- Individuals with rural education and backgrounds (powerlessness) working in urban areas/cities
- White folk (historically empowered) in senior public sector roles (empowered) who are encumbered to the whims/wishes/visions of the dominant political elite (powerlessness), who are almost exclusively black, and do not always have their best interests at heart (powerlessness).

It is important to document the experience of empowered powerlessness from the perspective of the black emerging leader, primarily because the story has not been adequately told in South Africa. From the perspective of social studies, giving voice to experiences brings legitimacy, visibility and validity to the groups' experience. For instance, Aspers (2009), Wertz (2005), and Scott and Howell (2008) all stress the importance of doing research from an emic point of view, giving primacy to the experience of the research participant. Failure to give voice to an experience is to perpetrate the myth that such an experience does not exist. Given the large numbers of emerging black professionals and executives in South Africa, it is an omission that their experiences in South Africa's corporate environment are neither documented nor told. Such a silencing further perpetrates the power imbalances which exist between established corporate executives (most of whom are still white and male), and the emerging black executives.

Therefore, Namhla Mniki-Mangaliso and Kurt April at the University of Cape Town decided to research a particular type of under-researched empowered powerlessness (i.e., emerging [younger and mainly first-generation]) African black executives who are part of the population majority and placed in top, senior executive positions in private- and non-profit organisations but without the necessary corporate experience and (real) authority, and in particular their relationships with their mainly (minority population) white boards of directors/trustees. Not all such appointments are organic, given the aggressive employment equity laws of the country. The starting assumption of this research was that these emerging executives are significantly disempowered in the executive milieu of workplace whiteness and unheard in upstream accountability relationships with their boards/trustees, while they remain quite powerful to their subordinates. The concept empowered powerlessness is used here to refer to this dichotomy between power and powerlessness.

Kivel (2002) explains that, in most cases, those who have power are often not conscious of it. In many ways, this understanding is similar to the concept of rank. Smit (2009, p. 91) defines rank as "the differentiated status afforded to an individual or a sub-group in a group as a result of the combination of power and privilege." Unlike Kivel (2002), Steyn's (2005) understanding is that power and domination is conscious and intentional. In her presentation on "White talk", she explains that, in the democratic South Africa, the white minority have intentionally sought to retain economic power through morally acceptable means of racial domination (Steyn, 2005). She goes further to explain that through mechanisms such as the use of language, discourse domination, and belittling the historical past, the white minority continues to entrench and protect their institutional power in corporate South Africa (Steyn & Foster, 2008). In our research, the board was assumed to have power and higher rank than the executive head and his/her team. The extent to which this is a factor of race/ethnicity, status, or both was explored in this research.

Themes identified in the stories and experiences of the participants were categorised into the following six components (in order of prevalence): undermined decision-making space, collusion and exclusion, not-good-enough-syndrome, not much I can do, lack of skills and experience, and co-opted silence. Undermined decision-making space refers to an experience where executives feel they are not able to make decisions because their superiors do not make such decision-making space available. Instances were cited where decisions were made "above the executive's head," even though the authority for that decision lies with the executive. Another form is when the board refuses to give approval to key decisions that need to be made for one to function optimally in their position. Another participant maintained that in most of the cases where his decisions as a black executive were not being accepted, the same decisions/proposals would be endorsed if they came from someone else, specifically white colleagues. Additionally, there was a tendency to micro-manage black executives under the guise of monitoring and supervising performance, because of lack of full trust in their competencies and experience.

The experience of collusion has been interlinked with experiences of exclusion by many of the research participants, as those parties who collude often do so to exclude and bypass the 'other' from important discussions and decisions. These two experiences combined are best expressed in the words of research participants:

I was an outsider--and the knowledge person did not want to share the knowledge. My efforts of trying to work with this person were not working, and she had the ear of the big boss. So, it was like almost operating in an environment of a broken triangle where I was the bottom part--the missing bottom...and...It is possible to think that you are actually friends with White colleagues in the work environment, however, you discover that the same white colleagues socialise together outside work in weekend [barbeques] where black people are not invited, but are discussed in less-than-positive terms.

Collusions often will not work if colleagues do not collude with their superiors, thus establishing a "them and us" scenario. Many of our research respondents expressed the fact that having a powerful superior, who is biased towards one party, creates an environment for collusion and exclusion of the "other."

Another occurrence common among participants who had experienced being powerlessness while in positions of power was the feeling that it did not matter how well they performed, they would never be good enough or perform on par with white colleagues, given the relatively short period that black folk have been allowed access into management roles in modern South Africa. One participant explained:

Young black executives are coming into companies that have not been doing well and losing business from the government because of a lack of transformation. They come in ... these young energetic [black] people are helping, often through double the effort, to turn this thing around, opening doors, creating new opportunities–but white corporate culture still says that they are still not good enough.

Similar responses from others have been attributed to the fact that the upper echelons of most companies are still white and, as some respondents put it: "... the pockets of black executives who are there ... well, some want to sit pretty and claim being the only black at the top rather than fight for real change" and "sometimes if I wanted to raise an issue [at strategic level], I will give it to someone who is white to raise it" because there would be a different reception for the input. It is "taken for granted that they know what they are talking about." Respondents expressed how boards often found any aspect of potential difference to question the credibility and performance of black executives (e.g., dress code [Western preferred], social norms [white cultural norms regarded as standard], communicative histories [common sayings, thought patterns, jokes, shared views, ideologies considered "normal"], religious affiliations [dominant white religions more acceptable] and sexual orientation [heterosexuality considered the norm]).

A number of participants experienced the feeling that there was not much they could do to effect change in situations where they were experiencing powerlessness. In all the cases where this feeling was experienced, executives would have tried a number of avenues to effect change; however, in the end they discovered none of these avenues were working and, in a sense, there was nothing really they could reasonably do to effect change. One participant claimed that "... you can push back on your own Director to intervene, but this has little impact because you know that the directive is coming from the white CEO's office,;" in other words, there was no recourse to affect change if the perpetrator was at the top. The end result often was the exiting of the frustrated black executive from the organisation.

Three participants spoke about having felt disempowered when they did not know enough about the job they were expected to do. This was the only instance mentioned by participants that reflected on their own internal judgement about their capacity, as opposed to being judged by others. A research participant explained that he felt disempowered when he started his role in finance and operations without a finance background. His solution was to quickly learn as much as possible about the areas he felt he did not know enough about. Another participant attested to this, stating that while her relationship with her CEO and board were great, she did feel overwhelmed in that she was COO at 27 years of age, and felt that her previous experience had not prepared her adequately for her current role.

She explained the additional home pressures: "I also have a young baby at home and I am married. This job needs me 24/ 7–so I get home after 8 or after 10. I don't need to be doing that right now." A different black participant had a similar experience in his first executive job, where he was CEO at the age of 30. He explained that there were no systems or policies in place, and he felt overwhelmed with the responsibility, particularly, as he felt that he could not turn to any of his white colleagues for fear of being questioned even further regarding his capabilities.

A CEO who led an executive recruitment and training company noted that she had seen instances where black executives have been co-opted by white business to sit in powerful positions while having no say in decisions. In her experience, the underlying assumption is that the executive then gets compensated generously for his/her silence through company perks. She explained, "sometimes they will say … okay, we will make you a CEO and give you all the perks that come with it, but don't challenge anything, don't challenge us on transformation, and just worry about your family … they are bought into the inner circle of white leadership, where they are singled out as special and different from other Black people." With a history of Apartheid, many black people find that they become adults with accompanying lack of self-esteem, lack of self-confidence and psychological cognitive dissonance (due to the dual truths they were told). Some of our research respondents claimed that they and others agree to these arrangements because they are tired of fighting, reach a point where they no longer care, they do not want to rock the boat, and they would rather focus on their families and their own wealth creation/stability. As a result of this, they show up to meetings, they become the face of the company and earn the money while, often, they are running their own businesses/initiatives on the side in order to "one day get out and stop sacrificing myself."

In conclusion, the empowered powerless phenomenon begins with a perpetrator who, as a result of racism, sexism, and/or ageism, has a fundamental mistrust in the abilities of the emerging top executive. As a result, the perpetrator is convinced that the executive is not good enough to play the role they are playing in the organisation. Feelings of superiority are an integral part of this belief system. The perpetrator may then do a number of things to create an uncomfortable and hostile environment for the black executive. He/she may directly undermine the executive's decision-making space; or he/she may silence the executive through co-option, collude against the executive, or exclude the executive from important work processes. All of these efforts fundamentally come to the same thing, which is undermined decision-making space. If we have a brief look at the key issues facing the USA and South Africa, we can see that even when the key strand that we discuss is ethnicity, ethnic disadvantage is experienced in different ways in organisations. As the challenges are different, they call for different and specifically tailored solutions.

DIVERSITY MANAGEMENT IN NORWAY: HOW TO MANAGE DIVERSITY IN NORWAY?

The case of Norway will focus on two diversity challenges: the lack of women in senior position and the use of gender quotas, and the knowledge gap on how to take advantage of the resources the diverse labour forces in Norway posses. Norway is ranked among the most equalitarian countries (WEF, 2008), and is often used when exemplifying successful policies at promoting equality between the sexes (The Nordic Council of Ministers, 2007). In fact, both strategies in terms of equality of access (such as equal opportunity/ affirmative action) and substantive benefits (such as welfare) have been in place for the last 30 years. Norway has a social democratic welfare approach (Esping-Andersen, 1990) with state policies designed around a weak breadwinner model and a strong commitment to gender equity (Melkas & Anker, 1997). Yet, although Norway has a strong focus on equality, with long traditions of using equal opportunity (EO) strategies, the labour market is characterised by strong patterns of vertical sex segregation. While the proportion of women in Norwegian politics is high, the patterns differ in other areas of the labour market such as academia and the private sector (Seierstad & Healy, 2012; Seierstad & Opsahl, 2011). There are a variety of governmental strategies in place, such as EO/ AA aimed at increasing the share of women in specific settings, in particular in senior positions. In fact, Norway is seen as a frontrunner in terms of strategies for improving women's situation in the labour market. Yet, you still find strong levels of vertical sex segregation.

Political strategies are vital for influencing the situation for women and men, not only related to the labour market, but in the domestic sphere and society as well. Hence, political strategies and state intervention are in use globally to counteract vertical sex segregation and the selection of men over women to get more equal and democratic societies, and to take advantage of all the human resources which exist. Strategies can be of different natures. While equality of access means that states can intervene in the public sphere by passing legislation that either promotes or inhibits women's access to participate in all occupations, substantive benefits take the approach that states can interfere in the private sphere by taking over some of the responsibilities of families (e.g., childcare, cash support) (Chang, 2000).).

In Norway, gender balance is a political goal (Teigen, 2003). A variety of strategies for promoting equality are in place, and a range of initiatives and directives have over the past three decades been introduced which aim to challenge and eliminate discrimination and inequality between the sexes. Legally regulated quota arrangements were first introduced in 1981 in the Gender Equality Act, which regulates the gender composition of publicly appointed boards, councils and committees. For 25 years this was the only type of quota procedure which was subject to legislation. The introduction of gender representation regulation on boards for public limited companies, requiring all boards to have a minimum of 40% of each sex by 2008, was the first type of regulation for the private sector. This is a radical step for challenging the lack of diversity in senior positions within organisations. Although there are legal guidelines for improving equality and diversity within organisations in terms of gender in Norway, Seierstad (2011) argues that this will not successfully be achieved without the support from the individual organisations. Moreover, it is questionable if radical changes in the labour market, especially in senior positions, will occur without legal requirements. In terms of gender and diversity, we can pointout several puzzles. For example, in relation to the introduction of the gender representation regulations for boards, the private sector was given the option of voluntary increase the share of women on boards. If they successfully increased the share of women, the gender representation regulations would be withdrawn. This did not occur; hence, in the private sector there was a need for state-controlled compulsory strategies to make the change.

The share of women on boards increased to approximately 40%. This indicates that the radical strategy of legislation was a successful tool for improving gender balance, which could guide international policymakers. Nevertheless, it is also evident that even though companies complied with the law and reached the minimum target, the women's share is not higher than the required minimum. In fact, from 2008 to 2011 there has been little movement in term of gender representation on boards. This could suggest that companies are still simply complying with the law, and not moving towards further equality between the sexes (Seierstad and Opsahl, 2011).

After the introduction of the gender representation law, the share of women increased to approximately 40%. In terms of the chair position, there have been little movements with still only approximately 4% of the chairs being women. Hence, the legal requirements have not yet changed the gender balance for the most senior positions. Maybe surprisingly, it has found strong support for the use of radical strategies on boards among women (Seierstad, 2011). The participants referred to homo-social reproduction (Kanter, 1997) and organisational barrier (Acker, 1990; 2006), not merit for them not having directorships before the law was introduced. Moreover, women directors questioned organisational cultures embracing diversity as they found that merit is not working and they identified barriers in the labour marked. Consequently, as the system has been gendered and biased, it was an acceptance of radical strategies, such as AA.

Nevertheless, once AA strategies are in place, merit is embraced as criteria and seen as important and beneficial from the utility side. There is a paradox in terms of the merit discourse: while there is a rejection of a meritocratic society, it is accepted that AA can create a system where merit becomes more of gender-neutral criteria. It is proven that women that got directorships as a result of the gender representation law has been asked to be in positions not affected by gender regulations, hence, organisations have seen the benefit of attracting a more diverse workforce at senior levels.

Women directors in Norway have "proven to be competent; hence, few of the arguments related to lack of human capital as was visible in the national debate before the introduction of quotas had been justified. The gender representation law has increased the focus on diversity beyond gender. In fact, there has been more focus on diversity in terms of age, background and ethnicity. After the introduction of the gender representation law, there has been an increased focus on diversity within organisations at all levels. This indicates that organisations are focusing more on the argument of diversity management and the business case for diversity.

Moreover, the Norwegian labour market is characterised by strong patterns of race segregation where the lack of people from ethnic minority backgrounds in senior positions, both in public and private sector organisations is apparent. Additionally, the unemployment rate for people from ethnic minority backgrounds is higher than for the population in total. This indicates that there is a need to focus on diversity within the labour market. Traavik (2006) argues there are two key challenges in terms of diversity in Norway. First, to make sure that the senior positions within organisations are diverse. Second, to increase knowledge on how to take advantage of the resources that the diverse labour forces in Norway possesses. It is obvious there are several areas where the Norwegian organisations are failing in terms of taking advantage of the populations' potential, where the diverse demographics at macro level are not found within the labour market. Further, the resilience of segregation in the labour market for gender, race as well as other minority groups, are seen as having essential implications for individuals, economic growth and efficiency (Clark et al., 2003), and labour market rigidities ((Anker, 1997).

In addition, the persistence of expectations and stereotypes of what is appropriate for specific groups to do has negative effects on education and training and can therefore result in inequalities, which might also be carried on into future generations. For any organisation, attracting the best candidates is crucial from a business perspective. Nevertheless, changes in the population require changes within the organisations in terms of organisational culture, leadership and strategies. What types of strategies to use to change labour market patters are debated. While AA/ EO strategies have a long tradition, diversity management, with the focus on individual organisations and the business case for diversity is a newer approach.

However, Norway is a relatively small country, with approximately five million people. Changes in terms of the increase of women in the labour market, women's situation in the labour market, globalisation, increased migration, EU's free movement of labour, as well as the aging population has yielded the need for organisations to rethink strategies in terms of how to manage their workforce. Some of the key challenges in terms of the lack of diversity in the Norwegian labour market are related to these areas: the lack of women in senior positions in the private sector; the lack of women in senior positions in academia; the lack of women in senior positions on boards; the gender pay gap; the lack of skilled labour, such as doctor, nurses, and engineers in the labour market, while you find unemployed nurses, doctors, and engineers of ethnic minority background;

the lack of people with minority backgrounds in senior positions in private sector, public sector, and in politics; higher unemployment rate among people with ethnic minority backgrounds than for the population in total and lastly older workers are left behind in the labour market despite ability and willingness to work (Seierstad & Healy, 2012; Teigen, 2003; Seierstad & Opsahl, 2011; Nordhaug & Nordhaug, 2004; Traavik, 2006).

It is also important for Norwegian organisations to rethink challenges in terms of diversity management and how to best take advantage of resources available. Arguments for focusing on equality and diversity are many. While AA/EO often focuses on the justice case for equality, diversity management is built around the business case. The discourses in terms of increasing the share of women in organisations have recently been centred on utility rationales. Utility justifications focus on the benefits of increasing the share of for example women, drawing in part on notions of human capital, and the business case for equality. Human capital arguments state that since the total potential of a population is about evenly distributed between men and women, the paucity of women in high status positions means the talent potential is not fully exploited (Hernes, 1987).

In Norway's case, with more women than men pursuing higher education, this is an important argument. Some aspects of this argument go further to claim that women have a special contribution to make (e.g., through their supposed emotional labour and capacities for connectivity that are complementary to the skills and capacities) (Teigen, 2003). The recent financial crisis, for example, has given new prominence to arguments that women possess qualities and characteristics necessary for organisational success in the 21st century (Lewis & Simpson, 2010). Hence, the focus is on the organisational advantage gained by including women (Hernes, 1987; Helgesen, 1990). This focus shifts from strategies as a tool to prevent discrimination towards seeing strategies and diversity management as a means of organisational enhancement by recruiting women. For example, Helgesen (1990) takes the position that because of gender differences in management styles, attitudes, experiences, and interests, more women in male-dominated areas will contribute to new perspectives and ways of solving problems, which will result in higher productivity and a better working environment. Therefore, to increase the share of women can be supported taking the position that it is important to correct for biased criteria of merit to enable the identification of talented among the disadvantaged, thereby adding them to the labour pool.

CONCLUSION

Exploring the three examples of the USA, South Africa, and Norway, this chapter provides an overview of how diversity is managed in different countries and what some of the key challenges of diversity management are in these countries. Firstly, for the USA, we showed that diversity management is still an evolving and growing value-based notion on how to run a company in today's globally interconnected world. However, many diversity management specialists tend to provide cookbooks of best practices, including a set of recipes and remedies to tackle the organizational opportunities of diversity. Yet, it is important to emphasise the human dimension of diversity and that management needs to understand the history of its people, the context the company operates in, and the future of its people. The country needs to establish the right mix of whole change systems, leadership, inclusivity, transparency, equity and responsiveness, paired with the anthropological tools of observing, analysing, scaling, and utility to assess the feasibility of many diversity policies and programmes. This will prove to be useful if diversity is to take place not at the surface but with substance, relevance and sustenance.

In the second country case, South Africa, we discussed the different kinds of empowered powerlessness phenomena. Empowered powerless is a result of feelings of superiority on side of the perpetrator and racism, sexism, and/or ageism, which translates into a fundamental mistrust in the abilities of the emerging top executive investigated in this section. There is a belief that the studied executives are deficient and unable to fully fulfil their organisational role. According to the study presented, black executives are confronted with an uncomfortable and hostile environment for the black executive. Moreover, their executive decision-making space is undermined: they are silenced through co-option, colluded against, or excludedfrom important work processes. Empowered powerlessness should therefore be an important consideration in diversity management and inclusion in the South African environment.

Lastly, in Norway, Traavik (2006) argues there are two key challenges in terms of diversity management. First, to make sure that the senior positions within organisations are diverse. Second, to increase knowledge on how to take advantage of the resources that the diverse labour forces in Norway possesses. Paradoxically, although there are strong business case arguments for having a more diverse labour force, it seems like organisations need some help in terms of acknowledging this benefit. There is a need to rethink the use of radical strategies. In fact, recently, the academic as well as political debates globally have highlighted the need and opened for the possibility of taking more radical steps to challenge vertical sex segregation. The introduction of gender representation regulations for boards in order to ensure gender diversity within senior positions was a successful strategy. Moreover, to take advantage of the resources in the labour force it is crucial to focus on diversity and diversity management within organisations. This underlines the importance of legal regulations as well as organisational diversity management strategies in order to successfully change the situation for specific groups and utilise the potential within the labour force (Noon, 2010).

Although it is crucial to highlight the strong utility and business case arguments for diversity, it is also important to remember the moral and justice case as barriers in the labour market are still preventing underrepresented groups maximising their potential within the labour market, both within senior levels and in the labour market in general.

In conclusion, it can be summarised that two important points surface when looking at the different country examples provided in this chapter. Firstly, international is a fallacy in international diversity management, as can be seen from our examples (Tatli et al., in press). Diversity management happens locally and needs to address different challenges in different circumstances and contexts. It is a false assumption that diversity can be managed internationally without acknowledging the importance of each specific country context and without tailoring diversity management measures and policies in a way that they address local challenges and requirements. One of the ways organisations seek to overcome cross-national contextual differences is to adopt an approach, which facilitates dialogue and cross-fertilisation of ideas and practices among country representatives (Ozbilgin et al., in press).

The business-case argument brings us to the second point. Although these three countries are facing very different challenges in terms of diversity management, we found there is one common subject emerging when looking closer at all three examples. In all three cases, we can find a call for the moral and justice case for diversity management, instead of the business-case alone. Similar research on global organisations demonstrates that rich repertoires of business cases for diversity management are emerging. In fact, business case definitions are wide and broad enough to capture unique national needs, organisations idiosyncracies and legacies. The expansion in the language of business case for diversity is also mirrored in the range of activities that global and international organisations adopt (Oner et al.,

2012; Karabacakoglu & Ozbilgin, 2010; Jonsen & Ozbilgin, in press).

REFERENCES

Acker, J. (1990). Hierarchies, jobs, bodies: A theory of gendered organizations. *Gender & Society*, *4*(2), 139–158. doi:10.1177/089124390004002002.

Acker, J. (2006). Inequality regimes: Gender, class, and race in organizations. *Gender & Society*, *20*(4), 441–464. doi:10.1177/0891243206289499.

Anker, R. (1997). Theories of occupational sex segregation: An overview. *International Labour Review*, *136*(3), 315–339.

Aspers, P. (2009). Empirical phenomenology: A qualitative research approach - The Cologne seminars. *Indo-Pacific Journal of Phenomenology*, *9*(2), 1–12.

Cauldron, S. (1998). Diversity watch. *Black Enterprise*, *29*, 91.

Chang, M. L. (2000). The evolution of sex segregation regimes. *American Journal of Sociology*, *105*(6), 1658–1701. doi:10.1086/210469.

Clark, R. Y. A., & Anker, R. (2003). Cross-national analysis of women in the labour market. In Garcia, B. A., & Pinelli, A. (Eds.), *Women in the Labour Market on Changing Economies: Demographic issues*. Oxford, UK: Oxford University Press.

Coleman, T. (1994). Managing diversity: Keeping it in focus. *Public Management*, *76*, 10–16.

Cox, T. (2001). *Creating the Multicultural Organization*. San Francisco, CA: Jossey-Bass.

Ely, R., & Thomas, D. (2001). Cultural diversity at work: The effects of diversity perspectives on work group processes and outcomes. *Administrative Science Quarterly*, *46*(2), 229–273. doi:10.2307/2667087.

Garcia, M. F., Posthuma, R. A., & Colella, A. (2008). Fit perceptions in the employment interview: The role of similarity, liking, and expectations. *Journal of Occupational and Organizational Psychology*, *81*(2), 173–189. doi:10.1348/096317907X238708.

Harvey, C., & Allard, J. (2002). *Understanding and Managing Diversity*. Upper Saddle River, NJ: Prentice Hall.

Hays-Thomas, R. (2004). Why now? A contemporary focus on managing diversity. In Stockdale, M. S., & Crosby, F. J. (Eds.), *The Psychology and Management of Workplace Diversity* (pp. 3–30). Malden, MA: Blackwell Publishing.

Helgesen, S. (1990). *The female advantage: Women's ways of leadership*. New York: Doubleday.

Hernes, H. (1987). *Welfare State and Women Power – Essays in State Feminism*. Oslo, Norway: Norwegian University Press.

Hubbard, E. (2004). *The Diversity Scorecard: Evaluating the Impact of Diversity on Organisational Performance*. San Francisco, CA: Elsevier.

Johnston, W. B., & Packer, A. E. (1987). *Workforce 2000*. Indianapolis, IN: Hudson Institute.

Jonsen, K., & Ozbilgin, M. F. (in press). *Models of Global Diversity Management, Diversity at Work: The Practice of Inclusion* (Ferdman, B. M., & Deane, B., Eds.). Hoboken, NJ: Jossey-Bass.

Kaiser, R., & Prange, H. (2004). Managing diversity in a system of multi-level governance: The open method of co-ordination in innovation policy. *Journal of European Public Policy*, *11*(2), 249–266. doi:10.1080/1350176042000194421.

Kanter, R. M. (1977). *Men and Women of the Corporation*. New York: Basic Books.

Karabacakoğlu, F., & Özbilgin, M. (2010). Global diversity management at Ericsson: The business case. In Costanzo, L. (Ed.), *Cases in Strategic Management*. London: McGraw-Hill.

Kellough, E. J. (2006). *Understanding Affirmative Action: Politics, Discrimination, and the Search for Justice*. Washington, DC: Georgetown University Press.

Kivel, T. (2002). *Uprooting racism: How white people can work for racial justice*. Gabriola Islands, CA: New Society Publishers.

Kochan, T., Bezurlova, K., Ely, R., Jackson, S., Aparna, J., & Jehn, K. et al. (2003). The effects of diversity on business performance: Report of the diversity research network. *Human Resource Management*, *42*(1), 3–22. doi:10.1002/hrm.10061.

Kossek, E. E., & Lobel, S. A. (1996). Introduction: Transforming human resource systems to manage diversity: An introduction and orienting framework. In Kossek, E. E., & Lobel, S. A. (Eds.), *Managing Diversity: Human Resource Strategies for Transforming the Workplace*. Cambridge, MA: Blackwell.

Kossek, E. E., Lobel, S. A., & Brown, J. (2006). Human resource strategies to manage workforce diversity: Examining "The Business Case". In Konrad, A. M., Prasad, P., & Pringle, J. K. (Eds.), *Handbook of Workplace Diversity*. Thousand Oaks, CA: Sage Publications. doi:10.4135/9781848608092.n3.

Lewis, P. & Simpson, R. (2010). Meritocracy, difference and choice: Women's experiences of advantage and disadvantage at work. *Gender in Management: An International Journal, 25*(3).

Noon, M. (2010). The shackled runner: Time to rethink positive discrimination? *Work, Employment and Society*, *24*(4), 728–739. doi:10.1177/0950017010380648.

Nordhaug, I., & Nordhaug, O. (2004). Omstillingtil et mangfoldingarbeidsliv. *Magma (New York, N.Y.)*, 4.

Oner, H., Surgevil, O., Kaya, E., & Özbilgin, M. (2012). Leveraging global diversity through management strategies at Ceva Logistics. In Scott, C. L., & Byrd, M. Y. (Eds.), *Handbook of Research on Workforce Diversity in a Global Society: Technologies and Concepts*. doi:10.4018/978-1-4666-1812-1.ch018.

Özbilgin, M., Jonsen, K., Tatli, A., Surgevil, O., & Vassilopoulou, J. (in press). Global diversity management. In Roberson, Q. (Ed.), *Oxford Handbook of Research on Diversity in the Workplace*. Oxford, UK: Oxford University Press. doi:10.4135/9781412982764.n23.

Ozbilgin, M., & Tatli, A. (2008). *Global Diversity Management: An Evidence-Based Approach*. London: Palgrave Macmillan.

Schneider, B. D., Smith, B., & Paul, M. C. (2001). P-E fit and the Attraction-Selection-Attrition Model of Organisational Functioning: Introduction and overview. In Erez, M., Kleinbeck, U., & Thierry, H. (Eds.), *Work Motivation in the Context of a Globalising Economy*. Mahwah, NJ: Lawrence Erlbaum.

Scott, W. K., & Howell, D. (2008). Clarifying analysis and interpretation in grounded theory: Using a conditional relationship guide and reflective coding matrix. *International Journal of Qualitative Methods*, *7*(2), 1–15.

Seierstad, C. (2011). *Exploring the Norwegian paradox of vertical sex segregation: Strategies and experiences in politics, academia and company boards*. PhD Thesis, University of London, London, U.K.

Seierstad, C., & Healy, G. (2012). Women's equality in the Scandinavian academy – A distant dream? *Work, Employment and Society*, *26*, 296–313. doi:10.1177/0950017011432918.

Seierstad, C., & Opsahl, T. (2011). For the few not the many? The effects of affirmative action on presence, prominence, and social capital of female directors in Norway. *Scandinavian Journal of Management*, *27*(1). doi:10.1016/j.scaman.2010.10.002.

Smit, H. (2009). *The depth facilitator's handbook: Transforming group dynamics*. Cape Town, South Africa: Moonshine Media.

South Africa business forecast report 2011, 3.

Steyn, M., & Foster, D. (2008). Repertoires for talking white: Resistant whiteness in post-Apartheid South Africa. *Ethnic and Racial Studies*, *31*(1), 25–51. doi:10.1080/01419870701538851.

Tatli, A., Vassilopoulou, J., Ariss, A., & Ozbilgin, M. (in press). The role of regulatory and temporal context in the construction of diversity discourses: The case of the UK, France and Germany. *European Journal of Industrial Relations*.

Teigen, M. (2003). *Kvoteringogkontrovers: Omlikestillingsompolitikk*. Oslo, Norway: Universiteteti Oslo.

Thomas, D. (2004). Diversity as a strategy. *Harvard Business Review*, *82*(9), 98–108. PMID:15449859.

Thomas, R. R. (1996). A diversity framework. In Chemers, M. M., Oskampand, S., & Costanzo, M. A. (Eds.), *Diversity in Organisations: New Perspectives for a Changing Workplace* (pp. 245–263). Thousand Oaks, CA: Sage Publications.

Thomas, R. R. (2005). *Building on the Promise of Diversity: How Can We Move to the Next Level in Our Workplaces, Our Communities, and Our Society*. New York: AMACOM.

Traavik, L. E. M. (2006). Ledelseavmangfold. *Magma (New York, N.Y.)*, 2.

Wertz, F. J. (2005). Phenomenological research methods for counselling psychology. *Journal of Counseling Psychology*, *52*(2), 167–177. doi:10.1037/0022-0167.52.2.167.

World Bank. (2012). *World Bank data*. Retrieved from http://www.worldbank.org, retrieved 11th September 2012

Chapter 3
Business Intelligence Solutions for Decision-Making in Global Organizations

Yasemin BAL
Yildiz Technical University, Turkey

Mert BAL
Yildiz Technical University,Turkey

ABSTRACT

Organizations have started to compete in a challenging and competitive environment with the effects of globalization. In today's world, organizations must manage many environmental factors. Technological developments are one of those factors to which organizations must manage and adapt themselves to gain competitive advantage. With increasing data flow, it has become more difficult for organizations to store this data and gain useful knowledge to manage their business operations and functions. This explosive growth in data and databases has generated an urgent need for new techniques and tools that can intelligently and automatically transform the processed data into useful information and knowledge. This situation is especially more difficult for global organizations that have various branches in different countries around the world. Parallel with these developments in information technology for business applications, management information systems and business intelligence solutions have gained more importance. This paper investigates the importance of using business intelligence solutions and techniques for decision making process in the perspective of business functions in global organizations. Business intelligence solutions and techniques will be introduced, followed by explanation of the use of these systems in decision making processes within the context of global organizations.

DOI: 10.4018/978-1-4666-3966-9.ch003

INTRODUCTION

Until the mid-1950s, organizations managed all the information they received from business functions, entities and environments, and related information flow via paper records. During the past 60 years, more and more business information and the flow of information among key business actors in the environment have been computerized (Laudon & Laudon, 2009). The 1990s brought a growing data glut problem to the world of science, business, and government. Capabilities for collecting and storing of all kinds have far outpaced abilities to analyze, summarize, and extract meaningful "knowledge" from this data (Fayyad, 1996). Depending on the increase of data stored in the databases of organizations, traditional statistical methods have become insufficient. Traditional methods of data analysis, based mainly on human dealing directly with the data, simply do not scale to handle large data sets. This explosive growth in data and databases has generated an urgent need for new techniques and tools which can intelligently and automatically transform the processed data into useful information and knowledge (Bal, Bal, & Demirhan, 2011).

There has also been a change in management thought to accept the importance of fast, effective provision of targeted information for management planning and control (Curtis & Cobham, 2002). Therefore, organizations have started to invest in information systems as a way to manage their internal production functions and to fulfill the demands of key actors in their environments. Firms invest in information systems for business objectives such as: achieving operational excellence (productivity, efficiency, agility); developing new products and services; attaining customer intimacy and service (continuous marketing, sales and service; customization and personalization); improving decision making; achieving competitive advantage; and ensuring survival (Laudon & Laudon, 2009). Parallel with the increase of data stored in databases of organizations in business applications, management information systems have gained in importance. Information systems transform the data to knowledge which is collected from the internal and external environment of organization, then protect, store, and transmit the knowledge to all management levels in order to facilitate the strategic decision making process and support managers for planning, implementing, and controlling functions.

Briefly, the systems which provide essential processed information to managers are called "information systems." Information systems have a vital role in organizations for eliminating uncertainty and providing efficiency in decision making. (Bal, Bal, Demirhan & Bozkurt, 2011). A Management Information System (MIS) is any system which provides information for management activities to be carried out within an organization. This information is selected and presented in a form suitable for managerial decision making and for the planning and monitoring of the organization's activities. Figure 1 illustrates the reliance of the provision of information at strategic, managerial and operational levels of an organization according to the hierarchical system (Curtis & Cobham, 2002). As seen in Figure 1, MIS can be employed in different levels of an organization for operational, tactical, and strategic decisions. Raw data can be transformed to information with the help of MIS and this MIS- generated information is used as input for decision making process in managerial activities.

Information systems, especially those utilizing Business Intelligence (BI) techniques, developed for specific needs of business functions which can facilitate all the processes in organizations and coordinate functions to aid managers in decision making processes. BI aims to support better business decision-making. The concept of business intelligence and BI techniques will be explained in the sections below.

Figure 1. Use of MIS in different levels of the organization

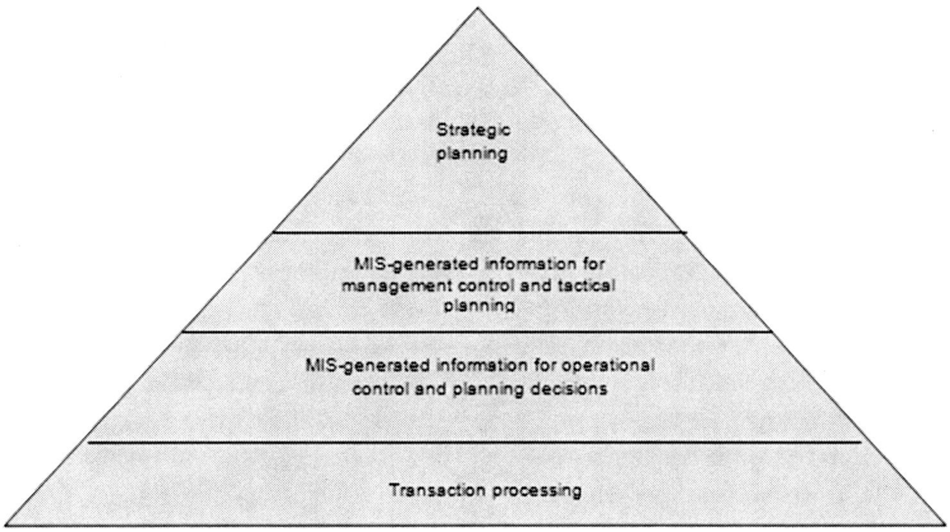

EVOLUTION AND DEFINITON OF BUSINESS INTELLIGENCE (BI)

The term business intelligence (BI) was developed by the Gartner Group in the mid-1990s. However, the concept is much older; it has its roots in MIS reporting systems of the 1970s. During that period, reporting systems were static; two dimensional and possessed no analytical capabilities (Turban, Sharda, & Delen, 2011). In the 1970s, there began to arise within enterprises increasingly complex needs to devise software applications called *management information systems* to ease access to useful and timely information for decision makers. From the late 1980s, personal computers with operating systems were introduced. Later developments brought to light new types of applications and architectures; executive information systems and strategic information systems were first introduced to support managers in the decision making process (Vercellis, 2009). These concepts expanded the computerized support to top-level managers and executives. Some of the capabilities introduced were dynamic multidimensional reporting, forecasting and prediction, trend analysis, and critical success factors. Then, the same capabilities and some new ones appeared under the generic term BI (Turban, Sharda, & Delen, 2011). From the early 1990s, network architectures and distributed information systems based on client server computing models began to be widely adopted (Vercellis, 2009).

BI is a strategic approach for systematically targeting, tracking, communicating, and transforming relevant weak signs into actionable information on which strategic decision making is based (Fitriana, Eriyatno, & Djatna, 2011). BI has been viewed as sets of powerful tools and approaches to improve business executive decision making and business operations, and also to increase the value of the enterprise (Zeng et al., 2006). BI has been promoted as enhancing decision making and ultimately improving business value (Vinekar, Teng, & Chennamaneni, 2009). There are various definitions for BI. Nagesh (2004) defines BI systems as those that combine operational data with analytical tools to present complex and competitive information to planners and decision makers. Stackowiak et al. (2007) define BI as the process of taking large amounts of data, analyzing that data, and presenting a high level set of reports which condense the essence of that data into the basis of business actions, enabling management to make fundamentally daily business decisions.

Zeng et al. (2006) defines BI as the process of collection, treatment, and diffusion of information that has an objective, the reduction of uncertainty in the making of all strategic decisions (Ranjan, 2009). Additionally, BI is defined as the process of providing decision makers with valuable information and knowledge by leveraging a variety of sources of data including structured and unstructured information. The information and data could reside within or outside of the organization, obtained from multiple sources, structured in different ways, and be either quantitative or qualitative in nature (Sabherwal & Fernandez, 2011). Biere (2003) defines BI as conscious and methodical transformation of data from any and all data sources into new forms to provide information that is business driven and results oriented. According to another definition, BI is a set of mathematical models and analysis methodologies which systematically exploit the available data to retrieve information and knowledge useful in supporting complex decision making process (Vercellis, 2009).

One of the primary purposes of BI is to improve the timeliness and quality of input to the decision process. Companies with well-designed BI systems available to their managers find their managers make better decisions on a variety of business issues. Higher quality managerial decision making allows companies to obtain a competitive advantage over firms which operate without the benefit of BI systems for their managers to use. BI systems provide managers with actionable information and knowledge at the right time, in the right location, and in the right form (Haag & Cummings, 2008). The BI system provides decision makers with information and knowledge extracted from data, through the application of mathematical models and algorithms (Vercellis, 2009). BI which is constantly renewed and enhanced can be seen as an important source of gaining and improving competitive advantage (Thierauf, 2001). BI is a process for increasing competitive advantage via the intelligent use of available information collection for users to make wiser decisions. It is fundamentally concerned with improving the effectiveness and efficiency of knowledge management and decision support. (Gao, Chang & Han, 2005). The intelligence phase of decision making is described as "searching for the environment for conditions calling for decisions." In this phase, raw data is obtained, processed, and examined for clues that may identify problems. Executives and managers begin their decision-making by seeking, collecting, processing, and analyzing information to identify and understand potential problems and opportunities for their organization (Vinekar, Teng & Chennamaneni, 2009).

BI changes the traditional flow of information. Instead of an individual going to a database, the database comes to the individual. BI helps managers focus on what is important, and decide how to react to problems and opportunities (Nickels, McHugh, & McHugh, 2010). Therefore, intelligence is defined as "customized information that is focused on identifying specific problems and opportunities." Information is usually standardized and detailed while intelligence is more sophisticated and looks at relationships within the information and provides a bigger picture for more holistic understanding (Vinekar, Teng, & Chennamaneni, 2009).

BI is collective information about the customers, competitors, business partners, the competitive environment, and internal operations which gives the organization the ability to make effective, important, and strategic business decisions. BI enables the organization to extract true meaning of information to take creative and powerful steps to ensure competitive advantage (Haag & Cummings, 2008). Figure 2 shows the difference between information and business intelligence. Raw data and information is taken from various functions of organization and this information is processed by different BI techniques to make judgments and

Figure 2. The difference between information and business intelligence

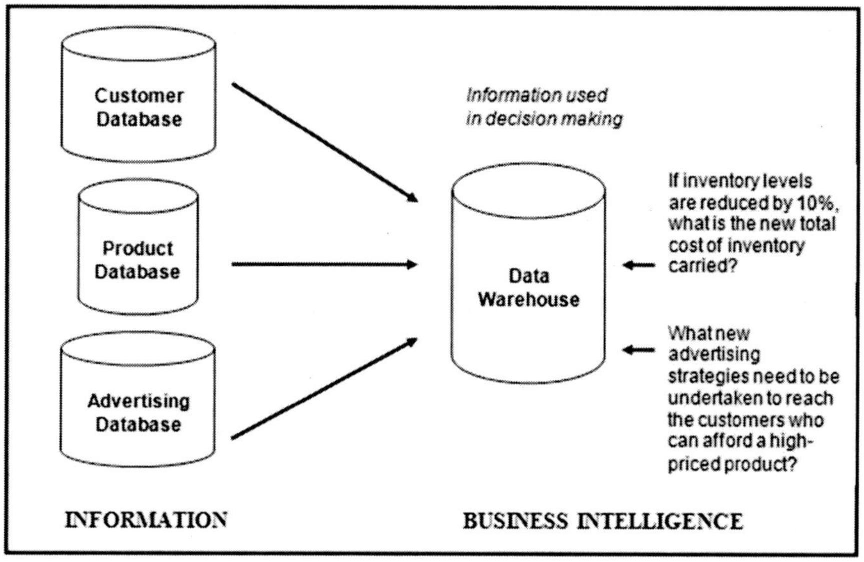

future estimations about organizational operations (Haag & Cummings, 2008). Today, a good BI-based enterprise information system contains all the information that managers require (Turban, Sharda & Delen, 2011).

BENEFITS OF BUSINESS INTELLIGENCE

Today, information and knowledge represent the fundamental wealth of an organization. Enterprises attempt to utilize this wealth to gain competitive advantage when making important decisions. Enterprise software and systems include Enterprise Resource Planning (ERP), Customer Relationship Management (CRM), and Supply Chain Management (SCM) systems. These systems convert and store the data in their databases; therefore, they can be used as a pool of data to support decisions and explore applicable knowledge. With the potential to gain competitive advantage when making important decisions, it is vital to integrate and implement decision support into the environment of their enterprise and work systems. BI can be embedded in these enterprise systems to obtain this competitive advantage (Ghazanfari, Jafari, & Rouhani, 2011). BI is becoming vital to many organizations, especially those which have an extremely large amount of data. Decision makers depend on detailed and accurate information when they have to make decisions. BI can provide decision makers with such accurate information, and with the appropriate tools for data analysis (Alnoukari, 2009). There are a number of benefits common to all businesses which deploy BI. It can eliminate much guesswork within an organization, enhance communication among departments while coordinating activities, and enable companies to respond quickly to changes in financial conditions, customer preferences and supply chain operations (Ranjan, 2009). BI solutions enable managers to use trends to anticipate what might occur in the future and to make sound decisions which lead to improved organizational performance and increase organizational efficiency. BI solutions also help to identify new opportunities for the organization by creating new insights and knowledge through the discovery of previously unknown patterns, correlation, and trends to prepare better for the future by providing support for the identification of new products and services (Sabharwal & Fernandez, 2011). Some of the benefits of BI are listed below (Kocbek & Juric, 2010).

- Help align the organization towards its key objectives
- Enables faster and fact-based decision making
- Meet or exceed customer expectations based on factual information
- Find latent problems by building a picture of unseen information
- Quickly recognize competitive advantages
- Combines multiple sources of data for decision making
- Efficient collection and distribution of essential data and statistics
- With superior BI tools, employees can also easily convert their business knowledge via analytical intelligence to solve many business issues
- BI permits organizations to identify their most profitable customers and the underlying reasons for those customers' loyalty
- Analyze potential growth customer profitability and reduce risk exposure through more accurate financial credit scoring of their customers.

BI solutions help organizations by enabling the dissemination of real time information in so-called "user-friendly" fashion. BI facilitates the reporting of information about the past and provides information to make decisions about the present and to plan for the future. BI solutions also contribute by enabling the creation of new knowledge based on information about the past. They also help organizations to be more responsive and anticipative when making decisions that are based more closely on all the latest information and facilitate better planning for the future (Sabharwal & Fernandez, 2011).

BUSINESS INTELLIGENCE TECHNIQUES

BI is a so-called "umbrella term" which refers to a variety of software applications which analyze a company's data and extract useful insights to help managers make better decisions. BI includes activities such as data mining which searches out and analyzes data from multiple sources within the enterprise, and occasionally from outside sources, to identify patterns and relationships which might be significant (Daft, 2008). The availability of real time information reduces the degree of uncertainty confronting business managers (Thierauf, 2001). BI has various techniques such as data mining, Online Analytical Processing (OLAP), predictive analytics, process mining, text mining, and complex event processing. These BI techniques will be explained briefly.

Data Mining

Data Mining (DM) is a discovery process of the hidden information from the data which is yet unknown and potentially useful. However, according to Raghavan and Sever, DM discovers the general patterns and relations hidden in the data (Sever & Oguz, 2003). DM is an iterative process which acts as a bridge the gap between logical decision-making and the data, and is possible the classification for finding the useful samples or using and combining the classification rules from the samples. This process combines the approaches used in different disciplines such as machine learning, statistics, database management systems, data warehousing, and constraint programming (Sever & Oguz, 2003). In DM applications, many methods to discover the useful patterns are available and each method has advantages and disadvantages over the others. However, if required, the advantages of different methods could be combined and hybrid methods can be created. The process of creating hybrid methods is a work of combining computational intelligence tools. Many algorithms are used to implement a DM process. The reason is that some technologies are better than others for different tasks, states, and subjects. At the core of data mining lays a model creation process which represents a data set.

A model creation process which represents a data set is generic for all DM products; however, the process itself is not generic. Some methods used in DM processes are rough sets theory, Bayesian networks, genetic algorithms, neural networks, fuzzy sets, and inductive logic programming. DM functions are used to determine the pattern types that may exist in the DM tasks. Generally, DM tasks are classified into two categories: descriptive and predictive. Descriptive mining tasks characterize the general properties of the data in the database. But, predictive mining makes inferences from the available data to make estimations (Han & Kamber, 2001). The samples of the DM functions and resulting discovered pattern types are classification, clustering, summarization, estimation, time series analysis, association rules, sequence analysis, and visualization.

Online Analytical Processing (OLAP)

On-Line Analytical Processing (OLAP) is a technology which encompasses applications requiring a multidimensional and hierarchical view of data. OLAP applications often require fast response time to complex grouping/aggregation queries on enormous quantities of data. Commercial relational database management systems use mainly multiple one-dimensional indexes to process OLAP queries that restrict multiple dimensions. However, in many cases multidimensional access methods outperform one-dimensional indexing methods (Theodoratos & Tsois, 2003). OLAP is an important component of business intelligence. OLAP has gained popularity as a method to support decision making in situations where raw data on measures such as sales or profit needs to be analyzed at different levels of statistical aggregation. In OLAP, queries are made against structures called OLAP cubes. The design of a cube is based on knowledge of the application area and the types of queries the users are expected to generate.

As commercial use of OLAP technology gains in sophistication, OLAP cube design techniques will become more important because of the increased frequency with which an enterprise will require the redesign of its OLAP. There are many reasons for this phenomenon. In practice, companies may often change their organizations. Thus, realignment of data warehouse schemata is needed quite often. Especially, dimensions and their hierarchies can change even regularly. For example, users may also want to speculate about the effects of changing the way their company has arranged its organization. Also, there may be needs to analyze data in ways which were not anticipated at the time the OLAP cubes were designed.

It is common practice for some OLAP users to frequently reorganize their OLAP cubes even though the nature and source of the underlying raw data has not changed (Niemi, Nummenmaa, & Thanisch, 2003). OLAP provides multidimensional, summarized views of business data and is used for reporting, analysis, modeling and planning for optimizing the business. Reporting software generates aggregated views of data to keep the management informed about the state of their business (Ranjan, 2009). Facts are usually measures of business processes of some kind (e.g., how many products are sold, how many patients are treated, how long something takes, etc.), and dimensions represent the different ways in which the data can be viewed and sorted (e.g., according to time, store, customer, product, etc.) (Pardillo, Mazon, & Trujillo, 2010). Common operations of OLAP can be listed as below (Volitich, 2008):

- **Slice and Dice:** Slicing refers to the ability to combine and re-combine the dimensions to view different slices of the information. The dice operation is to slice a data cube on more than two dimensions. Analysis across several dimensions and many categories of data items are used to uncover business behavior and rules. Analysts use this operation to answer the subsequent business question.

- **Drill Down/Up:** Specific technique in which the analyst navigates among different levels of data.
    - Up mean to move to less detailed information.
    - Down mean to move to more detailed information.
- **Pivot:** This technique changes dimensional orientation of report. For example, changing the dimensions from columns in row and vice versa of the table.
- **Nesting:** Display data dimension one dimension within another (Kocbek & Juric, 2010).

Predictive Analytics

Business predictive analytics model analyze historical events and data with goals to locate patterns of subtle data in relation to the surroundings which uses data in a dependent and independent manner. Prediction models often perform real time transactions and calculations to introduction data-driven decisions which lead to efficient and effective business (Indart, 2006). Business success depends on being able to understand and analyze the future and then to take correct actions where necessary. Business analytics and managers must be able to predict the future scenarios well enough to prepare plans in order to seize opportunities, neutralize threads, and mitigate risks. Predictive analytics here plays an essential role and helps to plan day-to-day operations in business. Predictive analytics, using obtained information about data from data warehouses with help of mathematical algorithm, predicts the trend of business processes. The results of predictive analytics are used to identify patterns, trends and forecast business activity flow.

The accuracy of forecasts depends on the complexity of data interdependence (Kocbek & Juric, 2010). Increasing the number of variables results in a less accurate forecast (Volitich, 2008). Methods and algorithms for predictive trends include; Machine learning techniques (Rough set theory, Neural networks, Naïve Bayes, K-nearest neighbors, Genetic algorithm, Support Vector Machines); Regression techniques (Linear Regression Model); Discrete choice models (Logistic regression, Probit regression, Multinomial logistic regression); Time series model; Classification and regression trees; Multivariate adaptive regression spines; Survival or duration analysis.

Process Mining

Process mining is applicable to a wide range of information systems. There are different Process Aware Information systems which produce event logs (Van der alst et.al., 2006). The goal of process mining is to extract information (e.g., process models) from these logs. Process mining has proven to be a valuable approach that provides new and objective insights into the way business processes are actually conducted within organizations. Taking a set of real executions as the starting point, these techniques attempt to extract non-trivial and useful process information from various perspectives, such as control flow, data flow, organizational structures, and performance characteristics. A common mining XML (MXML) log format was defined in to enable researchers and practitioners to share their logs in a standardized way. However, while process mining has reached a certain level of maturity and has been used in a variety of real-life case studies, a common framework to evaluate process mining results is still lacking. There is the need for a concrete framework that enables (a) process mining researchers to compare the performance of their algorithms, and (b) end users to evaluate the validity of their process mining results (Rozinat et al., 2007).

Process mining addresses the problem which most "process owners" have regarding very limited information about what is actually occurring in their organization. In practice, there is often a significant gap between what is prescribed or supposed to happen, and what actually takes place. Only a concise assessment of the organizational reality, which process mining strives to deliver, can help in verifying process models, and ultimately be used in a process redesign effort (Van der alst et al., 2006).

Text Mining

Text mining or Knowledge Discovery from Text (KDT) for the first time mentioned in Feldman and Dagan (1995) deals with the machine supported analysis of text. It uses techniques from information retrieval, information extraction, as well as Natural Language Processing (NLP) and connects them with the algorithms and methods of KDD, data mining, machine learning and statistics. Thus, one selects a similar procedure as with the KDD process, whereby not data in general, but text documents are in focus of the analysis (Hotho, Nürnberger, & Paass, 2005). With the widespread inclusion of documents, especially text, in business systems, business executives cannot get useful details from the large collection of unstructured and semi structured written materials based on natural languages within our traditional BI systems. It is the right time to develop the powerful tool to expand the scope of BI to gain more competitive advantages for business. Text mining is a variation of data mining and is a relatively new discipline. Like many new research areas, it is difficult to provide a generally agree-upon definition. Commonly, text mining is the discovery by computer of previously unknown knowledge in text by automatically extracting information from different written resources.

Noticeably, not like finding the ore from huge amount of rocks, the goal of text mining is to extract new, never-before encountered information, such as finding overall trends in textual data and detecting potential frauds (Gao, Chang, & Han, 2009). Text mining is the technology to extract knowledge from structured repositories and document warehouse enabling business intelligence operations. It is built on a number of techniques such as Clustering, Natural Language Processing/ Computational Linguistics, Categorization, and Information Retrieval Pattern Recognition.

Complex Event Processing

Complex Event Processing (CEP) (Luckham, 2002) provides an effective solution to process event streams in real time for today's dynamic business environment. Compared to the delayed-analysis methods used traditionally in relational databases, CEP involves continuous processing and analysis of high-volume and high-speed data streams such as RFID data. It also correlates distributed data to detect and respond to business-critical situations in real time. Thus, CEP helps to deal with a variety of data streams to deliver actionable information (Yao, Chu, & Li, 2011). CEP provides a new paradigm to collect and process data flowing through an organization in real time to automate and accelerate decision cycles while facilitating an agile approach to keep the underlying business logic adaptable to changing business requirements. Until today, the main research focus in CEP has been devoted to operational issues such as performance, query and rule implementations, event type models, or event correlation (Roth, Schiefer, Obweger, & Rozsnyai, 2010).

THE USE OF BI SOLUTIONS IN GLOBAL ORGANIZATIONS

Globalization has completely altered the way in which the world operates. Additionally, over the past few decades advancements in information technology have had a profound impact on the global landscape as well as on the progression of globalization. Innovation in information technology has been a major driving force behind globalization and that information technology has now become a key component of a corporation's global business strategy (Lawlor, 2007). Advances in technology are particularly important in driving market globalization (Cavusgil, Knight, & Riesenberger, 2008). According to Porter (1985), a firm belonging to the global category is one whose competitive position in one country is significantly affected by its position in other countries. The global firm targets the international market without distinguishing national or political boundaries. Thus, it ranks high on market integration. Its structural considerations also require high value-chain configuration and value-chain coordination.

Centralization is an integral part of this configuration because all foreign operations are controlled by the parent corporation. However, in global companies, decision-making is fairly decentralized (Duggal, 2002). Geographically distant country subsidiaries of a multinational company can be interconnected via intranets, facilitating the instant sharing of data, information, and experience across the firm's operations worldwide. The improvements in the era of technology help the flow of information and knowledge throughout the firm's worldwide operations. In addition, managers can make instant changes to strategies and tactics in the firm's value chain activities. The firm can respond in real time environmental changes and customer demands in market conditions almost as quickly as they occur (Cavusgil, Knight, & Riesenberger, 2008).

The increase of information technology has affected management greatly. All management process and management functions (e.g., planning, organizing, leading, and controlling) include making decisions. The marketing managers must decide what price to charge for a product, what distribution channels to use, and what promotional messages to emphasize. The manufacturing managers must decide how much of a product to make and how to make it. The purchasing manager must decide from whom to purchase inputs and what inventory of inputs to hold. The human relations manager must decide how much employees should be paid, how they should be trained, and what benefits they should be given. Top managers must decide how to allocate scarce financial resources among competing global projects, how best to structure and control the organization and what business level strategy the organization should be pursuing (George & Jones, 2006). IT managers should better understand the global implications of work in ethical, historical, sociological, technical, and political dimensions to make better and more profitable decisions (Duggal, 2002).

Information technology also eliminates some middle management functions and thus flattens organization structures (Nickels, McHugh, & McHugh, 2010). Rapid advances in information technology have been associated with a delayering (flattening) of the organizational hierarchy and move toward greater decentralization and horizontal information flows within organizations. By electronically providing managers with high-quality, timely, relevant and relatively complete information, modern management information systems have reduced the need for tall management hierarchies (George & Jones, 2006).

MIS and business solution techniques support managers during their managerial activities. MIS is an organized method for providing past, present, and projected information on internal operations, as well as external intelligence to support decision making (Boone & Kurtz, 2003). Taking into consideration managers must handle large amounts of data and information coming from the environment, it is possible to realize the importance of meaningful and useful data. Managers need information for three reasons: to make effective decisions, to control the activities of the organization, and to coordinate the activities of the organization. Multinational organizations must use global information systems which are systems that serve organizations and individuals in multiple countries. These organizations might unify policies throughout the organization unlike organizations that operate in a single country. Multinational organizations have the burden of ensuring their information systems and information flowing through the systems conforms with laws, cultures, standards, and any other factors which are specific to countries and regions (Oz, 2009).

In this case, the use of information technology in organizations has become essential, especially for global organizations competing in a challenging environment with various branches. Top managers of global organizations always operate in an environment where they compete with other organizations for scarce and valuable resources. Today's managers recognize that organizations exist and compete in a truly global market. Managers regard the global environment a source of important opportunities and threats that they must respond to (George & Jones, 2006). Additionally, to achieve control over any organizational activity, managers must have information. BI and MIS are used to control a variety of operations within organizations. Coordinating department and divisional activities to achieve organizational goals is another basic task of management. Coordination problems that managers face in managing their global supply chains to take advantage of national differences in the costs of products continue to increase.

To contend with global coordination problems, managers have been adopting sophisticated BI methods which help them to coordinate the flow of materials, semi-finished goods, and finished products throughout the world (George & Jones, 2006). With businesses utilizing new work flow software and with the development of transmission protocols, companies were well on their way to becoming faster, more effective, and more cost efficient. Along with this quickening of business processes, companies were now able to communicate with businesses in other countries because they knew they were using the same standards of transmission as their partners and this helped immensely in the progression of globalization (Lawlor, 2007).

The various BI techniques mentioned above are used in global organizations to coordinate and to control their activities among different branches and boundaries. The typical OLAP applications are used in business reporting for marketing, sales, business process management, forecasting, financial reporting and etc. (Kocbek & Juric, 2010). Predictive Analytics techniques are used in risk management, retail, insurance, fraud detection, financial services, healthcare, marketing, customer relationship management, telecommunications, customer retention, and cross-selling. Process mining can be used in the areas such as classical Workflow Management Systems (WMS), Enterprise Resource Planning (ERP), Case Handling Systems, Customer Relationship Management (CRM) systems, Hospital Information Systems, Supply Chain Management (SCM) Systems, and Business-to-Business (B2B).

Typically, these systems provide very detailed information about the activities that have been executed. Some of the fields in which text mining is used are security, biomedical sciences, social media monitoring, marketing, market segmentation, sentiment analysis, e-discovery, records management, and fraud detection. CEP is used in areas such as RFID Applications, Supply Chain Management, Business Activity Monitoring, Event Processing in Workflows, Fraud Detection, Telecommunications, Health Monitoring, Financial Trading, and Transportation. There are many successful applications of data mining process in many different areas such as market basket analysis, customer churn, customer retention, market segmentation, interactive marketing, direct marketing, trend analysis, cross-selling, fraud detection, and others. All of these BI techniques assist managers and facilitate the decision making process, especially in global organizations.

There are additional examples of global organizations which use various BI techniques effectively. The mobile phone company, Vodafone, needed to make better decisions based on real-time knowledge of its market, customers and competitors. It became essential for Vodafone to make a wholesale shift to analytical marketing using BI which could rapidly provide fact-based decision support. The goal was to help the company deliver the right message to the appropriate customers when they wanted it using the preferred channel. First, the company formed a customer knowledge and analysis department to conduct analysis, modeling market research, and competitive intelligence. The company implemented an enterprise data warehouse to obtain a single view of all of the information in the organization and also developed its analytical team. With this system, Vodafone's sales and marketing department are now able to perform analysis and achieve better customer offer optimization, campaign effectiveness analysis and customer service The most important benefit of the system is that the analysts can spend more time generating insights than managing data. The system also provides better information to decision makers to support the decision making process (Turban, Sharda, & Delen, 2011).

The Coca-Cola Company is a good example in the soft drink industry for global companies that employ BI solutions successfully. Coca-Cola wanted to develop a way to increase sales and find a cheaper way to test new products. In 2009, the company installed new self-serve soft drink dispensers with RFID technology in selected fast food restaurants. The new dispensers with almost 30 flavor cartridges enabled customers to create 100 different drinks. Customers used the dispensers by choosing a brand and flavoring options on the dispenser's LCD panel which runs on the Windows CE operating system. The RFID technology allowed Coca-Cola to test new drink flavor and concepts, observe what flavors and combinations customers choose, identify regional preferences and keep track of the amounts that customers drink. With this system, the company became able to use the flavors in multiple combinations and see the most popular combinations. Also, this process saved the company money (Turban, Sharda, & Delen, 2011).

Another example is Volkswagen AG in the automobile industry. The company uses BI to track, understand, and manage data in every department-from finance, production, and development, to research, sales and marketing, and purchasing. Users at all levels of the organization access supplier and customer reports relating to online requests and negotiations, vehicle launches, and vehicle capacity management and tracking. Another company using BI solutions successfully is Shell Services International in oil industry. With its BI solution, Shell was able to access information about revenues between fuel and non-fuel business. Understanding that 20% of their products were delivering 80% of their sales, Shell made significant improvements in margin and turnover. They also negotiated better deals with suppliers and improved product master file management, which helped them reduce working capital.

British Airways can be given as an example in the airline industry. Various company managers in British Airways suspected the carrier was suffering from a high degree of ticket fraud. To address this problem, the company rolled out BI. Analyzed the problem, the managers discovered that ticket fraud was not an issue at all. Instead, they discovered data quality issues or process problems. The company estimates their BI deployment has resulted in around US$100 million in cost savings and new revenues for the airline. In fast food industry, Pizza Hut significantly boosted sales revenue by using BI solutions. Based on 20 years of accumulated data on consumers and sales transactions, Pizza Hut discovered what kind pizza consumers prefer, how their preference varies on demographics, what kind of coupons they use, and the historical sales trends. Using BI tools to forecast its future sales, it formulated marketing strategies to better influence customers (Murugesan, 2010).

It is possible to increase the number of company examples that use BI solutions effectively in the global context. We have given only a few global company examples here in order to focus on the use and benefits of BI solutions in global organizations.

FUTURE RESEARCH DIRECTIONS

This chapter provides insights to this book in the context of the technological improvements and their use in organizations. Information technology has an important impact in decision making processes of all organizations especially in the global arena. MIS and BI techniques have been widely used in business functions. Various BI techniques support managers to make decisions in different levels of the organization and to facilitate this decision making process by providing useful and hidden information and judgment to managers. Especially in global organizations, this process is more difficult than in other firms which only have local operations. Organizations which pursue their activities across borders in various countries with different branches should design an effective system for coordinating and controlling these activities.

In this chapter, the concept of BI has been explained and its techniques are analyzed in the context of global organizations and their functions consistent with the theme of this book. As future research directions, it is possible to say MIS and BI will be more widely used in organizations and their importance will increase in parallel with their usage. In particular, empirical research should be conducted to reveal the usage of these techniques and their effectiveness in global organizations taking into account the managerial functions. This will permit recommendations to be developed to improve usage of these systems better in the future.

CONCLUSION

Organizations must pursue their activities under the influence of many environmental factors. Technological factors are one of the important developments facing organizations. With the effect of globalization and technological developments, organizations must effectively handle much data flow. Information systems facilitate the data keeping and decision making processes within organizations. Parallel to this thought, BI techniques and their use in global and large scale organizations are investigated in this study. Various BI techniques are used by different management levels of organizations to manage their activities and to make decisions. BI techniques have an importance for especially global organizations which have various branches overseas to control and coordinate their activities. Each of these BI techniques has advantages compared to each other according to the needs of organizations. A few examples from global companies that employ BI solutions effectively are given in the paper. We can see that these companies use various BI techniques and solutions in different business functions to increase their profits, facilitate their decision making processes, and coordinate their functions in the global context.

REFERENCES

Alnoukari, M. (2009). Using business intelligence solutions for achieving organization's strategy: Arab International University case study. *Internetworking Indonesia Journal*, *1*(2), 11–15.

Bal, M., Bal, Y., & Demirhan, A. (2011). Creating competitive advantage by using data mining technique as an innovative method for decision making process in business. *International Journal of Online Marketing*, *1*(3), 38–45. doi:10.4018/ijom.2011070104.

Bal, Y., Bal, M., Demirhan, A., & Bozkurt, S. (2011). A new paradigm in decision making process in business: Using soft computing methods. In *Proceedings of 2nd World Conference on Information Technology*. Antalya, Turkey.

Biere, M. (2003). *Business Intelligence for the Enterprise*. New York: Pearson Education.

Boone, L. E., & Kurtz, D. L. (2003). *Contemporary Business*. New York: Thomson Western Publishing.

Cavusgil, S. T., Knight, G., & Riesenberger, J. R. (2008). *International Business: Strategy, Management and the New Realities*. Upper Saddle River, NJ: Prentice Hall.

Curtis, G., & Cobham, D. (2002). *Business Information Systems: Analysis, Design and Practice* (4th ed.). Upper Saddle River, NJ: Prentice Hall.

Daft, R. L. (2008). *New Era of Management* (2nd ed.). New York: Thomson South Western Publishing.

Duggal, S. M. (2002). Global information technology management. *Informing Science*, 397–406.

Fayyad, U. M., Piatetsky-Shapiro, G., Smyth, P., & Uthurasamy, R. (1996). *Advances in Knowledge Discovery and Data Mining*. Palo Alto, CA: AAAI Press.

Feldman, R., & Dagan, I. (1995). Kdt-knowledge discovery in texts. In U.M. Fayyad & R. Uthurusamy (Eds.), *Proceedings of the 1st International Conference on Knowledge Discovery* (pp.112-117). Palo Alto, CA: AAAI Press.

Gao, L., Chang, E., & Han, S. (2005). Powerful tool to expand business intelligence: Text mining. *Transactions on Enformatika. Systems Sciences and Engineering-ESSE*, *8*, 110–115.

George, J. M., & Jones, G. R. (2006). *Contemporary Management* (4th ed.). New York: McGraw Hill.

Ghazanfari, M., Jafari, M., & Rouhani, S. (2011). A tool to evaluate the business intelligence of enterprise systems. *Scientia Iranica*, *18*(6), 1579–1590. doi:10.1016/j.scient.2011.11.011.

Haag, S., & Cunnings, M. (2008). *Management Information Systems for the Information Age*. New York: McGraw Hill.

Han, J., & Kamber, M. (2001). *Data Mining: Concepts and Techniques*. San Francisco, CA: Morgan Kaufmann Publishers.

Hotho, A., Nürnberger, A., & Paass, G. A. (2005). Brief survey of text mining. *GCDV Journal of Computational Linguistics and Language Technology*, *20*(1), 19–62.

Indart, B. (2006). Operationalizing business intelligence - Turning insight into action. *Business Intelligence Journal*, *11*(2), 35–38.

Kocbek, A., & Juric, M. B. (2010). Using advanced business intelligence methods in business process management. Retrieved June 12, 2012, from http://ailab.ijs.si/dunja/SiKDD2010/Papers/Kocbek_Final.pdf

Laudon, K. C., & Laudon, J. P. (2009). *Essentials of Management Information Systems* (8th ed.). New York: Prentice Hall.

Lawlor, B.R. (2007). *The Age of Globalization: Impact of Information Technology on Global Business Strategies*. Senior captone project.

Luckham, D. (2002). *The Power of Events: An Introduction to Complex Event Processing in Distributed Systems*. Berlin, Germany: Springer Verlag.

Murugesan, S. (2010). *Intelligence and value*. Retrieved on October 21, 2012, from http://alinement.net/component /content/ article/6-governance/62-intelligence-a-value

Nickels, W. G., McHugh, J. M., & McHugh, S. M. (2010). *Understanding Business* (9th ed.). New York: McGraw Hill.

Niemi, T., Nummenmaa, J., & Thanisch, P. (2003). Normalising OLAP cubes for controlling sparsity. *Data & Knowledge Engineering*, *46*, 317–343. doi:10.1016/S0169-023X(03)00035-1.

Oz, E. (2009). *Management Information Systems* (6th ed.). Boston, MA: Thomson Publishing.

Pardillo, J., Mazon, J. N., & Trujillo, J. (2010). Extending OCL for OLAP querying on conceptual multidimensional models of data warehouses. *Information Sciences*, *180*, 584–601. doi:10.1016/j.ins.2009.11.006.

Porter, M. (1985). *Competitive Advantage: Creating and Sustaining Superior Performance*. New York: Free Press.

Ranjan, J. (2009). Business ıntelligence: Concepts, components, techniques and benefits. *Journal of Theoretical and Applied Information Technology*, *9*(1), 60–70.

Roth, H., Schiefer, J., Obweger, H., & Rozsnyai, S. (2010). Event data warehousing for complex event processing. In P. Loucopoulos & J.L. Cavavero (Eds.), *Proceedings of the 4th IEEE International Conference on Research Challenges in Information Science* (pp.203-212). IEEE.

Rozinat, A., Alves de Medeiros, A. K., Günther, C. W., Weijters, A. J. M. M., & Van der Alst, W. M. P. (2007). Towards on evaluation framework for process mining algorithm. *BPM Center Report, BPM-07-06, Eindhoven University of Technology*. Retrieved June 10, 2012, from http://www.process-mining.org/_media/publications/bpm-07-06.pdf

Sabherwal, R., & Fernandez, I. B. (2010). *Business Intelligence: Practices, Technologies and Management*. Hoboken, NJ: John Wiley and Sons.

Sever, H., & Oğuz, B. (2003). *Veri Tabanlarında Bilgi Keşfine Formel Bir Yaklaşım: Kısım II-Eşleştirme Sorgularının Biçimsel Kavram Analizi ile Modellenmesi* (pp. 15–44). Bilgi Dünyası.

Stackowiak, R., Rayman, J., & Greenwald, R. (2007). *Oracle Data Warehousing and Business Intelligence Solutions*. Indianapolis, IN: Wiley Publishing.

Theodoratos, D., & Tsois, A. (2003). Processing OLAP queries in hierarchically clustered databases. *Data & Knowledge Engineering*, *45*, 205–224. doi:10.1016/S0169-023X(02)00180-5.

Thierauf, R. J. (2001). *Effective Business Intelligence Systems*. New York: Greenwood Publishing.

Turban, E., Sharda, R., & Delen, D. (2011). *Decision Support and Business Intelligence Systems*. Upper Saddle River, NJ: Pearson.

Van der Alst, W. M. P., Rubin, V., Van Dongen, B. F., Kindler, E., & Günther, C. W. (2006). Process mining: A two-step approach using transition systems and regions. *BPM Center Report, BPM-06-30, Eindhoven University of Technology*. Retrieved June 10, 2012, from http://wwwis.win.tue.nl/~wvdaalst/BPMcenter/reports/2006/BPM-06-30.pdf

Vercellis, C. (2009). *Business intelligence: Data mining and optimization for decision making*. London, UK: John Wiley and Sons.

Vinekar, V.T., & James, T.C., & Chennamaneni. (2009). The ınteraction of business ıntelliegence and knowledge management in organizational decision making. *Journal of International Technology and Information Management*, *18*(2), 143–159.

Volitich, D. (2008). *IBM Cognos 8: Business Intelligence The Official Guide*. New York: Mc Graw Hill.

Yao, W., Chu, C. H., & Li, Z. (2011). Leveraging complex event processing for smart hospitals Using RFID. *Journal of Network and Computer Applications*, *34*, 799–810. doi:10.1016/j.jnca.2010.04.020.

Zeng, L., Xu, L., Shi, Z., & Wang, M. (2006). Techniques, process and enterprise solutions of business ıntelligence. In *Proceedings of the IEEE International Conference on Systems, Man and Cybernetics* (pp.4722-4726). IEEE.

ADDITIONAL READING

Baltzan, P. (2011). *Business driven information systems*. New York: Mc Graw Hill.

Brown, C. V., DeHayes, D. W., Hoffer, J. A., Martin, E. W., & Perkins, W. (2012). *Managing information technology* (7th ed.). Upper Saddle River, NJ: Pearson Education.

Chen, Z. (2000). *Computational intelligence for decision support*. Boca Raton, CA: CRC Press.

Curtis, G., & Cobham, D. (2002). *Business information systems: Analysis, design and practice* (4th ed.). London: Pearson Education.

Gupta, J. N. D., Forgionne, G. A., & Mora, M. (Eds.). (2010). *Intelligent decision-making support systems: Foundations, applications and challenges*. Berlin, Germany: Springer Verlag.

Heaton, J. (2012). *Business intelligence: A project lifecycle approach using Oracle technology cookbook*. Birmingham, UK: Packt Publishing.

Hsu, K. C., & Li, M. Z. (2011). Techniques for finding similarity knowledge in OLAP reports. *Expert Systems with Applications*, *38*, 3743–3756. doi:10.1016/j.eswa.2010.09.033.

Inmon, W. H., & Nesavich, A. (2007). *Tapping into unstructured data: İntegrating unstructured data and textual analytic into business intelligence*. Boston, MA: Prentice Hall.

Jans, M., Van der Werf, J. M., Lybaert, N., & Vanhoof, K. (2011). A business process mining application for internal transction fraud mitigation. *Expert Systems with Applications*, *38*, 13351–13359. doi:10.1016/j.eswa.2011.04.159.

Kapoor, B. (2010). Business intelligence and its use for human resource management. *The Journal of Human Resource and Adult Learning*, *6*(2), 21–30.

Laursen, G. H. N., & Thorlund, J. (2010). *Business analytics for managers: Taking business intelligence beyond reporting*. Hoboken, NJ: John Wiley and Sons.

Magal, S. R., & Ward, J. (2009). *Essentials of business processes and information systems*. Hoboken, NJ: John Wiley and Sons.

Matsatsihis, N. F., & Siskos, Y. (2002). *Intelligent support systems for marketing decisions*. Boston, MA: Kluwer Academic Publishers.

Miller, G. J., Brautigan, D., & Gerlach, S. V. (2006). *Business intelligence competency centers: A team approach to maximizing competitive advantage*. Hoboken, NJ: John Wiley and Sons.

O'Brien, J., & Marakas, G. (2010). *Management information systems*. New York: McGraw Hill.

Sauter, V. L. (2010). *Decision support systems for business intelligence*. Hoboken, NJ: John Wiley and Sons.

Shmueli, G., Patel, N. R., & Bruce, P. C. (2010). *Data mining for business intelligence: Concepts, techniques and applications in Microsoft Office Excel with XLMiner*. Hoboken, NJ: John Wiley and Sons.

Tsiptsis, K., & Charianopoulos, A. (2009). *Data mining techniques in CRM: İnside customer segmentation*. London: John Wiley and Sons.

Turban, E., Sharda, R., & Delen, D. (2010). *Decision support and business intelligence systems* (9th ed.). New York: Prentice Hall.

Turban, E., Sharda, R., Delen, D., & King, D. (2010). *Business intelligence: A managerial approach* (2nd ed.). New York: Prentice Hall.

Van der Aaalst & Weijters, A.J.M.M. (2004). Process mining: A research agenda. *Computers in Industry*, *53*, 231–244. doi:10.1016/j.compind.2003.10.001.

Wu, J., & Coggeshall, S. (2012). *Foundations of predictive analytics*. Boca Raton, CA: CRC Press.

Chapter 4
Foreign Market Entry Mode Choice:
Internal and External Perspectives

Ho Yin Wong
Deakin University, Australia

ABSTRACT

The purpose of this chapter is to empirically examine firms' internal and external factors that can affect their foreign market mode choice. The model is comprised of internal factors such as control, domestic business experience, and industry type; and external factors in terms of culture of foreign markets and intensity of competition. A mail-out survey to Australian firms involved in international business generated 315 useful responses. The hypotheses were tested using direct logistic regression analysis. Among the five variables, industry type, domestic business experience, and intensity of competition were found statistically significant. While industry type and domestic business experience encourage non-export mode, intensity of competition favours export mode. The major contributions of this study are the discovery of a variable, domestic business experience that is new in the literature; and the reinforcement of the importance of examining both internal and external factors when making a foreign market entry mode choice.

INTRODUCTION

When firms enter international markets, two groupings of foreign market entry modes can be identified; namely, exporting and non-exporting. With export entry modes, a firm's products are manufactured in the home country or a third country, and then sent to the host country in a direct or indirect manner. Direct exports involve the firm performing various export tasks such as market research and logistics. Goods are then sold in overseas markets by agents or distributors.

DOI: 10.4018/978-1-4666-3966-9.ch004

Contrary to direct export, indirect export mode involves a firm selling overseas using export houses or trading firms to carry out these tasks. Non-export mode includes a range of deployment other than exporting, such as licensing, franchising, strategic alliances, and foreign direct investment. This mode is different from the export mode in a sense that some forms of knowledge transfer and investments are involved.

Foreign market entry mode choice plays an important role in global business and is widely researched without reaching a consensus. The challenge continues as to rationalisation of foreign market entry mode choice. Various models have been used to explain the factors that affect foreign market entry mode choice. Dunning's eclectic paradigm (1977; 1988; 1995) provides an integrative framework of the determinants of foreign market entry modes. The paradigm suggests that three independent variables of eclectic paradigm; ownership, internalization, and location advantages (OLI) are the key determinants in explaining why multinational firms expand their global businesses. The eclectic paradigm can explain why multinational firms expand their global operations, but it falls short in providing insights with regard to exactly what factors are involved to achieve one or more of these three advantages (Dunning, 2001), or whether the paradigm equally applies to firms in the service industry and small to medium sized companies (Wong & Merrilees, 2009a).

Another model in the existing literature, mainly contributed by Scandinavian scholars, is the Uppsala model (Johanson & Vahlne, 1990; Johanson & Vahlne, 1977; 2006; Johanson & Wiedersheim-Paul, 1975). The model proposes internationalisation is a process in which global firms increase their levels of international involvement as they gather more information and gain more knowledge about the foreign markets. It is a combination of the internationalisation theory and internalisation theory (Fina & Rugman, 1996). However, this model has been critiqued as lacking in generalisability and statistical representativeness, and as overlooking strategic factors.

To overcome the shortcoming of the above-mentioned two models, some researchers study the impact of strategic variables on the foreign market entry mode choice (Hill, Hwang, & Kim, 1990; Kim & Hwang, 1992; Wong & Merrilees, 2009a). This stream focuses upon the importance of strategic factors, rather than resource commitment or solely economic benefits, in foreign market entry mode choice.

While all three schools of thought have contributed literature on foreign market entry mode choice, research gaps still exist such as foreign cultural impacts and domestic business experience. This study is expected to provide empirical evidence to fill in these research gaps. The study's general question is, "What are the internal and external factors that affect foreign market entry mode choice?" The direction of this study is to examine firms' internal and external factors that can affect foreign market entry choice by: (1) critically reviewing the literature of foreign market entry choice, (2) identifying research gaps in the existing literature, (3) developing hypotheses, and (4) conducting an empirical survey to test the hypotheses.

BACKGROUND

Two major theoretical perspectives guide this study; resources and capabilities, and institutional perspectives. The resources and capabilities perspective emphasises the internal issues of the firms when making strategic decisions, while the institutional perspective stresses that firms' international marketing decisions depend on the elements of the external country environment such as culture (Wong & Merrilees, 2009a). These two theoretical perspectives have been used to understand the foreign market entry mode choice in the literature (Driscoll & Paliwoda, 1997; Dunning, 2001; Wong & Merrilees, 2009a). Literature review in the next section based on these two theoretical perspectives delineates the reasons for including these variables in the model for testing.

LITERATURE REVIEW

Internal Factors: Control

The concept of control in foreign market entry mode is concerned with having strategic and operational decision-making authority (Hill et al., 1990). In the foreign market entry mode choice literature, control plays an important role because it is a means of maximizing economic efficiency and return on investment in international markets (Anderson & Gatignon, 1986; Dunning, 1988).

Control allows firms to safeguard supplies of essential inputs to the production process, co-ordinate activities, ensure the quality of end products, and influence the logistical and marketing activities for the product in the target foreign market (Anderson & Gatignon, 1986; Dunning, 1988). Firms also make use of various levels of control for reduction of resource commitment with an aim to reducing some forms of risk while increasing their returns. Therefore, focusing on control is consistent with the classical risk-adjusted return perspective (Anderson & Gatignon, 1986). In conclusion, firms can determine their own fate about their branding activities if they maintain the decision-making control.

Empirically, a number of studies have analysed the firm performance in terms of different market entry modes (Nitsch, Beamish, & Makino, 1996; Pan & Chi, 1999; Simmonds, 1990; Wilson, 2001; Woodcock, Beamish, & Makino, 1994). Other works have tried to rationalise the choice of foreign market entry mode (Driscoll & Paliwoda, 1997; Erramilli & Rao, 1993; Gatignon & Anderson, 1988). The general consensus of the empirical works suggests that firms tend to choose non-export mode when control of operation is considered as an important factor.

Internal Factors: Experience

Experience refers to the extent to which a firm has been involved in its international operation (Erramilli, 1991; Klein, Frazier, & Roth, 1990), and include experience gained from the operation in a particular country or from the operation in the international environment in general. International experience of managers and thus of the firm plays an important role in entry mode choice (Benito & Gripsrud, 1992; Dunning, 1981). According to Stopford and Wells (1972), entry mode decision depends on the international experience of the company. Buckley and Casson (1985) argue that experience reduces the cost and uncertainty of serving a market and in turn increases the probability of firms committing resources to foreign market. Johanson and Vahlne (1977) assert uncertainty in international markets is reduced through actual operations in foreign markets, that is experiential knowledge, rather than through the acquisition of objective knowledge. Firms can accumulate new knowledge through network collaboration by drawing upon experiences from various parties involved in the collaboration (Liu & Hart, 2011). Inexperienced firms have been found to overstate the risks and costs of operating internationally and to understate the returns generated from international operation (Caves, 1982; Cavusgil & Nevin, 1981; Davidson, 1980). Consequently, these firms prefer to use exporting mode rather than investment entry mode until their accumulated experience grows to a certain level that reduces their internal uncertainty justifying shifting to entry mode other than exporting. In general, it is direct experience with international markets that increases the likelihood of committing a large amount of resources to foreign markets.

Local market knowledge transfer takes place even though it is a complicated process (Lord & Ranft, 2000). By using an incremental approach, Japanese firms have been found to build capabilities through experience gained from overseas markets (Chang, 1995; Lin, 2000). However, some studies find that experience is not a statistically significant factor in entry mode decisions (Kogut & Singh, 1988; Sharma & Johanson, 1987; Wong & Merrilees, 2009a). A major gap exists in the market entry literature with respect to experience. Studies have focused solely on the firms' international experience without looking at experience gathered from domestic operations. No empirical study has examined the impacts of domestic business experience, which is generated from domestic operation and is later utilised in global business venture, on foreign market entry mode choice. Business literature shows that firms' domestic experience affects their momentum towards repeated acquisition in a host country (Collins, Holcomb, Certo, Hitt, & Lester, 2009) and the timing of entering the foreign markets (Abreu, Mendes, & Santos, 2011). This study is expected to fill this gap in market entry mode choice literature.

Internal Factors: Services Industry

Another internal issue related to market entry model choice is derived from research on the service industry. Internationalisation of service firms differs from that of manufacturing firms due to the unique characteristics of services; namely, intangibility, inseparability, heterogeneity and perishability (Wong & Merrilees, 2009b; Zeithaml, Parasuraman, & Berry, 1985). Empirical findings show that service firms are different from manufacturing firms in choosing market entry mode (Erramilli, 1991; Erramilli & Rao, 1990; 1993; Wong & Merrilees, 2009a). Service firms require less investment in physical assets but more in human capital with the consequence of choosing non-export mode (Wong & Merrilees, 2009a). Service firms following their customers overseas are more likely to choose non-export mode (Erramilli & Rao, 1990). While the empirical findings broadly suggests that service firms tend to choose non-export mode, there is a lack of empirical evidence that includes both cultural and service variables within a logistic regression model.

External Factors: Intensity of Competition

The demand for firms' products and services in international markets is another consideration in deciding market entry mode. The size and growth of host markets have been found to be an important determinant of foreign investment (Khoury, 1979; Terpstra & Yu, 1988; Weinstein, 1977). Dunning (1993) argues that firms seek growth opportunities in international markets when growth in their home markets stagnates or declines. In contrast, some scholars propose that the main reason behind firms' internationalisation is to aggressively take advantage of rapid industry growth in the host country (Ray, 1998). In either case, firms may choose investment mode which provides greater long term profitability to them or the opportunity to establish long term market presence (Agarwal & Ramaswami, 1992).

Prices of the firms' products and services depend on the competitors' activities and the demand for the products and services in the overseas marketplace. From the point of view of strategic management, Harrigan (1985a; 1985b) suggests firms tend not to get involved in markets where the intensity of competition is high due to such a markets being less profitable. Therefore, firms opt to adopt exporting and licensing in a competitive market. However, firms entering a new oligopolistic or monopolistic market require sole ownership to compete effectively against the dominant firms (Root, 1994). In summary, firms have higher incentive to commit more resources to attractive markets, with the exception of cases exhibiting the strategic needs mentioned above.

Kim and Hwang (1992) empirically test the effects of demand and competitive conditions on firms' mode choice decisions and find that demand uncertainty and competitive intensity are not deterministic in influencing the choice of entry mode. However, a contradictory result, wherein firms facing intensity of competition tend to choose non-export mode has been presented (Wong & Merrilees, 2009a). The contradictory empirical results call for further study on the effect of intensity of competition on market entry mode choice.

External Factors: Socio-Cultural Conditions

Johanson and Vahlne (1977) propose that more economic interaction occurs between socio-culturally similar countries than between socio-culturally dissimilar countries. Socio-culturally similarity can be in the form of business and management practices, a common or similar language and belief, and cultural characteristics. Cultural characteristics are considered as the sum total of knowledge, beliefs, art, morals, laws and customs, and any other capabilities and baits acquired by humans as a member of society (Wertsch, 1985). Culture can be classified in four categories: power distance, individualism, masculinity/femininity, and uncertainty avoidance (Hofstede, 1980). Power distance is concerned with the attitude of the culture toward inequalities within a society. Individualism represents the extent of interdependence a society maintains among its members. Masculinity/femininity states the polar opposites of the dominant values in a society; masculinity driven by success and femininity concerning with caring for others. Uncertainty avoidance is an indication of how a society deals with the uncertainty of the future.

Australia scored low on power distance, high on individualism, high on masculinity and medium on uncertainty avoidance. The results are similar to those of the U.K. and US, but signify big differences when comparing to Asian countries such as Hong Kong and Singapore. Hofstede's culture classification has established a theoretical foundation to study the impacts of culture on business decisions such as foreign entry strategy decisions.

Kogut and Singh (1988) suggest cultural differences between home and host countries increase the level of risk in post-acquisition integration with consequence of leading firms to choose less risky entry mode. Their study, using the measurement of a composite index developed by Hofstede (1980), confirm that the greater cultural distance between the investing firm's home country and the host country, the more likely the firm would choose joint venture and green field investment rather than by acquisition. Gatignon and Anderson (1988), using an index developed by Ronen and Shenkar (1985), also posit that high socio-cultural distance relates to a less committed mode of entry. Evans, Mavondo and Bridson (2008) empirically found a negative association between psychic distance and entry strategy. Empirical evidence suggests that Australia managers make market entry mode decisions in different manners to their counterparts in the states and in the U.K. (Wong & Merrilees, 2009a).

In summary, previous studies provide empirical evidence that socio-cultural factors play a significant role in the choice of firm's foreign market entry mode. However, as Mayrhofer (2004, p. 89) suggests, "the influence of this variable (culture) on entry-mode choice is not clearly established in the international management literature." This study proposes to use a more contemporary cultural measure developed by Wong and Merrilees (2007) to examine the its impact on market entry mode choice.

HYPOTHESIS DEVELOPMENT

Managers' experience strongly affects how they make international marketing decisions (Benito & Gripsrud, 1992; Julian, 2003; Wong & Merrilees, 2006) and market entry strategy in particular (Benito & Gripsrud, 1992; Wong & Merrilees, 2009a). Uncertainty of overseas markets can be reduced and costs of running overseas operations can be driven down with firms' growing international experience (Buckley & Casson, 1985). Consequently, firms are more likely to commit more resources to the foreign markets in relation to their level of experience. When firms involve more in foreign markets, they are able to gain experiential knowledge, which reduces uncertainty in international markets (Johanson & Vahlne, 2006). Inexperience firms tend to underestimate the potential profits from international operations and overstate the risks and costs of international involvements with the consequences of choosing export mode (Driscoll & Paliwoda, 1997). Firms prefer export mode until there are justifications of doing otherwise (Wong & Merrilees, 2009a). Firms gain knowledge about doing business from their domestic markets. The knowledge in terms of capability development helps build up confidence with the consequence of choosing non-export mode. Thus,

Hypothesis 1: Firms with more business experience tend to prefer the non-export mode of entry to exporting.

Socio-cultural differences between a firm's home country and the targeted market can create uncertainty that in turn affects the selection of entry mode by the firm. Moreover, socio-cultural dissimilarity discourages investment due to the difficulties involved in the transfer of marketing skills, technology, and human resources to socio-culturally different markets (Davidson, 1980). Firms which are unfamiliar with a foreign market with dissimilar cultures endeavour to acquire large amount of information necessary to bridge the cultural gap between the firms' and foreign country. The perceived risks involved in international operations are lower when cultural backgrounds between the home and host countries are similar (Erramilli, 1996; Pan & Tse, 2000). As a result, firms tend to choose non-export mode in similar cultural environment. Thus,

Hypothesis 2: Firms more familiar with the cultural backgrounds of the host country tend to prefer the non-export mode of entry to exporting.

Different entry modes imply different levels of control of a firm. Foreign direct investment mode of entry are characterised by higher levels of control and exporting mode by lower ones. Control can facilitate firms in organising actions, implementing strategies, and handling any disputes among global operation units if conflicts arise (Dong, Zou, & Taylor, 2008). It can also make the implementation of global marketing strategies easier to integrate and coordinate (Zou & Cavusgil, 2002). With high control mode such as foreign direct investment, firms can oversee their global business strategies to ensure that they are carried out in desirable manners. However, control comes with a high cost. Exercising control can force firms to take responsibility and make decisions in uncertain or unfamiliar environments (Dong et al., 2008) and to commit resources with the consequence of increasing switching costs, reducing the firms' ability to change, and increasing risks (Anderson & Gatignon, 1986). When firms consider controlling their global business activities as not a particularly important issue, they tend to choose export mode. Thus,

Hypothesis 3: Firms with greater intention to control their global business tend to prefer the non-export mode of entry to exporting.

The competitive situations in the global markets can affect firms' strategic decisions. When the competitive situations are intensive in the host markets, firms may need to invest more resources to pass the threshold of and to hold a position in the overseas markets. Profit prospects in intensive competitive markets may not be as bright as those with less competition. Prices may have to be cut to maintain competitive advantage with the consequence of eroding profits (Wong & Merrilees,

2009a). Kim and Hwang (1992) argue that firms prefer market entry mode with low resource commitment in markets with greater intensity of competition. In addition, host governments are equipped with more alternatives, furnishing them with more bargaining power over the global firms in markets with greater competitive intensity (Taylor, Zou, & Osland, 2000). Facing intensive competition in the overseas markets, firms may choose a more conservative entry mode such as exporting. Thus,

Hypothesis 4: Firms tend to prefer the exporting mode of entry to non-exporting when facing intensive competition in the host markets.

The service industry is different from the manufacturing industry due to its unique aspects of in intangibility, perishability, heterogeneity, and inseparability of production and consumption. Owning to these unique aspects, service firms make strategic moves such as market entry mode choice different from manufacturing firms (Wong & Merrilees, 2009a). Resources and capability building between the service firms and manufacturing firms are also different. The former cultivate based more on human resources and less on physical equipment or inventory when internationalising their businesses (Blomstermo & Sharma, 2006; Bouquet, Hebert, & Delios, 2004; Erramilli & Rao, 1993). With the distinctiveness of services, the service firms may choose a different market entry mode from that of manufacturing firms. Thus,

Hypothesis 5: Service firms tend to prefer the exporting mode of entry to the non-exporting mode.

CONSTRUCT DEVELOPMENT

Export mode is defined as "a firm's products are manufactured in the domestic market or a third country, and then transferred either directly or indirectly to the host market" (Driscoll & Paliwoda, 1997, p. 61). It includes direct exporting and indirect exporting. Non-export mode represents foreign market entries other than exporting. Foreign direct investment, joint venture, franchising, and strategic alliance fall under this construct. A categorical variable with service firms coded zero and non-service firms coded one was used to measure the industry-type construct. Experience refers to the extent to which a firm possesses experience in running its business. This study uses an item "number of years in business" as a measure of a firm's experience. Wong and Merrilees (2007, p. 389) define control as "the use of authority over operational and strategic decision-making employed by international marketers to guide their inter- and intra-firm activities." Three items representing the control construct are taken from their study. Five items to capture the cultural aspect are borrowed from Wong and Merrilees (2007). Intensity of competition represents "the extent of competition in the overseas markets" (Wong & Merrilees, 2009a, p. 257). Four items from their study were used to measure the construct of intensity of competition. Control, culture, and intensity of competition were measured by a 7-point scale with anchors (1) and (7) signifying strongly disagree and strongly agree, respectively.

RESEARCH METHOD

Australian firms engaged in international business were the target population in this study. A random sample of every fifth firm listed in the Austrade database was invited to join the survey. A total of 2,882 questionnaires were mailed out. Out of that, there were 315 usable questionnaires received--a response rate of 13%, which is similar to the 10% response rate found in other industrial mail surveys (Hart, 1987).

The sampling units of this study include senior executives, such as CEOs, marketing managers, general managers, managing directors, and export managers. Since they are most likely to be involved in the international operations of their firms, they tend to be knowledgeable about international marketing decisions. Table 1 depicts the respondents' firm characteristics and informant characteristics. Of the 315 responses, 18% of respondents stated the choice of non-export market entry mode, 81% export market entry mode, and 1% missing data. In addition, 54% of the respondents reported engaging in the service sector, and 46% in the manufacturing sector.

Table 1. Sample Characteristics

A. Number of Staff	N	% of Firms
1 – 10	103	33
11 – 50	130	41
51 – 100	28	9
101 - 200	18	6
201 and more	32	10
Missing	4	1
Total	315	100
B. Foreign Sales as % of Total Sales	**N**	**% of Firms**
1 - 10	90	29
11 – 30	93	29
31 - 50	45	14
51 - 70	17	5
71 – 90	37	12
91 – 100	33	11
Total	315	100
Job Title of Informants	**N**	**%**
Owner	88	28
CEO	6	2
Managing director	65	20
General manager	39	12
Marketing manager	65	21
Manager	46	15
Missing	6	2
Total	315	100
Industry Type	**N**	**% of Firms**
Services	170	54
Non-services	145	46
Market Entry Mode	**N**	**% of Firms**
Export arrangements	258	81
Non-export arrangements	54	18
Missing	3	1
Total	315	100

DATA ANALYSIS

Non-response bias was tested with the method of comparing early (the first 50% of returned questionnaires) respondents and late respondents (the last 50% of returned questionnaires) proposed by Armstrong and Overton (1977). A series of t-tests was done to examine the potential non-response bias between the early and late respondent groups. All variables in the study were compared across the early and late respondent groups at the 0.05 significance level to determine if they are significantly different. There were no statistically significant differences found between the two groups. Thus, it can be concluded this study was not affected by non-response bias.

Reliability of the items was tested by using Cronbach Alpha's internal consistency reliability. The results, which are demonstrated in Table 2, show that all alpha coefficients are above the 0.70 recommended cut-off (Francis, 2007; Robinson, Shaver, & Wrightsman, 1991) after deleting one item from the construct of intensity of competition. Therefore, it can be concluded that the items are reliable in terms of measuring the designated variables.

Face, Discriminant, and Convergent Validity

The survey's questionnaire was shown to a professor and business practitioners to attain expert feedbacks with the aim of increasing face validity. From the experts' advice, items were modified to ensure that the items are good measures of the designated variables. Discriminant validity examines the extent of the distinctiveness of a construct whereas convergent validity represents items loading heavily on the designated construct

Table 2. Results of Cronbach's Alpha Internal Reliability Test

Construct	Initial # of Items	Initial Alpha	Items Deleted	Revised # of Items	Revised Alpha
Control	3	.84	none	3	.84
Culture	5	.73	none	5	.73
Intensity of Competition	4	.74	V12 (after validity test)	3	.78
Industry Group	1	n.a.	n.a.	n.a.	n.a.
Experience	1	n.a.	n.a.	n.a.	n.a.

and poorly on all other variables in exploratory factor analysis (Wong & Merrilees, 2009a). Table 3 depicts the results of discriminant and convergent validity of the items of control, culture, and intensity of competition.

To achieve convergent validity, item loadings on the designated variables should be over 0.50 (Hair, Anderson, Tatham, & Black, 1998). In the exploratory factor analysis, after dropping an item "our industry is very price competitive" due to its low loading on the construct of intensity of competition, evidence of convergent validity for all items emerged.

Three pieces of evidence show that the items achieve discriminant validity. Firstly, the loadings of the items in the exploratory factor analysis are low on the unintentional variables. Secondly, variables are entered in pairs in exploratory factor analysis using principal components with Varimax rotation, there were always two components

Table 3. Exploratory Factor Analysis for Control, Culture, and Intensity of Competition

Variables	Control	Culture	Intensity of Competition
Our firm wanted to have a considerable influence over the marketing of the products / services (V1)	**.89**	.01	-.05
Our firm wanted to control major decision-making of the foreign operation (V2)	**.87**	.05	.02
Our firm wanted to make all the decisions relating to the integrity of the brand (V3)	**.84**	.07	.03
In relation to the domestic market, interpersonal relationships in this foreign market are more important (V4)	.06	**.69**	.06
In relation to the domestic market, visual aspects such as packaging and colours are more important in this foreign market (V5)	.05	**.60**	.28
In relation to the domestic market, the culture in this foreign market is totally different (V6)	-.03	**.76**	-.01
In relation to the domestic market, the customers in the foreign market behave differently (V7)	.04	**.75**	-.08
In relation to the domestic market, the motivation of customers in the foreign is harder to understand (V8)	.04	**.71**	.05
In relation to the domestic market, there is a more competition in our industry in this overseas market (V9)	-.07	.17	**.82**
This overseas market is extremely competitive (V10)	.01	.05	**.91**
There is a lot of competition in our industry (V11)	.06	-.03	**.76**
Our industry is very price competitive (V12) **(deleted)**	n.a.	n.a.	n.a.

extracted for each pair of concepts. Finally, the average variance extracted (AVE) method proposed by Fornell and Larcker (1981) was done to examine the discriminant validity. AVE scores of all variables show higher values than the correlation coefficients between the paired variables. Results of the AVE test were shown in Table 4.

Logistic Regression Results

Logistic regression is used to estimate the effects of control, culture, intensity of competition, business experience, and industry type on the probability of selecting export-entry mode over non-export entry mode. Logistic regression is recommended when the dependent variable is binary, the independent variables are both categorical and continuous, and the assumption of multivariate normality has not been met (Hair et al., 1998). In this study, a positive coefficient of an independent variable in logistic regression represents that the baseline entry mode (non-export) is less likely to be elected. Conversely, a negative coefficient of an independent variable states that the baseline entry mode is more likely to be chosen.

A direct logistic regression analysis was performed using SPSS. A test of the full model with all five independent variables against a constant-only-model was statistically reliable with χ^2 (DF=5, n=315) = 21.39, p = 0.001. The results indicate that some of the coefficients are not zero, meaning that the independent variables

Table 4. Discriminant Validity Test Using AVE Method

Variables	AVE	Control	Culture	Intensity of competition
Control	.75	---	---	---
Culture	.50	.08	---	---
Intensity of competition	.69	-.01	.17	---

The lower diagonal shows the correlation coefficients between the variables.

are reliably distinguished between export and non-export market entry mode. An alternative method used to examine statistical significance, the Hosmer and Lemeshow goodness-of-fit test, also suggests that the logistic regression model is a goof fit, χ^2 (DF=8, n=315) = 9.01, p = .34 (A *non-significant* Hosmer and Lemeshow goodness-of-fit test statistic specifies a good model). Nagelkerke's R^2 = .11 signifies a relationship between the independent variables and the two groups of the market entry mode. Furthermore, the logistic regression model correctly classifies 82.5% of the market-entry mode choice.

The Wald criterion shows three of the independent variables are statistically significant. They are industry group, z = 9.26, p = .002, business experience, z = 5.62, p = .018, and intensity of competition, z = 3.75, p = .05. The negative coefficients for industry type and business experience in the logistic regression model show that service firms and firms with greater business experience are opt to choose non-export market-entry mode. However, the positive coefficient of intensity of competition signifies that firms with greater competition in the overseas market are likely to choose export market-entry mode. Control and culture were found not to furnish statistically significant contributions to predicting market entry mode choice, with z = 2.70, p = .10 and z = 0.94, p = .33 respectively. Based on these results, the logistic regression model appears to have reasonable explanatory and predictive abilities. Table 5 describes the results of the direct logistic regression analysis.

DISCUSSION AND CONTRIBUTIONS

The results can be classified into three categories for discussion of the contributions to the literature. Firstly, the variable of domestic business experience in the logistic regression model is new to the literature. The statistically significant result indicates that firms with more domestic business

Table 5. Results of a Direct Logistic Regression Analysis

Hypotheses	Variables	B	Wald	Sig	Results
H1	Business experience	-.01	5.62	.02	Supported
H2	Culture	.16	.94	.33	Rejected
H3	Control	-.20	2.70	.10	Rejected
H4	Intensity of competition	.25	3.75	.05	Supported
H5	Industry group	-1.04	9.26	.00	Supported

Dependent variable: Market entry mode choice (others=0; export=1)

experience are very likely to choose the non-export entry mode. The knowledge gained from running domestic operations is considered as a good gauge to run business in overseas markets. Equipped with domestic business experience, firms perceive risks entering overseas markets to be lower with the consequence of choosing non-export entry mode. The findings are parallel to those studies examining the impacts of international business experience on market entry mode choice (Chang, 1995; Lin, 2000; Wei, Liu, & Liu, 2004). Irrespective of where the knowledge comes from, that is domestic or overseas; firms increase confidence about entering the overseas markets as their business experiences grow.

Secondly, both intensity of competition and industry group achieve statistically significant results. However, they affect foreign market entry mode choice differently. When firms' competitive situation in overseas markets is intense, they tend to choose export mode so that less commitment needs to be made with the consequence of taking less risk. The findings in this study is contradictory to Kim and Hwang's (1992) study that intensity of competition was not a statistically significant factor in foreign market entry mode choice, or Taylor, Zou and Osland's (2000) work that greater competition in overseas markets led to non-export mode. However, a more recent empirical result from Wong and Merrilees (2009a) is comparable to this study's result, in that the greater intensity of competition in the overseas markets, the more the chance firms choose export entry mode. The industry group variable is highly significant statistically, showing that service firms opt to choose non-export market entry mode. The results in this study are similar to other empirical studies in the US and Australia (Erramilli & Rao, 1990; Wong & Merrilees, 2009a). The findings reinforce the unique characteristics of the service firms: human interactions are emphasised, and services are perishable.

The third category is concerned with two statistically insignificant variables, which are culture and control. With regard to culture, the findings in this study are different from other works such as Kogut and Singh (1988), Gatignon and Anderson (1988), Chen (2008), and Evans, Mavondo and Bridson (2008). The difference may be due to the fact that cultures in the global environment are perceived as more similar than twenty years ago. The statistically non-significant findings in this study concerning control are also contradictory to the existing literature (Driscoll & Paliwoda, 1997; Erramilli & Rao, 1993; Gatignon & Anderson, 1988; Kogut & Singh, 1988). With global business practices more concerned about integration and empowerment, international marketers may find that control is not as critical a strategic factor as it used to be in foreign market entry mode choice.

MANAGERIAL IMPLICATIONS

In general, the results suggest both internal and external factors play an important role in deciding foreign market entry-mode choices. The above model can be used in a practical manner by any firm evaluating various foreign market entry modes when going for international ventures.

The results with reference to internal perspectives suggest that firms need to consider the industry type of their business. For service firms, their choice may be relatively straightforward, with non-export mode being the preferred mode. Another internal factor which concerns international marketers is their domestic business experience. Firms tend to choose non-export mode when their domestic business experience grows. For newer firms without much domestic business experience, it is better for marketers to select the export mode and cultivate their organisational learning capability before adopting non-export mode. After accumulating years of domestic business experience, firms' capability of running their operations in overseas markets is likely to enhance. Some domestic business strategies and practices can be applied in overseas markets even though knowledge about these markets is limited. In other words, international marketers can standardise some of their marketing strategy and practices in the global business.

International marketers need to evaluate the extent of competition in the overseas market before they make an entry mode choice. The understanding of this external factor, intensity of competition, shed light on how brutal the overseas markets are likely to be. If the competition situation in overseas markets is too severe to manage efficiently and effectively, international marketers can avoid direct competition by choosing the export mode. This strategic move is reasonable considering that firms are able to gain useful knowledge with their domestic business operations without the need to go into overseas markets to gain experience.

Furthermore, control is found not to be a significant issue for firms operating globally in terms of entry mode choice. The deliverance from control in strategic choice provides international marketers more latitude to consider other issues such as competitive situations.

CONCLUSION

This study was motivated by the gaps in the literature of foreign market entry mode choice. A total of 315 internationally active Australian firms were surveyed. A direct logistic regression analysis was undertaken to explain the factors affecting their choice between export and non-export mode.

The three most important variables explaining this entry mode choice, in sequence of significance level, included: industry type, domestic business experience, and intensity of competition in overseas markets. Firms in service industries and greater overseas competition favour export mode, whereas greater domestic business experience favours non-export mode. The general conclusion of the results is that global firms need to consider both the internal and external factors when selecting a foreign market entry mode. Overlooking any one of these two aspects may lead to undesirable consequences.

Further studies are required in other countries in order to enhance the validity of the model. It is suggested the model in this paper be tested in developing countries such as Brazil, Russia, India, and China. With high internal purchasing power that can potentially support internationalisation more aggressively, companies in these emerging markets may opt for non-export modes. Moreover, further research on how individual factors such as risk taking attitude and networking ability can affect foreign market entry mode choice can provide further insights as to the rationalisation of foreign market entry mode choice.

REFERENCES

Abreu, M., Mendes, V., & Santos, J. A. C. (2011). Home country bias: Does domestic experience help investors enter foreign markets? *Journal of Banking & Finance*, *35*(9), 2330–2340. doi:10.1016/j.jbankfin.2011.01.032.

Agarwal, S., & Ramaswami, S. (1992). Choice of foreign market entry mode: Impact of ownership, location and internationalization factors. *Journal of International Business Studies*, *23*(3), 1–27. doi:10.1057/palgrave.jibs.8490257.

Anderson, E., & Gatignon, H. (1986). Modes of entry: A transaction cost analysis and propositions. *Journal of International Business Studies*, *17*(3), 1–26. doi:10.1057/palgrave.jibs.8490432.

Armstrong, S. J., & Overton, T. S. (1977). Estimating nonresponse bias in mail surveys. *JMR, Journal of Marketing Research*, *14*(3), 396–402. doi:10.2307/3150783.

Benito, G. R. G., & Gripsrud, G. (1992). The expansion of foreign direct investments: Discrete rational location choices or a cultural learning process? *Journal of International Business Studies*, *23*(3), 461–476. doi:10.1057/palgrave.jibs.8490275.

Blomstermo, A., & Sharma, D. D. (2006). Choice of foreign market entry mode in service firms. *International Marketing Review*, *23*(2), 211–229. doi:10.1108/02651330610660092.

Bouquet, C., Hebert, L., & Delios, A. (2004). Foreign expansion in service industries separability and human capital intensity. *Journal of Business Research*, *57*, 35–46. doi:10.1016/S0148-2963(02)00282-5.

Buckley, P. J., & Casson, M. C. (1985). *The economic theory of the multinational enterprise*. London: Macmillan.

Caves, R. E. (1982). *Multinational enterprises and economic analysis*. New York: St. Martin's Press.

Cavusgil, S. T., & Nevin, J. R. (1981). State-of-the-art in international marketing: An assessment. In Enis, B. M., & Roering, K. J. (Eds.), *Review of Marketing* (pp. 195–216). Chicago, IL: American Marketing Association.

Chang, S. J. (1995). International expansion strategy of Japanese firms: Capability building through sequential entry. *Academy of Management Journal*, *38*(2), 383–407. doi:10.2307/256685.

Chen, C. (2008). Entry mode selection for international construction markets: The influence of host country related factors. *Construction Management and Economics*, *26*, 303–314. doi:10.1080/01446190701882382.

Collins, J. D., Holcomb, T. R., Certo, S. T., Hitt, M. A., & Lester, R. H. (2009). Learning by doing: Cross-border mergers and acquisitions. *Journal of Business Research*, *62*(12), 1329–1334. doi:10.1016/j.jbusres.2008.11.005.

Davidson, W. H. (1980). The mode choice and change decision process and its impact on international performance. *International Business Review*, *2*(1), 97–120.

Dong, B., Zou, S., & Taylor, C. R. (2008). Factors that influence multinational corporations' control of their operations in foreign markets: An empirical investigation. *Journal of International Marketing*, *16*(1), 98–119. doi:10.1509/jimk.16.1.98.

Driscoll, A., & Paliwoda, S. J. (1997). Dimensionalizing international market entry mode choice. *Journal of Marketing Management*, *13*(1-3), 57–87. doi:10.1080/0267257X.1997.9964459.

Dunning, J. H. (1977). Trade location of economic activity and the MNE: A search for an eclectic approach. In Ohlin, B. (Ed.), *The International Allocation of Economic Activity*. London: Macmillan.

Dunning, J. H. (1981). *International production and the multinational enterprise*. London: Allen and Unwin.

Dunning, J. H. (1988). Explaining the international direct investment position of countries: Toward a dynamic or development approach. *Weltwirtschaftliches Archiv*, *117*(1), 30–64. doi:10.1007/BF02696577.

Dunning, J. H. (1993). *Multinational enterprise and the global economy*. Boston, MA: Addison Wesley.

Dunning, J. H. (1995). Reappraising the eclectic paradigm in an age of alliance capitalism. *Journal of International Business Studies*, *26*(3), 461–491. doi:10.1057/palgrave.jibs.8490183.

Dunning, J. H. (2001). The eclectic (OLI) paradigm of international production: Past, present and future. *International Journal of the Economics of Business*, *8*(2), 173–190. doi:10.1080/13571510110051441.

Erramilli, M. K. (1991). The experience factor in foreign market entry behaviour of service firms. *Journal of International Business Studies*, *22*(3), 479–501. doi:10.1057/palgrave.jibs.8490312.

Erramilli, M. K. (1996). Nationality and subsidiary ownership patterns in multinational corporations. *Journal of International Business Studies*, *27*(2), 225–248. doi:10.1057/palgrave.jibs.8490133.

Erramilli, M. K., & Rao, C. P. (1990). Choice of foreign market entry modes by service firms: Role of market knowledge. *Management International Review*, *30*(2), 135–150.

Erramilli, M. K., & Rao, C. P. (1993). Service firms' international entry mode choice: A modified transaction-cost analysis approach. *Journal of Marketing*, *57*(3), 19–38. doi:10.2307/1251852.

Evans, J., Mavondo, F. T., & Bridson, K. (2008). Psychic distance: Antecedents, retail strategy implications, and performance outcomes. *Journal of International Marketing*, *16*(2), 32–63. doi:10.1509/jimk.16.2.32.

Fina, E., & Rugman, A. (1996). A test of internalization theory and internationalization theory: The Upjohn company. *Management International Review*, *36*(3), 199–213.

Fornell, C., & Larcker, D. F. (1981). Evaluating structural equation models with unobservable variables and measurement error. *JMR, Journal of Marketing Research*, *18*(1), 39–50. doi:10.2307/3151312.

Francis, G. (2007). *Introduction to SPSS for Windows* (5th ed.). Sydney, Australia: Pearson Prentice Hall.

Gatignon, H., & Anderson, E. (1988). The multinational corporation's degree of control over foreign subsidiaries: An empirical test of a transaction cost explanation. *Journal of Law Economics and Organization*, *4*(Fall), 305–335.

Hair, J. F. J., Anderson, R. E., Tatham, R. L., & Black, W. C. (1998). *Multivariate data analysis* (5th ed.). Upper Saddle River, NJ: Prentice Hall.

Harrigan, K. R. (1985a). Exit barriers and vertical integration. *Academy of Management Journal*, *28*(3), 686–697. doi:10.2307/256124.

Harrigan, K. R. (1985b). Vertical integration and corporate strategy. *Academy of Management Journal*, *28*(2), 397–425. doi:10.2307/256208.

Hart, S. (1987). The use of the survey in industrial market research. *Journal of Marketing Management*, *3*(1), 25–38. doi:10.1080/0267257X.1987.9964025.

Hill, C. W. L., Hwang, P., & Kim, W. C. (1990). An eclectic theory of the choice of international entry mode. *Strategic Management Journal*, *11*(2), 117–128. doi:10.1002/smj.4250110204.

Hofstede, G. (1980). *Culture's consequence: International differences in work-related values*. Beverly Hills, CA: Sage.

Johanson, J., & Vahlne, J. E. (1977). The internationalization process of the firm: A model of knowledge development and increasing foreign market commitment. *Journal of International Business Studies*, *8*(1), 23–32. doi:10.1057/palgrave.jibs.8490676.

Johanson, J., & Vahlne, J.-E. (1990). The mechanism of internationalization. *International Marketing Review*, *7*(4), 11–24. doi:10.1108/02651339010137414.

Johanson, J., & Vahlne, J. E. (2006). Commitment and opportunity development in the internationalization process: A note on the Uppsala internationalization process model. *Management International Review*, *46*(2), 165–177. doi:10.1007/s11575-006-0043-4.

Johanson, J., & Wiedersheim-Paul, F. (1975). The internationalization of the firm - Four Swedish cases. *Journal of Management Studies*, *12*(October), 305–322. doi:10.1111/j.1467-6486.1975.tb00514.x.

Julian, C. C. (2003). Export marketing performance: A study of Thailand firms. *Journal of Small Business Management*, *41*(2), 213–221. doi:10.1111/1540-627X.00077.

Khoury, S. J. (1979). International banking: A special look at foreign banks. *Journal of International Business Studies*, *10*(3), 36–52. doi:10.1057/palgrave.jibs.8490642.

Kim, W. C., & Hwang, P. (1992). Global strategy and multinationals' entry mode choice. *Journal of International Business Studies*, *23*(1), 29–53. doi:10.1057/palgrave.jibs.8490258.

Klein, S., Frazier, G. L., & Roth, V. J. (1990). A transaction cost analysis model of channel integration in international markets. *JMR, Journal of Marketing Research*, *27*(2), 196–208. doi:10.2307/3172846.

Kogut, B., & Singh, H. (1988). The effect of national culture on the choice of entry mode. *Journal of International Business Studies*, *19*(3), 411–432. doi:10.1057/palgrave.jibs.8490394.

Lin, H. (2000). Choice of market entry mode in emerging markets: Influences on entry strategy in China. *Journal of Global Marketing*, *14*(1/2), 83–109. doi:10.1300/J042v14n01_05.

Liu, R., & Hart, S. (2011). Does experience matter? - A study of knowledge processes and uncertainty reduction in solution innovation. *Industrial Marketing Management*, *40*, 691–698. doi:10.1016/j.indmarman.2011.05.004.

Lord, M. D., & Ranft, A. L. (2000). Organizational learning about new international markets: Exploring the internal transfer of local market knowledge. *Journal of International Business Studies*, *31*(4), 573–589. doi:10.1057/palgrave.jibs.8490923.

Mayrhofer, U. (2004). International market entry: Does the home country a ffect entry-mode decisions? *Journal of International Marketing*, *12*(4), 71–96. doi:10.1509/jimk.12.4.71.53211.

Nitsch, D., Beamish, P. W., & Makino, S. (1996). Entry mode and performance of Japanese FDI in Western Europe. *Management International Review*, *36*(1), 27–34.

Pan, Y., & Chi, P. S. K. (1999). Financial performance and survival of multinational corporations in China. *Strategic Management Journal*, *20*(4), 359–374. doi:10.1002/(SICI)1097-0266(199904)20:4<359::AID-SMJ31>3.0.CO;2-9.

Pan, Y., & Tse, D. K. (2000). The hierarchical model of market entry modes. *Journal of International Business Studies*, *31*(4), 535–554. doi:10.1057/palgrave.jibs.8490921.

Robinson, J. P., Shaver, P. R., & Wrightsman, L. S. (1991). Criteria for scale selection and evaluation. In Robinson, J. P., Shaver, P. R., & Wrightsman, L. S. (Eds.), *Measures of Personality and Social Psychological Attitudes*. San Diego, CA: Academic Press.

Ronen, S., & Shenkar, O. (1985). Clustering countries on attitudinal dimensions: A review and synthesis. *Academy of Management Review*, *10*(3), 435–454.

Root, F. R. (1994). *Entry strategies for international markets*. Lexington, VA: Lexington Books.

Sharma, D. D., & Johanson, J. (1987). Technical consultancy in internationalization. *International Marketing Review*, *4*(4), 20–29. doi:10.1108/eb008339.

Simmonds, P. G. (1990). The combined diversification breadth and mode dimensions and the performance of large diversified firms. *Strategic Management Journal*, *11*(5), 399–410. doi:10.1002/smj.4250110506.

Stopford, J. M., & Wells, L. T. (1972). *Managing the multinational enterprise: Organiztion of the firm and ownership of the subsidiaries*. New York: Basic Books.

Taylor, C. R., Zou, S., & Osland, G. E. (2000). Foreign market entry strategies of Japanese MNCs. *International Marketing Review*, *17*(2), 146–163. doi:10.1108/02651330010322624.

Terpstra, V., & Yu, C. (1988). Determinants of foreign investment of US advertising agencies. *Journal of International Business Studies*, *19*(1), 33–46. doi:10.1057/palgrave.jibs.8490373.

Wei, Y., Liu, B., & Liu, X. (2004). Entry modes of foreign direct investment in China: A multinomial logit approach. *Journal of Business Research*, *58*(11), 1495–1505. doi:10.1016/j.jbusres.2004.10.002.

Weinstein, A. K. (1977). Foreign investment by service firms: The case of multinational advertising agencies. *Journal of International Business Studies*, *8*(1), 83–91. doi:10.1057/palgrave.jibs.8490681.

Wertsch, J. (1985). *Culture, communication, and cognition*. New York: Cambridge University Press.

Wilson, I. (2001). U.K. SMEs in China - Performance and market entry strategies. *Journal of International Marketing and marketing research*, *26*(3), 151-164.

Wong, H. Y., & Merrilees, B. (2006). Determinants of SME brand adaptation in global marketing. *International Journal of Entrepreneurship and Small Business*, *3*(3/4), 477–497.

Wong, H. Y., & Merrilees, B. (2007). Multiple roles for branding in international marketing. *International Marketing Review*, *24*(4), 384–408. doi:10.1108/02651330710760982.

Wong, H. Y., & Merrilees, B. (2009a). Foreign market entry mode choice of Australian firms. *International Journal of Trade and Global Markets*, *2*(3/4), 250–266. doi:10.1504/IJTGM.2009.028992.

Wong, H. Y., & Merrilees, B. (2009b). Service versus product brands: Understanding international adaptation. *Journal of International Business and Entrepreneurship Development*, *4*(3), 231–242. doi:10.1504/JIBED.2009.029014.

Woodcock, C. P., Beamish, P. W., & Makino, S. (1994). Ownership-based entry mode strategies and international performance. *Journal of International Business Studies*, *25*(2), 253–273. doi:10.1057/palgrave.jibs.8490200.

Zeithaml, V. A., Parasuraman, A., & Berry, L. L. (1985). Problems and strategies in service marketing. *Journal of Marketing*, *49*(2), 33–46. doi:10.2307/1251563.

Zou, S., & Cavusgil, S. T. (2002). The GMS: A broad conceptualization of global marketing strategy and its effect on firm performance. *Journal of Marketing*, *66*(October), 40–56. doi:10.1509/jmkg.66.4.40.18519.

Chapter 5
Measuring the Effects of Advertising Polysemy on Branding

Ulysses J. Brown III
Savannah State University, USA

Anshu Saxena Arora
Savannah State University, USA

Amit Arora
Georgia Southern University, USA

ABSTRACT

In the advertising research literature, polysemy is defined as different interpretations for the same advertising message. The multiple ad-interpretations can be attributable to complexities and diversities in culture and/or consumers' own demographics, perceptions, attitudes, lifestyles, values, behavior, and psychographics. We provide a bipolar and dichotomous perspective on advertising polysemy as positive and negative polysemy with research and practice examples from the print advertisements for alcoholic beverages and corporate social responsibility to explain the conditions that lead to the emergence of positive and negative polysemic contexts for the same message. Furthermore, the study explores how polysemy leads to better branding. The research investigates the concept of polysemy and the generation of idiosyncratic meanings, and examines the impact of advertising polysemy on consumer-based brand equity. The research proposes and measures the advertising polysemy and consumer-based brand equity conceptual framework supported by accommodation theory, consumer response theory, and theory of hierarchy of effects, leading to stronger ad-evoked feelings, ad and brand attitudes, and consumer-based brand equity.

DOI: 10.4018/978-1-4666-3966-9.ch005

INTRODUCTION

Advertising polysemy is defined as a subjective decoding of an advertisement shaped by the individual's sociocultural milieu (McCracken 1986; Ringberg & Reihlen, 2008). Puntoni, Schroeder, and Ritson (2010) defined advertising polysemy as the existence of at least two distinct interpretations for the same advertising message across audiences, or across time and situations. There are two broader types of polysemy–synchronic polysemy and diachronic polysemy, as discussed in the research by Puntoni, Schroeder, and Ritson (2010). The synchronic aspect of advertising polysemy can be explained through an example of the advertisement which means one thing to one group of consumers and something different to another group (Grier & Brumbaugh, 1999; Puntoni, Schroeder, & Ritson, 2010). For example, international advertising often has problems with synchronic polysemy. A "thumbs-up sign," which signifies affirmation in most Western nations, has offensive meaning in some countries, such as Russia and Poland if the palm of the hand is visible but is acceptable if the back of the hand is shown. Often the use of colors is interpreted differently in different cultures. In Japan, India, and many Asian countries, white is a color of mourning and purple is associated with death in many Latin American countries. This kind of unintended misinterpretation of the same advertising message by different cultural and/or sub-cultural groups is an example of synchronic polysemy. Heineken beer print ad's slogan is "Brewers don't have to be good talkers" with a sub headline–"When you make a great beer, you don't have to make a great fuss." The word "fuss" may have different interpretations for individuals from different cultures and countries and may lead to perceived synchronic polysemy. As a result, this Heineken ad could not be translated in a meaningful way into many other languages (Belch & Belch, 2009).

However, a diachronic dimension of advertising polysemy can also characterize multiplicity of meanings during an advertising reception, especially when exposed to the advertisement on multiple times–first impression of the ad and then subsequent impression about the same ad on repeated viewings (Kirmani 1997; Puntoni, Schroeder, & Ritson, 2010). For example, Absolut Vodka ads are very creative.

When we look deeper into polysemy from advertising perspective, we realize that at the end of multiple viewings and multiple ad interpretations of polysemic ads, there is always one predominant feeling which stays with every individual. This feeling is either a positive or negative ad-evoked feeling which further defines the individual's positive or negative ad and brand attitudes leading to either positive or negative branding for the advertised brand. We conceptualize two different advertising polysemy appeals – positive and negative. Positive advertising polysemy will evoke positive feelings for the ad and the brand leading to positive ad and brand attitudes and hence, positive branding. For example, the Old Spice Guy, Isaiah Mustafa, has received fame from endorsing Old Spice in the Super Bowl commercials, "The Man Your Man Could Smell Like." The commercial received 3.4 million views on YouTube in the first week that it was released. The personality based advertising successes like Jack from Jack in the Box, the King from Burger King, the Cavemen from Geico, the Most Interesting Man in the World from Dos Equis, and the latest Old Spice Guy–they all have distinct, likable characteristics, genuinely funny ad content, and an incredible online presence via videos, websites, and social networks to engage their fans.

On the other hand, there are some polysemic ads which evoke many feelings on multiple viewings of the advertisement, but the predominant feeling may be negative at the end, leading to negative ad and brand attitudes and negative impressions on branding. We call this "Negative Advertising Polysemy," which predominantly evokes negative feelings for both the advertisement and the brand, leading to negative ad and brand attitudes and hence, negative branding.

Although in theory all advertisements are potentially polysemic, in practice, each one of us attributes certain meanings to the advertisement. These meanings may vary on multiple viewings of the ad but in conclusion only one dominant meaning and/or feeling is attached to the advertisement. This dominant meaning or feeling or message received by the receiver (person) can be either positive leading to positive advertising polysemy or negative leading to negative advertising polysemy. In this research study, we investigate advertising polysemy as a dichotomous concept and conceptualize the existence of polysemy into two bipolar types – positive advertising polysemy and negative advertising polysemy. We further study the relationship of these two types of advertising polysemy as advertising appeals on consumer-based brand equity.

The goal of our paper is to understand advertising polysemy as an advertising appeal which advertisers can use as a creative strategy for changing and shaping consumer perceptions, attitudes and behavior. This research study addresses the following questions:

- How does the concept of positive and negative advertising polysemy impact the target consumers in the context of purposeful advertising polysemy and branding?
- How can advertisers use purposeful advertising polysemy (both positive and negative) for changing consumer perceptions and attitudes towards advertising and branding? In other words, can advertisers create brands and strengthen consumer-based brand equity by employing positive and negative advertising polysemic appeals to the print advertisements for alcoholic beverages and corporate social responsibility?

DEFINING POSITIVE AND NEGATIVE ADVERTISING POLYSEMY

There is a dearth of advertising polysemy research in the extant literature. As a result of increasing diversity in the marketplace, target marketing strategies are gaining importance (Grier & Brumbaugh, 1999). Viewers who feel they belong to the target market display more favorable attitude towards an ad than do viewers who feel excluded (Leigh, Rethans, & Whitney, 1987; Whittler & Spira, 2002). Polysemy occurs when people generate different basic understandings of the same message, not merely different attitudes (Condit, 1989). Puntoni, Schroeder, and Ritson (2010) defined advertising polysemy as the existence of at least two distinct interpretations for the same advertising message across audiences, or across time and situations and further categorized polysemy into two broader types–synchronic and diachronic polysemy. While these two polysemic types are existent both in theory and practice, the literature on advertising polysemy lacks a focus on how consumers feel after multiple viewings of the same advertisement. These feelings are subjective and may vary across individuals on account of their cultures, beliefs, perceptions, values, demographics and psychographics. It may also happen that while one individual likes an ad and has positive feelings for the ad, the other individual may completely dislike the same ad with completely negative feelings for it. This is the true definition of contextual based polysemy as an advertising concept and appeal. People do not experience advertising in isolation from their social and cultural world (McCracken, 1986; Buttle 1991). While polysemy relates to cultures, groups of individuals, beliefs, perceptions, values, demographics and psychographics, it is contextual at the same time and different contexts can provide different meanings to the same ad.

The feelings one draws from the advertisement on multiple viewings of the advertisement can be positive or negative, but in the end there always is one dominant feeling which stays with the individual in the context of the stated ad. This dominant feeling is, what we conceptualize, the end result of advertising polysemy as an advertising appeal. Hence, we have two types of advertising polysemic appeal–positive advertising polysemy and negative advertising polysemy.

Some individuals may experience negative advertising polysemy due to the advertisement layout and the portrayal of blood. These individuals may not like the ad on multiple viewings and may develop negative feelings for it. These negative feelings may negatively impact the ad-evoked feelings, ad and brand attitudes and, most importantly, branding. However, some others may experience feelings of eroticism and/or may see the underlying positive message from the ad. They may experience positive advertising polysemy due to the advertisement's message and/or the erotic feelings due to the portrayal of human skin shown in the ad. These positive feelings may positively impact the ad-evoked feelings, ad and brand attitudes and, most importantly, branding.

For the purpose of this research, we define polysemy as an independent advertising appeal for targeting specific consumer segments and "purposeful advertising polysemy" is defined as an intended advertising strategy used by the advertisers and the corporate world for targeting different consumer segments with the flexibility of reaching and appealing to all of them in a way to want them to buy the brand. Polysemy is a potential advertising strategy, which illustrates the existence of multiple ad meanings and interpretations in advertising messages resulting in effective advertising and branding. Purposeful polysemy is the intended polysemy used by the advertisers for their advertising messages to be popular and to increase brand popularity among the target audiences. Advertisers can use contextual based negative and positive advertising polysemy while designing their ad messages through any medium of communication–print, TV, billboards, radio, Internet, interactive and social media. Positive and negative advertising polysemy can be viewed as valuable tools for purposeful advertising polysemy to put forth the intended advertising message to the target audience more effectively.

While advertising polysemy has been researched to an extent (McCracken, 1986; Ringberg & Reihlen, 2008; Puntoni, Schroeder, & Ritson, 2010), the impact of advertising polysemy on branding has not received much attention. Advertisers and brand managers know brand personality plays a pivotal role in defining consumer attitudes and purchase intentions (Plummer, 1985). Brand personality and brand equity provide value to customers by enhancing their interpretation and processing of information, confidence in the purchase decision, and satisfaction (Aaker, 1991). According to Aaker (1991), brand equity can be generated in two manners: 1) financial equity of a brand which determines its value for accounting purposes, such as a merger, acquisition, or stock price; and 2) consumer-based brand equity which is derived from the perceptions of individual consumers, based on the differential effect of a marketing program on their attitudes toward the brand. In this research, we focus on consumer-based brand equity, which is measured by the cognitive and behavioral brand equity at the individual consumer level through a consumer survey (Yoo & Donthu, 2001).

We believe consumer-based brand equity consists of four dimensions: brand loyalty, brand awareness, brand associations, and perceived quality of brand, as proposed by Aaker (1991) and Keller (1993). Aaker defines brand loyalty as "the attachment that a customer has to a brand" and brand awareness is defined as "the ability for a buyer to recognize or recall that a brand is a member of a certain product category" (Aaker, 1991, p. 61). Aaker (1991) defines brand associations as "anything linked in memory to a brand" (p. 109) while Zeithaml (1988, p. 3) defines perceived quality as "the consumer's judgment about a product's overall excellence or superiority." Moorthy and

Zhao (2000) demonstrated a positive correlation between advertising expenditures and the perceived quality of consumer durable goods. Their study noted that previous negative experiences reduced the effect of advertising but suggested that advertising may play a more important role in brand equity than actual product performance. We believe that the positive and negative advertising polysemic appeals should enhance branding and customer satisfaction due to their impact on consumer advertisement and brand attitudes, and purchase intentions.

The following section discusses the development of the theoretical framework–advertising polysemy and consumer-based brand equity and highlights the existence of positive and negative polysemic advertising appeals and their impact on branding by changing and shaping consumer perceptions, attitudes and behavior.

THEORETICAL FRAMEWORK AND RESEARCH HYPOTHESES

Our review of the literature has provided us with a direction of researching positive and negative advertising polysemy as potential and valuable advertising tools and appeals for targeting consumers through purposeful and intended advertising polysemy, and further investigates the relationship of these polysemic appeals with branding. Meaning-based models of advertising (Mick & Buhl, 1992) suggests the consumer response to an advertisement depends on the meaning given to it in the context of the goals and values which are salient in the life of the consumer (Puntoni, Schroeder, & Ritson, 2010). According to Puntoni, Schroeder and Ritson (2010), the polysemic messages designed in the advertisements can have a targeting goal of reaching out to different consumer segments with the same advertising message, a positioning goal focusing on the core brand features, an aesthetic goal for generating and increasing interest and appeal of an ad and/or a social norms goal where the advertiser use the ambiguous message for promoting a controversial message without breaking advertising conventions or societal standards of appropriateness.

Accommodation theory (Anderson & Meyer, 1988) emphasizes the role of the audience as members of the social community, for instance friends, family, and social groups (Anderson & Meyer, 1988, p. 310) and offers a social action framework for investigating media effects. This theory uses two assumptions: (1) people are continuously making sense of meanings and this sense making is historically situated reflecting a particular moment in time; and (2) routine social actions and practices between self and others characterize human behavior (Anderson & Meyer, 1988, p. 210). According to this theory, advertising is well embedded and integrated into social experiences and these experiences are further modified by advertising on a routine basis (Buttle, 1991). This theory does not assume unlimited interpretation of the ad content, but the limits are defined by the readers' own thoughts, interpretations, including the "moment" (Sigman, 1987, p. 101) and conventional structure of ads (Buttle, 1991, p. 103). This leads to perceived ad-response polysemy, similar to O'Keefe's (2003) Protection Motivation Theory (PMT), which involves the creation of message variations aimed at influencing such perceptual states (e.g., messages that vary in their depiction of the severity of the threat) and the post-exposure assessment of both the perceptual state and persuasive outcomes.

Reader-response theory can be effectively applied to our research on positive and negative advertising polysemy. Reader-response or consumer-response (Hirschman & Thompson, 1997) approach links advertising texts and consumer response (Scott, 1994). Researchers (Mick & Buhl, 1992; Stern, 1989; Parker, 1998; Ritson & Elliot, 1999; Zhou & Belk, 2004) have used the reader or consumer-response theory for understanding consumers' advertising experiences and interpretations. McQuuarrie and Mick's (1999) research on persuasive advertising investigate the role of visual elements as rhetorical devices and examine the interpretation of advertisements through consumers' cultural knowledge and background. Classical conditioning theory has been studied by many scholars in the field of advertising, including (1) consumers' attitude towards the ad (Aad) and attitude towards the brand (Ab) (Mitchell & Olsen, 1981; Shimp, 1981); (2) consumers' prior attitude toward the brand (Stuart, Shimp, & Engle, 1987), and (3) consumers' perception of congruence between the ad (unconditioned stimulus) and the brand (conditioned stimulus) (Mitchell, Kahn, & Knasko, 1995; Shimp, 1981). Burke and Edell (1989) found that consumers will hold positive attitudes toward the advertised brand when the advertising elicits warm feelings to them. Glodberg and Gorn (1987), Mitchell (1986), Russo, Shah, and Park (1994), and Srull (1983) provide great support to the classical conditioning theory and conclude the advertisement evaluations and ad-evoked feelings were debilitated by negative effect and stimulated by positive effect.

Figure 1 provides our advertising polysemy and consumer-based brand equity conceptual framework, illustrating the presence of two polysemic advertising appeals (positive and negative advertising polysemy) leading to ad-evoked feelings, attitudes toward the ad (Aad), attitudes toward the brand (Ab), and most importantly, consumer-based brand equity, characterized by brand loyalty, brand awareness, brand associations, and perceived quality (as indicators of brand equity). The model links directly to perceived ad-response polysemy on account of PMT and consumer response theories. Our conceptual framework uses these theories through the application of consumers' interpretations of advertising, where consumers are conceived as readers of advertisements and advertisements are considered texts.

Ad-evoked feelings or Primary Affective Reactions (PARs) and their relationship with Aad and Ab have not been explicitly studied in the literature (Geuens & De Pelsmacker, 1998). Our research study investigates the ad-evoked feelings with respect to positive and negative advertising polysemic appeals. As discussed in the earlier sections, advertising polysemy can be both intended (purposeful polysemy) and unintended depending on the way consumers perceive the message in the ads. The advertisements may contain a positive message, but the subjective interpretation by various consumers and consumer groups may be negative, or vice versa. This leads to the emergence of positive and negative advertising polysemy. Advertisers are interested in the effectiveness of advertising meaning especially when the advertising meets the intended goals (Tellis & Ambler, 2007, p. 3). The occurrence of unintended meanings across an audience can happen due to the influence of cultural and ethnic differences on advertising interpretation,

Figure 1. Advertising polysemy and consumer-based brand equity framework

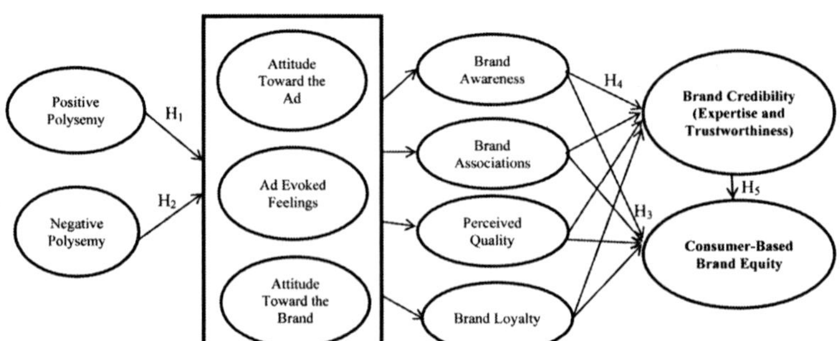

ethnic self-awareness, and consumer ontology (e.g., Borgerson & Schroeder, 2002; Grier & Brumbaugh, 1999; Keck & Mueller, 1994). Consumers today are highly knowledgeable about the products they use. They are overly alert to meanings and images associated with the products (Caru & Cova, 2007) since there can be a fair amount of polysemy used in advertising messages.

These polysemic messages may lead to either positive ad-evoked feelings of cheerfulness, carefree, honored, pleased, interested, happiness, adventure, confidence, among others, or negative ad-evoked feelings of irritation, indifference, caution, pessimism, regret, insult, and depression. Geuens and De Pelsmacker (1998) studied the impact of ad-evoked feelings on ad and brand cognitions and found positive relationships. They carried out a regression analyses of brand attitudes (Ab) as a function of affective and cognitive responses; Attitudes towards the advertisement (Aad) as a function of cognitive and affective responses; Ab as a function of Aad; and Ab as a function of Aad together with affective and cognitive responses (Geuens & De Pelsmacker, 1998). Walker and Dubitsky (1991) measured the impact of ad and brand attitudes on purchase intentions. None of these researches measured the indicators of ad-evoked feelings and/or attitudes towards the ads and brands. We propose that positive and negative polysemy lead to corresponding positive and negative ad-evoked feelings, and ad and brand attitudes. This leads to the formation of the following hypotheses:

H_{1A}: Positive polysemic advertising appeals are associated with positive ad-evoked feelings.

H_{1B}: Positive polysemic advertising appeals are associated with positive attitude towards the ad (Aad).

H_{1C}: Positive polysemic advertising appeals are associated with positive attitude towards the brand (Ab).

H_{2A}: Negative polysemic advertising appeals are associated with negative ad-evoked feelings.

H_{2B}: Negative polysemic advertising appeals are associated with negative attitude towards the ad (Aad).

H_{2C}: Negative polysemic advertising appeals are associated with negative attitude towards the brand (Ab).

Certain brands (e.g., Coca-Cola, McDonald's) are considered to possess high brand equity, resulting in higher market shares and prices than competing products (Badenhausen, 1996) and, as a result, they enjoy high levels of customer loyalty, name awareness, perceived quality, strong brand associations, and other assets (Aaker, 1991). Yoo and Donthu (2001) have coined the term "consumer-based brand equity" to refer to the set of four brand equity dimensions or indicators of brand awareness, brand associations, perceived quality and brand loyalty. Consumer-based brand equity is defined as "the value consumers associate with a brand, as reflected in the dimensions of brand awareness, brand associations, perceived quality and brand loyalty" (Pappu et al., 2006, p. 698) and in the present research, brand equity refers to consumer-based brand equity. Brand and ad attitudes reflect a consumer's private/internal evaluations and feelings about an object (Batra and Homer, 2004) and hence, positive brand and ad attitudes may result in favorable, strong, and unique associations in consumers' memories (Keller, 1993). This results in strong consumer branding. Although McCracken (1986; 1989) conceptualized the implications of meaning transfer for branding, the mechanisms he postulated have not been verified experimentally. There has been a considerable amount of researches available showing the impact of ad-evoked feelings on advertising responses (Aaker, Stayman, & Hagerty, 1986; Batra & Ray, 1986; Burke & Edell, 1989; Edell & Burke, 1987; Holbrook & Batra, 1987), but these research activities did not study the consequent effects of ad-evoked feelings on branding. We propose that positive and negative advertising polysemy play an important role in creating consumer-based brand equity.

Brand credibility is "the believability of the product position information contained in a brand, which depends on the willingness and ability of firms to deliver what they promise" (Erdem & Swait, 2004). According to Spry, Pappu and Cornwell (2011), brand credibility contains two dimensions–expertise and trust-worthiness. Expertise refers to the extent to which a source is perceived to hold valid assertions, whereas trustworthiness refers to the degree of confidence in the source's intent to communicate the assertions considered to be most valid (Hovland et al., 1953). Brand signaling theory suggests that credibility can build brand equity (Erdem & Swait, 1998). Credible brands enjoy lower information-gathering and information-processing costs, and lower perceived risk (Erdem & Swait, 2004). Advertising and branding scholars have studied the brand equity indicators of brand awareness, brand associations, perceived quality and brand loyalty in detail but have not investigated the linkages of these indicators with brand credibility. We propose positive relationships between brand equity indicators and brand equity; and brand equity indicators and brand credibility, which then lead to brand equity. This leads to the development of the following hypotheses:

H_3: Brand awareness, brand associations, perceived quality and brand loyalty are indicators and antecedents of consumer-based brand equity.

H_4: Brand awareness, brand associations, perceived quality and brand loyalty are indicators and antecedents of brand credibility.

H_5: Brand credibility is an indicator and an antecedent of consumer-based brand equity.

All hypotheses developed in this section and illustrated in our advertising polysemy and consumer-based brand equity conceptual framework in Figure 1 are tested in the subsequent sections.

RESEARCH DESIGN AND METHODOLOGY

Study 1 (Pre-Test With 191 Respondents)

Our primary goal in Study One is to develop an instrument to assess negative and positive polysemy. The sample consisted of 191 undergraduate respondents from a historically black university, all between 18 to 28 years old, and 102 of them were women (see Table 1). Approximately 95% of the participants were African Americans, and 53.4% were females. With respect to class rank, the majority of the participants were juniors and seniors. The study was confined to six print ads in two product categories: socially conscious ads and alcoholic beverages ads. These product categories were relevant to the subjects because of their interest in these product categories. All subjects were at or above the legal drinking age and encountered the advertising messages. These product categories have an availability of a large

Table 1. Study 1 - Demographical Characteristics, (N=191)

Sample Characteristics	% of Sample
Gender	
Female	53.4
Male	46.6
Ethnicity	
African-American	94.0
Other	6.0
College Rank	
Sophomore	5.2
Junior	42.4
Senior	50.4
Graduate	1.0
Other	1.0

number of print advertisements with a good mix of the positive and negative advertising polysemic appeals.

The six print ads were presented to a group of 191 students in random order to avoid any potential order effects bias. These six ads operationalize polysemy as "perceived ad response" (O'Keefe, 2003) by an individual. If the ads were representing tangible goods, then it was easier for the respondents to answer questions about buying the product or brand but for intangible goods' (socially-conscious) ads, the respondents were given the cue that if they support the ad/brand then it is similar to raising funds and donations for the brand. We developed a simple polysemic scale consisting of four items as shown in Figure 2 below.

We conducted an exploratory factor analysis on the 4-item polysemy scale and two factors, positive and negative polysemy, emerged from the analysis. The two-factor model explained 81.96% of the variance. Table 2 shows the results regarding the existence of positive and negative advertising polysemy factors.

Study 2 (Post-Test with 177 respondents)

We conducted further research involving measures of advertising polysemy, ad-evoked feelings, ad and brand attitudes, consumer-based brand equity, and brand credibility with a sample of 177 respondents (undergraduate students) at a historically black university, all between the ages of 17 to 50 years, and 104 of them were women (see Table 3). Of the 177 respondents, 91.8% were at or above the legal drinking age and encountered the ad messages. The study was confined to six print ads in two product categories–socially conscious ads and alcoholic beverages ads.

The research was executed in two stages as follows.

Stage I – Qualitative Stage: Initially 50 advertisements in two product categories were selected from the Ads of the World Website (http://adsoftheworld.com). Fifteen academic experts in marketing and advertising were recruited as a jury and were asked to assess the 50 ads on positive and negative advertising polysemic ap-

Figure 2. Measures of Polysemy

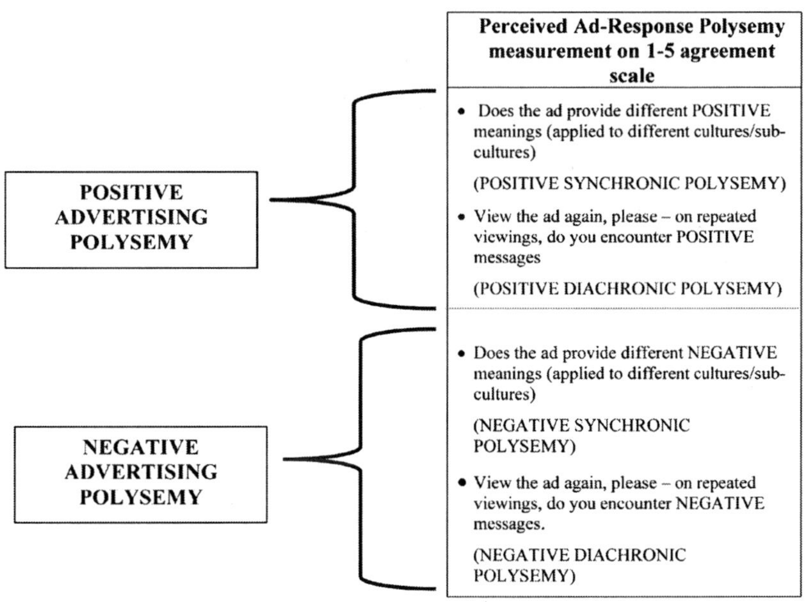

Table 2. Exploratory Factor Analysis – Advertising Polysemy

	Component	
	1	2
Does the ad provide a different but POSITIVE meaning when applied to different (your) culture/sub-culture?	**.552**	-.045
Does the ad provide a different but NEGATIVE meaning when applied to different (your) culture/sub-culture?	-.046	**.555**
View the ad again, at least view it 3 more times – on repeated viewings, do you encounter different POSITIVE messages?	**.548**	.025
View the ad again, at least view it 3 more times – on repeated viewings, do you encounter different but NEGATIVE messages?	.026	**.551**
Eigen Values	1.65	1.63
% of Variance	41.21	40.75
Cronbach alpha	0.78	0.81

peals. The experts had the required knowledge about synchronic and diachronic polysemy and analyzed the ads in the context of the definition of polysemy. A final set of six (6) ads emerged from this stage after conducting the frequency counts; the six ads fall into two categories: positive and negative advertising polysemy. Out of 6 final ads, three ads were found to be diachronic, two ads were synchronic, while one had both polysemic appeals. Also, these six ads were selected because they were believed to evoke both positive and negative advertising polysemy among different individuals. Hence, these polysemic ads included both positive and negative emotions. Appendix 1 shows the final selection of the six ads that were subsequently used in Stage II. Table 4 provides a detailed description of these six ads from different world regions, as selected in Stage I of the research process.

In Stage I, we used print ads from two product categories-socially responsible/conscious ads and alcoholic beverages ads, and they were randomly assigned to the different experimental treatments. When the real ads are tested, they are high on external validity but low on experimental control, and hence, it is important to attribute the ads to the correct experimental category to avoid confounds (Geuens & Pelsmacker, 1998). By careful selection and attribution of the 50 ads to two experimental appeal categories (positive advertising polysemy and negative advertising polysemy), the jury of 15 academic experts developed six (6) ads which best illustrated the correct two experimental categories because testing all 50 ads with a series of constructs on 191 respondents (Study 1) and then 177 respondents (Study 2) would be

Table 3. Study 2 - Demographical Characteristics, (N=177)

Sample Characteristics	% of Sample
Gender	
Female	60.1
Male	39.9
Ethnicity	
African-American	86.1
Other	13.9
College Rank	
Freshman	0.6
Sophomore	2.9
Junior	20.8
Senior	54.9
Graduate	20.2
Other	0.6

impossible leading to survey and ad fatigue in our focal population. We used the Geuens and Pelsmacker (1998) research design of measuring subject-based perception of the ads and selecting only the ads that were judged as diachronic and synchronic along with positive and negative polysemic advertising appeals, thus leading to our final selection of six print ads. The concept of positive and negative polysemy along with the presence of synchronic and diachronic polysemy was carefully considered when we examined the final set of six ads, and three were found to be diachronic, two were synchronic, and one falls into both categories.

Stage II - Quantitative Stage - The survey instrument involving all advertising and branding measures (as shown in Table 5) was administered via Web to 177 college students at a comprehensive historically black university in the southeastern part of the United States. All research participants were volunteers and the survey took approximately 20 minutes to complete. The six print ads were presented to a group of 177 students in random order to avoid any potential order effects bias. If the ads were representing tangible goods, then it was easier for the respondents to answer questions about buying the product or brand; for intangible goods (socially-conscious) ads, the respondents were given the cue that if they support the ad/brand then it is similar to raising funds and donations for the brand.

Common Method Variance Tests

Because all constructs were measured using self-report measures, we examined whether common method variance was a serious issue. As recommended by Podsakoff and Organ (1986), Harman's one-factor test was performed. In this test, all survey items were entered together into an unrotated factor analysis and the results were examined. If substantial common method variance is present, then either a single factor would emerge or one general factor would account for most of the total variance explained in the items (Podsakoff & Organ, 1986). After entering all items into the factor analysis model, 10 factors emerged from the analysis, and the first factor only accounted for 25.029% of the total variance. In addition, no general factor emerged from the factor analysis. Thus, common method variance was not deemed a serious issue in this study.

Measures

In the present study, Table 5 presents the descriptors for the measures of the constructs used to develop and test the hypothesized model shown in Figure 2. Unless stated otherwise, we used a Likert-type response format for the survey items. We developed positive and negative advertising polysemy scale consisting of 4-items, pretested on 191 respondents (Study 1) and then on 177 respondents (Study 2). The primary affective reactions or ad-evoked feelings were measured on a 16-item semantic differential scale, assessing respondents' feelings as a reaction to seeing the stimulus (Brooker & Wheatley, 1994). Attitude towards the ad (Aad) was measured by a 6-item Likert Scale (Baker & Kennedy, 1994), and attitude towards the brand (Ab) was measured by a 4-item Likert scale (Stayman & Aaker, 1988; Coulson, 1989; Homer, 1990). Brand awareness (3-items), perceived quality (4-items), brand loyalty (3 items) and overall consumer-based brand equity (4-items) were measured using Yoo and Donthu (2001) scales while brand associations (5-items) was measured using Aaker's (1991) instrument. Brand credibility encompasses expertise and trustworthiness (Erdem & Swait, 2004). Expertise and trustworthiness were considered sub-dimensions of a higher order brand credibility construct, which was based on past research (Erdem & Swait, 1998). Measures for brand credibility were obtained from brand signaling research (Erdem & Swait, 2004) and consisted of seven items encompassing expertise and trustworthiness on a seven-point scale.

Table 4. Description of six polysemic ads selected in Stage I of the research process

Ad #	Company	Advertising agency	Description	Polysemy	Product Category	World Region to which the ad belongs
1	Deutscher Tierschutz Bund e.V.	Frese & Wolff, Oldenburg, Germany	The focus of the ad is the animal rights protection in Germany. The sight of excessive blood may lead to misinterpretation, especially when seen repeatedly.	Yes Diachronic	Socially Responsible (Conscious) Ad	Germany, Europe
2	Absolut Vodka	French firm - Pernod Ricard (In-House agency)	The ad shows a pregnant male and outgoing female couple, with female holding the drink and male as the primary house maker. This depiction may lead to misinterpretation across different cultures and consumer-groups.	Yes Synchronic	Alcohol	France, Europe
3	Brazilian Bit Copa	Jung von Matt Alster, Hamburg, Germany	The ad shows an erotic alcoholic ad with painted woman breasts. This depiction may lead to misinterpretation across different cultures and consumer-groups.	Yes Synchronic	Alcohol	Brazil, South America
4	Italian animal rights group, the LAV	cOOkies adv, Milan, Italy	The Italian ad shows the cruelty to animals with the underlined message - the show mustn't go on. Support animal-free circuses. This depiction may lead to misinterpretation when viewed multiple times.	Yes Diachronic	Socially Responsible (Conscious) Ad	Italy, Europe
5	Beer Point pub: Hoegaarden in Belgium	Kinograf, Kiev, Ukraine	The ad shows funny (unusual) men drinking beer in an unusual way. This depiction may lead to misinterpretation when viewed multiple times.	Yes Diachronic	Alcohol	Ukraine, Europe
6	Kafa, UAE	Y&R, Dubai, UAE	The print ad is about verbal abuse to women. The ad has diachronic polysemy as the 'fear' appeal is pretty high leading to 'anger' on repeated viewings.	Yes (Both Diachronic and Synchronic)	Socially Responsible (Conscious) Ad	United Arab Emirates

Data Analysis

We tested the proposed polysemy model presented in Figure 1 using structural equation modeling to evaluate the research hypotheses by using the linear structural relations (LISREL) computer program (Jöreskog & Sörbom, 1999; Jöreskog, Sörbom, Du Toit, & Du Toit, 2003). The covariance matrix was used as the input for the structural model, and the maximum likelihood estimation procedure was employed to produce the model parameters. Since the data followed a non-normal distribution (kurtosis = 99.84, t-value = 35.82), bootstrapping techniques and the Bollen-Stine corrected p-value were employed to obtain unbiased model parameters (Arbuckle & Wothke, 1995; Bollen & Stine, 1992). To examine model fit, we utilized measures of absolute fit, close fit, and incremental fit to determine how well the data fit the hypothesized model (Hair, Anderson, Tatham, & Black, 1998).

The following fit indices were used to assess the fit of the nomological network developed in Figure 1. The Goodness-of-Fit Index (GFI) is a measure of absolute fit of the model by comparing the fitted model with the actual data, and ranges

Table 5. Advertising polysemy and branding measures' descriptors

Polysemy measurement on 1-5 agreement scale	Ad-Evoked Feelings or Primary Affective Reactions (PARs)	Attitude Towards the Ad (Aad)	Attitude Towards the Brand (Ab)	Brand Credibility	Brand Equity Dimensions / Indicators / Antecedents	Consumer-Based Brand Equity
• Does the ad provide different POSITIVE meanings (applied to different cultures/sub-cultures)........... (POSITIVE SYNCHRONIC POLYSEMY) • Does the ad provide different NEGATIVE meanings (applied to different cultures/sub-cultures)........... (NEGATIVE SYNCHRONIC POLYSEMY) • View the ad again, please – on repeated viewings, do you encounter POSITIVE messages......... (POSITIVE DIACHRONIC POLYSEMY) • View the ad again, please – on repeated viewings, do you encounter NEGATIVE messages......... (NEGATIVE DIACHRONIC POLYSEMY)	• Worried-carefree • Nervous-calm • Contemplative-impulsive • Critical-accepting • Cautious-adventurous • Dubious-confident • Pessimistic-hopeful • Callous-affectionate • Bad-good • Sad-happy • Insulted-honored • Indifferent-interested • Irritated-pleased • Unemotional-sentimental • Depressed-cheerful • Regretful-rejoicing	I like this ad a lot. I don't think this ad is interesting. I think this ad is very convincing. This ad is very appealing. This ad is easy to forget. This ad is not effective.	Do you like the advertised brand? Do you think this is a good brand? Do you feel favorably towards this brand? Would you recommend the advertised brand to others?	***Expertise*** 1. This brand reminds me of someone who's competent and knows what he/she is doing. 2. This brand has the ability to deliver what it promises. ***Trustworthiness*** 3. This brand delivers what it promises 4. This brand's product claims are believable 5. Over time, my experiences with this brand have led me to expect it to keep its promises, no more and no less 6. This brand has a name you can trust. 7. This brand doesn't pretend to be something it isn't	***Brand Awareness*** • I can recognize this brand among other competing brands. • I am aware of this brand. • Some characteristics of this brand come to my mind quickly. ***Brand Associations*** • It is likely that this brand offer good value for money • It is likely that this brand would be technically advanced. • I like this brand. • I trust this brand as a manufacturer of (product category). • I would feel proud to own this brand. ***Perceived Quality*** • It is likely that this brand is of high quality. • It is likely that this brand is of very consistent quality. • It is likely that this brand offer excellent features. • It is likely that this brand is very reliable. ***Brand Loyalty*** • I consider myself to be loyal to this brand. • This brand would be my first choice. • I will not buy other brands if this brand is available at the store.	• It makes sense to buy this brand instead of any other brands, even if they the same. • Even if another brand has same features as this brand, I would prefer to buy this brand. • If there is another brand as good as this brand, I prefer to buy this brand. • If another brand is not different from this brand in any way, it seems smarter to purchase this brand.

from 0-1. Values greater than 0.90 demonstrate the model fits the data well (Hair et al., 1998). The absolute fit measures, maximum likelihood ratio chi-square statistic (X^2), p-value, and GFI, provide a measure of the extent to which the covariance matrix estimated by the hypothesized model reproduces the Observed Covariance Matrix (James & Brett, 1984). The Root Mean Square Error of

Approximation (RMSEA) was considered as it provides an estimate of the measurement error. Another fit index, the Non-normed Fit Index (NNFI), was used to assess model fit; the NNFI assesses a penalty for adding additional parameters to the model. The Normed Fit Index (NFI) provides information about how much better the model fits than a baseline model, rather than as a sole function of the difference between the reproduced and observed covariance matrices (Bentler & Bonett, 1980). The Comparative Fit Index (CFI) has similar attributes to the NFI and compares the predicted covariance matrix to the observed covariance matrix and is least affected by sample size. The two-step approach to structural equation modeling was employed (Anderson & Gerbing, 1988). First, the measurement model was inspected for satisfactory fit indices. After establishing satisfactory model fit, the structural coefficients were interpreted.

Table 6. Means, standard deviations, and zero-order correlations

Variables	Mean	s.d.	1	2	3	4	5	6	7	8	9	10	11	12
1. Pos Poly	5.82	2.08	(.78)											
2. Neg Poly	9.32	1.84	-.14	(.80)										
3. Attitude Ad	16.44	3.59	.43*	.20	(.66)									
4. Ad Evoked	58.20	15.91	.54*	-.02	.61*	(.95)								
5. Attitude Brand	25.86	5.90	.60*	.10	.64*	.66*	(.85)							
6. Brand Aware	10.05	2.87	.22*	.21*	.22*	.20*	.39*	(.91)						
7. Brand Assoc	14.33	4.02	.51*	.04	.63	.60*	.76*	.35*	(.94)					
8. P Quality	11.79	3.39	.52*	.05	.55*	.56	.71*	.45*	.79*	(.95)				
9. Brand Loyalty	8.14	2.62	.44*	.20*	.60*	.57*	.68*	.17*	.67*	.58*	(.90)			
10. Brand Cred-E	5.87	2/89	.49*	.09	.46*	.49*	.68*	.39*	.72*	.74*	.63*	(.91)		
11. Brand Cred-T	14.50	3.85	.49*	.15*	.54*	.53*	.71*	.36*	.77*	.81*	.65*	.78*	(.93)	
12. Brand Equity	11.36	3.07	.48*	.21*	.57*	.55*	.74*	.28*	.68*	.76*	.70*	.73*	.83*	(.92)

$n = 177$ * $p \leq .05$
Pos Poly = Positive Polysemy
Neg Poly = Negative Polysemy
Attitude Ad = Attitude Toward the Ad
Ad Evoked = Ad Evoked Feelings
Attitude Brand = Attitude Toward the Brand
Brand Aware = Brand Awareness
Brand Assoc = Brand Association
P Quality = Perceived Quality
Brand Cred-E = Brand Credibility-Expertise
Brand Cred-T = Brand Credibility-Trustworthiness

RESULTS

The means, standard deviations, reliability estimates, and Pearson zero-order correlations are provided in Table 6. Correlations were in the intended direction with positive and negative polysemy demonstrating a significant relationship with most of the constructs in our model. For example, positive polysemy was significantly related to ad evoked feelings, brand awareness, brand association, perceived quality, brand loyalty, brand credibility-expertise, brand credibility-trustworthiness, and brand equity. Similarly, negative polysemy was related to brand awareness, brand loyalty, brand credibility-trustworthiness, and brand equity. In addition, brand credibility-trustworthiness and brand equity were significantly related to all variables in our model.

The measurement model had acceptable fit indices [χ^2 = 31.852(26), p=.198, CFI= .99, GFI= .97, NNFI= .99, NFI= .98, RMSEA= .036]. That is, the Chi-square statistic was at its minimum, and the p-value was nonsignificant. The GFI was above its recommended threshold level of greater than 0.90 (Hair et al., 1998), and the RMSEA was less than 0.08, indicative of an acceptable model (Steiger & Lind, 1980). The Chi-square divided by the degrees of freedom coefficient was less than three, which indicates acceptable model fit (Arbuckle & Wothke, 1995). The CFI, NFI, and NNFI all indicated an acceptable fit of the model to the data. Next, we discuss the structural coefficients of the hypothesized model.

Table 7 presents the structural coefficients for the model. Support was established for Hypotheses 1A, 1B, and 1C because the paths from positive polysemy to ad evoked feelings, attitude towards the ad, and attitude towards the brand were statistically significant and in a positive direction. Hypotheses 2A, 2B, and 2C were supported because the paths from negative polysemy to ad evoked feelings, attitude towards the ad, and attitude towards the brand were statistically significant. These hypotheses further established the nomological validity by examining the impact of our polysemy constructs (positive and negative polysemy) on various dependent measures of ad-evoked feelings, and attitudes towards ad and brand. Nomological validity refers to the degree to which the construct, as measured by a set of indicators, predicts other constructs that past theoretical and empirical work suggests it should predict (Netemeyer, Bearden, & Sharma, 2003).

Our model established partial support for Hypothesis H3 because brand awareness, brand loyalty, and perceived quality influenced brand equity. However, brand association did not influence brand equity. Partial support was established for Hypothesis 4 as perceived quality and brand loyalty influenced brand credibility-expertise; brand awareness and brand association were not significant predictors of brand credibility-expertise. Brand awareness and brand association influenced brand credibility-trustworthiness; perceived quality and brand loyalty did not predict brand credibility-trustworthiness in the model.

Some interesting results emerged from our research. Ad-evoked feelings and attitude towards brand were found to be strong indicators for brand awareness and perceived quality. Attitude towards brand, in particular, was found to predict all brand equity variables of brand awareness, brand associations, brand loyalty and perceived quality, but attitude towards the ad was not a predictor for either of these consumer-based brand equity variables. This means that advertisement and brand attitudes impact the consumer-based brand equity differently, whereby brand attitudes positively and strongly influence the brand equity variables more than ad attitudes. Consumers may like the ad, but if they do not have positive impressions about the brand, they will not form positive impressions about the brand equity parameters of brand awareness, brand associations, perceived quality and brand loyalty.

Hypothesis 5 was partially supported because the path from brand credibility-trustworthiness to consumer-based brand equity was statistically significant and in a positive direction. The path from brand credibility-expertise to brand equity was not significant. We did not find any gender differences in our model. That is, males and females did not report any significant differences regarding positive or negative advertising polysemy or other constructs in our model.

DISCUSSION

Polysemy has provided a new intriguing dimension in our research study. There is a dearth of advertising polysemy research in the extant literature. Advertising polysemy is an important concept which advertisers can use as a creative strategy for changing and shaping consumer attitudes, behaviors and perceptions. Polysemy can be useful as a branding agent to strengthen the appeal of alcoholic beverages and socially conscious messages. There is a paucity of advertising research that examines the influence of positive and negative polysemy on branding. Brand personality and brand equity provide value to consumers by enhancing satisfaction and reducing buyer's remorse. Thus, the aim of this study was to further explore the perceptions of consumers encountering polysemic ads and the role these encounters may have on ad evoked feelings and attitudes toward the ad and brand. Specifically, the current project investigated the antecedents of brand equity indicators, brand credibility, and brand equity, thereby leading a less-researched and significant research area of advertising polysemy into branding literature.

Our research seeks to understand how positive and negative advertising polysemy influences consumers, whether advertisers can use polysemy as a tool to influence the attitudes and behaviors of consumers, and thereby strengthen consumer-based brand equity, and how consumers' ad and brand attitudes respond to polysemic advertising. Using structural equation modeling to address our research questions, we found support for Hypotheses 1A, 1B and 1C, which stated that positive polysemy would be related to ad evoked feelings, attitude towards the ad, and attitude towards the brand. These findings are consistent with the advertising literature which focuses on emotional appeals (Geuens & De Pelsmacker, 1998). In a similar manner, support was established for Hypotheses 2A, 2B, and 2C because negative advertising polysemy was significantly related to ad evoked feelings, attitude towards the ad, and attitude towards the brand in our model.

Partial support was established for Hypothesis 3 because only brand awareness, brand loyalty, and perceived quality predicted consumer-based brand equity in our sample; brand associations did not significantly influence brand equity. Perceived quality and brand loyalty influenced brand credibility-expertise, but brand awareness and brand associations were not significant predictors; brand awareness and brand associations influenced brand credibility-trustworthiness, but perceived quality and brand loyalty were not predictors in the model, thus providing partial support for Hypothesis 4, which stated that brand equity indicators would influence brand credibility. Although researchers (Erdem & Swait, 1998; Spry, Pappu, & Cornwell, 2011) have examined brand equity indicators, the brand equity indicators-brand credibility nexus lacks attention.

We also found that brand credibility-trustworthiness influenced brand equity in the model, indicating partial support for Hypothesis 5. Brand credibility-expertise was not a significant predictor of brand equity. Brand credibility component of "trustworthiness" is the willingness of the brand to continuously deliver what has been promised and if brands do not deliver what is promised—their brand equity erodes (Erdem & Swait, 2004). Our research proves that trustworthiness impacts brand equity positively. However, brand credibility component of "expertise," defined as the believability of the product information contained in a brand, which requires that consumers perceive that the brand have the ability (i.e., expertise) to continuously deliver what has been promised (Erdem & Swait, 2004), was not found to impact

Table 7. Path coefficients for the model (unstandardized values)

Parameter	Path Coefficient	T-value	R^2	
Attitude Toward Ad			59%	
Positive Polysemy	1.90	8.74*		**H_{1B} & H_{2B}**
Negative Polysemy	1.70	5.39*		**Supported**
Ad Evoked Feelings			65%	
Positive Polysemy	9.17	9.26*		**H_{1A} & H_{2A}**
Negative Polysemy	1.24	2.16*		**Supported**
Attitude Toward Brand			92%	
Positive Polysemy	3.57	9.33*		**H_{1C} & H_{2C}**
Negative Polysemy	0.97	5.15*		**Supported**
Brand Awareness			21%	
Attitude Toward Ad	-.10	-1.09		
Ad Evoked Feelings	-.08	-2.06*		
Attitude Toward Brand	0.37	4.57*		
Brand Association			74%	
Attitude Toward Ad	0.03	0.29		
Ad Evoked Feelings	-.03	-1.23		
Attitude Toward Brand	0.70	8.23*		
Perceived Quality			28%	
Attitude Toward Ad	-.16	-1.02		
Ad Evoked Feelings	-.08			
Attitude Toward Brand	1.43	8.28*		
Brand Credibility-Expertise	-.44	-.88		
Brand Credibility-Trust-worthiness	0.53	1.96*		
Brand Loyalty			60%	
Attitude Toward Ad	0.08	1.22		
Ad Evoked Feelings	-.01	-.53		
Attitude Toward Brand	0.37	6.16*		
Brand Credibility-Expertise			62%	
Brand Awareness	0.02	0.41		**H_4**
Brand Association	0.05	1.08		**Partially**
Perceived Quality	.34	5.45*		**Supported**
Brand Loyalty	0.15	3.07*		
Brand Credibility-Trust-worthiness			74%	
Brand Awareness	0.16	2.03*		**H_4**
Brand Association	0.39	4.47*		**Partially**

continued on following page

Table 7. Continued

Parameter	Path Coefficient	T-value	R^2	
Perceived Quality	-.23	-1.11		**Supported**
Brand Loyalty	-.20	-1.70		
Brand Equity			63%	
Brand Awareness	-.42	-2.98*		**H_3**
Brand Association	-.31	-1.80		**Partially**
Perceived Quality	1.57	3.22*		**Supported**
Brand Loyalty	0.43	2.70*		

n = 191 respondents. *Significant at the 0.05 level.
The endogenous variables are underlined and the exogenous variables are listed underneath.

the consumer-based brand equity. Both the expertise and trustworthiness of a brand reflect the cumulative impacts of associated past and present marketing strategies and activities (Erdem & Swait, 2004).

Contrary to our conjecture, we did not find any gender differences in our model. That is, males and females did not report any significant differences across positive or negative advertising polysemy or between the other constructs in our model. We expected females to have a stronger reaction to the negative and positive polysemy ads as compared to their male counterparts. Although females did report higher levels of both negative and positive polysemy, these levels were not significantly different from males. In retrospect, we believe gender differences may indeed exist but that perhaps it is generational such that older gender differences may exist but not in the current millennial generation represented by our sample.

CONCLUSION AND SUGGESTIONS FOR FUTURE RESEARCH

The purpose of this research was to examine the influence of advertising polysemy on branding. Specifically, we examine the link between advertising polysemy and its influence on the brand equity indicators of brand awareness, brand associations, brand loyalty and perceived loyalty using a structural equation modeling framework. We found that positive and negative advertising influenced ad evoked feelings, attitude towards the ad, and attitude towards the brand in model. Further, brand awareness, brand loyalty, and perceived quality influenced consumer-based brand equity. Perceived quality and brand loyalty influenced brand credibility-expertise whereas only brand awareness and brand associations influenced brand credibility-trustworthiness. Brand credibility-trustworthiness influenced brand equity. Unexpectedly, we did not find any gender differences across the nomological network.

Our findings contribute to the existing body of knowledge because our study is the "first" to examine advertising polysemy (positive and negative) and its impact on ad evoked feelings, attitude towards the ad, attitude towards the brand, and the brand equity indicators. Another contribution of the current research is that our sample contained a large percentage of African Americans, which adds to the richness of the extant literature. The current research provides deeper insights into advertising polysemy and its impact on consumer-based brand equity with a special focus on African-American population. This sample may be of distinct interest for advertising agencies and marketing practitioners trying to employ innovative advertising techniques and strategies for targeting minority demographics.

Our study suggests that positive and negative polysemic appeals represent two distinct concepts which should not be considered as a continuum, but rather measured individually. This investigation fills an important gap in advertising scale literature, as to date no instrument has been available to formally measure the extent to which an ad employs positive or negative advertising polysemy. From a managerial perspective, the polysemy measurements will enable firms to understand better the nature of positive and negative advertising polysemy in advertising strategy.

The current research did have some limitations. First, the cross-sectional design of the study does not allow for causal inferences. We also believe longitudinal designs are needed in this area to examine the behavior of these constructs over time. Another limitation of the study was that all data were collected via self-report measures, which may lead to the problem of common method bias and may inflate the predictive relationships. However, we conducted the Harmon's One Factor test, which did not indicate that common method variance was problematic in our structural equation model. Lastly, we had a modest sample size. Despite these limitations, we believe that our study contributes to the existing body of knowledge because it provides a useful scale to examine both negative and positive advertising polysemy. Future research is needed to replicate these findings and examine the stability of our model coefficients across samples. Analyzing diverse samples may provide additional insight into consumer behavior that may be useful to advertisers and marketing firms.

Another future area of inquiry would be to examine the mediation effects of ad evoked feelings, attitude toward the ad and attitude toward the brand on the advertising polysemy-brand equity indicator relationship. It would also be interesting to examine this model with respect to generational samples to determine whether gender differences are indeed a function of generation with respect to advertising polysemy.

REFERENCES

Aaker, D. A. (1991). *Managing Brand Equity: Capitalizing on the Value of a Brand Name*. New York: The Free Press.

Aaker, D. A., Stayman, D. M., & Hagerty, M. R. (1986). Warmth in advertising: Measurement, impact, and sequence effects. *The Journal of Consumer Research*, *12*(4), 365–381. doi:10.1086/208524.

Andersen, J. P., & Meyer, T. P. (1988). *Mediated Communication. A Social Action Perspective*. Newbury Park, CA: Sage.

Anderson, J. C., & Gerbing, D. W. (1988). Structural equation modeling in practice: A review and recommended two-step approach. *Psychological Bulletin*, *103*(3), 411–423. doi:10.1037/0033-2909.103.3.411.

Arbuckle, J. L., & Wothke, W. (1995). *AMOS 4.0 User's Guide*. Chicago, IL: Smallwaters Corporation.

Badenhausen, K. (1996). Blind faith. *Financial World*, *165*(July 8), 50-65.

Baker, S. M., & Kennedy, P. F. (1994). Death by nostalgia: A diagnosis of context-specific cases. *Advances in Consumer Research. Association for Consumer Research (U. S.)*, *21*, 169–174.

Batra, R., & Homer, P. M. (2004). The situational impact of brand image beliefs. *Journal of Consumer Psychology*, *14*(3), 318–330. doi:10.1207/s15327663jcp1403_12.

Batra, R., & Ray, M. L. (1986). Affective responses mediating acceptance of advertising. *The Journal of Consumer Research*, *13*(2), 234–249. doi:10.1086/209063.

Belch, G. E., & Belch, M. A. (2009). *Advertising and Promotion – An Integrated Marketing Communications Perspective* (8th ed.). McGraw-Hill.

Bentler, P. M., & Bonett, D. G. (1980). Significance tests and goodness of fit in the analysis of covariance structures. *Psychological Bulletin*, *88*, 588–606. doi:10.1037/0033-2909.88.3.588.

Bollen, K. A., & Stine, R. A. (1992). Bootstrapping goodness-of-fit measures in structural equation models. *Sociological Methods & Research*, *21*, 205–229. doi:10.1177/0049124192021002004.

Borgerson, J. L., & Schroeder, J. E. (2002). Ethical issues of global marketing: Avoiding bad faith in visual representation. *European Journal of Marketing*, *36*(5/6), 570–594. doi:10.1108/03090560210422399.

Brooker, G., & Wheatley, J. J. (1994). Music and radio advertising: Effects of tempo and placement. *Advances in Consumer Research. Association for Consumer Research (U. S.)*, *21*, 286–290.

Burke, M. C., & Edell, J. A. (1989). The impact of feelings on ad-based affect and cognition. *JMR, Journal of Marketing Research*, *26*(1), 69–83. doi:10.2307/3172670.

Buttle, F. (1991). What do people do WITH advertising! *International Journal of Advertising*, *10*(April-June), 95–110.

Caru, A., & Cova, B. (2007). Consuming experiences: An introduction. In Caru, A., & Cova, B. (Eds.), *Consuming Experience*. London: Routledge.

Condit, C. M. (1989). The rhetorical limits of polysemy. *Critical Studies in Mass Communication*, *6*(2), 103–122. doi:10.1080/15295038909366739.

Coulson, J. S. (1989). An investigation of mood commercials. In Cafferata, P., & Tybout, A. M. (Eds.), *Cognitive and Affective Responses to Advertising*. Lexington, MA: Lexington Books.

Edell, J. A., & Burke, M. C. (1987). The power of feelings in understanding advertising effects. *The Journal of Consumer Research*, *14*(3), 421–433. doi:10.1086/209124.

Erdem, T., & Swait, J. (1998). Brand equity as a signaling phenomenon. *Journal of Consumer Psychology*, *7*(April), 131–157. doi:10.1207/s15327663jcp0702_02.

Erdem, T., & Swait, J. (2004). Brand credibility, brand consideration, and choice. *The Journal of Consumer Research*, *31*(1), 191–198. doi:10.1086/383434.

Fish, S. (1980). Literature in the reader: Affective stylistics. In Tompkins, J. (Ed.), *Reader-Response Criticism. From Formalism to Post-structuralism*. Baltimore, MD: The John Hopkins University Press.

Fiske, J. (1990). *Introduction to Communication Studies* (2nd ed.). London: Routledge.

Geuens, M., & De Pelsmacker, P. (1998). Product category involvement and the reaction of Belgian and Polish consumers to different advertising appeals. *European Advances in Consumer Research*, *3*, 33–41.

Goldberg, M. E., & Gorn, G. J. (1987). Happy and sad TV programs: How they affect reactions to commercials. *The Journal of Consumer Research*, *14*, 387–403. doi:10.1086/209122.

Grier, S. A., & Brumbaugh, A. M. (1999). Noticing cultural differences: Ad meanings created by target and non-target markets. *Journal of Advertising*, *28*(1), 79–93.

Hair, J. F. Anderson, R. E., Tatham, R.L., & Black, W.C. (1998). Multivariate Data Analysis. New York: MacMillan.

Hirschman, E., & Thompson, C. (1997). Why media matter: Toward a richer understanding of consumers, relationships with advertising and mass media. *Journal of Advertising*, *26*(1), 44–59.

Holbrook, M. B., & Batra, R. (1987). Assessing the role of emotions as mediators of consumer responses to advertising. *The Journal of Consumer Research*, *14*(3), 404–420. doi:10.1086/209123.

Holland, N. (1980). Unity identity text self. In Tompkins, J. (Ed.), *Reader-Response Criticism. From Formalism to Post-structuralism* (pp. 118–133). Baltimore, MD: The John Hopkins University Press.

Homer, P. M. (1990). The mediating role of attitude towards the ad: Some additional evidence. *JMR, Journal of Marketing Research*, *27*, 78–86. doi:10.2307/3172553.

Hovland, C. I., Janis, I. L., & Kelley, H. H. (1953). *Communication. and persuasion: Psychological studies of opinion change*. New-Haven, CT: Vale University Press.

James, L. R., & Brett, J. M. (1984). Mediators, moderators, and tests for mediation. *The Journal of Applied Psychology*, *69*(2), 307–321. doi:10.1037/0021-9010.69.2.307.

Jöreskog, K. G., & Sörbom, D. (1999). *LISREL 8: User's Reference Guide*. Lincolnwood, IL: Scientific Software International.

Jöreskog, K. G., Sörbom, D., Du Toit, S., & Du Toit, M. (2003). *LISREL 8: New Statistical Features*. Lincolnwood, IL: Scientific Software International.

Keck, G. L., & Mueller, B. (1994). Intended vs. unintended messages: Viewer perceptions of United States Army television commercials. *Journal of Advertising Research*, *34*(2), 70–78.

Keller, K. L. (1993). Conceptualizing, measuring, and managing brand equity. *Journal of Marketing*, *57*(January), 1–22. doi:10.2307/1252054.

Kirmani, A. (1997). Advertising repetition as a signal of quality: If it's advertised so much, something must be wrong. *Journal of Advertising*, *26*(3), 77–86.

Leigh, T. W., Rethans, A. J., & Whitney, T. R. (1987). Role portrayals of women in advertising: Cognitive responses and advertising effectiveness. *Journal of Advertising Research*, *27*(October-November), 54–62.

McCracken, G. (1986). Culture and consumption: A theoretical account of the structure and movement of the cultural meaning of consumer godos. *The Journal of Consumer Research*, *13*(1), 71–84. doi:10.1086/209048.

McCracken, G. (1989). Who is the celebrity endorser? Cultural foundations of the endorsement process. *The Journal of Consumer Research*, *16*(3), 310–321. doi:10.1086/209217.

McQuarrie, E., & Mick, D. G. (1999). Visual rhetoric in advertising: Text-interpretive, experimental, and reader-response analyses. *The Journal of Consumer Research*, *26*(1), 37–54. doi:10.1086/209549.

Mick, D. G., & Buhl, C. (1992). A meaning-based model of advertising experiences. *The Journal of Consumer Research*, *19*(3), 317–338. doi:10.1086/209305.

Mitchell, A. A. (1986). The effect of verbal and visual components of advertisements on brand attitudes and attitude towards the advertisement. *The Journal of Consumer Research*, *13*(June), 12–23. doi:10.1086/209044.

Mitchell, A. A., & Olson, J. C. (1981). Are product attribute beliefs the only mediator of advertising effects on brand attitude? *JMR, Journal of Marketing Research*, *18*(3), 318–332. doi:10.2307/3150973.

Mitchell, D. J., Kahn, B. E., & Knasko, S. (1995). There's something in the Air: Effects of congruent or incongruent ambient odor on consumer decision making. *The Journal of Consumer Research*, *22*(September), 229–238. doi:10.1086/209447.

Moorthy, S., & Zhao, H. (2000). Advertising spending and perceived quality. *Marketing Letters*, *11*(3), 221–233. doi:10.1023/A:1008135126025.

Netemeyer, R. G., Bearden, W. O., & Sharma, S. (2003). *Scaling Procedures: Issues and Applications*. Thousand Oaks, CA: Sage.

O'Keefe, D. J. (2003). Message properties, mediating states, and manipulation checks: Claims, evidence, and data analysis in experimental persuasive message effects research. *Communication Theory*, *13*(3), 251–274. doi:10.1111/j.1468-2885.2003.tb00292.x.

Pappu, R., Quester, P. G., & Cooksey, R. W. (2006). Consumer-based brand equity and country-of-origin relationships: Some empirical evidence. *European Journal of Marketing*, *40*(5/6), 696–717. doi:10.1108/03090560610657903.

Parker, B. (1998). Exploring life themes and myths in alcohol advertisements through a meaning-based model of advertising experiences. *Journal of Advertising*, *27*(1), 97–112.

Plummer, J. T. (1985). Brand personality: A strategic concept for multinational advertising. In *Marketing Educators' Conference* (pp. 1–31). New York: Young and Rubicam.

Podsakoff, P. M., & Organ, D. W. (1986). Self-reports in organizational research: Problems and prospects. *Journal of Management*, *12*(4), 531–544. doi:10.1177/014920638601200408.

Puntoni, S., Schroeder, J. E., & Ritson, M. (2010). Meaning Matters Polysemy in Advertising. *Journal of Advertising*, *39*(2), 51–64. doi:10.2753/JOA0091-3367390204.

Ringberg, T., & Reihlen, M. (2008). Communication assumptions in consumer research: An alternative socio-cognitive approach. *Consumption. Markets and Culture*, *11*(September), 173–189. doi:10.1080/10253860802190512.

Ritson, M., & Elliott, R. (1995). Advertising literacy and the social signification of cultural meaning. In F. Hansen (Ed.), European Advances in Consumer Research, 2, 113-117. Provo, UT: Association for Consumer Research.

Russo, F. K., Shah, R. H., & Park, C. W. (1994). The impact of emotional valence and intensity on ad evaluation and memory. *Advances in Consumer Research. Association for Consumer Research (U. S.)*, *21*, 583–588.

Scott, L. M. (1994). The bridge from text to mind: Adapting reader-response theory to consumer research. *The Journal of Consumer Research*, *21*(3), 461–480. doi:10.1086/209411.

Scott, L. M. (1994). The bridge from text to mind: Adapting reader-response theory to consumer research. *The Journal of Consumer Research*, *21*(3), 461–480. doi:10.1086/209411.

Shimp, T. A. (1981). Attitude towards the ad as a mediator of consumer brand choice. *Journal of Advertising*, *10*(Summer), 9–15.

Sigman, S. (1987). A Perspective on Social Communication. Lexington, VA: Lexington.

Spry, A., Pappu, R., & Cornwell, T. B. (2011). Celebrity endorsement, brand credibility and brand equity. *European Journal of Marketing*, *45*(6), 882–909. doi:10.1108/03090561111119958.

Srull, T. K. (1983). Affect and memory: The impact of affective reactions in advertising on the representation of product information in memory. *Advances in Consumer Research. Association for Consumer Research (U. S.)*, *10*, 520–525.

Stayman, D. M., & Aaker, D. A. (1988). Are all the effects of ad-induced feelings mediated by Aad? *The Journal of Consumer Research*, *15*(December), 368–373. doi:10.1086/209173.

Steiger, J. H., & Lind, J. C. (1980). *Statistically-based tests for the number of common factors.* Paper presented at the Annual Meeting of the Psychometric Society. Iowa City, IA.

Stern, B. (1989). Literary criticism and consumer research: Overview and illustrative analysis. *The Journal of Consumer Research*, *16*(3), 322–334. doi:10.1086/209218.

Stuart, E. W., Shimp, T. A., & Engle, R. W. (1987). Classical conditioning of consumer attitudes: Four experiments in an advertising context. *The Journal of Consumer Research*, *14*(3), 334–349. doi:10.1086/209117.

Tellis, G. J., & Ambler, T. (2007). Handbook of Advertising. In Tellis, G. J., & Ambler, T. (Eds.), *The Sage Handbook of Advertising* (pp. 3–16). London: Sage. doi:10.4135/9781848607897.n1.

Walker, D., & Dubitsky, T. M. (1991). *Do they like it? Does it matter? An ASI perspective*. Paper presented at the 36th Annual Conference of the Advertising Research Foundation. New York.

Whittler, T. E., & Spira, J. S. (2002). Model's race: A peripheral cue in advertising messages? *Journal of Consumer Psychology*, *12*(4), 291–301. doi:10.1207/15327660260382333.

Yoo, B., & Donthu, N. (2001). Developing and validating a multidimensional consumer-based brand equity scale. *Journal of Business Research*, *52*(1), 1–14. doi:10.1016/S0148-2963(99)00098-3.

Zeithaml, V. A. (1988). Consumer perceptions of price, quality, and value: A means-end model and synthesis of evidence. *Journal of Marketing*, *52*(3), 2–22. doi:10.2307/1251446.

Zhou, N., & Belk, R. (2004). Chinese consumer readings of global and local advertising appeals. *Journal of Advertising*, *33*(3), 63–76. doi:10.1080/00913367.2004.10639169.

Chapter 6
Exploring the Use of Performance Measurements in Arab Manufacturing Firms

Ahmed B. Abdel-Maksoud
United Arab Emirates University, UAE

ABSTRACT

This study focuses on two Arab developing countries following the view that scope, role, and positioning of management accounting differ across organisations and countries, and, in the same direction, the study draws on the recent literature on localisation of global management control systems. Furthermore, the study embeds the view that certain contextual variables such as country differences and organisational culture possess particular cultural characteristics, which in turn affect individuals to respond distinctively to Management Accounting Systems' (MAS) applications. The main objective of this study is to investigate whether or not there are significant associations between the use and levels of importance of operational non-financial performance indicators (ONFPIs) and the extent of a set of contextual variables including firms' and managers' characteristics and workforce involvement. The study reports and discusses findings of surveying manufacturing firms belonging to various industry sectors in Egypt and Saudi Arabia (SA) in mid-2005. Findings show that levels of importance of ONFPIs in Egyptians firms are higher than those in use at their Saudi peers' firms. In general, findings on significant positive associations between the levels of importance of ONFPIs and the incorporated contextual variables in the Egyptian firms seem to be in line with prior literature findings drawn from global practices. Interestingly, the effect of organisational culture seems to be witnessed in Saudi firms evident by the negative, rather than positive, associations between two variables belonging to managers' characteristics and workforce involvement and levels of importance of ONFPIs.

DOI: 10.4018/978-1-4666-3966-9.ch006

INTRODUCTION

Management Accounting Systems (MAS) can be considered as 'those parts of the formalised information system used by organisations to influence the behavior of their managers that leads to the attainment of organisational objectives' (Gerdin, 2005, p. 103). In this paper, performance measurement as a MAS instrument (Gerdin, 2005; Abdel-Kader & Luther, 2008) is investigated. Chenhall (2003) defines MAS as the systematic use of management accounting to achieve some goals. Bouwens and Abernethy (2000) argue that MAS can be designed to provide more sophisticated information which facilitates decision making within and coordination between functional departments.

The sophistication of MAS' techniques has received attention in the extant literature (Bjornenak, 1997; Malmi, 1999; Tillema, 2005), such as costing (e.g., activity-based costing), and performance measurements (e.g., balanced scorecard). The focal point of this study is on the accounting information MAS provide. Such information comprises accounting instruments and is provided to managers and employees for specific purposes–such as an operating decision or the planning and control of an operating task (Tillema, 2005). Performance measurement as a MAS' instrument is the core of this study.

The localisation of global management control systems has been a focal theme recently (Cruz, Scapens, & Major, 2011), where questions are raised whether management control systems are re-produced or rather reshaped by local managers when they are enacted at the local level. It is about analysing whether local managers are capable of resisting the homogenising pressures resulting from "travelling of accounting systems across interconnected times and spaces in contemporary world" (p.412). It is suggested research should focus on accounting as a "situated craft" (Chua, 2007, p. 487), as this could provide better explanations of "how 'skillful' practices are constituted locally in response to global accounting systems" (Cruz et al., 2011, p. 425). Cruz et al. argue that "heterogenisation of management control practices is an essential part of the process of homogenisation which is developed by the stretching of 'extra-local' or global management control systems. This heterogeneity in accounting is produced as locals are increasingly exposed to the homogeneity produced by corporate (global) management control systems" (p. 425). Homogeneity is often said to be a product of globalisation, as the latter is supposed to lead to increasingly homogenised practices (Cruz et al., 2011, p. 417). This study, in line with Cruz et al.'s (2011), contributes to a better understanding of the use and levels of importance of performance measurements (particularly non-financial) in the surveyed Arab firms.

Firm's MAS are said to be a significant element of their structures. Features of an appropriate accounting system depend upon firm's circumstances (Abdel-Maksoud, Dugdale, & Luther, 2005). The appropriateness of using sophisticated techniques depends on the circumstances in which they are being used, which advocates the use of the contingency theory perspective (Tillema, 2005) as adopted in this study. The contingency theory postulates that no single best or universal control system exists, but that effective systems must be designed to fit the organisational and environmental circumstances faced by firms. Previous studies highlight the role of contingency theory in accounting studies (Hartmann, 2000; Abdel-Maksoud et al., 2005; Al-Omiri & Drury, 2007). The variables most commonly identified in the contingency theory literature are environmental uncertainty, production technology, structure, corporate strategy, and size (Covaleski, Dirsmith, & Samuel, 1996; Hartmann, 2000; Chenhall, 2003; Abdel-Maksoud et al., 2005).

Furthermore, commentators propose other variables such as political, economic environment, and culture. Hopwood (2005, p. 576), for instance, argues that "the complex hybrids of national and supranational influences observed in accounting itself and in the wider operations of the capital markets, concluding that the political dynamics of change are now much more complex and remain very largely unexplored and not understood." Political environments could be extended further to include economic governance and legal systems (Aerts, 2005; Cormier, Magnan, & Van Velthoven, 2005; Peek, 2005). Also, awareness of the need to consider "cultural" remains evident in prior research studies, in particular cross countries, and has attracted many researchers in accounting field. Baskerville-Morley (2005) argues that debates on cross-cultural accounting research remain timely and Lehman (2005) observes that "accounting is a social practice with people, cultures, and myths performing the dance and concert that create relationships, collaborations, harmonies and conflicts" (p. 675).

Commentators argue that country differences possess particular cultural characteristics, which in turn affect individuals from within these cultures to respond distinctively to MAS' applications (Chenhall, 2003). However, Chenhall proposed other variables for consideration that offer promise in the study of culture of which organisational culture is amongst. "It is possible that a strong organisational culture may dominate national culture in the work situation. Little work has been completed in the area of organisational culture" (Chenhall, 2003, p. 154). To this extent, evidence permeates management accounting literature on various contextual variables that could influence the use of performance indicators in firms. For instance, it is said that the use of performance indicators reflects the management style of managers' concerned (CIMA, 1993; 1996). Also, commentators highlight the important role of operational staff, whereas it is argued that ideas for improving processes and performance for customers must increasingly come from operational staff that are closest to internal processes and the organisation's customers (Ibid). Hence, managers' characteristics and operational staff involvement could be seen as, amongst others, proxies for organisational culture.

This study has three main objectives; these are to investigate whether there are significant associations between the use and levels of importance of ONFPIs and the extent of: first, the surveyed firms' characteristics; second, managers' characteristics; and third, workforce involvement. Figure 1 depicts the relationships investigated in this study.

Figure 1. The investigated relationships in this study

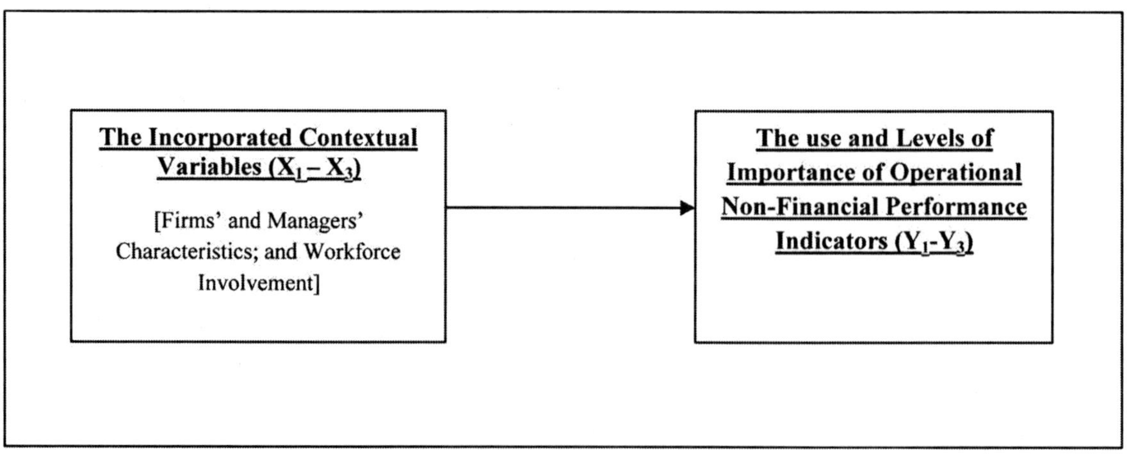

- It is noteworthy to indicate that the above figure depicts the bilateral relations investigated in this study. The direction of the arrow in the figure above does not implicate any causal relations.

Three contextual variables are depicted in Figure 1: firms' characteristics [comprised of company size and industry type]; managers' characteristics [managers' expertise and qualifications]; and workforce involvement [impact of operational staff suggestions and percentage of operational staff who receive feedback of performance].

BACKGROUND AND DEVELOPMENT OF HYPOTHESES

Operational Non-Financial Performance Indicators (ONFPIs)

Manufacturing performance measurement on operational control is said to be important in ensuring that production elements operate efficiently (Chenhall, 1997). Commentators advocate the use of manufacturing measures for operational control as to provide capability to recognise deviations in the manufacturing process and signal a need for process adjustments (Chenhall, 1997). Abdel-Maksoud et al. (2005) summarised the development of the use of operational performance measures as follows:

A statement by the International Federation of Accountants (IFAC, 1998) portrays the development of management accounting in sequential stages. In Stage I early management accountants concentrated on cost determination and financial control; then, by 1965, in Stage II their role expanded to include provision of information for management planning and control. By 1985, in the third stage, they aimed to reduce resource waste in business processes. In Stages I and II shop floor performance was formally reported through financial outcomes. So, through much of the 20th century, standard cost variances provided the principal monitoring of shop floor activity. Nonfinancial 'process' indicators, such as units completed, scrapped or rejected, were seen to fall within the domain of 'operations' and were not necessarily integrated into the financially dominated management control systems. But in IFAC's Stage III, shop floor performance measures of actual processes (rather than their financial consequences) start becoming integrated into the formal monitoring system (p.264).

Around the same era (i.e., 1980s-1990s), many commentators (Kaplan, 1983; Vollman, 1989; Drucker, 1990; Hall, Johnson, & Turley, 1991; Conti, 1993) were influential in arguing that traditional financial performance measurement systems were insufficient. They advocated the use of broader measures to assess operational performance where various authors (Maskell, 1989; Bhimani, 1993; Bromwich & Bhimani, 1994; Otley, 1997; Abdel-Maksoud et al., 2005) indicated operational control is best achieved by *non-financial measures*. Performance measurement literature suggests non-financial performance measures can be critical for providing useful operational information for planning and controlling purposes, in particular, change management in competitive environments (Bhimani, 1994; Otley, 1997; 1999; Hoque, Mia, & Alam, 2001; Pollanen & Maheshwari, 2007). In general, previous studies' findings highlight the importance of the operational level in the existing environment and show a particular emphasis among the surveyed firms on the use of non-financial performance measures. Literature identifies some broad categories of non-financial performance indicators, such as Customer Satisfaction (CS); Product Quality (PQ), and On-Time Delivery (OTD) to be particularly important in manufacturing firms (CIMA, 1993; 1996; Neely, Gregory, & Platts, 1995; Otley, 1997; Abdel-Maksoud et al., 2005).

This study investigates the relationships between the levels of importance of ONFPIs of the above three categories of ONFPIs and the three contextual (i.e., contingent) variables incorporated. A discussion of the incorporated variables and development of hypotheses is presented next.

Development of Hypotheses

Firms' Characteristics (X_1)

In performance measurement literature, mixed results regarding the use of performance measures have been attributed to organisational size (Poister & Streib, 1999). Baldwin (1997) provides evidence that when compared to larger entities, smaller companies have fewer tendencies to introduce advanced management technologies and practices. Commentators also argue that size has been found to be an important factor influencing the adoption of more complex administration systems (Alomiri & Drury, 2007; Abdel-Kader & Luther, 2008; Pollanen & Abdel-Maksoud, 2009). It is argued that larger organisations might have greater access to resources to experiment with the introduction of new MAS (Ibid).

Large organisations have resources to adopt more sophisticated management accounting practices than smaller organisations. Otley (1995) reported evidence of the impact of size on control techniques in studies of the role of MAS following merger or takeover. Also, Haldman and Laats (2002) argue that the sophistication level of cost accounting and budgeting systems tends to increase in line with a firm's size (Abdel-Kader & Luther, 2008, p. 7).

One would expect to see more use of ONFPIs in large firms where availability of resources intensifies as the firm goes larger in size. In this study, size of work force is used as a proxy for firm size. The following hypothesis is stated:

H_1: There is a significant positive association between firm size (X_{11}) and the use and levels of importance of operational non-financial performance indicators (ONFPIs) (Y) in the surveyed firms.

It is argued that industry-particular aspects are likely to affect the design of MAS, and previous contingency studies have collected empirical evidence across a range of industry sectors (Abdel-Kader and Luther, 2008). Different industries call for use of different ONFPIs; for example, industries with standard low-cost products might place more weight on measures of "efficiency and utilisation," while those with innovative products are expected to consider more measures of "customer satisfaction" (Pollanen & Abdel-Maksoud, 2009). The second hypothesis is as follows:

H_2: There is a significant association between the industry type a firm belongs to (X_{12}) and the use and levels of importance of ONFPIs (Y) in the surveyed firms.

Managers' Characteristics (X2)

This contextual variable incorporates two sub-variables: managers' expertise and qualifications. Managers who have long experience with their firms and/or higher levels of qualifications are expected to have more experience and knowledge of operations. It could be that managers with longer expertise with their firms would tend to use more ONFPIs, though literature is said to be rare on providing empirical evidence on such assumption (see, Pollanen & Abdel-Maksoud, 2009). This assumption builds upon Young (1997) who suggests management influences the success of implementing new innovations:

Because most innovations involve major organisational change, management can infer that if their organisation succeeds with one type of innovation, then there is a good chance of success for the next innovation (Young, 1997, p. 186).

The above seems to be in line with the organisational theory suggesting beliefs and behaviors of managers toward a particular innovation are shaped by their individual circumstances within the organisation (Anderson & Young, 1999).

H_3: There is a significant positive association between managers' expertise (X_{21}) and the use and levels of importance of ONFPIs (Y) in the surveyed firms.

This study also investigates whether there could be an association between managers' expertise and the levels of importance of ONFPIs in manufacturing firms in the countries surveyed.

H_4: There is a significant positive association between managers' levels of qualifications (X_{22}) and the use and levels of importance of ONFPIs (Y) in the surveyed firms.

Workforce Involvement (X_3)

Literature advocates the need for operational staff involvement in the new production technologies and the need to revise PIs as a consequence of novel manufacturing work methods and advanced forms of technologies (Kaplan, 1983; Drury, 1993; Bromwich & Bhimani, 1994; Brancato, 1995; Smith, 1997; Kaplan & Norton, 2001).

Employee empowerment is said to be crucial in enabling firms to deliver high quality and low cost products and services (Brancato, 1995). It is argued that firms need to be sensitive to employees' issues in implementing their performance measurement systems (Arena, Azzone, & Caimi, 2004). Arena and Azzone (2005) carried out a survey on 289 Italian firms and report significant correlations between delegation and the achievement of MAS objectives.

"World Class" performance became essential to firms' international competitiveness in the early 1990s (Jazayeri & Hopper, 1999). "World Class Manufacturer" (WCM) is based on the belief that competitive manufacturing requires an emphasis on customer service, high quality, timeliness, and employee involvement (Jazayeri & Hopper, 1999). It is said that, for any WCM, two areas are deemed to be crucial: structured management skilled in managing cultural changes, and workforce involvement (Schonberger, 1996; Jazayeri & Hopper, 1999). Workforce involvement researched in this study comprises two sub-variables: impact of operational staff suggestions, and percentage of operational staff who receive feedback of performance.

Kaplan (1983) suggests a common theme of the new manufacturing approaches is the attempt to fully utilise the talents of shop-floor staff by putting production under their control. Operational staff is encouraged to solve problems and improvise (Banker, Rajiv, Potter, & Schoreder, 1993). Jazayeri and Hopper (1999) argue that issues such as employee involvement and trust are both recognised as key elements for WCM success. It is argued that creative involvement of the workforce can be facilitated by developing responsible attitudes and ensuring that operational staff suggestions are, wherever possible, acted upon (Smith, 1997). Smith indicates that innovative solutions may be developed in identified problem areas by making the best use of the experience and intellect of operational staff. To move operational staff in this direction, it is necessary for supervisors and managers to motivate them and show interest in their suggestions (Abdel-Maksoud et al., 2005). In addition, Kaplan and Norton (2001) provide evidence on the existence of positive correlations between increased number of shop-floor suggestions and lower rework.

H_5: There is a significant positive association between impact of operational staff suggestions (X_{31}) and the use and levels of importance of ONFPIs (Y) in the surveyed firms.

However, it is argued that firms should provide regular feedback to employees as this facilitates employee learning and self-management (Hanser & Muchinsky, 1978; Juran & Gryna, 1980; Aoki, 1991; Abdel-Maksoud et al., 2005). Commentators consider reporting feedback as a useful motivator for operational staff (Maskell, 1992).

H_6: There is a significant positive association between percentage of operational staff who receive feedback of performance (X_{32}) and the use and levels of importance of ONFPIs (Y) in the surveyed firms.

RESEARCH METHOD

The Method

Interviews using structured questionnaire forms[1] were conducted to collect required data in mid-2005 from the surveyed firms in Egypt and Saudi Arabia. It is argued that questionnaire surveys are considered deceptively easy when reported in developed countries (e.g. US and UK) studies. However, questions like "whom to ask" and "what to ask" become important in research planning in other developing countries (Weetman, 2006). High-quality survey research needs a population which has good access and trusts pledges of confidentiality (Groves, 1989; Fleischman & Herz, 2005; Gerdin, 2005; Van der Stede, Young, & Chen, 2005). Structured interviews, accordingly, were used to collect data in Egypt and Saudi Arabia. Interviews were carried out by trained research assistants.

The questionnaire form included questions on the levels of importance of 11 ONFPIs belonging to the three evaluation categories (i.e., CS, PQ, and OTD), and six independent variables (belonging to firms' and managers' characteristics and workforce involvement). More details are presented in section "Measurement of Variable".

Sample Firms

Two large-scale surveys were carried out in mid-2005 to collect data from the surveyed Egyptian and Saudi firms. In surveying the Egyptian firms[2], the research sample frame was confined to the three biggest industrial areas in Egypt: Tenth of Ramadan, Burj El Arab, and Sixth of October. In each industry area, a so called "Investors' Society Office" exists where one can obtain some primary data on firms in that area. Each society office publishes a bulletin including data on firms operating within its domain. A total of 3,600[3] private firms are thought to be operating in the three areas (as per 2005 bulletins). A quota sampling was used in surveying 80 randomly selected manufacturing firms in each area composing a total sample of 240 firms[4]. Trained research assistants carried out structured interviews with managers of the surveyed firms[5] in each area. Each research assistant had a formal letter from the designated investors' society office requesting respondents' support. All efforts were made to ensure that the sample chosen from each area was representative. 239 interviews were completed successfully with managers of the surveyed firms.

In surveying the Saudi firms[6], the sample frame was confined to the three biggest industrial regions in Saudi Arabia: Makkah, Riyadh, and the Eastern Regions. These three regions contain 85% of manufacturing firms in Saudi Arabia with 78% of country's total industrial investments according to the country's Ministry of Economy and Planning Statistical Yearbook 2005. A total of 3,000 manufacturing firms were thought to be operating in these regions. A random sample of 300 firms[7] in the three regions was selected and trained research assistants carried out structured interviews. Again, efforts were made to ensure that the sample chosen from each area was representative. Only 144 interviews were completed successfully with managers of the surveyed firms[8].

Measurement of Variables

This study examines the relationships between the levels of importance of ONFPIs and six independent variables. The incorporated variables were adopted from previously validated instruments. Table 1 summarises the constructs, measurements together with descriptive statistics of the variables incorporated. Cronbach's alpha was used to test for the reliability of the variables incorporated.

Results in Table 1 show that the alpha results are, in general, at acceptable levels (Cramer & Howitt, 2004). It can be concluded the incorporated variables are reliable. The validity of the incorporated variables was reviewed in the piloting stage. Moreover, Guilford's (1954) objectivity/subjectivity of judgment analysis was applied on data collected in the two countries surveyed. The results as seen in the Appendix indicate high level of objectivity amongst respondents. In other words, the proportion of variance in respondents' judgment that is due to subjectivity is limited. These results provide support for the high reliability of country-specific data.

Findings

Findings conclude that levels of importance of ONFPIs in Egyptians firms are higher than those of their Saudi peers. The Egyptian respondents place moderate to very high importance on these measures (Average Means = 3 to 6), while their Saudi peers place low to average importance (Means are around 2) on two of the ONFPIs (i.e., customer satisfaction (CS) and product quality (PQ), and above average (Mean = 5) on ONFPIs of on-time delivery (OTD). Interestingly, the ranking of importance of the three ONFPIs categories is the same in both countries where ONFPIs of OTD comes first followed by CS and PQ, respectively.

Recall from Section 1, the main objective of this study is to investigate significant associations between three sets of contextual (i.e., independent) variables (X_1- X_3) and the use and levels of importance of ONFPIs of three categories ($Y_1 - Y_3$). A non-parametric statistical test (Kendall's Tau) was conducted using SPSS to test for significant associations between levels of importance of ONFPIs and firm's characteristics (X1) variables (i.e., size (X_{11}) and industry type (X_{12})). As size[9] and industry types of the surveyed firms were heterogeneous, the partial correlation test, controlling for the former variables, was applied in testing for associations between OFNPIs and managers' characteristics ($X_{21} - X_{22}$) and workforce involvement variables ($X_{31} - X_{32}$). Results are presented in Tables 2 and 3, for brevity, the acceptance and rejection of the study hypotheses depends on the results reported in these tables.

Results reveal that company size (X_{11}), against prior assumptions, has no significant correlations with ONFPIs of the three categories in both countries (H_1). Significant associations are found between the industry type a firm belong to (X_{12}) and ONFPIs of CS in both countries while a single significant association is reported with OTD in case of Saudi firms (H_2).

The Egyptian results show, in line with prior assumptions, significant positive correlations between managers' expertise (X_{21}) and two of the ONFPIs categories: CS and PQ (H_3). Interestingly, the Saudi results show significant negative correlations with the two categories. No significant correlations against assumptions are found to exist between managers' qualifications (X_{22}) and any of the ONFPIs categories in the two countries (H_4). One would have expected that more qualified managers are to place more importance on the use of non-financial performance indicators in developing countries, an assumption that is proven to be invalid herein.

Strong significant positive associations are found between the impact of operational staff suggestions (X_{31}) and the three categories of ONFPIs in the surveyed Egyptian firms which support the prior assumption (H_5). Again, Saudi findings show the contrary, where X_{31} has significant negative associations with two of the ONFPIs categories

Table 1. Variables Constructs and Descriptive Statistics

Variable	Source of Construct	Country	Construct Description					
Operational Non-Financial Performance Indicators (ONFPIs) (Y1-Y3)								
Customer Satisfaction (CS) (Y1)	Bhimani (1993); CIMA (1993); Drury *et al.* (1993); Chenhall and Langfield-Smith (1998); Otley (1999); Abdel-Maksoud, *et al.* (2005).		Respondents were asked to indicate whether three measures (complaints from customers, number of returns, and number of warranty claims) were applied and to rank them on an eight-point Likert scale, from 0 (not measured), 1 (no importance), 4 (moderate importance), up to 7 (critical importance), their level of importance. Respondents' rankings were added up to constitute a composite of CS.					
			N	Mean	Std. dev.	Min	Max	Cronbach's Alpha
		Egypt	239	4.07	1.74	0	7	.405
		SA	132	2.78	1.72	0	6	.644
Product Quality (PQ) (Y2)	Bhimani (1993); CIMA (1993); Drury (1996); Chenhall and Langfield-Smith (1998); Otley (1999); Abdel-Maksoud *et al.* (2005).		Respondents were asked to indicate whether four measures (scrap, defects and rework – percentage of total production, and batches- percentage adjusted) were applied and to rank them on an eight-point Likert scale. Again, a composite PQ was used in this study.					
			N	Mean	Std. dev.	Min	Max	Cronbach's Alpha
		Egypt	239	3.62	2.08	0	7	.728
		SA	135	2.01	.85	0	5	.813
On-Time Delivery (OTD) (Y3)	CIMA (1993); Drury (1996); Chenhall and Langfield-Smith (1998); Otley (1999); Abdel-Maksoud *et al.* (2005).		Respondents were asked to indicate whether four measures (percentage on-time delivery to customers; on-time production, and schedule adherence; and manufacturing cycle efficiency) were applied and to rank them on an eight-point Likert scale. A composite OTD was used.					
			N	Mean	Std. dev.	Min	Max	Cronbach's Alpha
		Egypt	239	6.08	1.25	0	7	.762
		SA	139	5.29	1.09	2	7	.770
Variable	**Source of Construct**	**Country**	**Construct Description**					
Firms' Characteristics (X1)								
X11: Size	CIMA (1993); and Abdel-Maksoud (2007).		Size of workforce was used as a measure of company size. Respondents were asked to indicate the size of workforce in their companies.					
			N	1-100 employees		101-2000	More than 2,000	
		Egypt	239	43.9%		54.9%	1.3%	
		SA	144	36.1		63.9	-	
X12: Industry type	Al-Omiri and Drury (2007)		The surveyed firms belong to various industry sectors in the two countries surveyed. For more details, kindly refer to "Sample Firms" Section.					
Managers' Characteristics (X2)								
X21: Managers' expertise	Pollanen and Abdel-Maksoud (2010)		Respondents were asked to indicate the length of period (number of years) they had in job.					
			N	1 – 2 Yrs	More than 2 Yrs			
		Egypt	226	14.2%	85.8%			
		SA	140	15.7	84.3			
X22:Managers' qualifications	Pollanen and Abdel-Maksoud (2010)		Respondents were asked to indicate whether they are members in professional bodies.					
			N	% with a membership	% with no membership			
		Egypt	239	0.0%	100.00%			
		SA	144	2.80%	97.20%			

continued on following page

Table 1. Continued

Variable	Source of Construct	Country	Construct Description					
Operational Non-Financial Performance Indicators (ONFPIs) (Y1-Y3)								
Workforce Involvement (X3)								
X31: Impact of operational staff suggestions	Abdel-Maksoud *et al.* (2005)		Consists of two questions to indicate, on a seven point Likert scale from 1 (not at all) up to 7 (extensively), respondents' evaluation of the impact of operational staff suggestions on quality improvement and cost reduction. A composite measure of these was used in this study.					
			N	**Mean**	**Std. dev.**	**Min**	**Max**	**Cronbach's Alpha**
		Egypt	239	4.45	1.70	1	7	.850
		SA	144	5.00	.978	2	7	.689
Variable	**Source of Construct**	**Country**	**Construct Description**					
Workforce Involvement (X3) (continued)								
X32:Percentage of operational staff who receive feedback	Abdel-Maksoud *et al.* (2005)		Consists of one question asking respondents to indicate, on a four-point scale from 1 (0% - 25%) up to 4 (76% - 100%), the percentage of their operational staff routinely receiving feedback of performance.					
			N	**0% - 25%**	**26% - 50%**	**51 – 75%**	**76% - 100%**	
		Egypt	239	39.3%	6.7%	5.9%	48.1	
		SA	143	25.9	9.1	59.5	5.5	

Table 2. Significant Correlations between the Contextual Variables and Levels of Importance of Operational Non-Financial Performance Indicators (ONFPIs)

Contextual Variables	Expected Sign	Country	ONFPIs of: Customer Satisfaction CS (Y1)	Product Quality PQ (Y2)	On-Time Delivery OTD (Y3)
X11: Company Size	+	Egypt	-	-	-
		Saudi Arabia	-	-	-
X12: Industry type (Detailed in Table 3)	+/-	Egypt	SIG	-	-
		Saudi Arabia	SIG	-	SIG
X21: Managers' expertise[1]	+	Egypt	.154*	.130*	-
		Saudi Arabia	- .164*	- .230**	-
X22: Managers' qualifications[1]	+	Egypt	-	-	-
		Saudi Arabia	-	-	-
X31: Impact of operational staff suggestions[1]	+	Egypt	.310**	.260**	.391**
		Saudi Arabia	-.205*	-.176*	-
X32: % of operational staff who receive feedback on performance[1]	+	Egypt	-	.112*	.380**
		Saudi Arabia	-	.178*	-

* and ** Significant at the 0.05 and 0.01 levels, respectively, (1-Tailed).

[1]These are partial correlations with Y_{11}-Y_{13} controlling for size and industry type.

Table 3. Significant Correlations between Industry Type and Levels of Importance of ONFPIs

	ONFPIs of:		
	Customer Satisfaction CS (Y1)	Product Quality PQ (Y2)	On-Time Delivery OTD (Y3)
X11: Industry type			
Egypt			
Food	.118*	-	-
Mineral and non-mineral	-.111*	-	-
Saudi Arabia			
Food	-	-	-
Wearing	.152*	-	-
Tanning	.191*	-	.145*
Chemical	-.149*	-	-

* and ** Significant at the 0.05 and 0.01 levels, respectively, (2-Tailed).

(i.e. CS and PQ), which adds to the fussiness of the reported findings in the Saudi firms. Percentage of operational staff receiving feedback (X_{32}) is found to have significant positive correlation, in line with assumptions, with two of the ONFPIs categories, PQ and OTD, in the surveyed Egyptian firms and only one category, PQ, in the Saudi firms (H_6).

Differences between Egyptian and Saudi findings reported above are interesting. One might tend to ascribe these differences to culture, which could be seen complying with prior literature on cultural effects across aspects of management control systems (Chenhall, 2003). For instance, the Vance, McClaine, Boje and Stage (1992) study incorporated various aspects of MCS (e.g., formality of controls, appraisal systems, and frequency of feedback) in Indonesian, Malaysian, Thai, and US firms, and shows significant differences not only between US and Asian firms, but also amongst the different Asian firms incorporated. However, this interpretation needs to be read cautiously, since literature provided mixed results in this field (Chenhall, 2003), and, more importantly, culture *per se* was not measured amongst the variables incorporated in this study. Further discussion of the reported findings and conclusions of findings reported in this section is presented in the section. The next section presents future research directions.

FUTURE RESEARCH DIRECTIONS

In line with Cruz et al.'s (2011) view, the author recommends further studies to be developed on contemporary performance measurement systems in use in Arab firms. Findings of this study could contribute in stimulating interested academics/researchers to carry out further investigations into localisation of global MAS' applications in Arab firms. For instance, the Saudi firms' tendency towards placing average levels of importance on ONFPIs of CS and PQ deserves attention. Also, the contrary to expectations results of the influence of managers' characteristics on levels of importance of ONFPIs in Egyptian and Saudi firms merit further investigations.

On the other hand, Weetman (2006) argues that "theories and models are often developed on premises that reflect Anglo-American or Anglo-Saxon cultures and institutions." I would like to encourage researchers to offer critical evaluation of such theories and models from results based on robust analysis of country-specific data. I would like to see papers recognise and discuss the country-specific context rather than set it to one side or assume it does not exist" (p. 379). The author, building upon Weetman's, suggests the inclusion of two critical aspects in any future studies on performance measurement in Arab firms: political, economic environment, and culture. Arnold (2005) argues economic governance is being internationalised and contrary, political and social rights remain localised. Commentators advocate Arnold's view as being important in making international comparisons particularly in corporate reporting (Weetman, 2006).

However, studies on the effect of culture on accounting practices in Arab firms are found to depend on Hofstede's (1980; 2001) dimensions of culture. Interpreting cultural effects on Arab managers building upon Hofstede's raises serious concerns. Hofstede's dimensions of culture have been criticised in management accounting literature (Baskerville, 2003, 2005), human resources literature (McSweeney, 2002) and information systems literature (Myers & Tan, 2002). In his work, Hofstede noted cultural homogeneity may be low among newer nations, albeit, he described Arab countries as only one nation, "Arab States," which included seven Arab countries[10]. The reported findings in this study reveal considerable differences between Egyptian and Saudi responses which impose concerns on adopting Hofstede's dimensions of culture in performance measurement studies in Arab firms. It is, hence, recommended to consider the inclusion of other cultural variables such as organisational culture in future studies. More importantly, it is crucial to check that the assumed cultural values of any Arab country under study are still apparent in contemporary relevant performance measurement studies on firms operating in that designated country (Chenhall, 2003).

DISCUSSIONS AND CONCLUSION

This study builds upon recent calls for more research to better understand various factors which explain the use of performance measurements, particularly ONFPIs which are amongst MAS' instruments. The study focuses on two Arab developing countries following the view that scope, role, and positioning of management accounting differ across organisations and countries (Weetman, 2006; International Federation of Accountants, 2008). "The 'country as context' provides scope for broader understanding of international differences and similarities...The pace of change in developing and emerging markets offers the potential to focus on issues that are different from those encountered in mature developed markets" (Weetman, 2006, p. 358). In the same direction, this study draws on the recent work of Cruz et al. (2011) on localisation of global management control systems.

However, it is argued that importing MAS as is and using them in developing countries may not be as valuable as in developed countries. These imported MAS are said to be developed in industrialised developed countries (Etemadih, Dilami, Baza, & Parameswaran, 2009), while it is argued that effective MAS in one environment might be ineffective or even dysfunctional in others (Tsui, 2001; Chow, Harrison, Lindquist, & Wu, 1997).

Commentators ascribed that to, among other reasons, cultural characteristics which are said to affect individuals to respond distinctively to various MAS' applications. However, Chenhall proposed other variables for consideration that offer premise in the study of culture of which organisational culture is one. To this extent, evidence permeates management accounting literature on various contextual variables that could influence the use of performance indicators in firms, of which managers' characteristics and workforce involvement are used as proxies for organisational culture in the current study.

This study aims to investigate whether the use and levels of importance of ONFPIs in Arab manufacturing firms (i.e., dependent variables) are associated with three contextual (independent) variables: workforce involvement, and firms' and managers' characteristics. Two Arab countries were surveyed in this study: Egypt and Saudi Arabia (SA). The choice of these two countries was due to their considerable political and economic impact in the Arab region and, most importantly, ease of access to data. In the context of MAS in Arab firms, no similar study, to the best of the author's knowledge, was carried out in Arab countries.

This study presents findings of large surveys of manufacturing firms in Egypt and SA. Interviews were carried out in mid-2005 using structured questionnaire forms to collect required data from 239 and 144 manufacturing firms, belonging to various industry sectors, in Egypt and SA respectively. Findings conclude that levels of importance of ONFPIs in Egyptian firms are higher than those at their Saudi peers' firms. Interestingly, the ranking of importance of the three ONFPIs categories is the same in both countries where ONFPIs of OTD comes first followed by CS and PQ, respectively.

Findings in the two countries from Section 3 support prior assumptions regarding significant associations between levels of importance of ONFPIs and the following four out of a total of six contextual sub-variables: industry type a firm belongs to (firms' characteristics); managers' expertise (managers' characteristics); and the two variables composing 'workforce involvement' (i.e., impact of operational staff suggestions and percentage of operational staff who receive feedback).

In general, findings on significant positive associations between the levels of importance of ONFPIs and the incorporated contextual variables in the Egyptian firms seem to be in line with prior literature findings drawn from global practices. Interestingly, though, the effect of organisational culture seems to be witnessed in Saudi firms evident by the negative, rather than priori assumed positive, associations between two variables belonging to managers' characteristics and workforce involvement (i.e., managers' expertise and impact of operational staff suggestions respectively) and levels of importance of ONFPIs of CS and PQ.

One possible interpretation of the negative associations between managers' expertise and levels of importance of ONFPIs of the two categories is that managers who have longer experience working for Saudi firms, the vast majority of respondents having more than two years of experience, tend to perceive negatively any use of what could be perceived as new/fashionable MAS' instruments such as ONFPIs. This could be understood if we look at it from the view that using such new instruments imposes an additional work burden on their shoulders with the risk of failing. This complies with Young (1997) who advocates that managers become highly sceptical and cynical about any change programmes in organisations that do not have organisational culture that allows embracing change.

The negative associations between impact of operational staff suggestions and levels of importance of ONFPIs of CS and PQ in Saudi firms remain confusing. The descriptive analysis shows tendency in Saudi firms to place more emphasis on "impact of operational staff suggestions" (Mean = 5). Accordingly, one would expect that Saudi firms would be keen on placing similar emphasis on ONFPIs (i.e., "what you measure is what you get"). Apparently, this is not the case here, which might lead to drawing a conclusion that Saudi firms might not be integrating their MAS with other managerial practices.

The above interpretations of Saudi findings, though, could be interpreted somewhat differently drawing on the work of Cruz et al. (2011). They conclude that "when global management control systems are localised (i.e., enacted), practice variations (heterogenisation) can occur. Moreover, this local variety results largely from the process of homogenisation which occurs as global systems are stretched across local contexts (cf. Robertson, 1995). … "We argue that local managers can reshape or reconstitute the global systems to achieve local, as well as corporate, objectives. For this purpose, we do not necessarily see global–local relationships exclusively in terms of multinational–national/ regional relationships" (Cruz et al., 2011, p. 413). Cruz et al. continue: "The locals did not simply reproduce the global management control system, instead they 'made it work for them', and in so doing they reshaped it"….. "our study illustrates that heterogenisation does not exist without homogenisation and, as Robertson (1992; 1995) argues, the processes of homogenisation construct the local. When exposed to the homogenising pressures of globalisation, locals learn from what it brings with it and, where necessary, they reshape/adapt it to the specificities of their context. In so doing, they construct the local as unique and differentiated from the global. This reflects Robertson's argument that localisation is part of globalisation in the sense that the local is in essence included within the global, thereby being a 'micro' manifestation of it. It also explains why he uses the term glocalisation to refer to ''the simultaneity and the interpenetration of what are conventionally called the global and the local or–in more abstract vein–the universal and the particular'' (Robertson, 1995, p. 30)" (Cruz et al., 2011, p. 424).

On the other hand, findings show consistent patterns in Egyptian and Saudi firms regarding the lack of significant relationships between levels of importance of ONFPIs and firm size (i.e., firms' characteristics) and managers' professional qualifications (i.e., managers' characteristics). The lack of a relationship between managers' qualifications and levels of importance of ONFPIs is not surprising as almost all of respondents in both countries hold no professional memberships.

Finally, findings reported in this study render themselves to certain limitations. First, there are the typical constraints in using a survey method (e.g., sampling and the use of structured questionnaires in data collection). Malmi and Graulund (2009) argue that researchers need to consider the situation in which the study of a random sample of organisations produces sufficient ground for a useful theory. Second, the assumption that all firms tend to optimise the use of their MAS is another limitation of this study; "from how things are we cannot infer how things ought to be. Frequent changes in exogenous variables accompanied by the fact that the time required for major changes in accounting and control systems has been shown to be long, and the fact that most ideas, methods, or principles in management accounting may be applied in a number of ways, and the evidence of accounting failures, all suggest that assuming that all firms optimise is bold at best and dangerous at worst (Luft & Shields, 2002)" (Malmi & Granlund, 2009, p. 610). Third, the contingency theory perspective adopted in this study, though advocated by many commentators, is criticised (Otley, 1980; Fisher, 1995; Chapman, 1997; Chenhall, 2003; Tillema, 2005) in particular when it comes to cross-sectional survey method. It is argued that the dominance of this method has resulted in a situation in which understanding of what explains MAS sophistication is incomplete (Tillema, 2005).

The above limitations put constraints on generalisation of findings reported in this study. However, it is noteworthy to cite Weetman (2006) who recommends placing more importance on country-specific studies as they reveal potential for comparative studies on a wider geographical basis. Weetman, though, argues that the achievement of such aim needs the academic research community (editors, reviewers and authors) to show flexibility in dealing with smaller data sets and greater uncertainty about the nature of MAS.

ACKNOWLEDGMENT

The author is grateful for the constructive and valuable comments of the anonymous reviewers. The author is also grateful for comments received from the anonymous reviewers and participants of the European Accounting Association Annual Conference (Italy, 2011) on a relevant earlier paper presentation. The author would like to extend his gratefulness to the College of Business and Economics at United Arab Emirates University for its "Faculty Summer Research Grant 2010" which facilitated the writing of this chapter.

REFERENCES

Abdel-Kader, M., & Luther, R. (2008). The impact of firm characteristics on management accounting practices: A UK-based empirical analysis. *The British Accounting Review*, *40*(1), 2–27. doi:10.1016/j.bar.2007.11.003.

Abdel-Maksoud, A. (2007). Shop-floor non-financial performance measures and the contingent variables. In Abdel-Maksoud, A., & Abdel-Kader, M. (Eds.), *Non-financial performance measurement and management practices in manufacturing firms: A comparative international analysis* (pp. 35–70). Oxford, UK: Elsevier.

Abdel-Maksoud, A., Dugdale, D., & Luther, R. (2005). Non–financial performance measurement in manufacturing companies. *The British Accounting Review*, *37*(3), 261–297. doi:10.1016/j.bar.2005.03.003.

Abegglen, J., & Stalk, G. (1985). *Kaisha: The Japanese Corporation*. New York: Basic Books.

Aerts, W. (2005). Picking up the pieces: Impression management in the retrospective attributional framing of accounting outcomes. *Accounting, Organizations and Society*, *30*, 493–517. doi:10.1016/j.aos.2004.07.001.

Al-Omiri, M., & Drury, C. (2007). A survey of factors influencing the choice of product costing systems in UK organizations. *Management Accounting Research*, *18*, 399–424. doi:10.1016/j.mar.2007.02.002.

Anderson, S. W., & Young, S. M. (1999). The impact of contextual and process factors on the evaluation of activity based costing systems. *Accounting, Organizations and Society*, *24*, 525–559. doi:10.1016/S0361-3682(99)00018-5.

Aoki, M. (1991). *Information, Incentives and Bargaining in the Japanese Economy*. New York: Cambridge University Press.

Arena, M., & Azzone, G. (2005). ABC, Balanced Scorecard, EVA: An empirical study on the adoption of innovative management accounting techniques. *International Journal of Accounting, Auditing and Performance Evaluation*, *2*(3), 206–225. doi:10.1504/IJAAPE.2005.007673.

Arena, M., Azzone, G., & Caimi, N. (2004). I sistemi di controllo di gestione nelle imprese italiane: diffusione e determinant. *Budget*, *58*, 47–57.

Arnold, P. (2005). Disciplining domestic regulation: The World Trade Organization and the market for professional services. *Accounting, Organizations and Society*, *30*, 299–330. doi:10.1016/j.aos.2004.04.001.

Baldwin, J. R. (1997). *The Importance of Research and Development for Innovation in Small and Large Canadian Manufacturing Firms, 11F0019MIE, No. 107*. Ottawa: Statistics Canada.

Banker, Rajiv D., Potter, G., & Schoreder, R. G. (1993). Reporting manufacturing performance measures to workers: An empirical study. *Journal of Management Accounting Research*, Fall, 33-53.

Bashiekh, A., & Abdel-Maksoud, A. (2008). Operational performance measures used and contemporary management practices deployed in manufacturing firms: The case of Kingdom of Saudi Arabia. *Arab Journal of Administrative Sciences*, *15*(1), 151–183.

Baskerville, R. (2003). Hofstede never studied culture. *Accounting, Organizations and Society*, *28*, 1–14. doi:10.1016/S0361-3682(01)00048-4.

Baskerville-Morley, R. (2005). A research note: The unfinished business of culture. *Accounting, Organizations and Society*, *30*, 389–391. doi:10.1016/j.aos.2004.08.002.

Baskerville-Morley, R. (2005). A research note: The unfinished business of culture. *Accounting, Organizations and Society*, *30*, 389–391. doi:10.1016/j.aos.2004.08.002.

Bhimani, A. (1994). Monitoring performance measures in UK manufacturing companies. *Management Accounting*, January, 34-36.

Bjornenak, T. (1997). Diffusion and accounting: The case of ABC in Norway. *Management Accounting Research*, *8*, 3–17. doi:10.1006/mare.1996.0031.

Bouwens, J., & Abernethy, M. (2000). The consequences of customization on management accounting system design. *Accounting, Organizations and Society*, *25*, 221–241. doi:10.1016/S0361-3682(99)00043-4.

Brancato, C. K. (1995). New corporate performance measures, Research Report No. 1118-95-RR. New York: The Conference Board.

Bromwich, M., & Bhimani, A. (1994). *Management accounting: Pathways to progress*. London: The Chartered Institute of Management Accountants.

Chapman, C. (1997). Reflections on a contingent view of accounting. *Accounting, Organizations and Society*, *22*, 189–205. doi:10.1016/S0361-3682(97)00001-9.

Chenhall, R. (2003). Management control systems design within its organizational context: Findings from contingency – based research and directions for the future. *Accounting, Organizations and Society*, *28*, 127–168. doi:10.1016/S0361-3682(01)00027-7.

Chenhall, R. (2003). Management control systems design within its organizational context: Findings from contingency-based research and directions for the future. *Accounting, Organizations and Society*, *28*, 127–188. doi:10.1016/S0361-3682(01)00027-7.

Chenhall, R. H. (1997). Reliance on manufacturing performance measures, total quality management and organisational performance. *Management Accounting Research*, *8*, 187–206. doi:10.1006/mare.1996.0038.

Chenhall, R. H., & Langfield-Smith, K. (1998). Factors influencing the role of management accounting in the development of performance measures within organisational change programs. *Management Accounting Research*, *9*, 361–386. doi:10.1006/mare.1998.0080.

Chow, C., Harrison, P., Lindiquist, T., & Wu, A. (1997). Escalating commitment to unprofitable projects: Replication and cross – cultural extension. *Management Accounting Research*, *8*(3), 347–361. doi:10.1006/mare.1996.0046.

Chua, W. F. (2007). Accounting, measuring, reporting and strategizing–Re-using verbs: A review essay. *Accounting, Organizations and Society*, *32*, 487–494. doi:10.1016/j.aos.2006.03.010.

CIMA. (1993). *Performance measurement in the manufacturing sector*. London: Charted Institute of Management Accountants.

CIMA. (1996). *Management accounting official terminology*. London: Charted Institute of Management Accountants.

Conti, T. (1993). *Building Quality: A Guide to Management*. London: Chapman and Hall. doi:10.1007/978-94-011-1546-9.

Cormier, D., Magnan, M., & Van Velthoven, B. (2005). Environmental disclosure quality in large German companies: Economic incentives, public pressures or institutional conditions? *European Accounting Review*, *14*(1), 3–39. doi:10.1080/0963818042000339617.

Covaleski, M., Dirsmith, M., & Samuel, S. (1996). Managerial accounting research: The contribution of organizational and sociological theories. *Journal of Management Accounting Research*, *8*, 1–35.

Cramer, D., & Howitt, D. (2004). *The sage dictionary of statistics, a guide for social scientists*. East Sussex, UK: Routledge.

Cuz, I., Scapens, R., & Major, M. (2011). The localisation of a global management control systems. *Accounting, Organizations and Society*, *36*, 412–427. doi:10.1016/j.aos.2011.08.001.

Drucker, P. E. (1990). *The emerging theory of manufacturing* (pp. 94–102). Boston, MA: Harvard Business Review.

Drury, C. (1996). *Management Accounting Handbook*. Oxford, UK: Butterworth-Heinemann.

Etemadih, H., Dilami, Z., Baza, M., & Parameswaran, R. (2009). Culture, management accounting and managerial performance: Focus Iran. *Advances in Accounting, incorporating. Advances in International Accounting*.

Fisher, J. (1995). Contingency-based research on management control systems: Categorization by level of complexity. *Journal of Accounting Literature*, *14*, 24–53.

Fleischman, G., & Herz, P. (2005). An empirical investigation of trends in barter activity in the Russian federation. *The International Journal of Accounting*, *40*, 39–63. doi:10.1016/j.intacc.2004.11.001.

Fullerton, R., & McWatters, C. (2002). The role of performance measures in relation to the degree of JIT implementation. *Accounting, Organizations and Society*, *27*, 711–735. doi:10.1016/S0361-3682(02)00012-0.

Gerdin, J. (2005). Managing accounting system design in manufacturing departments: An empirical investigation using a multiple contingencies approach. *Accounting, Organizations and Society*, *30*, 99–126. doi:10.1016/j.aos.2003.11.003.

Groves, R. (1989). *Survey errors and survey results*. New York: Wiley. doi:10.1002/0471725277.

Guilford, J. (1954). *Psychometric methods* (2nd ed.). London: McGraw-Hill.

Hall, R. W., Johnson, H. T., & Turley, P. B. (1991). *Measuring Up: Changing Pathways to Manufacturing Excellence, 111*. Homewood: Business One Irwin.

Hanser, L. M., & Muchinsky, P. M. (1978). Work as an information environment. *Organizational Behavior and Human Performance*, *21*, 47–60. doi:10.1016/0030-5073(78)90038-7 PMID:10306432.

Hartmann, F. G. (2000). The appropriateness of RAPM: Towards the further development of theory. *Accounting, Organizations and Society*, *25*, 451–482. doi:10.1016/S0361-3682(98)00036-1.

HassabElnaby, H. & Mosebach, M. (2005). Culture's consequences in controlling agency costs: Egyptian evidence. *Journal of International Accounting, Auditing & Taxation*, *14*, 19–32. doi:10.1016/j.intaccaudtax.2005.01.003.

Hofstede, G. (1980). *Culture's Consequences*. Beverly Hills, CA: Sage Publications.

Hofstede, G. (2001). *Cultures consequences: Comparing values, behaviours, institutions and organizations across nations* (2nd ed.). Thousand Oaks, CA: Sage Publications.

Hopwood, A. (2005). Editorial: After 30 years. *Accounting, Organizations and Society*, *30*, 585–586. doi:10.1016/j.aos.2005.06.002.

Hoque, Z., Mia, L., & Alam, M. (2001). Market competition, computer-aided manufacturing and use of multiple performance measures: An empirical study. *The British Accounting Review*, *33*(1), 23–45. doi:10.1006/bare.2000.0149.

International Federation of Accountants (IFAC). (1998). *International Management Accounting Practice Statement*. Management.

Jazayeri, M., & Hopper, T. (1999). Management accounting within world class manufacturing: A case study. *Management Accounting Research*, *10*, 263–301. doi:10.1006/mare.1999.0106.

Juran, J. M., & Gryna, F. M. (1980). *Quality Planning and Analysis*. New York: McGraw Hill.

Kaplan, R., & Norton, D. (2001). Using the balanced scorecard as a strategic management system: Building a scorecard can help managers links today's actions with tomorrow's goals. In Young, S. M. (Ed.), *Readings in management accounting* (pp. 190–198). Upper Saddle River, NJ: Prentice Hall.

Kaplan, R. S. (1983). Measuring performance: A new challenge for managerial accounting research. *Accounting Review*, *18*(4), 686–705.

Lehman, C. (2005). Accounting and the public interest: All the world's a stage. *Accounting, Auditing & Accountability Journal*, *18*(5), 675–689. doi:10.1108/09513570510620501.

Luft, J., & Shields, M. (2003). Mapping management accounting: graphics and guidelines for theory-consistent empirical research. *Accounting, Auditing & Accountability Journal*, *8*, 71–90.

Malami, T. (1999). Activity-based costing diffusion across organizations: As exploratory empirical analysis of Finnish firms. *Accounting, Organizations and Society*, *24*, 649–672. doi:10.1016/S0361-3682(99)00011-2.

Malmi, T., & Granlund, M. (2009). In search of management accounting theory. *European Accounting Review*, *18*(3), 597–620. doi:10.1080/09638180902863779.

Martin, J. (1992). *Cultures in organizations: Three perspectives*. Oxford, UK: Oxford University Press.

Maskell, B. (1989). Performance measurement for world class manufacturing-3. *Management Accounting*, 48–50.

Maskell, B. H. (1992). Performance measurement for world class manufacturing. *Corporate Controller*, January/February, 44-48.

McSweeney, B. (2002). Hofstede's Model of national cultural differences and their consequences: A triumph of faith – A failure of analysis. *Human Relations*, *55*(1), 89–118.

Myers, M. D., & Tan, F. (2002). Beyond models of national culture in information systems research. *Journal of Global Information Management*, *10*(1), 24–32. doi:10.4018/jgim.2002010103.

Neely, A., Gregory, M., & Platts, K. (1995). Performance measurement systems design: A literature review and research agenda. *International Journal of Operations & Production Management*, *15*(4), 80–116. doi:10.1108/01443579510083622.

Otley, D. (1980). The contingency theory of management accounting: Achievement and progress. *Accounting, Organizations and Society*, *5*(4), 413–428. doi:10.1016/0361-3682(80)90040-9.

Otley, D. (1997). Better performance management. *Management Accounting, 44*.

Otley, D. (1999). Performance management: A framework for management control systems research. *Management Accounting Research*, *10*, 363–382. doi:10.1006/mare.1999.0115.

Poister, T., & Streib, G. (1999). Performance measurement in municipal government: Assessing the state of the practice. *Public Administration Review*, *59*(4), 325–335. doi:10.2307/3110115.

Pollaned, R., & Abdel-Makoud, A. (2010). Deployment of contemporary management accounting practices in Canadian firms: A contingency approach. *International Journal of Managerial and Financial Management*. 2(2), 134-152.

Pollanen, R., & Maheshwari, B. (2007). Performance measurement and organizational change management. In Abdel-Maksoud, A., & Abdel-Kader, M. (Eds.), *Non-Financial Performance Measurement and Management Practices in Manufacturing Firms: A Comparative International Analysis* (pp. 273–303). Oxford, UK: Elsevier.

Robertson, R. (1992). *Glocalization: Social theory and global culture*. London: Sage Publications.

Robertson, R. (1995). Glocalization: Time-space and homogeneity–heterogeneity. In Featherstone, M., Lash, S., & Robertson, R. (Eds.), *Global modernities* (pp. 25–44). London: Sage Publications. doi:10.4135/9781446250563.n2.

Schonberger, R. J. (1996). *World class manufacturing: The next decade*. New York: The Free Press.

Smith, M. (1997). Putting NFIs to work in a balanced scorecard environment. *Management Accounting*, 32-35.

Tillema, S. (2005). Towards an integrated contingency framework for MAS sophistication: Case studies on the scope of accounting instruments in Dutch power and gas companies. *Management Accounting Research*, *16*, 101–129. doi:10.1016/j.mar.2004.12.001.

Tsui, J. (2001). The implication of culture on relationship between budgetary participation, management accounting systems, and managerial performance: An analysis of Chinese and Western managers. *The International Journal of Accounting*, *36*, 125–146. doi:10.1016/S0020-7063(01)00101-7.

Van der Stede, W., Young, S., & Chen, C. (2005). Assessing the quality of evidence in empirical management accounting research: The case of survey studies. *Accounting, Organizations and Society*, *30*, 655–684. doi:10.1016/j.aos.2005.01.003.

Vance, C. M., McClaine, S. R., Boje, D. M., & Stage, D. (1992). An examination of the transferability of traditional performance appraisal principles across cultural boundaries. *Management International Review*, *32*, 313–326.

Vollman, T. (1989). *Changing manufacturing performance measurements, Service Organizations*. Sarasota, FL: American Accounting Association.

Weetman, P. (2006). Discovering the international in Accounting and Finance. *The British Accounting Review*, *38*(4), 351–370. doi:10.1016/j.bar.2006.09.001.

Young, M. (1997). Principles for lasting change. *Journal of Cost Management*, *1*, 16–20.

ENDNOTES

1 The questionnaire form used was created in English then translated into Arabic. The form was tested in the piloting stage where many academics and managers in manufacturing firms in Egypt and Saudi Arabia were incorporated.

2 Data collection was funded by University of Sharjah, United Arab Emirates.

3 Unfortunately, no precise figure could be determined because of unavailability of accurate databases. This is partially due to lack of updated records on firms closing or changing activities in each area.

4 The surveyed firms belong to the following industry sectors: manufacturing of chemicals, petroleum, coal, rubber, and plastic products; manufacturing of fabricated metal products; manufacturing of basic metal and non-metallic mineral products; and manufacturing of food products.

5 The surveyed firms belong to the following industry sectors: manufacturing of chemicals, petroleum, coal, rubber, and plastic products; manufacturing of fabricated metal products; manufacturing of basic metal and non-metallic mineral products; and manufacturing of food products.

6 Data collection was funded by King AbdulAziz University, Saudi Arabia (see, Bashieskh and Abdel-Maksoud, 2008).

7 The choice of 300 firms as a sample was due to a funding constraint in the Saudi part of the study.

8 The surveyed firms belong to the following industry sectors: manufacturing of fabricated metal products, manufacturing of chemicals, petroleum, coal, rubber and plastic products; manufacturing of basic metal and non-metallic mineral products; manufacturing of food products; manufacturing of wood and wooden products; manufacturing of publishing and reproduction of record media; and manufacturing of wearing apparel, tanning, and dressing of leather.

9 Most of the surveyed firms, 55% and 64% in Egyptian and Saudi firms respectively, have a workforce size between 101 and 2000 employees. See, Table 1.

10 Including: Egypt, Saudi Arabia, Lebanon, Libya, Kuwait, Iraq and United Arab Emirates.

APPENDIX

Communalities in Analysis of Objectivity/Subjectivity of Judgments

Objectivity is defined as "the extent of agreement among observers" (Guilford, 1954, p. 251). Subjectivity, on the other hand, "arises in part from the fact that different dimensions enter into the determination of the judgments of an observer (*O*)" (Guilford, 1954, p. 253). The total variance in any *O*'s set of judgments is composed of three sources: common-factor, specific, and error variance (Guilford, 1954). "The proportion of any *O*'s variance that is objective in any set of judgments depends upon the extent to which his/her judgments are determined by common-factors. His/her proportion of common-factor variance is known as his/her communality" (Guilford, 1954, p.254).

To compute the communalities of respondents in their evaluation or judgments, the factor analysis statistical technique was applied using SPSS. Communalities are computed for respondents' evaluations of the variables incorporated in the study. In Egypt, results reveal that these communalities range from a minimum of (0.914) to a maximum of (0.998), while in Saudi Arabia, communalities ranged from (0.921) to (1.00).The high values of the communalities and the low range of these values indicate a high degree of objectivity among respondents in both countries.

Chapter 7
Making Agile Development and Offshoring Practice Successful on Global Software Development Project

Edward T. Chen
University of Massachusetts Lowell, USA

ABSTRACT

Two significant trends have been gaining momentum in software development: the utilization of Agile development methodologies, and the continuing trend of companies to outsource development work offshore. These two trends have changed the way companies develop software and business applications. This chapter seeks to evaluate how a company can successfully manage both trends in conjunction with each other on global business. The primary question addressed is whether the benefits derived from Agile development methodologies and the savings from outsourced software development efforts cancel each other out when applied together, or whether they create a synergy greater than the sum of the parts. In order to answer this question, this chapter intends to examine several relevant business practices and industry experiences. From lessons learned, we identify factors which seem to influence a successful combination of Agile methodology and offshoring in global software development projects.

INTRODUCTION

Companies have been adopting Agile development methodologies for a number of reasons, including shorter cycle times for delivering solutions, better team morale, better visibility, and more frequent interactions with business owners (Moe, Dingsoyr, & Dyba, 2009). Agile methodology helps companies deal with the unpredictable nature of development by focusing more on the people involved and less on the process employed (Pearlson & Saunders, 2010).

DOI: 10.4018/978-1-4666-3966-9.ch007

Companies have increasingly been moving software development works to offshore project teams. An obvious benefit of "offshoring" of development work is the dramatically lower costs. While companies can sometimes experience difficulty bringing international software development resources to the outsourcing countries such as United States, there appears to be no restrictions on the amount of software development work a company can send overseas (Battin, Crocker, Kreidler, & Subramanian, 2001; Pearlson & Saunders, 2010).

The following sections include a review of recent literature on the Agile methodologies and offshoring software development, discussion on the effectiveness of Agile methodologies, analysis on various factors and issues of offshoring software development work. The final section concludes the research findings with implications and suggestions for future research of Agile methodologies and offshoring practices.

AGILE DEVELOPMENT

Jones (2006) identifies that among the 30 most significant issues in software engineering which have persisted and haunted software development companies for over 30 years are:

- Only 50% of all the customer's requirements are known at the initiation of the project
- Once development is underway, there is a 2% scope increase every month (scope-creep)
- A total of 20% of the initial requirements are postponed for implementation and delivery only in the next release
- Documentation is very expensive (2nd most expensive activity)
- New customer requirements for post-delivery applications grows every year

Organizations used to following a structured life cycle for software product development find themselves at a crossroads between quickly meeting customer demands and keeping tight control over the development process. The traditional model for software product development, commonly known as the Waterfall Development Model, provides a well-defined process for software development teams to meet customer requirements. However, this model has limited some organizations' ability to deliver on customer's expectations in a timely fashion.

The Agile software development model took shape when IS researchers started to challenge the assumptions of the Waterfall model. They take inspiration from Lean Manufacturing methods to tackle some of the major software development problems (Cohen, Lindvall, & Costa, 2004). The Agile development model yields great benefits to organizations seeking to provide iterative and incremental releases to their customers. There are multiple ways to attain agility. Many methods have been suggested in the extant literature after they have been implemented successfully in the industry. Among those proposed Agile models, Scrum and Extreme Programming are two of the most popular Agile development methods (Succi, & Marchesi, 2001; Marchesi, Succi, Wells, Williams, & Wells, 2003).

The concepts behind Agile were created by a group of developers who gathered to develop an enhanced method for software development (Abrahamsson, Salo, Ronkainen, & Warsta, 2002; Cohen, Lindvall, & Costa, 2004; Conboy, 2009; Highsmith, 2001; Highsmith & Cockburn, 2001). They believe changing software requirements is unavoidable in the software development process. The processes used to develop software should allow for flexibility in handling changes as early as possible (Sharp & Ryan, 2011). To accomplish this challenge, Agile methods categorize the work load into small manageable pieces labeled User Stories. User stories are further grouped into discrete tasks and are addressed over time in iterations or "sprints." Each sprint generally lasts two to three weeks, although some sprints may take longer to develop. The work is generally completed during these sprints. Depending on the size of the sprint, the goals of the team, and the specific processes employed, the code which is developed may not be released for productive use until a number of sprints have been completed.

One of the implicit goals of Agile methodologies is to assign ownership and responsibility to the team or individual where it has the most direct impact and applicability (Highsmith, 2001). In Agile, the Product Owner is ultimately responsible for maintaining the Product Backlog, which is the list of work to be done and the priority of the items on the Backlog. They must be able to answer or find the answer for any questions the development team has about the Backlog items. Thus, the Product Owner should be a business expert familiar with the current processes and the function of proposed software. The final role of the Product Owner is to determine when sufficient work has been completed to merit a deployment. Agile places much emphasis on self-managing teams. In self-managing teams, members define their development processes and are responsible for developing and executing their individual tasks (Moe et al., 2009). The team works together to make decisions on what to work on and how to accomplish the work. Therefore, while the Product Owner defines the work to be done along with the priority, it is the project team that actually chooses what to work on, who will do which tasks, and how long they anticipate the work to be completed.

A long standing tenet of effective project management is to obtain time estimates from the source that will be doing the work. In Agile, a key benefit is that the individual doing the work is committing to a time estimate by the whole team, not just the project manager. This practice ensures the most accurate time estimate because other team members have similar domain knowledge. Team members know if they are padding the estimate with extra time or they may significantly underestimate the work load. Even if padding does occur, it will not be too long. The less experienced team member is able to identify the slip and help the team to correct the situation.

As Viaene and Van den Bunder (2011) describe, Agile methods allow for learning through a single iteration of a project. The lesson learned assists project managers to deliver value in the early stage of project life cycle. Mistakes or failures will be caught in the beginning to reduce the cost to the organization and lead the team to productive work through continuous learning. These short iterations also encourage experimentation and creativity within the development team. If an environment of risk-taking can be engendered, the team may advance solutions which the business or the planners do not originally contemplate (Bose, 2008).

IMPLICATIONS OF AGILE

One main concern with Agile methods is the lack of focus on the planning elements fundamental to most traditional software development methodologies. However, Agile methods are conducted with insight since a core concept is that change is inevitable. Change is incorporated into the continuous process rather than being viewed as an interruption or a break in the process (Highsmith, 2001). This is a crucial reason why Agile methods focus on short iterations. The product owner constantly prioritizes work in between iterations, but not during the entire development process so that change can be embraced in a very timely fashion.

Viaene and Van den Bunder (2011) conducted research on evaluating the key attributes of successful business analytics project managers. They discovered a strong bias towards execution and delivery can help a project team achieve the goals of timely delivery within budget and meet the requirements of the business. Again, this practice is not to minimize the planning efforts; rather, it guarantees a minimum of required planning is undertaken. It will eventually lead to an early adoption of useful software. Traditional software project managers have a propensity towards planning. The syndrome of "analysis by paralysis" has been known to be detrimental in situations where managers can easily become overloaded by vast amounts of information and fail to reach appropriate resolutions (Pearlson & Saunders, 2010).

A crucial component for the successful use of Agile in any organization is the effectiveness of the team (Carmel, 1999). Moe et al. (2009) divide barriers to the success of Agile into two categories—team-level barriers and organization-level barriers. Team-level barriers include commitment, leadership, and failure to learn at the individual level. Historically, developers are quite autonomous. Estimating or committing to team-level tasks can be disoriented to them. They tend to revert estimating and committing only for their individual tasks and not for the completion of the work of the team. Individual leadership becomes a barrier to success when the team is not effective at decision-making. Groupthink is a common problem in group decision-making tasks. However, individuals choose on which tasks to focus without coordinating with other team members. So-called "Groupthink" and a lack of group consensus can often lead to unnecessary work. A worst case scenario is the team must re-do the work which was completed independently. And the last team level barrier–a failure to learn–occurs when individuals do not adapt the key elements of Agile methodology. This is a typical example where a core set of activities must be done in the new manner; otherwise, the whole process will fail.

Moe et al. (2009) cite the example of a Product Owner who continually interrupted iterations which were already underway with new but unrelated requests to be completed during the same iteration. A fundamental principle of Scrum is that once the work in iteration is in progress, it shall not be changed. Any requests for change should be addressed in a future iteration. Teams can commit and stick to a schedule. If Product Owners ignore this principle, the result will be consternation within the team and prevent the team from accomplishing its commitments. The lingering low team morale could eventually cause further staffing problems (Hossain, Babar, & Paik, 2009).

The organization must effectively provide needed support to Agile teams. They cannot function in isolation from the rest of the company. Any barriers to success must be detached. Organization level barriers identified by Moe et al. (2009) include shared resources, organizational control, and a culture of specialization. It is common that organizations have resources allocated to multiple projects. This has also occurred with Agile teams. When a resource is shared across different projects, unforeseen issues in one project can cause delays in other projects. It is often left up to the individuals to determine on which project they will focus to the disadvantage of other projects. An effective organization should support this resource by having "scrum of scrum" meetings where the different teams would get together and mutually resolve organization level barriers. However, this is a higher-order Agile process and many companies may not have yet achieved it in their adoption of Agile (Hossain, Babar, & Paik, 2009). Organization control barrier often appears in monitoring or reporting requirements imposed by management that the Agile team deems unnecessary, duplicative, or even invasive. And the final organization level barrier is the culture of specialization.

Development teams gradually develop a desire to specialize or brand their skills. Organization can play a supporting role by allowing individuals to participate in senior meetings. Top management can permit individuals to hoard their knowledge and skill without sharing them with teammates. Organization can set up a policy to create a culture that rewards individuals who hold the keys to important information instead of rewarding the sharing of that information. Balancing the needs of the team to be cross-trained and the needs of individuals to have specialized training relevant to their domain of expertise is therefore crucial to success (Battin et al., 2001).

Methods to mitigate these barriers to success proposed by Moe et al. (2009) include: creating greater redundancy to aid in the sharing of information, reducing the workload and stress on dedicated individuals; providing self-managed teams with adequate authority to avoid other teams poaching their members; recognizing and rewarding the generalists and the specialists; working to instill trust and commitment; circumventing unnecessary controls or reporting requirements on the team; and striving to assign resources to only one project. Management ultimately decides where resources shall be allocated to the appropriate development project teams. If this is untenable, management should aid in the apportionment of resources to each project.

TECHNOLOGIES ENABLING OFFSHORING

Offshoring has become a fact of business in today's industry. In order to stay competitive, companies need to realize these opportunities and risks of offshoring and carefully evaluate their business operations and technologies to streamline business processes to produce efficiencies. In optimal situations, these efficiencies will produce positive firm value leading to increased shareholder wealth and, in most cases, increased compensation for management. When facing offshoring, many companies have followed its evolution and examined the factors that drive them to a decision to "insourcing" or "outsourcing" their IT services. If the decision is made to offshore the IT services, companies need to develop a set of metrics to judiciously evaluate the essential factors of choosing an offshore location.

Advances in technologies have made outsourcing and offshoring arrangements possible. Workers have to communicate with their colleagues and managers on project development. Without traditional face-to-face interactions of an in-house operation, remote communication necessitates a high degree of collaboration. Today, we are fortunate to have a vast array of emerging technologies to ease the flow of information across distances. Communications through the Internet have seen improvements in quality and reliability and at a lower cost. These advancements of technology have allowed offshoring to gain popularity as a business alternative.

OFFSHORING IT DEVELOPMENT

In recent years, offshore service companies have greatly improved the quality of their processes and the skills to project management efforts (Cusumano, MacCormack, Kemerer, & Crandall, 2009). Dyba and Sharp (2011) indicate the primary drivers behind offshoring are the reduction of costs, a need for additional knowledge, and a need for additional resources. A key component for the success of offshore teams as noted by Sarker and Sarker (2009) is the access to comparable high speed networks and communications systems at each offshore location similar to what the domestic teams utilize. They need to have access to the same software development systems such as code development and bug tracking tools. Same system setting enhances team cohesiveness and improves productivity. Having to maintain information in two different systems could lead to delay, wasted time, and potential error or faulty code.

Companies may approach a move to offshoring from many angles. A review of the research can help them avoid common pitfalls and anticipate a variety of needs and issues that may arise. Cusick and Prasad (2006) lay out some foundational principles and suggestions for companies looking to outsource IT services offshore. They suggest the use of an onsite team lead which remains with each project throughout its lifecycle. They consider the offshore development team to be a compliment to the onsite team. Companies most likely will keep the requirements and design functions onsite and give the detailed development work to the offshore developers. They also take the important step of bringing the offshore lead onsite during the analysis and design phases to help facilitate the clarification of specifications and translate the requirements into functioning code.

Cusick and Prasad (2006) also propound the use of sufficient infrastructure and development tools to foster success in offshoring. They indicate putting rules in place for the setup and maintenance of the infrastructure will ensure reproducibility to avoid problems that could be unique to the offshore environment. One way to ensure sufficient local knowledge of the code is to have domestic team members participate in quality assurance. They suggest all teams work from a common source control system, a common defect tracking tool, and a common reporting generator to ease updates and avoid duplication of effort. They propose a framework on which to build successful offshore codes. This framework includes a documented enterprise library and a set of detailed coding standards. The offshore team can begin learning early in the process if key metrics such as page load times are not met.

When making the decision to outsource, Prikladnicki, Audy, and Shull (2010) suggest that companies seeking to offshore possess three key capabilities: vendor management which encompasses strengths in controlling and coordinating vendor relationships; project management which incorporates controls for managing outsourced projects; and process management whereby a company is able to demonstrate skills. A performance system is developed to monitor and manage key performance indicators to keep offshoring sustainable over time.

IMPLICATIONS OF OFFSHORING

There are numerous disadvantages to offshoring highlighted by researchers including language difference, time zone difference, and cultural differences (Carmel & Agarwal, 2001; Hanisch, Thanasankit, & Corbitt, 2001; Shachaf, 2008). Each of these factors can have dramatic effect on productivity. Especially, the cultural difference can lead to misunderstandings that could end a beneficial arrangement. As also noted by Moe et al. (2009), offshore projects may fail if these three differences are not addressed appropriately.

Many companies do not anticipate the soft costs brought up by offshoring arrangement. Rottman and Lacity (2006) find that companies are willing to give domestic suppliers plenty of freedom and time in understanding the specifications, providing updates, and delivering on requirements. They will not do the same for offshore suppliers. For example, companies typically request updates from domestic suppliers every two weeks. It is not uncommon to see outsourcing managers ask international suppliers to provide daily updates. One effective way to mitigate this issue is to include an on-site manager from the offshore company to perform intermediary processes directly. The net cost may be lower than having other domestic counterparts performing those duties. Rottman and Lacity (2006) indicate the transaction costs for offshoring can reach 50% of the total project costs if not carefully managed. If the arrangement of an on-site manager from the offshore provider goes well, future projects can reap the benefits and help improve performance to recapture the savings.

Not all offshore outsourcing efforts are successful. Dyba and Sharp (2011) review recent literature of 59 studies and find that about 10% of offshoring IT projects have clear success. It outweighs the stories of clear failure, which is 3 percent among the studies. Most results fall somewhere in between clear success and clear failure. It is evident that the offshore outsourcing is not yet a fully mature business practice. Each case must be reviewed on an individual basis to determine the suitability of offshoring to the company and project at hand.

Managers should be aware of cultural differences when working with offshore teams. For example, people in India tend to be less willing to push back on requirements or say "no" to direct questions than people in the US. Managers must learn to ask questions in more open-ended ways and probe offshore teams more than they might do with domestic counterparts. Companies working with sensitive client information such as HIPAA related information will require offshore providers to ensure that all clients' data are masked (Cusick & Prasad, 2006).

COMBINING AGILE WITH OFFSHORING

There are some unique considerations to consider when a company seeks to implement an Agile development methodology with an offshore resource. Cusumano et al. (2009) suggest the selection of an Agile methodology should be the first stage of a project undertaking. Their research indicates that while offshoring can reduce quality and productivity, implementing the proper processes can result in team learning that will significantly mitigate those losses. They recommend that companies develop a continuous habit of reviewing their IT development processes to ensure they still fit the context in place. Companies can then take those factors into account when weighing the benefits of offshoring.

Dyba and Sharp (2011) find that complex development projects may not be beneficial from a "follow the sun" approach. They advocate some Agile principles such as short development cycles, frequent communication, regular face-to-face walk-through meetings, and exchange visits to enhance collaboration and understanding. They study how an offshoring relationship might evolve to help companies project typical growth patterns and changing needs in the relationship. They determine that offshoring relationship generally moves through five phases: (1) Trust, where potentially compatible companies are identified and trust begins to build; (2) Assess, where supplier capabilities are evaluated and initial agreements are drafted and enacted; (3) Prove, where operational capabilities and efficiencies are achieved in the offshore team; (4) Enhance, where ongoing operations are continually improved upon while expanding the scope of the relationship and the complexity of the project; and (5) Reengineer, where the offshore team is developed into an Agile responsive team.

Cusick and Prasad (2006) indicate not all projects lend themselves to the benefits of offshoring. They find new development projects of a medium size that are built on existing frameworks are the most successful in offshore efforts. They have learned that projects require integration with external entities can be much more difficult with offshore teams. They cannot replicate the whole infrastructure for those teams to utilize offshore just as they are local. Rottman and Lacity (20006) suggest including more oversight of the offshore team in a domestic outsourcing arrangement. They have weekly scheduled meetings and plenty of ongoing interactions with clearly defined lines of communication. Even in the modified waterfall methodology, some common elements are really foundational components of Agile. For example, the usage of regular design and code reviews, continuous communications during iterations, timely escalation of issues, and the frequent delivery of code so that any issues can be addressed quickly (Cusick & Prasad, 2006).

Many organizations moving to offshore their IT development work have run into an issue when it comes to integrate the offshore code with the domestic code and other systems. Cusick and Prasad (2006) are able to mitigate this common problem by instituting an interim delivery of code halfway through the development effort. Agile methods address this integration issue directly by delivering functioning code at the end of almost every sprint (Holmstrom, Fitzgerald, Agerfalk, & Conchuir, 2006).

PEOPLE FACTORS

A key success factor of Agile methodology is the successful management of people. One of the main tenets of Agile is people over process.

The impact of the role people play cannot be overlooked. Conboy, Coyle, Wang and Pikkarainen (2011) find a number of people areas which Agile methods can elicit and moderate. The first one they illuminated is the fear developers may have of exposing deficiencies in their skill levels. Since Agile is all about constant communication and daily updates, any weaknesses a developer may have could be uncovered. If developers are lacking a certain skill, they may need to spend some time learning it. They probably would not want to explain to the team or business owners. However, they would have to explain when the time expires. Interestingly, in those surveyed companies, some developers show reticent and feel inadequate. Conversely, other developers use the opportunity to impress and even bully other team members. To address these people issues, the authors recommend creating an atmosphere where developers can feel safe to expose shortcomings. Some companies allow team members to share information in a more private environment and others have separate meetings for junior members to work with more experienced mentors to help coach them and allay any concerns.

Another key people factor identified by Conboy et al. (2011) is the need for developers to be very well-rounded and play roles in many other areas such as a tester, an architect, and a good communicator. The processes invoked by Agile require more people skills of the participants. No longer can a developer be handed a set of requirements and spend weeks only coding diligently or learning quietly. They are expected to participate in the team, share what they are working on, and ensure any code they delivered has been sufficiently unit tested. And once work on hand is complete, developers are likely expected to help out in other tasks and possibly test other developer's code. Some developers are concerned that this focus on so many different functional areas could make them lose their edge in their selected area of specialization. Conboy et al. (2011) suggest that developers have a chance to continue training and maintaining specialized skills. This can be accomplished by blocking out a certain amount of a developer's time to be dedicated to training.

The crucial need for developers to maintain and enhance their skills is highlighted in work done by Lee and Mirchandani (2010). They find business executives and education professionals need to remain updated on the knowledge and skills required for their constituents to meet current and future trends in technology. They note five areas in particular which are expected to see significant growth and change in the near future: wireless applications and communications; mobile commerce applications and technology; information systems security; web applications and technology; and data management. They also point out the five most important skills in the future: information systems security; data management; web applications and technology; project management and other business knowledge; and wireless applications and communications. It is interesting to note that even in a review of IT skills, the topic of business knowledge and project management skills develops.

Any discussion of personnel issues is incomplete without an evaluation of the employee review process. Changes required by people using Agile methodologies can have unforeseen impacts on other areas of the business. Conboy et al. (2011) note most companies evaluate employee performance on an individual basis. However, Agile teams are evaluated on team performance criteria. Therefore, an individual who spends much of his or her time helping other team members to be successful in furtherance of the project goals may have lower individual performance results. This dichotomy poses a significant challenge to company adopting Agile methodology. Thus, management needs to make sure both team and individual understand the performance measurement procedures. Any wins for the team should reflect on its individual performance measures as well. If this is not specified clearly and handled carefully, team members will quickly engage in the conflict and work to highlight their own performance over the team. Team morale will deteriorate and team synergy will quickly diminish which is detrimental to the project. Implementing metrics which take the team successes into account help avoid this unfavorable situation. Other methods can include promoting 360 degree feedback mechanisms so members can be rewarded for their contributions to the team. Establishing a team-based bonus programs can be very motivating to team members.

Given the team nature of Agile, other areas of limited knowledge can be exposed among team members such as general business knowledge of the project undertaken. Developers are often used to being insulated from the complexities and vagaries of general business and are historically handed discrete units of work. In an Agile environment, the open discussion can lead to embarrassing revelations about someone's lack of knowledge as to how the business actually works. As Conboy et al. (2011) highlight, if this is exposed to business stakeholders or clients, they could lose faith that the Agile team has the ability to successfully meet their needs. They suggest training such teams on business basics. One particularly innovative solution is to actually have the client provide the training to the team. This involvement of clients in the results of the team provides clients the opportunity to show the team the important aspects of their business that they want to highlight.

Conboy et al. (2011) reveal those characteristics beneficial to the success of Agile programs shall be contemplated during the hiring process. It is particularly problematic for hiring graduates directly out of school. Students generally have not had many chances to develop Agile-related skills. A few companies create mock meetings where applicants can demonstrate how they perform in an Agile team. One company cited even puts applicants into real project meetings. However, Agile is a people-oriented development method. It may be sufficient to simply screen for traditional people skills to determine how likely a candidate may perform well in such an Agile environment.

DISCUSSION AND IMPLICATIONS

The adoption of Agile development methodologies can be very complicated. There are instances of failures in moving to teams with offshore resources. The high amount of customized processes created in Agile projects presumably makes their process work as opposed to adopting a pure Scrum methodology. The increased pressure on employees to deliver work in a short period and the lack of documentation developed during the course of the project often cause confusion among participants. Lack of training is noted and can clearly doom any initiative (Sarker & Sarker, 2009).

Sarker and Sarker (2009) also highlight that frequent synchronous meetings can help facilitate the hand-off work from multiple locations. This is precisely what Agile methodology advocates. Managers should be cognizant of team members' local time zones to minimize the impact on the balance of work and life. For example, a meeting first thing in the morning East Coast time in United States is generally acceptable to teams in India, where it is the end of a business day. It would be harder for domestic teams on the West Coast of United States. Team members have to participate likely pre-dawn. Under telecommuting policy, many companies allow employees greater flexibility of joining those meetings from home.

As we saw in the discussion on offshoring, many of the same requirements companies use to stay involved with international suppliers are the same requirements that Agile development advocates. The constant communication, verification of understanding, and delivery of work in small chunks become habitual under the Agile development methodology actually benefits outsourcing. Therefore, it appears from the research that companies can implement offshoring using

Agile methodologies just as easily and perhaps more naturally than they can in trying to use any other software development methodologies.

Sharp and Ryan (2011) conclude that 8 of the 11 Agile manifesto principles are directly involved in the effectiveness of offshore teams utilizing Agile methodologies. Their study leads to the development of a framework for setting up the structure of an Agile offshore team along three dimensions: agility, "virtualness," and structure. The agility component relates to the nature of the Agile manifesto in its emphasis on individual interactions, functioning software, responsiveness and working directly with clients. The "virtualness" component relates to how similar or different team members are along two axes, Temporal Distribution and Boundary Spanning. Temporal Distribution is the similarity or difference of both time zones and whether or not the teams are working concurrently. Some development teams in offshore locations actually work nights so that they are working the same hours as domestic teams. The Boundary Spanning element of the virtualness component describes how much or how little the teams cross cultural, functional, and organizational boundaries (Mitchell & Zigurs, 2009; Shachaf, 2008). Undoubtedly, this is a component also emphasized by Agile methodologies. Having the team solve its own problems is a sign of a mature functional team.

Finally, the structure component of the framework is the most often overlooked. Structure contains elements such as team processes, core norms, and team composition. Any well designed team should take all of these factors into consideration. The effective implementation of an Agile methodology appears to reinforce the process and procedures that have been demonstrated to be successful in other types of teams. If these principles are implemented, monitored, and followed appropriately, offshore Agile teams can deliver successful IT services (Hackman, 2002; Mintzberg, 1979; Mintzberg, 1983; Prasad & Akhilesh, 2002).

CONCLUSION

Organizations which follow the traditional waterfall model can consider Agile development methodology when they are constantly riddled with the puzzle of "unknown future requirements." Such organizations could be wary of developers and other members of the team not liking the Agile methodology. Agile methodology may create a sense of pressure and burden such as asking for too many outputs or prototypes within a short duration. Agile methodology has little documentation to drive the development process. An innovative practice they are historically not used to. Organizations should have a dialogue with their senior developers to figure out which portions of Agile can be immediately implemented, which ones need to be phased in, and which ones are not suitable for the team or its products in the current situation. Targeting superficial deadlines creates unnecessary pressure on the development team. This type of critical path scheduling may eventually lead to developer burn out and poor quality of work.

The foundation of Agile development process is to provide incremental software code to customer in each iteration. An organization seeking to adopt an Agile methodology must first determine if its customers are willing to participate in this effort. The organization needs to specifically understand if the customers can afford to frequently upgrade their software without causing any disruptions in their routine operations. The customers' rapid feedback makes up an important component of the iterative process. It can be a detrimental drawback if the customer is unwilling to provide any feedback.

Agile methods work best when the team members are in physical proximity as this improves the communication amongst team members. The immediate question that arises in this age of multi-site development and offshoring is how can a distributed or virtual team be Agile successfully when there is a lack of sufficient communication?

Research has shown that even though implementing Agile in virtual teams can be daunting and difficult, Agile models have been successfully practiced in distributed teams. Agile methods are not rigid; rather they are very flexible. Organizations can become as Agile as they want to within their existing organizational framework without having to make dramatic changes to their structure and culture.

Agile has been discussed as a software development model. The reality of the situation is however changing slowly but steadily. It is apparently that software maintenance has become a very quintessential activity. Software maintenance has in fact become even more dominant effort than the software development itself. Thus, more research is needed to investigate how Agile models will augur for software maintenance teams. Future research can be performed to determine if Agile teams can use the maintenance period to cycle back to waterfall model where they can invest the resources in detailed design and documentation of the entire product.

Technology plays an important role in our lives. Its significance continues to grow with further advancements in information technologies. During the past two decades, we have experienced remarkable progress in regards to the Internet connectivity leading to high speed and broadband connections. New IT technologies like Web 2.0 and cloud computing have provided reliable high speed and quality connections enabling real-time transmission of information flows. The Internet has become the foundation for a vast array of social media tools, which are also playing an important role in Agile development among virtual teams.

As we have seen from the prior research, much has been done to evaluate the effectiveness of Agile methodologies and the impacts of offshoring separately. From this chapter, it is clear that many of the tenets of Agile directly support the recommendations found in successful offshoring. Companies considering offshoring should seek to implement at least some of the Agile components. Those companies already using Agile can foresee a relatively smooth transition in a move to offshoring. As relatively little has been published to date that incorporates both of those components to form a synergy in IT development, further research is recommended to directly evaluate the effectiveness of using Agile with offshoring.

REFERENCES

Abrahamsson, P., Salo, O., Ronkainen, J., & Warsta, J. (2002). *Agile Software Development Methods: Review and Analysis*. Espoo, Finland: VTT Publications.

Battin, R. D., Crocker, R., Kreidler, J., & Subramanian, K. (2001). Leveraging resources in global software development. *IEEE Software*, *18*(2), 70–77. doi:10.1109/52.914750.

Bose, I. (2008). Lessons learned from distributed agile software projects: A case-based analysis. *Communications of the Association for Information Systems*, *23*(34), 619–632.

Carmel, E. (1999). *Global software teams: Collaborating across borders and time zones*. Upper Saddle River, NJ: Prentice-Hall.

Carmel, E., & Agarwal, R. (2001). Tactical approaches for alleviating distance in global software development. *IEEE Software*, *18*(2), 22–29. doi:10.1109/52.914734.

Cohen, D., Lindvall, M., & Costa, P. (2004). An introduction to agile methods. *Advances in Computers*, *62*, 1–66. doi:10.1016/S0065-2458(03)62001-2.

Conboy, K. (2009). Agility from first principles: Reconstructing the concept of agility in information systems development. *Information Systems Research*, *20*(3), 329–354. doi:10.1287/isre.1090.0236.

Conboy, K., Coyle, S., Wang, X., & Pikkarainen, M. (2011). People over process: Key challenges in Agile development. *IEEE Software*, *28*(4), 48–57. doi:10.1109/MS.2010.132.

Cusick, J., & Prasad, A. (2006). A practical management and engineering approach to offshore collaboration. *IEEE Software*, *23*(5), 20–29. doi:10.1109/MS.2006.118.

Cusumano, M. A., MacCormack, A., Kemerer, C. F., & Crandall, W. (2009). Critical decisions in software development: Updating the state of the practice. *IEEE Software*, *26*(5), 84–87. doi:10.1109/MS.2009.124.

Dyba, T., & Sharp, H. (2011). A whisper of evidence in global software engineering. *IEEE Software*, *28*(4), 15–18. doi:10.1109/MS.2011.70.

Hackman, J. R. (2002). *Leading teams: Setting the stage for great performances*. Boston, MA: Harvard Business School Press.

Hanisch, J., Thanasankit, T., & Corbitt, B. (2001). Exploring the cultural and social impacts on the requirements engineering process - Highlighting some problems challenging virtual team relationships with clients. *Journal of Systems and Information Technology*, *5*(2), 1–19. doi:10.1108/13287260180000763.

Highsmith, J. (2001). *History: The Agile manifesto*. Retrieved February 1, 2012 from http://agilemanifesto.org/history.html

Highsmith, J., & Cockburn, A. (2001). Agile software development: The business of innovation. *IEEE Computer*, *34*(9), 120–122. doi:10.1109/2.947100.

Holmstrom, H., Fitzgerald, B., Agerfalk, P. J., & Conchuir, E. O. (2006). Agile practices reduce distance in global software development. *Information Systems Management*, *23*(3), 7–18. doi:10.1201/1078.10580530/46108.23.3.20060601/93703.2.

Hossain, E., Babar, M. A., & Paik, H. (2009). Using scrum in global software development: A systematic literature review. *4th IEEE International Conference on Global Software Engineering*. Limerick, Ireland.

Jones, C. (2006). *Positive and Negative Innovation in Software Engineering*. Retrieved February 10, 2012 from www.compaid.com/caiinternet/ezine/capers-posneg.pdf

Lee, K., & Mirchandani, D. (2010). Dynamics of the importance of IS/IT skills. *Journal of Computer Information Systems*, *50*(4), 67–78.

Marchesi, M., Succi, G., Wells, D., Williams, L., & Wells, J. D. (Eds.). (2003). *Extreme Programming Perspectives*. Reading, MA: Addison-Wesley.

Mintzberg, H. T. (1979). *The structuring of organizations*. Englewood Cliffs, NJ: Prentice-Hall.

Mintzberg, H. T. (1983). *Structure in fives: Designing effective organizations*. Englewood Cliffs, NJ: Prentice-Hall.

Mitchell, A., & Zigurs, I. (2009). Trust in virtual teams: Solved or still a mystery? *The Data Base for Advances in Information Systems*, *40*(3), 61–83. doi:10.1145/1592401.1592407.

Moe, N. B., Dingsoyr, T., & Dyba, T. (2009). Overcoming barriers to self-management in software teams. *IEEE Software*, *26*(6), 20–26. doi:10.1109/MS.2009.182.

Pearlson, K. E., & Saunders, C. S. (2010). *Managing and Using Information Systems* (4th ed.). Hoboken, NJ: John Wiley & Sons, Inc..

Prasad, K., & Akhilesh, K. B. (2002). Global virtual teams: What impacts their design and Performance? *Team Performance Management*, *8*(5/6), 102–112. doi:10.1108/13527590210442212.

Prikladnicki, R., Audy, J. L. N., & Shull, F. (2010). Patterns in effective distributed software development. *IEEE Software*, *27*(2), 12–15. doi:10.1109/MS.2010.48.

Rottman, J. W., & Lacity, M. C. (2006). Proven practices for effectively offshoring IT work. *MIT Sloan Management Review*, *47*(3), 56–63.

Sarker, S., & Sarker, S. (2009). Exploring agility in distributed information systems development teams: An interpretive study in an offshoring context. *Information Systems Research*, *20*(3), 440–461. doi:10.1287/isre.1090.0241.

Shachaf, P. (2008). Cultural diversity and information and communication technology impacts on global virtual teams: An exploratory study. *Information & Management*, *45*(2), 131–142. doi:10.1016/j.im.2007.12.003.

Sharp, J. H., & Ryan, S. D. (2011). Global Agile team configuration. *Journal of Strategic Innovation and Sustainability*, *7*(1), 120–134.

Succi, G., & Marchesi, M. (Eds.). (2001). *Extreme Programming Examined*. Reading, MA: Addison-Wesley.

Viaene, S., & Van den Bunder, A. (2011). The secrets to managing business analytics projects. *MIT Sloan Management Review*, *53*(1), 64–70.

Chapter 8
A Synthesis of Globalisation, Business Culture and E-Business Adoption in Vietnam

Huong Le
Deakin University, Australia

Fung K. Koo
University of Sydney, Australia

Jason Sargent
Swinburne University of Technology, Australia

ABSTRACT

The pace and intensity of social change in modern society is increasing, particularly through advances in modern technology and the remarkable innovations in information and communications technology (ICT), as well as through social movements, especially globalisation (Synott, 2004). This chapter will discuss the concept of globalisation and its impact on the economies, cultures, and international business in developing countries and, in particular, Vietnam. The chapter provides an insight into how national culture and technology affects business operations, including current issues in technological readiness for e-business adoption in Vietnam. By applying theories of globalisation to explain changes and progress in Vietnamese economic development, the chapter also provides a better understanding of the complex mix of culture, technology, and business operations in Vietnam. Recommendations are also made for the development of an appropriate environment for e-business in small to medium enterprises that will further strengthen the country's international business operations.

INTRODUCTION

The pace and intensity of social change in modern society has increased through advances in modern technology and the remarkable innovations in information and communications technology (ICT), as well as through social movements, especially globalisation (Synott, 2004). Synott (2004) points out the term 'globalisation' has been adopted to define the complex changes occurring at the present time. The author emphasises that some of the contemporary changes indicated above

DOI: 10.4018/978-1-4666-3966-9.ch008

can be attributed to the profound influence of the technology revolution, namely, mobile phones, computers, the Internet, and television. The current world-wide phenomenon of globalisation and, in particular, the effects of economic, cultural, and global changes in business, which were major forces for contemporary change in all societies in the late twentieth century, are the main focus of this chapter.

There is an established body of literature and research reports on a variety of topics in relation to the economic reforms and transition in Vietnam (e.g., Beresford, 1988; 1989; Beresford & Tran, 2004; Dang & Beresford, 1998; Taylor, 2004; Van Arkadie & Mallon, 2003). For example, Meyer, Tran, and Nguyen (2006) investigate the economy, culture, society, investment strategies and policies in Vietnam and implications for foreign investment in Vietnam; Truong, Heijden and Rowley (2010) study human resource management in Vietnam in the context of economic reform and globalisation, and argue that a better way to manage human capital should be found in Vietnam; Beresford and Tran (2004) discuss the sustainability of economic development in Vietnam. However, to the authors' knowledge, little has been done with regard to the relationship between globalisation, culture and technology in the Vietnamese context although the country has experienced substantial change as part of global economic integration and technological development in the last 20 years. The growth in the Vietnamese economy and international business reflects the process of global economic integration, indicating the importance of a better understanding of Vietnam's own business operation style, characteristics and prejudices. Therefore, Vietnam is adopted as a case study to understand the interrelationship between globalisation, culture and technological adoption in this country.

Specifically, this chapter answers the question of how national culture and technology affect business operations, including current issues in technological readiness for e-business adoption in Vietnam. This chapter will discuss the concept of globalisation and related theories, and review the debate on the overall effects of globalisation on the economies, cultures and international business in developing countries and, in particular, in Vietnam. Using four main approaches of globalisation as a theoretical framework, this chapter will also discuss how culture and technology affect business operations in Vietnam through an analysis of relationships between national culture and business practices, and an adoption of e-business by Small to Medium Enterprises (SMEs) in Vietnam.

Our analysis shows the concept of globalisation cannot simply be applied to a developing market without the requisite thorough understanding of the host country's culture, business environment, and government policies to optimise business success. This chapter contributes to the theoretical and practical understanding of interrelationships between globalisation, culture, and technological development and their impacts on an emerging economy such as Vietnam. This chapter also discusses the implications for the long-term growth of the Vietnamese economy and for success in international business operations in Vietnam, as well as other developing countries with similar cultures experiencing rapid economic development.

GLOBALISATION AND THE GLOBAL ECONOMY

Globalisation in its most basic form refers to the widening and speeding up of global interconnections (Held, McGrew, Goldblatt, & Perraton, 1999), and to the increasing interdependence of different parts of the world (Seitz, 2002; Sklair, 1999b). There are several major elements in globalisation. First, there is integration of the financial and currency markets, or, in other words, the enhanced integration of economies across the world (Bacchus, 2004; Burbules & Torres, 2000; Fenna, 2004; Ngok & Kwong, 2003). Second, globalisation involves the incorporation of production, trade and capital development across national borders through global corporations (Fenna, 2004; Webber, Wang, & Zhu, 2002). In addition, the functions of international agencies and organisations, for example, the World Bank, and the World Trade Organisation (WTO), need to adjust national economic, social and environmental policies, which form the third element of globalisation. The final element of globalisation is the effect of the imposition of market relations on the social and cultural life in countries formerly protected from such market pressures (Webber et al., 2002).

Sklair (1999a) categorises globalisation into four main approaches/models: the world-systems approach, the global culture approach, the global society approach, and the global capitalism approach. The world-systems approach was rooted in the earlier work of Wallerstein (1974), and stresses the division of the world into three hierarchical levels of core countries, semi-peripheral countries and the peripheral countries, in terms of their altering positions in the international division of labour in the capitalist global system. The key issues with this approach, as Wallerstein (1974; 2011) argues, are the unequal economic relations between the core and the peripheral countries in which various policies provide benefits predominantly for the firms in the core countries. The second approach of globalisation–global culture–emphasises the hazards that "a homogenising mass media-based culture poses for national identities" (Sklair, 1999a, p. 151). This idea is based on the very rapid growth and spread of mass media communication, particularly television, and the emergence of what is called 'the global village,' that has occurred over the last few decades. The notion of 'the global village' indicates that 'everyone in the world can be exposed to the same images, almost instantaneously' (Sklair, 1999a, pp. 151–152).

The third approach of globalisation–a global society–is a unique stage in world development, which is claimed to be both positive and comprehensive, and creates an ideal arrangement for the production of world-views. The fourth approach of globalisation–global capitalism–as Sklair argues, represents the increasing dominance of capitalism as a global social and economic system. This approach, partly described above, has created a significant context for political and economic change in the world (Sklair, 1999a). In an assessment of the different models of globalisation, we are of the view that except for a global society, which is more difficult to find evidence for, the three other models of globalisation best explain the changes to the business operations and socio-economic development in Vietnam. These models will form the theoretical framework for our chapter.

Concomitantly with the trend toward globalisation, economic restructuring is occurring in the world. Burbules and Torres (2000) indicate economic globalisation occurs in the milieu of a new international division of labour, and of economic combinations of national economies through which common trade and market agreements emerge. Further, new exchange relations and engagements between countries, and amongst various social sectors within each country, are emerging. At a time when services and information are becoming more significant than manufacturing, new areas have emerged, particularly in the developed countries. The authors further indicate there is also a growing capacity to connect markets on an immediate basis, and to shift capital across nations as a result of the escalating internationalisation of trade. Simultaneously, labour markets are being restructured and hourly wages are being superseded in various settings by piecework remuneration, while the power of unions is being undermined by relaxation or non-enforcement of labour legislation. Such factors as the rise of surplus labour, the intensification of competition, decreasing profit margins, less-protective labour contracts and the institutionalisation of 'team concept' strategies, are decreasing capital-labour conflict (Burbules & Torres, 2000).

In line with labour restructuring, there is a shift from a strict Fordist model of production to a model based on flexible use of the labour market and inventories, and on the decreasing costs and escalating speed of delivering information and products from one location to another across the globe (Burbules & Torres, 2000). Thus, de-skilling and redundancy of large workforces produce a labour market comprised of a small, highly-skilled and well-paid sector coupled with a large, low-skilled and low-paid sector as a result of the growing significance of capital-intensive production (Burbules & Torres, 2000). However, at the same time, Burbules and Torres (2000) indicate the percentage of part-time, female and flexible workers has increased as a proportion of the labour force. In addition, the service sector has become larger and more important at the expense of the primary and secondary sectors.

Restructuring and changes in economic theories are engines for change in many aspects and sectors of society. Such change is reflected in deep fiscal crises and reductions in public sector dominance as a consequence of the curtailing of some welfare states, including privatisation of social, housing and health services, and education (Burbules & Torres, 2000). This change is also evident in the implementation of neo-liberal policies wherein the state has withdrawn from its responsibility for administering public resources to support social justice. Other changes in economics include those in trade relations, the formation of 'free trade' regions, changes in banking and credit processing, and the greater presence of international lending agencies such as the World Bank and the International Monetary Fund (IMF). Additionally, there is the growth of global (transnational) corporations, global mobility of labour and companies, the spread of new technology, and new patterns of consumption, as well as advertising and marketing strategies to boost that consumption (Burbules & Torres, 2000). All of these factors are changing the social and economic situations within countries profoundly, and Vietnam is not immune from these global changes.

It is evident that social change through globalisation positively influences levels of economic success in the world. Economists see globalisation as a key to global economic development. Countries involved in the globalisation process have also experienced a faster rate of economic growth in international trade and Foreign Direct Investments (FDI) which have grown substantially since the 1970s (Bacchus, 2004). China and Vietnam are examples of emerging economies which have achieved dramatic economic growth in their economies through their involvement in the globalisation process since the 1990s. For example, in Vietnam, the average growth in GDP in 2009 and 2010 was almost 7% per annum (Central Intelligence Agency, 2011), and this figure was higher in previous years (Le, 2008).

Arguably, globalisation, with all the above features, also negatively impacts on socio-economic development through the connections between countries. Global competitive pressures have pushed governments 'to curtail state spending and interventions; for, despite different partisan commitments, all governments have been pressed in the same direction' (Held et al., 1999, p. 13). As a result of globalisation, western ideas of modern state and capitalist markets have widely conditioned the development of many societies and civilisations across the globe. Accordingly, traditional patterns of power and authority have been transformed, and, at the same time, new forms of governance and resource allocation have been generated. There is also an ever-increasing cultural, financial, and technological gap between the 'more-developed' and 'less-developed' nations (Burbules & Torres, 2000).

In the competitive battle between countries for resources and markets, there are also increased debt burdens and/or economic dependence of the less powerful countries on the more powerful states (Central Intelligence Agency, 2011; Synott,

2004). Subsequently, the former may become indebted to the World Bank if they cannot properly service their debts. If so, this will only deepen existing concerns about the fact that the imposition of structural adjustment policy widens the gap between the rich and the poor, resulting in high unemployment rates (Welch, 2003), and environmental and ecological issues (Synott, 2004). Arguably, world-systems theory remains valid in this context through an imposition of policies to the advantage of the core countries.

The seemingly inexorable spread of technological developments such as telecommunications, Internet and television, is likely to sweep aside national and local cultures, to be replaced by Westernisation and/or popular culture (Sklair, 1999a). Given that global culture promotes cultural exchanges between countries, such developments potentially pose problems such as Americanisation, homogenisation, repluralisation, commodification, globalism and 'glocalism' (Dewey, 2004; Wyszomirski, 2000), leading to more cultural fragmentation (Burbules & Torres, 2000; Sklair, 1999a) for local societies. This trend is not surprising. The decline of classical and traditional arts and a lack of audiences for these art forms have been occurring in Vietnam for some time due to the force of Western and popular entertainment forms (Le, 2008; 2009). In return, the arts sector has struggled to adapt to the changes, both in terms of financial viability and in adapting to the new socio-economic context (Le, 2004; 2008).

Despite the above changes, countries have adopted various ways to respond to global trends. As a result of global integration, political and economic reforms which reflect the rise of global capitalism (for example, decentralisation, privatisation and deregulation) have occurred in many developing countries (Mok & Welch, 2003a). During the 1970s and 1980s, many former communist and currently communist nations adopted at least some market mechanisms to reform their economies (Fogel & Zapalska, 2001; Seitz, 2002), including Vietnam. For example, China and Vietnam have implemented 'open door' market policies, at the same time they are pursuing a socialist political system. This process is sometimes known as a transitional economy, and may prompt a structural adjustment program supported by the World Bank's adjustment loans (Commins, Gevers, Randa, & World Bank, 2001). Market-oriented reform entails the introduction of the market into the economic domain. Elements of the market economy have led to significant changes in China's economic growth, for example, and a rising ethos of free enterprise, the valuing of individual initiatives, and the pursuit of profit (Ngok & Kwong, 2003).

The opening up of and integration into the global market in the case of China and Vietnam were also meant to encourage direct investments from foreign and transnational corporations, facilitate the transfer of Western technology, and increase the production of goods for export (Ngok & Kwong, 2003). Despite the continuing dominance of the state industrial sector in China, collective enterprises, individually-owned businesses, joint ventures, and foreign-owned firms (sometimes more efficient than those in the state-owned sectors) have rapidly gained ground. Meanwhile, public sector activities have been reduced while foreign direct investment and private economic activities are being encouraged in a climate of increasing deregulation (Ngok & Kwong, 2003). All of the features of reform that indicate the influences of globalisation and structural adjustment policies in China have parallels with Vietnam, as both nations share similar political systems and have reformed their economies. The global economic changes outlined above provide a theoretical basis for explaining changes in Vietnamese society, which have been heightened by technological developments since the late 1980s.

The following section will discuss influences of culture and technology on business operations in light of the economic reform in Vietnam.

GLOBALISATION, NATIONAL CULTURE, AND E-BUSINESS IN VIETNAM

In light of globalisation, notable changes in the economies of some socialist countries have been taking place since the late 1970s and 1980s. Part of this reform was to adopt aspects of market approaches in parallel with the state approach (Seitz, 2002), which reflects the increasing effects of global capitalism on socialist nations such as Vietnam and China.

Vietnam has remained a socialist country even after the collapse of the Soviet Union in 1991. Before the economic reforms in 1986, the Socialist Republic of Vietnam (SRV) was organised under a subsidised economic system (UNDP, 2002; Van Arkadie & Mallon, 2003). In the subsidised period, the power to lead development processes and all perspectives of the socio-economic situation was concentrated in the communist government (NCSSH, 2001). This economic model, as Seitz (2002) highlights, is the state approach widely adopted by most Eastern European countries before the 1990s.

However, Vietnam has undergone an important social change in its recent history, a fact which has increasingly influenced its socio-economic growth. There are many reasons for economic reforms in Vietnam. First, wars against foreign incursions and American economic embargoes caused severe internal economic difficulties in the 1970s and 1980s (RIAP, 2003). Second, the collapse of communism in many socialist countries seriously affected Vietnam's overall economy in the early 1990s, resulting in sharp decreases in trading with and foreign aid received from the Soviet bloc (World Bank, 2011). Third, Vietnam's opening up of its doors to the global economy was also driven by China's economic reforms in the late 1970s.

Responding to the economic reform climate which was occurring in many countries under the spread of globalisation, the Vietnamese government adopted a market approach called a market-oriented economy (or, in Vietnamese – *doi moi*) in 1986 (Warner, 2001). The new Constitution, approved in 1992, recognised the Communist Party of Vietnam as the leading strength of the state, which would manage within the principles of the Constitution and the laws of the country (UNDP, 2002). The UNDP report shows the Vietnamese economic and political structure and situation was changing significantly as a result of market liberalisation policies. This reform is regarded as a key means for Vietnam to integrate into the global economy, while pursuing socialist mechanisms. The 'open door' policy is seen as a feature of global capitalism and is a combination of market and state principles (Seitz, 2002). Vietnam now has a mixed economy, also known as a 'factor-driven economy' (Harman, Hayden, & Pham, 2010). The economic reforms have notably affected Vietnam's economic growth, business operation and many aspects of life.

Global Capitalism: Economic Reforms in Vietnam

Economic Reforms: Is There Any Difference?

The debate on Vietnamese economic development often focuses on two key strands: substantial improvements to Vietnam's economic conditions as a result of globalisation, and the remnants of the subsidised system. One of the most important changes resulting from *doi moi* was the abolition of the centrally-planned economy for production and goods distribution (Van Arkadie & Mallon, 2003), which was replaced by implementation of the open door policy allowing Vietnam to integrate into the international economy (Warner, 2001; World Bank, 2011). Privatisation (*xa hoi hoa* in Vietnamese) has occurred in every sector. To achieve economic growth and poverty reduction, the Vietnamese government specified that "its structural reform priorities were to change

Vietnam's trade and financial policies, liberalise the climate for private investment, increase the efficiency of public enterprises, and improve governance" (Auffret & World Bank, 2003, p. 2). Recognition of the private sector and development of a multi-sector economy with many categories of ownership and many forms of business organisations were emphasised (World Bank, 2011). This has created a mixed economy in Vietnam, something which the government has consistently pursued. As a result, the number of private industrial establishments has substantially increased.

Equally important was the identification of the need for the reform of State-Owned Enterprises (SOEs). The reform of the state enterprise sector was not only motivated by the need to shift priorities to move towards a multi-sector economy, but also by the necessity of enhancing the efficiency of the sector (World Bank, 2011). The report indicates SOEs were given greater financial autonomy and responsibility for setting input and output prices as well as production, marketing, investment and personnel decision-making. With the reduction of state input, many SOEs were dissolved or merged with others, resulting in a dramatic decrease in the number of SOEs since the late 1980s (Warner, 2001), and substantial decline between 2002 and 2005 (World Bank, 2011). However, the 2011 World Bank report indicates the number of SOEs increased in 2009, posing a question as to why state ownership was still dominant in the Vietnamese economy.

Despite the declining number of SOEs, Warner (2001) reveals that "the sector continues to pose a serious threat to macroeconomic stability and prospects for sustainable growth" (p. 6). The reasons are that SOEs still account for a large percentage of GDP and outstanding bank credit, and remain dominant, even 25 years after *doi moi* (World Bank, 2011), which means the SOEs' financial performance carries significant implications for the efficiency and influence of the Vietnamese banking system (Warner, 2001, p. 7). Again, it is noted here that while reducing the role of the state is seen by some as a positive reflection of economic globalisation, worker redundancy is a negative side of market capitalism (Seitz, 2002) in the current globally competitive environment (Burbules & Torres, 2000). This is still an emerging trend in Vietnam, which may increase when Vietnam fully integrates its economy into the global market. As can be seen, global economic integration, an increase in privatisation and a reduced role by the state are elements of economic globalisation in Vietnam, reflecting principles of global capitalism.

As a result of this adjustment and economic globalisation, Vietnam's economy and living standards have improved sharply. In the 1990s, Vietnam experienced very high economic growth rates, and has become one of the fastest transitioning economies in the world (World Bank, 2011). Since then, the GDP of Vietnam has remained consistently high, with an average annual increase of 7.3% in the period from 1990 to 2010 (World Bank, 2011). In addition, incomes have risen and poverty has decreased significantly (ADB, 2003; World Bank, 2011). Yet, challenges to the transition from central planning to a market economy require Vietnam to implement on-going structural adjustments in every aspect of society, particularly the economy and legislative system. The above analysis indicates that the more Vietnam restructures its economy under market principles, the sooner it will gain from the process of integration into the global economy.

Notwithstanding the success of *doi moi*, Vietnam is still in the process of improving living conditions and reducing poverty (ADB, 2003; SRV, 2002). Additionally, Vietnam is still very dependent on foreign aid as well as on external loans from international lending agencies. Overall, however, Vietnam's economic growth has not yet reached a sustainable level of stability (SRV, 2002; World Bank, 2011). Despite some achievements, NCSSH's report (2001) indicates free market transactions and individual autonomy for running a business were almost stamped out, a process which encouraged 'red-tape subsidised' central planning mechanisms, and hindered the development in lower socio-economic areas of individual capabilities and people's active participation. The report also stresses the necessity for Vietnam to reform further, and to refine, reformulate and adjust its policies and legislation, while effectively implementing reforms to promote rapid and sustainable growth in order to achieve successful integration into the global market (SRV, 2002) and facilitate business operations and FDI in Vietnam.

Business Environment in Vietnam: The World Systems Approach

Another important aspect of global economic restructuring is reform and/or emergence of new policies to accommodate a new business environment, for example, the liberalisation of foreign trade and investment, or, in other words, the reform of trade policy (Taylor, 2004; World Bank, 2011). There are two main objectives of trade reform (Auffret & World Bank, 2003). First, it aims to make the shift from a subsidised economy to an open market-based economy, and second, to promote export-oriented industries. Since the launching of *doi moi*, the progress in trade reform has been remarkable.

Since becoming involved in the global economy, Vietnam has attracted enormous direct investment from Western countries (Pickle & Dinh, 2009). From virtually zero in the 1980s (Dollar, 2001), the flow of FDI into Vietnam has grown progressively since the 1990s, with Japan a leading source (Meyer et al., 2006). This has occurred especially since Vietnam became an official member of the World Trade Organisation in 2007 (The China Post, 2008). Further, in line with the expansion of the global economy, Vietnam's exports and imports have expanded along with those in the rest of the world, and Vietnam has shifted away from the former Soviet Union and Eastern Europe (Dollar, 2001; SRV, 2002). Nonetheless, faster liberalisation of trade reform may cause conflicts with other structural reforms such as SOEs and tax administration, due to the apparently slower pace of restructuring in those sectors (Auffret & World Bank, 2003). The above research indicates consistent results in the progress of trade reform in Vietnam as part of the structural adjustment policies. This adjustment is also happening in other developing countries in the Asia-Pacific region, and in Eastern European and Latin American countries (Mok & Welch, 2003b).

Parallel to the pressure for globalisation, the implementation of structural adjustment policies to improve economic growth in Vietnam has also been driven by lending agencies such as the World Bank, the Asian Development Bank (ADB), and the International Monetary Fund (IMF). These institutions require a reduction in public spending and an expansion of privatisation and decentralisation as part of liberalisation (Williamson, 1990). Given Vietnam's general endorsement of such preconditions for loans, it has been receiving extensive donor support from the above organisations for its efforts to build reform programs through more organised systems of economic and financial management and state enterprise management (Warner, 2001). The presence of these bodies and other support from the international community are the key means of supervising and enhancing on-going economic reforms in Vietnam. In this context, the world-systems model reflects an unequal exchange between the core and the peripheral countries (Surborg, 2009), which is the case for Vietnam, and the structural adjustments required by the lending agencies.

Given the above progress in global business, Vietnam was recently ranked 103 out of 183 economies for ease of starting and carrying on a business (World Bank, 2012), indicating the country still has many complex regulations and policies which hinder an entrepreneur from establishing a business. Additionally, there was a continuing decline in the Growth Competitiveness Index of Vietnam, especially in relation to national policy and business effectiveness (Truong et al., 2010). The threat of losing investors and its competitiveness in the global market is present due to complex business procedures, inflation, and the loss of international reserves (World Bank, 2011). The above issues underline an urgent need for the government to seek out good solutions.

Influenced by both global culture and global capitalism, it is likely that Vietnam's local culture is gradually adapting to the Western business style and will possibly be undermined when Western business models and culture are applied by international business in Vietnam. The next section, therefore, discusses Vietnamese business operations and endeavours to find out how culture plays an important role in the Vietnamese business market, using the national model of Hofstede (1980) as a conceptual framework. The section aims to provide an insight into developing significant relationships with Vietnamese business counterparts, and the key factors for successful global management when setting up a business in Vietnam, or in other developing countries with similar socio-economic backgrounds.

Global Culture: National Culture and Business Practices in Vietnam

National culture can be described as "the collective programming of the mind which distinguishes the members of one human group from another" (Hofstede, 2001, p. 9). Hofstede's framework tends to dominate cultural research in Information Systems (Barton, Corbitt & Nguyen, 2009; Thanasankit & Corbitt, 1999) as well as in the international management and international business field. We also review how Hofstede's (1980) dimensions of culture (power distance, uncertainty avoidance, individualism versus collectivism, masculinity versus femininity, and short-term versus long-term orientation) are presented in Vietnamese business behaviours and practices.

National Culture and Business Culture in Vietnam

Pickle and Dinh (2009) show one of the essential issues necessary to consider before entering a global market is culture. Culture is defined as a group-level circumstance in which beliefs, attitudes, values, norms, and behavioural expectations are shared and learned among community members, all of which affect the development and implementation of negotiation plans or strategies (Salacuse, 2010). To a great extent, Vietnam is similar to many Southeast Asian countries and represents a challenge for foreign managers. Differences in cultures, manners, expectations and perspectives can, potentially, create an unpredictable situation that affects managerial business effectiveness (Neupert, Baughn, & Dao, 2005; Pickle & Dinh, 2009). This suggests that a good understanding of Vietnamese culture when doing business is important, although many countries largely rest their focus on the idea of a "global culture."

In cultural terms, Vietnam's most powerful neighbour, China, has been shaped by influences from Confucianism, Buddhism, and Chinese culture more generally. Yet, Vietnamese culture, in various subtle ways, has its own specific traits (Meyer et al., 2006). The authors indicate, having been under Chinese rule for 1000 years, traces of Chinese culture in Vietnam still remain in the Confucian practices of showing respect towards their ancestors, hierarchy in the family, and a male-dominated culture. Further, Chinese Confucian philosophy emphasises the value of relationships, responsibility and obligation which are still viewed as crucial components of Vietnamese society (Central Intelligence Agency, 2011). Both Vietnam and China have been criticised for being part of the socialist camp for many decades. Historical influences and their geographic proximity mean that some elements of Chinese cultural and business practices have merged with Vietnam's (Do, Quilty, Milner, & Longstaff,

2007; Ralston, Nguyen, & Napier, 1999; Truong & Nguyen, 2002). As Vietnam was colonised by the French in the mid-1800s, the French were the second significant impact on Vietnamese culture, bringing the Latin language system, Western arts, other French technology, architecture, and verbal and non-verbal communication skills.

Vietnamese culture can be classified as high power distance, high collectivism, low to moderate uncertainty avoidance, long-term orientation and high context (Hofstede, 1980; Truong & Nguyen, 2002). As a collectivist society, personal needs must be subordinated to the needs of family or organisation (Nguyen, Takanashi, & Aoyama, 2012; Truong & Nguyen, 2002). Family or community concerns, therefore, will usually come before business or personal needs (Smith & Pham, 1996; Truong & Nguyen, 2002). However, in many individualistic Western societies such as the United States, people are encouraged to be independent and look out for themselves (Pickle & Dinh, 2009). Paradoxically, in a "high-context" culture, words spoken may differ from their intended meaning or not be explicit; however, non-verbal behaviour, attitude, gestures, situation and place moderate the true meaning of spoken words (Meyer et al., 2006; Smith & Pham, 1996). Saving face is an extremely important element in Vietnamese society, which explains why any explicit public criticism or reproachful comments can result in losing face and cause embarrassment (Truong & Nguyen, 2002). Indeed, it is not uncommon for Vietnamese people to agree with something in order to maintain a harmonious atmosphere, although they might have no intention of implementing it. From cross-cultural perspectives, the above attributes offer huge potential for misunderstandings between Vietnamese and Western business counterparts, and create barriers to technological transfer, as experienced between Japan and Vietnam (Nguyen et al., 2012).

The debate is on the level of uncertainty avoidance in Vietnam. Theoretically speaking, Vietnam is a low uncertainty avoidance society (Hofstede, 2012). In reality, however, it is a moderate uncertainty avoidance society in which flexibility is a common value even in regard to timeframes and law/legal compliance (Nguyen et al., 2012). Vietnamese business negotiations generally take a longer view of time since they tend to examine any proposals carefully, including consulting a group before reaching an agreement, to reduce uncertainty, risk and ambiguity. The process can be relatively slow due to the high level of bureaucracy. Therefore, patience remains the ultimate Confucian virtue in personal life as well as in business (Truong & Nguyen, 2002).

In a comparison between the negotiation styles of American and Vietnamese university students, Pickle and Dinh (2009) reveal the importance of cultural context in the problem-solving approach. In a high-context, collectivist and feminine culture such as Vietnam, it is suggested that negotiation is relationship-oriented, and tends to focus on a long-term single source arrangement. This implies that collaborative attitudes in negotiations will more likely lead to mutual satisfaction. In contrast, in a low-context culture and highly individualistic society such as America, people tend to concentrate on final outcomes.

In accordance with Marxist ideology, Smith and Pham (1996) contend Vietnamese society is externally egalitarian but exhibits paternalistic and male-dominant attitudes in most business and official activities. While Vietnamese women tend to have minor roles in the family and society, especially in regard to managerial positions (Le, Rentschler, & Frederick, 2010), foreign women professionals are treated with respect, particularly if they possess high status or strong professional reputations in their company. Business women lacking such status might find it harder to be taken seriously in Vietnam. This cultural context shows a strong relationship with Confucian attitudes towards the male-female hierarchy in families and society (Do et al., 2007).

Despite Vietnam's strong macroeconomic performance, networking, reverse commissions, and even bribes are still common business practices (Do et al., 2007; Tenev, Calier, Chaudry, &

Nguyen, 2003). State ownership is still dominant and informal business practices and land leasing are still issues causing confusion to foreign investors (World Bank, 2011). In addition, the informality mentioned above creates administrative and financial burdens for business. Businesses with dissimilar ownership types and sizes are treated unequally, which develops incentives to form suboptimal contractual arrangements and promotes informality. Eventually, private and smaller enterprises experience greater difficulties in accessing bank financing, purchasing/leasing land, and obtaining other critical resources (Tenev et al., 2003). Since corruption was recognised as a threat to the investment environment, the Vietnamese government endorsed the regional Anti-Corruption Action Plan in July 2004 (Meyer et al., 2006). However, questions remain about how effective this program is in practice.

Our analysis above demonstrates Hofstede's model of national culture provides a good explanation of the characteristics of Vietnamese business culture, arguing that while Vietnamese society is being further influenced by global culture, the country has maintained its own culture which substantially influences business practices in Vietnam. Therefore, a good understanding of the culture is important for business success.

Globalisation reflects changes in technology, economics and culture, both nationally and internationally (Synott, 2004). The expansion of globalisation in the 21st century is heavily reliant on technological development, and the Internet has noticeably altered the world's economies (Rayport & Jaworski, 2001). The following section, therefore, will discuss electronic business (e-business) adoption and critical issues for successful e-business adoption in Vietnam.

E-Business Adoption in Vietnam

In a broader context of global economic integration, improvement in investment climates in developing countries is facilitated by access to, and quality of, ICT (Qiang, Clarke, & Halewood, 2006). The infrastructure, particularly the increase in the ICT infrastructure of a country, has a positive impact on the adoption of new technologies (Ling, 2001). ICT infrastructure can "improve the connectivity between firms, suppliers, and clients as well as provide business opportunities, especially for companies which are physically distant from urban centers" (Qiang et al., 2006, p. 57). Dahlman (2008) also indicates ICT is a crucial component for monitoring the desires and buying behaviour of consumers, and transferring that information smoothly along to production units. In recognition of the role of ICT in economic development, in the early 2000s the Vietnamese government set a target of industrialising and modernising the country through emphasis on ICT development (Institute of Labour, Science and Social affairs (ILSSA, 2004). The development of ICT in Vietnam clearly reflects its embracing of a global capitalism approach.

For the purposes of this discussion, the definitions of electronic commerce and digital commerce are analogous. The dissimilarities, however, between electronic commerce (e-commerce) and e-business require elucidation. E-commerce denotes commercial transactions mediated through the Internet, which includes all kinds of computer-mediated activities involved in supporting profit-making (McKay & Marshall, 2004). E-commerce encompasses the organisational activities which are electronically based and can support a firm's market exchanges (Rayport & Jaworski, 2001) and is not just "anything digital" that a firm does (Laudon & Traver, 2010). Kelly (1999) described the digital commerce scenery in "New rules for the New Economy" as being global, supporting intangible things, that is, information, ideas, and relations, and as being strongly interwoven. These elements create a new form of marketplace and society. In this new economy, service, information, and intelligence have replaced physical goods as the primary sources of value formation for customers (Rayport & Jaworski, 2001). An e-business, therefore, according to McKay and Marshall (2004), "creatively and intelligently utilises and exploits the capabilities of IT and Internet technologies to create efficiencies, to achieve effectiveness gains such as flexibility and responsiveness, and to create strategic opportunities through competitive uses to alter market and industry structures" (p. 5).

E-business plays a key role in the world's economy today. This expansive view of e-business can be seen when marketing via the Internet is given as an example. In the case of Vietnam, many Vietnamese organisations/firms seem to be at an early stage of Internet use as an effective marketing tool. For example, in a study of Vietnamese performing arts organisations' use of the web as a marketing tool, Le and Sargent (2010) find arts organisations are lagging behind their Western counterparts in making use of opportunities to take up the Internet as a marketing tool. As such, in the early 2000s, none of 137 professional performing arts organisations nation-wide had a website to promote their activities (Le, 2005).

For Vietnamese firms to further integrate into the global market, the Vietnamese government is highlighting the importance of e-commerce. The government set a goal of having more firms conducting e-commerce by 2010 under their Overall Plan on Developing E-commerce (People's Daily, 2006). For example, the government supports the growth of SMEs after *doi moi* (Le, Rowe, Truex, & Huynh, 2012) by encouraging the SME sector to be open to new techniques, especially the Internet and e-commerce which are regarded as essential business management tools (Le & Filiatrault, 2006). However, more than 90% of local firms are classified as Small and Medium Enterprises (SMEs) in Vietnam, with poor management skills, infrastructure bases, technology, and cross-border business experience. Meanwhile, less than 10% of those local firms have a strong sense of urgency or readiness for the impacts of globalisation (TBKTSG cited in Truong, et al., 2010). This situation poses a real challenge for foreign investors.

However, substantial progress has been made in using the Internet to facilitate commerce and business in Vietnam, with 17,500 corporates having a website by 2005 (Surborg, 2009). As one of the government's crucial economic strategies in Vietnam is to alter its targets from agricultural production to the service industry, online banking has become part of the overall e-commerce strategic plan in Vietnam (Chong, Ooi, Lin, & Tan, 2010). Surborg (2009) provides evidence the Internet now has a greater role in property trading and the banking sector in Vietnam. Yet, e-commerce and the adoption of online banking in Vietnam are still in their infancy due to the limited e-commerce infrastructure (Chong et al., 2010; Le & Filiatrault, 2006), and especially through not being fully equipped to process online payments and order form services. Although the Vietnamese government is willing to invest money in e-commerce infrastructure, successful e-business still relies strongly on consumers' perceptions and willingness to adopt the technology (Chong et al., 2010; Fleenor & Raven, 2002; Le & Filiatrault, 2006).

In addition, many other pertinent issues related to the business and cultural environments in Vietnam and the adoption of e-business have been identified. According to Le et al. (2012), in a large-scale empirical study on e-commerce adoption by SMEs in Vietnam, these issues included enterprises and consumers alike not being confident to participate in e-business due to the slow growth and deployment of ICT infrastructure, intellectual property (IP) issues and privacy rights, as well as the lack of use of online banking and financial infrastructure. For example, financial policies (i.e., tax policies – VAT) were criticised for being vague, and insufficient understanding of the specific nature of technological innovation was also identified (Tran, 2002). In addition, business transactions and availability of information over the Internet were still ruled and controlled by the government (Le et al., 2012, p. 2). These restrictions clearly affect the ability to learn to embrace and take advantage of openness and the freer transfer of information, which are requisite conditions for the effective implementation and use of online technologies.

Government laws concerning security and privacy issues have remained ambiguous in many users' minds, which will affect users' perceptions of the trustworthiness of Internet banking. Chong et al. (2010) also emphasise the perceptions of usefulness, trust and government support are all directly associated with the intention to utilise internet banking in Vietnam; trust was defined as the extent to which a user believes that using Internet banking is secure and free from privacy threats. This is particularly essential in Vietnamese culture wherein monetary transactions are commonly conducted face-to-face, and where some people have limited experience with Internet transactions. Apart from user's perceptions and IT infrastructure, other cultural behaviour, for example, risk aversion and lifestyle differences, may have an impact on Web success (Singh, Jayashankar, & Singh, 2001). At the same time, logistics and practical issues, such as differences in tariffs, currencies, language, customs regulations, and return rates on international shipments, make it more challenging to conduct e-business in Vietnam (Fleenor & Raven, 2002).

Limited resources can pose another challenge to the adoption of new technology in Vietnam. Grandon and Pearson (2004) suggested the scarcity of resources might prove difficult for a firm to adopt any new technology, as human, technological, cultural, and structural preparations are influential to both facilitating or delaying the initial adoption and subsequent institutionalisation of e-commerce. Tran's report (2002) provides evidence that a shortage of well-trained local technicians, engineers and overall skilled human resources in industrial firms hinders technological innovation in Vietnam. Indeed, Vietnamese enterprises have not successfully taken up technological innovations because of the combination of a shortage in those resources and the work habits and culture of SME managers (Le & Filiatrault, 2006). Further, the attitude of managers towards the use of ICT, their knowledge of IT, the structure and culture of the organisation, and the economy and infrastructure, are important factors affecting the adoption of ICTs (Chieochan, Lindley, & Dunn, 2000). Overall, a lack of management capability to lead firms in a competitive global market is evident (Tran, 2002).

The adoption of e-business more widely in Vietnam could be associated with the limited number of Internet users and subscribers, as Le et al. (2012) indicate, the Internet is an indicator of the power of e-commerce buyers and suppliers in Vietnam. The global access of the Internet facilitates cost-efficient ways of opening up new markets, drawing in new customers, and delivering products and services, as well as developing good coordination between business partners and suppliers (Zhu & Kraemer, 2005). Growth of Internet utilisation has been progressive in Vietnam compared with one of the world's fastest growing economies such as China. The number of Internet users in Vietnam increased from 2.25% in 2003 to 23.12% of the population in 2008, equivalent to more than 19 million people (Surborg, 2009). Vietnam was ranked 18th in a list of the number of Internet users for Quarter 1 of 2012 (Miniwatts Marketing Group, 2012) (see Appendix A). Le et al. (2012) surmise that having access to the Internet and credit or debit cards would pressure SMEs to offer more transactions on the Web. Paradoxically, with its young population, increasing wealth, and high economic growth, Vietnamese consumers tend to be eager to embrace new technology and apply it quickly in their life and work; it appears this alignment has yet to filter through to the mindset of SME owners.

The potential issue of e-business ethics has often been overlooked. In the traditional model of business ethics, firms worked more independently to compete with other firms in a fairly aggressive business environment (Fleenor & Raven, 2002). However, the contemporary e-business environment creates a challenge for the Vietnamese market, characterised by high power distance and moderate uncertainty avoidance. The reason is that e-business globally often collaborates with foreign firms, which requires opening themselves up to different kinds of investigation and sharing important and confidential information (Bacheldo, 2000; Fleenor & Raven, 2002). In business ethics, the network relationship becomes highly-valued and, at the same time, trust turns into a crucial element, without which firms may be intentionally excluded from e-business opportunities (Fleenor & Raven, 2002).

Basing upon the above discussion, we will propose recommendations to tackle the issue in the next section.

Implications and Recommendations

Echoing Hofstede's (1980; 2001) national culture framework, our analysis reflects the need to develop strategies to strike a balance between individualistic and the traditional collectivist values, high and low power distance and uncertainty avoidance, masculinity versus femininity, and long-term and short-term orientations. Based on national characteristics, we propose the following implications to improve the effectiveness of running a SME business in Vietnam in the context of globalisation, which could also be applicable to other similar developing countries.

As Fleenor and Raven (2002) argue, culture and sensitivity to cultural differences take a significant position for succeeding in international e-business. Foreign firms considering business engagement with Vietnam may experience a different legal structure and a business culture that is more in common with other Southeast Asian countries. Therefore, development of good personal relationships with prospective business partners and with the local authorities, and a comprehensive analysis of the institutional structure governing the targeted industry are important steps for setting up a business in Vietnam and for overcoming bureaucratic impediments (Fleenor & Raven, 2002). Understanding key differences between individualistic and collectivist cultures could help all stakeholders improve the negotiation process. Given the importance of technological transfers from a developed to a developing country, Nguyen et al. (2012) suggest that to successfully manage cross-cultural differences and national cultural dimensions (i.e., in Japanese and Vietnamese joint-ventures), staff training, team-work, managerial commitment and support, and a shift to a hybrid corporate culture should be enhanced.

In relation to the adoption of e-business, it is crucial for managers to encompass suitable regulatory and legal systems, together with an emphasis on e-signature, secure digital communications and safe payment systems (Dahlman, 2008). Further, there is a need for both national and international enterprises to understand how Internet-based communication fits into a country's culture to enable the development of successful global business and customer relations (Grosse, 2007). Sites targeting customers such as the Vietnamese should appear to be welcoming to them, and a well-translated site is more likely to yield a significant profit increase. While developing countries such as Vietnam may struggle with creating effective e-business strategies to avoid the loss of global competitiveness, adoption of a collaborative and corporate competition model is required to manage the new challenges to traditional business ethics (Fleenor & Raven, 2002). Successful e-business involves appropriate objective setting, appropriate staffing recruitment, technological knowledge development and training, technology enablement, redesign of business processes and regulations, identification of security issues, effective e-business migration, cooperation with other organisations, good management development and maintenance, and the integration of all those plans (Bakry & Bakry, 2001).

Other ways in which the government could improve the economic transition process have emerged. To facilitate online banking services in

Vietnam, the government could assist in improving the confidence of Internet users through the establishment of clear cyber laws. The government could also help the banking industry by improving Internet infrastructure (i.e., mobile wireless networks), which would encourage customers to use online banking and increase Vietnamese banks' competitiveness (Chong et al., 2010). Advertising campaigns, privacy guarantees, company guarantee policies and statements may also be helpful strategies to build trust and gain the confidence of users in online banking (Wei, Marthandan, Chong, Ooi, & Arumugam, 2009). This also suggests the Vietnamese government should prioritise the further evaluation of the country's competitiveness policy, and enhance the quality of the country's workforce throughout the entire electronic economic structure. At the same time, a clear legal system, which has mutual benefits for all stakeholders, is important for future international business operations in Vietnam.

CONCLUSION AND FUTURE RESEARCH DIRECTIONS

In this chapter, we provide an analysis of the inter-relationship between culture, technology and business operations in the context of globalisation in Vietnam, arguing that culture and technology have significant influences on business operations in Vietnam. Three models of globalisation—the world systems approach, the global culture approach, and the global capitalism approach—prove their validity in explaining changes in the Vietnamese business context, including economic reforms, influence of global culture and relationships between developed and developing countries. We maintain that the concept of globalisation through foreign investment and international business cannot be simply applied to any developing market; it requires a thorough understanding of the host country's culture, its business environment and the government policies to optimise the possibility of business success.

For developing countries, the implication of globalisation is that to respond rapidly and adequately to new threats and opportunities, they need to develop greater capability than ever before to adapt to global changes (Dahlman, 2008). In the Vietnamese context, the economic reform was driven largely by the external pressures from globalisation, and broadly paralleled the reform climate in many developing countries. Vietnam's involvement in globalisation can be seen through structural adjustment in every sector, and the opening up of its markets to the world in an attempt to boost economic growth. Vietnam has also implemented decentralisation, deregulation and privatisation, as well as reforms in trade, taxation and the banking system. In particular, the reduction in the role of government, thereby increasing the role of the private sector, has been noticeable.

In this chapter we also discuss dimensions of the national culture of Vietnam which have important implications for business operations. Therefore, in a broader context it is crucial for both the host countries and the potential foreign investors to attempt to make sense of the multi-faceted and complex fabric of local-global relations. Ideas, for instance, such as hybridisation and creolisation, might be useful to conceptualise what happens when people from different business cultures and practices interact in the global world.

We also explore the adoption of e-business by SMEs in Vietnam, and the role of government in developing e-commerce in the current context. The analysis shows that while Vietnam has made substantial progress in introducing e-commerce into the country, traditional ways of doing business and the level of technological development still hinder the adoption of e-business and online transactions.

In summary, despite the differences between the Vietnamese socialist system and the market mechanisms, and the challenges of the progressive expansion of the global market, the Vietnamese government and the Vietnamese people have embraced globalisation. This is evidenced by the economic success of Vietnam after the economic reforms, the willingness to open its doors to the global economy, and its progress in the development of ICT and e-business. In order for Vietnam to select an appropriate e-business model that will strengthen its international economic integration, it is important to identify the conditions promoting e-business development, and to develop relevant trustworthy policies on the conducting of e-business to facilitate online payments and security systems. To take advantage of the further development of technology, a number of questions are posed: How can government policy in Vietnam become more sensitive to global long-term perspectives on further enhancing the quality of the Vietnamese workforce? How can Western ethical standards be incorporated into e-business in Vietnam? How can other developing countries manage changing business cultures and practices to facilitate business globally?

REFERENCES

ADB. (2003). Vietnam Development Report 2004: Poverty (Joint Donor Report to the Vietnam Consultative Group Meeting). Hanoi, Vietnam: Vietnam Development Information Centre.

Auffret, P. & World Bank. (2003). *Trade Reform in Vietnam: Opportunities with Emerging Challenges* (World Bank Policy Research Working Paper No. 3076). Hanoi, Vietnam: World Bank.

Bacchus, M. K. (2004). Reducing international conflicts by improving economic conditions of the poor through education. *SangSaeng*, *9*, 10–15.

Bacheldo, B. (2000). Worldwide e-Commerce: It's more than a Web Site. *Informationweek*, *785*, 47–48.

Bakry, S. H., & Bakry, F. H. (2001). A strategic view for the development of E-Business. *International Journal of Network Management*, *11*(2), 103–112. doi:10.1002/nem.395.

Barton, S. M., Corbitt, B., & Nguyen, L. (2009). Academic social networks affecting the adoption of e-learning in Turkey. *International Journal on E-Learning*, *8*(4), 561–575.

Beresford, M. (1988). *Vietnam: Politics, economics, and society*. London, New York: Pinter.

Beresford, M. (1989). *National unification and economic development in Vietnam*. London, UK: Macmillan.

Beresford, M., & Tran, A. N. (2004). Reaching for the dream: Challenges of sustainable development in Vietnam. Copenhagen, Denmark: Nordic Institute of Asian Studies (NIAS).

Burbules, N. C., & Torres, C. A. (2000). Globalisation and education: An introduction. In Burbules, N. C., & Torres, C. A. (Eds.), *Globalisation and Education: Critical Perspectives* (pp. 1–26). New York: Routledge.

Central Intelligence Agency. (2011). *The World Factbook - East & Southeast Asia: Vietnam.* Retrieved January 2, 2012, from https://www.cia.gov/library/publications/the-world-factbook/geos/vm.html

Chieochan, O., Lindley, D., & Dunn, T. (2000). Factors affecting the use of information technology in Thai agricultural cooperatives: A work in progress. *Electronic Journal on Information Systems in Developing Countries*, *2*(1), 1–15.

Chong, A. Y., Ooi, K., Lin, B., & Tan, B. (2010). Online banking adoption: An empirical analysis. *International Journal of Bank Marketing*, *28*(4), 267–287. doi:10.1108/02652321011054963.

Commins, S., Gevers, C., Randa, J., & World Bank. (2001). *Adjustment from Within: Lessons from the Structural Adjustment Participatory Review Initiative* (World Bank Report).

Dahlman, C. (2008). Technology, Globalisation, and International Competitiveness: Challenges for Developing Countries. In O'Connor, D., & Kjöllerström, M. (Eds.), *Industrial Development for the 21st Century* (pp. 29–84). Hyderabad, India: Orient Longman Zed Books and United Nations.

Dang, P., & Beresford, M. (1998). *Authority relations and economic decision-making in Vietnam: An historical perspective*. Copenhagen, Denmark: NIAS.

Dewey, P. (2004). From arts management to cultural administration. *International Journal of Arts Management*, *6*(3), 13–22.

Do, T., Quilty, M., Milner, A., & Longstaff, S. (2007). Business culture issues in Vietnam: Case studies market, working paper series, Volume 2: No.2. Retrieved July 2, 2012, from http://dspace.anu.edu.au/handle/1885/44441

Dollar, D. (2001). *Reform, Growth, and Poverty in Vietnam.* Paper presented at the Conference on Economic Growth and Household Welfare: Policy Lessons for Vietnam. Hanoi, Vietnam.

Fenna, A. (2004). *Australian Public Policy* (2nd ed.). Frenchs Forest, Australia: Pearson Education Australia.

Fleenor, P., & Raven, P. (2002). Barriers to Effective E-Business in Developing Countries. *International Business & Economics Research Journal*, *1*(4), 39–47.

Fogel, G., & Zapalska, A. (2001). A comparison of small and medium-size enterprise development in Central and Eastern Europe. *Comparative Economic Studies*, *43*(3), 35–68. doi:10.1057/ces.2001.13.

Grandon, E. E., & Pearson, J. M. (2004). Electronic commerce adoption: An empirical study of small and medium US businesses. *Information & Management*, *42*, 197–216. doi:10.1016/j.im.2003.12.010.

Grosse, C. U. (2007). Web-Based Communication of Global Companies: Do Languages and Culture Matter? *Global Business Languages*, *12*(7), 67–83.

Harman, G. S., Hayden, M., & Pham, T. N. (2010). Higher education in Vietnam: Reforms, challenges and priorities. In Harman, G. S., Hayden, M., & Pham, T. N. (Eds.), *Reforming Higher Education in Vietnam: Challenges and Priorities* (1st ed., pp. 1–14). Dordrecht, The Netherlands: Springer. doi:10.1007/978-90-481-3694-0_1.

Held, D., McGrew, A., Goldblatt, D., & Perraton, J. (1999). *Global Transformations: Politics, Economics and Culture*. Oxford, UK: Polity Press.

Hofstede, G. (1980). *Culture's Consequences: International Differences in Work-Related Values*. Beverly Hills, CA: Sage Publications.

Hofstede, G. (2001). *Culture's Consequences*. Thousand Oaks, CA: Sage Publications.

Hofstede, G. (2012). National Culture. Retrieved June 10 2012, from http://geert-hofstede.com/countries.html

Institute of Labour, Science and Social affairs (ILSSA). (2004). *Determining the Impact of Information and Communication Technology on Decent Work in the Asian and Pacific Region: Viet Nam Report*. Hanoi, Vietnam: ILO/JIL Networking of National Institute for Labour Studies.

Kelly, K. (1999). *New Rules for the New Economy: 10 Radical Strategies for a Connected World*. New York: Penguin Books.

Laudon, K. C., & Traver, C. G. (2010). *E-Commerce 2010 – Business, Technology, Society*. New York: Pearson.

Le, H. (2004). Changes in Arts Organisations under the Open Market Economy in Vietnam. *International Journal of Knowledge. Culture and Change Management*, *4*, 1539–1547.

Le, H. (2005). *Performing Arts Management in a Climate of Adjustment: Case Studies from Vietnam and Australia. Unpublished PhD*. Sydney, Australia: University of Sydney.

Le, H. (2008). Economic Reforms, Cultural Policy: Opportunities and Challenges to the Arts and Culture in Vietnam in the Age of Globalization. *Journal of Arts Management. Law & Society*, *38*(1), 5–18.

Le, H. (2009). Performing arts management in a climate of adjustment: Case studies from Vietnam and Australia. *Asia Pacific Journal of Arts and Cultural Management*, *6*(2), 488–503.

Le, H., Rentschler, R., & Frederick, H. (2010). Breaking through the 'glass ceiling': Gender and arts leaders in Vietnam. *International Journal of the Arts in Society*, *5*(2), 1–14.

Le, H., & Sargent, J. (2010). The use of the web as a marketing tool by selected arts organisations in Vietnam: A preliminary investigation. *TMC Academic Journal*, *4*(2), 50–63.

Le, V. H., & Filiatrault, P. (2006). *The Adoption of E-commerce in SMEs in Vietnam: A Study of Users and Prospectors*. Paper presented at the PACIS 2006 Proceedings. Kuala Lumpur, Malaysia.

Le, V. H., Rowe, F., Truex, D., & Huynh, M. Q. (2012). An Empirical Study of Determinants of E-Commerce Adoption in SMEs in Vietnam: An Economy in Transition. *Journal of Global Information Management*, *20*(3), 23–54. doi:10.4018/jgim.2012070102.

Ling, C. Y. (2001). *Model of factors influences on electronic commerce adoption and diffusion in small and medium sized enterprises*. Paper presented at the European Conference on Information Systems (ECIS).

McKay, J., & Marshall, P. (2004). *Strategic management of e-business*. Milton, Australia: John Wiley & Sons.

Meyer, K. E., Tran, Y. T. T., & Nguyen, H. V. (2006). Doing business in... Vietnam. *Thunderbird International Business Review*, *48*(2), 263–290. doi:10.1002/tie.20095.

Miniwatts Marketing Group. (2012). *Internet World Stats: Usage and Population Statistics; Top 20 Internet countries – 2012 Q1 with highest number of users*. Retrieved July 9, 2012, from http://www.internetworldstats.com/top20.htm

Mok, K.-H., & Welch, A. R. (2003a). Globalisation, structural adjustment and educational reform. In Mok, K.-H., & Welch, A. R. (Eds.), *Globalisation and Educational Restructuring in the Asia Pacific Region* (pp. 1–31). Basingstoke, UK: Palgrave Macmillan. doi:10.1057/9781403990488.

Mok, K.-H., & Welch, A. R. (Eds.). (2003b). *Globalisation and Educational Restructuring in the Asia Pacific Region*. Basingstoke, UK: Palgrave Macmillan. doi:10.1057/9781403990488.

NCSSH. (2001). National Human Development Report 2001: Doi Moi and Human Development in Vietnam. Hanoi, Vietnam: The Political Publishing House.

Neupert, K., Baughn, C., & Dao, T. (2005). International management skills for success in Asia: A needs-based determination of skills for foreign managers and local managers. *Journal of European Industrial Training*, *29*(2), 165–180. doi:10.1108/03090590510585118.

Ngok, K.-l., & Kwong, J. (2003). Globalisation and educational restructuring in China. In Mok, K.-H., & Welch, A. R. (Eds.), *Globalisation and Educational Restructuring in the Asia Pacific Region* (pp. 160–188). Basingstoke, UK: Palgrave Macmillan.

Nguyen, N. T. D., Takanashi, C., & Aoyama, A. (2012). Can Efficient Technology Transfer Be Achieved through a Hybrid Corporate Culture? A Study on Japanese Manufacturing Subsidiaries in Vietnam. *International Journal of Business and Management*, *7*(7), 24–39.

People's Daily. (2006). Few firms in Vietnam keen on e-commerce: Survey. Retrieved July 3, 2012, from http://english.peopledaily.com.cn/200602/09/eng20060209_241189.html

Pickle, L., & Dinh, T. T. V. (2009). A comparative study of Vietnamese and American customers' behaviour in negotiation style. *Global Journal of International Business Research*, *2*(2), 37–50.

Qiang, C. Z., Clarke, G. R., & Halewood, N. (2006). *The Role of ICT in Doing Business*. Washington, DC: World Bank.

Ralston, D. A., Nguyen, V. T., & Napier, N. K. (1999). A Comparative Study of the Work Values of North and South Vietnamese Managers. *Journal of International Business Studies*, *30*(4), 655–672. doi:10.1057/palgrave.jibs.8490889.

Rayport, J., & Jaworski, B. (2001). *E-Commerce*. New York: McGraw-Hill.

RIAP. (2003). *BICA Report 2003 (Building Institutional Capacity in Asia - Project commissioned by the Ministry of Finance, Japan): Re-defining the Border between Public and Private in Southeast Asia: Malaysia, Philippines, Vietnam, Thailand and Indonesia*. Sydney, Australia: Research Institute for Asia and the Pacific, The University of Sydney.

Salacuse, J. W. (2010). Teaching International Business Negotiation: Reflections on Three Decades of Experience. *International Negotiation*, *15*, 187–228. doi:10.1163/157180610X506956.

Seitz, J. L. (2002). *Global Issues: An Introduction* (2nd ed.). Oxford, UK: Blackwell Publishers.

Singh, T., Jayashankar, J. V., & Singh, J. (2001). E-Commerce in the U.S. and Europe - Is Europe Ready to Compete? *Business Horizons*, *44*(22), 6–16. doi:10.1016/S0007-6813(01)80017-3.

Sklair, L. (1999a). Competing conceptions of globalisation. *Journal of World-systems Research*, *5*(2), 143–163.

Sklair, L. (1999b). Globalisation. In Taylor, S. (Ed.), *Sociology: Issues and Debates* (pp. 321–345). Basingstoke, UK: Macmillan Press.

Smith, E. D. J., & Pham, C. (1996). Doing business in Vietnam: A cultural guide. *Business Horizons*, *39*(3), 47–51. doi:10.1016/S0007-6813(96)90007-5.

SRV. (2002). *The Comprehensive Poverty Reduction and Growth Strategy (CPRGS) (No. 2685/VPCP-QHQT)*. Hanoi: Vietnam.

Surborg, B. (2009). Is it the 'Development of Underdevelopment' all over again? Internet Development in Vietnam. *Globalizations*, *6*(2), 225–247. doi:10.1080/14747730902854182.

Synott, J. (2004). *Global and International Studies: Transdisciplinary Perspectives*. Southbank, Australia: Social Science Press.

Taylor, P. (Ed.). (2004). *Social Inequality in Vietnam and the Challenges to Reform*. Singapore: Institute of Southeast Asian Studies.

Tenev, S., Calier, A., Chaudry, O., & Nguyen, Q. T. (2003). *Informality and the playing field in Vietnam's business sector*. Washington, DC: IFC, World Bank, and MPDF.

Thanasankit, T., & Corbitt, B. (1999). Cultural context and its impact on requirements elicitation in Thailand. *Electronic Journal on Information Systems in Developing Countries*, *1*(1), 15–32.

The China Post. (2008). Foreign direct investment in Vietnam triples in 2008. *The China Post*. Retrieved from http://www.chinapost.com.tw/business/asia/vietnam/2008/12/27/189529/Foreign-direct.htm

Tran, N. C. (2002). *Learning Technological Capability for Vietnam's Industrial Upgrading: Challenges of Globalisation*. Hanoi, Vietnam: National Institute for Science and Technology Policy and Strategy Studies (NISTPASS).

Truong, Q. Heijden, B. I. v. d., & Rowley, C. (2010). Globalisation, competitiveness, and human resource management in a transitional economy: The case of Vietnam. *International Journal of Business Studies*, *18*(1), 75–100.

Truong, Q., & Nguyen, T. V. (2002). Management Styles and Organisational Effectiveness in Vietnam. *Research and Practice in Human Resource Management*, *10*(2), 36–55.

UNDP. (2002). *Briefing Report for Vietnam* (No. UNDP/POST/VIE/Rev12). Hanoi, Vietnam: Office of the United Nations Resident Coordinator, Vietnam.

Van Arkadie, B., & Mallon, R. (2003). *Viet Nam: A Transition Tiger?* Canberra, Australia: Asia Pacific Press at the Australian National University.

Wallerstein, I. M. (1974). *The modern world-system*. New York: Academic Press.

Wallerstein, I. M. (2011). *The Modern World-system: The Second Era of Great Expansion of the Capitalist World-economy, 1730's-1840's*. University of California Press.

Warner, B. (2001). *Vietnam: Economic and Financial Management* (Working paper 1). Canberra, Australia: The Australian Government's Overseas Aid Program. The Australia Agency for International Development (AusAID).

Webber, M. J., Wang, M., & Zhu, Y. (2002). Knocking on WTO's door. In Webber, M. J., Wang, M., & Zhu, Y. (Eds.), *China's Transition to a Global Economy* (pp. 1–13). New York: Palgrave Macmillan. doi:10.1057/9781403918604.

Wei, T. T., Marthandan, G., Chong, A. Y. L., Ooi, K. B., & Arumugam, S. (2009). What drives Malaysian m-commerce adoption? An empirical analysis. *Industrial Management & Data Systems*, *109*(3), 370–388. doi:10.1108/02635570910939399.

Welch, A. R. (2003). Globalisation, structural adjustment and contemporary educational reforms in Australia: The politics of reform, or the reform of politics? In Mok, K.-H., & Welch, A. R. (Eds.), *Globalisation and Educational Restructuring in the Asia Pacific Region* (pp. 262–301). Basingstoke, UK: Palgrave Macmillan.

Williamson, J. (1990). What Washington means by policy reform? In Williamson, J. (Ed.), *Latin American Adjustment: How Much Has Happened?* Washington, DC: Institute for International Economics.

World Bank. (2011). *Vietnam development report 2012: Market economy for a middle-income Vietnam (Joint Donor Report to the Vietnam Consultative Group Meeting No. 65980)*. Hanoi: Vietnam.

World Bank. (2012). *Doing business in a more transparent world 2012 - economic profile: Vietnam - comparing regulation for domestic firms in 183 economies* (Working paper). Washington, DC: World Bank.

Wyszomirski, M. J. (2000). *Negotiating the Global Maze Artfully*. Paper presented at the 2000 Barnett Arts and Public Policy Symposium. Columbus, OH: Ohio Arts Council and Ohio State University College of the Arts.

Zhu, K., & Kraemer, K. L. (2005). Post-adoption variations in usage and value of e-business by organizations: Cross-country evidence from the retail industry. *Information Systems Research*, *16*(1), 16–24. doi:10.1287/isre.1050.0045.

APPENDIX

Figure 1. Source: (Miniwatts Marketing Group, 2012)

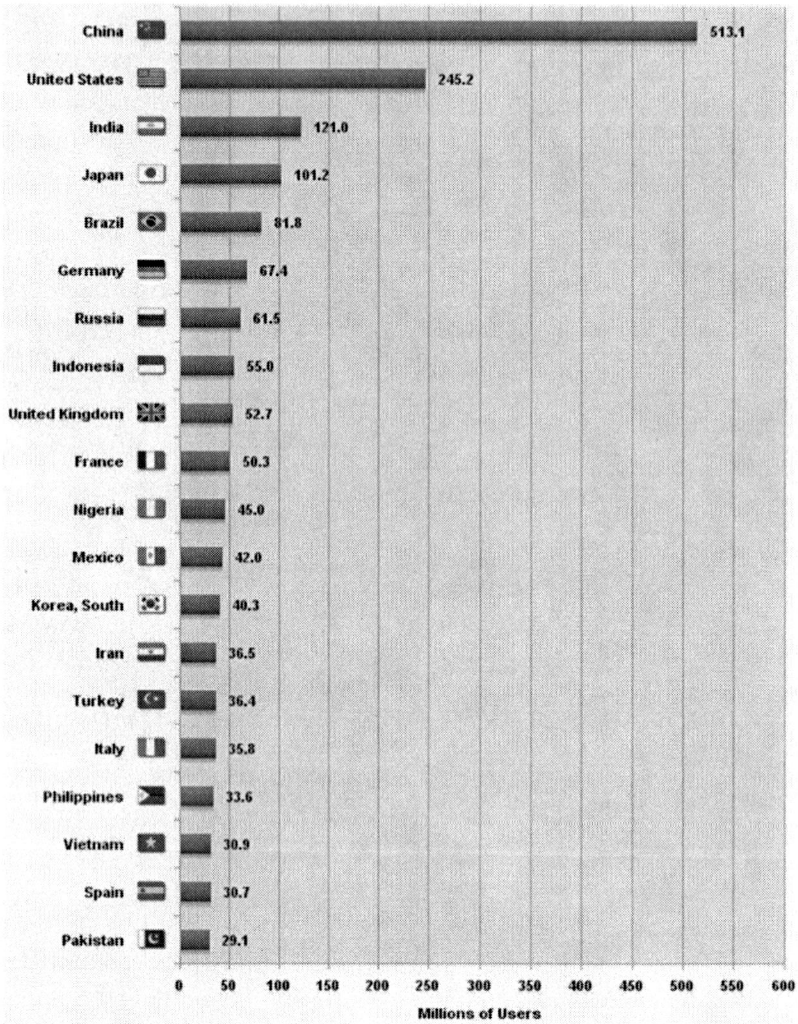

ABBREVIATIONS

ADB: Asian Development Bank
FDI: Foreign direct investment
ICT: Information and communications technology
IMF: International Monetary Fund
IT: Information technologies
NCSSH: National Centre for Social Sciences and Humanities
RIAP: Research Institute for Asia and the Pacific
SOE: State Owned Enterprises
SME: Small and Medium Enterprises
SRV: Socialist Republic of Vietnam
TBKTSG: Thoi Bao Kinh Te Sai Gon
UNDP: United Nations Development Program

Chapter 9
Optimizing International Joint Venture (IJV) Ownership Structures:
A Technology and Knowledge Transfer-Linked Productivity Growth Perspective

Alexander Wollenberg
Universidad EAFIT, Colombia

ABSTRACT

This chapter portrays a quantitative framework regarding entry mode choice and ownership structures by measuring performance under given ownership structures as the degree of efficiency in technology transfer, and knowledge exchange in the form of a residual productivity growth variable. This method has been shown to be a proxy for or an indirect measure of transaction costs, in that ownership structures are validated by the growth in technology/knowledge-based productivity that they caused. In the process, the chapter discusses hierarchical entry modes and adjustment of ownership structures with respect to minimizing transaction costs incurred in the transfer and internalization of complementary assets, both tangible and intangible. Previous research has dealt with subsidiary performance mainly in terms of financial measures (e.g., profitability, ROA, ROE, ROI), instability, and lifespan. By contrast, this chapter extends existing research by providing a specific quantitative framework for optimizing technology/knowledge-based productivity growth. The second important contribution of the chapter is the linkage of the quantitative results to their applicability and potential for implementation in Japanese equity-based subsidiaries in Latin America over the lifetime of the subsidiaries. Other factors important in the implementation and internalization of new technologies and knowledge have also been analyzed quantitatively and linked to case studies qualitatively. The chapter further analyzes adaptations to regional

DOI: 10.4018/978-1-4666-3966-9.ch009

contexts and parent companies of nationalities other than Japanese. Therefore, the model presented in the chapter addresses IJV ownership structures which are optimal to productivity growth linked to new technologies and knowledge and by adaptation of variables, and discusses results for emerging markets in Latin America, such as Peru, Colombia, and the newly industrialized Brazil. The chapter also highlights advantages and disadvantages of forming IJVs with a local partner of different levels of technological sophistication, and the degree of managerial and equity involvement to allow the local partner.

PRODUCTIVITY AND OWNERSHIP

Several studies have been conducted on ownership and productivity. Those conducted on a micro-economic level have tended to remain conceptual due to the difficulty of access to large-scale company or subsidiary-level data, particularly panel (time-series) data. Yet other studies have tended to remain industry- or sector-based, such as private and state ownership. Therefore, most studies which have employed a productivity growth concept (e.g., Total Factor Productivity or TFP) have tended to analyze industry-level or country-level data.

A highly relevant study with regard to firm-level data was conducted by Fukao et al. (2005). They included a micro-level firm panel data of both foreign and domestically-owned companies in Japan's manufacturing sector over a seven-year period and conducted a TFP analysis. Their sample size was 236, and their findings indicated foreign-owned companies' technology-based productivity was approximately 8% higher than that of local firms. Furthermore, the growth rate of technology-based productivity also exceeded that of domestic enterprises, and they showed that local companies which were later acquired by foreign companies had higher technology-based productivity growth rates. Their findings were supported by data on expenditure on Research and Development (R&D) per worker and capital per worker ratio which were both higher. Interestingly, Fukao et al. (2005) also found that foreign-owned companies had significantly lower growth rates of tangible assets, suggesting foreign-owned companies rely much more on the exchange of knowledge-based assets.

Several studies have already considered ownership and its effects on technology-based productivity in more detail. For instance, Blomstrom and Sjoholm (1999) have found majority ownership allows the subsidiary to receive more sophisticated technologies from the parent firm. However, Jefferson et al. (2000) has suggested minority ownership allows the local partner greater contact with technologies, and therefore helps technology diffusion, barring large technological or knowledge gaps. Similarly, Dougherty and Guckin (2001) highlight that value-added activities in Chinese Standards of Excellence (SOEs) tend to rise when partnering with a foreign firm due to technology and knowledge spillovers, which therefore raises the overall technology-induced productivity for the IJV. However, their study is conceptual and not nationality-specific. I will first review those studies which treated the issue of ownership and technology-based productivity.

Blomstrom and Sjoholm (1999) approach the problem of productivity growth from the perspective of technological spillover effects by Multinational Corporations (MNCs) entering a foreign market where their market entrance distorts the existing local market equilibrium. Local companies are then forced to react to protect their market share. Nonetheless, the authors argue these effects have had a positive influence on local firms with respect to absorption of new technologies. Where technological gaps were too large, however, the authors found a moderating effect on productivity because of the "limited scope for learning" by the local partner.

Their study leaves several issues unanswered. First, they only present statistical proof that productivity is compromised due to the local partner's limited absorption capacities. Second, they do not provide a framework for such absorption capacities.

However, the importance of their contribution is that productivity growth is linked to technological capabilities. Importantly, they discuss attempts to separate these technological capabilities from labor and capital-induced productivity. Importantly, Blomstrom and Sjoholm (1999) make a case for equity-based (hierarchical) IJVs by arguing hierarchical IJVs facilitate knowledge spillovers by pooling their proprietary assets. However, other research has strongly criticized this fact as a liability of joint ventures (e.g., Mowery et al., 1996; Inkpen & Dinur, 1998).

Perkins (1996) discovered ownership was highly significant in explaining growth in TFP. His study uses firm-level data of 3,000 foreign and domestic companies in China including Sino-foreign IJVs, SOEs, Wholly-Owned Subsidiaries (WOSs), collectives, and township enterprises during the period 1980-1994. He found productivity growth was much higher in firms with a non-state partner, and that the ability to retain control, or keep majority ownership had a positive effect on labor productivity. Among the subsidiaries surveyed, IJVs, and WOSs in China recorded the highest productivity growth.

Wei et al. (2002) tested the relationship between ownership and productivity growth in state-owned enterprises, domestic non-state-owned enterprises, and foreign-owned enterprises. Wei et al.'s (2002) findings indicate SOEs experience lower productivity growth than do domestic non-SOEs and foreign-owned enterprises. IJVs tended to outperform WOSs on productivity growth, which the authors attributed to the local partners' sharing of intangible assets, including tacit knowledge, connections, and access to the local market, thereby enhancing IJV productivity. Wei et al.'s (2002) study was groundbreaking in that it linked the long-term contribution of the local partner's intangible assets to that of the subsidiary productivity growth, therefore solidifying the argument that a local partner is indeed necessary. Therefore, Wei et al.'s (2002) research extends Perkins' (1996) and Blomstrom and Sjoholm's (1999) studies with regard to the former in that productivity indeed depends on ownership and with regard to the latter–that state ownership and foreign ownership should be split so as to achieve higher productivity rates.

Other Factors in Relation to Productivity Growth

Griffith (1999) addresses the problem of parent company nationality, ownership, and productivity in high-tech manufacturing IJVs in which the UK is the host country. His findings indicate foreign-owned subsidiaries are more productive and have greater unit output per worker than domestic firms. In fact, one can find support for simple productivity-related performance measures from the works of Gerschenkron (1962) and Nelson and Phelps (1966), who argued differences in technological knowledge and ability across countries have been seen as possible sources of differences in productivity levels. Thus, Dunning's (1988) eclectic theory, and its concept of ownership advantages, could also apply to productivity-related measures (Dunning, 1988; Brouthers et al., 1996; Madhok, 1996). Griffith (1999) specified his findings into output per worker and value-added per worker and found differences in nationalities regarding value-added per worker. Certain nationalities, such as US- and German-owned IJVs in the UK had higher value-added per worker than did French-owned IJVs. His study, however, did not include any Japanese IJV partners.

With respect to emerging economies, scholars have found that non-transparency, high discretionary powers of officials, opaque legislation, and weak enforcement of Intellectual Property Rights (IPR) can alter the relationship between productivity rates and ownership. Several studies have argued that foreign ownership has a positive effect on productivity in high value-added manufacturing industries (Delios & Beamish, 1999; Li et al., 2002; Asiedu & Esfahani, 2001). Studies have thus far not identified to which extent foreign ownership in high value-added industries has resulted in higher levels of technology-based productivity growth and therefore lower transaction costs.

Prior work on productivity has identified the relationship between ownership and productivity growth to the extent that foreign ownership raises productivity in the long term within both the subsidiary and the foreign partner company. Productivity rates may be low in the short term due to the liability of being foreign (Delios & Beamish, 1996). Further work (e.g., Oulton, 1998; Moon & Lado, 2000) has shown productivity is higher in industries which have a high value-added component. These subsidiaries are often found in the electronics, precision-mechanical, and chemical industries. Studies have also shown that in these industries IJVs occasionally exhibit higher technology-induced productivity than do WOSs, although causes and reasons have not been discussed. Several studies have addressed the utility of a local partner and inferred a link between tacit knowledge spillovers from the local to the foreign partner which may impact productivity in the long term (Perkins, 1996; Griffith, 1999; Wei et al., 2002).

In support of the previous studies, Okamoto and Sjoholm's (2000) study of the automotive industry in Indonesia indicates majority foreign-owned subsidiaries tend to display higher technology-induced productivity than do locally-owned firms. Therefore, I expect majority foreign ownership to be essential for technology transfer. Further quantitative analysis will seek to find ownership combinations within Japanese majority ownership for the specific case of Sino-Japanese high-tech joint ventures by linking their technology/knowledge-induced productivity growth to ownership levels. In so doing, I take Okamoto and Sjoholm's (2000) study and methodology further by using panel data for a much longer period (17 years) and conducting regression analyses. Importantly, the above studies have only shown links between minority and majority ownership. They have not addressed variations within majority ownership.

POLITICAL FACTORS

Political factors in China have significantly shaped the landscape for potential IJV partners (Luo, 2000). The Chinese economy is characterized by strong governmental interference, poorly specified guidelines for ownership (entry mode) approval as well as poorly specified property rights. State-owned enterprises, however, have the location-based advantages of access to scarce resources, materials, capital, networks (*guanxi*) and information. SOEs also have an advantage over local privately owned firms in terms of their government connections, *guanxi*, access to capital, market presence, industry experience, production and innovation (R&D) facilities, and economies of scale. For these reasons, an SOE or SOE-affiliated enterprise may contribute more to an IJV than a WOS would be able to achieve.

Within the context of Latin American countries, the following variables would merit further consideration, and a model for entry mode could be modified to address some of the following issues. For example, factors in Latin America which could be used as independent or control variables with regard to entry modes could include demographic issues such as segmentation of the population, GDP per capita growth rates, purchasing power, market size and competitors, as well as political and economic systems. The latter could be represented by competitiveness or corruption indexes.

Other factors could be similarities in religion, language, and culture. The latter distinguishes Latin America from Asia markedly. While Spanish and Portuguese are predominant in Latin America (Portuguese being very similar to Spanish as well), differences in languages are much more pronounced in Asia. In Southeast Asia, the predominant languages are Thai, Vietnamese, Malay, Burmese, as well as several dialects of Chinese spoken by the Chinese diaspora such as Mandarin, Hokkien, and Cantonese. In addition to the former, Chinese dialects tend to be significantly different from one another when spoken, much more so than Spanish and Portuguese. It is the writing system which communicates meaning to all Chinese, not the spoken word. Despite these differences, however, Asia has achieved remarkable economic growth rates.

Religions tend to vary across Asia as well. While most of northeast Asia is Buddhist or Shintoist (e.g., Japan), many countries in Southeast Asia are Muslim and represent a large share of the population and market. These countries are Indonesia, Malaysia, Brunei, and Bangladesh (although the latter is more part of South Asia than Southeast Asia). Therefore, foreign firms entering countries in Latin America through hierarchical modes could be able to achieve synergies and productivity growth with fewer transaction costs and/or a shorter period of time.

REVIEW OF PREVIOUS METHODS

This section is concerned with developing the concept for measuring the performance of Japanese subsidiaries in China, and based on technology/knowledge-induced productivity growth as a performance measure, the entry mode or ownership strategy that should be chosen.

According to Prasad and Wei (2007), a natural measure of performance is a productivity ratio – the ratio of outputs to inputs, in which a larger value of the ratio is associated with better performance. However, performance is a relative concept and several methods regarding performance measurement and its dependent entry mode or ownership strategies exist. All studies are based on the underlying concept of an efficient and least costly method to define ownership structures.

Studies can be defined into two broad categories: a) studies in which ownership structures/entry mode were the outcome of a composition of a subsidiary's combined assets (ownership advantages) and/or environmental factors; and b) studies in which the performance of a subsidiary was the (outcome) of ownership decisions. Generally, in category a) ownership was the dependent variable while in category b) ownership was the independent variable. My study attempts to combine both approaches. In the first part, my method would fall into category b) in which a statistical relationship is established linking ownership and ownership change to a performance variable which I refer to as technology/knowledge-based productivity. In other words, out of a sample of 1,800 subsidiaries (IJVs), a relationship is initially shown in which subsidiary performance depends on ownership-related variables. In a further subpart of the quantitative chapter, ownership is then adjusted to show its influence IJV performance.

Previous studies can be further divided into two more groups–namely, those studies which have addressed performance and ownership unidimensionally–thus from the point of view of the benefit for the technology owner or parent company; while the other broad group of studies has been concerned with assessing performance multi-dimensionally (i.e., from the point of view of all stakeholders). For the case of IJVs–multidimensional studies take into account the foreign and local IJV partners' tangible and intangible assets. Multi-dimensional studies have been better at linking the ownership with (performance measures) firm-linked or endogenous attributes such as financial measures, capital productivity, labor productivity, asset specificity, or bargaining power, and exogenous factors such as a host country's environment, including infrastructure, presence of other MNEs. In addition, those studies that used ownership as an independent variable, tended to link ownership to financial indicators most frequently.

Most research has tended to treat ownership as a dependent variable and to focus on parent firm capabilities in determining an ownership structure. Uni-dimensional studies, which look only at the parent company, tend to be concerned with the choice between (non-equity, contractual) and hierarchical (equity) entry modes, while multidimensional studies tend to focus more specifically on the levels of ownership and consider both equity partner's capabilities. Multi-dimensional studies are also less concerned with financial performance indicators and tend to focus on factor inputs in subsidiaries; therefore, they are more inclined to use productivity factors and the choice of ownership (e.g,. Burgel & Murray, 2000; Moon & Lado, 2000). Moreover, uni-dimensional studies tend to focus on financial performance such as sales, profits, return on assets (ROA) and return on investment (ROI) while multi-dimensional studies shifted their focus to factor inputs and often resulted in productivity measures for capital or labor (Oulton, 1998).

The table below summarizes the most important literature which has linked ownership to firm-level performance indicators. Studies have been categorized as either uni-dimensional or multi-dimensional. I further categorized existing research into whether ownership was treated as a dependent or independent variable. Table 1 summarizes these findings.

Studies which are uni-dimensional and where ownership is the dependent variable emphasize financial performance and use the transaction cost approach (Burgel & Murray, 2000; Moon & Lado, 2000). However, in cases where ownership is an independent variable, uni-dimensional studies tend to extend beyond transaction cost theory by extending financial performance indicators into productivity and efficiency measures. Studies which employ measures such as capital and labor productivity and technical efficiency as a result of a parent company's ownership choice include those by Oulton (1998) and Li et al. (2002).

Multi-dimensional studies, on the other hand, expand the focus to include the resource-based view where partner capabilities and complementary assets become a central issue. The exchange of these assets at the lowest transaction cost becomes a central focus of multi-dimensional studies. These studies make the claim that shared ownership is preferred to sole ownership or non-hierarchical (non-equity) entry modes where it is necessary to overcome the disadvantage of being foreign, mainly in the institutional and experiential sense. Scholars that have published multi-dimensional studies including Delios and Beamish (1997), Asiedu and Esfahani (2002), and Gomes-Casseres (1989; 1992) argue from the point of view that shared equity ownership lowers the transaction costs for acquiring these intangible assets.

The transaction cost approach is the direction taken by most scholars including those in uni-dimensional studies. The difference between ownership as a dependent and independent variable is that with the former the impact of non-firm specific factors in addition to firm-specific factors can be measured, such as the host country environment, host country risk, or other externalities such as improvements in infrastructure. The importance for ownership is that any change in these variables can cause a change in ownership – the dependent variable. The most important concept to the effects of changes in ownership that has emerged from studies which use ownership as a dependent variable is the concept that intangible assets are not static and that they have an impact on ownership over time, which therefore calls for the case that ownership be revised periodically. However, when ownership is revised and adjusted, the role of the ownership variable changes. Ownership then becomes an independent variable which will influence an IJV's performance in the future. Thus, if knowledge is non-static and dependent on ownership adjustment, then how can the effects of a change in ownership on knowledge/capabilities be measured quantitatively? This is where many studies have shown limitations.

As a non-static concept, it is not sufficient to capture changes in knowledge by measures such as R&D intensity, or percentage of engineers

Table 1. Ownership as dependent and independent variable in previous studies

Dimension of studies / Role of ownership variable	Uni- dimensional	Main findings	Multi- dimensional	Main findings
Dependent	*(a)* Burgel and Murray (2000); *(b)* Moon and Lado (2000)	*(a)* Organizational capabilities considered, entry mode depends on subsidiary age and experience; high degree of tacit knowledge leads parent company to choose local partner *(b)* suggest longitudinal research designs in the study of ownership change caused by technological progress, changes in knowledge	*(e)* Asiedu and Esfahani (2001); *(f)* Hagedoorn and Narula (1996); *(g)* Delios and Beamish (1999)	*(f)* if learning rates are similar for both partners, alliances can be sustained *(g)* high asset specificity causes high owner to assume high ownership share, requirements for complementary assets moderate ownership share *(e)* found negative link between foreign ownership share and importance of local partner's contributed assets; importance of local partner's assets increases due to non-static view of knowledge
Independent	*(c)* Li *et al.* (2002); *(d)* Oulton (1998)	*(c)* measure effect of foreign ownership on capital efficiency (ROA) and technology intensity *(d)* foreign ownership raises capital and labor productivity	*(h)* Grossman and Hart (1986); *(i)* Rasiah (2004)	*(h)* mention ownership as means to purchase 'residual rights' at lower transaction costs, ownership depends on extent of residual rights *(i)* subsidiaries with high local ownership exhibit greater reliance on local partner's network

Source: Own compilation of various sources

employed in a subsidiary. These measures do not capture the internalization and absorption effects of new technologies and knowledge by the subsidiary – (therefore, they are insufficient to address the view of knowledge transfer and absorption, which by definition is a non-static process).

Subsidiary-level data availability, however, has often been a significant problem. I begin with the papers in which ownership was used as an independent variable. Studies in this stream tend to precede those in which ownership was used as a dependent variable.

METHODOLOGY

The following section will form the quantitative concept which is used to analyze technology-based productivity growth based on data from the *Toyo Keizai Kaigai Shinshutsu Kigyo Soran* which had been compiled in electronic form ranging from 1986 to 2003. There were over 16,000 subsidiaries in the entire dataset, of which 1,881 subsidiaries yielded relevant data. I have chosen companies from electronics-related industries that manufacture end products and assemble components.

Applying an economics-related concept, the article seeks to make an important cross-discipline contribution to current business research. Quantitative business research has relied heavily on statistical methods, but application of micro-economic frameworks has been rare. Furthermore, the article also seek to make a contribution to the field of economics since most economics-related papers eschew application of the theoretical concepts they develop, due in part to a lack of firm-level data. In doing so, I combine approaches from both the fields of business research and economics. The advantage of my study is I have complete micro-level time-series subsidiary data for 1,881 Japanese subsidiaries (WOSs and IJVs) in China covering a 17-year period from 1986 to 2003, obtained from each annual issue of the *Toyo Keizai Kaigai Shinshutsu Kigyo Soran from 1986 to 2003*.

Residual values are used in order to estimate productivity growth within subsidiaries. In other words, a low residual value would indicate low productivity growth. It can thus be inferred that some factors within the subsidiary are obstructing the transfer and absorption of knowledge and/or technology, which could be due to an inappropriate ownership structure or other factors that have an impact on ownership choice, such as experience in foreign market entries or subsidiary age. Employee ratio between Japanese and local employees can also be a factor and a direct result of the control structure (Felipe, 1997). The method used or its variations have until now mostly been applied in macroeconomic studies (Felipe, 1997; Li et al., 2002) and several microeconomic studies on industry scale (Perkins, 1996; Blomstrom & Sjoholm, 1999). Economists (Solow, 1956; Felipe, 1997; Barro & Sala-i-Martin, 1997; Barro, 1998) mathematically proved the measurement approach's feasibility to private sector companies, including factories, units within a firm, service industries, and non-profit organizations--as long as micro-level data was available. In this section, a background and overview of the quantitative methods further employed is provided.

Technology/Knowledge-Based Productivity Growth

In its simplest form, productivity can be defined as the ratio of outputs that a firm produces to the inputs that it uses. Therefore,

$$Productivity = \frac{Outputs}{Inputs} \tag{1}$$

Equation (1) is the most basic example of productivity, where the production process involves a single input and a single output. However, in practical terms, this is seldom the case. Thus, when there is more than one input, a method for aggregating these inputs into a single index or inputs must be used to obtain a ratio measure of productivity. Therefore, when one refers to productivity, the reference is to Total Factor Productivity (TFP), which is a productivity measure that involves all factors of production. Other measures of productivity, such as labor productivity, capital productivity, and land productivity are often referred to as partial measures of productivity. These partial productivity measures, however, are not an indication of overall productivity when considered in isolation. Therefore, I do not follow partial productivity measures in this article.

When one considers productivity comparisons through time, however, an additional source of productivity change is possible. It is commonly referred to as technical change (Coelli et al., 1998; 2005). This measure involves advances in technology and/or improved management. An introduction of new technology, for instance, can extend the productivity potential of the firm/subsidiary beyond previous limits, thus resulting in productivity growth.

Weights

One of the important assumptions scholars make about productivity is it is a technical concept which refers to a ratio of outputs to inputs (Barro,

1998; Felipe, 1997; Coelli et al., 2005). When more than one factor is taken into account, the problem of how to weight each factor becomes critical to the equation. Therefore, weights of labor and capital become important. They are often indicated by the coefficients α (*alpha*) and β (*beta*), respectively. In an ideal scenario, these weights could be measured. Due to difficulties, however, some scholars have addressed these as aggregate values, derived from a large pool of economic data. Another problem is that data has been biased in favor of companies based in developed industrial countries. Nonetheless, values were assigned to the factors of labor and capital. Under the Hicks-neutral technique and the Hicks-technique, fixed values of α=0.4 and β=0.6 or α=0.35 and β=0.65 have commonly been assigned, respectively.

The disadvantage of fixed weights is that they are generic by assuming constant returns to scale. With enough micro-level subsidiary data, however, individual weights can be assigned to each subsidiary within a given time period. The dataset enables me to do so. Therefore, the assumption of constant returns to scale and usage of generic values can be avoided, thereby making calculations more accurate.

In its simplest form, the problem of weighing can be solved by relating the productivity ratio to the basic aggregate production function, where output is a function of capital, labor, and technology. I have already discussed the difficulty of quantifying the last part – technology - and therefore treat it as a residual value.

In its simplest form, the aggregate production function can be written as:

$$Q_t = F(K_t, L_t, t) \qquad (2)$$

(Felipe, 1997).

The next section will discuss in closer detail the concept of growth accounting as a method for computing the TFP. Behind the TFP is the (neoclassical) production function:

$$Y = F(A, K, L) \qquad (3)$$

(Barro, 1998).

A is the level of technology, K is the capital stock, and L is the quantity of labor. In Barro's (1998) version, the growth rate of output can be partitioned into components associated with factor accumulation and technological progress.

If technological progress appears in a Hicks-Neutral way, output becomes a function of technology-induced productivity and a function of capital and labor.

$F\left(A, K, L\right)$ becomes:

$$Q_t = A_t F(K_t, L_t) \qquad (4)$$

A division by $F\left(K_t, L_t\right)$ will then yield:

$$A_t = \frac{Q_t}{F\left(K_t, L_t\right)} \qquad (5)$$

In Equation (2), output was shown to be the dependent variable of a function of capital, labor, and time, where time as a shift factor is a proxy for the effects of productivity and technical progress/change. Barro (1998) and Felipe (1997) both assume that "*t*" is separable from *K* and *L*, a finding from which they create a new variable: *A*, or technical progress at a discrete point in time.

In its simplest form, productivity is a function of output, capital, and labor, which is derived from the aggregate production function of

$$A = \frac{Q}{\alpha_L \beta_K}, \qquad (6)$$

whereby A denotes a technology-based productivity measure at a discrete point in time.

Per this equation, A_t is referred to as exogenous and Hicks-Neutral technical progress, and is a measure of how output changes at different time intervals. Therefore, the measure of productivity can be interpreted as an index of factors other than labor and capital, which contribute to the generation of output but which cannot be accounted for in discrete terms. Solow (1959), Barro (1998), and Felipe (1997) highlight that these factors are managerial capabilities, organizational competence, diffusion of technology, intersectoral transfer of resources, and research and development (R&D). Therefore, it is a combined and implied measure of technology and knowledge transfer.

Equation (2) by itself is impractical since it requires knowledge of the marginal products. But, according to Barro (1998), it can be measured by observed factor prices. Thus, if K and L have "paid their social marginal products", so that $F_K = R$ (R is the rental price of capital, thus the interest rate or depreciation rate) and $F_L = w$ (wage rate), then Barro (1998) suggests the standard of the rate of technological progress can therefore be calculated from Equation (2) as a residual, according to the following notation:

$$g = \frac{\dot{Y}}{Y} - s_k\left(\frac{\dot{K}}{K}\right) - s_l\left(\frac{\dot{L}}{L}\right) \tag{7}$$

Variables s_k and s_l are factor payments of capital and labor, respectively.

If adapted to the variables used in this article, g can be used in the following notation:

$$g = \frac{\dot{A}}{A}$$

$$g = \frac{\dot{b}_t}{b_t}, \tag{8}$$

as the variable b_t is used to denote technical change. This formula illustrates the residual of technology growth, which one can also call the growth rate, or change in TFP, where technological progress is the result of subtracting changes in the shares of capital and the shares of labor. This article closely follows this method.

Estimation (*Thornqvist* Index)

A significant advantage of the aforementioned method (growth accounting–TFP) method is it makes it possible to calculate the growth rates for technology-induced productivity between specific time intervals, which therefore makes it suitable for panel data. By using panel data, one can get more accurate results for both the weights of labor with respect to time and technology-induced growth (TFP growth) as a result. For empirical purposes, however, Equation (2) also raises a conceptual problem. Although the equation represents output per unit of joint inputs, it is much more difficult to assign a meaningful interpretation to it as well as to the meaning of the level of technology, which in itself can be subject to speculation (Felipe, 1997). Studies have tended to use such measures as technology intensity (assets per employee) (Li et al., 2002) or R&D intensity (R&D expenditure relative to sales) (Makino and Delios, 1996), but these are static figures and are not based on absorption rates of new technology or knowledge, and therefore say little about a firm's technology/knowledge-based productivity growth, thus the efficacy of technology or knowledge transfer. The partial productivity in the growth accounting method index, however, addresses the problem more suitably by accounting for the weighted productivities of labor and capital, leaving a residual value for growth in productivity (Felipe, 1997).

Coelli et al. (1998; 2005) have developed a framework for measuring productivity and productivity change as part of a performance measurement. "Productivity is essentially a level concept and measures of productivity can be used in comparing performance of firms at a given time. In contrast, productivity change refers to movements in productivity performance of a firm or an industry over time" (Coelli et al., 2005).

The *Thornqvist* Index has become a commonly used measure of technology-induced productivity change (Coelli et al., 2005). In the *Thornqvist* Index, observed productivity improvements could be the result of improvements in technical efficiency and/or in the underlying production technology (Coelli et al., 2005). I have specifically chosen the *Thornqvist* Index and subsequently refer to it as such or as technology/knowledge-based productivity growth interchangeably.

CASE STUDY

The following conducted between a Japanese and Chinese manager in an equity joint venture illustrates some of the issues of diffused ownership and significant differences in capabilities, but in which the local partner retains a relatively large ownership share.

Case characteristics:

- **Year of Subsidiary Formation:** 1995
- **Ownership Structure:** 65% (Japanese); 35% (Chinese)
- **Productivity Growth:** High
- **Feasibility of Changing Ownership Structure:** Medium
- **Instability:** Low
- **Type of IJV relationship:** Non-arm's length

Background of the International Joint Venture (IJV)

The IJV was formed in 1995 between a Japanese electronics company that specializes in automotive and aviation GPS and mobile communications equipment, and a Chinese SOE which specializes in navigation and telecommunications equipment. The IJV was set up at an ownership ratio of 65% and 35% for the Japanese and Chinese partners, respectively. Ownership in this IJV has not changed since that time, and productivity growth has been high.

Significance of the Case

The significance of this case is that despite no change in ownership, productivity has risen over time, which shows that the partner's value of contribution to the IJV relative to its ownership share began to match more closely over time. The case is an example of a conventional non-arm's length relationship with diffused ownership structures. The local partner has high ownership and is actively involved in management.

The ownership the local partner received at the time of IJV set-up was high relative to its level of contribution in the early stages of the IJV. In other words, the IJV partner was overcompensated (relative to its initial contribution to the IJV). Despite the local partner's high ownership share, the Japanese company still transferred key knowledge necessary to upgrade the local partner's know-how and production capabilities, including drawings of integrated circuits in incremental steps. The incentive for the partner to remain loyal to the IJV was therefore established; in other words, the partner did not become complacent in receiving profits. Instead, the local partner upgraded its own capabilities which would enable it to become the main supplier of semiconductor and other high-tech components to the IJV. Therefore, the overcompensation from the high ownership share eventually became worthwhile in retaining the local partner's loyalty, in contrast to the previous case study.

The high value for productivity growth ultimately resulted from a carefully planned and incremental technology transfer to the local partner who helped the Japanese parent company almost fully localize its component supply chain in China. The learning effect in this subsidiary eventually went further leading to the set-up of a new R&D subsidiary. The initial overcompensation of the IJV partner with regard to the ownership share was successful in combination with the planned and incremental technology and knowledge transfer to the subsidiary, so that it became unnecessary to renegotiate the ownership share in the later life of this IJV, which also means that no further inefficiencies arose from ownership renegotiation.

The IJV was founded on an initial understanding to gradually and systematically upgrade the local partner's skills through a technology contract in which the partner would receive technological assistance by using expatriate Japanese technical personnel/engineers without charge to the IJV. This was different from the other cases in which the local subsidiary was required to pay a fee for engineers who were sent from the Japanese parent company, and which both IJV partners split according to their equity. The setup and required assets that the local partner would provide made such no-fee engineer-import arrangement possible. An important expectation of the local partner was that it would increase its supply of component types to the JV and help the JV achieve full- or near-to-full localization rates within a 10-year time frame, following which the Japanese parent company planned to transfer most R&D functions to China and ultimately localize its entire supply chain in China including the supply of yet-to-be-developed components through the R&D process. In the meantime the JV partner was to learn the production technology together with some sensitive know-how.

Local IJV Partner

The local partner is an SOE and a market leader in China in GPS and OEM communications equipment. At the time of IJV formation, this SOE already had four IJVs with US and European MNCs, and the current case was its first IJV with a Japanese company.

Therefore, the Chinese partner had relatively high product complementariness and greater knowledge symmetry with the Japanese company. It was already capable of supplying about 10% among all types of GPS navigation components that the Japanese partner required at the IJV setup stage; eventually the localization rate with regard to these components was to be raised to above 80%. The areas which needed improvement were the quality of existing products and new product development. The localization rate of 10% could have been higher, but some quality issues had to be resolved first.

Technology Protection

Although the Japanese parent company transferred first-generation equipment to the newly formed IJV, it did not attempt to protect knowledge by keeping the local partner arm's length. Active involvement in management, such as employing Chinese staff at both upper management and lower management levels (i.e., line supervisors) was done in the interest of imparting new knowledge. Moreover, the Japanese parent company arranged for technical staff to supervise new production equipment and processes when they were introduced, and offer free technical assistance in the same form when problems arose. The goal was to localize activities at the highest level–the R&D level. In the meantime, the Japanese parent needed the local partner to provide regular contributions necessary to operate in China, such as the contribution of HR functions, clearing bureaucracy (customs, taxes, etc.), and liaising with the government. The regular introduction of new technologies motivated the local partner to learn and make counter-contributions in the form of new or improved components.

Productivity Growth

Technology/knowledge-induced productivity growth in this IJV has attained a high level. Both partners later agreed to create a new R&D subsidiary from the existing IJV at the wish of the Japanese parent company. A new wholly-owned subsidiary would allow the Japanese partner to engage in R&D without a local partner but with some of the local partner's employees trained previously in the IJV. This option, the GM explained, would enhance the protection of know-how, or tacit technical knowledge, since asset specificity between the two IJV partners had become low as a result of their close cooperation.

The engineering background of Chinese managers often enables them to learn and internalize Japanese technology and implement it in the production process, particularly within the open culture of this IJV. Furthermore, the local partner's management participation has compensated for the insufficient management skills, which have limited the local partner's ability to "engage in fundamental changes that concern managerial tasks such as work processes and delegating decision making and responsibility" (Nguyen & Meyer, 2005, p. 48). Therefore, participation at all management levels has ultimately compensated for the lack of management skills and aided in the implementation of production and innovation processes. As a result, technology/knowledge-based productivity has risen over the years.

Objectives for Ownership

By giving the local partner high ownership and preserving a flexible ownership agreement, the incentive structure of the IJV remained largely intact throughout the life of the IJV. For the Japanese partner, it meant that majority ownership enabled it to retain control of the joint venture, technologies, and strategy in the short term. In the long-term, the Japanese partner could focus on developing the joint venture, increasing product lines, and increasing the local partner's capability to act as supplier and provider of other tangible and intangible assets. For the Chinese partner, the ownership structure meant that at IJV setup time and the short term, they could contribute what they were competent in such as tangible assets which included finding and negotiating land, building factory space, providing utilities, labor, and contacts to local and national governments. In addition, the local partner was also able to supply a limited range of components. As for intangible assets, the local partner's most important contribution at the time of IJV setup included mainly contacts to national and local governments and negotiating favorable tax terms for the production.

Interview Results: Japanese Partner

Tangible Assets

Securing contributions from the Chinese partner has been long-term and systematic planning of upgrading the IJV partner's capabilities from the time of IJV formation. The Japanese partner has actively pursued a higher value-added strategy towards the subsidiary and acknowledged that the key in securing an effective relationship was to upgrade both partners' capabilities. The IJV in this case study was the Japanese parent company's second IJV in China and overseas; therefore it had limited experience in foreign market entries.

Another IJV was located in southern China, but had been built on an export-oriented and low-value added strategy several years earlier. The company's goal had been to localize component production in the long-term. Therefore, the current IJV required a number of the local partner's simple tangible assets at setup time and more sophisticated tangible assets later. These included operating permits, land, labor, factory space, and tax concessions initially, while locally-produced and locally-sourced components would be sourced locally later . The latter, however, could only be attained after exchange and absorption of tacit knowledge (intangible assets) had taken place successfully. The significance is that the shift from simple tangible assets to value-added sophisticated tangible assets required internalization of intangible assets (e.g., tacit knowledge). The General Manager (GM) not only wanted to localize production, but also wanted to eliminate the strategy of exporting finished products to Japan and re-importing them to China to be used mostly by other foreign MNCs. Most of the products the subsidiary was producing at the time were intermediate industrial products.

The subsidiary's full export orientation was part of an IJV setup requirement by the government, which signals its weak bargaining power vis-à-vis the Chinese government and the local IJV partner. In the future, however, all production was to be sold in China directly. While the Chinese industrial market continued to increase rapidly, the subsidiary also began to diversify its production to include products for individual consumers. The subsidiary eventually shifted from a full export orientation to a partial export orientation for both industrial and individual consumers.

The GM was aware the utility of these simple tangible assets would eventually decline and the partner overcompensated if a future flow of increasingly value-added contributions from the local partner was not maintained in order to justify the ownership share. According to the GM (2007), "We wanted to ensure the local partner would continue to be of value to us after their initial contributions when we set up the company." Doing so, however, would not be possible without the transfer of high technology, to which the GM delivered the following comment:

Our customers are MNCs that demand the latest technology and best product quality... We have a strong reputation which we have to maintain... We had already decided at the negotiation stage that in the future we would be setting up R&D facilities here... We were going to implement it systematically, and we needed a competent local partner... We could not afford to lose a good local partner. (General Manager A, 2007)

Furthermore, the GM added that over time component production would be incrementally localized as the Chinese partner learned new production technologies.

Intangible Assets

The shift from a reliance on the partner's simple tangible assets to higher value-added tangible assets and their requisite intangible assets had been a set strategy since the time of IJV set up. Therefore, the local partner knew its role from the start, and knowledge uncertainty was minimized. Moreover, the non-fixed ownership structure in this case simplified the process of any change in ownership that would reflect the local partner's higher value-added contributions.

Even though the Japanese partner in this IJV did not intend to change the ownership in the future, the GM also did not rule it out for the sake of preserving a harmonious and long-term oriented relationship with the local partner. According to the GM, the reliance on the local partner's intangible assets had transgressed the increasingly important roles of dealing with government agencies and sourcing local suppliers to one in which the local partner had been increasingly made part of the Japanese parent company's R&D network. Despite the fear about weak intellectual property protection in China, the GM believed that so long as they created incentives for the partner to stay, the problem of knowledge leakage could be kept to a minimum. Ownership and new knowledge were indispensable in maintaining the local partner's loyalty. The local partner, whose engineers were eventually to be employed in a separately-created R&D subsidiary first received experience and training to increase their capabilities in quality control, product knowledge, and knowledge of the production process with the eventual goal of product development for the industrial market.

The company's customers were large MNCs which also exported their products and therefore had high quality demands. The GM believed that to transfer know-how necessary for the production of high-quality, advanced industrial goods, the subsidiary should first expose local staff to product development in consumer goods when the skill level had been reached. Unlike industrial customers, among whom the company had been highly regarded, the subsidiary was still relatively unknown among end-users, which made it less risky to test the acceptance of locally developed products with end-users first.

We decided to transfer our consumer goods development to China first, while maintaining industrial R&D in Japan. We had decided to enter the consumer goods when we set up the JV. Setting our JV up in China was a method to test locally developed consumer goods among consumers in China and assess the potential for further R&D localization for our industrial goods. We were new in the consumer market, so we could afford to experiment since we had no reputation to lose... We will assess our R&D subsidiary first and its success in the R&D of consumer goods, but it will take a few years until we reach a decision on whether we will conduct R&D for our core industrial products there. (General Manager A, 2007)

The main mechanism for transfer was the use of experienced transfer teams and temporary expatriate engineers together with extensive education and training (three to four months) of managerial and engineering personnel in the parent company in Japan from early on in the project. Considerable on site involvement by engineers from headquarters in Japan has also been critical for the successful transfer of essential tacit knowledge and problem-solving skills. According to the GM,

We wanted to establish a culture of innovation, but we had to start almost from scratch. The (local) engineers had some training and theoretical knowledge but did not know how to apply it... They also had no idea how to use the research budget, so we had to create this knowledge first. We tried to increase their knowledge systematically. (General Manager A, 2007)

Ownership

According to the GM, the IJV was set up on the premise the ownership structure had to be adjustable in order to reflect the partner's contributions in the future. When the IJV was formed, the goal of localizing production and expanding sales in the Chinese market directly (as opposed to re-importing) was already in existence.

However, at the time of setup, the GM also mentioned that the Japanese parent company did not consider entering the Chinese market immediately because the Japanese partner wanted to accumulate experience in China first, including experience with the Chinese partner. Furthermore, the GM believed the Chinese consumer market did not have the purchasing power and quality orientation for high-quality and high value-added end products at the time of IJV setup. Therefore, he believed it would be useful in the meantime to learn from the Chinese partner and expand the Chinese partner's technological skills and tacit knowledge.

He also mentioned that in the course of time, the Japanese parent company expected the Chinese partner's contributions to shift to more value-added tangible and intangible assets in connection with the upgrading of the partner's capabilities along with the gradual increase in capabilities of manufacturers within China. The GM explained with regard to reflecting each partner's contributions through the ownership share,

We gave up a higher share as a bonus to the Chinese... Their share did not initially reflect their contributions or their value-added to our joint venture, but we hoped to create goodwill and gain the partner's trust through it. We entered China for the long-term and we were sure that in the future we would gain the appropriate value-added contribution from our local partner. (General Manager A, 2007)

The ownership structure was thus used a tool to motivate the Chinese partner; or, as the GM maintained–it would eventually deliver higher value-added contributions from the partner in the future. At the time of the interview, the ownership share did not have to be changed yet.

Government Influence

Government influence was perceived by the GM as strong:

The government seemed eager to get us to form a JV with them [SOE]. The government should not even have tried so hard because our trading company already advised us to form a JV with this particular SOE before. We had a clear plan for the JV partner to become part of our production network and possibly R&D network later. First, we needed the partner to set up our production facilities speedily and with all the necessary production equipment. (General Manager A, 2007)

The General Manager further added,

Taxes and duties were complex, opaque, and illogical... This has not improved much in recent years despite China's entry into WTO, we will always need the partner for negotiating the arbitrary duties on components and equipment... Sometimes the import and depreciation tax we are assessed depends on the mood of the official. At least we are now able to localize more of our production thanks to our partner. As for new production equipment, we will still need to import it for a long time, and we cannot cope without our partner in this regard. (General Manager A, 2007)

The quote shows the extent to which the GM depends on the local partner to negotiate with the government. Even though localization of production has taken some pressure off tax negotiations for components supplies on one hand, increased localization had resulted in more frequent equipment imports, where the Japanese partner had a difficulties in negotiating import taxes. The quote above also implies that localizing anything but final component production is unlikely, and that despite strong tax pressures, the company would not consider sourcing or developing any production equipment locally. As a required intermediate step, production technologies remain the core of technological know-how, and these will not be localized, despite higher tax liabilities (GM, 2007). This indicates strong unwillingness and inability with regard to local technological capabilities to transfer production equipment, in spite of the fact that transferring production equipment would mean time and cost savings. However, it is not likely because of the variety of contractors involved. The GM mentioned,

We do not know of any local company that could make the equipment to our specifications within the time, advancement, and quality we require. At this time, we would not develop the design of production equipment with our partner, since we would be giving essential know-how away... In the future, we will still receive it from Japan... (General Manager A, 2007)

Accordingly, the Chinese partner will remain an essential link between the IJV and the government. In this sense government connections–an intangible asset contributed from the start of the JV, (thus a simple intangible asset) have and will likely remain important throughout the life of the JV. The above quote highlight the pressure companies can face to transfer and impart know-how to China and discourage the sole importation of key technologies. The Japanese partner, by contrast, chose to protect the know-how.

In addition, the transfer of sophisticated intangible assets, such as technological knowledge, has perpetuated the Japanese partner's reliance on the simple intangible assets that the local partner can provide, such as government connections. Therefore, the local partner's role has retained and possibly increased in importance. The Japanese partner has required more of the Chinese partner's tacit knowledge over time. With regard to obtaining the local partner's intangible assets, the strategy by the Japanese parent company to concede a higher ownership ratio to the Chinese partner in the beginning was therefore justified. The local partner did not have reason to claim that the value of their contributions to the IJV exceeded the value of their ownership share.

Knowledge Transfer

According to the summary of the interview results in the table, it can be seen that tacit knowledge transferred to the local partner increased over time from a reported level of "medium." According to Kremic (2003), a higher rate of knowledge absorption by the technology transferee over time is the result of increasing absorption of tacit knowledge that could be internalized only after explicit knowledge had been absorbed. Therefore, the indication from the data in the previous chapter and the self-reported results stated by the GM indicate that the transfer of explicit knowledge resulted in tacit knowledge being implemented more efficiently later. According to the GM,

We wanted to train our engineers and managers to be capable of conducting R&D later. They already had the skills to modify products for the local market; we also knew they had the potential for further R&D... But local staff had weak managerial skills... they could not manage the R&D budget... we could not trust them to spend the R&D budget wisely... We spent a long time teaching them... (General Manager A, 2007)

The above quote highlights the importance of a wide range of tacit knowledge which ranges from product-specific knowledge (modification of products, R&D) to managerial knowledge such as managing the R&D budget. The linkage between skills upgraded from absorbing tacit knowledge and skills upgraded from learning explicit knowledge became evident in the retention of local engineers. The GM further mentioned that,

We also wanted our engineers to be challenged and avoid letting them feel underused by limiting them doing product modifications; this is why we let them manage the R&D budget... We did not want them to feel that they were just wasting their time here when they could have acquired other skills from other companies... We had already invested in their training... (General Manager A, 2007)

He also explained retaining these engineers was important since they had already invested in their training, and they had reached a higher skill level. State-of-the-art R&D, however, could not be conducted in the IJV for fear of leakage of proprietary knowledge. A newly created wholly-owned subsidiary for R&D had, therefore, been spun off from the IJV one year before the interview. The GM mentioned that engineers and managers were transferred to the newly set-up WOS, where product design was initially conducted. As for technology leakage through staff turnover, the GM had the following to say:

We cannot control staff turnover or knowledge leaking through engineers that leave the company. However, we pay them a high salary, we give them job autonomy, and continuous training programs in Japan...So we don't think they will go back to working at an SOE...They cannot take any technical drawings outside the premises, but whatever they memorize and take out, we cannot help...(General Manager A, 2007)

The above quote highlights that engineer retention plays an important role. As for knowledge transfer, although this case shows that R&D is most likely achieved in WOSs, it also highlights that newly-formed R&D-focused WOS had been formed from an IJV that had laid the necessary infrastructure in both tangible and intangible assets for R&D activities to occur in the future. With regard to knowledge transfer, this type of IJV with its ownership structure has been useful.

Knowledge Uncertainty Towards Chinese Partner

With regard to knowledge uncertainty about the misappropriation of the Japanese partner's technology, the manager mentioned two concerns. The first concern was leakage of technology through structural market failure; in other words, government action (Dunning, 1999). Structural market failure outweighed concerns about leakage through company-internal channels. For both, however, fears about technology leakage seem to be greatest in the first two years of operation. According to the manager:

The largest potential for leakage of our intellectual property (proprietary knowledge) was during the establishment phase. We had to obtain a business license, and in the process of applying for it we were required to submit drawings, which were then reviewed by government departments. We do not know who gets to see the drawings... (General Manager A, 2007)

Such structural failure was perceived as the first instance where commercially sensitive information could be leaked. In order to obtain a business license, the company had no choice but to abide. As for the leakage of technological knowledge within the subsidiary, the GM was more confident of the Japanese side's ability to control it, citing ownership structure as a useful tool:

From what we heard from other managers, we knew that the Chinese partner would try to study our products and techniques within the first two years of operation... We wanted the partner to learn but didn't want them to use this knowledge against us. So we tried from the start to make sure their goals were the same as ours so they would have no incentive to act against us. (General Manager A, 2007)

The GM further elaborated on the determination of the Chinese partner's equity share and its role in reducing uncertainty about the local partner's behavior:

If the Chinese side had a lower than 30% share, we felt they would not be of use to our JV. In the short term, we had their cooperation because they had contributed part of the land, capital, management staff, and engineers, and together with their ownership share, they would have a strong incentive to ensure our company would succeed... In the long term, we thought they would be interested in seeing their profits increase and participate in management, so we decided to give them a proper ownership share. (General Manager A, 2007)

The quote shows the Japanese partner had given consideration to the motivation of the Chinese partner when determining the ownership share. As for the technology aspect, the manager further mentioned that the local partner would "benefit from the continuous upgrading of production technologies and skills unless they [local partner] since they knew that we were in the process of localizing most of our production and R&D... why should they go elsewhere?" The Japanese GM thus believed there was interest alignment between both partners, and that uncertainty and that ownership and systematic technology transfer would ensure continued non-adverse behavior by the local IJV partner.

CONTRIBUTIONS

The chapter has provided several important contributions to the research on entry mode choice, ownership structures, and quantitative modeling using econometric and qualitative approaches.

With regard to entry mode choice and ownership structures, the chapter has developed a quantitative framework which measures performance under given ownership structures as the degree of efficiency in technology transfer and knowledge exchange in the form of a residual productivity growth variable. This method has been shown to be a proxy for or an indirect measure of transaction costs, in that ownership structures are validated by the growth in technology/knowledge-based productivity that they caused.

The second important contribution of the chapter has been the linkage of the quantitative results to their applicability and potential for implementation in Japanese equity-based subsidiaries in China within the framework of a qualitative discussion that has addressed issues of initial entry mode choice and ownership restructuring over the lifetime of the subsidiaries.

The case study has also provided a link between types of subsidiary structures and associated quantitative outcomes of productivity growth due to technology transfer and knowledge exchange, and therefore information about the cost of their transaction. With regard to quantitative modeling, the article has employed an approach that had previously been developed by economists for documenting macroeconomic progress.

PRACTICAL IMPLICATIONS

The chapter has shown that specific ownership structures are important and receive consideration by Japanese managers with long-term capability development strategies in subsidiaries when their parent companies chose entry modes. Companies that did not pay much attention to ownership structures may have become aware of the importance of ownership structures over time as they accumulated experience with their IJV partners and underwent the dynamic process of learning by accumulating and exchanging experience and knowledge while operating in China. Ownership structures are an important motivational tool for both partners to ensure that processes within subsidiaries proceed smoothly.

For Japanese or Asian managers in Latin America, the qualitative findings can thus help anticipate the type of IJV partner that might be encountered depending on government suasion and the Japanese company's own ability and bargaining power in negotiating a desired ownership structure. Therefore, Japanese managers could better anticipate the behavior of the local IJV partner and choose a framework for an IJV relationship accordingly. The quantitative part can give suggestions about the extent of technology/knowledge-based productivity growth that can be expected from forming an IJV with a particular ownership structure and relationship and thus provide some information about the distribution of ownership to which an IJV can be structured or adjusted in the future to achieve optimal productivity levels. Furthermore, the chapter also with local partners of different levels of technological sophistication, and accordingly, the degree of managerial and equity involvement to allow the local partner.

For policymakers in Latin America, the chapter can provide guidance on how to advise Japanese high-tech companies with little experience in emerging markets and what they should consider before setting up IJVs in such circumstances.

The framework regarding IJV relationships could provide other guidance for policymakers in Latin America to introduce local companies to Japanese companies based on new technologies and managerial knowledge required from the foreign firm. The chapter could also provide guidance on what to expect with regard to the acquisition of new technologies and acquisition of knowledge from the Japanese or foreign partner. Such information could be useful in specifying a role for the local company within, such as becoming a supplier or creating higher value-added by taking on certain R&D functions. As a result, more appropriate ownership structures and contract terms could be negotiated prior to IJV setup.

REFERENCES

Abel, A. B., & Eberly, J. C. (1994). A Unified Model of Investment Under Uncertainty. *The American Economic Review*, *84*(5), 1369–1384.

Agarwal, S., & Ramaswami, S. N. (1992). Choice of Foreign Market Entry Mode: Impact of Ownership, Location and Internalization Factors. *Journal of International Business Studies*, *23*(1), 1–27. doi:10.1057/palgrave.jibs.8490257.

Anderson, E., & Gatignon, H. (1986). Modes of Foreign Entry: A Transaction Cost Analysis and Propositions. *Journal of International Business Studies*, *17*(3), 1–26. doi:10.1057/palgrave.jibs.8490432.

Asiedu, E., & Esfahani, H. S. (2001). Ownership Structure in Foreign Direct Investment Projects. *The Review of Economics and Statistics*, *83*(4), 647–662. doi:10.1162/003465301753237731.

Asiedu, E., & Esfahani, H. S. (2001). Ownership Structure in Foreign Direct Investment Projects. *The Review of Economics and Statistics*, *83*(4), 647–662. doi:10.1162/003465301753237731.

Barkema, H. G., & Vermeulen, F. (1997). What Differences in the Cultural Backgrounds of Partners Are Detrimental for International Joint Ventures? *Journal of International Business Studies*, *28*(4), 845–864. doi:10.1057/palgrave.jibs.8490122.

Barro, R. J. (1998). Notes on Growth Accounting. *National Bureau of Economic Research*. Working Paper 6654. Retrieved on December 6, 2011, from http://www.nber.org/papers/w6654

Bartlett, C. A., & Ghoshal, S. (1989). *Managing across borders: The transnational solution*. Cambridge, MA: Harvard University Press.

Baum, J. A. C., & Ingram, P. (1998). Survival-Enhancing Learning in the Manhattan Hotel Industry, 1898-1980. *Management Science*, *44*(7), 996–1016. doi:10.1287/mnsc.44.7.996.

Beamish, P. W. (1988). *Multinational joint ventures in developing countries*. London, UK: Routledge.

Beamish, P. W., & Banks, J. C. (1987). Equity Joint Ventures and the Theory of the Multinational Enterprise. *Journal of International Business Studies*, *18*(2), 1–16. doi:10.1057/palgrave.jibs.8490403.

Beamish, P. W., & Killing, J. P. (Eds.). (1997). *Cooperative Strategies: Asian Pacific Perspectives*. San Francisco, CA: New Lexington Press.

Belderbos, R., & Sleuwaegen, L. (1996). Japanese Firms and the Decision to Invest Abroad: Business Groups and Regional Core Networks. *The Review of Economics and Statistics*, *78*(2), 214–220. doi:10.2307/2109923.

Blomstrom, M., & Sjoholm, F. (1999). Technology transfer and spillovers: Does local participation with multinationals matter? *European Economic Review*, *43*(4-6), 915–923. doi:10.1016/S0014-2921(98)00104-4.

Brouthers, K. D. (2002). Institutional, Cultural and Transaction Cost Influences on Entry Mode Choice and Performance. *Journal of International Business Studies*, *33*(2), 203–221. doi:10.1057/palgrave.jibs.8491013.

Brown, D., & Porter, R. (1996). *Management Issues in China* (*Vol. 1*). London, UK: Routledge.

Buckley, P. J. (1988). The Limits of Explanation: Testing the Internalization Theory of the Multinational Enterprise. *Journal of International Business Studies*, *19*(2), 181–193. doi:10.1057/palgrave.jibs.8490382.

Buckley, P. J., & Casson, M. (1976). *The future of the multinational enterprise*. London, UK: Macmillan.

Buckley, P. J., & Casson, M. C. (1998). Analyzing Foreign Market Entry Strategies: Extending the Internalization Approach. *Journal of International Business Studies*, *29*(3), 539–562. doi:10.1057/palgrave.jibs.8490006.

Burgel, O., & Murray, G. C. (2000). The International Market Entry Choices of Start-Up Companies in High-Technology Industries. *Journal of International Marketing*, *8*(2), 33–62. doi:10.1509/jimk.8.2.33.19624.

Chang, J. (2007). International Expansion Path, Speed, Product Diversification and Performance Among Emerging-Market MNEs: Evidence from Asia-Pacific Multinational Companies. *Asian Business & Management*, *6*(4), 331–354. doi:10.1057/palgrave.abm.9200228.

Chang, S. J. (1995). International Expansion Strategy of Japanese Firms: Capability Building through Sequential Entry. *Academy of Management Journal*, *38*(2), 383–407. doi:10.2307/256685.

Chang, S. J., & Rosenzweig, P. M. (2001). The Choice of Entry Mode in Sequential Foreign Direct Investment. *Strategic Management Journal*, *22*(8), 747–776. doi:10.1002/smj.168.

Chen, H. C., & Shih, H. T. (2005). *High-Tech Industries in China*. Cheltenham, UK: Edward Elgar Publishing.

Child, J. (1996). *Management in China during the age of reform*. Cambridge, MA: Cambridge University Press.

China Statistical Yearbook. 1988-2006. Beijing, China: China Statistical Information and Consultancy Service Centre.

Coelli, T., Rao, D. S. P., O'Donnell, C. J., & Battese, G. E. (1998). *An introduction to efficiency and productivity analysis* (1st ed.). New York: Springer. doi:10.1007/978-1-4615-5493-6.

Delios, A., & Beamish, P. W. (1999). Geographic Scope, Product Diversification, and the Corporate Performance of Japanese Firms. *Strategic Management Journal*, *20*(8), 711–727. doi:10.1002/(SICI)1097-0266(199908)20:8<711::AID-SMJ41>3.0.CO;2-8.

Delios, A., & Henisz, W. (2003). Political Hazards, Experience, and Sequential Entry Strategies: The International Expansion of Japanese Firms, 1980-1998. *Strategic Management Journal*, *24*(11), 1153–1164. doi:10.1002/smj.355.

Dhanaraj, C., & Beamish, P. W. (2003). Effect of equity ownership on the survival of international joint ventures. *Strategic Management Journal*, *25*(3), 295–305. doi:10.1002/smj.372.

Dougherty, S. M., & McGuckin, R. H. (2004). *The Effects of Federalism and Privatization on Productivity in Chinese Firms*. National School of Development Working Paper 2036. Peking University. Retrieved on December 6, 2011, from http://www.ccer.pku.edu.cn/download/2036-1.pdf

Dunning, J. H. (1976). Trade, location of economic activity and the MNE: A search for an eclectic approach. P.O. Ohlin, P.M. Hesselborn, Wijkman (Eds.), *Proceedings of Nobel Symposium - The International*

Dunning, J. H. (1998). Location and the Multinational Enterprise: A Neglected Factor? *Journal of International Business Studies*, *29*(1), 45–66. doi:10.1057/palgrave.jibs.8490024.

Felipe, J. (1997). *Total Factor Productivity in East Asia: A Critical Survey*. Asian Development Bank. Economic Development and Resource Center Report Series No. 65. Retrieved on December 6, 2011, from http://www.adb.org/Documents/EDRC/Reports/ER065.pdf

Gomes-Casseres, B. (1992). *International trade, competition, and alliances in the computer industry*. Working Paper 92-044. Boston, MA: Harvard Business School Press.

Grossman, G. M., & Helpman, E. (1994). Endogenous Innovation in the Theory of Growth. *The Journal of Economic Perspectives*, *8*(1), 23–44. doi:10.1257/jep.8.1.23.

Grossman, S. J., & Hart, O. D. (1986). The Costs and Benefits of Ownership: A Theory of Vertical and Lateral Integration. *The Journal of Political Economy*, *94*(4), 691–719. doi:10.1086/261404.

Guillen, M. F. (2002). Business groups and economic development: A resource-based view. M. Kotabe, P.S. Aulakh (Eds.) Emerging issues in international business research. Cheltenham, UK: Edward Elgar Publishing.

Gupta, A. K., & Govindarajan, V. (1991). Knowledge Flows and the Structure of Control within Multinational Corporations. *Academy of Management Review*, *16*(4), 768–792.

Hejazi, W., & Safarian, A. E. (1999). Trade, Foreign Direct Investment, and R&D Spillovers. *Journal of International Business Studies*, *30*(3), 491–511. doi:10.1057/palgrave.jibs.8490080.

Hennart, J. F., & Park, Y. R. (1994). Location, Governance, and Strategic Determinants of Japanese Manufacturing Investment in the United States. *Strategic Management Journal*, *15*(6), 419–436. doi:10.1002/smj.4250150602.

Hymer, S. H. (1976). *The International Operations of National Firms: A Study of Direct Foreign Investment*. Cambridge, MA: MIT Press.

Inkpen, A. C., & Beamish, P. W. (1997). Knowledge, Bargaining Power, and the Instability of International Joint Ventures. *Academy of Management Review*, *22*(1), 177–202.

Inkpen, A. C., & Dinur, A. (1998). Knowledge Management Processes and International Joint Ventures. *Organization Science*, *9*(4), 454–468. doi:10.1287/orsc.9.4.454.

International Monetary Fund (2003). *World Economic Outlook. World Economic and Financial Surveys*. Retrieved on December 6, 2011, fromhttp://www.imf.org/external/pubs/ft/weo/2003/01/pdf/chapter1.pdf

Johanson, J., & Vahlne, J. E. (1977). The Internationalization Process of the Firm – A Model of Knowledge Development and Increasing Foreign Market Commitments. *Journal of International Business Studies*, *8*(1), 23–32. doi:10.1057/palgrave.jibs.8490676.

Klimenko, M., & Saggi, K. (2007). Technical Compatibility and the Mode of Foreign Entry with Network Externalities. *The Canadian Journal of Economics. Revue Canadienne d'Economique*, *40*(1), 176–206. doi:10.1111/j.1365-2966.2007.00404.x.

Lu, J. W., & Beamish, P. W. (2006). Partnering strategies and performance of SMEs' international joint ventures. *Journal of Business Venturing*, *21*(4), 461–486. doi:10.1016/j.jbusvent.2005.02.002.

Luo, Y. (2001). *Strategy, Structure, and Performance of MNCs in China*. Westport, CT: Quorum Books.

Luo, Y. (2002). *Multinational Enterprises in Emerging Markets*. Copenhagen, Denmark: Copenhagen Business School Press.

Maitland, E., Rose, E. L., & Nicholas, S. (2005). How Firms Grow: Clustering as a Dynamic Model of Internationalization. *Journal of International Business Studies*, *36*(4), 435–451. doi:10.1057/palgrave.jibs.8400140.

Makino, S., & Delios, A. (1996). Local Knowledge Transfer and Performance: Implications for Alliance Formation in Asia. *Journal of International Business Studies*, *27*(5), 905–927. doi:10.1057/palgrave.jibs.8490156.

Marcotte, C., & Niosi, J. (2005). Small and Medium-sized Enterprises Involved in Technology Transfer to China: What do their Partners Learn? *International Small Business Journal*, *23*(1), 27–47. doi:10.1177/0266242605048871.

Nelson, R. R., & Phelps, E. S. (1966). Investment in humans, technological diffusion, and economic growth. *The American Economic Review*, *56*(1), 69–75.

Poell, R. F., Chivers, G. E., Van Der Krogt, F. J., & Wildemeersch, D. A. (2000). Learning-Network Theory: Organizing the Dynamic Relationships between Learning and Work. *Management Learning*, *31*(1), 25–49. doi:10.1177/1350507600311004.

Polanyi, M. (1958). *Personal knowledge; Towards a post-critical philosophy*. Chicago, IL: University of Chicago Press.

Proexport Colombia (2010). Foreign Direct Investment Report in Colombia. Retrieved on July 26, 2012, from http://www.bnamericas.com/cgi-bin/getresearch?report=157029.pdf&documento=1120796&idioma=I&login

Qiu, Y. (2005). Problems of Managing Joint Ventures in China's Interior: Evidence from Shaanxi. *SAM Advanced Management Journal*, (Summer), 46-57.

Solow, R.M. (1956). A Contribution to the Theory of Economic Growth. *The Quarterly Journal of Economics, 70*(1)\, 65-94.

Solow, R. M. (1957). Technical Change and the Aggregate Production Function. *The Review of Economics and Statistics*, *39*(3), 312–320. doi:10.2307/1926047.

Solow, R. M. (2000). *Growth theory: An exposition*. New York: Oxford University Press.

UNCTAD. (1996). *Trade and Development Report: Responding to the New Global Environment*. Retrieved on December 6, 2011, from http://vi.unctad.org/resources-mainmenu-64/digital-library?act=show&doc_name=tdr96-ch3

Vanhonacker, W. (1997). Entering China: An Unconventional Approach. *Harvard Business Review*, *75*(2), 130–140. PMID:10165447.

Wang, Y. (2007). Understanding Contractual Joint Ventures in China. *Journal of Chinese Economic and Business Studies*, *5*(1), 75–90. doi:10.1080/14765280601109394.

World Bank. (2012). GDP growth. Retrieved on July 26, 2012, from http://data.worldbank.org/indicator/NY.GDP.MKTP.KD.ZG/countries

World Economic Forum. (2012). The Global Competitiveness Report 2011-2012. Retrieved on July 26, 2012, from http://www3.weforum.org/docs/WEF_GCR_Report_2011-12.pdf

Yan, Y. (1999). *International Joint Ventures in China: Ownership, Control, and Performance*. New York: St. Martin's Press. doi:10.1057/9780333983898.

Yu, J., & Meyer-Ohle, H. (2008). Working for Japanese Corporations in China: A Qualitative Study. *Asian Business & Management*, *7*(1), 33–51. doi:10.1057/palgrave.abm.9200250.

Yusuf, S., & Weiping, W. (1997). *The dynamics of urban growth in three Chinese cities*. New York: Oxford University Press.

Zacharakis, A. L. (1997). Entrepreneurial Entry into Foreign Markets: A Transaction Cost Perspective. *Entrepreneurship Theory and Practice*, *21*(3), 23–40.

Chapter 10
Promoting Global Virtual Teams Across the Globe:
Cross-Cultural Challenges and Synergies

Norhayati Zakaria
University of Wollongong in Dubai, UAE

Ghadeer Al Safi
University of Wollongong in Dubai, UAE

ABSTRACT

This chapter presents a preliminary understanding of cross-cultural challenges and synergistic experiences of multicultural students engaged in Global Virtual Teams (GVTs). In this case study, we introduce the GVT structure as a novel learning platform which utilizes Computer Mediated Communication (CMC) tools as part of its virtual-based learning. We administer the case study with 30 students (n=30) in the United of Emirates (UAE) who engage in GVTs across the globe—encompassing 26 universities and 22 countries. Qualitative data is collected in the form of documents—reflective reports of the students' experiential learning over a 10-week period. We content analyse the reports based on the thematic analysis with two distinctive categories—cultural challenges and cultural synergies based on the first seven weeks of the experiential learning process. In this study, we find that students experienced challenges such as managing technical difficulty, language barriers, deteriorating motivations, geographical distance, time differences, and non-committed and unresponsive attitude. However, students also experience synergies from the GVTs such as strong relationships and continued friendships, formation of emergent leadership, learned diverse managerial styles and competencies skills, varied use of varied CMC tools, and international exposure to diverse cultures without the need to travel abroad.

DOI: 10.4018/978-1-4666-3966-9.ch010

INTRODUCTION

Global Virtual Teams (GVTs) are becoming the most widespread and innovative working structure in Multinational Corporations (MNCs). GVTs are composed of people from different cultural backgrounds, working at a distance, collaborating using varied communication technologies to achieve their goals, and who often have no historical work relationship (Mohd Yusof & Zakaria, 2012). The availability of new information and communication technologies combined with increasing pressure for globalization is driving the growth of GVTs. In addition, a new social context also arises in GVTs, since the ability to share knowledge is no longer constrained by geographical distance and time.

When considering GVTs, one must recognize such teams differ in many aspects from traditional teams. GVTs fundamentally diverge on two distinct dimensions – the sophistication of their communication tools, and the time spent working apart (Griffith & Neale, 2001; Powell et al., 2004; Fuller, Hardin, & Davidson, 2006; O'Leary & Cummings, 2007). The purest GVT is the one which collaborates while team members are situated in different locales, totally working apart, and depending entirely on computer-mediated communication tools. Thus, there are some inevitable challenges in building a sustainable learning and knowledge-sharing base between diverse members of GVTs. For instance, it is clearly noted in several studies that this type of virtual collaboration results in heightened challenges for organizations to manage due to cross-cultural differences and such teams also differ on managerial requirements and strategies from the onset and throughout the team's life cycle (Maznevski & Chudoba, 2000; Furst, Reeves, Rosen & Blackburn, 2004; Montoya, Massey, & Lockwood, 2011). Yet the advantages of such teamwork continue to be promoted in multinational organizations because of its significant work structure (Araujo & Chidambaram, 2008; David, Newell, & Resende-Santos, 2008; Griffith & Neale, 2001).

Distributed Work Structure

Empirical studies have examined the emergent structure of GVTs, but limited research has fully examined the impact of culture on GVT effectiveness (Evaristo, 2003; Gillam & Oppenheim, 2006; Shachaf, 2008; Zhang, Lowry, Zhou & Fu, 2007; Zhang & Lowry, 2008). The understanding of what is the cross-cultural challenges and how cultural factors influence the effectiveness of GVTs around the world has not received sufficient attention, particularly from scholars in interdisciplinary fields such as information technology and information systems, CMC, cross-cultural management, and international management. The increasing use of GVTs in MNCs strongly implies these and similar emerging work structures are, and will continue to be, heavily dependent on electronically collaboratory tools such as e-mail, videoconferencing, teleconferencing, instant messaging, chat, and many more (Zakaria & Abdul Talib, 2011; Weimann, Hinz, Scott, & Pollock, 2010).

With these tools, additional problems and challenges will emerge when managing a distributed work structure, including the many complex dimensions of cultural values. For instance, problems with communication and collaboration using CMC will surface because not all people are comfortable working with others through a medium with limited non-verbal cues such as email. Yet many people find email an efficient tool to operate across the globe despite its technological limitations (DeLuca & Valacich, 2006). Indeed, with the rise of the global market and the global information society, it is likely that workers will encounter more, and more different, cultures than ever before.

In this chapter, the purpose of our study is to examine the significance of working in GVTs as a new educational platform in providing practical knowledge. We will explore the phenomenon of collaborating with team members who are totally 'strangers' to each other—thus introducing twofold of experiential learning and experiences—cross-cultural challenges encountered and synergies obtained. Based on the idea of 'working with a stranger,' we thus recognize the team members in our case study were engaged in a pure virtual environment. Thus, we anticipate the students will experience learning in GVT which is lived through and, as a result, allows students to obtain knowledge and information. Additionally, it also allows students to obtain experiences while undergoing the process itself, benefitting from the 'hands-on' value. For example, members have never met with one another face-to-face at any point of time–be it prior, during, or after project completion. In essence, this study aim at focusing on the challenges and best practices of virtual-based learning to explore GVTs as a novel educational environment in which to understand participant recruitment, effort coordination, learning and transfer of training to real-life settings, student feedback and challenges, and use of large-scale student collaboration projects for teaching, research, and inter-institutional and professional networking.

BACKGROUND OF STUDY

A Case of Virtual-Based Project

Since this project is the first of its kind in the United Arab Emirates (UAE), our goal was to understand to what extent virtual-based learning imparts practical knowledge to students who can then capitalize on such experience in a future work setting such as in the MNCs. This virtual-based learning project was first launched in the Autumn semester of 2011 in which the team members came from 22 countries and 26 universities[1] (refer to Table 1), thus truly reflecting the cross-cultural component. The primary objective was to offer a 'hands-on' as well as global and virtual experience to the students.

The project was administered by the faculty and instructors on a voluntary basis and participation in the project was completely free for the students and their institutions. In this project, student teams were assigned to a hypothetical consulting company; their company was then approached by a hypothetical multinational corporation with a request to conduct a market analysis and provide suggestions for their next 'big' idea. The following are some of the well-known MNCs used in the study:

- ALDI Einkauf GmbH & Co. oHG., one of the world's largest retailers, www.aldi.com
- BP p.l.c., one of the world's leading oil and gas companies, www.bp.com
- Google Inc., the world's largest IT company, www.google.com
- HSBC Holdings p.l.c., the world's second largest banking and financial services group, www.hsbc.com
- McDonald's Corporation, world's largest restaurant chain, www.mcdonalds.com
- Toyota Motor Corporation, world's largest automobile manufacturer, www.toyota.com
- VF Corporation, world's largest clothing company, www.vfc.com/

Table 1. Participating Countries for the Cross-Cultural Project

Participating Countries	Participating Countries
1. Austria	2. Romania
3. Colombia	4. Lithuania
5. Ecuador	6. Mexico
7. France	8. New Zealand
9. Germany	10. Poland
11. Ghana	12. Romania
13. Indonesia	14. Slovakia
15. India	16. Spain
17. Japan	18. UAE
19. Korea	20. UK
21. Kosovo	22. USA-HI, USA-IL, USA-MA, USA-NC, USA-NJ

- Walt Disney Company, world's largest media conglomerate and entertainment company, www.disney.com

Each of these companies offers a wide range of products and has clients in just about every country around the world. All these companies are public and details on their history, products, corporate structure and earnings are readily available on the Internet. For this project, each GVT was free to choose any one of the abovementioned companies. They were then asked to develop a business proposal for a product or service in which the company of their choice should invest. Teams were free to choose any product or service, whatever offered the greatest economic potential for their client. The product or service could be produced or offered in any location, not necessarily limited to the countries represented by the members of the team.

For the final assignment, teams needed to submit a business plan which provided a general description of the product/service and its development and marketing strategy. The business proposal had to detail the following areas: product/service, target market, production site or service personnel location, market entry mode, staffing, marketing, payment arrangements, capital requirements and other likely challenges. Teams also had to provide an economic justification for the product or service.

QUALITATIVE METHODOLOGY

Case Study

To explore the phenomenon of virtual-based learning in a specific educational setting, we decided to employ a case study methodology. According to Yin (2009), a case study is most appropriate when the researchers need to develop an in-depth or rich understanding of an observed behavior or environment. The case study approach is also an effective methodology when a researcher wishes to gain new insights into a phenomenon. In our research, we wanted to obtain a preliminary understanding of GVTs as a novel platform and structure of working at a distance with diverse cultural backgrounds team members using varied form of CMC.

Data Collection

We collected data in the form of reflective reports written by a total of thirty (30) students based on their early stages in the first seven weeks out of ten weeks of participation in the cross-cultural project. The students underwent five phases or milestones of virtual-based learning experiences which include pre-project survey, establishing contact with teammates, agreement of company and idea for business proposal and write-up of reflective report on GVT experience, business proposal report, and post-project survey. Each milestone carried different report requirements and allocated marks.

In this study, we used a set of qualitative questions to elicit data from the respondents (students) where the purpose was to obtain a preliminary understanding of their first-hand and unique virtual experience in working across a distance and with the diverse cultural backgrounds of the six other team members from 26 participating universities around the globe. The questions were given to the students to enable them to reflect their learning experiences in the GVT environment over the seven week period. Students were asked the following questions specifically on cross-cultural teamwork to explore their perceptions of the synergies as well as the challenges they experienced in this new learning platform:

- What were the most effective cross-cultural teamwork experiences during the project preparation, and why?

- What were the challenges/problems (if any) during the team collaboration and why?
- How did each member contribute to the preparation of the team project?
- What did you learn during the virtual collaboration?
- How could the virtual-based learning been improved—e.g., what would you do differently next time?

Content Analysis

For this study, we conducted content analysis based on their cross-cultural reflections report once they developed the novel idea for their business proposal, and before they submitted their finalized business proposal report. Content analysis is a common and widely used methodology in qualitative study to obtain in-depth understanding of the subject matter through rich descriptions of an observed phenomenon (Krippendorff, 2003). However, it can also be used in the quantitative study with the purpose of evaluating and interpreting the phenomenon under study numerically (i.e., using numbers and figures [Nuendorf, 2001; Weber, 1990]). In this study, we chose to conduct content analysis qualitatively. Specifically, the objective is to provide a detailed description of the GVT experience in relation to cultural challenges and synergistic values. For the data analysis, we first reviewed and content analyzed all 30 essays to obtain the general themes and patterns of the reported experiences. Then we coded the experiences into the abovementioned two categories. To further narrow down the themes, we further sorted the experiences into specific aspects of either challenge or synergistic value. The coding process was developed based on two hierarchical layers:

- **First Layer:** Challenges encountered and synergies obtained
- **Second Layer:** Sub-challenges and sub-synergies

RESULT

Overall, our study found that students reported bilateral experiences when working in GVTs. On one hand, participants experienced varied challenges such as managing technical difficulty, language barriers, deteriorating motivational level over the time span of ten weeks, geographical distance, time differences, and non-committed/unresponsive attitude. But, students also expressed their optimism regarding the multicultural experiences obtained through GVTs, such as of developed relationships and continued friendships even after the semester ends, formation of emergent leadership-- practicing leadership without a formal appointment, learned diverse managerial styles and competencies skills such as planning, organizing and coordinating, varied use of varied CMC tools other than email such as Facebook, Skype, Instant Messaging, Twitter, etc., work in GVT structure, and international exposure to diverse cultures without the need to travel abroad.

Cross-Cultural Challenges

Challenges are inevitable in any group interaction, but this is particularly so when members of the group come from various backgrounds and where the members have no real face-to-face communication or historical background of working together. Our study identified several obstacles faced by GVTs in this cross-cultural project (refer to the summarized finding in Table 2).

First, students expressed difficulty with managing the requisite technology. For example, cases of non-working e-mail addresses delayed initial contact between participants. A few team-members experienced power cuts or outages in their countries which, coupled with inconsistent internet access and fluctuating internet speeds, served as bottlenecks to project progress. Although the majority of the participants were comfortable using common social networking tools such as Facebook, some expressed privacy concerns and

Table 2. Thematic Analysis based on Cross-Cultural Challenges

Cross-Cultural Challenges	Quotations from Documents
1. Managing technical-oriented difficulty— non-working email addres	• "An initial issue faced was couple was members responded late, and one of the members email address was invalid and we could not get in touch."
2. Language barrier	• "Some members have a very hard time understanding and communicating in basic English, which led to a team member not being able to even communicate his proposal of a business idea due to his bad English"
3. Decline of motivation over time	• "Another difficulty was how the excitement seemed to wane as the weeks went by and very little had been done."
4. Non-committed and indifferent attitude, irregular responses	• "Some members barely knew anything about what had to be done and how it is to be done."
5. Geographical distance—working with strangers	• "The international project seems very interesting at the first blank, but it's very complicated to communicate by the people around the world."
6. Time zone differences--Coordinating meeting	• "It is difficult to get everybody online together because of the time difference"

as a result some of them had reservations. They asked the team to choose an alternative mode of communication and collaboration that suited their own preference of working together.

Another difficulty commonly cited by participants in this cross-cultural project was the inconvenience of dealing with different time-zones because the team members originated from seven different countries. Arranging video-conferencing or mere online chat meetings proved to be problematic and challenging. Although a handful of teams managed to schedule meeting times that satisfied everyone, most teams had to contend with waiting for members to reply to messages at their own convenience.

Apart from the time zone differences, another barrier was language. English as a universal language was naturally the language used for communication amongst team members. However, as it was common for a single team to harbor first, second and even third-language speakers, variations in language made it challenging to ensure that everyone was on the same page. Not only did this sometimes cause misunderstanding of the content of messages, but it also discouraged struggling speakers from expressing their ideas and opinions openly.

Students also clearly stated their motivation seemed to decline over time. For example, some of them said that keeping all team members constantly motivated was a difficult task, and even more so over a long duration and without the aid of tangible interaction. Most teams reported very high enthusiasm levels at the start of the project, which eventually declined as they neared the end of the project. A few participants showed non-committal attitudes, evident through irregular responses and indifference during brain-storming sessions. Yet this did not seem to significantly demotivate the participants, who continued working as a team with committed members.

Due to the various countries participating in this project, each member of each team reported to his or her own instructor. This led to misunderstanding of the elements of the project and related deadlines, despite there being a single instructions file which was to be used by all instructors. Issues such as mismatches in time orientation resulted in delayed submission of the proposal, though the milestones were clearly outlined in the first few weeks of the class.

Cross-Cultural Synergies

Generally, students reported being deeply satisfied with their experiences despite the challenges and obstacles along the way (refer to the summarized finding in Table 3). Students felt very fortunate to have had the opportunity to be exposed cross-

Table 3. Thematic Analysis based on Cross-Cultural Synergies

Cross-Cultural Synergies	Quotations from Documents
1. Developed relationships and friendship	• "Rapport building and collaboration came to us naturally as most of my team members shared the same type of enthusiasm and openness to a global atmosphere."
2. Practiced leadership without a formal appointment	• "Our group dynamic is great, in normal circumstances one person assumes leadership based on a variety of characteristics, but since this project has so many elements, there has already been a few leaders from a group as little as 7.
3. Learned new and different management skills	• "People in the group have different skills that when put together is our main strength."
4. Utilized varied form of CMC tools, i.e. Skype, Facebook, Instant messaging	• "Facebook had proved to be an essential tool for group work to be successful, helping us get in touch easier and even vote better and fasting using its embedded voting application."
5. Exposed internationally without travelling across the globe	• "The best thing about working with six different people around the world is that, first; I have never worked with so many different nationalities at once." • I've developed some knowledge about different countries and people whom I've never seen."
6. Acquired competence in working with GVTs structure	• "I also started to learn the way of communicating with different people residing in different parts of the world" • "You get to know their way of working and culture, which makes it easier for yourself to work at your workplace in the future."

culturally without the need to travel. Although Dubai is a melting pot of various cultures, the range of backgrounds in the population is still relatively limited. The experiment exposed participants to individuals from countries with whom they had not previously interacted. Working with new cultures added an extra flavor to the team experience, broadened participants' minds by educating them on lifestyles and work processes different from their own, and most importantly helped dispel previously-held stereotypes about the cultures they were dealing with.

What many participants found the most rewarding segment of the project was the opportunity to form friendships with their team-mates which extended beyond the scope of the project. Most communication between team members seemed to be casual and free-flowing, reflecting informal relationships even from the start of the project. A majority of the participants reported still having their team-members listed as a Facebook friend, with a few continuing to remain in touch with each other after the semester ends.

Students also learned new and different management styles and skills. A GVT necessitates careful planning and management of resources. As a result of the experiment, students gained good practice in handling a wide range of people which will prove useful in their future professional lives. Participants were educated through practical means on how to delegate tasks effectively by making the best use of members' strengths and weaknesses and following up on progress. Apart from basic management skills, student also learned a number of technical competencies. For example, all participants were comfortable using computer-mediated communication tools to contact their teammates, attesting to the technology-driven generation to which they belong. There were no difficulties related to technical know-how with any of the tools chosen, whether it was social networking, e-mail, video-conferencing, voice chat or document sharing.

The most important thing students observed was some of them emerged as leaders in this virtual environment. In the beginning, no leaders were assigned after the random appointment of teams. This left each team with the responsibility of selecting its own leader, whether through actual appointment or spontaneous leadership through natural abilities. A significant number of the students from Dubai showed initiative in leading their teams, which gave them the upper hand in propelling the project forward and keeping the project's progress in control.

FUTURE RESEARCH DIRECTIONS

With the widespread use of computer mediated communication technology tools, GVTs are becoming the most popular and innovative learning structure in many educational institutions. Such teams are composed of members from different cultural backgrounds, working at a distance, collaborating using varied communication technologies to achieve their goals, and often with no historical work relationship. Based on our case study, we found many challenges stem from such a learning structure, yet students also see many advantages to GVTs in the context of the learning environment. With this preliminary understanding, the study has provided us with insights into both the challenges and synergies present when using GVTs as a learning platform. We suggest future research should be undertaken to understand several additional or deeper aspects, such as:

- What are the motivating factors for an educational institution to employ GVTs as part of its practical learning environment?
- How might GVTs provide an opportunity to harness cross-cultural experience among students?
- How might GVTs provide a learning platform for students that will promote collaboration without geographical barriers?

CONCLUSION

This case study offers many valuable insights into whether or not and how educational institutions might promote GVTs as part of learning in order to capture the synergistic values of cross-cultural experiences, as well as give students experience in handling the challenges of a working environment that is prevalent in corporate settings. We have conducted a thematic analysis to identify what students perceived as the challenges and synergistic values of the cross-cultural collaboration project. Although this was the first time the students had participated in a GVT, our exploratory understanding concludes that students reported bilateral experiences encompassing challenging issues such as managing technical difficulty, language barriers, decline of motivation, geographical distance, time differences, non-committed and unresponsive attitude, but they also felt optimistic about several aspects such as formation of relationships and friendships, emergent leadership, managerial competencies, varied use of CMC, work in GVT structure, and international exposure to diverse cultures.

REFERENCES

Araujo, A. L., & Chidambaram, L. (2008). A Dynamic Perspective of Trust in Virtual Teams: The Role of Task, Technology, and Time. *International Journal of Networking and Virtual Organizations*, *5*(1), 4–16. doi:10.1504/IJNVO.2008.015995.

David, G. C., Newell, S., & Resende-Santos, J. O. (2008). Integrated collaboration across distributed sites: The perils of process and the promise of practice. *Journal of Information Technology*, *23*(1), 44–54. doi:10.1057/palgrave.jit.2000126.

DeLuca, D., & Valacich, J. S. (2006). Virtual teams in and out of synchronicity. *Information Technology & People*, *19*(4), 323–344. doi:10.1108/09593840610718027.

Evaristo, R. (2003). The management of distributed projects across cultures. *Journal of Global Information Management*, *11*(4), 58–70. doi:10.4018/jgim.2003100104.

Fuller, M., Hardin, A., & Davison, R. (2006). Efficacy. *Journal of Management Information Systems*, *23*(3), 209–235. doi:10.2753/MIS0742-1222230308.

Furst, S. A., Reeves, M., Rosen, B., & Blackburn, R. S. (2004). Managing the life cycle of virtual teams. *The Academy of Management Executive*, *18*(2), 6–20. doi:10.5465/AME.2004.13837468.

Gillam, C., & Oppenheim, C. (2006). Reviewing the Impact of Virtual Teams in the Information Age. *Journal of Information Science*, *32*(2), 160–175. doi:10.1177/0165551506062328.

Griffith, T. L., & Neale, M. A. (2001). Information processing in traditional, hybrid, and virtual teams: From nascent knowledge to transactive memory. In Staw, B., & Sutton, R. (Eds.), *Research in organizational behavior* (pp. 379–421). Stamford, CT: JAI Press. doi:10.1016/S0191-3085(01)23009-3.

Javenpaa, S. L., & Leidner, D. E. (1998). Communication and trust in global virtual teams. *Organization Science*, *10*(6), 791–815. doi:10.1287/orsc.10.6.791.

Krippendorff, K. (2003). *Content Analysis: An Introduction to Its Methodology*. Thousand Oaks, CA: Sage Publications.

Maznevski, M. L., & Chudoba, K. M. (2000). Bridging space over time: Global virtual team dynamics and effectiveness. *Organization Science*, *11*(5), 473–492. doi:10.1287/orsc.11.5.473.15200.

Mohd Yusof, S. A., & Zakaria, N. (2012). Exploring the State of Discipline on the Formation of Swift Trust within Global Virtual Teams. In *Proceedings of 45th Hawaii International Conference on System Sciences*. Hawaii: IEEE.

Montoya, M., Massey, A. P., & Lockwood, N. S. (2011). 3D Collaborative Virtual Environments: Exploring the Link between Collaborative Behaviors and Team Performance. *Decision Sciences*, *42*(2), 451–476. doi:10.1111/j.1540-5915.2011.00318.x.

Neuendorf, K. A. (2001). *The Content Analysis Guidebook*. Thousand Oaks, CA: Sage Publications.

O'Leary, M. B., & Cummings, J. N. (2007). The spatial, temporal and configurational characteristics of geographic dispersion of teams. *Management Information Systems Quarterly*, *31*(3), 433–452.

Powell, A., Piccoli, G., & Ives, B. (2004). Virtual teams: A review of current literature and directions for future research. *The Data Base for Advances in Information Systems*, *35*(1), 6–36. doi:10.1145/968464.968467.

Shachaf, P. (2008). Cultural diversity and information communication technology impacts on global virtual teams: An exploratory study. *Information & Management*, *45*, 131–142. doi:10.1016/j.im.2007.12.003.

Weber, R. P. (1990). Basic Content Analysis (Quantitative Applications in the Social Sciences) (2nd. ed.). Thousand Oaks, CA: Sage Publications.

Weimann, P., Hinz, C., Scott, E., & Pollock, M. (2010). Changing the Communication Culture of Distributed Teams in a World Where Communication is Neither Perfect nor Complete. *The Electronic Journal Information Systems Evaluation*, *13*(2), 187–196.

Yin, R. (2009). *Case Study Research: Design and Methods* (4th ed.). Thousand Oaks: Sage Publications.

Zakaria, N., & Abdul Talib, A. N. (2011). What Did You Say? Cross-Cultural Analysis of the Distributive Communicative Behaviors of Global Virtual Teams. In *Proceedings of International Conference on Computational Aspects of Social Networks*. Salamanca, Spain: IEEE.

Zhang, D., & Lowry, P. J. (2008). Issues, Limitations and Opportunities in Cross-Cultural Research on Collaborative Software in Information Systems. *Journal of Global Information Management*, *16*(1), 61–92. doi:10.4018/jgim.2008010103.

Zhang, D., Lowry, P. J., Zhou, L., & Fu, X. (2007). The Impact of Individualism-Collectivism, Social Presence and Group Diversity on Group Decision making under Majority Influence. *Journal of Management Information Systems*, *23*(4), 53–80. doi:10.2753/MIS0742-1222230404.

KEY TERMS AND DEFINITIONS

Case Study: A research methodology that is often used to obtain in-depth insights about a phenomenon, individual or organization. It is a powerful method when such phenomenon offers unique and interesting aspects to investigate.

Culture: Shared values, beliefs, attitudes, norms and practices of a group people who work together. Culture is a collective phenomenon and it affects people at a group level, and not an individual level.

Content Analysis: It is widely used in qualitative method to analyze secondary data in the form of text such as interview transcriptions, newspapers, books, and/or manuscripts.

Computer Mediated Communication Technology: Use of computer technology with strong function for communication and collaboration at workplace.

Experiential Learning: Learning experiences that is lived through and as a result allows people to obtain knowledge and information. In addition, it also allows people to obtain experiences while undergoing the process itself, benefitting from the 'hands-on' value.

Global Virtual Teams: A global virtual team is a geographically dispersed team, has diverse cultural backgrounds, communicates and collaborates using information communication technologies, and has no prior history of working together.

ENDNOTES

1. To protect the confidentiality and identity of the universities who participated in this project, we will not disclose the name of the universities. However, we are only able to disclose the participating countries in this cross-culture project as to highlight the range of team members' diversity and degree of cultural distance of the participating countries in terms of cross-cultural differences.

Chapter 11
Industrial and Organizational (I/O) Psychology:
The Roles and Purposes of I/O Practitioners in Global Businesses

Ben Tran
Alliant International University, USA

ABSTRACT

An Industrial and Organizational (I/O) psychologist is commonly referred to as an I/O practitioner and as an I/O consultant. I/O psychology is the branch of psychology concerned with the application of psychological principles in the workplace. To practitioners, I/O psychology is the application or extension of psychological methods and principles to the solution of organizational and workplace problems, both in the domestic and international arenas. Most commonly, I/O psychology is concerned with those problems caused by human performance and those which affect human performance within organizational contexts. As such, I/O psychologists employ psychological measurement and research findings related to human abilities, motivation, perception, and learning in seeking to improve the fit between the needs of the work organization and those of the people who populate it. Thus, an I/O psychologist plays a paramount role in successful global ventures by addressing two key factors—culture and behavior—resulting in positive return-on-investment (ROI).

DOI: 10.4018/978-1-4666-3966-9.ch011

INTRODUCTION

The globalization of markets refers to the merging of historically distinct and separate national markets into one huge global marketplace. Falling barriers to cross-border trade have made it easier to sell internationally. It has been argued for some time the tastes and preferences of consumers in different nations are beginning to converge on some global norm, thereby helping to create a global market (Levitt, 1983). Used here, globalization refers to the shift toward a more integrated and interdependent world economy. Globalization has two main components: the globalization of markets and the globalization of production.

In globalization, challenges emerge in the process as firms engage in international trade or investment. The action of firms engaging in international trade or investment is known as international business. A firm does not need to become a multinational enterprise, investing directly in operations in other countries, to engage in international business, although multinational enterprises are international businesses. All that a firm must do is export to or import from products in other countries. As the world shifts toward a truly integrated global economy, more firms, both large and small, are becoming international businesses. As organizations increasingly engage in international businesses, it means managers need to recognize the task of managing an international business differs from that of managing a purely domestic business in numerous ways. At the most fundamental level, the differences arise in culture, political systems, economic systems, legal systems, and levels of economic development. Despite all the talk about the emerging global village, and despite the trend toward globalization of markets and production, many of these differences are very profound and enduring. One of the key factors that organizations quite often ignore is the role and purpose of an industrial and organizational (I/O) psychologist in international businesses.

International business has been well-analyzed and studied through the perspectives of business and international business practitioners and business and international business programs within academic settings. However, there is a lack of perspective and voice from industrial and organizational practitioners regarding the detrimental role industrial and organizational practitioners play in international business. The purpose of this chapter is two-fold: 1) to delve into the roles and purposes of I/O psychology in international business; 2) to address one of the most detrimental barriers in international business which has evaded organizations and international business practitioners—culture. In so doing, this chapter will cover: international business, the roles and purposes of I/O psychology in international business, the history of I/O psychology, and recommendations for international businesses and international organizations that do not have an internal department of industrial and organizational practitioners.

The purpose of this chapter serves two intentions, with the primary one being scholar-practitioners who have qualified reference material regarding the subject matter, and the secondary one being business executives and undergraduate/graduate business students who require the same reference material. I proposed this chapter also serves an additional intention, being scholars-scholars focused on those scholars who will reflect upon the referenced knowledge and information, and further contribute to this area via future research, and thus utilized by future scholars and practitioners. Taking these three intentions into consideration, I objectively realized and acknowledged that the degrees and levels of acceptance from these candidates[1] in turn, do and will indeed vary. Upon objectively accepting the fact that these candidates' knowledge regarding industrial and organizational psychology as a field of study, and industrial and organizational psychologists as practitioners in the field of business and global business ventures, a detailed but brief background of industrial and organizational psychology necessary.

The reason for the necessity for a detailed but brief background of industrial and organizational psychology is detrimental is because the history (and system) of any field is more often than not deemed unnecessary, thus it lacks coverage in academia. For example, the histories of business[2] as a field of study, and the history of psychology, particularly industrial and organizational psychology as a field of study, more often than not, are excluded in academia. As George Santayana, a prominent philosopher once said, "Those who cannot learn from history are doomed to repeat it." To avoid misunderstandings and misassumptions regarding the nature of industrial and organization psychology, who industrial and organizational practitioners are, and how industrial and organizational practitioners can and do contribute to global business ventures, a detailed but brief background of the field is necessary.

INTERNATIONAL BUSINESS: STRATEGIC HUMAN RESOURCE MANAGEMENT

In the arena of international business, Strategic Human Resource Management (SHRM) has existed for a relatively short period of time (Devanna, Fombrum, & Tuchy, 1981; Lengnick-Hall, & Lengnick-Hall, 1988; Wright, 1998). However, several of the concepts underlying SHRM have some longer history. For example, notions of utility in personnel selection (Brogden, 1949) were created more than 50 years ago to depict how and when a selection device would demonstrate value in improving the quality of the workforce over what was then currently the case. Similarly, the logic utility and cost/benefit analysis have become the basis for assessing the value of any intervention affecting the organization's so-called human capital. However, the difference is the unit of analysis is not just the pool of applicants or a personnel initiative, but rather that of the organizations themselves.

Expatriates

Businesses typically develop in four phases: domestic, international, multinational, and global (Adler & Gunderson, 2007). Today, there are fewer organizations competing solely on a domestic basis, and more are operating globally in one form or another. Electronic media and decreased transportation costs allow even small businesses to compete internationally (Furnham, 1977), and increased competitive pressures frequently require a global presence even if a firm seek to remain primarily domestic. This expanding global reach of many organizations has increased interest in the issues of expatriate management (Black & Gregersen, 1999; Toh & DeNisi, 2005).

Expatriates are home country nationals sent abroad by the parent company to live and work temporarily in another country (Tran, 2008). In the initial stages of international expansion, it is quite common to send expatriates to oversee the development of appropriate systems and procedures consistent with the parent company's approach and outlook. While subsequent decisions on the extent of use of expatriates are a function of the nature of the business, the country in which the subsidiary operates, and the culture of the parent country, they still require in even advanced stages of international development a home country presence in many cases. Therefore, for many organizations sending expatriates abroad to develop global competencies is consistent with their overall SHRM plan. In general, expatriates find the position to offer developmental experiences and report having gained tangible skills that are value-added for their organizations. Oddou and Mendenhall (1991) surveyed expatriates and discovered 90% report an increase in their global perspectives, 80% report being able to communicate more effectively with people from culturally diverse backgrounds, and 80% are better able to comprehend business trends.

Nevertheless, original work on the management of expatriates focused to a great extent on the cost of a *failure* in a global assignment. Failure was typically defined as an *early return* to the home country prior to the time originally planned (Tran, 2008). Early returns were generally estimated to be very high, around 25%-40%, or even higher per year (Tran, 2008). Furthermore, it was frequently argued these early returns were very expensive (Harris & Brewster, 1999), and this was the basis for a focus on the cross-cultural adjustment of the expatriate and his/her family to the international assignment (Copeland & Griggs, 1985; Mendenhall & Oddou, 1985; Tran, 2008).

Cross-Cultural Adjustment

Over the past 30 years of research on cross-cultural adjustment, a large number of substitute definitions of *cross-cultural adjustment* have been used. Cross-cultural adjustment has been defined as the individual's affective psychological response to the new environment and its variables (Black, 1990). Therefore, the cross-cultural adjustment is an internal, psychological, emotional state which should be measured from the perspective of the individual experiencing foreign culture (Black, 1990; Searle & Ward, 1990). However, cross-cultural adjustment is defined as the process of adaptation to living and working in a foreign culture. It is the perceived degree of psychological comfort and familiarity a person has with the new host culture (Black, 1988; Black & Mendenhall, 1991). Recent conceptualizations of the contrast have focused attention on three specific facets of cross-cultural adjustment.

The first facet is work adjustment involving the adaptation to new job tasks, work roles, and the new work environment. Work adjustment is aided by similarities in procedures, policies, and task requirements between the parent company and host subsidiary abroad (Black, Gregersen, Mendenhall, & Stroh, 1999). The second facet is interaction adjustment, which involves the comfort achieved in interacting with host nationals in both work and non-work situations. Black et al., (1999) argued that interaction adjustment is the most difficult of the three facets to achieve. The third facets is general adjustment, which involves the overall adaptation to living in the foreign culture (Black, 1988) and comprises factors such as housing conditions, health care, and cost of living (Black & Stevens, 1989).

The process of cross-cultural adjustment can be stressful because there is the insecurity and ambiguity of not knowing what is appropriate, coupled with a potential inability to understand feedback from the environment due to a lack of knowledge of language or culture (Black & Gregersen, 1991; Louis, 1980). During the process of cross-cultural adjustment, uncertainty in the environment is reduced (Black, 1988; Black & Gregersen, 1991; Church, 1982). In relation to the criterion of premature termination of an assignment, an expatriate who is unable to adjust would be feeling insurmountable stress and would feel the need to return home (Tung, 1981). In relation to the criterion of work performance, cross-cultural adjustment enables expatriates to develop effective working relationships with host nationals, and to interpret their host national colleagues' behaviors, gestures, and stories. In some preliminary research, cross-cultural adjustment has been found to be a predictor of success in expatriate assignment (Black, Gregersen, & Mendenhll, 1992).

Examination of the international selection literature reveals a mismatch between theory and practice, with extensive lists of theoretical criteria relating to effective international expatriates, most of which resemble a cross-cultural *wish list* in respect of the vast array of skills and abilities required. Selection processes are equally depicted as both formal and professional. However, the level of theory of international expatriate selection reflects actual practice has been questioned (Brewster, 1991). More often than not, the selection process is decided by senior management, line managers in the country of origin, and line managers in the destination country—not by human resources through a set of formal assessment and selection processes (Brewster, 1991; Tran, 2008).

Selection criteria: The theory. Research into selection criteria for international assignments shows a split between theory and practice. In surveys asking for general views on what makes effective expatriates, the criteria mentioned as being critical differ from those reported as being used in practice. Phillips (1992) suggests there is little or no difference between the personal qualities required for success in managing domestic or international business, but successful development of international business demands a higher level of skills and qualities. This is because expatriates working abroad will be involved in a wider range of activities, roles and responsibilities than those required in the home market, which are technical competence at work, personality traits/attributes, and interpersonal social skills and personal and family situations (Forster & Johnsen, 1996; Harris & Brewster, 1999; Tung, 1982; Torbiorn, 1982).

Selection criteria: The practice. Given the emphasis on interpersonal skills in management theory, it is somewhat surprising to find evidence in the research into current practices of Multinational Corporations (MNCs) of the continuing adoption of more traditional criteria for selection of expatriates. Brewster's 1988 survey of international personnel executives from European multinational corporations identified the following top criteria used to select expatriates: technical expertise, language, family support, potential, knowing company systems, experience, marital status, medical status, independence, and motivation. Likewise, in the Ashridge survey (1989-1990), the top factors were identified as: technical skills/expertise for the job, potential, knowledge of company systems, understanding the market and customers, language, necessary part of career path, family support, knowledge/understanding of culture good (Barham & Devine, 1991). Nevertheless, the only criteria MNCs seek is technical expertise, whereas human resource does not assess for any of the other factors identified.

INDUSTRIAL AND ORGANIZATIONAL PSYCHOLOGY

An industrial and organizational (I/O) psychologist in the USA is commonly referred to as an I/O consultant and as an I/O practitioner. I/O psychology is the branch of psychology concerned with the application of psychological principles in the workplace (Figure 1). To practitioners[3], I/O psychology is the application or extension of psychological methods and principles to the solution of organizational and workplace problems, both in the domestic and international arenas. Most commonly, I/O psychology is concerned with those problems caused by human performance and those which affect human performance within organizational contexts. As such, I/O psychologists employ psychological measurement and research findings related to human abilities, motivation, perception, and learning in seeking to improve the fit between the needs of the work organization and those of the people who populate it. To researchers, I/O psychology is known as the study of human behavior in organizations. The behaviors of interest contribute to the effectiveness of organizational functioning, the satisfaction and well-being of those who populate the organizations, or both. These behaviors and the people who exhibit them exist in a dynamic open system (Katz & Kahn, 1978). I/O psychology differs from other psychology subfields in the settings where it is practiced, in its content, and in its approach. However, it does not differ in its reliance on the scientific method for its theories and research. I/O psychology is second only to clinical psychology in the number of practitioners. I/O psychologists are mostly found in four sectors of the economy: industry, universities, government, and consulting firms.

Settings

I/O psychology is defined more clearly by where it happens than by what I/O psychologists actually do. I/O psychology is practiced in work settings, just as school psychology is practiced in educational settings. But even though the context in which research and application are carried out may be unique, I/O psychology makes use of the findings of many other branches of psychology. In fact, much work of the I/O psychologist involves adapting or extending the basic principles of other specialty areas of psychology to the work setting.

Selection, assessment, and training. According to Tran (2008), international corporations that are involved in global business ventures and either do not have an I/O practitioner or do not utilize an industrial and organizational practitioner are experiencing detrimental failures. Specifically, Tran (2008) assessed U.S. high-tech companies which are based in the country and have locations outside of the U.S., or are involved in global business ventures. Based on Tran's study (2008), U.S. high-tech companies who are utilizing their expatriates based solely on these expatriates' networks and these expatriates' direct supervisor's and mentor's recommendations, and not through the corporation's I/O practitioners, are experiencing failed ventures. One dimension of these failures is the enormous price that corporations pay due to selecting inappropriate expatriates (Tung, 1981).

Research estimates U.S. firms lose US$2 billion annually in direct costs associated with failed overseas assignments. The direct costs of expatriate problems include loss of business and company reputation, failed negotiations, expatriate depression and loss of self-esteem, and family dysfunction (Black, 1988; Borstorff, Harris, Field, & Giles, 1997). Direct costs of returning a failed expatriate home and finding a replacement range between US$50,000 and US$200,000 (Black & Mendenhall, 1990). Some claim the cost is even higher ranging from US$55,000 to US$250,000 (Copeland & Briggs, 1985; Tung, 1982; Wederspahn, 1992; Zeira & Banai, 1985).

The significant rate of premature returns of expatriates resulting from poor initial selection is very costly for both the company and the expatriate (Baliga & Baker, 1985; Black, 1988; Black & Mendenhall, 1990; Borstorff, Harris, Field, & Giles, 1997; Copeland & Briggs, 1985; McDonald, 1993; Poe, 2002; Talbott, 1996; Tung, 1981; 1982; 1988; Wederspahn, 1992; Zeira & Banai, 1985). Research indicated 25% to 40% of expatriates posted in developed countries return early (Black, Gregersen, Mendenhall, & Stroh, 1999; Shay & Tracey, 1997); other studies indicate the rates are even higher, with 15% to 70% returning early (Copeland & Griggs, 1985; Mendenhall, Dunbar, & Oddou, 1987). That number is closer to 70% for individuals posted in developing countries (Black et al., 1999; Shay & Tracey, 1997).

Global business ethics. Some companies without an I/O practitioner on board who recognizes cultural differences simply accept whatever prevails in the host country. This is an error as it exposes the company—and its reputation—to corruption and public affairs disasters, and because it misses the opportunity to find the "glue" which cements morale and cooperative strategy. In the face of such conflicting and confusing circumstances, the application of Integrative Social Contracts Theory (ISCT)[4] categories to global problems is helpful (Donaldson & Dunfee, 2001). ISCT can provide a practical guide for corporations operating globally.

In particular, according to Donaldson and Dunfee (2001), ISCT demonstrates how cutting the Gordian knot of international business ethics means utilizing two key aspects of ISCT: hypernorms and microsocial contracts. First, it is important to make use of hypernorms, especially the structural hypernorm of necessary social efficiency[5]. Second, many problems dissolve when relevant microsocial contracts are carefully identified and the proper priority is established among them. The Interactive type alone satisfies

ISCT by acknowledging both universal moral limits and the ability of communities to set moral standards of their own. It balances better than the other types a need to retain local identity with the acknowledgement of values that transcend individual communities.

Content and System Approach

The content of I/O psychology helps define it as a branch of psychology more than anything else. The I/O psychologist possesses three primary areas of interest: personnel psychology, organizational psychology, and human factors (also known as ergonomic or human engineering) psychology. However, in practice the people who do the actual work and operate in the work environment define a larger entity which might best be labeled the sociotechnical system (Daft, 2001, p. 225; Hollway, 2000; Jones, 2004, p. 310). Changes made in one part of the system usually affect other parts of the system. Changing the design of a task so that it is more complex is a human factor activity and may have a substantial impact on the satisfaction that a worker derives from that task (an organizational issue), and who might do best at that task, (a personnel psychology matter). For example, consider the simple act of computerizing what had previously been a manual task. On the surface, this might appear to be a human factor change since it is a modification of the tools of the job. However, the new technology also changes other aspects of the work. Additionally, the introduction of the computer changes the skill and ability mix necessary for success on the job. Unless the worker is capable of interacting effectively with the hardware and software of the computer system, he or she is likely to experience performance problems and accompanying feelings of frustration. Finally, supervisors might interact with employees by sending messages via e-mail rather than by talking directly with them, losing a personal element. In short, computerizing a function is actually much more complex and dynamic than it seems on the surface.

The fact that the three areas of I/O psychology are not mutually exclusive is both a burden and an opportunity for I/O psychologists. The opportunity lies in having several options for dealing with real-world problems. The psychologist might suggest changing the methods used to select or train workers. Any or all of these methods might be effective in reducing accidents or improving productivity. In all likelihood, the most effective intervention would combine elements of all approaches.

*Occupational information network (o*net).* A major contribution of industrial and organizational psychology to human behavior at work has been in the form of taxonomies and structures for describing the world of work (e.g. Dictionary of Occupational Titles). In the early 1990s, the U.S. Department of Labor convened a panel of industrial and organizational psychologists to plan the development of a database which would eventually replace the Dictionary of Occupational Titles as the primary information source for jobs in the U.S. economy. This panel designed a plan for a content model that could describe jobs according to both person and job requirements (Advisory Panel for the Dictionary of Occupational Titles, 1993; Campion, Gowing, Lancaster, & Pearlman, 1994). In fact, the ultimate goal was to obtain content model ratings on all occupations in the U.S. economy to make the O*NET maximally useful (Borman, Klimoski, & Ilgen, 2003; Peterson, Mumford, Borman, Jeanneret, & Fleishman, 1999; Peterson, Mumford, Borman, Jeanneret, Fleishman, Levin, Campion, Mayfield, Silver, & Dye, 2001; Tran, 2008).

Culture. Culture can explain differences in business dress and its meaning. Culture is a way of life for a group of people. In 1952, researchers identified more than 160 definitions of culture (Kroeber & Kluckhohn, 1991). Taylor (1871a; 1871b, p. 1) proposed one of the earliest definitions as "that complex whole which includes knowledge, belief, art, morals, law, custom, and any other capabilities and habits acquired by man as a member of society." Ferraro's (1994, p. 17) more recent and simpler definition is "everything that people have, think, and do as members of society." Knowing the basic assumptions of a culture provides insight into the principles on which the other levels rest[6].

INDUSTRIAL AND ORGANIZATIONAL PSYCHOLOGY'S TECHNOLOGICAL INFLUENCES IN GLOBAL BUSINESS

I/O psychology's technological influences in global businesses occur in two ways: industrial and organizational. The first is computer-based job analysis instrument. The second is leadership in a changing workplace.

Industrial Psychology's Technological Influences in Global Business

The Work Profiling System (WPS) (Saville & Holdsworth Limited, 2001) is an example of how the data collection and interpretation process of job analysis can be streamlined, reducing costs to the organization, minimizing distractions to the subject matter experts (SMEs), and increasing the speed and accuracy of the process. Additional information about the system can be found on the website of SHL USA, the consulting firm which developed and administers the WPS (http://www.shlusa.com). According to Landy and Conte (2004), the WPS uses three databases which are interrelated through an expert computer system employing sophisticated algorithms to weigh and integrate information from databases. The first database is derived from responses to a structured questionnaire for assessing the actual work performed in the job in question. The second database is constructed from a comprehensive model of the human attributes necessary to perform those tasks. The third database includes relevant assessment methods to tap the human attributes identified as important for the job.

According to Landy and Conte (2004), computer-based job analysis systems provide a number of advantages (Caric, Tuba, & Moisil, N. Y.). The first is time and convenience to the employer. SMEs need not be assembled in one spot at one time as is often the case with traditional job analysis. SMEs can work from their desks at their own pace and submit their responses electronically. The second advantage is the efficiency with which the expert system can create reports. The reports can serve a wide range of purposes, from individual goal-setting and performance feedback to elaborate person-job matches to support selection and placement strategies. Finally, since systems like this use the same taxonomies and processes across jobs, they make it easier to understand job similarities and career paths, thus facilitating vocational counseling and long-term strategic HR planning in the form of replacement charts for key positions. Of course, possible shortcomings of such systems are similar to those shortcomings which would be apparent with more traditional paper- and pencil-based systems. If the data being collected is poor, or if the task or human attribute taxonomies are flawed or irrelevant, then the results, reports, and decisions made on the basis of that system will also be flawed or irrelevant.

ORGANIZATIONAL PSYCHOLOGY'S TECHNOLOGICAL INFLUENCES IN GLOBAL BUSINESS

Changes in the workplace in the past two decades have been substantial. One consequence of the changes is a very different work environment for leaders, workers, and expatriates. Some of the more salient changes with respect to the challenge of global businesses are teams/groups, virtual teams, and telecommuting.

Teams/Groups. Teams and groups are increasingly popular in today's workplace. There are fewer and fewer single contributors. While individual interactions between a worker and a manager still take place, there are also interactions between managers and teams/groups. It is no longer sufficient for a leader to concentrate on influencing individual work group members one by one. The team or group is a separate entity and must be considered independent of its members.

Virtual Team. Virtual teams present additional challenges beyond those found in a more traditional team scenario. A virtual team consists of geographically or organizationally dispersed members brought together through "a combination of telecommunications and information technologies to accomplish an organizational task (Townsend, DeMarie, & Hendrickson, 1998, p. 17). As Bell and Kozlowski (2002) highlighted, this presents novel challenges for a leader, including the socialization of new team members and monitoring of the progress of the teams as they conduct their work. Bell and Kozlowski (2002) hypothesized that as the work of a virtual team becomes more complex, the communications will need to be more frequent and intense.

By definition, much of this increased communication will not take place in a face-to-face scenario. This will make the monitoring function of the leader increasingly difficult and will also require virtual teams to become more self-managing than leader directed. For example, software programmers, software engineers, and quality assurance (QA) individuals from Adobe, Microsoft, Google, and Yahoo, often work in virtual teams, and quite often work in more than one virtual team in global companies.

Telecommuting. The discussion of virtual teams anticipates a related issue. An increasing number of employees work from home part or all of the workweek. This is referred to as telecommuting or dispersed work (Adams, 2001). As with virtual teams, telecommuting will present monitoring and communication challenges for leaders. When Lyndon Johnson was majority leader in the U.S. Senate and then U.S. President, he used his imposing physical presence as a way to influence individuals (Caro, 2002). Johnson would not have been able to use that advantage had he been communicating by telephone, electronic-mail, or fax. Dispersed work comes in many different forms (Adams, 2001). Additionally, there are drop-in work centers located close to employees' homes, and locations which provide access to the internet that will convert electronic devices (such as a laptop, notebook, and tabulate) into a personal work station. Many offices now have *unassigned* work spaces for use by employees who travel often and use regional or branch facilities to complete their work.

BRIEF HISTORY OF INDUSTRIAL AND ORGANIZATIONAL PSYCHOLOGY

The history of industrial and organizational (I/O) psychology consists of two perspectives: macro and micro. From a macro perspective, according to Landy and Conte (2004), the evolution of I/O psychology in the U.S. parallels the development of I/O psychology in other countries such as England (Chmiel, 2000; Shimmin & Wallis, 1994), Australia, Germany, the Netherlands (Shimmin & van Strien, 1998; van Drunen & van Strien, 1999; van Strien, 1998), and eastern European countries such as Romania (Pitariu, 1992; Rosca & Voicu, 1982). Unfortunately for many countries, there is no English version of the development of I/O psychology. However, for interested readers one of the first modern American I/O psychologists, Morris Viteles, did an excellent job of describing the status of I/O psychology around the world during the period 1922 – 1932 (Viteles, 1926; 1928; 1930; 1932). Arthur Kornhauser (1929) also provided a description of I/O psychology in England and Germany.

From a micro perspective, the focus of the history of I/O psychology is the U.S. Although psychology as a science was born in the late 19th century, various specialty areas, including I/O psychology, appeared somewhat later. Bryan and Harter[7] (1897) published the first paper describing the study and application of psychology to work activities, while learning Morse code telegraphic, coined the term industrial psychology by mistake which was thus the birth of industrial psychology. Thereafter, in the beginning of the 1960s, organizational psychology began to enter the area of industrial psychology and as such, special emphasis was given to the organizational inputs in the industrial situation. In the 1970s, the division of industrial psychology was renamed as the division of industrial and organizational psychology[8].

There are four founding figures in I/O psychology: Hugo Munsterberg[9], Frederick Winslow Taylor[10], Walter Dill Scott[11], and Lillian Gilbreth[12]. Wilhelm Wundt[13] was seldom mentioned and Frank Bunker Gilbreth[14] was rarely mentioned in the history of I/O psychology. The first and the most reputable, Hugo Munsterberg, was one of the earliest practitioners of I/O psychology, and an original founder of the American Psychological Associate in 1892. By 1910, Munsterberg had written the first text in I/O psychology. The first Doctor of Philosophy (Ph.D.) granted in I/O psychology was presented in 1915 to Lillian Gilbreth by Brown University. I/O psychologist has three primary areas of interest: personnel psychology, organizational psychology, and human factors (ergonomics or human engineering) psychology.

The field of I/O psychology is relatively new compared to the field of psychology in general and other scientific disciplines such as physics. Most of the early researchers were trained as experimental psychologists, who then began fitting their applied interests into their experimental background. In general, industrial psychology focuses on the measurement of job requirements and individuals' knowledge, skills, and abilities, and performance so as to match individuals with suitable jobs. Organizational psychology is more theoretical and considers psychological processes such as motivation and work attitudes. Organizational psychologists also study phenomenon which occur at a level higher than the individual, such as group and organizational climates, as well as organizational change and development. Studying phenomenon at these higher levels of analysis or focus is called macro research while studying phenomenon that occurs at an individual level is called micro research (Figure 2).

Personnel Psychology

Personnel psychology was the first of the three I/O subfields to appear. Personnel psychology is also commonly known as occupational psychology (Hollway, 2000) and occupational psychology was once known as vocational psychology (Hollway, 2000, p. 6). The emergence of this subfield was the result of several forces, the foremost being psychology's increased interest in measuring and recording individual differences. In other words, personnel psychology determines whether or not individuals possess the knowledge, skills, abilities and personality, also commonly known as other characteristics (Schneider & Schmitt, 1986, p. 53; Tran, 2008), needed to perform various types of work effectively. This subarea of I/O psychology is concerned with the broad topic of employment testing and with such related topics as job training, test validation, interviewing, and employment discrimination. Personnel psychologists see the job or work environment as the given and the population of individuals who might be workers as the variable factor. Personnel psychologists' goal is to find the workers who have the right attributes to fit the demands of the job.

When the United States entered World War I, intelligence testing was introduced as a method of identifying those recruits with the greatest likelihood of becoming successful officers, as well as steering non-officers into specialties for which they were best suited (Yerkes, 1921). The respectability acquired by psychological testing from this wartime application carried over into industry following the war, and modern personnel psychology emerged. By 1932, there were dozens of texts describing the goals and methods of personnel psychology (Burtt, 1929; Viteles, 1932). Similar pressures for mass testing exerted by World War II further enhanced the importance of personnel testing, which retains a prominent role in I/O psychology today.

Organizational Psychology

Organizational psychology is concerned with how people adapt emotionally and socially to working in complex motivation, job satisfaction, leadership, organizational culture, teamwork, and related topics (Hollway, 2000; Salvendy, 2012). From this perspective, the concern of the I/O psychologist is to understand the factors which contribute to the right emotional fit between people and their work. Eighty years ago, managers believed money was the only work motivator. The modern I/O psychologist concentrates on making the job itself more interesting, rather than getting workers to forget how boring the work actually is by paying them higher wages. Other topics pursued by organizational psychologists are the relationships between work and non-work, such as family life (Watanabe, Takahashi, & Minami, 1997; Zedeck, 1997), the creation of cohesive workgroups within increasingly ethnically diverse workplaces, and the complexities of leadership in a dynamic workplace.

As mentioned above, the prevailing belief in the early part of the 20th century was that money was the only motivator in business and industry, a belief formalized by the theory of Frederick Winslow Taylor (1911), variously known as scientific management (Drucker, 1974; Hollway, 2000), or Taylorism. The Taylorists' views were eventually undermined by some influential experiments conducted at a Western Electric facility near Chicago in 1930 (Hollway, 2000; Roethlisberger & Dickson, 1939). Thereafter, a new paradigm was introduced to replace scientific management, and the human relations movement was launched (Drucker, 1974; Hollway, 2000). This movement proposed that many factors beyond pay level contributed to the satisfaction and productivity of workers and that these factors can be identified in the attitudes that workers hold toward various aspects of their work. The implication was that supervisors should be more sensitive to the feelings of workers as a way of improving productivity. The human relations movement gave birth to 60 years of interests in job satisfaction, work motivation, and leadership, areas of study that remain important today (Drucker, 1974; Hollway, 2000). In other words, organizational psychology is concerned with the human relations aspects of work. Organizational psychologists are interested in how organizational factors influence workers' social and emotional functional.

Work motivation. Employers and I/O psychologists have a particular interest in motivational principles as they apply in the work setting. As such, the two most popular theories of work motivation in the 1960s were Frederick Herzberg's (1966) job enrichment theory and the application of B. F. Skinner's (1969) reinforcement theory to work settings. Herzberg proposed the nature of the work is motivating in and of itself beyond any rewards. Herzberg prescription for increasing the motivation of a worker is to enrich the job by challenges. He conceded that external rewards such as money and praise are also necessary to attract and keep a worker, but ultimately, he proposed that motivation depends on whether the job is interesting. The implications of Skinner's reinforcement theory are just the opposite. Reinforcement theory postulates that jobs acquire interest only through their associates with extrinsic or external rewards. Attempts to motivate workers are based on ensuring that desired work behavior is followed by meaningful rewards.

Two additional theories of work motivation which have attracted interest are expectancy theory and self-efficacy theory. Expectancy theory (Porter & Lawler, 1968; Vroom, 1964) has a cognitive aspect. It is based on the premise that people operate based on a prediction of what rewards they will receive for certain work behaviors. Unlike reinforcement theory, which assumes that associations are stamped in automatically, expectancy theory asserts that individuals make mental calculations about what is being asked of them and the probability of their receiving something they desire for specified performance, and then take action based on these estimates. Albert Bandura's (1995) self-efficacy theory proposes individuals gradually develop confidence, or a lack of confidence, about their ability to overcome obstacles and successfully complete difficult tasks. This confidence can be diminished or enhanced by their actual work experiences. Another motivational theory which has received considerable attention relatively recently is goal-setting theory (Locke, 1968; 1970). This theory is potent in its simplicity as it proposes the best way to increase effort is to set specific, challenging goals for a worker. According to goal-setting theory, even if one does not reach the desired goal, one will perform better and work harder than if one has not set specific goals.

Job satisfaction. Closely associated with work motivation is job satisfaction. Recently, the term *quality of working life* has been used as a synonym for job satisfaction. Presumably, people wish to gain satisfaction from their work and to avoid dissatisfaction. Therefore, more research has been conducted on these topics than on nearly any other subject in I/O psychology. Thousands of studies have led to the basic conclusion that the primary sources of job satisfaction are interesting and challenging work, pleasant co-workers, adequate pay and other financial benefits, opportunities for advancement, effective and supportive supervisors, and acceptable company policies.

Work teams. Until 30 years ago, the concept of a work team was an unusual one for companies in the United States. Although work teams were used extensively by European companies, they were the exception in North America as U.S. companies decided to radically reduce their workforces. This decision usually meant eliminating many mid-level management positions, so fewer people were expected to do more work with less supervision. As a result, teams began to emerge as the new paradigm for effective organizations. This change improved both work motivation and job satisfaction through participative goal setting and job enrichment. Since the shift towards team work, I/O psychologists have devoted much effort to understanding team formation processes, the advantages of teams, and the optimal conditions for team functioning (Guzzo & Dickson, 1996).

Additionally, with the emergence of the Internet, I/O psychologists are required more and more frequently to help facilitate the effective operation of virtual teams. Virtual teams are very similar to traditional work teams in that all members work on the same project. The main difference is these members work from various locations. In some cases, they may be separated by thousands of miles and many time zones. The use of virtual teams is increasing due to the globalization of commerce. While technological advances have made virtual teams a valuable and convenient option, several possible disadvantages must also be considered. Virtual teams can experience problems resulting from time differences, local/cultural differences, and inadequate face-to-face interaction (Gibson & Cohen, 2003). Thus, I/O psychologists who work in this arena must study the most effective ways virtual teams can be implemented and managed.

Leadership. A more traditional area of interest for organizational psychologists has been the study of leadership. In recent years, I/O psychologists have been particularly interested in transformational and charismatic leadership. The term transformational is used because change and adaptation to change are emerging as the hallmarks of the successful modern company. The transformational leader is one who has a compelling vision of what one wants to accomplish and transforms followers' beliefs, values, and needs (Bass, 1990; 1995). Transformational leaders seek to realize their goals by making workers or followers more aware of the importance of what they are doing, persuading them to put the good of the organization or team ahead of their own self-interest, and appealing to their achievement and mastery needs (Hughes, Ginnett, & Curphy, 1996). Charismatic leadership depends more on the sheer force of a leader's personality than it does on the appeal of the leader's vision. Charismatic leaders elicit trust in others, are willing to take personal risks, and are sensitive to others' needs (Conger & Kanungo, 1994). Charismatic leaders are able to get followers to suspend disbelief and to accept challenges that they would ordinarily reject.

A more recent topic in this area is the concept of emancipatory leadership described by Corson (2000). Emancipatory leadership's guiding principle is that leadership should reflect the constituency it serves. Emancipatory leaders make sure those affected by leadership's decision making play a role in those decisions and are responsible for their implementation. The power and presence of leaders are minimized while democracy and inclusion are maximized. Emancipatory leaders understand their own boundaries and biases. They strive to empower their employees rather than to rule them. Moreover, they resist stereotypes and limits which impede the progress of members of minority groups. This leadership model has been proposed to be ideal in situations where an organization is undergoing change related to increasing diversity.

Another emerging line of research suggests leaders' emotional intelligence has a considerable impact on leadership effectiveness. According to Jennifer George (2000), emotional intelligence—the ability to understand and manage moods in oneself and others—contributes to effective leadership in organizations. For example, Zhou and George (2003) review research suggesting the emotional intelligence of leaders plays a critical role in fostering creativity in workers. In any event, as organizations continue to evolve and change, leadership will remain a critical area of interest for organizational psychologists as well as for society overall (Hogan & Kaiser, 2005).

Organizational culture and climate. Every organization, no matter how small or large, has a personality. In simple terms, it is this personality and the value system of the organization which is referred to as culture in organizational psychology jargon (Denison, 1996). The culture of the organization is manifested in its rituals, language, traditions, symbols, and unwritten rules. I/O psychologists are primarily interested in how employees, as opposed to clients or customers, experience organizational culture. Employees' perceptions of their organizational culture can create variations in workplace climate. Climate consists of shared perceptions among workers about specific aspects of the workplace environment that can affect workers' behavior and social interactions. As such, the primary issue for I/O psychologists is to understand how this culture is developed, maintained, and changed – and the resulting climate for employees.

Balancing work and other spheres of life. Another emerging trend in organizational psychology is increased interest on how employees balance work obligations and their personal lives. Balancing work and other spheres of life is also commonly known as work-life-balance (Bloom, Kretschmer, & Van Reenen, 2006; Lockwood, 2003; Watanabe, Takahashi, Minami, 1997; Zedeck, 1997). Research in this area often focuses on the design and evaluation of programs intended to reduce stress at work. Ultimately, the goal is to develop programs which enhance employees' work life and their family life.

A review of the work-family literature (Eby, Casper, Lockwood, Bordeaux, & Brinley, 2005) revealed this research has focused on nine topics: 1) work-family conflict, 2) work role stress, 3) work-family assistance, 4) work schedules, 5) job-related relocation, 6) career and job related outcomes, 7) gender and the relationship between work and family domains, 8) the challenges of dual-earner couples, and 9) relationships among life domains. Although the work-family interface has traditionally fallen within the realm of organizational psychology, it is also relevant to other branches of I/O psychology. For example, personnel psychologists may be interested in how family obligations tend to affect workers' performance, while human factors psychologists may be interested in how different works schedules correlate with workers' productivity and their quality of life outside work. For instance, Fritz and Sonnentag (2005) examined the impact of weekend downtime on health and job performance. Fritz and Sonnentag (2005) found that time off from work, the extent of work-related hassles, and the level of non-work stress are significant correlates of subsequent work-week performance, as well as of employee health.

Human Factor Psychology

Human factors[15], ergonomics[16] [HFE (Dul, Bruder, Buckle, Carayon, Falzon, Marras, Wilson, & van der Doelen, 2012; Meister, 1999), or human engineering psychology (Salvendy, 2012), examines the way in which work environments can be designed or modified to match the capabilities and limitations of human beings (Hollway, 2000; Meister, 1999). The human factor approach, according to Helander (1997, p. 4), uses the "knowledge of human (capabilities) to design systems, organizations, jobs, machines, tools, and consumer products for safe, efficient, and comfortable human use." The term *human factors* is synonymous with *human factor engineering* or *human factors psychology*. Human factors overlaps with related disciplines such as ergonomics, the study of the physical demands of work, such as reaching, stretching, lifting, and carrying.

The two most critical elements of HFE are the human and technology aspects. Without these, there is no HFE (Meister, 1999, p. 6). The human is represented in HFE by one's performance in specific contexts in relation to individual technological variables. As such, the major difference between the human and technology is that the latter is a construction of the former. This means the human impress on the technology is everywhere, and the more complex the technology the greater the impression. Complex technology has existed for thousands of years (James & Thorpe, 1994), but only recently have people become concerned about its effect on the human. Early industrial engineers such as Taylor and the Gilbreths were largely interested in improving the productive outputs of the worker. Only recently has a humanistic influence developed that views the human as more than a unit of production. HFE—in its sociotechnical, macroergonomic, and organizational development interests—has become to a limited extent the ombudsman in the effort to restrain the potentially negative effects of unbridled technology (Hancock, 1997; Meister, 1999).

From this perspective, the human being is the constant and the job or work environment is the variable in the behavior equation. The concept of the work environment is used broadly and includes the actual physical setting in which the work takes place, the tools and resources used in conducting the work, and the arrangement or design of the work tasks. Thus, the challenge to the human factors psychologist is to design or redesign a work environment so it best fits the capabilities and allows for the limitations of the humans who will inhabit it. Unlike personnel psychology in which the individual is being tested or selected to fit the job, human factors psychologists fit the work technology or environment to human capabilities to promote efficiency, effectiveness, and safety.

Research and application of modern human factors psychology began during the Second World War. Airplanes, ships, submarines, and weapons had undergone a radical transformation since World War I, resulting in greater attention to developing technical systems which could be used effectively by humans. Of particular concern was the fact that far more accidents involving aircraft occurred than had ever been experienced in World War I. This situation was due largely to the fact that military aircraft had become much more complex. Human error, rather than equipment failure, seemed to play the major role in most such accidents. Modern human factors psychology was born out of this sort of need to design the best and safest combination of human and machine. Much of the complex equipment used today, particularly in high-technology areas such as aviation, nuclear power, and computers, shows the influence of the human factors specialist.

CULTURE IN ACTION: ORGANIZATIONS

Unfortunately, culture does not exist when it comes to a fixed universal understanding, for there is little consensus within, let alone, across disciplines. Often culture is applied so broadly, such that merely as social pattern, it means very little. Highly specific, idiosyncratic definitions, also abound where the term is used in various context in support of any agenda. When culture first appeared in the Oxford English Dictionary around 1430 it meant *cultivation* or *tending the soil*, based on the Latin culture.

Into the 19th century, *culture* was associated with the phrase *high culture*, meaning the cultivation or *refinement of mind, taste, and manners*. This generally held to the mid-20th century when its meaning shifted toward its present American Heritage English Dictionary definition: "The totality of socially transmitted behavior patterns, arts, beliefs, institutions, and all other products of human work and thought" (Tharp, 2009). British anthropologist Sir Edward Burnett Tylor[17] is widely credited with the first (1871) modern definition of culture: "that complex whole which includes knowledge, beliefs, arts, morals, laws, custom, and any other capabilities and habits acquired by man as a member of society." Undoubtedly this definition influenced the shift toward current dictionary definitions. According to Tharp (2009), subsequent to this new interpretation and vision of a complex whole, academics attempted to build upon this by creating universal lists of all of the elements of culture, the most exhaustive of which, first published in 1938, lists 79 major divisions and 637 subdivisions. While comprehensive and still useful for social science researchers today, it is ineffective for most general applications, as well as corporations and other organizations.

While the complexities of the culture concept were being debated in the mid-20th century, surveys of its different definitions yielded a few common threads which are helpful in organizational research. Most simply, culture involves three basic human activities: what people think, what people do, and what people make. Further, several common properties arise: culture is shared, learned, transmitted cross-generationally, symbolic, adaptive, and integrated. Additionally, culture is learned, actively or passively, and is transmitted cross-generationally through formal or informal social interaction. Culture is also adaptive in that it can and does change in response to various influences and conditions. No culture is truly static, for culture is integrated in the sense that it permeates society, and becomes part of the social machinery. Culture is the ever-present, ethereal medium, in which members live and through which they act.

In 1973, anthropologist Clifford Geertz published *The Interpretation of Cultures*, in which he wrote: "Culture is the fabric of meaning in terms of which human beings interpret their experience and guide their action" and that culture is "an ordered system of meaning and of symbols in terms of which social interaction takes place." This semiotic notion of culture gained great popularity in the postmodern movement of the 1980's, when the relatively mature discipline of organizational behavior, first began to talk broadly about *organizational culture*. Geertz's anthropological definition was the most cited in the literature at that time and still has great purchase in contemporary research.

Organizational Culture

The *modern organizational culturalism* was born in 1979, although the term *organizational culture* appeared by chance in the English-speaking literature of the 1960s (Morcillo & Garces, N. Y.). However, the field of organizational behavior and the related discipline of management science began investigating organizations in terms of culture as early as the 1930s. The final phase of the famous Hawthorne studies at the Western Electric Company marked the first systematic attempt to use a concept of culture to understand the work environment (Drucker, 1974; Hollway, 2000). While an important step forward in qualitative research, the investigation was rather blunt, and the understanding of organizational culture remained fairly primitive during the following decades. Most mid-century attempts at understanding were conducted by scholars steeped in quantitative psychology and sociology, though by the 1970s, researchers more explicitly and emphatically appropriated the theories and methods of anthropology.

The late-century upsurge of interest in organizational culture is credited largely to the economic conditions of the 1970s when international competition had heightened and more foreign companies were opening factories in the United States. Specifically, the success of the Japanese in many industries sparked curiosity about whether their differing corporate values, attitudes, and behaviors were responsible for their often superior performance. The 1982 publication of Tom Peters and Robert H. Waterman, Jr.'s, *In Search of Excellence*, stirred both popular and professional interest through its suggestion that organizations with strong cultures were more effective. Thereafter, corporate culture was offered as an asset which could be managed to improved business performance.

While *In Search of Excellence* is definitely the most popular book on the subject, three others were seminal to the development of the field: 1) *Theory Z: How American Business Can Meet the Japanese Challenge* (Ouchi, 1981), 2) *The Art of Japanese Management: Applications for American Executives* (Pascale & Athos, 1982), and 3) *Corporate Cultures: The Rites and Rituals of Corporate Life* (Deal & Kennedy, 1982). Since the early 1980s, academic and applied exploration of organizational culture has increased steadily, and even now there is little indication of abatement as changes in data management, work organization, values, lifestyles, demographic, knowledge-intensive work, outsourcing, and a host of other social, economic, and technological factors continue to impact the relationship between organizations, workers, and the workplace.

Understanding Organizational Culture

Definitions of organizational culture are almost as numerous as those of culture—a 1998 study identified 54 different definitions within the academic literature between 1960 and 1993. One helpful, though general, definition offered by Edgar Schein of Massachusetts Institute of Technology's Sloan School of Management is that organizational culture (Schein, 1996; 1998) is: a pattern of shared basic assumptions which the group learned as it solved its problems of external adaptation and internal integration, that has worked well enough to be considered valid, and therefore, to be taught to new members as the correct way to perceive, think, and feel in relation to those problems. Delving deeper, three common attributes seem to arise across the varying perspectives within sociology, psychology, anthropology, and management science. One is that the concept of shared meaning is critical. Second is the notion that organizational culture is constructed socially and is affected by environment and history. Third is the common feature among the many definitions is that organizational culture has many symbolic and cognitive layers—culture is thick and resides at all levels (Daft, 2001; Jones, 2004; Morgan,

1997; Schneider & Barsoux, 1997; Shafritz & Ott, 2001; Shafritz, Ott, & Jang, 2005). To help understand these symbolic and cognitive layers, Schein (1992) has categorized the places where culture is found into three fundamental categories: observable artifacts, espoused values, and basic underlying assumptions (Daft, 2001; Jones, 2004; Morgan, 1997; Schneider & Barsoux, 1997; Shafritz & Ott, 2001; Shafritz, Ott, & Jang, 2005).

CULTURE IN ACTION: INTERNATIONAL (INDUSTRIAL/ ORGANIZATIONAL) PSYCHOLOGY

International or global psychology is an emerging branch of psychology focusing on the worldwide enterprise of psychology in terms of communication and networking, cross-cultural comparison, scholarship, practice, and pedagogy. Often, the terms international psychology[18], global psychology, and cross-cultural psychology are used interchangeably, but their purposes are subtly and importantly different: Global means worldwide, international means across and between nations, cross-cultural means across cultures. In contrast, the term *multicultural* is more often used to refer to ethnic and other cultural differences existing within a given nation rather than to global or international comparisons. This entry focuses predominantly on international psychology.

Psychology's (international and domestic) paradigm on culture differs from organizations' paradigm on culture. From a psychology's paradigm, many writers, including anthropologists, sociologists, and psychologists, have written about culture, providing a variety of definitions and descriptions (Keith, 2010). Heine (2008) described a two-part definition of culture: 1) information which has been learned from others, that is capable of influencing behavior, and 2) a group of people who share context and experience (Berry, 1979; Erez, 1997; Erez & Earley, 1993; Hofstede, 1991; Kagitcibasi & Berry, 1989; Kluckhohn, 1954; Shweder & LeVine, 1984). Matsumoto (2009) offered a comprehensive definition which shares key characteristics with that of Triandis, Kurowski, Tecktiel, and Chan (1993), who defined culture in terms of objective and subjective characteristics that increase the odds of survival, provide satisfaction for people sharing an environmental context, and are shared via language.

Cross-Cultural Psychology

The field of cross-cultural psychology finds itself today in somewhat the same positions as the discipline of psychology soon after the turn of the 20th century when Hermann Ebbinghaus (1908/1973) observed that psychology has a long past, yet its real history is short (p. 3). Just as there was widespread interest in the subjects we now call psychology long before the field was given a name, so it was that many writers were interested in culture and cultural relationships, long before the modern concern with the connection between culture and psychology. As such, Kagitcibasi and Berry (1989, p. 494) defined cross-cultural psychology as "the study of similarities and differences in individual psychology and social functioning in various cultures and ethnic groups." Cross-cultural psychologists originally set out to seek universal principles that would apply across cultures (Sinha, 2002). Thus, cross-cultural psychology traditionally involved testing Western theories in other cultures (Laungani, 2002; Yang, 2000), with the notion that culture was independent of the individual and separable from psychological activities and principles (Greenfield, 2000).

Cultural Psychology

Researchers identified as cultural psychologists are less likely than cross-cultural psychologists to be interested in traditional experimental or quasi-experimental approaches, and more likely to view culture as internal to the person (Triandis, 2000). Cultural psychology uses method and studies problems arising from the everyday activities of particular cultures, with less emphasis on cross-cultural comparison (Greenfield, 2000). Therefore, the methods of cultural psychologists are often ethnographic in nature, meaning they involve extensive observation and rich description of a culture (Heine, 2008). The focus is on uncovering relationships between a culture and the psychological characteristics of people living in the culture, with the corresponding view that psychological processes derive from the interplay between the person and one's culture (Shiraev & Levy, 2010).

RECOMMENDATIONS[19]

It stands to reason the first step in any initiatives taken by corporations is a top-down approach, supported by the decision makers. In so doing, companies are encouraged to consult with their I/O practitioner(s), if not, then their organizational consultants (OC), organizational psychologists (OP), organizational development practitioners (OD), if they have such in-house practitioners. Otherwise, company managers should contract with an external consultant if financially convenient, or consult with one's in-house department of human resources. Such initiatives do not exist just on paper, but must be implemented and continuously evaluated for change and improvement (Tran, 2012). Multinational corporations (MNCs) who are involved in global ventures are not naïve or "green" when it comes to utilizing their I/O practitioners (Tran, 2008). According to Tran (2008), MNCs more often than not are under-minding, under-utilizing, and under-valuing their in-house I/O practitioners. Common U.S.-based MNCs with locations abroad, and conducts global ventures, with their own in-house I/O practitioners[20], include but are not limited to: Adobe Systems, Inc.[21], Cisco Systems, Inc., Eli Lilly and Company, Google, Inc., Hewlett-Packard (HP)[22], International Business Machine (IBM), Microsoft Corporation, Oracle Corporation[23], and Yahoo! Inc.

Recommendation One: Successful international ventures. MNCs wanting consistency in culture across their subsidiaries need to export the parent company's culture by staffing expatriates in key positions of its foreign subsidiaries. MNCs employing this tactic believe expatriates can significantly impact the subsidiaries' cultures (Kobrin, 1988). Selecting expatriates for foreign assignments would be quite simple for MNCs if success in domestic assignments were predictive of success in foreign assignments. Unfortunately, the failure rate of expatriates is extraordinarily high despite the fact it is generally the more successful domestic employees who are sent abroad (Tung, 1981). The high failure rate is understandable since many MNCs use the same employee selection procedures to select both expatriates and domestic employees with the same job title (Tran, 2008).

Generally, when no formal or standardized selection method is used, the company relies on past results derived from existing personnel selection processes. The *personnel selection processes* are the methods by which organizations use to evaluate potential employees' knowledge, skills, and abilities to determine whether there is a good fit between an available position and a candidate. These are the commonly used sets of criteria which identify successful domestic candidates; these sets of criteria are well-known and have been used for a long time but again, primarily for domestic candidates. Knowledge, skills, and abilities will be referred to as KSAs; while the criteria including "other" attributes will be referred to as KSAOs:

1. Knowledge is usually defined as the degree to which a candidate is required to know certain technical material.
2. Skill indicates adequate performance on tasks requiring the use of tools, equipment, machinery, etc.
3. Abilities are physical and mental capacities to perform tasks not requiring the use of tools, equipment, or machinery.
4. Other characteristics include personality, interest, or motivational attributes that in-

dicate a candidate will learn certain tasks, rather than whether they can do those tasks (Schneider & Schmitt, 1986: 53).

Recommendation Two: Appropriate selection program[24]. The appropriate selection program consists of three stages. Stage one is Selection, defined as how to make a fair and relevant choice among the applicants by accessing their strengths and weaknesses, presented in Figure 1. In the selection process, no technical criteria need to be given more weight than they are at present. The two methods in the selection process that the international human resource personnel (IHRP) needs include implementation, self-selection, and recruitment. In the Selection stage, there are five important factors that the IHRP need to take into consideration when forming a selection committee:

1. The selection committee must be very carefully selected and trained
2. One of the members of the selection committee must:
   a. Possess knowledge of the culture and language to which a potential expatriate will be sent
   b. Possess knowledge of the culture and language to which a potential expatriate will be sent via expertise (derived and/or acquired through research and/or academic knowledge and training)
3. It is inappropriate that individuals who have no overseas experience should have served, or serve on, the selection committee (unless the second factor has been met)
4. Interpersonal skills, such as achieving rapport, questioning approaches, and prompting and probing are crucial in interviewing the potential recruit and deciding about "fit" between recruit and overseas assignment

Figure 1. Selection Stage

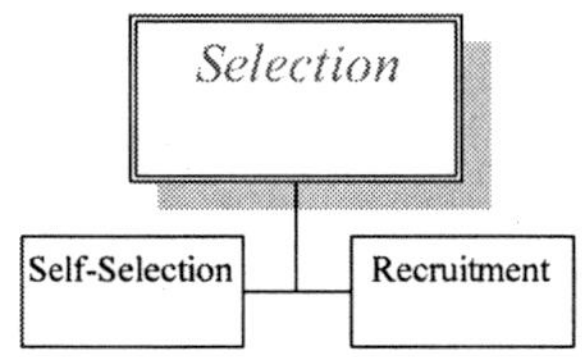

The selection committee must have diverse representation, in both gender and ethnicity, unless it violates the second factor

Stage 1A: self-selection. The first method in the selection stage is self-selection, presented in Figure 2. In the self-selection stage, the IHRP must consider that the potential overseas worker may not necessarily be aware of his or her motivations for accepting an overseas opportunity. The objective of the organization is to confirm that the skill and motivation of the potential recruit must be compatible with the organization. However, the candidate must eventually decide if he or she is ready or possesses the necessary skill, experience, or attitude for an international assignment.

It is as important for the expatriate and the firm alike that the candidate fits the assignment in question since both will suffer from a bad fit. In the first self-selection method, the potential expatriate can voluntarily elect to participate in one of two, or both types of self-assessment. The first type of self-assessment is the paper-and-pencil format. The second type of self-assessment is an electronic format. The organization must provide both types (paper-and-pencil and electronic) of self-selection assessments on its intranet that is accessible to all interested candidates. These as-

Figure 2. Stage 1A: Self-Selection

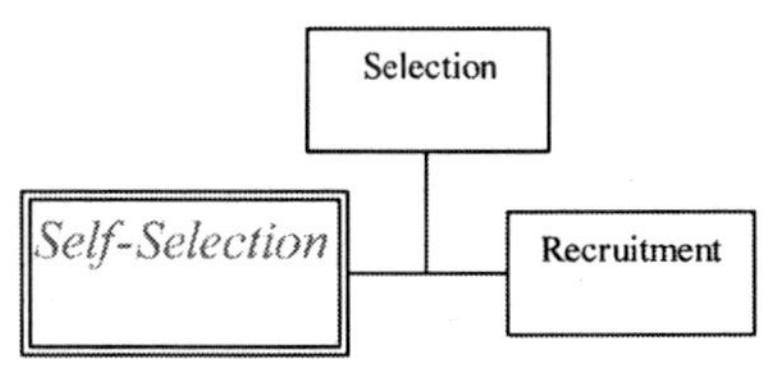

sessments must be available in alternative formats and compliable with assistive technology.

Stage 1A$_1$: Paper-and-Pencil in Self-Selection. For the paper-and-pencil self-assessment format presented in Figure 3, the general idea is that the longer a worker is happily employed, the greater the worker's commitment and loyalty to the firm. Thus, a potential expatriate can assess and determine whether he or she is ready or has the necessary skill, experience, or attitude to go on an international assignment. The organization must provide the paper-and-pencil self-selection format on its internet in such a fashion that it is accessible to all interested candidates to obtain and print out into hard copies. The purposes of the paper-and-pencil format of the self-assessment include:

1. Some individuals may prefer the paper-and-pencil format due to the sense of less intimidation (no time limit imposed)
2. Personal preferences

Stage 1A2: Electronic in Self-Selection. For the electronic self-assessment format, presented in Figure 4, the general idea is the longer a worker is happily employed, the greater the worker's commitment and loyalty to the firm. Thus, a potential expatriate can assess and determine, whether one is ready or has the necessary skill, experience, and/or attitude to go on an international assignment. The organization must provide the electronic self-selection format on its internet in such a fashion that it is accessible to all interested candidates. The organization must provide the electronic format

Figure 3. Stage 1A$_1$: Paper-and-Pencil in Self-Selection

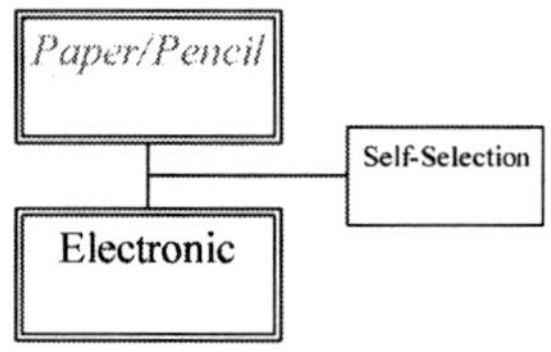

Figure 4. Stage 1A$_2$: Electronic in Self-Selection

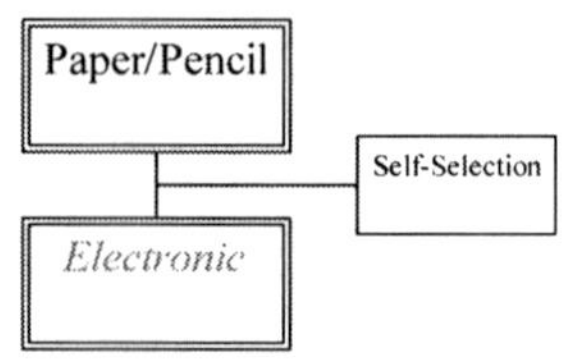

in such a fashion that it is available in alternative formats and is compatible with assistive technology. The purposes of the electronic format of the self-assessment:

1. Some individuals may prefer the electronic format due the desire to achieve real-time result (no waiting needed)
2. Personal preferences

Stage 1B: Recruitment. Recruitment refers to the process of finding the right people for the right job or function. During the recruitment stage, presented in Figure 5, recruiters must very carefully select and train. Recruiters must have the ability to not only sell, but possesses the ability to do outreach (promote and establish visibility), maintain relationship with interested candidates, and be accessible for support (question-and-answer). Recruiters have to be knowledgeable, be able to handle questions, and be able to direct interested candidates to answers that the recruiters cannot address themselves. Recruiters must be professional, genuine, and helpful. There are three types of recruiting methods: newsletters/newsgroups, workshops/meetings, and informational packages.

Figure 5. Stage 1B: Recruitment

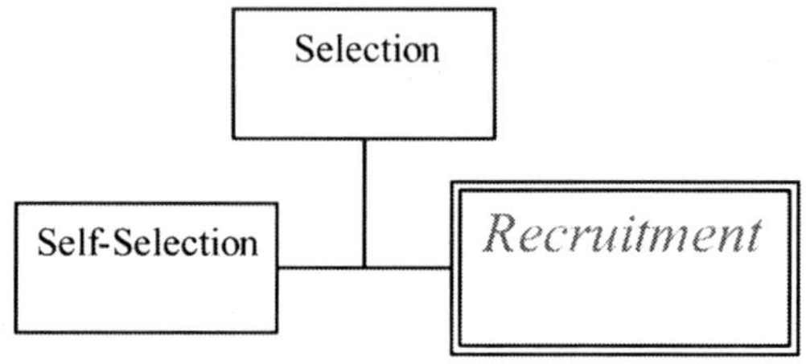

Stage $1B_1$: Newsletters/Newsgroups in Recruitment. Newsletters, presented in Figure 6, are defined as any and all printed documents giving news or information of interest to a special group of interested individuals. However, newsgroups are defined as an area on a computer network, especially the Internet or Intranet which are devoted to the discussion of a specified topic. The organization can utilize the avenues of the newsletters and newsgroups to the following:

- Send out weekly and monthly messages regarding expatriate opportunities and contact information
- Emphasis on the purpose and benefit of expatriate opportunities
- Include a list of locations that are available for expatriates

Stage 1B2: Workshops/Meetings in Recruitment. Workshops, presented in Figure 7, are defined as educational seminars or series of meetings emphasizing interaction and exchange of information among a usually small number of participants. Meetings, on the other hand, are defined as an assembly or gathering of people, as for a business, social, or special interest purpose. The organization can utilize the avenues of the workshops and meetings to the following:

Figure 6. Stage $1B_1$: Newsletters/Newsgroups in Recruitment

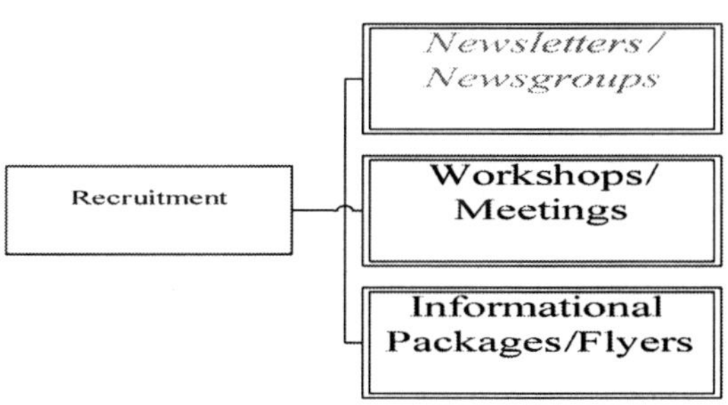

Figure 7. Stage $1B_2$: Workshops/Meetings in Recruitment

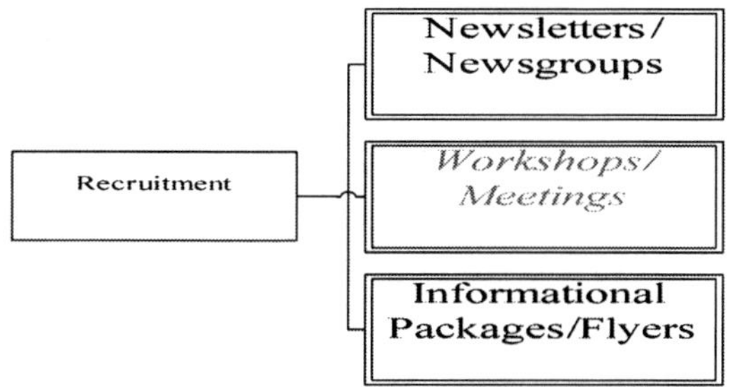

- Conduct monthly and quarterly expatriate workshops and meetings (and network opportunities such as mentorship)
- Invite expatriates and retried expatriates to share their experience and opportunities gained since their assignments

Stage 1B3: Informational Packages/Flyers in Recruitment. Informational packages are defined as any and all bundled of, propositions of, or any offers composed of several items of information which pertains to the same purpose. However, flyers, presented in Figure 8, are defined as any and all pamphlets or circulars for mass distribution for the sole purpose of advertising a message printed on one or both sides with an advertising message. The organization can utilize the avenues of informational packages and flyers to the following:

- Provide accessible informational packages on the organization's intranet that are available in alternative formats and are compatible with assistive technologies
- Send individual hard copy flyers to employees' mailboxes

At the end of the selection process, prior to proceeding to the next stage presented in Figure 9, the pre-departure, the progress should appear similar to the figure below.

Recommendation Three: Appropriate assessment prior to pre-departure. Stage two is assess-

Figure 8. Stage 1B$_3$: Informational Packages/ Flyers in Recruitment

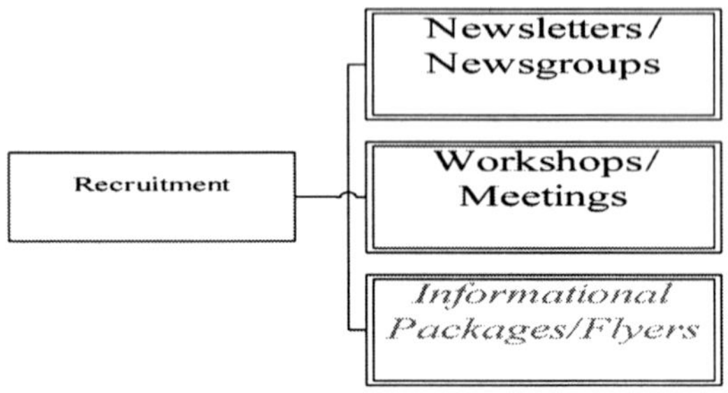

ment prior to pre-departure. Pre-Departure is defined as a stage where the potential expatriate has been recruited but has yet to be selected. The status of the selection of the individual as an expatriate for an assignment is pending, depending on the results of the assessment and the assessment of the expatriate as a whole. An assessment is defined as the act or result of judging the worth or value of something or someone. In doing so, assessment is the process of documenting, usually in measurable terms, knowledge, skills, attitudes, and beliefs. The assessment is the most crucial step in the pre-departure stage. Multinational corporations (MNCs) which are equipped with their own Department of Assessment can conduct the necessary assessments. The assessments will assist in the determination of the goodness-of-fit between an available and interested potential expatriate and the available assignment which needs to be filled.

MNCs interested in receiving an alternative objective opinion, or smaller corporations which are less equipped, can contract out to assessment centers. Assessment Centers are most suitable to use when a potential candidate has been identified but not selected, or that the position the candidate is seeking is very different from the current position the candidate holds, since assessment centers allow for evaluation of skills which might not be possible to observe in the workplace. Individuals are usually assessed in small groups by trained management personnel, professional psychologists, and sometimes even both. Assessment comes in two forms, quantitative formal assessment tests, and qualitative formal interviews.

Stage 2A: Quantitative Formal Assessment. Quantitative assessment has also been referred to as objective assessment, which is a form of questioning possessing one single correct answer. Quantitative assessments are designed to test the individual in three paramount areas: cross-cultural training, international/intercultural communication skills, and other characteristics, as demonstrated in Figure 10.

Figure 9. Pre-Departure

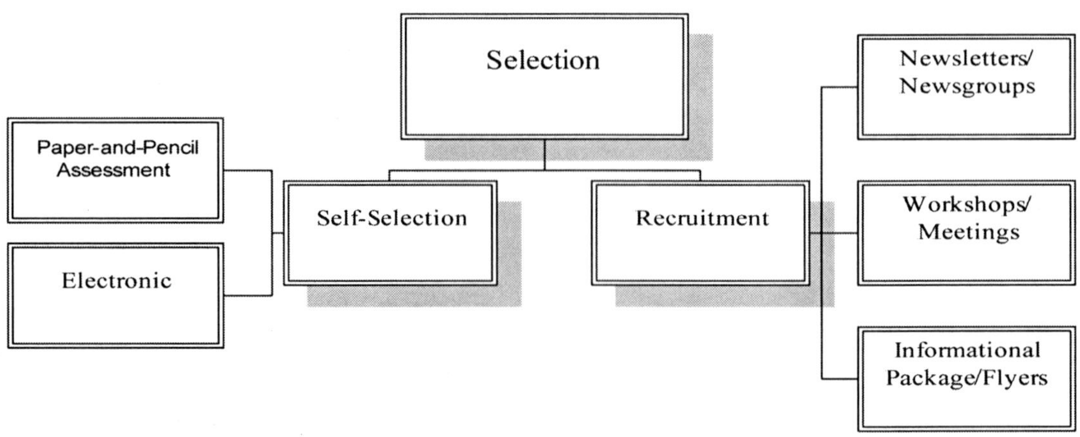

Figure 10. Stage 2A: Quantitative Formal Assessment

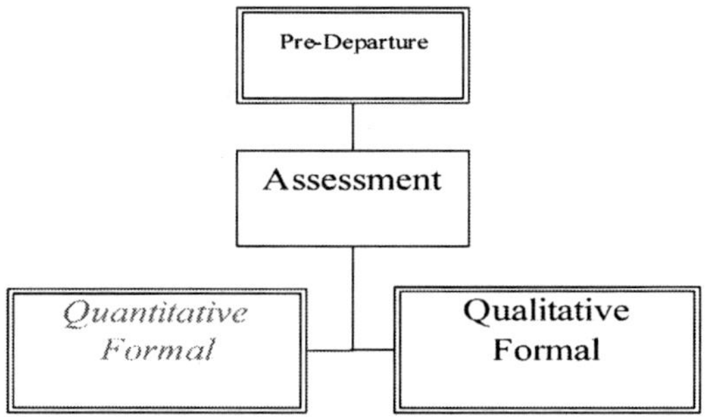

Stage 2A$_I$: CCT, IIC, and O in Quantitative Formal Assessments. Quantitative formal assessment test evaluates the candidate's personal traits (Big Five personality inventory) determined to be important in adjusting to the new culture. These include adaptability, flexibility, the liking for new experiences, and good interpersonal (communication) skills. Testing to see if the candidate has competences related to managing diversity is as important if not more important than the candidate's technical competences. Last but not least, assessments of the candidate's willingness to accept the overseas opportunity, the candidate's readiness are also important. Thus, the following three quantitative criterions[25], presented in Figure 11, must be assessed to determine if there is a good fit between the potential candidate and the available expatriate assignments:

1. Cross-Cultural Training
2. International/Intercultural Communication
3. Diversity/Other Characteristics

Stage 2B: Qualitative Formal Assessment. Qualitative assessment, presented in Figure 12, has also been referred to as Subjective assessment, which is a form of questioning which may have more than one correct answer (or more than one way of expressing the correct answer).

However, Qualitative assessment includes an interview with the candidate and possibly the candidate's spouse to ascertain if they have the ability to adjust to foreign cultures. The interview in itself should be focused on the candidate's past behaviors which might provide evidence of the presence or absence of the characteristics in the interviewer's favor. Interviews can be most useful when assessing a candidate's communication and interpersonal skills, and also, sometimes, general intelligence. The interview should include, as presented in Figure 13:

1. An expatriate (current or retired)
2. An international human resource personnel
3. Direct supervisor
4. An expert
5. Host Supervisor (Optional)

At the end of the Pre-departure process, prior to proceeding to the next stage (the Post-departure) the progress should appear similar to the figure below. Based on individual assessment results, the organization must then determine if the individual is a good fit for the expatriate assignment; therefore, the organization must then develop appropriate and necessary training for the individual. Training is defined as "any intervention aimed at increasing the knowledge or skill of the individual." This can help the individual cope better personally, work more effectively with others, and perform better professionally. Another definition of training is an organized educational experience with the objective of helping expatriates learn about, and therefore adjust to, their new home in a foreign land. Training can involve many techniques and methods, ranging from the experiential (role-playing) to the documentary (reading literature).

Recommendation Three: Post-Departure support. Post-Departure is defined as the stage in which the expatriate has been relocated to the host country after being awarded the assignment. An expatriate requires mentoring prior to Post-Departure. Mentoring is defined as an individual who provides one's expertise to less experienced individuals to assist the protégé advance one's career and build networks. Mentorship must be

Figure 11. Stage 2A_I: CCT, IIC, and O in Quantitative Formal Assessments

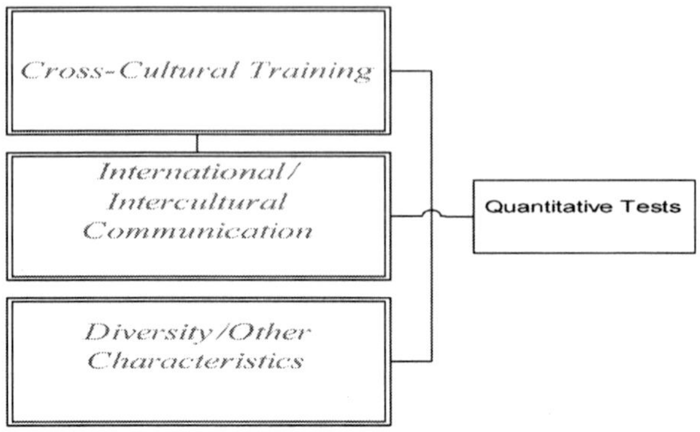

Figure 12. Stage 2B: Qualitative Formal Assessment

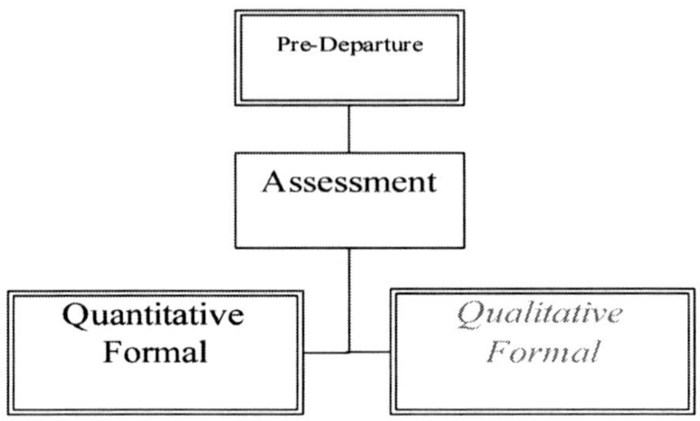

Figure 13. Stage 2B: Expatriate, IHRP, Director Supervisor, Expert, and Host Supervisor

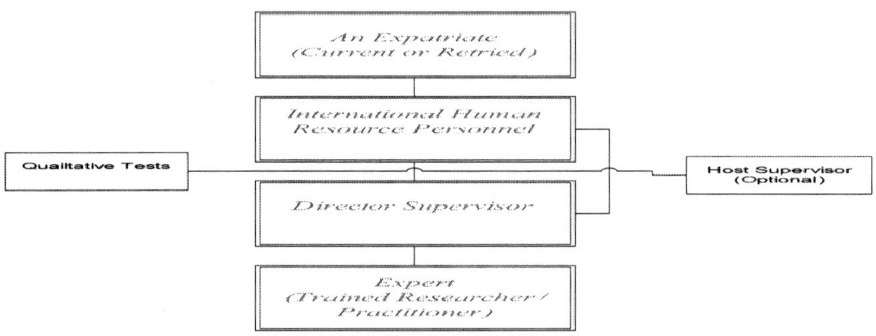

implemented Pre-Departure (prior to the assignment) and Post-Departure (during the assignment). The expatriate's mentor serves as a so-called "buddy" or colleague. The buddy, presented in Figure 14, not only keeps the expatriate informed and "in-the-loop" about the situations at the base location, but also advises the expatriate on the assignment(s) at hand.

Stage 3A: Expatriate Mentor. As previously defined, an expatriate mentor, presented in Figure 15, is an individual who provides one's expertise to less experienced individuals to assist the protégé advance his or her career and to build networks. The mentor serves as a "buddy" as defined above. The buddy not only keeps the expatriate informed and "in-the-loop" about situations at the

Figure 14. Buddy

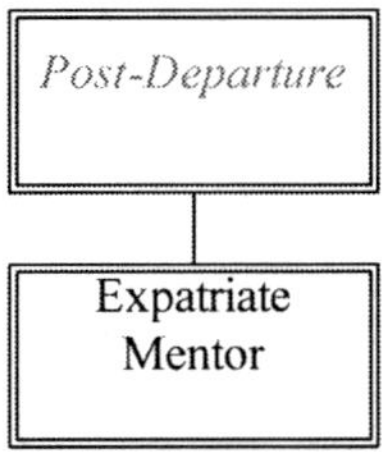

base location, but also advises the expatriate on the assignment(s) at hand. The expatriate mentor also assists the expatriate in finding and selecting a "host country mentor" and an "expatriate community."

Stage 3A$_1$: Host Country Mentor in Expatriate Mentor. The host country mentor, presented in Figure 16, is defined as an individual who is a native of the host country but is an employee of the company to which the expatriate works for in the home country. The host country mentor is similar to a "big brother" to the expatriate while on assignment. If necessary, the host mentor will assist and introduce the expatriate to the local expatriate community for additional support. At the end of the Post-Departure process, the progress should resemble the figure below; otherwise, the organization may need to address and resolve the situation immediately.

Stage 3A$_2$: Expatriate Community in Expatriate Mentor. The expatriate community is defined as a social group of expatriates sharing an environment, normally with shared interests, with the purpose of a sense of family, and home away from home. The expatriate community serves as a source of emotional, psychological, and mental support both the expatriate's mentor and what the host country's mentor does not provide, as presented in Figure 17. An expatriate community does not provide work or assignment related support, but does support what is not work and assignment related. Expatriate community, in a rough and indirect form, is a source of "comfort" environment, and something relative. Therefore, at the end of the Post-Departure process the progress should resemble the figure below, and the whole process should resemble the figure which follows thereafter (Figure 3).

Recommendation Four: Assessing the other characteristics (O). Knowledge, skills, and abilities will be referred to as KSAs; while the criteria including "other" attributes will be referred to as KSAOs:

1. Knowledge is usually defined as the degree to which a candidate is required to know certain technical material.
2. Skill indicates adequate performance on tasks requiring the use of tools, equipment, machinery, etc.
3. Abilities are physical and mental capacities to perform tasks not requiring the use of tools, equipment, or machinery.
4. Other characteristics include personality, interest, or motivational attributes that indicate a candidate will learn certain tasks, rather than whether they can do those tasks (Schneider & Schmitt, 1986, p. 53).

Figure 15. Stage 3A: Expatriate Mentor

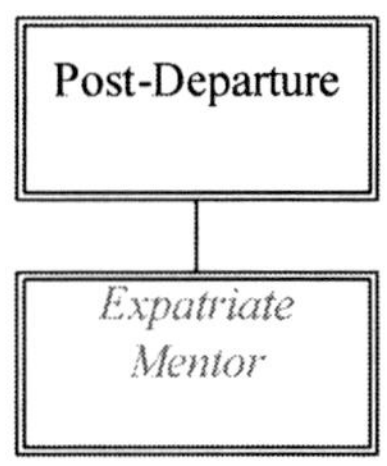

Figure 16. Stage 3A$_1$: Host Country Mentor in Expatriate Mentor

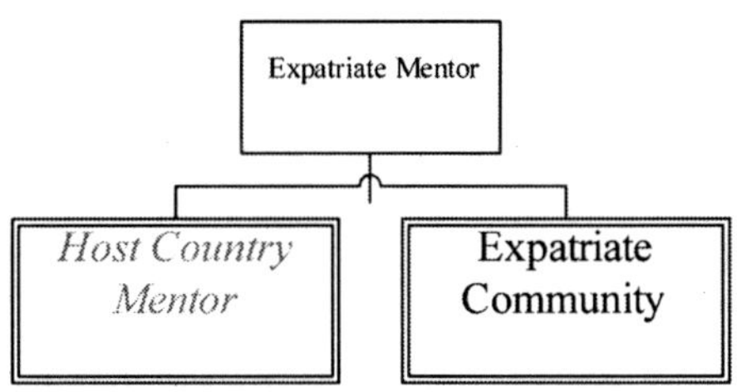

Figure 17. Stage $3A_2$: Expatriate Community in Expatriate Mentor

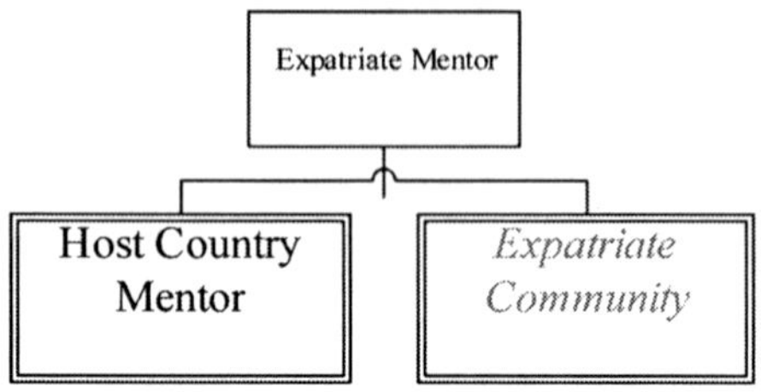

Based on the definition, purpose, and usage, KSAs are only applicable to the assessment and selection of domestic employees and are not sufficient for the assessment and selection of expatriate candidates (Peterson, Mumford, Borman, Jeanneret, Fleishman, Levin, … Dye, 2001). The detrimental outcome (Baliga & Baker, 1985; Black, 1988; Black, Gregersen, Mendenhall, & Stroh, 1999; Black & Mendenhall, 1990; Borstorff, Harris, Field, Giles, 1997; Copeland & Briggs, 1985; McDonald, 1993; Mendenhall, Dunbar, & Oddou, 1987; Poe, 2002; Shay & Tracey, 1997; Talbott, 1996; Tung, 1981; 1982; 1988; Wederspahn, 1992; Zeira & Banai, 1985) of selecting an expatriate based solely on KSAs cannot continue if MNCs plan to expand and succeed globally (Bjorkman & Schaaps, 1994; Caligiuri, 2000; Hodgetts & Luthans, 1993; Katz & Seifer, 1996; The Conference Board, 1992; Webb, 1996; Windham International, 1998; Zeira & Banai, 1987). Specifically, MNCs should use the expatriate-specific manual to assess a potential candidates' other characteristics (O). The other characteristics consist of the following:

1. The expatriates desire to prematurely terminate the assignment resulting from the supervisor-rated performance on the expatriate assignment,
2. Stable competencies, and
3. Intercultural/international business communication skills.

CONCLUSION

Globalization has become a so-called "buzzword" in management jargon, and it is unnecessary to investigate extensively to discover exhortations about the internationalization of management practice in the business press (Walter, 2007). As such, Judge and Simon (2007) say there are challenges to a full convergence of perspective. First, there is the issue of language as English is the language of the top professional journals; however, English is the native language of only a small minority of the world's population. While it is true English is the most common second language learned, it is naïve to assume that a second language is not is as readily absorbed as a native language.

Even in 2006 more than 8 of 10 articles published were from researchers in English-speaking countries. This language barrier will continue to pose challenges in the globalization of I/O research, even as great strides are being made. Second, culture is a complicated matter and it poses significant problems for I/Ol psychology research. For example, it is difficult to even define and measure national culture (Hofstede, 2002; Spector, Cooper, & Sparks, 2001), and to compare and contrast two culture or more cultures is a complicated proposition. Moreover, there is some evidence supporting the statement that while cultural stereotypes are widely held, they are belied by greater within-country than between-country differences (Terracciano, Abdel-Khalek, Adam, Adamovova, Ahn, Ahn, … McCrae, 2005).

I/O psychology is the study of human behavior in organizations as well as the behaviors of interest contributing to the effectiveness of organizational functioning, the satisfaction and well-being of those who populate the organizations, or both. These behaviors and the people who exhibit them exist in a dynamic open system (Katz & Kahn, 1978). As such, significant scientific advances in the field of I/O psychology are documented in detail in several available reviews (Anderson,

Ones, Sinangil, & Viswesvaran, 2001; Borman, Ilgen, & Klimoski, 2003; Dunnette & Hoough, 1990; 1991; 1992; Rogelberg, 2007; Triandis, Dunnette, & Hough, 1994). Although scientific advances are important in areas central to the field such as assessment, validation, motivation, leadership, performance appraisal, training, data-analytic techniques, and research methodology, one constant in the field has been its support of the scientist—the practitioner model (Bass, 1974; Dunnette, 1990; Lapointe, 1990; McHenry, 2007; Murphy & Saal, 1990; Rupp & Beal, 2007).

Unfortunately, there are concerns with the effective implementation of the scientist-practitioner model because there is a serious disconnect between the knowledge that academics are producing and the knowledge which practitioners are consuming (McHenry, 2007; Rynes, Colbert, & Brown, 2002). As a result, many organizations fail to adopt the practices that I/O psychology research suggests are most effective (Dipboye, 2007), and so the scientist-practitioner gap persists (Aguinis & Pierce, 2008; Anderson, 2007; Cascio, 2007; 2008; Gelade, 2006; Hodgkinson, 2006; Markides, 2007; Rynes, 2007; Rynes, Bartunek, & Daft, 2001), despite efforts to reduce it. According to Cascio and Aguinis (2008), it seems ironic to be asking questions related to the broader relevance of I/O psychology research because the field, from its inception, was created to address, inform, and help solve important human-capital challenges. For example, consider the recent account of some of the classic applications of organizational psychology, along with rich detail about the difficulties of practice implementation provided by Highhouse (2007).

That same sense of mission is true today, as Rogelberg (2007, p. xxv) noted, "in general the goals of I/O psychology are to better understand and optimize the effectiveness, health, and well-being of both individuals and organizations." Likewise, the mission statement of the Society for Industrial and Organizational Psychology (SIOP) is to enhance human well-being and performance in organizational and work settings by promoting the science, practice, and teaching of I/O psychology (SIOP, 2007). Thus, I/O psychology is the branch of psychology concerned with the application of psychological principles in the workplace and so I/O psychologist plays a paramount role in successful global ventures, by addressing two key factors—culture and behavior—resulting in positive return-on-investment (ROI).

REFERENCES

Adams, J. D. (2001). Managing dispersed work effectively. *OD Practitioner*, *33*(1), 381–391.

Adler, N. J., & Gunderson, A. (2007). *International dimensions of organizational behavior*. Boston, MA: PWS-Kent.

Advisory Panel for the Dictionary of Occupational Titles. (1993). *The new dot: A database of occupational titles for the twenty-first century*. Washington, DC: U.S. Department of Labor, Employment and Training Administration.

Aguinis, H., & Pierce, C. A. (2008). Enhancing the relevance of organizational behavior by embracing performance management research. *Journal of Organizational Behavior*, *29*, 139–145. doi:10.1002/job.493.

Anderson, N., Ones, D. S., Sinangil, H. K., & Viswesvaran, C. (2001). *Handbook of industrial, work and organizational psychology*. London: Sage.

Baliga, G. & Baker, J. C. (1985). Multinational corporation policies for expatriate managers: Selection, training, and evaluation. *Advanced Management Journal*, 31-38.

Bandura, A. (1995). Exercise of personal and collective efficacy in changing societies. In Bandura, A. (Ed.), *Self-efficacy in changing societies*. New York: Cambridge University Press. doi:10.1017/CBO9780511527692.003.

Barham, K., & Devine, M. (1991). *The quest for the international manager: A survey of global human resource Strategies*. London: Ashridge Management Guide/Economist Intelligence Unit.

Bass, B. M. (1974). The substance and the shadow. *The American Psychologist, 29*, 870–886. doi:10.1037/h0037515.

Bass, B. M. (1990). *Bass and stogdill's handbook of leadership: Theory research, and managerial applications*. New York: Free Press.

Bass, B. M. (1995). Theory of transformational leadership redux. *The Leadership Quarterly*, 6.

Bell, B. S., & Kozlowski, S. W. J. (2002). A typology of virtual teams: Implications for effective leadership. *Group & Organization Management, 27*, 12–49. doi:10.1177/1059601102027001003.

Berry, J. W. (1979). In Berkowitz, L. (Ed.). Advances in experimental social psychology: *Vol. 12. A cultural ecology of social behavior*. Orlando, FL: Academic Press.

Bjorkman, I., & Schaaps, A. (1994). Outsiders in the Middle Kingdom. *European Management Journal, 12*(2), 147–153. doi:10.1016/0263-2373(94)90005-1.

Black, J. S. (1988). Work role transitions: A study of American expatriate managers in Japan. *Journal of International Business Studies, 19*, 277–294. doi:10.1057/palgrave.jibs.8490383.

Black, J. S. (1990). The relationship of personal characteristics with adjustment of Japanese expatriate managers. *Management International Review, 30*, 119–134.

Black, J. S., & Gregersen, H. B. (1991). The other half of the picture: Antecedents of spouse cross-cultural adjustment. *Journal of International Business Studies, 22*(3), 3, 461–477. doi:10.1057/palgrave.jibs.8490311.

Black, J. S., & Gregersen, H. B. (1999). The right way to manage expats. *Harvard Business Review*, (March-April): 52–62.

Black, J. S., Gregersen, H. B., & Mendenhall, M. (1992). *Global assignments: Successfully expatriating and repatriating international managers*. San Francisco, CA: Jossey-Bass.

Black, J. S., Gregersen, H. B., Mendenhall, M. E., & Stroh, L. K. (1999). *Globalizing people through international assignments*. MA: Addison-Wesley.

Black, J. S., Gregersen, H. B., & Stroh, L. K. (1999). *Globalizing people through international assignment*. Reading, MA: Addison-Wesley.

Black, J. S., & Mendenhall, M. E. (1990). Cross-cultural training effectiveness: A review and a theoretical framework for future research. *Academy of Management Review, 15*(1), 113–136.

Black, J. S., & Stevens, G. K. (1989). The influence of the spouse on American expatriate adjustment and intent to stay in pacific rim overseas assignments. *Journal of Management, 15*, 529–544. doi:10.1177/014920638901500403.

Bloom, N., Kretschmer, T., & Van Reenen, J. (2006). *Work-life balance, management practices and productivity*. Retrieved on June 13, 2012, from http://www.stanford.edu/~nbloom/WorkLifeBalance.pdf

Borman, W. C., Ilgen, D. R., & Klimoski, R. L. (2003). Handbook of psychology: *Vol. 12. Industrial and organizational psychology*. New York: Wiley.

Borman, W. C., Klimoski, R. L., & Ilgen, D. R. (2003). Stability and change in industrial and organizational psychology. In W. C. Borman, D. R. Ilgen, & R. J. Klimoski (Eds.), Handbook of psychology, Vol. 12: Industrial and organizational psychology. New York: John Wiley and Sons.

Borstorff, P. C., Harris, S. G., Field, H. S., & Giles, W. F. (1997). Who'll go? A Review of factors associated with employee willingness to work overseas. *Human Resources Planning*, *20*(3), 29–40.

Bransford, J., Vye, N., Stevens, R., Kuhl, P., Schwartz, D., & Bell, P. ... Sabelli, N. (2005). Learning theories and education: Toward a decade of synergy. In P. Alexander & P. Winne (2nd ed.), Handbook of educational psychology. Mahwah, NJ: Erlbaum.

Brewster, C. (1991). *The management of expatriates*. London: Kogan Page.

Brogden, H. E. (1949). When testing pays off. *Personnel Psychology*, *2*, 171–183. doi:10.1111/j.1744-6570.1949.tb01397.x.

Bryan, W. L., & Harter, N. (1897). Studies in the physiology and psychology of the telegraphic language. *Psychological Review*, *4*, 27–53. doi:10.1037/h0073806.

Burtt, H. E. (1929). *Psychology and industrial efficiency*. New York: Appleton.

Caligiuri, P. M. (2000). The Big Five Personality Characteristics as Predictors of Expatriate's Desire to Terminate the Assignment and Supervisor-Rated Performance. *Personnel Psychology*, *53*(1), 67–88. doi:10.1111/j.1744-6570.2000.tb00194.x.

Campion, M., Gowing, M., Lancaster, A., & Pearlman, K. (1994). *United states department of labor database of occupational titles reinvention project: DOT transition team final report*. Washington, DC: U.S. Department of Personnel Management.

Cari, M., Tuba, M., & Moisil, I. (N. Y.). *Web-based testing and self-assessment system implemented with open technologies*. Retrieved on August 18, 2012, from http://www.wseas.us/e-library/conferences/2010/Corfu/EDUCATION/EDUCATION-50.pdf

Caro, R. A. (2002). *Master of the senate: The years of Lyndon Johnson*. New York: Knopf.

Cascio, W. F. (2007). Evidence-based management and the marketplace for idea. *Academy of Management Journal*, *50*, 1009–1012. doi:10.5465/AMJ.2007.27151942.

Cascio, W. F. (2008). To prosper, organizational psychology should bridge application and scholarship. *Journal of Organizational Behavior*, *29*, 455–468. doi:10.1002/job.528.

Cascio, W. F., & Aguinis, H. (2008). Research in industrial and organizational psychology from 1963 to 2007: Changes, choices, and trends. *The Journal of Applied Psychology*, *93*(5), 5, 1062–1081. doi:10.1037/0021-9010.93.5.1062 PMID:18808226.

Chmiel, N. (2000). History and context for work and organizational psychology. In Chmiel, N. (Ed.), *Introduction to work and organizational psychology: A european perspective*. Malden, MA: Blackwell.

Church, A. (1982). Sojourner adjustment. *Psychological Bulletin*, *91*, 540–572. doi:10.1037/0033-2909.91.3.540.

Conger, J., & Kanungo, R. N. (1994). Charismatic leadership in organizations: Perceived behavioral attributes and their management. *Journal of Organizational Behavior*, *15*, 439–452. doi:10.1002/job.4030150508.

Copeland, L., & Briggs, L. (1985). *Going international*. New York: Random House.

Corson, D. (2000). Emancipatory leadership. *International Journal of Leadership in Education*, *3*(2), 93–120. doi:10.1080/136031200292768.

Daft, R. L. (2001). *Organization theory and design* (7th ed.). South-Western College Publishing.

Deal, T. E., & Kennedy, A. A. (1982). *Corporate cultures: The rites and rituals of corporate life*. New York: Basic Books.

Denison, D. (1996). What is the difference between organizational culture and organizational climate? In Cartwright, S., & Cooper, C. (Eds.), *The handbook of organizational culture*. London: John Wiley & Sons.

Devanna, M., Fombrum, N., & Tichy, N. (1981). Human resources management: A strategic perspective. *Organizational Dynamics*, *10*, 51–67. doi:10.1016/0090-2616(81)90038-3.

Dipboye, R. L. (2007). Eight outrageous statements about HR science. *Human Resource Management Review*, *76*, 96–106. doi:10.1016/j.hrmr.2007.04.001.

Donaldson, T., & Dunfee, T. W. (2001). When ethics travel: The promise and peril of global business ethics. In J. S. Osland, D. A. Kolb, & I. M. Rubin (7th ed.), The organizational behavior reader. Upper Saddle River, NJ: Prentice Hall.

Drucker, P. F. (1974). *Management: Tasks, responsibilities, practices*. New York: Harper & Row Publishers, Inc..

Dul, J., Bruder, R., Buckle, P., Carayon, P., & Falzon, P., Marras, …van der Doelen, B. (2012). A strategy for human factors/ergonomics: Developing the discipline and profession. *Ergonomics*, *55*(4), 377–395. doi:10.1080/00140139.2012.661087 PMID:22332611.

Dunnette, M. D. (1990). Blending the science and practice of industrial and organizational psychology: Where are we and where are we going? In Dunnette, M. D., & Hough, L. M. (Eds.), *Handbook of industrial and organizational psychology* (2nd ed., *Vol. 1*). Palo Alto, CA: Consulting Psychologists Press.

Dunnette, M. D., & Hough, L. M. (1990). *Handbook of industrial and organizational psychology* (2nd ed., *Vol. 1*). Palo Alto, CA: Consulting Psychologists Press.

Dunnette, M. D., & Hough, L. M. (1991). *Handbook of industrial and organizational psychology* (2nd ed., *Vol. 2*). Palo Alto, CA: Consulting Psychologists Press.

Dunnette, M. D., & Hough, L. M. (1992). *Handbook of industrial and organizational psychology* (2nd ed., *Vol. 3*). Palo Alto, CA: Consulting Psychologists Press.

Ebbinghaus, H. (1973). *Psychology: An elementary text-book*. New York: Arno Press. (Original work published 1908).

Eby, L. T., Casper, W. J., Lockwood, A., Bordeaux, C., & Brinley, A. (2005). Work and family research in io/obl: Content analysis and review of the literature (1980-2002). *Journal of Vocational Behavior*, *66*(1), 124–197. doi:10.1016/j.jvb.2003.11.003.

Erez, M. (1997). A culture-based model of work motivation. In Earley, P. C., & Erez, M. (Eds.), *New perspective on international industrial/organizational psychology*. San Francisco, CA: The New Lexington Press.

Erez, M., & Early, P. C. (1993). *Culture, self-identity, and work*. New York: Oxford University Press. doi:10.1093/acprof:oso/9780195075809.001.0001.

Ferraro, G. P. (1994). *The cultural dimension of international business* (2nd ed.). Upper Saddle River, NJ: Prentice Hall.

Forster, N., & Johnsen, M. (1996). Expatriate management policies in UK companies new to the international scene. *International Journal of Human Resource Management*, *7*(1), 177–205. doi:10.1080/09585199600000124.

Fritz, C., & Sonnentag, S. (2005). Recovery, health, and job performance: Effects of weekend experiences. *Journal of Occupational Health Psychology, 10*(3), 187–199. doi:10.1037/1076-8998.10.3.187 PMID:16060723.

Furnham, A. (1997). *The psychology of behavior at work*. East Sussex, UK: Taylor and Francis.

Geertz, C. (1973). *The interpretation of cultures*. New York: Basic.

Gelade, G. A. (2006). But what does it mean in practice? *Journal of Occupational and Organizational Psychology, 79*, 153–160. doi:10.1348/096317905X85638.

George, J. M. (2000). Emotions and leadership: The role of emotional intelligence. *Human Relations, 53*, 1027–1055. doi:10.1177/0018726700538001.

Gibson, C. B., & Cohen, S. G. (2003). *Virtual teams that work: Creating conditions for virtual team effectiveness*. San Francisco, CA: Jossey-Bass.

Greenfield, P. M. (2000). Three approaches to the psychology of culture: Where do they come from? Where can they go? *Asian Journal of Social Psychology, 3*, 223–240. doi:10.1111/1467-839X.00066.

Guzzo, R. A., & Dickson, M. W. (1996). Teams in organizations: Recent research on performance and effectiveness. *Annual Review of Psychology, 47*, 307–338. doi:10.1146/annurev.psych.47.1.307 PMID:15012484.

Hancock, P. A. (1997). *Essays on the future of human-machine systems*. Minneapolis, MN: Author.

Harris, H., & Brewster, C. (1999). The coffee-machine system: How international selection really works. *International Journal of Human Resource Management, 10*(3), 488–500. doi:10.1080/095851999340440.

Heine, S. J. (2008). *Cultural psychology*. New York: W. W. Norton.

Helander, M. (1997). The human factors professions. In Salvendy, G. (Ed.), *Handbook of human factors and ergonomics* (2nd ed.). New York: John Wiley.

Herzberg, F. (1966). *Work and the nature of man*. Cleveland, OH: World Publishing.

Highhouse, S. (2007). Applications of organizational psychology: Learning though failure or failure to learn? In Koppes, L. L. (Ed.), *Historical perspectives in industrial and organizational psychology*. Mahwah, NJ: Erlbaum.

Hodgetts, R. M., & Luthans, F. (1993). U.S. Multinational's Expatriate Compensation Strategies. *Compensation and Benefits Review, 25*(1), 57–62. doi:10.1177/088636879302500111.

Hodgkinson, G. P. (2006). The role of joop (and other scientific journals) in bridging the practitioner-researcher divide in industrial, work, and organizational (i/o) psychology. *Journal of Occupational and Organizational Psychology, 79*, 173–178. doi:10.1348/096317906X104013.

Hofstede, G. (1991). *Culture and organizations: Software of the mind*. London: McGraw-Hill.

Hofstede, G. (2002). The pitfalls of cross-national survey research: A reply to the article by spector et al. on the psychometric properties of the hofstede values survey module 1994. *Applied Psychology, 51*, 170–173. doi:10.1111/1464-0597.084_2.

Hogan, R., & Kaiser, R. B. (2005). What we know about leadership. *Review of General Psychology, 9*(2), 169–180. doi:10.1037/1089-2680.9.2.169.

Hollway, W. (2000). *Work psychology and organizational behaviour: Managing the individual at work*. Thousand Oaks, CA: Sage.

Hughes, R. L., Ginnett, R. C., & Curphy, C. G. (1996). *Leadership: Enhancing the lessons of experience*. Chicago, IL: Irwin.

James, P., & Thorpe, N. (1994). *Ancient inventions*. New York, NY: Ballentine.

Jones, G. R. (2004). *Organizational theory, design, and change: Text and cases* (4th ed.). Upper Saddle River, NJ: Pearson Prentice Hall.

Judge, T. A., & Simon, L. S. (2007). The globalization of industrial-organizational psychology: A comparative analysis. *Psychology of Human Resources*, *5*, 6–13.

Kagitcibasi, C., & Berry, J. W. (1989). Cross-cultural psychology: Current research and trends. *Annual Review of Psychology*, *40*, 493–531. doi:10.1146/annurev.ps.40.020189.002425.

Karwowski, W. (1991). Complexity, fuzziness and ergonomic and incompatibility issues: The control of dynamic work environments. *Ergonomics*, *34*(6), 676–686. doi:10.1080/00140139108967345.

Karwowski, W. (2001). *International encyclopedia of ergonomics and human factors*. London: Taylor and Francis.

Katz, D., & Kahn, R. L. (1978). *The social psychology of organizing* (2nd ed.). New York: Wiley.

Katz, J. P., & Seifer, D. M. (1996). It's a Different World Out There: Planning for Expatriate Success Through Selection, Pre-departure Training and On-site Socialization. *HR. Human Resource Planning*, *19*(2), 32–54.

Keith, K. D. (2010). Introduction to cross-cultural psychology. In K. D. Keith (Ed.), Cross-cultural psychology: Contemporary themes and perspectives. Wiley-Blackwell.

Kluckhohn, C. (1954). *Culture and behavior*. New York: Free Press.

Kobrin, S. J. (1988). Expatriate reduction and strategic control in American multicultural corporations. *Human Resource Management*, *27*, 63–75. doi:10.1002/hrm.3930270104.

Kornhauser, A. W. (1929). Industrial psychology in England, Germany and the United States. *The Personnel Journal*, *8*, 421–434.

Kroeber, A. L., & Kluckhohn, F. (1991). Culture: A critical review of concepts and definitions, peabody museum papers, (Vol. 47, no. 1). In N. J. Adler (Ed.), International dimensions of organizational behavior. Boston, MA: PWS-Kent.

Landy, F. J., & Conte, J. M. (2004). *Work in the 21st century: An introduction to industrial and organizational psychology*. Boston, MA: McGraw-Hill.

Lapointe, J. B. (1990). Industrial/organizational psychology: A view from the field. In Murphy, K. R., & Saal, F. E. (Eds.), *Psychology in organizations: Integrating science and practice*. Hillsdale, NJ: Erlbaum.

Laungani, P. (2002). Cross-cultural psychology: A handmaiden to mainstream western psychology. *Counselling Psychology Quarterly*, *15*, 385–397. doi:10.1080/0951507031000069392.

Lengnick-Hall, C. A., & Lengnick-Hall, M. (1988). Strategic human resource management: A review of the literature and a proposed typology. *Academy of Management Review*, *13*(3), 454–470.

Levitt, T. (1983). The globalization of markets. *Harvard Business Review*, *5*(6), 92–102.

Locke, E. A. (1968). Toward a theory of task motivation and incentives. *Organizational Behavior and Human Performance*, *3*, 157–189. doi:10.1016/0030-5073(68)90004-4.

Locke, E. A. (1970). Job satisfaction and job performance. *Organizational Behavior and Human Performance*, *5*, 484–500. doi:10.1016/0030-5073(70)90036-X.

Lockwood, N. R. (2003). Work/life balance: Challenges and solutions. *HRMagazine*, *48*(6), 2–11.

Louis, M. R. (1980). Surprise and sense making: What newcomers experience in entering unfamiliar organizational settings. *Administrative Science Quarterly*, *25*, 226–251. doi:10.2307/2392453 PMID:10247029.

Markides, C. (2007). In search of ambidextrous professors. *Academy of Management Journal*, *50*, 762–768. doi:10.5465/AMJ.2007.26279168.

Matsumoto, D. (2009). Teaching about culture. In Gurung, R. A. R., & Prieto, L. R. (Eds.), *Getting culture: Incorporating diversity across the curriculum*. New York: Stylus.

McDonald, G. M. (1993). Et go home? The successful management of expatiate transfer. *Journal of Managerial Psychology*, *8*(2), 18–29. doi:10.1108/02683949310032758.

McHenry, J. (2007). *We are the very model*. Presidential address delivered at the annual meeting of the Society for Industrial and Organizational Psychology. New York.

Meister, D. (1999). *The history of human factors and ergonomics*. Mahwah, NJ: Lawrence Erlbaum Associates.

Mendenhall, M. E., Dunbar, E., & Oddou, G. R. (1987). Expatriate selection, training, and career-pathing: A review and critique. *Human Resource Management*, *26*, 331–345. doi:10.1002/hrm.3930260303.

Mendenhall, M. E., & Oddou, G. R. (1985). The dimensions of expatriate acculturation: A review. *Academy of Management Review*, *10*(1), 39–47.

Morcillo, P. & Garces, I. (N. Y.). *The cultural organization model: A review of the organizational culture literature*. Retrieved on June 14, 2012 fromhttp://patriciomorcillo.com/publicacion4.pdf

Morgan, G. (1997). *Images of organization* (2nd ed.). Sage Publications, Inc..

Murphy, K. R., & Saal, F. E. (1990). What should we expect from scientist-practitioners? In Murphy, K. R., & Saal, F. E. (Eds.), *Psychology in organizations: Integrating science and practice*. Hillsdale, NJ: Erlbaum.

Oddou, G., & Mendenhall, G. (1991). Succession planning for the 21st century: How well are we grooming our future business leaders? *Business Horizons*, *34*, 26–34. doi:10.1016/0007-6813(91)90078-A.

Ouchi, W. (1981). *Theory Z: How American business can meet the Japanese challenge*. Boston, MA: Addison-Wesley. doi:10.1016/0007-6813(81)90031-8.

Pascale, R. T., & Athos, A. G. (1982). *The art of Japanese management: Applications for american executives*. Warner Books.

Peters, T., & Waterman, R. H. Jr. (1982). *In search of excellence: Lessons from America best-run companies*. New York: HarperCollins.

Peterson, N. G., Mumford, M. D., Borman, W. C., Jeanneret, P. R., & Fleishman, E. A. (1999). *The occupation information network*. Washington, DC: American Psychological Association.

Peterson, N. G., Mumford, M. D., Borman, W. C., Jeanneret, P. R., Fleishman, E. A., & Levin, K. Y. et al. (2001). Understanding work using the occupational information network: Implications for practice and research. *Personnel Psychology*, *54*, 451–492. doi:10.1111/j.1744-6570.2001.tb00100.x.

Phillips, N. (1992). *Managing international teams*. London: Pitman.

Pitariu, H. D. (1992). I/O psychology in Romania: Past, present and intentions. *The Industrial-Organizational Psychologist*, *29*(4), 29–33.

Poe, A. C. (2002). Selection savvy. *HRMagazine*, *47*(4), 77–83.

Porter, L. W., & Lawler, E. E. (1968). *Managerial attitudes and performance*. Homewood, IL: Dorsey Press.

Roethlisberger, F. J., & Dickson, W. J. (1939). *Management and the worker*. Cambridge, MA: Harvard University Press.

Rogelberg, S. G. (2007). Introduction. In Rogelberg, S. G. (Ed.), *Encyclopedia of industrial and organizational psychology* (*Vol. 1*). Thousand Oaks, CA: Sage.

Rosca, A., & Voicu, C. (1982). *A concise history of psychology in roamnia*. Bucharest: Editura Stiintifica Psychologica si Enciclopedia.

Rupp, D. E., & Beal, D. (2007). Checking in with the scientist-practitioner model: How are we doing? *The Industrial-Organizational Psychologist*, *45*, 35–40.

Rynes, S. L., Bartunek, J. M., & Daft, R. L. (2001). Across the great divide: Knowledge creation and transfer between practitioners and academics. *Academy of Management Journal*, *44*, 340–355. doi:10.2307/3069460.

Rynes, S. L., Colbert, A. E., & Brown, K. G. (2002). HR professionals' beliefs about effective human resource practices: Correspondence between research and practice. *Human Resource Management*, *41*, 149–174. doi:10.1002/hrm.10029.

Salvendy, G. (2012). *Handbook of human factors and ergonomics* (4th ed.). Wisley. doi:10.1002/9781118131350.

Saville & Holdsworth Limited. (2001). *The work profiling system (WPS) technical manual*. Boulder, CO: Author.

Schein, E. (1996). *Organizational culture and leadership* (2nd ed.). Jossey-Bass.

Schein, E. (1998). *Process consultation revisited: Building the helping relationship*. Boston, MA: Addison Wesley Longman.

Schneider, B., & Schmitt, N. (1986). *Staffing organizations* (2nd ed.). New York: HarperCollins Publishers, Inc..

Schneider, S. C., & Barsoux, J. L. (1997). *Managing across cultures*. Prentice Hall.

Searle, W., & Wards, C. (1990). The predication of psychological and sociocultural adjustment during cross-cultural transitions. *International Journal of Intercultural Relations*, *14*, 449–464. doi:10.1016/0147-1767(90)90030-Z.

Shafritz, J. M. Ott, J. S., & Jang, Y. S. (2005). Classics of organization theory (6th ed.). Belmont, CA: Thomson-Wadsworth.

Shafritz, J. M., & Ott, J. S. (2001). *Classics of organization theory* (5th ed.). San Diego, CA: Harcourt College Publishers.

Shay, J., & Tracey, J. B. (1997). Expatriate managers: Reasons for failure and implications for training. *The Cornell Hotel and Restaurant Administration Quarterly*, *38*, 30–35. doi:10.1177/001088049703800116.

Shimmin, S., & van Strien, P. J. (1998). History of the psychology of work and organization. In Drenth, P. J. D., Thierry, H., & de Wolff, C. J. (Eds.), *Handbook of work and organizational psychology*. Hove, UK: Psychology Press.

Shimmin, S., & Wallis, D. (1994). *Fifty years on occupational psychology*. Leicester, UK: British Psychological Society.

Shiraev, E. B., & Levy, D. A. (2010). *Cross-cultural psychology: Critical thinking and contemporary applications* (4th ed.). Boston, MA: Allyn and Bacon.

Shweder, R. A., & LeVine, R. A. (1984). *Culture theory: Essays on mind, self and emotion*. New York: Cambridge University Press.

Sinha, D. (2002). Culture and psychology: Perspective of cross-cultural psychology. *Psychology and Developing Societies*, *14*, 11–25. doi:10.1177/097133360201400102.

Skinner, B. F. (1969). *Contingencies of reinforcement*. New York: Appleton Century Crofts.

Society for Industrial and Organizational Psychology. (2007).*Mission statement*. Retrieved June 15, 2012, from http://www.siop.org

Spector, P. E., Cooper, C. L., & Sparks, K. (2001). An international study of the psychometric properties of the hofstede values survey module 1994: A comparison of individual and country/province level results. *Applied Psychology*, *50*, 269–281. doi:10.1111/1464-0597.00058.

Talbott, S. P. (1996). Building a global workforce starts with recruitment. *The Personnel Journal*, *3*, 9–12.

Taylor, E. B. (1871a). *Origins of culture*. New York: Harper & Row.

Taylor, E. B. (1871b). *Primitive culture*. New York: J. P. Putman's Sons.

Terracciano, A., Abdel-Khalek, A. M., Adam, N., Adamovova, L., Ahn, C. K., & Ahn, H. N. et al. (2005). National character does not reflect mean personality trait levels in 49 cultures. *Science*, *310*, 96–100. doi:10.1126/science.1117199 PMID:16210536.

Tharp, B. M. (2009). *Defining culture and organizational culture: From anthropology to the office*. Retrieved on June 14, 2012, from http://www.haworth.com/en-us/Knowledge/Workplace-Library/Documents/Defining-Culture-and-Organizationa-Culture_5.pdf

The Conference Board. (1992). *Recruiting and Selecting International Managers (report no. 998)*. New York: The Conference Board.

Toh, S. M., & DeNisi, A. (2005). A local perspective on expatriate success. *The Academy of Management Executive*, *19*(1), 132–145.

Torbiorn, I. (1982). *Living abroad: Personal adjustment and personnel policy in the overseas setting*. New York: Wiley.

Townsend, A. M., DeMarie, S. M., & Hendrickson, A. R. (1998). Virtual teams: Technology and the workplace of the future. *The Academy of Management Executive*, *12*, 17–29.

Tran, B. (2008). *Expatriate selection and retention*. Doctoral dissertation, Alliant International University, San Francisco, CA.

Tran, B. (2012). Gendered technology-based organizations: A view of the glass cliff through the window of the glass ceiling. In Jemielniak, D., & Marks, A. (Eds.), *Managing dynamic technology-oriented businesses: High-tech organizations and workplaces*. Hershey, PA: IGI Global. doi:10.4018/978-1-4666-1836-7.ch015.

Triandia, H. C., Dunnette, M. D., & Hough, L. M. (1994). *Handbook of industrial and organizational psychology* (2nd ed., *Vol. 4*). Palo Alto, CA: Consulting Psychologists Press.

Triandis, H. C. (2000). Dialectics between cultural and cross-cultural psychology. *Asian Journal of Social Psychology*, *3*, 185–195. doi:10.1111/1467-839X.00063.

Triandis, H. C., Kurowski, L., Tecktiel, A., & Chan, D. (1993). Extracting the emics of cultural diversity. *International Journal of Intercultural Relations*, *17*, 217–234. doi:10.1016/0147-1767(93)90026-5.

Tung, R. L. (1981). Selection and training of personnel for overseas assignments. *The Columbia Journal of World Business*, *16*, 21–25.

Tung, R. L. (1982). Selection and training procedures of United States, European, and Japanese multinationals. *California Management Review*, *25*, 57–71. doi:10.2307/41164993.

Tung, R. L. (1988). Career issues in international assignments. *The Academy of Management Executive*, *11*, 241–244. doi:10.5465/AME.1988.4277265.

van Drunen, P., & van Strien, P. J. (1999). Psychology in the Netherlands: Recent trends and current situation. *European Psychologist*, *4*, 263–271. doi:10.1027//1016-9040.4.4.263.

van Strien, P. J. (1998). Psychotechnics in the Netherlands. *Revista de Historia de la Psicología*, *19*, 121–141.

Viteles, M. S. (1926). Psychology in industry. *Psychological Bulletin*, *23*, 631–680. doi:10.1037/h0070328.

Viteles, M. S. (1928). Psychology in industry. *Psychological Bulletin*, *25*, 309–340. doi:10.1037/h0072719.

Viteles, M. S. (1930). Psychology in industry. *Psychological Bulletin*, *27*, 567–635. doi:10.1037/h0073024.

Viteles, M. S. (1932). *Industrial psychology*. New York: W. W. Norton.

Vroom, V. H. (1964). *Work and motivation*. New York: John Wiley & Sons.

Walter, M. (2007). Just how good is globalization? *Wall Street Journal*.

Watanabe, S., Takahashi, K., & Minami, T. (1997). The emerging role of diversity and work-family values in a global context. In Earley, P. C., & Erez, M. (Eds.), *New perspective on international industrial/organizational psychology*. San Francisco, CA: The New Lexington Press.

Wederspahn, G. (1992). Costing failures in expatriate human resource management. *Human Resource Planning*, *15*, 27–35.

Wright, P. M. (1998). Introduction: Strategic human resource management research in the 21st century. *Human Resource Management Review*, *8*(3), 187–191. doi:10.1016/S1053-4822(98)90001-8.

Yang, K. S. (2000). Monocultural and cross-cultural indigenous approaches: The royal road to the development of a balanced global psychology. *Asian Journal of Social Psychology*, *3*, 241–263. doi:10.1111/1467-839X.00067.

Yerkes, R. M. (1921). *Memories of the national academy of sciences: Psychological examining in the United States army* (*Vol. 15*). Washington, DC: U.S. Government Printing Office. doi:10.1037/10619-000.

Zedeck, S. (1997). Commentary on diversity and work-family values. In Earley, P. C., & Erez, M. (Eds.), *New perspective on international industrial/organizational psychology*. San Francisco, CA: The New Lexington Press.

Zeira, Y., & Banai, M. (1985). Selection of expatriate-managers in multinational corporations: The host environment point of view. *International Studies of Management and Organization*, *15*, 33–51.

Zhou, J., & George, J. M. (2003). Awakening employee creativity: The role of leader emotional intelligence. *The Leadership Quarterly*, *14*, 545–568. doi:10.1016/S1048-9843(03)00051-1.

ADDITIONAL READING

Aamodt, M. G. (2009). *Industrial/organizational psychology* (6th ed.). Belmont, CA: Wadsworth Publishing.

Aguinis, H. (2009). *Performance management* (2nd ed.). Upper Saddle River, NJ: Prentice Hall.

Allwood, C. M., & Berry, J. W. (2006). Origins and development of indigenous psychologies: An international analysis. *International Journal of Psychology*, *41*, 243–268. doi:10.1080/00207590544000013.

Barnett, M. L. (2007). (Un)learning and (mis) education through the eyes of bill starbuck: An interview with pandora's playmate. *Academy of Management Learning & Education*, *6*, 114–127. doi:10.5465/AMLE.2007.24401709.

Berry, J. W., Poortinga, Y. H., Segall, M. H., & Dasen, P. R. (2002). *Cross-cultural psychology: Research and applications* (2nd ed.). Cambridge, UK: Cambridge University Press.

Boxall, P. (1998). Achieving competitive advantage through human resource strategy: Toward a theory of industry dynamics. *Human Resource Management Review*, *8*(3), 265–288. doi:10.1016/S1053-4822(98)90005-5.

Bridger, R. S. (2008). *Introduction to ergonomics* (3rd ed.). CRC Press.

Brislin, R. (2000). *Understanding culture's influence on behavior* (2nd ed.). Fort Worth, TX: Harcourt College Publishers.

Burnham, J. C. (2009). *Accident prone: A history of technology, psychology, and misfits of the machine age*. Chicago, IL: University of Chicago Press. doi:10.7208/chicago/9780226081199.001.0001.

Bush, P. M. (2011). *Ergonomics: Foundational principles, applications, and technologies (Ergonomics design and management: Theory and applications)*. CRC Press.

Cascio, W. F., & Aguinis, H. (2010). *Applied psychology in human resource management* (7th ed.). Upper Saddle River, NJ: Prentice Hall.

Cohen, A. B. (2009). Many forms of culture. *The American Psychologist*, *64*, 194–204. doi:10.1037/a0015308 PMID:19348520.

Dowling, P. J., Festing, M., & Engle, A. (2007). *International human resource management: Managing people in a multinational context*. South-Western College Publishing.

Francesco, A. M., & Gold, B. A. (1998). *International organizational behavior: Text, readings, cases, and skills*. Upper Saddle River, NJ: Prentice Hall.

Gatewood, R., Feild, H. S., & Barrick, M. (2010). *Human resource selection* (7th ed.). South-Western College Publishing.

Gratton, L., Hailey, H., Stiles, P., & Truss, C. (1999). *Strategic human resource management*. New York: Oxford University Press. doi:10.1093/acprof:oso/9780198782049.001.0001.

Jex, S. M., & Britt, T. W. (2008). *Organizational psychology: A scientist-practitioner approach* (2nd ed.). New York: Wiley.

Koppes, L. L. (2006). *Historical perspectives in industrial and organizational psychology*. Hillsdale, NJ: Lawrence Erlbaum Associates.

Latham, G. P. (2011). *Work motivation: History, theory, research, and practice* (2nd ed.). Sage Publications, Inc..

Lawson, R., & Shen, Z. (1997). *Organizational psychology: Foundations and applications*. Oxford, UK: Oxford University Press.

Lepak, D. P., & Snell, S. A. (1998). Virtual HR: Strategic human resource management in 21st century. *Human Resource Management Review*, *8*(3), 215–234. doi:10.1016/S1053-4822(98)90003-1.

Miller, R. L. (2008). Community psychology. In S. F. Davis & W. Buskist (Eds.), 21st century psychology: A reference handbook. Thousand Oaks, CA: Sage.

Morrison, T., Conaway, W. A., & Borden, G. A. (1994). *How to do business in sixty countries: Kiss, bow, or shake hands*. Avon, MA: Adams Media Corporation.

Noe, R. (2009). *Employee training & development* (5th ed.). New York: McGraw-Hill/Irwin.

Osland, J. S., Kolb, D. A., & Rubin, I. M. (2001a). *The organizational behavior reader* (7th ed.). Upper Saddle River, NJ: Prentice Hall.

Osland, J. S., Kolb, D. A., & Rubin, I. M. (2001b). *Organizational behavior: An experiential approach* (7th ed.). Upper Saddle River, NJ: Prentice Hall.

Poortinga, Y. H. (2005). The globalization of indigenous psychologies. *Asian Journal of Social Psychology*, *8*, 65–74. doi:10.1111/j.1467-839X.2005.00157.x.

Riggio, R. E. (2012). *Introduction to industrial and organizational psychology* (6th ed.). Upper Saddle River, NJ: Prentice Hall.

Rogers, E. W., & Wright, P. M. (1998). Measuring organizational performance in strategic human resource management research: Problems, prospects, and performance information markets. *Human Resource Management Review*, *8*(3), 311–331. doi:10.1016/S1053-4822(98)90007-9.

Sathe, V. (1985). *Culture and related corporate realities*. Homewood, IL: Richard D. Irwin.

Schultz, D., & Schultz, S. E. (2009). *Psychology and work today* (10th ed.). Prentice Hall.

Segall, M. H., Lonner, W. J., & Berry, W. J. (1998). Cross-cultural psychology as a scholarly discipline: On the flowering of culture in behavioral research. *The American Psychologist*, *53*, 1101–1110. doi:10.1037/0003-066X.53.10.1101.

Shapiro, D. L., Kirkman, B. L., & Courtney, H. G. (2007). Perceived causes and solutions of the translation problem in management research. *Academy of Management Journal*, *50*, 249–266. doi:10.5465/AMJ.2007.24634433.

Shaw, J. D., Delery, J. E., Jenkins, G. D., & Gupta, N. (1999). An organizational level analysis of voluntary and involuntary turnover. *Academy of Management Journal*, *41*(5), 511–525. doi:10.2307/256939.

Spector, P. E. E. (1997). *Job satisfaction: Application, causes, and consequences*. Thousand Oaks, CA: Sage Publications, Inc..

Taylor, S., Beechler, S., & Napier, N. (1996). Toward an integrative model of strategic international human resource management. *Academy of Management Review*, *21*(4), 959–985.

Triandis, H. C. (1977). Cross-cultural social and personality psychology. *Personality and Social Psychology Bulletin*, *3*, 143–158. doi:10.1177/014616727700300202.

Triandis, H. C. (1980). Introduction. In H. C. Triandis & W. W. Lambert (Eds.), Handbook of cross-cultural psychology: Vol. 1, Perspectives. Boston, MA: Allyn and Bacon, Inc.

Vicente, K. (2004). *The human factor: Revolutionizing the way people live with technology*. London: Routledge.

Wickens, C. D., & Hollands, J. G. (1999). *Engineering psychology and human performance* (3rd ed.). Upper Saddle River, NJ: Prentice Hall.

Wickens, C. D., Lee, J. D., Liu, Y., & Gordon-Becker, S. (2003). *Introduction to human factors engineering* (2nd ed.). Prentice Hall.

Windham International and National Foreign Trade Council, Inc. (1998). *Global relocation trends: 1998 survey report*. New York: Windham International.

Wright, P. M., & McMahan, C. C. (1992). Thetoretical perspectives for strategic human resource management. *Journal of Management*, *18*, 295–320. doi:10.1177/014920639201800205.

Zedeck, S., & Goldstein, I. L. (2000). The relationship between i/o psychology and public policy: A commentary. In Kehoe, J. F. (Ed.), *Managing selection in changing organizations*. San Francisco, CA: Jossey-Bass.

KEY TERMS AND DEFINITIONS

Cross-Cultural Psychology: Is the study of similarities and differences in individual psychology and social functioning in various cultures and ethnic groups.

Globalization of Markets: Refers to the merging of historically distinct and separate national markets into one huge global marketplace.

Human Factors (Ergonomics or Human Engineering) Psychology: Examines the way in which work environments can be designed or modified to match the capabilities and limitations of human beings.

Industrial and Organizational Psychology: Is the branch of psychology concerned with the application of psychological principles in the workplace.

International (Global or Cross-Cultural) Psychology: Is an emerging branch of psychology that focuses on the worldwide enterprise of psychology in terms of communication and networking, cross-cultural comparison, scholarship, practice, and pedagogy.

Multinational Corporations (MNCs): Are U.S. international corporations that are based in the U.S., have their own internal industrial and organizational practitioners, but have locations abroad and conducts international business ventures with other countries.

Organizational Culture: Is a pattern of shared basic assumptions that the group learned as it solved its problems of external adaptation and internal integration, that has worked well enough to be considered valid, and therefore, to be taught to new members as the correct way to perceive, think, and feel in relation to those problems.

Organizational Psychology: Is concerned with how people adapt emotionally and socially to working in complex motivation, job satisfaction, leadership, organizational culture, teamwork, and related topics.

Personnel Psychology (Occupational Psychology): Was once known as vocational psychology and is interest in measuring and recording individual differences. In other words, personnel psychology deals with determining whether people have the knowledge, skills, abilities and personality, also commonly known as other characteristics.

Strategic Human Resource Management (SHRM): Is the logic utility and cost/benefit analysis process for assessing the value of any intervention affecting the organization's so-called human capital.

ENDNOTES

1 Candidates, used here, refer to any and all types and levels of scholar-practitioners, business executives, undergraduate/graduate business, and scholars-scholars.

2 A random research among the international community regarding commonly recognized universities located in the United States of America demonstrated that the Hass School of Business at University of California, Berkeley, Krannert School of Management at Purdue University, Marshall School of Business at University of Southern California, Stanford University's School of Business, Yale University, and The Fuqua School of Business at Duke University, just to randomly name a few business schools/program, do not offer a course in history and system.

3 Practitioners, used here, is based on Gelande's (2006) definition, namely, those who make recommendations about the management or development of people in organizational settings or advises those who do.

4 ISCT is pluralism and relativism. It allows for tolerance without amoralism by combining two previously unconnected traditions of social contract thinking—the hypothetical or *macro* contract and the extant or *micro* contract. Under ISCT, business communities cannot claim that their set of ethics norms is necessarily universal: they must exercise tolerance of some approaches from different communities.

5 The hypernorm of *necessary social efficiency*, or *efficiency* hypernorm, speaks to the need for institutions and coexistent duties designed to enable people to achieve basic or *necessary* social goods. These are goods desired by all rational people, such as health, education, housing, food, clothing, and social justice.

6 There are a handful of frameworks for examining cultures. Among these handful frameworks, the following four frameworks for examining cultures are often utilized by I/O practitioners: 1) Kluckhohn and Strodtbeck's Variations in Values Orientations, 2) Hofstede's Dimensions of Cultural Values, 3) Thrompenaars' Seven Dimensions of Culture, and 4) Hall's High- and Low-Context Cultural Framework (Francesco & Gold, 1998).

7 Reference was found and retrieved from Bransford, Vye, Stevens, Kuhl, Schwartz, Bell, Meltzoff, Barron, Pea, Reeves, Roschelle, and Sabelli's (2005) work.

8 The American Psychological Association (APA) has 56 divisions. The Society for Industrial and Organizational Psychology is division 14.

9 Hugo Munsterberg (1863-1916) was a Professor of Psychology at Harvard University. Munsterberg was known as one of four and most recognized founding figures of Industrial and Organizational Psychology.

10 Frederick Winslow Taylor (1865-1915) was trained as an engineer and known for inventing scientific management.

11 Frederick Winslow Taylor (1865-1915) was trained as an engineer and known for inventing scientific management.

12 Lillian Gilbreth (1878-1972) was trained as an engineer and was also known for being the mother of modern management. Gilbreth's maiden name is Lillian Evelyn Moller.

13 Wilhelm Wundt (1832-1920) was a German physician, psychologist, physiologist, philosopher, and professor, known today as one of the founding figures of modern psychology. He is widely regarded as the father of experimental psychology. Experimental psychology gave birth to I/O psychology during the WWI and WWII when experimentations were practiced.

14 Frank Bunker Gilbreth (1868-1924) was the husband of Lillian Gilbreth. With his wife and professional partner, Lillian, Gilbreth introduced the application of psychology to industrial management. He also developed intricate studies of motion that he adapted for use by injured soldiers and the physically disabled, as well as laborers. His work established that psychology and education are integral parts of successful management.

15 Human factors are comprised of many disciplines: Clinical Psychology, Experimental Psychology, Anthropometrics, Computer Science, Cognitive Science, Safety Engineering, Medical Science, Occupational Medicine, Exercise Physiology, Organizational Psychology, Educational Psychology, and Industrial Engineering.

16 Ergonomics, the study of work, was originally defined and proposed by the Polish

scientist B. W. Jastrzebowski (Karwowski, 1991, 2001). The term ergonomics was first coined by an Englishman, K.H.F. Murrell, who derived it from its Greek semantic roots. However, the Polish Ergonomics Society affirms a prior usage by the scientist W.B. Jastrezbowski whose 1857 thesis has an evident claim on priority of the word itself. Ergonomics is a term commonly used in the UK whereas human factors is a term commonly used in the US.

17 Sir Edward Burnett Tylor was an English anthropologist regarded as the founder of cultural anthropology. Taylor's most important work, *Primitive Culture* (1871), influenced in part by Darwin's theory of biological evolution, thus, developed the theory of an evolutionary, progressive relationship from primitive to modern cultures. Tylor was knighted in 1912. He is best known today for providing, in this book, one of the earliest and clearest definitions of culture, one that is widely accepted and used by contemporary anthropologists.

18 The American Psychological Association (APA) has 56 Divisions. International psychology is Division

19 The following four recommendations were adapted from Dr. Ben Tran's doctoral dissertation titled *Expatriate Selection and Retention*, at the Marshall Goldsmith School of Management [now known as California School of Professional Psychology (CSPP)] at Alliant International University.

20 I/O practitioners, used here, include organizational consultants (OC), organizational psychologists (OP), and organizational development practitioners (OD). While there are minor differences among these practitioners, MNCs commonly utilize these practitioners, and refer to them interchangeably.

21 Adobe Systems, Inc. acquired Macromedia on December 3, 2005.

22 Hewlett-Packard acquired Compaq Computer Corporation in 2002.

23 Oracle Corporation acquired Sun Microsystems, Inc. on January 27, 2010.

24 Recommendations two thru four were adapted from the *Expatriate Selection and Retention Handbook* in Dr. Ben Tran's doctoral dissertation titled *Expatriate Selection and Retention*, at the Marshall Goldsmith School of Management [now known as California School of Professional Psychology (CSPP)] at Alliant International University in San Francisco, California. Dr. Tran's dissertation was chaired by Dr. Jyotsna Sanzgiri and Dr. John Kantor. Dr. Jyotsna Sanzgiri has been an educator, researcher, and practitioner in the field of organizational behavior and change for more than 30 years. Benedictine University named her "one of the most distinguished women practitioners in the field of Organization Development, locally and globally." Dr. Sanzgiri continues to present at the National Academy of Management and the National Organization Development Conferences. Most recently, Dr. Sanzgiri was an invited delegate to the International Conference on Psychology and Business in Capetown, South Africa. Dr. Sanzgiri publishes regularly in the areas of cross-cultural and international approaches to practice in national and international journals. Dr. Sanzgiri is the founder and former Program Director of the Organizational Psychology program in the California School of Professional Psychology at Alliant International University in San Francisco, California. Dr. Sanzgiri received her Master of Business Administration (MBA) from Tulane University and her Doctor of Philosophy (Ph.D.) in Business Administration from the

University of Pittsburgh. Dr. John Kantor has been an educator, research, and practitioner in the field of Industrial and Organizational Psychology for many years. Dr. Kantor is an Associate Program Director of the Organizational Psychology Programs & Program Director of the Leadership PhD at Alliant International University in San Diego, California. Dr. Kantor has a Master of Business Administration (MBA) and received his Doctor of Philosophy (Ph.D.) in Industrial and Organizational Psychology from California School of Professional Psychology in San Diego, California. Dr. Sanzgiri is a tenured professor and Dr. Kantor is an Associate Professor at the California School of Professional Psychology at Alliant International University in California.

25 For an elaborate detail on the selection of criterions and the evolution of the ESRH, please refer to Dr. Ben Tran's doctoral dissertation titled *Expatriate Selection and Retention*.

APPENDIX

Figure 1A. The History of Industrial and Organizational Psychology

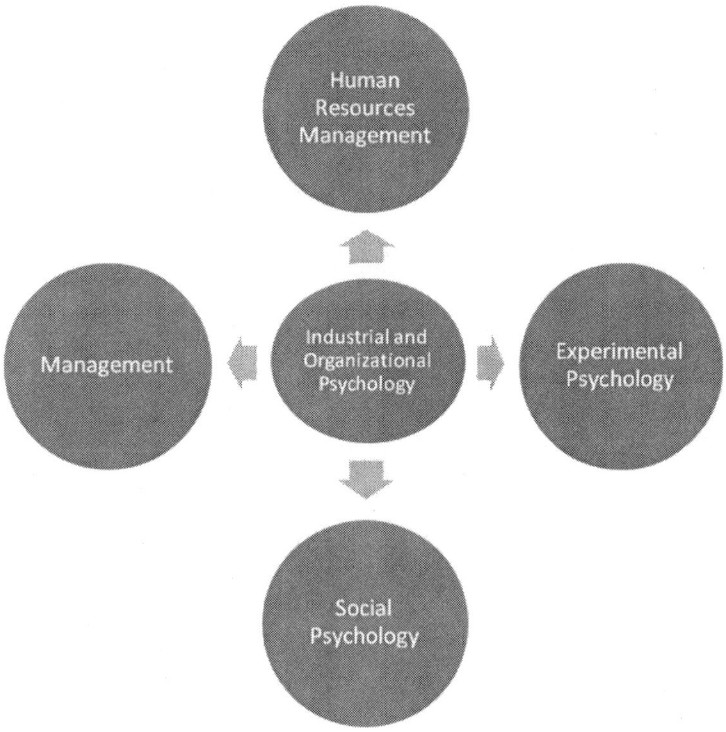

Figure 2A. Industrial and Organizational Psychology

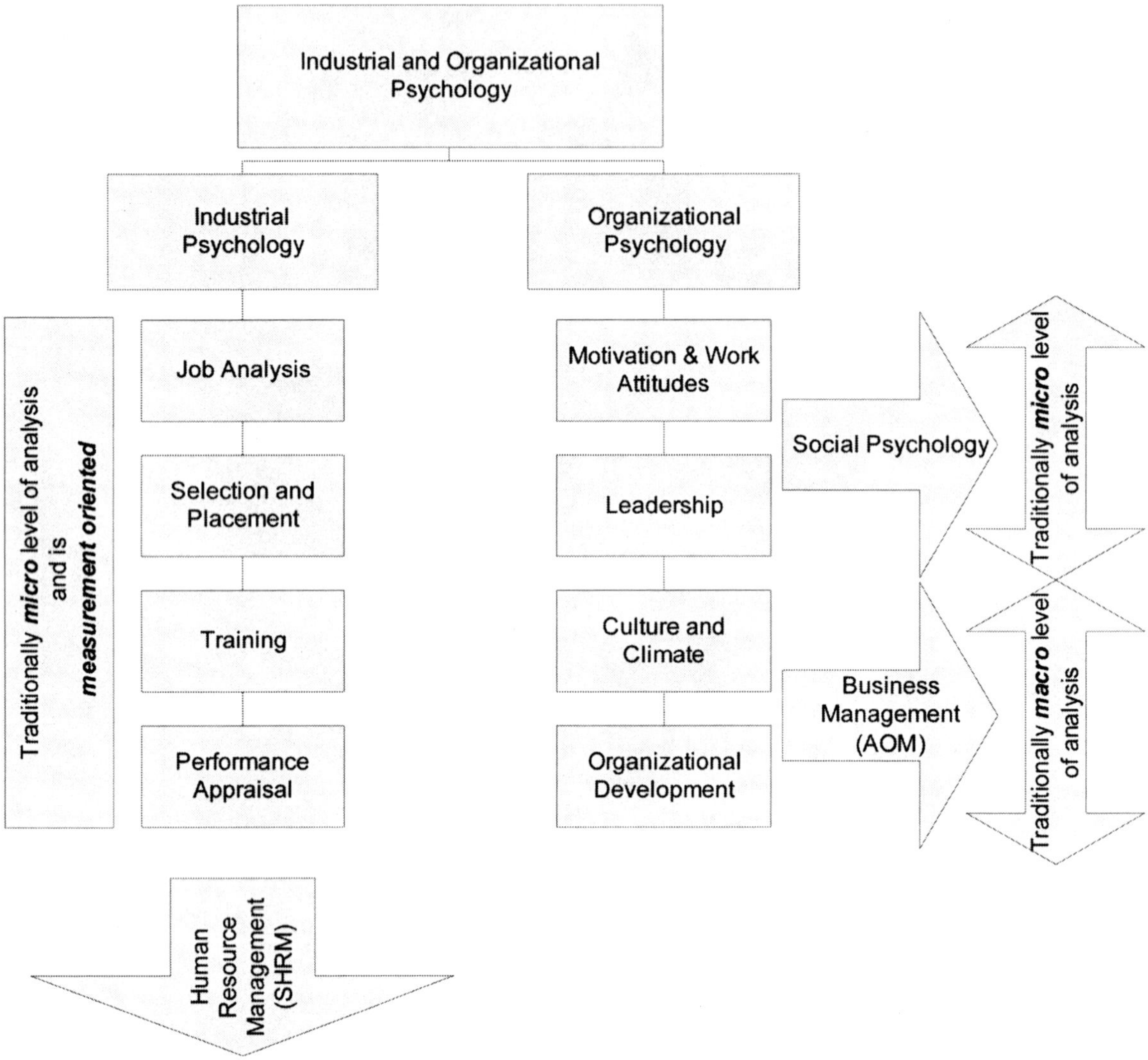

Figure 3A. Expatriate Selection and Retention Handbook

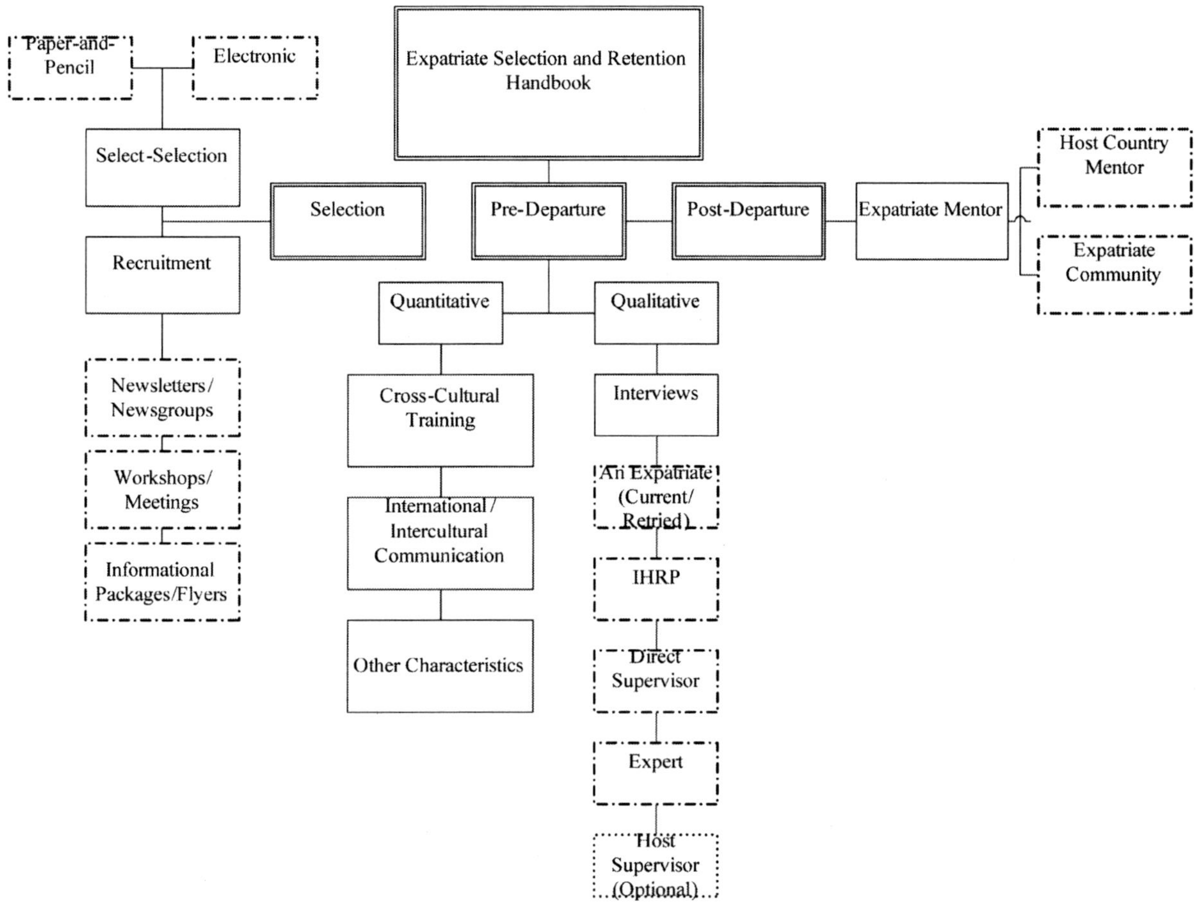

Chapter 12
Towards an Integrated Approach for Leading and Managing Transcultural Virtual Teams

M. Reza Hosseini
University of South Australia, Australia

Nicholas Chileshe
University of South Australia, Australia

ABSTRACT

*Many industries have observed the rise of Virtual Teams (VTs) as highly productive team structures taking advantage of members scattered around the globe while being able to accomplish assigned tasks by communicating through internet based technologies. Nonetheless, the looked-for achievable gains of VTs working heavily rest on meeting the requirements prescribed by the antecedents and critical success factors associated with specific idiosyncrasies of VTs such as the multiculturalism dominating their working environment. In this regard, it is widely recognized that when it comes to adopting VTs, the managerial/leadership matters are among the main challenges facing organisations. The major parts of foregoing issues are stemmed from the limitations of mediums of communications exacerbated by cultural diversity and disparity of members. This chapter first aims at critically analysing the different approaches of managing and leading virtual teams and ascertaining the main influential variables. This is followed by presenting a management/leadership model for VTs based on a dynamic integrated approach, thus labelled, '**Le**ading and **Man**aging **Vi**rtual **T**eams' (LeManViT).*

DOI: 10.4018/978-1-4666-3966-9.ch012

INTRODUCTION

Many novel team working structures have been emerged due to the push from the industry to improve the performance (Atrostic & Nguyen, 2005). The pressure on organisations to use more effective team working structures have been mounted considerably by the invasive globalization (Duarte & Snyder, 2006) and decentralisation trend (Algesheimer et al., 2011). Likewise, researchers have conducted a noticeable number of studies aimed at harnessing the capabilities of technology for satisfying the requirements of different industries in team working. Outcomes of the foregoing publications and the reports of successful cases within various industries have catalysed the trend of merging technology into team working procedures (Rezgui & Zarli, 2006; Bal & Teo, 2000; Reed & Knight, 2010). Specifically, many methods relied on Information and Communication Technologies (ICTs) have been introduced in recent years as effective strategies to improve different aspects of team performance and facilitate getting along with the globalization invasion (Duyshart et al., 2003; Nesbit, 2002; Hosseini et al., 2012; Peansupap, 2004). Utilizing internet based technologies have received special attention within organizations in which team members might happen to be located in different geographical areas (Joseph, 2005; Abudayyeh et al., 2001; Ahmad et al., 2002; Skibniewski & Abduh, 2000; Sriprasert & Dawood, 2002; Yacine, 2007). As the result, we have witnessed the emergence of Virtual Teams (VTs) as effective, efficient, and innovative team structure comprising of members scattered over different locations and time zones while working and communication through ICTs. On the one hand, the existing literature recommends adopting VTs in organizations due to many advantages they bring about for the organization. On the other hand, industries seem to be obliged to embark on using VTs as an available option to overcome the fierce competitive globalized business atmosphere eventually (Chen & Messner, 2010; Algesheimer et al., 2011; Yacine, 2007). On top of that, forecasts and predictions by the experts, practitioners and governmental institutes from many countries overwhelmingly show an increasing trend for using VTs as a part of future organizations' structures (Duarte & Snyder, 2006; Chang, 2011; Mukherjee et al., 2012).

Nonetheless, the major parts of literatures widely argue that any kind of VT comes with some particular challenges. Should the challenges not managed properly, the VTs have the potential for presenting worse effectiveness than that of the traditional ones. The positive outcome of VTs heavily relies on addressing the issues and resolving these challenges in due course. Any negligence in recognizing, addressing and taking appropriate measures to resolve the inherent challenges will jeopardize the efforts and investments by any organization to adopt virtual teams (Camarinha-Matos & Afsarmanesh, 2003; Gignac, 2005; Zenun et al., 2007; Chang, 2011). Therefore, any kind of effective strategy encompassing utilizing ICTs in teams with dispersed members requires a deeper understanding along with identification of the various critical factors that may not be found or be as important in traditional teamwork.

Above all, there is a common belief in the literature that research on utilizing VTs is not mature enough for providing the industry with necessary information (Van Pelt, 2010; Algesheimer et al., 2011; Booth, 2011; Martins & Schilpzand, 2011; Schweitzer & Duxbury, 2010). As the result, along with obvious necessity of further research, there is also a need for considering all the aspects of VTs in the industry and synthesizing the fragmented results of previous studies (Martins & Schilpzand, 2011). Otherwise, the industry will be deprived of considerable benefits VTs are able of offering for organizations due to the lack of knowledge (Joseph, 2005: Zhang et al., 2008). Nevertheless, some of the challenges of implementing VTs have been addressed in the literature more frequently. Obviously, the emphasis is on variables playing crucial role in successful adopting of VTs. Concisely, the main challenges of VTs could be summarised as the managerial/leadership issues due to the limitations of ICTs as the main medium exacerbated by antecedents of VTs namely cultural diversity and disparity of members. In alignment with the objective of the book, this chapter aims to describe the different aspects of the challenges of VTs in terms of managing and leading extracted from the cutting-edge research. It is followed by discussions presenting a new viewpoint by the authors stating the dire necessity of addressing the challenges of managing VTs based on an integrated approach, thus labelled, **Le**ading and **Man**aging **Vi**rtual **T**eams' (LeManViT). The proposed integrated approach considers resolving all the issues of managing VTs utilizing the most appropriate package of best practices of managing and leadership of VTs. In this regard, the fitted package of managing a VT will be selected based on the specific structure, defined affecting variables and the dimensions of virtuality designed for the team. However, any discussion on VTs requires a thorough knowledge of the conceptual definition of VTs in the literature and the affecting factors. Hence, the following sections of the chapter endeavour to enlighten the readers of the book about the definitions and labels used followed by the historical background and the updated status of industry in managing and leading VTs. The matters are selected based on a bias towards issues reflecting the different aspects of having members from various cultures in a team while having technology as the prime channel for working and communicating.

THEORETICAL DEFINITION

Before considering identification of the challenges affecting the virtual teams, it is necessary to explore the various approaches towards the definition of 'virtual teams' as offered in literature, and suggest a working definition of 'virtual teams' as used within this chapter.

Various Approaches to Theoretical Definition of 'Virtual Teams'

A quick scan of the titles of well-known articles shows one the fact that there is no unique widely accepted label for teams working virtually amongst the extant published works. Their rapid proliferation is the outcome of a combination of driving forces including the inevitable necessity for changes dictated from the industry and the advancements within the ICTs. Hence, the concepts related to VTs are still evolving and the terminology has not been fixed yet (Powell et al., 2004; Martins & Schilpzand, 2011). As the result of the ever evolving concept of VTs, there is not even one common definition for the virtual teams which has been agreed upon by the researchers (Chen & Messner, 2010; Martins & Schilpzand, 2011; Schweitzer & Duxbury, 2010; Mawanda, 2012). Reviewing the literature reveals that the number of available definitions nearly equals the number of researchers presenting the definitions. In this regards, we consider three approaches towards defining virtual teams in the literature as illustrated in Table 1.

The confusion in the literature in presenting a theoretical definition for VTs is obvious since there are different hypothesis and even many approaches for determining whether a team could be assumed as a virtual team. It is due to the lack of appreciation on the dimensions associated with the virtuality of a team. On the other hand, the conceptual definition is the basis of further research and discussions on the subject. Therefore, any ambiguity in this area could directly end up in the vagueness in all the issues regarding VTs. Concerning this problem, some researchers have endeavoured to resolve the issue (Schweitzer & Duxbury, 2010) by investigating the directions and variables of virtuality. Investigating the dimensions of virtuality of the team is still under research. Therefore, for the purpose of the chapter we mention degree of virtuality as the concept reflecting the degree of dependency on ICTs for

Table 1. Different approaches for defining and distinguishing Virtual teams adapted from Hosseini and Chileshe (2013)

Number of Approaches	Approach Principles	References
1	Presenting a truly distinctive definition for VTs in comparison to conventional teams	(Fuller et al., 2012, Chen and Messner, 2010, Chinowsky et al., 2003)
2	Distinguishing virtual teams by defining them as team structures demonstrating some specific attributes	(Hertel et al., 2005, Bal and Teo, 2000, Kirkman et al., 2002)
3	Challenging the traditional concept of virtual teams by introducing the concept of dimensions and degree of virtuality for teams	(Mukherjee et al., 2012, Schweitzer and Duxbury, 2010, Gibson and Gibbs, 2006, Kirkman and Mathieu, 2005, Peñarroja et al., 2013)

communications and the level of disparity between the members in terms of spatial distance, time zones, and difference of cultural backgrounds.

Virtual Teams Definition

It is the author's view that, investigating any correlation between the attributes of a VT and the related variables relies on incorporating the structure of the VT in terms of virtuality. Nonetheless, agreeing with the third category of definitions and based on the fact that all the teams are to some extent virtual these days, we consider the term of VTs for this chapter as a team demonstrating high degrees of virtuality. Therefore, all our discussions might be based on the below definition for VTs:

Groups of geographically, organizationally and/or time dispersed intelligent workers with different skills and in different positions of the hierarchy heavily relied on ICTs to accomplish tasks which for all are held accountable (Hosseini & Chileshe, 2013).

We defined the abovementioned definition as the corner stone for all our discussions. In addition, we considered any kind of organizational structure or working team meeting the attributes described in the above definition as a VT.

HISTORICAL OVERVIEW OF THE CONCEPT

Roots of the migration of the organization to virtual structures were in early works of the economists such as Oliver Williamson in 1970s. He suggested that firms should utilize externally purchased services as much as possible to decrease the costs by exploiting skills outside the firms. In his theory, utilizing skilful complementary services from outside would decrease the overall manufacturing costs along with eliminating poor performance units (Camarinha-Matos et al., 2005).

Gignac (2005) explores the background of VTs from a historical perspective. He opines that the birth of this team structure is the direct outcome of the inevitable end of the dominance of industrial culture and the commencement of the knowledge culture governance. In his theory, the phenomenon of virtual teams has been built on the emergence of knowledge workers concept introduced by Peter Druker in 1959. This new form of worker is not responsible for producing tangible goods like the traditional worker. The knowledge worker uses and manipulates information to produce more information and deliver knowledge. While work teams were in use in the U.S. as early as the 1960s, the idea of VT structure witnessed a more evident impact with the booming of outsourcing wave in 1980. The concept of outsourcing became very commonplace when managers experienced the remarkable ability of outsourcing phenomenon in reducing the organizational overhead (Camarinha-

Matos et al., 2005). Hertel et al. (2005) argued that the notion of virtual teams is not a phenomenon of the recent decades and there are numerous examples of collaboration between people across large distances from earlier times. Concisely, it seems that no single researcher has the title of the inventor of the virtual teams. In addition, virtual teams have not been built on a specific theory or model designed specifically for them. Our historic review showed that the concept and related methods are fostered through an evolutionary process (Ebrahim et al., 2009; Powell et al., 2004; Chinowsky et al., 2003).

As stated in the previous section, due to the ever evolving concept of virtual teams, there could be found no widely accepted definition or label for the virtual teams which has been agreed upon by the researchers in the related areas. Even researchers have revised the approaches for distinguishing and defining the VTs under the influence of the mentioned evolving concept of VTs.

TECHNOLOGY AS THE MAIN COMMUNICATION CHANNEL IN VTS

All the conceptual definitions of virtual teams presented by different researchers have one aspect in common. They all hold the view that one of the main attributes of the virtual teams that make them truly distinctive from conventional ones is the heavy reliance on the technology to perform their tasks specifically ICTs. It is not overstated that virtual teams cannot work and will have no existence excluding ICTs from the scene (Peters & Manz, 2007; LaLonde, 2011; Booth, 2011). Even many studies have regarded the degree of dependence on ICTs as an index for determining the degree of virtuality of VTs (Gibson & Gibbs, 2006). Although some studies have argued that the degree of reliance of VTs on ICTs is a controversial matter among scholars (Curseu et al., 2008), and more than being a characteristic for VTs, heavy reliance on ICTs is one of the consequences of working in virtual environment for teams (Schweitzer & Duxbury, 2010). Nevertheless, the fast pace of technology towards better ICTs has helped VTs in numerous forms (Kirkman et al., 2004; Montoya-Weiss et al., 2001; Rezgui, 2001), but heavily dependency of virtual teams to ICTs for communications (Booth, 2011) makes them extremely vulnerable to any problem with regard to technological issues. In addition, decreased quality of communications via ICTs is another concern regarding VTs (Hertel et al., 2005). Hence, the potential of a company in terms of its ability to provide necessary communication technologies when considering of adopting VTs in any stage is of crucial importance. Therefore, the awareness of the project manager of the state of the ICTs in the organization should be considered as a very influential element. The case is more important for some sectors of the industry such as construction since many construction projects are supposed to be executed in remote areas with less facilities and more ICTs disruptions. In addition, some of the members of VTs might be based in places with less developed ICTs infrastructure. All the foregoing issues should be taken into account when considering embarking on utilizing VTs and managing them successfully. In this respect, some studies also state the direct effect of ICTs on the performance of VTs (Martins et al., 2004). On top of that choosing the right ICTs tool for the specific communication goals is also another important factor in VTs success (Karoui et al., 2010). Therefore, there is a necessity for VT managers for being fully aware of the different patterns of information in their projects, the types of knowledge necessary to be exchanged, and the best channels in terms of ICTs tools for VTs. The latter issues will be discussed in detail in coming sections of the chapter.

VIRTUAL TEAMS MEMBER SELECTION CHALLENGES

Either conventional or a highly virtual team, the members will be the cornerstone of success for the team (Jones et al., 2000). The choice of appropriate team members could distinguish a successful virtual team from an unsuccessful one (Ebrahim et al., 2009; Goodbody, 2005) and is one of the challenging stages of forming a VT (Harvey et al., 2004). The required technical knowledge of team members totally depends on the goals defined for the team and finding the right person in accordance to the defined criterion is one of the managerial vital tasks (Hunsaker & Hunsaker, 2008). However, due to the disparity between the members and having ICTs as the main medium between co-workers of the team, there are some other skills that should be possessed by virtual team members (Salas et al., 2000; Bellamy et al., 2005; Cannon-Bowers et al., 1995; Hertel et al., 2005) although some studies argue about the dominance of non-technical skills issues in comparison to task-related skills in selecting VT members (D'Souza & Colarelli, 2010). There is also some viewpoints regarding ascertaining the essential attributes of VTs team members regarding the socio-emotional characteristics of members followed by debatable arguments over the preferences of some cultures over other cultures in terms of effectiveness in virtual teams. In addition, the type of effect of the diversity of team members on the effectiveness of the team is still unclear (Hertel et al., 2005). On the other hand, a study in construction industry mandated that team members would experience some alternations in their skills and character as the result of utilizing ICTs playing the role of main mediums during the life-cycle of the team (Bellamy et al., 2005).

ISSUES ASSOCIATED WITH CULTURAL DIVERSITY OF VIRTUAL TEAMS

A number of issues associated with cultural diversity of virtual teams as identified in literature can be categorised into the following four areas:

- Cultural diversity
- Cultural related factors
- Team cohesiveness
- Team identity

The following section presents a brief discussion of each of the areas identified.

Cultural Diversity

People from very different backgrounds and experiences bring with themselves different behaviours, work cultures, routings and assumptions about the organization, and team working to VTs (Kayworth & Leidner, 2002; Powell et al., 2004; Kozlowski & Ilgen, 2006). Studies argue that the cultural diversity matters of virtual teams have a dramatic effect on the function and outcome of any virtual team and should be considered seriously, when it comes to manage a virtual team (Hitson, 2008: Piccoli et al., 2004: Connaughton & Shuffler, 2007: Zimmermann, 2011). Based on the vital importance of these items, some authors have conducted explicit researches to find out the effect of matters regarding cultural diversity on virtual teams and determining the cultural aspects with an influence on the performance of teams (Prasad & Akhilesh, 2002; Harvey et al., 2004; Trent, 2003; Hartenian, 2003; Zimmermann, 2011; Dekker et al., 2008) . In this regard, dimensions associated with cultural diversity has been describes by different hypothesis.

Cultural Related Factors

Cultural related factors are believed to have the main influence on team composition, but other attributes such as difference in functional background and team size are other factors which could affect team composition as well (Duarte & Snyder, 2006; Goodbody, 2005). Some studies also argue that managers should address the cultural issues of virtual teams by selecting members who are able to work independently and negotiate cultural differences successfully (D'Souza & Colarelli, 2010; Harvey et al., 2004). Nevertheless, we would argue that cultural differences might be a source of problem, but the virtual environment and dependence of relationships on ICTs acts as a double-edged sword. Namely, in some aspects, ICTs alleviate the problem of cultural differences. Therefore, cultural diversity is a less effective factor in VTs in comparison to their co-located counterparts.

Team Cohesiveness and Team Identity

Two other main issues mentioned in the literature as problematic aspects of diversity in VTs are matters related to team cohesiveness (Martins & Schilpzand, 2011; Powell et al., 2004) and team identity (O'Leary & Mortensen, 2011; Shapiro et al., 2002; Hertel et al., 2005), which suffer from disagreement between the researchers. The type of influence virtuality of the team has on these variables and the effect they have on the performance of the VT is still not clear. Nevertheless, determining the best practices for managers to foster positive points and eliminate adverse effects of cultural diversity would facilitate managing VTs.

CHALLENGES OF MANAGING AND LEADING VIRTUAL TEAMS

The following key challenges are suggested as critical for the managing and leading virtual teams and are illustrated in Figure 1. The following section presents a brief discussion of each of the challenges identified.

Leadership Strategy in Virtual Teams

Matters regarding the leadership of virtual teams suffer from vagueness in many grounds. Maybe the salient reason is the existing controversy over the phenomenon of leadership in general management and specially managing projects (Toor & Ofori, 2008; Brodbeck, 2001) as one can find many different viewpoints and theories in this respect. On the one hand, some researchers maintain that leadership has a crucial effect on effectiveness of VTs (Jarvenpaa & Tanriverdi, 2003; Kayworth & Leidner, 2002) and even is one of the most challenging issue of managing VTs (Hertel et al., 2005; Bell & Kozlowski, 2002; Bal & Teo, 2001; Malhotra et al., 2007). On the other hand a recent study showed that VTs performance is not directly affected by the type leader-member relationship in virtual teams (Goh, 2010). Nevertheless, generally some researchers argue that direct autonomous controlling methods are not effective for virtual teams (Hertel et al., 2005: Powell et al., 2004). In addition, the existing literature emphasizes on the specific necessary attributes that a VT leaders should demonstrate as an effective team leader (Bal & Teo, 2001). On top of that, the most effective leadership strategy appropriate for VTs has been studied by many researchers (Malhotra et al., 2007; Van Pelt, 2010) while it is still a matter of debate (Mukherjee et al., 2012; Mawanda, 2012).

There could be found many contradicting suggested leadership approaches for VTs including leadership by monitoring the personnel by ICTs, self-managing strategy, and managing by using objective-feedback (Hertel et al., 2005). Although some studies have addressed leadership for developing a framework for managing VTs in some industries as the construction (Chinowsky et al., 2003; Chen & Messner, 2010), we argue that the knowledge on VTs leadership is still in need of further research.

Figure 1. Key challenges of managing and leading VTs

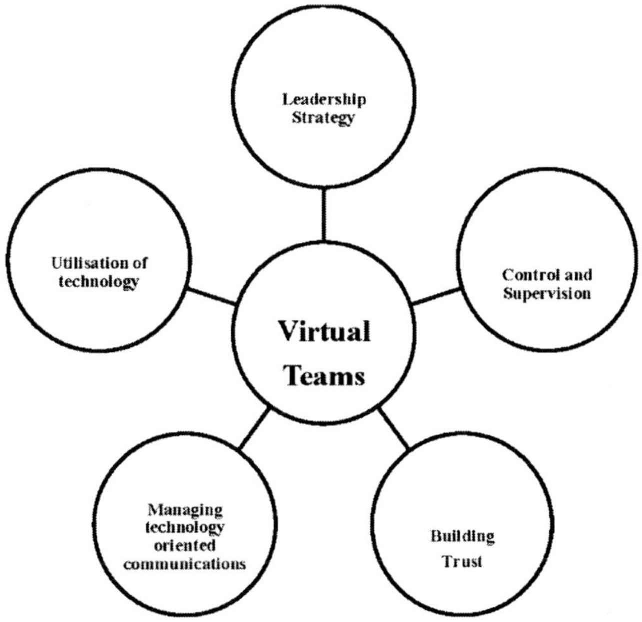

Control and Supervision Via ICTs

Missing an appropriate tool for measuring performance and exercising supervision would be among one of the challenges organizations face when adopting virtual teams (Haywood, 1998; Piccoli et al., 2004; Bell & Kozlowski, 2002). Some studies stated that supervisory methods based on empowerment of the team would facilitate increasing the performance of VTs (Walvoord et al., 2008; Kirkman et al., 2004).

Other studies show that teams with higher performances could be recognized by their level of dedication to teams' goals, cohesiveness among team members, and demonstrating equilibrium between respect and unity for individual differences (Ebrahim et al., 2009). Another element as the index of performance by VTs could be regarded as customer satisfaction (Kirkman et al., 2004). Studies have mentioned some other performance evaluation tools for VTs such as decision quality, the number of ideas emerged from the team, and the time that the team spends on making a decision (Powell et al., 2004; Piccoli et al., 2004).

It seems that the tools introduced for evaluating the effectiveness of VTs in the literature are mostly the same as the yardsticks used for conventional teams. Nevertheless, the criteria developed for traditional teams are not able to measure the performance of VTs carefully, since they ignore the main areas of superiority of VTs over traditional ones and the driving forces behind utilizing VTs (Schweitzer & Duxbury, 2010).

The issue of supervision and measuring the performance of VTs is inseparable from factors related to the management style, leadership strategy, and control method of the team which all of them are the matters of controversy (Hertel et al., 2005).

Building Trust in Transcultural Virtual Teams

From all the issues, building trust amongst the members is the area related to managing VTs that we can assume as the most frequently addressed issue of VTs in existing researches. On the other hand, trust is the factor with a noticeable effect on the performance of VTs members according to many studies (Henttonen & Blomqvist, 2005; Malhotra et al., 2007; Khan, 2012). Interestingly, based on longitudinal studies, the mechanism of development of trust among VTs members and its influence on their performance alters during the lifecycle of a team (Kanawattanachai & Yoo, 2002) and also depends on variables such as the cultural background of team members (Yusof & Zakaria, 2012). Even some studies claimed that effectiveness degree of trust on the performance of VTs is not constant and changes based on the conditions (Jarvenpaa et al., 2004). Generally, there is partial conscience amongst the researchers regarding the positive impacts of trust on performance of VTs (Martins & Schilpzand, 2011). However, some studies doubted if there is a significant correlation between the foregoing variables (Jarvenpaa et al., 2004). Choosing the best practices of building trust among the members of VTs in different phases of the virtual teams' lifecycle is an important issue that managers should take into account.

Managing Technology Oriented Communications in Transcultural Virtual Teams

Researches show that VTs struggle to coordinate their work because of the loss of time on trying to accurately interpret communication and coordinate activities via ICTs (Maynard et al., 2012). Briefly, communication is one of the great challenges VTs face with even if they are equipped with the most advances technological tools and devices (Walvoord et al., 2008; Rosen et al., 2007; Lin et al., 2008; Duarte & Snyder, 2006; Goodbody, 2005). Although the communication device namely the type of ICTs used has a great effect on the richness of the knowledge shared between the team members (Malhotra & Majchrzak, 2012). Another issue brought up by the extant literature is that each project sets patterns of its own and selects specific communication tools for developing communications. Interestingly, research showed that once established changing the pattern and tools takes a lot of effort. Therefore, laying down appropriate rules, strategies and selecting appropriate technology for communication at initial stages is vital for the efficacy of the VT (Martins & Schilpzand, 2011; Huysman et al., 2003). Of the challenges related to communications is whether organizing face-to-face meetings at the beginning of the VT or periodically is necessary. Some research emphasizes that face-to-face meetings can enhance the communications and trust (Pauleen, 2003). In addition, it lessens the communication difficulties due to the distance between the team members (Kayworth & Leidner, 2000; Ramesh & Dennis, 2002). In general, a major part of the research believes in the positive effect of face-to-face meetings physically or via video-conferences on general efficiency of VTs (Martins & Schilpzand, 2011). Conversely, some researchers mandate the idea that face-to-face meetings highlight the cultural differences between the members and adversely affects the quality of communication between team members (Bjørn & Ngwenyama, 2009). On the other hand, studies also emphasize that non-job-related or social communications between members of the VTs is one of the factors that managers should consider when it comes to managing VTs (Hertel et al., 2005: Martins & Schilpzand, 2011). These sorts of communications have critical influence on the effectiveness of the virtual teams (Shin, 2005; Lin et al., 2008) particularly in order to build the cohesion of the team (Powell et al., 2004). Interestingly, one of the methods of fostering non-job-related relationships between the members in the literature is mentioned as holding face-to-face meetings in different stages of the team creation (Cascio & Shurygailo, 2003; Mittleman et al., 2000; Goodbody, 2005) along with chatting sessions and utilizing humour in contacts between co-workers in a VT (Kayworth & Leidner, 2002).

Utilizing Technology for Developing Transcultural Virtual Teams

There is a widespread agreement on the necessity of training and education for VTs, since they argue there is a positive relationship between the training of team members and the performance of the team by enhancing the abilities of team members. The necessity of training include matters such as improving the capabilities of members in utilizing technology (Kayworth & Leidner, 2000; Grosse, 2002). The training plan should incorporate the objective of fostering the cohesiveness and relationships between team members, and facilitating resolving cultural issues (Anderson et al., 2007; Fuller et al., 2007; Anawati & Craig, 2006; Hill, 2007). Some researchers also have tried to develop a framework for best practices of training VTs (Rosen et al., 2006). In this regard, Lumsden et al. (2009) raised the issue of ever changing training requirements of VTs members with emphasize on dependency of training modules on the specific conditions of the team. On the other hand, we came across other studies (Hertel et al., 2005) arguing that very significant correlation between training of team members and effectiveness of the team is not recognizable in conducted studies. The effectiveness of training of VTs members via ICTs relied media which has a lower quality is also debatable based on some recent research (Martins & Schilpzand, 2011). As a result, defining the best methods of training for each phase of the lifecycle of the team, along with selecting the best technological tools for training, is another area in need of full attention by managers of VTs.

COMBINED EFFECT OF TECHNOLOGY DOMINANCE AND CULTURAL DIVERSITY ON VIRTUAL TEAMS

Different professionals with different unfamiliar nationalities and organizational backgrounds unite in a virtual team for achieving common goals. They lack the shared language and behavioural patterns (Gudykunst et al., 1988). Their interpretation of the events and each other's reactions could be different and misleading (Shachaf, 2008). They also experience problems for dividing the task, coordinating the work, resolving conflicts, and setting common rules. Coming up with a feasible coherent scheme for the team, incorporating all the cultural values, organizational beliefs and visions of the members while utilizing ICTs as the main medium with less richness seems problematic in VTs (Booth, 2011; Pauleen, 2004). Therefore, virtual teams are simultaneously under the influence of the combined effect of cultural diversity and the attributes of ICTs as the main medium for communications. Existing literature has presented different and sometimes contradicting views regarding the kind of effect the foregoing factors have on the performance of the VTs (Shachaf, 2008). While some have emphasized on the direct effect of cultural diversity on virtual environment performances (Dafoulas & Macaulay, 2002), we came across some studies questioning the existence of clear correlating between cultural diversity of members working in VTs utilizing ICTs (Martins et al., 2004; Walsham, 2002).

Individually, each one of abovementioned variables seems to act as a double edges sword brining about positive and negative effect on the outcome of the VTs (Shachaf, 2008). On the one hand, studies stated that technologically mediated communications in transcultural teams is able to promote equality and flexibility of routines (Draghici, 2008) and better decision makings (Shachaf, 2008). On the other hand, ICTs are less "rich" in comparison to traditional face-to-face communication methods and often lead to feelings of isolation (Shachaf, 2008) and de-individuation (Godar & Ferris, 2004). Even Draghichi (2008) opines that generalising the effect of cultural diversity and ICTs on VTs is not rational since every individual acts differently. Nevertheless, when it comes to taking into account the combined effect of ICTs and cultural diversity in VTs, one can find few published work available (Shachaf, 2008; Myers & Tan, 2003). In this regard, some studies have showed that many conflicts and misunderstandings erupted due to cultural diversities could be alleviated and mitigated by utilizing appropriate ICTs tools, although the media selection itself is affected strongly by the culture of people utilizing it (Shachaf, 2008).

Concerning utilizing technology effectively, many authors hold the view that members of the VTs should eagerly accept ICTs as the main medium for performing their tasks. Hence, the technology acceptance and the kind of technology fitting specific cultures are the main variables of great importance when concerning the relationship between cultural diversity and technology utilization in VTs. Theory of Acceptance and Use of Technology (UTAUT) (Venkatesh et al., 2012) and TAM (technology acceptance model) (Lai & Li, 2005) define the factors which affect the technology implementation by different people. Many studies have explored the effect of cultural dimensions on accepting technology (Im et al., 2011; Im et al., 2008). In this regard, the undeniable effect of task type and national cultural background has been proved by researchers (Venkatesh et al., 2012). In terms of considering the combined effect of technology and cultural diversity in order to have the highest performance possible, we argue that the manager of the virtual team faces the challenge of harnessing the ICTs for mitigating the adverse effects of cultural differences between the members. Meeting this objective entails selecting members from compatible cultures, selecting the technological tools accepted by the members and coming up with the best combination of media channels to alleviate the cultural conflicts between members of the team. All the above decisions should be taken based on an integrated sequential procedure that will be described in the following subsequent sections of the chapter.

DISCUSSIONS

The undeniable importance of the proper fit between the type of communication media selected and task type defined for VTs have been mentioned frequently in the relevant literature (Hertel et al., 2005). In addition, some authors maintained that using ICTs by itself could not necessarily be advantageous or damaging for virtual teamwork. Actually, the outcome of their utilization strongly depends on the fit to the objective of the communication in VTs (Maznevski & Chudoba, 2000).

In terms of the effect of cultural backgrounds on performance of VTs, some combinations of cultures can have advantages for virtual teamwork. As an example, individualistic cultures might help to cope with isolated work conditions while collectivistic cultures might help with actively overcoming isolation by seeking contacts with other team members. Regarding the necessity of selecting compatible team members, integration of cultural sensitivity as selection criteria of team members has been mentioned as one of the methods of overcoming the cultural conflicts in VTs (Hertel et al., 2005) and even some web-based tools for selecting compatible team members have been introduced (Hertel et al., 2006). Many studies also has emphasized on the effect of alignment between technological aspects of the work on the performance of virtual teams (Cao & Dowlatshahi, 2005) . In this regard, Bjørn and Ngwenyama (2010) have even introduced new strategies for managing virtual teams in terms of technology by proposing the *technology alignment* hypothesis. The authors of the foregoing paper state that applying compatible technologies is not simply a process of providing VTs with the relevant technology and making it usable. They maintain the view that also comes with it serious considerations for selecting the fitted strategies. It is because all the foregoing features have strong correlations with the socio-emotional aspects and task procedures of VTs with a profound effect on the VT's performance.

It seems that the combined effect and the composition of different variables in a VT, which acts as a coherent system defines the final performance of the team rather than the effect of single items individually. Hence, despite some challenges in managing VTs, the manager of the VT is still capable of designing the best effective composition for the team taking into account that some of the variables of the team are somehow out of the control of the manager. We argue that the duty of the VT manager could be described as completing a puzzle in which some of the elements are available based on the organizational goals defined for VTs. The important stage of doing this role is to select the best elements compatible with the variables out of the control of the manager taking into account the combined effects of all the influential elements and the interactions between them. Even the leadership strategy and the kind of relationship developed by the manager between the members are defined by basic variables in the VT. The selection of best strategy or fitted variable for having the highest possible performance in VTs are possible only by awareness of the state of the other factors and variables of the team which some are defined in previous stages of team's lifecycle. Therefore, managing a virtual team composed of people from different cultures by using technology as the main medium for communications is a sequential procedure. In the mentioned process, outcome of selection of variables in each stage will define the state of the successive stage. Logically, the state of each stage includes some variables determined by the attributes of variables in the predecessor stage. The following section of the chapter proposes a general procedure for VTs managers in a systematic procedure in order to implement the most appropriate managerial and leadership strategy for the specific conditions of any VT.

THE LEADING AND MANAGING VIRTUAL TEAMS (LEMANVIT) INTEGRATED APPROACH FRAMEWORK

Figure 2 shows the proposed leading and managing virtual teams (LeManViT) framework. It consists of the following steps:

1. **Key Member Selection:** The key members of the VT will be selected based on the tasks delegated to the team, which defines their necessary technical skills. Organizational goals, cost considerations and the business environment variables such as the availability of the resources have direct effect on selection of key members of the team.
2. **Defining Team Design:** The next step would be designing the team based on the attributes of the selected key members. In this stage, the degree of virtuality of the team will be defined including the disparity of team members and the level of virtuality in terms of their spatial, time differences and the level they depend on ICTs for their cooperation. It is obvious that the remaining members will be chosen from cultures and by attributes compatible with the key members of the team taking into account all the factors with an effect for forming a coherent team capable of resolving conflicts and develop trust.
3. **Selecting Most Appropriate Strategies:** Having been aware of the details of the team design, the most fitted packages of management will be implemented during the lifecycle of the team based on the variables set in previous steps. Therefore, as stated before, managing virtual teams effectively is a dynamic process affected by many factors that are all internally related and connected. As team proceeds in its lifecycle, the requirements such as type

Figure 2. Implementing integrated sequential management strategy for VTs

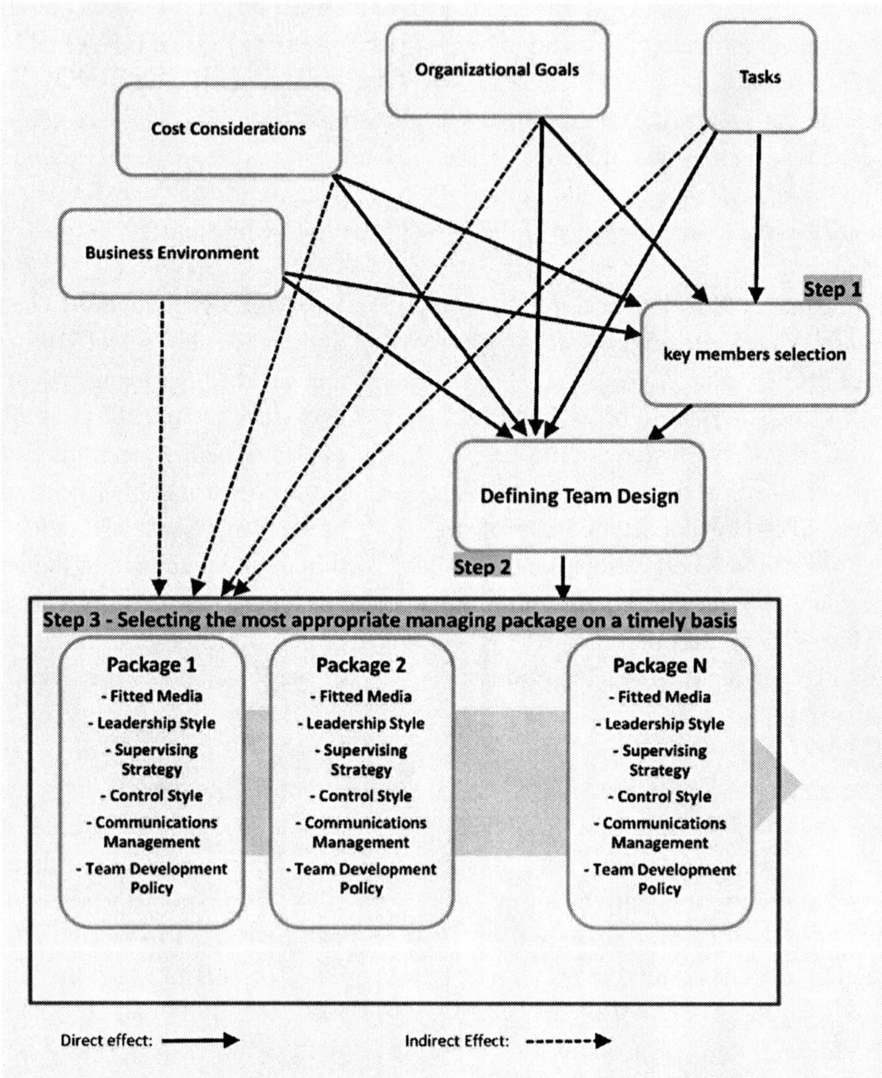

of communications and training necessities change. Hence, the manager should select and pick the most appropriate package fitted for each timely cross-section in team's lifecycle. As the results, implementing different leadership styles, control policies and supervisory strategies deems necessary as time passes. The packages to be considered would comprise the following:

- Fitted media
- Leadership style
- Supervising strategy
- Control style
- Communications management
- Team development policy

The above steps are now explained with some illustrated examples.

Illustrative Examples of 'LeManViT' Application

As mentioned in the previous section, the variables related to leading and managing VTs are so closely dependent and correlated which could not be addresses in isolation as independent aspects. The authors hold the view that leading and managing a VT is in practice a package including all the relevant issues in which each part influences the other aspects of the package and their combined composition design as a coherent whole determines the performance of the team. In this regard, the selection of the unique package we should adopt for effectively managing a VT under any specific condition heavily relies on a set of large number of variables. Some of the foregoing variables are beyond the control of the manager and traditionally might be defined in higher levels of the organization or based on the pervasive conditions in the business environment. Examples could be the objective and the kind of tasks and goals defined for the VT, the driving forces behind implementing VT instead of traditional teams, cost saving policies, technical issues of the tasks delegated to VTs, and others. In some aspects, the selection process is limited. For instance, the kind of skills required (Hunsaker & Hunsaker, 2008) and the location the skills are available along with cost and revenue policies of the organization define who the key members of the VT would be. The latter step is somehow a kind of limited shortlist selection with few available options in which the major part of vital variables are out of the control of the manager of the VT. Successively, the attributes of the key members of the VT including their cultural aspects, the degree of virtuality and level of disparity between team members, cost policies, and the type of tasks and goals of the VT will shape the most effective design applicable to the team. Selecting the most effective managing/leadership package for the VT is only possible after being aware of the design of the team in detail. The organizational cost saving policies and the kind of task and goals defined for the team will affect all the aspects of managing the VT and all the selection procedures made by the manager through the team's lifecycle. We argue that there is only one unique package of management for the predetermined VT design capable of bringing about the highest possible performance based on the specific conditions ruling over the team. Put it another way, the VT management puzzle will miss merely one particle filing the other elements. The task of the manager will encompass selecting, and picking the fitted element correctly. The package of managing/leading the VT will include defining all the aspects of managing, leading, supervising, controlling, training, developing, along with communication management of the VT. We state again that elements composing the VTs also interact and any package definition takes combining compatible elements as a coherent set beforehand. As examples, the leadership style a manager selects will dictate the kind of technology and the communications channels required for implementing the leadership strategy along with the necessary training topics for team development. The package selected will also determine the most effective supervision strategy implemented by the manager.

It should be noted that, the proposed Figure 2 only illustrates a summary of the process proposed by the authors for managing and leading a VT from an integrated sequential perspective. It should be mentioned that issues incorporated in the diagram include only some of the aspects of managing VTs in order to enlighten the minds of readers of the general philosophy of the concept introduced.

CONCLUSION AND FURTHER RESEARCH OPPORTUNITIES

The issues surrounding the harnessing of the capabilities of technology for satisfying the requirements of different industries in terms of team working are well documented. To enhance the effective delivery of virtual teams, a number of 'challenges' and 'drivers' such as technologically and culturally oriented need specific consideration. However, despite the identification of the numerous variables associated with the effective leading and management of virtual teams, these are not captured in a more holistically manner. This chapter sought to present these factors through a conceptual integrated approach with special consideration given to the resolving of some of the issues associated with the management of virtual teams. The basic premise of the proposed model (LeManViT) in the chapter is through the utilization of the most appropriate packages of managing and leadership of VTs.

A number of potential areas requiring further research were also identified. In the main, these were linked with the identification and selection of appropriate management strategies for managing and leading virtual teams. A summary of this discussion can be found in the following sub section dealing with 'further research opportunities'.

Future Research Opportunities and Recommendations

Our belief based on regarding the management and leadership of VTs as a dynamic package provides the future researchers with a fertile ground in this field. Most of the previous researchers have considered all the issues related to managing and leading virtual teams as isolated matters and have studied them in fragmented studies without considering the interactions and internal correlations. The future research should focus on selecting the management strategies considering it from a holistic perspective taking into account all the issues of VTs as correlated matters having effects on each other and the whole system. Therefore, the future research trend should mostly study the correlations between the variables affecting the performance of VTs, along with developing best strategies related to different aspects of managing VTs as coherent packages taking into account all the variables affecting selecting the managing package as a coherent whole. Presenting general strategies prescribed for all the conditions of virtual teams does not provide us with effective management strategies for VTs.

REFERENCES

Abudayyeh, O., Temel, B., Al-Tabtabai, H., & Hurley, B. (2001). An Intranet-Based Cost Control System. *Advances in Engineering Software*, *32*, 87–94. doi:10.1016/S0965-9978(00)00094-6.

Ahmad, I., Azhar, S., & Ahmed, S. (2002). *Web-Based Construction Project Management: Scope*. Potential And Trends.

Algesheimer, R., Dholakia, U. M., & Gurău, C. (2011). Virtual Team Performance In A Highly Competitive Environment. *Group & Organization Management*, *36*, 161–190. doi:10.1177/1059601110391251.

Anawati, D., & Craig, A. (2006). Behavioral Adaptation Within Cross-Cultural Virtual Teams. *Professional Communication. Ieee Transactions On*, *49*, 44–56.

Anderson, A., Mcewan, R., Bal, J., & Carletta, J. (2007). Virtual Team Meetings: An Analysis Of Communication And Context. *Computers in Human Behavior*, *23*, 2558–2580. doi:10.1016/j.chb.2007.01.001.

Atrostic, B. K., & Nguyen, S. V. (2005). It And Productivity In Us Manufacturing: Do Computer Networks Matter? *Economic Inquiry*, *43*, 493–506. doi:10.1093/ei/cbi033.

Bal, J., & Teo, P. (2000). Implementing Virtual Teamworking. Part 1: A Literature Review Of Best Practice. *Logistics Information Management*, *13*, 346–352. doi:10.1108/09576050010355644.

Bal, J., & Teo, P. K. (2001). Implementing Virtual Teamworking: Part 2--A Literature Review. *Logistics Information Management*, *14*, 208–222. doi:10.1108/09576050110390248.

Bell, B. S., & Kozlowski, S. W. J. (2002). A Typology Of Virtual Teams. *Group & Organization Management*, *27*, 14–49. doi:10.1177/1059601102027001003.

Bellamy, T., Williams, A., Sher, W., Sherratt, S., & Gameson, R. (2005). Preliminary Examination Of Ict Collaborative Design And Management. In *The Construction Industry*. Newcastle, UK: The University Of Newcastle's Digital Repository.

Bjørn, P., & Ngwenyama, O. (2009). Virtual Team Collaboration: Building Shared Meaning, Resolving Breakdowns And Creating Translucence. *Information Systems Journal*, *19*, 227–253. doi:10.1111/j.1365-2575.2007.00281.x.

Bjørn, P., & Ngwenyama, O. (2010). Technology Alignment: A New Area In Virtual Team Research. *Professional Communication. Ieee Transactions On*, *53*, 382–400.

Booth, B. (2011). Examining The Critical Factors Of Success. In *Virtual Team Performance. Ph.D. 3442987*. Prescott Valley, AZ: Northcentral University.

Brodbeck, F. (2001). Leadership In Organizations, Psychology Of. In Neil, J. S., & Paul, B. B. (Eds.), *International Encyclopedia Of The Social &Amp; Behavioral Sciences*. Oxford, UK: Pergamon. doi:10.1016/B0-08-043076-7/01404-2.

Camarinha-Matos, L., Afsarmanesh, H., & Ollus, M. (2005). *Virtual Organizations: Systems And Practices*. New York: Springer Verlag. doi:10.1007/b102339.

Camarinha-Matos, L. M., & Afsarmanesh, H. (2003). Elements Of A Base Ve Infrastructure. *Computers in Industry*, *51*, 139–163. doi:10.1016/S0166-3615(03)00033-2.

Cannon-Bowers, J. A., Tannenbaum, S. I., Salas, E., & Volpe, C. E. (1995). Defining Competencies And Establishing Team Training Requirements. *Team Effectiveness And Decision Making In Organizations*, *333*, 380.

Cao, Q., & Dowlatshahi, S. (2005). The Impact Of Alignment Between Virtual Enterprise And Information Technology On Business Performance In An Agile Manufacturing Environment. *Journal of Operations Management*, *23*, 531–550. doi:10.1016/j.jom.2004.10.010.

Cascio, W. F., & Shurygailo, S. (2003). E-Leadership And Virtual Teams. *Organizational Dynamics*, *31*, 362–376. doi:10.1016/S0090-2616(02)00130-4.

Chang, C. M. (2011). New Organizational Designs For Promoting Creativity: A Case Study Of Virtual Teams With Anonymity And Structured Interactions. *Journal of Engineering and Technology Management*, *28*, 268–282. doi:10.1016/j.jengtecman.2011.06.004.

Chen, C., & Messner, J. I. (2010). A Recommended Practices System For A Global Virtual Engineering Team. *Architectural Engineering And Design Management*, *6*, 207–221. doi:10.3763/aedm.2010.0121.

Chinowsky, P. S., & Rojas, E.M. (2003). *Virtual Teams: Guide To Successful Implementation. Journal of management in engineering, 19, 98-106.*

Connaughton, S. L., & Shuffler, M. (2007). Multinational And Multicultural Distributed Teams. *Small Group Research*, *38*, 387–412. doi:10.1177/1046496407301970.

Curseu, P. L., Schalk, R., & Wessel, I. (2008). How Do Virtual Teams Process Information? A Literature Review And Implications For Management. *Journal of Managerial Psychology*, *23*, 628–652. doi:10.1108/02683940810894729.

D'souza, G. C., & Colarelli, S. M. (2010). Team Member Selection Decisions For Virtual Versus Face-To-Face Teams. *Computers in Human Behavior, 26*, 630–635. doi:10.1016/j.chb.2009.12.016.

Dafoulas, G. & Macaulay, L. 2002. Investigating Cultural Differences In Virtual Software Teams. *The Electronic Journal Of Information Systems In Developing Countries, 7*.

Dekker, D. M., Rutte, C. G., & Van Den Berg, P. T. (2008). Cultural Differences In The Perception Of Critical Interaction Behaviors In Global Virtual Teams. *International Journal of Intercultural Relations, 32*, 441–452. doi:10.1016/j.ijintrel.2008.06.003.

Draghici, A. (2008). Influence Of Multi-Culturality. In *Virtual Teams*. Berlin, Heidelberg: Springer Berlin Heidelberg.

Duarte, D. L., & Snyder, N. T. (2006). *Mastering Virtual Teams: Strategies, Tools, And Techniques That Succeed*. Jossey-Bass.

Duyshart, B., Walker, D., Mohamed, S., & Hampson, K. (2003). An Example Of Developing A Business Model For Information And Communication Technologies (Ict) Adoption On Construction Projects–The National Museum Of Australia Project. *Engineering, Construction, and Architectural Management, 10*, 179–192. doi:10.1108/09699980310478430.

Ebrahim, N. A., Ahmed, S., & Taha, Z. (2009). Virtual Teams: A Literature Review. *Australian Journal Of Basic And Applied Sciences, 3*, 2653–2669.

Fuller, C. M., Marett, K., & Twitchell, D. P. (2012). An Examination Of Deception In Virtual Teams: Effects Of Deception On Task Performance, Mutuality, And Trust. *Professional Communication. Ieee Transactions On, 55*, 20–35.

Fuller, M. A., Hardin, A. M., & Davison, R. M. (2007). Efficacy In Technology-Mediated Distributed Teams. *Journal of Management Information Systems, 23*, 209–235. doi:10.2753/MIS0742-1222230308.

Gibson, C. B., & Gibbs, J. L. (2006). Unpacking The Concept Of Virtuality: The Effects Of Geographic Dispersion, Electronic Dependence, Dynamic Structure, And National Diversity On Team Innovation. *Administrative Science Quarterly, 51*, 451–495.

Gignac, F. (2005). *Building Successful Virtual Teams*. Boston, MA: Artech House.

Godar, S. H., & Ferris, S. P. (2004). *Virtual And Collaborative Teams*. Hershey, PA: IGI Global.

Goh, S. H. (2010). Leader-Member Relationships. In *Virtual World Teams. Ph.D. 3462304*. Tallahassee, FL: The Florida State University.

Goodbody, J. (2005). Critical Success Factors For Global Virtual Teams. *Strategic Communication Management, 9*, 18–21.

Grosse, C. U. (2002). Managing Communication Within Virtual Intercultural Teams. *Business Communication Quarterly, 65*, 22–38. doi:10.1177/108056990206500404.

Gudykunst, W. B., Ting-Toomey, S., & Chua, E. (1988). *Culture And Interpersonal Communication*. New York: Sage Publications, Inc..

Hartenian, L. S. (2003). Team Member Acquisition Of Team Knowledge, Skills, And Abilities. *Team Performance Management, 9*, 23–30. doi:10.1108/13527590310468033.

Harvey, M., Novicevic, M. M., & Garrison, G. (2004). Challenges To Staffing Global Virtual Teams. *Human Resource Management Review, 14*, 275–294. doi:10.1016/j.hrmr.2004.06.005.

Haywood, M. (1998). *Managing Virtual Teams: Practical Techniques For High-Technology Project Managers*. Boston, MA: Artech House.

Henttonen, K., & Blomqvist, K. (2005). Managing Distance In A Global Virtual Team: The Evolution Of Trust Through Technology-Mediated Relational Communication. *Strategic Change*, *14*, 107–119. doi:10.1002/jsc.714.

Hertel, G., Geister, S., & Konradt, U. (2005). Managing Virtual Teams: A Review Of Current Empirical Research. *Human Resource Management Review*, *15*, 69–95. doi:10.1016/j.hrmr.2005.01.002.

Hertel, G., Konradt, U., & Voss, K. (2006). Competencies For Virtual Teamwork: Development and Validation Of A Web-Based Selection Tool For Members Of Distributed Teams. *European Journal of Work and Organizational Psychology*, *15*, 477–504. doi:10.1080/13594320600908187.

Hill, G. M. (2007). *The Complete Project Management Office Handbook*. Boca Raton, FL: Auerbach. doi:10.1201/9781420046823.

Hitson, M. C. (2008). *An Analysis Of Leadership Methodology And Job Satisfaction Among Virtual Team Members. D.M. 3324077*. University Of Phoenix.

Hosseini, M. R., & Chileshe, N. (2013). Global Virtual Engineering Teams (Gvets): A Fertile Ground For Research In Australian Construction Projects Context. *International Journal Of Project Management*. Retrieved from Http://Dx.Doi.Org/10.1016/J.Ijproman.2013.01.001

Hosseini, M. R., Chileshe, N., Zuo, J., & Baroudi, B. (2012). Approaches For Implementing Ict Technologies Within Construction Industry. *Australasian Journal Of Construction Economics And Building The Conference Series*, *1*(2), 1–12.

Hunsaker, P. L., & Hunsaker, J. S. (2008). Virtual Teams: A Leader's Guide. *Team Performance Management*, *14*, 86–101. doi:10.1108/13527590810860221.

Huysman, M., Steinfield, C., Jang, C. Y., David, K., In't Veld, M. H., Poot, J., & Mulder, I. (2003). Virtual Teams And The Appropriation Of Communication Technology: Exploring The Concept Of Media Stickiness. *Computer Supported Cooperative Work (Cscw)*, *12*, 411–436. doi:10.1023/A:1026145017609.

Im, I., Hong, S., & Kang, M. S. (2011). An International Comparison Of Technology Adoption: Testing The Utaut Model. *Information & Management*, *48*, 1–8. doi:10.1016/j.im.2010.09.001.

Im, I., Kim, Y., & Han, H.-J. (2008). The Effects Of Perceived Risk And Technology Type On Users' Acceptance Of Technologies. *Information & Management*, *45*, 1–9. doi:10.1016/j.im.2007.03.005.

Jarvenpaa, S. L., Shaw, T. R., & Staples, D. S. (2004). Toward Contextualized Theories Of Trust: The Role Of Trust In Global Virtual Teams. *Information Systems Research*, *15*, 250–267. doi:10.1287/isre.1040.0028.

Jarvenpaa, S. L., & Tanriverdi, H. (2003). Leading Virtual Knowledge Networks. *Organizational Dynamics*, *31*, 403–412. doi:10.1016/S0090-2616(02)00127-4.

Jones, R., Stevens, M., & Fischer, D. (2000). Selection In Team Contexts. *Managing Selection In Changing Organizations: Human Resource Strategies*, 210-241.

Joseph, G. (2005). Global Virtual Engineering Team Utilization. In *The Engineering, Procurement, And Construction (Epc) Industry. State College*. PA: Pennsylvania State University.

Kanawattanachai, P., & Yoo, Y. (2002). Dynamic Nature Of Trust In Virtual Teams. *The Journal of Strategic Information Systems, 11*, 187–213. doi:10.1016/S0963-8687(02)00019-7.

Karoui, M., Gürkan, A., & Dudezert, A. (2010). Virtual Team Collaboration: A Review Of Literature. *And Perspectives.*

Kayworth, T., & Leidner, D. (2000). The Global Virtual Manager: A Prescription For Success. *European Management Journal, 18*, 183–194. doi:10.1016/S0263-2373(99)00090-0.

Kayworth, T. R., & Leidner, D. E. (2002). Leadership Effectiveness In Global Virtual Teams. *Journal of Management Information Systems, 18*, 7–40.

Khan, M. S. (2012). Role Of Trust And Relationships In Geographically Distributed Teams: Exploratory Study On Development Sector. *International Journal Of Networking And Virtual Organisations, 10*, 40–58. doi:10.1504/IJNVO.2012.045210.

Kirkman, B. L., & Mathieu, J. E. (2005). The Dimensions And Antecedents Of Team Virtuality. *Journal of Management, 31*, 700–718. doi:10.1177/0149206305279113.

Kirkman, B. L., Rosen, B., Gibson, C. B., Tesluk, P. E., & Mcpherson, S. O. (2002). Five Challenges To Virtual Team Success: Lessons From Sabre, Inc. *The Academy Of Management Executive (1993-2005)*, 67-79.

Kirkman, B. L., Rosen, B., Tesluk, P. E., & Gibson, C. B. (2004). The Impact Of Team Empowerment On Virtual Team Performance: The Moderating Role Of Face-To-Face Interaction. *Academy of Management Journal*, 175–192. doi:10.2307/20159571.

Kozlowski, S. W. J., & Ilgen, D. R. (2006). Enhancing The Effectiveness Of Work Groups And Teams. *Psychological Science in the Public Interest, 7*, 77–124.

Lai, V. S., & Li, H. (2005). Technology Acceptance Model For Internet Banking: An Invariance Analysis. *Information & Management, 42*, 373–386. doi:10.1016/j.im.2004.01.007.

Lalonde, K. (2011). Communication Among Virtual Teams. [The College Of St. Scholastica.]. *Ms*, 1493595.

Lin, C., Standing, C., & Liu, Y.-C. (2008). A Model To Develop Effective Virtual Teams. *Decision Support Systems, 45*, 1031–1045. doi:10.1016/j.dss.2008.04.002.

Lumsden, G., Lumsden, D., & Wiethoff, C. (2009). Communicating. In *Groups And Teams: Sharing Leadership*. Wadsworth.

Malhotra, A., & Majchrzak, A. (2012). How Virtual Teams Use Their Virtual Workspace To Coordinate Knowledge. *Acm Trans. Manage. Inf. Syst., 3*, 1–14.

Malhotra, A., Majchrzak, A., & Rosen, B. (2007). Leading Virtual Teams. *The Academy Of Management Perspectives Archive, 21*, 60–69. doi:10.5465/AMP.2007.24286164.

Martins, L. L., Gilson, L. L., & Maynard, M. T. (2004). Virtual Teams: What Do We Know And Where Do We Go From Here? *Journal of Management, 30*, 805–835. doi:10.1016/j.jm.2004.05.002.

Martins, L. L. & Schilpzand, M. C. (2011). Global Virtual Teams: Key Developments, Research Gaps, And Future Directions. *Research In Personnel And Human Resources Management, 30.*

Mawanda, H. J. (2012). *Beyond Technology, An Analysis Of The Perceived Impact Of Transformational Leadership And Contingent Rewards As Extrinsic Motivation On Virtual Team Member Satisfaction And Leadership Effectiveness: A Quantitative Study. Ph.D. 3503075*. Minneapolis, MN: Capella University.

Maynard, M. T., Mathieu, J. E., Rapp, T. L., & Gilson, L. L. (2012). Something(S) Old And Something(S) New: Modeling Drivers Of Global Virtual Team Effectiveness. *Journal of Organizational Behavior*, *33*, 342–365. doi:10.1002/job.1772.

Maznevski, M. L., & Chudoba, K. M. (2000). Bridging Space Over Time: Global Virtual Team Dynamics And Effectiveness. *Organization Science*, 473–492. doi:10.1287/orsc.11.5.473.15200.

Mittleman, D. D., Briggs, R. O., & Nunamaker Jr., J. F. (2000). Best Practices In Facilitating Virtual Meetings: Some Notes From Initial Experience. *Group Facilitation: A Research And Applications Journal*, *2*, 5-14.

Montoya-Weiss, M. M., Massey, A. P., & Song, M. (2001). Getting It Together: Temporal Coordination And Conflict Management In Global Virtual Teams. *Academy of Management Journal*, 1251–1262. doi:10.2307/3069399.

Mukherjee, D., Lahiri, S., & Billing, T. K. (2012). Leading Virtual Teams: How Do Social, Cognitive, And Behavioral Capabilities Matter? *Management Decision*, *50*, 6–6. doi:10.1108/00251741211203560.

Myers, M. D., & Tan, F. B. (2003). Beyond Models Of National Culture In Information Systems Research. *Advanced Topics In Global Information Management*, *2*, 14.

Nesbit, P. L. (2002). Opportunities And Developments Of Hrm Within The E-Business Environment. *Employment Relations Record*, *2*, 41–52.

O'leary, M., & Mortensen, M. (2011). *Go (Con) Figure: Subgroups*. Imbalance, And Isolates In Geographically Dispersed Teams.

Pauleen, D. (2004). *Virtual Teams: Projects, Protocols And Processes*. Hershey, PA: IGI Global.

Pauleen, D. J. (2003). Lessons Learned Crossing Boundaries In An Ict-Supported Distributed Team. *Journal of Global Information Management*, *11*, 1–19. doi:10.4018/jgim.2003100101.

Peansupap, V. (2004). An Exploratory Approach To The Diffusion Of Ict In A Project Environment.

Peñarroja, V., Orengo, V., Zornoza, A., & Hernández, A. (2013). The Effects Of Virtuality Level On Task-Related Collaborative Behaviors: The Mediating Role Of Team Trust. *Computers in Human Behavior*, *29*, 967–974. doi:10.1016/j.chb.2012.12.020.

Peters, L. M., & Manz, C. C. (2007). Identifying Antecedents Of Virtual Team Collaboration. *Team Performance Management*, *13*, 117–129. doi:10.1108/13527590710759865.

Piccoli, G., Powell, A., & Ives, B. (2004). Virtual Teams: Team Control Structure, Work Processes, And Team Effectiveness. *Information Technology & People*, *17*, 359–379. doi:10.1108/09593840410570258.

Powell, A., Piccoli, G., & Ives, B. (2004). Virtual Teams: A Review Of Current Literature And Directions For Future Research1. *The Data Base for Advances in Information Systems*, *35*, 6–36. doi:10.1145/968464.968467.

Prasad, K., & Akhilesh, K. (2002). Global Virtual Teams: What Impacts Their Design And Performance? *Team Performance Management*, *8*, 102–112. doi:10.1108/13527590210442212.

Ramesh, V., & Dennis, A. R. (2002). The Object-Oriented Team: Lessons For Virtual Teams From Global Software Development (pp. 212-221).

Reed, A. H., & Knight, L. V. (2010). Effect Of A Virtual Project Team Environment On Communication-Related Project Risk. *International Journal of Project Management*, *28*, 422–427. doi:10.1016/j.ijproman.2009.08.002.

Rezgui, Y. (2001). Review Of Information And The State Of The Art Of Knowledge Management Practices In The Construction Industry. *The Knowledge Engineering Review*, *16*, 241–254. doi:10.1017/S026988890100008X.

Rezgui, Y., & Zarli, A. (2006). Paving The Way To The Vision Of Digital Construction: A Strategic Roadmap. *Journal of Construction Engineering and Management*, *132*, 767. doi:10.1061/(ASCE)0733-9364(2006)132:7(767).

Rosen, B., Furst, S., & Blackburn, R. (2006). Training For Virtual Teams: An Investigation Of Current Practices And Future Needs. *Human Resource Management*, *45*, 229–247. doi:10.1002/hrm.20106.

Rosen, B., Furst, S., & Blackburn, R. (2007). Overcoming Barriers To Knowledge Sharing In Virtual Teams. *Organizational Dynamics*, *36*, 259–273. doi:10.1016/j.orgdyn.2007.04.007.

Salas, E., Burke, C. S., & Cannon-Bowers, J. A. (2000). Teamwork: Emerging Principles. *International Journal of Management Reviews*, *2*, 339–356. doi:10.1111/1468-2370.00046.

Schweitzer, L., & Duxbury, L. (2010). Conceptualizing And Measuring The Virtuality Of Teams. *Information Systems Journal*, *20*, 267–295. doi:10.1111/j.1365-2575.2009.00326.x.

Shachaf, P. (2008). Cultural Diversity And Information And Communication Technology Impacts On Global Virtual Teams: An Exploratory Study. *Information & Management*, *45*, 131–142. doi:10.1016/j.im.2007.12.003.

Shapiro, D. L., Furst, S. A., Spreitzer, G. M., & Von Glinow, M. A. (2002). Transnational Teams In The Electronic Age: Are Team Identity And High Performance At Risk? *Journal of Organizational Behavior*, *23*, 455–467. doi:10.1002/job.149.

Shin, Y. (2005). Conflict Resolution In Virtual Teams. *Organizational Dynamics*, *34*, 331–345. doi:10.1016/j.orgdyn.2005.08.002.

Skibniewski, M. & Abduh, M. Web-Based Project Management For Construction: Search For Utility Assessment Tools. 2000. 56-77.

Sriprasert, E., & Dawood, N. (2002). *Next Generation Of Construction Planning And Control System: The Lewis Approach*. Taylor & Francis.

Toor, S. R., & Ofori, G. (2008). Leadership For Future Construction Industry: Agende For Authentic Leadership. *International Journal of Project Management*, *26*, 620–630. doi:10.1016/j.ijproman.2007.09.010.

Trent, R. J. (2003). Planning To Use Work Teams Effectively. *Team Performance Management*, *9*, 50–58. doi:10.1108/13527590310482235.

Van Pelt, S. (2010). *The Complexities Of Leading Virtual Teams: A Phenomenological Study*. University Of Phoenix.

Venkatesh, V., Thong, J., & Xu, X. (2012). Consumer Acceptance And Use Of Information Technology: Extending The Unified Theory Of Acceptance And Use. *Technology (Elmsford, N.Y.)*.

Walsham, G. (2002). Cross-Cultural Software Production And Use: A Structurational Analysis. *Management Information Systems Quarterly*, 359–380. doi:10.2307/4132313.

Walvoord, A. A. G., Redden, E. R., Elliott, L. R., & Coovert, M. D. (2008). Empowering Followers In Virtual Teams: Guiding Principles From Theory And Practice. *Computers in Human Behavior*, *24*, 1884–1906. doi:10.1016/j.chb.2008.02.006.

Yacine, R. (2007). Exploring Virtual Team-Working Effectiveness In The Construction Sector. *Interacting with Computers*, *19*, 96–112. doi:10.1016/j.intcom.2006.07.002.

Yusof, S. A. M., & Zakaria, N. (2012). *Exploring The State Of Discipline On The Formation Of Swift Trust Within Global Virtual Teams* (pp. 475–482). IEEE. doi:10.1109/HICSS.2012.272.

Zenun, M., Loureiro, G., & Araujo, C. (2007). The Effects Of Teams' Co-Location On Project Performance. *Complex Systems Concurrent Engineering*, 717-726.

Zhang, Y., Gregory, M., & Shi, Y. (2008). Global Engineering Networks (Gen): Drivers, Evolution, Configuration, Performance And Key Patterns. *Journal Of Manufacturing Technology Management*, *19*, 299–314. doi:10.1108/17410380810853740.

Zimmermann, A. (2011). Interpersonal Relationships In Transnational, Virtual Teams: Towards A Configurational Perspective. *International Journal of Management Reviews*, *13*, 59–78. doi:10.1111/j.1468-2370.2010.00284.x.

Chapter 13
The Role of Market Orientation in Internationalization of SMEs

Rosmeriany Nahan-Suomela
Vaasa University of Applied Sciences, Finland

Satu Lautamäki
Vaasa University of Applied Sciences, Finland

ABSTRACT

A rapidly changing business environment generates a growing demand for enterprises to understand their markets. Knowledge about markets is a strategic resource and enterprises are advised to invest in understanding their markets, competitors, and customers. Market orientation is widely studied as a concept describing how enterprises generate and respond to market knowledge. Market orientation is a cultural factor which we analyze in the framework of organizational culture. We examine market orientation as a cultural factor, as adopting a new type of culture inside and outside an organization can be particularly challenging for Small- and Medium-Enterprises (SMEs). SMEs have not been considered as very active participants in global business, where market knowledge is of utmost importance. For example, Keskin (2006) finds that market orientation is an antecedent of learning orientation in SMEs and market intelligence guides their learning processes. This chapter examines both theoretically and empirically how market orientation as a cultural factor is related to the internationalization processes of SMEs. This hopefully helps us to understand how SMEs can develop their businesses to a global level. We will present a qualitative study of four Finnish SMEs representing different phases of internationalization. Finally, discussion on the results and future research directions will be presented.

DOI: 10.4018/978-1-4666-3966-9.ch013

INTRODUCTION

In marketing literature, emphasis on market knowledge is termed as market orientation. Many scholars have contended with clarifying and understanding the meaning of market orientation as a concept. Knowledge about markets is a strategic resource for enterprises that are advised to invest in understanding their markets, competitors, and customers. Competitive advantage increasingly depends on an enterprise's ability to use the market knowledge, but not only on its access to it (Deshpandé, Farley, & Webster, 1993). It is also often claimed that if enterprises fail to develop their market orientation, they are likely to experience a failure in their business performance. Enterprises which are able to increase their level of market orientation will improve their market performance (Day, 1994; Kohli & Jaworski, 1990; Slater & Narver, 2000; Nielsen et al., 2003; Verhees & Meulenberg, 2004).

Research on market orientation has concentrated on large enterprises--not on SMEs; neither has market orientation been fully examined in the context of internationalization. In addition, there would be a need for managerial suggestions on how to implement market orientation in practice (Bradshaw, Maycock & Öztel, 2008). For instance, Dougherty (1990) discovered market, customer (related to product usage), and competitor information were essential in the successful product development projects. Verhees & Meulenberg (2004) also discovered that customer knowledge is related positively to small enterprise performance. This leads us to investigate what type of market knowledge would be most important for small- and medium-sized enterprises in their internationalisation process. We also look at methods Small- and Medium-Enterprises (SMEs) are likely to use in collecting this information, because in fact, most small enterprises do not conduct market research or set long term market planning (Meziou, 1991; Pelham & Wilson, 1996).

Doing business at an international level brings uncertainty of the future development of the market. In terms of developing business operations from an international-to global level, SMEs have not been considered as very active participants. Market orientation can be a powerful factor which changes this situation, because in global business, generation and dissemination of market knowledge is of utmost importance. However, market orientation is also a cultural factor. In this chapter, the concept of culture is examined in the framework of organizational culture and its relationship with market orientation. Adopting a new type of culture inside and outside an organization can be particularly challenging for SMEs. To understand how SMEs can move from an international to a global context, our goal is to understand how SME managers perceive market knowledge and, more specifically, how market orientation as part of organizational culture is related to their internationalization processes.

Narver & Slater (1990) have examined market orientation from a cultural perspective. According to them, market-oriented enterprises are embodied with a culture in which personnel value being customer oriented, competitor oriented and participating in interfunctional coordination. This means employees in such a culture put a priority and gather market intelligence about customers and competitors and collaborate between various departments in the enterprises. The main argument of their research is that market orientation is closely connected with organizational culture, in other words, being market oriented is a part of the enterprise's culture and reflects the values which are shared by organizational members. Additionally, Farrell (2000) states an enterprise should consider the creation of a market-orientation as a fundamental part of the organization's culture. So, market orientation is a cultural factor, which we will analyze in the framework of organizational culture.

Lafferty & Hult (2001) have produced a synthesis of the concept of market orientation based on earlier conceptual studies. According to them, the concept of market orientation can be approached from five perspectives; namely,

a) decision making perspective, b) strategic perspective, c) customer orientation perspective, d) market intelligence perspective and e) culturally based behavioral perspective. We will use their synthesis to compare enterprises in different phases of internationalization and see if the enterprises describe their market orientation from different perspectives. We also aim to contribute to the growing body of empirical work on the internationalization of SMEs, which lags behind the research on large multinational firms. A case study approach is used in this study to analyze how market orientation becomes interpreted by managers from Finnish SMEs and in which way market orientation facilitates their internationalization processes.

INTERNATIONALIZATION OF SMALL AND MEDIUM-SIZED ENTERPRISES

In the global economy, markets are characterized with strenuous international competition and growing demands of customers, which concern also SMEs. They seek actively opportunities abroad and at the same time they are forced to internationalize their activities to maintain their position in the market. According to the extant literature, there are two major streams on the process of internationalization of small and medium-sized enterprises (SMEs). In the first stream, perspective of internationalization is an incremental process through which an enterprise builds on its experience and knowledge about specific market gained in one phase, before moving to the next phase of larger market involvement (Bilkey & Tesar, 1977; Johanson & Vahlne, 1977; Johanson & Wiedersheim-Paul, 1975).

Internationalization literature is largely concerned with how the channels through which an enterprise enters foreign markets evolve over time, and it takes the perspective of a single enterprise operating in some generalized environment. It infers that outcomes are largely the result of the actions of a single enterprise in relation to its skills, resources, experience, and attitudes. The internationalization of an enterprise is seen as stages in the process and the factors that lead to shift between stages (Bilkey & Tesar, 1977; Johanson & Vahlne, 1977; Johanson & Wiedersheim-Paul, 1975). These studies suggest that internationalization is an incremental process through which an enterprise builds its experience and knowledge about specific market gained in one phase, before moving to the next phase of broader market involvement. This perspective focuses on internal organizational factors especially during the incremental process of learning in the earlier phase of internationalization. The theoretical models with this perspective consider internationalization as a process and can be regarded as behaviorally oriented. In the Uppsala (U) model by Johanson & Vahlne (1977) and Johanson & Wiedersheim-Paul (1975), the emphasis is on learning theory and it emphasizes the internationalization process as a step by step development. Based on the authors' arguments, the gradual pattern of the firm's internationalization process can be referred to (1) the lack of knowledge by the firm and (2) uncertainty related to the decision to internationalize.

However, there has been some criticism by several researchers regarding the Uppsala model (Andersen, 1993; Nordström,. 1991; Turnbull, 1987), who have argued the model lacks explanatory power and does not consider the process: why or how the process takes place or how to predict the movement from one phase to the next. They have also stated the analysis of environment such as the impact of industry and competition are not properly addressed. The limitations of the Uppsala model have been confirmed by different surveys and case studies which show some enterprises do not follow the traditional stage pattern in their internationalization process. On the contrary, there are enterprises which are involved in international markets right from their establishment. Such enterprises have been called "born globals" (Knight & Cavusgil, 2004; Knight, Madsen, & Servais,

2004). Another stumbling block for the first stage models (Johanson & Vahlne, 1977; Johanson & Vahlne, 1990; Johanson & Wiedersheim-Paul, 1975) was they were based on small samples which were a considerable impediment to generalization (Oviatt & McDougall, 1997; 1995).

Much of the research has used theories from different disciplines such as international business, management, entrepreneurship and sociology. This leads us to examine the second stream of the existing literature on internationalization of SMEs. In the second stream, research is based on international entrepreneurship literature. In this stream, it is argued SMEs can be international either from their inception or from established small enterprises. Oviatt & McDougall (1994, p. 49) explained a definition of an International New Venture (INV) as "a business organization that, from inception, seeks to derive significant competitive advantage from the use of resources and the sale of outputs in multiple countries." McDougall's definition of INV has been discussed because if implication of age at internationalization is used, the definition of INV can create a problem, as some new ventures are created through restructuring of existing enterprises. In this case, they have benefitted resources and networks from their parent corporations. In contrast to this, the evolution of enterprise's mission and resources are related to managerial capacity which to some extent is defined by the pre-launch experience. Then, is it the age that creates the advantages associated with internationalization, or is it the enterprise's entrepreneurial activities (Zahra, 2005)?

McDougall & Oviatt (2000) as well as Zahra & George (2002) have suggested it is the actions that INVs undertake which appear to be the major source of competitive advantage. The definition of INVs can be applied equally well to both INVs and established enterprises. In other words, it focuses more on the entrepreneurial qualities of enterprises rather than on their age of internationalization. Using insights from research on entrepreneurship has been useful for considering an enterprise's entrepreneurial characteristics when discussing internationalization. The present study also rests on this. The relevance of entrepreneurs or managers in this case has been emphasized in the literature, which has found a positive relationship between international development of business operations and entrepreneur's international orientations (Zahra, Hayton, Marcel, & O'Neill, 2001).

INTEGRATING MARKET ORIENTATION WITH INTERNATIONALIZATION

There is a large body of research literature on the concept of market orientation. The majority of definitions have distinguished three core components of market orientation; namely, customer focus, profitability, and interdepartmental coordination of market knowledge (Kohli & Jaworski, 1990; Desphandé et al., 1993; Lafferty & Hult, 2001). In addition, some researchers state competitor knowledge should be also perceived as an element of market orientation (Day, 1994), while other researchers claim that competitor knowledge may be "almost antithetical to a customer focus" (Desphandé et al., 1993, p. 27). Another concept closely related with market orientation is market knowledge, which Li & Calantone (1998) describe as relevant market information systematically structured and organized in a company.

There are clearly different perspectives behind the market orientation definitions, which Lafferty & Hult (2001) have pointed out by making a synthesis of the main research perspectives. They conclude there are five different perspectives: decision-making, strategic, customer orientation, market intelligence, and culturally-based behavioral perspectives. According to the decision-making perspective, the role of the top management is vital because managers guide the decision-making and sharing of information within the enterprise. The strategic perspective emphasizes that market knowledge is a tool to develop and implement business strategy. A Customer-orientation perspective means customer interests are given the highest priority and to which market information is continuously responded. Market intelligence perspective defines market orientation as the way to collect, communicate, and respond to the present market needs as well as to anticipate new needs in the markets.

Additionally, the culturally based behavioral perspective is widely used in the marketing literature. It defines market orientation as an organizational culture which produces superior value for customers as well as superior performance for the enterprise (Narver & Slater, 1990). Bjerke (2006) has investigated relationship between market orientation and organizational culture among hospitals in the Midwestern states of Iowa, Minnesota and Wisconsin In the U.S. Her findings indicated a strong relationship between the degree of market orientation and organizational culture characteristics. Results of her study suggested the CEO/administrator would benefit from incorporating organic cultural elements such as low complexity, low centralization, low formalization, extensive lateral communication process and flexibility, factors which have been confirmed earlier by Deshpandé et al. (1993) and Slater & Narver, (1995).

Earlier research evidence shows there is a link between overall market orientation and competitive ability of an enterprise. It is also suggested that it is easier for small enterprises to build competitive advantage on market orientation than it is for larger enterprises because the former are more flexible. Further, according to Anderson and Boocock (2002), self-directed, work-based, and informal learning is dominant in small enterprises as they allow more flexibility and adaptability. However, the resources they can devote to market intelligence are scarce (Verhees & Meulenberg, 2004), and their information systems are usually simple (Appiah-Adu & Singh, 1998). Small firms are suggested to reinforce formalization in decision making and to disseminate the market intelligence properly (Pelham & Wilson, 1996). In addition, SMEs are more reluctant than larger enterprises to embrace the concept of market orientation in their strategy formulation (Meziou, 1991). In fact, most small enterprises do not conduct market research or set long term market planning.

Kohli & Jaworski (1990) refer to market orientation in terms of generation and dissemination of market intelligence. Narver & Slater (1990) emphasize an enterprise's orientation towards its customers and competitors. These are activities which are easier to undertake when customers are known and close rather than unknown or far way. In addition, managers will understand better their customer needs as well as discuss competitors' strategies when those customers and competitors are familiar to the company. Yet, there is scarcity of research clarifying the conditions for those business activities that take place in foreign markets, or investigating how market orientation differs when moving from domestic to foreign markets. Kropp, Lindsay & Shoham (2006) expanded the market orientation-performance relationship to incorporate small enterprises that internationalize their operations rapidly in several markets abroad.

Globalization of markets and industries make competition very intense both in domestic and international markets. This is experienced especially by SMEs who have to compete both in domestic and international markets with Multinational Entities (MNEs). According to McDougall & Oviatt (2000) and Moen & Servais (2002), SMEs must manifest particular resources comprising orientation and competencies that will put forward their positions to achieve superior international performance. There is a variation of existing research on process of internationalization among SMEs. Some SMEs proceed directly from the primary stages to the final ones, such as born globals (Chetty & Campbell-Hunt, 2004; Gabrielsson & Kirpalani, 2004; Madsen & Servais, 1997). In the research of Knight et al. (2004), the international performance of born globals is enhanced by managerial emphasis on foreign customer focus and marketing competence in the implementation of market orientation. The marketing competence implies skillful handling of product adaptation, the marketing planning process, control of marketing activities, product differentiation, as well as pricing, advertising and distribution. Besides the importance of marketing factors that appear to drive international success of born globals, it is also stated that age, size and limited resources are no longer barriers to early and substantial internationalization of the firm.

Fast growing internationalizing small enterprises learn not only "by doing but also by imitating successful ventures, networking with other companies, and hiring skilled personnel" (Ruokonen & Saarenketo, 2009, p. 22). Therefore, market orientation can be considered as a key managerial characteristic which is spread to other managerial areas and contributing to the gathering and analysis of market intelligence. Pelham & Wilson (1996) mention that managers of small enterprises have a unique opportunity to seek competitive advantage through their market orientation since they are in a better position to reinforce company-broad market-oriented perspectives (Knight & Cavusgil, 2004; Vikøren, 1990). However, as international aspects of operations are included, it is a challenge for SMEs to collect market intelligence from global markets. In addition, responding competitively to customer needs may be difficult because of intense global competition.

The founding managers of small enterprises play a critical role in directing them towards domestic and international markets. The founders of fast growing internationalizing enterprises are often active entrepreneurs who have a global mindset which gives them an international perspective, vision, proactiveness, and ability to search for opportunities abroad (Fletcher, 2000; Oviatt & McDougall, 1995; Moen, 2002; Nummela, Saarenketo, & Puumalainen, 2004). Research has also shown that having certain competencies can facilitate the development of an enterprise's internationalization strategy (Li, Li, & Dalgic, 2004). This study contributes to this line of research by describing how market orientation as a cultural factor facilitates the internationalization of an enterprise. In addition, we propose to bring novel insights by assuming the role of market orientation is different at different phases of internationalization. We will use the synthesis of market orientation concept presented by Lafferty & Hult (2001) to compare enterprises in different phases of internationalization and see if enterprises describe their market orientation differently. The concept of culture is examined in the framework of organizational culture, in order to understand the role of market orientation as a cultural factor in the internationalization of SMEs.

As the literature review demonstrates, there is a wide variety of studies about either market orientation or internationalization of SMEs, but there still is a strong need to integrate these two concepts. This is an area we will focus on the next subchapter, where the empirical study is presented and discussed.

QUALITATIVE STUDY ON SME INTERNATIONALIZATION

The empirical study was conducted by interviewing managers at four small- and medium-sized business-to-business enterprises in Finland (for general information on the case companies, see Table 1). The enterprises attended a research project, where the focus was on defining future customers and creating product concepts for these customers. During the one-year research project, altogether 10 managers were interviewed in different project phases.

The method applied in our empirical study is *phenomenography*. It is a qualitative research approach which aims at describing, analyzing, and understanding experiences which the respondents have for a particular phenomenon, not the researcher's reflection of these experiences. Bowden (2005) also states that in phenomenog-

Table 1. General information on the case companies.

Company	Year of establishment	Industry	Yearly turnover (million euros)	Number of employees
A	1996	Machinery manufacturing	1,2	16
B	1916	Apparel and textile manufacturing	28	140
C	1977	Material handling	7	30
D	1945	Auto manufacturing	26,8	139

raphy, the object of the study is not the phenomenon itself, but the relationship between the respondent and the phenomenon. In our study, this means to analyze how the interviewed managers perceive the internationalization process of their company.

According to the methodological guidelines, phenomenography does not attempt to evaluate the correctness of experiences, but rather to discover various meanings that respondents associate with the scrutinized subject. These meanings are usually found by having an open, in-depth interview which has no pre-determined structure, and the interview continues until the respondent has nothing to add. The main results are often presented as meaning categories, and especially the aim is to find out the underlying reasons behind the meanings (Booth, 1997; Hasselgren & Beach, 1997; Marton, 1986).

Personal, qualitative interviews were conducted by a group of researchers. Researchers asked the interviewed managers to describe how they understand their business context, markets, and customer needs presently and in the future. The interviews were started by questions related to the company background, ownership and history, after which the main product areas and product development were discussed, both presently and in the future. After these, the interviews proceeded into questions concerning the strategic areas of business, market areas and their development, competitors, customers and their needs as well as strategies and competencies related to these. Finally, the business environment was discussed with questions about the main changes and possible directions as well as requirements and possibilities supported by various factors, such as environmental regulations, laws, sustainability, culture, societal issues, and technology.

All interviews were tape-recorded and transcripts based on the tapes were written. Our analysis of these interviews is based on a content analysis of the transcripts. The respondents' insights about markets were analyzed and preliminary meaning categories were deduced and revised. The meaning categories were first compared between the enterprises to see if there are major differences in how each enterprise experiences issues related to their markets. Our main interest lies in comparing not only the meaning categories between the enterprises but also the phases of internationalization of each enterprise. Figure 1 presents the main differences between the enterprises, in terms of their phases of internationalization as well as through the main experiences of market orientation in each of them.

Enterprise A is at pre-internationalization stage where there are no export activities. The enterprise is interested in developing them in the future, and it admits that "in order to learn about the international operations you have to follow what is happening in the world. This learning phase becomes timely for the personnel when the exporting starts." However, at this point, they clearly see that the business sense of the CEO is driving them forward. So, we could assume that at the early stage of internationalization, managerial competences are

Figure 1. How market orientation facilitates internationalization.

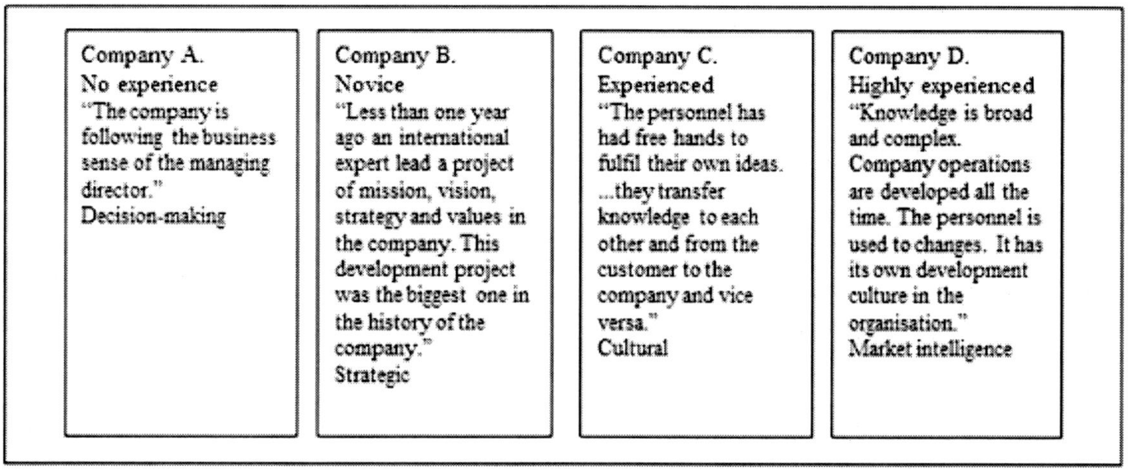

vital. This could be termed as decision-making perspective, following the synthesis by Lafferty & Hult (2001).

Enterprise B has some years of some years of experience of internationalization, mainly in the Scandinavian countries. Its internationalization strategy has been focused on finding and developing an international network of business partners and working as a subcontractor or supplier to them. The managers see it as a challenge to create a new organizational culture to meet the objectives set. So, they do not see decision-making as a challenge, but rather how to put the strategy into action, how to combine and get the right competences into the company and how to achieve the strategic goals. When defining the view point of market orientation in this company, we would use the term strategic perspective (Lafferty & Hult, 2001).

Enterprise C exports 80% of its products to international markets, mainly within Europe, but also to South America and Asia. It has sales offices in some European countries, but mostly it works as a business partner or a subcontractor for local distributors. This means getting the personnel become enthusiastic and competent about understanding customer needs. The enterprise already does so that they invite their customers and end-user to come to the factory at the production phase, which helps everyone in the company to become involved with their customers. The enterprise admits, that "It depends very much on the personnel how smart solutions the company is able to develop to the customers. Therefore the level of know-how of the personnel has to be kept on a high level." At this stage, when the enterprise is active in international activities, the focus may be on cultural perspective (Lafferty & Hult, 2001).

Enterprise D is very active and perhaps also dependent on foreign markets as the Finnish market for its products is very limited and there is strong competition in the domestic context. The enterprise exports more than 80% of its products into European countries, and it also has sales offices in the Scandinavian countries. This means everyone in the enterprise is involved in generating, disseminating, and responding to market needs now and in the future. The enterprise has a vision to become the top manufacturer in the world, the personnel is involved in a new developmental culture and there a lot of market-sensing activities going on. For this firm, it is important to be active and flexible to customer preferences. At this stage of internationalization, the focus could be defined as market intelligence (Lafferty & Hult, 2001).

Our goal was not only to separate the perspectives between the enterprises, but also to analyze what type of common categories of market knowledge exists. After analyzing the interview transcripts, three common categories of market knowledge were coded (in order of importance): 1) market-driven strategy; 2) competition; and 3) customer focus. Some subcategories were defined within each of these main categories (See Figure 2). Some additional meanings were also expressed by the managers, but these did not form clear new, shared categories. We will briefly analyze the three main categories which present the most prevailing thoughts on market knowledge among the managers.

Mostly, the managers shared their thoughts about business strategy based on market-driven factors: "We have to know where the business will be in ten years in order to develop our own strategy." In addition, managers considered that internationalization and differentiation have become basic strategies set by the external forces. Although earlier studies have not explicitly described strategy as part of market orientation, this category was perceived as the strongest one by the managers. Based on this finding, we could propose that market orientation in SMEs means gathering general market information which will be used for developing business strategies.

The second meaning category was connected with competitive factors: "Competitors are moving so fast that you cannot catch them with traditional methods. You really have to find your position in order to survive." Related to this theme, managers discussed how competition can turn into cooperation with other manufacturers. As a third subcategory of competitive environment, managers talked about competitive advantage: "We have

Figure 2. Common categories of market knowledge.

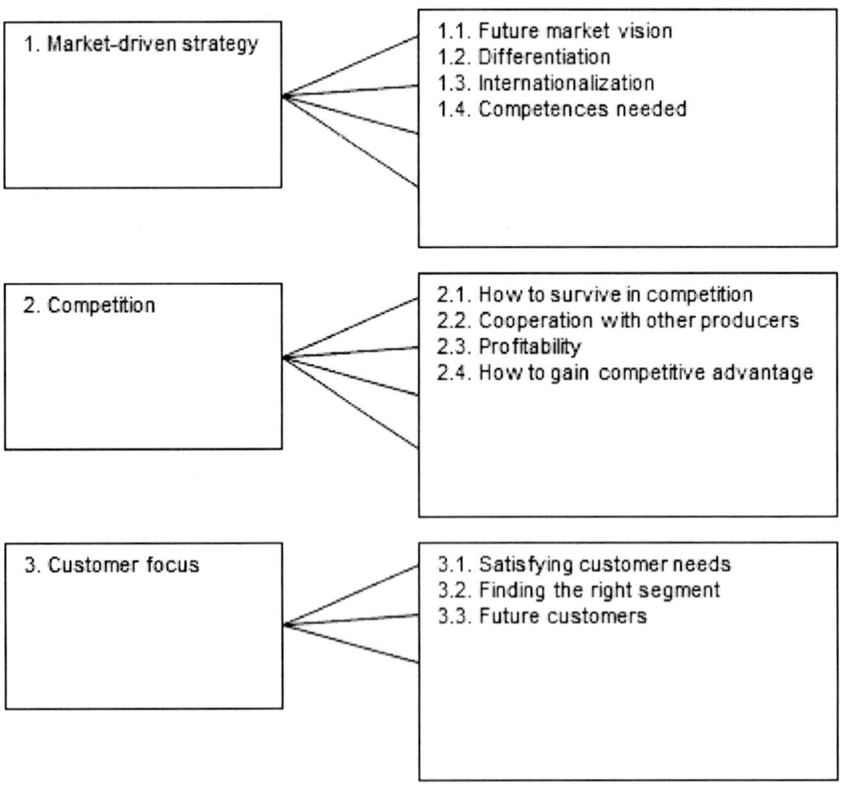

developed many unique product characteristics which no other enterprise has, and we have to believe that these will provide us a competitive advantage." Profitability, which in theoretical studies has been described as an element of market orientation, also aroused as an essential factor. However, managers did not discuss it as a separate theme but associated it with competition: "Competitors are moving their production to cheaper countries, competitors are bigger and bigger companies, things like these make you really think about profitability."

Customer focus became apparent as the third main category; first, it refers to ideas related to customer satisfaction: "We know that customers want to have easy-to-use products, and this is where we have been successful in satisfying their needs." Another subcategory related to customer focus was labeled segmentation, which was commonly described by managers: "It is very important to find the right niche segment, because competitors are growing and we should specialize in a particular customer segment." A third interesting theme was defined when company managers talked about their future customers: "We already have knowledge about the future customer needs, and we continuously develop new product features to fit these needs but the challenge is to know when the customers are ready to adapt new, innovative features."

MANAGERIAL IMPLICATIONS

Based on the case studies, we can ponder how market orientation can support the internationalization of SMEs. Are there certain elements that are vital to understand and what are these elements? Based on data collected from four case companies, we found that an enterprise with no or little experience of internationalization appeared to emphasize the managerial competences. Managers first develop their own insights about the markets and this knowledge is mostly used when planning corporate actions and strategies. In this situation managers use their earlier and existing experiences and network in planning the strategic direction of the firm. This can also be linked with the research on the entrepreneurial dimension of internationalization (Zahra, 2005).

Second, managers in enterprises which had some experience with internationalization, seemed to focus on how to put things into action, either through strategic or cultural actions. These enterprises can be described as learning organizations which aim to develop new type of competences and get the whole organization to support the actions. In earlier studies, internationalization process has been often described as a learning process (e.g. the Uppsala model), which our study also seems to confirm.

Third, managers who are willing to take risks and to innovate also improve relations both internally and externally. Especially managers in a highly experienced enterprise understand market knowledge as market intelligence which drives everything in the organization. The key dimension can be called commitment: in order to reach the advanced stages of internationalization, both managers and personnel have to be committed and enough resources must be given to market-oriented actions. Commitment has been also defined as a key term in the internationalization research area (Johanson & Vahnle, 1977).

Although the case studies showed different competences are vital in different stages of internationalization, there were also similarities among the case companies, and they especially seemed to share the customer orientation perspective (Lafferty & Hult, 2001). Managers admitted that they need to be constantly aware of their markets in order to better serve their customers, but also in order to be profitable and survive in the competition. This idea is shown in the following expression by one of the managers: "The company tries to collect information and carry out R&D actively all the time, because otherwise you can lose the grip." In all, managers were interested in developing networks of expertise and business partnership, they talked about the importance of learning, they claimed to have a good level of knowledge of their competitors, but they were willing to constantly know more of their customers.

When reflecting all these issues, we can state they are deeply rooted in the cultural context: internationalization of SMEs is a learning process where market orientation is "the principle cultural foundation of the learning organization" (Slater & Narver, 1995, p.67). In addition, Armario, Ruiz & Armario (2008) state that market orientation is a dynamic competence which influences the organizational culture. In order to develop from pre-international to international and further to global business, SMEs have to understand and develop market orientation as part of their cultural foundation, which helps them to efficiently gather and share information on foreign markets and to develop their international competitiveness.

FUTURE RESEARCH DIRECTIONS

For future research direction, firstly, it should be noted that a qualitative research approach is called for, taking into consideration the change process and how the elements of market orientation influence the internationalization process of SMEs. It would be important to investigate in which way activities of enterprises can be influenced by changes caused by the status and the dynamic nature of an enterprise–environmental adaptations as interpreted by managers. In addition, the relationship between market orientation and national culture could be further studied by doing a comparative study of enterprises representing different national cultures.

For instance, Kirca, Jayachandran & Bearden (2005) examined the relationship between market orientation and performance by using Hofstede's (2001) model of national culture dimensions. They found out that there are higher correlations between market orientation and performance in cultures with low uncertainty avoidance and low power distance. Our case companies were from Finland, which represents low power distance, but medium high uncertainty avoidance (Hofstede, 2001). However, we focused on examining how market orientation is related with the level of internationalization, not with performance, so our results are not fully comparable with the study of Kirca et al. (2005).

Secondly, the concept of internationalization process should be extended to the pre-internationalization process: what happens before enterprises start conducting business abroad, who initiates, what, how and why? This can be studied by looking at the role of change agents in the internationalization of the firm from a dynamic point of view. Finally, enterprises are urged to move from being market-driven to market-driving (Jaworski, Kohli & Sahay, 2000). Thus, it is no longer sufficient to seek objective market information and to react with modified products or services. This is especially true in the international markets: enterprises must change markets by taking advantage of customer information, especially by interpreting or even developing future customer needs. In order to drive markets, companies must develop their managerial competences, do correct actions on the strategic and cultural level and become committed to market knowledge in order to gain a strong foothold on the international markets.

In addition, the case studies give support for a resource-based approach into internationalization of SMEs, which is somewhat different from the traditional process or entrepreneurial views of internationalization. Resource-based approach is a quite recent perspective, not still based on explicit theoretical foundations. The concept of resource generally refers to tangible or intangible factors, which companies have to own and develop in order to build competitive advantage. However, there are a lack of studies which would define which types of resources are relevant in the internationalization (Ruzzier, Hisrich & Antoncic, 2006). Our case studies give some insight about the resources needed in internationalization: in order to proceed from pre-internationalization to global business, development of managerial, strategic and cultural competences is needed. Further research interest could be given to this theme as an aim to construct a theoretical model of various competences and their integration with the global business.

CONCLUSION

The purpose of this chapter was to understand how SME managers perceive market knowledge and, more specifically, how market orientation is related to the internationalization process of the enterprise. The limitations of this study can be found to the relation of amount and quality of data available. Generalizations should not be made because this study was based only on four enterprises from four different industries. Earlier research findings have shown market orientation has a positive effect on performance (Slater & Narver, 2000). We can assume that this condition is also true in the international context. As a matter of fact, market orientation may even have a stronger impact on the performance at international markets. Although we did not study the relationship between market orientation and performance, we can state that market orientation is beneficial for enterprises going abroad to do business, because it is a proactive way of using market knowledge, systematically developing the competences and commitment to fit with the changing markets. Also, these dimensions of proactiveness, competence development and commitment have been often described as keys of internationalization (Fletcher, 2000; Oviatt & McDougall, 1995; Moen, 2002; Nummela et al., 2004).

Based on our company cases, we could assume the internationalization process begins with entrepreneurial skills of managers, followed by the organizational learning, and finally ending with an all-embracing commitment. However, there seemed to be two main elements which are present across all stages of internationalization: building professional networks and managing change in the organization. These elements were admitted as relevant, no matter which stage of internationalization enterprises studied were at. Network building often starts at the management level, but gradually widens into the whole organization.

Commitment from the top is required in organizational change and the change management is in this case under the responsibility of the managers. A study by Nielsen et al. (2003, p. 1818) discussed change management in a form of "supported empowerment" as an indication of path to performance in an organization. This is also confirmed in our study. The case enterprises talked about training activities which have been or will be offered across the organization. Certainly, organizational change needs other tools as well, but these enterprises appeared to emphasize the role of training to improve personnel's competence which had given them good results. Managers also stated they had quite a lot of information from the markets, but the challenge is how to interpret it.

SMEs often state that all people are potential customers, which clearly shows a lack of in-depth customer knowledge. Companies know the rational needs of present customers, and use customer feedback to improve their products. However, the emotional or symbolic needs of customers are not widely known or discussed in SMEs. Also, in the literature of internationalization, experiential knowledge has been claimed to have a more important role than objective knowledge (Johanson & Vahnle, 1977). In all, when entering into global business, market orientation becomes very dynamic in nature, which demands commitment at every organizational level. Thus, market orientation in global business is a highly influential cultural factor, which should be studied further.

REFERENCES

Andersen, O. (1993). On the internationalization process of firms: A critical analysis. *Journal of International Business Studies*, *24*(2), 209–231. doi:10.1057/palgrave.jibs.8490230.

Anderson, V., & Boocock, G. (2002). Small firms and internationalization: Learning to manage and managing to learn. *Human Resource Management Journal*, *12*(3), 5–24. doi:10.1111/j.1748-8583.2002.tb00068.x.

Appiah-Adu, K., & Singh, S. (1998). Customer orientation and performance: A study of SMEs. *Management Decision*, *36*(6), 385–395. doi:10.1108/00251749810223592.

Armario, J. M., Ruiz, D. M., & Armario, E. M. (2008). Market Orientation and Internationalization in Small and Medium-Sized Enterprises. *Journal of Small Business Management*, *46*(4), 485–511. doi:10.1111/j.1540-627X.2008.00253.x.

Bilkey, W. J., & Tesar, G. (1977). The export behavior of smaller Wisconsin manufacturing firms. *Journal of International Business Studies*, *9*(Spring/Summer), 93–98. doi:10.1057/palgrave.jibs.8490783.

Bjerke, V. A. (2006). *Assessing the relationship between market orientation and organizational culture in Midwestern hospitals: An empirical study*. Doctoral dissertation, Capella University, Ann Arbor, MI: ProQuest Information and Learning Company.

Booth, S. (1997). On phenomenography, learning and teaching. *Higher Education Research & Development*, *16*(2), 135–159. doi:10.1080/0729436970160203.

Bowden, J. (2005). Reflections on the phenomenographic research process. In Bowden, J., & Green, P. (Eds.), *Doing Developmental Phenomenography*. Melbourne, Australia: RMIT University Press.

Bradshaw, R., Maycock, C. & Öztel, H. (2008). Exploring SME market orientation: An organizational learning perspective. *Education + Training*, *50*(8), 764-777.

Chetty, S., & Campbell-Hunt, C. (2004). Internationalisation strategy and its impact on learning during the process. *Journal of Asia-Pacific Marketing*, *3*(2), 38–52.

Day, G. S. (1994). The capabilities of market-driven organizations. *Journal of Marketing*, *58*(4), 37–52. doi:10.2307/1251915.

Deshpandé, R., Farley, J. U., & Webster, F. E. Jr. (1993). Corporate culture, customer orientation, and innovativeness in Japanese firms: A quadrad analysis. *Journal of Marketing*, *57*(1), 23–37. doi:10.2307/1252055.

Dougherty, D. (1990). Understanding new markets for new products. *Strategic Management Journal*, *11*, 59–78.

Farrell, M. A. (2000). Developing a market-oriented learning organization. *Australian Journal of Management*, *25*(2), 201–222. doi:10.1177/031289620002500205.

Fletcher, D. (2000). Learning to think global and act local: Experiences from the small business Sector. *Education + Training*, *42*(4), 211–219. doi:10.1108/00400910010373651.

Gabrielsson, M., & Kirpalani, V. H. M. (2004). Born globals: How to reach new business space rapidly. *International Business Review*, *13*(5), 555–571. doi:10.1016/j.ibusrev.2004.03.005.

Hasselgren, B., & Beach, D. (1997). Phenomenography: A good-for-nothing brother of phenomenology? Outline of an analysis. *Higher Education Research & Development*, *16*(2), 191–202. doi:10.1080/0729436970160206.

Hofstede, G. (2001). *Culture's Consequences: comparing values, behaviors, institutions, and organizations across nations*. Thousand Oaks, CA: Sage Publications.

Jaworski, B. J., Kohli, A. K., & Sahay, A. (2000). Market-driven versus driving markets. *Journal of the Academy of Marketing Science*, *28*(1), 45–54. doi:10.1177/0092070300281005.

Johanson, J., & Vahlne, J.-E. (1977). The internationalization process of the firm - A model of knowledge development and increasing foreign commitments. *Journal of International Business Studies*, *8*(1), 23–32. doi:10.1057/palgrave.jibs.8490676.

Johanson, J., & Vahlne, J.-E. (1990). The mechanism of internationalization. *International Marketing Review*, *7*(4), 11–24. doi:10.1108/02651339010137414.

Johanson, J., & Wiedersheim-Paul, F. (1975). The internationalization of the firm - Four Swedish cases. *Journal of Management Studies*, *12*(3), 305–322. doi:10.1111/j.1467-6486.1975.tb00514.x.

Keskin, H. (2006). Market orientation, learning orientation, and innovation capabilities in SMEs. *European Journal of Innovation Management*, *9*(4), 396–417. doi:10.1108/14601060610707849.

Kirca, A. H., Jayachandran, S., & Bearden, W. O. (2005). Market orientation: A meta-analytic review and assessment of its antecedents and impact on performance. *Journal of Marketing*, *69*(2), 24–41. doi:10.1509/jmkg.69.2.24.60761.

Knight, G., Madsen, T. K., & Servais, P. (2004). An inquiry into born-global firms in Europe and the USA. *International Marketing Review*, *21*(6), 645–665. doi:10.1108/02651330410568060.

Knight, G. A., & Cavusgil, S. T. (2004). Innovation, organizational capabilities, and the born global firm. *Journal of International Business Studies*, *35*(2), 124–141. doi:10.1057/palgrave.jibs.8400071.

Kohli, A. K., & Jaworski, B. J. (1990). Market orientation: The construct, research propositions, and managerial implications. *Journal of Marketing*, *54*(2), 1–18. doi:10.2307/1251866.

Kropp, F., Lindsay, N. J., & Shoham, A. (2006). Entrepreneurial, market, and learning orientations and international entrepreneurial business venture performance in South African firms. *International Marketing Review*, *23*(5), 504–523. doi:10.1108/02651330610703427.

Lafferty, B. A., & Hult, G. T. M. (2001). A synthesis of contemporary market orientation perspectives. *European Journal of Marketing*, *35*(1/2), 92–109. doi:10.1108/03090560110363364.

Li, L., Li, D., & Dalgic, T. (2004). Internationalization process of small and medium-sized enterprises: Toward a hybrid model of experiential learning and planning. *Management International Review*, *44*(1), 93–116.

Li, T., & Calantone, R. J. (1998). The impact of market knowledge competence on new product advantage: Conceptualization and empirical examination. *Journal of Marketing*, *62*(4), 13–29. doi:10.2307/1252284.

Madsen, T. K., & Servais, P. (1997). The internationalisation of born globals: An evolutionary process? *International Business Review*, *6*(6), 561–583. doi:10.1016/S0969-5931(97)00032-2.

Marton, F. (1986). Phenomenography. A research approach to investigating different understandings of reality. *Journal of Thought*, *21*(3), 28–49.

McDougall, P., & Oviatt, B. (2000). International entrepreneurship: The intersection of two research paths. *Academy of Management Journal*, *43*(5), 902–906. doi:10.2307/1556418.

Meziou, F. (1991). Areas of strength and weakness in the adoption of the marketing concept by small manufacturing firms. *Journal of Small Business Management*, *29*(4), 72–78.

Moen, Ø. (2002). The born globals: A new generation of small European exporters. *International Marketing Review*, *19*(2), 156–175. doi:10.1108/02651330210425015.

Moen, Ø., & Servais, P. (2002). Born global or gradual global? Examining the export behavior of small and medium-sized enterprises. *Journal of International Marketing*, *10*(3), 49–72. doi:10.1509/jimk.10.3.49.19540.

Narver, J. C., & Slater, S. F. (1990). The effect of a market orientation on business profitability. *Journal of Marketing*, *54*(4), 20–35. doi:10.2307/1251757.

Nielsen, J. F., Høst, V., Jaensson, J.-E., Kock, S., & Selnes, F. (2003). Market orientation in Nordic banks: Does nationality matter? *European Journal of Marketing*, *37*(11/12), 1818–1841. doi:10.1108/03090560310495474.

Nordström, K. (1991). *The internationalization process of the firm - Searching for new patterns and explanations*. Doctoral dissertation. Stockholm School of Economic, Stockholm, Sweden.

Nummela, N., Saarenketo, S., & Puumalainen, K. (2004). A global mindset – A prerequisite for successful internationalization? *Canadian Journal of Administrative Sciences*, *21*(1), 51–64. doi:10.1111/j.1936-4490.2004.tb00322.x.

Oviatt, B., & McDougall, P. (1994). Toward a theory of international new ventures. *Journal of International Business Studies*, *25*(1), 45–64. doi:10.1057/palgrave.jibs.8490193.

Oviatt, B., & McDougall, P. (1997). Challenges for internationalization process theory: The case of international new ventures. *Management International Review*, *37*, 23–40.

Oviatt, B. M., & McDougall, P. P. (1995). Global start-ups: Entrepreneurs on a worldwide stage. *The Academy of Management Executive*, *9*(2), 30–44.

Pelham, A., & Wilson, D. T. (1996). A longitudinal study of the impact of market structure, firm structure, strategy and market orientation culture on dimensions of performance. *Journal of the Academy of Marketing Science*, *24*(1), 27–43. doi:10.1007/BF02893935.

Ruokonen, M., & Saarenketo, S. (2009). The strategic orientations of rapidly internationalizing software companies. *European Business Review*, *21*(1), 17–41. doi:10.1108/09555340910925166.

Ruzzier, M., Hisrich, R. D., & Antoncic, B. (2006). SME internationalization research: Past, present, and future. *Journal of Small Business and Enterprise Development*, *13*(4), 476–497. doi:10.1108/14626000610705705.

Slater, S. F., & Narver, J. C. (1995). Market orientation and the learning organization. *Journal of Marketing*, *59*(3), 63–74. doi:10.2307/1252120.

Slater, S. F., & Narver, J. C. (2000). The positive effect of a market orientation on business profitability: A balanced replication. *Journal of Business Research*, *48*(1), 69–73. doi:10.1016/S0148-2963(98)00077-0.

Turnbull, P. (1987). A challenge to the stages theory of internationalization process. In Rosson, P. S., & Ford, S. D. (Eds.), *Managing export entry and expansion* (pp. 21–40). New York: Praeger Publishers.

Verhees, F. J. H. M., & Meulenberg, M. T. G. (2004). Market orientation, innovativeness, product innovation, and performance in small firms. *Journal of Small Business Management*, *42*(2), 134–154. doi:10.1111/j.1540-627X.2004.00102.x.

Vikøren, B. M. (1990). Market orientation: A sustainable small scale advantage? *Entrepreneurship & Regional Development*, *2*(4), 335–343. doi:10.1080/08985629000000021.

Zahra, S., & George, G. (2002). International Entrepreneurship: The Current Status of the Field and Future Research Agenda. In Hitt, M., Ireland, D., Sexton, D., & Camp, M. (Eds.), *Strategic Entrepreneurship: Creating an Integrated Mindset* (pp. 255–288). Oxford, UK: Blackwell Publishers.

Zahra, S. A. (2005). A theory of international new ventures: A decade of research. *Journal of International Business Studies*, *36*(1), 20–28. doi:10.1057/palgrave.jibs.8400118.

Zahra, S. A., Hayton, J., Marcel, J., & O'Neill, H. (2001). Fostering entrepreneurship during international expansion: Managing key challenges. *European Management Journal*, *19*(4), 359–369. doi:10.1016/S0263-2373(01)00037-8.

KEY TERMS AND DEFINITIONS

International New Ventures (INVs): Oviatt & McDougall (1994, p. 49) have defined an international new venture (INV) as "a business organization that, from inception, seeks to derive significant competitive advantage from the use of resources and the sale of outputs in multiple countries." The definition of INVs in this article can be applied equally well to both INVs and established enterprises.

Internationalization: Carrying out international activities is typically referred to as internationalization. By using insights from research on entrepreneurship, an enterprise's entrepreneurial characteristics have been useful when discussing internationalization. In other words, it focuses more on the entrepreneurial qualities of enterprises rather than on their age of internationalization. The present study also rests on this. The relevance of entrepreneurs or managers in this case has been emphasized, which has found a positive relationship between international development of business operations and entrepreneur's international orientations.

Market Knowledge: This concept is closely related with market orientation, introduced by Li & Calantone (1998) who describe it as relevant market information systematically structured and organized in a company. SMEs (Small- and Medium-sized Enterprises): The definition of small- and medium-sized enterprises adopted in this article is based on the European Community standard. A small enterprise has fewer than 50 employees, less than 7 million euros in revenue, and less than 5 million euros in assets. The upper limit for a medium enterprise is fewer than 250 employees, less than 40 million euros in revenue, and less than 27 million euros in assets.

Market Orientation: A synthesis of market orientation of Lafferty and Hult (2001) is used in this article. They conclude that there are five different perspectives: decision-making, strategic, customer orientation, market intelligence, and culturally based behavioral perspectives. Generally, market orientation means that enterprises are actively generating, disseminating, and using market knowledge in their business operations. In addition, market orientation is understood as a cultural factor, for instance, Armario, Ruiz, & Armario (2008) state that market orientation is a dynamic competence which influences the organizational culture.

Chapter 14
The Role of Culture in Developing Disruptive Innovation in Domestic Firms

Birton J. Cowden
Saint Louis University, USA

Morris Kalliny
Saint Louis University, USA

ABSTRACT

National culture influences how people perceive the world, and subsequently, what actions they take. Research has shown that this also follows in the actions taken by firms that reside in those national cultures. The actions identified in this paper look at domestic firms' pursuit of disruptive innovation. Disruptive innovations are unique types of innovation that require different thinking from the firm. We discuss the two ways a firm can pursue disruption and how culture might affect that pursuit. Specifically, Hofstede's (1980) five cultural dimensions of uncertainty avoidance, power distance, long-term orientation, individualism, and masculinity will provide a guiding light on the values needed for a firm to develop disruptive innovations. Additionally, it will be further argued of the coexistence of disruptive business models and the opportunities of the bottom of the pyramid markets.

INTRODUCTION

Existing literature on innovation has elaborated on the different types of innovations a firm may pursue. One type of innovation which has not received much attention is disruptive innovation, specifically in an international business context (Sandberg & Hansen, 2004). Disruptive innovations are simple adaptations to existing technologies that appeal to customers who were not attracted to previous products (Christensen, 1997). To develop such innovation, the firm must

DOI: 10.4018/978-1-4666-3966-9.ch014

seek change and question current practices. The literature clearly shows that certain cultures are more apt to seek change while others may be resistant to change. This leads to the question, what role, if any, does culture play in a firm's pursuit of disruptive innovation?

Hofstede's five cultural dimensions (Hofstede, 1980; Hofstede & Bond, 1988) are well documented in terms of their ability to assist in understanding cultural differences. Researchers have used Hofstede's cultural dimensions to review the relationship between new product development and national culture. For example, Waldman, Luque, Washburn, and House (2006) build their study on the assumption that societal-level values predict the values at the firm level. From Nakata and Sivakumar (1996), it can be seen that national culture will have an influence over the direction of research and development (R&D) inside the firm. For instance, Morris, Davis, and Allen (1994) find that certain levels of individualism lead to more corporate entrepreneurship. Similarly, Shane (1992; 1993) finds individualistic- and low-power distance societies have more patents and trademarks. The key discovery of Jones and Davis (2000) is that national cultures affect innovation and the location factor for innovation should be a major consideration for any firm. Thus, when analyzing different types of innovation, it is important to understand culture.

To identify true national culture effects, this chapter will look at the perspective from domestic firms rather than Multinational Companies (MNCs). This is not to say these cultural relations do not hold true for other types of firms with their innovation. MNCs operate in several different countries, all with unique cultures. Operating in different cultures could potentially form a cosmopolitan perspective or create a cornucopia of all of the mixed cultures put together (Cantwell & Piscitello, 2000). Thus, keeping the perspective on domestic firms allows the ability to capture the truest form of the cultural effects. Additionally, to maintain a competitive advantage over MNCs, domestic firms must be more adaptive to local needs (Bartlett & Ghoshal, 1989). This requires a more in depth knowledge of the national culture, from the internal processes and decision to the exchange with customers.

Johne (1984) states there are two phases of product development: initiation where the idea is generated and tested, and implementation where the product is fully developed and launched into the market. For the purpose of this study, only the first phase will be examined to see the effect that culture has on a firm's intention to pursue either disruptive or sustaining technologies. Pursuing disruption is a priority and mindset which the firm must adopt (Jalinek & Schoonhoven, 1993); otherwise, it will not pursue it. Thus, this chapter is not focused on implementation and market adoption of the disruptive innovation. Others have already explored in depth the diffusion and adoption of innovations in different nations (Dwyer, Mesak, & Maxwell, 2005; Steenkamp, Hofstede, & Michel, 1999). It is more relevant for this chapter to examine if different domestic firms which sit in different cultures even seek to pursue a disruptive strategy. The intent of proactiveness in disruption provides more of the firm-level actions.

This chapter seeks to expand on the concept of national cultural effects on developing disruptive innovations. We will also expand disruptive innovation in an international setting by looking at cross-cultural differences. Understanding disruption in this context and identifying cultural differences further reduce the mystique of disruptive innovations which has kept many firms from actively pursuing such a strategy. While this chapter takes a domestic firm perspective, MNCs can also utilize such a study to be aware of cultural affects in pursuing disruptive innovations in certain subsidiaries or when partnering with certain domestic or foreign firms. As described above, firms act differently when developing disruptive innovation, which validates the need to look at specific types of innovation when providing pertinent implications. This view is also shared by Veryzer (2005).

The remainder portion of the chapter is organized as follows: we will begin by reviewing what disruptive innovation is and the different forms it can take. Hofstede's five cultural dimensions will then be reviewed. Propositions will follow each cultural dimension stating its effect on disruptive innovation. The chapter will conclude by providing an avenue on how to test the suggested propositions.

LITERATURE REVIEW

Disruptive Innovation

Schumpeter (1942) states all innovations require some degree of creative destruction. As stated above, disruptive innovations are simple adaptations to existing technologies that appeal to customers who were not attracted to previous products (Christensen, 1997). Disruptive innovation is shown to be very beneficial for long-term competitive success (Christensen & Raynor, 2003). Sustaining innovations are incremental improvements on existing technology that allows the firm to move up the market to sell higher margin products to its best customers. Christensen (2006) states that the theory of disruption stemmed from discovering anomalies from Henderson and Clark's (1990) architectural versus modular classification of innovation. Architectural innovation stemmed from anomalies that could not be explained by Tushman and Anderson's (1986) classification of competency-enhancing versus competency-destroying innovation. Perhaps the best form of viewing disruptive innovation is the matrix put together by Chandy and Tellis (1998). By looking at high to low newness of the technology and the customer need fulfillment per dollar four types of product innovations are introduced: incremental innovation, market breakthrough, technological breakthrough, and radial innovation. Low on both is represented by incremental innovation, which aligns directly with the idea of sustaining innovation. Low on newness of technology, but high on customer need fulfillment is market breakthrough, which is most appropriate place for disruptive innovation.

Bower and Christensen (1995) state the difference between a sustaining idea and a disruptive idea can be determined by the department proposing the new innovation. Finance and Marketing typically will favor sustaining innovation with known markets, while the technology gurus will see the potential in disruptive innovations. Paap and Katz (2004) argue disruptive innovation can be in any part of the business model: what the firm sells, how it sells it, distributes and supports it, who it sells to, and who it competes against.

Tushman and O'Reilly (1997) and Christensen (1997) find that non-sustaining innovation is predominantly introduced by new entrants into a market, while existing firms typically win the battle on sustaining innovation in the marketplace. They all agree existing firms become losers to new entrants with disruptive innovation because existing firms are not set up to be flexible, nor are they willing to potentially cannibalize any part of the existing company. Gillette learned this lesson at the height of its success by almost being toppled by Wilkinson Sword's stainless steel blade, which could last three times longer than Gillette's carbon steel blade (Tellis & Golder, 2003). From this lesson, Gillette learned it was better to disrupt itself even at a cost of cannibalizing existing products, rather than having someone else disrupt established products and losing control of the market.

There are two strategies for pursuing disruptive innovation: creating a new market through a new technology or creating a new business model at the low end of an existing market (Christensen, Johnson, & Rigby, 2002). Three litmus tests can be used to see if a technology will be disruptive in a new market. First, does the innovation help consumers do what they have already been trying to do, but more effective and efficient? Second, does the innovation target customers looking for a simple product? Third, is the innovation aimed at consumers who have not consumed the product or service due to lack of money or skills?

As Veryzer (1998) argues for discontinuous innovation, disruptive technologies can be further subdivided into being technologically disruptive and commercially disruptive. Technological disruption is the packaging of existing technology in a new format that has more implications for Business-to-Business (B2B) transactions. This technology development might not lead directly to Business-to-Customer (B2C) transactions, but might enhance a supply chain or an input for a new product that can be sold commercially. The other type, commercial disruption, is more consumer market focused. This is a new product that is the integration of mostly existing technologies (and perhaps some new technologies) which was never combined for a new purpose and can be taken directly to customers. This change will have an effect on how people consume other goods or services and will disrupt or create a new market of goods and service providers. These two subcategories do not need to be mutually exclusive as some technologies can contain both elements as B2B offerings transform into B2C offerings.

The second type of disruption comes from creating a low-end business model in an existing market. Two litmus tests can be used to determine if disruption can occur by creating a new business model (Christensen et al., 2002). First, are the existing products more than good enough? This test to see if existing products over-serve their customers with very little value added. If so, there is room in the market to provide a low-end product that adds the most value to more sets of people. The second litmus test asks can a different business model be created. More specifically, is there a way to create a unique business model that adds value in a new way, while also being able to make a profit? Thus, having a disruptive business model is not dependent on the technology, but more so the business practices.

A more recent example of a disruptive business model is that of Wikipedia, which is a free online encyclopedia edited by its users. The group which owns Wikipedia (Wikimedia) is a nonprofit organization with a mission to allow free access to information. They are able to handle expenses through private donations, grants, and corporate sponsorships. By keeping things open and free, Wikipedia's business model has disrupted the existing publishers of encyclopedias that depended on the sales of physical books to users. These publishers have since moved to an online format, but have had slow adoption due to their lack of collaboration of the content.

Culture

Hofstede (1980, p. 25) defines national culture as the "collective programming of the mind which distinguishes the members of one group or category of people from those of another." Hofstede (1980) surveyed IBM employees from all around the world. From this survey, he found four cultural dimensions that differentiate each culture. The original four cultural dimensions are uncertainty avoidance (UA), power distance (PD), individualism-collectivism (IND-COL), and masculinity-femininity (MAS-FEM). A few years later, a fifth cultural dimension was added, Confucian dynamism or long-term orientation vs. short-term orientation (LTO-STO) (Hofstede & Bond, 1988).

Teece, Pisano, and Shuen (1997) believe the ability to innovate is a dynamic capability of a firm. A core capability is a set of skills and processes that strategically differentiates a company from others (Prahalad & Hamel, 1990). Leonard-Barton (1992) adopts a knowledge-based view of the firm to develop a set of four dimensions that defines a firm's product development. They include: employee knowledge and skills, technical systems, managerial systems, and values and norms. In her conceptual model, the first three dimensions form a Venn diagram with the circles intersecting the fourth dimension, values and norms. Thus, all four are interrelated and interdependent. This intersection is where corporate and national culture begin to merge (Schneider, 1988). From other studies, it is well documented that human resources and values are affected by national culture. For instance, Usunier (1996) finds that national culture provides a frame of reference of how to interpret the world and influences perceptions. Similarly, Nakata and Sivakumar (2001) find that national culture influences how people interpret experiences. Thus, it can be seen that national culture drives the perception of the firm, which influences its actions.

Similarly, Christensen et al. (2002) state that for a firm to make disruptive strategies work, it needs to pay attention to human resources and corporate processes and values. For human resources, it is not suggested to select a successful manager in the mainstream business to lead the disruptive business, where flexibility and or efficiency are needed. Values and processes must also change to enter a new market or put forth a new business model. Thus, it can be seen that culture has a significant influence on the major inputs of successful disruptive innovation.

All five of Hofstede's cultural dimensions will be evaluated against the development of disruptive technologies. While Hofstede's cultural dimensions have received some criticism (Shenkar, 2001), Kirkman et al. (2006) criticizes that the data was collected during the late 1960s and early 1970s, but has yet to be updated to reflect any possible changes in the culture. McSweeney (2002) criticizes Hofstede's study design of surveying IBM employees and then extrapolating those findings to represent the culture of the entire country. However, Hofstede's dimensions have been validated by many studies (Sondergaard, 1994) and still are the most used form of looking at cultural differences. This continued popularity stems for the dimensions' are able to be clearly understood by managers (Kirkman, Lowe, & Gibson, 2006), which aligns with the intent of this paper to remove the mystique of pursuing disruptive innovation for existing firms. At the very least, using Hofstede's measures as a proxy to show cultural differences among employees in a firm like IBM is beneficial to an article such as this that is trying to determine the linkage of the firm's setting and the innovation it pursues. Additionally, Hofstede's measures are used for congruence purposes with other papers that look at the market acceptance and consumer behavior side of this phenomenon (Yeniyurt & Townsend, 2003).

This chapter will rely on Leonard-Barton's interaction among values and norms, managerial systems, and employee knowledge and skills within a firm. As stated above, these factors play a key role in the interaction of national culture and the development of disruptive innovation. Each cultural dimension has an effect on how a firm's values and norms, managers, and employees will approach innovation. However, this approach will most likely be different than previous studies based on the unique characteristics that are needed to make disruptive innovations, as defined above.

PROPOSITIONS

Uncertainty Avoidance

Uncertainty avoidance can be defined as a society's acceptance of uncertainty, ambiguity, and risk (Hofstede, 1980). Some cultures are content with unstructured lives and are classified as having weak uncertainty avoidance, while others that require structure are classified as having strong uncertainty avoidance. Weak uncertainty avoidance cultures are more accepting of change and different ideas. Strong uncertainty avoidance cultures are threatened by change and create more institutions to provide more structure and reduce risk (Hofstede, 1983). Pursuing a disruptive strategy is fraught with uncertainty and risk. There are uncertainties involved when trying to think up and develop something that is new or unproven. For most firms, the first task is to scan the environment to see what others have done or are doing currently in a given market. From this, many businesses use previous examples as templates to follow in order to reduce risk and the learning curve. Without such a template, risk must be accepted in order for a disruptive technology to be pursued. Similarly, many innovation decisions rely on profit potential. However, the most uncertain aspect of a disruptive technology is an undefined market. Because it is new, no one has proof if there is a market, and if there is, how big it is.

For example, it is logical to think that IBM took a large gamble on an unknown market for personal computers. Minicomputers and workstations disrupted mainframes, but would people really want or need these types of machines in their home? Thus, the value of uncertainty affects the actions of managers and employees in the types of innovations that are thought of and the types of innovations that are accepted to be developed. Risk adverse management will not support projects that explore the unknown. This uncertainty does not only pertain to the actual operation endeavors of disruptive innovation, but also the perceived risk by the managers (Downey, Hellriegel, & Slocum, 1977). This leads to the following conclusion:

Proposition 1: Domestic firms in low uncertainty avoidance cultures are more likely to develop more disruptive technologies than domestic firms in high uncertainty avoidance cultures.

Power Distance

Power distance can be defined as a society's acceptance of power inequality (Hofstede, 1980). Some cultures are more accepting of power inequalities and prefer centralized authority. These cultures are classified as high power distance. Cultures which could be classified as having low power distance do not seek hierarchies and feel more comfortable allowing decisions to be made with a flatter structure. Christensen and Raynor (2003) argue that incumbent firms have three options to proactively pursue disruptive innovation: they can change the processes and values of the current organization, create an independent organization, or acquire a different organization. From the authors' point of view, it is recommended to pursue the second option of creating an independent organization to take control of the disruptive innovation. Thus, developing disruptive strategies does not appear to be a centralized process. Teece (2007, p. 1323) also suggests when discussing dynamic capabilities that "more decentralized organizations with greater local autonomy are less likely to be blindsided by market and technological developments." Firms developing disruptive strategies must also allow their people to question current authority in order to make a positive change (Christensen, Johnson, & Rigby, 2002). This leads to the following conclusion:

Proposition 2: Domestic firms in low power distance cultures are more likely to develop more disruptive technologies than domestic firms in high power distance cultures.

Long-Term Orientation

Long-term orientation vs. short-term orientation refers to a society's perspective on priorities (Hofstede & Bond, 1988). Short-term oriented cultures focus more on the past and present, and put more emphasis on upholding traditions. Long-term oriented cultures look more to the future to be motivated on what could be or how things could be better.

Cultures with a past-time orientation are likely to emphasize respect for tradition and belief that the way things have always been done in the past is the way they should continue; therefore, they are not easily open to change or innovation. These cultures emphasize things that are past oriented such as cultural heritage, history, tradition, past accomplishments and preservation of the past. Change in these cultures does not come easily and is often fought and resisted. In contrast, cultures having present-time orientation are likely to emphasize the present and hold it as most important. These cultures tend to "pay little attention to what has happened in the past and regard the future as both vague and unpredictable. Planning for the future or hoping that the future will be better than either the present or the past simply is not their way of life," (Kluckhohn & Strodtbeck, 1961, p. 14). Thus, these cultures are described as short-term oriented where their focus is more on the present rather than the past or the future. Future-time orientated cultures tend to focus on the future. This is not to say that they do not respect the past or not live in the present, but rather to state their main focus is concerned with the future.

The main objective of disruptive innovations is to be able to provide more value than there is currently. A firm must be able to look to the future and try to determine how it can make things better. This leads to the following conclusion:

Proposition 3: Domestic firms located in long-term oriented cultures are more likely to develop more disruptive technologies than domestic firms located in short-term oriented cultures

Individualism/Collectivism

Traindis (2004) concluded that the dimension of individualism/collectivism is the most important dimension in studying culture. This dimension has extensively been used and investigated in many disciplines (Cukur, De Guzman, & Gustavo, 2004; Gudykundst, Matsumoto, Ting-Tconey, Nishida, Kirn, & Seyman, 1996; Han & Shavitt, 1994; McCarty & Hattwick, 1992; Mueller, 1987). Individualism and collectivism are defined by the relationship ties and responsibility of care a person has in a society (Hofstede, 1980). Individualistic cultures believe that everyone should take care of themselves and do not identify themselves as being a part of any one group. Collectivistic cultures, however, believe it is the responsibility of everyone in the group to take care of each other and their main identity is being a part of that group (Hofstede, 1983). In collectivistic societies, people are integrated into strong and cohesive in-groups which care for them in exchange for a high degree of loyalty. Collectivists are more willing than individualists to sacrifice their personal goals for group's goals (Perea & Slater, 1999). Additionally, social norms are very important in guiding the behavior of individuals in collectivist societies (Prior & Whalen, 1997).

One could argue that creating a disruptive innovation can be seen as very individualistic. As stated above, Morris et al. (1994) find that individualistic cultures tend to have more entrepreneurial firms. Being more entrepreneurial creates a mindset to look on how to capitalize on new opportunities, which could lead to disruption. However, others could argue that collectivists can also create disruptive innovations to better meet the needs of the group. For example, Japanese teams are documented as working well together to build consensus about a project (Kennard, 1991), and Sony, a Japanese firm, is well documented as disrupting the market via the Sony Walkman. Collectivistic innovation could also come in the form of innovation through local networks. Birkinshaw, Bessant, & Delbridge (2007) focus on how to create new networks for discontinuous innovation. Examples of these networks would be idea networks, corporate venturing networks, lead user groups, cross-industry alliances, communities of practice, supplier networks, and open innovation networks. Another study sees that the new frontier for innovation for the firm is to create experiences through networks of external partners and customer communities (Prahalad & Ramaswamy, 2003). This leads to the following conclusion:

Proposition 4: There will not be a significant difference positively or negatively in the number of developments of disruptive technologies between domestic firms in individualistic and collectivistic cultures

Masculinity/Femininity

Masculinity and feminism refers to the roles of gender in society. Masculine cultures put men as leaders and women in support roles. Feminine cultures are not necessarily the opposite of masculine cultures, but have less defined roles and separation of power between the two sexes. Masculine cultures are said to value achievement and be more concerned about status then feminine cultures (Newman & Nollen, 1996). Feminine cultures tend to put relationships first and generally think about other people and things besides themselves, like the environment (Hofstede, 1983). Men are expected to be assertive, tough, and focused on material success while women are expected to be more modest, tender, and concerned with quality of life. According to Hofstede's (1984) description, this dimension refers to the extent to which cultures strive for ego-goals and competitiveness where masculinity stands for achievement, heroism, assertiveness, and material success. In contrast, femininity stands for relationships, modesty, caring for the weak, and the quality of life. De Mooij (1998, p. 82) states the femininity/masculinity dimension "discriminates between cultures particularly with respect to values related to winning, success, and status."

Thus, one could argue the pursuit of achieving something disruptive is very masculine. However, some have argued that disruptive strategies can play a major role in corporate environmental sustainability, which is more prone to feministic qualities. For instance, Hart (2005) makes the claim that disruptive strategies is how companies can enter emerging markets while also helping people at the bottom-of-the-pyramid. This conflict can also be seen in research about the cultural effects of teams during product development. For instance, success of projects in high masculine cultures show the need for the leader to play the role as a gatekeeper and set clear goals (Barczak & Wilemon, 1992). Alternatively, Thwaites (1992) finds the softer people issues, which are considered to be more feminine, or explain more of the success of project. This leads to the conclusion:

Proposition 5: There will not be a significant difference positively or negatively in the number of developments of disruptive technologies between domestic firms in masculine and feminine cultures

Business Models

While it is believed the above propositions hold for disruptive technologies, it is questioned if culture plays a role in the second type of disruption, disruptive business models. The nature of this type of disruption is less dependent on the individual efforts of the personnel in R&D or in the executive decision-making process, and more dependent on market mechanisms. For instance, if most of the firms in the market cater to high-end consumers, then reusing existing technology to provide a product or service to the low-end of the market is driven by market demand and the competitive environment. When markets are saturated from the low end to the high end, it does not leave much room for a niche player to disrupt the market. If it is more demand driven, then culture plays a less significant role in this type of disruption. If this were the case, businesses in certain cultures would never see competition, which is rare unless forced by a country's formal institution. This leads to the following conclusion:

Proposition 6: Domestic market conditions will have more explanatory power on the number of local firms that pursue disruptive business models than the difference in national culture effects.

As stated above, this type of disruption is market-driven. Therefore, it would be logical that many firms which pursue this type of disruption prosper in places where demand exists, but is currently not being served. The quintessential scenario for this has been coined Bottom-of-the-Pyramid (BOP) markets. A traditional perspective is to review the annual income amount of these individuals and assume they cannot afford a company's service or product. It has been demonstrated the poor do buy luxury items and that one must look at the aggregate demand of these people rather than the individual (Prahalad & Hammond, 2002). Additionally, London and Hart (2004) determine that business can thrive in these markets if they change their business models to fit these markets rather than trying to force fit a standard western model.

A prime example of this is the micro-financing and phone plans provided by Grameen Bank of Bangladesh (Bayes, von Braun, & Akhter, 1999). Grameen Bank of Bangladesh disrupted the whole notion of banking by establishing a micro-financing business model. The tradition way in banking when providing a line of credit is to only provide credit to a person who can provide collateral of a value which would relative equal to the loan provided by the bank in case that person defaults on the loan. This essentially left a large poor population without the ability to get a loan. Grameen Bank saw that the poor had a need to secure loans and built a whole new business model that removed the traditional barriers for the poor. Grameen Bank offers micro-financing without the need for collateral. Grameen Bank provides the poor with small amount loans, enforced by trust, not contracts.

This trust is built around social capital and making entire groups responsible for the potential loans they can receive. Grameen Bank has also begun providing telecommunication services to those in the area that normally could not afford traditional communication plans. Again, it developed a low-end disruptive business model to attract those customers which were previously non-consumers. For its most trusted customers, Grameen Bank has offered leased cellular phones, which have been referred to as village pay phones. The cellular phones are essentially free and customers only need to purchase pre-paid phone cards for the minutes they plan to use.

Many more examples exist of how business models are changed to successfully attract a lower end customer, and more opportunities exist to get traditional services and products to BOP markets. This untapped demand is ripe for disruption and the market is completely unsaturated. However, as London and Hart (2004) show, many MNCs have been unable to adapt their processes to these markets and very few have been unable to extract value. This provides a potential weakness that domestic firms can exploit. Additionally, research has shown that firms in emerging markets can actually springboard MNCs because these new firms can adopt the newest technologies and are not inhibited by past investments (Luo & Tung, 2007). This leads to the following conclusion:

Proposition 7: Firms located in bottom-of-the-pyramid markets will be most competitive against MNCs through introducing disruptive business models

CONCLUSION

Disruptive innovation is a relatively new characterization for innovation, and so far most of the research has reviewed what it is and how it works. This chapter expands this concept further by looking at where it occurs. International business has greatly explored almost all aspects of general innovation, but has rarely put the focus on different types of innovation, such as disruptive innovation. Additionally, disruptive innovation has been maintained more in the USA setting. Thus, this chapter is the first to explore how national culture might affect which firms are most likely to pursue disruption. This is important because this informs managers of key locations or personnel that should lead the charge to pursuing disruption.

This chapter can provide different insights to domestic and international firms. By understanding more about the cultural effect on disruptive innovation, domestic firms which recognize the need for disruption might be better served by partnering with another firm set in a culture that is more apt to developing disruptive innovation. Similarly, MNCs can also benefit from this study by identifying which subsidiaries they should put in charge of developing disruptive innovations or what external partners in different locations might be best to collaborate with on disruptive projects. This could also lead to implications on the hiring practices management and R&D personnel that would lead disruptive projects.

Lastly, this has implications for venture capitalists that might be looking to invest in disruptive innovation in different countries. By knowing how the differences in culture affect a firm's pursuit into disruptive innovation, a venture capitalist will be able to better narrow his or her search for the best bets on disruption. For instance, based on the above propositions, a country with smaller power distance and weaker uncertainty avoidance would be more prone for disruption than counterparts on the opposite side of the scale. As an example, this might mean that disruption would be more apt from Great Britain than from France, or Jamaica will be more disruptive than Guatemala. Thus, even for this topic as other in international business, location still matters (Dunning, 2009).

This chapter also further defines the boundaries of disruptive innovation in an international context. By identifying the national culture effect on a firm's pursuit of disruptive innovation, more research can be developed to examine cross-national perspectives of how firms treat disruptive innovation and how it is implemented. Future work can also be done on the effect culture has on the consumer adoption of disruptive innovation. Additionally, this work could lead to research on the diffusion of disruptive innovations to different regions.

This chapter provides a conceptual interaction between national culture and disruptive innovation. A deeper understanding of how firms do and can pursue such endeavors' is still lacking, which has led to companies still being reluctant to pursuing a disruptive strategy (Hamel, 2000). Understanding the cultural effects will further reduce the mystique of pursuing disruptive strategies. When this occurs, both the firm and the consumer benefit.

REFERENCES

Barczak, G. J., & Wilemon, D. (1992). Successful New Product Team Leaders. *Industrial Marketing Management*, *21*(February), 61–68. doi:10.1016/0019-8501(92)90034-Q.

Bartlett, C. A., & Ghoshal, S. (1989). *Managing across Borders: The Transnational Solution*. Boston, MA: Harvard Business School Press.

Bayes, A., von Braun, J., & Akhter, R. (1999). Village Pay Phones and Poverty Reduction: Insights from a Grameen Bank Initiative in Bangladesh. In *Discussion Papers on Development Policy*. Bonn, Germany: University of Bonn.

Birkinshaw, J., Bessant, J., & Delbridge, R. (2007). Finding, Forming, and Performing: Creating Networks for Discontinuous Innovation. *California Management Review*, *49*(3), 67–84. doi:10.2307/41166395.

Bower, J. L., & Christensen, C. M. (1995). Disruptive Technologies: Catching the Wave. *Harvard Business Review*, *73*(1), 43–53.

Cantwell, J. A., & Piscitello, L. (2000). Accumulating Technological Competence: Its Changing Impact on Corporate Diversification and Internationalisation. *Industrial and Corporate Change*, *9*(1), 21–51. doi:10.1093/icc/9.1.21.

Chandy, R. K., & Tellis, G. J. (1998). Organizing for Radical Product Innovation: The Overlooked Role of Willingness to Cannibalize. *JMR, Journal of Marketing Research*, *35*(4), 474–487. doi:10.2307/3152166.

Christensen, C. M. (1997). *The Innovator's Dilemma*. New York: HarperCollins Publishing, Inc..

Christensen, C. M. (2006). The Ongoing Process of Building a Theory or Disruption. *Journal of Product Innovation Management*, *23*(1), 39–55. doi:10.1111/j.1540-5885.2005.00180.x.

Christensen, C. M., Johnson, M. W., & Rigby, D. K. (2002). Foundations for Growth: How to Identify and Build Disruptive New Businesses. *Sloan Management Review*, *43*(3), 22–31.

Christensen, C. M., & Raynor, M. E. (2003). *The Innovator's Solution*. Boston, MA: Harvard Business School.

Cukur, C. S., De Guzman, M., & Gustavo, C. (2004). Religiosity, Values, and Horizontal and Vertical Individualism/Collectivism: A Study of Turkey, the United States and the Philippines. *The Journal of Social Psychology*, *144*(6), 613–635. doi:10.3200/SOCP.144.6.613-634 PMID:15565828.

De Mooij, M. (1998). *Global Marketing and Advertising: Understanding Cultural Paradoxes*. Thousand Oaks, CA: Sage Publications.

Downey, H. K., Hellriegel, D., & Slocum, J. W. (1977). Individual Characteristics as Sources of Perceived Uncertainty Variability. *Human Relations*, *30*(2), 161–174. doi:10.1177/001872677703000205.

Dunning, J. H. (2009). Location and the Multinational Enterprise: A Neglected Factor? *Journal of International Business Studies*, *40*(1), 5–19. doi:10.1057/jibs.2008.74.

Dwyer, S., Mesak, H., & Maxwell, H. (2005). An Exploratory Examination on the Influence of National Culture on Cross-National Product Diffusion. *Journal of International Marketing*, *13*(2), 1–27. doi:10.1509/jimk.13.2.1.64859.

Gudykundst, W., Matsumoto, Y., Ting-Tconey, T., Nishida, T., Kirn, K., & Seyman, S. (1996). The Influence of Cultural Individualism-Collectivism, Self Construal, and Individual Values on Communication Styles across Cultures. *Human Communication Research*, *22*(June), 510–543. doi:10.1111/j.1468-2958.1996.tb00377.x.

Hamel, G. (2000). *Leading the Revolution*. Boston, MA: Harvard Business School Press.

Han, S., & Shavitt, S. (1994). Persuasion and Culture: Advertising Appeals in Individualistic and Collectivistic Societies. *Journal of Experimental Social Psychology*, *30*(4), 326–350. doi:10.1006/jesp.1994.1016.

Hart, S. L. (2005). Innovation, Creative Destruction and Sustainability. *Research Technology Management*, *48*(5), 21–27.

Henderson, R. M., & Clark, K. B. (1990). Architectural Innovation: The Reconfiguration of Existing Systems and the Failure of Established Firms. *Administrative Science Quarterly*, *35*(1), 9–30. doi:10.2307/2393549.

Hofstede, G. (1980). *Culture's Consequences: International Differences in Work Related Values*. Beverly Hills, CA: Sage.

Hofstede, G. (1983). The Cultural Relativity of Organizational Practices and Theories. *Journal of International Business Studies*, *14*(2), 75–89. doi:10.1057/palgrave.jibs.8490867.

Hofstede, G. (1984). *Culture's Consequences: International Differences in Work-Related Values*. London: Sage.

Hofstede, G., & Bond, M. H. (1988). The Confucius Connection: From Cultural Roots to Economic Growth. *Organizational Dynamics*, *16*(4), 5–21. doi:10.1016/0090-2616(88)90009-5.

Jalinek, M., & Schoonhoven, C. B. (1993). *The Innovation Marathon*. San Francisco, CA: Jossey-Bass.

Johne, F. A. (1984). How Experienced Product Innovators Organize. *Journal of Product Innovation Management*, *4*(12), 210–223. doi:10.1016/S0737-6782(84)80002-8.

Jones, G. K., & Davis, H. J. (2000). National Culture and Innovation: Implications for Locating Global R&D Operation. *Management International Review*, *40*(1), 11–39.

Kennard, R. B. (1991). From Experience: Japanese Product Development Process. *Journal of Product Innovation Management*, *8*(September), 184–188. doi:10.1016/0737-6782(91)90025-T.

Kirkman, B., Lowe, K., & Gibson, C. (2006). A Quarter Century of Culture's Consequences: A Review of Empirical Research Incorporating Hofstede's Cultural Values Framework. *Journal of International Business Studies*, *37*(3), 285–320. doi:10.1057/palgrave.jibs.8400202.

Kluckhohn, F. R., & Strodtbeck, F. Z. (1961). *Variations in Value Orientations*. West Port, CT: Greenwood Press.

Leonard-Barton, D. (1992). Core Capabilities and Core Rigidities: A Paradox in Managing New Product Development. *Strategic Management Journal*, *13*(Summer), 111–125. doi:10.1002/smj.4250131009.

London, T., & Hart, S. L. (2004). Reinventing Strategies for Emerging Markets: Beyond the Transnational Model. *Journal of International Business Studies*, *35*(5), 350–370. doi:10.1057/palgrave.jibs.8400099.

Luo, Y., & Tung, R. L. (2007). International Expansion of Emerging Market Enterprises: A Springboard Perspective. *Journal of International Business Studies*, *38*(4), 481–498. doi:10.1057/palgrave.jibs.8400275.

McCarty, J., & Hattwick, P. (1992). Cultural Value Orientations: A Comparison of Magazine Advertisements from the United States and Mexico. *Advances in Consumer Research. Association for Consumer Research (U. S.)*, *19*, 34–38.

McSweeney, B. (2002). Hofstede's Model of National Cultural Differences and Their Consequences: A Triumph of Faith - A Failure of Analysis. *Human Relations*, *55*(1), 89–118.

Morris, M. H., Davis, D. L., & Allen, J. W. (1994). Fostering Corporate Entrepreneurship: Cross-Cultural Comparisons of the Importance of Individualism Versus Collectivism. *Journal of International Business Studies*, *25*(1), 65–89. doi:10.1057/palgrave.jibs.8490849.

Mueller, B. (1987). Reflections of Culture: An Analysis of Japanese and American Advertising Appeals. *Journal of Advertising Research*, *27*(June/July), 51–59.

Nakata, C., & Sivakumar, K. (1996). National Culture and New Product Development: An Integrative Review. *Journal of Marketing*, *60*(1), 61–72. doi:10.2307/1251888.

Nakata, C., & Sivakumar, K. (2001). Instituting the Marketing Concept in a Multinational Setting: The Role of National Culture. *Journal of the Academy of Marketing Science*, *29*(3), 255–275. doi:10.1177/03079459994623.

Newman, K., & Nollen, S. D. (1996). Culture and Congruence: The Fit between Management Practices and National Culture. *Journal of International Business Studies*, *27*(4), 753–779. doi:10.1057/palgrave.jibs.8490152.

Paap, J., & Katz, R. (2004). Anticipating Disruptive Innovation. *Research Technology Management*, *47*(5), 13–22.

Perea, A., & Slater, M. (1999). Power Distance and Collectivist/Individualist Strategies in Alcohol Warnings: Effects by Gender and Ethnicity. *Journal of Health Communication*, *4*, 295–310. doi:10.1080/108107399126832 PMID:10790786.

Prahalad, C. K., & Hamel, G. (1990). The Core Competence of the Corporation. *Harvard Business Review*, *68*(3), 79–91.

Prahalad, C. K., & Hammond, A. (2002). Serving the World's Poor, Profitably. *Harvard Business Review*, *80*(9), 48–57. PMID:12227146.

Prahalad, C. K., & Ramaswamy, V. (2003). The New Frontier of Experience Innovation. *MIT Sloan School of Management*, *44*(4), 12–18.

Prior, J. B., & Whalen, N. J. (1997). A Typology of Sexual Harassment: Characteristics of Harassers and the Social Circumstances under Which Sexual Harassment Occurs.W. O'Donohue (Ed.), In Sexual Harassment: Theory, Research, and Treatment. Boston, MA: Allyn & Bacon.

Sandberg, B., & Hansen, S.-O. (2004). Creating and International Market for Disruptive Innovations. *European Journal of Innovation Management*, *7*(1), 23–32. doi:10.1108/14601060410515619.

Schneider, S. C. (1988). National Vs. Corporate Culture: Implications for Human Resource Management. *Human Resource Management*, *27*(2), 231–246. doi:10.1002/hrm.3930270207.

Schumpeter, J. (1942). *Capitalism, Socialism, and Democracy*. New York: Harper.

Shane, S. (1992). Why Do Some Societies Invent More Than Others? *Journal of Business Venturing*, *7*(January), 29–46. doi:10.1016/0883-9026(92)90033-N.

Shane, S. (1993). Cultural Influences on National Rates of Innovation. *Journal of Business Venturing*, *8*(January), 59–73. doi:10.1016/0883-9026(93)90011-S.

Shenkar, O. (2001). Cultural Distance Revisited: Towards a More Rigorous Conceptualization and Measurement of Cultural Differences. *Journal of International Business Studies*, *32*(3), 519–536. doi:10.1057/palgrave.jibs.8490982.

Sondergaard, M. (1994). Research Note: Hofstede's Consequences: A Study of Reviews, Citations and Replications. *Organization Studies*, *15*(3), 447–456. doi:10.1177/017084069401500307.

Steenkamp, J.-B. E. M., Hofstede, F. T., & Michel, W. (1999). A Cross-National Investigation into the Individual and National Culture Antecedents of Consumer Innovativeness. *Journal of Marketing*, *63*(April), 55–69. doi:10.2307/1251945.

Teece, D. J. (2007). Explicating Dynamic Capabilities: The Nature and Microfoundations of (Sustainable) Enterprise Performance. *Strategic Management Journal*, *28*(8), 1319–1350. doi:10.1002/smj.640.

Teece, D. J., Pisano, G., & Shuen, A. (1997). Dynamic Capabilities and Strategic Management. *Strategic Management Journal*, *18*(7), 509–534. doi:10.1002/(SICI)1097-0266(199708)18:7<509::AID-SMJ882>3.0.CO;2-Z.

Tellis, G. J., & Golder, P. N. (2003). First to Market, First to Fail? Real Causes of Enduring Market Leadership. In Katz, R. (Ed.), *The Human Side of Managing Technological Innovation*. New York: Oxford University Press.

Thwaites, D. (1992). Organizational Influences on the New Product Development Process in Financial Services. *Journal of Product Innovation Management*, *9*(June), 303–313. doi:10.1111/1540-5885.940303.

Traindis, H. (2004). The Many Dimensions of Culture. *The Academy of Management Executive*, *19*(1), 88–95. doi:10.5465/AME.2004.12689599.

Tushman, M. L., & Anderson, P. (1986). Technological Discontinuities and Organizational Environments. *Administrative Science Quarterly*, *31*(3), 439–465. doi:10.2307/2392832.

Tushman, M. L., & O'Reilly, C. A. (1997). *Winning through Innovation: A Practical Guide to Leading Organizational Change and Renewal*. Cambridge, MA: Harvard Business School Press.

Usunier, J. C. (1996). *Marketing across Cultures*. London: Prentice Hall.

Veryzer, R. W. (1998). Discontinuous Innovation and the New Product Development Process. *Journal of Product Innovation Management*, *15*(4), 304–321. doi:10.1016/S0737-6782(97)00105-7.

Veryzer, R. W. (2005). The Roles of Marketing and Industrial Design in Discontinuous New Product Development. *Journal of Product Innovation Management*, *22*(1), 22–41. doi:10.1111/j.0737-6782.2005.00101.x.

Waldman, D. A., Luque, M. S. d., Washburn, N., & House, R. J. (2006). Cultural and Leadership Predictors of Corporate Social Responsibility Values of Top Management: A Globe Study of 15 Countries. *Journal of International Business Studies*, *37*(6), 823–837. doi:10.1057/palgrave.jibs.8400230.

Yeniyurt, S., & Townsend, J. D. (2003). Does Culture Explain Acceptance of New Products in a Country?: An Empirical Investigation. *International Marketing Review*, *20*(4), 377–396. doi:10.1108/02651330310485153.

Chapter 15
Work-Groups Conflict at PetroTech-Italy, S.R.L.: The Influence of Culture on Conflict Dynamics

Angelo A. Camillo
Woodbury University, USA

Francesca Di Virgilio
University of Molise, Italy

Loredana Di Pietro
University of Molise, Italy

Massimo Franco
University of Molise, Italy

ABSTRACT

Field experts take numerous approaches to modeling how culture influences groups in dealing with interpersonal conflict and its dynamics. Researchers investigate cultural traits that may predict a range of cultural conflict behaviors. In addition, anecdotal evidence shows that researchers continue to take up a constructivist approach of identifying the centrality of cultural influence that causes work related conflicts. This study attempts to determine the different types and levels of conflicts within a multicultural workforce by considering various factors such as ethnicity and geographic and lingual diversities within the global context. The scope is to find possible solutions to reduce and/or eliminate group related and, to a certain extent, individual conflicts within the work place, which have become a matter of concern for any international organization. The findings reveal systematic conflicts between and within work-groups and suggest that regardless of type, relationship, and process, conflicts are detrimental to the operation and total outcome. Those conflicts have a negative impact on performance in the production, especially when they escalate. Displays of interpersonal hostility (yelling, name-calling, throwing things at people and making derogatory inferences about others' own cultures) prevent productive work in all groups, which are inefficient and do not seem motivated to complete their tasks. Increased bickering and hostile behaviour inhibits talking about and working on the immediate task. To a certain extent, the situation could be described as a "toxic working environment." A key finding reveals through interviews

DOI: 10.4018/978-1-4666-3966-9.ch015

and participative and non-intrusive observations demonstrated that members of these work-groups are psychologically distressed when there are frequent arguments about interpersonal issues. Consequently, the intrinsic problems which escalate over a five year period, together with extrinsic economic problems due to the global economic downturn, cause the company to have high cost of labor and material. With less than expected sales and, operational destruction due to distress about going concern, PTI is put to challenge. Hence, PTI faces a serious test in solving the existing group conflicts. Failure to improve the working relationships could jeopardize the strategic going concern of the company.

INTRODUCTION AND SIGNIFICANCE OF THE STUDY

Culture has been identified as having a significant influence on conflict dynamics, but there are limitations in existing research. In this study, we wanted to determine the different types and levels of conflicts within a multicultural workforce. Specifically, we were given the opportunity to study whether group conflicts exist in workgroups at a global company operating in the host country of Italy, and if they may create constructive and destructive dynamics in conflict. Due to time constraints and amount of time dedicated in collecting data we focused on determining the problem and not to offer a solution. Therefore we organized the study in two parts; this first investigation is Part 1, which identifies the problems. Part 2 will be a subsequent investigation in which we will analyze all results and offer possible solution scenarios. Therefore, this part of the study offers useful findings about the problems evolving conflicts at workplace. We then suggest that the instructor use the teaching notes available at the end of the chapter to engage participants in a constructive discourse about how conflicts originate, how they can be prevented, and offer a hypothetical scenario as to how they (students/participants) could resolve them.

CONTEXTUAL HIGHLIGHTS

To understand "Conflict Dynamics," it is important to understand how conflicts originate and evolve. Considering various factors such as ethnicity, geographic and lingual diversities within the global context, conflicts become a matter of concern for any international organization. The term "group dynamics" describes the positive and negative forces within groups of people and it can be referred to as "team chemistry." Team chemistry can be described as the spontaneous reaction of people, especially a mutual sense of attraction or understanding that create the patterns of interaction among team members that determine team spirit, harmony, cohesion, and morale. In this scenario "conflict" can be described as the disagreement or clash between ideas, principles, or people working together toward a common goal. The term "group conflict" can be described as the "normal, predictable occurrence and condition of disagreement involving group members at work." Lastly, within the context of *global conflict dynamics* we interpret the term "dynamics" as the relationships of power between "culturally diverse" people in a group.

In this same context, we explain the meaning of "Cultural fluency," which involves recognizing and acting respectfully from the knowledge that communication, ways of naming, framing, and taming conflict, approaches to meaning-making, and identities and roles vary across cultures. Within this framework, conflict dynamics can be understood as an "escalation" of a disagreement or clash between ideas, principles, or people working together toward a common goal. We then interpret "conflict escalation" as the increase in the magnitude of disagreements, including, but not limited to, hostilities or possible verbal or even physical violence. We believe that conflict escalation depends on the way group members involved in groups' interactions react in response to others. When management fails to identify and manage basic disagreements, conflicts can evolve and escalate to the point of becoming potentially harmful to the firm. Indeed, conflict can derail companies' strategic objectives. Many conflicts at the workplace originate because of unfulfilled needs within the area of control, recognition, affection, or respect for one another.

In humans, it is a normal occurrence to react hastily and even ferociously when faced with circumstances threatening their fundamental needs. Therefore, when management fails to recognize conflicts or avoids dealing with basic groups' disagreements, serious conflicts emerge which then escalate to the point that spill over from the original issue and begin to affect other interactions. Consequently, if conflicts are not resolved they can turn into polarization which can be characterized by severe negative emotions and uncontrollable behaviors. At that point group members may no longer be able and willing to listen, understand, and accept one another. Consequently, their relationships are broken and become difficult to repair.

COMPANY BACKGROUND

PetroTech Inc., is an international industry leader primarily involved in the design and manufacturing of petrochemical products. Petrochemical business is very competitive. The largest petrochemical industries are located in the USA and Western Europe; however, major growth in new production capacity is in the Middle East and Asia. Petrochemicals are chemicals made from petroleum (crude oil) and natural gas. They are organic and inorganic compounds and mixtures which include, but are not limited to, organic chemicals, cyclic intermediates, plastics and resins, synthetic fibers, elastomers, organic dyes, organic pigments, detergents, surface active agents, carbon black, and ammonia. Figure 1 depicts the crude oil refining process at different stages.

The Italian subsidiary *PetroTech-Italy, s.r.l. (PTI)* was established in 1992 and is located in the region of Molise in south-central Italy. It specializes in three major areas of the industry: mass transfer technology, separations technology and specialty plant services. It offers a line of mass transfer products, including 1) distillation trays; 2) random; 3) severe services (grid); and 4) structured packing for tower internals for distillation, absorption, stripping and extraction columns. Products are available in a wide range of metals, plastics, thermoplastics, and fiber--reinforced plastics. PTI business model was designed to secure contracts from wholesale customers or affiliates, or by acting as intermediaries between the company and customers. In this operation, there are three production lines for continuous production of 24 hours on three shifts of 8 hours each.

All production activities occur through automatic and manual processes such as punching machines, bending machines, laser welding, and are conducted within the department "workshop" which covers an area of 3,500 square meters or approximately 4,186 sq. yards (Figure 4). The activities of storage and semi-finished sheet metal, assembly and testing samples, packing, and shipping are done outside the workshop, in a yard, in the approximate area of 2,000 square meters or approximately 2,392 sq. yards. PTI has been recognized as a strong competitor among the Italian petrochemical players. In December of 2011, the end if its fiscal year, it had a share capital of (Euro) €46.5 million (± US $59.0 million). The 2011 sales revenues were (Euro) €13,5 million (± US $59.0 million) with a further (Euro) €350.000 (± US $457,000) of investment. Figure 2 shows a linear decline in revenue beginning in 2009 and an overproduction in 2011 (Figure 3).

Figure 1. The process of oil refining for primary products used in the production of derivatives such as petrochemical by-products

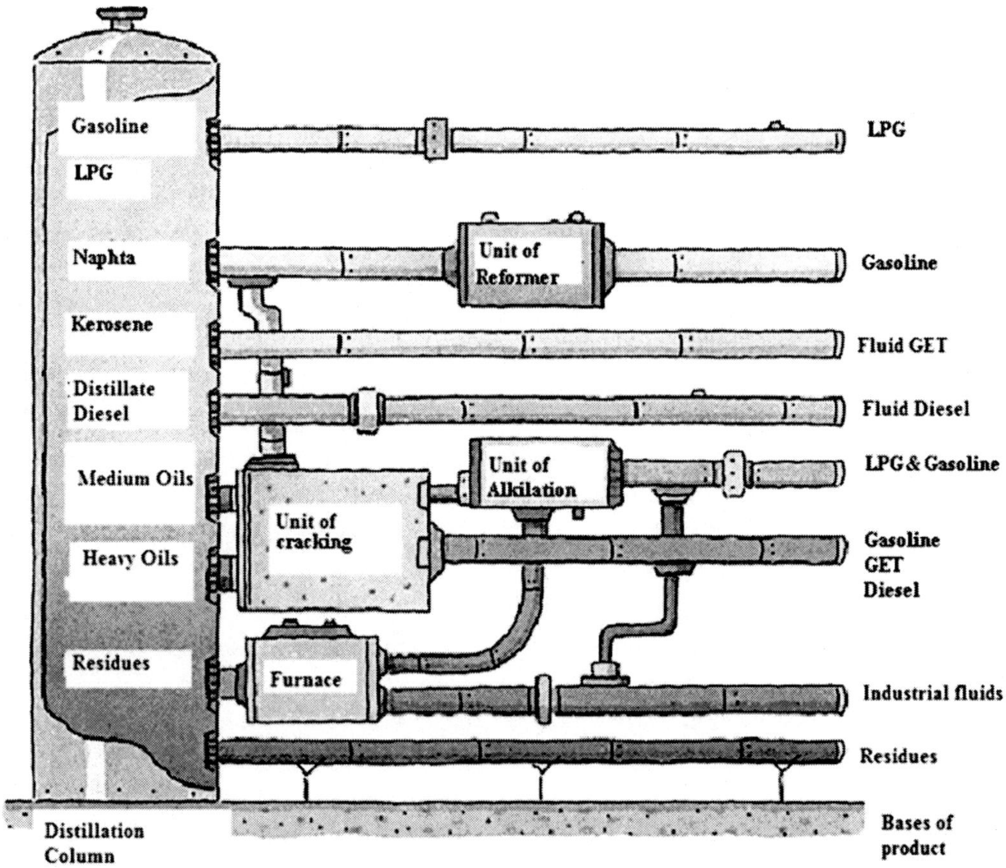

Figure 2. Sales revenues and production (m3) of the last 4 years

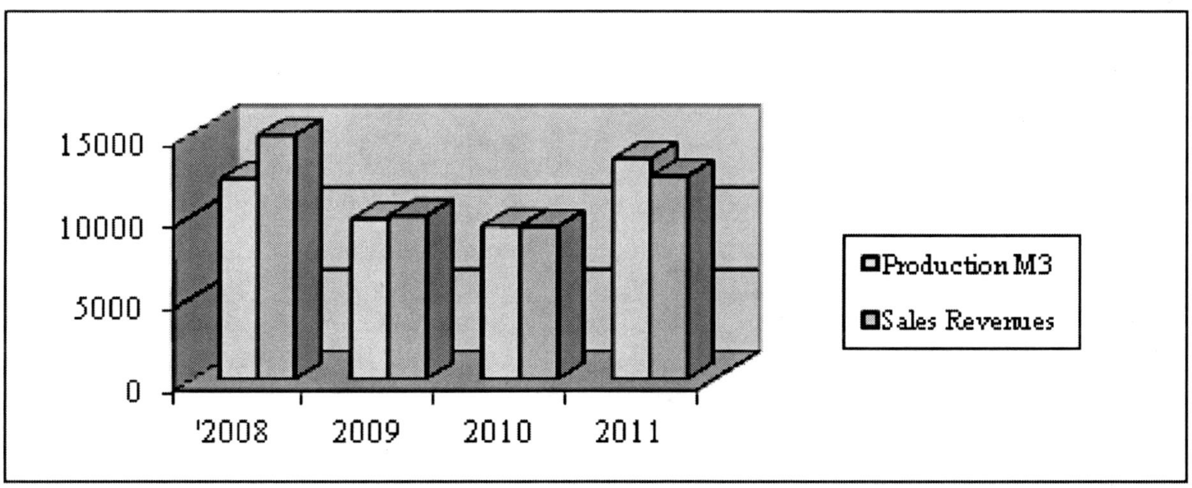

WORK GROUPS AND MANAGEMENT DEMOGRAPHICS

The production at PTI is staffed by a diverse work force which reflects the current demographics of workers in Italy. According to the National Italian Institute of Statistics (ISTAT), the aggregate number of immigrants in 2010 was 4.57 Million representing five continents. The highest number of immigrants however is represented by the countries of origin of of Rumania (21.2%), Albania (10.6%), and Morocco (9.9%). The region of Molise, where PTI operates, hosts about 8,900 immigrants, mainly from the countries named above. It is important to mention that Albanian and Moroccan immigrants are mostly Muslims, while Romanians are mostly Protestants and the local Italian workforce is overwhelmingly Catholic. The engineering departments and management are staffed by Italian nationals and their activities are separate from the main workshop. The middle and top management team is organized (in order of reporting structure) as follows:

1. Mr. Gregory McCall, Vice President European Division (not involved in the investigation, reports to the U.S. Heard Quarter)
2. Mr. Giovanni Mariano, Financial Comptroller (not involved in the investigation, reports to the VP)
3. Mr. Giuseppe Conti, General Manager (not involved in the investigation)
4. Davide Santorini: Operations Manager
5. Mr. Mario Rossi: Production Manager
6. Lucia Scarpati: Junior Management Executive In charge of Procurement
7. Alessandra Pedroni: Human Resources Manager (reports to the General Manger)

Traditionally, the top management has no direct involvement with the operation. For the company's internal performance and overall financial results the General Manager relies on the information provided by the middle and top management.

TURBULENT TIMES AT PTI

Since its inception in 1992, **PTI** enjoyed a dynamic growth both in sales and in profit after taxes. However, over the past six years, around 2006, the management has seen a rather negative change in the operation and so in its dynamic financial performance. This negative-growth trend became

Figure 3. Investment of the last four years

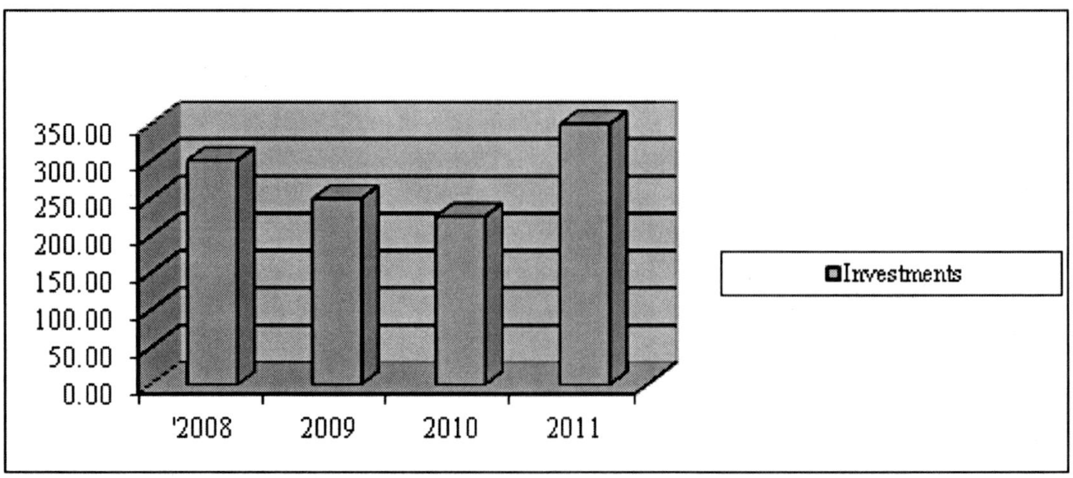

more critical during the global economic crisis in 2009 with increasingly high cost. A trend analysis by the Chief Financial Officer (CFO) at PTI's Head Quarter triggered the decision to launch an investigation into the operation at *PetroTech Inc.* in Italy. Consequently, its parent company in the U.S. suggested PTI management review every possible contributing factor which had led to a slow growth and not only at the recent economic downturn as an indicator. Following the parent company's advise PTI management hired the Avanti Consulting Group (ACG) a consulting firm with expertise in the field of petrochemicals' products based in Milan. ACG had to determine the contributing factors that caused PTI's negative growth. ACG investigation revealed several contributing factors which were key to the overall results and made numerous recommendations.

One recommendation was to launch a deep investigation in the internal operations and specifically in the production department. All Stakeholders agreed to pursue this investigation which was considered top priority. After the investigation, they identified serious group-work anomalies which could have been catalyst to low productivity, high cost, or labor and material. In addition, they also determined serious communications anomalies between the management and work-groups. The team strongly suggested to consult with experts specializing in organization behaviour to look for immediate solution. PTI management followed the consultants' advise and hired Sergio Martino, Ph.D., an expert in the field of Human Resources (HR) with specialization in Organizational Behaviour (OB) and Group Conflict Dynamics. Dr. Martino analyzed the consultants' reports and suggested the design of a scenario that would lead to the in depth identification of problems. Suggestions for possible solutions will be formulated and presented in Part 2 of the project.

The Investigation Design

Under the guidance of Dr. Sergio Martino, the design of the investigation process was prepared. The document provided a useful guidance and reference tool to conduct the investigation and to produce a valuable report conducive to solving the problems. The main task of the design was to assign key people to help with the investigation and to compile an inventory of key variables necessary for the investigation.

The Investigating Team

1. In consultation with Dr. Martino, the top management of PTI assigned the following people to conduct the investigation:
    a. Team leader: Mario Rossi, Production Manager of Internal Control
    b. Lucia Scarpati: Junior Management Executive
    c. Davide Santorini: Operation Teams' Leader
    d. Alessandra Pedroni: Human Resources Manager
2. Time Frame: January to June of 2011
3. Physical Location of the investigation: Production department

The production department lay-out is presented in Figure 4 below and Figure 5 depicts the complexity of the production line, from raw material to finished product.

Workflow of the Production Group Diagram

The diagram in Figure 5 depicts the workflow of a production group for a specific product in the production line. In each step of the production the product is checked for quality assurance. As the product is in conformity with the specifications guidelines, it will pass to the next step in the

Figure 4. Production Department lay-out

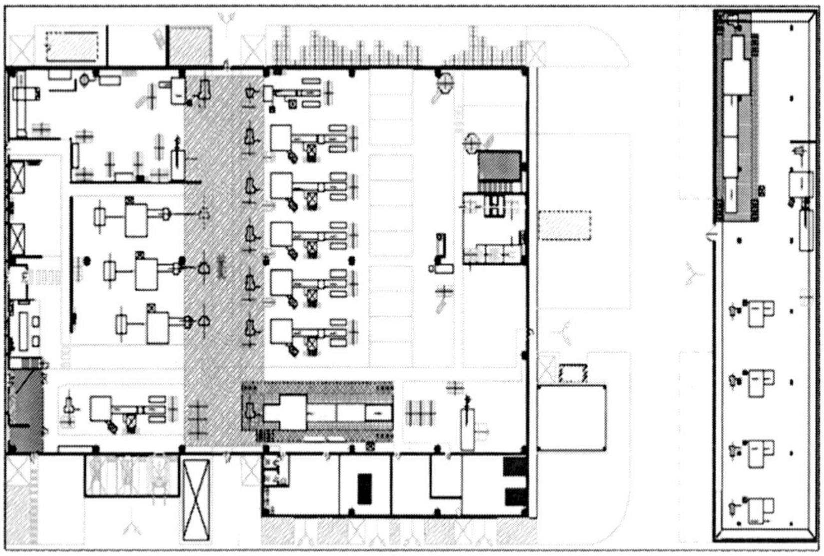

process. If the product does not meet the required specifications it will be rejected and returned to the previous job for correction, further rejection, or elimination form the production line. This process requires work-groups to be in perfect synergy.

Groups Demographic Characteristics of the Work-Groups' Members

This production at PTI is staffed by a diverse workforce which reflects the current demographics of workers in Italy. According to the National Italian Institute of Statistics (2011), the aggregate number of immigrants in 2010 was 4.57 Million from all five continents. The highest number of immigrants, however, was represented by Romania (21.2%), Albania (10.6%), and Morocco (9.9%). The region of Molise, where PT operates, hosts about 8,900 immigrants, mainly from the countries named above. It is important to mention that Albanians and Moroccan immigrants are mostly Muslims, while Romanians are mostly Protestants. The engineering departments and management are staffed by Italian nationals and their activities are separate from the main workshop. The official language of communication as per PTI's policy is Italian between all work-groups and management. In fact, proficiency in Italian is a prerequisite for employment. Accordingly, there was no record of language difficulties across all work-groups and between groups members and management. Whether the foreign workers' own language was being used among those of the same nationality while they interact colloquially during working hours or break time is not known and was not part of the study. Although PTI encourages comradeship at the workplace, it is not within the scope of its Human Resources policy to encourage fraternization outside the work place. Whether group members themselves and management included fraternize during off time outside the company was not known and was not part of the study.

Groups Structure

The entire production consist of three lines which are staffed with 12 production groups. All 12 production groups are composed of 12 operators each including one foreman (group leader). All group members are men. Table 1 shows the demographic characteristics of groups based on average level of education, average age, and average tenure with

Figure 5. Workflow of a production group

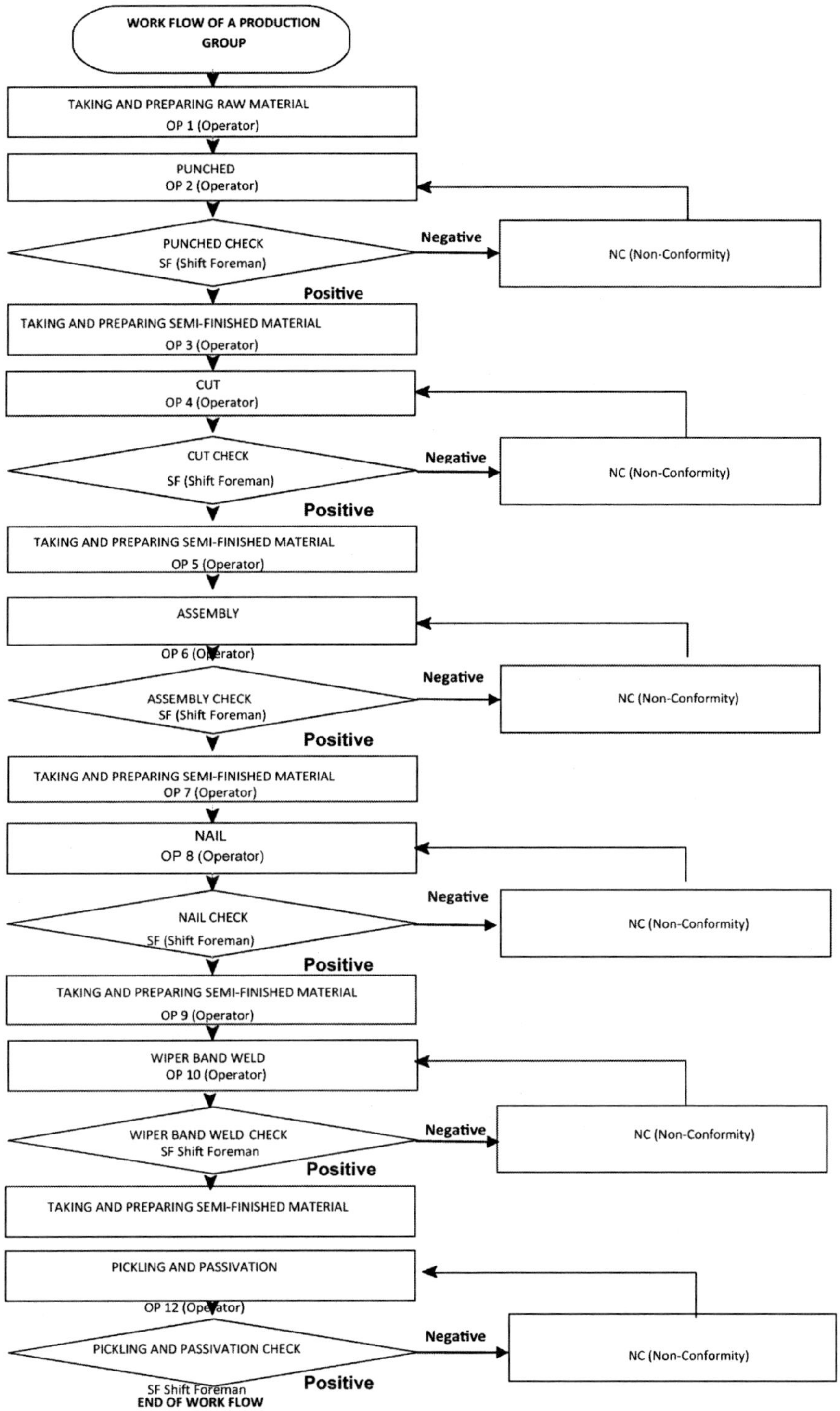

Table 1. Demographic characteristics of work-group

Work Groups	Average level of education (years)	Average age	Average tenure in the company (years)	Average tenure within the group (years)
WG1	13.05	33.25	9.25	9.05
WG2	13.75	31.05	11.25	10.90
WG3	13.45	29.30	10.45	10.00
WG4	12.90	32.75	9.85	9.85
WG5	13.15	31.95	9.05	9.05
WG6	12.75	32.25	11.50	11.00
WG7	12.90	35.05	10.25	9.25
WG8	12.90	33.15	10.75	10.75
WG9	13.55	29.95	9.95	9.95
WG10	13.05	33.25	9.25	8.25
WG11	13.75	31.05	11.25	11.00
WG12	13.45	28.10	8.45	8.45

the company, as well as average tenure within the group. Table 2 shows the percent of foreign workers in each work-group.

Every group works on one of the three production lines to produce a single product. The organization's definition of work-groups and Human Resource reports indicated that employees batched together to perform tasks were viewed by others as a work-group members. Every group performs the same routine and repetitive tasks. Work-group members share responsibility for workflows and exchange information about codes and formats of various products. There is evidence of a high level of interdependence among members of the work-groups which is consistent throughout the company's work-groups.

Table 2. Percent of foreign workers in each work-group

Work Groups	Italian	% Italian	Foreign: Romanians, Albanians, Moroccans, others	% Foreign	Total
WG1	6	50%	6	50%	100%
WG2	4	33%	8	67%	100%
WG3	6	50%	6	50%	100%
WG4	5	42%	7	58%	100%
WG5	5	42%	7	58%	100%
WG6	8	67%	4	33%	100%
WG7	8	67%	4	33%	100%
WG8	6	50%	6	50%	100%
WG9	7	58%	5	42%	100%
WG10	5	42%	7	58%	100%
WG11	4	33%	8	67%	100%
WG12	7	58%	5	42%	100%

Company Culture, Diversity, and Level of Interdependence of Group Members

PetroTech Inc., and PTI promote a high level of interdependence in all their international operations. In fact, at PTI there exists a high level of interdependence among members of the production work-groups which is consistent throughout the parent company's work-groups. PTI recognizes that it lives in an interdependent world with conflicts and overlapping interests. Therefore the company believes that people who do not have the authority to act interdependently may be good individual producers, but they won't be good leaders or team players and may be detrimental to the process of achieving optimal synergy. PTI strongly supports that synergy within multicultural work-groups and believes that synergy is created only when relationships are at optimal level and when group members work in concert together. This is especially important in a diverse setting with people of different cultures in order to create an outcome of more value than the sum of what each individual member inputs.

Existing Key Performance Measurements

Departmental production records and supervisor ratings are used to measure work-group performance (GP). The departmental production records were developed by the company's Quality Assurance Department, and used for over five years with biannual updates from system analysts to maintain standardized performance measures. For the work-groups, group performance (GP) was measured by a production index; the amount (cubic meter/or cubic yards equivalent) of metal sheet produced in one hour [GP = 0.22 m^3/h (or 0.29 $Yards^3$/h); GP = 1.76 m^3/8hrs (or 2.30 $Yards^3$/8hrs)]. Performance measures are comparable across work-groups because outcome records such as production indexes are standardized.

Methodology Design and Data Collection

To collect the necessary information which would have determined exactly the cause of the problem, Dr. Martino proposed using existing data from previous investigations and experience on work-group members interdependence, conflicts and conflicts dynamics, and group synergy. From the historical data Dr. Martino determined that relationship conflict (RC), task conflict (TC), and process conflict (PC), may have had a positive or negative impact on work-group performance (GP), synergy, and ultimately on productivity and related outcomes. Consequently, Dr. Martino suggested the design and implementation of a process to study conflict and group performance at PTI. The process through which data had to be collected involved a qualitative investigation with the group members using a multiple heterogeneous instruments to understand participants' behaviours and situations of conflict. The methods included internal document analysis, participant observations and semi-structured interviews.

Review of Internal Documentation

The investigating team, together with Dr. Martino, began collecting data by reviewing a series of formal documents which included the official management program, training programs, internal communications company website, business reports and organizational charts. The analysis revealed that members were batched together to perform tasks and were viewed by others as a group. It also allowed to better contextualize the interview data, providing information on the overall history, structure, production, ethnicity, people's culture, and culture of the company.

Each product had a specific identification code. Each order was given a code that included one of the product and a 5-digit number (for example the order 16.53798). The codes of orders already placed orders in the inter-company and supplied in advance to the company. The alphanumeric codes are placed between the identification number of the product and what the job entails (for example 16R53798) and have a specific meaning:

- R for "replacement," a contract that has already been made and should only be replicated. All specifications (quantity of raw material to order, designs, timing, and mode of production) are already available to the company. These orders, therefore, are where delivery times are short due to economies of learning.
- U for "urgent", it is a contract to be implemented very quickly and quota requirements dictated by compelling the market to be given the highest priority to production and shipping.
- Z for "backcharges", an order that must be replicated due to a non-compliance (CN) received by the customer. The company, in these cases, will assume the costs of the CN.
- C for "critical" is committed involving the use of special materials (e.g., titanium), hard to find on the market and then bound to the times and modes of supply.

Additional documents revealed that the company employed 154 people, 144 of whom are operators making up 12 production groups. The remaining 10 employees comprised upper and middle management and were in charge of the following business departments: General Management, Production (Maintenance and Packaging), Administration (Job executive, Information Technology, Human Resources, Accounting & Internal Control and Logistic), Work Security, and Quality Assurance.

Participative Observation

A consulting agreement gave Dr. Martino unrestricted access to the premises as well as the capacity to establish informal contacts with the employees. During the fieldwork, Dr. Martino spent three days a week in the plant, following the work schedule of the personnel from 8 a.m. to 2 p.m. or from 2 p.m. to 8 p.m. on alternate weeks. Each group worked interdependently between 66% and 81% of the shift/day, with the remainder of the shift/day spent on individual tasks. He eventually became familiar with management, operators, and leaders of various work-groups. Assisted by the investigating team, Dr. Martino began the collection of data through participative observation to assess group size by asking supervisors to report how many members their group had. This measure served as a control variable. The number provided always matched the number of respondents per work-group. All employees were full time employees (40 hours per week) and had an open-ended contract regulated on the basis of national law. During the period of participative observation, Dr. Martino gained full familiarity with the company.

Semi-Structured Interviews

Interviews were conducted face-to-face with members of each group (excluding the leaders). This method yields a high response rate and the information gathered meets the criteria of reliability, validity, and correctness. All interviews were conducted in 2 steps for a total of 288 interviews ranging from 25 minutes to 60 minutes (mean duration = 38.17 minutes). All interviews were carried out in a private meeting room and were voice recorded. The initial interview was conducted with individual group members in a non-directive style asking general questions about a typical workday. Sample questions included "what is the name of your group?" and "describe your typical work day, including breakfast, lunch, and dinner." These questions built the relationship with the participants and formed a basis for subsequent, more focused interviews. During this first stage that we attempted to identify group members' ethnicity by simply asking "I hear you have a foreign accent, may I ask what country you are from?" The second step of the interviews

Table 3. Episodes of Conflict Types

Episodes of Conflict Types		
Conflict Type	**Transcribed interview texts**	**Transcribed field notes**
Task	"We usually fight about work matters-interpreting our reports, disagreeing about formal rules" "We usually fight about which numbers to use to identify work orders" "Sometimes people get irritated at each other about work matters for example about how insert a metal sheet"	They began to discuss the problem but soon were in a fight about which viewpoint was right. They definitely took sides. The comments made were based on facts about the work process, but it seemed that they focused on their area of expertise (production).
Relationship	"he is arrogant and presumptuous" "There are some of us that don't get along, and so we don't talk at all" "I don't think he is a good operator, he is unable to have a relationship with the others". That show the kind of work moral he has.	Two of the group members were fighting again. They argue back and forth about the production issue. It is an ongoing exchange with snide comments about their personalities (i.e., "you are so stupid, that makes no sense at all" or "only an idiot would say that!"). They are constantly bickering.
Process	"I don't think we have personal problems, but we fight about the reorganization of the work. There is some conflict regarding who should do what" "Some phases of the work process are critical, so there is conflict on how work is divided and who is responsible for what"	The group was discussing which operator would be moved, and couldn't make a decision. They realized that they were going to change the responsibilities: "Like I said from the start, it might be just all of us from the whole process deciding on an issue. I'm not sure if it's his responsibility to continue to make these tasks" "I think Manuel can complete it". And so on.

occurred simultaneously with the observation and focused on questions concerning specific topics Dr. Martino suggested to investigate. It was during this step that participants were asked to identify and describe specific conflict situations and common problems encountered in their work-group. Because of the sensitive nature of conflict, Dr. Martino used special techniques such as asking questions in third person to elicit open communication information, and protect the participant's own identity. This scenario allowed for the collection of data about attitude (e.g., "Let's imagine there is an employee in your work-group named Christian. How would Christian describe a conflict that has recently taken place in your work-group?", or, "Describe a conflict that a typical employee in your work-group would experience."). Participants were also asked to indicate the degree of relationship, task, and process conflict in each work-group (e.g., "How much disagreement has there been in your group?"). A simple scale for conflict was used: frequently (the conflicts interfere with productivity and work on a regular basis) and rare (it is rare that conflicts occur).

Data Analysis and Synthesis

From all observations, a total of 432 episodes of conflict (a conflict episode occurred on average once every two days in each group) were analyzed. For each episode, Dr. Martino took extensive notes, writing down all possible behaviours witnessed, the chronology of the events, and discussions among work-group members. Field notes and the informants' descriptions of conflict occurrences were later cross-referenced with the informants who provided examples of behavior connected with each type of conflict (see Table 3).

From semi-structured interviews, Dr. Martino analyzed the data using systematic interpretive techniques (i.e., linguistic text analysis, context ratings). These procedures analyze topics and themes from transcribed interviews by using a multi-step approach that involves developing categories for coding content. The interviews were transcribed from the recorded tapes and the notes taken during observation into a text analysis program--Atlas TI Software. The program indexes the terms both alphabetically and by frequency of occurrence. To categorize the interview texts, keyword lists were created containing words, often synonyms, relating to the variable of interest (see Table 4).

Work-group frequency counts indicate how often terms were mentioned by group members. Dr. Martino scanned the relationship conflict episodes in the production group for negative effect terms and found mentions of terms such as destroy, difficult and dislike to be extremely high (see Table 5).

Toward the end of the four months investigation, Dr. Martino conducted one follow-up interview with each of the participants to clarify and validate their prior comments and to allow them to check the accuracy of his interpretations. He then conducted four additional follow-up interviews: one with a member of production group number 4; two with 2 members of production group number 6; and one with a member of production group number 9. These interviews served to make additional clarifications and confirm data interpretation. After the interviews were completed, Dr. Martino debriefed each participant, paying special attention to those who had revealed particularly sensitive conflict situations. Participants were reminded of the confidentiality of both the interview and the data being collected. When participants asked what other group members had said, they were given no specific information. In another interview, an operator described process conflicts in responsibility delegation and suggested a better organization of activities.

In fact, top management involvement was non-existent. In regards to leadership and problem solving interventions the participants expressed disappointment emphasizing that no one cared. They were given production guidelines and standard of performances but the management preferred to manage from the desk and not in the operation.

The data collected revealed participants had similar representations and experienced similar conflicts. Of the 144 group members, 129 recognized all three types of conflict. Of the remaining 15 operators, 6 identified task conflict and 9 mentioned relationship conflict. Conflict categories across individuals and within groups were identified using questions from the interviews such as: "What types of conflict occur in your work-group?" For example, process conflict was called "reorganization disagreements" or "uncorrected distributions of resources" as opposed to "work differences" and "personal antipathy" for work-group members. The conflict was further described as "disagreements about responsibilities" and "disagreements about how best to utilize

Table 4. Example from the Keyword List

General conflict	Performance	Relationship conflict	Process conflict	Task conflict
Agree	Achievement	Banter	Allocate	Differ
Alike	Attitude	Complain	Delegate	Disagree
Argue	Bad	Conflict	Direct	Discuss
Complete	Competent	Destroy	Divide	Ends
Conflict	Constructive	Destructive	Order	Goals
Confusion	Correct	Difficult	Organize	Ideas
Contest	Effective	Dislike	Plan	Opinion
Control	Efficient	Enemy	Procedure	Task
Decide	Improve	Fight	Process	Viewpoint
Discuss	Perform	Personality	Responsibility	Work
Dispute	Productive	Pressure	Schedule	
Diverse	Promote	Problem	Way	
Misconception	Results	Relationship	What	
Oppose	Reward	Social	Why	
Problem	Success			
Trouble	Useful			

*Table 5. Text analysis frequencies and contextual rating scores**

Variables	PG1	PG2	PG3	PG4	PG5	PG6	PG7	PG8	PG9	PG10	PG11	PG12
Relationship conflict												
Destroy	(25)	(9)	(7)	(11)	(3)	(6)	(23)	(9)	(19)	(18)	(3)	(4)
Difficult	(32)	(6)	(5)	(28)	(5)	(7)	(25)	(13)	(16)	(19)	(5)	(6)
Dislike	(18)	(5)	(10)	(12)	(7)	(6)	(19)	(3)	(15)	(15)	(6)	(8)
Task Conflict												
Ideas	(5)	(8)	(11)	(15)	(9)	(13)	(3)	(15)	(4)	(12)	(20)	(19)
Opinion	(4)	(9)	(10)	(15)	(13)	(15)	(6)	(11)	(6)	(17)	(15)	(14)
Viewpoint	(3)	(11)	(14)	(20)	(11)	(17)	(7)	(10)	(8)	(9)	(12)	(13)
Process Conflict												
Allocate	(17)	(8)	(4)	(23)	(9)	(11)	(29)	(7)	(18)	(21)	(12)	(9)
Order	(21)	(7)	(9)	(16)	(8)	(12)	(21)	(8)	(14)	(17)	(10)	(4)
Organize	(10)	(2)	(3)	(11)	(4)	(6)	(17)	(4)	(20)	(14)	(12)	(7)

*The number in parentheses is the group frequency count, which is the number of times a keyword was mentioned by all group members. The analyses are based on examples from the 432 episodes of conflict.

people." One member of work-group number 7 described process conflict as: "...disagreements about who does what...", or, "...scarce competencies in my group and too much in other groups...". Surprisingly, this subsequent-confirmatory interviews did not reveal "cultural conflict" as being a key indicator for problem creation and escalation.

Key Findings

Table 6 shows the synthesis of the results according to task type, conflict type and performance level or productivity. According to the expected productivity each group was expected to produce at least 0.22 m^3 per hour or 0.29 $Yards^3$ per hour. Clearly group 4, 7 and 10 attest that when conflicts are high, the productivity efficiency is lowest at 0.17* m^3/h or .222 Yards $^3/h$ output. In contrast when conflicts are low the productivity efficiency is high see results for groups 5, 6, and 8, and 12 respectively: 0.24* m^3/h or .314 $Yards^3/h$, 0.24* m^3/h or .314$Yards^3/h$, 0.23* m^3/h or .301 $Yards^3/h$, and 0.23* m^3/h or .301 $Yards^3/h$. In sum five groups: 1, 4, 7, 9, and 10 out of 12 or 41.67% have underperformed below the minimum requirement of .22 cubic meter or .29 cubic yards per hour.

Table 7 shows the frequency and percent of conflict episodes confirmed by each technique applied. It also illustrates the repeat rate of the same conflict episodes as identified by both techniques.

Summary and Conclusion

After nearly five months of data collection, analysis, and synthesis of the results, Dr. Marino has prepared a summary and is ready to compile the final report for the top management at PTI. The summary of his findings is presented below.

The findings of this investigation revealed systematic conflicts between and within work-groups. Regardless of type, relationship and process conflict are detrimental to the operation and total outcome. Those conflicts have a negative impact on performance in the production, especially when they escalate. Displays of interpersonal hostility (yelling, name-calling, throwing things at people and making derogatory inferences about others'

Table 6. Tabulated description of key findings

	Task Type	Conflict Type			Average Performance* 0.22 m^3/h / or .288Yards^3/h
Groups	R	Relationship	Task	Process	Value
PG1	R	H	L	H	0.20* m^3/h or 0.262Yards^3/h
PG2	R	L	H	L	0.22* m^3/h or 0.288Yards^3/h
PG3	R	L	H	L	0.22* m^3/h or 0.288Yards^3/h
PG4	R	H	H	H	0.18* m^3/h or .235Yards^3/h
PG5	R	L	H	L	0.23* m^3/h or .301Yards^3/h
PG6	R	L	H	L	0.24* m^3/h or .314Yards^3/h
PG7	R	H	L	H	0.17* m^3/h or .222Yards^3/h
PG8	R	L	H	L	0.23* m^3/h or .301Yards^3/h
PG9	R	H	L	H	0.19* m^3/h or .249Yards^3/h
PG10	R	H	H	H	0.18* m^3/h or .235Yards^3/h
PG11	R	L	H	L	0.22* m^3/h or 0.288Yards^3/h
PG12	R	L	H	L	0.23* m^3/h or .301 Yards^3/h

LEGEND:
PG 1-12 = Production Groups
R = routine
H = high;
L = low
* = average value [total value (all group values added) divided by the number of groups observed:12]

own cultures) prevented productive work in all groups, which were inefficient and did not seem motivated to complete its tasks. Increased bickering and hostile behaviour inhibited talking about and working on the immediate task. To a certain extent the situation could be described as a "toxic working environment."

The results suggest that not all conflicts are equally disruptive. In fact, task conflict appears to be not so disruptive as relationship conflict. Relationship conflict was high in five of the 12 groups. The interviews and observations demonstrate that members of these work-groups are psychologically distressed when there are frequent arguments about interpersonal issues. During an

Table 7. Episodes of conflict confirmed by two techniques

		Episodes Confirmed by		
		Observation	Interviews	2 Techniques*
	Number of Episodes			
Task	98	78%	94%	87%
Relationship	181	88%	86%	78%
Process	153	92%	76%	57%
Total	432			

*2 Techniques.= the same episode identified by two techniques

interview, one member of work-group number 4 stated: "…hey, calm down, it's not about you, it's about this damn project"; at another time, the member stated: "I don't care if we agree; I don't like your behaviour." These statements suggest that relationship conflicts may have a higher degree of occurrence and happen before task related conflicts. We therefore can infer that in this scenario relationship conflicts may be precursors to task related conflicts which together turn into "conflict dynamics", or escalation of the problems. In fact, interpersonal problems create intense dislike and frustration; the resulting distress and animosity encourages withdrawal. On-site non-intrusive observation shows that the language used was harsh and behavioural responses were strong (slamming doors and yelling or making derogatory inferences about others' own culture and moral).

The interviews illuminate an additional result: relationship conflict is intensified by a high level of interdependence among members. The increased interaction, the interdependent nature of the job, and the physical set-up of the group, which promotes close interaction but caused infringements on people's personal space, are all factors that increase relationship conflict. In addition, personal and company culture, coupled with a diverse "male exclusive" workforce, make it difficult for any of the groups to achieve synergy. In fact, the impact of relationship conflict on group-related outcomes is exacerbated when group members must work closely together to achieve success. The findings, however, revealed that the interactions within group members and between groups included disagreements which were followed by inappropriate language used by one member to another of different ethnic background (e.g., "that is how those people's upbringing is! No work moral, just work for the money they send to their home country!"). Nevertheless, we found no evidence that such comments, which we recorded following the conflicting episodes, have had a strong effect on the overall production quality and output. We also noted foreign nationals' group members were not integrated into the Italian people's culture and into the PTI's culture.

This was attested by several observations made during the non-intrusive interviews (e.g., the type of food they consumed, the religious beliefs and devotions such as prayers timing during working hours/break time, etc.). Thus, the results suggest an ethnocentric behaviour by all members which may have had a possible negative effect on other group members in terms of acceptance, collaboration, and job performance. We also observed that name calling, yelling, and throwing things were not equally done by each and all group members. This could explain that each culture may react differently to a specific situation. There were instances when a group member yelled at another but the "member who was attacked" in that that specific occurrence did respond with the same tone of voice of with physical action. Whether these types of actions and reactions (or no reactions) can be attributed to one's specific cultural background could not be determined; in fact, the episode may have been purely situational. We examined all results and extrapolated the most significant findings to draw the best scenario.

In our opinion, the data analyzed leads us to infer that the seniority of the group members, whether foreign nationals or Italians, may have contributed to an "unintended partial integration" of the foreign members into the Italian culture in general both, at the work place and in the society outside work. However we cannot confirm this phenomenon and offer the readers a purely speculatory interpretation. Undoubtedly the results here show a negative impact on 5 specific cases. Groups 1, 4, 7, 9, and 10 out of 12 or 41.67% have underperformed below the minimum requirement of .22 cubic meter or .29 cubic yards per hour. Underperforming translates to higher labor cost in relationship to sales, and high material cost due to defects and rejections in the production line. Interestingly, the finding revealed that these problems were not identifiable before 2006.

We can only speculate and attribute this phenomenon to the fact that high sales produced desirable profits and may have masked possible operational problems prior to 2006. It is possible that these problems have always existed, however, they never escalated to the point that profits were directly affected. Then we can assume that as the group members' seniority increased, conflicts may have increased as well. Consequently, the intrinsic problems which escalated in 2006, together with extrinsic economic problems since 2008, have caused the company to have high cost of labor and material. Thus, with less sales, the financial performance and distress about going concern PTI has been put to challenge. In sum, one thing is true and correct--PTI faces serious challenges in solving the existing group conflicts. Failure to improve the working relationship could jeopardize the strategic going concern of the company.

Suggestions for possible solutions scenarios will be presented in Part 2 of the study. For this Part 1, the following scenario and teaching notes provide a useful framework to engage the instructor and students/participants in a productive discourse as to how "they" would have prevented these types of conflicts and what the long-term solution and recommendations are for PTI.

SUGGESTIONS FOR DISCUSSION ABOUT POSSIBLE SOLUTION SCENARIO

Dr. Martino reports his findings to the top management of PTI however he has an important questions to ask in order to offer a viable solution. "How did all this happen?". To find out he had to interview the entire management in the organization chart. Armed with the written consent in the consulting agreement, Dr. Martino interviews all managers face-to-face and concludes that several errors have been made from 1992 to roughly 2005. First, the company had been very successful with a linear – dynamic growth. This caused the management to feel comfortable and become sedentary in their management decision making process without a long term planning for contingency in case the unexpected would have happened. Then the management believed in a company culture that allowed for maximum interdependence especially among a culturally diverse, yet "male exclusive," workforce. Although the labor force was not represented by a labour organization, there was little or no interactive relationship between management and group members. Work-groups simply followed management directives, produced products according to contracts and specifications and after years of working together they had developed a working relationship that was not healthy. The management also failed to look into the behaviour of the multicultural groups' members to determine how they would get along? In fact the relationships may have deteriorated as the seniority was increasing. In summary, necessary changes had to take place for PTI to become competitive and financially healthy again. Hence Dr. Martino makes the following recommendations to be implemented immediately and to be observed over a 12 month period.

1. PTI top management to meet with work-groups' members and discuss the problems, the findings from the investigation and propose an agenda for change.
2. The management to develop a corrective action plan to reduce and or eliminate all conflicts successfully within a 12 months period.
3. All Key Performance Indicators must be used to measure future performance and to contrast and compare the results with the previous 6 fiscal years, from 2005 to 2011.
4. A training plan for all employees and management to be implemented which will include:
   a. improving the working relationship between groups and within groups,
   b. improving the working relationship between management and employees,
   c. implementation of effective interpersonal and managerial communication,

d. plan to improve productivity, work processes, and work-flow
e. a plan to develop innovative ideas for total transformation
f. a plan that will help blend diverse mentalities and personal views into the working environment for a mutually beneficial outcome.
g. A plan that will lead to optimum synergy between and within work-groups and management

REFERENCES

National Italian Institute of Statistics. (2011). The resident foreign population in Italy. *Istat.it*. Retrieved from http://www.istat.it/it/archivio/39726

Chapter 16
Knowledge Management and Its Challenges in Global Business

Harish C. Chandan
Argosy University, USA

ABSTRACT

Knowledge Management (KM) is an organization-wide, strategic change management initiative dealing with people, processes, and Information Communication Technology (ICT) to achieve a competitive advantage through learning, productivity improvement, and innovation. Based on the current literature review of KM and its challenges in global business, a general framework for KM in terms of leadership, organization, and ICT is proposed. The role of leadership includes developing an international strategy for KM, executing strategic change management, practicing a mix of transformational and transactional leadership style, and developing KM performance metrics. The organizational parameters include learning, processes, culture, and organizational structure. ICT plays a crucial role in the learning and processes to acquire, store, share, and apply knowledge. Some of the KM challenges in global business include global leadership competencies and strategy, project-based flexible global virtual teams, global knowledge integration, and working with ICT gaps across different economies.

INTRODUCTION

Knowledge Management (KM) is an organization-wide, strategic change management initiative dealing with people, processes and ICT to achieve a competitive advantage through productivity improvement. Productivity improvements come from innovation and process improvements rooted in organizational learning and knowledge sharing. KM in a global business has additional implications in terms of global leadership competencies, integrating explicit and implicit knowledge of

DOI: 10.4018/978-1-4666-3966-9.ch016

global virtual teams across cultures and working with ICT gaps among subsidiaries in various countries. The goal of KM is to obtain the most pertinent information in the best context to the correct person at the optimum time for the right business purpose (Nohria, 2000; Lehaney et al., 2003). Based on the resource-based view of a business, knowledge is the most important strategic resource leading to competitive advantage (Nonaka, 1994).

The ability to acquire, integrate, store, share, and apply knowledge becomes the most important capability for building and sustaining competitive advantage (Zack, 1999). Knowledge has been referred to as "the genetic material" of firms. Knowledge and expertise resides in people, products, processes, and routines in an organization. Knowledge is embrained, embodied, encultured, embedded, and encoded in the organization. "Embrained" refers to the conceptual skills and abilities; "Embodied" refers to acquiring knowledge by doing; "Encultured" refers to acquiring knowledge through socialization; "Embedded" refers to organizational routines; "Encoded" refers to signs and symbols and is a part of organizational culture (Blacker et al., 1993; Blacker, 1995). Knowledge is the source of wealth. Applied to tasks we already know, it becomes productivity. Applied to tasks that are new, it becomes innovation (Drucker, 1991).

The popularity of KM with academics and practitioners has increased since the discussion first started in the 1990's. The literature on challenges for KM in global business is not as extensive as that for KM but is increasing as globalization progresses. Five top ranked peer-reviewed, refereed KM journals include the journal of knowledge management, journal of intellectual capital, knowledge management research and practice, International journal of knowledge management and the learning organization (Serenko & Bontis, 2004). The market value of an organization consists of the tangible assets and intangible assets. Intangible assets include knowledge and expertise of the employees and knowledge in processes, products and routines. Intangible assets are part of the intellectual capital that consists of human capital, structural capital and relational capital (Edvinson & Malone, 1997). A significant part of a company's value may consist of intangible assets such as the value of its workers' knowledge and expertise or the intellectual capital. A knowledge worker is one who works primarily with information or one who develops and uses knowledge in the workplace (Drucker, 1959; Davenport, 2005). Knowledge Workers are now estimated to outnumber all other workers in North America by at least a four to one margin (Haag et al., 2006). A knowledge worker's primary task is "non-routine" problem solving that requires a combination of convergent, divergent, and creative thinking (Reinhardt et al., 2011). Managing the productivity of knowledge workers across cultures is the main focus of KM and its challenges in global business.

Based on the literature review, a general framework for KM and its challenges in global business is proposed in terms of leadership, organization, and information communication technology (ICT). The role of leadership includes developing an international strategy for KM, developing global competencies, practicing a mix of transformational and transactional leadership style, and creating a learning organization. Knowledge assessment, identification of knowledge gaps, knowledge integration, creating a learning environment, and establishing measures of effective KM, including rewards, are some of the leadership challenges for a global business. The organizational parameters include processes, culture, structure and learning. The organizational processes include acquiring, storing, sharing and applying knowledge where ICT plays a key role. Cultural sensitivity and competence is essential for knowledge integration in project-based flexible global virtual teams. Organizational learning and working with ICT gaps across different economies play a crucial role in effective KM. In this chapter, KM is discussed in general first and then its challenges in global business are reviewed.

A KM system begins with the assessment of the data, information, knowledge, and expertise in an organization. The competitive advantage value increases steadily as the raw data is converted into information, knowledge and expertise, Figure 1 (Kakabadse et al., 2003). The value increases even more when the information is applied to solve a problem or innovate a process, product, or service. Data is unstructured, unrelated collection of facts and observations. When the data is analyzed in a given context, it becomes information. Information is data with context, categorization, relevance and purpose. Information conveys trends and patterns. Information represents an understanding of relationships among pieces of data in a given context. Not all information is knowledge. Information converted to a new application to get value is knowledge. Knowledge deals with know-how and represents an understanding of patterns in the data and information. Knowledge deals with the experience or individual memory that is used to make decisions about the new inputs (Davenport & Prusak, 2000).

Expertise is knowledge with insight. Knowledge represents an understanding of patterns in the data in a given context whereas the expertise is to understand the underlying principles that apply to multiple contexts. People integrate the new knowledge with their past experience to develop an expertise which is most valuable for a competitive edge for the business. Expertise is even more valuable than Knowledge. Expertise resides in people's heads. It is implicit and difficult to codify.

Organizational knowledge consists of individual knowledge and expertise, group knowledge, structural knowledge and organizational memory. KM involves an assessment of all types of organizational knowledge and identifying knowledge gaps. KM involves managing organizational learning, sharing knowledge and developing organizational memory. It requires managing a mixture of explicit and implicit knowledge (Nonaka, 1994; Botha, 2008). The explicit knowledge can be documented and communicated using ICT. Implicit knowledge and expertise reside in an organization as an individual memory in the minds of the employees. It cannot be captured in physical and communicable form. Implicit knowledge also gets internalized into organizational processes and routines.

Formal and informal mentoring of an aspiring expert by an expert is one of the time-tested ways of

Figure 1. Nature of Knowledge

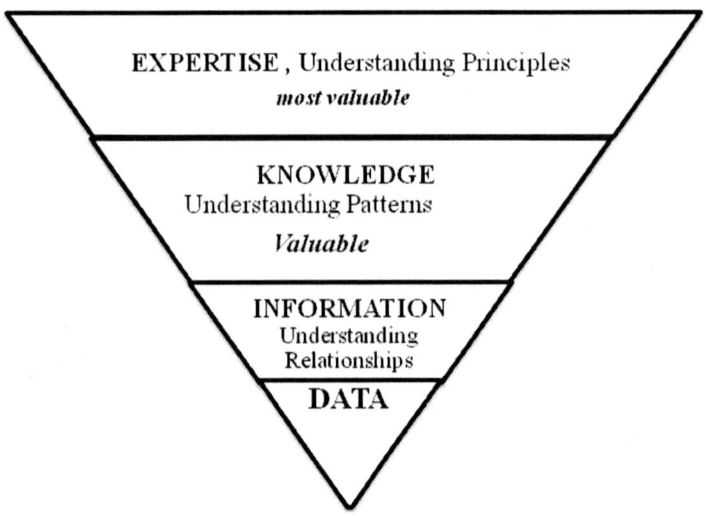

transferring the implicit knowledge and expertise. Employees have to feel secure in sharing implicit knowledge in that they will still be valuable to the organization. KM involves knowing where the data, information, knowledge, and expertise reside within and outside the organization so that the right people can be connected at the right time. The knowledge manager also has to know what the organization does not know. This can guide training of the individuals to acquire the missing knowledge or hiring to acquire the knowledge needed to meet strategic goals.

Humans and ICT help convert data into information. ICT helps to organize data across multiple departments and functions into information. Once the data is analyzed in a given context, it becomes useful information with increasing value. ICT plays an important role in implementation of knowledge management. The role of technology has to be to support people in the organization since people create knowledge. "Every business organization that wants to prosper in the knowledge society should fuse synergistically information communication technology (ICT) as knowledge creation tools and human beings with collaborative knowledge-creation capabilities to become a knowledge creating company" (Nonaka & Takeuchi, 1996). Using appropriate technology, knowledge management facilitates acquiring, storing, sharing, and applying the knowledge of the employees of an organization in a way to improve its performance. The ICT employed for KM has to fit with the organizational processes, culture, structure, and learning in the organization.

KM: DEFINITIONS AND MODELS

Many definitions of KM have been reported in the literature, but there is no universally agreed upon definition. This may be due the fact that KM is situational and context-specific. "Every business organization that wants to prosper in the knowledge society should fuse synergistically information technology as knowledge-creation tools and human beings with collaborative knowledge creation capabilities to become a knowledge-creating company"(Nonaka, 1991; Nonaka & Takeuchi, 1995; Nonaka & Takeuchi, 1996; Nonaka & Konno, 1998; Nonaka et.al., 2000; Nonaka & Takeuchi, 2011). KM is about knowledge exploitation, whereas knowledge creation or learning is all about exploration. Organizations need both exploitation for productivity and exploration for innovation (Kakabadse et al., 2003). KM is a process to discover, develop, utilize, deliver, and absorb knowledge from inside and outside the organization through an appropriate management process to meet current and future needs (Ouintas et al., 1997). The manager's role in KM is "the coordination and exploitation of organizational knowledge resources in order to create benefit and competitive advantage" (Drucker, 1991; 1993; 1999).

KM involves managing the corporation's knowledge through a systematically and organizationally specified process for acquiring, organizing, sustaining, applying, sharing, and renewing both the implicit and explicit knowledge of employees to enhance organizational performance and create value (Allee, 1997; Alavi & Leidner, 2001; Davenport & Prusak, 2000). A total of 73% of 260 UK and European corporations voted for the business definition of KM as the "collection of processes that govern the creation, dissemination, and utilization of knowledge to fulfill organizational objectives (Murray & Meyers, 1997). KM is "a systematic and integrative process of coordinating organization-wide in pursuit of major organizational goals" (Rastogi, 2000). KM is a process that helps organizations find, select, organize, disseminate, and transfer important information and expertise necessary for activities (Gupta et al., 2000).

KM is a process of knowledge creation, validation, presentation, distribution, and application (Bhatt, 2001). KM is getting the right information to the right people at the right time, helping people create knowledge and sharing and acting on information. KM is the creation, extraction, transformation and storage of the correct knowledge and information in order to design better policy, modify action and deliver results (Horwitch & Armacost, 2002). KM is the organized and systematic process of generating and disseminating information, as well as using tacit and explicit knowledge to achieve a competitive advantage in the marketplace. KM processes include creation, usage, storage, sharing, transferring, and retrieving knowledge with a goal to improve business performance. In a project management context, KM can be viewed as knowledge stock, enabling environment and knowledge practices. KM enables the creation and alignment of technical design knowledge, organizational change knowledge, and business value knowledge. These three types of project-based knowledge are critical to achieving desired business outcomes (Reich et al., 2012).

Based on the above literature review, there is no universal agreement on the definition of KM since its implementation is situational and context-specific to the project, industry sector, and the organization. However, the essence of the various definitions of KM in the literature is that it is a business process through which an organization acquires, stores, shares, and applies explicit and tacit knowledge to create value by leveraging, improving, and refining its competencies. KM begins with recognition from the leadership of its strategic and competitive advantage for the organization. Leadership has to incorporate the KM into the business strategy. To implement this strategy, the leadership has to focus on the organization. Organizational learning and knowledge sharing culture has to be created in the organization. ICT helps the organization to acquire, store, collaborate, and apply knowledge. A consistent theme in the many definitions of KM is that it provides a framework that builds on past experience and creates new mechanisms for exchanging and creating knowledge (Kakabadse et al., 2003).

Five KM models have been proposed: network model, cognitive model, communities of practice model, philosophical model, and quantum model (Kakbadse et al., 2003). The network model views knowledge building as social networking and knowledge is seen as distributed in internal and external networks. The networking perspective of KM focuses on acquisition, sharing, and knowledge transfers. Information and Communication (ICT) tools facilitate to build and maintain networks to share and transfer knowledge. Network models of KM are integrative in approach as they develop network structures and ways to control the flow of information. The network model has a strategic intention of tapping across levels within the organization and industry (Swan & Newell, 2000).

The cognitive model is based on the view that knowledge is a valuable strategic asset and has to be managed for competitive advantage. SECI model (socialization, externalization, combination, and internalization) is an example of a cognitive model of KM (Nonaka & Takeuchi, 1995; Nonaka & Konno, 1998). In the Cognitive model, ICT tools help with codification, storage, retrieval, and transfer of knowledge. The focus is on standardization, replication, and continuous review of processes to improve them. To avoid this model becoming an obstacle for change, one has to balance exploitation and exploration (Swan & Newell, 2000).

The communities of practice (CP) model views the knowledge being mutually and socially constructed within broad communities of practice. This is the traditional apprenticeship approach to transferring tacit knowledge from the expert to the new employee. Knowledge has been traditionally passed from one generation to the next through apprenticeship. The CP model also works well for selection and implementation of knowledge which requires that the explicit knowledge be re-interpreted, re-created, and appropriated alongside locally-situated, contextually specific, often tacit knowledge about organizational practices and processes (Swan & Newell, 2000).

The philosophical model is based on the interactive dialogue within a strategic context. It values ongoing inquiry into internal processes and competing firms. It is an attempt to think deeper on how one thinks and acts and about the nature of knowledge within the organizations (Murray, 2000). Knowledge in organizations is both tacit and explicit. The philosophy-based model of KM is practiced by the higher level executive teams in learning organizations. It has roots in Socratic dialogue and has low dependence on technology. The quantum model of KM is based on quantum computing that provides simultaneous and virtual scenarios of decision outcomes from complex, inter-related, dynamically changing and sometimes even conflicting pieces of information. Quantum computing is being able to make a rational assessment of complex situations that may be beyond the comprehension of the human intellect. This is not fact-driven but scenario-driven. This is the highest form of knowledge (i.e., the wisdom). It is achieved through a deep rational analysis, intuition, emotions and empathy (Tissen et al., 2000).

The quantum model of KM is simultaneously interactive and integrative of all levels of the organization. It attempts to solve complex, conflicting, and paradoxical problems in way that makes sense and is beneficial to the organization and society. Organizations have to adopt the KM model that best fits with their corporate strategy context. No one model is best for all organizations. The situational nature of KM makes it difficult to design a system that fits every organization.

KM CONCEPTUAL FRAMEWORK: LEADERSHIP, ORGANIZATION AND ICT

Based on the current literature on KM and its challenges in global business, a conceptual framework of leadership, organization and ICT is proposed, Figure 2. These three elements of our framework are inter-related in the sense that the leadership and ICT influence the organizational processes, learning, culture and structure. KM initiative begins with the leadership making it a priority and including it in the business strategy of the

Figure 2. Conceptual Framework of KM and Its Challenges in Global Business

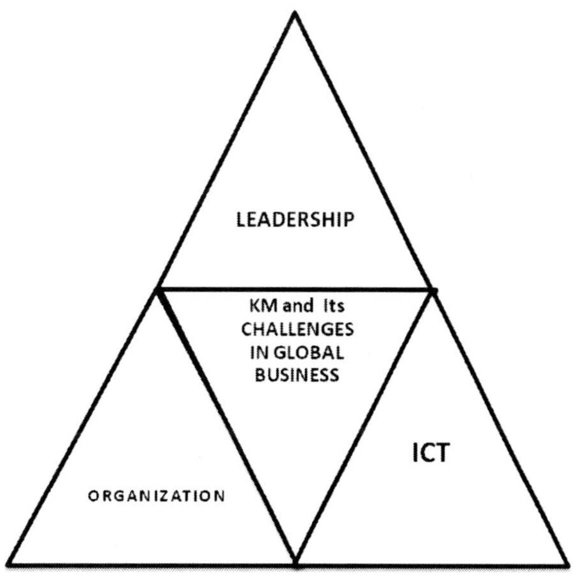

organization. The role of leadership in KM include developing a global KM strategy, implementing strategic change management through appropriate leadership style, and developing KM performance metrics, Figure 3.

Leadership

The leadership must support a continuous improvement in strategy, policies, and structure which facilitate KM. The leadership must obtain "buy-in" from the employees regarding this strategic change initiative. The leadership has to create a learning environment and inspire a knowledge culture by leadership style. The leader has to know what the organization does not know to meet the strategic goals so that learning opportunities can be provided. Appropriate ICT for knowledge acquisition, storage and sharing has to be put in place for members of global virtual teams. The leadership has to develop strategic management performance metrics to encourage knowledge integration across cultures.

The leadership has to communicate to the employees that the business strategy includes KM. The leader has to ensure that the people are onboard with the business strategy objectives. The employees have to know what problems they need to work on. The leader creates a shared vision, acts as a coach and a steward (Senge, 1990). Along with creating a shared vision, the leader created shared values and purpose. KM processes cannot be managed by the traditional management approach of the manager controlling the flow of information (Nonaka et al., 2000). The role of leadership is changing from a knowledge gatekeeper to knowledge creation and sharing for all employees. They have to create a culture where sharing knowledge is encouraged. (Politis, 2001).

The leader needs to create a learning environment using an appropriate leadership style. A transformational leadership is more conductive to a learning organization. The transactional leadership builds upon the exchange of reward (or punishment) for performance (or lack of performance) of desired behavior. The employees may comply but transactional leadership fails to generate

Figure 3. Role of Leadership in KM

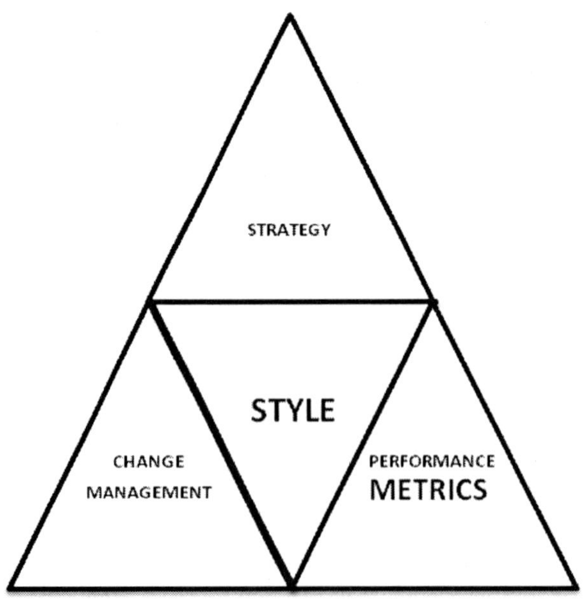

enthusiasm and commitment. A transactional leader emphasizes existing routines and values and focuses on improving the process efficiency. A transactional leader gets things done based on existing procedures. She provides employees with formal systems and training programs that disseminate existing learning to guide future actions and decisions (Vera & Crossan, 2004). Transformational leadership inspires trust, loyalty and admiration, leading to the group interests taking precedence over individual interests (Bass, 2000). Transformational leadership focuses on intangible qualities like vision, shared values, and ideas. It builds relationships, and gives a broader meaning to separate activities. A transformational leader is able to enlist employees in the change process. Transformational leadership can affect the process and goal of an organization's learning (Lam, 2002). A transformational leader motivates employees to question existing routines and break through learning boundaries. He encourages the employees to share their learning within and across departments (Vera & Crossan, 2004). They have to establish an open environment with trust where people have channels of discussion, a flow of ideas and knowledge sharing. The leadership needs to develop and implement a culture of learning and innovation. People need to learn new information, need time to reflect. They need to question the existing processes and develop better ones. The knowledge work is heuristic in nature and requires right brain creative thinking. The knowledge worker is typically intrinsically motivated and needs task and technique autonomy. Internal marketing is a strategic management philosophy that enhances the intellectual capital of a firm by attracting, developing and motivating employees and creating a knowledge-sharing culture (Lee & Chen, 2005). Internal marketing integrates marketing concepts and human resource functions and treats employee job satisfaction on par with customer satisfaction.

The leadership has to inspire a learning organizational culture and provide organizational and individual support for KM across cultures. The leadership has to inspire a knowledge culture. Leadership behaviors and organizational culture are considered to be two major barriers to creating and leveraging knowledge (Politis, 2004). The charismatic and contingent reward leadership has greater influence on knowledge exchange, knowledge socialization and knowledge internalization than the transformational and transactional leadership (Nguyen & Mohamed, 2011). This is similar to Politis (2001) and Crawford's (2005) contention that transformational and transactional leadership behaviors are positively related to knowledge acquisition attributes and KM inventory (Chang & Lee, 2007; Lam, 2002) reported similar findings for KM and innovation. The leadership has to support and promote cross-functional project teams, KM training, education, mentoring and story telling. Cross-functional teams help with creation of new knowledge, knowledge sharing, creation of informal knowledge networks and innovation. Informal networks are an important part of communities of practice and organizational learning. The leadership has to initiate and support formal and informal mentoring. Mentoring is an effective way to transfer tacit knowledge from an expert to a new employee and retain the expertise within the company. Leaders can shape organizational vision and transfer knowledge and change organizational culture through story telling. Stories capture knowledge and routines of the past and enable employees to adapt it to the present conditions

Ethics has to be a part of KM strategy. An ethical leader of a multinational firm ensures that their people adhere to values and ethics across cultures. Leaders must acquire practical wisdom, or what Aristotle called phronesis. This is the experiential knowledge that enables people to make ethically sound judgments. Apprenticeship and mentoring can be used to cultivate practical wisdom in others (Nanaka & Takeuchi, 2011). Ethics and corporate social responsibility can be integrated into knowledge management and innovation technology (Guadamillas-Gomez & Donate-Manzanares, 2011).

Organization

Organization is the second element in our KM framework of leadership, organization, and ICT. Four interrelated organizational parameters of learning, processes, culture, and structure influence KM in global business, Figure 4. The learning environment contributes to the intellectual capital of the organization. The intellectual capital of the organization has to be recognized, nurtured and increased by ongoing learning opportunities and training. The organizational processes that involve learning include acquisition, storage, sharing and application of knowledge. The leadership has to assess the existing implicit and explicit intellectual capital, promote an organizational structure and a knowledge culture to increase the intellectual capital on an ongoing basis. KM is rooted in organizational learning which has to fit with the organizational culture and structure in order to contribute to organizational effectiveness and competitive edge (Davenport & Prusak, 2000; Zheng et al., 2010).

Organizational Learning

Organizations consist of individual people and "communities of practice." Communities of practice are "a group of professionals informally bound to one another through exposure to a common class of problems, common pursuit of solutions, and thereby themselves embodying a store of knowledge" (Botha et al., 2008). This collective social practice links individual together across official organizational boundaries and departments. These informal networks create knowledge through social interaction.

An organization needs to be a learning organization to constantly acquire new information internally and externally. Computer-based training is becoming popular for employees to acquire new information. Organizational learning creates new data, information, knowledge, and expertise. Organizational learning is the "bridge between working and innovating" (Brown & Duguid, 1991). It is the cycle of conceiving what to improve, acting to achieve continuous improvement of the processes and outcomes, and reflecting on the lessons learned (Botha et al., 2008). Learning leads to conceptions of new ideas. Acting on the new ideas and reflecting on them leads to more new ideas. The organization has to reflect both on success and failure. Reflecting on failure may provide the richest learning experience (Senge, 1990).

A learning organization sets its goal based on its KM strategy and is a place where people continually expand their capacity to create the results they truly desire, where new and expansive patterns of thinking are nurtured, where collective aspiration is set free, and where people are continually learning to see the whole realty together. The five dimensions of a learning organization include systems thinking, personal mastery, mental models, building a shared vision and team learning. Organizational learning involves information acquisition, distribution, interpretation, knowledge integration and institutionalization or organizational memory.

Organizational learning is a product of organizational inquiry where one looks at the difference between the prescribed processes and the practiced processes and looks for a better mouse-trap. The organizational inquiry starts the learning process leading to single loop learning, double loop learning, and "learning about how to learn." Single loop learning consists of one feedback loop where a single process is changed based on the feedback. Learning from one feedback loop leads to double loop learning where one makes a systemic change to support the change in the single process. Finally, learning about how learning takes place leads to changes in the organizational structure and behavior. To improve an organization continuously, all of the three types of learning have to occur (Argrys & Schon, 1978).

Organizational learning involves both implicit and explicit knowledge. Implicit knowledge is in

Figure 4. Organizational Parameters for KM

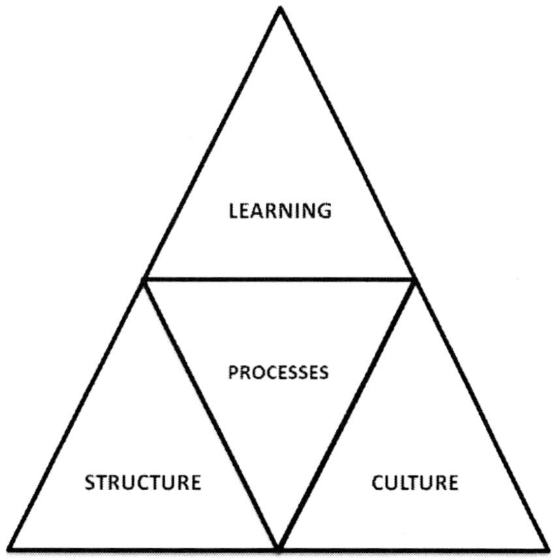

the minds of people and the processes. Implicit knowledge is internal and cannot be codified. Explicit knowledge is external and can be codified. Both kinds of knowledge are created and shared in the organization. Organizational learning involves transferring knowledge within and between explicit and implicit knowledge. There are four ways that implicit and explicit knowledge can be combined and converted: socialization, externalization, combination, and internalization. Socialization transfers implicit knowledge to implicit through internship, observation, guidance and practice. Externalization refers transferring implicit knowledge into explicit. Explicit knowledge can be codified and transferred to others through ICT. Different forms of explicit knowledge can be put together through combination. New explicit learning becomes implicit knowledge when it is internalized through reflection. This is a never-ending spiral of tacit and explicit knowledge, (Nonaka & Takeuchi, 1996). Knowledge created by individuals and teams gets amplified and crystallized into organizational knowledge. A learning organization develops a memory. This organizational memory forms the basis for new learning, problem solving, responding to opportunities and innovation in the context of changing organizational goals and processes and external environment.

Organizational learning adds to the intellectual capital of the organization. Intellectual capital consists of human capital, structure capital, and relational capital. Human capital refers to the implicit knowledge of employees including their expertise. Structural capital refers to innovation capital and process capital. Relational capital refers the goodwill and business relationships that exist in an organization. The success of KM had the strongest correlation with the structural capital although human and relational capitals were also related (Salmaninezhad & Daneshwar, 2012; Lambe, 2011). Organizations have to avoid superstitious learning where success or failure may be attributed to reasons without objective reflection.

A successful learning organization is able to acquire new knowledge and skills and apply these to create value in much the same way as individual human beings do. To be useful, the learning has to be double-loop (Argyris & Schon, 1978). In the first loop, one gains experience by learning a new set of rules to improve quality and productivity. In the second loop, one learns from the experience by questioning the existing rules in the context of market orientation and improving them. Learning orientation and transformational leadership were found to positively influence each of the five sub processes of organizational learning. Also, participative decision making and openness was found to positively influence information acquisition, interpretation, and integration (Flores et al., 2012; Sarin & McDermott, 2003).

Processes

KM requires four organizational processes: Acquire, Store, Share, and Apply (ASSA). These processes have two sides: people and technology. Both people and technology are equally important and are interrelated. Botha et al.'s (2008) KM process model includes knowledge creation and sensing, knowledge organizing and capture, and knowledge sharing and dissemination. Acquiring knowledge involves organizational learning. Individual learning through training and internships leads to organizational memory and intellectual capital.

Storing data and information in a centralized location in an organization contributes to the organizational history and memory. The data sources in the organization include the individuals, teams, communities of practice and processes. The data in the organizational memory has to be stored in a centralized warehouse with proper indexing, categorization and access. The goal of storing information in a centralized system allows access to different departments. Storing knowledge is crucial to knowledge sharing, reuse, and knowledge creation through application. A data warehouse can have internal and external knowledge. The external knowledge includes competitive intelligence and environmental scanning. Data mining tools and techniques can be used to search the stored data for patterns that may lead to new insights. This converts data into information and knowledge with increasing value. Data warehouse is usually the driver of data-driven decision support systems (DSS). Knowledge sharing can occur only if data is stored and can be accessed by the entire organization. Organization's current decision making is influenced by the history of stored information (Walsh & Ungson, 1991).

For effective KM, knowledge sharing plays a crucial role (Gamble & Blackwell, 2001). An organization has to effectively leverage the expertise or knowledge of its employees by sharing. Managers need to develop ways to capture knowledge of individual employees and share it throughout the organization using ICT (Leonardi & Treem, 2012). KM is about making the right information available to the right people in the right organization at the right time. Knowledge sharing can be both a pull or push process. Knowledge sharing is a pull process when the knowledge worker seeks the knowledge or expertise. Knowledge sharing is a push process when the manager makes information available to the knowledge worker through technology or arranged collaboration. Collaboration involves diffusion and sharing of knowledge. The sharing comes from debate and interaction. Collaborative-filtering software makes it easier for geographically dispersed groups to access one another's knowledge base. Knowledge sharing leads to creation of new knowledge. The willingness of employees to share knowledge is facilitated by the element of reciprocity in the organizational culture (Davenport & Prusak, 2000). Individuals are willing to share knowledge when they perceive a current or future return on sharing the knowledge. The return can be a tangible reward or an intangible enhancement of reputation. The internal competition interferes with knowledge sharing. Technology makes it easier for people to share knowledge. Sharing tacit knowledge requires socialization (Davenport & Prusak, 2000). Tacit knowledge can be shared through mentoring and networking. Technology can also help in externalization of tacit knowledge to some extent through codification (Botha et al., 2008). A positive correlation was found between trust, sharing information freely, and working closely with others or developing friends at work and successful implementation of KM technology (Park et al., 2004).

Applying existing knowledge to solve current problems is a source of innovation and competitive advantage (Wellman, 2009). New knowledge is created by applying the existing explicit knowledge with the implicit knowledge of employees. Leadership has to create and support a culture that values and rewards the applying existing knowledge to solve new problems. Cross-functional project teams are one way to apply the existing knowledge for innovation. Applying knowledge is mainly a human function although technology can be programmed to spot trends and patterns. Human intuition offers ways to apply knowledge in innovative ways. These four processes of acquiring, storing, sharing, and applying knowledge play a key role in effective KM in a global business.

Culture

KM is influenced by the organizational culture (Mueller, 2012). The conventional wisdom concerning the successful practice of KM deals with a knowledge creating and sharing culture. The relevant levels of culture include national culture, organizational culture, organizational climate, organizational sub-cultures, and team culture (King, 2008; Ang & Massingham, 2007; Salmaninezhad & Daneshwar, 2012; Zhang, 2012). KM has been studied in the framework of the organizational structure, membership, relationship, and strategy (Magnier-Watanabe & Senoo, 2008). This framework provides useful insights for KM in multinational companies or domestic companies going abroad.

There is a relationship between KM and organizational culture, national culture, technology, and leadership style (Nguyen & Mohamed, 2011; Shafei et al., 2011; Palanisamy, 2008; Rai 2011). The four dimensions of organizational culture include participative decision-making, openness, learning orientation, and transformational leadership. Diffusion of knowledge occurs through sharing the knowledge across the entire organization instead of staying within the organizational silos. Employees share their knowledge freely when they feel valued by the organization in terms of good working environment and opportunities for personal and professional growth (Cruz et al., 2009). The best leadership style to motivate employees to share their tacit knowledge is the delegating style (Singh, 2008). Employee commitment also plays a role in employee motivation to share their knowledge (Hislop, 2003). KM is affected by the internal marketing: market research, market segmentation, communications, perspectives, development, and rewards. Internal marketing promotes the establishment of outstanding relations between management and employees, and its goal is to increase employee satisfaction as well as innovative customers' satisfaction (Lee & Chen, 2005). An organizational culture where change is anticipated and accepted is helpful for effective KM implementation.

Both process-oriented and open communication system organizational cultures significantly influenced perceived ease of use, perceived usefulness, perceived behavioral control, and subjective norms. In other words, employees who perceive their work environment to be process-oriented have higher levels of perceived usefulness, perceived ease of use, and perceived behavioral control than employees who perceive their work environment to be results-oriented. In addition, employees who perceive their work environment to be more employee-oriented have higher levels of perceived behavioral control than employees who perceive their work environment to be more job-oriented. Furthermore, employees who perceive their work environment to be more open have higher levels of subjective norms than employees who perceive their environment to be more closed (Ciganek et al., 2008). Knowledge-centered organizational culture contributes to innovation (Donate & Guadamillas, 2010). KM practices are guided by the type of industry and collaborating parties (Biasutti, 2012). In the context of networked innovation between multiple actors, two models of networked innovation can be distinguished according to KM needs: networks focusing on the transaction of explicit knowledge and intellectual property, and networks focusing on the co-creation of new knowledge and business opportunities. Within networked innovation, a strategic approach to KM is a key element of success. Firms are able to manage knowledge within networked innovation when they understand their partners' business models and strategic intents, for example their motivation to collaborate. KM, organizational culture and intranets are being combined to create virtual human resources development practices for employee performance improvement (Bennett, 2009).

Structure

A bureaucratic organization has vertical structure, individual membership, systematic relationships and a reactive strategy. A task-force type of organization has horizontal structure, collective membership, ad hoc relationships, and innovative strategy. It was found that a vertical structure, individual membership, systematic relationship, and reactive strategy were positively related to focused knowledge acquisition, private knowledge storage, prescribed knowledge diffusion, and exploitative knowledge application respectively. High power distance, individualism, masculinity and high uncertainty avoidance were found to be positively related to focused knowledge acquisition, private knowledge storage, prescribed knowledge diffusion, and exploitative knowledge application respectively. They also found that organizational characteristics exert a stronger influence on knowledge management than the national culture (Magnier-Watanabe & Senoo, 2010).

In a firm, both formal and informal organizational structures exist. Informal networks are created when people interact on projects. They represent the way people actually interact. Knowledge flow within a firm depends on the formal and informal networks. A firm should be viewed as community of communities. The organizational structure depends upon the firm's processes and products or services. Decentralized structures are more effective for KM (Chen & Huang, 2007; Claver-Cortes et al., 2007).

In summary, the four interrelated organizational parameters of learning, processes, culture, and structure influence KM in global business. KM is rooted in organizational learning which has to fit with the organizational processes, culture and structure in order to contribute to organizational effectiveness and competitive edge (Davenport & Prusak, 2000; Zheng et al., 2010).

INFORMATION AND COMMUNICATION TECHNOLOGY (ICT)

ICT is the third element in our proposed conceptual framework for KM and its challenges in global business. It is interrelated with the other two KM elements of leadership and organization. ICT plays a significant role in the leadership communication, organizational learning and KM processes to acquire, store, share and apply knowledge, Figure 5

Global leadership and strategy implementation, global knowledge integration and managing global virtual teams have to take into account the global ICT gaps that exist between different economies. ICT was found to be a precondition requirement for effective KM (Ahmed & Schroeder, 2011; Nurluoz & Birol, 2011). KM was found to partially mediate in the relationship between technology and organizational effectiveness (Kuo et al., 2011). ICT plays a key role in establishing a knowledge–sharing culture, storage, and diffusion of knowledge (Yaghoubi et al., 2011; Leonardi & Treem, 2012; Lopez-Nicolas & Merono-Cerdan, 2009). Establishing company intranets and virtual communities for knowledge sharing helps in converting knowledge into value

Figure 5. Role of ICT in KM Processes

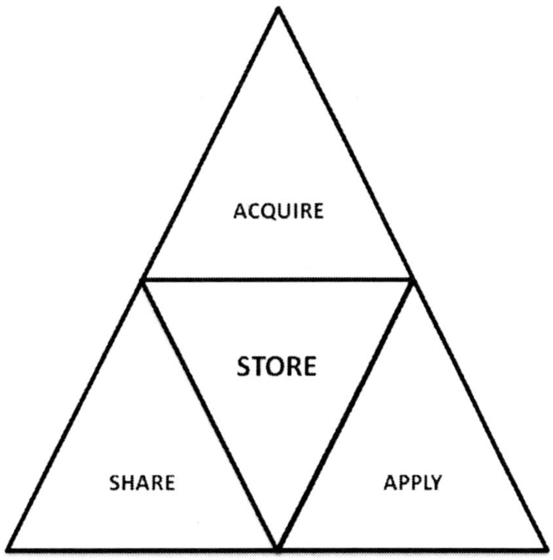

creation and innovation (Volpel & Hahn, 2005; Lai & Lin, 2012; Smedley, 2010). ICT has to be context specific and should be in tune with the people side.

ICT includes technology for information management and communication within the global organization. ICT based KM tools include groupware systems, intranet and extranet document management systems, data warehousing, data mining, decision support systems (DSS), online analytical processing (OLAP), and content management systems (Bali et al., 2009). For a successful KM initiative, the organizational data has to be stored in a centralized warehouse with proper indexing and categorization. Data mining, data visualization, and OLAP can be used to search and analyze the stored data for patterns and insights. DSS helps to make decisions quickly. Document management systems help in publishing, storage, indexing, and retrieval of documents containing explicit knowledge.

ICT plays an important role in storing data. The goal of storing information in a centralized system allows access to different departments. A data warehouse can have internal and external knowledge (e.g., competitive intelligence) stored in it. Data mining tools and techniques can be used to search the stored data for patterns that may lead to new insights. Data warehouse is usually the driver of data-driven decision support systems (DSS). The role of DSS is to access and manipulate data and enhance the manager's knowledge through knowledge discovery. A DSS answers queries based on what the expert inputs, but does not carry out further analysis. The goal of warehousing data is to reduce the time for decision making by using online analytical processing system (OLAP), data mining, and data visualization. Groupware is the technology designed to help people collaborate. These include communication tools, conferencing tools, and collaborative management tools that help manage group activities.

The content management systems (CMS) manage the content of intranet and extranet. The extranet is an extension of the intranet to the company's external network to enhance transfer of information and collaboration with the partners. CMS are very useful for KM since they create, manage and distribute content on the internet website, intranet and extranet. Intranet is essentially a within-the-firm Internet. It has the same functionality as the Internet. It uses TCP/IP (Transmission control protocol/internet protocol). It allows the creation of networks within the firm with common Internet applications that allows one to communicate across different operating systems (Hislop et al., 2000). Firewalls prevent outsiders to gain access. Intranet can act as a platform for groupware applications and publishing. The intranet homepage has seven roles, including news, navigation, key tools, key information, community and culture, internal marketing, and knowledge sharing, collaboration, innovation management. Intranet implementation has to be in accordance with the needs, objectives and processes of the organization.

The Document Management Systems (DMS) help in publishing, storage, indexing and retrieval of documents. Groupware systems support KM by increasing collaboration and knowledge creation. These systems include communication tools, conferencing tools and collaborative management tools. The collaborative management tools include project management systems, workflow systems and information management systems. Document management systems help extract knowledge from old documents including past e-mails. The groupware has to meet the organizational needs and objectives.

In today's knowledge economy, knowledge workers depend on information to create new products and services. The external sources of such information include customers, suppliers, competitors, partners, recognized outside experts and consultants. Three kinds of knowledge are necessary for each of the categories - knowledge about, knowledge from and knowledge for. Internet, intranet and extranet are good sources of such knowledge. Internet and firm's website are a good source of gathering information about external to the company. Intranet is a small-scale version of the Internet that operates entirely within the firm. The extranet is an extension of the intranet to the firm's external network including partners, suppliers. This knowledge has to be aligned with the business strategy to gain competitive advantage. Not all information is knowledge. Knowledge is the information that has a potential for value for the business in terms of solutions to existing problems or innovation in products, services and processes.

Developing knowledge management system (KMS) in a global business presents many challenges. For successful implementation of KMS, employee acceptance is crucial. One of the challenges is the perceived loss of behavioral control. When employees are asked to put their tacit knowledge into a KMS, they tend to feel a loss of ownership of the knowledge that they previously controlled (Delong & Fahey, 2000). Giving up control of their tacit knowledge may be perceived as marginalizing their worth as an employee and potential loss of their job. Organizational culture influences the employee acceptance of knowledge management systems. Four constructs have been used in the literature to study technology acceptance -perceived usefulness, perceived ease of use, perceived behavioral control and subjective norms (Venkatesh et al., 2003). These four constructs influence employee's behavioral intentions to use KMS. Subjective norms involve organizational support from coworkers, supervisors and managers. In the absence of subjective norms, employees hesitate to share their tacit knowledge.

KM CHALLENGES IN GLOBAL BUSINESS

The global economy is influencing the way global businesses manage their institutional knowledge. The KM challenges in global business can be summarized in terms of the proposed conceptual framework of leadership, organization, and ICT. The role of global leadership is to formulate a global strategy, integrate global knowledge in global virtual teams within the constraints of global ICT gaps in different economies, Figure 6.

Four strategies have been identified for competing across borders: multinational, global, international, and transnational. The multinational strategy involves autonomous foreign subsidiaries that enable local market adaptation. Global strategy involves regulation of the foreign subsidiary by the headquarters enabling economic efficiency. International strategy involves knowledge exploitation through diffusion and adaptation enabling rapid development and innovation. Transnational strategy utilizes global principles and practices them locally enabling local flexibility and global benefit. Based on a series of semi-structured interviews with senior managers from 11 firms in three continents, there are three global KM strategies based on governance. They include headquarter (HQ) commissioned and executed, HQ commissioned and regionally executed, regionally commissioned and locally executed. Sharing and managing knowledge across borders is more effective when one thinks globally and acts locally (Desouza & Evaristo, 2003). One of the complexities of knowledge sharing in a large global organization included the tension between "local" production of knowledge and global sharing. Exclusive focus on certain types of knowledge can be counter-productive. KM needs to be "integrative and flexible enough to facilitate dynamic interplay between different forms of knowledge across the space and time" (Davis et.al., 2005). The degree of tacitness or codifiability determines how to integrate and share knowledge across the national borders (Kogut & Zander, 1992a; 1992b).

At the beginning of the KM initiative, the leadership needs to identify what knowledge exists and where including people, processes and resources. The knowledge assessment consists of identifying what is known and what knowledge needs to be acquired. Identifying knowledge gaps is crucial to the KM strategy execution. This process of identifying knowledge assessment and gaps in the global context presents unique challenges. Identifying knowledge gaps, dealing with tacit knowledge, cross-cultural knowledge sharing, developing rewards, and effective measures of KM, developing new organizational structures and global competition. Kalkan (2008) reported six main KM challenges for global business. They include coping with increased competition, developing a working definition of knowledge, adaptation to cultural complexity, attention to human resources, developing new organizational structures and utilization of IT to deal with tacit knowledge.

KM is an organization-wide process involving all employees in an organization. The leadership has to develop a KM strategy and communicate it to all employees A global survey of KM regarding how a KM strategy can be developed that will enable its successful implementation revealed that strategy is key to the KM process. However, it is often not communicated well to workers. Soft issues, such as organizational culture, is one of the most important factors in formulating KM strategy. This global survey found that organizations are still struggling to use KM tools and techniques. The organizational knowledge is not yet well-structured and easy to retrieve and use. The survey also found that the communities of practice for the sharing of tacit knowledge are used extensively throughout the world for knowledge work but it is not clear if they add value to the organization's intellectual capital (Coakes et al., 2010).

The role of leadership in KM is to promote organizational learning (Garvin, 1993). This assessment of knowledge in processes, work groups, and systems is challenging. Articulation and communication of topics of knowledge to be exchanged increases the chances of efficient knowledge transfer between geographically dispersed entities (Gassmann & Von Zedtwitz, 2003). This assessment helps the leader to know what knowledge exists in the organization and where. This also identifies what knowledge that needs to be acquired from outside the organization for a given project. The leadership has to involve the human resources team within the organization in the KM process. The leadership has to communicate the vision to global virtual teams and ensure that the teams work on projects that will increase the global competitiveness. The leader has to develop measures of effective KM and institute rewards for knowledge sharing globally. Traansfer of knowledge between groups that share the same norm is easier, indicating that creating a learning organizational culture is a challenge (Gassmann & Von Zedtwitz, 2003).

A mix of transformational and transactional leadership style promotes organizational learning (Singh, 2011). Transactional leadership style helps improve the efficiency of the organizational learning (Bass, 1997). The KM leader develops and effectively communicates the global strategic vision, motivates others, acts as a change agent, coaches others, models good practices, and carries out the knowledge agenda (Debowski, 2006). In a global business, organizational culture plays an important role in the success of any change initiatives required for KM. Global virtual teams present unique challenges in terms of knowledge sharing. Acquiring knowledge or organizational learning is facilitated by organizational values of openness, supportiveness, trust and respect for the employees. Knowledge management is affected by the organizational structure, membership, relationship and strategy.

The leadership has to communicate the KM vision to employees, providing the right technology, motivating them to use it, promote knowledge sharing, externalize the employees' tacit knowledge, embracing change and managing the tacit knowledge of global virtual employees. Many organizations do not adequately transmit to the employees the vision of the business and what areas employees need to create new knowledge. In addition, the leadership does not communicate clearly the value of the employees' knowledge and new learning to the organization. This leads to employees not being fully engaged in KM processes. Communicating the vision and goal of the company helps employees to focus their efforts in the right place. Employees need to know what to invent. The leadership has to motivate people to use it. Technology is no good if people don't use it. People adapt new technology that is easy to use and people perceive it to be useful (Venkatesh et al., 2003).Training and mentoring help with making the technology easy to use. Another leadership challenge consists of promoting and facilitating knowledge sharing without controlling it. Technology makes sharing easy but people must want to do it and should be rewarded for it.

The organizational processes, culture, structure, learning, and intellectual capital presents challenges. Selection of appropriate information and communication technologies across countries of varying economic development status to achieve effective KM is another challenge. Developing KM effectiveness measures and rewards across cultures offers another challenge. Another organizational challenge is figuring out how to tap into the tacit knowledge of employees and turn it into explicit knowledge for the organization without making employees feel insecure. The sixth challenge is to create a culture of anticipating and embracing change. KM is an organizational change effort. Employees have to buy into this change for it to succeed. As organizations become more global, they are employing more and more global virtual teams. Capturing and integrating the tacit knowledge of global virtual team members is a new challenge.

Since knowledge is embedded in the organization's processes, work groups, and systems, it is a challenge to identify and codify it. Knowledge transfer is easier between groups that share the same organizational culture. The determinants of knowledge transfer were found to be systemic nature of the project, type of innovation being pursued, knowledge conversion modes and the extent to which resources are bundled together. Other challenges were found to be the number of virtual groups, the degree of industrialization of different countries represented, relative costs of running the virtual teams, advances in ICTs, and

Figure 6. KM Challenges in a Global Business

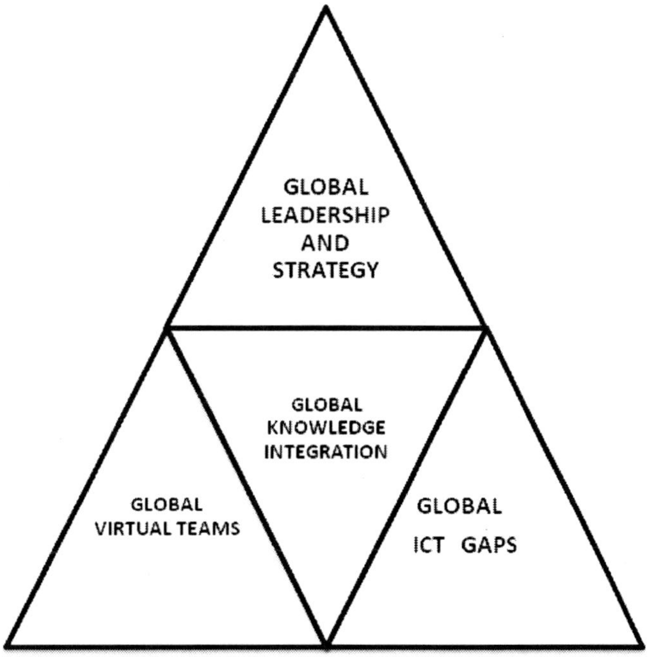

degree of decentralization of the global virtual teams (Gassmann & Von Zedtwitz, 2003).

Hierarchical-bureaucratic structures prevent knowledge-sharing, application, learning, and innovation. Effective KM in a global business stems from work in multidisciplinary groups with a high degree of autonomy and acting in environments characterized by fluctuation, creative chaos, requisite variety, and redundancy (Nonaka & Takeuchi, 1995). The dynamics of project-based globally dispersed teams is different from that for the collocated teams. Cross-cultural knowledge sharing requires developing knowledge, sensitivity, and skills about other cultures. Visible rewards for knowledge sharing and measures of effective knowledge sharing help with this difficult process across cultures. Hierarchical and bureaucratic organizations prevent knowledge sharing and innovation. Innovative organizational structures based on multidisciplinary groups with a high degree of autonomy and acting in environments characterized by fluctuation, creative chaos, requisite variety, and redundancy, promote knowledge sharing and innovation (Nonaka & Takeuchi, 1995). A global business has to deal with increased global competition.

Technologies to support KM in global business include group collaboration systems for sharing knowledge, office systems to distribute knowledge, artificial intelligence systems to codify knowledge, and knowledge work systems to create knowledge. In addition, business process management, content management, web content management, and knowledge applications management are also available. Technology for sharing and distributing knowledge helps to alleviate the unique issues of time and space for a transnational organization. However, a successful KM in global business requires a sociotechnical approach where social aspects of knowledge creation, storage, and sharing need to be considered also. Implementing technology has to take into account the people, task, process, and environment (Coakes, 2006). Making the right technology infrastructure and training available to employees. Having the right technology is crucial to KM implementation. The technology has to fit in the organizational structure and culture. Employee training to effectively use the technology promotes technology acceptance and use. Implicit knowledge can be codified and easily shared globally using ICT. However, the tacit knowledge is difficult to codify and is difficult to share via traditional role of ICT. Video conferencing is one way to see the tacit knowledge in action. This "video internship" can be supplemented with face-to-face international internships with opportunity to socialize and pick up tacit knowledge.

In summary, the KM challenges for a global business can be described in the conceptual framework of leadership, organization and technology. The leadership has to develop awareness, knowledge and skills for the global diverse and multicultural environment. The leader has to develop global competencies including cross-cultural communication and integrating global virtual teams. The leadership has to develop a strategy for implicit and tacit knowledge assessment, cross-cultural knowledge integration, and knowledge transfer across the global virtual teams and developing measures of KM effectiveness. In addition to knowledge in people, the leader has to assess the knowledge that exists in the organizational processes across national boundaries. In a global business, the main KM challenges include identifying knowledge gaps, dealing with tacit knowledge across cultures, cross-cultural knowledge sharing, developing rewards and effective measures of KM, developing new organizational structures and global competition. Integrating knowledge among global virtual team members requires the leadership to develop sensitivity, awareness and skills in managing across cultures.

SUMMARY

A conceptual framework of leadership, organization, and ICT is proposed for KM and its challenges in global business. KM is both an organizational process and a management goal. KM is context-specific to the industry sector, organizational strategy, and project. KM is effective and adds value when it is integrated into the day-to-day business processes of the organization. KM is a strategic change initiative for the entire organization involving people, processes, and ICT. Explicit and implicit knowledge resides in documents, people's minds, products, processes, and routines. The leadership has to develop an international KM strategy and communicate their vision to the employees and get their buy-in this change-initiative. The organizational parameters that influence KM include organizational structure, culture, learning and processes. The leadership has to create a structure that supports a learning culture in the organization. A knowledge-centered organizational culture leads to innovative performance. Organizational values of openness, supportiveness, trust and respect for the employees promote organizational learning. The four processes of KM consist of knowledge acquisition, storage, sharing, and application of knowledge. ICT plays a key role in getting the right information to the right people at the right time. The main objective of KM is to identify, gather, generate, store, share, and deploy knowledge to improve knowledge worker productivity, improve process efficiency, and create innovation and value by leveraging, improving, and refining its competencies. KM is situational and context-specific. How knowledge is acquired, stored, shared and applied depends on the context of the industry and organization. KM programs are typically tied to specific organizational objectives and are intended to lead to the achievement of specific targeted results such as improved performance, competitive advantage, or higher levels of innovation. An effective knowledge management in an organization leads to employee job satisfaction and commitment and leads to a competitive advantage. The Chief Knowledge Officer (CKO) is becoming a dedicated executive position in the multinational corporations to effectively manage knowledge in a global business. To achieve a competitive edge from knowledge management, the CKO has to focus on the three interrelated KM elements (leadership, organization, ICT). The role of leadership in KM includes strategy, style, change management, and performance metrics. The organizational parameters for KM include learning, processes, culture, and structure. ICT plays a key role in the organizational processes to acquire, store, share, and apply knowledge. KM challenges in a global business include global leadership and strategy, managing global virtual teams and global knowledge integration in spite of the global ICT gaps in different economies. KM makes employees more productive through learning and innovation. KM is rooted in organizational learning which has to fit with the organizational processes, culture, and structure in order to contribute to organizational effectiveness and competitive edge (Davenport & Prusak, 2000; Zheng et al., 2010; Bloodgood & Chilton, 2012).

REFERENCES

Ahmed, S., & Schroeder, R. G. (2011). Knowledge management through technology Strategy: Implications for Competitiveness. *Journal of Manufacturing Technology Management*, *22*(1), 6–24. doi:10.1108/17410381111099789.

Alavi, M. & Leidner, D. E. (2001). Review: Knowledge Management and Knowledge

Allee, V. (1997). Twelve Principles of Knowledge Management. *Journal of Training and Development*, *51*(11), 4–71.

Ang, Z., & Massingham, P. (2007). National Culture and the Standardization versus Adaptation of Knowledge Management. *Journal of Knowledge Management*, *11*(2), 5–21. doi:10.1108/13673270710738889.

Argyris, C., & Schon, D. (1978). *Organizational Learning: A Theory of Action Perspective*. Reading, MA: Addison-Wesley.

Bali, R., Wickramsinghe, N., & Lehaney, B. (2009). *Knowledge Management Primer*. London: Routledge.

Bass, B. M. (1997). Does the Transactional and Transformational Leadership paradigm transcend Organizational and National Boundaries? *The American Psychologist*, *52*(2), 130–139. doi:10.1037/0003-066X.52.2.130.

Bass, B. M. (2000). The Future of Leadership in Learning Organizations. *Journal of Leadership & Organizational Studies*, *7*, 18–40. doi:10.1177/107179190000700302.

Bennett, E. E. (2009). Virtual HRD: The Intersection of Knowledge Management, Culture, and Intranets. *Advances in Developing Human Resources*, *11*(3), 362–374. doi:10.1177/1523422309339724.

Bhatt, D. (2001). Knowledge Management in Organizations: Examining the Interaction between Technologies, Techniques and People. *Journal of Knowledge Management*, *5*(1), 68–75. doi:10.1108/13673270110384419.

Biasutti, M., & Heba, E. D. (2012). Using Wiki in Teacher Education: Impact on Knowledge Management Processes and Student Satisfaction. *Computers & Education*, *59*(3), 861–872. doi:10.1016/j.compedu.2012.04.009.

Blacker, F. (1995). Knowledge, Knowledge Work and Organizations: An Overview and Interpretation. *Organization Studies*, *15*(6), 1021–1046. doi:10.1177/017084069501600605.

Blacker, F., Reed, M., & Whitaker, A. (1993). Editorial: Knowledge Workers and Contemporary Organization. *Journal of Management Studies*, *30*(6), 851–862. doi:10.1111/j.1467-6486.1993.tb00469.x.

Bloodgood, J. M., & Chilton, M. A. (2012). *Performance Implications of Matching Adaptation and Innovation Cognitive Style with Business Environment, Knowledge Management and Knowledge Management Technology*. Chandice Publishing Ltd..

Brown, J. S., & Duguid, P. (1991). Organizational Learning and Communities of Practice –Towards a Unified View of Working. *Organization Science*, *2*(1). doi:10.1287/orsc.2.1.40.

Chang, S. C., & Lee, M. S. (2007). A Study on Relationship among Leadership, Organizational Culture, the Operation of Learning Organization and Employees' Job Satisfaction. *The Learning Organization*, *14*, 155–185. doi:10.1108/09696470710727014.

Chen, C., & Huang, J. (2007). How Organizational Climate and Structure Affect Knowledge Management – the Social Interaction Perspective. *International Journal of Information Management*, *27*(2), 104–118. doi:10.1016/j.ijinfomgt.2006.11.001.

Ciganek, A. P., Mao, E., & Srite, M. (2008). Organizational Culture for Knowledge Management Systems: A Study of Corporate Users. *Journal of Knowledge Management*, *4*(1), 1–15. doi:10.4018/jkm.2008010101.

Claver-Cortes, E., Zaragoza-Saez, P., & Pertusa-Ortega, E. (2007). Organizational Structure Features Supporting Knowledge Management Processes. *International Journal of Knowledge Management*, *11*(4), 45–57. doi:10.1108/13673270710762701.

Coakes, E. (2006). Storing and Sharing Knowledge – Supporting the Management of Knowledge Made Explicit in Transnational Organizations. *The Learning Organization*, *13*(6), 579–593. doi:10.1108/09696470610705460.

Coakes, E., Amar, A. D., & Grandos, M. L. (2010). Knowledge Management, Strategy, and Technology: A Global Snapshot. *Journal of Enterprise Information Management*, *23*(3), 282–304. doi:10.1108/17410391011036076.

Crawford, C. B. (2005). Effects of Transformational Leadership and Organizational Position on Knowledge Management. *International Journal of Knowledge Management*, *9*, 6–16. doi:10.1108/13673270510629927.

Cruz, N. M., Perez, V. M., & Cantero, C. T. (2009). The Influence of Employee Motivation on Knowledge Transfer. *International Journal of Knowledge Management*, *13*(6), 478–490. doi:10.1108/13673270910997132.

Davenport, T. H. (2005). *Thinking for a Living: How to Get Better Performance and Results from Knowledge Workers*. Boston, MA: Harvard Business School Press.

Davenport, T. H., & Prusak, L. (2000). *Working Knowledge: How Organizations Manage What They Know*. Boston, MA: Harvard Business School Press. doi:10.1145/347634.348775.

Davis, J. E., Subrahmanian, E., & Westerberg, W. (2005). The "Global" and the "Local" in Knowledge Management. *International Journal of Knowledge Management*, *9*(1), 101–112. doi:10.1108/13673270510582992.

De Long, D. W., & Fahey, L. (2000). Diagnosing Cultural Barriers to Knowledge Management. *The Academy of Management Executive*, *14*(4), 113–127.

Debowski, S. (2006). *Knowledge Management*. Hoboken, NJ: John Wiley & Sons.

Desouza, K., & Evaristo, R. (2003). Global Knowledge Management Strategies. *European Management Journal*, *21*(1), 62–67. doi:10.1016/S0263-2373(02)00152-4.

Donate, M. J., & Guadamillas, F. (2010). The Effect of Organizational Culture on Knowledge Management Practices and Innovation. *Knowledge and Process Management*, *17*(2), 82. doi:10.1002/kpm.344.

Drucker, P. F. (1959). *Landmarks of Tomorrow*. New York: Harper.

Drucker, P. F. (1991). The New Productivity Challenge. *Harvard Business Review*, *69*(6), 69–76. PMID:10114929.

Drucker, P. F. (1993). *Post-Capitalist Society*. Oxford, UK: Butterworth/Heinemann.

Drucker, P. F. (1999). *Management Challenges fir the 21st Century*. New York: Harper Collins.

Edvinson, L., & Malone, M. S. (1997). *Intellectual Capital: Realizing Your Company's True Value by Finding its Hidden Brainpower*. New York: Harper Business.

Flores, L. G., Zheng, W., Rau, D., & Thomas, C. H. (2012). *Organizational Learning: Sub Process Identification, Construct Validation, and an Empirical Test of Cultural antecedents, 38*(2), 640-667.

Gamble, P. R., & Blackwell, J. (2001). *Knowledge Management: A State of the Art Guide*. Kogan Page Ltd..

Garvin, D. (1993). Building a Learning Organization. *Harvard Business Review*, *71*(4), 78–91. PMID:10127041.

Gassmann, O., & Von Zedtwitz, M. (2003). Trends and Determinants of Managing Virtual R&D teams. *R & D Management*, *33*(3), 243–262. doi:10.1111/1467-9310.00296.

Guadamillas-Gomez, F., & Donate-Manzanares, M. J. (2011). Ethics and Corporate Social Responsibility Integrated into Knowledge Management and Innovation Technology. *Journal of Management Development*, *30*(6), 569–581. doi:10.1108/02621711111135170.

Gupta, B., Iyer, L. S., & Aronson, J. E. (2000). Knowledge Management: Practices and Challenges. *Industrial Management & Data Systems*, *100*(1), 17–21. doi:10.1108/02635570010273018.

Haag, S., Cummings, M., McCubbrey, D., Pinsonneault, A., & Donovan, R. (2006). *Management Information Systems For the Information Age* (3rd ed.). Whitby, Canada: McGraw Hill Ryerson.

Hislop, D. (2003). Linking Human Resource Management and Knowledge Management via Commitment. *Employee Relations*, *25*(2), 182–202. doi:10.1108/01425450310456479.

Hislop, D., Newell, S., Scarbrough, H., & Swan, J. (2000). Networks, Knowledge and Power: Decision Making, Politics and the Process of Innovation. *Technology Analysis and Strategic Management*, *12*(3), 399–411. doi:10.1080/713698478.

Horwitch, M., & Armacost, R. (2002). Helping Knowledge Management be All it can be. *International Journal of Business Strategy*, *23*(3), 26–32. doi:10.1108/eb040247.

Ichijo, K., & Nonaka, I. (Eds.). (2007). *Knowledge Creation and Management: New Challenges for Managers*. New York: Oxford University Press.

Kakabadse, N. K., Kakabadse, A., & Kouzmin, A. (2003). Reviewing the Knowledge Management Literature: Towards a Taxonomy. *International Journal of Knowledge Management*, *7*(4), 75–91. doi:10.1108/13673270310492967.

Kalkan, V. D. (2008). An Overall View of Knowledge Management Challenges for Global Business. *Business Process Management Journal*, *14*(3), 390–400. doi:10.1108/14637150810876689.

King, W. R. (2008). Questioning the Conventional Wisdom: Culture-Knowledge Management Relationships. *International Journal of Knowledge Management*, *12*(3), 35–47. doi:10.1108/13673270810875840.

Kogut, B., & Zander, U. (1992a). *Knowledge of the Firm, Technology Transfer, and the Theory of the Multinational Corporation*. Working Paper, Institute of International Business, Stockholm School of Economics, Stockholm, Sweden.

Kogut, B., & Zander, U. (1992b). Knowledge of the Firm, Combinative Capabilities and the Replication of Technology. *Organization Science*, *3*(3), 383–397. doi:10.1287/orsc.3.3.383.

Kuo, T. S., Chi, H., & Dorjgotov, B. (2011). Mediation Effect of Knowledge Management in the Relationship Between Technology and Organizational Effectiveness – An Empirical Study of Mongolian Academy of Sciences. *Journal of Human Resource and Adult Learning*, *7*(1), 1–10.

Lai, Y. L., & Lin, F. J. (2012). The Effects of Knowledge Management and Technology Innovation on New Product Development Performance – An Empirical Study of Taiwanese Machine Tool Industry. *Proceed. –. Social and Behavioral Sciences*, *40*, 157–164.

Lam, Y. L. J. (2002). Defining the Effect of Transformational Leadership on Organizational Learning: A Cross-Cultural Comparison. *School Leadership & Management*, *22*, 439–452. doi:10.1080/1363243022000053448.

Lambe, P. (2011). The Three Tribes: Knowledge Management, Learning and Intellectual Capital – Towards a Common Agenda. *Keynote Presentation, 8th International Conference on Intellectual Capital, Knowledge Management &Organizational Learning – ICICKM 2011*. Bangkok, Thailand: IKI SEA

Lee, C., & Chen, W. J. (2005). The Effects of Internal Marketing and Organizational Culture on Knowledge Management in the Information Technology Industry. *International Journal of Management*, *22*(4), 661–672.

Lehaney, B., Clark, S., & Coakes, E. (2003). *Beyond Knowledge Management*. Hershey, PA: IGI Global. doi:10.4018/978-1-59140-180-3.

Leonardi, P. M., & Treem, J. W. (2012). Knowledge Management Technology as a Stage for Strategic Self-Presentation: Implications for Knowledge Sharing in. *Information and Organization*, *22*, 37–59. doi:10.1016/j.infoandorg.2011.10.003.

Lopez-Nicolas, C., & Merono-Cerdan, A. L. (2009). The Impact of Organizational Culture on the Use of ICT for Knowledge Management. *Electronic Markets*, *19*, 211–219. doi:10.1007/s12525-009-0020-4.

Magnier-Watanabe, R., & Senoo, D. (2008). Organizational Characteristics as Prescriptive Factors of Knowledge Management Initiatives. *International Journal of Knowledge Management*, *12*(1), 21–36. doi:10.1108/13673270810852368.

Magnier-Watanabe, R., & Senoo, D. (2010). Shaping Knowledge Management: Organization and National Culture. *Journal of Knowledge Management*, *14*(2), 214–227. doi:10.1108/13673271011032364.

Mueller, J. (2012). The Interactive Relationship of Corporate Culture and Knowledge Management: A Review. *Review of Managerial Science*, *6*(2), 183–201. doi:10.1007/s11846-010-0060-3.

Murray, P. (2000). Designing Business Benefits from Knowledge Management. In Despres, C., & Chauvel, D. (Eds.), *The Present and the Promise of Knowledge Management*. Boston, MA: Butterworth-Heinemann.

Murray, P., & Meyers, A. (1997). The Facts about Knowledge. *Information Strategy*, *2*(7), 29–33.

Nguyen, H. N., & Mohamed, S. (2011). Leadership Behaviors. *Organizational Culture and Knowledge Management Practices*, *30*(2), 206–221.

Nohria, N., Prichard, C., Hull, R., Chumer, M., & Willmostt, H. (Eds.), *ManagingKnwowledge: Critical Investigations of Work and Learning*. Macmillan Business.

Nonaka, I. (1991). The Knowledge Creating Company. *Harvard Business Review*, 96–104.

Nonaka, I. (1994). A Dynamic Theory of Organizational Knowledge Creation. *Organization Science*, *5*(1), 14–37. doi:10.1287/orsc.5.1.14.

Nonaka, I., & Konno, N. (1998). The Concept of 'Ba': Building a Foundation for Knowledge Creation. *California Management Review*, *40*(3), 40–54. doi:10.2307/41165942.

Nonaka, I., & Takeuchi, H. (1995). *The Knowledge Creating Company*. New York: Oxford University Press.

Nonaka, I., & Takeuchi, H. (1996). Theory of organizational knowledge creation. *International Journal ofTechnology Management*, *11*(7-8), 833.

Nonaka, I., & Takeuchi, H. (2011). The Wise Leader. *Harvard Business Review*, *89*(5), 58–67. PMID:21548419.

Nonaka, I., Toyama, R., & Konno, N. (2000). SECI, "Ba" and Leadership: A Unified Model of Dynamic Knowledge Creation. *Long Range Planning*, *33*, 5–34. doi:10.1016/S0024-6301(99)00115-6.

Nurluoz, O., & Birol, C. (2011). The Impact of Knowledge Management and Technology: An Analysis of Administrative Behaviors. *The Turkish Online Journal of Educational Technology*, *10*(1), 202–208.

Ouintas, P., Lefrere, P., & Jones, G. (1997). Knowledge Management: A Strategic Agenda. *Long Range Planning*, *30*(3), 91–385.

Palanisamy, R. (2008). Organizational Culture and Knowledge Management in ERP Implementation: An Empirical Study. *Journal of Computer Information Systems*, *48*(2), 100–119.

Park, H., Ribiere, V., & Schulte, W. D. Jr. (2004). Critical Attributes of Organizational Culture that Promote Knowledge Management Technology Implementation Success. *Journal of Knowledge Management*, *8*(3), 106–117. doi:10.1108/13673270410541079.

Politis, J. D. (2001). The Relationship of Various Leadership Styles to Knowledge Management. *Leadership and Organization Development Journal*, *22*, 355–364. doi:10.1108/01437730110410071.

Politis, J. D. (2002). Transformational and Transactional Leadership Enabling (Disabling) Knowledge Acquisition of Self-Managed Teams: the Consequence for Performance. *Leadership and Organization Development Journal*, 23.

Politis, J. D. (2004). Transformational and Transactional Leadership Predictors of the 'Stimulant' Determinants to Creativity in Organizational Work Environments. *Electronic Journal of Knowledge Management*, *2*, 23–34.

Rai, R. K. (2011). *Knowledge Management and Organizational Culture: A Theoretical Integrative Framework.*, *15*(5), 779-801.

Rastogi, P. N. (2000). Knowledge Management and Intellectual Capital – The New Virtuous Realty of Competitiveness. *Hum Systems Manage*, *19*(1), 39–49.

Reich, B. H., Gemino, A., & Sauer, C. (2012). Knowledge Management and Project-based Knowledge in IT Projects: A Model and Preliminary Empirical Results. *International Journal of Project Management*, *30*, 663–674. doi:10.1016/j.ijproman.2011.12.003.

Reinhardt, W., Schmidt, B., Sloep, P., & Drachsler, H. (2011). Knowledge Worker Roles and Actions – Results of Two Empirical Studies. *Knowledge and Process Management*, *18*(3), 150–174. doi:10.1002/kpm.378.

Salmaninezhad, R. A., & Daneshwar, M. (2012). Relationship Between Intellectual Capital and Knowledge Management – Case Study: Tehran Science & Technology Park. *Interdisciplinary Journal of Contemporary Research in Business*, *3*(10), 135–143.

Sarin, S., & McDermott, C. (2003). The Effect of Team Leader characteristics on learning, knowledge application and performance of cross-functional new product development teams. *Decision Sciences*, *34*, 707–739. doi:10.1111/j.1540-5414.2003.02350.x.

Senge, P. M. (1990). The Leader's New Work: Building Learning Organizations. *Sloan Management Review*, 7–23.

Serenko, A. & Bontis. (2004). Meta Review of Knowledge Management and Intellectual Capital Literature: Citation Impact and Research Productivity Rankings. *Knowledge and Process Management*, *11*(3), 185–198. doi:10.1002/kpm.203.

Shafei, R., Ghaderzadeh, H., Salavati, A., & Lavei, S. (2011). *Survey of Relationship between Knowledge Management and Organizational Culture Dimensions in Public Organizations - A Case of Iranian Public Organizations,* 2(11), 355-370.

Singh, S. K. (2008). Role of Leadership in Knowledge Management. *International Journal of Knowledge Management*, *12*(4), 3–15. doi:10.1108/13673270810884219.

Smedley, J. (2010). Modeling the Impact of Knowledge Management Using Technology. *OR Insight*, *23*, 233–250. doi:10.1057/ori.2010.11.

Swan, J., & Newell, S. (2000). Linking Knowledge Management and Innovation. In H.R. Hansen, M. Bichler, & H. Mahrer, (Eds), Proceedings *of the 8th European Conference on Information Systems* (pp. 591-598)., Vienna, Austria: Vienna University of Economics and Business Administration.

Systems, M. Conceptual Foundations and Research Issues. *Management Information Systems Quarterly*, *25*(1), 36–107.

Tissen, R., Andreiessen, D., & Depres, F. L. (2000). *The Knowledge Dividend*. London: Prentice Hall.

Valkokari, K., Paasi, J., & Rantala, T. (2012).. . *Knowledge Management and Practice*, *10*(1), 27–40. doi:10.1057/kmrp.2011.39.

Venkatesh, V., Morris, M. G., Davis, G. B., & Davis, F. D. (2003). User Acceptance of Information Technology: Towards a Unified View. *Management Information Systems Quarterly*, *27*(3), 425–478.

Vera, D., & Crossan, M. (2004). Strategic Leadership and Organizational Learning. *Academy of Management Review*, *29*, 222–240.

Volpel, S. C., & Han, Z. (2005). Managing Knowledge Sharing in China: The Case of Siemens ShareNet. *International Journal of Knowledge Management*, *9*(3), 51–63. doi:10.1108/13673270510602764.

Walsh, J. P., & Ungson, G. R. (1991). Organizational Memory. *Academy of Management Review*, *16*(1), 57–91.

Wellman, J. L. (2009). *Organizational Learning*. Basingstoke, UK: Palgrave Macmillan. doi:10.1057/9780230621541.

Yaghoubi, N. M., Yazdani, B. O., Ahoorani, N., & Banihashemi, S. A. (2011). Information Technology Infrastructures and Knowledge Management: Towards Organizational Excellence. *Computer and Information Science*, *4*(5), 20–27. doi:10.5539/cis.v4n5p20.

Zack, M. H. (1999). Developing a Knowledge Strategy. *California Management Review*, *41*(3), 125–145. doi:10.2307/41166000.

Zhang, Z. (2012). A Social Software Strategy for Knowledge Management and Organization Culture. *OR Insight*, *25*(2), 60–79. doi:10.1057/ori.2011.14.

Zheng, W., & Yang, B., McLean, & G. N. (2010). Linking Organizational Culture, Structure, Strategy, and Organizational Effectiveness: Mediating Role of Knowledge Management. *Journal of Business Research*, *63*, 763–771. doi:10.1016/j.jbusres.2009.06.005.

Chapter 17
Culture and Websites Interaction:
Issues and Perspectives

Ramazan Nacar
Istanbul Technical University, Turkey & Yalova University, Turkey

Sebnem Burnaz
Istanbul Technical University, Turkey

Nimet Uray
Istanbul Technical University, Turkey

ABSTRACT

With the increasing globalization of the business world, websites have become ever more important tools in international business. After the invention of websites, researchers have begun to analyze the websites as they have for traditional communication channels. Websites, as the communication medium of global firms, are not culturally neutral mediums. Website components should be analyzed very carefully in terms of their interaction with cultural issues to come up with culturally adapted websites. In this chapter, 114 studies on culture and websites are critically reviewed, and selected papers among them from a variety of areas such as marketing, communications, management, information technologies, and others, are analyzed in detail to consolidate the existing knowledge and approaches. This chapter aims to analyze how scholarly research on the interaction of culture and websites has developed. The studies are categorized according to the framework developed and selected. Forty of them are discussed in detail under some subcategories. A number of conceptual and methodological issues that deserve more attention are discussed to fulfill the high potential of websites. A state-of-the-art review of several innovative advances in culture and websites is provided to stimulate new streams for future research, and future research recommendations are proposed at the end of the chapter.

DOI: 10.4018/978-1-4666-3966-9.ch017

INTRODUCTION

In the new millennium, companies affected by the globalization are more eager to extend their geographical reach to take advantage of global business opportunities (Leung et al., 2005). As the globalization process takes place within the companies, their websites also need to be operated worldwide, although it is not easy to communicate with different time zones and different places with 24-hour access (Robbins & Stylianou, 2003; Burgmann, Kitchen, & Williams, 2006). In fact, websites are truly global because wherever they are hosted, they are globally accessible and can easily cross national borders (Singh, Zhao, & Hu, 2005; Fletcher, 2006; Sinkovics, Yamin, & Hossinger, 2007; Usunier & Roulin, 2010). Additionally, they are important channels for companies to reach their consumers (Maynard & Tian, 2004; Gevorgyan & Manucharova, 2009). Audiences of websites have increased more than five times between 2000-2011, and now 32.7% of the world population could access the Internet, which equates to more than 2.2 billion people worldwide (Internet World Stats, 2012). With these figures, websites could easily reach to potential consumers more than any other distribution or communication channel.

Since the invention of websites in 1994, studies have been mostly conducted on design and usability of websites. However, the focus was not only engineering of websites, but also finding new avenues for globally communicating and disseminating information on the websites (Faiola & Matei, 2006). Easy and 24-hour access from all over the world, public relations, messages, hypertexts, images, sales promotions, direct marketing, interactive customer services, technical support, among others, make websites vital communication channels for global companies (Robbins & Stylianou, 2003; Cho & Cheon, 2005). The interactivity of websites, which traditional forms of communication do not possess, is an attractive feature of this new communication medium. Especially for product-based multinationals (Okazaki, 2004; Tong & Robertson, 2008), websites provide an easier market penetration for global companies than do traditional channels. Moreover, with its unlimited and ever changing content and other visual elements, websites can provide a visual experience of brands for potential customers (Ferreira, 2007; Baack & Singh, 2007). They improve international marketing efforts and overall business success (Sinkovics, Yamin, & Hossinger, 2007).

In addition to the increasing globalization of the business world, the influence of culture on global business has become even more critical. Globalization forces companies to operate and organize their business across borders. Therefore, companies must communicate, manage, and execute many of their activities through newly developed communication technologies to a heterogeneous group of stakeholders. For instance, information and communication technologies (ICTs) are now crucial parts of global business. ICTs, websites in particular, are means used to communicate with global consumers both at home and in host markets, promoting and facilitating companies' branding and communicating efforts (Martinez-Lopez, Sousa & Gázquez-Abad, 2011).

From the very beginning of the World Wide Web, its global usage has increased exponentially, and it has become an important channel for international communication. Due to its global audience nature, the number of international participants and transactions increase each day as the World Wide Web evolves. Despite the fact they are associated with "worldwide" and "global," websites are still under the impact of cultural constraints. Therefore, interest in the impact of culture on websites has tremendously increased as the world business becomes more globalized.

Functions of websites such as e-commerce, control of information flow, information disclosure, and reduced communication expenses, all must be considered with firms' image and performance at the same time (Luna, Peracchio,

& Juan, 2002; Maynard & Tian, 2004). The rapid growth of websites and their cross-cultural existence brought many challenges for scholars and practitioners in terms of how to communicate within different environments (Faiola & Matei, 2006). Mostly, companies prefer to develop single websites in English for the entire world. However, when they engage in global operations, they need to prepare country-specific websites where just simple translation of domestic websites is no longer sufficient (Kalin, 1997; Nacar & Burnaz, 2011). Translation is one problem; however, there are numerous cultural issues when operating websites for global companies. In order to serve global consumers through websites, companies should understand global consumers' needs and overcome cultural barriers. They should also balance the need for brand consistency and the need for website adaptation to local cultural values (Martinez-Lopez, Sousa, & Gázquez-Abad, 2011). Therefore, the means a company presents itself on the website is significant for both academic researchers and business practitioners.

Operating a global website or adapting website to local culture is a complex and cost-increasing issue. Serving consumers from different cultures through websites is a major problem and as the company crosses more cultural boundaries this problem becomes even more critical. Consumers in different countries might often understand the same thing in different ways (Cho & Cheon, 2005; Liao, Proctor, & Salvendy, 2007).

Several studies on the importance and value of websites have been published for about 15 years. Since research could be cyclical, it seems crucial to reveal and examine how scholarly research has progressed and shaped the interaction of culture and websites. By reviewing 114 studies and focusing on 40 of them in detail, this chapter covers the interaction between culture and websites by grouping the studies within some broad categories. Culture and websites research includes a wide variety of concepts and has a multidisciplinary basis which makes the area valuable and important. The research field related with culture and websites include diverse areas such as business, communications, design, corporate image, branding, advertising, information technologies, computer-mediated communication, etc. Due to the multifaceted and complex nature of culture and websites studies, an interdisciplinary literature survey is conducted which is expected to provide a state-of-the-art review of several advances in culture and websites interaction.

This chapter provides a contribution for scholars and practitioners interested in culture and websites by classifying the structures, issues, concepts and methodologies and by identifying the key journals, articles and authors in the field. This will provide an understanding about the center of excellence on culture and websites interaction along with the most important journals, the most influential articles and authors in the field. An overview of the research streams and research gaps is also provided. An extensive reference list on culture and websites is placed at the end since literature search is not limited only to journal articles but also book chapters and conference proceedings as well.

This chapter integrates concepts from a variety of areas, such as the ones listed above, and suggestions for future research are offered to encourage further improvements. The chapter is expected to provide a significant contribution to managers of newly globalized companies as it will enhance the utilization of websites as an integrated marketing communication (IMC) tool.

THEORETICAL BACKGROUND

The Impact of Globalization

Websites are accessible to everyone from all over the world, thus the tendency of companies is to standardize them. Although websites can force homogenization of consumer culture, they are still under the impact of local and traditional culture which forces them to stay heterogeneous. Further, since websites contain not only the required and essential elements for commerce, but also embedded cultural values and company objectives such as branding elements (Martinez-Lopez, Sousa, & Gázquez-Abad, 2011), they are expected to be culture specific or culture dependent.

The business world continues to globalize and technology has contributed to the globalization of business more than anything else. Especially new communication technologies foster globalization where culture as the constraining factor determines the limits of globalization. However, technology reshapes itself and creates alternative ways to overcome these cultural restrictions. In fact, the relationship between technology, globalization, and culture is mutually interdependent.

The increase in information technologies is changing the rules of work place and transforming the way of companies do business, present themselves and directly communicate with their constituents and consumers (Robbins & Stylianou, 2003; Yun, Park, & Ha, 2008; Pollach, 2011); the physical distance is no more a constraint for many global companies (Leung et al., 2005). Consumers' active participation in the communication process also provided new opportunities to develop new relationships between consumers and companies (Yun, Park & Ha, 2008). In the globalization process, the interaction among many local cultures is facilitated by technologies, particularly by information and communication technologies such as websites.

As Hannerz (1990, p. 237) proposed, world culture is emerging as a result of "increasing interconnectedness of varied local cultures as well as through the development of cultures without a clear anchorage in any one territory." In addition, Appadurai (1990) stated that five paths of global cultural flow, including mediascapes (print media, websites, etc.), facilitate a global consumer culture. Technology, especially computer-mediated communications and websites, is facilitating cultural convergence (Leung et al., 2005; Martinez-Lopez, Sousa, & Gázquez-Abad, 2011).

Formerly, international marketers forecasted that culturally different markets will converge in one-world culture through standardized activities (Hermeking, 2006). With the growth of websites which are ubiquitous in nature, this view become even stronger; companies expected that they could communicate in a new, standardized way where all consumers speak electronic language unrelatedly with region, country, culture or class. However, this is not always the case; consumers still feel cultural and contextual even in the parallel virtual or online environment. Internet, websites, or virtual space is not culture-free (Fang & Rau, 2003; Robbins & Stylianou, 2003; Sinkovics, Yamin, & Hossinger, 2007; Zahedi & Bansal, 2011).

Cultural Resistance

Culture, as the soft side of international business and marketing, has a major impact on websites (Luna, Peracchio, & Juan, 2002; Leung et al., 2005; Gevorgyan & Manucharova, 2009). Different features of culture direct consumers to understand, infer, and assess similar things in different ways (Fu & Wu, 2010; Kittler, Rygl, & Mackinnon, 2011); consumers mostly interpret information and knowledge on websites through their cultural lenses (Leung et al., 2005). Therefore, to develop culturally appropriate websites as an efficient communication tool, companies have to understand patterns of consumers' design preferences and they also have to be able to reflect these preferences on their websites (Singh, Zhao, & Hu, 2005; Gevorgyan & Porter, 2008; Fu & Wu, 2010).

Many studies emphasized that culturally sensitive websites are more usable, accessible, and interactive because consumers could easily categorize, process and interpret these websites and their contents (Singh, Zhao & Hu, 2005). As in the McCracken's (1993) meaning transfer; verbal, thematic and visual signs on websites communicate various meanings to consumers (referred as semiotics theory). Also, these meanings of signs communicating brands, firms, websites, and others, may vary across cultures (Alden, Steenkamp, & Batra, 1999) and culturally appropriate websites are essential requirements for success in local markets (Okazaki, 2004; Tixier, 2005; Fletcher, 2006; Baack & Singh, 2007; Sinkovics et al., 2007). However, although global companies focus on adaptation, there is no standard approach in localization regarding the multicultural content of websites (Ferreira, 2007).

Cultural habits, norms and values of consumers directly influence the design and structure of global websites. Most recent studies on cross-cultural websites reveal that culture influences the way consumers think, act and feel which in turn influences the usability, efficiency and performance of websites. Culturally-adapted websites increase the navigational performance, ease of information access and learnability of consumers. As culture affects the consumers, companies have to learn about culture and cultural dimensions before they build and organize their websites. This will not only include translating website from one language to another one; but there is more to do in terms of navigation, content and context of websites. When companies build global websites, they usually deal with colors, text translations, visual appearance, images, icons, etc., however they should also manage their global websites within the guidance of cultural dimensions such as social hierarchy, individualism, gender roles, time-orientation, etc.

The fast growth of technology has made the Internet a worldwide service, leading researchers to study "culturally sensitive" websites (Fletcher, 2006; Faiola & Matei, 2006). It is a fact that many multinational companies localize their websites and develop country-specific websites in order to meet local markets' cultural needs (Cyr & Trevor-Smith, 2004; Fletcher, 2006; Jagne & Smith-Atakan, 2006).

Abundance of Cultural Perspectives

There is an increase in the number of studies dealing with websites which focus on the effect of culture on acceptance and placement of websites in global setting (Martinez-Lopez, Sousa, & Gazquez-Abad, 2011). However, the first challenge in studying culture is about definitions, conceptualizations, and dimensions used to measure it (Leidner & Kayworth, 2006). It is observed three types of cultural models in terms of dimensionality: single, multiple and historical-social. Single or dyadic characterization of culture includes the studies of high-low context (Hall, 1960), mono-polychromic (Lewis, 1992), high-low trust (Fukuyama, 1995), ideocentric-allocentri (Triandis, 1995), and mono-polymorphic (Bottger, Hallein, & Yetton, 1995). Multiple dimension models consist of pragmatism-idealism and rationalism-humanism (Lessem & Neubauer, 1994), free will-determinism and accumulation of wealth-just enough (Kluckhohn & Strodbeck, 1961), five dimensions of Newman, Summer and Warren (1977), seven dimensions of Hampden-Turner and Trompenaars (1994), and four dimensions of Hofstede (1980) (Singh, Zhao, & Hu, 2003).

Among these studies, works of Hofstede (1980), the GLOBE-project proposed by House et al. (2004), studies of Trompenaars (1993), Hall (1976), and Schwartz (1992) are the leading ones which are mostly used to conceptualize cross-cultural communication differences. However, except for Hall's dimensions, other conceptualizations do not directly relate culture with communication (Kittler, Rygl, & Mackinnon, 2011). Hall stated that "culture is communication and communication is culture" (Hall, 1992, p. 212) (Kittler, Rygl, & Mackinnon, 2011).

Two communication styles, low and high context, proposed by Hall (1976) is analyzed by many researchers to understand cross-cultural differences. In high-context cultures, communication is indirect and vague and mostly receivers capture the meaning from the context; while in low-context, communication is direct and unambiguous, receiver is provided to understand what is meant. Countries are positioned in two groups based on Hall's concept of context (Hermeking, 2006). For example, some low-context countries include Switzerland, Germany, Scandinavia, and the USA; by contrast, Japan, China, Arab countries, and Greece are among the high-context countries. Because these two communication styles differ, it is considered that consumers within these contexts also differ and understand the same message in different ways; hence, it is essential to recognize these differences in order to develop effective websites (Fu & Wu, 2010).

Among different cultural frameworks, Hofstede's work is the most dominant one. In order to research websites, many studies either tested or replicated parts of Hofstede's dimensions (Pauwels, 2012). Hofstede's four cultural dimensions (power distance, individualism/collectivism, masculinity/femininity, and uncertainty avoidance), where each dimension reflects a distinct cultural value, have been widely used (Baack & Singh, 2007). The fifth dimension, time orientation, is added later to measure Asian cultures. The origins of these dimensions lie on general workplace, family and school relationships; however, they are used subsequently for other contexts (Li et al., 2009).

One of the biggest advantages of Hofstede's model is that it lessened the complexities of culture and treated culture composed of five dimensional concepts (Gevorgyan & Porter, 2008). Although Hofstede's dimensions are widely used, his work is highly criticized in terms of epistemological and methodological characteristics such as measuring culture uniquely through surveys, equating/reducing culture to the idea of a monolithic national culture, using old data of employees of one multinational (IBM) to extrapolate to national culture, and focusing on only four, later five dimensions (Baack & Singh, 2007; Pauwels, 2012).

The Interplay between Culture and Websites

Many studies in cross-cultural behavioral and cognitive psychology researched the way consumers behave, think, and assign value. There is accumulated knowledge and know-how about how to treat consumers to generate a strong communication and interaction with them. Thus, if companies want to attract local customers through websites, they have to adapt at least some key components of their websites (Tong & Robertson, 2008; Martinez-Lopez, Sousa, & Gazquez-Abad, 2011). Websites should adapt their content and structure to local cultural values, even though website adaptation is costly for companies (Luna et al., 2002; Cyr & Trevor-Smith, 2004). Thus, understanding culture is also vital for computer-mediated communication (Leung et al., 2005; Faiola & Matei, 2006). The studies on culture and websites explore cultural backgrounds of consumers and focus on integrating different cultural backgrounds into specific web design elements (Gevorgyan & Manucharova, 2009). Table 1 below illustrates the key characteristics of websites that make them cultural documents and the cultural implications those are used to communicate with culturally sensitive consumers.

Linguistic and graphical details are important for companies which operate in global markets to adapt their websites according to local tastes (Kalin, 1997; Robbins & Stylianou, 2003). For example, a standard term could be named as different in another culture; also a symbol or icon or color of a command could not be easily understood in another culture. Many academicians have studied the aesthetic design of website adaptation; however, content preparation has not been widely studied. Content preparation could be handled in two main dimensions: the information content to be provided and the structure of how this information is to be presented (Liao et al., 2008).

Table 1. Cultural implications of key web characteristics

Characteristic	Cultural implication of the characteristic
The web is a general open network having global accessibility	The web is viewed by people across culture thus lending itself to vast cultural variability
Internet interactive nature of the web	The interactive nature of the web makes it an ideal medium to create culturally sensitive dialogue
Web is characterized by hyperlinks and self-search option	Hyperlinks and self-search options rely on consumer motivation to browse, therefore if web content is not customized for global customers on individual bases the interactive efforts might be wasted
Web technologies can help capture customer data that can be used for mass customization	Using customer databases and software country specific profiles can be created and used to make the websites culturally adapted
Media convergence and broad-band technology make web an ideal medium to interact with audio, video, graphic and text	Media convergence on the web can be used to develop country-specific themes, pictures, videos, and sounds to create localized websites
On the web the capacity to hold the visitors attention "the flow state" is an important challenge	The websites that are culturally congruent or closely match the social perceptions of users are more likely to engage the users

Source: Singh, Zhao, & Hu (2005)

As the Internet becomes a major and popular source of information, it also has to be suitable for customers' cultural backgrounds (Tong & Robertson, 2008). Websites offer numerous opportunities for global companies to provide world-wide access to information about a company and its brands. The informational and branding capabilities of websites are known as the essential part of IMC (Martinez-Lopez, Sousa & Gazquez-Abad, 2011). Similarly, creating uniform brand image is one of the key components of Global Marketing Strategy (GMS) and websites with their global reach are mostly used to serve this purpose of displaying consistent brand image. Serving a global website is a convenient and effective way to reach customers throughout the world, however, it is essential to localize and adapt websites according to local cultural values in order to attract and retain more local consumers. Two mainstream schools of thought in international marketing, namely standardization and adaptation, force companies to decide whether to serve in a cost effective, corporate image focused and uniform way or in a way that is suitable for local values.

The longstanding debate of standardization and adaptation in international business and marketing also exist and valid for websites (Okazaki, 2004; Sinkovics, Yamin, & Hossinger, 2007; Okazaki & Skapa, 2008). Since websites are considered as global communication channels for companies which cross over national borders (Fletcher, 2006), this debate can become even more heated. This dichotomy has puzzled companies in the global arena (Singh, Zhao, & Hu, 2005). Running a standardized website for global brand consistency or running websites those are adapted to local tastes are two distinct options for companies (Tixier, 2005; Martinez-Lopez, Sousa, & Gazquez-Abad, 2011). A "*one size fits all*" approach leads global companies to use the same websites in all countries mainly by simply translating them, without any attempt for adaptation to the relevant cultural context. However, the same message in a uniform style does not produce the same meaning in every country, because cultural backgrounds of countries are distinct (Okazaki, 2004; Okazaki & Skapa, 2008).

When communication is standardized, website content is translated keeping the structure same. On the other hand, when a website is localized or adapted, not only language is adapted but also other components of website are adapted according to cultural, technical and administrative features. In so-called "glocalization," there is a balance between two polar strategies and when website adaptation constraints of both are taken into consideration (Tixier, 2005), glocalization is at the compromise position between two extremes (Fletcher, 2006). Selecting the appropriate strategy strongly depends on cost reduction, scale and scope effects, brand building, meeting consumer demand, and culture-bound preferences (Sinkovics, Yamin, & Hossinger, 2007; Okazaki & Skapa, 2008). Although there are alternatives for global companies in terms of standardization and adaptation, there is no clear and general conclusion on this topic (Harris, 1994).

As summarized above, technology, information technologies and computer-mediated communication have concurrent effects on both cultural divergence and convergence (Leung et al., 2005). This chapter will review and analyze previous major studies focusing on these effects in different fields.

METHODOLOGY

The data or in another term, academic papers, were collected through an extensive literature search with a combination of different keywords and different databases. To collect comprehensive data, we employed a two-step approach. As the first step, the studies were examined with a combination of such keywords as "culture," "web," "web site," "website," "cultural," "cross-culture," "cross-cultural," "cross-nation," "cross-national," and "country." These keywords were searched into title, keywords and abstract of papers separately, which generated tens of different searches. By searching into title, keywords, and abstract, the most relevant studies were collected. This initial search resulted in 157 papers.

At the second step, these 157 papers are content-analyzed by reading and cross-checking their abstracts to understand that we had collected right and appropriate papers for our chapter. Among them, 43 papers focus on organizational culture, deal with governmental websites in detail, and analyze websites within very technical terms which is beyond the scope of this chapter, were omitted. After all, we had 114 papers to review, those mostly focus on international business, international marketing, global branding, advertising, cross-cultural communication, computer-mediated communication, human-computer interaction, and others. The main users of the websites are considered to be consumers, not employees or citizens. The searches are done within the ABI Complete, ACM Digital Library, Cambridge Journals Online, Computers & Applied Sciences Complete, Directory of Open Access Journals, Econlit, Emerald Journals, Expanded Academic ASAP, IEEE Electronic Library Online, İktisat İşletme ve Finans, JSTOR, Oxford Journals Online, Psychology & Behavioral Sciences Collection, SAGE Premier, ScienceDirect: Subscribed Content (360 Search), Springer LINK Contemporary, Taylor & Francis Online, Web of Science, Wiley-Blackwell databases. Actually, these databases are not selected by the authors, but the search process took place with combined database search and it resulted with the databases listed above. The field is notably interdisciplinary, with papers published mainly in business, management, marketing, computer-mediated communications, advertising, and human-computer interaction disciplines.

A total of 114 studies (journal article, book chapter or conference proceeding) on culture and websites are reviewed. All these studies are peer-reviewed and indexed studies. Among 114 studies, 40 of them are selected from leading journals (mostly SSCI indexed) for detailed review according to the relevance of their research topic to the present chapter.-For each study, author name(s), journal/book/conference name, publication date, type of the study, research methodology, purpose, topic of interest, type of website, sampling used, cultural dimensions and countries are recorded in tables (see Table 2, Table 3, Table 4, Table 5, Table 6, Table 7, Table 8, and Table 9).

Table 2. Overview of Selected 40 Papers on Culture and Websites Interaction

Author(s) (Year)	Journal	Type of paper	Research Methodology	Methodology / Data collection	Purpose / Concern	Topic of interest	Type of website	Cultural dimensions used	Countries covered
Singh, Zhao and Hu (2003)	J of Global Information Management	Empirical	Content analysis	40 US companies' websites in domestic and Chinese market are content analyzed	Addressing the localization deficit in literature and providing marketers and web designers with insights into website localization	IMC	General / Company websites	Hofstede - 4 dimensions and Hall dimensions	US, China
Singh and Matsuo (2004)	J of Business Research	Empirical	Content analysis	45 Japanese and 48 US websites are content analyzed in the same sector, all webpages in websites	Proposing a framework to measure cultural values embedded in Web sites and testing it using a content analysis of U.S. and Japanese company Web sites	IMC	General / Company websites	Hofstede - 4 dimensions and Hall - 2 dimensions	Japan, US
Singh, Zhao and Hu (2005)	International Marketing Review	Empirical	Content analysis	93 Websites from 4 countries are content analyzed (25 Japanese, 26 US, 21 Indian and 21 Chinese)	Exploring the depiction of cultural values on international websites	IMC	General / Company websites	Hofstede - 4 dimensions and Hall dimensions	4 countries (China, India, Japan, US)
Baack and Singh (2007)	J of Business Research	Empirical	Content analysis and consumer perceptions	Two step study, first step: content analysis of 274 websites from 15 countries and second step: 169 attendees fill out questionnaires after visiting a Taiwanese website for evaluating adaptation degree	Testing the applicability of the cultural frameworks of Hofstede and Schwartz to study the reflection of culture in web communications	IMC	General / Company websites	Hofstede and Schwartz dimensions	15 countries (Saudi Arabia, Bahrain, Egypt, Brazil, China, France, Germany, Hong Kong, Italy, Japan, Malaysia, Mexico, Portugal, Spain, Taiwan, Thailand, US)
Okazaki and Rivas (2002)	Internet Research	Empirical	Content analysis	20 MNCs' websites in 3 countries (60 websites in total) are content analyzed, websites are selected from product based websites	Constructing a research framework for cross-cultural comparison of corporate web pages	S-A, IMC	Product-based	Hofstede - 1 dimension	Japan, Spain, US

Table 3. Overview of Selected 40 Papers on Culture and Websites Interaction, continued

Author(s) (Year)	Journal	Type of paper	Research Methodology	Methodology / Data collection	Purpose / Concern	Topic of interest	Type of website	Cultural dimensions used	Countries covered
Okazaki (2004)	Internet Research	Empirical	Content analysis	150 product-based Japanese websites are content analyzed in a comparison with Spain and US	Determining whether Japanese MNCs' web communication strategies are standardized or localized	S-A, IMC	Product-based	NA	Japan, Spain, US
Okazaki (2005)	European J of Marketing	Empirical	Content analysis	206 websites of 64 US brands for UK (57), France (49), Germany (57) and Spain (43) are content analyzed	Exploring US brands' website standardization	S-A, IMC	General / Company websites	NA	5 countries (US, UK, France, Germany, Spain)
Okazaki and Skapa (2008)	European J of Marketing	Empirical	Content analysis	34 MNCs' websites from 100 Top Global Brands are content analyzed in a comparison with German, Polish and Czech websites	Examining American MNC's web site standardization in Poland and the Czech Republic	S-A, IMC	General / Company websites	NA	4 countries (US, Germany, Poland, Czech Republic)
Cyr and Trevor-Smith (2004)	J of the American Society for Information Science and Technology	Empirical	Focus groups - Content analysis	Focus groups for survey instrument development and observations from 90 municipal websites	Exploring issues of user interface design and experience, including culturally preferred design elements	HCI	General / Company websites	NA	Germany, Japan, US
Cyr, Head and Larios (2010)	International J of Human-Computer Studies	Empirical	Consumer perceptions - Experiments	Laboratory experiment, Eye-tracking, survey and interviews, 90 participants from 3 countries (30 for each), only one website (SonyStyle websites)	The effects of color on trust, satisfaction and e-loyalty	HCI	E-commerce	NA	Canada, Germany, Japan
Luna, Peracchio and Juan (2002)	J of the Academy of Marketing Science	Empirical	Literature review - Experiments	Proposing a cognitive framework and then testing it with 3 experiments	Examining some of the site content characteristics that can lead website visitors to an optimal navigation experience	IMC	NA	NA	Spain, US

Table 4. Overview of Selected 40 Papers on Culture and Websites Interaction (continued)

Author(s) (Year)	Journal	Type of paper	Research Methodology	Methodology / Data collection	Purpose / Concern	Topic of interest	Type of website	Cultural dimensions used	Countries covered
Zhao, Massey, Murphy and Fang (2003)	Prometheus	Empirical	Content analysis	100 Chinese and American websites (50 websites for each) are content analyzed	Testing the proposition that the technology of the Internet and Web offers a basis for culturally-neutral, computer-mediated communication	CMC	General / Company websites	Hofstede - 2 dimensions and Hall's dimensions	China, US
Tixier (2005)	Thunderbird International Business Review	Empirical	Interview	64 interviews from 4 US and 1 French company for each sector, 300 websites	Examining how various sectors of industry actually localize their Internet sites in the United States and France	S-A, IMC	General / Company websites	NA	US, France
Burgmann, Kitchen and Williams (2006)	Marketing Intelligence & Planning	Empirical	Content analysis	Observations from 105 websites (15 Banking and 90 higher education websites) with a 1-7 scale	Exploring the impact of culture on online international marketing	IMC	General / Company websites	Hofstede - 2 dimensions	Germany, Greece, UK
Faiola and Matei (2006)	J of Computer-Mediated Communication	Empirical	Consumer perceptions - Experiments	53 questionnaires from 1615 invitations, attendees visited websites and completed a post-task questionnaire, also tracked while completing tasks within websites (Prototype website)	Exploring web designers' cultural cognitive styles and their impact on user responses	CMC	General / Company websites	NA	US, China
Fletcher (2006)	J of Communication Management	Conceptual	Literature review	Literature review into the variables that impact on both culture and cross-cultural comparison of website content, design and structure	Highlighting the need for cultural sensitivity in designing websites	CMC	NA	NA	Australia
Hermeking (2006)	J of Computer-Mediated Communication	Empirical	Literature review, discussion and content analysis	Discussion, literature review, 6 website observations (Amazon, ABB, Sony, Coca-Cola, Mercedes-Benz and Lancia)	Discussing cultural influences on website design, related structural design criteria, basic conditions, and complementary criteria	HCI	General / Company websites	Hofstede and Hall dimensions	6 countries (France, Germany, UK, US, Japan, Italy)

Table 5. Overview of Selected 40 Papers on Culture and Websites Interaction (continued)

Author(s) (Year)	Journal	Type of paper	Research Methodology	Methodology / Data collection	Purpose / Concern	Topic of interest	Type of website	Cultural dimensions used	Countries covered
Steenkamp and Geyskens (2006)	J of Marketing	Empirical	Consumer perceptions and attitudes	Data from 8886 consumers from 23 countries, involving 30 websites of 16 consumer packaged goods companies, country data from secondary data	Examining how country characteristics affect the perceived value of a brand manufacturer's website	IMC	General / Company websites	Hofstede - 1 dimension, National identity	23 countries (listed in the study)
Liao, Proctor and Salvendy (2007)	Behaviour & Information Technology	Conceptual	Literature review - Model proposition	Literature review and model proposition	Proposing a conceptual model on content preparation for cross-cultural e-commerce	HCI	E-commerce	Hofstede - 5 dimensions	NA
Sinkovics, Yamin and Hossinger (2007)	J of Electronic Commerce Research	Empirical	Content analysis	300 websites of 100 German corporates are content analyzed both the domestic and target country versions by 2 independent researchers	Exploring 100 German companies' websites by employing a cultural value analysis	S-A, IMC	E-commerce	Hofstede - 4 dimensions and Hall - 2 dimensions	Germany, US, UK, Latin America
Gevorgyan and Porter (2008)	J of Website Promotion	Empirical	Consumer perceptions	Questionnaires from 67 American and 62 Chinese students, convenience sampling	Examining whether internet users' cultural backgrounds influence how they perceived importance of specific web design features	IMC	General / Company websites	Hofstede - 2 dimensions	China, US
Gevorgyan and Manucharova (2009)	J of Computer-Mediated Communication	Empirical	Content analysis and consumer attitudes	Pretests, two focus groups for instrument development, 370 questionnaires and 6 coders rated websites, 1055 favorite websites (700 American and 442 Chinese, minus 87 overlaps)	Examining the effects of Internet users' cultural backgrounds on the attitudes toward Web design elements	CMC	General / Company websites	Hofstede - 2 dimensions	US, China

Table 6. Overview of Selected 40 Papers on Culture and Websites Interaction (continued)

Author(s) (Year)	Journal	Type of paper	Research Methodology	Methodology / Data collection	Purpose / Concern	Topic of interest	Type of website	Cultural dimensions used	Countries covered
Nacar and Burnaz (2011)	Qualitative Market Research: An International J	Empirical	Content analysis	108 MNCs' web sites are content analyzed	Analyzing the appropriateness of the information content and organization of web sites for Turkish local cultural values	IMC	General / Company websites	NA	Turkey
Fang and Rau (2003)	Ergonomics	Empirical	Experiment - Consumer perceptions	8 Taiwanese and 7 American participated in the study (only Yahoo! Website)	Investigating the effects of cultural differences in using Web searching tools	HCI	General / Company websites	NA	US, China
Robbins and Stylianou (2003)	Information & Management	Empirical	Content analysis	90 corporate (16 countries and 20 different industries) websites from Fortune Global 500 corporations	Developing a conceptual model to differentiate website content from design	CMC	General / Company websites	NA	16 countries (UK, US, Finland, Netherlands, Norway, Sweden, France, Italy, Venezuela, Germany, Switzerland, India, Korea, Malaysia, Taiwan, Japan)
Maynard and Tian (2004)	Public Relations Review	Empirical	Content analysis	Observations of 100 global brands' Chinese websites	Identifying branding and glocalization strategies of global brands	S-A (Gloc.)	General / Company websites	NA	13 countries (China, US, Germany, Japan, UK, France, Italy, Switzerland, Netherlands, Sweden, Bermuda, Finland, Korea)

Table 7. Overview of Selected 40 Papers on Culture and Websites Interaction (continued)

Author(s) (Year)	Journal	Type of paper	Research Methodology	Methodology / Data collection	Purpose / Concern	Topic of interest	Type of website	Cultural dimensions used	Countries covered
Cho and Cheon (2005)	J of Advertising	Empirical	Content analysis	200 corporate websites (50 for each country) are content analyzed in terms of inter-activity	Cross-cultural examination of interactivity of websites	IMC	General / Company websites	Hofstede - 2 dimensions and Hall's dimensions	4 countries (US, UK, Japan, South Korea)
Leidner and Kayworth (2006)	MIS Quarterly	Conceptual	Literature review	The development of criteria for the types of studies to be included in our analysis, a literature search strategy, and an analysis scheme outlining the documentation and coding of the various studies, 82 articles reviewed	Providing a review of this literature in order to lend insights into our under-standing of the linkages between IT and culture	CMC	NA	Hofstede's, Hall's and Trompenaar's etc. all dimen-sions	NA
Kim and Lee (2006)	International J of Consumer Studies	Empirical	Consumer perceptions and attitudes	Questionnaires with 278 US and 347 Korean, A retail website (JCPenney)	Comparing Internet users in terms of their perceptions of retail website quality	IMC	E-com-merce	NA	US, Korea
Würtz (2006)	J of Computer-Mediated Com-munication	Empirical	Content analysis	Observations from McDon-ald's websites of 9 countries and qualitative analysis	Exploring and identifying the strategies used by high-context cultures in utiliz-ing the Internet for communica-tion and market-ing purposes	IMC	General / Company websites	Hall's dimen-sions	9 countries (Japan, China, Korea, Germany, Denmark, Nor-way, Finland, US)
Lituchy and Barra (2008)	J of Engineering and Technology Management	Empirical	Case study - Observations	A qualitative case-study is used, 5 researchers analyzed 10 airline and 11 hotel websites	Examining how international differences affect website design	CMC	E-com-merce	NA	NA
Yun, Park and Ha (2008)	J of Interactive Marketing	Empirical	Content analysis	Observations from 200 retail websites	Examining the nature of online consumer-gener-ated communica-tions	CMC	General / Company websites	NA	US, South Korea

Table 8. Overview of Selected 40 Papers on Culture and Websites Interaction (continued)

Author(s) (Year)	Journal	Type of paper	Research Methodology	Methodology / Data collection	Purpose / Concern	Topic of interest	Type of website	Cultural dimensions used	Countries covered
Li, Hess, McNab and Yu (2009)	ACM SIGMIS Database	Empirical	Consumer perceptions and attitudes	Subjects from two countries evaluated country-specific versions of a personal web portal (MyYahoo) with TAM model in a laboratory study (371 US and 273 Chinese)	Investigating the influence of national cultural values on acceptance of a personal web portal	CMC	Product-based (portal)	Hofstede - 5 dimensions	US, China
Fu and Wu (2010)	Online Information Review	Empirical	Content analysis	A means-end comparison procedure, 217 websites with the phrasal containing credit card are content analyzed according to 30 variables of credit cards	Understanding whether the differentiation of culture connotations is directly reflected in the design of web advertisements and whether the text content of web ads is a reliable indicator of different context cultures	CMC	General / Company websites	Hall's dimensions	4 countries (China, Taiwan, UK, US)
Kim and Kuljis (2010)	J of Computing and Information Technology	Empirical	Content analysis	Observations from 40 charity websites	Exploring the effects of culture on web design	HCI	General / Company websites	Hofstede - 4 dimensions	UK, South Korea
Usunier and Roulin (2010)	J of Business Communication	Empirical	Content analysis	597 B2B Web sites in 57 countries are content analyzed	Investigating how communication styles influence Web site design and content	IMC	General / Company websites	Hall's dimensions	57 countries (listed in the study)
Martinez-Lopez, Sousa and Gazquez-Abad (2011)	J of Marketing Theory and Practice	Empirical	Conceptual model - ad hoc qualitative study	An integrative conceptual model is built with propositions and an ad hoc exploratory qualitative study was developed	Discussing the likely cultural rapprochement of markets as a consequence of the mass use of the Internet worldwide	IMC	NA	NA	NA
Pollach (2011)	J of Business Communication	Empirical	Consumer attitudes	521 surveys (250 Europe and 271 Asia)	Investigating people's interest in the content of corporate websites	CMC	General / Company websites	NA	19 countries (compared Europe and Asia)

Table 9. Overview of Selected 40 Papers on Culture and Websites Interaction (continued)

Author(s) (Year)	Journal	Type of paper	Research Methodology	Methodology / Data collection	Purpose / Concern	Topic of interest	Type of website	Cultural dimensions used	Countries covered
Zahedi and Bansal (2011)	J of Management Information Systems	Empirical	Two step, interpretive qualitative approach and content analysis	Interpreting qualitatively Grounded Theory to develop a new theory and then testing it quantitatively; Hospital, university and bank websites (opposed to e-commerce websites), 245 websites for the first step and 728 websites for the second step	Exploring the cultural content of website images and developing a theory for Web-image signifiers	HCI	General / Company websites	Hofstede - 5 dimensions	14 countries (Costa Rica, Greece, Guatemala, Hong Kong, Jamaica, Japan, Mexico, Nigeria, Pakistan, Sweden, Taiwan, UK, US, Yugoslavia) for the first step and 39 countries for the second step
Pauwels (2012)	J of Computer-Mediated Communication	Conceptual	Literature review / Framework	Literature review / Framework proposal	how to decode/disclose the cultural information both in the form and content of websites	NA	NA	NA	NA

J: Journal, **CMC**: Computer-mediated communication, **HCI**: Human-computer interaction, **IMC**: Integrated marketing communications, **S-A**: Standardization – Adaptation, **Gloc**: Glocalization, **NA**: Not available

MAJOR RESEARCH ON CULTURE AND WEBSITES

There are numerous academic studies on culture among which some of them already became classics. Various cross-cultural studies analyzed the impact of culture on consumers' response to varying marketing stimuli but this was not the case for websites. Standardization and adaptation of websites are studied in the areas such as human-computer interactions (HCI), computer mediated communication (CMC), integrated marketing communication (IMC), other consumer and marketing applications, and others. Despite the growing use of websites as important IMC channels, there is a lack of a comprehensive study that critically reviews the existing and leading literature on culture and website interaction. Thus, a closer evaluation of these studies reveals a potential gap to be filled. In the following sections, first, a quick overview of general characteristics of 114 papers will be provided and then a selected 40 papers will be reviewed in detail.

Characteristics of Papers Under Consideration

A total of 114 papers are written by 208 different authors and the leading authors of this area are "Singh" (7), "Cyr" (5), "Kim" (4), "Okazaki" (4), "Zhao" (4), "Lee" (3), and "Wu" (3) (numbers in parenthesis indicates the papers of the author within 114 papers). For the author groups, the leading groups are "Luna, Peracchio & Juan" (2), "Okazaki" (2), "Robbins & Stylianou" (2), and "Singh, Zhao, & Hu" (2) (numbers in parenthesis indicates the papers of the author group within 114 papers). No date limitation is put while searching databases, but all the papers appear as published after 2000. The number of papers peaked in 2006, 2007, and again in 2010.

Of the 114 papers, 101 (88.6%) of them are published as "journal articles," 9 (7.9%) of them as "book chapter," and 4 (3.5%) of them as "conference proceedings." The papers focusing on culture and websites are published in 83 different sources: the leading publications are listed as "Journal of Computer-Mediated Communication" (7), "Usability and Internationalization" (5), "International Marketing Review" (4), "Internet Research" (4), "Journal of Global Information Management" (3), "Journal of Management Information Systems" (3), and "Online Information Review" (3) (numbers in parenthesis indicates the papers of publications within 114 papers). Overall, communication and marketing journals, especially those with a focus on integrated marketing communication and computer-mediated communication, dominate the list of the most influential journals.

Among the 114 papers, 103 (90.4%) of them are "empirical" and 11 (9.6%) of them are "conceptual" papers. 91 (79.8%) papers used "single research methodology," where 23 (20.2%) of them used "mixed and multiple research methodology" such as experiments with content analysis, interviews with surveys, content analysis with surveys, among others. Without any doubt, "content analysis" is the most dominant research method used to analyze websites; 52 (45.6%) papers used "content analysis" as the research method. Thirty-five (30.7%) papers measured "consumer perceptions and attitudes" through "questionnaires/surveys," thus, surveys are the second leading research method. These two are followed by "experiments" (14 papers/12.3%) and "literature reviews" (14 papers/12.3%). In addition, 95 (83.3%) papers have "single topic of interests" and 10 of them (8.8%) have "multiple topic of interests" and also 9 of them (7.9) could not be categorized among the current categorization list. The leading topics of interest of papers are "computer-mediated communication" – 43 (37.7%) papers–, "integrated marketing communication" – 39 (34.2%) papers–, "human-computer interaction" – 20 (17.5%) papers–, "standardization vs. adaptation" – 11 (9.6%) papers–, and "branding" – 2 (1.8%) papers.

In terms of types of websites analyzed, 19 (16.7%) of the papers did not indicate any "type of website." Seventy (61.4%) papers analyzed "general/company websites," 19 (16.7%) papers analyzed "e-commerce websites," and 6 (5.3%) papers analyzed "product-based websites." Among the reviewed 114 papers, 81 (71.1%) of them stated "the number of websites" they analyzed. A regular paper analyzed an average of 162 websites ranging from 1 website to 4,000 websites (the later is a technical one in which 4,000 websites were analyzed with a special program). As stated above, some papers measured "consumer perceptions and attitudes." Only 12 (10.5%) papers stated "the number of consumers surveyed." A regular paper surveyed an average of 1,742 consumers ranging from 45 consumers to 8,886 consumers.

Interestingly, among 114 papers, only 52 (45.6%) papers stated the "cultural dimensions" they used. Other papers either did not use any cultural dimension or did not explicitly state them. Among 52 papers, 33 (63.5%) of them used "single cultural dimension" (either Hall's or Hofstede's dimensions) and 19 (36.5%) of them used "more than one cultural dimension." "Hofstede's dimensions" are the most dominant perspective to measure culture. Forty-nine (94.2%) papers used "Hofstede's dimensions," followed by "Hall's dimensions" in 19 (36.5%) papers, "Trompenaars' dimensions" in 5 (9.6%) papers, and "Schwartz's dimensions" in only 1 (1.9%) paper. Four (7.7%) papers used "cultural dimensions of Hofstede, Hall, Trompenaars, etc." in the same study. Among other cultural dimensions used, Hofstede deserves special attention. Among the 49 papers that used "Hofstede's dimensions," 17 (34.7%) of them used "5 dimensions," 17 (34.7%) papers used "4 dimensions," 1 (2.0%) paper used "3 dimensions," 8 (16.3%) papers used "2 dimensions," and 6 (12.2%) papers used only "1 dimension."

In terms of countries analyzed, among 114 papers, 97 (85.1%) of them stated "the number of the countries they analyzed." A regular paper analyzed an average 7 countries ranging from 1 country to 57 countries. Among the number of countries, 38 (39.2%) papers compared "2 countries" and this could be considered as the generic number for this area. These 97 papers analyzed 85 different countries around the world. The most popular country is "the US" with 66 (57.9%) papers, followed by "China" in 34 (29.8%) papers, "Germany" in 32 (28.1%) papers, "UK" in 30 (26.3%) papers, and "Japan" in 28 (24.6%) papers. Of the 97 papers which noted the number of countries analyzed, one used "Arab countries" and another one used "Latin America" as one country.

The extensive review of studies on culture and website interaction has led the researchers to make a selection for further detailed analysis. Among 114 studies reviewed, 40 of them are selected from leading journals (mostly SSCI indexed) mainly according to the relevance of their research focus to the present chapter.

Detailed Review of Selected Research Papers

Previous leading empirical studies in the area which are at most a decade old are reviewed for the purpose of this chapter. The research question, "how are cultural dimensions, values and norms reflected on websites?" is examined in depth. Thus, the relationship between cultural dimensions and websites is explored and the contribution of cultural dimensions to the field and reassessment of current theories on websites are analyzed. The accumulated knowledge on culture and websites will provide an understanding of the interaction between culture and websites and enable to identify key concepts and future projections.

It is aimed to critically review the current status of culture and websites research and provide a systematic review of previous leading empirical studies with respect to evaluation and comparison criteria, topic of interest, type of website analyzed, cultural dimensions used, comparison approaches, methods, geographies covered, among others. As the first step, the papers overviewed are classified and summarized. For this purpose, a new and integrated framework is developed and the review is based on this framework. In line with the aim of the chapter, the comprehensive framework is used to explain issues of culture and websites in details. Also, a number of conceptual and methodological issues that deserve attention are discussed. It is not the focus of this chapter to advocate standardization or adaptation of websites. By reviewing current literature on culture and websites, the co-existence of two different approaches will be presented. The basic questions answered by previous studies are mostly as follows: Does culture matter online? How does a company present itself on website? What different web communication strategies are employed? How is reputation and brand essence managed on website?

Previous research on culture and websites explored issues such as website interactivity, website usage, interface design, website usability, website quality, navigation and their perception by global consumers (Singh, Zhao, & Hu, 2005; Hermeking, 2006). According to Pollach (2011), there are two lines of research in this field: one is how a firm presents itself on website, the other one is the effectiveness of website. When the research area is categorized into more detailed parts, 4 different research streams could be identified. These research streams focus on characteristics of consumers from different cultures; company strategies in terms of standardization/adaptation dichotomy (e.g., Okazaki, 2004); content, design and structure of websites from different cultures and cultural recognition of web designers to understand how they develop web design. As seen from different research streams, the area is interdisciplinary in nature and for that reason some research streams may partially overlap with other ones.

Tables 2 through 9 provide a detailed overview of the key features of selected 40 papers on culture and websites. For each paper, information is provided on the name of journal/book/conference, type of paper, research methods used, research methodology, sample size, purpose of paper, topic of interest, type of website, cultural dimensions used and countries covered. There is no paper on culture and websites before the year of 2000; it is encouraging to see that the interest on culture and websites has increased over time, as evidenced by all the publications having appeared after 2000.

Tables 2 through 9 indicate clearly there is an emerging body of culture and websites research. Nevertheless, there are still a number of conceptual and methodological issues that need to be addressed if this area is to fulfill its high potential for global companies and also for international business and marketing theory. In the next sections, conceptual issues (topic of interest, cultural dimensions used, type of websites) and methodological issues (type of papers, research methodology, sampling, sample size, countries covered) will be discussed to present the current situation based on a comprehensive framework and detect potential progress areas.

Conceptual Issues

In this section, topic of interest, cultural dimensions used and type of website studied in the selected papers will be analyzed in details.

Topic of Interest

Okazaki and Rivas (2002), Okazaki (2004; 2005), and Okazaki and Skapa (2008) treated websites as corporate communication and promotion channels, especially for advertising and promotional campaigns. The main focus of their study was standardization of corporate websites; they were proponents of standardization and seek evidence for it. In addition to these, Okazaki and Skapa (2008) based their research on Global Marketing Strategy (GMS) theory. As opposed to Okazaki and Rivas (2002) and Okazaki (2004; 2005); Singh, Zhao and Hu (2003; 2005) and Singh and Matsuo (2004) advocated the use of country-specific websites, or in other terms, adaptation of websites to local culture. For them, country-specific websites are more usable, rich and interactive thus lead to high web traffic than others. All the studies of Singh, Zhao and Hu (2003; 2005), Singh and Matsuo (2004), and Baack and Singh (2007) are related with integrated marketing communications topic and analyzed websites with this perspective.

In other research by Maynard and Tian (2004) and Tixier (2005), hybrid strategy is advocated and "glocalization of websites" is seen as the best alternative. Not as the opponent or proponent of neither standardization nor adaptation, Sinkovics, Yamin, and Hossinger (2007) also focus on standardization and adaptation of websites with an integrated marketing communication perspective.

Apart from studies listed above, Cyr and Trevor-Smith (2004), Cyr, Head and Larios (2010), Liao, Proctor and Salvendy (2007), Fang and Rau (2003), Zahedi and Bansal (2011), Hermeking (2006), and Kim and Kuljis (2010) have analyzed websites from the perspective of human-computer interaction (HCI). Cyr and Trevor-Smith (2004) analyzed website design consisting of symbols and graphics, color preferences, site features (links, maps, search functions, page layout), language, and content, while Cyr, Head and Larios (2010) analyzed color as a website design element--these two studies being truly interdisciplinary. Zahedi and Bansal (2011) conducted a study for similar purposes; they analyzed web images to develop a theory for web image signifiers.

Integrated Marketing Communication (IMC) is a topic of interest which is highly studied by researchers. The exemplary and leading ones are summarized briefly in Tables 2 through 9. Luna, Peracchio, and Juan (2002) analyzed websites with an IMC perspective and answered how to design websites in both content and structure based cultural congruity. Martinez-Lopez, Sousa and Gazquez-Abad (2011) analyzed their conceptual model with a qualitative study to discuss how websites affect cultural convergence with an IMC viewpoint. Also, Cho and Cheon (2005) analyzed three dimensions of interactivity, namely consumer-message, consumer-marketer, and consumer-consumer interactivity.

Another topic of interest for researchers is computer-mediated communication (CMC). These studies mostly focused on web design and perception of web design elements. Leading studies of CMC are conducted by Robbins and Stylianou (2003), Fletcher (2006), Faiola and Matei (2006), and Gevorgyan and Manucharova (2009).

Cultural Dimensions Used

Out of selected 40 papers, a total of 19 did not use any cultural dimension or did not indicate the cultural dimensions they used. The bulk of research on culture and websites takes Hall's model and/or Hofstede's key dimensions of culture as its prime conceptual framework (Pauwels, 2012). Detailed analysis showed that 8 papers used only Hofstede's dimensions varying from only 1 dimension to all 5 dimensions (Zahedi & Bansal, 2011; Burgmann, Kitchen, & Williams, 2006; Okazaki & Rivas, 2002). Okazaki and Rivas (2002) focused on individualism/collectivism dimension of Hofstede. Gevorgyan and Porter (2008), Gevorgyan and Manucharova (2009), and Burgmann, Kitchen, and Williams (2006) used two dimensions, namely power distance and uncertainty, that are identified as under-researched by those researchers. Liao, Proctor and Salvendy (2007) used all the dimensions of Hofstede in their conceptual model. They did not test the model or Hofstede's dimension; however, they used them to construct theoretical structure. Li et al. (2009) and Zahedi and Bansal (2011) also used all dimensions of Hofstede to categorize countries and explain differences. Besides, Kim and Kuljis (2010) used only 4 dimensions of Hofstede.

Among the total sample, three papers used Hall's dimensions merely (Würtz, 2006; Fu & Wu, 2010; Usunier & Roulin, 2010). For them, Hall's dimensions are less criticized, more flexible to measure culture, and more appropriate to analyze websites.

Both Hofstede's and Hall's dimensions are used in combination in seven papers (Hermeking, 2006; Sinkovics, Yamin, & Hossinger, 2007; Singh, Zhao, & Hu, 2003; 2005). Singh, Zhao and Hu (2003) used four dimensions of Hofstede and two dimensions of Hall. To extend their analysis to websites, they generated web-specific cultural elements. Accepted as the most typical studies in the field, Singh, Zhao and Hu (2003; 2005), Singh and Matsuo (2004) and Sinkovics, Yamin and Hossinger (2007) used four dimensions of Hofstede and Hall's dimensions.

In a similar vein, Zhao et al. (2003) and Cho and Cheon (2005) used Hofstede's two dimensions plus Hall's dimensions. Zhao et al. (2003) used individualism/collectivism and time orientation, whereas Cho and Cheon (2005) used power distance and individualism/collectivism. Hermeking (2006) used all the dimensions of Hofstede and Hall in order to comprehensively explain and discuss cultural influences.

Moreover, three papers used Hofstede's dimensions with other cultural variables, namely Schwartz's dimensions, Trompenaars' dimensions and national identity by Baack and Singh (2007), Leidner and Kayworth (2006) and Steenkamp and Geyskens (2006), respectively. Steenkamp and Geyskens (2006) used only one dimension of Hofstede and added national identity as a cultural construct in their study. However, Baack and Singh (2007) criticized that many studies in this area were based on one cultural framework and then they used both Hofstede's and Schwartz's dimensions together. This made their study unique among not only selected 40 papers but also 114 papers reviewed for the present chapter. They stated that only Hofstede's or Schwartz's dimensions would not be appropriate to measure culture, rather, an amalgamation of both would serve better than their separate use.

In fact, culture is not static, especially under many effects of a changing world and when considering the dynamics of an emerging economy under transition, culture itself presents dynamism. Also, the impact of culture on different behavioral patterns could be contingent depending on the nature of the subject matter under analysis. There are several cross-cultural studies as listed above which compare countries by correlating the analyzed variables with Hofstede's scores; this tendency is widely observed especially in standardization/adaptation literature. However, Nacar and Burnaz (2011) focused on a specific country, Turkey, in which foreign multinationals operate.

Rather than comparing home and host countries of foreign multinationals based on certain dimensions, they found more appropriate to assess on what terms and to what degree these companies could adapt or standardize their global communication channels, namely their websites. This approach has its basis in the literature, under the concept of "thing centeredness" (Applbaum & Jordt, 1996). In the study conducted by Nacar and Burnaz (2011) the cultural values of dimensions were drawn directly from Turkish and global websites of companies, not from general and macro cultural scores. The research conducted by Okazaki (2004; 2005) and Okazaki and Skapa (2008) offer similar examples; they referred to Hofstede's dimensions but did not use them in their analyses.

Type of Website

Among selected 40 papers, five papers analyzed e-commerce websites (Cyr, Head & Larios, 2010; Liao, Proctor, & Salvendy, 2007; Sinkovics, Yamin, & Hossinger, 2007; Kim & Lee, 2006; Lituchy & Barra, 2008). Different from other studies, Lituchy and Barra (2008) focused on airline and hotel companies' websites.

A total of 27 papers analyzed company websites; Okazaki (2005), Okazaki and Skapa (2008), Singh, Zhao and Hu (2003; 2005), Singh and Matsuo (2004), and Baack and Singh (2007) are among them. Cyr and Trevor-Smith (2004) and Kim and Kuljis (2010) did not focus on company websites, but municipal and charity websites, respectively. This makes their studies original in terms of analyzing non-profit organizations' websites. Zahedi and Bansal (2011) analyzed websites from three distinct domains, namely universities, hospitals, and banks. On the other hand, while Tixier (2005) analyzed company websites from 13 different sectors, Burgmann, Kitchen, and Williams (2006) focused only on banking and higher education websites.

Among the papers reviewed, only three analyzed product-based websites prepared directly for specific products. Only one paper analyzed a prototype website; Faiola and Matei (2006) studied a prototype website designed by Chinese and US designers and evaluated later by the consumers. Five other papers did not indicate the type of websites analyzed. It is seen that mostly empirical studies analyzed B2C websites, however, Usunier and Roulin (2010) analyzed B2B company websites, and this is the only study that analyzed this type of website.

Methodological Issues

In this section, types of papers, research methodology and data collection, sample size and countries covered in selected 40 papers will be analyzed in detail.

Type of Paper

The detailed review reveals that only four papers are conceptual while the remaining 36 papers are empirical. Key features of conceptual studies are summarized in this section; however, empirical studies are studied in the next section. Developing and studying conceptual papers are important because majority of studies are exploratory in nature, especially the studies that content-analyzed websites. Few studies examine particular hypotheses or base their work on a particular conceptual model. In order to decrease exploratory nature of this area, more conceptual studies those develop new models or offer the improved ones, need to be encouraged.

In his conceptual article, Pauwels (2012) provided the foundations of a 6-phased multimodal framework for analyzing websites from both a medium specific and socio-cultural perspective. He did not analyze any country or website; he proposed the procedure to analyze cultural information on websites. In a similar vein, Leidner and Kayworth (2006) reviewed literature to understand the link between culture and IT and did not analyze any country or website.

After an extensive literature review, Liao, Proctor and Salvendy (2007) proposed a conceptual model which shows how to prepare content for cross-cultural e-commerce websites. This model takes cognitive abilities, cognitive styles, cultural patterns, and infrastructural and economic development into consideration. Fletcher (2006) also reviewed literature by focusing on the effects of culture on website content, design and structure and he concluded there is need for culturally-sensitive websites.

Research Method and Data Collection

Many of the studies on culture and websites asserted that global consumers prefer locally adapted websites and "culture matters" websites (Martinez-Lopez, Sousa, & Gazquez-Abad, 2011). New scales were developed to measure cultural dimensions of websites (Gevorgyan & Manucharova, 2009). Okazaki and Rivas (2002) developed a new framework based on traditional advertising content and Okazaki and Rivas (2002) and Okazaki (2004) cross-culturally compared corporate websites using this framework which includes information content, cultural values, and creative strategies. Content analysis was used to measure differences. Information content classification is based on the seminal study of Resnik and Stern (1977) which is replicated by almost all the studies in communication and advertising content studies.

Similar to Okazaki and Rivas (2002), Nacar and Burnaz (2011) also analyzed information content, including language and organization of websites in their studies and developed an original assessment sheet. While Okazaki and Rivas (2002) and Okazaki (2004) used information content, cultural values and creative strategies as the framework, Okazaki (2005) Okazaki and Skapa (2008) used four functions of website content, namely transaction, communication, relationship and interactivity.

Singh, Zhao and Hu (2005) analyzed whether websites are culturally neutral or cultural documents and explored how cultural values are depicted on websites. They claimed it would enable to understand whether to communicate through standardized or localized websites with global consumers. Based on the previous research, they used a cultural value framework for website analysis. They compared four nations (China, India, Japan, and the USA) and two different industries (electronic and automotive) using this framework. In addition, Baack and Singh (2007) analyzed 15 nations with Hofstede and Schwartz's cultural typologies adapted for web communications and consumer preferences for a culturally adapted website were explored. They used factor analysis which is not so common in this field.

Maynard and Tian (2005) analyzed websites of top global brands in Chinese culture in order to understand the glocalization strategies of them. They used content analysis to explore the theory of glocalization and examined local presence on websites of top global brands. Liao, Proctor and Salvendy (2007) stated that information quality is an important criterion for e-commerce success which directly influences online shopping experience, purchase intention, and website revisit intention. For e-commerce websites, competitors are just one-click away, thus companies have to make consumers experience positively. However, their study showed that companies give the biggest importance to visually attractive and enjoyable websites but disregard information content of websites.

Luna, Peracchio and Juan (2002) analyzed the impact of culture on websites by examining website navigation behavior and the persuasion, revisit and purchase intentions of consumers. They proposed a cognitive framework and tested with 3 separate experiments. In a similar study, Fang and Rau (2003) also tested their proposed hypothesis with two separate experiments and explored usability of web search tools by comparing consumers in China and the USA. To see industry effects, Singh, Zhao and Hu (2003) analyzed only one sector and compared the US with China. Another study of the same authors dated 2005 has a similar perspective. Nacar and Burnaz (2011) did not include any specific country in their analysis; instead they focused on top global brands operating in Turkish market. They used Turkey as the domestic market and compared it with other foreign market websites. In order to set a basis for global brand comparison, they also compared Turkish companies' domestic and global websites.

Cyr, Head, and Larios (2010) analyzed the effect of color on perceptions of trust, satisfaction and e-loyalty. A multi-method approach is also used such as eye-tracking, survey and interviews. This could be considered as a distinct study which analyzes the effect of website color on consumer perceptions and compares results for 3 countries. Gevorgyan and Porter (2008) and Gevorgyan and Manucharova (2009) used the same content analysis instrument and same web design elements as in the studies of Singh, Zhao, and Hu (2003) and Singh and Matsuo (2004); namely graphics, symbols, colors, site elements (maps, links, etc.), and textual content. Besides, Gevorgyan and Manucharova (2009) used multi-method approach.

First, pretests and focus groups were conducted to develop and improve instruments, and then consumers were surveyed and favorite websites for consumers were content analyzed. Gevorgyan and Porter (2008) focused on user-centric studies that examine design preferences and perceptions. Hermeking (2006) used a multi-method approach;

the author extensively reviewed the literature, discussed various topics of cultural influences on website design and finally content analyzed six corporate websites. Robbins and Stylianou (2003) developed a new model that differentiated website content from design and tested it by content analyzing 90 corporate websites. Design component is used for presentation and navigational features while content component is used for various types of information. From a semiology perspective, Zahedi and Bansal (2011) developed a new theory for web-image signifiers based on the "Grounded Theory" and tested it quantitatively. They used a two-step study; first they interpreted grounded theory qualitatively and developed web-image signifiers' theory, and then they content analyzed websites.

Faiola and Matei (2006) proposed a model based on the framework of Vygotsky and Nisbett, called cultural cognition theory. They explored web designers' cultural cognitive styles and their impact on user responses. Faiola and Matei (2006) proposed a new model called cultural cognition theory which is original in the field and used it to understand web designer cultural cognitive styles and proposed that cultural cognitive style of web designers could create cultural biases. Cho and Cheon (2005) analyzed and compared cultural influences on utilization of three dimensions of website interactivity. Cho and Cheon (2005) analyzed interactivity of websites for more effective persuasion, engagement, and interaction with consumers. Also based on consumer behavior, Li et al. (2009) proposed and tested a model that explores the influence of each cultural dimension on technology beliefs and adoption intentions of consumers. Also, Pollach (2011) analyzed individuals' interest in the content of corporate websites. The data are collected through surveys.

Burgmann, Kitchen, and Williams (2006) content analyzed websites of two different sectors--namely banking and education. They content analyzed websites from three countries and two different industries and compared results based on Hofstede's dimensions. Kim and Lee (2006) used an existing website quality scale called WebQual, and analyzed retail sector website quality with this scale. To explore how companies localize their websites, Tixier (2005) content analyzed 300 websites and interviewed managers from US and French companies. Steenkamp and Geyskens (2006) analyzed how country characteristics moderate the effects of the perceived value that consumers derive from visiting websites. While collecting data, they used web surveys from company websites. Yun, Park, and Ha (2008) narrowed the scope of their research to only retail sector and content analyzed only retail company websites. The main focus of their research is to examine nature of online consumer-generated communication.

Würtz (2006) analyzed nine countries to explore and identify the strategies when customizing a website to appeal to different cultures being either high or low context. Although he used content analysis, Würtz's (2006) study diverges from other studies in terms of focusing on the qualitative approach. Similarly, in another qualitative, Lituchy and Barra (2008) analyzed how international differences affect website design, implementation and usage. They performed empirical research, a qualitative case-study. This is the only study that used a case study approach among the papers under investigation. Fu and Wu (2010) used Means-End Chain (MEC) theory to analyze how culture is reflected on web advertisements for credit cards. They did not directly analyze websites; instead they focused on web advertisements. This is the first study that used MEC theory in culture and websites area.

To extend findings of previous studies, Sinkovics, Yamin, and Hossinger (2007) replicated the methodology of Singh et al. (2005) and analyzed German companies. They used Hofstede's and Hall's dimensions and content analyzed websites of German companies in domestic, US, UK, and Latin America markets. The papers under analysis have used a wide variety of research methods and research methodology. Some studies used only a single research method such as case study, experiment, interview, content analysis, literature review, and others. Some other studies used combinations of research methods such as case studies with observations, content analysis with case studies, content analysis with experiments, focus groups with content analysis, experiments with surveys, content analysis with an interpretive qualitative study, etc.

Content analysis is the most common method used in this area due to its objective, systematic, and quantitative analysis of communication contents. Okazaki and Rivas (2002), Okazaki (2004; 2005), Okazaki and Skapa (2008), and Singh, Zhao, and Hu (2003; 2005), Singh and Matsuo (2004), and Baack and Singh (2007) are the leading authors those utilized content analysis in their website research. However, Baack and Singh (2007) stated there are many shortcomings of content analysis as well. They adapted a new method and used content analysis with experimental design. They validated results of content analysis with experimental research. In terms of reliability and validity, Okazaki and Rivas (2002) and Gevorgyan and Manucharova (2009) applied a series of pre-tests to see whether the framework they used was appropriate or not. Moreover, Cyr and Trevor-Smith (2004) conducted a focus group study to improve content analysis instrument. Participants of the focus group categorized content analysis instrument into eight categories--namely language, layout, symbols, content and structure, navigation, links, multimedia, and colors.

Sample Size

One of the methodological weaknesses of studies is their relatively small sample size. For instance, Hermeking (2006) analyzed only six websites, similarly, Würtz (2006) analyzed only one company website but in nine different countries. Even though Cyr, Head, and Larios (2010), Faiola and Matei (2006), and Fang and Rau (2003) used experimental research, they only analyzed one website. For the experimental research, 90 consumers participated from three countries, 53 consumers from two countries and 15 consumers participated from two countries, respectively. Li et al. (2009) also used experimental research where 371 US and 273 Chinese consumers have participated. In the Gevorgyan and Porter's (2008) study, a total sample included 67 US and 62 Chinese consumers.

Okazaki and Rivas (2002) and Okazaki (2004) analyzed 60 and 150 product-based Japanese websites, respectively. Okazaki (2005) content analyzed 206 websites of 64 US companies in four European countries. Okazaki and Skapa (2008) analyzed 34 US firms' websites and compared with three European countries. Singh, Zhao, and Hu (2003) analyzed 40 US-based corporate websites and compared domestic ones with China-specific ones. Singh, Zhao, and Hu's (2005) other study content analyzed 25 Japanese, 26 US, 21 Chinese, and 21 Indian websites-- 93 websites in total. Singh and Matsuo (2004) compared 45 Japanese websites with 48 US websites. Baack and Singh (2007) content analyzed 274 websites and experimentally analyzed a Taiwanese website.

Kim and Kuljis (2010) analyzed 40 websites, Lituchy and Barra (2008) analyzed 21 websites from 2 sectors, and Robbins and Stylianou (2003) analyzed 90 websites, respectively. Nacar and Burnaz (2011) analyzed 108 corporate websites with a comparison of Turkey with foreign countries. In a similar vein, Maynard and Tian (2004) also analyzed 100 global companies' Chinese websites. Cyr and Trevor-Smith (2004) and Burgmann, Kitchen and Williams (2006) focused on three countries; the first group of researchers analyzed 90 websites, the latter analyzed 105 websites. Zhao et al. (2003) studied 100 websites from China and the US. Cho and Cheon (2005) and Yun, Park, and Ha (2008) analyzed 200 corporate websites while Fu and Wu (2010) examined 217 websites. Sinkovics, Yamin and Hossinger (2007) analyzed 300 corporate websites and Tixier (2005) observed 300 websites. Usunier and Roulin (2010) analyzed

597 websites, being one of the highest numbers of websites that was content analyzed.

However, Zahedi and Bansal (2011) used a two-step study; first they analyzed 245 websites and then 728 websites, reaching 973 websites in total. Kim and Lee (2006) conducted surveys from 278 US and 347 Korean consumers, while Pollach (2011) collected 521 surveys. Steenkamp and Geyskens (2006) analyzed 30 websites with 8,886 consumer data; they reached this big sample through web surveys on company websites.

Countries Covered

Among the papers under review, 35 papers indicated the names of countries they analyzed. In 27 papers (US), in 13 papers (Japan), in 12 papers (China), in 11 papers (Germany), and in 10 papers (UK). Within 35 papers, 10 papers focused on Triad countries (US, Europe, and Japan) and 23 papers compared Triad countries with non-Triad ones. There are only two papers that did not focus on Triad countries (Australia [Fletcher, 2006] and Turkey [Nacar & Burnaz, 2011]).

Okazaki and Rivas (2002) and Okazaki (2004) compared Japanese websites with US and Spanish websites. They stated the selection of these countries is based on their difference in cultural, economic, and geographical positions. However, Okazaki (2005) and Okazaki and Skapa (2008) analyzed US companies' standardization strategies in Europe; the former one compared UK, France, Germany, and Spain and the latter compared new EU members Poland and Czech Republic with Germany,used as a control country. The reason Okazaki and Skapa (2008) selected new EU members was that there is no many empirical research for these countries and they enjoy rapid economic growth. Not only for these authors but for others as well, countries are chosen mainly to demonstrate differences between countries.

Many studies compared only two countries (Singh, Zhao, & Hu, 2003). Singh, Zhao, and Hu (2003), Fang and Rau (2003), Gevorgyan and Porter (2008), Zhao et al. (2003), Faiola and Matei (2006), and Li et al. (2009) compared the US and China that are the most commonly contrasted countries in this area of research. Singh, Zhao, and Hu (2005) expanded country coverage and compared China, India, Japan and the US. Fu and Wu (2010) also analyzed China and the US, but they added Taiwan and UK to their research. Singh and Matsuo (2004) selected another country, Japan, to compare with the USA.

Baack and Singh (2007) analyzed 15 countries, Robbins and Stylianou (2003) analyzed 16 countries, and Steenkamp and Geyskens (2006) analyzed 23 countries from all over the world.

Cyr and Trevor-Smith (2004) studied Germany, Japan, and the US. Hermeking (2006) analyzed 6 countries (US, UK, France, Germany, Japan and Italy); Burgmann, Kitchen, and Williams (2006) analyzed 3 countries (Germany, Greece, and the UK); Würtz (2006) analyzed nine countries. Burgmann, Kitchen, and Williams (2006) compared Germany, Greece, and the UK.

Cho and Cheon (2005) analyzed the USA, UK, Japan, and South Korea; they have compared two east and two west countries in terms of country composition. Furthermore, Yun, Park, and Ha (2008) compared the US and South Korea; Kim and Kuljis (2010) compared the UK and South Korea; Kim and Lee (2006) compared the US and Korea. Fletcher (2006) reviewed related literature on this topic, but while reviewing he related some initial findings with Australia and interpreted them within Australian context. Luna, Peracchio, and Juan (2002) conducted experiments in the US and Spain but did not contrast the results of each country. Interestingly, Lituchy and Barra (2008) did not report any country name in their empirical study.

Tixier (2005) stated many companies do not know what to do in the globalization process and going back and forth from globalization to localization. Thus, they analyzed localization efforts of different sectors in the USA and Europe, particularly in France. Tixier analyzed France and compared it with the USA; however, he generalized the findings for the USA and Europe as a whole. This approach comprises an important limitation; although it is located in Europe, it is questionable that France could represent all of Europe, since, for instance, Hofstede's rankings of European countries differ. Pollach (2011) analyzed 19 countries; however, he compared countries as in two groups, namely Europe and Asia. Despite the conducted research in Austria and Singapore, he analyzed participants' nationalities as the country values.

Sinkovics, Yamin, and Hossinger (2007) compared Germany with the US, UK, and Latin America and they treated Latin America as a single country, which could lead again to some drawbacks.

Usunier and Roulin (2010) analyzed 57 countries which is the highest number of countries analyzed. They analyzed the effect of communication styles (high-low context) on content and design of websites by content analyzing B2B websites from 57 countries in different sectors.

In order to expand geographical coverage of websites studies, Nacar and Burnaz (2011) analyzed the Turkish market and compared global brands' local websites with their Turkish counterparts. They mainly evaluated Turkish cultural values, but did not use any specific country while they were comparing Turkey with other countries; instead, they compared Turkey as the domestic market with foreign countries.

Zahedi and Bansal (2011) analyzed 14 countries in their first study and added 26 countries in their second phase, resulting to a sum of 39 countries. In terms of countries covered, studies assessed websites mainly from China, USA, and Europe, which locked up online standardization and adaptation studies within these geographical areas. The majority of the existing studies focus on the US culture and US companies which makes the research in this area geographically limited.

Peripheral Studies

Among 114 papers under consideration, only 40 of them are labeled as essential by the authors, the remaining 74 papers are listed as peripheral or secondary studies based on the classification purposes of the study. Basically, there are four main reasons why the remaining papers are treated as peripheral studies and not analyzed in details within the scope of the present study. First of all, although related with the subject matter of this study, those papers did not specifically focus on the interaction of culture and websites. For instance, some topics considered by those papers are as follows: consumers trust within Iranian context (Meskaran, Abdullah, & Ghazali, 2010), luxury e-branding within website context (Lin, 2012), corporate communication with the public audience (Jo & Jung, 2005), online customer satisfaction (Lee, Joshi and Bae, 2009), banner advertising effectiveness (Möller & Eisend, 2010), privacy and trust perceptions and behavioral intentions in e-commerce websites (Liu, Marchewka, & Ku, 2004), online branding (Murphy & Scharl, 2007), unethical behavior of websites (Huang, 2001), corporate social responsibility (Kampf, 2007), interactivity and advertising appeals (Yu, Paek, & Bae, 2008), corporate website recruiting (Puck, Mohr, and Holtbrügge, 2006), perceived risk (Martin, Camarero, & Jose, 2011), e-service quality and e-satisfaction (Sabiote, Frias, & Castaneda, 2012), trust, satisfaction and e-loyalty (Cyr, 2008), online brand community (Ahn, Kwon, & Sung, 2010), customer satisfaction, trust, and loyalty in e-commerce settings (Kassim & Abdullah, 2010), website design, trust, satisfaction, and e-loyalty (Cyr, Kindra, & Dash, 2008). Among these papers, website design, trust, satisfaction, and e-loyalty are the leading and most popular topics.

Second, similar studies of the same authors were selected for detailed review; however, papers that were published in less scholar journals (not indexed in high-prestige and rigor indexes) were grouped as secondary (Singh, Fassott, Zhao, &

Boughton, 2006; Robbins & Stylianou, 2002; Singh, Baack, Kundu, & Hurtado, 2008; Cyr, Bonanni, Bowes, & Ilsever, 2005; Usunier, Roulin, & Ivens, 2010).

Third, many of those papers analyzed technical components of websites using technical analysis (e.g., images [Shen, Prior, Chen, & You, 2007], color [Kondratova & Goldfarb, 2006; 2007] and web download time [Rose, Evaristo, & Straub, 2003]). Finally, some papers among them were either conference proceedings or were at their early stages of research or not directly satisfied rigorousness and relevance issues. All of those studies are not cited here since they are not classified as the leading studies, but they should be considered as preliminary studies in this area.

DISCUSSION AND CONCLUSION

This chapter aims to identify, analyze and interpret the major papers about culture and websites in the last decades through an extensive literature review. Thus, the analysis of the previous studies gives an opportunity to assess the impact of selected papers, journals, and key authors on the knowledge on the interaction between culture and websites as a research field and provide some important insights for the future studies. Data on the outline, structure and key topics in the research field were collected from various databases which summed up in 114 studies and selected 40 of them are analyzed in depth. Due to the interdisciplinary nature of the subject, the researchers from many different disciplines have devoted their attentions to analyze the interaction between culture and websites. However, the majority of these studies is seen to be published in communication and business journals and related other sources.

In today's high-technology environment, communications become global and websites have the capability to be available for the whole world; they are just one click away from the furthest consumer. This encourages many multinational companies to use single and standard websites to communicate with their customers throughout the world. However, this so-called opportunity might turn out a threat and may damage multinationals' competitive power more than predicted. Undoubtedly, with increasing use of the internet, every kind of borders has been diminishing and the digital age is beginning to dominate the scene where traditional approach is losing its relevance. Consumers move from catalogue to online environments and the number of product-based websites is increasing day by day (Okazaki, 2004).

With its global access and less geographical, regulatory and cultural constraints as compared to traditional media forms, websites are today's vital communication mediums for global business. Thus, global brands have to position and locate themselves in local markets by using today's most popular and effective communication channels, namely websites. However, the usage of websites will raise some important questions that should be taken into consideration. One of the key questions that company management should deal with is as follows: "Should the global brands focus on developing a single, standard website as the cultural constraints decrease?"

Meanwhile, technology, especially information technologies and computer-mediated communication, have concurrent effects on both cultural divergence and convergence (Leung et al., 2005). Converging and diverging tendencies inevitably become obvious both in global marketing and in the use of the new communication technologies. These tendencies directly affect the use of new information technologies (Maynard & Tian, 2004), especially websites. Therefore, while websites are affecting cultural issues, cultural issues also affect websites. Undoubtedly, the most important result of the analysis presented in this chapter is that the majority of the studies under consideration support the idea that culture and websites are mutually interdependent. In addition, from the perspective of consumer culture, many of the studies on culture and websites concluded that websites enable the companies to eliminate some other borders, but not cultural borders totally and it is observed that global consumers still prefer locally adapted websites.

Cultural adaptation will increase the success of websites which will then affect competitiveness of companies in local markets. As an important marketing communication channel, websites also contribute to the brand image of companies. Thus, a perspective that integrates IMC and branding strategic priorities will be useful to incorporate the impact of culture in various elements of website. As a result, it is essential to develop websites which are sensitive to cultural norms, values, and beliefs in terms of both design and content. However, most of the previous studies did not provide any guidance, theory, or framework for how to adapt websites to local culture (Singh, Zhao, & Hu, 2005; Gevorgyan & Manucharova, 2009).

Culture and websites research is truly international in that many different countries from all continents are included. Although there is a bias toward Triad countries, it is encouraging to see that research has also been conducted in other parts of the world. One of the important weaknesses of the cross cultural studies in the related field is that the number of countries compared in the majority of those studies is very limited. Only a few studies examined more than 10 countries. Although, the common approach in these studies is to compare mostly two countries, two-country based analysis restricts the generalizability of the results.

However, there are a considerable number of studies using a variety of cultural dimensions in their analyses of the interaction between culture and websites. However, they mostly provide a little depth of cultural analysis. Culture has been studied by researchers from different domains, and thus defined in many ways (Liao, Proctor, & Salvendy, 2007). Even though there is large number of cultural models, current studies on cultural adaptation are mostly based on the frameworks of Hofstede's and Hall's dimensions (Okazaki, 2004). Singh, Zhao, & Hu (2003) reported that although they have recognized the shortcomings of these models, they also preferred to use Hofstede and Hall dimensions due their high level of usage in the literature. They stated that commonly used and tested models in the literature make them highly valid and legitimate to use as compared to other models. Moreover, these models are also defined as parsimonious and analytically flexible enough to measure culture. However, the use of only particular dimensions could generate drawbacks in terms of decreasing the diversity and dynamism of culture, as a result of reductionist approach. Certainly, reductionist studies also provide many important insights about culture and websites, however, the area has reached to a mature stage, and thus there is strong need to approach culture from different perspectives.

Studies in this area mostly used Hofstede and/or Hall's cultural dimensions. Most of the studies in the literature about cultural adaptation of websites correlated their findings with Hofstede's scores. Thus they are criticized all as blindly following the literature (Hermeking, 2006). However, methodological problems and conclusions from Hofstede's study which are not universally accepted produce other debates (Baack & Singh, 2007). The best-known criticism of Hofstede's study in this area is McSweeney's study of 2002 (Avery et al., 2008). McSweeney offered criticisms under two major headings: the heterogenic nature of cultures, where IBM-based cultural dimensions could fail to identify culture appropriately, and the dynamic nature of culture, where Hofstede's study is too old, as many cultures have changed since that time. Even though it is not free of criticism, Hofstede's study has been used mostly as the main framework to study cultural topics.

The possible use of one cultural framework as the theoretical basis is a gap in the literature, and it is strongly recommended to use multiple cultural frameworks. Moreover, it will be more appropriate to study cultural issues with more dynamic perspectives, rather than just focusing on static frameworks (Martinez-Lopez, Sousa,

& Gazquez-Abad, 2011). Although Hofstede's cultural typology is highly criticized in terms of methodology and context, Singh, Zhao, and Hu (2003) reported that due to wide use and gained support of this model, the overlap of Hofstede's dimensions with other cultural models, valid nature for regional differences and empirical development of Hofstede's dimensions have made them appropriate to be used in order to measure cultural differences for websites.

Nacar and Burnaz (2011) used a different approach to analyze the effects of culture on websites. In their study, Turkish cultural identities for websites are determined by examining local e-content. Actually, in the literature, a "thing centeredness" approach (Applbaum & Jordt, 1996) is mainly used, especially for culture, which has unknown variables, an ambiguous nature, and similar problems. Additionally, there have been many studies regarding the adaptation of print and broadcast media according to different cultural dimensions, but it is obvious that there are few studies adopting a similar approach for websites. Statistical tests used in the previous studies on this research area are limited to only Chi-square and t-tests, additionally inter-coder reliability statistics are run for the reliability analysis. Therefore, more rigorous statistical tests are required to test the effect of culture on websites. However, while increasing the rigor of analysis, relevancy should not be dismissed.

Content analysis is widely used as the norm analysis method of this area. The exploratory nature of the studies limits the generalizability of specific findings. For this reason, descriptive or causal researches can perfectly support this research area. Although it is not easy to apply experimental studies, their intensity of usage has to be increased in order to describe the cause and effect relations between culture and website characteristics more clearly. One of the major decisions multinationals face in using websites is how to organize and present the website content to fit local needs and values. Although adaptation becomes a major concern, there is no standard for the multicultural content of websites. There are several cross cultural studies which compare countries by correlating the analyzed variables with Hofstede's scores. Rather than comparing home and host countries of foreign multinationals based on certain dimensions, the authors believe that it is more appropriate to assess on what terms and to what degree these companies could adapt or standardize their global communication channels, namely their websites.

In conclusion, depending on the strategy of firms either global strategy or multi-domestic strategy, the use of websites in interaction with the relevant culture will differ. In the former one, global performance is a crucial factor, whereas in the latter, local performance and competition have utmost importance. Thus, our recommendation for companies, even if it is complex, difficult, and cost-increasing, is to run both a global website which is truly standard all over the world and different multi-domestic websites which are adapted to each local culture. Undoubtedly, culturally sensitive and adapted websites could persuade consumers more than standardized ones, whereas standardized websites will enhance more integrated communication approach required to transmit more consistent messages to the consumers in terms of effective branding and corporate communications.

Recommendations for Future Research

The present research is limited by the database and the keywords used for the search during the literature survey. Also, this study used a qualitative analysis based on the existing literature by interpreting studies and research streams in the field. However, future research could employ bibliometric analysis which is quantitative in nature and uses more databases. The type of websites should be expanded by including the new contexts and forms to increase the generalizability of studies. Thus, it is recommended that future studies should incorporate the analysis of social media websites such as YouTube and Facebook. Rather than analyzing corporate websites, analyzing consumer and firm generated social media will be more appropriate to understand and analyze the effects of culture on websites and how cultural issues are reflected on websites.

Many studies mainly approach the topic from the company's point of view and neglect the consumer side. Future researchers having interest in this area could also give more importance to consumer perspective and investigate how consumers perceive adaptation practices of foreign multinationals through websites in their countries.

Moreover, all the variables taken into consideration in the present study are mainly utilitarian, so adaptation of websites could also be investigated taking a hedonic perspective or relying on both a utilitarian and a hedonic basis.

Last but not least, studies should diversify their research perspective. Many studies in this area have an etic focus and compare the websites which then lead to obvious difference between countries where making comparison is the main purpose. In etic research, the main focus is finding out indifferences, thus if the researcher focuses on differences it is evident that he or she will come up with differences. However, future studies guided by an emic approach could provide more insights about one specific culture and focus but on the meaning and characteristics of one culture rather than on the possible differences between cultures.

REFERENCES

Ahn, H., Kwon, M. W., & Sung, Y. (2010). Online Brand Community across Cultures. *International Journal of e-Business Management, 4*(1), 34-52.

Alden, D. L., Steenkamp, J.-B. E., & Batra, R. (1999). Brand Positioning Through Advertising in Asia, North America, and Europe: The Role of Global Consumer Culture. *Journal of Marketing, 63*(1), 75–87. doi:10.2307/1252002.

Appadurai, A. (1990). Disjuncture and Difference in the Global Cultural Economy. *Theory, Culture & Society, 7*, 295–310. doi:10.1177/026327690007002017.

Applbaum, K., & Jordt, I. (1996). Notes toward an application of McCraken's 'cultural categories' for cross-cultural consumer research. *The Journal of Consumer Research, 23*(3), 204–218. doi:10.1086/209478.

Avery, A., Baradwaj, B., & Siner, D. (2008). An examination of Hofstede's cultural factors in explanation of differences in Citibank international retail banking web sites. *Journal of Business and Economics Studies, 14*(2), 73–90.

Baack, D. W., & Singh, N. (2007). Culture and web communications. *Journal of Business Research, 60*, 181–188. doi:10.1016/j.jbusres.2006.11.002.

Burgmann, I., Kitchen, P. J., & Williams, R. (2006). Does culture matter on the web? *Marketing Intelligence & Planning, 24*(1), 62–76. doi:10.1108/02634500610641561.

Cho, C.-H., & Cheon, H. J. (2005). Cross-Cultural Comparisons of Interactivity on Corporate Web Sites. *Journal of Advertising, 34*(2), 99–115. doi :10.1080/00913367.2005.10639195.

Cyr, D. (2008). Modeling Web Site Design Across Cultures: Relationships to Trust, Satisfaction, and E-Loyalty. *Journal of Management Information Systems, 24*(4), 47–72. doi:10.2753/MIS0742-1222240402.

Cyr, D., Bonanni, C., Bowes, J., & Ilsever, J. (2005). Beyond Trust: Web Site Design Preferences Across Cultures. *Journal of Global Information Management*, *13*(4), 25–54. doi:10.4018/jgim.2005100102.

Cyr, D., Head, M., & Larios, H. (2010). Colour appeal in website design within and across cultures: A multi-method evaluation. *International Journal of Human-Computer Studies*, *68*, 1–21. doi:10.1016/j.ijhcs.2009.08.005.

Cyr, D., Kindra, G. S., & Dash, S. (2008). Web site design, trust, satisfaction and e-loyalty: The Indian experience. *Online Information Review*, *32*(6), 773–790. doi:10.1108/14684520810923935.

Cyr, D., & Trevor-Smith, H. (2004). Localization of Web Design: An Empirical Comparison of German, Japanese, and U.S. Website Characteristics. *Journal of the American Society for Information Science and Technology*, *55*(13), 1199–1208. doi:10.1002/asi.20075.

Faiola, A., & Matei, S. A. (2006). Cultural Cognitive Style and Web Design: Beyond a Behavioral Inquiry into Computer-Mediated Communication. *Journal of Computer-Mediated Communication*, *11*, 375–394. doi:10.1111/j.1083-6101.2006.tb00318.x.

Fang, X., & Rau, P.-L. P. (2003). Culture differences in design of portal sites. *Ergonomics*, *46*(1-3), 242–254. doi:10.1080/00140130303535 PMID:12554409.

Ferreira, G. (2007). Consumer perceptions of global branding and iconization. *Dissertation of Doctor of Management in Organizational Leadership in University of Phoenix*. Phoenix, AZ: ProQuest Information and Learning Company.

Fletcher, R. (2006). The impact of culture on web site content, design, and structure: An international and a multicultural perspective. *Journal of Communication Management*, *10*(3), 259–273. doi:10.1108/13632540610681158.

Fu, C.-S., & Wu, W.-Y. (2010). The means-end cognitions of web advertising: A cross-cultural comparison. *Online Information Review*, *34*(5), 686–703. doi:10.1108/14684521011084573.

Gevorgyan, G., & Manucharova, N. (2009). Does Culturally Adapted Online Communication Work? A Study of American and Chinese Internet Users' Attitudes and Preferences Toward Culturally Customized Web Design Elements. *Journal of Computer-Mediated Communication*, *14*, 393–413. doi:10.1111/j.1083-6101.2009.01446.x.

Gevorgyan, G., & Porter, L. V. (2008). One Size Does Not Fit All: Culture and Perceived Importance of Web Design Features. *Journal of Website Promotion*, *3*(1), 25–38. doi:10.1080/15533610802052589.

Hall, E. T. (1976). *Beyond Culture*. New York: Doubleday.

Hannerz, U. (1990). Cosmopolitans and Locals in World Culture. In Featherstone, M. (Ed.), *Global Culture: Nationalism, Globalization and Modernity* (pp. 237–252). Thousand Oaks, CA: Sage Publications.

Harris, G. (1994). International Advertising Standardization: What Do the Multinationals Actually Standardize? *Journal of International Marketing*, *2*(4), 13–30.

Hermeking, M. (2006). Culture and Internet Consumption: Contributions from Cross-Cultural Marketing and Advertising Research. *Journal of Computer-Mediated Communication*, *11*, 192–216. doi:10.1111/j.1083-6101.2006.tb00310.x.

Huang, J.-H. (2001). Consumer Evaluations of Unethical Behaviors of Web Sites: A Cross-Cultural Comparison. *Journal of International Consumer Marketing*, *13*(4), 51–71. doi:10.1300/J046v13n04_04.

Internet World Stats. (2012, July 29). *Internet Usage Statistics*. Retrieved August 3, 2012, from http://www.internetworldstats.com/stats.htm

Jagne, J., & Smith-Atakan, A. (2006). Cross-cultural interface design strategy. *Universal Access in the Information Society*, *5*, 299–305. doi:10.1007/s10209-006-0048-6.

Jo, S., & Jung, J. (2005). A cross-cultural study of the World Wide Web and public relations. *Corporate Communications: An International Journal*, *10*(1), 24–40. doi:10.1108/13563280510578187.

Kampf, C. (2007). Corporate social responsibility: WalMart, Maersk and the cultural bounds of representation in corporate web sites. *Corporate Communications: An International Journal*, *12*(1), 41–57. doi:10.1108/13563280710723741.

Kassim, N., & Abdullah, N. A. (2010). The effect of perceived service quality dimensions on customer satisfaction, trust, and loyalty in e-commerce settings: A cross cultural analysis. *Asia Pacific Journal of Marketing and Logistics*, *22*(3), 351–371. doi:10.1108/13555851011062269.

Kim, I., & Kuljis, J. (2010). Manifestations of Culture in Website Design. *Journal of Computing and Information Technology*, *18*(2), 125–132.

Kim, S., & Lee, Y. (2006). Global online marketplace: A cross-cultural comparison of website quality. *International Journal of Consumer Studies*, *30*(6), 533–543. doi:10.1111/j.1470-6431.2006.00522.x.

Kittler, M. G., Rygl, D., & Mackinnon, A. (2011). Beyond culture or beyond control? Reviewing the use of Hall's high-/low-context concept. *International Journal of Cross Cultural Management*, *11*(1), 63–82. doi:10.1177/1470595811398797.

Kondratova, I., & Goldfarb, I. (2006). Cultural Interface Design: Global Colors Study. In Meersman, Z. T. R. (Ed.), *OTM Workshops* (pp. 926–934). Montpellier, VT: Heidelberg Springer.

Kondratova, I., & Goldfarb, I. (2007). Color Your Website: Use of Colors on the Web. In N. Aykin (Ed.), *Proceedings of the 12th HCI International Conference* (pp. 123–132). Beijing, China: Heidelberg Springer.

Lee, K., Joshi, K., & Bae, M. (2009). A Cross-National Comparison of the Determinants of Customer Satisfaction with Online Stores. *Journal of Global Information Technology Management*, *12*(4), 25–51.

Leidner, D. E., & Kayworth, T. (2006). A Review of Culture in Information Systems Research: Toward a Theory of Information Technology Culture Conflict. *Management Information Systems Quarterly*, *30*(2), 357–399.

Leung, K., Bhagat, R. S., Buchan, N. R., Erez, M., & Gibson, C. B. (2005). Culture and international business: Recent advances and their implications for future research. *Journal of International Business Studies*, *36*, 357–378. doi:10.1057/palgrave.jibs.8400150.

Li, X., Hess, T. J., McNab, A. L., & Yu, Y. (2009). A Cross-Country Study of the Effects of National Cultural Values on Acceptance of a Personal Web Portal. *ACM SIGMIS Database*, *40*(4), 62–87. doi:10.1145/1644953.1644959.

Liao, H., Proctor, R. W., & Salvendy, G. (2007). Content preparation for cross-cultural e-commerce: A review and a model. *Behaviour & Information Technology*, *27*(1), 43–61. doi:10.1080/01449290601088424.

Lin, E.-Y. (2012). A Cross-Cultural Study of Luxury e-Branding: Standardization vs. Adaptation, Product Category, and Country-of-Origin. *Marketing Review*, *9*(1), 91–120.

Lituchy, T. R., & Barra, R. A. (2008). International issues of the design and usage of websites for e-commerce: Hotel and airline examples. *Journal of Engineering and Technology Management*, *25*, 93–111. doi:10.1016/j.jengtecman.2008.01.004.

Liu, C., Marchewka, J. T., & Ku, C. (2004). Americana dn Taiwanese Perceptions Concerning Privacy, Trust, and Behavioral Intentions in Electronic Commerce. *Journal of Global Information Management*, *12*(1), 18–40. doi:10.4018/jgim.2004010102.

Luna, D., Peracchio, L. A., & Juan, M. D. (2002). Cross-Cultural and Cognitive Aspects of Web Site Navigation. *Journal of the Academy of Marketing Science*, *30*(4), 397–410. doi:10.1177/009207002236913.

Martin, S. S., Camarero, C., & Jose, R. S. (2011). Dual effect of perceived risk on cross-national e-commerce. *Internet Research*, *21*(1), 46–66. doi:10.1108/10662241111104875.

Martínez-López, F. J., Sousa, C. M., & Gázquez-Abad, J. C. (2011). A Cultural Constructivist Analysis of the Internet's Role in the International Approximation of Markets. *Journal of Marketing Theory and Practice*, *19*(1), 57–79. doi:10.2753/MTP1069-6679190104.

Maynard, M., & Tian, Y. (2004). Between global and glocal: Content analysis of the Chinese Web Sites of the 100 top global brands. *Public Relations Review*, *30*, 285–291. doi:10.1016/j.pubrev.2004.04.003.

McCracken, G. (1993). The Value of the Brand: An Anthropological Perspective. In Bowl, D. A. (Ed.), *Brand Equity and Advertising: Advertising's Role in Building Strong Brands* (pp. 125–139). Hillsdale, NJ: Lawrence Erlbaum Associates.

McSweeney, B. (2002). Hofstede's 'Model of National Cultural Differences and Consequences: A Triumph of Faith - A Failure of Analysis. *Human Relations*, *55*(1), 89–118.

Meskaran, F., Abdullah, R., & Ghazali, M. (2010). A Conceptual Framework of Iranian Consumer Trust in B2C Electronic Commerce. *Computer and Information Science*, *3*(2), 126–139.

Möller, J., & Eisend, M. (2010). A Global Investigation into the Cultural and Individual Antecedents of Banner Advertising Effectiveness. *Journal of International Marketing*, *18*(2), 80–98. doi:10.1509/jimk.18.2.80.

Murphy, J., & Scharl, A. (2007). An investigation of global versus local online branding. *International Marketing Review*, *24*(3), 297–312. doi:10.1108/02651330710755302.

Nacar, R., & Burnaz, S. (2011). A cultural content analysis of multinational companies' web sites. *Qualitative Market Research: An International Journal*, *14*(3), 274–288. doi:10.1108/13522751111137505.

Okazaki, S. (2004). Do multinationals standardise or localise? The cross-cultural dimensionality of product-based Web sites. *Internet Research*, *14*(1), 81–94. doi:10.1108/10662240410516336.

Okazaki, S. (2005). Searching the web for global brands: how American brands standardise their web sites in Europe. *European Journal of Marketing*, *39*(1/2), 87–109. doi:10.1108/03090560510572034.

Okazaki, S., & Rivas, J. A. (2002). A content analysis of multinationals' Web communication strategies: Cross-cultural research framework and pre-testing. *Internet Research*, *12*(5), 380–390. doi:10.1108/10662240210447137.

Okazaki, S., & Skapa, R. (2008). Global web site standardization in the new EU member states: Initial observations from Poland and the Czech Republic. *European Journal of Marketing*, *42*(11/12), 1224–1245. doi:10.1108/03090560810903655.

Pauwels, L. (2012). A Multimodal Framework for Analyzing Websites as Cultural Expressions. *Journal of Computer-Mediated Communication*, *17*, 247–265. doi:10.1111/j.1083-6101.2012.01572.x.

Pollach, I. (2011). The Readership of Corporate Websites. *Journal of Business Communication*, *48*(1), 27–53. doi:10.1177/0021943610385657.

Robbins, S., & Stylianou, A. (2002). A Study of Cultural Differences in Global Corporate Web Sites. *Journal of Computer Information Systems*, *42*(2), 3–9.

Robbins, S. S., & Stylianou, A. C. (2003). Global corporate web sites: An empirical investigation of content and design. *Information & Management*, 205–212. doi:10.1016/S0378-7206(02)00002-2.

Rose, G. M., Evaristo, R., & Straub, D. (2003). Culture and Consumer Responses to Web Download Time: A Four-Continent Study of Mono and Polychronism. *IEEE Transactions on Engineering Management*, *50*(1), 31–44. doi:10.1109/TEM.2002.808262.

Sabiote, C. M., Frias, D. M., & Castaneda, J. A. (2012). E-service quality as antecedent to e-satisfaction: The moderating effect of culture. *Online Information Review*, *36*(2), 157–174. doi:10.1108/14684521211229011.

Shen, S.-T., Prior, S. D., Chen, K.-M., & You, M.-L. (2007). Chinese Web Browser Design Utilising Cultural Icons. In N. Aykin (Ed.), *Proceedings of the 12th HCI International*

Singh, N., Baack, D. W., Kundu, S. K., & Hurtado, C. (2008). U.S. Hispanic Consumer E-Commerce Preferences: Expections and Attitudes toward Web Content. *Journal of Electronic Commerce Research*, *9*(2), 162–175.

Singh, N., Fassott, G., Zhao, H., & Boughton, P. D. (2006). A Cross-cultural analysis of German, Chinese and Indian consumers' perception of web site adaptation. *Journal of Consumer Behaviour*, *5*, 56–68. doi:10.1002/cb.43.

Singh, N., & Matsuo, H. (2004). Measuring cultural adaptation on the Web: A content analytic study of U.S. and Japanese Web sites. *Journal of Business Research*, *57*, 864–872. doi:10.1016/S0148-2963(02)00482-4.

Singh, N., Zhao, H., & Hu, X. (2003). Cultural adaptation on the Web: A study of American companies' domestic and Chinese websites. *Journal of Global Information Management*, *11*(3), 63–80. doi:10.4018/jgim.2003070104.

Singh, N., Zhao, H., & Hu, X. (2005). Analyzing the cultural content of web sites: A cross-national comparision of China, India, Japan, and US. *International Marketing Review*, *22*(2), 129–146. doi:10.1108/02651330510593241.

Sinkovics, R. R., Yamin, M., & Hossinger, M. (2007). Cultural Adaptation in Cross Border e-Commerce: A Study of German Companies. *Journal of Electronic Commerce Research*, *8*(4), 221–235.

Steenkamp, J.-B. E., & Geyskens, I. (2006). How Country Characteristics Affect the Perceived Value of Web Sites. *Journal of Marketing*, *70*, 136–150. doi:10.1509/jmkg.70.3.136.

Tixier, M. (2005). Globalization and Localization of Contents: Evolution of Major Internet Sites Across Sectors of Industry. *Thunderbird International Business Review*, *47*(1), 15–48. doi:10.1002/tie.20039.

Tong, M. C., & Robertson, K. (2008). Political and Cultural Representation in Malaysian Websites. *International Journal of Design*, *2*(2), 67–79.

Usunier, J.-C., & Roulin, N. (2010). The Influence of High- and Low-Context Communication Styles on the Design, Content, and Language of Busines-to-Business Web Sites. *Journal of Business Communication*, *47*(2), 189–227. doi:10.1177/0021943610364526.

Usunier, J.-C., Roulin, N., & Ivens, B. S. (2010). Cultural, National, and Industry-Level Differences in B2B Web Site Design and Content. *International Journal of Electronic Commerce*, *14*(2), 41–87. doi:10.2753/JEC1086-4415140202.

Würtz, E. (2006). Intercultural Communication on Web sites: A Cross-Cultural Analysis of Web sites from High-Context Cultures and Low-Context Cultures. *Journal of Computer-Mediated Communication*, *11*, 274–299. doi:10.1111/j.1083-6101.2006.tb00313.x.

Yu, H. J., Paek, H.-J., & Bae, B. (2008). Cross-cultural comparison of interactivity and advertising appeals on antismoking web sites in the United States and South Korea. *Internet Research*, *18*(5), 454–476. doi:10.1108/10662240810912738.

Yun, G. W., Park, S.-Y., & Ha, L. (2008). Influence of Cultural Dimensions on Online Interactive Review Feature Implementations: A Comparison of Korean and U.S. Retail Web Sites. *Journal of Interactive Marketing*, *22*(3), 40–50. doi:10.1002/dir.20116.

Zahedi, F. M., & Bansal, G. (2011). Cultural Signifiers of Web Site Images. *Journal of Management Information Systems*, *28*(1), 147–200. doi:10.2753/MIS0742-1222280106.

Zhao, W., Massey, B. L., Murphy, J., & Fang, L. (2003). Cultural Dimensions of Website Design and Content. *Prometheus*, *21*(1), 75–84. doi:10.1080/0810902032000051027.

Chapter 18
Qualitative Research: Ex Cultura

M. Gordon Hunter
University of Lethbridge, Canada

ABSTRACT

This chapter presents a conceptual discussion about investigating management issues relating to global business operations. Current global business operations provide an opportunity to conduct Ex Cultura research. This term represents the situation where researchers conduct investigations beyond their own culture. A Grounded Theory approach within a qualitative perspective is proposed so that newly emerging themes may be identified. These themes may not be known before hand because of the Ex Cultura environment. Two methods are suggested; the first method, Personal Construct Theory and the RepGrid technique, documents what the research participant thinks about a particular research question. The other method, Narrative Inquiry and the Long Interview technique, documents what a research participant has done relative to a research question. Both methods document the research participant's interpretation of their personal experiences. Further, the methods support Ex Cultura research into management issues involved in global business operations.

INTRODUCTION

Global operations seem to be the standard taken by many businesses. Product manufacture may be established close to raw material and/or less expensive labour. Some businesses may search out skilled personnel as a way to decide where to establish their operations. The distribution function is located in relation to the end market. Governments, in order to stimulate their respective economies, may create tax regimes which facilitate the establishment of global business operations within their nation.

DOI: 10.4018/978-1-4666-3966-9.ch018

Usually, the establishment of global business operations is carried out by large corporations. They have the necessary resources to begin and maintain such ventures. Indeed, the business model of some large corporations necessitates expansion beyond the country in which they originally began operations. However, small businesses now may also be able to provide products and services on a global basis. The advent of the Internet which facilitates e-commerce has provided vast market opportunities for businesses of all sizes.

The globalization of business leads to operations in many different cultures. Management researchers, as a consequence, may now conduct investigations which incorporate a cultural perspective. These management researchers will have the opportunity to conduct their studies outside of their own culture–as is suggested in the title of this chapter–*Ex Cultura*. It is thus incumbent upon management researchers to consider and adopt methods which will respond to the inherent cultural diversity in global business operations. This is the main thesis of this document.

This chapter takes a conceptual approach to presenting two methods for conducting qualitative investigations by *Ex Cultura* researchers within the purview of global business operations. The next section presents an overview of a cross-cultural perspective by renowned cross-cultural researcher, Hofstede. Then, a qualitative perspective is outlined. Qualitative research is proposed because it promotes an in depth investigation of a subject in its natural surroundings. This interpretive approach facilitates identifying emerging themes in a relatively under-researched or novel (to the researcher) area such as cross-cultural investigations. A description of Grounded Theory is also included in this section. An investigation is initiated relative to an interesting research question. Data are gathered relative to the question, usually through interviews. The transcripts of these interviews are analyzed to identify emerging themes which are compared across a series of interviews employing Ground Theory Method.

Grounded Theory provides the context for the two proposed methods. The objective of both the proposed methods is to document the research participant's personal interpretations of their past experiences. The first method based on Personal Construct Theory (PCT) (Kelly, 1955; 1963) attempts to document what the research participant thinks about a subject through the administration of a Repertory Grid which facilitates the elicitation of a person's individual constructs. The second method, proposed here, is based on Narrative Inquiry (Girden, 2001; Scholes, 1981; Swap et al., 2001; Tulving, 1972), which documents what a research participant has done through an approach known as the Long Interview Technique (McCracken, 1988). Following the description and analysis of these two methods, relative to conducting cross-cultural research, a series of issues are described which the researcher must address when planning and conducting these types of investigations. The chapter concludes by returning to the initial idea of conducting management research of global business operations.

CROSS-CULTURAL PERSPECTIVE

It is obvious cross-cultural qualitative researchers will include research participants from cultures which may not be from their own culture. A series of publications (Webber, 1969; Yang, 1986; Ronen, 1986; Berry, 1990; Headland et al., 1990; Triandis, 1972; Early & Mosakowski, 1995) have presented a perspective on cultures which may be employed to develop comparisons across a number of cultures. These publications are generally attributed to Hofstede. This chapter will not delve into some of the issues that others have raised regarding Hofstede's work. But an overview of his cultural comparisons is presented.

Hofstede (1980; 1983; 1988; 1990; 1993) suggested culture represents the "...collective programming of the mind...." Thus, individuals will adopt assumptions about how to act based upon the cultural environment in which they spend the majority of their informative years. A further contention would suggest that long term experience in another culture will have an impact upon an individual's assumptions about how to behave in interpersonal relationships. Originally, Hofstede (1980) proposed four dimensions upon which culture may be differentiated. Subsequent investigations identified two more dimensions. These dimensions are included in Table 1.

Hofstede's subsequent investigations (1983; 1988; 1990; 1993) also determined that some management practices could be compatible with some cultural assumptions, while other practices may not be compatible, causing interpersonal conflict. The incompatibility with underlying assumptions about how to act may undermine management practices and inhibit quality performance. Further, successful management practices in one culture may not meet with success when an attempt is made to implement the practice in another culture. It is these types of issues which lead to the exciting investigation possibilities of *Ex Cultura* research.

GENERIC QUALITATIVE RESEARCH

Qualitative research is an interpretive approach to investigating subjects in their natural surroundings. Thus, qualitative researchers attempt to make sense of phenomena in terms of their meanings attributed by research participants. Qualitative researchers document the meanings that research participants use to describe their experience relative to a research question.

Qualitative research methods are designed to help researchers understand people and what they say and do. They are designed to help researchers understand the social and cultural contexts within which people live (Myers, 2009, p. 5).

The use of a qualitative research approach necessitates the consideration of some important issues. First, it is possible to investigate a subject in some detail. The level of detail allows the researcher to become intimately involved with the specific situation. Also, the researcher may interact with the research participant almost to the extent of establishing a co-researcher relationship. Second, because of this co-researcher relationship, which may be established, the possibility for the introduction of researcher bias is introduced. Thus, the researcher must ensure that the process of gathering and analyzing data is not only appropriate but is proven and accepted. Third, research participants must be allowed

Table 1. Hofstede's Cross-Cultural Dimensions. (Adapted from Hofstede, 1980; Hofstede et al., 2010; Hofstede & Minkov, 2010)

DIMENSION	DESCRIPTION
Individualism – Collectivism	Individualist cultures emphasize independence, while Collectivist cultures emphasize mutual dependence and obligations
Power Distance	High Power Distance cultures accept an unequal distribution of power, while Low Power Distance cultures strive for an equal distribution
Uncertainty Avoidance	Strong Uncertainty Avoidance cultures have formal codes of behaviour, while Weak Uncertainty Avoidance cultures are less controlled
Masculinity – Feminism	Masculine cultures emphasize achievement, while Feminine cultures emphasize caring
Orientation	Short-term orientation exhibits concern for establishing absolute truth and respect for traditions, while long-term orientation considers truth depends on context and traditions may be adapted to changing conditions.
Indulgence – Restraint	Indulgent cultures allow the gratification of basic human drives, while restrained cultures regulate these drives through strict social norms.

to solely determine the content and descriptive nature of their responses. The chosen technique must support this approach. Because research participants choose the content of their responses it will be possible for the researcher to identify new ideas or determine different understandings of certain situations.

Qualitative researchers work very closely with research participants. The researcher will visit the research participants in their natural surroundings and attempt to document their interpretations of their own personal experiences. The researcher and the research participant work together to record the comments of the research participant about a specific research question. Two aspects are paramount. First, the answer to the research question should be important and prove potentially valuable to as wide an audience as possible. Second, the research participant should possess sufficient personal direct experience relating to the research question that an opinion or interpretation may be formed regarding specific aspects related to the question. The researcher and research participant work as a team documenting interpretations of personal experiences. Because of this close working relationship concerns may arise relating to bias, reliability, and verification.

Bias may result from the way data are gathered. Qualitative researchers generally gather data by conducting in-depth one-on-one interviews. Bias may be introduced in an interview simply by the way a question is posed. Rather than asking a question in a non-evaluative way, the researcher may state or imply a personal opinion when posing a question. This, in turn, may result in a biased response from the research participant. Also, the research participant may strive to respond to a question in a way that attempts to anticipate what is thought to be the "correct" answer or what is thought to be the researcher's desired answer. Thus, the researcher must take care to identify these potential issues. The researcher must guard against introducing bias into the interview question and the overall data gathering process. This potential for bias may be reduced through the development and consistent use of a standard interview guide. The two methods proposed in a subsequent section address the issue of bias. In all cases questions should be posed in a non-evaluative manner.

Reliability may be evaluated via replication. The reliability of research results, "...relates to the extent to which our observations are stable, dependable, and can be replicated" (Pervin, 1989, p. 271). The last phrase of this comment responds to the reliability issue in qualitative research. Thus, if another researcher employs the same data gathering method and obtains the same results, then both investigations would be considered more reliable.

Verification may also be assessed by replication. Initially, the results of an investigation into a research question may be presented. Subsequent investigations which replicate the methods of the initial research project may support or refute the initial project's results. The more subsequent replications provide support for the conclusions of prior investigations the more the results of all of the projects can be verified.

Thus, the response to the concerns about bias, reliability, and verification should be addressed through the development and use of a data gathering process which is appropriate for answering the research question. The next section presents a description of two data gathering processes which address these issues.

If qualitative researchers attempt to gather data with minimal bias and no preconceptions, then the concepts of Grounded Theory may apply. Grounded Theory is defined as, "...the discovery of theory from data systematically obtained from social research" (Glaser & Strauss, 1967, p. 2). Grounded Theory also defines a "Category" as a conceptual element of the theory, which emerges from the data; and a "Property" as a conceptual element of a category, which emerges from the data. The data analysis process involves three types of coding (Strauss & Corbin, 1990). First, "open" coding involves assigning the data to categories that are identified from the data by the researcher. Second, "axial" or "theoretical" coding involves identifying relationships between the categories. These relationships support the identification of an overall theoretical framework. Third, "selective" coding involves ensuring that all available data are associated with an emerging category and that core categories are identified to support the conceptualization of the theoretical framework.

As an approach to research, Grounded Theory may be used in two ways. On one hand, it may be used as a research philosophy. Thus, the researcher approaches a research question with no *a priori* research framework or theoretical context. A research question, considered interesting, is posed and data are gathered relative to the question. Subsequent data analysis, as explained below, is employed to support the researcher's contention about how the data may be used to respond to the research question. On the other hand, Grounded Theory may be used as a technique for analyzing data, which involves the process of constant comparison. The theory suggests that categories and properties are concepts that are identified by the researcher and evolve from the constant comparison of the data. A category emerges from the data and may stand by itself as a conceptual element. A property is an attribute of a category. For example, the category "Communication" may have properties of "written" and "verbal." The constant comparison process may support existing categories or generate new ones. "By comparing where the facts are similar or different, we can generate properties of categories that increase the categories' generality and explanatory power" (Glaser & Strauss, 1967, p. 24).

Grounded Theory Method focuses on the constant comparison of data to identify emerging themes. It is common practice to identify emerging themes when conducting qualitative research (Miles & Huberman, 1994). Throughout the interview process and data analysis the qualitative researcher must, "… be open to possibilities afforded by the text rather than projecting a predetermined system of meanings onto the textual data" (Thompson, 1997, p. 441). Grounded Theory Method facilitates the development of a framework relative to the research question. Eventually, theoretical saturation (Strauss & Corbin, 1990) is attained and no new categories and properties emerge from the data. The researcher then knows that it will not be necessary to conduct any further interviews.

PERSONAL CONSTRUCT THEORY AND NARRATIVE INQUIRY

This section presents a description of two methods which are proposed for conducting *Ex Cultura* research. Personal Construct Theory (Kelly, 1955; 1963) documents what a research participant thinks about a personal experience. Narrative Inquiry (Girden, 2001; Scholes, 1981; Swap et al., 2001; Tulving, 1972) documents what a research participant has done and again records a personal experience. The research participant's personal experiences are sufficient for them to form an opinion and are related to a specific research question.

Personal Construct Theory (PCT)

Kelly (1955; 1963) developed Personal Construct Theory based upon his work as a clinical psychologist to help assess his patients' interpersonal relationships. He determined that individuals would develop a personalized system for dealing with current or future situations, which is based upon their own interpretations of their past experiences. These personal interpretations of previous experiences are directly informed by Hofstede's (1980) programming of the mind. That is, an individual's cultural environment will affect their interpretations of their experiences and their interpersonal relationship behaviours.

An individual's personal construct system may be documented using the technique known as the Role Construct Repertory Test, or RepGrid. "[RepGrids] ... provide a way of doing research into problems ... in a more precise, less biased, way than any other research method" (Stewart & Stewart, 1981, p. vii). It is also suggested by these authors that the RepGrid technique, "... enables one to interview someone in detail, extracting a good deal of information ... and to do this in such a way that input from the observer is reduced to zero" (Stewart & Stewart, 1981, p. 5). The two main components of the RepGrid are elements and constructs. Elements are entities within the research domain upon which the research participant may be able to form an opinion. The constructs are the research participant's interpretation of the elements within the same research domain.

RepGrids bring structure to the interview while allowing flexibility and reducing researcher bias. It is important to determine the interpretations of the research participants. Thus, this technique emphasizes a method for gathering consistent data from the research participant while allowing the participant to determine the subject matter and content of the data. This aspect is one of the advantages of the RepGrid technique. RepGrids generate a large amount of rich, in-depth, qualitative and narrative data relating to a research participant's explanation of an elicited construct. The documentation of the research participant's explanations as interview notes forms the basis of the research data. Detailed comments are recorded for each pole of the elicited construct. The researcher may determine a system of hierarchies, for each construct, which depicted the relationships, within the interview notes, between an elicited construct, at the RepGrid level, and a details action statement, at the interview note level. The interview notes may be obtained via the technique of Laddering whereby the researcher probes further regarding the research participant's detailed interpretations of a general comment.

The RepGrid technique has been employed in research areas beyond those for which it was originally designed. It has been used for general problem construction and market research (Bannister & Mair, 1968; Corsini & Marsella, 1983; Eden & Jones, 1984; Eden & Wheaton, 1980; Fransella, 1981; Shaw, 1980); and for knowledge acquisition for expert systems (Botton et al., 1989; Latta & Swigger, 1992; Phythian & King, 1992). Also, the RepGrid technique has been employed in a series of information systems research projects (Hunter, 1993; Hunter & Beck, 1996; Hunter, 1997; Hunter & Beck, 2000). The research question related to determining how members of various groups construe the skills and personal characteristics of "excellent" systems analysts. That is, the research attempted to document the personal construct system of research participants within the domain of discourse relating to their experiences working with systems analysts.

Narrative Inquiry

Narrative Inquiry documents, "... a segment of one's life that is of interest to the narrator and researcher" (Girden, 2001, p. 49). It entails "... the symbolic presentation of a sequence of events connected by subject matter and related by time" (Scholes, 1981, p. 205). The Narrative Inquiry approach facilitates documenting stories that are contextually rich and temporally bounded. The contextually rich concept suggests that those events, which are experienced first hand, are the ones that are most vividly remembered (Tulving, 1972). As Swap et al. (2001) suggest, employing an approach where research participants relate stories about their personal experiences "... would be more memorable, be given more weight, and be more likely to guide behavior" (Swap et al., 2001, p. 103). The second concept, temporally bounded, suggests that narratives should have a beginning and an ending, along with a chronological sequemce of intervening events. Research suggests that the sequential aspect of relating events contributes to the appropriateness of the narrative (Bruner, 1990; Czarniawska-Joerges, 1995; Vendelo, 1998).

Narrative Inquiry has been employed to investigate behavioral science (Rappaport, 1993), Fiction and film (Chatman, 1978), and strategic management (Barry & Elmes, 1997). It has been employed to investigate various aspects of information systems by Boland and Day (1989), and Hirschheim and Newman (1991). Further, Hunter and Tan (2001) employed Narrative Inquiry to identify the major career path impacts of information systems professionals. They interviewed a number of information systems professionals at various stages of their careers to determine why these individuals changed jobs. In order to ground the discussion in the research participants' personal experiences, individual resumes were employed as the main instrument to guide the interview and to elicit the narratives. The resume was employed to assist research participants to reflect upon their work experiences and report these experiences in a sequential account of events as they transpired throughout their careers. The resume approach has been used previously in information systems research (Young, 2000). The resume is readily available and an untapped source of data (Dex, 1991), as well as acting as a milestone reference to assist human memory recall (Baker, 1991). While the resume guided the interview, the next paragraph describes a generic technique upon which the interview was organized.

McCracken's (1988) Long Interview Technique may be used to provide some structure to the interview, yet allowing research participants to reflect on their personal experiences in a relatively unbiased and free-flowing manner. The four-step technique involves the following:

- Gaining an awareness of the relevant literature
- Introspectively understanding one's own awareness of the research question
- Conducting the interview during which research participants have an opportunity to tell their story
- Conducting analyses of the interview data to identify emerging themes.

The research participants are encouraged, through the research method, to thoroughly describe their interpretations of a specific experience. This process identifies important factors grounded within that experience.

The Long Interview Technique (McCracken, 1988) may be used in association with Narrative Inquiry. During the course of the interview research participants are asked to reflect upon past work experiences. Initially, "grand tour" (McCracken, 1988) questions are asked. These questions are general in nature and non-directive in manner, allowing the research participant to specify much of the substance or perspective of the interview. The main part of the interview relates to documenting the narratives of the research participant relative to the research question. The research participant is guided through a chronological discussion of events relative to the area under investigation. Throughout this section of the interview, "floating prompt" (McCracken, 1988) questions were asked. The nature of these questions depends upon the content of each interview, and, generally, relate to the researcher's decision to pursue a thread of discussion in more detail. Specific, or "planned prompt" (McCracken, 1988) questions were asked near the end of the interview in order to address issues gleaned from the literature or previous investigations.

Laddering

As described in both of the above research methods, a process of Laddering may be employed to obtain more in-depth responses from the research participant. The elaboration of the research participants' interpretations may be obtained via the technique of Laddering (Stewart & Stewart, 1981) whereby the researcher probes for more detail regarding a research participant's interpretations of a general comment. The technique incorporates a series of "how" questions to elicit more detail and to increase the researcher's understanding of the terms employed by the research participant to elaborate upon a construct. Laddering supports the unbiased search for a detailed understanding of a research participant's interpretation of a situation. The application of the process of Laddering will allow the researcher to probe further into the research participant's interpretation of their experiences. Thus, it is possible to allow the research participant the fullest amount of freedom while still maintaining a structured method for gathering qualitative data.

DISCUSSION OF ISSUES

This section presents a series of issues which must be addressed when conducting *Ex Cultura* research. These issues involve a consideration for various approaches to conducting the research, data gathering, involving co-researchers, and the language of interviews.

Development of Constructs

When conducting *Ex Cultura* research it is important to identify if the research method takes an emic or an etic approach. These concepts originated within linguistic research (Pike, 1954; Berry, 1990; Headland et al., 1990). Essentially, an emic approach is based upon constructs developed in one culture. Conversely, an etic approach is based upon universal constructs developed by comparing data from many cultures. The issue of which approach to adopt is further complicated by the introduction of another term, "pseudo-etic" (Triandis, 1972) which suggests constructs from a limited number of cultures could be used to logically deduce those constructs and their relationships which are considered universal. Thus, the most effective research approach will be one, which incorporates both emic and etic elements. That is, *Ex Cultura* researchers may replicate emic studies in other cultures from which it may be possible to evolve an etic model of universal constructs. Further, as Early and Mosakowski (1995) suggest,

...What seems to be the most useful approach to conducting IM [International Management] and ICO [Intercultural Organizational] research is to focus on the pseudo-etic approach to develop quasi-universal constructs which may be subsequently challenged to more universal tests of validity (Earley & Mosakowski, 1995, p. 9).

A truly etic study would require conducting an international investigation on a very large scale. This exciting challenge would require participation of a large number of researchers or a very long time for one researcher.

Convergence vs. Divergence

Another issue in conducting *Ex Cultura* research involves the competing hypotheses of convergence and divergence (Ronen, 1986; Webber, 1969; Yang, 1986). The convergence hypothesis suggests that cultures throughout the world are becoming similar. One explanation in support of the convergence hypothesis is the development and use of common technologies such as the Internet which facilitates *Ex Cultura* communication among many cultures. Another explanation relates to the internationalization of education and the consequent influencing of common attitudes and values. These two forces seem to be particularly relevant to the development of the global information technology profession.

Alternatively, the divergence hypothesis suggests that societies tend to resist changes to their culture and strive to retain their distinctiveness. This manuscript will not attempt to present a resolution to this issue. It is important, however, that researchers conducting *Ex Cultura* investigations indicate and support the perspective they propose to adopt. Therefore, at one and the same time there appears to be forces at work which will bring uniformity and standardization to the activities of global business operations in different cultures, and also forces which would encourage and reinforce differences in the approach to work.

Making Research Participant Contacts

Qualitative research usually involves conducting one-on-one interviews. Because of the distance involved in *Ex Cultura* research, the logistics become much more complex. It is more complicated to make contacts, organize travel arrangements, and schedule interviews. Perhaps the most difficult of these three items is making contacts. Beyond involving a local co-researcher, a knowledgeable facilitator with the appropriate contacts will be helpful. In either case, it will take a long time to develop a relationship with this initial contact. Organizing travel and interviews is less complex but requires some planning to fit the schedule commitments of the individuals involved in both the home and visiting countries.

Striving to Provide the "Right" Answer

When conducting qualitative interviews, researchers must continually be aware of whether the participant is attempting to respond by giving their interpretation of what they think the researcher wants to hear. Essentially, the research participant may strive to provide the "right" answer. These types of responses can arise in any situation. They may occur when the researcher and participant are from the same culture. But, they seem to arise more often when the two individuals are from different cultures. Thus, the researcher should strive to re-enforce the importance of the participant's comments and that there is neither a right nor a wrong answer. Indeed, the answer provided by the research participant is the "right" answer as it is their interpretation of their experiences.

Telling the Good News

Research participants will desire to only tell the good news. It is difficult to encourage participants to discuss any negative aspects of their current situations or past experiences. One approach that may help here is the development of a trusting relationship with the research participant over a long period of time. Eventually, as the research participant becomes more comfortable, it may be easier for them to discuss some of the negative interpretations of their experiences.

Involving Co-Researchers

An *Ex Cultura* qualitative project will take a very long time if one researcher is involved. Establishing contacts and obtaining participant commitment will be very difficult especially when trying to make these arrangements from afar and a different culture. Alternatively, if many researchers are involved concern arises about project co-ordination and researcher commitment. When more than one researcher is involved in a project, it becomes important to ensure a coordinated approach. This is especially the case when conducting qualitative *Ex Cultura* research. All researchers must understand and agree with the research objectives. It is also important that an interview protocol be developed and employed consistently throughout the project. This will facilitate subsequent data analysis.

One of the major concerns originating from Group Theory (McGrath et al., 2000) is member co-ordination. This concern becomes even more important when the members are geographically and culturally separated. Researcher commitment is imperative when more than one researcher is involved. If priorities change during a project, valuable data may be lost if a researcher does not complete their part of the project. Employing the concepts of team building early in the project may contribute to resolving this issue. It is important to ensure all researchers are able to identify the benefits of completing the project and sharing the data. A positive and open attitude towards another culture will also be helpful.

Language of the Interviews

If research is being conducted in another culture, in all likelihood another language will be involved. Thus, it may be necessary for either the researcher or the participant to speak a language which is not their mother tongue. This may make expressing interpretations or understanding an explanation more difficult. Alternatively, a translator may be employed. However, this will increase the logistical complexity. Also, a translator may be less familiar with the content of the conversation and word selection may affect the meaning of the participant's comments.

CONCLUSION

Beyond the issues discussed above, the in-depth interviews will be a source of rich data. Research participant's comments will give the researcher a valuable perspective on the subject under investigation from another culture. Comments in the interview will provide further elucidation and perhaps a new understanding of how a situation may be perceived in a different culture. Research participant's interpretations will be a valuable supply of data for subsequent analysis.

Qualitative research allows the research participant to decide on the content and descriptive nature of the response to the researcher's questions. This may allow new ideas to be discovered or different understandings to be documented by the researcher. While qualitative research provides some interesting methodological approaches, it is important to ensure the specific technique adopted is one which reflects a consideration for the specific objectives of the project. This approach to conducting research will ground the data within the culture of the research participant. This will allow subsequent analysis to be based upon the content of the comments initiated by the research participant.

Therefore, when conducting qualitative research, it is incumbent upon the investigator to gather data in a systematic way to address the above concerns. The RepGrid technique has been proven (Stewart & Stewart, 1981) to be an acceptable method to document the personal constructs of research participants. The Long Interview technique (McCracken, 1988) supports an open unbiased investigation. It allows the researcher to document a research participant's interpretation of an event.

Finally, these techniques respond to the concern for qualitative researcher bias by allowing the research participants to determine the response and to provide their own comment elaboration. The techniques lend structure to the qualitative data gathering process while allowing flexibility in the research participants' responses. Incorporating these techniques will support the grounding of interview data within the environment as interpreted by the research participant. The use of both techniques will support conducting *Ex Cultura* management research in global operations.

REFERENCES

Baker, M. (1991). *Research in Marketing*. London: MacMillan.

Bannister, D., & Mair, J. M. M. (1968). *The Evaluation of Personal Constructs*. New York: Academic Press, Inc..

Barry, D., & Elmes, M. (1997). Strategy Retold: Towards a Narrative View of Strategic Discourse. *Academy of Management Review*, *22*(2), 429–452.

Benbasat, I., & Zmud, R. W. (1999). Empirical Research in Information Systems: The Practice of Relevance. *Management Information Systems Quarterly*, *23*(1), 3–16. doi:10.2307/249403.

Berry, J. W. (1980). Introduction to Methodology. In Triandis, H. C., & Berry, J. W. (Eds.), *Handbook of Cross Cultural Psychology* (*Vol. 2*). Boston, MA: Allyn and Bacon.

Boland, R. J. Jr, & Day, W. F. (1989). The Experience of Systems Design: A Hermeneutic of Organization Action. *Scandinavian Journal of Management*, *5*(2), 87–104. doi:10.1016/0956-5221(89)90017-1.

Botten, N., Kusiak, A., & Raz, T. (1989). Knowledge Bases: Integration, Verification, and Partitioning. *European Journal of Operational Research*, *42*(2), 1. doi:10.1016/0377-2217(89)90315-9.

Bruner, J. (1990). *Acts of Meaning*. Cambridge, MA: Harvard University Press.

Chatman, S. (1978). *Story and Discourse: Narrative Structure in Fiction and Film*. Ithaca, NY: Cornell University Press.

Corsini, R., & Marsella, A. J. (1983). *Personality Theories, Research and Assessment*. Itasca, IL: Peacock Publishers, Inc..

Czarniawska-Joerges, B. (1995). Narration or Science? Collapsing the Division in Organization Studies. *Organization*, *2*(1), 11–33. doi:10.1177/135050849521002.

Dex, S. (1991). *Life and Work History Analyses*. London: Routledge.

Earley, P. C., & Mosakowski, E. (1995). A Framework for Understanding Experimental Research in an International and Intercultural Contextd. In Punnett, B. J., & Shenkar, O. (Eds.), *Handbook of International Management Research*. Hoboken, NJ: Blackwell Publishers, Inc..

Eden, C., & Jones, S. (1984). Using Repertory Grids for Problem Construction. *Journal of Operations Research*, *35*(9), 779–798.

Eden, C., & Wheaton, G. (1980). *In Favour of Structure, Centre for the Study of Organisational Change and Development*. Working paper. University of Bath, Bath, UK.

Fransella, F. (Ed.). (1981). *Personality - Theory, Measurement and Research*. New York: Methuen and Co..

Girden, E. R. (2001). *Evaluating Research Articles – From Start to Finish* (2nd ed.). Thousand Oaks, CA: Sage Publications.

Glaser, B. G., & Strauss, A. L. (1976). *The Discovery of Grounded Theory: Strategies for Qualitative Research*. New York: Aldine De Gruyter.

Headland, T. N., Pike, K. L., & Harris, M. (1990). *Emics and etics: The insider/outsider debate*. Newbury Park, CA: Sage Publications.

Hirschheim, R., & Newman, M. (1991). Symbolism and Information Systems Development: Myth, Metaphor and Magic. *Information Systems Research*, *2*(1), 29–62. doi:10.1287/isre.2.1.29.

Hofstede, G. (1980). *Culture's Consequences: International Differences in Work-Related Values*. Beverly Hills, CA: Sage Publications.

Hofstede, G. (1983). The Cultural Relativity of Organizational Practices and Theories. *Journal of International Business Studies*, (Fall): 75–89.

Hofstede, G. (1993). Cultural Constraints in Management Theories. *The Academy of Management Executive*, *7*(1), 81–94.

Hofstede, G., & Bond, M. H. (1988). The Confucius Connection: From Cultural Roots to Economic Growth. *Organizational Dynamics*, *16*(4), 4–21. doi:10.1016/0090-2616(88)90009-5.

Hofstede, G., Hofstede, G. J., & Minkov, M. (2010). *Cultures and Organizations: Software of the Mind* (2nd ed.). New York: McGraw-Hill.

Hofstede, G., & Minkov, M. (2010). Long- versus Short-term Orientation: New Perspectives. *Asia Pacific Business Review*, *16*(4), 493–504. doi:10.1080/13602381003637609.

Hofstede, G., Neuijen, B., Ohayv, D. D., & Sanders, G. (1990). Measuring Organizational Cultures: A Qualitative and Quantitative study Across Twenty Cases. *Administrative Science Quarterly*, *35*, 286–316. doi:10.2307/2393392.

Hunter, M. G. (1993). A Strategy for Identifying "Excellent" Systems Analysts. *The Journal of Strategic Information Systems*, *2*(1), 15–26. doi:10.1016/0963-8687(93)90019-7.

Hunter, M. G. (1994). "Excellent" Systems Analysts: Key Audience Perceptions. *Computer Personnel*, April, 15-31.

Hunter, M. G. (1997). The Use of RepGrids to Gather Interview Data about Information Systems Analysts. *Information Systems Journal*, *7*(1), 67–81. doi:10.1046/j.1365-2575.1997.00005.x.

Hunter, M. G., & Beck, J. E. (1996). A Cross-Cultural Comparison of "Excellent" Systems Analysts. *Information Systems Journal*, *6*(4), 261–281. doi:10.1111/j.1365-2575.1996.tb00018.x.

Hunter, M. G., & Beck, J. E. (2000). Using Repertory Grids to Conduct Cross-Cultural Information Systems Research. *Information Systems Research*, *11*(1), 93–101. doi:10.1287/isre.11.1.93.11786.

Hunter, M. G., & Tan, F. (2001). Information Systems Professionals in New Zealand: Reflective Career Biographies. In *Proceedings of International Conference of the Information Resources Management Association* (pp. 132-133). Toronto, CA.

Kelly, G. A. (1955). *The Psychology of Personal Constructs*. New York: Norton.

Kelly, G. A. (1963). *A Theory of Personality*. New York: Norton.

Latta, G. F., & Swigger, K. (1992). Validation of the Repertory Grid for Use in Modelling Knowledge. *Journal of the American Society for Information Science American Society for Information Science*, *42*(2), 115–129. doi:10.1002/(SICI)1097-4571(199203)43:2<115::AID-ASI2>3.0.CO;2-I.

Lee, A. S. (1999). Rigor and Relevance in MIS Research: Beyond the Approach of Positivism Alone. *Management Information Systems Quarterly*, *23*(1), 29–33. doi:10.2307/249407.

McCracken, G. (1988). *The Long Interview*. New York: Sage Publications.

Miles, M. B., & Huberman, A. M. (1994). *Qualitative Data Analysis: A New Sourcebook of Methods* (2nd ed.). Newbury Park, CA: Sage Publications.

Myers, M. D. (2009). *Qualitative Research in Business and Management*. Los Angeles, CA: Sage Publications.

Pervin, L. A. (1986). *Personality – Theory and Research* (5th ed.). New York: John Wiley and Sons.

Phythian, G. J., & King, M. (1992). Developing an Expert System for Tender Enquiry Evaluation: A Case Study. *European Journal of Operational Research*, *56*(1), 15–29. doi:10.1016/0377-2217(92)90289-L.

Pike, R. (1954). *Language in relation to a united theory of the structure of human behaviour*. Glendale, AZ: Summer Institute of Linguistics.

Rappaport, J. (1993). Narrative Studies, Personal Stories and Identity Transformation in the Mutual Help Context. *The Journal of Applied Behavioral Science*, *29*(2), 239–256. doi:10.1177/0021886393292007.

Reason, P., & Rowan, J. (Eds.). (1981). *Human Inquiry – A Sourcebook of New Paradigm Research*. Chichester, UK: John Wiley and Sons.

Robey, D., & Markus, M. L. (1998). Beyond Rigor and Relevance: Producing Consumable Research about Information Systems. *Information Resources Management Journal*, *11*(1), 7–15.

Ronen, S. (1986). *Comparative and Multinational Management*. New York: John Wiley.

Scholes, R. (1981). Language, Narrative, and Anti-Narrative. In Mitchell, W. (Ed.), *On Narrativity* (pp. 200–208). Chicago: University of Chicago Press.

Shaw, M. L. G. (1980). *On Becoming a Personal Scientist - Interactive Computer Elicitation of Personal Models of the World*. London: Academic Press.

Stewart, V., & Stewart, A. (1981). *Business Applications of Repertory Grid*. London: McGraw-Hill.

Strauss, A., & Corbin, J. (1990). *Basics of Qualitative Research: Grounded Theory Procedures and Techniques*. Newbury Park, CA: Sage Publications.

Swap, W., Schields, M., & Abrams, L. (2001). Using Mentoring and Storytelling to Transfer Knowledge in the Workplace. *Journal of Management Information Systems*, *18*(1), 95–114.

Thompson, C. J. (1997). Interpreting Consumers: A Hermeneutical Framework for Deriving Marketing Insights from the Texts of Consumers' Consumption Stories. *JMR, Journal of Marketing Research*, *34*, 438–455. doi:10.2307/3151963.

Triandis, H. C. (1972). *Analysis of subjective culture*. New York: Wiley Interscience.

Tulving, E. (1972). Episodic and Semantic Memory. In Tulving, E., & Donaldson, W. (Eds.), *Organization of Memory* (pp. 381–404). New York: Academic Press.

Vendola, M. T. (1998). Narrating Corporate Reputation: Becoming Legitimate Through Storytelling. *International Journal of Management and Organization*, *28*(3), 120–137.

Webber, R. H. (1969). Convergence and Divergence. *The Columbia Journal of World Business*, *4*(3), 75–83.

Yang, K. S. (1986). Will Societal Modernization Eventually Eliminate Cross-Cultural Psychological Differences. In Bond, M. H. (Ed.), *The Cross-Cultural Challenge to Social Psychology*. Newbury Park, CA: Sage Publications.

Young, J. (2000). *The Career Paths of Computer Science and Information Systems Major Graduates*. Unpublished doctoral thesis. University of Tasmania, Tasmania, Australia.

Chapter 19
The Effects of Culture on Planning and Technology in the Internationalisation of Medellín's SMEs

Luis Bustamante
University of Medellín, Colombia

ABSTRACT

As an emerging market, global business is of greatest importance in Colombia and several efforts are implemented to keep up with the international competitive environment. However, these efforts should be accompanied with the development of entrepreneurial capabilities in a wide range of ambits, among others, cross-cultural management. This chapter describes cultural influences in internationalisation activities of Medellin's small and medium enterprises based on original research results using descriptive multi-case methods within five companies and documentary review of business publications. It starts with an overview of the Colombian SME and cross-cultural management theories; then, the cultural influences on planning and internationalisation are listed, suggesting that systematic plans during internationalisation are not followed and technology tools are not properly seized due to management styles, a changing business environment, and small education levels.

DOI: 10.4018/978-1-4666-3966-9.ch019

INTRODUCTION

Unless you know everything what you need is thinking. Edward de Bono (Maclure & Davies, 1991, p. xii)

Business opportunities materialise in any national environment committed to provid proper conditions to investment and entrepreneurial activity. These conditions mostly rely on various actors whose interaction determines the environment's prospective or at least that's expected; for this reason governmental role is highly accepted as important in a company's performance as an organiser of the national environment towards business matters, among others. Since 2002 the Colombian government has been implementing several policies and programmes to attract foreign direct investment and improve a company's relative competitiveness (Posada, 2012). Tax incentives, export promotion agencies, free trade agreements, financing opportunities, and multiple others efforts have configured an interesting market for foreign direct investment.

Recent research on the business environment does not confirm a solid relation between the conditions of the business environment and incubation of companies (Struwig & Meru, 2011). According to Rugman, Oh, & Lim (2012), the competitiveness of multinational firms rely on several factors, such as Firm-Specific Advantages (FSAs) and Country-Specific Advantages (CSAs); both are articulated to generate appropriate business conditions not only from an external perspective, but also from an internal company approach. This also applies for SMEs around the world; they are called to develop their own set of capabilities and seize tools which proved to work in bigger entrepreneurial scenarios to face internationalisation. Specifically, Colombian SMEs are facing greater challenges given the governmental policies of economic integration and promotion of internationalisation activities and the relative informality in the sector's economic entrepreneurial action.

Recent economic events and governmental policy in Colombia encourages companies to improve their competitiveness. Soon, more international companies will penetrate the local market, forcing SMEs to look abroad and start internationalisation processes and national culture will propose difficulties (Leung, Bhagat, Buchan, Erez, & Gibson, 2005). Certainly, no company can escape from globalisation processes[1] (Deresky, 2005). This means every manager will eventually face the challenge of obtaining results and leading the organisation towards sustainability, profitability, and growth (Sallenave, 2002), and minimise culture consequences in entrepreneurial action. Constant changes of the Colombian business environment raise several questions on firms' performance and managerial capabilities to achieve competitiveness from different theoretical and practical perspectives.

This chapter objective is to describe cultural influences in internationalisation activities of Medellin's small and medium enterprises and the non-software technological tools integrated based on original research results. The first part presents a briefing on the SME in Colombia and the cross-cultural management approaches used in research. Then, cultural influences are linked with the use and appropriation of technology. Afterwards future research directions are proposed to encourage academic debate.

BACKGROUND

SME in Colombia

Defined by law, SMEs represent 92.6% of Colombian companies (Ministry of Commerce, Industry and Tourism of Colombia, 2008). In the target geographic area of research, there are over 14,000 medium, small, and micro enterprises according to countries regulation stated in Law 905 of 2004 (as follows, also presented in Box 1):

Article 2°. Definition. For all purposes, the term micro, including small, family owned enterprises, and medium enterprises, means every unit of economic exploitation bya natural or legal person, in business, agricultural, industrial, commercial or services activities, rural or urban, responding to two (2) of the following parameters:

For classification by combination of these parameters, the decisive factor is total assets

According to the Colombian Ministry of Commerce, Industry and Tourism (2008, p. 4), SMEs employ nearly 80.8% of the country's work force. They had been the object of a study for their economic importance from different perspectives (Marulanda, 2004; Martínez, 2009; Velásquez, 2004; Calle & Tamayo, 2005; Rodríguez, 2003; Howald, 2001). In terms of internationalisation activities, Colombian SMEs don't represent a meaningful portion of the country's total trade activities. Although internationalisation is not only represented by export and import activities, 94% of Medellin's SMEs did not export in 2011-12 (ANIF, 2012, p. 71), which reveals that going abroad is not in the agenda of their managers.

Usually, companies start their internationalisation by entering closer markets in what is commonly explained by the theory of internationalisation stages (Cavusgil, 1980; Gankema, Snuif, & Zwart, 2000), but the current situation of Colombian business environment does not allow this. Our relations with neighbours are deteriorated, and companies are beginning to seek new business horizons. Nevertheless, more than 50% of 2007 exports went to Venezuela and Ecuador (Ministerio de Comercio, Industria y Turismo, 2008, p. 70). This means that soon the process of internationalisation in Colombian companies may not be easily described by traditional theories which only provide partial explanations of the phenomenon, as Leonidas & Katsikeas (1996) stated.

Box 1. Parameters of Article 2° of Law 905 of 2004 summary

Companies Factors	Medium	Small	Micro-enterprise
Staff	Between 51 and 200 workers	Between 11 and 50 workers	Not exceeding 10 workers
Total assets	Between 5.001 and 30.000 legal monthly minimum salary	Between 501 and fewer than 5.000 legal monthly minimum salary	Less than 500 legal monthly minimum salary

Just like other SMEs in the world, Colombian companies have their own set of problems which have reduced their capabilities to internationalise. "These small, family-owned businesses have historically suffered from a series of constraints that impeded their growth and financial success: the inability to break beyond the local market, inadequate management, low or non-existent profit margins, and lack of access to technology and credit" (Torres, 2007, p. 155). As expected, if micro-enterprises improve their competitiveness, this will impact an important amount of the employed work force. Thus, questioning the possibility of improving micro-enterprise competitiveness from any perspective is important in Colombia.

Cross-Cultural Management

Cross-cultural management occupies a relatively important position in terms of international business research (Griffith, Cavusgil, & Xu, 2008). However, Colombian enterprises, apart from marketing activities, haven't realised the real importance of creating and applying cultural knowledge. Most of the efforts in international management education are based on logistics and marketing training. This would not be such an obstacle if the country had not started partnering with non-natural allies for international trade such as Turkey, South Korea, Singapore, and Japan, which poses greater difficulties.

Academic literature recognises different approaches to cross-cultural management and defines it as "development and application of knowledge about cultures in the practice of international management, when the people involved have different cultural identities. These people may or may not belong to the same business unit" (Mead, 2005, p. 16). These approaches may vary according to their locus of time explanation of cultural issues, as presented in Table 1.

Knowledge management and system thinking approaches focus on future events, while older approaches are based on past events. Although both are necessary, SMEs require theoretical proposals that derive into prospective tools to face different competitive scenarios. These tools must be as simple as possible, since a great majority of Colombian SMEs are run by people with poor qualifications.

Classical approaches to cross-cultural management have several criticisms in discussion, specifically to Hofstede's dimensions (Mc Sweeney, 2002; Myers & Tan, 2002; Hofstede, 2002; Hofstede, 2003; Baskerville-Morley, 2005), mainly related to the training proposal and the methodology of construction (Cavusgil & Das, 1997), as presented in Table 2. According to Earley & Peterson (2004), training has improvement opportunities if it makes lesser relations between individuals and their culture; design specific training methods for every manager; don't rely on analogical learning which is not as effective in every trainee; and find better ways to facilitate the broad cognitive background needed to start a possible formation course. As per the methodological issues, Mead (2005) states that assuming national territory as cultural unit may lead to dangerous generalisations; the results of the research may be imprinted with ethnocentrism and there is a chance of deviation in questionnaires on which the results are based.

For these reasons, and the fact that cross-cultural management is mostly applied and regularly used in large companies (Adler, 1997; Dowling, Welch, & Schuler, 1999; Schneider & Barsoux, 1997), a different approach to the issues is required. SMEs do not have the same firm-specific advantages as large companies do, and traditional approaches must be adapted or replaced by other proposals. Knowledge management (Søderberg & Holden, 2002) and systems thinking (Senge, 2004) would probably be more appropriate combined with methodological designs which privilege case studies. In cross-cultural management, Thomas (2008, p. 19) distinguishes six different possible types of them: domestic, replication, indigenous, comparative, international, and intercultural studies explained in Table 3.

Table 1. Cross-cultural management approaches

Approach	Focus	Further reading
Classical	Cultures' values	Hofstede (1980)
Anthropological	Ethnic groups	Ong Fon Sim (1993) Boulanger (1996)
Psychological	Contextual factors Multilevel theory	Fontaine & Richardson (2005) Klein & Koslowski (2000)
Stereotypes	Stereotypes	Jongeward (1999) Hewstone (2003)
Knowledge management	Culture as tacit knowledge	Holden (2002)
Systems thinking	Structure of inter-cultural relation systems	Senge (2004) Sterman (2000)

Source: Adapted from Fontaine (2007)

Table 2. Typical criticism on classical cross-cultural management approaches

Training Issues	Methodological Issues
Close individual-culture relations Same training for everyone Analogical learning Cognitive background	National territory as cultural unit Ethnocentrism Deviation in questionnaires

Source: Constructed from Mead (2005) and Earley & Peterson (2004)

Table 3. Types of Cross-Cultural Management Studies

Category	Description	Cultural assumptions	Research questions
Domestic	Management studies in a single country	Culture is ignored, or universality of theory is assumed.	How can we explain and predict the behaviour of people in organisations?
Replication	Management study repeated in another country	Universality is questioned; there is no theory available to predict the effect of culture.	Does this theory that applies in culture A also apply in culture B?
Indigenous	Individual Management studies conceived and executed in one or many cultures	Cultural differences are assumed to exist, indigenous theory is needed to explain behaviour.	How can we explain and predict the behaviour of people in organisations in country X?
Comparative	Management studies conducted in two or more countries	Similarities and differences exist; there may or may not be a theory available to predict the effect of culture.	What similarities and differences exist in the behaviour of people in organisations? Is this theory universal?
International	Studies of multinational organisations	Similarities and differences exist, or culture is ignored.	How do organisations that operate in multiple countries function?
Intercultural	Studies of intercultural interactions in organisations	Specific aspects of culture are part of the theoretical framework underlying the study.	How is this theory influenced by cultural differences, and how is it universal?

Source: Thomas (2008, p. 19)

Knowledge management and systems thinking approach to cross-cultural management is consequent with the definition of international management by Gooderham & Nordhaug (2004, p. 1): "generation and transfer of knowledge across initial settings, organisations, and countries"; because it can be articulated to the cultural intelligence system[2] to propose a cross-cultural management process, presented in Figure 1.

Throughput may be filled by different theoretical constructions. However, the cultural intelligence system seems to be a clever response to the blank, presented in Figure 2. It is already defined as a system; it recognises the importance of transforming tacit knowledge into explicit applications and emphasises in possible categories of skills to be developed. Thomas et al. (2008, p. 127) define cultural intelligence as "a system of interacting knowledge and skills, linked by cultural metacognition, that allows people to adapt to, select, and shape the cultural, aspects of their environment."

This system is composed of three main elements: knowledge, skills, and metacognition (Thomas, et al., 2008). The first element is shaped by expertise and observation; it facilitates effective responses based on previous experiences and attitudes, choosing the most appropriate actions among them. The second refers to easily interact with other individuals and to develop perceptual, relational, and adaptation skills. Finally, metacognition refines the response acting as a self-controlling element and creates a connection for all elements.

Not every interaction of a company is related to cross-cultural management and that must be differenced by the leaders of the organisations. In terms of Colombian SMEs compared to large companies, they would probably have fewer situations to apply cross-cultural management. But this does not excerpt them to build every capability required to compete abroad in internationalisation. Large debate is still needed to effectively materialise the different approaches of cross-cultural management especially the latest into SMEs practices.

Figure 1. Cross Cultural management process (with cultural intelligence)

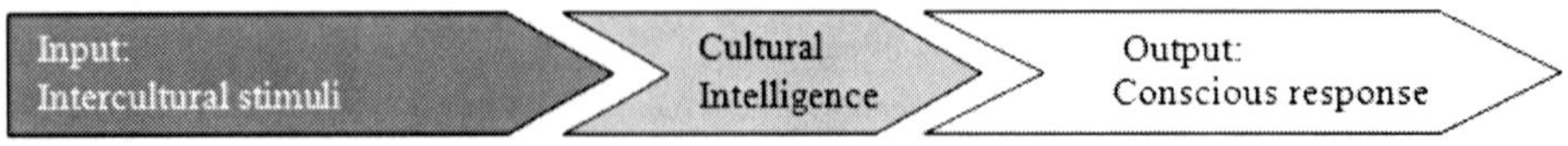

Source: Bustamante & Aguilar (2012)

CULTURAL INFLUENCES FOR INTERNATIONALISATION ON PLANNING AND TECHNOLOGY APPLICATIONS OF COLOMBIAN SMES

Research Method[3]

Background

This chapter is based on the original results of two separate research projects supported by the University of Medellín between 2011 and 2012. The first one, developed in 2011 and entitled *Cross Cultural Management Challenges in Internationalization Activities of Medellin's SMEs*, aimed to analyse by identifying and describing internationalisation activities to typify cross-cultural management challenges found in Medellin's SMEs. The second started in January 2012 analysed the use of ICTs in international negotiation processes in the internationalisation of productive organisations of Medellín. The project named "Information and communication technologies in negotiation: Tool or obstacle to the internationalisation of productive organizations in Medellin?" was running at the submission of this chapter; however, it had already accomplished the first specific objective: to identify in documentary sources ICT applications that influence international negotiation processes of Colombian companies. Both projects are strongly related to each other since most problems of the national business environment are a common finding in local research[4].

Data Collection Instruments

The projects were designed to collect data using simple electronic questionnaires following the proposals of Stawarski & Phillips (2008) in order to retrieve a significant amount of data. The first project had the specific objective of describing

Figure 2. Cultural Intelligence System

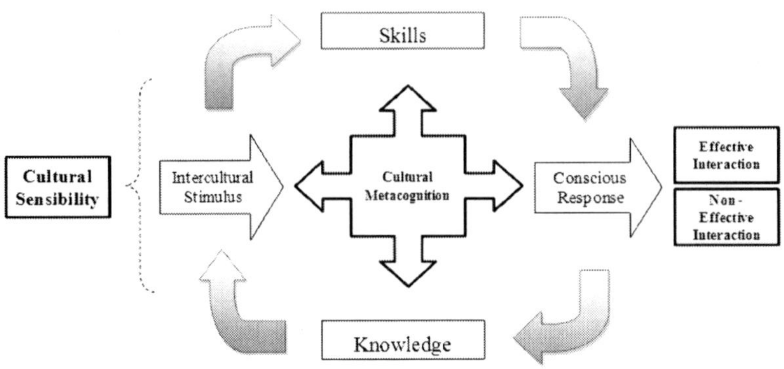

internationalisation activities, but since these were so broad in definition and practice, it was preferred to group them according to Fayol's administrative process. This is planning, organising, directing, coordinating, and controlling activities (Fayol, 1974). These categories served as a guide for designing the questionnaire complemented with a documentary analysis of international business management academic literature; the following generic internationalisation activities according to the administrative process were identified in this task, as presented in Table 4.

These activities were translated into a questionnaire consisting of 33 multiple choice, Likert-type scale, semantic differential scale, and pre-coded open questions, with an attachment of 9 open ended questions. Different efforts were implemented to reach ten micro-enterprises in the service industry using a 15,000 company database retrieved from the Chamber of Commerce of Medellín. Two e-mail waves were sent and ten business centres were visited in order to ensure enough responses. However, after several efforts during eight months of fieldwork, companies' cooperation was very poor and only five companies correctly replied to the questionnaire. This forced the research to improve the multi-case approach using meta-analysis tools partially ordered meta-matrixes (Miles & Huberman, 1994). The characteristic of respondents are described in the next sub-section.

The second project, in execution at the submission of this document, had a first goal of identifying, by means of a documentary analysis, ICT applications in international negotiation of companies in Medellín. An online form was designed to record the information of the most important local business publications such as *Revista Dinero*, *Portafolio*, *La República*, *El Colombiano*, *Revista Enter*, and an international publication: *Business Week*. Since the project is oriented towards international negotiation, three search terms procurement, negotiation, and distribution were used to cover the generic stages of negotiation planning, dialogue, and closure[5]. Articles were analysed in mentions of procedures, manuals, software, processes, training, and systematisation or expertise record. From empiric observations, it was decided to inquiry not only on software but in non-software applications, as mentioned. The documentary study took six months and reviewed publications from the last 10 years for a total of 80 relevant entries that served as a basis for sketching an inventory of ICT applications used in Colombian companies[6].

Characteristic of Respondents

Within the first research project, a questionnaire was distributed among a discretional selection of 400 enterprises from a 15,000 database of the Chamber of Commerce of Medellín to reach a target of 10 companies. These enterprises were selected to fit the following criteria: 1) allow access to information, 2) advanced stages of internationalization, 3) experience in global processes, 4)

Table 4. Generic internationalisation activities in academic literature

Planning	Organising	Directing	Coordinating	Controlling
▪ Planning research ▪ Executing research ▪ Selecting relevant information ▪ Analysing information ▪ Formulating plans ▪ Socialising plans	▪ Design of internationalisation activities ▪ Training human talent ▪ Test internationalisation activities	▪ Team building ▪ Establishing rules ▪ Socialising objectives ▪ Doubts solving ▪ Executing internationalisation activities	▪ Lead teams ▪ Motivating human resource ▪ Communicating developments ▪ Executing plans	▪ Monitoring developments ▪ Correcting deviations ▪ Retrieving feedback into plans

convenient location and access, 5) relationships with non-natural markets neither culturally similar, and, 6) service industry.

The latter respondents are characterised by having small staff less than five people in most cases. Four of them were constituted as S.A.S.[7], a relatively new figure in Colombia, which allows flexibility for creating and closing companies with a broad spectre of economic activities. Most of the studied companies were in the information technologies industry. Also, 60% were founded less than three years ago and 80% are located in the entertainment and business area of *El Poblado*.

Data Analysis

For the research conducted in Medellín (Colombia), a knowledge management, systematic approach to cross-cultural management was preferred in order to make tacit knowledge explicit. Three reasons motivated this decision: first, culture is a fuzzy concept in popular conception; second, directly asking for cultural elements may lead to misconceptions; and third, traditional approaches require big samples of companies to be studied.

Data analysis, apart from descriptive statistics of the questionnaires, was based on a partially ordered meta-matrix which permits to multiply information when a descriptive data collection does not have enough entries (Miles & Huberman, 1994). The matrix was configured by crossing generic internationalisation activities with cross-cultural management proposals, specifically Hofstede's, for its wide acceptance and Cultural Intelligence for its interesting unique approach related to knowledge management. Also, emergent categories of analysis are considered. In the example presented in Table 5, a reduced model of the meta-matrix is presented. The vertical axis includes only one activity of the administrative process, and the horizontal axis only the knowledge perspective of cross-cultural management; in addition, the complete matrix includes categories of analysis for cross-cultural skills.

Each relation in the matrix represents a possible cross-cultural management challenge that was latterly contrasted with empirical and theoretical data to determine if it was ascertainable. As a result, eleven cross-cultural management challenges that affect the internationalisation activities of Medellín's SMEs were described. These presume influences on planning and technology management described in section *3.2. Results and Discussion*. Table 6 lists the chal-

Table 5. Example of the partially ordered meta-matrix used for planning activities

Administrative Process		**Knowledge**					
	Long Term Orientation	**Power Distance**	**Masculinity**	**Individualism**	**Uncertainty Avoidance**	**Dependence on Others**	**Others**
Planning Activities							
Planning research							
Executing research	**Relation 3**						
Selecting relevant information							
Analysing information			**Relation 4**				
Formulating plans							
Socialising plans					**Relation 5**		
Others							

Table 6. Cross-cultural management challenges in internationalisation activities of Medellin's SMEs

Knowledge related challenges	Skills related challenges
Challenge 1: Uncertain but indifferent *Sub-Challenge:* Uncertainty avoidance **Challenge 2:** Anarchy in entrepreneurial action *Sub-Challenge:* Uncertainty avoidance **Challenge 3:** Your vision, my vision *Sub-Challenge:* Long term orientation **Challenge 4:** I'm the one who commands *Sub-Challenge:* Dependence on others **Challenge 5:** I'm the boss *Sub-Challenge:* Masculinity **Challenge 6:** No time for knowledge *Emergent Sub-Challenge:* Elements of culture	**Challenge 7:** First what comes first *Sub-Challenge:* Skills for adaptation **Challenge 8:** Closed management system *Sub-Challenge:* Skills for adaptation **Challenge 9:** First and last attempt *Sub-Challenge:* Skills for motivation **Challenge 10:** We'll see tomorrow *Sub-Challenge:* Skills for perception **Challenge 11:** Let's focus *Sub-Challenge:* Skills for relations

Source: Bustamante & Aguilar (2012)

lenges and shows a representative name associated to the situation.

Every challenge received a name to ease its apprehension and is described as much as data analysis permitted. These results are only valid for companies with a real commitment to foreign markets (Johanson & Vahlne, 2009); however, there's a necessity of broadening the scope of each challenge with further research to transfer the project's product. A brief of every challenge is presented in Table 7.

Results and Discussion

Internationalisation processes are influenced by national culture just like any other entrepreneurial activity as it was stated by Hofstede[8], Hall (1976), Fontaine (2007), and others. These realities also apply to SMEs. Most of the studied companies presented basic internationalisation processes based on non-regular export and import activities. The latter analysis revealed that proposed cross-cultural management challenges are basically the result of deficient planning and poor application of enterprise technology within internationalisation activities. This can be summarised in the overlapping clusters figure presented in Figure 3 (Hodson, 1991).

The first step to the internationalisation of Medellín's SMEs is to beat the lack of vision and start serious planning activities to configure a globalised enterprise set, develop and apply different technologies, and build skills to appropriate the international environment into the daily entrepreneurial action (Bustamante, Arboleda, & Gutiérrez, 2010). The lack of planning in internationalisation activities is an effect of Colombian culture in entrepreneurial action that can be solved by appealing to different approaches to cross-cultural management and technology applications.

Theoretical evidence suggests that the seizing and applying of ICTs may improve the performance of companies (Alvadbi, Keramati, & Razmi, 2007). This may as well impact on the mentioned cross-cultural management challenges if we approach to this area from knowledge management perspectives (Holden, 2002; Dalkir, 2011; Senge, 2004). However, two obstacles derive from this approach. First, in Medellín, most executives think of knowledge management and technology only as software applications, and, secondly, companies are modified to use software instead of adding value, and ignoring strategic planning processes thus spoiling any chance of developing competitive advantages (Hill & Jones, 2000).

The documentary study analysis revealed 91% of the articles related to internationalisation activities were dedicated to non-software applications. A huge percentage of the articles refer to business

Table 7. Briefing on the cross-cultural management challenges identified

Challenge	Brief Description
Challenge 1: Uncertain but indifferent	Worries about ambiguous and uncertain situations persist, according to the questionnaire results and as a constant of Colombian cultural programming. However, people in charge of internationalisation activities of studied companies do nothing to prepare against them.
Challenge 2: Anarchy in entrepreneurial action	Internationalisation activities are executed without establishing rules, it is evidenced that they are mostly empirically developed.
Challenge 3: Your vision, my vision	Culturally programmed mindsets define human range of vision and since these are different for staff in local companies and foreign partners causes difficulties of coordination.
Challenge 4: I'm the commander	The performance of human resource is closely dependant on the manager's presence. When staff in charge of internationalisation activities is left alone, they have difficulties to adapt to environment changes and control their performance.
Challenge 5: I'm the boss	Building teams is a difficult because of the role of the owners; they represent a figure of prestige and personal achievement whit fewer motivation to associate.
Challenge 6: No time for knowledge	Elements such as language, education, aesthetics and values are recognised as possible causes for misunderstandings in internationalisation activities. However, evidence shows lack of knowledge and preparation to face culture elements.
Challenge 7: First what comes first	Owners are not focused on effective cross-cultural relations, but accomplishing goals in other aspects of the organisation.
Challenge 8: Closed management system	Companies do not verify execution of tasks to correct any deviation. Apparently environmental stimuli are not taken as input for entrepreneurial action which is a requisite in cross-cultural management.
Challenge 9: First and last attempt	A single person is subject and object of motivation and internationalisation is a complex process that requires effort and dedication. Evidence suggests a lack of motivation in owners to tolerate frustration.
Challenge 10: We'll see tomorrow	In 80% of studied companies employees are not trained for identifying and responding to situational changes or to adapt to cultural differences. Managers focus on today's task over future challenges.
Challenge 11: Let's focus	Staff in charge of internationalisation activities does not incorporate cultural elements into conversations with foreign companies rather than focusing in transactional details of the business.

Source: Bustamante & Aguilar (2012)

processes, as shown in Table 8; however, since most of the internationalisation activities derive from spontaneous opportunities, it is not possible to confirm if these processes are established or at least designed prior to the execution of internationalisation activities. This could possibly lead to poor outcomes as Li, Li, and Dalgic (2004) confirm with their experiential learning theoretical perspective of SMEs internationalisation.

Other results of the documentary study indicate that negotiation is not as important as other business phases such as procurement and distribution; it only receives 10% of entries (See Table 9). From a negotiation perspective, this could mean that establishing business relations may be more dif-

Table 8. Technology applications in internationalisation of Colombian companies according to business publications

Element	Articles	Percentage
Procedure	6	4%
Manual	0	0%
Software	14	9%
Process	107	68%
Training	10	6%
Systematisation or experience registry	5	3%
Other	25	16%

Figure 3. Main problems of internationalisation and entrepreneurial action derived from culture

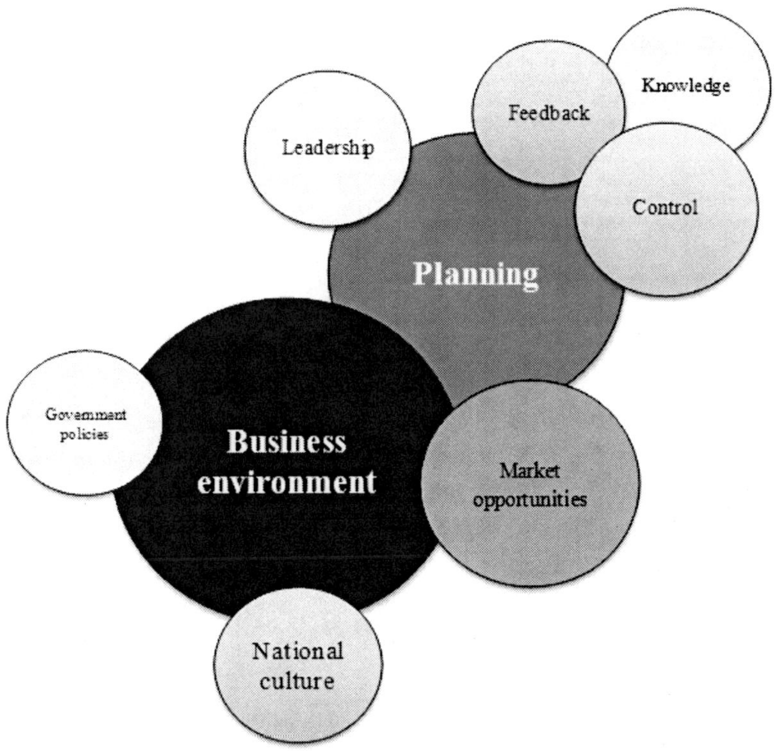

Source: Bustamante & Aguilar (2012)

ficult due to cultural tendency of short-term results related to Colombian managers' style. In terms of internationalisation theory (Welch & Luostarinen, 1988; Root, 1994; Rialp, 1999; Galván, 2003), transactional business may not be enough to generate steady links with partners abroad and demonstrate commitment and knowledge generation of foreign markets to advance in internationalisation stages (Johanson & Vahlne, 2009).

Other cultural influence on planning processes is associated to the relative importance given of each plan of the company. In studied Colombian SMEs, a commercial plan is more important than any other. Sales is the first worry of the managers; survival is a priority which could mislead to transactional business. A production plan, as presented in Table 10, is relegated to the last place; it is not clear if they answer to market needs with contingency production frameworks or if they had already designed market-oriented production processes.

This apparent transactional focus for survival alters international negotiation, especially for partnering. As a communication process and mandatory condition for establishing long-term relationships, negotiation is always influenced by culture (Danciu, 2010). Besides, since organisational leaders in 80% of studied companies are only responsible for internationalisation activities,

Table 9. Article results for each query term

Query term	Articles	Percentage
Procurement	67	43%
Distribution	75	48%
Negotiation	15	10%

Table 10. Relative importance of business plans for every functional area

Plan	Relative Importance
Commercial	4,6
Marketing	4,0
Human Resource	4,0
Informatics and Technologic	4,0
Financial	3,6
Logistic	3,4
Production	3,2

rules are not clearly established and little control is made on advances of the execution. You cannot control what you have not planned in advance.

To summarize, transactional business focus, hardly any planning, centralisation of responsibilities, and some elements of Colombian culture make global business difficult. In response, managers opt for incorporating technology to improve a company's internationalisation results. For example, experiences on the usage of ICT in the negotiation processes during internationalisation of Medellín's SMEs demonstrate that most of the applications are used but not appropriated to seize all possibilities and create value. Companies invest in software expecting this to solve all their problems, when in reality, software can only solve humanly made and introduced inquiries. This leads to a machine bureaucracy (Mintzberg, 1979; 1992), which generates difficulties to identify a company's problems, innovate, and appropriate technology correctly.

No technology application can solve detected problems on planning readiness, commonly used tools, and little appropriation. These obstacles require organisational changes at every level, including a deep understanding of Colombian business culture. Survey results indicate that 60% of studied companies do not plan their internationalisation activities, while a small 20% make plans with less than six months of anticipation. Only 20% have between six months and a year to define their paths of action. Although Colombians are averse to uncertainty, they do not tend to manage alternative ways to face it, then manifesting this behaviour into business administration.

Documental study also pointed out that the business process is the most used tool over software and other applications. Processes are important in order to standardise and generate improvement and innovation opportunities (Prahalad & Krishnah, 2008). However, these are not correctly implemented resting innovation capacity and thus being irrelevant for internationalisation performance. In either case, whether a company uses software or non-software technology applications, the real problem is the appropriation-use dilemma. The mere fact of using a tool does not mean that it is fully seized and positively related to the achievement of a goal. Technology must be subordinated and at the same time assist the design of business strategy (Alierta, 2011), especially during internationalisation processes, in order to become a real tool for Medellín companies.

MANAGERIAL IMPLICATIONS

As presented, the Colombian business environment represents several challenges for any firm or any skilled practitioner. In particular, international managers in the country must be aware of several inward and outward forces and realities related to technology investment, personnel training, free trade policies, and knowledge management. These different elements are much more related than they seem, and generate forces to drive competitiveness towards global standards, in many cases out of the reach of SMEs.

Firstly, technology investment in Colombia should be decision based on multiple criteria, including staff's capabilities and support services. SMEs require quick, easy solutions for their problems, which do not represent a major change in company's focus. Most managers confuse performance improvement with software application and this is not necessarily true. Cases on the implementation of corporate enterprise resource planning (ERP) tools and other major changes that end up moving to previous software platforms are abundant in the business literature. Also, specific regulations in Colombia may be against *good practices* to protect other governmental interests. An example on this is the prevention of money laundering, therefore financial regulation in the country is rigid and in some cases result in several extra procedures of earnings registry and follow-up.

Another important issue in Colombia is related to personnel training. Elementary and secondary education reaches only 37.1% of the potential population (Colombian Ministry of Education, 2012). College education is sometimes considered a privilege; in 2010, only 37.2% of the population enrolled into College education (Colombian Ministry of Education, 2012), and technical education was preferred among the lower bases of society. A company must have a training policy of the staff in order to seize its full potential and most SMEs ignore this issue. These firms primarily focus on survival strategies, which in the entrepreneurial rationale, have more sense to ensure the long term functioning of the company. However, international competition and competitiveness require more than survival strategies. It could be fixed by applying knowledge management approaches to understand the free trade policy and seize the forthcoming opportunities and, of course, the treats of international competition.

Current governmental policies encourage the establishment of free trade agreements with several countries all around the globe. The upcoming agenda includes Australia, Russia, and African countries such as Kenya, South Africa, and China (Romero & Ramírez, 2012). This continuously transforms the business environment, attracting potential customers and competitors. According to the government, there are ongoing FTAs with the United States, Mexico, Salvador, Guatemala, Honduras, CARICOM, the Andean Community, MERCOSUR, Cuba, Chile, Canada, the EFTA, and a treaty with the European Union is subscribed pending for ratification. Negotiations are currently made with South Korea, Panamá, Turkey, Israel, Japan, Costa Rica, and the Alliance of the Pacific (Colombian Ministry of Commerce, 2012).

The country is gaining terrain in international trade as security and infrastructure conditions improve. These circumstances mean that managers must develop serious planning schemes to seize future opportunities as every FTA comes into vigour; otherwise competitors may establish entry barriers to protect their positions in the market.

Anticipating future events and designing correct strategies to prevent negative impacts and boost positive endings only result from knowledge management (KM) perspectives, especially by strengthening the latter steps of the KW process which ensure future intellectual capability (Dalkir, 2011). However, KW approaches in Colombia are very rare and limited to medium-sized and big companies. This is not because firms do not want to implement these advanced management techniques, as one might guess, but is a consequence of the previously presented issues: technology investment, personnel training, and free trade policies that change the face of the business environment.

CONCLUSION

The previous analyses of the Colombian business environment from planning, technological, and cultural perspectives may seem too hard for the real appealing of the market. As any investor recognises, high profits come from hard work and a correct interpretation of the market conditions. There are some important elements to be improved, but the foreign direct investment indexes do not lie Colombia is in the mainstream of the emergent markets in Latin America, even with the difficult situations after the global 2008 crisis

FDI continues to grow (Posada, 2012). Some last items should be highlighted:

To strengthen the relative competitiveness of Colombian SMEs for global business, it is important to change the internationalisation paradigm from experiential learning processes to systematic planning. Future research directions should focus on the implementation of transforming processes for SMEs in Colombia developing not only basic competencies but skills on cross-cultural management and technology management in emerging markets.

Studies on SMEs, not only in Colombia but in the world, mostly diagnose the same difficulties: limited financial resources, scarce managerial skills, and informal execution (Baird, Lyles, & Orris, 1994; Papadopoulos, 1987). Nevertheless, few effective solutions have appeared in the country to face the challenges of internationalisation and the establishment of global business. Strategies such as increased governmental role, financing opportunities, export promotion agencies, networking arrangements, among others, should be companied with internationalisation processes that cover every other sphere of human interaction. In other words, Colombia has to configure a globalised environment and educate citizens of the world if it is willing to provide conditions for internationalising every human endeavour.

Finally, when incorporating technology applications to solve any business problem, whether it is software based or not, it is necessary to evaluate its use and appropriation with the intention of determining if it is an effective alternative to the issue. Also, human resource training should be addressed with the aim of seizing their full potential. Simply relying on technology applications to improve business performance may leave aside the importance of defining a business model, establishing leaderships, and allowing people to print their particular seal to the organisational framework.

REFERENCES

Adler, N. (1997). *International dimensions of organizational behavior*. Cincinnati, OH: South Western.

Alierta, C. (2011). The Promise of Technology. In W. E. Forum, *The Global Information Technology Report 2010-2011* (p. 435). Geneva, Switzerland: World Economic Forum Editors.

Alvadbi, A., Keramati, A., & Razmi, J. (2007). Assessing the impact of information technology on firm performance considering the role of intervening variables: Organizational infrastructures and business processes reengineering. *International Journal of Production Research*, *45*(12), 2697–2734. doi:10.1080/00207540600767780.

ANIF. (2012). *Informe de Resultados Gran Encuesta PYME 2012-1*. Bogotá: ANIF.

Baird, I., Lyles, M., & Orris, J. (1994). The choice of international strategies by small business. *Journal of Small Business Management*, *48*(1), 48–59.

Baskerville-Morley, R. (2005). A research note: The unfinished business of culture. *Accounting, Organizations and Society*, *30*(4), 389–391. doi:10.1016/j.aos.2004.08.002.

Bazerman, M., & Neale, M. (1992). *Negotiating Rationally*. New York: The Free Press.

Boulanger, C. (1996). Ethnicity and practice in Malaysian unions. *Ethnic and Racial Studies*, *19*(3), 660–679. doi:10.1080/01419870.1996.9993929.

Bustamante, L., & Aguilar, S. (2012). *Retos de gestión intercultural en las actividades de internacionalización de microempresas de Medellín*. Medellín, Colombia: Universidad de Medellín.

Bustamante, L., Arboleda, A., & Gutiérrez, J. (2010). Cultura, política industrial y competitividad internacional de PyMEs en Colombia. *Revista Ad-Minister*, (16), 83-98.

Calle, A., & Tamayo, V. (2005). Estrategia e internacionalización en las pymes: Caso Antioquia. *Cuadernos de Administración, 18*(30), 137–164.

Cavusgil, T. (1980). On the Internationalization Process of Firms. *European Research, 8*(6), 273–281.

Cavusgil, T., & Das, A. (1997). Methodological issues in empirical cross-cultural research: A survey of the management literature and a framework. *Management International Review, 37*(1), 71–96.

Colombian Ministry of Commerce. (2012). *Acuerdos suscritos, vigentes y en negociación.* Retrieved October 29, 2012, from http://www.tlc.gov.co/

Colombian Ministry of Education. (2012). *Estadísticas del Sector Educativo en Colombia.* Retrieved October 29, 2012, from http://menweb.mineducacion.gov.co/seguimiento/estadisticas/

Colombian Ministry of Education. (2012, September). *Resumen de indicadores de Educación Superior.* Retrieved October 29, 2012, from http://www.mineducacion.gov.co/sistemasdeinformacion/1735/w3-article-212350.html

Dalkir, K. (2011). *Knowledge management in theory and practice.* Cambridge, MA: MIT Press.

Danciu, V. (2010). The Impact of the Culture on the International Negotiations: An Analysis Based on Contextual Comparisons. *Theoretical and Applied Economics, 17*(8), 87–102.

Deresky, H. (2005). *International Management. Managing across Borders and Cultures.* Upper Saddle River, NJ: Prentice Hall.

Dowling, P., Welch, D., & Schuler, R. (1999). *International human resource management. Managing people in a multinational context.* Cincinnati, OH: South-Western.

Earley, C., Ang, S., & Tan, J. (2006). *CQ: Developing Cultural Intelligence at Work.* Palo Alto, CA: Stanford University Press.

Earley, C., Murnieks, C., & Mosakowski, E. (2007). Cultural Intelligence and the Global Mindset. In M. Javidan, R. Steers, & M. Hitt (Eds.), The Global Mindset (Advances in International Management, vol. 19, pp. 75-103). Oxford, UK: JAI Press.

Earley, P. (2002). Redefining Interactions across Cultures and Organizations: Moving Forward with Cultural Intelligence. *Research in Organizational Behavior, 24*(1), 271–299. doi:10.1016/S0191-3085(02)24008-3.

Earley, P., & Ang, S. (2003). *Cultural intelligence: Individual interactions across cultures.* Stanford, CA: Stanford University Press.

Earley, P., & Mosakowski, E. (2004). Toward culture intelligence: Turning cultural differences into a workplace advantage. *The Academy of Management Executive, 18*(3), 151–157. doi:10.5465/AME.2004.28561784.

Earley, P., & Peterson, R. (2004). The Elusive Cultural Chameleon: Cultural Intelligence as a New Approach to Intercultural Training for the Global Manager. *Academy of Management Learning & Education, 3*(1), 100–115. doi:10.5465/AMLE.2004.12436826.

Fayerweather, J., & Kapoor, A. (1976). *Strategy and Negotiation for the International Corporation.* Cambridge, MA: Ballinger. doi:10.1002/tie.5060180210.

Fayol, H. (1974). *Administración Industrial y General.* México: Herrero Hnos. Svcs. S.A..

Fisher, R., Ury, W., & Patton, B. (1991). *Getting to yes: Negotiating agreement without giving in.* New York: Penguin.

Fon Sim, O. (1993). Chinese ethnicity: Its relationship to some selected aspect of consumer behaviour. *Malaysian Management Review, 28*(2), 29–43.

Fontaine, R. (2007). Cross-cultural management: Six perspectives. *Cross-Cultural Management. International Journal (Toronto, Ont.)*, *14*(2), 125–135.

Fontaine, R., & Richardson, S. (2005). On cultural values in Malaysia: Malays, Chinese and Indians compared. *Journal of Cross Cultural Management*, *12*(4), 63–77. doi:10.1108/13527600510798141.

Galván, I. (2003). *La formación de la estrategia de selección de mercados exteriores en el proceso de internacionalización de las empresas*. Retrieved August 25, 2009, from http://www.eumed.net/tesis/igs/

Gankema, H., Snuif, H., & Zwart, P. (2000). The internationalization process of small and medium-sized enterprises: An evaluation of stage theory. *Journal of Small Business Management*, *38*(4), 15–27.

Ghauri, P., & Usunier, J. (2003). *International Business Negotiations*. New York: Pergamon.

Gooderham, P., & Nordhaug, O. (2004). *International management: Cross-boundary challenges*. Malden, MA: Wiley-Blackwell.

Griffith, D., Cavusgil, T., & Xu, S. (2008). Emerging themes in international business research. *Journal of International Business Studies*, *39*(7), 1220–1235. doi:10.1057/palgrave.jibs.8400412.

Hall, E. (1976). *Beyond culture*. New York: Doubleday.

Hewstone, M. (2003). Intergroup contact: Panacea for prejudice? *The Psychologist*, *16*(7), 352–355.

Hill, C., & Jones, G. (2000). *Administración estratégica: Un enfoque integrado*. México: McGraw-Hill.

Hodson, R. (1991). The Active Worker: Compliance and Autonomy at the Workplace. *Journal of Contemporary Ethnography*, *20*(1), 47–78. doi:10.1177/089124191020001003.

Hofstede, G. (1979). Value Systems in Forty Countries: Interpretation, Validation and Consequences for Theory. In Eckensberger, L., Looner, W., & Poortinga, Y. (Eds.), *Cross Cultural Contribution to Psychology*. Lisse, The Netherlands: Swets & Zeitlingerd.

Hofstede, G. (1980). *Culture's Consequences International Differences in Work Related Values*. Beverly Hills, CA: Sage.

Hofstede, G. (1983). Dimensions of National Culture in Fifty Countries and Three Regions. In Deregowski, J., Dzieurawiec, S., & Annios, R. (Eds.), *Explications in Cross Cultural Psychology*. Lisse, The Netherlands: Swets & Zeitlinger.

Hofstede, G. (1984). The Cultural Relativity of the Quality of Life Concept. *Academy of Management Review*, *9*(3), 389–398.

Hofstede, G. (1997). *Cultures and Organizations: Software of the Mind*. New York: McGraw-Hill.

Hofstede, G. (2002). Dimensions do not exist: A reply to Brendan McSweeney. *Human Relations*, *55*(11), 1355–1361.

Hofstede, G. (2003). What is culture? A reply to Baskerville. *Accounting, Organizations and Society*, *28*(7–8), 811–813. doi:10.1016/S0361-3682(03)00018-7.

Holden, N. (2002). *Cross Cultural Management: A Knowledge Management Perspective*. Harlow, UK: Pearson.

Howald, F. (2001). *Obstáculos al desarrollo de la pyme causados por el estado en Colombia: el caso del sistema tributario*. Santiago, Chile: McGraw-Hill.

Johanson, J., & Vahlne, J. (2009). The Uppsala internationalization process model revisited: From liability of foreignness to liability of outsidership. *Journal of International Business Studies*, 1411–1431. doi:10.1057/jibs.2009.24.

Jongeward, C. (1999). Shifting the ground of the familiar: Using autobiography and intercultural learning in a time of transition. *CJSAE*, *13*(1), 21–40.

Klein, K., & Kozlowski, S. (2000). *Multilevel Theory, Research and Methods in Organizations: Foundations, Extensions and New Directions*. San Francisco, CA: Jossey-Bass.

Kremenyuk, V. (2002). *International Negotiation. Analysis, Approaches, Issues*. San Francisco, CA: Jossey-Bass.

Leonidas, L., & Katsikeas, C. (1996). The export development process: An integrative review of empirical models. *Journal of International Business Studies*, *27*(3), 517–551. doi:10.1057/palgrave.jibs.8490846.

Leung, K., Bhagat, R., Buchan, N., Erez, M., & Gibson, C. (2005). Culture and international business: Recent advances and their implications for the future. *Journal of International Business Studies*, *36*(4), 357–378. doi:10.1057/palgrave.jibs.8400150.

Li, L., Li, D., & Dalgic, T. (2004). Internationalization process of small and medium-sized enterprises: Toward a hybrid model of experiential learning and planning. *Management International Review*, *44*(1), 93–117.

Maclure, S., & Davies, P. (1991). Learning to think: Thinking to learn (Eds.). Oxford, UK: Pergamon Press.

Martínez, P. (2009). Proceso del desarrollo exportador de la PYME Colombiana. *Cuadernos de Gestión*, *9*(1), 47–66.

Marulanda, E. (2004). *La Competitividad de las Pymes, Como ingresar exitosamente en el mercado globalizado. El Empresariado Colombiano y el TLC*. Bogotá, Colombia: CONFECAMARAS.

Mc Sweeney, B. (2002). Hofstede's model of national cultural differences and their consequences: A Triumph of faith - A failure of analysis. *Human Relations*, *55*(1), 89–118.

Mead, R. (2005). *International management: Cross-cultural dimensions*. London: Blackwell.

Miles, M., & Huberman, M. (1994). *Qualitative data analysis: An expanded source book*. Thousand Oaks, CA: Sage Publications.

Ministerio de Comercio. Industria y Turismo. (2008). *Reporte de Mipymes No. 03*. Retrieved July 22, 2009, from http://www.mincomercio.gov.co/econtent/Documentos/mipymes/2008/ReporteMipymes03.pdf

Ministry of Commerce. Industry and Tourism of Colombia. (2008). *Reporte de Mipymes No. 03*. Retrieved July 22, 2009, from http://www.mincomercio.gov.co/econtent/Documentos/mipymes/2008/ReporteMipymes03.pdf

Mintzberg, H. (1979). *The structuring of organizations*. Englewood Cliffs, NJ: Prentice Hall.

Mintzberg, H. (1992). *Structure in fives: Designing effective organizations*. Upper Saddle River, NJ: Prentice Hall.

Myers, M., & Tan, F. (2002). Beyond models of national culture in information systems research. *Journal of Global Information Management*, *10*(1), 24–32. doi:10.4018/jgim.2002010103.

Papadopoulos, N. (1987). Approaches to international market selection for small and medium sized enterprises. In Rosson, P., & Reid, S. (Eds.), *Managing Export Entry and Expansion* (pp. 128–158). New York: Praeger Publishers.

Posada, M. (2012, June 13). *Colombia's FDI Profile*. Retrieved October 29, 2012, from http://www.vcc.columbia.edu/files/vale/documents/Colombia_IFDI_-_FINAL_-_13_June_2012.pdf

Posada, M. (2012, June 13). *Inward FDI in Colombia and its policy context, 2012*. Retrieved August 7, 2012, from http://www.vcc.columbia.edu/files/vale/documents/Colombia_IFDI_-_FINAL_-_13_June_2012.pdf

Prahalad, C., & Krishnah, H. (2008). *The New Age of Innovation*. New York: McGraw Hill.

Rialp, A. (1999). *Los Enfoques Micro-organizativos de la Internacionalización de la Empresa: Una Revisión y Síntesis de la Literatura. Información Comercial Española* (ICE), *October*(781), 17-128.

Rodríguez, A. (2003). *La realidad de la pyme colombiana: desafío para el desarrollo*. Bogotá, Colombia: FUNDES.

Romero, M., & Ramírez, J. (2012, July 5). *Conozca los próximos tratados de libre comercio de Colombia*. Retrieved October 29, 2012, from http://www.portafolio.co/negocios/conozca-los-proximos-tratados-libre-comercio-colombia

Root, F. (1994). *Entry Strategies for International Markets*. New York: Lexington Books.

Rugman, A., Oh, C., & Lim, D. (2012). The regional and global competitiveness of multinational firms. *Journal of the Academy of Marketing Science*, *40*(2), 218–235. doi:10.1007/s11747-011-0270-5.

Sallenave, J. (2002). *La Gerencia Integral*. Bogotá, Colombia: Editorial Norma.

Schneider, S., & Barsoux, J. (1997). *Managing across cultures*. London: Prentice-Hall.

Senge, P. (2004). *La quinta disciplina: El arte y la práctica de la organización abierta al aprendizaje*. Barcelona, Spain: Granica.

Søderberg, A., & Holden, N. (2002). Rethinking Cross Cultural Management in a Globalizing Business World. *International Journal of Cross Cultural Management*, *2*(103), 103–121.

Stawarski, C., & Phillips, P. (2008). *Data Collection: Planning for and Collecting All Types of Data*. San Francisco, CA: John Wiley & Sons.

Sterman, J. (2000). *Business Dynamics: System Thinking and Modeling for a Complex World*. New York: McGraw-Hill.

Struwig, M., & Meru, A. (2011). The Relationship between Business Environment and Business Incubation. *China-USA Business Review*, *10*(9), 880–892.

Thomas, D. (2006). Domain and development of cultural intelligence: The importance of mindfulness. *Group & Organization Management*, *31*(1), 78–99. doi:10.1177/1059601105275266.

Thomas, D. (2008). *Cross-Cultural Management: Essential Concepts*. Los Angeles: Sage Publications.

Thomas, D., & Inkson, K. (2003). *Cultural Intelligence. People Skills for the Global Business*. San Francisco, CA: Berrett-Koehler Publishers.

Thomas, D., & Inkson, K. (2004). Cultivating your cultural intelligence. *Security Management*, *48*(8), 30–33.

Thomas, D., Stahl, G., Ravlin, E., Poelmans, S., Pekerti, A., & Maznevski, M. et al. (2008). Cultural Intelligence: Domain and Assessment. *International Journal of Cross Cultural Management*, *8*(2), 123–143. doi:10.1177/1470595808091787.

Torres, G. (2007). The New "Export-Culture" in Latin America. *Global Business Languages*, *12*(Article 12), 149-165.

Velásquez, F. (2004). La estrategia, la estructura y las formas de asociación: Fuentes de ventaja competitiva para las pymes colombianas. *Estudios Gerenciales*, *93*, 73–97.

Welch, L., & Luostarinen, R. (1988). Internationalisation: Evolution of a Concept. *Journal of General Management*, *14*(2), 34–55.

Wild, J., Wild, K., & Han, J. (2001). *International Business: An Integrated Approach*. Upper Saddle River, NJ: Prentice Hall.

ENDNOTES

1 Wild, Wild, & Han (2001, p. 6) define globalisation as "the tendency of economic, cultural, political and technological interdependence among economies and national institutions".

2 Several academics have based their proposals on the work of Christopher Earley (Earley P., 2002; Earley & Ang, 2003; Earley & Peterson, 2004; Earley & Mosakowski, 2004; Earley, Ang, & Tan; Earley, Murnieks, & Mosakowski, 2007); and David Thomas (Thomas & Inkson, 2004; Thomas & Inkson, 2003; Thomas, 2008; Thomas, 2006; Thomas, et al., 2008).

3 Research in Colombia has some *sui generis* characteristics: 1) It may not be conducted by Ph.D.s because few professors have graduated from doctoral programmes, 2) most research is made based on small samples, discretional selections or specific cases because companies are not keen to cooperate with the academy, and 3) it is majorly funded by universities or governmental institutes.

4 Among others these are: informality, deficient planning, scarce financing opportunities, lack of trust for cooperation, poor human resource politics, and short global thinking.

5 Further reading on the negotiations stages and the debate on it can be found in Fayerweather & Kapoor (1976), Ghauri & Usunier, (2003), Bazerman & Neale (1992), Fisher, Ury, & Patton (1991), and Kremenyuk (2002), among others.

6 It is important to highlight that applications that are mentioned in business publications represent a certain level of awareness of a certain company capability by managers. For that reason these applications were evident and relevant for a business article. Otherwise it would not be easy to identify these applications and to analyse the implications of each in company' performance.

7 Simplified Stock Company or Spanish for *Sociedad por Acciones Simplificada*

8 The major acceptance of his proposals derives from three decades of work (Hofstede, 1979; Hofstede, 1980; Hofstede, 1983; Hofstede, 1984; Hofstede, 1997).

Chapter 20
Evaluating UK Intra-National Outsourcing to North Staffordshire

Anthony S. Atkins
Staffordshire University, UK

Bernadette Sharp
Staffordshire University, UK

Lyn Atkins
Staffordshire University, UK

ABSTRACT

Outsourcing is a widespread practice in the modern global economy, with decisions motivated by expectation of various advantages of which cost reduction is often the primary factor. Recent trends have been towards Business Process Outsourcing (BPO) and offshore outsourcing, and more recently Knowledge Process Outsourcing (KPO) has emerged as an established area of the market. Despite the potential attractions, there are a range of risks associated with outsourcing, and these are demonstrated by the substantial number of arrangements that fail to meet expectations. For example, Glick (2004) cites research by Gartner that indicated £4bn was wasted on poorly managed contracts by European businesses in the previous year. This highlights the business significance of outsourcing decisions and shows that the impact of major outsourcing decisions is likely to be strategic in that the competitive position of a company is influenced by the outcomes. The argument for use of a systematic decision support system to assist with outsourcing decisions is persuasive. The Holistic Approach Business, Information, Organisation (HABIO) Framework offers a holistic approach which takes account of interrelated strategies and complex considerations that may vary according to the circumstances and priorities of the decision-maker. It also facilitates monitoring decisions over the life of the outsourcing arrangements, thereby supporting timely anticipation and response to significant changes in the economic, political, or social environment. The HABIO model could be used in consideration of intra-national outsourcing decisions to areas such as North Staffordshire where decline in industries traditionally associated with the locality created needs and opportunities for regeneration.

DOI: 10.4018/978-1-4666-3966-9.ch020

INTRODUCTION

In order to be successful in today's global markets, companies and organisations must pursue strategies that enable them to maintain a competitive advantage over their rivals. Various strategies can be used to support differentiation but cost reduction is, perhaps, the most obvious. Cost reduction has often been a powerful driver towards decisions on outsourcing, which is a widespread practice in our modern global economy. Indeed one of the main drivers for offshore outsourcing has been lower labour costs. Predictions from Forrester Research Inc. indicated that over 3 million white-collar jobs will move from the U.S. to low-cost countries by 2015 (Engardio et al., 2003). Examples of outsourced activities are found in both the private and public sectors and in both manufacturing and service industries. A 2004 report suggested that outsourcing already accounted for one third of IT spending globally and was a growing market (Cap Gemini, 2004).

There are numerous definitions of outsourcing; for example, Linder (2004) described it as "purchasing on-going services from an outside company that a company currently provides, or most organisations normally provide, for themselves." Lei and Hitt (1995) defined outsourcing as "reliance on external sources for manufacturing components and other value-adding activities." Outsourcing can take place intra-nationally, within the country of the parent company, or it can involve moving the outsourced activity internationally, often referred to as offshore outsourcing.

Recent trends in outsourcing projects have often involved offshore outsourcing or Business Process Outsourcing (BPO). The growth of low-cost communications and the Internet are supportive of offshore outsourcing to developing economies. The GAO Study (2004) cites improvements in global telecommunications, the falling costs of data transmission, and growing infrastructure in developing countries. The attraction of lower labour costs has resulted in many UK companies outsourcing to countries in Asia and Eastern Europe. The UK has not been alone in taking opportunities for cost reduction; this is shown in the prediction that by 2015, 3.3 million U.S. jobs will be outsourced overseas (Mangan, 2004). Falk and Wolfmayr (2005) recognise the debate around the impact on employment in the 15 EU countries from trade with low-wage economies, also that growth in international outsourcing and competition from imports are often blamed for a falling demand for labour in European manufacturing. With respect to BPO it has been suggested that outsourcing is now seen as a service where total, defined business processes are given to expert service providers who manage the process and ensure the total integration between outsourced business processes and in-house processes (Kruse & Berry, 2004). However, BPO has usually involved outsourcing of defined business processes that are non-core to the parent company, rather than its core activities. In The Economist (2008), it is noted that the concept of core competence was introduced into management literature in 1990 by Prahalad and Hamel. In summary, some of the key features of core competence are the collective learning in the organisation, which grows as it is applied and shared, and. includes not only skills associated with technology and production, but also communication and commitment to working across organisational boundaries. It was also noted that this drive to identify core competencies and thereby activities that a parent organisation was uniquely well qualified to carry out itself coincided with the time of growing popularity of outsourcing.

Looking ahead and commenting on developments in Knowledge Process Outsourcing (KPO), Druce (2009) indicates that KPO represents the next stage in the evolution of the outsourcing market. KPO differs from BPO in that KPO implies outsourcing of core business functions that demand high levels of specialist knowledge and expertise.

It is reasonable to expect that as developments in outsourcing move into areas of core function, decisions are becoming more critical than ever to strategic objectives and to the ultimate success or failure of the organisation. There is a potential advantage to be gained from sound outsourcing decisions. However, effective planning and management of outsourcing strategies are essential, because on the other side of the debate around such considerations is that there are also substantial risks. These opportunities and dangers will be discussed as a baseline for consideration of North Staffordshire as a location for UK intra-national outsourcing and outsourced service providers.

OPPORTUNITIES AND RISKS FROM OUTSOURCING

There are various factors and circumstances that can make outsourcing decisions attractive. Outsourcing can free up assets and reduce costs in the immediate financial period (Harland et al., 2005). It can be advantageous in allowing the parent firm to concentrate on its core business. As recognised in The Economist (2008), Prahalad and Hamel outlined three tests to be applied to determine whether something is a core competence: a core competence provides potential access to a wide variety of markets, it makes a significant contribution to the perceived customer benefits of the end product, and it is difficult for competitors to imitate because it is a complex harmonisation of individual technologies and production skills.

Research conducted on large companies in the recession period of the early 1990s found that "focus on core business" was considered very important by 54% of the firms responding to the survey (Geroski & Gregg, 1997). In a similar vein, where external service providers specialise in particular activities and processes they may offer benefits in terms of specialist skills or resources and greater economies of scale. Outsourcing can resolve problems associated with meeting peaks in demand, thus making the parent company able to be more flexible and responsive to fluctuations in the market and this is particularly applicable to companies that experience predictable seasonal variations in demand for their products or services for example peaks in demand around holidays and festivals. It has been suggested that outsourcing can offer mutual benefit to clients and service providers in that partnerships may assist learning and cross-fertilisation between them (Rubery et al, 2002). Looking outside the parent organisation may mean access to a specialist, expert service provider and this may be a particular consideration with KPO. Cost reduction has often been a primary attraction for outsourcing from countries where labour costs are relatively high, however there are other attractions. Locating overseas in different time zones from the parent company may be seen as value adding in assisting in the provision of 24-hour per day services. Companies may see offshore outsourcing as a way of increasing their global presence and visibility and this may also provide an opportunity to reinforce brand familiarity in countries where markets are emerging or growing. There are also arguments that outsourcing from high-cost countries supports lower domestic inflationary pressures and offers additional employment opportunities in host nations. These opportunities indicate the potential benefits of outsourcing however the practice does not always yield the business success anticipated.

Although outsourcing is considered to be a powerful management tool (Johnson 1997), an incorrect decision can have a devastating effect on an organisation, both economically and politically. For example, Glick (2004) cites research by Gartner that indicated £4bn was wasted on poorly managed contracts by European businesses in the previous year, and the analyst estimated that as many as 80% of outsourcing deals were unsuccessful. This underlines the various risks associated with outsourcing, some of these come within the parent organisation and these threats can arise from loss of internal expertise, skill and technical knowledge; from failure to successfully manage change; or from trade union opposition. There is also a caveat concerning how an outsourcing decision will effectively support the strategic management principles adopted by the organisation. Further threats from outside the organisation can be those more specifically concerning the external service provider as well as threats associated with customers' perceptions and reactions to outsourced products and services.

Within the organisation loss of internal expertise or aspects of core competence could alter the bargaining position of service users and service providers, and where an activity is provided by an external organisation for a prolonged period of time there is further risk particularly if the external provider is updating and/or developing the product or service in response to market demands or technological opportunities. As an example where technology changes the service user may suffer loss of relevant expertise and so come into a more dependent position with the service provider. In a similar vein when the outsourcing arrangement involves KPO there can be additional concerns; Druce (2009) makes reference to quality and security. Apart from the loss of internal expertise there is the risk of loss of knowledge spill-over to and from the local area (Kyle, 2004). Where there are local universities and research and development there may be benefits from knowledge transfer, but this spill-over becomes less effective with geographical distance. Loss of internal expertise and support from local research and development could put at risk a company's future innovations and speed of market responsiveness, which would then impact on its competitiveness. In a similar vein, Byham (1997) notes the level of benefit that an organisation gains from outsourcing depends very heavily on the partner it selects. It is clear that selection of a partner with excellent skills in the area required will bring much more benefit than selection of a partner with less skill in the particular activity.

Outsourcing represents change for a parent organisation and managing change typically includes the challenge of overcoming workforce fears and resistance, in order to win their compliance and commitment. People in a workforce often fear change particularly if it is seen as threat to job security or the value of current skill sets. Mumford et al. (2006) highlight people and management factors as a risk. Another aspect of change management includes recognition that distributed development of advanced technology requires an organisation structure that will support increased communication, testing and control requirements.

The possibility of conflict and need to seek agreement with trade unions is a further consideration in outsourcing decisions, particularly where trade unions are strong and could influence timescales and outcomes. In some cases organisations may have multiple trade unions to consult and seek agreement with.

The challenges of achieving and maintaining competitive advantage today take place within the context of global market and rapid technological change. In the 1990s, Hamel and Prahalad (2005) outlined the concept of strategic intent; this usually incorporates stretched targets which means competing in innovative ways. In order to compete successfully in the global market organisations need to do more than assess current technical advantages of competitors, they also need to be aware of the inventiveness and stamina of potential competitors. In order to achieve these aims it is clear that strategic management must be seen as a dynamic process in an ever-changing environment, and this is the context in which outsourcing decisions are made.

Taking a view that includes both the outsourcing company and the partner organisation, there are new challenges to effective communication when outsourcing takes place, and when the service provider is offshore these can include language, culture, and time zone differences. If outsourced service providers do not meet targets regarding delivery or quality of service then the client company faces risks to its reputation and future business. Where there is high labour turnover in an outsourced service-provider company this could be a further threat to quality. Another risk is that a service provider could become a competitor particularly where the parent organisation loses skills or expertise or the host company is able to innovate independently. Efficient and dependable output could be put at risk by political or economic instability in host countries, for example if there were civil unrest or currency fluctuations.

It is clear that a company's success depends on attracting customers and maintaining their esteem, therefore any negative customer perceptions of outsourcing decisions are potentially threatening. Such perceptions may include expectations that local jobs will be lost, concerns over lower wage costs of offshore workers, or that that the quality of products, services or components supplied may change. Where financial services are outsourced offshore, companies may face negative customer perceptions about confidentiality and security, which could impact on sales.

In assessing the risks associated with outsourcing it is pertinent to consider the reasons for reports of low levels of significant benefit realisation. Lonsdale (1999) and Cox (1996) offer the following reasons: focusing on short-term benefits, lack of formal outsourcing decision-making processes, and more complex total supply networks. Another obstacle shown up in an Australian survey was formulating and quantifying requirements (Beaumont & Sohal, 2004).

Outsourcing decisions need to be made with due consideration of the advantages and risks, and some of the dangers appear greater when the service provider is offshore. According to the German Engineers' Association, about one in five outsourcing companies return production to Germany after only a few years (Leidel, 2008). Similarly, a recent survey by the Engineering Employers Federation (EEF), the industry body for engineering and manufacturing employers, and accountants BDO indicated that in the past two years one in seven companies had moved manufacturing to the UK from abroad (BBC, 2009). The EEF's survey, which included 300 manufacturers, showed that the reasons for returning production to the UK included cost savings not meeting expectations, poor quality, higher freight costs and the slow speed of products to market. This survey also indicated nearly 70% of companies said the UK was a competitive location for manufacturing, and this compared with 43% two years previously. In recent years some UK banks have realised they can use locally based call centres as a primary marketing strategy (Watts, 2005).

Whilst recognising the widespread use and positive potential of outsourcing it is clear that there are various risk factors and evidence of applications that have failed to meet expectations and/or resulted in serious financial losses. Decisions concerning outsourcing are therefore both complex and potentially critical in outcome. The complexity is enhanced by the dynamic socio-economic, technical and political environments in which modern organizations exist.

THE HABIO FRAMEWORK AS A DECISION SUPPORT SYSTEM FOR OUTSOURCING

The Holistic Approach Business, Information, Organisation (HABIO) Framework (Atkins et al, 2010a; Ho & Atkins, 2009; Ho & Atkins, 2006a; Ho et al, 2006b; Ho & Atkins, 2006c) offers a decision support system for outsourcing, based on systematic and holistic analysis of relevant considerations. It also allows for maintenance of historical records of decisions taken, thereby facilitating audit and reference. A HABIO web tool has recently been developed. The web tool (Atkins et al., 2010b) facilitates routine use of the concepts and is user-friendly for non-experts. The HABIO framework and web tool supports the strategic assessment of outsourcing options by providing a comparison of outsourcing projects and companies. Reuse over time enables monitoring for any changes that may occur and the web tool includes a facility to view the history. This is important in that it supports a structured approach to anticipation and identification of relevant changes so that responses can be initiated and a competitive position maintained. The HABIO Framework was developed recognising the Information Systems Strategy Triangle (ISST) by Pearlson (2001). Figure 1 illustrates the Framework sited within the ISST.

It shows the inter-related strategic perspectives (business, information and organisational) each with a weighting allocated to reflect its relative importance to the evaluating organisation. Within each strategic perspective relevant considerations are represented by cards; for example, in the organisational strategy perspective cards for internal expertise, legislations, risk management, historical precedent, internal policies and union

Figure 1. HABIO Framework within the ISST (Atkins et al 2010b)

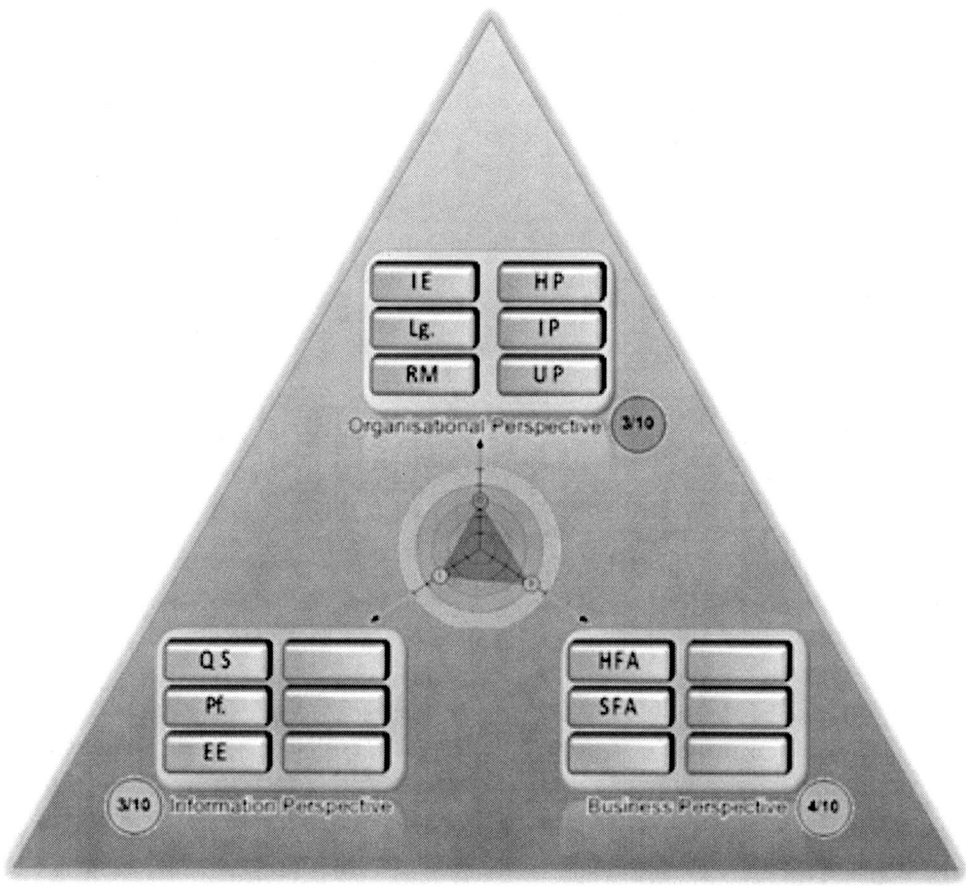

LEGEND

Organisational Perspective	Information Perspective	Financial Perspective
IE Internal Expertise	QS Quality of Service	HFA Hard Financial Analysis
L g. Legislations	Pf. Performance	SFA Soft Financial Analysis
RM Risk Management	EE External Expertise	
HP Historical Precedent		
IP Internal Policies		
UP Union Pressures		

pressures may be evaluated. Scores for each card are measured using a scale or grid. Where scores can be measured by comparison with baseline a scale is used, and where two or more factors have to be taken into account a grid is required. With grids multiple criteria can be plotted and the recently developed HABIO web tool automatically calculates and displays the overall score for the grid. The framework has flexibility in that cards can be added or deselected. Figure 1 shows some "spare" cards in the information perspective and the business perspective. These could be customised and allocated to reflect additional considerations, whilst equally other cards could be added in the organisational perspective. Figure 2 focuses in on the scales and grids which lie behind the cards and enable scores to be established for each consideration. Figure 3 provides an enlarged view of a scale and a grid to clarify how scores on a scale such as quality of service are established by comparison with a baseline and how and overall score on a grid such as external expertise is derived from scores for relevant criteria which the user can define. The ability to select and remove cards allows decision takers to tailor the framework to their specific needs. For example, in evaluating a UK regeneration area as an intra-national outsourcing option location against alternatives the decision taker may wish to accommodate scoring for additional considerations such as environmental "green" impact, specific local incentives, or aspects of customer perception or value added to communities. When all the cards have been scored, the weighted scores for all three perspectives are calculated and their sum is expressed as a percentage of the maximum possible. This allows companies or projects to be selected on the basis of systematic and holistic quantification of comparative scores. The web tool allows for the export of automatically calculated results to an Excel spread sheet for quick and easy comparison of weighted scores.

This framework as been applied in two large commercial organisations' outsourcing decisions for customer service and IT infrastructure functions. This indicated that the approach was found to be effective and that drivers relevant to outsourcing are increasingly considerations of strategic factors rather than cost reduction alone (Atkins et al, 2010a; Ho & Atkins, 2009; Ho & Atkins, 2006a; Ho et al, 2006b; Ho & Atkins, 2006c).

The HABIO principle of a holistic approach to outsourcing decisions will be used in discussion of UK intra-national outsourcing to North Staffordshire, an area that has suffered from the decline in the UK coal mining and local ceramics industries, but which is now subject to regeneration. In this sense, North Staffordshire has had both a negative and positive experience of environmental change. The following section III will apply consideration of the benefits and risks to North Staffordshire and in doing so it will recognise the holistic principle of the HABIO approach.

UK INTRA-NATIONAL OUTSOURCING TO NORTH STAFFORDSHIRE

Located centrally within the UK, North Staffordshire is actively ambitious to move away from its current levels of economic inactivity and output shortfall. Historically it was an area famous for its pottery and coal mining industries, both of which required skilled workers; it has a proud industrial heritage having enjoyed international recognition for pottery products in particular. It is keen to enable the workforce to have the skills required by modern employers, enable businesses to offer better and higher paid jobs, attract new types of employment and encourage business start-ups. The area-includes a central heartland that is largely urban, sandwiched between a more rural south western part and on the other side an area that includes part of the High Peak National Park. It covers the areas of Stoke-on-Trent City

Figure 2. Strategic Perspective with cards showing scales and grids for HABIO scores (Atkins et al 2010b)

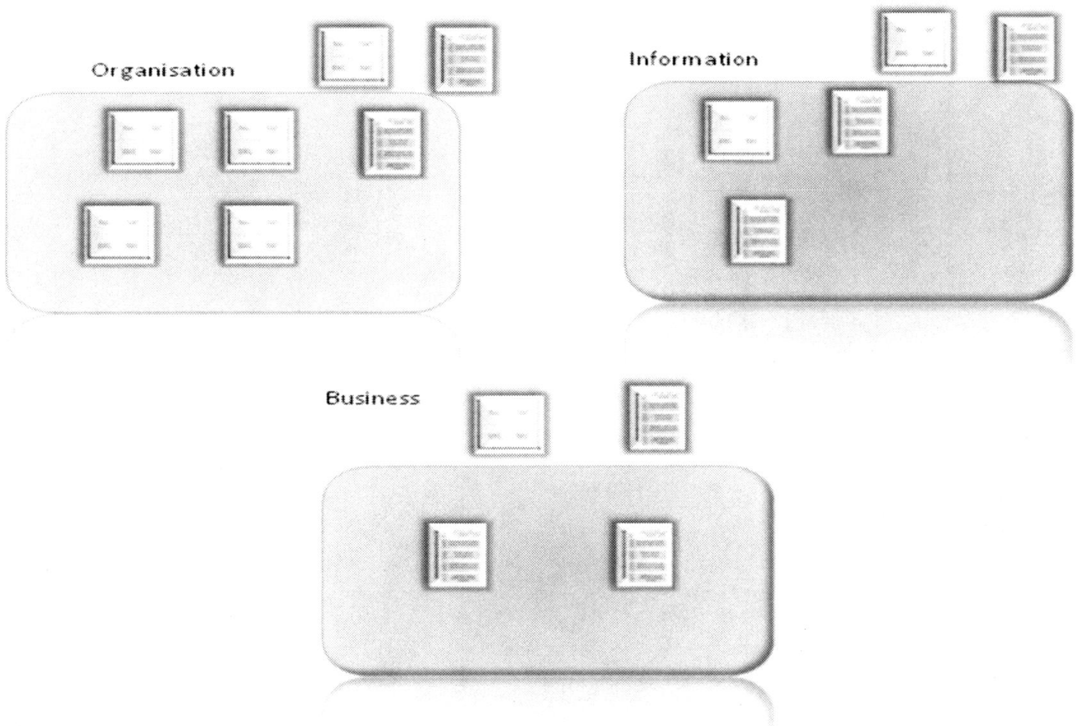

NOTE: Spare cards can be created, drawn in and customised to reflect issues such as "green" considerations

Council, Staffordshire Moorlands District Council and Newcastle Borough Council.

As a potential location for UK intra-national outsourcing, North Staffordshire can be considered in terms of the issues that have been identified and discussed. Like any investment, strategic decisions on outsourcing will have effects over a period of time. Decisions must therefore take into account anticipated change and developments such as those associated with regeneration potentials as well as current factors.

An evaluation of the expertise available in the area highlights a number of factors. The immediate area has two universities, Keele and Staffordshire. There are also local colleges and Staffordshire University Regional Federation (SURF) is an example of a partnership initiative with local colleges. The universities and colleges promote education and the development of skills to offer employers. In addition to the universities in Staffordshire, those at Manchester, Birmingham and Wolverhampton are all within easy access. As a potential location for intra-national outsourcing including KPO the indications are that North Staffordshire is well positioned for knowledge overspill from universities, cross-fertilisation of ideas and it is active and ambitious to be part of growing knowledge businesses by promoting and retaining skills and knowledge. This infrastructure offers potential opportunities for companies to pursue modern management philosophies like continuous improvement of processes, products and services, and to enhance core competence and support strategic intent.

Figure 3. Enlarged View of Scale and Grid (Atkins et al 2010b)

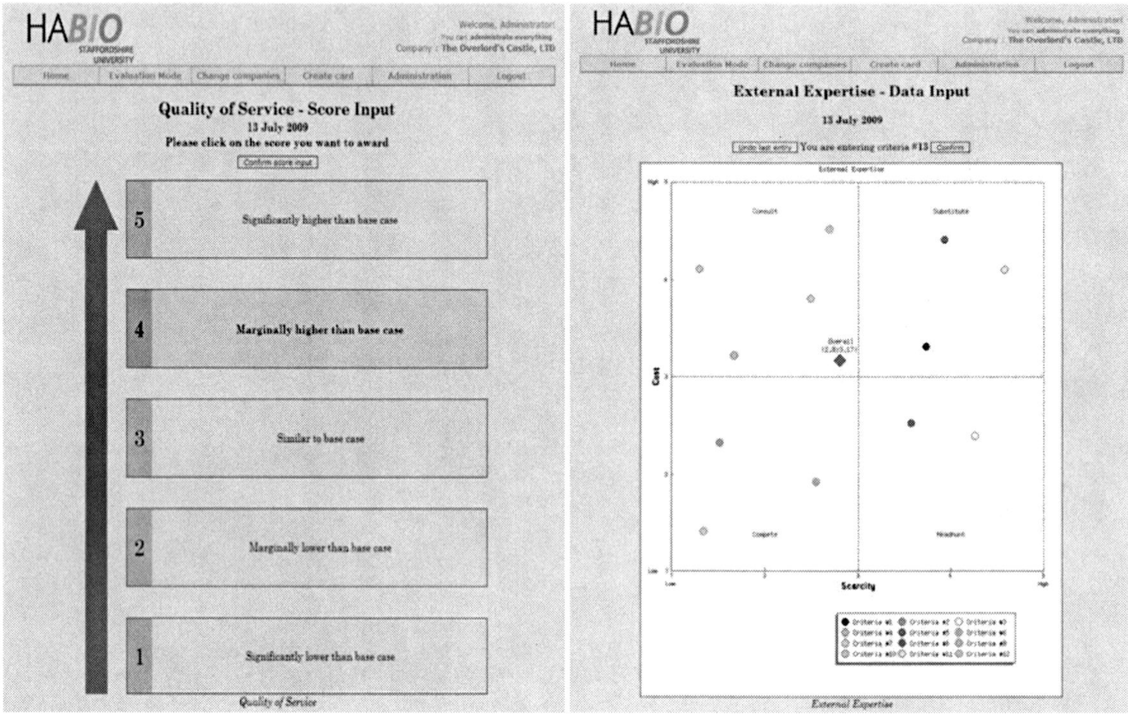

In terms of quality of life, North Staffordshire currently offers relatively low cost housing and further development is foreseen. A further attraction of North Staffordshire is that it includes part of the High Peaks National Park, an area of natural beauty that attracts walkers, cyclists and sight-seers.

Communication has been recognised as a risk factor for outsourcing decisions. The central UK location of North Staffordshire is offered as a positive consideration in terms of communication and access. Its central urban heartland around the city of Stoke-on-Trent and Newcastle-under-Lyme are easily accessible from the M6 motorway, and Stoke is on a direct rail line for Birmingham, London and Manchester. There are international airports at Birmingham, Manchester and Nottingham. A BBC News (2010a) reports that Network Rail has proposed a new high-speed railway line between London and Scotland which would allow travel from London to Birmingham in 45 minutes, down from 1 hour and 22 minutes. In December 2010 it was reported that the Transport Secretary confirmed the government broadly agreed the chosen HS2 rail route and that plans would be put out for consultation in 2011 (BBC News, 2010b).

Outsourced activity located in North Staffordshire would be subject to the English legal system including law related to intellectual property protection. The culture would also be familiar to UK firms considering intra-national outsourcing to the area. These factors help to minimise communication risks that can arise from differences. It can also be expected to be a politically stable long term environment. Quality of service and performance are important considerations in outsourcing decisions but there can be risks in these areas which have been described. Intra-national outsourcing in North Staffordshire would offer closeness to UK parent companies, also proximity to UK markets which will assist with delivery times. The positive arguments around expertise, communication, political stability and vision for sustainable growth are also offered as supportive contributions to the achievement of quality output and performance.

In terms of customer perception, intra-national outsourcing offers a more local service to UK customers. It overcomes possible negative customer perceptions regarding communication associated with different first languages or cultural differences. Any negative perceptions from those customers who fear loss of domestic employment are avoided by location within the UK and choice of a regeneration area invites local loyalty from both customers and employees. Closely related to customer perception is the concept of adding value to the local community, which is particularly potent in an area where some regeneration activity has been demonstrated and where further increases economic activity would assist employment. Locating in an area which has undergone loss due to contraction of its traditional industries could further support local loyalty.

Turning to cost, North Staffordshire has lower property costs than many parts of the UK, which would represent a lower cost for outsource service providers. Outsourcing decisions should take account of any Government support or initiatives for locating production activity in regeneration areas, which may offer benefit not only at the immediate time but also during the lifetime of the outsourcing decision. Areas of regeneration may also offer a support to new business opportunities, for example through initiatives like the Government's Regional Growth Fund which has recently provided over £5million towards securing new jobs at Wedgewood site at Barlaston, Stoke-on-Trent. Environmental considerations have become a matter of increased interest for organisations and individuals in recent years. In the context of outsourcing, "green" solutions can have a positive value in terms of customer perception and image of the organisation, on top of the direct benefit to the environment. North Staffordshire is currently a low carbon area compared with the rest of England, (North Staffordshire Regeneration Partnership Business Plan 2009-2012, 2009) however this is within a context of low levels of economic activity.

The considerations highlighted for decision-making on intra-national outsourcing to North Staffordshire are ones which could be used in conjunction with the HABIO framework and automated web tool. Individual decision makers could add to or deselect criteria that take account of the factors highlighted above and so tailor the system to their own specific circumstances and requirements. The HABIO decision support system adds value in ensuring quantifiable, auditable decisions that can furthermore be monitored over time to take account of environmental change

CONCLUSION

Outsourcing is widespread in modern, highly developed economies. There are various potential benefits and risks of outsourcing which have been discussed Outsourcing decisions are complex because of the need to take account of possible benefits and dangers and because of the dynamic nature of the socio-economic, technical and political environments in which organisations operate. The strategic importance of sound outsourcing decisions and effective monitoring is demonstrated by the incidence of decisions that fail to deliver their anticipated benefits. This is underscored by recent trends further emphasising the importance of strategic outsourcing compared to traditional outsourcing. Furthermore the emergence of Knowledge Process Outsourcing (KPO) substantiates the trend towards strategic outsourcing. The challenges of strategic management in today's global market and dynamic competitive environment would suggest added advantage to outsource locations which can benefit from knowledge overspill and established infrastructure. Strategic decision support systems are needed to assist outsourcing decision makers. The HA-

BIO Framework provides a holistic and flexible decision support tool and the HABIO web tool facilitates systematic use, routine maintenance of records, and audit trails.

The HABIO framework has been applied in two large commercial organizations one that used outsourcing in a UK retailer customer service-call centres and another in IT aspects of commercial banking. These case study approaches indicated that the framework was found to be effective and that drivers behind the use of outsourcing are increasingly considerations of strategic factors rather than cost reduction alone.

The HABIO concepts are flexible to differing organisations and situations and can be used to appraise various outsourcing decisions, such as one to outsource intra-nationally within the UK, for example to areas such as North Staffordshire where regeneration is in progress. The case for North Staffordshire has been examined, including the various benefits it can offer. The use of HABIO would enable individual organisations to evaluate the possibilities against their own specific needs. The recently developed HABIO web tool supports routine use of the concept and automatic maintenance of records by non-experts.

The HABIO framework uses a graphical style of "grids and scales" which can be customised to specific outsourcing opportunities allowing the inclusion and deletion of "cards." This provides a quick visual review in an executive summary format that is concise and intuitive for both operation and senior management. The use of a weighting system allows companies to set priorities according to their particular organisational circumstances.

The HABIO framework has been extended to construct ontology to build an intelligent reasoning component to provide the stakeholders with a series of what-if scenarios for evaluating the various score cards and their implications on outsourcing decisions. Future work will link the intelligent reasoning system, which is a stand-alone component, to the information system to provide a real time support for monitoring the impact of outsourcing decisions against performance and outside influences (e.g., economic fluctuation) on a continuous basis.

ACKNOWLEDGMENT

This work was conducted under the auspices of the Research Informed Teaching (RIT) project, at the Faculty of Computing, Engineering and Technology at Staffordshire University.

REFERENCES

Atkins, A. S., Sharp, B., & Atkins, L. (2010b). Decision Support System for Strategic Outsourcing Risk Reduction. In *Proceedings of the 4th International Conference on Software, Knowledge, Information Management and Applications*. Paro, Bhutan.

Atkins, A. S., Sharp, B., Hickey, D. S., & Ho, L. (2010a). HABIO Management of Outsourcing: Systems, Capabilities and Cybernetics. *Technia-International Journal of Computing Science & Communication Technologies*, *2*(2), 407–413.

BBC NEWS. (2010a). *New high-speed rail plan unveiled*. Retrieved on October 26, 2012, from http://news.bbc.co.uk/1/hi/8221540.stm

Beaumont, N., & Sohal, A. (2004). Outsourcing in Australia. *International Journal of Operations & Production Management*, *24*(7), 688–700. doi:10.1108/01443570410541993.

Byham, W. C. (1997). *The Outsourcing Question*. Pittsburgh, PA: Development Dimensions International.

Cap Gemini. (2004). *The Outsourcing Report: Making Choices – Insights into Successful Outsourcing*.

Cox, A. (1996). Relational competence and strategic procurement management. *European Journal of Purchasing and Supply Management*, *2*(1), 57–70. doi:10.1016/0969-7012(95)00019-4.

Druce, L. (2009). *Knowledge process outsourcing offers significant growth opportunities*. Retrieved on October 26, 2012, from http://searchcio.techtarget.com/sDefinition/0,sid182_gci212731,00.html

Engardio, P., Bernstein, A., & Kripalani, M. (2003). The New Global Job Shift. *Business Week*.

Falk, M., & Wolfmayr, Y. (2005). *The Impact of International Outsourcing on Employment: Empirical Evidence from EU Countries*. Vienna, Austria: Austrian Institute of Economic Research WIFO.

Geroski, P. A., & Gregg, P. (1997). *Coping with recession: UK Company Performance in Adversity*. Cambridge, MA: NIESR.

Glick, B. (2004). *Does your Outsourcing agreement measure up*? Retrieved on February 16, 2010, from http://www.computing.co.uk/computing/features/2072394/does-outsourcing-agreement-measure?vnu_lt=ctg_art_related_articles

Hamel, G., & Prahalad, C. K. (2005). Strategic Intent. *Harvard Business Review*, 148–161. PMID:10303477.

Harland, C., Knight, L., Lamming, R., & Walker, H. (2005). Outsourcing: Assessing the risks and benefits for organisations, sectors and nations. *International Journal of Operations & Production Management*, *25*(9), 831–850. doi:10.1108/01443570510613929.

Ho, L., & Atkins, A. S. (2006a). IT Outsourcing: Impacts and Challenges. In Walters, B., & Tang, Z. (Eds.), *IT Enabled Strategic Management – Increasing Returns for the Organization* (pp. 244–274). Hershey, PA: Idea Group Inc. doi:10.4018/978-1-59140-908-3.ch012.

Ho, L., & Atkins, A. S. (2006c). Outsourcing Decision-Making: A Review of Strategic Frameworks and Proposal of a Multi-Perspective Approach. In Kehal, H. S., & Singh, V. (Eds.), *Outsourcing and Offshoring in the 21st Century: A Socio-Economic Perspective* (pp. 165–196). Hershey, PA: Idea Group Inc. doi:10.4018/978-1-59140-875-8.ch008.

Ho, L., & Atkins, A. S. (2009). IT Portfolio Management: A Holistic Approach to Outsourcing Decisions. In Tan, A. (Ed.), *Handbook on Strategic Information Technology and Portfolio Management* (pp. 100–112). Hershey, PA: IGI Global. doi:10.4018/978-1-59904-687-7.ch005.

Ho, L., Atkins, A. S., Prince, I., & Sharp, B. (2006b). Alignment of a Strategic Outsourcing Framework to Practitioner Case Studies. In *Proceedings of European and Mediterranean Conference on Information Systems (EMCIS)*. Alicante, Spain.

Johnson, M. (1997). *Outsourcing in brief*. Oxford, UK: Elsevier Butterworth-Heinemann.

Kruse, G. & Berry, C. (2004). Outsourcing: The How-to Guide. *IEE Manufacturing*, August/September, 36-39.

Kyle, M. (2004). Does Locale Affect R and D Productivity? The Case of Pharmaceuticals. In FRBSF Economic Letter 32.

Lei, D., & Hitt, M. (1995). Strategic restructuring and outsourcing: The effect of mergers and acquisitions and LBO's on building firm skills and capabilities. *Journal of Management*, *21*(5), 835–859. doi:10.1177/014920639502100502.

Leidel, S. (2008). *German Companies Eye Moving Production Back Home*. Retrieved on October 26, 2012, from http://www.dw-world.de/dw/article/0,2144,3462948,00.html

Linder, J. C. (2004). *Outsourcing for radical change*. New York: American Management Association.

Lonsdale, C. (1999). Effectively managing vertical supply relationships: a risk management model for outsourcing. *Supply Chain Management: An International Journal*, *4*(4), 176–183. doi:10.1108/13598549910284499.

Mangan, K. (2004). This political hot potato is a course in demand. *The Chronicle of Higher Education*, A12-A13. May 14.

Mumford, E., Hickey, S., & Matthies, H. (2006). *Designing Human Systems – An agile approach to ETHICS*. Morrisville, NC: Lulu Press.

News, B. B. C. (2009). *Firms move production back to UK*. Retrieved on October 26, 2012, from http://news.bbc.co.uk/go/pr/fr/-/2/hi/business/8434458.stm

News, B. B. C. (2010b), *London-to-Birmingham high speed train route announced*. Retrieved on October 26, 2012, from http://www.bbc.co.uk/news/uk-politics-12035524

North Staffordshire Regeneration Partnership Business Plan 2009-12. (2009). *"Stoke-on-Trent City Centre Partnership Business Plan 2009-2012*. Retrieved on October 26, 2012, from http://www.atcm.org/uploads/DOCS/553-Stoke_CCP_Bcapital_Plan_09_-_12_low_resolution.pdf

Pearlson, K. E. (2001). *Managing and using Information Systems: A Strategic Approach*. New York: John Wiley & Sons.

Rubery, J., Earnshaw, J., Marchington, M., Cooke, F., & Vincent, S. (2002). Changing Organisational Forms and the Employment Relationship. *Journal of Management Studies*, *39*(5), 645–672. doi:10.1111/1467-6486.00306.

Study, G. A. O. (2004). *International Trade*. Retrieved on October 26, 2012, from www.gao.gov/new.items/d04932.pdf

The Economist. (2008). *Core Competence*. Retrieved on October 16, 2012, from http://www.economist.com/node/12231124

Watts, R. (2005). *Subcontinental drift*. Retrieved on October 26, 2012, from http://www.telegraph.co.uk/finance/2903629/Subocontinental-drift.ttml

Chapter 21
Managerial Communication in the Global Cross-Cultural Context

Angelo Camillo
Woodbury University, USA

Loredana Di Pietro
University of Molise, Italy

ABSTRACT

Managerial Communication today is an integral component of many business related disciplines (strategic management, leadership, strategic marketing, business ethics, etc.). However, within the context of global business management, Managerial Communication follows under the broad umbrella of "Business Communication." Communication with internal and external stakeholders demands careful consideration regardless of the industry. Having a managerial communication policy in place allows for strategic information dissemination as well as the protection of transmission of confidential data. This chapter discusses the topic of communication in general with emphasis on managerial communication within the cross-cultural context. The result of a qualitative study used in this chapter confirms that efficient communication strategies and effective communications policy implementation can propel a firm to success. Within this framework and that of managerial leadership effectiveness, managerial communication does not refer to media communication or journalism for that matter; instead, it focuses solely on managerial communication within the context of global business management.

DOI: 10.4018/978-1-4666-3966-9.ch021

INTRODUCTION

In a broad sense, Managerial Communication today is an integral component of many business related disciplines (strategic management, leadership, strategic marketing, international negotiation, business ethics, etc.). Cross-cultural communication however encompasses every area of communication. This topic is usually integrated in courses under the discipline of Media Communication which does not follow within the scope of this chapter. A global search on the topic of Cross-cultural communication within the global business context reveals that the discipline is under researched, hence the need for a chapter in this text. In fact in 2010 the UNESCO (United Nations Education Scientific and Cultural Organization) established a program in Multilingual, Transcultural Communication in the Digital Age (UNESCO, 2010). It's scope is to strengthen research in the field in multilingual and transcultural communication, including multilingual computing methods, e-learning, multilingual web content management, and related methods; and to promote the development of a multilingual social web, harnessing semantic web technologies, and strengthening transcultural communication patterns using a wide range of language resources and technologies, multilingual computing methods, multilingual e-learning, and cultural diversity management procedures (UNESCO).

However, within the global business management context, Managerial Communication follows under the broad umbrella of "Business Communication" which is at the core of this chapter. In fact, when researching global competitive advantage a major research question comes to mind: Why are some competitors more successful than others? Further, why do some executives consistently make the right decisions, while others invariably fail? This chapter provides an explanation by asserting that one of the most significant attributes to global managerial success is "effective managerial communication." In an attempt to exploit the true meaning of managerial communication, we theorize that when humans interact they create relationships. We base our theories and applications using a polycentric approach by thinking of "communication" as being more universal in nature than ethnocentric based. And, because we are different in nature, different people act and react differently. Since we are actively interacting, we adapt and learn the rules of the surroundings which condition the interaction, whether it is at the work place, at school, or on the golf course, or other places. By interacting we acquire each other's culture and integrate our exchanged behavior, knowledge, experience, among others; thus, we become multicultural. Consequently, we adapt to the way we interact and communicate, and according to each given situation. Hence, when adaptation is not possible, we fail.

Indeed, failure due to lack of effective communication with all stakeholders leads to lower productivity, lower profitability and short-term survivorship. Increased managerial communication effectiveness however, enables practitioners at all management levels to realize the benefits of proper communication. In order to achieve effective communication a firm must have well defined communication's policies and plans in place. Communication policies are designed to enable a member of an organization to understand the finer points of internal communication with employees and external communication with business associates (Stevens, 2005). Through appropriate training and effective policy implementation companies aim to develop communication skills which can be applied to all levels of the organization, but especially at middle to upper management levels.

However, policies and plans can only be developed and implemented with effective and continuous training, by using new and more efficient supporting tools such developing communication's technologies, and by having effective communication leadership.

To support this objective, certain fundamental elements are necessary. The management must have the ability to manage and deliver what it promises and must possess a high level of Communication Competence including, but not limited to, communication skills, language proficiency, cross-cultural awareness, intelligence, expertise, adaptability, understanding, etc. (Hammer, 1989, pp. 247-261; Cushner & Brislin, 1996; Earley & Ang, 2003; Arasaratnam & Doerfel, 2005; Abbe, Gulick, & Herman, 2007).

Within this framework Managerial Communication can be described as "an integrative theory-practice methodology that enables the management to sensibly apply the knowledge acquired to any situations, within the perspective of business communication." In other words, it is the process that interconnects knowledge with competent practice (Ting-Toomey, 1999). Furthermore, Managerial Communication can be interpreted as "the skill to efficiently communicate activities/ messages to stimulate an anticipated reaction in a specific situation." Specifically, competent management needs to master the art of interaction and apply it efficiently with the people and the environment, and at the same time fulfil its own communication goals using this capability (Chen & Starosta, 1998: pp. 241–2).

BACKGROUND

Meaning and Application of Managerial Communication

Scholastically, managerial communication, within the framework of applied business communication is considered a discipline (Gross, 2011) and a research topic in the field of social sciences (Calhoun, 2011) which has reached the classroom of many business schools around the globe. In fact, many graduate business programs now include "Managerial communication and also strategic-managerial communication" in their curriculum. Strategic communication is instructed as a foundational management competence instrumental in amplifying general performance at personal, company, financial, and strategic strata. It is applied to key managerial fields of study which include crisis management, multicultural leadership, ethical communication, informational vs. persuational leadership and team building amongst others. Practitioners have long seen the necessity of effective communication.

In the early 1980s the topic of "managerial communication" engaged scholars in finding its clear definition. In 1986 Henderson proposed "A Conceptual Explication and Model for Guiding Future Research" (Henderson, 1986). Since then many definitions have emerged. To a certain extent managerial communication today can be defined as "the communication between manager and subordinates." In a broader sense it can also include external stakeholders, including but not limited to customers and suppliers (Ellis & Hopkinson, 2010). However, Managerial Communication is considered an applied and essential discipline that continues to engage scholars in research and has become one of the most important elements of concern within the context of global management.

Nevertheless, the goal of communication within the global business context is comprehensive in that it intends to develop and disseminate relevant knowledge, which will increase the effectiveness and efficiency of managers and employees in the contemporary multicultural and diverse business environment. Transcultural communication is still in the developmental stage today. The scope, however, is to integrate it within the area of managerial communication, which already expands beyond the walls of the global organization. It involves interaction between two or more diverse individuals who must communicate in a business situation whether it is Manager to Employee (M2E); Business to Business (B2B); Business to Customer/Guest, (B2CG), or in a "non-verbal" and "impersonal setting" such as social media across the globe (MIT, 2009; Monash University, 2010; Cornell University, 2011). Good communication practices in the working environment are developed over time through experience and education. Too often miscommunication can lead to create conflict. It is important, therefore, that firms not only have communications training and manuals at their disposal, but also that they master the art of "Managerial communication."

In an ideal world, a message sender could easily predict how others will perceive his or her message. In such a world, television commercials would be optimally placed, and no one would be offended by an inter-office e-mail. In such a world there would be no language barriers, no political, religious, gender, or cultural constraints. Unfortunately, the business world does not deal with such utopias, and consequently business leaders must be organized and prepared with well-formulated communication policies in place to avoid possible pitfalls.

Communicating strategically involves several basic elements: Purpose, Message Sender (Encoder), Message Configuration, Message Receiver (Decoder), Channel of Communication, and Expected Outcome. When properly applied, communication should be an easy task to accomplish. However, all too frequently, we hear that a company's major hurdle to success is communication. Consequently, talented managers with expertise in their field often fail in their duties simply because they lack the ability to communicate effectively. They also run the risk of delegating ineffectively because of their own inability to communicate effectively. A marketing manager who has innovative ideas about how to capture more customers, for instance, will be passed over if he/she is unable to make his/her suggestions clear and compelling. Many strategic plans may never be implemented if there is lack of communication ability (Thatam, 2008). Having a well defined policy is, therefore, key. Such a plan will have one goal in mind: to communicate an idea, request, accomplishment, event, or even a failure. In other words, effective communication is neither a function of trial and error nor is it a matter of doing what comes naturally. Effectiveness in managerial communication requires managers to establish clear goals and then apply principles and insights to make wise choices about language and behavior in the communication process.

This chapter describes general communication with real-life examples how prominent companies have a communications policy in place and how they use the results to raise awareness about the criticality of communication issues within organizational settings, especially during this current era of dynamic interconnectivity due to IT evolution. It also addresses the responsibility of executives who manage complex international businesses and have a need to communicate effectively with diverse cultures in foreign lands. Therefore, the focus is on the importance of effective communication, both oral and written, while emphasizing the criticality of culture and cultures in business communication. Overall it explores ways in which intrapersonal, interpersonal, intercultural, group and organizational communication is experienced within both companies and cultures. Within this framework and that of managerial leadership effectiveness, managerial communication does not refer to media communication or journalism for that matter; instead, it focuses solely on managerial communication within the context of global business management.

Past, Present, and Future Applicability of Managerial Communication

Interest has been shown in the art of communication since the classical age. The Greeks developed specific communication methods and techniques that conferred it the status of a science. In the contemporary age, the communication theory has experienced an impressive growth, and become a major preoccupation for many specialists in extremely different domains (psychology, philosophy, marketing and public relations, management, etc.). Managerial communication today has a special status, derived from an organizational framework simply known as "business communications" in which it is performed, from its goals, purpose and role (Gheorghe et al., 2009). For example, Carlson's (1951) classic study was based upon nine senior Scandinavian managers recording the details of each activity they engaged in. Subsequent researchers have empirically documented the volume, hierarchical direction, and purposes of managerial communication (Landsberger, 1961; Kelly, 1964; Horne & Lupton, 1965; Stinchcombe, 1974). Lawrence and Lorsch (1967) found that managerial communications and influence from lower and middle levels of management increased the quality of the decision making process. Also, Vroom and Yetten (1973) have investigated managerial communication and decision-making among managers and their impact on the quality of decision making and implementation. Vroom (1964), in his studies of both autocratic and participative decisions, found that communication amongst diverse work groups required a greater investment of time but produced a higher acceptance of decisions and increased the probability that the decision would be executed efficiently. Astley and Zammuto (1992) more explicitly centralize managerial communication in the sense-making processes that both create and disseminate managerial knowledge, thereby making and shaping communities and organizations. For them, "managers espouse their own theories about the way their world works, and the conceptual language they use establishes a context within which organizational life is constructed and reconstructed."

Weick (1995) argues that the basis of managerial action is not the world as objectively given but, rather, the world as people understand it to be. Rejecting traditional approaches to management scholarship that assume objectivity and rationality as human characteristics, Weick (1995) considers interpretation of communication in general as the underpinning of human nature. Several empirical studies of communication during mergers have provided support for the positive effects of managerial communication on employee attitudes and behaviours, especially in relationship with diverse work groups (Covin et al., 1996; Schraeder, 2001; Zorn et al., 2000).

Other researchers have provided empirical support for the positive effects of communication on organizational performance. For example, Miller, Johnson, and Grau (1994) found that communication was a significant factor in reducing employees' anxiety and increasing their willingness to participate in planned activities. Similarly, Wanberg and Banas (2000) examined the role of communication in a longitudinal study of government reorganization. They found that employees who received adequate information about the organization plan demonstrated more positive attitudes toward the organization. More recent organizational researchers have suggested that communication is particularly important in organizational change processes (Zorn et al., 2000; Armenakis & Harris, 2002).

The role of organizational communication in a change context is generally defined as a process through which companies announce, explain, or prepare employees for change (Armenakis & Harris, 2002). This process perspective suggests that when employees receive sufficient and appropriate communication in a change context (i.e., appropriate justification for, and information about, the change and timely feedback), they will have more favourable attitudes towards the change which, in turn, should result in positive organizational outcomes (Goodman & Truss, 2004).

Effective communication within an organization has also been identified as a significant factor in helping employees understand the need for change, as well as the personal effects of a proposed change (Armenakis & Harris, 2002). This becomes even more critical in a global organization operating in any given host country. Increasing employees' understanding of the change process may also reduce the level of uncertainty and resistance toward the change and, thus, help promote employees' involvement in and acceptance of the change (Goodman & Truss, 2004). The importance of effective communication is noted also by Weick, Sutcliffe and Obstfeld (2005) who argue that it is talk that brackets action and thus gives meaning. Harvard Business School focused on the meaning and application of effective "Communication" and emphasized that "Face-to-Face Communication" be used for clarity and impact by the "Results-Driven Manager" (HBS, 2004)

However, over time the concept of managerial communication has been ascribed numerous and very different meanings. Its exact meaning is still intensely debated. There are several definitions of managerial communication: 1) it is an applied, interdisciplinary field focusing on language and behavior within an organizational context (Brownell, 2003); 2) it focuses on cross-cultural communication across various contexts: interpersonal, group, organizational and, in some instances, mediated (Kraut et al., 1982; Kraut et al., 2002); 3) it includes all relevant forms and channels of communication that managers may select in accomplishing their purposes, including written, oral, nonverbal, and mediated (Cornelissen, 2004); 4) its research supplies the principles and insights that help practitioners to apply knowledge derived from all other disciplines as they seek to increase their effectiveness (Clampitt, 2005).

In an organizational approach, managerial communication represents the decisive means by which the manager fulfils his/her tasks and duties and employs the competences and skills pertaining to his/her role in the company and in relations with business partners (Gheorghe et al., 2009). The manager sends information to the members of an organization and its business partners, and their response influences his/her subsequent decisions and behavior. The quality of communication channels depends on the functionality of the communication system. This system needs to be conceived as a dynamic organism, capable of adapting to the information needs of the company at any moment, at any level, responding to any problems which may influence and condition its normal functioning (Johansson & Heide, 2008; Gheorghe et al., 2009).

Within a company, the individual and the group performance of the employees largely depend on the quality of managerial communication. The manager communicates for the purpose of sending and receiving information, triggering adequate answers and, implicitly, influencing the receptors' decisions and their response to the transmitted messages. The efficient management of communication is a weighty responsibility for any manager, and the way he/she fulfils it is fundamental to business success. Managers need to inform all employees with of company missions and goals, and related costs and targets. However, a manager is also interested in conveying information on task fulfilment, and suggestions and opinions on the well-being of the company, as seen by employees. At the same time, the members of the managerial team must exchange information with regard to any technical, economic and social problems affecting the company. Within the global business framework and the scope of this chapter managerial communication becomes an important element of the interaction between all players. Thus, a system of reciprocal cooperation is created, which facilitates the fundamental objectives of the company.

Published literature (Dance, 1970; Campbell & Level Dale, 1985; Clampitt, 2005; Stefanescu & Popa, 2008) emphasizes many modes of communication, however; two modes stand out as the most important: formal and informal communications. Formal communication can be defined as a set of rules that all stakeholders in the organization strictly adhere to. It is a structured flow of information formally conveyed to members within and outside the organization. The structure enables the flow of communication in a way that guarantees the transfer of a specific knowledge effectively, effortlessly, precisely, timely and confidentially. In other words the structure is the only formal channel of communication. Formal communication within the organization includes but is not limited to: departmental meetings, conferences, telephone calls, e-mails, text messages, company news releases, media interviews and, specialist publications.

Informal communication cannot be as readily defined since its content is derived from unplanned events that may occur under specific circumstances. Informal communication is based on the realization that individuals or group members cannot be effective without personal interaction amongst its members. Therefore, informal communication is personal, unofficial, and mostly verbal. While it is unplanned for, past experience shapes informal communication.

When formal communication is non-existent informal communication occurs organically between individuals and within a team. When a crisis occurs, key players who have not been trained in communications develop and sporadically implement an immediate communication plan based on successful past experiences. When emergencies happen, a manager is able to promptly begin communicative interactions, fostering effective crisis management (McKinney et al., 2005)

Managerial communication acts as an integrated relationship with those inside the company, as well as those outside the company. Competitive companies have understood this, and have promoted communicative competence as a philosophy assumed by management and the organization as a whole. In many companies, communication is considered to be, and is used as one of the most valuable instruments of strategic management. Conversely, the defective transmission of information, communication breakdowns and lack of transparency and honesty frequently account for business failures.

Examples of the criticality of using especially managerial communication are prevalent in the international political arena. The online version of The Hill Times, a Canadian weekly newspaper, reports that the current Prime Minister of Canada, Stephen Harper, has taken communiqués to a new level. The Hill Times reports that Mr. Harper's office and departments employ approximately 1,500 communications staffers (Ryckewaert, 2011). Quite a high number considering that Canada's population is about one tenth of that of the USA.

Approaches to Managerial Communication

Over time, multiple approaches to communication have been built. According to literature (Dance, 1970; Campbell & Level Dale, 1985; Clampitt, 2005; Copley, 2004; Stefanescu & Popa, 2008), there are four approaches that are the most significant and prevalent in managerial practice: The one-way communication model, the circuit communication model, the interactive communication model and the behavioural model.

The one-way communication approach is a classic model (Schramm, 1955; Campbell & Dale Level, 1985). Managers who choose this approach (from transmitter to receptor or from encoder to decoder), which Clampitt (2005) called "the arrow approach" (p. 1), start from the presupposition that the receptor's feedback is not needed as long as the information and decisions transmitted were clearly formulated, in a language that is adequate and unambiguous. This idea relies on the belief that if the message is clear for the transmitter, it must be equally clear to the receptor. The latter will act in complete accordance with the content of the message received. By adopting this type of communication, the manager considers that, by using a clear and precise language, the decision that he/she transmits will be correctly understood and complied with by the receiver, without any feedback required. This type of communication is a model that proves defective, as it generates problems at the organizational level. Employees often complain about the lack of information or about the fact that the information reaches them distorted. In the absence of a response, this sort of information can no longer be corrected. The inadequate distribution of the information from the upper level of management to the lower levels was critiqued by Peter Drucker (1993); when taking up the one-way communication model, a manager invariably ignores the receptor.

Communication is incomplete if information is misunderstood. Many theorists consider that we may speak of communication only when the receiver gives feedback. Under the conditions of the ever increasing complexity of company activities, the efficiency of managerial communication process is not fully sustained by adopting a one-way communication model. Organizational practice has shown that efficient managerial communication relies on a plurality of factors. Among them, employee feedback to messages received from management attests to communication comprehension and makes possible the adaptation of employee behavior to managerial expectations. Overlooking employee responses can have negative effects upon the success of the communication process, and consequently upon the company in general.

Another approach of managerial communication is circuit communication, which supposes the existence, in all cases, of the receptor's response (reaction) to the received message. Unlike the "arrow" approach, this type of communication starts from the presupposition that the manager must know all problems facing subordinates are facing in fulfilling assigned tasks, and all their opinions and views on activities they carry within the company. The success of this type of managerial approach depends on the manager's skills in psychology and of his/her ability to stimulate the employee devotion towards the company. The disadvantage of approaching this sort of communication comes from the large amount of time spent in discussions and debates, which may negatively reflect on the effectiveness and efficacy of the company.

Interactive communication is yet another way of approaching communication. Interactive communication supposes an exchange of ideas between those who communicate, each having, in turn, the role of receptor and transmitter. This model of communication is particularly characteristic of organizations in which employees' creative skills are appreciated and their participation in problem solving is stimulated. Interactive communication relies on group creativity, the valorisation of proposals, suggestions and ideas expressed by members of the organization. Its aim is to identify solutions generated by the exchange of ideas. The effectiveness of this type of communication is conditioned by the compatibility of those who communicate; their shared level of knowledge, experience, values and behaviours.

In 1985, Campbell and Level proposed a more complex model of communication–the behavioural model. The two researchers analyzed the managerial communication process by studying transmitter expectations of receptor reactions to a message. The anticipation of likely employee responses to a message helps the manager structure and adapt the message in order to illicit a positive response. The determination of the receiver's behavior subsequent to the communication must be, in the two researchers' view, the transmitter's first goal. He/she should also take into account the outside interferences that might occur and which may prejudice the communication process.

Although companies have gone through massive changes with respect to the way they approach managerial communication, none of the models presented above is remotely close to perfection. Each has, as shown, both advantages and disadvantages. In essence, any communication must be approached in a manner that best suits the set purpose, and the communication competence of all concerned. He/she must ensure the smooth transit of the communication process through all channels, both formal and informal, and both inside and outside the company.

Development of the Managerial Communication Competence

Although communication may at first glance appear simple and uncomplicated, it is, in fact, a complex undertaking. Clampitt (2005) argues that communication within the firm is an important skill for all managers, irrespective of their seniority. Effective communication requires training and development. Often, organizations do not invest sufficient money, time, and effort in developing effective communications skills, which in turn results in communication failure.

Many researchers have placed communicational competence at the very core of managerial success. Reflecting on the qualities that underpin managerial success, Maxwell (2002) ranks the manager's ability to communicate efficiently first in importance, with a rating of 38% (p. 101). It is notable that Maxwell gives other components a markedly lower grade: creativity– 31%, management knowledge – 19%, relationships – 12% (Maxwell, 2002). In turn, Drucker (1977) urges managers to improve their communicative competence, so that they may be noted for their "ability to communicate with people and to introduce to them their own thoughts and ideas in such a way as to get them to understand and be persuaded" (p. 262). Furthermore, "this ability to express oneself may be the most important aptitude one can have" (Drucker, 1977).

A manager's ability to constantly improve his/her communication skills is fundamental to the operation of any company. In the process, the true understanding of "managerial communication" and its application becomes most critical for any manager. The result is a positive-communicative aptitude that fosters a climate of open mindedness and trust and repels conflict and tension. Additionally, the ability to convey unpleasant news or information with diplomacy, to divert conflict tactfully and to solve problems with authority is key aspect of effective communication.

Published literature (Johansson & Heide, 2008; Gheorghe et al., 2009) shows that too often communication by managers fails because of lack of proper training, lack of follow-up, follow through, and lack of consequence for those who do not perceive the communication to be relevant or important. Accordingly, managers often abdicate the responsibility for communicating effectively to their internal communications department and lack the confidence to facilitate discussion within their teams (Clampitt, 2005). Communication is far from simple and experienced communicators recognize, therefore, the need to be persistent until their messages have been clearly received, understood, and dealt with accordingly. The results of an investigation into persistent and redundant communication revealed that clarity in messaging was not the goal for redundant communication (Girard, 2011). Even if a powerful manager is clear and direct with an employee-team member, it is still the redundancy that counts in order to get the core of the message delivered as intended.

Strategic communication, policy-making, and guidance for consistent information activity both internally and externally, are of increased interest to researchers. It is key that sensitive information be safeguarded effectively (e.g., computer hackers are now able to use social media to gain competitive advantage). WikiLeaks (Johnson, 2011) provides a vivid example of a seemingly weaker social media stakeholder empowered to compel concessions from an apparently stronger adversary (Castells, 2007). Certainly, companies ignore the power of social media within the context of communication at their peril. The top management however should be rather concerned that leaks can be detrimental to any company and therefore the need to be prepared should be a priority.

The Role of Information Technology in Contemporary Communication's Practice

Advances in information technology are allowing organizations to: (1) distribute information at increased rates of speed; (2) make more information available than ever before; (3) allow broader and more immediate access to this information; (4) encourage participation in the sharing and use of information; and, (5) integrate systems and functions in unprecedented ways.

The political tumult since 2011 in the Middle East has illustrated the key role of social media.

Similarly, global corporations are using social media to disseminate all manner of information whether marketing related or human resources related (Shah, et al. 2005). The most popular social media outlets such as Facebook, Twitter, and various other Web 2.0 technologies, are being used to communicate with individuals internally and externally across the globe.

Although using social media to communicate can be challenging, executives often use it effectively to stay in touch with all concerned in a timely and effective fashion (Lenhart & Fox, 2006). Oracle's CEO, Jonathan Benoit (Oracle, 2011); Bill Marriott, Chairman & CEO of Marriott International; and John Mackey, Whole Foods CEO use internal and external blogs. The phenomenon delivers measurable benefits to all stakeholders (Drezner & Farrell, 2004). Internal blogs can, for example, facilitate the collation of workplace data. This information can be used to aid performances evaluations and for many other applications. Data collected on external parties such as guests/customers can be used in the application of competitive analytics, Customer Relations Management (CRM), Customer Experience Management (CEM), and other marketing related applications. With unparalleled access to stakeholders, IT communication must avoid any breach of privacy and unlawful collection of personal information.

Use of Effective Communication to Create Competitive Advantage

Earlier in the chapter we discussed that when researching competitive advantage a major research question comes to mind: why are some competitors more successful than others? And why do some executives consistently make the right decisions, while others invariably fail? Studies in the field of managerial communication reveal that failure to effectively communicate leads to lower productivity, lower profitability and short-term survivorship. In response to continuous failure, Fortune 500 companies have been hiring experts in the field of corporate communication in order to gain competitive advantage. A global search for job opportunities in "Corporate Communication" revealed that most job descriptions include some common themes: "Identifying, anticipating and prioritizing communication needs, providing, strategic insight and direction for organizational communication within the organization; developing a concerted stakeholder engagement effort, especially among business leaders, complete with metrics and aligned with the company's 'change management' program; partnering with the company's leadership team at a strategic level, coaching and counselling them, influencing leadership thinking in communication outreach; developing executive communications strategies for members of the company's leadership team; leading, developing and executing internal organizational and employee communication programs to engage employees and heighten their level of commitment to the new operating model's goals and objectives; managing issues and crisis situations that may arise, in coordination with senior management" (Johnson & Johnson, 2011).

Even the most talented managers, who attempt to lead an organization without effective communication, especially without the concept of managerial communication, will ultimately fail while their more communicatively astute counterparts succeed. Many strategic plans may never be implemented due to lack of communication from managers. Increased managerial communication effectiveness enables practitioners at all management levels to realize the benefits of proper communication (Munter, 2011).

Highlights from a Case Study

Yates (2006) writes that the Global Practice Director for Communication Consulting with Watson Wyatt has conducted a six year research study titled

"Becoming a ROI Builder: Delivering Effective Employees' Communication." The results for which Watson Wyatt Worldwide surveyed more than 750 companies representing more than 12 million employees aimed at determining the best practices in organizational communication and at identifying the "critical communication areas" companies should be concerned with. The results of the study confirmed that "communication effectiveness" is a leading indicator of financial performance. In fact, companies with "superior employee communication" policies provided a 47% higher total return to shareholders over a five year period (2002–2006) compared with those firms at the bottom of the communication effectiveness scale (Yates, 2006). The study also found that companies which implement or improve their communication practices by one significant deviation can achieve a 15.7% increase in market or shareholder value. Hence, improving communication effectiveness can provide added shareholder value for small and large companies alike. The results also determined that the areas in which top performing companies excel are: customer focus, employee engagement, cross-cultural managerial communication, change management, measuring effectiveness, and employer brand (Yates, 2006).

Highlights from an Industry Leader

On March 25, 2011, Carmine Gallo (Gallo, 2011) renowned communications coach and former reporter and anchor for CNN and CBS television, published an article in Forbes Magazine titled "Starbucks CEO: Lesson in Communication Skills." In the article Gallo states: "Howard Schultz taught me a valuable lesson in communication skills: 'what you stand for is more important than what you make'" (Forbes, 2011). According to the article, Schultz states that Starbucks is the quintessential "experience brand" and that this experience comes to life via its employees. "The only competitive advantage we have is the relationship we have with our people and the relationship they have built with our customers." "We're not in the coffee business. It's what we sell as a product but we're in the people business—hiring hundreds of employees a week, serving 60 million customers a week, it's all human connection" (Forbes, 2011).

The original idea behind the dynamic growth of Starbucks was not to involve investors in a new coffee chain, instead he wanted to create a "Third Place" between home and work; a place that sells "Human Connection." This message resonated with the consumer who embraced the idea of human connection first and that of the coffee second. This vision behind the brand helped Shultz create the most successful coffee company in modern economic times. Thus, it is not what a company may produce and sell, and not even the quality of the product, which unarguably could be challenged by competitors; instead it is about the way a message behind a product is communicated. Starbucks continues to benefit from its effective communication skills, effectively positioning its coffee products in the consumer's mind (Starbucks, 2011).

A QUALITATIVE FIELD INVESTIGATION ON MANAGERIAL COMMUNICATION

Methodology of the Study

In support of the criticality of managerial communication discussed earlier in the chapter, we present and discuss the findings of a qualitative study on the topic of communication in general. The study uses philosophical and ethnographic research methodology to investigate and to assess the status- quo of contemporary managerial communication policy implementation within firms. The study applies qualitative methodology using interpretative techniques to analyze the non-intrusive collection of data. This data is obtained from a convenience sample of companies across industries listed in the Fortune 500 directory and from companies that provide communications' related services.

The methodology uses the techniques of coding and frequency, and trend and pattern analysis. Coding is an analytical process in which data is categorized to facilitate the detailed analysis of critical variables which have variety, richness, and individual character. Coding is also used to distinguish between a set of variables, followed by an additional in-depth interpretive coding in which more specific trends and patterns can be interpreted. Thus coding allows for summarizing the prevalence and relevance of codes, discussing similarities and differences among them. In addition, it uses recursive abstraction, a methodology where datasets are summarized; those summaries are then further summarized, until a subset of useful data is obtained (Denzin & Lincoln, 2005; Loseke & Cahil, 2007; Holliday, 2007).

Data Collection

Data from previous studies was extrapolated principally from published scholarly literature and partially from practitioners' trade literature. The qualitative data was obtained from previously arranged semi-structured phone interviews and face-to-face structured interviews with participants. Information was assessed accurately and consistently by asking all subjects the same questions, and from referring to company websites. Like personal interviews, telephone interviews enable a researcher to gather information rapidly and they allow for personal contact between the interviewer and the respondent. During the interview, participants also had the opportunity to answer open ended questions which allowed them to contribute their personal point of view.

About 100 firms representing America's largest and most successful corporations listed in the Fortune 500 directory were selected and contacted via e-mail and by phone to participate in the study (CNN, 2011). We specifically selected companies based on their success, which in turn infers competitive advantage and that "communication" in general may be an integral part of their strategic planning. We determined that a convenience sample of 100 firms was appropriate for this exploratory study. From the sample, 27 representatives agreed to participate. Participants were asked a set of questions that included whether their company had a communications policy in place; the policy content; to what extent the policy was implemented (e.g., corporate level or at other levels of the organization chart); whether a communications plan was effectively implemented, and had information they could freely provide.

RESULTS

Summary from Published Literature

The synthesis of the findings from published literature revealed that firms across industries cannot neglect the importance of a well formulated and implemented communication policy when operating in this century of high-tech evolution. A well executed communication's policy has a direct correlation with a company's success. Furthermore, the implementation of a managerial communication plan allows for maximum efficiency of information dissemination as well as the protection of confidential and highly sensitive data which is vital to maintaining advantage over a competitor. Also of key importance is the methodology in which data is disseminated and the degree of confidentiality as to who should receive the information and what to do with it, for example using company blogs, Facebook, intranet, internet mail, written internal memorandum, and others. Table 1 shows the factors a firm should consider in the formulation of a managerial communication plan identified in an earlier study on Managerial Communication for an industry specific investigation (Camillo & Di Pietro, 2011).

Once the factors to be considered in the formulation of a communication plan have been

Table 1. Factors a firm should consider in the formulation of a managerial communications plan

Factors (Not rank specific)
Good communication skills and proper etiquette by managers are essential
The value of learning about culture and cultures
Effectively practicing Managerial Communication
Must have a communications plan in place
Define the scope and the goal of the plan
Deciding on the critical components of the communication plan
Who should be in charge of disseminating what information
Who should receive the information
What should be the content of the information include
The criticality of the timing on when information should be released
What methodology should be used to relay the information
Determine how to store, track, retrieve, and, if necessary delete the disseminated information
Plan for unintended consequences and how to deal with them
Implement an effective control mechanism that can monitor all company information to avoid distortion, tempering, and manipulation of the original information by intruders
Clear the Managerial Communication's initiative with legal department before implementing the final plan.

identified, a logistics of the critical components must be developed (see Table 2).

Much debate pervades the education sector on managerial communication. Since it was first introduced in the classroom, academicians have argued about whether the subject should be catalogued and taught as a discipline, or be part of the social sciences or simply regarded as an integral tool for the practitioner in the field. In addition scholars and practitioners in the field have yet to agree on a convention about the definition; distinction, meaning, and application of various terms used almost interchangeably within the context of managerial communication (see introduction section in this chapter for additional highlights.) Nevertheless, top business schools today offer communications classes both, general and specific, as a requisite for those majoring in journalism or mass communication and as an elective for those students enrolled in MBA programs.

Regardless of prevailing managerial communications debates, published literature and recent events (including that of the WikiLeaks release of sensitive U.S. Department of Defence documents) (Johnson, 2011), offer compelling evidence that not only is there a need for companies to implement an effective communications policy support by a dynamically updated training plan, but there is also a need to formulate a policy that is effective in protecting confidential data.

Summary from Structured Interviews

Data obtained from the structured interviews was transcribed, coded and analyzed for frequency and pattern. Results were synthesized applying recursive abstraction, summarized, tabulated and are presented below. The first questions participants were asked was: "Does your company have a communications department? If yes, does it have a communication's policy in place?" What are the most important factors included in your communication's policy? Does your policy cover internal and external communication? Please provide an example of what your internal and external communication's policy (e.g., a meeting [internal] or a press release [external]) includes? Table 3 lists the most essential elements participants believed a firm should consider in policy creation.

Communications policies require efficient practicality and compelled adherence by all stakeholders. Not only must everything be recorded at any time for any given situation but the rules must be followed without exception. Table 4 shows the outline of an actual meeting agenda which highlights the importance to produce a record about anything concerning an important company meeting. In this scenario a financial matter is discussed. Lot is at stake before the final financial results can be communicated to all stakeholders. The company stock value, the effect of the financial

Table 2. Critical components and logistics of a communication plan

Who is responsible for the plan and dissemination of information?	What should the plan include?	When should the plan be implemented	How should the plan be developed	Where – through which channel should the information be disseminated	Who are the Stakeholders
Management Appointed spokes person	Policy and plan Type of communication: internal-external; how much and level of confidentiality	At inception or by timely adoption Specific Timing, frequency On going	Self developed, hiring an expert, adoption from parent company, research	At specified location, either with public access or private At all designated physical locations and in cyber space Directly: memo, email, presentation Indirectly: accessible on intranet, website Personal: relayed to others in person In writing: electronically, voice and video recording, or by other means such as witness observation and taking notes	All management, employees and customers All persons as appointed by management

performance results will have on customers, employees and business associates outside the company. (In order to protect the identity of the company and the identity of the meeting participants, the names have been omitted.)

Participants indicated several internal factors that are critical to management in the formulation and implementation of a communication policy and plan (see Table 5). The results in Table 5 concur with the industry specific factors determined in previous study, see Table 1.

Summary of the Results

In this era of rapid fire technological advances, managers must understand the complexity of managerial communication and must decide to what extent a communications policy should be implemented. In the case of a company that operates globally there is a need to change and adapt the communications policy to reflect the diversity and local culture of the host country's nationals. Hence, education and continuous training programs have to be in place especially if firms operate as multinationals or conglomerates. One must also consult with legal experts to insure that no potential legal infringements exist. In the case of an international or multinational company, both countries' host and home countries' legal aspects must be considered before a policy can be freely

Table 3. Essential elements to consider when creating a communication's policy

Essential Elements of Communication
1. Purpose
2. Message Sender (Encoder)
3. Message Configuration (timing, content, level of confidentiality)
4. Message Receiver (Decoder)
5. Channel of Communication (electronic, type written, in person)
6. Expected Outcome

Table 4. Sample communication meeting schedule regarding quarterly performance results

Q1-Quarterly Meeting – North America Division
▪ **Purpose:** quarterly performance results and strategic planning review
▪ **Date and Time:** April 16st. 20xx
▪ **Venue:** Head Office Executive Boardroom
▪ **Present:** VP Finance, Divisional Managers
▪ **Participants excused:** (List all absentees)
▪ **In attendance:** (List all attendees)
▪ **Agenda items:**
1. Approval of previous meeting minutes
2. Discussion of matters pending or arising from previous meeting
3. Discussion of agenda items in order of priority:
a. As planned by the meeting chair
b. As submitted by meeting attendees
c. As submitted by absentees
d. Items from the Board of Directors, Shareholders, other Executives/Stakeholders
4. Financial performance review
5. Sales and Marketing Strategies feed-back
6. New Business Development
7. Divisional Activities at regional and Strategic Business Unit (SBU) Level
8. Production – Inventory – Backlog, etc…
9. Logistics and Distribution
10. Quality Assurance Report
11. New Projects – R&D report
12. Ethics report
13. CSR (Corporate Social Responsibility) Report
14. Human Resources Issues
15. Union Issues (if applicable)
16. Communications and Media Relations report
17. Other Business Issues
18. Date of next meeting and deadline for submitting new agenda items
19. Time meeting was adjourned
20. Signed: Minutes taken by…

implemented. The findings from companies that have a communication policy in place reveal six common elements they value the most before a plan is implemented (see Table 4). These elements revolve around the information that needs to be disseminated as highlighted below:

- **Purpose:** Define the purpose of the policy and determine whether messages disseminated based on this policy will be clearly understood by all stakeholders. Assess the decoder's perception about the creditability of your company and the validity of the message being sent.
- **Message Sender (Encoder):** Encoding means translating information into a message in the form of symbols that represent ideas or concepts into the coded message that will be communicated. Encoding involves the use of specific language, types of words, and graphic, visual or auditory representations. Thus, encoding translates ideas into messages that others can interpret and understand. When encoding a message, the sender decides what to transmit based on what he/she believes about the receiver's (decoder's) knowledge and assumptions, along with additional information he/she wants the receiver (decoder) to have. It is important for the sender to use symbols that are familiar to the intended receiver. The sender should always create a scenario to mentally visualize the communication from the receiver's point of view (Munter, 2011).
- **Message Configuration:** Strategic formulation of the message being disseminated. What is the message? Negative, positive, informative, persuasive, reinforcement, to raise awareness about something new or something to be concerned about? Does the message carry a further message to a

Table 5. Factors a firm should consider in the formulation of a managerial communications policy

Factors
• Management responsible for the policy must possess good communication skills
• Effective practicing of managerial communication
• Understand the demographics of the stakeholders: different cultures and beliefs, diversity…
• Understand for whom the policy is being developed: employees, customers…
• Demonstrate good ethics
• Must have an effective and well formulated communications policy and plan in place
• Decide who should be in charge of developing and implementing the policy and plan
• Define the scope and the goal of the policy and plan
• Determine what the policy and plan should include
• Decide who should be in charge of disseminating what information
• Determine who the stakeholders are
• When should be the information disseminated
• What is the information about and what should the information include
• What channel of communication should be used
• How should the information be filed, stored, tracked, retrieved, classified, or deleted
• Have a contingency plan for unexpected response or action against the firm
• Have an effective monitoring system in place for accurate feed-back and corrective action if necessary
• Be ready to
• Prepare to counter negative criticism and take action for "Damage Control"
• Always consult with the legal representative before implementing a policy, a plan or before responding to negative criticism or action by stakeholders.

sub-audience? Does the encoder require feedback? Level of confidentiality? Is this the right timing?

- **Channel of Communication:** A communication channel is the means used to convey a message. Channels can be oral, written, visual, auditory, electronic, internal or external mail distribution, or via telephone. Various media such as television, websites, blogs, radio, etc. also exist. The effectiveness of each channel fluctuates depending on the characteristics of the communication. For example, when immediate feedback is necessary, oral communication channels are more effective because any uncertainties can be corrected instantaneously. In a situation where the message must be delivered to a wider audience, other channels should be considered.
- **Message Receiver (Decoder):** The receiver is the individual (or individuals) to whom the message is intended to be received. Once the message is received, examined, and interpreted, the decoder assigns some type of meaning to it. Successful communication takes place when the receiver correctly decodes and interprets the sender's message. The extent to which the decoder comprehends the message will depend on several factors; familiarity with the topic, the creditability of the sender, validity of the message based on prior relationship and trust. The receiver's interpretation of the message is influenced by the experiences, attitude, knowledge, skills, perception, and his/her culture. It is, in a way, the reverse of what the encoder attempts to determine before a message is disseminated.
- **Expected Outcome, Feedback:** These are important components of the communication process. Feedback and expected outcome are crucial in the evaluation of the effectiveness of the message. Feedback provides an opportunity for the sender to determine if the message correctly served its purpose. Did it produce the expected outcome and does corrective action needs to be taken to reduce or eliminate confusion? Misunderstandings and eventual failure to effectively communicate is caused by several factors: inappropriate channel of communication, incorrect grammar, of-

fensive language, words that may be misconstrued, miss-translation, among others. Regardless of the policy in place, communication within an organization can only be successful and effective if the communication process is flawlessly implemented and carried out. Ineffective communication can be averted if the organization thinks of communication as a process of continuous improvement The results of this qualitative investigation offer useful insights into the criticality of having a communications policy and plan in effect at all levels of the organizational chart. The section below highlights this study's findings and proposes useful recommendations for the practitioner in the field as well as for educators who wish to include the critical components of a managerial communications policy into their curriculum and for graduating business major students about to join the workforce.

SOLUTIONS AND RECOMMENDATIONS

Managerial communication is a vast field which affects every individual that works within the organization. Despite its unstable or non-standardized position in the academic world, research in the field of communication is of great importance. The need for a solid communication infrastructure within an organization is key at every level. Having a communications department contributes to the overall competitive strategy of the company. Not only is good managerial communication dependent on the communication adroitness of individual managers, it also pivots on the response and of subordinates. However the problem will continue to persist until an agreement for a solution can be mitigated in regards to the criticality and complexity of communication in general. Specifically, scholars and practitioners in the field should agree whether the subject should be catalogued and taught as a discipline, or be part of the social sciences or simply regarded as an integral tool for the practitioner in the field. Furthermore the definition, distinction, meaning, and application of various terms used almost interchangeably within the context of managerial communication, must be discussed and agreed on conventionally in order to have common understanding of the application across the board (see introduction section in this chapter for additional highlights.) The results will be mutually beneficial to all stakeholders. In this way a communications plan will be taught, learned in the classroom and applied in the field the same as a budget, or any other component of the strategic planning. Therefore, a communications plan can be described is a tool that helps an individual, such as a manager decide how he/she intends to have the organization understand the team's plans, strategies and operations objectives. In an era of advanced technological innovation we can relay a message in person, by email, by texting, over a social network site such as Facebook, Twitter, or simply indirectly through gossip. Too often messages reach unintended audiences. Consequences derived from miscommunications can be detrimental to an entire organization especially in the international arena. Yet, incidents such as this do happen on a regular basis. It is also worth noting that once electronic messages have been sent, they can be stored by anyone in perpetuity. In sum, future studies should audit the effectiveness of communication policies by applying measurement matrices, surveys, and focus groups especially in relationship with evolution of information technology. The development of a model for global standardization of corporate communication would be beneficial to the entire international business community. Business schools should require that managerial communication be included in their curriculum at undergraduate and graduate levels, in required disciplines such as journalism and related disciplines such as marketing, accounting, finance and in management and leadership courses.

LIMITATIONS OF THE STUDY

To conduct this study about 100 companies listed in the Fortune 500 directory on CNN.com (CNN, 2011) were contacted. There were several challenges. Ironically, as the study was about communication, the main challenge was finding the right department or person who could confirm if the firm had a communication policy in place. Although several firms' representatives had agreed to participate in the interviews, eventually they could not due to company's proprietary-confidentiality policies. Nevertheless, we were able to determine that most companies had a communication link or webpage on their corporate website, dedicated to various audiences (e.g., shareholders, employees, customers, etc.). Usually this was established through public relations departments. Although several attempts were made to communicate using electronic mail, no personalized reply was ever received; instead only automated email responses were received. This confirms that the complexity and criticality of communication in the modern era will remain a hot topic for discussion. Company information can be received from them (pushed) as they determine worthy and necessary; however, it cannot be received (pulled) by simply contacting a communications department or individual. Clearly this is an area companies can improve upon.

CONCLUSION

An extensive review of the literature and data obtained from selected companies provided valuable information about the status-quo of contemporary communication. In sum, effective Managerial communication is a vital skill for everyone in business today but especially for managers at all levels of global companies. Great communicators have a key advantage in building managerial influence especially while starting their careers. Knowing how to communicate effectively in every business situation is not only important but critical to business success. From sensitively articulated employee feedback to persuasive announcements to customers, today's executive must be a frontline communicator.

In order to master the art of communication a manager has to apply the following proficiencies:

- Understand the optimal 'medium' to present information.
- Learn the best timing to deliver of key messages.
- Master the art of self-editing.

Grasping the best timing for "bad news" is paramount in the business world, especially during economic downturns when employees face job loss; knowing when to communicate forthcoming layoffs is a tricky task. With a comprehensive communication policy in place, many scenarios can be planned for making it easier for management to deliver grave tidings.

This study is a subsequent study of an industry specific study (Camillo & Di Pietro, 2011) and which investigates managerial communication cross nationally and across industries and contributes to extant business research by raising awareness about the criticality of managerial communication. It illustrates the need for further study of this discipline in business schools and provides useful insights regarding the factors and logistics needed to create and implement a communication policy and plan.

REFERENCES

Abbe, A., Gulick, L. M. V., & Herman, J. L. (2007). *Cross-cultural competence in Army leaders: A conceptual and empirical foundation.* Washington, DC: U.S. Army Research Institute. doi:10.1037/e551892009-001.

Ali, M. (2011). *Chartis Launches Reputation-Guard®, Reputational Risk Insurance*. Press Release. New York: ChartisChartis. Retrieved from http://www.chartisinsurance.com/searchresults/search_295_195443.html

Allen, J. (2011). *$16 muffins, $8 coffee served in Justice Audit*. Retrieved on September 21, 2011, from http://www.reuters.com/article/2011/09/21/us-usa-justice-muffins-idUSTRE78J7B020110921

Arasaratnam, L. A., & Doerfel, M. L. (2005). Intercultural communication competence: Identifying key components from multicultural perspectives. *International Journal of Intercultural Relations*, *29*, 137–163. doi:10.1016/j.ijintrel.2004.04.001.

Armenakis, A., & Harris, S. (2002). Crafting a change message to create transformational readiness. *Journal of Organizational Change Management*, *1*(2), 169–183. doi:10.1108/09534810210423080.

Astley, W. G., & Zammuto, R. F. (1992). Organization science, managers and language games. *Organization Science*, *3*(4), 443–460. doi:10.1287/orsc.3.4.443.

Britannica. (2012). *Fernando Ortiz*. Retrieved June 27, 2012, from http://www.britannica.com/EBchecked/topic/848801/Fernando-Ortiz

Brownell, J. (2003). Applied Research in Managerial Communication. *The Cornell Hotel and Restaurant Administration Quarterly*, *44*(2), 39–49. doi:10.1016/S0010-8804(03)90017-6.

Calhoun, C. (2011). Communication as Social Science (and More). *International Journal of Communication*, *5*, 1479–1496.

Camillo, A. A., & Di Pietro, L. (2011). The Importance of Managerial Communication for Hospitality Organizational Settings in the Era of High-Tech Evolution. *Hosteur*, *20*(2), 19–27.

Campbell, D. P., & Level Dale, A. (1985). A Black Box Model of Communication. *Journal of Business Communication*, *22*(3), 37–47. doi:10.1177/002194368502200304.

Carlson, S. (1951). *Executive Behavior*. Stockholm, Sweden: Strombergs.

Castells, M. (2007). Communication, power and counter-power in the network society. *International Journal of Communication*, *1*(1), 238–266.

Chen, G. M., & Starosta, W. J. (1998). *Foundations of Intercultural Communication*. Boston, MA: Allyn and Bacon.

Clampitt, P. (2005). *Communicating for Managerial Effectiveness*. New York: Sage Publications.

CNN. (2011). *Money, Annual Ranking of America's Largest Corporations. Fortune 500 companies*. Retrieved from http://money.cnn.com/magazines/fortune/fortune500/2011/full_list/)

Copley, P. (2004). *Marketing Communications Management. Concepts and Theories, Cases and Practices*. Oxford, UK: Elsevier.

Cornelissen, J. (2004). *Corporate communications. Theory and Practice*. London: Sage Publications Cornell University (2011). *Managerial Communication. An introduction to key library resources for Hotel Administration*. Retrieved from http://guides.library.cornell.edu/HADM3365)

Covin, T., Sightler, K., Kolenko, T., & Tudor, R. (1996). An investigation of post-acquisition satisfaction with the merger. *The Journal of Applied Behavioral Science*, *32*(2), 125–141. doi:10.1177/0021886396322001.

Cushner, K., & Brislin, R. W. (1996). *Intercultural interactions: A practical guide*. Thousand Oaks, CA: Sage.

Dance, F. (1970). The concept of communication. *The Journal of Communication*, *20*, 201–210. doi:10.1111/j.1460-2466.1970.tb00877.x.

Denzin, N. K., & Lincoln, Y. S. (2005). *The Sage Handbook of Qualitative Research*. Thousand Oaks, CA: Sage Publications.

Drezner, D., & Farrell, H. (2004). *The power and politics of blogs*. Paper presented at the American Political Science Association Conference. Chicago, IL.

Drucker, P. (1977). *People and Performance*. New York: Harper`s College Press.

Drucker, P. (1993). *Inovatia si sistemul antreprenorial*. Bucharest: Editura Enciclopedica.

Earley, P. C., & Ang, S. (2003). *Cultural intelligence: Individual interactions across cultures*. Stanford, CA: Stanford University Press.

Ellis, N., & Hopkinson, G. (2010). The construction of managerial knowledge in business networks: Managers' theories about communication. *Industrial Marketing Management*, *39*, 413–424. doi:10.1016/j.indmarman.2007.08.011.

Forbes. (2011, December). *Starbucks CEO: Lesson in Communication Skills*. Retrieved from http://www.forbes.com/sites/carminegallo/2011/03/25/starbucks-ceo-lesson-in-communication-skills/)

Gallo, C. (2011*). The communications coach for the world's most admired brands*. Retrieved from http://gallocommunications.com/

Gheorghe, P., Gardan, D., & Geangu, P. (2009). *The Importance of Managerial Communication in Establishing the Company Marketing Communication*. Paper presented at the International Conference on Administration and Business, ICEA – FAA. Bucharest, Romania.

Girard, K. (2011). *It's Not Nagging-Why Persistent, Redundant Communication Works*. Paper presented at the Research and Ideas, Working Knowledge Conference. Boston, MA.

Goodman, J., & Truss, C. (2004). The medium and the message: Communicating effectively during a major change initiative. *Journal of Change Management*, *4*(3), 217–229. doi:10.1080/1469701042000255392.

Gross, L. (2011). Communication as the Discipline of the 21st Century. *International Journal of Communication*, *5*, 1497–1498.

Hall Edward, T. (1959). *The Silent Language*. New York: Doubleday.

HBS. (2004). *Face-to-Face Communications for Clarity and Impact by the Results-Driven Manager*. Boston, MA: Harvard Business School Press.

Henderson, L. S. (1986). Unraveling the Meaning of Managerial Communication: A Conceptual Explication and Model for Guiding Future Research. *Academy Of Management Best Papers Proceedings*, 219-223.

Holliday, A. R. (2007). *Doing and Writing Qualitative Research*. London: Sage Publications.

Horne, J., & Lupton, T. (1965). The work activities of middle managers: An exploratory study. *Journal of Management Studies*, *1*(21), 14–33. doi:10.1111/j.1467-6486.1965.tb00563.x.

Johansson, C., & Heide, M. (2008). Speaking of change: Three communication approaches in studies of organizational change. *Corporate Communications: An International Journal*, *13*(3), 288–305. doi:10.1108/13563280810893661.

Johnson, C. (2011). *Case Against Wiki Leaks Part Of Broader Campaign*. Retrieved from http://www.npr.org/2011/05/11/136173262/case-against-wikileaks-part-of-broader-campaign

Johnson & Johnson. (2011). *Director, Corporate Communications Job, Health Care Systems Inc*. Retrieved from http://www.careers.jnj.com/region

Kelly, J. (1964). The study of executive behavior by activity sampling. *Human Relations, 17*, 277–287. doi:10.1177/001872676401700310.

Kraut, R. E., Egido, C., & Galegher, J. (2002). Patterns of contact and communication in scientific research collaboration. In Galegher, J., & Kraut, R. (Eds.), *Intellectual Teamwork: Social and technological foundations of group work*. New York: Lawrence Earlbaum Associates.

Kraut, R. E., Lewis, S. H., & Swezey, L. W. (1982). Listener responsiveness and the coordination of conversation. *Journal of Personality and Social Psychology, 43*, 718–731. doi:10.1037/0022-3514.43.4.718.

Landsberger, H. (1961). Horizontal Dimension in Bureaucracy. *Administrative Science Quarterly, 6*, 299–322. doi:10.2307/2390705.

Lawrence, P. R., & Lorsch, J. W. (1967). *Organization and Environment: Managing Differentiation and Integration*. Cambridge, MA: Harvard University Press.

Leeds-Hurwitz, W. (1990). Notes in the History of Intercultural Communication: The Foreign Service Institute and the Mandate for Intercultural Training. *The Quarterly Journal of Speech, 76*(3), 262–281. doi:10.1080/00335639009383919.

Lenhart, A., & Fox, S. (2006). *Bloggers: A portrait of the Internet's new story tellers*. Washington, DC: Pew Internet & American Life Project.

Loseke, D. R., & Cahil, S. E. (2007). Publishing qualitative manuscripts: Lessons learned. In Seale, C., Gobo, G., Gubrium, J. F., & Silverman, D. (Eds.), *Qualitative Research Practice: Concise Paperback Edition* (pp. 491–506). London: Sage.

Maxwell, J. C. (2002). *Cele 21 de legi supreme ale liderului*. Bucharest, Romania: Editura Amaltea.

Mckinney, E. H. Jr, Barker, J. R., Davis, K. J., & Smith, D. (2005). How Swift Starting Action Teams Get off the Ground: What United Flight 232 and Airline Flight Crews Can Tell Us About Team Communication. *Management Communication Quarterly, 19*(2), 198–237. doi:10.1177/0893318905278539.

Miller, V., Johnson, J., & Grau, J. (1994). Antecedents to willingness to participate in a planned organizational change. *Journal of Applied Communication Research, 22*, 59–80. doi:10.1080/00909889409365387.

MIT Massachusetts Institute of Technology. (2009). Advanced Managerial Communication. Retrieved from http://ocw.mit.edu/courses/sloan-school-of-management/

Monash University. (2010). *Managerial Communication*. Retrieved on November 20, 2011, from http://www.monash.edu.au/Munter, M. (2011). *Guide to Managerial Communication* (8th ed.). Upper Saddle River, NJ: Prentice Hall.

Oracle. (2011, August). *Oracle open world*. Retrieved from http://blogs.oracle.com/oracleopenworld/. (2011, September 12).

Rogers, E. M., Hart, W. B., & Miike, Y. (2002). Edward T. Hall and the History of Intercultural Communication: The United States and Japan. *Keio Communication Review, 24*, 1–5.

Rogers Everett, M., & Steinfatt Thomas, M. (1999). *Intercultural Communication*. Prospect Heights, IL: Waveland Press.

Ryckewaert, L. (2011). *PM Harper takes communications strategy to new level*. Retrieved on November 30, 2011, from http://www.hilltimes.com/news/2011/11/21/pm-harper-takes-communications-strategy-to-new-level/28868

Schraeder, M. (2001). Identifying employee resistance during the threat of a merger: An analysis of employee perceptions and commitment to an organization in a pre-merger context. *The Mid-Atlantic Journal of Business*, *37*(4), 191–204.

Schramm, W. (1955). *The Process and Effects of Mass Communication*. Urbana, IL: University of Illinois Press.

Shah, D. V., Cho, J., Eveland, W. P., & Kwak, N. (2005). Information and expression in a digital age: Modelling Internet effects on civic participation. *Communication Research*, *32*(5), 531–565. doi:10.1177/0093650205279209.

Starbucks, (2011). Starbucks *to Present at Morgan Stanley Global Consumer Conference*. Retrieved on December 3, 2011, from http://investor.starbucks.com/phoenix.zhtml?c=99518&p=irol-irhome

Stefanescu, C., & Popa, L. (2008). *Managerial Communication*. Paper No. 7172. Retrieved on October 19, 2011, from http://mpra.ub.uni-muenchen.de/7172/

Stevens, B. (2005). What communication skills do employers want? Silicon Valley recruiters respond. *Journal of Employment Counseling*, *42*(1), 2–9. doi:10.1002/j.2161-1920.2005.tb00893.x.

Stinchcombe, A. L. (1974). *Creating Efficient Industrial Administration*. New York: Academic Press.

Thatam, S. A. (2008). *Strategic Communication: A Primer*. UK: Advanced Research and Assessment Group.

Ting-Toomey, S. (1999). *Communicating across cultures*. New York: Guilford.

UNESCO. (2010). Transcultural Communication in the Digital Age. Retrieved on October 9, 2012, from http://www.unesco.org/en/university-twinning-and-networking/access-by-region/europe-and-north-america/austria/unesco-chair-in-multilingual-transcultural-communication-in-the-digital-age-902/

Vicini, J. (2011). *Government did not pay $16 for muffins after all*. Retrieved on November 18, 2011, from http://www.reuters.com/article/2011/09/30/us-usa-justice-muffins-idUSTRE78T54220110930

Vroom, V. H. (1964). *Work and Motivation*. New York: Wiley.

Vroom, V. H., & Yetton, P. W. (1973). *Leadership and decision making*. Pittsburgh, PA: University of Pittsburgh Press.

Wanberg, C. R., & Banas, J. T. (2000). Predictors and outcomes of openness to changes in a reorganizing workplace. *The Journal of Applied Psychology*, *85*(1), 132–142. doi:10.1037/0021-9010.85.1.132 PMID:10740964.

Weick, K. (1995). *Sensemaking in organizations*. London: Sage Publications.

Weick, K., Sutcliffe, K. M., & Obstfeld, D. (2005). Organizing and the process of sensemaking. *Organization Science*, *16*(4), 409–421. doi:10.1287/orsc.1050.0133.

Whiting, J. W. M. (1986). George Peter Murdock (1897–1985). *American Anthropologist*, *88*(3), 682–686. doi:10.1525/aa.1986.88.3.02a00120.

Wholefoods. (2011). *John Mackey's Blog*. Retrieved from http://www2.wholefoodsmarket.com/blogs/jmackey/. (2011, October 9).

Yates, K. (2006). Internal communication effectiveness enhances bottom-line results. *Journal of Organizational Excellence*, *25*, 71–79. doi:10.1002/joe.20102.

Zorn, T., Page, D., & Cheney, G. (2000). Nuts about change: Multiple perspectives on change-oriented communication in a public sector organization. *Management Communication Quarterly*, *13*(4), 515–566. doi:10.1177/0893318900134001.

ADDITIONAL READING

Edfelt, R. B. (2010). *Global comparative management: A functional approach*. Thousand Oaks, CA: Sage.

Hamlin, S. B. (1989). The Art of Q & A. In *How to Talk So People Listen: The Real Key to Job Success*. New York: Harper Paperbacks.

Hattersley, M., & McJannet, L. J. (1996). Giving and Receiving Feedback. In *Management Communication: Principles and Practice*. New York: McGraw-Hill.

Mclean, S. (2010). *Business communication for success*. Irvington, NY: Flatworld Knowledge Publishing.

Munter, M. (1995). Consult/Join Meetings. In *Guide to Managerial Communication: Effective Business Writing and Speaking* (5th ed.). Upper Saddle River, NJ: Prentice Hall.

Schein, E. (1988). *The Process of Building and Maintaining a Group*. Upper Saddle River, NJ: Prentice Hall.

KEY TERMS AND DEFINITIONS

Communication Plan: The art and science of reaching target audiences using marketing communication channels such as advertising, public relations, experiences, or direct mail. It is concerned with deciding who to target, when, with what message, and how. The communication plan serves as a guide to the communication efforts throughout the duration of the project. It is a living and working document and is updated periodically as the audience needs change.

Communication Policy: A strategic information dissemination and a protection of transmission of confidential data.

Electronic Communication: Communication by advanced technologies.

Information Technology: A term that encompasses all forms of technology used to create, store, exchange, and use information in its various forms (business data, voice conversations, still images, motion pictures, multimedia presentations, and other forms, including those not yet conceived). It's a convenient term for including both telephony and computer technology in the same word.

Managerial Communication: Decisive means by which the manager fulfils his/her tasks and duties and employs the competences and skills pertaining to his/her role in the company and in relations with business partners. The manager sends information to the members of an organization and its business partners, and their response influences his/her subsequent decisions and behavior.

Chapter 22
Local Embeddedness and Expatriates' Effectiveness for Knowledge Transfer within MNCs:
A Cultural Perspective

Fiona Xiaoying Ji
Ohio University, USA

Mary L. Connerley
University of Northern Iowa, USA

ABSTRACT

The development of expatriates' social relationships in a local environment is critical given that social ties are considered the key players of a Multinational Corporation's (MNC) network and a prerequisite for knowledge transfer within the organization. By building on the national and organizational culture literature, we develop a conceptual model to better understand how expatriates can effectively build local embeddedness. Our conceptual arguments include how four groups of culture-related factors predict expatriates' local embeddedness, expatriates' cross-cultural experience, expatriates' cultural orientation, local national culture, and MNCs' organizational culture. Finally, we also investigate under what conditions expatriates' social ties within the MNC can influence the expatriates' effectiveness in knowledge transfer.

DOI: 10.4018/978-1-4666-3966-9.ch022

INTRODUCTION

During the last 20 years with increased globalization, the number of international assignments undertaken by employees has increased. A growing stream of research has viewed expatriates as boundary spanners and has examined their role in creating, disseminating and leveraging knowledge within Multinational Corporations (MNCs) (Bolino, 2007; Kostova & Roth, 2003). A key notion addressed in this literature stream is that in addition to effective selection and training provided by MNCs, expatriation success depends on job-related knowledge transfer conducted by expatriates as well. For example, expatriates will consider future job-related prospects when they determine how much to contribute to knowledge transfer after they return back as part of their long-term career building. However, we know little about factors influencing the likelihood of expatriate effectiveness in knowledge transfer within the MNC. Moreover, barriers of long-term knowledge creation have been reported, such as low satisfaction of these international assignees, "Field Failure" in host countries, and high turnover after returning back to headquarters (Bolino & Feldman, 2000; Sanchez, Spector, & Cooper, 2000; Takeuchi, Tesluk, Yun, & Lepak, 2005).

In this chapter, we extend understanding on existing expatriate literature by developing the concept of "local embeddedness," and we argue that expatriates' proactive behaviors built in a local context can enhance their performance for further knowledge creation within the MNC. We argue that local embeddedness, defined as the degree to which an individual has developed local ties in a host country, can enhance expatriates' capabilities to seek, acquire and integrate knowledge in local subsidiaries. Studies identify that social ties, social networks and relational embeddedness can facilitate knowledge sharing between different entities within the MNC (Hansen, 1999; Schulz, 2003); therefore, expatriates as boundary spanners can facilitate knowledge network building and development for the MNC (Kostova & Roth, 2003). Despite an abundance of research on social networks in international management, however, we know little about what may influence why and how expatriates build local social relationships for further knowledge transfer. Accordingly, our goal is to address the following interrelated questions: First, what are the antecedents for expatriates' local embeddedness? Second, once this embeddedness is formed, under what conditions can it influence expatriates' effectiveness of knowledge transfer?

With respect to the first question, this chapter specifically focuses on culture-related antecedents. With the development of a global economy, people from different countries are more likely today to speak the same language compared to earlier generations. However, even with more bi- and tri-lingual speakers, different cultures still impact translation and meaning of the language. For example, although Chinese citizens may speak English and understand the meaning of their American counterparts' language, their interpretation of certain terms and symbols will be influenced by their own cultural experiences. Therefore, a comprehensive understanding of the essence of different cultures is critical to understanding the social interaction process between expatriates and local employees.

Please refer to Figure 1 for the conceptual framework of the paper.

In this chapter, we offer contributions to three primary areas: 1) extending cross-cultural research by examining culturally related antecedents to expatriates' embeddedness in a local culture; 2) Adding to the literature on MNC's knowledge transfer by offering insights into the influence of the culture and practices of MNCs on expatriates' embeddedness; and 3) Extending expatriate research which has historically been focused on adjustment to include embeddedness.

First, cross-culture research remains an important focus in international management literature (Ralston, Holt, Terpstra & Yu, 1997; Suddaby, Elsbach, Greenwood, Meyer, & Zilber, 2010).

Figure 1. Conceptual framework

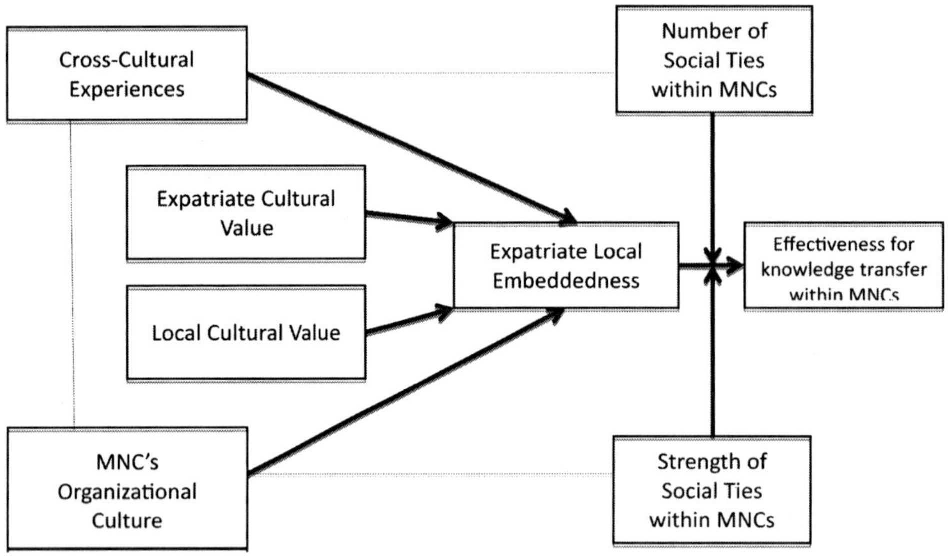

Multiculturalism has moved from an emerging trend to a concrete reality (Selmer, 1995). The parent company, through creating common norms in the MNC, addresses the problem of subsidiaries' local institutional impact (Forsgren, Holm, & Johanson, 2005; Nahapiet & Ghoshal, 1998; Nohria & Ghoshal, 1997). In this chapter, we will examine four groups of culturally related antecedents to expatriates' local embeddedness: expatriates' cross-cultural experience and acculturation; cultural values of the expatriate; local national culture; and MNC's organizational culture. Much of the early research on expatriates focused on the individual level or on the relationship between the expatriates and their headquarters (Kostova & Roth, 2003). The emphasis on multi-level attributes can help develop a holistic view of expatriates' local embeddedness by taking into account different culturally related aspects such as local national culture and organizational culture.

Second, this work can contribute to the knowledge transfer literature by identifying and examining factors that analyze expatriates' incentives to engage in mutual learning and in turn advance the overall strategic learning effectiveness of the MNC. Scholars studying knowledge transfer in MNCs have begun to shift the research attention away from a hierarchical view of the MNC headquarters and its subsidiaries toward a reconceptualization of the MNC as a web of diverse, differentiated inter and intra-firm relationships (Monteiro, Arvidsson, & Birkinshaw, 2008; O'Donnell, 2000). More researchers see the MNC as a social community of practices, in which both headquarters and its subsidiaries create, disseminate and leverage knowledge in a global context (Gupta & Govindarajan, 2000; Kogut & Zander, 1993). In this context, knowledge transfer across subsidiaries in different cultures becomes important for knowledge creation within the MNC. We need to better understand how to use expatriates as an integration mechanism for both expatriates' learning and transferring knowledge to local employees in cross-cultural units within the MNC, thus we expect to develop a further understanding of expatriates' roles from a strategic point of view for the MNC (Jassawalla & Sashittal, 2009).

Third, we examine expatriates' local embeddedness in order to extend previous expatriate research that emphasized local adjustment. Adjustment studies can only propose the preconditions that determine the success of an expatriate in certain international assignments. In addition, adjustment cannot guarantee expatriates' social interaction with local employees which is considered the key condition under which tacit knowledge transfer can overcome the barriers, especially in an ambiguous environment for communication (Tsai, 2002). Furthermore, local embeddedness may be related to whether expatriates can learn from the local assignment and transfer the intellectual assets following assignment to other units of the MNC (Oddou, Osland, & Blakeney, 2009). Thus, the stage of expatriates' local development will be related to that of further career advancement within the MNC.

THEORETICAL BACKGROUND

Local Embeddedness for Knowledge Transfer in MNCs

Granovetter (1985) highlighted that economic activities of firms are embedded in both ongoing economic and social relationships which affect and are affected by managers' decisions. The concept of embeddedness has been classified in many ways, including social, structural, cognitive, political, and cultural (Uzzi, 1997; Zukin & DiMaggio, 1990). Nahapiet and Ghoshal (1998) categorized embeddedness into three dimensions: structural embeddedness, relational embeddedness and cognitive embeddedness. Since structural embeddedness is considered as an "impersonal configuration of linkage between people or units" (Nahapiet & Ghoshal, 1998, p. 244) and we use expatriates' personal linkage as our unit of analysis, we suggest the use of relational and cognitive embeddedness as the two dimensions that make up our "local embeddedness of expatriates" construct. Local embeddedness of expatriates involves their social interaction with local employees from a relational perspective of embeddedness proposed by Uzzi (1997). This includes trust and trustworthiness (Kostova & Roth, 2003; Tsai & Ghoshal, 1998), norms and sanctions (Forsgren, 2004; Yli-Renko, Autio, & Sapienza, 2001), expectations (Granovetter, 1985), and identity and identification (Vora & Kostova, 2007). In addition, we propose this construct also involves psychological and cognitive characteristics. The cognitive dimension of embeddedness is defined as "shared representations, interpretations, and systems of meaning among parties" (Nahapiet & Ghoshal, 1998, p. 244), and can be reflected by shared codes and languages. Both the relational and cognitive nature of embeddedness helps a focal individual seek, acquire and absorb knowledge (Nahapiet & Ghoshal, 1998). Therefore, consistent with previous literature, local embeddedness is defined in our study as the degree to which an individual has developed local ties in a host country separate from organizational ties within a MNC network.

Although international management literature argues that MNCs send an expatriate overseas for knowledge development (Bolino, 2007), and that the overseas assignment can allow individuals to initially or further develop the requisite international skills which become intellectual assets of MNCs (Reiche, 2012), local knowledge is not easily acquired given the specialized and intangible nature of the knowledge (Cross & Cummings, 2004; Odou et al., 2009). For example, expatriates who expect that their responsibility will be to control subsidiary operations will be less concerned with developing knowledge such as social skills and abilities compared to expatriates who will be expected to lead a team of managers towards a common goal within the MNC. Therefore, we suggest that firms take into consideration local embeddedness when they are selecting and developing expatriates, especially when the focus is on knowledge transfer through the international assignment. Furthermore, executives in MNCs can seek, acquire and integrate knowledge embedded in expatriates and repatriates to achieve competitive advantage over firms that do not support the development of local embeddedness.

We outline a framework for understanding the nature of expatriates' local embeddedness by employing three key literatures – attitude, cross-cultural adjustment and social identity. First, attitude theory suggests that individuals' behaviors are predicted by their beliefs and affective factors (Eagly & Chaiken, 1998, p. 8). This capability requires a positive attitude from expatriates towards local subsidiaries and other cultural groups. The attitude can be learned, built through personal norms and values, and considered as all aspects of responding to the object including emotions, cognitions and behaviors in a consistent manner (Ajzen, 2001). Accordingly, the attitude towards a subsidiary and its employees and the behaviors of building social relationships and identification with local people can be based on their norms embedded in the national culture and the MNC shared culture, expectations on local assignments and also impacted by their affect triggered by local environments.

Second, cross-cultural adjustment literature examines expatriates' ability to adapt to the local environment. This literature argues that expatriates' adjustment predicts their psychological well-being in local environments (Bruning, Sonpar, & Wang, 2012). Scholars have stated that successful expatriates who have developed an effective adjustment process do not quit their assignments prematurely and perform effectively by completing their roles in the local subsidiary. Building local embeddedness takes both time and effort of expatriates, but without the adjustment of expatriates, social relationships with local employees remains impossible. If expatriates experience high discomfort during international assignments, their affective attributes will impede their attitudes towards local subsidiaries, therefore, they are less likely to become cognitively bounded to local subsidiaries.

Third, Vora and Kostova (2007) argued that expatriates often conduct behaviors differently according to their "dual identification" to both a subsidiary and a MNC. To better examine expatriates' identification into a local embeddedness construct, we employ their underlying arguments that an individual's motive to identify him or herself into a group is needed for positive self-esteem or self-enhancement, and needed for reducing uncertainty. According to social identity theory, individuals may view themselves, among other things, based on self-categorization, or cognitive grouping of oneself based on similarity to a class of stimuli and dissimilarity to some other stimuli. Thus a "dual identification" proposed by Vora and Kostova (2007) can predict different consequences including knowledge transfer, role commitment and other important outcomes.

Boundary Conditions

In this chapter, we focus on the relationship between expatriates and local employees. This model examines those expatriates who are assigned to the top positions in the local subsidiaries. Because we emphasize a network associated with expatriate activities and knowledge transfer within the organization from a strategic management perspective, we focus on subsidiary managers' level and leave the international assigned employees working in virtual teams from this conceptual work. In future research, expatriates' social relationships with supervisors, subordinates, peers, and even with local partners can be incorporated into the full model.

CONCEPTUAL MODEL AND PROPOSITIONS

An integration of perspectives on expatriates' local embeddedness is used to explain how culture-related antecedents drive expatriates' local embeddedness through positive attitude, local identification and capacity to build and develop local social relationships.

Expatriates' Cross-Cultural Experience

The first aspect of the model proposes that expatriates' cross-cultural experiences are more likely to be associated with their local embeddedness through efficacy of social interaction with local employees.

Cross-cultural experience. Cross-cultural experience helps expatriates acquire essential skills and knowledge demanded for effective international managerial behaviors in numerous transitional situations (Selmer, 1995). During cross-cultural assignments, expatriates' learning from experience provides the foundation for success of expatriates' knowledge transfer in an interculture environment. In addition, international assignees who have more previous international assignments or multiple overseas postings are more valuable within organizations since they have a broader set of experience on which to draw (Bolino, 2007). Expatriates' attitudes towards this learning experience could be important for determining their resistance, incentive and motivation for developing and maintaining interpersonal ties with local employees. The expatriates' expectations are largely formed from their understanding of the mutual benefit to the organization and to themselves, for example the benefit of successful accomplishment of the assignment and further development for repatriation. They have more capacity to help establish and expand MNC's international business, and thus they perceive themselves as valuable strategic assets to their MNC. Therefore, they are more likely to have motivation to build local relationships.

Moreover, expatriates with a broader range of cross-cultural experiences are more likely to develop new skills from current assignments to build additional opportunities to develop their cross-cultural skills and abilities. However, previous literature found that the longer expatriates stay overseas, the more likely they are to experience the "out of sight, out of mind problem" back home (Stroh, Black, Mendenhall, & Gregersen, 2005; Stroh, Gregersen, & Black, 1998). Although such expatriates face the challenge and risk of being isolated as permanent expatriates, they are more likely to seek knowledge and relationships in the local environment rather than miss out on such opportunities resulting from poor adjustment (Bolino, 2007). Not only do repatriates have a better understanding than their domestic counterparts of how MNCs are perceived abroad, they are more likely to have a better understanding of the relationship between the corporate headquarters and overseas subsidiaries. Those persons often have first-hand knowledge of particular cultures and can provide detailed information to the local employees. This knowledge enhances their ability to recognize and evaluate global benefits, which helps them to build dual identities to both local subsidiaries and headquarters. Therefore, the more cross-cultural experience they have through international assignments, the more likely they will build relationships with local employees.

Acculturation experience. In terms of specific experience, acculturation is defined as "a multi-dimentional psychological phenomenon that is reflected in psychological changes that occur in individuals as a result of their interaction with a new and different culture" (Stahl & Bjorkman, 2006, p.154). This psychological construct is viewed as the product of cultural learning that occurs between members from two or more culturally different groups. People succeeding in this process always experience attitudinal and behavioral changes. This change is brought about under conditions of direct contact between individuals of each society. Individuals of a foreign or minority culture learn the language, habits, and values of a standard or dominant culture by the cultural process of acculturation. Expatriates who have previous acculturation experience, either through international assignment or in their domestic context, are more likely to be open to new cultural experiences. Additionally, level of acculturation is associated with the time spent by expatriates in other cultures. Therefore, the more expatriates have previous acculturation experiences, the more likely they have the capability to adjust to new cultural environments and to interact with local employees in order to better adjust themselves to the new culture.

Proposition 1a: Expatriates with more previous cross-cultural experience (length and diverse scopes of assignments) are more likely to be locally embedded.

Proposition1b: Expatriates with more acculturation experience are more likely to be locally embedded.

Expatriates' Cultural Value

Hofstede (1980) defined value as a mental program, which every person receives during his or her childhood through exposure to family, education, religion, and indoctrination of political ideology. This is how basic values from national culture are developed. Expatriates' national culture value can impact their capability to be adapted to a new cultural environment, which will lead them to engage in different behaviors to adjust to an assignment in a new country (van Vianen, De Pater, Kristof-Brown, & Johnson, 2004).

Individualism and Collectivism. The dimension of individualism and collectivism has been discussed as the major dimension of cultural variability and as having a direct impact on behavior (Hwang & Francesco, 2010). Individualism refers to the broad value tendencies of people in a culture to emphasize individual identity over group identity, and collectivism represents the broad value tendencies of people in a culture to focus on group identity over individual identity (Hofstede, 1980). Scholars in communication research propose that members of collectivistic cultures emphasize group-based information to predict each other's behavior (Gudykunst Ting-Toomey, & Nishida, 1996). As members of individualistic cultures, expatriates value independence and achievement and learn personal preferred ways for how members of their culture are expected to view themselves. However expatriates from collectivistic cultures learn different major values such as harmony and solidarity and learn different ways to consider themselves such as through interaction with others. Thus people educated and embedded in collectivistic cultures experience strong influence on their behavior across situations such as work group and university settings.

Expatriates with a culture value of collectivism have self-concepts as being fundamentally connected to other human beings and interdependent with the surrounding context rather than being independent. And this self-concept affects expatriates' processes involved in social thinking (Bhagat, Kedia, Harveston, & Triandis, 2002). Accordingly, expatriates from collectivist cultures are more likely to focus on interactions with local employees once they are living away from their home country and family allowing them to build social relationships with local groups.

Power distance. The second dimension of Hofstede' s national culture values is power distance which is defined as "the extent to which the less powerful members of institutions and organizations accept that power is distributed unequally" (Hofstede & Bond, 1984, p. 419). People from high power distance cultures accept power as part of society (Gudykunst et al., 1996). Expatriates from high power distance cultures view power as a basic fact in society while those from low power distance cultures use power only when it is legitimate. Accordingly, we propose that expatriates from high power distance cultures are likely to build their self-esteem through legitimate power when they are assigned to local subsidiaries, which may lead to a reduced likelihood of building social relationships with local employees because identification to headquarters can satisfy their needs more. Besides, Gudykunst et al. (1996) suggest that cultural rules require less cooperation with outgroup members for those from high power distance cultures than in low power distance cultures.

Uncertainty avoidance. In addition to individualism-collectivism and power distance, uncertainty avoidance is a third dimension of culture variability. Uncertainty avoidance is critical in understanding how expatriates treat unfamiliar people in a local environment. People high in uncertainty avoidance have a lower tolerance for "uncertainty and ambiguity" which results in higher levels of anxiety, greater need for formal rules and absolute truth and less tolerance for people with different ideas or behaviors (Gudykunst et al., 1996). Tolerance for ambiguity and the extent to which ambiguous situations are seen as threatening encompass the notion of a generalized level of comfort with uncertainty. Therefore, expatriates with high uncertainty avoidance tend to ignore strangers in local environments and tend not to initiate social interaction. The interaction with local people is especially avoided in informal situations where there are no clear rules and norms to guide behaviors (Gudykunst et al., 1996). Gudykunst et al. (1996) found that people from high uncertainty avoidance cultures appear to engage in more vocalization of anger toward outgroups and are less capable of controlling this anger. This negative affect may be associated with a negative attitude towards international assignments with job duties associated with high uncertainty.

Thus, expatriates with an uncertainty-orientation can transition to new environments more easily. The more comfortable expatriates are the more likely they are to embed in the local culture allowing a deeper understanding of information. Expatriates uncomfortable with uncertainty are more likely to reject ideas that are different (Hofstede, 1980), thus reducing the likelihood of becoming locally embedded.

Proposition 2a: Expatriates who are more collectivistic are more likely to be locally embedded than those who are more individualistic.

Proposition 2b: Expatriates low on power distance are more likely to be locally embedded than those high on power distance.

Proposition 2c: Expatriates low on uncertainty avoidance are more likely to be locally embedded than those high on uncertainty avoidance.

Local Culture Value

Host country factors can also play a critical role in determining success of expatriates, especially from a local social tie perspective (Toh & DeNisi, 2005). It is important to acknowledge that the expatriates' peers, subordinates and managers are likely to be positioned to gauge and evaluate expatriates' performance and are also positioned to provide direction and feedback. The cultural backgrounds of local employees may reflect differently toward expatriates' social relationships with them, thus resulting in differential levels of motivation and success of local embeddedness by expatriates.

Individualism and Collectivism. First, collectivist cultures tend to be characterized by networks of stable relationships where members of the local culture spend time in more stable groups (Hofstede, 1980). These groups tend to be relatively small and entering new groups tends to be very difficult (Yamazaki & Kayes, 2004). For example, expatriates assigned to subsidiaries in Japan often have a difficult time becoming embedded because it is part of the Japanese culture for people to rarely interact with individuals from outside their groups unless they have been first introduced by an intermediary connected to both. Social identity theory explains psychological and social processes that influence the treatment of local employees towards expatriates (Van der Vegt, Van der Vliert, & Huang, 2005). If nationality becomes a salient attribute of expatriates, local employees will conduct behaviors consistent with in-group and out-group distinction.

Power distance. In a country of cultures low in power distance, subordinates are less likely to be dependent on bosses. Therefore, the relationship between expatriates and local employees is more likely to be interdependent in a low power distance country. In high power distance societies, local employees view their superiors (in our case, expatriates) as being more powerful than they are and have a tendency to behave submissively in their presence. Hofstede and Bond (1984) found that superiors in high power distance societies are more autocratic in their leadership style, more task oriented and less people oriented. Local employees in high power distance cultures (countries such as Singapore, Hong Kong, and China) tend to think of their organizations as traditional families. The subsidiary managers, considered to be like the head of the family, are expected to protect the members physically and economically in exchange for unwavering loyalty. Managers are expected to make decisions autocratically and paternalistically. Chains of command are important mechanisms for communicating across strata and are seldom violated by employees (Hofstede & Bond 1984).

However, in low power distance countries, subordinates expect that their superiors are more participative and consultative because they hold the belief that all should share the power. Working relationships tend to be relatively informal and egalitarian. Accordingly, when those local employees work with expatriates who have motivation to build social relationships, they are less likely to resist.

Uncertainty avoidance. In a country categorized as having high uncertainty avoidance, people tend to build rules and rituals for every possible situation to better handle the ambiguity (Gudykunst et al., 1996). Thus, interaction with out-group members may be avoided, since the rituals tend to exist in uncertainty avoidance cultures, which provide clear scripts for interactions and allows individuals to attune their behavior with out-group members. The scripts for interaction are always much more complex in high uncertainty avoidance cultures than in low uncertainty avoidance cultures. New relationships will present new culture risk. In cultures with a low tolerance for ambiguity, managers are expected to take fewer decision-making risks (Javidan, Stahl, Brodbeck, & Wilderom, 2005). Conversely, cultures with a high tolerance for ambiguity (low uncertainty avoidance) are more accepting of uncertainty and willing to take on risk to a greater extent (Hofstede, 1980). Thus, local employees from low uncertainty cultures are more likely to support expatriates' social tie formation as they work to become embedded.

Proposition 3a: Expatriates are more likely to be locally embedded in a country with a culture classification of individualism compared to a country classification of collectivism.

Proposition 3b: Expatriates are more likely to be locally embedded in a country with a culture classification of low power distance compared to a country with a classification of high power distance.

Proposition 3c: Expatriates are more likely to be locally embedded in a country with a culture classification of low uncertainty avoidance compared to a classification of high uncertainty avoidance.

Organizational Culture in MNCs

The organizational culture represents all the shared values and norms held by the employees within the organization (Bartlett & Ghoshal, 1998; Nohria & Ghoshal, 1997). It can be considered the glue that binds units within the organization together. In this chapter, we consider two perspectives: degree of organizational culture within the MNC and the concept of global culture.

Degree of organizational culture. Degree of culture represents whether a MNC uses culture control over subsidiaries and the level of strength of culture perceived by both expatriates and local nationals. Nohria and Ghoshal (1997) proposed normative integration as a distinctive control mechanism to use shared values and norms as a means to reduce the impact of the diversity of subsidiaries to achieve the resources integration objective. The parent company creates common norms in the MNC to address the problem of subsidiaries' local institutional impact (Forsgren, Holm, & Johnson, 2005; Kostovo & Roth, 2003; Nahapiet & Ghoshal, 1998; Nohria & Ghoshal, 1997). Social control or cultural control such as socialization mechanisms can make knowledge transfer more efficient and effective within the MNC (Nohria et al., 1997). Organizational culture provides social norms and values surrounding both expatriates and local nationals. These values and norms indicate correct ways of relating to others. Organizational cultural values are in turn reflected in actual behavioral patterns. The strong societal environment built by the MNC encompasses socialization processes for all employees, including both the content transmitted to members of the culture and the strength and vigor with which the society transmits that content. Therefore when subsidiaries share the same norms and values provided by a strong MNC culture, expatriates and local employees are less likely to perceive the other party as strangers and thus are more likely to embed locally.

Global culture. Global culture instills a global perspective to all of the subunits with a headquarters-centric, formalized, low differentiation norm. Although different languages may be spoken throughout a MNC, the firm, which develops a strong global culture, shares the single organizational language for communication all over the world. They are also creating a sense of inter-dependence by educating staff in each country about their operations worldwide. From many expatriates' perspectives, an organization with a strong global culture is more likely to provide cross-cultural opportunities for them to better adapt to an international assignment. They also develop environments in which employees' cross-cultural skills can flourish. This global culture also represents MNC's practices in rotating expatriates around the world to obtain new culture skills and knowledge. This facilitates shared value formation for both expatriates and subsidiary employees. Therefore a MNC's global culture can also impact both expatriates' and local employees' "dual identification" which will support expatriates' local embeddedness (Vora & Kostova, 2007).

Proposition 4a: The stronger the organizational culture shared between a focal subsidiary and other units of a MNC, the more likely expatriates are to be locally embedded.

Proposition 4b: With a global culture shared within a MNC, expatriates are more likely to be locally embedded compared to expatriates in a MNC with a decentralized culture.

Expatriates' Social Ties in a MNC Network

In the propositions developed thus far, we have examined how an expatriate's previous cross-cultural experiences, individual culture value, host national culture value and firm culture impact the likelihood that he/she will become locally embedded. We next propose that the social ties the expatriates build within a MNC network will moderate the relationship between their local embeddedness and performance.

In the literature, social ties within a MNC are defined as the "extent to which work processes are interrelated so that changes in the state of one element affect the state of the others." (Newburry Belkin, & Ansari, 2008). This interdependence of expatriates can be developed as they collectively accomplish the tasks with people in other parts of the MNC network. Interdependence can also be encouraged by socialization activities such as training or social communication. For example, headquarters can promote the exchange and generation of valuable knowledge throughout the MNC network by enabling forums that assist with the development of informal relations among managers (Ghoshal, Korine, & Szulanski, 1994). Cross-unit social events or alternatively, the use of teams, task forces, or conferences promote horizontal and diagonal communication and interactions among different subunits (Tsai, 2002). These integrative channels foster both task and social relationships among expatriates, as well as opportunities to access knowledge and resources, both of which positively affect expatriates' social network building within the MNC (Ghoshal et al., 1994; Schulz, 2003).

There are two social ties attributes associated with benefits of expatriates within the MNC: number and strength.

Number of social ties. First, more social ties built within the MNC can provide focal expatriates a central position, which can further create more value for expatriates as boundary spanners. This will allow expatriates to acquire more information, which will likely be a source of valuable information for the MNC. Meanwhile, they are more likely to utilize the knowledge gained through local embeddedness to create new knowledge to be transferred throughout the MNC. Second, more social ties bring benefits to the focal expatriate in terms of the familiarity with both mangers in other subsidiaries and their operations, which further raise their capability to transfer best practices to a local subsidiary. Those social ties are often the primary means for individuals to learn the appropriate codes of conduct within the MNC. The higher the communication depth and the frequency with which expatriates communicate with others within the MNC, the more likely they are able to communicate themselves so that shared codes, norms and routines can be developed. Third, social ties built within the MNC network accent the importance in the networks of strong, crosscutting, personal relationships developed over time that provide the basis for trust, cooperation and collective action for a knowledge transfer community (Nahapiet & Ghoshal, 1998).

Strength of social ties. The strength of social ties is associated with trust, identity and shared norms built within the MNC. First, the expatriate embedded in the internal social networks in the MNC can gain advantages through transferring and creating new knowledge, sharing common codes and norms, and enhancing their capacity (Nahapiet & Ghoshal, 1998). Thus, expatriates' internal social ties are more likely to affect the motivation and communication that facilitates their learning through international assignments. For example, by learning from local interactions in a host country, an expatriate manager can better understand the types of knowledge valuable to both the local subsidiary and other units within the MNC (Schulz, 2003). Through further interaction within the MNC, the focal expatriate can share mental models and this common knowledge will be beneficial for future expatriates. Second, the importance of affective and cognitive natures is amplified in the MNC especially given the geographical, cultural and linguistic barriers involved in the interaction. When an international assignment is completed, it is not easy to transfer the knowledge embedded in a local context to a larger audience within the MNC. However, the greater the extent to which expatriates are linked to the MNC through informal social ties with managers in other units, the more likely they can balance both subsidiary and headquarters' identities. These factors positively influence the likelihood of effective knowledge transfer from expatriates as boundary spanners (Gupta & Govindarajan, 2000; Schulz, 2003).

Proposition 5a: Expatriates' number of social ties in the MNC will positively moderate the relationship between their local embeddedness and their performance.

Proposition 5b: Expatriates' strength of social ties in the MNC will positively moderate the relationship between their local embeddedness and their performance.

DISCUSSION AND IMPLICATIONS

This chapter makes several important contributions to the existing international management literature. First, the framework that investigates expatriates' local embeddedness provides a foundation for advancing research on knowledge transfer within MNCs. MNCs can seek, acquire and integrate knowledge embedded in expatriates and repatriates to achieve competitive advantages over firms which do not support this embeddedness. The literature states the MNC's intangible assets are provided by those subsidiaries, as a "subsidiary-specific advantage" (Rugman & Verbeke, 2001). However, in order to transfer those intangible assets, MNCs confront complex tasks and challenges to integrate knowledge embedded in individuals who are situated in different locations (Kostova, 1999; Reiche, 2011). We argue that knowledge is not easily exchanged between cross-cultural units because of "stickiness" of knowledge. Kostova's (1999; 2003) studies showed that the knowledge transfer to subsidiaries is differentiated depending on the "Institutional Duality" which each subsidiary faces. Therefore, expatriates require skills and capabilities to seek, acquire, and aspire local knowledge through interaction with local employees. And local knowledge is mostly tacit knowledge, which is highly personal, difficult to communicate, and not always valued or easily traded in an exchange relationship. Sometimes it is embedded within an individual's cognitive processes and highly influenced by the values or norms he/she possesses (Bhagat et al., 2002). Because of effective relationships, expatriates who are locally embedded are likely to discuss and use individual knowledge and expertise and combine them into their knowledge base. Thus, expatriates can be considered as an integration mechanism for both transferring knowledge from and to local employees in cross-cultural units within the MNC (Reiche, 2011).

Second, this work advances our knowledge on cross-cultural aspects of MNCs. In the knowledge transfer literature; a relational perspective of social capital has been studied as an antecedent for effective knowledge transfer (Cross & Cummings, 2004). However, there remains a lack of systematic information to explain how this can be applied in more complex and cross-cultural environments such as within a MNC network. Although culture value has been examined with expatriate adjustment, how different levels of culture can impact expatriates' local embeddedness and further career development has not been well explored. In this chapter, we build our arguments of local embeddedness on attitude and social identification literature to better understand how cultural value can impact local embeddedness for knowledge transfer within the MNC. Moreover, this is a multi-level model, which helps to develop a holistic view of different factors impacting expatriates' local embeddedness by incorporating the role of expatriates, local employees, the MNC and culturally related antecedents. We consider this approach useful since it allows for a more thorough and innovative examination of the importance of different antecedents on embeddedness for knowledge transfer.

Third, the construct of local embeddedness also extends the current expatriate adjustment literature. Although current literature considered expatriates' communication adjustment as one perspective, adjustment can only capture expatriates' comfort in such local interactions without explaining how expatriates can be motivated to build social relationships with local employees. Bolino (2007) argues that expatriates returning from international assignments bring back new skills and information, which can contribute to organizational resources. However, it may be up to the MNC's culture to determine if this new learning will be utilized. Recent literature of repatriation raises an additional concern (Jassawalla & Sashittal, 2009). Without explicit analysis of expatriates' knowledge acquired and integration with local employees, the benefit of the expatriation experience may never be realized by the MNC. We argue that expatriates' importance is not only in their own knowledge sharing in a MNC network, but also in their new strategic decision making ability and the impact that this might have on not only their own performance, but the performance of both the subsidiary and the MNC overall (Jassawalla & Sashittal, 2009).

Our chapter also provides some managerial implications. The conceptual framework introduced in this paper provides information on how headquarters can enhance organizational learning through subsidiaries by international assignments while taking into account different cultural contexts. Nohria and Ghoshal (1997) proposed a normative integration as a distinctive control mechanism, within which shared values and norms are used as a means to reduce the impact of the diversity of subsidiaries and to achieve the resource integration objective. However, at a time when more organizations are realizing benefits from the alternative perspectives that diversity brings, care must be taken to allow the subsidiaries to be similar enough to allow transfer of knowledge, but not so similar as to lead to group think and other negatives associated with a "melting pot" or assimilation mentality. MNCs want to develop managers who understand the strategic intent of the MNC and are familiar with the resources and capabilities that support this strategic intent (Jassawalla & Sashittal, 2009). They must establish an organizational culture that supports and retains diverse and knowledgeable employees.

CONCLUSION

Knowledge, learning, and innovation are at the heart of understanding competitive advantage and firm performance (Johnston, 2005). The model and propositions presented in this paper provide direction for future theoretical and empirical studies. However, this chapter, like all others, has its limitations. The embeddedness construct may go beyond dyadic social relationships such as political and cultural perspectives of embeddedness (Zukin & Dimaggio, 1990). In addition, as mentioned earlier, this relational construct only focuses on expatriates with local employees as a whole without distinguishing a network of local subordinates, local supervisors and/or peers. Further studies can capture a more comprehensive picture of expatriates' local embeddedness. Additionally, the current chapter focused on only one cultural framework (Hofstede, 1980). Although there are many similarities across different cultural frameworks, future research may want to include other frameworks, such as GLOBE (House et al., 1999) which was developed using a set of cultural values and practices to measure national culture. Finally, individual personality and subsidiary strategic status will likely influence expatriates' local embeddedness, but these issues are beyond the scope of this culture-related framework. In future studies, scholars might consider how those factors combine with national culture and organizational culture to determine the influence on expatriates' local embeddedness and knowledge transfer. It is possible a person's cultural roots may overshadow the influence of individual personality, thus the interaction between those factors may offer a rich area of study on selection and training of expatriates for different local cultural environments.

REFERENCES

Ajzen, I. (2001). Nature and operation of attitudes. *Annual Review of Psychology*, *52*, 27–58. doi:10.1146/annurev.psych.52.1.27 PMID:11148298.

Bartlett, C. A., & Ghoshal, S. (1998). *Managing across borders: The transnational solution* (2nd ed.). Boston, MA: Harvard Business School Press.

Bhagat, R., Kedia, B. L., Harveston, P. D., & Triandis, H. C. (2002). Cultural Variations in the Cross-Border Transfer of Organizational Knowledge: An Integrative Framework. *Academy of Management Review*, *27*(2), 204–221.

Bolino, M. C. (2007). Expatriate assignments and intra-organizational career success: Implications for individuals and organizations. *Journal of International Business Studies*, *38*, 819–835. doi:10.1057/palgrave.jibs.8400290.

Bolino, M. C., & Feldman, D. C. (2000). Increasing the skill utilization of expatriates. *Human Resource Management*, *39*(4), 367–379. doi:10.1002/1099-050X(200024)39:4<367::AID-HRM7>3.0.CO;2-7.

Bruning, N. S., Sonpar, K., & Wang, X. (2012). Host-country national networks and expatriate effectiveness: A mixed-methods study. *Journal of International Business Studies*, *43*(4), 444–450. doi:10.1057/jibs.2012.5.

Cross, R., & Cummings, J. N. (2004). Tie and network correlates of individual performance in knowledge-intensive work. *Academy of Management Journal*, *47*(6), 928–937. doi:10.2307/20159632.

Eagly, A. H., & Chaiken, S. (1998). Attitude Structure and Function. In D. T. Gilbert, S. T. Fiske, & G. Lindzey (Eds.), The Handbook of Social Psychology (4th ed.), 54. New York: McGraw-Hill.

Forsgren, M. (2004). The Use of Network Theory in MNC Research. In Mahnke, V., & Pedersen, T. (Eds.), *Knowledge Flows, Governance and the Multinational Enterprise*. New York: Palgrave Macmillan.

Forsgren, M., Holm, U., & Johanson, J. (2005). *Managing the Embedded Multinational: A Business Network View*. Northampton, MA: Edward Elgar Publishing, Inc..

Ghoshal, S., Korine, H., & Szulanski, G. (1994). Interunit Communication in Multinational Corporations. *Management Science*, *40*(1), 96–110. doi:10.1287/mnsc.40.1.96.

Granovetter, M. (1985). Economic Action And Social Structure: The Problem of Embeddedness. *American Journal of Sociology*, *91*(3), 481–510. doi:10.1086/228311.

Gudykunst, W. B., Ting-Toomey, S., & Nishida, T. (1996). *Communication in Personal Relationships Across Cultures*. Thousand Oaks, CA: Sage Publications.

Gupta, A. K., & Govindarajan, V. (2000). Knowledge Flows Within Multinational Corporations. *Strategic Management Journal*, *21*, 473–496. doi:10.1002/(SICI)1097-0266(200004)21:4<473::AID-SMJ84>3.0.CO;2-I.

Hansen, M. T. (1999). The Search-Transfer Problem: The Role of Weak Ties in Sharing Knowledge across Organization Subunits. *Administrative Science Quarterly*, *44*(1), 82–111. doi:10.2307/2667032.

Hofstede, G. (1980). *Culture's consequences*. Beverly Hills, CA: Sage Publications.

Hofstede, G., & Bond, M. (1984). Hofstede culture dimensions- An independent validation using rokeach value survey. *Journal of Cross-Cultural Psychology*, *15*, 411–437. doi:10.1177/0022002184015004003.

House, R., Hanges, P., Ruiz-Quintanilla, S., Dorfman, P., Javidan, M., & Dickson, M. (1999). Cultural influences on leadership and organizations: Project GLOBE. In Mobley, W., Gessner, M., & Arnold, V. (Eds.), *Advances in global leadership* (pp. 171–233). Stamford, CT: JAI.

Hwang, A., & Francesco, A. M. (2010). The influence of individualism-collectivism and power distance on use of feedback channels and consequences for learning. *Academy of Management Learning & Education*, *9*(2), 243–357. doi:10.5465/AMLE.2010.51428546.

Jassawalla, A. R., & Sashittal, H. C. (2009). Thinking strategically about integrating repatriated managers in MNCs. *Human Resource Management*, *48*(5), 769–792. doi:10.1002/hrm.20313.

Javidan, M., Stahl, G. K., Brodbeck, F. C., & Wilderom, C. P. M. (2005). Cross-border transfer of knowledge: Cultural lessons from Project Globe. Academy of Management Executive, 19 (2), 59-76. doi: 10.5465/AME.2005.16962801.

Johnston, S. 2005. Headquarters and Subsidiaries in Multinational Corporations. New York,: PALGRAVE MACMILLAN

Kogut, B., & Zander, U. (1993). Knowledge of The Firm and The Evolutionary Theory of The Multinational Corporation. *Journal of International Business Studies*, *24*(4), 625–645. doi:10.1057/palgrave.jibs.8490248.

Kostova, T. (1999). Transnational Transfer of Strategic Organizational Practices: A Contextual Perspective. *Academy of Management Review*, *24*(2), 308–324.

Kostova, T., & Roth, K. (2003). Social Capital in Multinational Corporations and a Micro-Macro Model of its Formation. *Academy of Management Review*, *28*(2), 297–317.

Monteiro, L. F., Arvidsson, N., & Birkinshaw, J. (2008). Knowledge Flows Within Multinational Corporations: Explaining Subsidiary Isolation and Its Performance Implications. *Organization Science*, *19*(1), 90–107. doi:10.1287/orsc.1070.0264.

Nahapiet, J., & Ghoshal, S. (1998). Social Capital, Intellectual Capital, and The Organizational Advantage. *Academy of Management Review*, *23*(2), 242–266.

Newburry, W., Belkin, L. Y., & Ansari, P. (2008). Perceived career opportunities from globalization: Globalization capabilities and attitudes towards women in Iran and the US. *Journal of International Business Studies*, *39*(5), 814–832. doi:10.1057/palgrave.jibs.8400335.

Nohria, N., & Ghoshal, S. (1997). *The differentiated Network: Organizing multinational corporations for value creation*. San Francisco, CA: Jossey-Bass Publishers.

O'Donnell, S. W. (2000). Managing Foreign Subsidiaries: Agents of Headquarters, or An Interdependent Network? *Strategic Management Journal*, *21*, 525–548. doi:10.1002/(SICI)1097-0266(200005)21:5<525::AID-SMJ104>3.0.CO;2-Q.

Ralston, D. A., Holt, D. H., Terpstra, R. H., & Yu, K. C. (1997). The impact of national culture and economic ideology on managerial work values: A study of the United States, Russia, Japan, and China. *Journal of International Business Studies*, *28*(1), 177–207. doi:10.1057/palgrave.jibs.8490097.

Reiche, B. S. (2011). Knowledge transfer in multinationals: The role of inpatriates' boundary spanning. *Human Resource Management*, *50*(3), 365–389. doi:10.1002/hrm.20423.

Reiche, B. S. (2012). Knowledge benefits of social capital upon repatriation: A longitudinal study of international assignees. *Journal of Management Studies*, *49*(6), 1052–1077. doi:10.1111/j.1467-6486.2012.01050.x.

Rugman, A. M., & Verbeke, A. (2001). Subsidiary-specific advantages in multinational enterprises. Strategic Management Journal, 22(3), 237-250.

Sanchez, J. I., Spector, P. E., & Cooper, C. L. (2000). Adapting to a boundaryless world: A developmental expatriate model. *The Academy of Management Executive*, *14*(2), 96–106.

Schulz, M. (2003). Pathways of Relevance: Exploring Inflows of Knowledge into Subunits of Multinational Corporations. *Organization Science*, *14*(4), 440–459. doi:10.1287/orsc.14.4.440.17483.

Selmer, J. (1995). *Expatriate Management*. Westport, CT: Westport Greenwood Publishing Group.

Stahl, G. K., & Bjorkman, I. (2006). *Handbook of Research in International Human Resource Management*. Northampton, MA: Edward Elgar Publishing.

Stroh, L. K., Black, J. S., Mendenhall, M. E., & Gregersen, H. B. (2005). *International Assignments: An Integration of Strategy, Research, and Practice*. Mahwah, NJ: Lawrence Erlbaum Associates.

Stroh, L. K., Gregersen, H. B., & Black, J. S. (1998). Closing the gap: Expectations versus reality among repatrates. *Journal of World Business*, *33*(2), 111–124. doi:10.1016/S1090-9516(98)90001-3.

Suddaby, R., Elsbach, K., Greenwood, R., Meyer, J., & Zilber, T.B. (2012). Organizations and their institutional environments-bringing meaning, values, and culture back in: Introduction to the special research forum. *Academy of Management Journal*, *53*(6), 1234–1240. doi:10.5465/AMJ.2010.57317486.

Takeuchi, R., Tesluk, P. E., Yun, S. H., & Lepak, D.P. (2005). An integrative view of international experience. *Academy of Management Journal*, *48*(1), 85–100. doi:10.5465/AMJ.2005.15993143.

Toh, S. M., & DeNisi, A. S. (2005). A local perspective to expatriate success. *The Academy of Management Executive*, *19*(1), 132–146.

Tsai, W. (2002). Social Structure of "Coopetition" Within a Multiunit Organization: Coordination, Competition, Intraorganizational Knowledge Sharing. *Organization Science*, *13*(2), 179–191. doi:10.1287/orsc.13.2.179.536.

Tsai, W., & Ghoshal, S. (1998). Social Capital and Value Creation: The Role of Intrafirm Networks. *Academy of Management Journal*, *41*(4), 464–476. doi:10.2307/257085.

Uzzi, B. (1997). Social structure and competition in interfirm networks: The paradox of embeddedness. *Administrative Science Quarterly*, *42*(1), 35–67. doi:10.2307/2393808.

Van der Vegt, G. S., Van der Vliert, E. V. D., & Huang, X. (2005). Location-Level Links Between Diversity and Innovative Climate Depend on National Power Distance. *Academy of Management Journal*, *48*(6), 1171–1182. doi:10.5465/AMJ.2005.19573116.

van Vianen, A. E. M., De Pater, I.E., Kristof-Brown, A. L., & Johnson, E.C. (2004). Fitting in: Surface- And Deep- Level Cultural Differences and Expatriates Adjustment. *Academy of Management Journal*, *47*(5), 697–709. doi:10.2307/20159612.

Vora, D. & Kostova, T. (2007). A model of dual organizational identification in the context of the multinational enterprise. *Jounral of organizational Behavior, 28*, 327-350.

Yamazaki, Y., & Kayes, D. C. (2004). An Experiential Approach to Cross-Cultural Learning: A Review and Integration of Competencies for Successful Expatriate Adaptation. *Academy of Management Learning & Education, 3*(4), 18. doi:10.5465/AMLE.2004.15112543.

Yli-Renko, H., Autio, E., & Sapienza, H. (2001). Social capital, knowledge acquisition, and knowledge exploitation in young technology-based firms. *Strategic Management Journal, 22*, 587–613. doi:10.1002/smj.183.

Zukin, S., & Dimaggio, P. (1990). *Structures of Capital: The social organizaion of the economy.* New York: Cambridge University Press.

Chapter 23
Networking Through Cultures: Communicative Strategies in Transnational Research Teams

Oxana Karnaukhova
Southern Federal University, Russia

ABSTRACT

Transnational communication is a natural effect escorting activities of research teams throughout the world. We understand this phenomenon not as a new-born process mediated by technologies, but the process of cross-border dissemination of opinions, information, ideas, and toolkits. We also recognize that while so-called "new" information and communications technologies (ICTs) have created their own specific problems and concerns, it should be remembered that all forms of communication are capable of causing tensions and latent conflicts (Cupach, 1997; Ribeiro, 1998). The study concerns networking and ICT-mediated collaboration in transnational research teams with Russian participation affected by cultural differences. The core interest lies in investigation of communicative strategies and effects of visual and interactive techniques, including video-conferencing, participatory social media, podcasting, and others--and, to collaboratively construct, interpret, and theorize participants' accounts of cooperation.

INTRODUCTION

In the globalised world, we find at least three dimensions within which contemporary international project management exists. The first one is the theoretical collision around notion of culture. The second dimension is transculturality, which is defined as being "in-between." The final dimension linked with the previous one is ICT-mediated communication which reflexes cultural differences in the process of decision-making, technology acceptance, and more. Most people have some opinion, drawn from their own culture's folk psychology, regarding the concept

DOI: 10.4018/978-1-4666-3966-9.ch023

of culture. However, after close inspection of the true meaning of culture, a very complex phenomenon reveals itself. As a result, there is no consensus among researchers on a definition of culture (Smith & Bond, 1999; Triandis, 1996). At least several dimensions of culture could be found in extant literature: on culture and cultural differences in management (Adler, 1997), social psychology (Smith & Bond, 1999), and linguistic anthropology (Duranti, 1997).

Beginning with the fact that the word "culture" refers not only to masterpieces in literature, arts, and music, it must also be limited to something which differs one community from another. Culture emerges and is sustained by social relations within specific contexts. Although previously the objectivist view of culture has been predominant, during the past 20 years the symbolic view of culture has become commonplace. Hofstede (1997) defines culture as "the collective programming of the mind which distinguishes the members of one group or category of people from another." This is used as an every-day definition in project management, so we contend with preferably cultural differences, explaining management' faults in transnational project team-building. While researchers view the problem through "cultural glasses," they must consult with the people involved and to make sure that the same thing is estimated similarly across cultures in order to achieve a consensus on various questions.

However, following Kim and Markus (1999), cultures could be theorized as constantly changing, open systems of behaviors, attitudes, and norms. They also include institutions the people within a culture continuously reinforce through diverse ways of engagement and participation, including networking. Together with lifting global migrations we discover the most popular word, "transculture," emphasizing the moment of crossing barriers, imagined or real. Though transculture depends on the efforts of separate individuals to overcome their identification with separate cultures, on another level, it is a process of interaction between cultures themselves in which more and more individuals have found themselves "outside" of any particular culture, and "outside" of its national, age, political, and other limitations. It means being located beyond any particular mode of existence, or in this case, finding one's place on the border of existing cultures.

This realm *beyond* all cultures is located *inside* of transculture and belongs to this state of not-belonging (Epstein, 1995). Transculture is usually perceived as the mode of existence liberated from culture itself; however, transculture is not a rarified and isolated construct which is separated from real national cultures. Rather, it is more about the game which is essentially derivative and forbids the creation of new signs and values, so transculture aspires entirely to the sphere of creativity. The transcultural world lies not apart from, but within all existing cultures, like a multi-dimensional space, where communication exists between those of all cultures and sharing all possible experiences.

Transculturality is enforced by new information technologies. In the digital era, access to and familiarity with technology has become an important resource for successful cooperation. Media frames, feasible from Goffman's (1974) notion of schemas, define an issue through selection, exclusion, emphasis and elaboration – in other words, frames define communication. ICT studies typically consider frames at an issue-specific or generic (thematic) level, including values, human interests and motivations, communicative strategies. For further consideration of media technology usage and framing, we will exploit cultural dimensions, defined as the core dimensions by leading researchers (Trompenaars, Hampden-Turner, 1998, Hall, 1989; Hofstede, 1997): "individualism/collectivism," "power distance," "masculinity/femininity," "uncertainty avoidance," "time perception (monochronic/polychronic)," and "high context/low context."

These dimensions are the most influential and feasible in the context of transnational project team cooperation. First, these dimensions focus on human values, and precisely are more directly linked to organizational process and communication. Second, we suppose the first four dimensions are the most recognizable in studying cross-cultural issues in project management. Finally, the most important dimension is high/ low context. Hall (1989) depicted this dimension as an umbrella for other cultural dimensions, as it is revealed as the reason for a divergence between societies in several aspects of communication. It becomes clear in the context of cross-cultural studies of communicative strategies (Smith & Bond, 1999).

There are some criticism about the influence of new media technologies on social interaction and collaboration. For instance, Van de Donk (2004) argues the Internet will complement, not replace, existing communication tactics. However, an approach has proposed so-called "slacktivism" or a meaningless activism (Morozov, 2009). Some other scholars have questioned whether virtual interaction could prompt any level of trust among participants needed to support sustainable cooperation mode (Diani, 2000). Without trust, members are not deeply dedicated, so while a movement's support might grow quickly initially, that support is likely to soon diminish. Also virtual ties alone, without "real" face-to-face interaction, are doubtful to be strong enough to successfully mobilize or sustain interactions, as real relationships are considered more valuable and effective than impersonal ICT-mediated communication (Diani, 2000; Ribeiro, 1998).

The differences in how people from different cultures perceive their worlds and how they communicate (face-to-face mode or ICT-accepted) are to influence decision making processes and strategies of cooperation in multiple ways. As soon as transnational project teams are the most visible case for investigation of cultural differences in networking, the process of communication mode selection in the globalized media environment is of our interest. We could assume that doubts on the role of the internet and ICT mediation of communication reflex social and cultural localization of researchers. Therefore, we will attempt to extend the ideas of cultural preset in communication preferences of transnational team participants.

NETWORKING AND ICT: THE RUSSIAN CONTEXT

The close connection between culture and technology acceptance is not a brand new idea in the interdisciplinary studies of project management. Within this trend, some basic approaches for analysis have been recommended. Among them: Structuration Theory (Turner, 1991; Walsham, 2001), Value-Based Approach (Leidner & Kayworth, 2006) and Social Identity Theory (Ashforth & Mael, 1989). Considering networking as a conventional venue of coordinating relevant transactions we propose, that on one hand, coherent and dense networks enable actors to achieve their goals effectively because of cooperative behavior of members, high trust embedded in relationships and informal social mechanisms, which control opposing behavior (Coleman, 1988). However, sparse and dispersible networks facilitate participants' access to new information, opportunities and resources promoting the success of instrumental actions (Burt, 1997).

The instrumental value of networks is contingent upon the socio-cultural context, behavioral patterns and communicative strategies of individuals and project teams, mediated by ICT which is considered a buffer or an insulator for communication. As a result of the ICT usage, contacts provide network benefits that are in some degree additive rather than overlapping (Burt, 1997). ICT (social media, etc.) looks like structural holes, in terms of Burt, provoking a disconnection or extremely weak relationship between two contacts. Therefore, networking mediated by ICT is universal and could be observable in any networks including American, Eastern, European, or Russian contexts. Transnational research teams benefit from a network based on ICT usage. A crucial advantage as obtained from such a sparse networks is timely access to wide-range information from dispersed sources. Distantly tied networks, being a result of transculturality, generate more diverse and creative ideas since people appear in the intersections of social and cultural worlds. Disperse networks promote greater structural autonomies that enable participants to act upon new opportunities and neutralize harmful effects. Language skills enable to keep track of the latest Internet technology and research trends. At the same time, although international project teams can adopt the IT they may not appropriately use it. Even overall acquiring of IT as the necessary tool for project communication it is often thought insufficient to implement it effectively. That is why understanding cultural differences in accepting and using IT by project team is an important issues in the case of Russian participatory projects.

The most feasible break is between statistic data on ICT usage and the real implementation of it in every-day project communication. As an ICT-dynamic country, Russia is one of the largest "social media user and lover" nations compared to other countries in Europe. In 2011, more than 50% of the Russian population accessed the Internet, or approximately 61.5 million people (Internet World Stats, 2011). This Internet population makes Russia the second largest in Europe and the largest in Eastern Europe. About 80% of Russian Internet users have at least one account in social media, amounting to 32% of the overall population of the Russian Federation. Although recently born, Russian social media, social networking, and online media are developing. Russia's relatively high Internet access ratio reveals how social media can tremendously affect both social life and business. Based on data from Comscore (2011), Internet users in Russia–spending an average of 22 hours to surf and view an average of three pages per person of online content per month–were also found to be the most engaged users among Europe (Comscore, 2011). Russia has the third largest population of Facebook users in the world.

In addition to Facebook, another popular social media platform is "VKontakte"–the national internet platform. A total of 81% of users list social networking as the goal to visit the Internet, while 72% of Internet users are registered on the network VKontakte. Recently, personal blogs have also gained popularity. While 66% of users read blogs weekly, approximately 24% obtain information gained from social media before making a decision. The favorite blog atmosphere in Russia is "Livejournal.com" in its local "ru" sector. Finally, 48% of users employ mobile phones to be in permanent contact.

Venkatesh (2003) and colleagues have indentified the motivation for decision-making regarding the acceptance and use of information technologies as follows:

1. Individual reactions to using information technology;
2. Intentions to use information technology; and
3. Actual use of information technology.

The selection of ICT platforms for effective communication is based on goals and tasks of a project team, but it can be assumed the fourth element is cultural specificity.

Methodological Approach

To cast new light on debating differences influential for IT usage, it is necessary to inquire about cultural practices, behavioral patterns, and motivation affecting Russian participants in transnational research teams, and to promote opportunities to develop sufficient and sustainable cooperation in project teams. There is a wide range of methodological approaches and tools to explain and predict IT use in transnational team cooperation. Interdisciplinary studies of this topic began at the beginning of 1990s. Straub, Rose, and Srite have already explored the impact of cultural factors on the behavior of IT use. There are two main methodological approaches, considering links of culture, communicative strategies and information system' usage–Social (Cultural) Network Analysis (SNA or CNA), proposed by Sieck, Rasmussen, and Smart (2010), and the Technology Acceptance Model of Davis (1989). The method relevant for research purposes was borrowed from the Technology Acceptance Model (TAM) with some extensions. It is represented as an interdisciplinary synthesis of methods drawn from the Theory of Reasoned Action explaining behavior across behavioral intentions (Ajzen & Fishbein, 1980). The model answers the question regarding reasons and purposes to specific IT use. Davis has introduced two main correlating elements, such as perceived usefulness and perceived ease of use. These elements influence intentions to use IT and the selection of a specific platform. As soon as cultural differences are acknowledged as a determinant in cooperation mediated by the IT, the TAM is extended to integrate cultural specificity as an element in intentions to use IT and communicate.

This chapter began defining culture as a network of knowledge, where there is some level of agreement among members in the group, and specific ways of information transactions. Such a network could be replaced by the term of cultural model, which is activated within specific situations to drive thinking and decision making, and could barely be changed under suitable conditions. The dynamics across sociocultural networks is especially interesting for investigation of shared understanding among multinational teams, as well as anticipating effects in communication acts. As founders of the TAM demonstrate, it encompasses both qualitative, exploratory analysis, and quantitative, confirmatory analysis. The exploratory TAM will be used in which concepts and other elements are extracted from qualitative sources, such as interviews and open source media (web news, blogs, e-mail).

When qualitatively measured models reflect the "universe" of ideas for the cultural group, they seek to capture all relevant ideas mentioned. Six Centres of the European Union in Russia have been chosen as the cornerstone case. In-depth interviews with research project leaders of the North-West, South-West and East Russian Centres, including those with top managers, were considered as relevant and sufficient for further content-analysis. These interviews were supported by interviews with project managers, leading research teams in Russian academia. The number of in-depth interviews totals 15. Additionally, the data from reports freely accessed and taken from social media platforms are used for content analysis.

Content analysis was chosen as the method of analysis because it is regarded as a useful measurement technique for in-depth interviews. This analysis is useful in that it allows to process texts that are significant, meaningful, informative and representational. Content analysis recognizes that the data are read and interpreted by others who make sense of them by referencing them to their personal context. As a result, the use of content analysis that can handle large volumes of data provides an opportunity to create data that is relevant to all users.

For purposes of the research the survey was developed using an online survey tool, Survey Monkey, which is accessed from anywhere via the Internet. Participants have enough time to complete the survey, but they access the online survey once. Demographic information was considered as important and was also obtained. Participants were invited through e-mail directly, and information about the study was also spread through platform of Facebook and VKontakte. The online survey was available for two months before the data analysis and still could be accessed on-line.

The data collection has been organized around follow research questions:

Q1: Do individuals of the high-context culture have a less strong perception of IT usefulness than those of low-context cultures?

Q2: Do individuals in low power distance cultures accept IT more than do individuals in high power distance cultures?

Q3: Does power distance moderate the relationship between norms and behavioral intentions?

Q4: Does individualism/collectivism moderates the relationship between norms and behavioral intentions?

Cultural Dimensions, Communication Strategies and Decision-Making Process: The Case of the Russian Participatory Model

The study describes how respondents belonging to Russian culture apply decision processes and use decision aids in the case of interactions with European partners. Results showed not only that the participants from different nations (cultures) used differing decision processes, such as weighing alternative choices, information seeking, and willingness to accept trade-offs, they also used decision aids differently. One dimension which may differ across cultures is the set of factors that determine who makes the decision as well as the values and interests served by the decision. According to some respondents there could be seen three structural and relational elements of transnational research project teams ("building blocks"), which explain networking activity. They are follows: the content (including access to information), network governance (such as trust relations), and network structure (power relations and hierarchy).

In Russia, projects are often planned based on federal, local, or corporate norms and standards which usually refer to material resource productivity, costs and available human resources per unit of activity volume (volume of work to be done). Usage of these norms affects the planning of project activities. As one of respondents remarked, the main difference between the approaches of Russian and so-called Western networking activities is such: if activity volumes and resource productivity are used as the inputs in planning processes, activity duration can be estimated only after the assigned resources were chosen and project schedule calculated. That is why project management in the Russian context usually offers a set of separate knowledge areas that, in fact, should not be separated. In the Russian counterpart, the content is reorganized in a more instructive, process-oriented way. All respondents assure that project participants act within the framework of existing networks that serve as the institutional contexts for actions of players. When individual players act, some social and cultural attributes influence the existing patterns of network structure.

All of the survey participants are active players of transnational research projects. They are dedicated to the active interactions with their European partners as well as to networking with each other. Some of them constitute that "sparse and heterogeneous networks of researchers facilitate greater product (result) diversity because of diverse information sources, greater opportunities and resources, and different knowledge content found in such networks." Within the overall communication strategy and project management, the factor of trust is important. It logically leads to early and rapid detection of faults, and hence to high efficiency activity programming. When network participants are strongly connected to each other, relationships are multiplex–information exchange, learning, and emotional contacts "co-exist" in each tie. Multiplex relationships facilitate flows of knowledge that help to finish tasks in a timely mode. In the Russian cultural context, trust is an element of emotional relations, crucially important for cooperation. So in this course "analysis" is indicated as a communication point and used for clarifying relations.

Using IS platforms participants learn to communicate with colleagues who do not know each other and who are different in their cultural background, education and knowledge. As a respondent of the age 37 remarks, one of the initial disadvantages of networking within an Internet platforms is "the lack of information about informal rules of using ICT," but later broad result scope may turn into assets. ICT usage facilitates diversity through timely access to disperse information and relevant sources, prompts actors to discover new opportunities and resources, to feel them as translators of knowledge. ICT platforms demonstrate the transitivity mechanism through connecting directly two previously unconnected ties. According to a 50-year old respondent, "Now I see benefits of using Skype. You could solve problems and discuss ideas in the on-line regime, as if you are sitting face-to-face with your colleagues."

Answering the research question on perception of IT usefulness by those from high-context cultures and low-context cultures, the following can be assumed: Being representatives of high-context culture Russian participants of transnational project teams still prefer face-to-face communication. As the survey showed, Skype is popular as soon it imitates personal communication. The ICT-mediated communication, implying very explicit content, is considered not to be very useful as a means of communication. It cannot inform the receiver on the context of the message, questioning trust relations as a compulsory element of successful communication. In this case, Russian participants probably seek to know more about the message through traditional mechanisms that physical means imply (face expression, intonation of the voice, body movements, etc.). Interestingly, the highest popularity of the VKontakte network seems less useful for transnational team communication then Facebook. VKontakte is perceived useful for communication within the national system of interaction. Usage of the domestic national platform supports the idea about inability to overcome cultural differences. Some respondents assume that "There are some crucial differences in cross-cultural interaction. They appear to be inevitable… Only Russian could understand Russian…."

Answering the second research question on IT acceptance by representatives of low/high power distance cultures, we remark that Russian culture is considered a high power-distance culture, and hypothetically IT could threaten the hierarchy as it suggests decentralization. Indeed, in low power-distance cultures, individuals are more interdependent regardless of their ranks in the hierarchy; therefore, they are more interested in IT as it does not contradict their perception of power distribution. Though the Russian social reforms resulted in the destruction of existing institutions and networks, the internal hierarchy in Russian networks is still based on power and status, and this generates greater relational distance among participants. Recently intentions to use or not use ICT platforms depended on power distance among Russian participants. The idea of ICT implementation had to come from a top manager who is responsible for overall team collaboration policy and moderation of the ICT-mediated communication. As one of the reviewees remarks: "It is important who will be the moderator of our Facebook page and who will be responsible for the database…." In high power-distance cultures such as Russia's, reliance on the opinions of superiors is definitely marked when accepting the IT platforms. Moreover, many projects provided together with Russian participants communication through Internet networks are not supposed to disagree with existing norms.

Individuals adopting the monochronic time are worried about the monitoring of time and prefer do one thing at a time; therefore, they can view IT as a way in which to have control over time. Contrarily, Russian participants in the transnational teams hold more fluid attitude toward time. They are able to engage in many things at once and pay more attention to interpersonal relationships than to schedules. This is the reason they are expected to view IT as a constraint since "it could threaten freedom to spare time" (respondent of age 34).

Russia belonging to a collectivist type of culture provides specific cognitive patterns which affect the relationship between norms and behavioral intentions. That means a holistic overall approach, together with interdependence, intentions to maintain deep, long-duree, and personalized relationships with high value and distinct boundaries, to communicate with high-context information, are process-oriented and highly sensitive to interruptions. These characteristics influence the decision-making process. In detail, the decision-making process on the usefulness of IT depends on the opinion of all members of the group. Additionally, the basic communicative strategy is to maintain the team cohesiveness. This is why the predominant reason to organize communication through ICT is the opinion of the other team players.

Finally, findings from this study indicate two basic intentions in behavior. The first one is a simple consumption, which is imagined as engagement in participatory network. The second one is the perception that it is necessary to go beyond their internet activities and use on-line network as a place for creation and team action.

CONCLUSION

Project managers often encounter cultural differences which interfere with the successful conclusion of projects. It is feasible in the multicultural world where transcultural contacts and constant communications are natural effects of cooperative activities. Leading studies provided by Hall (1987), Trompenaars, Hampden-Turner (1997), Hofstede (2000) and others provide understanding cultural differences in motivations to use IT allows a better capturing of cultural influence on transnational networks, acceptance of information technologies especially the impact of low/ high context cultures on intention to use IT. This research is governed by the need to define more clearly existing communication practices in the transnational teams with Russian participation. It promotes better understanding of possible coherence between ICT development and cultural transitions within the management of research projects, which require complex negotiations and information exchange between players. The study is considered the pilot research of cultural differences in communicative strategies. This research extended TAM (Davis, 1989) in the Russian cultural context. The findings demonstrate the existence of cultural differences in terms of ICT acceptance and decision-making process.

The precise findings are as follows. It appears Russian participants do not consider ease- of-use as the most powerful motivation to exploit ICT platforms for communication. It is clear there is an external stimulus for ICT usage, such as emotional pressure from the communication environment. The most popular platform is Skype as soon it replaces the real conversation and provides on-line conferencing activities. Facebook is considered as less useful. Professional network LinkedIn is practically unknown for most of the reviewees, as its benefits are unclear. Therefore, usefulness influences attitudes of team members and their satisfaction as well. It can be assumed that functionality is among the preferences. The ICT-mediated communication of transnational project teams is, indeed, influenced by culture. In the case of Russian team members, we could see preferences in ICT acceptance for cooperation goals as follows: usefulness in the sense of the need to use ICT takes the first place; satisfaction by the results of ICT-mediated communication takes the second position; finally, behavior intentions are correlated with cultural dimensions, well-known since Hofstede's research.

It can also be assumed Russian participants are seen to mix private and business matters, to see relational uncertainty as threatening, to consider trust relations as important, and to prefer to work in teams close to the cultural origin. Hierarchy followed by power distance in the communication process is one of the visible characteristics of the communicative strategy and ways of networking, chosen by Russian participants.

REFERENCES

Adams, D. A., & Nelson, R. R. (1992). Perceived usefulness, ease of use, and usage of Information Technology: A replication. *Management Information Systems Quarterly*, *16*(2). doi:10.2307/249577.

Adler, N. J. (1997). *International Dimensions of Organizational Behaviour*. Boston, MA: PWS-Kent.

Agarwal, R. (1999). *Individual acceptance of information technologies*. Retrieved from http://www.pinnaflex.com/pdf/framing/CH06.pdf

Ajzen, I., & Fishbein, M. (1980). *Understanding attitudes and predicting social behavior*. Englewood Cliffs, NJ: Prentice-Hall.

Ashforth, B. E., & Mael, F. (1989). Social Identity Theory and the Organization. *Academy of Management Review*, *14*(1), 20–39.

Bagozzi, R. P. (2007). The Legacy of the Technology Acceptance Model and a Proposal for a Paradigm Shift. *Journal of the Association for Information Systems*, *8*(4).

Burt, R. S. (1997). A note on social capital and network content. *Social Networks*, *19*, 355–373. doi:10.1016/S0378-8733(97)00003-8.

Coleman, J. C. (1988). Social capital in the creation of human capital. *American Journal of Sociology*, *94*, S95–S120. doi:10.1086/228943.

Comscore. (2011). *ComScore Releases Overview of European Internet Usage in September 2011*. Retrieved from http://www.comscore.com/Press_Events/Press_Releases/2011/11/comScore_Releases_Overview_of_European_Internet_Usage_in_September_2011

Cupach, W. R., & Canary, D. J. (1997). *Competence in Interpersonal Conflict*. Long Grove, IL: Waveland Press.

Davis, F. D. (1989). Perceived usefulness, perceived ease of use and user acceptance of information technology. *Management Information Systems Quarterly*, *13*(3). doi:10.2307/249008.

Diani, M. (2000). Social movement networks virtual and real. *Information Communication and Society*, *3*(3), 386–401. doi:10.1080/13691180051033333.

Duranti, A. (1997). Linguistic Anthropology. Cambridge, MA: Cambridge University Press.

Epstein, M. (1995). *After the Future: The paradoxes of postmodernism and contemporary Russian culture*. Retrieved from http://www.emory.edu/INTELNET/ af.culturology.html

Goffman, E. (1976). *Replies and responses*. LIS.

Hall, E. T., & Hall, R. M. (1987). *Hidden Differences. Doing Business with the Japanese*. New York: Anchor Press Doubleday.

Hannerz, U. (1996). *Transnational connections. Culture, people, places*. LondonRoutledge.

Hofstede, G. (1997). *Cultures and organizations: Software of the mind*. London: McGraw Hill.

Internet World Stats (2011). Retrieved from http://www.internetworldstats.com/stats.htm

Kim, H., & Marcus, H. R. (1999). Deviance or Uniqueness, Harmony or Conformity? A Cultural Analysis. *Journal of Personality and Social Psychology*, *77*(4), 785–800. doi:10.1037/0022-3514.77.4.785.

Leavy, P. (2011). *Essentials of Transdisciplinary Research*. Walnut Creek, CA: Left Coast Press.

Leidner, D., & Kayworth, T. (2006). A review of culture in information systems research: Toward a theory of information technology culture conflict. *Management Information Systems Quarterly*, *30*(2), 357–399.

Morozov, E. (2009). Texting toward utopia: Does the Internet spread democracy? *Boston Review*, March/April. Retrieved from http://bostonreview.net/BR34.2/morozov.php

Myers, M. D., & Tan, F. B. (2002). Beyond models of national culture in information systems research. *Journal of Global Information Management*, *10*(1). doi:10.4018/jgim.2002010103.

Ribeiro, G. L. (1998). Cybercultural politics. In Alvarez, S. E., Dagnino, E., & Escobar, A. (Eds.), *Cultures of politics, politics of cultures: Revisioning Latin American social movements*. Boulder, CO: Westview Press.

Rose, G., & Straub, D. (1998). Predicting general IT use: Applying TAM to the Arabic World. *Journal of Global Information Management*, *6*(3).

Schwartz, S. H., & Bilsky, W. (1990). Toward a Theory of the Universal Content and Structure of Values: Extensions and Cross-Cultural Replications. *Journal of Personality and Social Psychology*, *58*(5). doi:10.1037/0022-3514.58.5.878.

Sieck, W. R., Rasmussen, L. J., & Smart, P. R. (2010). Cultural Network Analysis: A Cognitive Approach to Cultural Modeling. In Verma, D. (Ed.), *Network Science for Military Coalition Operations: Information Extraction and Interaction*. Hershey, PA: IGI Global. doi:10.4018/978-1-61520-855-5.ch011.

Smith, P. B., & Bond, M. H. (1999). *Social psychology across cultures*. Boston, MA: Allyn and Bacon.

Srite, M., & Karahanna, E. (2006). The Role of Espoused National Cultural Values in Technology Acceptanc. *Management Information Systems Quarterly*, *30*(3), 679–704.

Thurlow, C., Lengel, L., & Tomic, A. (2004). *Computer Mediated Communication: Social Interaction and the Internet*. London: Sage.

Thurlow, C., & Mroczek, K. (Eds.). (2011). *Digital Discourse: Language in the New Media*. New York: Oxford University Press. doi:10.1093/acprof:oso/9780199795437.001.0001.

Triandis, H. C. (1996). The psychological measurement of cultural syndromes. *The American Psychologist*, *51*, 407–415. doi:10.1037/0003-066X.51.4.407.

Trompenaars, F., & Hampden-Turner, C. (1997). *Riding the Waves of Culture: Understanding Diversity in Global Business*. Boston, MA: Nicholas Brealey Publishing.

Turner, J. H. (1991). Structuration Theory. InThe Structure of Sociological Theory.

Van de Donk, W., Loader, B. D., Nixon, P. G., & Rucht, D. (2004). *Cyberprotest: New Media, Citizens and Social movements*. London: Routledge.

Venkatesh, V., Morris, M. G., Davis, G. B., & Davis, F. D. (2003). User acceptance of information technology: Toward a unified view. *Management Information Systems Quarterly*, *27*(3).

Walsham, G. (2001). *Making a World of Difference: IT in a Global Context*. Chichester, UK: Wiley.

Chapter 24
Cultural Influence on Global Assessment of Higher Education Service Quality:
The Case of Central Queensland University, Australia

Parves Sultan
Central Queensland University, Australia

Ho Yin Wong
Deakin University, Australia

ABSTRACT

This study compares students' cultural influence on global assessment of higher education service quality. In particular, this study surveyed the full-time students (that is at least 24 credit points of study in a semester) studying at the Central Queensland University (CQU), Australia. CQU has ten campuses and is one of the largest universities in Australia, with more than 14,000 students, in which 3,000 students are enrolled as full-time students and 11,000 as part-time students. An online survey was undertaken, and 227 responses from full-time students were returned for data analysis. Exploratory factor analysis and confirmatory factor analysis were performed to determine valid and reliable dimensions of perceived service quality. Tests of differences such as ANOVA and t-test were conducted to examine the differences of perceived service quality in terms of four cultural dimensions; namely, power distance, individualism, uncertainty avoidance, and masculinity. Findings show that different cultures perceive service quality differently; especially administrative service quality and physical facilities service quality.

DOI: 10.4018/978-1-4666-3966-9.ch024

INTRODUCTION

Australian higher education institutions are popular destinations for both domestic and international students. However, the Bradley, Noonan, Nugent & Scales (2008) report states there is a clear sign that the quality of the educational experience is declining in Australia. One of the significant recommendations of this study emphasises course experience as perceived by the students (Bradley, et al., 2008). Current studies develop a number of measures of service quality in commercial service settings. Of these service quality measures, most of the studies have used either the SERVQUAL (perception–minus–expectation) measure (Parasuraman, Zeithaml, & Berry, 1985, 1988) or the SERVPERF (perception–only) measure (Cronin & Taylor, 1992, 1994). Although there are debates in relation to superiority of these service quality measures, the SERVPERF measure of service quality has been termed as an effective measure for the purpose of explaining variance in dependent constructs (Cronin, Brady, & Hult, 2000; Parasuraman, Zeithaml, & Berry, 1994; Zeithaml, Berry, & Parasuraman, 1996). Therefore, the present research is centred upon the SERVPERF measure.

Although the service quality measure in higher education is relatively new, the HEdPERF measure (Abdullah, 2005) and the PHEd measure (Sultan & Wong, 2010a) may be considered as comprehensive scales, as these measures include a broad range of service attributes in the context of higher education. The HEdPERF measure and the PHEd measure were conceptualised on the perception–only scale. However, there is little evidence as to how one's culture affects service quality assessment in a global higher education context. This study is expected to fill in this research gap by furnishing empirical evidence.

The direction of this study is to compare students' cultural influence on global assessment of higher education service quality. Particularly, the objectives of this study are:

1. To study the impacts of one's culture on service quality assessment in a global higher education context.
2. To examine if there is any significant difference between two or more cultures in terms of service quality assessment in a global higher education context.
3. To understand the implications of this difference in terms of service delivery.

LITERATURE REVIEW

Service Quality and Its Dimensions in Higher Education

Service quality is defined as the totality of features and characteristics of a product or service that bears on its ability to satisfy stated or implied needs (Johnson & Winchell, 1988). Perceived service quality is based on one's experience and is a function of attitude (Sultan & Wong, 2010a). Service quality has also been viewed as a critical determinant of competitiveness (Lewis, 1989), as a source of lasting competitive advantage through service differentiation (Moore, 1987), and as a driver of corporate financial and marketing performance (Buttle, 1996).

The higher education service quality has been the predominant area of research to both academics and practitioners for the last decade. Table 1 shows the service quality dimensions in higher education across various countries and cultures developed between 1997 and 2010. There are two major approaches to determine service quality, the supply-side approach and the demand-side approach (Gatfield, Barker, & Graham, 1999). A handful of studies (Abdullah, 2005, 2006a, 2006b, 2006c; Angell, Heffernan, & Megicks, 2008; Gatfield, et al., 1999; Kwan & Ng, 1999; LeBlanc & Nguyen, 1997; Sultan & Wong, 2011) examined service quality dimensions within the higher education sector from the students' perspective, essentially a demand-side perspective

Table 1. Service quality dimensions in higher education across various countries and cultures

Author, Date	No. of Items	Dimensions	Country/University
(Sultan and Wong, 2010a)	67 Items	Dependability, effectiveness, capability, efficiency, competencies, assurance, unusual situation management and semester–syllabus	Japan
(Rojas-Me´ndez, et al., 2009)	18 Items	Instructors, program director, secretaries, service attitude and competence development.	Chilean University
(Stodnick and Rogers, 2008)	18 Items	Reliability, Assurance, Tangibles, Empathy and Responsiveness	One course, Southwestern University, USA
(Angell, et al., 2008)	18 Items	Academic, leisure, industry links and cost	One university, UK
(Smith, et al., 2007)	22 Items	Reliability, Assurance, Tangibles, Empathy and Responsiveness	IT Department, one university, UK
(Abdullah, 2006c)	41 Items	Non–academic, academic, reputation, access, program and understanding	Malaysia
(Abdullah, 2005, 2006a, 2006b)	35 Items	Non–academic, academic, reliability and empathy	Malaysia
(Gatfield, et al., 1999)	26 Items	Academic instruction, campus life, guidance, recognition	One Australian University
(Kwan and Ng, 1999)	31 Items	Course content, concern for students, facilities, assessment, medium of instruction, social activities and people.	China and Hong Kong
(Li and Kaye, 1998)	27 Items	Reliability, Assurance, Tangibles, Empathy and Responsiveness	One university, UK
(Joseph and Joseph, 1997)	—	Program, academic reputation, physical aspects, career opportunities, location, time and other	New Zealand
(LeBlanc and Nguyen, 1997)	38 Items	Contact personnel/faculty, contact personnel/administration, responsiveness, reputation, curriculum, physical evidence and access to facilities	Business School, one university, Canada

of determining service quality. These studies have identified several dimensions in the context of higher education institutions across various countries and cultures. The current study takes a view from a demand-side perspective in determining service quality and its key dimensions, and examines the role of cultural differences in global assessment of higher education service quality.

In any higher education institution, academics are perceived to be highly important to students (Angell, et al., 2008; Gatfield, et al., 1999). In general, good teaching practices, after-hour consultancy, problem solving, fair grading, course content and easy access to faculty were perceived by the students as some common and desirable teaching characteristics in current studies (Gatfield, et al., 1999; Sultan & Wong, 2010a).

The administrative aspect of service quality is essential to enabling students to fulfil their study obligations, and is perceived as a set of several key attributes including: ability and willingness of administrative staff to support students, equal treatment, safeguarding confidentiality of information, prompt and effective services, positive attitudes, and good communication skills (Abdullah, 2005).

Research also demonstrates a number of dimensions (see Table 1) apart from academic and non-academic (or administrative) aspects of service quality in higher education. These dimensions vary across study perspectives, nations, and cultures. However, the commonalities in those dimensions are that they are based on facilities available to students and auxiliary services' management. Gatfield et al. (1999) suggest nationality could be an important factor in designing and operationalising academic instruction programmes. They stated that "it is inevitable that universities should adopt a common programme for Australian and international students to achieve uniform academic standards and to achieve a measure of economy of scale" (Gatfield, et al., 1999, p. 249). Current literature has yet to adequately address the extent to which culture or nationality influence the assessment of service quality at global higher education institutions.

Culture and Its Dimensions

Culture is an important factor in global business because it shapes how people perceive the outside world and affects what people do. With the highly human interactive nature of service industries, individuals' cultural backgrounds can be an important factor in determining service standards from the service providers' perspective and influencing perceived service standards from the point of view of the service receivers. Service quality dimensions are subjective and relativistic. People with different cultural backgrounds may have different values and beliefs that affect their perception with regard to service quality (Furrer, Liu, & shudharshan, 2000). Thus, people's cultural backgrounds can be an important factor that affects the perception of service quality.

Culture is rather hard to understand and define, considering that it is an extremely abstract concept that is programmed in individuals' minds. Culture is complex, multifaceted phenomenon that is expressed through behaviours, language, and traditions (Dedic & Pavlovic, 2011). It is considered as an umbrella concept which includes elements such as shared values, beliefs and norms that can collectively distinguish a particular group of people from others (Pizam & Reichel, 1997). Not only does the international business discipline study culture, but also other disciplines such as sociology, anthropology, psychology, and even arts and communications. The diversity of approaches in studying culture makes it harder to understand completely the nature of culture (Groeschel & Doherty, 2000). Doubts have been cast that culture cannot be generalised on a national basis due to the fact that individuals within one national do not necessarily all hold the same value (Dedic & Pavlovic, 2011). Nevertheless, Steenkamp (2001) argues that when a culture within a country is quite homogenous and there are cultural differences between countries, it is reasonable to use national boundaries and citizenship of a certain country as a proxy measure for culture.

This argument emphasises that not all people within a national boundary are the same in terms of cultural values, but "there are forces pushing to a meaningful degree of within country commonality" (Steenkamp, 2001, p. 36). These forces are embedded in a nation's social, education, religion, media, and even political (Hofstede, 1980) and legislative systems. The consequence of these forces congregates similar values systems shared by the majority of group members in a nation. Some prominent classifications based on these values systems include the empirical works of Hofstede (1980, 1991) and Trompenaars (1994).

In this study, we use Hofstede's influential work (Hofstede, 1980) as a theoretical background to examine the cultural impacts on the perception of service quality. Even though Hofstede's cultural study has received criticism, his study is still one of the most widely used cultural studies in international marketing and management (Laroche, Ueltschy, Abe, Cleveland, & Yannopoulos, 2004; Sodergaard, 1994). Hofstede (1980, p. 25) defines culture as "the collective programming of the mind which distinguishes the members of one group or category of people from those of another." This definition emphasises that culture is not something which is easily obtained, but a slow reception process of individuals within a society.

Hofstede's study gathered 80,000 questionnaire data from IBM employees in 66 countries across seven occupations (Furrer, et al., 2000). After analysing the data with factor analysis, he found four distinctive dimensions of national culture; those are individualism, power distance, masculinity, and uncertainty avoidance.

Individualism indicates "the relationship between the individual and the collectivity that prevails in a given society" (Hofstede, 1980, p. 148). Capturing people's social behaviour toward the group, individualism describes the extent to which welfare of the individual is valued more than the group. It can be considered as the degree of social/community integration (Jones, 2007). Individualistic culture emphasises "I" rather than "we". The individuals tend to be motivated by personal preferences, needs and rights, and for personal goals. Not only do they express self-interest seeking behaviour, but also promote this behaviour. On the other end of a bipolar continuum is collectivism, which is the tendency of people to belong to groups and to take care of each other in exchange for loyalty. In collectivistic cultures, the groups' interests are more important than the individuals', and there is a tendency that people are motivated by the norms and duties set by the in-group. According to Trandis, Bontempo and Villareal (1988), individualistic cultures are more likely to support competition, independence, self-orientation, freedom, self-confidence, and fairness; while collectivistic cultures favour cooperation, interdependence, other-orientation, harmony, conformity, friendship, forgiveness, and social usefulness.

Power distance is the extent to which members of groups accept power inequality between classes. The classes can be found in terms of the level of hierarchy in workplaces and distance between social levels. High power distance cultures tend to be more hierarchical, and group members expect the power to be distributed unequally on the bases of one's position, authority, competence, and resources (Hofstede, 1991). Power is placed at the top and is predominantly centralised. Relying on the instructions from authority and organisations, members in high power distance cultures show great tolerance for the absence of autonomy. Low power distance cultures, on the other hand, tend to value quality and fairness. Individuals lean away from blindly obeying the orders from the top. Power is more evenly allocated among group members.

Uncertainty avoidance is defined as "the extent to which a society feels threatened by uncertain and ambiguous situations" (Hofstede, 1980, p. 45). It is concerned with the way in which people deal with the future. Hofstede recognises that people are aware of the unpredictable nature of the future as part of human lives. The focus is how people in different cultures handle this nature in different ways. High uncertainty avoidance cultures tend not to tolerate ambiguity and risk. Rejecting new ideas or behaviours, individuals in high uncertainty avoidance cultures are characterised by their intention of reducing risk and ambiguity. They prefer security, known and stable situations, and stay within a comfort zone. Low uncertainty avoidance cultures, in contrast, are more willing to accept the fact that risks are unavoidable and that life must go on regardless of this. Ambiguity does not create the same level of anxiety or stress, compared to high uncertainty avoidance, when the individuals try new ideas or new products. In general, they are more willing to take risk and to tolerate deviance from existing patterns.

Masculinity is "a situation in which the dominant values in society are success, money, and things" (Hofstede, 1980, pp. 419-420). At the other end of the continuum is femininity, a term used to describe "a situation in which the dominant values in society are caring for others and the quality of life" (Hofstede, 1980, p. 420). Masculinity is concerned with tough traits such as assertiveness, achievement, competition, authority, caring less about the welfare of others, and performance. People in masculinity cultures tend to be more possession-oriented. An empirical study found that they own more expensive watches and clothing (Smith, Dugan, Peterson, & Leung,

1998). Feminine cultures, on the other hand, are relationship oriented. People in feminine cultures tend to emphasise the importance of cooperation, a friendly atmosphere, quality of life, and people. Conflicts are less likely to occur.

Impact of Culture on Perceived Service Quality

In service industries, service providers and customers interact extensively in economic activities. It is mainly due to the unique natures of services; namely, intangibility, inseparability, heterogeneity and perishability (Wong & Merrilees, 2009; Zeithaml, Parasuraman, & Berry, 1985). Contrary to product marketing, wherein the focal point is a product, an exchange in a service industry relies more on human delivery. Service marketers need to take pre-emptive and adjustment actions to position their services, in terms of service quality, that are perceived by their target customers matching their characteristics Imrie, Cadogan, & McNaughton, 2002). Culture's influence comes into play at this stage because of the human involvement in providing services and perceiving service quality. While service quality measurement instruments such as SERVQUAL and SERVPERF are being developed and refined, academics have called for studies examining the potential impacts of cultural influences on service quality (Anderson & Fornell, 1994; Dedic & Pavlovic, 2011).

One early attempt to understand the impacts of culture on service quality is the conceptual paper proposed by Malhotra, Ulgado, Agarwal, and Baalbaki (1994). They hypothesised that there were differences between developed and developing countries in terms of service quality dimensions and external factors. However, the major limitation of this chapter is the lack of empirical evidence. Winsted (1997), in an empirical study, found that the U.S. and Japanese cultures from the perspective of service encounter were significantly different. Nevertheless, her work was critiqued as not rendering a theoretical framework about culture and service encounter satisfaction (Mattila, 1999). Mattila (1999) examined the impact of culture on customer evaluations of luxury hotels. It was found that Asian and Western customers were different in terms of choosing personalised service and pleasant physical environment. The Western customers tend to rely on the tangible cues from the physical environment and rate the hedonic dimension of the consumption experience higher than their Asian counterparts.

The major limitation of Mattila's study lies in the fact that the Western and Asian samples are not well defined. Within Western countries, customers in the USA are very different from German customers. Thus, the study in fact used the U.S. customers as a proxy indicator of western customers. A more recent empirical study of Ladhari, Pons, Bressolles and Zins (2011) established that the Canadians and French are different in perceiving bank service quality. Similar to Mattila's (1999) work, the sample of their study is limited to only a handful of cultural backgrounds. A more comprehensive study was done by Crotts and Erdmann (2000), who examined consumers' evaluation of travel services from passengers of five different countries; namely, Brazil, Germany, Japan, Taiwan, and the UK. The passengers were classified into high, medium and low groups based on Hofstede's (1980) cultural dimensions. The results show that these three groups are statistically significantly different, except in one aspect: departure time.

While all these studies shed light on the cultural impacts on consumer behaviour, there is a lack of comprehensive, large scale study of the impacts of various cultures on service quality assessment. Most of the existing literature, except for the Crotts and Erdmann (2000) study, use a correlational data analysis method with the consequence of not being able to identify exactly which items within the dimensions of service quality are different among various cultures. In addition, there is little empirical evidence as to how one's culture influences service quality assessment in a global higher education context. This research proposes to fill this gap.

RESEARCH HYPOTHESES

Impact of Power Distance on Perceived Service Quality

Power distance mirrors how a culture deals with inequality. Cultures with high power distance have more respect for authority because they believe that power and authority are facts of life (Hofstede, 1991). Consequently, students classified as high power distance culture are more likely to tolerate sub-standard service quality provided by service providers. Their cultural background emphasises that obedience to authority such as academic and non-academic staff is anticipated; and teachers can be acceptably autocratic. On the contrary, students classified as low power distance culture tend to respect individuality with the consequence of accentuating decisions. Expecting autonomy in the service process, they expect the university to deliver good service quality in such areas as learning experience, physical facilities, and academic support. Due to cultural background differences in terms of power distance, students may have very different service quality perceptions about the same service provisions. Thus,

H1: With respect to service quality perception, students with high power distance cultures are different to those with low power distance cultures.

Impact of Individualism/Collectivism on Perceived Service Quality

The dimension of individualism or collectivism is concerned with how close the ties are between individuals within a given culture. People with a high level of individualistic culture tend to be more concerned with themselves and make decisions based on their own needs (Hofstede, 1991). They possess greater self-confidence, self-drive, and self-responsibility principles, and they demand others to be efficient and are more demanding than people are in collectivist cultures (Furrer, et al., 2000). Having high expectations on service quality and expecting service providers to deliver services right, they have low tolerance on below-par services. Collectivistic cultures, on the other hand, emphasise harmony within a group. Customers with high collectivistic cultures are more likely to blend in and avoid conflict. They opt not to express dissatisfaction of service quality that is not up to their expectations because it may create conflict with the group. Owing to different cultural backgrounds in terms of power distance, students may perceive the same service quality differently. Thus,

H2: With respect to service quality perceptions, students with high individualistic cultures are different to those with low individualistic cultures.

Impact of Uncertainty Avoidance on Perceived Service Quality

This cultural dimension centres on how cultures deal with uncertainty. High uncertainty avoidance cultures are less tolerant of unusual ideas, as they prefer specific details. Customers with high uncertainty avoidance cultures would use tangible cues as a proxy of service quality (Donthu & Boonghee, 1998). Used as a means of reducing risk, physical facilities such as academic buildings, campus environment, and library setups are visible evidence and indicators of service quality. Timely feedbacks and more personal contacts can be considered as factors that can minimise risk and lessen ambiguity with the consequence of signalling service quality. In contrast, low uncertainty avoidance cultures tend to accept difference and deviance. Customers with this cultural background are less unlikely to rely on physical facilities as the surrogates of service quality. In general, the cultural differences in uncertainty avoidance create dissimilar perceptions with regard to service quality. Thus,

H3: With respect to service quality perception,students with high uncertainty avoidance cultures are different to those with low uncertainty avoidance cultures.

Impact of Masculinity/Femininity on Perceived Service Quality

This cultural dimension focuses on the extent to which a society emphasises achievement on the one hand, and nurture and caring on the other. Masculine and feminine cultures can be considered as having "tough" and "tender" values, respectively (Schumann et al., 2010). Customers with masculinity cultures tend to perceive big and fast things as beautiful (Hofstede, 1991). As a result, service quality is consideredgood when physical buildings and set-ups are splendid. The same is true when feedback is fast and problems can be solved in a short period of time. Contrary to masculine cultures, feminine cultures stress sympathy for the weak, and perceive small and slow things as beautiful. Customers classified with feminine cultures have a tendency to cooperate with others and try to create a sociable and pleasant learning environment. It is suggested that even the gender of service providers can generate different service quality perceptions (Furrer, et al., 2000). The orientations of masculine and feminine cultures possess such big differences. Thus,

H4: With respect to service quality perception,students with masculinity cultures are different to those with feminine cultures.

CONSTRUCT DEVELOPMENT

The construct development process followed the current literature and focus group findings. Three focus group discussions were conducted at the Rockhampton campus of CQU to get more insights about perceived service quality. A description of the focus groups technique can be in found the research method section.

Relevant literature describes service quality as a set of satisfying features (Johnson & Winchell, 1988). The focus group findings, however, reveal that perceived service quality is a cognitive process of quality assessment, meaning that service quality assessment is a psychological result of perception, learning, reasoning and understanding of the service attributes. In this context, one respondent stated that:

I think we add–up the issues like recent experience, present performance and our interests in a subconscious manner....

In regards to critical service quality aspects, the focus group findings reveal three critical aspects--namely academic, administrative, and facilities. Academic service quality refers to those service attributes that provide core academic values including teaching quality and ability, course development, and teacher–student relationships. The following are some specific quotes:

To me the delivery of lecture should be good and lecturers should be interactive, so that I can understand what I am learning.

I think the quality of lecturers and how entertaining they are is most important. The lecture should not be boring, and after lecture availability is also important.

...they should have research expertise and intellectual capacity to conduct research and supervise the research students.

The academic activities in a university context are the core values. The academic aspect of perceived service quality as evidenced from focus group findings is consistent with the current literature (Abdullah, 2005, 2006a, 2006b, 2006c; Angell, et al., 2008; Gatfield, et al., 1999). The current empirical support further intensifies the essential role of academic aspect in a value-laden university context.

Administrative service quality has similar importance in overall assessment of service quality in the context of a higher education. Administrative service quality refers to those service attributes that provide support services for smooth functioning of academic activities. This may include skills and abilities of the administrative and support staff and their relationships with students. A shortfall in administrative service quality may result in poor evaluation of overall service quality assessment. As stated by respondents:

Sometimes staff takes time to reply to our query, and send us the common web links to search instead of addressing the queries. They should know what they are doing.

...student recruitment procedures, overall people and process of delivery are also vital as quality aspects"

The findings reveal that a customised and timely reply to a query, as well as assistance in regards to admission and relevant administrative activities, could play a positive role in perceived quality evaluations. In the higher education service quality literature, most studies find aspects (or dimensions) concerning academic activities (Rojas-Mendez et al., 2009; Angell et al., 2008; Gatfield et al., 1999). Although some studies (Abdullah 2005; 2006a; 2006b; 2006c) find a non-academic aspect of perceived service quality, the non-academic aspect in those studies combines administrative and academic support. The current study finds a separate aspect--administrative aspect--as one of the core aspects of perceived quality evaluation. The empirical findings of this study state that administrative support service quality is equally important for overall assessment of service quality.

Facilities service quality refers to those service attributes that are required to create a competitive higher education environment. Students refer to facilities service quality as library facilities, entertainment facilities, career counselling, transport facilities, dining facilities, access to computer and other facilities including access to workshops, seminars and conferences. The following are some direct quotes:

...of course the critical aspects are library facilties and then is career counselling.

I face specific problem with transport services.

We do not have a good dining facility here.

The other important issues are whether the university holds workshops and invites renowned people to deliver speeches.

...accessibility to entertainment centres and resources.

Current literature (LeBlanc & Nguyen, 1997; Kwan & Ng, 1999) finds "access to facilities" as a dimension of perceived service quality using factor analysis. Thus, the focus group findings of this study are also consistent with the current literature. Overall, the three critical aspects of service quality, academic, administrative and facilities are related to specific service attributes of a university that students encounter during their study. Finally, the operationalisation of the service quality construct includes seven items from Abdullah (2006c), four items from Fornell et al. (1996), one item from Cronin and Taylor (1992), seven items from Sultan and Wong (2010a), and seven items from the focus group findings. All the items measuring the three dimensions of service quality are listed in Appendix A.

RESEARCH METHOD

The present study adopts methodological triangulation, where both qualitative and quantitative research methods were employed. Methodological triangulation has been receiving growing interest in marketing research for its contribution to knowledge development (see, for example, Dahlstrom, Nygaard, & Crosno, 2008; Freling & Forbes, 2005; Stavros & Westberg, 2009). The major benefit of incorporating both approaches into the research method is that the weakness of one approach is compensated for by the strengths of the other.

Qualitative Research Method

This research employed a focus group technique because this technique provides flexibility, direct interaction, large amount of data, and is user friendly, easy to understand, and time and cost effective (Stewart, Shamdasani, & Rook, 2007). Although there is no rule of thumb about the number of members in a focus group, one study suggested that "a group consisting of 5–10 respondents is appropriate" (Krueger & Casey, 2000, p. 10), Literature suggests that several (3–4) groups are convened depending on distinct population segments (Morgan, 1988; Stewart, et al., 2007). In this research, three focus group discussions were held with 19 full-time students studying at the CQU, Rockhampton, Australia, using convenience and purposive sampling techniques following the suggestions of the current studies (Babbie, 2007; Brown, Varley, & Pal, 2009; Oldfield & Baron, 2000; Punch, 2005). Table 2 shows the demographic profiles of these students. Content analyses procedures were followed to analyse the focus group data to find the key themes of perceived service quality and relevant indicators of the respective themes following the suggestions of the studies (Krippendorff, 2004; Neuendorf, 2005; Sarantakos, 1997).

Quantitative Research Method

The scale development process followed the suggestion of (Churchill, 1979), and included 26 items in, the final survey. The items were validated through expert opinion. The expert panel included two senior academics experienced in qualitative and quantitative research methods in marketing, and one senior practitioner from the marketing division, CQU.

An online click–only survey link was sent to all the student population of CQU who were studying at one of its ten campuses in Australia. Thus, a random technique was adopted (Bethlehem, 2010; Bryman & Bell, 2007). The online questionnaire is methodologically and financially appealing to those who study and work with student populations. Although an online survey increases the likelihood of participation compared to paper surveys and its processing fees are usually lower, the online survey receives low response rates in practice (Sax, Gilmartin, & Bryant, 2003). However, owing to a "required completion answer" constraint, there was no missing data. The incomplete cases and the cases having less than six months of studying experience were deleted. This resulted in 227 usable questionnaires. The layout design of the online survey questionnaire followed the suggestions of Dillman, Smyth, & Christian, 2009.

To make data analysis manageable, we followed Crotts and Erdmann's (2000) research approach to classify students with various cultural backgrounds. Based on their nationalities, students were divided into three categories--namely high, medium, and low in terms of the four cultural dimensions. Note that there is no low masculinity culture in the 227 responses. Table 3 depicts these three categories by nations.

In the next stage, the data set was analysed statistically in order to establish valid and reliable scales. First, the Exploratory Factor Analysis (EFA) was performed, followed by reliability tests, in order to find dimensions or factors of perceived

Table 2. Demographics of the respondents

No	Age	Gender	Nationality	Level of Study	Program of Study	Duration of Studyat the CQU
R1.	19	Female	Japan	Undergraduate	Arts	07 Months
R2.	20	Male	Australia	Undergraduate	Information Tech	10 Months
R3.	20	Male	Australia	Undergraduate	Business Studies	09 Months
R4.	21	Male	Australia	Undergraduate	Business Studies	09 Months
R5.	21	Male	Australia	Undergraduate	Information Tech	10 Months
R6.	26	Male	Australia	Postgraduate	Business Studies	07 Months
R7.	26	Male	China	Postgraduate	Business Studies	07 Months
R8.	26	Male	China	Postgraduate	Business Studies	07 Months
R9.	27	Male	India	Postgraduate	Business Studies	07 Months
R10.	27	Male	India	Postgraduate	Business Studies	07 Months
R11.	27	Male	India	Postgraduate	Business Studies	07 Months
R12.	33	Female	Singapore	Postgraduate	Business Studies	07 Months
R13.	34	Female	Australia	Postgraduate	Business Studies	07 Months
R14.	33	Female	Bangladesh	Doctoral	Education	06 Months
R15.	34	Male	Bangladesh	Doctoral	Accounting	07 Months
R16.	34	Male	Pakistan	Doctoral	Law	07 Months
R17.	38	Male	Botswana	Doctoral	Accounting	>03 years
R18.	38	Female	China	Doctoral	Information Tech	>01 year
R19.	38	Male	Pakistan	Doctoral	Information Tech	>03 years

service quality. Second, convergent and discriminant validity were established following the suggestions of the extant literature (Hair, Black, Babin, & Anderson, 2010; O'Leary-Kelly & Vokurka, 1998). Finally, the Analysis of Variance (ANOVA) test and t-test (only for the masculinity dimension) were conducted to determine cultural differences in assessing service quality.

DATA ANALYSIS

Respondents represent a variety of nationalities and gender. Details of the respondent characteristics are shown in Table 4. The respondents are skewed towards Australian students. About 78% of respondents are from Australia and 11% from India. The results also reveal more female students (72%) replied to the survey than their male counterparts (28%).

The potential impacts of non-response bias were examined by comparing early respondents with late respondents; a method proposed by Armstrong and Overton (1997). No statistically significant differences were found. Both confirmatory and exploratory analyses were used to determine the discriminant validity of the items. Confirmatory factor analysis was undertaken with structural equation modeling to examine the suggested three service quality dimensions.

After deleting three items on academic service quality, four on administrative service quality, and one on physical facilities service quality; a measurement model achieved satisfactory results $\chi^2(132) = 417.72$, $p < .001$; GFI = .92; NFI = .94; RMSEA = .06. An exploratory factor analysis using principle component analysis with varimax rotation method was done to further study the discriminant validity of the items. As the rotated

Table 3. Four cultural dimensions by country

Nationality	Power Distance	Individualism	Uncertainty Avoidance	Masculinity
Australia	Low	High	Medium	High
China	High	Low	Low	High
India	High	Medium	Low	Medium
Indonesia	High	Low	Medium	Medium
Japan	Medium	Medium	High	High
Kenya	Medium	Low	Medium	Medium
Malaysia	High	Low	Low	Medium
New Zealand	Low	High	Medium	Medium
Pakistan	Low	High	Medium	High
South Africa	Medium	High	Medium	Medium
United Kingdom	Low	High	Medium	High

Source: adapted from Hofstede (1980)

component matrix in Table 5 demonstrates, the items clearly form three distinctive dimensions.

Table 4. Description of the samples by gender and nationality

Gender	Frequency	Percent
Female	163	71.8
Male	64	28.2
Total	227	100
Nationality		
Australia	177	78
China	6	2.6
India	25	11
Indonesia	2	.9
Japan	2	.9
Kenya	1	.4
Malaysia	1	.4
New Zealand	1	.4
Pakistan	4	1.8
South Africa	5	2.2
United Kingdom	6	2.6
Total	227	101.2*
*more than 100 due to decimals rounding up		

Reliability of the items was tested with Cronbach Alpha test. As shown in Table 6, all coefficient alphas are well above the 0.70 suggested cut-off level (Francis, 2001; Robinson, Shaver, & Wrightsman, 1991). Item-to-total correlations are also above the recommended 0.20 level (Nunnally & Bernstein, 1994).

ANOVA tests and independent sample t-test were performed to compare the three dimensions of perceived service quality in terms of the four cultural dimensions. Table 7 shows the results of the tests.

DISCUSSION

In general, the findings support the four hypotheses. The results indicate items with statistically significant and statistically insignificant differences. The results from the perspective of the four cultural dimensions provide insights on the differences amongst the various cultural backgrounds in relation to perceived service quality. In terms of the power distance dimension, students from low power distance cultures have higher perceived administrative service quality than the medium and high power distance cultures, whereas a

Table 5. Exploratory Factor Analysis Results

	Academic Service Quality	Administrative Service Quality	Physical Facilities ServiceQuality
SQ_1	.69		
SQ_2	.83		
SQ_5	.73		
SQ_6	.79		
SQ_7	.69		
SQ_24	.65		
SQ_8		.84	
SQ_9		.82	
SQ_10		.77	
SQ_11		.74	
SQ_13		.79	
SQ_27		.74	
SQ_17			.64
SQ_18			.71
SQ_19			.68
SQ_20			.69
SQ_21			.77
SQ_22			.55

high power distance cultural background leads to higher perceived physical facilities service quality than the medium and low categories. From the perspective of the individualistic dimension, students from high individualistic cultures perceive administrative service quality much higher than those from lower individualistic cultures (i.e., feminine culture). The uncertainty avoidance dimension shows that students from high uncertainty avoidance cultures have higher perceived values in physical facilities service quality than their medium and low uncertainty avoidance counterparts. In terms of masculinity, students from high masculinity cultures show higher perceived scores than the medium cultures in administrative service quality, and lower perceived scores in the physical facilities service quality.

From the service quality perspective, there are mixed findings. The insignificant results were found in academic service quality. Not even one item of academic service quality was found statistically significant in all four cultural dimensions, suggesting that students do not perceive any differences in academic service quality irrespective of their cultural backgrounds. Conversely, in administrative service quality, four out of six items were found statistically different in the power distance and masculinity dimensions; and all six

Table 6. Reliability test results

Factor/Item	*Coefficient Alpha Reliability*
Academic Service Quality	0.91
	Corrected correlation item-total
SQ_1	.72
SQ_2	.77
SQ_5	.72
SQ_6	.82
SQ_7	.75
SQ_24	.74
Administrative Service Quality	0.93
	Corrected correlation item-total
SQ_8	.83
SQ_9	.86
SQ_10	.80
SQ_11	.74
SQ_13	.80
SQ_27	.78
Physical Facilities Service Quality	0.82
	Corrected correlation item-total
SQ_17	.46
SQ_18	.63
SQ_19	.64
SQ_20	.59
SQ_21	.74
SQ_22	.49

Table 7. Results of ANOVA tests and Independent t-test

Power Distance					
	High	**Medium**	**Low**	**F**	**p-value**
Academic Service Quality					
SQ_1	5.52	5.13	5.63	1.245	.29
SQ_2	5.29	5.25	5.52	.79	.46
SQ_5	5.23	5.25	5.11	.15	.86
SQ_6	5.19	5.13	5.33	.28	.75
SQ_7	5.19	5.25	5.37	.34	.72
SQ_24	5.39	5.38	5.46	.73	.93
Administrative Service Quality					
SQ_8	5.42	5.25	5.88	3.58	.03*
SQ_9	5.39	4.88	4.8	4.50	.01**
SQ_10	5.16	5.00	5.66	3.88	.02*
SQ_11	5.55	4.88	5.56	1.36	.26
SQ_13	5.26	5.00	5.53	1.64	.20
SQ_27	5.52	4.88	5.72	2.95	.05*
Physical Facilities Service Quality					
SQ_17	5.74	5.25	5.30	1.72	.18
SQ_18	5.61	5.13	4.91	4.29	.02*
SQ_19	5.61	5.00	5.02	3.85	.02*
SQ_20	4.97	5.25	5.41	1.87	.16
SQ_21	5.19	5.25	5.03	.41	.66
SQ_22	5.10	5.25	5.23	.16	.85
Individualism					
	High	Medium	Low	F	p-value
Academic Service Quality					
SQ_1	5.63	5.64	5.08	2.12	.12
SQ_2	5.52	5.40	5.00	1.53	.22
SQ_5	5.12	5.40	4.85	.96	.39
SQ_6	5.32	5.36	4.92	.76	.47
SQ_7	5.37	5.32	4.92	.95	.39
SQ_24	5.46	5.56	5.08	.90	.41
Administrative Service Quality					
SQ_8	5.88	5.60	4.92	5.50	.01*
SQ_9	5.80	5.44	5.00	4.24	.02*
SQ_10	5.66	5.36	4.62	6.18	.00**
SQ_11	5.56	5.76	4.77	3.42	.04*
SQ_13	5.53	5.44	4.69	3.73	.03*
SQ_27	5.71	5.68	4.92	3.58	.03*

continued on following page

Table 7. Continued

Power Distance					
	High	Medium	Low	F	p-value
Physical Facilities Service Quality					
SQ_17	5.30	5.84	5.31	2.11	.12
SQ_18	4.92	5.68	5.15	4.27	.02*
SQ_19	5.01	5.76	5.08	5.04	.01*
SQ_20	5.41	5.24	4.62	2.84	.06
SQ_21	5.05	5.44	4.54	3.00	.05*
SQ_22	5.23	5.32	4.77	.97	.38
Uncertainty Avoidance					
	High	Medium	Low	F	p-value
Academic Service Quality					
SQ_1	5.50	5.59	5.67	.12	.89
SQ_2	5.50	5.48	5.47	.00	.99
SQ_5	5.50	5.09	5.33	.68	.51
SQ_6	5.00	5.28	5.44	.38	.69
SQ_7	5.00	5.35	5.36	.10	.91
SQ_24	6.00	5.42	5.56	.51	.60
Administrative Service Quality					
SQ_8	6.00	5.85	5.50	1.63	.20
SQ_9	5.50	5.75	5.56	.50	.61
SQ_10	5.50	5.62	5.31	1.22	.30
SQ_11	6.00	5.54	5.50	.18	.84
SQ_13	6.00	5.51	5.28	.91	.41
SQ_27	6.00	5.68	5.56	.31	.73
Physical Facilities Service Quality					
SQ_17	6.00	5.30	5.61	1.19	.31
SQ_18	5.50	4.91	5.56	4.30	.02*
SQ_19	5.50	4.99	5.61	4.80	.01*
SQ_20	5.50	5.39	5.08	1.03	.36
SQ_21	6.00	5.02	5.22	1.24	.29
SQ_22	5.50	5.20	5.28	.12	.88
Masculinity					
	High	Medium	Low	t-value	p-value
Academic Service Quality					
SQ_1	5.63	5.43	n.a.	1.16	.25
SQ_2	5.52	5.26	n.a.	1.33	.19
SQ_5	5.13	5.17	n.a.	.21	.84
SQ_6	5.31	5.26	n.a.	.26	.79

continued on following page

Table 7. Continued

Power Distance					
	High	**Medium**	**Low**	**F**	**p-value**
SQ_7	5.34	5.34	n.a.	.02	.98
SQ_24	5.46	5.34	n.a.	.61	.55
Administrative Service Quality					
SQ_8	5.86	5.40	n.a.	2.38	.02*
SQ_9	5.79	5.29	n.a.	2.55	.01*
SQ_10	5.66	5.06	n.a.	3.02	.00**
SQ_11	5.57	5.34	n.a.	1.08	.28
SQ_13	5.53	5.20	n.a.	1.80	.08
SQ_27	5.73	5.29	n.a.	2.35	.02*
Physical Facilities Service Quality					
SQ_17	5.31	5.60	n.a.	1.59	.12
SQ_18	4.96	5.34	n.a.	1.68	.09
SQ_19	5.02	5.51	n.a.	2.40	.02*
SQ_20	5.41	5.00	n.a.	1.86	.06
SQ_21	5.05	5.11	n.a.	.31	.75
SQ_22	5.21	5.23	n.a.	.09	.93
Notes: no respondent is from low masculine cultures. As a result, t-test was done for the masculinity dimension.					
*significant at .05 level; **significant at .01 level.					

items were different in the individualism dimension. However, no item was found different in the uncertainty avoidance dimension. Results for the physical facilities service quality are mixed. Two items in power distance, three in individualism, two in uncertainty and one in masculinity were found different.

This study has two major implications. These are categorized as the core aspects or dimensions of perceived service quality, and the cultural influence on the assessment of perceived service quality. In a university context, the empirical evidence of this study suggests students perceived service quality as three categories--namely academic, administrative, and physical facilities. These categories are related to specific attributes of the higher education institution that students encounter during their studies. Students perceive academic service quality as a set of teaching, lecturer's interest in solving academic issues, interactive and entertaining lectures, after–lecture availability for student consultation, and lecturers' intellectual ability and understanding of the course. While administrative service quality consists of courteous, helpful, skilled and active administrative staff keeping accurate academic records and responding to students' queries, physical facility service quality includes a set of location of the university, up-to-date classroom and lab facilities, library facilities, infrastructure facilities, and the scenic beauty of the university. These core dimensions of perceived service quality in a higher education context could generate valuable insights, especially, in regards to resource allocation. Although there is a current practice of student satisfaction survey at the end of a term which provides an indication of students' attitudes toward the course and the lecturer, a broader perspective of this survey could further provide important insights about these three dimensions of service quality in a higher education context.

The results suggest students' cultural backgrounds have a significant effect on perceptions of service quality, especially on *administrative* and *physical facilities* service quality. In contrast, the results suggest that international and domestic students as classified under each of the four dimensions of culture have no significant difference in perceptions of *academic* service quality. The key features of academic service quality across cultural dimensions and nations have equal importance to students. As an example, an Indian student from a high power distance culture, where power is more hierarchical and centralised, would not likely perceive *academic* service quality much differently than an Australian student from a low power distance culture, although the Indian student would likely perceive *administrative* service quality to be considerably lower than that noted by the Australian.

The results show that students from different cultural backgrounds perceive administrative and physical facilities services quality differently. For example, students with high individualism culture (e.g., Australia, United Kingdom, New Zealand, etc.) would expect to have greater personal attention from their staff. Personal greetings, attention, freedom and fairness could motivate these students. Conversely, group orientation, collective activities and group task could motivate Chinese, Japanese, Indonesian and Malaysian students. Thus, educational institutions should keep the key features of cultural dimensions in mind when allocating resources. In other words, understanding the right target market and allocating resources accordingly are vital for managers. Managers of multi-cultural and global institutions would be remiss if they focused solely on a particular set of programs for a set of students with homogeneous weights for each of the cultural dimensions.

CONCLUSION

A marketing approach to examine students' perceptions of service quality in the context of higher education can improve service functions, and attract and retain students in a global context. Ignoring the nature and importance of service quality is not advantageous for universities in the higher education industry, especially when the many students are coming to Australia from multiple countries with varying cultural norms.

This chapter is among the first attempts to examine the differences of cultural backgrounds with regard to service quality in the higher education context. The results show that there is no statistically significant difference among the four cultural dimensions with regard to perceived academic service quality. However, perceived administrative service quality is very different in individualistic culture, and to a lesser extent in high power distance and masculinity cultures. The findings of the physical facility service quality are varied. Statistically significant differences can be found in all four cultural dimensions.

It is recommended future research could investigate other education areas such as technical and community colleges. Since this study concentrates only on an Australia university, the findings from this study could be compared with studies in other countries so that the findings can be generalized. Moreover, new qualitative research could focus on exactly why certain cultures perceive service quality differently. In addition, it would be useful to study the moderating effect of reputation of universities to better detect the relationships between service quality and culture. Finally, the impacts of the fifth cultural dimension - time orientation - on higher education service quality need to be further examined empirically. Service quality in higher education is an important issue and is an ever changing area. More research is required to fully understand the dynamic of cultural influence in this area.

REFERENCES

Abdullah, F. (2005). HEdPERF versus SERVPERF: The quest for ideal measuring instrument of service quality in higher education sector. *Quality Assurance in Education*, *13*(4), 305–328. doi:10.1108/09684880510626584.

Abdullah, F. (2006a). Measuring service quality in higher education: HEdPERF versus SERVPERF. *Marketing Intelligence & Planning*, *24*(1), 31–47. doi:10.1108/02634500610641543.

Abdullah, F. (2006b). Measuring service quality in higher education: Three instruments compared. *International Journal of Research & Method in Education*, *29*(1), 71–89. doi:10.1080/01406720500537445.

Abdullah, F. (2006c). The development of HEdPERF: A new measuring instrument of service quality for the higher education sector. *International Journal of Consumer Studies*, *30*(6), 569–581. doi:10.1111/j.1470-6431.2005.00480.x.

Anderson, E. W., & Fornell, C. (1994). A customer satisfaction research prospectus. In Rust, R. T., & Oliver, R. L. (Eds.), *Service Quality: New Directions in Theory and Practice* (pp. 241–268). Thousand Oaks, CA: Sage. doi:10.4135/9781452229102.n11.

Angell, R. J., Heffernan, T. W., & Megicks, P. (2008). Service quality in postgraduate education. *Quality Assurance in Education*, *16*(3), 236–254. doi:10.1108/09684880810886259.

Armstrong, S. J., & Overton, T. S. (1977). Estimating nonresponse bias in mail surveys. *JMR, Journal of Marketing Research*, *14*(3), 396–402. doi:10.2307/3150783.

Babbie, E. (2007). *The Practice of Social Research*. Belmont, CA: Wadsworth.

Bethlehem, J. (2010). Selection Bias in Web Surveys. *International Statistical Review*, *78*(2), 161–188. doi:10.1111/j.1751-5823.2010.00112.x.

Bradley, D., Noonan, P., Nugent, H., & Scales, B. (2008). *Review of Australian Higher Education (E. a. W. R. Department of Education, Trans.)*. Canberra, Australia: Department of Education, Employment and Workplace Relations.

Brown, C., Varley, P., & Pal, J. (2009). University course selection and services marketing. *Marketing Intelligence & Planning*, *27*(3), 310–325. doi:10.1108/02634500910955227.

Bryman, A., & Bell, E. (2007). *Business Research Methods*. Oxford, UK: Oxford University Press.

Buttle, F. (1996). SERVQUAL: Review, critique, research agenda. *European Journal of Marketing*, *30*(1), 8–32. doi:10.1108/03090569610105762.

Churchill, G. A. (1979). A paradigm for developing better measures of marketing constructs. *Journal of Marketing*, *16*(2), 64–73.

Cronin, J., Brady, M., & Hult, G. (2000). Assessing the effect of quality, value, and customer satisfaction on consumer behavioral intentions in service environments. *Journal of Retailing*, *76*(2), 193–218. doi:10.1016/S0022-4359(00)00028-2.

Cronin, J., & Taylor, S. (1992). Measuring service quality: A re-examination and extension. *Journal of Marketing*, *56*(3), 55–68. doi:10.2307/1252296.

Cronin, J., & Taylor, S. (1994). SERVPERF versus SERVQUAL: Reconciling performance-based and perceptions-minus-expectations measurement of service quality. *Journal of Marketing*, *58*(1), 125–131. doi:10.2307/1252256.

Crotts, J. C., & Erdmann, R. (2000). Does national culture influence consumers' evaluation of travel services? A test of Hofstede's model of cross-cultural differences. *Managing Service Quality*, *10*(6), 410–419. doi:10.1108/09604520010351167.

Dahlstrom, R., Nygaard, A., & Crosno, J. (2008). Strategic, metric and methodological trends in marketing research and their implications for future theory and practice. *Journal of Marketing Theory and Practice*, *16*(2), 139–152. doi:10.2753/MTP1069-6679160204.

Dedic, G., & Pavlovic, D. K. (2011). A tale of two nations empirical examination of influence of national culture on perceived service quality. *International Journal of Management Cases*, *13*(3), 92–104.

Deshpande, R. (1983). Paradigms Lost: On Theory and Method in Research in Marketing. *Journal of Marketing*, *47*(Fall), 101–110. doi:10.2307/1251403.

Dillman, D. A., Smyth, J. D., & Christian, L. M. (2009). *Internet, Mail and Mixed-mode Surveys: The Tailored Design Method*. Hoboken, NJ: John Wiley & Sons.

Donthu, N., & Boonghee, Y. (1998). Cultural influences on servcie quality expectations. *Journal of Service Research*, *1*(2), 178–186. doi:10.1177/109467059800100207.

Francis, G. (2001). *Introduction to SPSS for Windows* (3rd ed.). Sydney, Australia: Pearson Education Australia.

Freling, T. H., & Forbes, L. (2005). An examination of brand personality through methodological triangulation. *Journal of Brand Management*, *13*(2), 148–162. doi:10.1057/palgrave.bm.2540254.

Furrer, O., & Liu, B. S. C., & shudharshan, D. (2000). The relationships between culture and service quality perceptions: Basis for cross-cultural market segmentation and resource allocation. *Journal of Service Research*, *2*(4), 355–371. doi:10.1177/109467050024004.

Gatfield, T., Barker, M., & Graham, P. (1999). Measuring Student Quality Variables and the Implications for Management Practices in Higher Education Institutions: An Australian and international student perspective. *Journal of Higher Education Policy and Management*, *21*(2), 239–252. doi:10.1080/1360080990210210.

Groeschel, S., & Doherty, L. (2000). Conceptualising culture. *Cross Cultural Management -. International Journal (Toronto, Ont.)*, *7*(4), 12–17.

Hair, J. F., Black, W. C., Babin, B. J., & Anderson, R. E. (2010). *Multivariate Data Analysis: A Global Perspective*. New York: Pearson Prentice Hall.

Hofstede, G. (1980). *Culture's consequence: International differences in work-related values*. Beverly Hills, CA: Sage.

Hofstede, G. (1991). *Cultures and Organizations: Software of the Mind*. London: McGraw-Hill.

Imrie, B. C., Cadogan, J. W., & McNaughton, R. (2002). The service quality construct on a global stage. *Managing Service Quality*, *12*(1), 10–18. doi:10.1108/09604520210415353.

Johnson, R., & Winchell, W. (1988). Educating for quality. *Quality Progress*, *2*(1), 48–50.

Jones, M. L. (2007). *Hofstede - Culturally questionable?* Paper presented at the Oxford Business & Economics Conference. Oxford, UK.

Krippendorff, K. (2004). *Content analysis: An introduction to its methodology*. London: Sage.

Krueger, R. A. A., & Casey, M. A. A. (2000). *Focus Groups: A Practical Guide for Applied Research*. London: Sage.

Kwan, P. Y. K., & Ng, P. W. K. (1999). Quality indicators in higher education: Comparing Hong Kong and China's students. *Managerial Auditing Journal*, *14*, 20–27. doi:10.1108/02686909910245964.

Ladhari, R., Pons, F., Bressolles, G., & Zins, M. (2011). Culture and personal values: How they influence perceived service quality. *Journal of Business Research*, *64*, 951–957. doi:10.1016/j.jbusres.2010.11.017.

Laroche, M., Ueltschy, L. C., Abe, S., Cleveland, M., & Yannopoulos, P. P. (2004). Service quality perceptions and customer satisfaction: Evaluating the role of culture. *Journal of International Marketing*, *12*(3), 58–85. doi:10.1509/jimk.12.3.58.38100.

LeBlanc, G., & Nguyen, N. (1997). Searching for excellence in business education: An exploratory study of customer impressions of service quality. *International Journal of Educational Management*, *11*(2), 72–79. doi:10.1108/09513549710163961.

Lewis, B. R. (1989). Quality in the service sector-a review. *International Journal of Bank Marketing*, *7*(5), 4–12. doi:10.1108/02652328910134590.

Malhotra, N. K., Ulgado, F. M., Agarwal, J., & Baalbaki, I. B. (1994). International Services Marketing: A Comparative Evaluation of the Dimensions of Service Quality between Developed and Developing Countries. *International Marketing Review*, *11*(2), 5–15. doi:10.1108/02651339410061937.

Mattila, A. S. (1999). The role of culture in the service evaluation processes. *Journal of Service Research*, *1*(3), 250–261. doi:10.1177/109467059913006.

Moore, C. D. (1987). Outclass the competition with service distinction. *Mortgage Banking*, *47*(11), 24–32.

Morgan, D. L. (1988). *Focus groups as qualitative research*. London: Sage.

Neuendorf, K. A. (2005). *The Content Analysis Guidebook*. London: Sage.

Nunnally, J. C., & Bernstein, I. H. (1994). *Psychometric Theory* (3rd ed.). New York: McGraw Hill.

O'Leary-Kelly, S. W., & Vokurka, R. J. (1998). The empirical assessment of construct validity. *Journal of Operations Management*, *16*(4), 387–405. doi:10.1016/S0272-6963(98)00020-5.

Oldfield, B., & Baron, S. (2000). Student perceptions of service quality in a UK university business and management faculty. *Quality Assurance in Education*, *8*(2), 85–95. doi:10.1108/09684880010325600.

Parasuraman, A., Zeithaml, V. A., & Berry, L. L. (1985). A conceptual model of service quality and its implications for future research. *Journal of Marketing*, *49*(4), 41–50. doi:10.2307/1251430.

Parasuraman, A., Zeithaml, V. A., & Berry, L. L. (1988). SERVQUAL: A multiple-item scale for measuring consumer perceptions of service quality. *Journal of Retailing*, *64*(1), 12–40.

Parasuraman, A., Zeithaml, V. A., & Berry, L. L. (1994). Reassessment of expectations as a comparison standard in measuring service quality - Implications for further research. *Journal of Marketing*, *58*(1), 111–124. doi:10.2307/1252255.

Pizam, A., & Reichel, A. (1997). Nationality versus industry cultures: Which has greater effect on managerial behaviour? *International Journal of Hospitality Management*, *16*(2), 127–145. doi:10.1016/S0278-4319(97)00001-7.

Punch, K. F. (2005). *Introduction to Social Research: Quantitative and Qualitative Approaches*. London: Sage.

Robinson, J. P., Shaver, P. R., & Wrightsman, L. S. (1991). Criteria for scale selection and evaluation. In Robinson, J. P., Shaver, P. R., & Wrightsman, L. S. (Eds.), *Measures of Personality and Social Psychological Attitudes*. San Diego, CA: Academic Press.

Sarantakos, S. (1997). *Social Research*. Melbourne, Australia: Macmillan Education Australia Pty Ltd..

Sax, L. J., Gilmartin, S. K., & Bryant, A. N. (2003). Assessing response rates and non-response bias in web and paper surveys. *Research in Higher Education*, *44*(4), 409–432. doi:10.1023/A:1024232915870.

Schumann, J. H., Wangenheim, F., Stringfellow, A., Yang, Z., Blazevic, V., & Praxmarer, S. et al. (2010). Cross-cultural differences in the effect of received word-of-mouth referral in relational service exchange. *Journal of International Marketing*, *18*(3), 62–80. doi:10.1509/jimk.18.3.62.

Smith, P. B., Dugan, S., Peterson, M. F., & Leung, K. (1998). Individualism: Collectivism and the handling of disagreement - A 23 country study. *International Journal of Intercultural Relations*, *22*(3), 351–367. doi:10.1016/S0147-1767(98)00012-1.

Sodergaard, M. (1994). Hofstede's consequences: A study of reviews, citations and replications. *Organization Studies*, *15*(3), 447–456. doi:10.1177/017084069401500307.

Stavros, C., & Westberg, K. (2009). Using triangulation and multiple case studies to advance relationship marketing theory. *Qualitative market research. International Journal (Toronto, Ont.)*, *12*(3), 307–320.

Steenkamp, J. E. M. (2001). The role of national culture in international marketing research. *International Marketing Review*, *18*(1), 30–44. doi:10.1108/02651330110381970.

Stewart, D. W., Shamdasani, P. N., & Rook, D. W. (2007). *Focus groups: Theory and practice*. London: Sage.

Sultan, P., & Wong, H. Y. (2010a). Performance-based service quality model: An empirical study on Japanese universities. *Quality Assurance in Education*, *18*(2), 126–143. doi:10.1108/09684881011035349.

Sultan, P., & Wong, H. Y. (2011). Service quality in a higher education context: Antecedents and dimensions. *International Review of Business Research Papers*, *7*(2), 11–20.

Trandis, H., Bontempo, R., & Villareal, M. (1988). Individualism and collectivism: Cross-cultural perspectives on self-group relationships. *Journal of Personality and Social Psychology*, *54*(2), 323–338. doi:10.1037/0022-3514.54.2.323.

Trompenaars, F. (1994). *Riding the Waves of Culture*. New York: Irwin.

Winsted, K. F. (1997). The service experience in two cultures: A behavioral perspective. *Journal of Retailing*, *73*(3), 337–360. doi:10.1016/S0022-4359(97)90022-1.

Wong, H. Y., & Merrilees, B. (2009). Service versus product brands: Understanding international adaptation. *Journal of International Business and Entrepreneurship Development*, *4*(3), 231–242. doi:10.1504/JIBED.2009.029014.

Zeithaml, V. A., Berry, L. L., & Parasuraman, A. (1996). The behavioral consequences of service quality. *Journal of Marketing*, *60*(2), 31–46. doi:10.2307/1251929.

Zeithaml, V. A., Parasuraman, A., & Berry, L. L. (1985). Problems and strategies in service marketing. *Journal of Marketing*, *49*(2), 33–46. doi:10.2307/1251563.

APPENDIX

Table 8.

Academic Service Quality
SQ_1 I find that academics at this University are knowledgeable
SQ_2 Lecturers show sincere interest in solving my academic problems
SQ_3 My academic performance is recorded correctly (deleted after factor analysis)
SQ_4 Lecturers provide feedback about my progress (deleted after factor analysis)
SQ_5 I receive adequate time for consultation with lecturers
SQ_6 I find that lecturers are skilled in teaching
SQ_7 The academic backgrounds of the lecturers are excellent
SQ_24 My overall evaluation of the service quality provided by the teaching staff of this University is good
SQ_26 The teaching staff meet my requirements (deleted after factor analysis)
Administrative Service Quality
SQ_8 I find that the administrative staff is courteous
SQ_9 I find that the administrative staff is prompt to provide service
SQ_10 I find that the administrative staff keeps accurate records
SQ_11 The admission department of this University is very helpful
SQ_12 I find that the University's career counselling service is very helpful (deleted afterfactor analysis)
SQ_13 I find that the administrative staff is skilled
SQ_14 The overall environment of this University is friendly (deleted after factor analysis)
SQ_23 My overall evaluation of quality with regard to support functions of this University isgood (deleted after factor analysis)
SQ_25 My overall evaluation of the service quality provided by the administrative staff of this University is good (deleted after factor analysis)
SQ_27 The administrative staff meet my requirements
Physical Facilities Service Quality
SQ_15 I find that classroom learning is very practical (deleted after factor analysis)
SQ_17 The location of the University is ideal
SQ_18 I find that this University has up-to-date equipment
SQ_19 I find that the classroom facilities are adequate
SQ_20 I find that the library facilities are adequate
SQ_21 I find that this University has good infrastructure
SQ_22 I find that the scenic beauty of this University is excellent

Chapter 25
Quality Management:
An Evolutionary Cross-Cultural Perspective

Alessandra Vecchi
University of London Arts, England

Louis Brennan
Trinity College Dublin, Ireland

ABSTRACT

The purpose of this chapter is to address the extent to which quality management is "culture-specific." The chapter presents the results of a survey administered across 21 countries that seeks to examine quality priorities and practices by adopting the Global Leadership and Organizational Behaviour Effectiveness (GLOBE) framework (House et al., 2004). Drawing on previous research (Vecchi & Brennan, 2011), data was collected in 2009 as part of the fifth iteration of the International Manufacturing Strategy Survey (IMSS). The methodology involved the use of a self-administered questionnaire to director/head of operations/manufacturing in best practice firms within the sector of firms classified by ISIC codes (rev.3.1) Divisions 28-35. From this study, it emerges that adopting the GLOBE framework provides an invaluable insight into understanding quality management across countries. While some previous research portrays quality management as a comprehensive management paradigm with elements and relationships that transcend cultural and national boundaries, the current study provides evidence that the adoption of certain quality practices across different countries can follow distinctive patterns.

INTRODUCTION

Since the 1990s, many quality models have been widely adopted by firms, such as the Deming Prize in Japan, the Malcolm Baldrige National Quality Award in the USA, and the European Quality Award in Europe as frameworks for implementing Total Quality Management (TQM). The widespread assumption is that these are operational frameworks that reproduce TQM by capturing its main constituent parts and replicate its core ideas in a clear and accessible language (Cua et al., 2001). However, TQM is an approach to management embracing both social ("soft TQM") and techni-

DOI: 10.4018/978-1-4666-3966-9.ch025

cal dimensions ("hard TQM"). The social aspect focuses on human resource management and emphasises leadership, teamwork, training, and employee involvement. The technical dimension reflects an orientation toward improving production methods and operations and seeks, through a systematic process, to make possible the constant improvement of goods and services to the customers. The management of these two sets of issues cannot be performed in isolation. Soft and hard TQM should be interrelated and mutually support each other reflecting the holistic character of TQM initiatives (Anwar & Jabnoun, 2006).

The commonly cited problems in the implementation of manufacturing programs are those related to the soft dimension. In particular, cultural resistance to change, lack of training and education (Crawford et al., 1988), lack of coordination of the different departments, and confusion in the relationship between manufacturing subsystems (Safayeni et al., 1991) have been portrayed as being detrimental to the successful implementation of manufacturing programs. These studies provide evidence of the importance of the institution of common practices based on a shared understanding that will facilitate the successful implementation of any TQM initiative. Moreover, according to socio-technical systems theory the joint optimization of practices that are socially and technically oriented should lead to good performance (Emery, 1990). For example, Rehder (1989) argues for the importance of building manufacturing competitiveness upon the integration and coordination of strategy, structure, culture, and human resource subsystems within a complex, changing environment. He shows that the concept of a balanced socio-technical system is reflected in all subsystems of successful Japanese transplants. Given the increasing importance of TQM and the close interrelation between its social and technical dimensions managers need to understand how and what dimensions of national culture influence operation decisions and whether these are likely to change over time.

Previous work on quality management attempts to address the issue of convergence or divergence of quality practices across countries by adopting Hofstede's national cultural framework. While existing research mainly adopts Hofstede's dimensions of national culture, GLOBE captures more comprehensively and less ambiguously the elements of national culture. Drawing on our previous work (Vecchi & Brenan, 2011) this paper thus examines quality management by using GLOBE's nine cultural dimensions (House et al., 2004). The purpose of this study is to address the extent to which quality management is "culture-specific" from an evolutionary perspective (Zbaracki, 1998; Ravichandram, 2000).

To this end, we explore the extent to which the different dimensions of national culture influence quality management over time in a global context. Specifically, we consider whether over a timeframe of three years (2006-2009) there is a difference in quality priorities and practices across national cultures followed by a consideration of the managerial implications of the results of our study. The chapter is organised as follows. In Section 2, we provide an overview of the literature of quality management from an evolutionary cross-cultural perspective. In Section 3, we explain national culture and explore its relationship to TQM by contextualising several hypotheses. In Section 4, the methodology is described, while in Section 5 we present the data analysis and the main findings. The final section presents the main conclusions of this study and the managerial implications arising from the findings.

QUALITY MANAGEMENT RESEARCH FROM AN EVOLUTIONARY CROSS-CULTURAL PERSPECTIVE

A significant strand of the literature seeks to assess the diversity of quality practices amongst countries. The increased complexity of today's business environment and heightened international competition make it necessary for firms to improve quality performance by aligning their quality practices in their attempt to capitalise on all possible traditional and non-traditional sources of competitive advantage. In line with this trend, the literature has devoted considerable attention to the issue of quality management and this includes a series of empirical studies of quality management across countries which report contrasting conclusions. Traditionally in the field of comparative management research, there have been three main approaches: the empirical work has been aimed towards testing the "convergence" hypothesis (Form, 1979), the "divergence" hypothesis (Child & Kieser, 1979) and the "culture-specific" hypothesis (Hofstede, 1980).

The "Convergence" Hypothesis

The "convergence" hypothesis (Form, 1979) asserts that learning will lead managers from different cultures to adopt the same efficient management practices. Competitive pressures will eliminate those who resist convergence. In addition with the increased dissemination of information about best quality practices around the world, one would expect similarities across countries where each country's respondents would be expected to embrace the same approach as their overseas counterparts. Over time, numerous studies have attempted to substantiate the evidence for convergence in the field of quality management research (Zhao et al., 1995; Abdul-Aziz et al., 2000; Chin et al., 2002; Ismail & Ebrahimpour, 2003; Rungtusanatham et al., 2005).

The "Divergence" Hypothesis

The "divergence" hypothesis (Child & Kieser, 1979) questions the universal applicability of any standardised business practice. According to this perspective, any organisational practice must be adapted to the national context to maximize its effectiveness. The different extent to which organisational practices are adapted to the national context results in the observed divergence of practices across nations. In the field of quality management research several studies have attempted to substantiate the evidence for the "divergence" and within this perspective the role of culture is acknowledged but often plays a very marginal role (Raghunathan et al., 1997; Subba Rao et al., 1997; Corbett et al., 1998; Tata et al., 2000).

The "Culture-Specific" Hypothesis

Similarly to the "divergence hypothesis", the "culture-specific" argument (Hofstede, 1980) shares the view that organisational practices must be adapted to the national context to maximize their effectiveness. While the divergence hypothesis considers all possible factors (political, economic, social, legal, etc) which might cause differences in the implementation of management practices, the culture specific hypothesis restricts itself to explaining difference solely in terms of culture. In particular, this view contends that even if managers located in different societies face similar imperatives for change, deeply embedded cultural factors will still affect the way managers approach quality and react to the need for change. In particular, Hofstede identifies four main cultural dimensions; namely, power distance, individualism, uncertainty avoidance, and masculinity (Hofstede, 1980). Although there is extensive evidence on how these cultural dimensions affect specific organisational outcomes (Garg & Ma, 2005; Wacker & Sprague, 1998; Flynn & Saladin, 2006; Snell & Hui, 2000), there has been limited effort dedicated to the development of a comprehensive framework to assess the impact of these cultural dimensions on quality management (Krosolid, 1999; Sousa-Poza et al., 2000; Lagrosen, 2002; Lagrosen, 2003; Kyoon Yoo et al., 2005).

By adopting Hofstede's model, Garg and Ma (2005) have attempted to link national culture to organisational performance. Their findings show there are significant differences in management systems, leadership and style within the national cultures of three types of organisations (foreign-owned, joint ventures, and Chinese-owned and operated firms). In relation to the effects of culture on the use of information within organisations, Wacker and Sprague (1998) attribute great importance to masculinity. In particular, they found that the type of information used to support decision making in masculine national cultures was dependent on its expected effectiveness in gaining advantage over competitors. By contrast, feminine countries tend to use information more extensively to support decision making. Flynn and Saladin (2006) show that while in countries characterised by high power distance, power as well as decision-making tend to be centralised, countries characterised by uncertainty avoidance have an emotional need for rules.

Vice-versa, national cultures which score low in uncertainty avoidance dislike formal rules, setting them only when it is necessary. This leads to more emphasis on formal methods for gathering and analysing external information. Differently, Snell and Hui (2000) emphasise the importance of individualism: while members of individualist countries are autonomous and confident, tending to rely primarily on their own ideas, members of collectivist countries are more likely to rely on information provided by others in formulating their opinions.

In the field of quality management research, a few studies have looked at national culture and mostly by using Hofstede's four main cultural dimensions. One of the major efforts in this area can be attributed to Krosolid (1999), who contends the development of quality management has followed two distinct paths: the deterministic school and the continuous improvement school. He further argues that the dominance of these two schools is different according to different national cultures. In a similar fashion, Sousa-Poza et al. (2000) assess the application of Total Quality Management (TQM) in the USA, Switzerland, and South Africa to investigate the relationship between national culture and the implementation of TQM. Their results show that in each country, several distinct relationships between the dimensions of TQM implementation and national culture exist. They therefore imply that the application of TQM should take into account different characteristics of national cultures. In a major study, Mathews et al., (2001) studied quality management practices in the UK, Finland, and Portugal. Their evidence indicates that the existing differences in quality management practices could be related to national culture.

They find there is a substantial variation in all aspects of quality management, from the reasons stimulating the adoption of the quality management programme to the problems faced. The dimensions of uncertainty avoidance and power distance appear particularly powerful in explaining the national differences observed. In general, the study finds that "*management approaches mirror the culture in which they develop*" (Mathews et al., 2001, p. 706). Cultures that are consistent with the imperative of TQM develop styles that will support the underpinning values of quality management. Others which are less consistent may adopt the tools and the approaches but not the philosophy that TQM requires.

An Evolutionary Perspective

In our previous research, we have identified two main notions underpinning the cross-cultural approach to TQM (Vecchi & Brennan, 2009; Vecchi & Brennan 2011). The notion of *better fit* recalls the idea of congruence by which, according to Newman & Nollen (1996), management practices need to be congruent and consistent with national cultural expectations to enable firms to achieve superior performance. An emblematic example is illustrated by Lagrosen (2002) who, by using Hofstede's model, shows how quality management assumes different connotations across different countries with power distance and uncertainty avoidance playing an important role. Countries characterised by high uncertainty avoidance were found to have a preference for a clear organisational structure and clearly laid out rules. A subsequent study conducted by Lagrosen (2003) also shows that countries characterised by low uncertainty avoidance and high collectivism tend to have greater customer orientation, while countries characterised by high uncertainty avoidance tend to focus less on business process. Flynn & Saladin (2006) argue that besides *better fit* there is also a *compensation* mechanism that might occur to overcome some of the perceived limitations of the national culture. For example, Snell & Hui (2000) note high power distance countries tend to rely more on procedure and routines as the national culture is inadequate in the formulation of systematic approaches that would allow employees to do their jobs without intervention.

Additionally, further evidence indicates that masculinity plays a crucial role in determining the overall quality strategy. Masculine countries seem to focus more on the internal operations whilst feminine countries display more concern for the environment as well as sharper customer focus (Kyoon Yoo et al., 2005). Anwar and Jabnoun (2006) take a step further by conceptualising a contingency model using Hofstede and by relating TQM to the characteristics of national culture. According to the model, quality control (i.e., supervision, inspection and control) can be implemented more effectively by countries characterised by high power distance. Quality assurance (i.e., planned and systematic actions) can be implemented more effectively by countries characterised by high uncertainty avoidance. Continuous improvement (i.e., commitment to improvement and learning) can be implemented more effectively by countries characterised by low power distance and low uncertainty avoidance. Total customer satisfaction (i.e., teamwork and empowerment of internal customers) can be implemented more effectively by countries characterised by low uncertainty avoidance, low power distance, and low collectivism.

Despite the fact there is well-established evidence in the literature supporting the importance of better fit and compensation, there is still substantial lack of knowledge about their dynamics over time–does national culture produce a consistent visible set of outputs in terms of quality priorities and quality practices over time? As such, there is the opportunity of applied research by applying an evolutionary perspective (Zbaracki, 1998; Ravichandram, 2000) in order to gain a fuller understanding of the impact of national culture on TQM from a dynamic point of view. Zbaracki (1998) introduces an evolutionary model assessing the evolving rhetoric and reality of TQM in five organizations to show how institutional forces can distort the technical reality of TQM. In particular, the author performs an assessment of the social construction of TQM to trace the relationship between the technical practices and rhetoric of TQM. The model shows that managers consume a rhetoric of success about TQM, use that rhetoric to develop their TQM program, and then filter their experiences to present their own rhetoric of success.

TQM AND ITS RELATIONSHIP TO NATIONAL CULTURE

Quality management research with an international focus has primarily focussed on differences between countries, regions or different organisational cultures while generally overlooking the issue of national culture. The few exceptions (Krosolid, 1999; Sousa-Poza et al., 2000; Mathews et al., 2001; Lagrosen, 2002; Gallear & Ghobadian, 2004; Kyoon Yoo et al., 2005; Anwar & Jabnoun, 2006) have been limited in the scope of their coverage. Thus, there is a need to study whether quality is, or should be, managed differently in different national cultures. In particular, the literature review suggests that a comparative holistic approach, involving a systematic comparison of similarities and differences that could considerably improve our understanding of quality management implementation in a global context, is missing.

The purpose of this study is to address the extent to which quality management is "culture-specific." To this end, we explore the extent to which the different dimensions of national culture influence quality management in a global context. Specifically we consider if there is a difference in quality priorities and practices across national cultures and how these might change over time. One of the most problematic issues confronting the researcher in quality management is the search for an appropriate definition (Fynes, 1998). More precisely, defining "quality" as a construct is difficult given the number of possible alternatives available (Hardie & Walsh, 1994). Reeves & Bednar (1994) suggest a four-way taxonomy of quality definitions that incorporates excellence, value, conformance to specifications, and meeting and/or exceeding customer requirements. The diversity that these definitions embrace, they contend, implies that "the quality construct space is so broad and includes so many components that there would be little utility in any model that tried to encompass them all" (p.441). Conversely, they argue that "the complexity and multiple perspectives historically associated with the concept have made theoretical and research advances difficult" and that ultimately the "search for a universal definition of quality and a statement of law-like relationships has been unsuccessful" (p. 441). In addressing this problem, Flynn et al. (1994) argue that a crucial issue in theory development is the articulation of the distinction between quality management practices (input) and quality performance (output), which has been blurred under the broad heading of quality. More recent studies also place emphasis on priorities (Voss, 2005)–manufacturing strategies may be articulated through competitive priorities which are then operationalised through improvement goals as well as action programs and demonstrated by performance improvement (Lindberg et al., 1998; Voss, 2005).

Drawing on our previous work (Vecchi & Brennan, 2009; 2011), this paper endorses the view that a fuller understanding of quality can be reached only by embracing these concomitant perspectives, namely *priorities and practices*. In particular we wish to explore the means by which *priorities* are transposed into *practices*, and how these practices are likely to be affected by national cultures. The review of the literature reveals that culture has a powerful effect on the performance and long-term effectiveness of the firm (Krosolid, 1999; Sousa-Poza et al., 2000; Mathews et al., 2001; Lagrosen, 2002; Gallear & Ghobadian, 2004; Kyoon Yoo, et al., 2005; Anwar & Jabnoun, 2006; Davison & Al-Shaghana, 2007) therefore an evolutionary perspective (Zbaracky, 1998) was deemed as appropriate to assess the extent to which quality priorities and practices have changed over time.

Differently from existing research we adopt GLOBE (House et al., 2004). GLOBE's intent is to explore the cultural values and practices in a wide variety of countries and to identify their impact on organisational practices and leadership attributes. To this end, House et al., (2004) examine national cultures in terms of nine dimensions:

1. *Uncertainty Avoidance* is defined as the extent to which members of a society strive to avoid uncertainty by reliance on social norms, rituals and bureaucratic practices to mitigate the unpredictability of future events.
2. *Power Distance* is defined as the degree to which members of society expect and agree that power should be equally shared.
3. *Institutional Collectivism* reflects the degree to which societal practices encourage and reward collective distribution of resources and collective action.
4. *In-Group Collectivism* reflects the degree to which individuals express pride, loyalty and cohesiveness in their organisations.

5. *Gender Egalitarianism* is the extent to which a society minimises gender role differences and gender discrimination.
6. *Assertiveness* is the degree to which individuals in societies are assertive, confrontational and aggressive in their social relationships.
7. *Future Orientation* is the degree to which individuals in societies engage in future-oriented behaviours such as planning, investing in the future, and delaying gratification.
8. *Performance Orientation* refers to the extent to which a society encourages and rewards group members for performance improvement and excellence.
9. *Humane Orientation* is the degree to which individuals in organisations or societies encourage and reward individuals for being fair, altruistic, friendly, generous, caring and kind to others.

On the basis of the nine cultural dimensions listed above, the GLOBE study identifies ten societal clusters: South Asia, Anglo, Arab, Germanic Europe, Latin Europe, Eastern Europe, Confucian Asia, Latin America, Sub-Sahara Africa, and Nordic Europe.

National culture provides a fruitful area for research in quality management. We argue that extending this line of enquiry to quality management issues holds great potential to gain a fuller insight on whether quality should be managed differently across different national cultures. In particular, the paper attempts to provide a fuller appreciation of the mechanisms of either *better fit* or *compensation*. Adopting the GLOBE framework can provide a fuller appreciation of these two mechanisms, thus helping firms to better align their quality priorities towards the attainment of improved quality practices. To this end, drawing on previous work (Vecchi & Brennan, 2011) we attempt to test the following ten hypotheses in relation to quality priorities and quality practices as presented in Table 1.

In particular, our previous analysis indicated that quality priorities tend to vary across GLOBE's cultural dimensions. The dimensions of uncertainty avoidance, institutional collectivism and performance orientation have a highly significant impact on quality priorities. Our analysis also indicated that quality practices tend to vary considerably across GLOBE's cultural dimensions. In particular, performance orientation, uncertainty avoidance, power distance and institutional collectivism have a highly significant impact on quality practices. In this sense, our previous study tends to support the "culture-specific" perspective by also raise the interesting issue of whether this perception of relative emphasis stems from a *better fit* between practice or priority and the national cultural dimension positioning or from a *compensation* by which firms engage in quality practices as a deliberate attempt to compensate for specific limitations of any of their cultural dimensions.

For example, while previous research adopting Hofstede has shown that high collectivism is often associated with more extensive quality management implementation (Snell & Hui, 2000; Anwar & Jabnoun, 2006), our findings showed that this is the case for in-group collectivism, but not for countries when characterised by institutional collectivism (Vecchi & Brennan, 2011). This discrepancy was explained on the basis that countries characterised by low institutional collectivism may engage more with quality management as a result of *compensation*; vice-versa, countries characterised by high in-group collectivism may engage more with quality management as a result of *better fit*.

In contrast to existing research (Mathews et al., 2001; Anwar & Jobnoun, 2006) which claims that there is no single national culture that is conducive to better quality management, our findings showed the contrary (Vecchi & Brennan, 2011) . In particular both the holistic and the prescriptive nature of our previous study allowed us to identify those countries in our survey that seem to be more

Table 1. Impact of GLOBE cultural dimensions on quality management

GLOBE cultural dimensions	Hypotheses developed from IMSS IV
Low Uncertainty avoidance countries (are more likely to):	• Prioritize superior product quality and superior conformance quality • Ascribe importance to product quality and reliability as improvement goals • Engage in quality improvement and control programs • Engage in equipment productivity programs
High Uncertainty Avoidance countries (are more likely to):	• Account for a greater proportion of their quality costs with external costs • Place greater importance on quality in supplier selection
Low Power Distance countries (are more likely to):	• Place greater importance on quality in supplier selection
High Power Distance countries (are more likely to):	• Ascribe importance to product quality and reliability as improvement goals • Account for a greater proportion of their quality costs with inspection costs • Engage in environmental performance programs
Low Collectivism Institutional countries (are more likely to):	• Prioritize superior conformance quality • Ascribe importance to manufacturing conformance and product quality and reliability as improvement goals • Engage in equipment productivity programs • Engage in environmental performance programs
High Collectivism In Group countries (are more likely to):	• Ascribe importance to product quality and reliability as improvement goals • Engage in equipment productivity programs • Engage in environmental performance programs
High Gender Egalitarianism countries (are more likely to):	• Ascribe importance to product quality and reliability as improvement goals
Low Future Orientation countries (are more likely to):	• Engage in equipment productivity programs • Engage in environmental performance programs
Low Performance Orientation countries (are more likely to):	• Prioritize superior product quality and superior conformance quality • Ascribe importance to product quality and reliability as improvement goals • Place greater importance on quality in supplier selection • Engage in environmental performance programs
High Humane Orientation countries (are more likely to):	• Account for a greater proportion of their quality costs with preventive costs
Source: Vecchi & Brennan, 2011	

suited to quality management. More specifically, countries that are characterised by low uncertainty avoidance, low institutional collectivism, and low performance orientation seemed to place more emphasis on quality priorities. Countries that are characterised by low uncertainty avoidance, high power distance, low institutional collectivism, low future orientation, and low performance orientation seem to place more emphasis on quality practices. Overall, in terms of quality management, countries characterised by low uncertainty avoidance, high power distance, low institutional collectivism, high in-group collectivism, low gender egalitarianism, high assertiveness, low future orientation, low performance orientation, and low human orientation seem better placed to deal with quality management. The purpose of the current study is therefore to assess whether our previous findings as depicted in Table 1 still apply or if there are significant discrepancies in terms of quality priorities and practises within the timeframe considered.

Methodology

The papers use three independent survey studies; it employs primary data from both the fourth and the fifth iteration of the International Manufacturing Strategy Survey (IMSS IV and IMSS V) and secondary data from the GLOBE survey (House et al., 2004). As discussed below, several factors suggest the combined use of these datasets.

The main unit of analysis of the IMSS survey were firms and its main respondents were managers. IMSS IV was carried out in 2006. A total of 711 firms in 24 countries responded representing a response rate of some 20%. The fifth iteration of the IMSS survey was conducted in 2009 by adopting the same data collection instrument that was adopted in 2006. The more recent iteration involved a total of 677 firms in 19 countries. In both instances, the directors of operations were contacted. Similarly, GLOBE was conducted in 62 countries by involving 951 firms (House et al., 2002). The main respondents were 17,000 managers. By contrast, Hofstede's study was conducted by involving 40 IBM subsidiaries, between 1967 and 1973, and later expanded through replications to 53 subsidiaries (Hofstede, 2001). In this case the unit of analysis were the subsidiaries of a single company and the main respondents were employees from different categories – two managerial and five non-managerial. Overall, given its rationale, its unit of analysis, its research design in terms of respondents, its international focus, the IMSS was deemed as a valuable instrument to assess the extent to which quality management is "culture-specific". In turn, the GLOBE instrument has been deemed as an appropriate methodological tool to assess the results of the IMSS survey in order to provide insights on the issue of quality management across countries.

This study focuses on the part of the IMSS survey that addresses quality management. Questions pertaining to quality priorities and practices are listed in the Appendix. Most questionnaire items were in the form of perceptual measures where respondents were asked to rate specific priorities and practices in terms of use or importance on five-point Likert scales. These scales can be treated as quasi-ratio scales (Gaski & Etzel, 1986). The constructs' validity of quality priorities, quality practices and quality performance along with their content validity and construct measurement have been widely discussed elsewhere (Frohlich & Westbrook, 2001; Frohlich & Dixon, 2001; Grossler & Grubner, 2006; Vereecke & Muylle, 2006; Vecchi & Brennan, 2009; 2011). For the purpose of this analysis, the five-point Likert scales were treated as three-point Likert scales and the associated distribution frequencies were calculated in relation to individual items for quality priorities and quality practices.

This paper specifically examines quality priorities and quality practices across the 19 IMSS V countries, classified according to GLOBE's nine cultural dimensions. In order to benchmark quality management on a global scale, a complete list of the 19 IMSS countries as well as their classification between "low" and "high" (by taking into account the median) according to the nine types of dimension scores and societal cluster is provided in Table 2 in the Appendix.

The quality priorities and practices are compared across 19 countries, according to GLOBE's nine cultural dimensions by using the Kruskall-Wallis test to assess possible significant differences. Consistent with Bryman & Cramer (2001), the choice of conducting non-parametric tests was mainly driven by the fact that our sample is biased by the presence of high-performing firms and any assumptions on the distribution of their scores would be highly hazardous.

The hypotheses previously developed (Vecchi & Brennan, 2011) in relation to IMSS IV and outlined in Table 1 were then tested for IMSS V based on the results obtained from comparative analysis of quality priorities and practices across the GLOBE's nine cultural dimensions. In particular, hypotheses were accepted where significant differences (either at significance level of $p<0.01$ or $p<0.001$) in terms of priorities and practices were observed.

DATA ANALYSIS AND MAIN FINDINGS

Table 3 in the Appendix contains the percentage distribution scores and the results of the analysis for IMSS V in relation to the first five dimensions of national culture: uncertainty avoidance, power distance, institutional collectivism, in-group collectivism and gender egalitarianism while Table 4 in the Appendix does so for the remaining four dimensions of national culture: assertiveness, future orientation, performance orientation, and human orientation. The findings are discussed below in relation to our original hypotheses previously developed and outlined in Table 1 and according to the nine GLOBE cultural dimensions.

- **Uncertainty Avoidance:** In terms of quality priorities, from IMSS IV it emerged that low uncertainty avoidance countries attributed more importance to superior product quality and superior conformance quality. Product quality and reliability was also considered more important when considering improvement goals. In this context, quality was seen as an immediate priority, a *better fit* only for those low uncertainty avoidance countries that can benefit from a reasonable level of certainty in their business environment. As for quality practices, low uncertainty avoidance countries attributed more importance to quality in supplier selection as well as to current use of all action programs except for future use of equipment productivity programs and continuous improvement programs. Our findings from IMSSV reveal that there are no significant differences in terms of priorities. In terms of practices, countries characterised by low uncertainty avoidance place more emphasis on internal quality costs and environmental programmes. Countries characterised by high uncertainty avoidance place more emphasis on quality improvement and control programmes. Overall the current findings validate the previous ones by showing how countries characterised by low uncertainty avoidance appear to place more emphasis than their counterparts on quality management. From the above analysis, we accept the hypothesis that uncertainty avoidance has an impact on quality management.
- **Power Distance:** In relation to quality priorities, the latest findings from IMSS V show no significant differences attributable to power distance. On the contrary, from IMSS IV it emerged that high power distance countries attributed more importance to product quality and reliability. In terms of quality practices, from the current iteration it emerges that low power distance countries tend to be more engaged with quality management than their counterparts. In the 2006 iteration despite external costs accounting for a greater share of quality, low power distance countries seemed less committed to quality programmes. By contrast, from the current iteration it emerges that they tend to place more emphasis on quality in suppliers' selection, engage more extensively in quality inspection and control programmes, equipment productivity programmes as well as environmental programmes. In this sense our recent findings represent a change from our previous ones where high power distance countries seemed more concerned with quality management. From the above analysis, we accept the hypothesis that power distance has an impact on quality management.
- **Institutional Collectivism:** In relation to quality priorities, the latest findings from IMSS V show no significant differences. On the contrary, from IMSS IV it emerged that countries characterised by low institutional collectivism attributed relatively more importance to superior quality. As for quality practices, countries characterised by low institutional collectivism placed relatively more importance on quality when selecting suppliers and were also more committed current use of equipment productivity programs and use of environmental performance programs. This was explained by a mechanism of *compensa-*

tion where countries characterised by low institutional collectivism needed to rely more on action programs to overcome the ineffectiveness that a weaker collective action inevitably entails. From IMSS V, it emerged that countries characterised by low institutional collectivism still attribute relatively more importance to quality when selecting suppliers while those countries characterised by high institutional collectivism are more committed current use of continuous improvement programmes. From the above analysis, we accept the hypothesis that institutional collectivism has an impact on quality management.

- **In-Group Collectivism:** In relation to quality priorities, from both iterations of the IMSS survey it emerges that countries characterised by high in-group collectivism seem more concerned with quality. In IMSS IV they rated improvement in product quality and reliability as a more important improvement goal. Likewise, in IMSS V they tend to rate more highly superior conformance quality as an important changing priority for their customers. Again, this emphasis could reflect a *better fit* given that strategic planning is consistent with collectivism. As for quality practices, from both iterations it emerges that countries characterised by high in-group collectivism show relatively more commitment towards the use of equipment productivity programs and environmental performance programs. The higher commitment and less myopic approach of high collectivist countries to action programs could be explained by a *better fit* given that strategic planning is consistent with collectivism. Additionally from IMSS V, they seem to engage more extensively with quality improvement and control programmes by attributing more importance to quality when selecting suppliers. In this sense, the more recent iteration of the IMSS survey seem to support our previous findings. From the above analysis, we accept the hypothesis that in-group collectivism has an impact on quality management.
- **Gender Egalitarianism:** From the more recent findings gender egalitarianism does not seem to have an impact on quality priorities. From IMSS IV it emerged that countries displaying higher gender egalitarianism attributed relatively more importance to product quality and reliability as improvement goals. There were no significant differences in quality practices between countries on this cultural dimension with the exception of the level of commitment towards the future use of environmental performance programs where countries with low gender egalitarianism report relatively more commitment towards their future use. By contrast, from IMSS V it emerges that countries characterised by high gender egalitarianism seem far more engaged with quality practices. They attribute more importance to quality in suppliers' selection and engaged more extensively in quality improvement and control programmes, equipment productivity programmes, environmental performance programmes and continuous improvement programmes. From the above analysis, we accept the hypothesis that gender egalitarianism has an impact on quality management. However, if we assume that high gender egalitarianism could be an indication of low masculinity (as meant by Hofstede) our findings support Wacker and Sprague (1998), according to whom feminine countries tend to rely more extensively on external information, in this case in the use of quality programmes. In the same way, our findings offer some support for the view that low masculinity countries should be more environmentally

concerned (Kyoon Yoo et al., 2005). From the above analysis, we accept the hypothesis that gender egalitarianism has an impact on quality management.

- **Assertiveness:** Our previous analysis did not offer any evidence that assertiveness significantly affects quality priorities. Conversely, the more recent findings from IMSS V highlight that countries characterised by low assertiveness attribute more importance to superior conformance quality as a changing priority of their customers while countries characterised by high assertiveness tend to place greater emphasis on manufacturing conformance as improvement goals. As for quality practices, differently from IMSS IV, the findings from IMSS V also highlight a higher emphasis on quality when selecting suppliers by countries characterised by low assertiveness. From both iterations there tends to be a more extensive engagement in the use of quality improvement and control programs by countries displaying high assertiveness. From the above analysis, we accept the hypothesis that assertiveness has an impact on quality management. Although assertiveness is often associated with masculinity (Wacker & Sprague, 1998; Kyoon Yoo et al., 2005), our findings show that assertiveness has a significant impact on quality priorities and on quality practices. From the above analysis, we accept the hypothesis that assertiveness has an impact on quality management.
- **Future Orientation:** While our previous analysis failed to reveal any significant differences in quality priorities amongst countries, from the current iteration of IMSS it emerges that countries characterised by low future orientation ascribe more importance to superior conformance quality as a changing priority of their customers. As for quality practices, from both iterations it emerges that countries characterised by low future orientation are likely to show more commitment towards the use of equipment productivity programs, use of environmental performance programs. According to the most recent findings they also ascribe more importance to quality when selecting suppliers. This could be explained by a mechanism of *compensation* where countries characterised by low future orientation need to rely more on action programs to overcome their lack of long term planning. From the above analysis, we accept the hypothesis that future orientation has an impact on quality management.
- **Performance Orientation:** According to the most recent iteration of the IMSS survey we found that performance orientation does not have any impact on quality priorities. By contrast, from IMSS IV it emerged that low performance orientation countries attributed relatively more importance to superior product quality and superior conformance quality. As for quality practices, from IMSS IV it emerged that low performance orientation countries attributed more importance to quality when selecting suppliers. They also showed more commitment towards the use of environmental performance programs. By contrast, from IMSS V it emerges that while low performance orientation countries seem more engaged with continuous improvement programmes, high performance orientation countries place relatively more emphasis on quality when selecting suppliers. From the above analysis, we accept the hypothesis that performance orientation has an impact on quality management.
- **Human Orientation:** From both iterations it emerges that there are no significant differences in quality priorities among countries on human orientation. In relation to quality practices, from both iterations

of the IMSS survey it emerges that countries with lower human orientation incur a greater proportion of quality costs in corrective quality costs in IMSS IV, whereas they tended to incur a greater proportion of quality costs in internal quality costs in IMSS V. By contrast, from the most recent findings it emerges that countries characterised by high humane orientation seem more extensively engaged with quality improvement and control programmes, equipment productivity programmes and continuous improvement programmes. Therefore, from the above analysis, we accept the hypothesis that humane orientation has an impact on quality management.

DISCUSSION AND CONCLUSION

Table 5 in the Appendix provides an evolutionary perspective of the findings in relation to the previous iteration of the survey. To this end, we have relied on the standard font to highlight the findings for IMSS IV, the bold font to highlight the findings of IMSS V and the grey shading to indicate convergent findings between the two iterations. Table 6 in the Appendix provides a summary of the main findings stemming from the assessment of quality priorities and practices of the most recent iteration of the IMSS survey. Grey shading has been used to indicate convergent findings between the two iterations.

Overall, in line with previous studies (Vecchi & Brennan, 2009; 2011) our analysis indicates that quality priorities do not tend to vary significantly across GLOBE's cultural dimensions. Quality practices tend to vary to a much greater extent. In particular, during IMSS V we highlighted the importance of uncertainty avoidance, institutional collectivism and performance orientation, the current iteration of the survey further highlight the importance of in-group collectivism in significantly shaping quality priorities. Additionally, amongst the respondents' perceptions of changing priorities of customers superior conformance quality seems to be particularly sensitive to the different dimensions of national culture.

Differently from existing research (Mathews et al., 2001; Anwar & Jobnoun, 2006) which claims that there is no single national culture that is conducive to better quality management, our findings show the contrary. In particular both the holistic and the prescriptive nature of our evolutionary framework allow us to identify those countries in our survey that seem to be more suitable to implement quality management. In line with our previous study (Vecchi & Brennan, 2011) the current analysis also indicates that quality practices tend to vary considerably across GLOBE's cultural dimensions. While during IMSS IV, performance orientation, uncertainty avoidance, power distance, and institutional collectivism seemed to have a highly significant impact on quality practices, the most recent findings also highlight the importance of gender egalitarianism and future orientation. According to the findings, amongst quality costs, countries characterised by low uncertainty avoidance and low human orientation tend to incur a greater proportion of quality costs in internal quality costs. From the findings it emerges that those countries ranking low across all the cultural dimensions (apart from uncertainty avoidance, in-group collectivism and human orientation) tend to ascribe significantly higher importance to quality when selecting suppliers than their counterparts. As for the engagement in quality programmes, from the most recent iteration of the IMSS survey, several trends have emerged: countries characterised by low gender egalitarianism and high human orientation seem to be more committed to quality improvement and control programmes; countries characterised by low power distance and low gender egalitarianism tend to be more extensively engaged with equipment productivity programs; countries characterised by high in-group collectivism, low gender egalitarianism and low future orientation seem to be more committed to environmental performance programmes; countries characterised by low gender egalitarianism and high human orientation tend to be more extensively engaged with continuous improvement programs.

The "culture-specific" perspective contends that even if managers located in different societies face similar imperatives for change, deeply-embedded cultural factors will still affect the way managers approach quality and react to the need for change. By providing some empirical evidence to support this perspective our findings also raise the interesting issue of whether this perception of relative emphasis on quality changes over time and requires an evolutionary approach. In particular, the variations reported in quality priorities and practices across the different dimensions of national culture lend support to the "culture-specific" perspective. While the variations reported in quality priorities and practices across the two different iterations of the IMSS survey offer evidence of increasing convergence around quality priorities over time this does not appear to be the case for quality practices where there remains considerable differences attributable to differences in cultural dimensions. These findings not only yield interesting questions concerning the reasons behind such a change but they also further highlight the value of applying an evolutionary framework. More specifically, our analysis of the data leads us to endorse the idea that through an accumulation of scientific knowledge relevant to the applicability of quality management across national settings, we can also help managers to better understand how to timely transfer best quality management practices from one country to another in their quest to enhance their market responsiveness. Additionally, we are able to identify which element in terms of priorities and practices should be modified during the transfer process to maximise the opportunity to achieve improved quality practices. In this sense, more attention to the cultural impacts on quality management and performance may reap rich rewards in terms of effective implementation of quality practices and accordingly outstanding quality performance.

This study uses national culture as a means of explaining differences in quality management. As illustrated in Table 6, the results of this study reveal that some cultures implement specific quality programs more than others. This suggests that different aspects of national culture appear to have facilitating or inhibiting consequences for the implementation of quality management. While the results have clearly indicated the significant relationship between cultural dimensions and quality management, several limitations need to be addressed in future research to confirm our findings.

First, the partial validation of only some of our original hypotheses calls for further research on why this might be the case. In particular our study highlights the extent to which over time the relative emphasis on quality across different cultural dimensions can change. This raises the interesting issue of whether a similar change can be detected by performing a longitudinal analysis of quality priorities and practices across the relevant societal clusters.

Second, the underlying assumption is that national culture is the same for all plants within a particular country. However, it is possible that different corporate, organisational, industrial and/or sectoral cultures may co-exist within the same firm and might conflict and counterbalance the national one. Furthermore, today in many IMSS countries such as Canada, Israel and Belgium different ethnic or national cultures co-exist (Au, 2000). This is likely to be intensified as the result of increased human mobility that globalisation entails. In particular, within the same country different sub-cultures might persist, but they might also still stand apart for religious reasons (e.g., Ireland), because of their language (e.g., Belgium) or their ethnicity (e.g., US, France, Turkey). In this sense, the nine dimensions of national cultures could be far from being reliable proxies for cultural homogeneity for a given national culture. In particular, future research embracing an evolutionary approach needs to focus on the true blending of cultures and managerial values that may affect quality management.

Finally, since our sample is biased towards best-performing firms, future research should target all kinds of firms regardless of their performance. This should provide a more robust representation of the state-of-the-art of quality management across different national cultures.

REFERENCES

Abdul-Aziz, Z., Chan, J. F. L., & Metcalfe, A. V. (2000). Quality Practices in the Manufacturing Industry in the UK and Malaysia. *Total Quality Management*, *11*(8), 1053–1064. doi:10.1080/095441200440322.

Anwar, S. A., & Jabnoun, N. (2006). The development of a contingency model relating national culture to total quality management. *International Journal of Management*, *23*(2), 272–280.

Bryman, A., & Cramer, D. (2001). *Quantitaive Data Analysis*. London: Routledge.

Child, J., & Kieser, A. (1979). Organisational and Management Roles in British and German Companies: An Examination of the Culture-Free Thesis. In C.J. Lammus & D.J. Hickson (Eds.), *Organisations Alike and Unlike*. London: Routledge.

Chin, K. S., Sun, H., Xu, Y., & Hua, H. (2002). A Comparative Study of Quality Management Practices in Hong Kong and Shanghai Manufacturing Industries. *International Journal of Management*, *19*(4), 576–581.

Corbett, L. M., Adam, E. E., Harrison, N. J., Lee, T. S., Rho, B. H., & Samson, D. (1998). A Study of Quality Management Practices and Performance in Asia and the South Pacific. *International Journal of Production Research*, *36*(9), 2597–2607. doi:10.1080/002075498192724.

Crawford, K. M., Blackstone, J. H. Jr, & Cox, J. F. (1988). A study of JIT implementation and operating problems. *International Journal of Production Research*, *26*(9), 1561–1568. doi:10.1080/00207548808947966.

Cua, K. O., McKone, K. E., & Schroeder, R. G. (2001). Relationships between implementation of TQM, JIT, and TPM and manufacturing performance. *Journal of Operations Management*, *19*(1), 675–694. doi:10.1016/S0272-6963(01)00066-3.

Davison, L., & Al-Shaghana, K. (2007). The link between Six-Sigma and quality culture – An empirical study. *Total Quality Management Journal*, *18*(3), 249–265. doi:10.1080/14783360601152269.

Emery, F. (1990). The nine-step model. In Trist, E. L., & Murray, H. (Eds.), *The Social Engagement of Social Science, A Tavistock Anthology: The Socio-Technical Perspective* (*Vol. 2*). Philadelphia, PA: University of Pennsylvania Press.

Flynn, B. B., & Saladin, B. (2006). Relevance of Baldridge constructs in an international context: A study of national culture. *Journal of Operations Management*, *24*(5), 583–603. doi:10.1016/j.jom.2005.09.002.

Flynn, B. B., Schroeder, R. G., & Sakakibara, S. (1994). The Impact of Quality Management Practices on Performance and Competitive Advantage. *Decision Sciences*, *16*(5), 659–691.

Form, W. (1979). Comparative industrial Sociology and the convergence hypothesis. *Annual Review of Sociology*, *5*, 1–25. doi:10.1146/annurev.so.05.080179.000245.

Frohlich, M., & Robb Dixon, J. (2001). A taxonomy of manufacturing strategies revisited. *Journal of Operations Management*, *19*(5), 541–558. doi:10.1016/S0272-6963(01)00063-8.

Frohlich, M., & Westbrook, R. (2001). Arcs of integration: An international study of supply chain strategies. *Journal of Operations Management*, *19*(5), 185–200. doi:10.1016/S0272-6963(00)00055-3.

Fynes, B. (1998). Quality Management Practices: A Review of the Literature. *Irish Business and Administrative Research*, *19/20*(2), 113–138.

Gallear, D., & Ghobadian, A. (2004). An empirical investigation of the channels that facilitate a Total Quality culture. *Quality Management Journal*, *15*(8), 1043–1067.

Garg, R., & Ma, J. (2005). Benchmarking culture ad performance in Chinese organisations. *Benchmarking: An International Journal*, *12*(3), 260–274. doi:10.1108/14635770510600375.

Gaski, J. F., & Etzel, M. J. (1986). The index of consumer sentiment toward marketing. *Journal of Marketing*, *50*(4), 71–81. doi:10.2307/1251586.

Grossler, A., & Grubner, A. (2006). An empirical model of the relationships between manufacturing capabilities. *International Journal of Operations & Production Management*, *26*(5), 458–485. doi:10.1108/01443570610659865.

Hardie, N., & Walsh, P. (1994). Towards a Better Understanding of Quality. *International Journal of Quality & Reliability Management*, *11*(4), 54–60. doi:10.1108/02656719410057953.

Hofstede, G. (1980). *Culture's Consequences: International Differences in Work-related Values*. London: Sage.

Hofstede, G. (2001). *Culture's Consequences: Comparing Values, Behaviours, Institutions and Organizations Across Countries*. Thousands Oaks, CA: Sage.

Hofstede, G. (2006). What did GLOBE really measure? Researchers' minds versus respondents' minds. *Journal of International Business Studies*, *37*(1), 882–896. doi:10.1057/palgrave.jibs.8400233.

House, R. J., Hanges, P. J., Javidan, M., & Dorfman, P. W. (2002). Understanding cultures and implicit leadership theories across the globe: An introduction to project GLOBE. *Journal of World Business*, *37*(1), 3–10. doi:10.1016/S1090-9516(01)00069-4.

House, R. J., Hanges, P. J., Javidan, M., Dorfman, P. W., & Gupta, V. (2004). *Culture, Leadership and Organizations: The GLOBE Study of 62 Societies*. Thousand Oaks, CA: Sage.

Ismail, S., & Ebrahimpour, M. (2003). Examination and Comparison of the Critical Factors of Total Quality Management (TQM) Across Countries. *International Journal of Production Research*, *41*(2), 235–268. doi:10.1080/0020754021000022212.

Krosolid, D. (1999). *In Search of Quality Management – Rethinking and Reinterpreting*. Linkoping, Sweden: Linkoping University.

Kyoon Yoo, D., Subba Rao, S., & Hong, P. (2005). A comparative study on cultural differences and quality practices – Korea, USA, Mexico and Taiwan. *International Journal of Quality & Reliability Management*, *23*(6), 607–624.

Lagrosen, S. (2002). Quality management in Europe: A cultural perspective. *The TQM Magazine*, *14*(5), 275–283. doi:10.1108/09544780210439707.

Lagrosen, S. (2003). Exploring the impact of culture on quality management. *International Journal of Quality & Reliability Management*, *20*(4/5), 473–482. doi:10.1108/02656710310468632.

Lindberg, P., Voss, C., & Blackmon, K. (1998). *International Manufacturing Strategies: Context, Content, and Change*. London: Kluver Academic.

Madu, C. N., Kuei, C., & Lin, C. (1995). A Comparative Analysis of Quality Practice in Manufacturing Firms in the U.S. and Taiwan. *Decision Sciences*, *26*(5), 621–635. doi:10.1111/j.1540-5915.1995.tb01443.x.

Mathews, B. P., Ueno, A., Kekale, T., Repka, M., Lopes Pereira, Z., & Silva Graca, S. (2001). European quality management practices, the impact of national culture. *International Journal of Quality & Reliability Management*, *18*(7), 692–707. doi:10.1108/EUM0000000005776.

Newman, K. L., & Nollen, S. D. (1996). Culture and congruence: The fit between management practices and national culture. *Journal of International Business Studies*, *27*(4), 753–779. doi:10.1057/palgrave.jibs.8490152.

Pagell, M., Katz, J. P., & Sheu, C. (2005). The importance of national culture in operations management research. *International Journal of Operations & Production Management*, *25*(4), 371–394. doi:10.1108/01443570510585552.

Raghunathan, T. S., Subba Rao, S., & Solis, L. E. (1997). A Comparative Study of Quality Practices: USA, China and India. *Industrial Management & Data Systems*, *97*(5), 192–202. doi:10.1108/02635579710367270.

Ravichandram, T. (2000). Quality management and systems development: An organizational system perspecitive. *Management Information Systems Quarterly*, *24*(3), 381–415. doi:10.2307/3250967.

Reeves, C. A., & Bednar, D. A. (1994). Defining Quality: Alternatives and Implications. *Academy of Management Review*, *19*(3), 419–445.

Rehder, R. R. (1989). Japanese transplants: In search of a balanced and broader perspective. *The Columbia Journal of World Business*, *24*(4), 17–28.

Rungtusanatham, M., Forza, C., Koka, B. R., Salvadora, F., & Nie, W. (2005). TQM across multiple countries: Convergence hypothesis versus national specificity arguments. *Journal of Operations Management*, *23*(1), 43–63. doi:10.1016/j.jom.2004.10.002.

Safayeni, F., Purdy, L., van Engelen, R., & Pal, S. (1991). Difficulties of Just-in-Time implementation: A classification scheme. *International Journal of Operations & Production Management*, *11*(7), 27–36. doi:10.1108/EUM0000000001272.

Snell, R. S., & Hui, S. K. K. (2000). Towards the Hong Kong learning organization: An exploratory case study. *Journal of Applied Management Studies*, *9*(2), 150–175. doi:10.1080/713674364.

Souza-Poza, A., Nystrom, H., & Wiebe, H. (2000). A cross-cultural study of the differing effects of corporate culture on TQM in three countries. *International Journal of Quality & Reliability Management*, *18*(7), 744–761. doi:10.1108/EUM0000000005778.

Subba Rao, S., Raghunathan, T. S., & Solis, L. E. (1997). A Comparative Study of Quality Practices and Results in India, China and Mexico. *Journal of Quality Management*, *2*(2), 235–250. doi:10.1016/S1084-8568(97)90005-5.

Tata, J., Prasad, S., & Motwani, J. (2000). Benchmarking Quality Management Practices: U.S. Versus Costa Rica. *Multinational Business Review*, *8*(2), 37–42.

Vecchi, A., & Brennan, L. (2009). Quality management: A cross-cultural perspective. *Cross-Cultural Management: An International Journal*, *16*(2), 149–164. doi:10.1108/13527600910953900.

Vecchi, A., & Brennan, L. (2011). Quality management: A cross-cultural perspective based on GLOBE. *International Journal of Production and Operations Management*, *3*(5), 527–553. doi:10.1108/01443571111126319.

Vereecke, A., & Muylle, S. (2006). Performance improvement through supply chain collaboration in Europe. *International Journal of Operations & Production Management*, *26*(11), 1176–1198. doi:10.1108/01443570610705818.

Voss, C. (2005). Alternative paradigms for manufacturing strategies. *International Journal of Operations & Production Management*, *25*(12), 1211–1222. doi:10.1108/01443570510633611.

Voss, C., & Blackmon, K. (1998). Differences in manufacturing strategy decisions between Japanese and Western manufacturing plants: The role of strategic time orientation. *Journal of Operations Management*, *16*(2), 147–158. doi:10.1016/S0272-6963(97)00034-X.

Wacker, J. F., & Sprague, L. G. (1998). Forecasting accuracy: Comparing the relative effectiveness of practices between seven developing countries. *Journal of Operations Management*, *16*(2), 271–290. doi:10.1016/S0272-6963(97)00042-9.

Yoo, D. K., Rao, S. S., & Hong, P. (2006). A comparative study on cultural differences and quality practices – Korea, USA, Mexico and Taiwan. *International Journal of Reliability and Quality Management*, *23*(6), 607–624. doi:10.1108/02656710610672452.

Zbaracky, M. (1998). The rhetoric and reality of Total quality Management. *Administrative Science Quarterly*, *43*(3), 602–636. doi:10.2307/2393677.

Zhao, X., Maheshwari, S. K., & Zhang, J. (1995). Benchmarking Quality practices in India, China and Mexico. *Benchmarking for Quality Management & Technology*, *2*(3), 20–32. doi:10.1108/14635779510099220.

APPENDIX

IMSS Questions:

Quality Priorities

Consider the importance of the following attributes to win orders from your major customers, presented in Box 1.

How important are the following improvement goals for your manufacturing function for the next 3 years (Box 2)?

Quality Practices

What is the approximate proportion of quality costs (adding up to 100%) (Box 3)?

What criteria do you use for selecting your key/strategic suppliers (Box 4)?

Indicate degree of the following action programmes undertaken over the last three years and planned efforts for the coming three years (Box 5).

Box 1.

	Current importance				
	Not important				Very important
superior **product design and quality**	1	2	3	4	5
superior **conformance quality**	1	2	3	4	5

Box 2.

	Not important				Very important
Improving **manufacturing conformance**	1	2	3	4	5
Improving **product quality and reliability**	1	2	3	4	5

Box 3.

Quality cost	
Inspection/control costs (sampling, supervision, lab tests)	____ %
Internal quality costs (e.g. scrap, losses)	____ %
Preventive costs (training, documentation, preventive maintenance, etc.)	____ %
External quality costs (e.g. warranty costs, returns, etc.)	____ %
	100 %

Box 4.

	Level of Importance				
	None				High
Quality of products/services offered	1	2	3	4	5

Box 5.

	Degree of use last 3 years None High
Undertaking programs for quality improvement and control (e.g. TQM programs, 6σ projects, quality circles, etc.)	1 2 3 4 5
Undertaking programs for the improvement of your equipment productivity (e.g. Total Productive Maintenance programs)	1 2 3 4 5
Undertaking programmes to improve environmental performance of processes and products (e.g. environmental management system, Life-Cycle Analysis, Design for Environment, Environmental certification)	1 2 3 4 5
Implementing Continuous Improvement Programs through systematic initiatives (e.g. kaizen, improvement teams, etc.)	1 2 3 4 5

Table 2. IMSS V country classification by GLOBE societal cluster and cultural dimensions

IMSS V Country	Societal cluster	Uncertainty Avoidance	Power Distance	Collectivism Institutional	Collectivism Group	Gender Egalitarianism	Assertiveness	Future Orientation	Performance Orientation	Human Orientation
Belgium	Germanic Europe	H	H	L	L	L	H	H	H	L
Brazil	Latin America	L	H	L	H	L	H	L	L	L
Canada	Anglo	H	L	H	L	H	L	H	H	H
China	Confucian Asia	H	L	H	H	L	L	L	H	H
Denmark	Nordic Europe	H	L	H	L	H	L	H	H	H
Estonia	Eastern Europe	L	H	L	H	H	L	L	L	L
Germany	Germanic Europe	H	H	L	L	L	H	H	H	L
Hungary	Eastern Europe	L	H	L	H	H	L	L	L	L
Ireland	Anglo	L	H	H	H	L	L	H	H	H
Italy	Latin Europe	L	H	L	H	L	L	L	L	L
Japan	Confucian Asia	H	L	H	H	L	L	L	H	H
Mexico	Latin America	L	H	L	H	L	H	L	L	L
The Netherlands	Germanic Europe	L	L	H	L	H	H	H	H	L
Portugal	Latin Europe	L	H	L	H	H	L	L	L	L
Spain	Latin Europe	L	H	L	H	L	H	L	L	L
Switzerland	Latin Europe	L	H	L	H	H	L	L	L	L
Taiwan	Confucian Asia	H	L	H	H	L	L	L	H	H
UK	Anglo	H	H	L	L	H	H	H	H	L
US	Anglo	L	L	L	L	L	H	H	H	H

Table 3. Quality Priorities, Practices and Performance and GLOBE cultural dimensions

	Uncertainty Avoidance				Power Distance				Collectivism Institutional				Collectivism Group				Gender Egalitarianism			
Quality Priorities	**Low**	**High**	**Tot**	**Sig**	**Low**	**High**	**Tot**	**Sig.**	**Low**	**High**	**Tot**	**Sig.**	**Low**	**High**	**Tot**	**Sig.**	**Low**	**High**	**Tot**	**Sig.**
Change of priorities of customers																				
Superior product quality	85	84	84		85	84	84		87	84	84		80	86	84		86	84	84	
Superior conformance quality	82	77	79		80	79	79		84	77	79		68	83	79	***	83	78	79	
Improvement goals in the next 3 years																				
Manufacturing conformance	34	35	35		36	34	35		34	35	35		34	35	35		39	39	35	
Product quality and reliability	38	39	39		43	38	39		36	37	39		36	40	39		47	37	39	
Quality Practices																				
Quality costs																				
Inspection/control costs	34	37	35		37	35	35		36	35	35		36	35	35		39	35	35	
Internal quality costs	25	21	23	***	20	23	23		18	24	23		24	22	23		18	24	23	
Preventive costs	23	26	25		25	25	25		25	25	25		25	25	25		25	25	25	**
External quality costs	18	18	18		19	18	18		16	19	18		16	19	18		19	18	18	
Quality & supplier selection	42	37	39		50	36	39	***	57	34	39	***	31	42	39	**	50	37	39	***
Quality improvement & control programs																				
Current use	41	45	44	**	55	41	44	**	45	43	44		34	47	44	**	60	40	44	***
Equipment productivity programs																				
Current use	37	40	39		50	36	39	***	41	38	39		31	42	39	**	57	35	39	***
Environmental performance programs																				
Current use	36	27	31	**	38	29	31	**	36	29	31		18	35	31	***	44	28	31	***
Continuous improvement programs																				
Current use	46	55	52		60	60	52	**	45	53	52	**	45	54	52		65	49	52	***
Significance: ** p<0.01; ***p<0.001																				

Table 4. Quality Priorities, Practices and Performance and GLOBE cultural dimensions

	Assertiveness				Future Orientation				Performance Orientation				Humane Orientation			
Quality Priorities	**Low**	**High**	**Tot**	**Sig**	**Low**	**High**	**Tot**	**Sig.**	**Low**	**High**	**Tot**	**Sig.**	**Low**	**High**	**Tot**	**Sig.**
Change of priorities of customers																
Superior product quality	85	84	84		85	83	84		88	84	84		83	86	84	
Superior conformance quality	83	77	79	**	82	75	79	**	84	77	79		77	82	79	
Improvement goals in the next 3 years																
Manufacturing conformance	28	38	35	**	36	33	35		34	35	35		35	34	35	
Product quality and reliability	34	41	39		41	36	39		36	40	39		38	40	39	
Quality Practices																
Quality costs																
Inspection/control costs	35	36	35		35	36	35		34	36	35		35	36	35	
Internal quality costs	24	22	23		23	22	23		25	22	23		24	20	23	**
Preventive costs	25	24	25		24	26	25		25	25	25		24	27	25	
External quality costs	17	19	18		19	17	18		16	19	18		18	19	18	
Quality & supplier selection	52	32	39	***	45	32	39	***	57	34	39	***	37	42	39	
Quality improvement & control programs																
Current use	44	43	44		47	39	44		45	43	44		39	52	44	***
Equipment productivity programs																
Current use	40	39	39		43	34	39	**	41	38	39		36	44	39	**
Environmental performance programs																
Current use	32	30	31		39	20	31	***	36	29	31		30	31	31	
Continuous improvement programs																
Current use	46	55	52	**	52	51	52		45	53	52	**	46	60	52	***
Significance: ** p<0.01; ***p<0.001																

Table 5. Impact of GLOBE cultural dimensions on quality management from an evolutionary perspective

	Uncertainty Avoidance		Power Distance		Collectivism Institutional		Collectivism In/Group	Gender Egalitarianism		Assertiveness		Future Orientation		Performance Orientation		Humane Orientation	
	L	H	L	H	L	H	H	L	H	L	H	L	H	L	H	L	H
Quality Priorities																	
Change of priorities of customers	Superior product quality Superior conformance quality				Superior conformance quality		**Superior conformance quality**							Superior product quality Superior conformance quality			
Improvement goals in the next 3 years	Product quality and reliability			Product quality and reliability	Manufacturing conformance Product quality and reliability		Product quality and reliability		Product quality and reliability					Product quality and reliability			
Quality Practices																	
Quality costs	**Internal**	External	External	Inspection				**Preventive**	**Preventive**							**Internal**	Preventive
		Quality & supplier selection	**Quality & supplier selection**		**Quality & supplier selection**			**Quality & supplier selection**		**Quality & supplier selection**		**Quality & supplier selection**		**Quality & supplier selection**			
Quality improvement & control programs	Current							**Current**		Current							**Current**
Equipment productivity programs	Current		**Current**		Current		Current	**Current**				Current					
Environmental performance programs				Current	Current		**Current**	**Current**				**Current**		Current			
Continuous improvement programs								**Current**									**Current**

Table 6. Impact of cultural dimensions on quality priorities and practices

GLOBE cultural Dimension	Findings
Low Uncertainty avoidance Cultures (are more likely to):	• Ascribe importance to internal quality • Engage in environmental performance programs
High Uncertainty avoidance Cultures (are more likely to):	• Engage in quality improvement and control programmes
Low Power Distance Countries (are more likely to):	• Place greater importance on quality in supplier selection
High Collectivism In Group countries (are more likely to):	• Ascribe importance to superior conformance quality as improvement goals • Ascribe importance to quality in suppliers' selection • Engage in quality improvement and control programmes • Engage in equipment productivity programs • Engage in environmental performance programs
High Gender Egalitarianism countries (are more likely to):	• Ascribe importance to quality in suppliers' selection • Engage in quality improvement and control programmes • Engage in equipment productivity programs • Engage in environmental performance programs
Low Assertiveness countries (are more likely to):	• Ascribe importance to superior conformance uality as a changing priority of their customers • Ascribe importance to manufacturing conformance as an improvement goal • Ascribe importance to quality when selecting suppliers
High Assertiveness countries (are more likely to):	• Engage in equipment productivity programs
Low Future Orientation countries (are more likely to):	• Ascribe more importance to superior conformance quality • Ascribe more importance to quality when selecting suppliers • Engage in equipment productivity programs • Engage in environmental performance programs
Low Performance Orientation countries (are more likely to):	• Engage in continuous improvement programs
High Performance Orientation countries (are more likely to):	• Place greater importance on quality in supplier selection
Low Humane Orientation countries (are more likely to):	• Account for a greater proportion of their quality costs
High Humane Orientation countries (are more likely to):	• Engage in quality improvement and control programs • Engage in equipment productivity programs • Engage in continuous improvement programs

Chapter 26
Tourism E-Booking and 'E-Purchasing': Changes in a 5-Year Period

Nataša Slak Valek
I-Shou University, Taiwan

Eva Podovšovnik Axelsson
University of Primorska, Slovenia

ABSTRACT

Information technology plays a significant role in tourism, but mainly as an informational tool. Ideally, the information search process on the Internet should try to encourage consumers to book and purchase travel services and products prior to leaving for their vacation, but cultural differences in booking on-line are found. The present study research problem is to understand the complex of e-booking and e-purchasing travel behaviors among Slovenes, since no research between Slovene tourists was done before. In details, the relationship between e-booking and paying travel accommodation and travel transportation on the Internet in the period of five years is investigated. The results show slow changes and an increase in booking and buying travel transportation, while booking and paying tourism accommodation gains greater interest during a five-year period.

INTRODUCTION

Information Communication Technology (ICT) and tourism are two of the most dynamic motivators of the emerging global economy; the Internet is becoming more sophisticated across all of these areas (Buhalis, 2003). There are more diverse levels of consumers and increased competition, and many computer users have explored the Internet and participated in online activities such as shopping, communicating with other computer users, and entertainment (Kim et al., 2004). The

DOI: 10.4018/978-1-4666-3966-9.ch026

increasing use of the Internet since the mid-1990s has created a variety of new business opportunities which include many in the airline and tourism industries (Harison & Boonstra, 2008).

If the past 20 years have seen an emphasis on technology, then since 2000 we have been witnessing the truly transformational effect of communications technologies (Buhalis & Law, 2008). Some analysts predicted there will be no need for travel agents in the future as consumers turn to the Internet to make their travel arrangements (Lang, 2000), but a decade later travel agents still exist. This raises an interesting question about the effect of cultural differences on tourists' preferences of booking and buying their travel accommodation and transportation.

With the enormous amount of information potentially available to travelers, the Internet constitutes an important platform for information exchange between the consumer and industry suppliers (e.g., hotels, transportation sectors, attractions), intermediaries (e.g., travel agents), controllers (e.g., governments and administrative bodies), as well as many non-profit organizations, such as destination marketing organizations (Werthner & Klein, 1999). In fact, airlines have increasingly adopted the Internet as a platform to generate new streams of profits (Harison & Boostra, 2008). The Internet is not just a communication tool on which to transfer contents previously conveyed by other media, but demands new, appropriate communication and customer relation strategies, because of its contextual product distribution function (Singer et al, 2010). Tourism destinations and businesses need to acquire data about their potential and present tourists (Slak, Valek, & Axelsson, 2012). For tourism agents and tourism destinations using web-reservation systems for booking different tourism services such as accommodation, transportation, and even activities at the destination, it is vital to know how tourists act and react on the Web.

Despite the growing importance of the Internet as an information source for travelers, there is a general lack of information on usage differences among travelers from different countries (Huang, 2003). That tourists mainly search for information on the Internet has been confirmed by many researchers (Bonn, Furr, & Susskind, 1998; Weber & Roehl, 1999; Ho et al., 2012). The advantages of online tourism information search include the relatively low cost, customized information, ease of product comparison, interactivity, virtual community formation, and 24-hour accessibility (Wang, Head, & Arthur, 2002). Ho et al. (2012) analyzed different web-search strategies and found that of five most common search strategies, each individual search tactic may not be sophisticated (Ho et al., 2012).

Further, social media, a recent online development, is becoming increasingly important in the online tourism domain (Xiang & Gretzel, 2010). It is widely recognized that Word-of-Mouth (WOM), both positive and negative, has the potential to influence consumer information searches and purchase and buying decisions (Sparks & Browning, 2011). As digital WOM, Facebook and Twitter can influence a tourist's final decision, as tourism destination images may be formed through online information and comments (Li et al., 2009).

Nevertheless, there are significant differences in access and usage between cultures, countries and socio-economic groups, which can make cross cultural differences between Internet users (Park & Jun, 2003). According to the Internet World Stats (2012), Asia is the strongest region by the number of internet users (44.8% of Asians), followed by Europe (22.1%), and North America (12.0%). By the same research, a total of 71% of residents are Internet users in Slovenia. Since no chapter to date has examined Slovenian tourists, the present chapter is prepared to present results of Slovene tourists using the Internet for purchasing a trip. On the other hand, Eurostat (2012) reported that two-thirds of Europeans used the Internet on average at least once a week, while one-quarter have never used it. The same research reported 64% of Slovenians use the Internet regularly, which is below the European average numbers (Eurostat, 2012). Taking into consideration those data, Slovenians should represent a big potential as "e-bookers," but in fact little is known about the real e-bookers and e-buyers between Slovenian tourists. Therefore, we have opted to deeply research how Slovenians act on the Internet while booking and buying the accommodations and travel transportation.

BOOKING ACCOMMODATIONS ON-LINE

There is a growing need to understand how various elements of online information search and review influence consumer behavior (Vermeulen & Seegers, 2009), especially in e-booking the accommodations and travel transportation. Apart from information searching, Internet users can also make bookings or purchase products and services (Heung, 2003) and Internet use has potentially important consequences for travel behavior (Kenyon, 2010). Smith and Jenner (1998) note travel products and services are perfectly suited to online selling because they possess the necessary characteristics that can function in the electronic environment. Online travel sales increased by 17% from 2007 to 2008 and reached EUR 58.4 billion in the European market in 2008, or 22.5% of the market (Marcussen, 2009). In 2008, the breakdown of the market by type of service was as follows: air travel, 54%; hotels (and other accommodations), 19.5%; package tours, 15%; rail, 7.5%; rental cars (and car ferries), 4%. New tools and opportunities have reduced the "distance" between producers and potential customers, who have more opportunities to know the providers of tourists (Singer et al, 2010). This is why selling holidays as packages and as individual needs (such as transportation or the accommodation) by Internet is expected to increase.

In 2005, a total of 50% of "Generation Y" Internet users had booked travel arrangements online, and, in 2008, that number rose to 65%. During the same time, the percentages of "Generation X" and older generations to make online travel reservations remained about the same (Jones & Fox, 2009). In 2005, the Internet was used by 37% of Americans for travel planning, and 30% of American adults (64.8 million) purchased travel products through the Internet.. Among those who purchased travel products online in 2005, a total of 36 million purchased airline tickets, 32 million purchased accommodations, 13.4 million purchased cultural events, and 8.8 million purchased travel packages (TIA, 2005). Similarly, respondents in the Jun et al. (2007) study were more likely to use the Internet or online channels for their travel information search during the pre-trip stage than for their travel product purchases. When Pearce and Schott (2011) analyzed domestic pre- and at- the destination booking, they discovered nearly half of the domestic accommodations booked were reserved by phone (48%) and 36% online, while a similar share of international accommodations are booked online (47.3%).

BOOKING TRANSPORTATION ON-LINE

Today, telecommunication changes the travel methods, affects an individual's choice of travel method, and may even eliminate the necessity of some travel or generate new demand for certain types of travel. By doing so, it affects people's lifestyles (Yoshii & Sasaki, 2010). It is clear that Internet use could have important implications for the understanding of travel behavior and, therefore, for transport policy, including policies to manage car use and to tackle mobility-related social exclusion (Kenyon, 2010). Not only booking a rented car by Internet, but buying airline tickets has become a "normal" process in traveling. Airline customers are coming back to purchase online tickets primarily because of the satisfaction of the online booking process and a positive attitude towards using the online booking system (Apostolou & Economides, 2008). The Jun et al. (2007) study highlights the spatial and temporal complexity of distribution and drawing attention to the timing and location of distribution functions, and differentiating activities that occur pre-trip and in transit from those carried out at the destination. Booking the transportation is undoubtedly a pre-trip activity since a mean of transport is needed for coming to the tourism destination; this could be a car, aircraft, ship, among others. The possibility exists for booking the transportation as a mean for the activities at the destination, as renting a bicycle, motorcycle, boat, among others.

Pearce and Schott (2011) found advance bookings for transport to the destination are made for virtually all outbound trips but only 41.8% of domestic trips. The same study reported that two-thirds of transport reservations for domestic destinations are booked online, while bookings for international travel are shared relatively evenly between online bookings (42.9%) and those made in person (40.9%). Online is dominantly used for information searches and purchasing accommodations, car rentals and flights, when attraction information, activities and events search and purchase was on low interests for "on-line tourists" (Jun et al., 2007). On-line purchase of the transportation is interesting as much as e-booking the accommodations, which should gain the same interest between academics and tourism marketing planners.

The present study research problem is to understand the complex booking-travel behaviors. In detail, the relationship between booking and paying travel accommodations and the relation between booking and paying travel transportation was investigated. The purpose of the study was to identify Slovenian tourists who search tourism information on the Internet in comparison with those who in fact make a booking and directly pay their travel accommodations and transportation using the Internet. The study is prepared in contest of analyzing data of the five-year period from 2005 to 2010.

DATA AND MODEL OF WORK

The research methodology was prepared and based on quantitative survey data. The data were received by the Statistical Office of the Republic of Slovenia (SORS). The target population was Slovenian citizens (aged 15 and above). The data were collected each year throughout the period between 2005 and 2010. The sampling frame is the directory of private telephone subscribers in the Republic of Slovenia. The sample is stratified systematically. Strata were defined by statistical region (12 regions) and type of settlement within the region (6 types). Each stratum was independently sampled. The SORS also prepared the necessary weights, according to the population data. In total, the following were analyzed: 24,627,796 trips Slovenians made in the period from 2005 to 2010 (in 2005, 3,900,823; in 2006 4,764,483; in 2007, 3,657,721; in 2008, 3,729,083; in 2009, 4,331,722; and in 2010; 4,243,964).

The research model which was prepared according to the theoretical background explained in the previous chapter is presented in Figure 1.

The following hypothesis was tested in our work:

H1: The period of travelling influences the use of the Internet for travel purposes.

All the data were weighed according to the weights and methodological implications prepared by the SORS. The methodological implications of the obtained data are shown in the representativeness of the obtained data. The SORS developed the weighing and validation of obtained data. If there are between 0 and 12 units in each cell for non-weighed data, the results are not representative, which are signed as: If there are between 12 and 75 units in each cell for non-weighed data then we have to report limited representativeness of the obtained data. In the tables we present this data with the sign M. If more than 75 units are in each cell for non-weighed data, we can assume the obtained results are representative of the Slovenian

Figure 1. Model of work

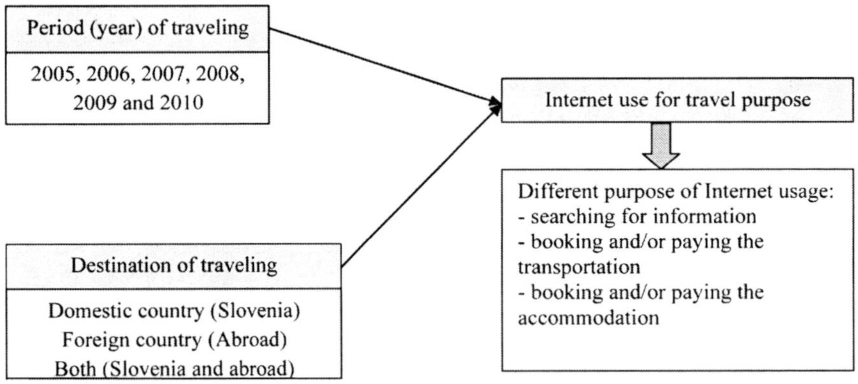

population. The analysis of variance was used to test the research hypothesis.

The analysis is based on using the Internet for travel purposes. This chapter has reached four different ways to use the Internet for travel purposes: booking travel transportation, paying travel transportation, booking travel accommodations, and paying travel accommodations. Additionally, the present chapter contends with the calculation of the ratios between the accommodation and transportation booked, and additionally also paid by the Internet. In doing so, the chapter deals with the issue of the actual sales according to the demand for organizing Internet trips. This is a very important issue for marketing and planning for the future of e-booking and e-paying of tourism services.

PRESENTATION OF THE SAMPLE

In the following example, the presentation of the sample is given. In Figure 2, the number of trips made by Slovenians to Slovenia abroad and the combination of travelling to Slovenia and abroad through the years is presented.

As seen from Figure 2, Slovenians mostly tend to travel abroad. The number of trips made by Slovenians abroad remained stable during the period from 2005 to 2010 with a slight fall in the years from 2007 to 2009. The number of trips made to Slovenia increased in 2006 and fell drastically in 2007, having an increase up to 2009 and then again a decrease. The number of trips made by Slovenians to Slovenia and abroad had a peak in 2006 before decreasing up to 2008, and from 2009 returning to the peak from 2006.

The total number of trips made by Slovenians increased between 400,000 trips made in 2005 to 500,000 trips made in 2006. The global financial crisis which affected Europe and Slovenia also started to take its toll in 2007 when the total number of trips diminished to 365,000. A year later, the number of total trips made by Slovenians slightly increased to 373,000, when in 2009 and 2010, the number of trips grew again to more than 420,000 trips per year.

RESULTS

The chapter focuses on Internet use for Slovenians who travel which is presented in Figure 3. The results are segmented by the year of travelling between 2005 and 2010. The research hypothesis stated that the period (year) of travelling influences the use of the Internet for different travel purposes. In this chapter, the focus was on identifying the percentage of trips made by Slovenians for which different internet activity was used. For each

Figure 2. Number of trips made by Slovenians by destination and year of travel (Source: SORS, 2005-2010)

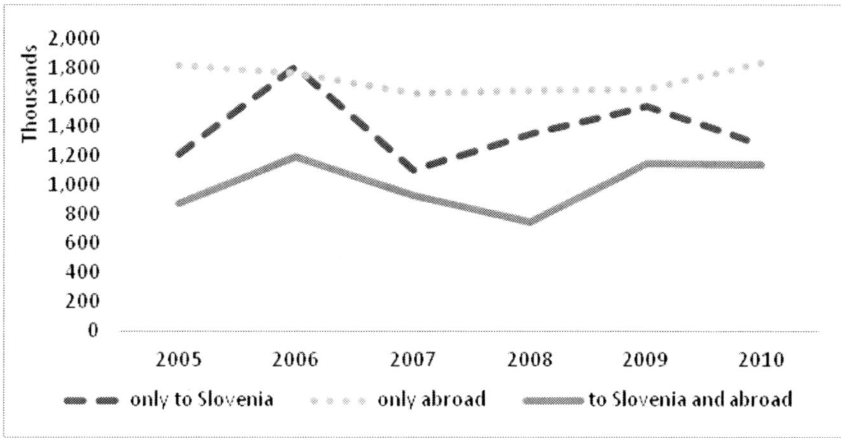

analysis, the analysis of variance was used to test if the results were statistically significant or not. The results are presented in Table 1 in the Appendix. The dependent variables (different types of Internet use) were statistically significant at the 0.000 level when testing their significance by the independent variable (year). In the following, the results are further explained.

In the first part of the questionnaire, the respondents were asked about their general use of the internet for the mentioned travel: "Have you used the internet for organizing this vacation or trip?" The possible answers were yes and no. In Figure 3 the results are shown.

From Figure 3, an increase in Internet use for trips Slovenians completed during the period between 2005 and 2010 is seen, with only one statistically significant downfall from 2005 to 2006. All the differences among the pair of years were statistically significant at the 0.00 level. From 2005 to 2006, the number of trips Slovenians made without using the Internet for travel purposes increased from 316,000 to 391,000, while after 2006 it remained stable up to 2010 (between 267,000

Figure 3. Percentage of internet users for organizing a trip by years (Source: SORS, 2005-2010)

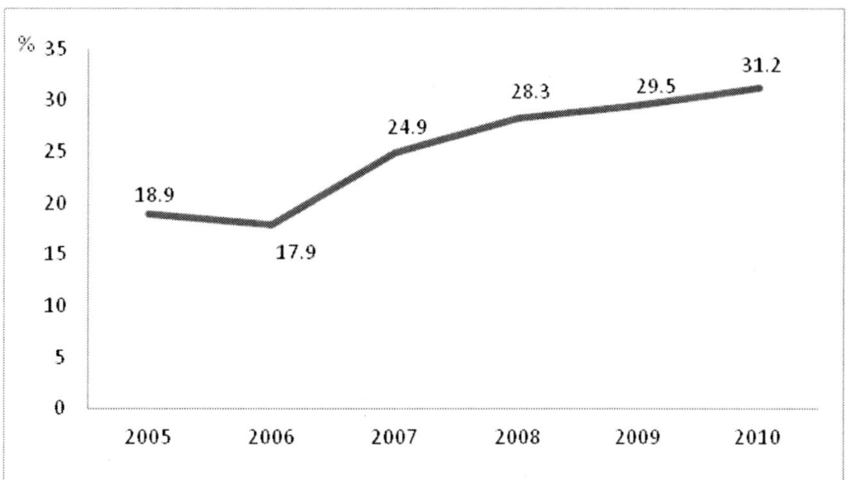

and 305,000). From 2005 to 2010, the number of trips Slovenians made using the Internet for travelling has increased from 73,900 up to 132,000. The respondents were also asked about the kind of activity for which they used the Internet in their travel. At the beginning, they were asked, "Have you used the Internet to obtain the information about the country, region, or city of travel?" The possible answers were Yes and No. The results are presented in the figure below.

The number of trips Slovenians made without using the Internet to get general information about their vacation remained stable from 2005 to 2010 (about 40,000 to 50,000 per year), while the number of those who used the Internet to get information about the vacation increased significantly from 700,000 in 2005 to 1,280,000 in 2010. The percentage of trips Slovenians made using the Internet to gather information about the travel ranged between 94% in 2005 to 96% in 2007. The increase from 2005 to 2006 was statistically significant at the 0.00 level, followed by a statistically significant decrease from 2006 to 2007, and followed again by a statistically significant increase in the following years.

In the next part of the research, the use of the Internet for booking and paying the travel transportation was analyzed. The ratio between paying and booking the travel transportation with the use of the Internet was calculated in order to understand how many trips booked on the internet were also an actual purchase. The results are shown in Figure 5 and 6.

The number of trips Slovenians made using the Internet for booking the transportation increased every year, from 57,000 trips in 2005, 132,000 in 2007, and finished to be more than 126,000 in 2010. Interestingly, the number of trips Slovenians made without booking their transportation by the Internet has also increased from 682,000 trips in 2005 to 1,197,000 trips in 2010. However, the number of trips Slovenians made using the Internet for buying or paying the travel transportation changed from 39,000 trips in 2005, 32,000 trips in 2006, to 88,000 trips in 2007, and 95,000 trips in 2010. As seen in Figure 5, the percentage of booking and buying the travel transportation through the Internet was between 4% and 15% in the period from 2005 to 2010.

All the differences between the years were statistically significant at the 0.05 level. The percentage of those travel transportations that were booked through the internet in 2005 and 2006 was 7%, while in 2007 it doubled. After 2007, we can see the decrease to 8.6%, followed by a raise to 11.4% in 2009, and a decrease to 9.5% in 2010. All the differences among the years were statistically significant at the 0.00 level. The percentage of the travel transportation that was bought using the Internet dropped from 5.3% in 2005 to 4% in 2006. In 2007 the percentage got the biggest raise to 9.7%, followed by a drop to 6.9% in 2008, followed by a raise to 8.4% in 2009, and dropped again to 7.2% in 2010.

All the differences among the years were statistically significant at the 0.00 level. When analyzing the ratio of the travel transportation which was booked and bought using the Internet, we can see that in 2005 it was 68.7%. In 2006, the lowest percentage of those who booked the travel transportation also bought it using the Internet (52.4%). In 2007 the ratio was 67%, and in 2008 the ratio was the highest--80% of all those who booked the travel transportation also bought it through the Internet. In 2009 and 2010, the percentage dropped slowly but not below 73%.

The last part of our investigation focused on the use of the Internet for booking and buying the travel accommodations. The ratio between buying and booking the travel accommodations with the use of the Internet was calculated. The results are shown in the figure below.

All the differences between years were statistically significant at the 5% level.

The number of trips Slovenians made using the internet to book the travel accommodations constantly increased from 18,000 in 2005 to 45,000 in 2010. All the differences among the years were

Figure 4. Percentage of internet users for gathering information about the trip by years (Source: SORS, 2005-2010)

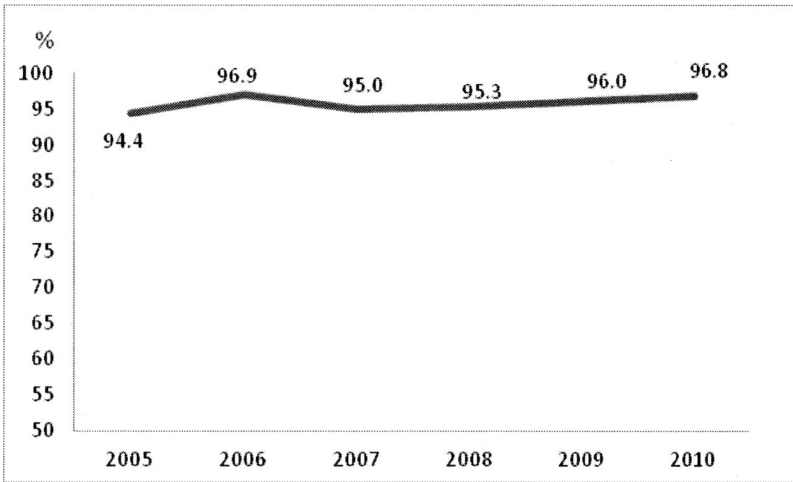

statistically significant at the 0.00 level. While analyzing the number of trips Slovenians made using the Internet to pay the travel accommodation, several increases can be seen: in 2005 the number was 66,000, in 2006 a slight downfall can be noted (53,000), resulting in an increase to 87,000 in 2007; 137,000 in 2008, and exceeding 170,000 in 2009 and 2010. All the differences among the years were statistically significant at the 0.00 level. The percentage of those trips that were made booking the travel accommodation using the Internet in 2005 and 2006 was 25%, while in 2007 it raised to 31%. After 2007 we can see the decrease to 29.5%, followed by a raise to 32.5% in 2009 and to 34.5% in 2010. The percentage of those trips that were made buying the travel ac-

Figure 5. Percentage and the ration of Internet users for booking and paying travel transportation by years (Source: SORS, 2005-2010)

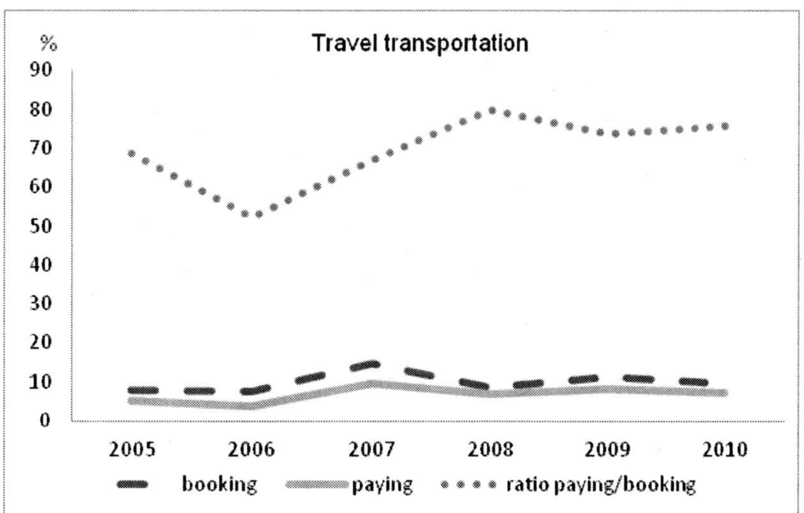

Figure 6. The percentage of Internet users for booking and paying travel accommodations by years (Source: SORS, 2005-2010)

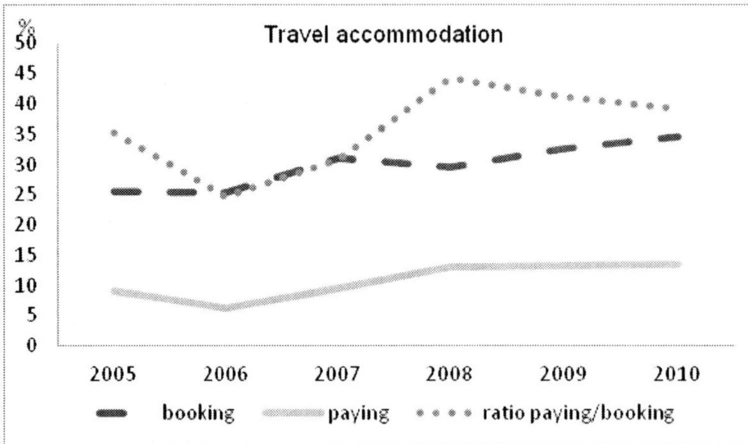

commodations using the internet in 2005 dropped from 9.% in 2005 to 6.2% in 2006. In 2007 the percentage got the biggest raise to 9.6%, followed by a raise to 13% in 2008, 2009, and 2010. All the differences among the years were statistically significant at the 0.00 level.

When analyzing the ratio of those travel transportations which were booked and bought using the Internet, we can see that in 2005 it was 35.3%. In 2006, the lowest percentage of those who booked the travel transportation also bought it (24.7%). In 2007, the ratio was 30.8%; in 2008, the ratio was the highest, namely 44.2% of all those who booked the travel transportation also bought it through the Internet. In 2009 and 2010, the percentage slightly dropped to approximately 40%. All the differences among the years were statistically significant at the 0.00 level.

ANALYSIS AND DISCUSSION

The Internet enhances the information search process and encourages consumers to purchase travel products prior to leaving for their vacation (Jun et al, 2007), but differences could be found between backgrounds and cultures. Each EU nation has a distinct national-culture, which is likely to have a different influence on travelers' information search behavior, but only a few studies examined the impact of national culture on travelers' external information search behavior (Gursoy & Umbreit, 2004).

Since Slovenia is a European country, but used to be a part of the former Communist Yugoslavia where many cultures were mixed between each other, a question about Slovenian Internet user habits was derived. Do Slovenes book and buy their travel accommodations by Web or are they still very cautious about that, like main residents from communist countries? Our results suggest that, like many other consumer product decisions, travelers conduct an information search before they make their vacation and destination selections. Thus, tourism destinations Internet pages with the reservation system included should promote and encourage tourists to not only check the information, but to book and buy their accommodations and travel transportation using that certain Web page. This is why tourism destinations with their reservation systems, hotels, and rent-a-car firms and other suppliers of tourism services and products should be more interested in tourism behaviors when using the Internet to promote their services in different cultures. The tourism supplier success on the Web is achieved when its customers book and buy the service offered on the web site.

Our research also confirms tourists review information on the Internet and tourism destinations Web pages (e.g., visitljubljana.com, exploreminnesota.com, tourismthailand.org). When Jun et al. (2007) analyzed pre-travel behavior on the Internet, they discovered the number of respondents who purchased a travel product was lower than the number of respondents who searched for information for a travel product. However, although the data was collected in 2001, it was published in 2007. Our interests derived in changes which occurred using the Internet to travel information during the period of 2005-2010, just after Slovenia officially joined the European Union (EU) in 2004.

While the EU encourages the preservation of the national-culture of member states, the long-term goal of the EU is to form a single European market (European Union, 1999), which means the development of similar purchasing habits between the EU countries. Nevertheless, between Slovenes, there were no big differences in the period of five years uncovered; 94.5% of Slovenians searched for travel information on the Internet in 2005, and 96.7% in 2010. There is an increase in about 2%, but in 2005 many Slovenians still actually used the Internet as an informational tool for travelling.

The main changes have been noticed in using the Internet to organize trips, travel, or vacation. Slovenians using the Internet to organize their trips amounted to 19% of the population in 2005, but in 2010 more than 30% of Slovenians used the Internet for their travel purposes. This finding could be connected in the distribution of the Internet in Slovenia during a period of five years; indeed, in 2005 Eurostat reported that 48% of Slovenian households had Internet access, but in 2011 this proportion increased to 73%. With increasing the household access to the Internet, it became a more frequently used tool for organizing the travelling and vacations. However, the Internet is not the only channel for tourism information searching (Ho et al., 2012). Hyde (2008) models pre-vacation decision-making for a tour vacation as comprising three phases: information search, vacation planning, and vacation booking, and shows that while these three concepts are unique phases, they are related to each other.

Despite the growing importance of the Internet as an information source for international travelers, and as a marketing tool and way of doing business, there is a general lack of information on how these travelers use the Internet for information, and booking and purchase of travel products and services (Huang, 2003). This is why our research is based on analyzing the changes in proportion of Slovenians who not only search for information, but also book and buy their travel service via the Internet. In 2011, a total of 58% of all Internet users in the 27 nations comprising the EU have bought or ordered goods or services over the Internet for private purposes in the last 12 months, compared with 57% in 2010, and 54% in 2009.

However, the share of e-shoppers among Internet users varied considerably between Member States where Slovenia recorded the highest increases comparing the data of 2010 and 2011 (Eurostat, 2011). Taking this data into consideration, one would expect an increase in booking and buying travel services (accommodations and transportation) via the Internet. However, there is discussion about checking for the information different from purchasing on the Internet. Trust is required when using the Internet for booking and buying. Marcussen (1999) suggested that services like travel and tourism are ideal for selling over the Internet because they do not incur any transportation costs. Despite the fact that online services provide convenience to travelers for information searches and purchasing, many tourists still prefer traditional ways of purchasing transportation tickets and accommodation, which impedes the growth of Internet shopping for travel purchase (Heung, 2003). In fact, our data shows that despite the continued growth in on-line purchasing, many

Slovenian consumers are still somehow reluctant to make an on-line purchase or booking.

In a 5-year period, little change in booking and purchasing travel transportation on-line is noticed. In 2005, a total of 7.7% of Slovenian trips that required booking of the transportation (flight, rent-a-car, etc.) were made via the Internet, while in 2010 this percentage increased to only 9.5%; less than a 2% increase may be noticed during a 5-year period. When coming to analyze data about "paying" the transportation by Web, the percentages are even lower; 5.2% in 2005 and 7.2% in 2010. When this is compared to the data about searching information the difference is obvious.

Ruiz-Mafé et al. (2009) stated that out of every 10 airline ticket buyers, 8 involved the Internet to obtain information on times and prices, but only 3 finally bought the ticket online. Tourism suppliers with the reservation system web sites should be interested in why such a big difference is noticed. At the beginning of the "Era of the Internet," many forecasts have predicted a big increase in using the Internet in every-day life, as buying and shopping by the Web (Butler & Peppard, 1998; Shon et al., 2003, Buhalis & Law, 2008), a fact which will dramatically change our lives, and this is why marketing workers in tourism expected self-evident results. However, in a period of five years analyzed in this study when Internet use should have shown rapid growth, little difference is noticed in on-line purchasing of tourism services. This finding suggests that tourism marketing workers and website creators should try to improve their systems to attract tourism consumers. Websites can foster positive experiences among consumers and increase online purchasing of tourism services as well as the degree of loyalty to the airlines' sites (Park & Gretzel, 2007). Ease of use is also important and if an Internet user considers a website easy to use then this positively influences perception of the site's usefulness and can lead to purchases (Ruiz-Mafé et al., 2009).

Complementary services, such as car rental and hotel bookings, are also now offered on airline websites, contributing substantial streams of revenues (Harison & Boostra, 2008). In fact, our results show better results while analyzing booking and buying tourist accommodations. From all the trips Slovenians made in 2005, 25.5% booked their accommodations using the Web (domestic and international travel) and almost 9% were paid via the Internet, while up to 2010 those numbers increased. In 2010, a total of 34.5% of trips were booked and 13.5% paid the accommodation through the Web. Comparing all the results, it can be said that Slovenians prefer to book and buy their travel accommodation using the Internet, while booking and buying travel transportation is still scary and needs more attention by the web-creator.

CONCLUSION

This study analyzes Slovene tourists' preferences in searching information, booking and buying travel accommodations and transportation. Since the use of the Internet has increased over the years, the present research focused on changes of using the internet for purchasing travel services over a period of five years. The results show slow increase in booking and buying travel transportation, while booking and paying tourism accommodations have gained greater interest. The nature and extent of travel booking and purchase prior to departure or at the destination will depend on where that destination is and what types of trip are being undertaken--fundamental points which have often been overlooked in previous studies (Pearce & Schott, 2011).

Future research on booking and buying the accommodations and travel transportation should be conducted to examine this issue. One possible avenue is an analysis by the hotel's stars or the type of accommodation (hotel, tourism farms, apartment, etc.), the level of vehicles class rented (economy, compact, intermediate, etc.) and type of flight tickets (business, first, economy class) purchased by tourists. Additional attention to design is needed when Web reservation systems try to attract tourists from different cultures. Organizations should study the culture in detail before investing resources (Gursoy & Umreit, 2004). As Stewart and Vogt (1999) claimed, "travelers developed plans before their trip, but these plans were often changed, especially with regard to on-site activities; travelers tended to over plan, actuating fewer elements than they planned; the amount of information searched for and purchasing patterns differed by travel products; and repeat visitors made more congruent plans than first-time visitors.."

REFERENCES

Apostolou, G., & Economides, A. A. (2008). *Airlines websites evaluation around the world. The Open Knowledge Society. A Computer Science and Information Systems Manifesto, First World Summit*. Athens, Greece: WSKS.

Bonn, M. A., Furr, H. L., & Susskind, A. M. (1998). Using the Internet as a pleasure travel planning tool: An examination of the sociodemographic and behavioral characteristics among Internet users and non-users. *Journal of Hospitality & Tourism Research (Washington, D.C.)*, *22*(3), 303–317. doi:10.1177/109634809802200307.

Buhalis, D. (2003). eTourism: Information technology for strategic tourism management. London: Prentice Hall.

Buhalis, D., & Law, R. (2008). Progress in information technology and tourism management: 20 years on and 10 years after the Internet—The state of eTourism research. *Tourism Management*, *29*(4), 609–623. doi:10.1016/j.tourman.2008.01.005.

Butler, P., & Peppard, J. (1998). Consumer purchasing on the Internet: Processes and prospects. *European Management Journal*, *16*(5), 600–610. doi:10.1016/S0263-2373(98)00036-X.

Eurostat (2012). Internet use in households and by individuals in 2011. Retrieved on August 4, 2012, from http://epp.eurostat.ec.europa.eu/cache/ITY_OFFPUB/KS-SF-11-066/EN/KS-SF-11-066-EN.PDF

Gursoy, D., & Umreit, T. (2004). Tourist information search behavior: Cross-cultural comparison of European Union member states. *Hospital Management*, *23*(1), 55–70. doi:10.1016/j.ijhm.2003.07.004.

Ho, C.-I., Lin, M.-H., & Chen, H.-M. (2012). Web users' behavioural patterns of tourism information search: From online to offline. *Tourism Management*, *33*(6), 1468–1482. doi:10.1016/j.tourman.2012.01.016.

Hyde, K. F. (2008). Information processing and touring planning theory. *Annals of Tourism Research*, *35*(3), 712–731. doi:10.1016/j.annals.2008.05.001.

Internet World Stats. (2009). Internet usage statistics: World internet users and population stats. Retrieved on August 8, 2012, from http://www.internetworldstats.com/stats.htm

Jones, S., & Fox, S. (2009). *Generations Online in 2009*. Washington, DC: Pew Internet & American Life Project.

Jun, S. H., Vogt, C. A., & MacKay, K. J. (2007). 'Relationships between travel information search and travel product purchase in pretrip contexts'. *Journal of Travel Research*, *45*, 266–274. doi:10.1177/0047287506295945.

Kenyon, S. (2010). The impacts of Internet use upon activity participation and travel: Results from a longitudinal diary-based panel study. *Transportation Research Part C, Emerging Technologies*, *18*(1), 21–35. doi:10.1016/j.trc.2009.04.014.

Kim, W. G., Lee, C., & Hiemstra, S. (2004). Effects of an online virtual community on customer loyalty and travel product purchases. *Tourism Management, 25*, 343–355. doi:10.1016/S0261-5177(03)00142-0.

Lang, T. (2000). The effect of the Internet on travel consumer purchasing behavior and implications for travel agencies. *Journal of Vacation Marketing, 6*(4), 368–385. doi:10.1177/135676670000600407.

Li, X., Pan, B., Zhang, L., & Smith, W. W. (2009). The effect of online information search on image development: Insights from a mixed-methods study. *Journal of Travel Research, 48*(1), 45–57. doi:10.1177/0047287508328659.

Marcussen (2003). Trends in European Internet Distribution. *Travel and Tourism Services Centre for Regional and Tourism Research*. Retrieved on August 9, 2012, from http://www.crt.dk/uk/staff/chm/trends.htm

Park, C. L., & Jun, J.-K. (2003). A cross-cultural comparison of Internet buying behavior: Effects of Internet usage, perceived risks, and innovativeness. *International Marketing Review, 20*(5), 534–553. doi:10.1108/02651330310498771.

Ruiz-Mafe, C. et al. (2009). Drivers and barriers to online airline ticket purchasing. *Journal of Air Transport Management, 15*(6), 294–298. doi:10.1016/j.jairtraman.2009.02.001.

Schmalleger, D., & Carson, D. (2008). Blogs in tourism: Changing approaches to information exchange. *Journal of Vacation Marketing, 14*(2), 99–110. doi:10.1177/1356766707087519.

Shon, Z. Y., Chen, F. Y., & Chang, Y. H. (2003). Airline e-commerce: The revolution in ticketing channels. *Journal of Air Transport Management, 9*, 325–331. doi:10.1016/S0969-6997(03)00040-1.

Singer P., Ferri M-A., Aiello L., & Cacia C. (2010). Internet as a "point of synergy" between communication and distribution: Hypothesis of model applied to tourism. *International Journal of Digital Content Technology and its Applications, 4*(7), 23-37.

Slak Valek, N., & Podovšovnik Axelsson, E. (2012). Understanding Internet use among passive and active tourists. Is there a need for a different web approach? *Innovative Issues and Approaches in Social Science, 5*(1), 88–106.

Smith, C., & Jenner, P. (1998). Tourism and the Internet. *Travel & Tourism Analyst, 1*, 62–81.

Sparks, B. A., & Browning, V. (2011). The impact of online reviews on hotel booking intentions and perception of trust. *Tourism Management, 32*(6), 1310–1323. doi:10.1016/j.tourman.2010.12.011.

Stewart, S., & Vogt, C. (1999). A Case-Based Approach to Understanding Vacation Planning. *Leisure Sciences, 21*, 79–95. doi:10.1080/014904099273165.

Vermeulen, I. E., & Seegers, D. (2009). Tried and tested: The impact of online hotel reviews on consumer consideration. *Tourism Management, 30*(1), 123–127. doi:10.1016/j.tourman.2008.04.008.

Wang, F., Head, M., & Arthur, N. (2002). E-tailing: An analysis of web impacts on the retail market. *The Journal of Business Strategy, 19*(1), 73–93.

Weber, K., & Roehl, W. S. (1999). Profiling people searching for purchasing travel products on the World Wide Web. *Journal of Travel Research, 37*(3), 291–298. doi:10.1177/004728759903700311.

Werthner, H., & Klein, S. (1999). *Information technology and tourism: A challenging relationship*. Vienna, Austria: Springer. doi:10.1007/978-3-7091-6363-4.

Xiang, Z., & Gretzel, U. (2010). Role of social media in online travel information search. *Tourism Management*, *31*(2), 179–188. doi:10.1016/j.tourman.2009.02.016.

Yoshii, T., & Saski, K. (2010). Information/Communication Technologies and Travel Behaviour. *Transportation Research Part C, Emerging Technologies*, *18*(1), 1–2. doi:10.1016/j.trc.2009.04.021.

APPENDIX

Table 1. Analysis of variance (the use of the Internet by year)

ANOVA						
		Sum of Squares	**df**	**Mean Square**	**F**	**Sig.**
Using the Internet to search for information	Between Groups	451,118	5	90,224	2267,230	,000
	Within Groups	245143,652	6160216	,040		
	Total	245594,770	6160221			
Using the Internet to book the transportation	Between Groups	3238,049	5	647,610	7229,389	,000
	Within Groups	551833,159	6160216	,090		
	Total	555071,208	6160221			
Using the Internet to pay the transportation	Between Groups	1944,842	5	388,968	5923,164	,000
	Within Groups	404535,333	6160216	,066		
	Total	406480,174	6160221			
Using the Internet to book the accomodation	Between Groups	6993,734	5	1398,747	6652,699	,000
	Within Groups	1295201,084	6160216	,210		
	Total	1302194,818	6160221			
Using the Internet to pay the accomodation	Between Groups	4371,920	5	874,384	8815,430	,000
	Within Groups	611018,902	6160216	,099		
	Total	615390,822	6160221			

Chapter 27
Entry Strategies and Distribution Channels of Italian SMEs in the Chinese Market

Patrizia de Luca
University of Trieste, Italy

Donata Vianelli
University of Trieste, Italy

Fabio Claudio Marzano
University of Trieste, Italy

ABSTRACT

The present chapter explores the internationalization process of Italian SMEs in the Chinese market, focusing on entry and distribution choices, in the framework of facilitating factors and perceived difficulties. The following main research questions were formulated: how do Italian SMEs enter the Chinese market and distribute their products? Which are the main facilitating factors and difficulties perceived by Italian companies selling in the Chinese market? This exploratory study that is part of an extensive field research was conducted through two steps: a quantitative research, based on a structured questionnaire; and a qualitative research, with open-ended interviews. The findings could provide marketing executives useful insights in developing entry and distribution strategies for SMEs in the Chinese market.

INTRODUCTION

The interest of the international business literature for emerging markets is particularly evident in the case of China (Fetscherin et al., 2010), and it is expected to expand in an economic context characterized by a growing polarization of world markets' performance. In this environment, advanced economies such as Europe and the USA face high uncertainty in post-crisis growth; however, emerging markets forecast a continuous development of Gross Domestic Product (GDP) (Fardoust et al., 2010). In this economic context where emerging economies become a driving force

DOI: 10.4018/978-1-4666-3966-9.ch027

for the advanced ones, entering these markets and distributing products and services become a necessity more than a simple opportunity. Despite a strong "Made in Italy" (Bucci et al., 2011), exports of Italian products in China have difficulty taking off, with a value of just over eight billion Euros (Ice, 2011). This issue concerns overall Small- and Medium-Enterprises (SMEs), which are often considered inexperienced when it comes to internationalization, but often even larger companies cope with some problems (Johnson & Tellis, 2008; Yeh & Bounds, 2006). Companies which are successful in this market recognize that entry modes and distribution channels are important key factors (de Luca et al., 2011; Solberg, 2006; Bello & Gilliland, 1997).

The present chapter explores the internationalization process of Italian companies in the Chinese market, focusing on entry and distribution choices in the framework of facilitating factors and perceived difficulties. The importance of China and that of other emerging markets in general, has only recently become more and more evident as there is a growing polarization of global market performance. There are, on one hand, advanced economies such as Europe and the USA, which are characterized by a weak and unstable recovery from the severe economic crisis. On the other hand, there are emerging markets, such as China, who are experiencing an impressive growth.

In this context, for many Italian companies, especially those of small or medium dimensions, dealing with internationalization is a risky process, especially in culturally distant markets such as China. The great opportunities for development and the concrete facilitating factors are not always enough to deal with the considerable entry difficulties and high investment risks adequately. For products made in Italy such as food & beverage, fashion, furniture, and automation, China is the second export country outside the European Union (EU) after the USA. The Italian export to China is growing but still very low compared to other European countries (Pegan, 2011). In this complex business context, some research questions arise. How do Italian SMEs enter the Chinese market and distribute their products? Which are the main facilitating factors and difficulties perceived by Italian companies selling in the Chinese market? To contribute to the knowledge on these issues, the chapter aims to answer to these research questions.

Research has an exploratory purpose and integrates a quantitative and qualitative approach. This mixed methods research (Creswell, 2003; Thashakkori & Teddlie, 1998; 2003) has become increasingly common in recent years, also in management studies (Bryman, 2006). According to the scheme developed by Green et al. (1989), the justifications for combining quantitative and qualitative research refers to "complementarities," because this mixed method "seeks elaboration, enhancement, illustration, clarification of the results from one method with the results from another" (Green et al., 1989, p. 259). On this basis, information was collected using both structured questionnaires (quantitative research) and open-ended interviews (qualitative research). A sample of Italian SMEs, on a wide range in terms of size and business sectors, was considered. After the quantitative phase, some open-ended interviews were used in order to obtain in-depth contributions to the explanation of data gathered through the structured questions.

The findings could provide marketing executives useful insights in developing entry and distribution strategies for Italian SMEs in the Chinese market.

DISTRIBUTION IN CHINA: BACKGROUND

Several economic, political, and social transformations have characterized the country in recent decades. They have contributed, first of all, to a more than tenfold increase in GDP since 1978. In 2010, China became the second-largest economy in the world after the USA on the basis of Purchasing Power Parity (PPP). In U.S. dollar values, the Chinese agricultural and industrial output exceeds those of the same sectors in the U.S. With regards to the value of services, China is in second position after the US. At the moment, per capita income is below the world average (CIA, 2012). These relevant transformations have also affected the distribution system. This developed above all in the last decade (Ling & Jaffe, 2007), especially for the "open door" policy, that conducted to some relevant change: a first evolution in 1992, the access to World Trade Organization in 2001, and the complete opening to foreign investment in 2004. Nevertheless, the country still presents some peculiarities. Also, with regards to distribution, China is a complex and challenging market which mixes the old and the new. In this context, it is important to improve knowledge about distribution in China.

Following an early study by Wortzel (1985), which provided a classification of consumer goods offered in the Chinese market and a description of distribution channels, literature on distribution in China has made important contributions. Many researchers have focused their attention towards the description of the channels' structure in the Chinese market (Luk, 1998; Jiang & Prater, 2002; Jaffe & Yi, 2007) and distribution strategies developed by foreign companies (Goldman, 2001; Chaney & Gamble, 2008; Uncles, 2010). Some studies analyze variables related to the selection of Chinese partners and the relational mechanisms internal to distribution channels (Liu & Wang, 1999; Dong et al., 2008). These issues are significantly relevant in cases of cultural distant countries showing a direct impact on the effectiveness of entry (Solberg, 2008). Cultural distance affects the implementation of marketing (de Mooij, 2010) and management strategies (Hill, 2009; Alon et al., 2012), increases conflict (Shoham et al., 1997), requires higher cooperation and flexibility in the trade relation (Balabanis, 1998), and influences trust and communication between partners as well as the willingness to invest in the relationship (Ivens, 2006). Cultural differences may be an important impediment to the development of distributor relationships in China by western companies and, in this specific analysis, by Italian SMEs. Hofstede's (2001) cultural dimensions indexes, which have been widely used in academic research, report significant differences between China and Western countries which can be summarized in the Kogut and Singh (1988) cultural closeness index.

In this context, a short description of the distribution system in the foreign country can be interesting. The Chinese distribution system is very complex, above all in the urban areas where distribution systems typical of a pre-industrial and planned economy, coexist with international retailers that are leaders at a global level (Ling & Jaffe, 2007). This situation is rapidly changing and it could condition the management and the results of the foreign companies in China. Furthermore, it is industry specific, and it is characterized by a constant evolution, based on changing trends of life and consumption styles in the Chinese society (McEwen et al., 2006). These aspects are very significant, for example, in the case of the typical products made in Italy such as food & beverage, fashion, and furniture.

Social and economic changes and the presence of new retailers have determined the transformation of the food & beverage market. Supermarkets, introduced in the early 1990s, can be state-owned or foreign-owned companies. They propose a large assortment at lower prices than small traditional stores. This phenomena resulted in a further growth of retail sales, above all for ready-to-eat food products, already increased of an annual rate of 14% during the 1980s and 1990s (Gilmour & Gale, 2002). In the last 20 years, 60,000 supermarkets entered the Chinese market reaching a market share of 35% on the retailing sales (ICE Shanghai, 2009). Additionally, hypermarkets have increased in number (New Zealand Trade & Enterprise, 2007), playing a double role as a retailer for final consumers and a cash & carry for small retailers (Musso, 2008). Convenience stores, recently introduced as an evolution of the traditional shops, are growing, especially through franchising. Prevalently Chinese-owned, they generally work around the clock and offer a large assortment of local food and integrated services.

Foreign retailers contributed to the development of the fashion market, positively influenced also by the growing income and luxury consumption. Beginning in Hong Kong, they rapidly expanded in first and secondary level cities in China, working with specialized stores in large malls, important locations to convey the image of Italian and French brands. However, local manufacturers, particularly able to imitate and learn from foreign competitors, are trying to develop their own Chinese retail brands with the intent to enter in foreign markets in the next future. In China, the expansion is achieved mainly through the acquisition of national chains or by franchising contracts. If in the past the attention of foreign investors was focused mostly on the big cities of the first level, like Beijing and Shanghai, recently their interest is shifting also to second level cities and to the urban areas with a high economic growth.

Finally, Beijing and Shanghai are the most important markets for almost every company operating in the furniture industry, both foreign and national ones. In particular, though Chinese companies usually produce for other major foreign brands, they have at the same time a commercial presence in these cities (e.g., through subsidiaries, branches, and showrooms). Most of the big buyers, both wholesaler and retailers, request the supply of goods directly to the manufactures, while others buy from agents or distributors. In the case of small retailers, the most diffused distribution formats are specialized stores mostly located within malls dedicated to high-end furniture. On the contrary, low and medium-end products are often sold in hypermarkets specializing in furniture.

ITALIAN SME'S IN CHINA: AN EMPIRICAL RESEARCH

The enormous Chinese market represents a relevant outlet for Italian companies. It is the second largest EU market after the USA, and the seventh in general for the exports made in Italy. The Italian export to China is rising (in 2011 + 16.2% in 2010), but it is still low: over eight billion Euros in 2011 (ICE, 2012). Table 1 offers some data about the position of China and Italy relevant to import-export. China occupies a considerable position for Italy, both as supplier (3rd position)

Table 1. Italy and China position as supplier and customer countries

Position of Italy as supplier and customer country for China					
	2007	2008	2009	2010	2011
	pos.	pos.	pos.	pos.	pos.
Italy as supplier for China	21°	20°	20°	20°	20°
Italia as customer for China	11°	11°	12°	10°	11°
Position of China as supplier and customer country for Italy					
	2007	2008	2009	2010	2011
	pos.	pos.	pos.	pos.	pos.
China as supplier for Italy	3°	3°	3°	3°	3°
China as customer for Italy	14°	14°	11°	8°	7°

Fonte: Vianelli, de Luca & Pegan (2012), p. 33

and customer country (from 14th position in 2007 to the 7th position in 2011).

To explore the internationalization process of Italian companies in the Chinese market, this study focuses on entry and distribution choices, considering facilitating factors and perceived difficulties. The following research questions were formulated: how do Italian SMEs enter the Chinese market and distribute their products? Which are the main facilitating factors and difficulties perceived by Italian companies selling in the Chinese market? The answers to these questions can suggest theoretical and managerial implications useful for the analysis of international marketing strategies in emerging markets.

Method

A database of 1,183 companies was built using secondary data, through trade journals, internet, and trade associations in the relevant Italian industries (Fortis, 2005; ISTAT, 2008; Ministero dello Sviluppo Economico & Interprofessionalnetwork, 2010). Considering that about 2,000 Italian companies operate in the Chinese market (Osservatorio Italia-Cina, 2011), the database can well represent the variety of the total population.

A self-administered questionnaire, in Italian language, pre-tested on a convenience sample of ten key companies, was prepared. To obtain an adequate response rate, researchers phoned the companies with the goal to obtain the willingness to cooperate and to identify the name of the most appropriate respondent in the firm. After this phase, a total of 879 SMEs agreed to cooperate. An e-mail with an introductory letter and the link to the questionnaire (surveymonkey.com©) was sent. The data were collected in a period of nine months, from November 2009 to July 2010. A total of 130 questionnaires were collected, with a response rate of over 14%. The sample represents a wide range of Italian SMEs, in terms of size (from less than €2 million to €10 million for Small companies and from €11 million to €500 million for Medium companies), and sectors of activity (food, fashion, furniture, mechanics, services, etc.). For data analysis, the statistical package SPSS 18 was used.

After the quantitative phase, we used open-ended interviews because of their relevance in giving important contributions to the explanation of data gathered through the structured questions. In the sample of 130 units, we selected a sub-sample of 25 companies respecting the purposive sampling approach (Kerlinger, 1986). Furthermore, we conducted two interviews with the Institute of Italian Foreign Trade and the Italian Chamber of Commerce in China, and four interviews with relevant Chinese distributors. With the help of the companies participating in the qualitative phase of the research, seven Chinese distributor partners operating in the representative industries of Italy (food, fashion, furniture, and mechanics) were identified. Four of them agreed to collaborate in our study. The total duration of audio recordings of the interviews was 45 hours. These data were analyzed using a deductive content analysis, based on a theoretical framework as guidance for initial codes (Hsieh & Shannon, 2005; Elo et al., 2008).

Findings

The Choice of Entry Mode

The choice of entry mode taken into consideration by the Italian companies during the study was heavily influenced by the availability of financial and managerial resources devoted to investing in China. The methods used range from exploratory to collaborative up to direct investment, but as the degree of control (and therefore effectiveness) over the internationalization activities increases, so too does the risk and the financial effort required, presenting a highly critical variable, especially for SMEs. The results of the sample of companies analyzed are given in Table 2.

For most of the companies, export is the main choice (53.7%), through distributors (30.9%),

Table 2. The choice of entry mode

Entry mode	N°	% on the specific entry mode	% on the total
EXPORTS	***110***	***100.0%***	***53.7%***
Distributor (in China)	34	30.9%	16.6%
Importer (in China)	28	25.5%	13.7%
Independent agents (in China)	26	23.6%	12.7%
Dealers (in China)	15	13.6%	7.3%
Italian exporter	7	6.4%	3.4%
COLLABO-RATIONS	***48***	***100.0%***	***23.4%***
Joint Venture	25	52.1%	12.2%
Franchising	12	25.0%	5.9%
Licencing	11	22.9%	5.4%
DIRECT INVEST-MENTS	***47***	***100.0%***	***22.9%***
WFOE - Wholly Foreign Owned Enterprise	25	53.2%	12.2%
Commercial branch	12	25.5%	5.9%
Branch (manufacturing and commercial)	6	12.8%	2.9%
FICE - Foreign Invested Commercial Enterprise	3	6.4%	1.5%
Manufacturing branch	1	2.1%	0.5%
Total	**205**	**-**	**100.0%**

followed by importers (25.5%) and independent agents (23.6%), all operating in the Chinese market. The leading option among the collaborative agreements, selected by 23.4% of the companies, was found to be that of joint ventures (52.1%), followed by franchising and licensing, which reached 25% and 22.9%, respectively. Joint ventures were especially popular with companies which carry out both manufacture and sales activities in China and that want to exercise greater control. Franchising has a typically distributive application but is suffering from very recent legislation (only authorised since 2004).

The WOFE (Wholly-Owned Foreign Enterprise) was the most frequent entry choice in cases of direct investment (53.2%). This being a type of joint stock Corporation in which all the shares are held by the foreign investor, control of the company is maximised as there is no need for partners who would otherwise be involved in deciding the strategies and company policies.

The next most popular choices were commercial branches (25.5%) and commercial and manufacturing branches (12.8%). The remaining option of Foreign Invested Commercial Enterprises (FICE) has a marginal weight of just 6.4%, which is partly due to its recent introduction into Chinese legislation (end of 2004). FICE is comprised of commercial companies which can distribute imported and locally manufactured products at the wholesale and retail level (Huang, 2003).

Within the range of the various choices, it can nevertheless be noted the complexity of the Chinese market in terms of number of targets and geographical areas of reference puts the companies in a position of having to choose more than one entry method (205 choices made by 130 companies). To cite just a few examples, many companies opted for a multi-channel strategy that requires a variety of intermediaries. Others, conversely, opted not only to export their own high-end global brands, but also to invest in local brands aimed at a medium- and high-end targets. Still others combined direct investments to develop shops belonging to them with a franchising network which allows them to extend their distribution coverage.

As highlighted above, the increased risk and financial effort present a variable that can significantly influence the choice of entry method. If we place the selected entry methods in relation to the size of the company (Table 3), we clearly see the SMEs tend to prefer export methods (56.8%), as they are less costly from both a financial and organisational perspective. Large companies, on the other hand, show a strategic balance that involves the various possible entry methods in almost equal measure with the aim of achieving multiple market goals, without the influential factor of the financial barrier.

The Choice of Distribution Channel

The sales channel preferred by the companies analysed (Table 4) is that of independent foreign distributors, such as importers or wholesalers (29.2%), followed by Chinese national agents, representatives and brokers (16.2%). Direct export implemented using an intermediary based in the foreign country greatly outweighs indirect export which plays a merely marginal role: Italian intermediaries or agents or foreigners resident in Italy are only secondary, such as the Internet and export consortia. The channel with the most weight after direct exports is that which reflects a choice in investment or a contractual collaboration in some other form. In fact, companies prefer direct foreign investments (13.5%), franchising (8.6%) and company-owned sales points (4.9%), and direct sales (6.5%), this latter being typical of *business to business* sectors.

The Internet is not yet a relevant distribution channel for Italian companies. This aspect could be a weakness in the future, considering the growing role of Internet in the Chinese market (Vianelli, de Luca & Pegan, 2012). On the basis of some recent market data, in the period 2010 – 2011, the online retail market in China passed from 10 to 20 billion Euros (Euromonitor International, 2011). Online sales are rapidly growing, but they are still low (2% of the total) (Atsmon & Magni, 2010; Atsmon et al., 2010), as in the present study on Italian companies.

If we relate the choice of sales channel to the size of the company (Table 5), it appears the channels preferred by big companies are direct investments and company-owned sales points, which are unpopular with SMEs, however, due to the investments required to establish them. Independent foreign distributors were adopted by the SMEs and large companies in equal measures, as were Chinese agents, representatives and brokers, as well as franchising sales points.

The analysis of sales points suffers from the marked differences among companies' sectors. Each sector, whether it is foodstuffs, furnishings, or fashion, is characterised by a prevailing distributive form.

In general (Table 6), a clear prevalence emerges for the use of specialised sales points (28.4%) and the presence of own brand products in large stores (26.7%). Supermarkets have a weight of 11.2% of the total and, as is obvious, represent one of the preferred channels for companies in the food sector especially. Despite their widespread presence throughout the region and their dominance as the prevailing forms of distribution in China, convenience stores, kiosks, and outdoor markets are almost never taken into consideration; this finding is consistent with the elevated position-

Table 3. Company size and entry mode

Entry mode		Company size		Total
		SME	Large Company	
Exports	N°	75	14	**89**
	%	56.8%	38.9%	**53.0%**
Collaborations	N°	31	11	**42**
	%	23.5%	30.6%	**25.0%**
Direct investments	N°	26	11	**37**
	%	19.7%	30.6%	**22.0%**
Total	**N°**	**132**	**36**	**168**
	%	**100.0%**	**100.0%**	**100.0%**

Table 4. The choice of distribution channel

Distribution channel	N°	%
Independent foreign distributors that buy from the company (importers, wholesalers, etc.)	54	29.2%
Chinese agents, representatives or brokers (paid on commission)	30	16.2%
Direct foreign investment (own facilities abroad, such as branches, subsidiaries etc.)	25	13.5%
Franchising sales points	16	8.6%
Direct sales	12	6.5%
Own sales points	9	4.9%
Italian intermediaries that buy products from the company and manage the sales in China (trading companies, export house)	7	3.8%
Foreign intermediaries resident in Italy (buying offices of foreign chains)	7	3.8%
Italian agents, representatives or brokers (paid on commission)	6	3.2%
Commercialisation companies (independent or joint) with offices in Italy	5	2.7%
Internet	4	2.2%
Export consortia	3	1.6%
Other	7	3.8%
Total	**185**	**100,0%**

ing of made in Italy brands as well as the greater organisational difficulties involved in achieving this extremely fragmentary type of channel.

The Main Facilitating Factors and Difficulties Perceived

With regard to the aspects facilitating the entry, the results of the factor analysis are in Table 7.

Two factors were extracted which cumulatively explain around 60% of the total variance. The first factor was generated by the variables that predominantly concern the "relational dimension" which specifically consists of the existence of relationships with a partner of a commercial, consulting or institutional partner able to provide assistance and support to the company, including financial. The second factor is identified by a group of variables which essentially refer to the company's "internal dimension," such as the overall vision, know-how, international experience, entrepreneurial spirit, and brand awareness on overseas markets.

Based on the average values assumed by the two factors, we can see that the internal resources, rather than the external relational ones, assume primary importance as a facilitating factor for the companies interviewed (average factors of 5.21 and 3.92, respectively).

Working against these facilitating factors, a series of entry difficulties were met by the 130 companies already based in China. The factor analysis applied to these data revealed a latent structure formed of four principle factors (Table 8) which cumulatively explain approximately 62% of the total variance. Based on the variables that comprise it, the first factor is referable to the dimension of "relationships with partners" of a commercial, institutional and consulting nature; the second factor is identified by the variables relating to a general "strategic direction"; the third is essentially attributable to the "market" based aspects; finally, the fourth factor is identified by the problems derived from "legislation."

By using the average values of the variables that make up the individual factors, we find that the companies interviewed attribute primary importance to difficulties in relationships with partners (average factor = 4.29), particularly in relation to difficulties in establishing relationships with reliable partners (average variable = 4.89) and identifying them adequately (average variable = 4.62). These are followed by issues relating to the market (average factor = 4.24), above all with regard to problems in understanding and adapting to the language and local culture (average variable

Table 5. Company size and distribution channel

Distribution channel		Company size		Total
		SME	Large company	
Independent foreign distributors that buy from the company (importers, wholesalers, etc.)	N°	38	8	46
	%	32.8%	23.5%	30.7%
Chinese agents, representatives or brokers (paid on commission)	N°	19	5	24
	%	16.4%	14.7%	16.0%
Direct foreign investment (own facilities abroad, such as branches, subsidiaries etc.)	N°	15	8	23
	%	12.9%	23.5%	15.3%
Franchise sales points	N°	11	4	15
	%	9.5%	11.8%	10.0%
Direct sales	N°	7	4	11
	%	6.0%	11.8%	7.3%
Own sales points	N°	4	3	7
	%	3.4%	8.8%	4.7%
Italian intermediaries that buy products from the company and manage the sales in China (trading companies, export house)	N°	4	0	4
	%	3.4%	0.0%	2.7%
Foreign intermediaries resident in Italy (buying offices of foreign chains)	N°	5	0	5
	%	4.3%	0.0%	3.3%
Italian agents, representatives or brokers (paid on commission)	N°	4	0	4
	%	3.4%	0.0%	2.7%
Commercialisation companies (independent or joint) with offices in Italy	N°	3	1	4
	%	2.6%	2.9%	2.7%
Internet	N°	3	1	4
	%	2.6%	2.9%	2.7%
Export consortia	N°	3	0	3
	%	2.6%	0.0%	2.0%
Total	N°	116	34	150
	%	100.0%	100,0%	100,0%

= 4.80). Legislative matters (average factor = 3.95) are especially significant in relation to the complexity of the regulatory constraints (average variable = 4.06).

Lastly, strategic direction comes in fourth place (average factor = 3.04), with particular reference to the allocation of financial resources invested in the Chinese market (average variable 3.45).

If we compare these results with entry difficulties perceived by other companies not yet selling on the market, highlighted in a previous research, with a sample of 109 companies (de Luca, Vianelli, & Marzano, 2011), we can note some interesting results. The factor analysis applied to the data revealed a latent structure formed of four principle factors, which cumulatively explain approximately 66% of the total variance.

Table 6. The choice of distribution formats

Distribution formats	N°	%
Specialised sales points	33	28.4%
Large stores/Department stores	31	26.7%
Supermarkets	13	11.2%
Small traditional shops	9	7.8%
Hypermarkets	8	6.9%
Discount stores	4	3.4%
Convenience store	3	2.6%
Kiosks/Bazaar/Outdoor markets	2	1.7%
Other	13	11.2%
Total	**116**	**100.0%**

In this case, the first factor–named "commercial and institutional relationships"–is again attributable to the relational dimension, however, with the addition of regulatory aspects. The second factor is determined by the variables connected to the difficulties derived from the "market," with reference to local tastes, culture and language and the identification of the target mist suited for the product in question. The third factor is that of "internal resources," connected to issues of international experience and financial sources. Finally, the fourth factor can be identified in terms of the "strategic direction," as it includes aspects connected to competitive difficulties, to the decision to operate mainly on other markets, and an anti-risk spirit.

By using the average values of the factors, the data shows that the companies interviewed attribute priority importance to difficulties derived from the combination of "commercial and institutional relationships" (average factor = 4.35), particularly in relation to difficulties in establishing relationships with reliable partners (average variable = 4.83) and in identifying institutions and commercial partners that are able to offer the company suitable support (average variable = 4.67).

The Relationship with Commercial Partners

From the analysis of the drivers and of the more critical difficulties met by Italian companies in entering the Chinese market, it can be seen just how important and at the same time how difficult it is to establish trustworthy relationships with the local partners. It is not easy to find a partner who can be trusted and who at the same time possesses the required managerial talents. And it is not easy to keep tabs on them, putting at risk the activities of the company, especially when it is noted for its well-known brand name and must manage a clear, high profile image position globally.

For this reason, we decided to look close at the characteristics of this relationship, with the purpose of identifying the more problematic aspects, and of providing useful points of reflection to overcome the difficulties then defined. With this in mind, two distinct phases were investigated: the first, through a factor analysis, the principal dimensions characterizing relations between partners were investigated. Following this, based on the information collected, the opinions of some Italian companies operating in China and a selection of local operators were collected in a qualitative survey.

Using the information obtained through the factor analysis (Table 9), four latent dimensions were identified in order of importance: "Financial Capabilities", "Marketing Skills", "Sales Skills" and "Relational Skills". Below are several excerpts from the interviews conducted.

As pointed out in Table 9, financial capabilities identify the willingness, readiness and ability to financially support the activities of Italian companies. It is, in fact, very difficult to find intermediaries who are ready to invest in communication, in marketing activities, and in developing and training sales networks. They are not willing to do so because they expect the Italian companies to invest alone, and they rarely accept a shared investment logic such as is usually done in other

Table 7. Factor analysis: Facilitating factors

Items	Relational dimension	Internal dimension	Alfa	Mean score factors	Mean score items	SD
Relationships with government and institutional bodies able to provide assistance and support	0.894		0.834	3.92	3.32	2.129
Numerous pre-existing informal and personal relationships with several partners in the Chinese market	0.840				4.54	2.030
Pre-existing and formalised business contracts in the Chinese market	0.832				4.25	2.040
Relationships with consultancy firms able to provide assistance and suppor	0.629				3.04	1.962
The availability of additional financial resources to invest in the Chinese market	0.604				4.47	1.858
The company's overall vision		0.818	0.763	5.21	5.15	1.785
The company's know how		0.738			5.47	1.492
Previously consolidated international experience in other countries		0.733			5.10	1.576
The company's entrepreneurial spirit		0.709			5.31	1.667
A brand already known internationally		0.613			5.02	1.830
Explained variance (%)	31.319	28.475	–	–	–	–
Eigenvalues	4.039	1.941	–	–	–	–

Note: Bartlett's homogeneity test was found to be significant (.000, < 0.05). The KMO (Keiser Meyer Olkin) measure of sampling adequacy is equal to 0.794 (> 0.50). Cronbach's alpha reliability coefficient is equal to 0.833. Extraction method: Analysis of the principal components. Rotation method: Varimax with Kaiser normalisation. The rotation reached the convergence criteria in 3 iterations

foreign countries. Quite the opposite, the Chinese partners consider the investment made by Italian companies to be an indicator of credibility and of long-term involvement.

From the many qualitative interviews it emerged that the Italian companies insist on market penetration without, however, being disposed to accept responsibility for the investment necessary for communication, training, or the adaptation of the product. For example, as highlighted by a Chinese businessman operating in the fashion sector, even if he was willing to deal with Italian products, not necessarily with famous brands, the main problem he has to face is that often small Italian companies are not willing to invest and do not want to adapt collections to the tastes and physical structure of Chinese consumers. Similarly, another Chinese entrepreneur, talking about footwear, points out that even if Italian shoes are beautiful, no one will buy them if the brand is unknown, even if they are "the best shoes on earth." In other terms, the need of investing in the creation of brand value is a concept that Italians do not seem to understand but it is expected by the Chinese partner.

The lack of marketing capacity represents another aspect which is frequently noted as being problematic partners' relations. Companies considered in the research, in fact, complain about the scarce product knowledge and the limited managerial capacity of their Chinese partners. At the same time, it is difficult to find partners who already manage products of complimentary level of price and image and who have therefore acquired a significant experience in distributive channels coherent with a product labelled "Made in Italy." For example, a furnishing company reports their Chinese partner was managing a set

Table 8. Factor analysis: difficulties perceived by Italian companies selling in China

Items	Relationship with partners	Strategic direction	Market	Legislation	Alfa	Mean score factors	Mean score items	SD
Difficulties in establishing relationships with reliable partners on the Chinese market	0.848				0.839	4.29	4.89	1.66
Difficulties in controlling activities carried out by intermediaries	0.811						4.55	1.70
Difficulties in identifying institutions/commercial partners that can provide adequate informative/operational support	0.764						4.62	1.60
Difficulties in establishing relationships with consultancy firms able to provide assistance and support	0.544						3.15	1.61
Difficulties in establishing relationships with government and institutional bodies able to provide assistance and support	0.491						4.24	1.81
Difficulties due to the company's lack of international experience		0.759			0.789	3.04	2.69	1.61
Difficulties due to the limited additional financial resources required to invest in the Chinese market		0.744					3.45	1.89
Difficulties generally linked to a company strategy more orientated towards other markets		0.71					3.21	1.57
Difficulties linked to an entrepreneurial spirit adverse to taking risks		0.689					2.82	1.53
Difficulties in finding a suitable target for our product			0.696		0.696	4.24	4.07	1.65
Difficulties in obtaining information on the taste and trends in the local market			0.682				3.76	1.57
Difficulties linked to very high competitive pressure			0.658				4.33	1.83
Difficulties understanding and adapting to the language and local culture			0.626				4.80	1.83
Difficulties caused by too many regulatory/legislative constraints				0.814	0.519	3.95	4.06	1.72
Difficulties due to the risk of violating the rights to intellectual property				0.451			3.8	1.84
Explained variance (%)	18.756	16.607	14.881	11.625	-	-	-	-
Eigenvalues	5.230	1.765	1.270	1.015	-	-	-	-

Note: Bartlett's homogeneity test was found to be significant (.000, < 0.05). The KMO (Keiser Meyer Olkin) measure of sampling adequacy is equal to 0.804 (> 0.50). Cronbach's alpha reliability coefficient is equal to 0.869. Extraction method: Analysis of the principal components. Rotation method: Varimax with Kaiser normalisation. The rotation reached the convergence criteria in 6 iterations

Table 9. Factor analysis: Difficulties perceived by Italian companies in selection and management of the distribution partner in China

Items "It is easy to find a partner that…"	Sales skills	Marketing skills	Financial capabilities	Relational skills	Alfa	Mean score Factors	Mean score Items	SD
Has an adequate market share	0.880				0.95	4.33	4.46	1.58
Has an efficient sales network	0.763						4.30	1.62
Has a stable product (and client) portfolio	0.752						4.60	1.48
Guarantees a good geographical cover-age	0.670						4.43	1.73
Has experience in the target market	0.625						4.18	1.60
Guarantees a good service before and after sales	0.623						4.46	1.60
Is on time with deliveries	0.562						4.11	1.46
Has established good relations with the area's economics institutions	0.539						3.90	1.47
Is available to buy large quantities of product to sell	0.527						4.70	1.70
Has at his disposal good logistics and warehouse infrastruc-tures	0.473						4.13	1.55
Has a good product knowledge		0.702			0.87	4.59	4.69	1.69
Sells product lines of similar quality/ brand image		0.690					4.53	1.65
Has good managerial skills		0.668					4.70	1.43
Is able to implement a marketing plan		0.643					4.53	1.55
Has a good reputa-tion among his past and present clients		0.487					4.20	1.32
Can guarantee the brand's safety		0.423					4.89	1.75
Is available to invest in the development and training of sales networks			0.805		0.84	4.97	4.74	1.62

continued on following page

Table 9. Continued

Items "It is easy to find a partner that..."	Sales skills	Marketing skills	Financial capabilities	Relational skills	Alfa	Mean score Factors	Mean score Items	SD
Is available to invest in your product's communication			0.799				4.76	1.68
Is able to financially support the marketing and sales activity in the Chinese market			0.604				5,35	1.55
Is available to eliminate from his portfolio the competitors' products			0.354				5.03	1.48
Has a consolidated relationship experience with other foreign companies				0.575	0.76	4.16	3.98	1.50
Speaks English well or, in general, with whom communication is effective				0.486			4.33	1.81
Explained variance	23.9%	17.4%	15.6%	9.1%				
Eigenvalues	12.113	1.507	1.282	0,925				

Extration method: Principal Axis Factoring; Rotation method: Varimax with Kaiser normalization; 6 iterations.

of three major brands of western-manufactured mattresses, which were not in competition between them. The experience did not last long because the partner was unable to fully understand the product, or how there could be three solutions to the problem of proper rest yet be complementary to each other: therefore he could not take care of image positioning.

Just as important, in addition, are factors connected with the sales' capacities. Many managers highlight there is little enthusiasm for purchasing a minimum stock of products and that the turnover of products and brands is high, resulting in an excessive fragmentation of the product portfolio. Furthermore, sales networks and logistic infrastructures are often inefficient and the geographical coverage risks to be limited. Pre and post-sales services are also very weak. This is an aspect which is particularly felt by Italian companies which have to intervene directly if they wish to guarantee the level of service requested for high quality products. Several companies seem to have understood just how fundamental it is to work in synergy with their partners in order to have success in China. An entrepreneur operating in the furniture industry underlines that to be successful they have to support constantly their partners not only providing technical and sales assistance but also staff training and marketing resources, for example teaching how to manage the corporate image in the showroom for their single-brand stores, or their corner in the case of multi-brand dealers.

Finally, another critical factor which emerges from the factorial analysis is that of Relational Skills. These are strongly influenced by the linguistic and cultural diversity, which often makes the dialogue between companies and their distributing partners difficult and full of misunderstandings. As a company in the mechanical field emphasises, the use of an interpreter is not enough, because there is always the risk of adding a filter to dialogues without understanding the mood of the counterparts, and there is always that feeling of expressing and receiving something which is watered down.

SOLUTIONS AND RECOMMENDATIONS

Manifold are the issues highlighted in the research which shows how critical the internalization process of Italian SMEs is in the Chinese market. In general, Italian companies are faced with problems related to the weak governance of the distribution channel, the deep cultural differences, the limited financial resources and the high competitiveness of the Chinese market.

In consideration of modes of entry and distribution channels, a low grade of control of the market is observed. The widespread use of Chinese distributors and importers can rarely assure the valorization of made in Italy products. These choices are justified, as pointed out by the literature, by the limited size of the Italian companies which are generally smaller than the corresponding companies of other developed countries. They often face scarce financial, managerial and organizational resources that force them to execute less risky internationalization strategies, like exportations, which are highly externalized, but at the same time unable to guarantee the control of the distribution channel.

Nevertheless, for those who aspire towards greater control over the market, it is highly important to aim for more challenging forms of entry, perhaps following a route towards growth and involvement that expands over time, for example, starting by establishing a joint venture with Chinese partners or opening representative offices in the region before exposing the company to the high risks that the incorporation of a wholly owned subsidiary may generate.

Again, a valid alternative to the indirect entry methods would be to create a synergy between companies by sharing financial resources and technologies, coming to an agreement over local distribution, or even developing shared marketing strategies to promote and raise awareness of Italian products with greater impact.

Given the facilitating factors, we can observe how companies feel it necessary to look within to find the resources required to enter and successfully compete on the Chinese market. This could signal a lack of recognition of the role of both Italian and Chinese internationalisation support services. However, at the same time it could also demonstrate a high degree of individualism which drives Italian companies to "do it themselves" in the Chinese market with all the risks that may arise as a result.

Regarding the entry difficulties, the issues connected to relationships with a distribution partner seem to be the main barrier met or at least perceived by those interviewed. This represents the weak link in the whole distribution chain, and often generates difficulties in keeping it under control. Finding a good partner with whom to develop a business is not an easy task: companies are often faced with problems connected to reliability, low confidence or the limited managerial and marketing skills of the partner. These aspects are particularly problematic for products with a symbolic and qualitative value such as those made in Italy.

Another problem which emerged during the research is, as expected, the cultural and linguistic aspect. Referring to the data processed, we notice that the companies already present there attribute a big importance to this aspect. More specifically, the complexity of the situation the companies face after entering the Chinese market actually exceeds expectations.

Finally, ranked in third place in the order of importance, is the perception of very high competitive pressure. This is indeed highly probable in a market such as China that is very attractive for national and foreign investments.

FUTURE RESEARCH DIRECTIONS

This study highlights several factors which should be addressed in future research. First, this study fails to capture the dynamic nature of entry strategies. Hence, future analysis should be focused on the evolution of the choices related to modes of entry and distribution channels, from the very beginning to a more mature phase of the companies' presence in the Chinese market. Second, the sample is made up of small and medium Italian companies: a future replication of the research to SMEs of other nationalities could significantly enrich the results of this analysis. The next stage of this research should also be to determine the role of governmental institutions in facilitating the entry strategies of SMEs in the Chinese market, promoting internationalization and creating competitive platforms that improve the future growth not only in China but also in other relevant emerging markets.

CONCLUSION

Internationalization is a very complex and risky process for many Italian companies, above all those of small and medium dimensions, particularly in culturally distant markets such as China. There are significant opportunities for development but the existing facilitating factors are often insufficient in front of the considerable entry difficulties and high investment risks. In general, Italian companies are faced with problems related to the weak governance of the distribution channel, the deep cultural differences, the limited financial resources and the high competitiveness of the Chinese market.

In the specific area of this study, with regards to the entry modes, because of the complexity of the Chinese market in terms of the number of targets and geographical areas of reference, the companies have to choose more than one entry method, among exports, collaborations and direct investments. The main distribution channels consist of independent foreign distributors, which buy from the company, such as importers or wholesalers, Chinese agents, representatives or brokers, paid on commission, and branches or subsidiaries, that are direct foreign investment. In this context, a clear prevalence emerges for the use of specialised sales points and the presence of own brand products in large stores. Supermarkets have an important role and represent one of the preferred channels for companies especially in the food sector. Despite their pervasive presence throughout the market, convenience stores, kiosks and street markets are rarely taken into consideration. In any case, this result is consistent with the high positioning of made in Italy brands as well as the difficulties involved in achieving this particularly fragmentary type of channel.

Regarding the facilitating factors, the internal resources (such as the overall vision, know how, international experience, entrepreneurial spirit and brand awareness on overseas markets), rather than the external relational ones (mainly the existence of relationships with a commercial, consulting or institutional partner able to provide assistance and support to the company), assume primary importance for the interviewed companies. In front of these facilitating factors, a series of entry difficulties were met by the same companies, mainly regarding the relationships with partners, the strategic direction, and the market based aspects and the legislation.

Despite the limitation of this study, the result offers "food-for-thought" on the commercialisation and sale of made in Italy products in China that can be useful for all economic operators interested in the Asian market in various ways.

First of all, our results show clear suggestions for SMEs which want grow their business in the Chinese market. The distributive channel must be more controlled, and all the financial and managerial resources a company can provide must be put in place. This implies the existence of a strong entrepreneurial spirit that is certainly part of the Italian company culture. Nevertheless, the entrepreneurial effort must be accompanied by significant investments to guarantee commercial control of the company and, consequently, the continuing defense and valorization of a brand which reflects the values of made in Italy.

Further, the figures presented may lead the various institutions that try to support the growth of Italian companies abroad, to reflect on the necessity of finding different paths to support companies at various stages of the process of entering and developing within the Chinese market.

REFERENCES

Alon, I., Jaffe, E. D., & Vianelli, D. (2012). *Global Marketing: Contemporary Theory, Practice, and Cases*. London: McGraw Hill Higher Education.

Atsmon, Y., Dixit, V., Magni, M., & St-Maurice, I. (2010). China's new pragmatic consumers. *McKinsey Quarterly*, October.

Atsmon, Y. & Magni, M. (2010). China's Internet obsession. *McKinsey Quarterly*, March.

Balabanis, G. (1998). Antecedents of cooperation, conflict, and relationship longevity in an international trade intermediary's supply chain. *Journal of Global Marketing*, *12*(2), 25–46. doi:10.1300/J042v12n02_03.

Bello, C. D., & Gilliland, D. I. (1997). The effect of output controls, process controls, and flexibility on export channel performance. *Journal of Marketing*, *61*(1), 22–38. doi:10.2307/1252187.

Bryman, A. (2006). Integrating quantitative and qualitative research: How is it done? *Qualitative Research*, *6*(1), 97–113. doi:10.1177/1468794106058877.

Bucci, A., Codeluppi, V., & Ferraresi, M. (2011). *Il made in Italy*. Rome, Italy: Carrocci Editore.

Chaney, I., & Gamble, J. (2008). Retail store ownership influences on Chinese consumers. *International Business Review*, *17*, 170–183. doi:10.1016/j.ibusrev.2008.02.008.

CIA. (2012). The *World Factbook – China*. Retrieved from https://www.cia.gov/library/publications/the-world-factbook/geos/ch.html

Creswell, J. W. (2003). *Research Design: Qualitative, Quantitative, and Mixed Methods Approaches* (2nd ed.). Thousand Oaks, CA: Sage.

de Luca, P., Vianelli, D., & Marzano, F. C. (2011). L'internazionalizzazione delle imprese italiane nel mercato cinese: Fattori propulsivi e difficoltà percepite. *Micro & Macro Marketing*, *3*, 33–51.

de Mooij, M. (2010). *Global Marketing and Advertising: Understanding Cultural Paradoxes* (3rd ed.). Thousand Oaks, CA: Sage Publications.

Dong, M. C., Tse, D. K., & Cavusgil, S. T. (2008). Efficiency of governance mechanisms in China's distribution channels. *International Business Review*, *17*, 509–519. doi:10.1016/j.ibusrev.2008.07.001.

Elo, S., Elo, K., & Kyngas, H. (2008). The qualitative content analysis process. *Journal of Advanced Nursing*, *62*(1), 107–115. doi:10.1111/j.1365-2648.2007.04569.x PMID:18352969.

Euromonitor International (2011). *Internet Retailing in China*. December.

Fardoust, S., Kim, Y., & Sepulveda, C. P. (2010). *Postcrisis Growth and Development: A Development Agenda for the G-20*. Washington, DC: World Bank.

Fetscherin, M., Voss, H., & Gugler, P. (2010). 30 Years of foreign direct investment to China: An interdisciplinary literature review. *International Business Review*, *19*, 235–246. doi:10.1016/j.ibusrev.2009.12.002.

Fortis, M. (2005). *Il Made in Italy nel nuovo mondo: Protagonisti, sfide, azioni*. Bologna, Italy: Il Mulino.

Gilmour, B., & Gale, F. (2002). Transportation and Distribution: Will Bottlenecks be Eliminated? In Gale, F. (Ed.), *China's Food and Agriculture: Issue for the 21st Century*.

Goldman, A. (2001). The transfer of retail formats into developing economies: The example of China. *Journal of Retailing*, *77*, 221–242. doi:10.1016/S0022-4359(01)00044-6.

Greene, J. C., Caracelli, V. J., & Graham, W. F. (1989). Toward a Conceptual Framework for Mixed-method Evaluation Designs. *Educational Evaluation and Policy Analysis*, *11*(3), 255–274.

Hill, J. S. (2009). *International Business*. Thousand Oaks, CA: Sage Publications.

Hofstede, G. (2001). *Culture's Consequences: Comparing Values, Behaviors, Institutions and Organizations across Nations*. Thousand Oaks, CA: Sage Publications.

House, R. J., Hanges, P. J., Javidan, M., Dorfman, P. W., & Gupta, V. (Eds.). (2004). *Culture, Leadership and Organizations: The GLOBE Study of 62 Societies*. Thousands Oaks, CA: Sage Publications.

Hsieh, H. F., & Shannon, S. E. (2005). Three Approaches to Qualitative Content Analysis. *Qualitative Health Research*, *15*(9), 1277–1288. doi:10.1177/1049732305276687 PMID:16204405.

ICE. (2011). *L'interscambio commerciale tra l'Italia e il resto del mondo nel 2010*. Retrieved March 30, 2011, from http://www.ice.gov.it/statistiche/interscambio_def.pdf

ISTAT. (2008). *Internazionalizzazione delle medie e grandi imprese*. Anni 2001-2006 e previsioni 2007-2009. Retrieved October 7, 2011 from http://www.3.istat.it/salstampa/ comunicati/nob_calendario/20080318_00/testointegrale20080318.pdf

Ivens, B. S. (2006). Identifying differences in foreign customers' relational behavior: An exploratory study using multidimensional scaling. In Solberg, C. A. (Ed.), *Advances in international marketing. Relationship between exporters and their foreign sales and marketing intermediaries* (*Vol. 16*, pp. 245–266). Oxford, UK: Elsevier. doi:10.1016/S1474-7979(05)16010-4.

Jaffe, E. D., & Yi, L. (2007). What are the drivers of channel length? Distribution reform in the People's Republic of China. *International Business Review*, *16*, 474–493. doi:10.1016/j.ibusrev.2007.04.001.

Jiang, B., & Prater, E. (2002). Distribution and logistics development in China. The revolution has begun. *International Journal of Physical Distribution & Logistics Management*, *32*(9), 783–798. doi:10.1108/09600030210452459.

Johnson, J., & Tellis, G. J. (2008). Drivers of Success for Market Entry into China and India. *Journal of Marketing*, *72*(May), 1–13. doi:10.1509/jmkg.72.3.1.

Kerlinger, F. N. (1986). *Foundations of behavioural research* (3rd ed.). New York: Holt.

Kogut, B., & Singh, H. (1988). The Effect of National Culture on the Choice of Entry Mode. *Journal of International Business Studies*, *19*(3), 411–432. doi:10.1057/palgrave.jibs.8490394.

Ling, Y., & Jaffe, E. D. (2007). Economic development and channel evolution in The People's Republic of China. *Asia Pacific Journal of Marketing and Logistics*, *19*(1), 22–39. doi:10.1108/13555850710720885.

Liu, H., & Wang, Y. P. (1999). Co-ordination of international channel relationships: Four case studies in the food industry in China. *Journal of Business and Industrial Marketing*, *14*(2), 130–150. doi:10.1108/08858629910259008.

Luk, S. (1998). Structural changes in China's distribution system. *International Journal of Physical Distribution & Logistics Management*, *28*(1), 44–67. doi:10.1108/09600039810205953.

McEwen, W., Fang, X., Zhang, C., & Burkholder, R. (2006). Inside the Mind of the Chinese Consumer. *Harvard Business Review*, *84*(3), 68–76. PMID:16846190.

Ministero dello Sviluppo Economico & Interprofessionalnetwork (Ed.). (2010). *Dossier Cina. L'impresa verso i mercati internazionali*. Rome, Italy. Retrieved September 30, 2011, from http://www.sviluppoeconomico.gov.it/pdf_upload/documenti/Dossier_Cina.pdf

Musso, F. (2008). *La Cina come mercato: prospettive, vincoli, illusioni*. Paper presented at the Conference Cina e oltre. Piccola e media impresa fra innovazione e internazionalizzazione. Lodi, Italy.

New Zealand Trade & Enterprise. (2007). *Market Profile for Food and Beverage Retail in China*. Retrieved from www.ntze.govt.nz

Osservatorio Italia Cina. (2011). *La Cina nel 2011*. Milano, Italy: Fondazione Italia Cina.

Pegan, G. (2011). Il made in Italy in Cina: Un quadro di sintesi. In Vescovi, T. (Ed.), *Libellule sul drago. Modelli di business e strategie di marketing per le imprese italiane in Cina*. Padova, Italy: Cedam.

Shanghai, I. C. E. (2009). Il *mercato cinese dei prodotti agroalimentari e del vino*. Retrieved from www.ccio.it

Shoham, A., Rose, G. M., & Kropp, F. (1997). Conflict in international channels of distribution. *Journal of Global Marketing*, *11*(2), 5–22. doi:10.1300/J042v11n02_02.

Solberg, C. A. (Ed.). (2006). *Advances in international marketingRelationship between exporters and their foreign sales and marketing intermediaries* (*Vol. 16*). Oxford, UK: Elsevier.

Solberg, C. A. (2008). Product complexity and cultural distance effects on managing international distributor relationships: A contingency approach. *Journal of International Marketing*, *16*(3), 57–83. doi:10.1509/jimk.16.3.57.

Thashakkori, A., & Teddlie, C. (1998). *Mixed Methodology: Combining Qualitative and Quantitative Approaches*. Thousand Oaks, CA: Sage.

Thashakkori, A., & Teddlie, C. (2003). *Handbook of Mixed Methods in Social and Behavioral Research*. Thousand Oaks, CA: Sage.

Uncles, M. D. (2010). Retail change in China: Retrospect and prospects. *International Review of Retail, Distribution and Consumer Research*, *20*(1), 69–84. doi:10.1080/09593961003594501.

Vianelli, D., de Luca, P., & Pegan, G. (2012). *Modalità d'entrata e scelte distributive del made in Italy in Cina*. Milano, Italy: Franco Angeli.

Wortzel, H. V. (1985). The logistics of distribution in China. *International Journal of Physical Distribution & Materials Management*, *15*(5), 51–60. doi:10.1108/eb014618.

Yeh, A., & Bounds, A. (2006). Ferrero Rocher dispute calls for diplomacy. Retrieved October 3, 2011, from http://www.ft.com/cms/s/0/766d0fe4-8c8c-11db-9684-0000779e2340.html#axzz1aMkwSkWO

Chapter 28
A Comparative Analysis of Functionalities of Salesforce.com, mySAP.com, and SiebelCRM

Vandana Ahuja
Jaypee Institute of Information Technology, India

ABSTRACT

Customer Relationship Management or CRM is an enterprise-wide initiative which belongs to all areas of an organization. It reflects the comprehensive strategy and process of acquiring, retaining, and partnering with selective customers to create superior value for the company and the customer. In the era of IT-enabled relationship management, organisations have a host of CRM software products from which they can choose. These products come with different functionalities and support the different functions of a firm, thereby changing the face of global business today. In the era of so-called Cloud computing, support for web-based functionalities is the prime requisite for any CRM Software. This chapter attempts to compare functionalities of three well-established CRM Tools for Organisations: Salesforce.com, mySAPCRM and Siebel CRM.

INTRODUCTION

Contemporary globalism has ushered in an era in which the words *Business* and *Technology* are inseparable. Customer Relationship Management (CRM) Technology offers the business world a host of solutions for process and revenue optimisation. Functionally, CRM applications can be categorised into three main segments: Sales Applications (Sales Force Automation Solutions), Marketing Applications (Campaign Management), and Customer Service and Support (CSS) Applica-

DOI: 10.4018/978-1-4666-3966-9.ch028

tions. Availability of a diverse range of software applications helps to streamline enterprise functions and save invaluable time and resources for organisations. Issues under consideration at the time of CRM tool selection include Functionalities, Legacy System Integration, Technologies used in the tool, performance under critical solutions, security issues, and scalability. Decisions have been made easier in the era of the Cloud. As business applications are moving to the Cloud, the shift from traditional software models to the Internet has steadily gained ground. With the advent of Cloud computing, companies pay for what they need, as the shared infrastructure implies usage of the services like a utility, wherein companies pay only for what they need with options for scalability and automatic upgrades.

Each CRM solution should essentially have three main components: *Operational CRM* involves process management technologies; *Analytical CRM* involves business performance management technologies; and *Collaborative CRM* involves business collaboration management technologies. This chapter evaluates significant functions which any CRM Software needs to perform for an organisation, and further proceeds to conduct detailed studies of three well-established CRM Tools for Organisations: Salesforce.com, mySAPCRM and Siebel CRM, and subsequently compares the tools.

BACKGROUND

Customer Relationship Management

Customer Relationship Management or CRM is an enterprise-wide initiative which belongs to all areas of an organization (Singh, Agarwal, 2003). It reflects the comprehensive strategy and process of acquiring, retaining, and partnering with selective customers to create superior value for the company and the customer.

The goals of CRM include:

1. Building long term and profitable relationships with chosen customers.
2. *Getting closer to those customers with every point of contact with them* (Shainesh & Sheth, 2006).

CRM is an enterprise-wide approach to understanding and influencing customer behavior through meaningful communication to improve customer acquisition, customer retention, customer loyalty, and corporate profitability. CRM can be viewed as an application of one-to-one marketing and relationship marketing, responding to an individual customer on the basis of what the customer says and what else is known about that customer (Pepper et al., 1999). It is a management approach which enables organizations to identify, attract, and increase retention of profitable customers by managing relationships with them (Hobby, 1999), and further identifying strategically significant customers (Buttle, 2008). In the academic community, the terms "relationship marketing" and CRM are often used interchangeably (Parvatiyar & Sheth, 2002). The heart of marketing is relationships and nurturing long term relationships should be the goal of marketing practice (Berry et al., 2006). Five macro-environmental factors responsible for the growth of relationship orientation in marketing (Sheth, 2000) include:

- Rapid technological advancements, especially in the field of information technology
- The adoption of total quality programs by companies.
- The growth of the service economy
- Organizational development processes leading to the empowerment of individuals and teams
- An increase in competitive intensity leading to concern for customer retention

Increased competition reduces brand loyalty, thus making the job of marketers more complex. Further, customers also become indifferent to the myriad marketing messages being thrust upon them. As a result, marketing needs to be more well-directed and specific because customers, whether consumers or businesses, do not want more choices. They want exactly what they want, when, where, and how they want it, and technology now makes it possible for companies to provide it to them (Joseph et al., 1995). Customers have hidden or overt preferences which marketers can reveal by building a learning relationship. Earlier, marketers were attempting to interpret consumer needs on the basis of their buying behaviours. With the arrival of consumer generated media discussed in the next section, marketers have another avenue available to them to learn more about the consumer. The objective is to keep the consumers satisfied and keep them loyal towards the company or brand. CRM, which has also been described as 'information-enabled relationship marketing' (Ryals, Payne, 2001), comprises processes used by organizations to manage consumer relationships which also include collecting, storing and analyzing data, and is often termed as data-driven marketing. CRM attempts to provide a strategic bridge between information technology and marketing strategies aimed at building long-term relationships and profitability. This requires 'information-intensive strategies' (Glazer, 2002). It is vital to maintain appropriate Customer Information Management (CIS) systems by acquiring customer databases and consolidating customer feedback.

Four main CRM strategic capabilities (Gordon, 2002) include:

- **Technology:** This enables the desired functionality for the CRM practice
- **People:** Skills, abilities and attitudes of the people responsible for the CRM initiative
- **Process:** The processes the company has identified to enable or to ensure the CRM objectives are fulfilled-these include the transactional interactions with the customers
- **Knowledge and Insight:** To ensure stronger and deeper relationships with the correct set of customers, companies need to identify the right approaches which will enable them to gain knowledge to gain insight for enhancing the customer value significantly.

CRM is a strategic approach (Mukherjee, 2007) concerned with creating improved shareholder value through the development of appropriate relationships with key customers and customer segments. CRM unites the potential of relationship marketing strategies (Jayachandran, et al., 2005) and Information Technology (IT) to create profitable, long-term relationships with customers and other key stakeholders. CRM provides enhanced opportunities to use data and information to both understand customers and co-create value with them. This requires a cross-functional integration of processes, people, operations, and marketing capabilities that is enabled through information, technology, and applications (Payne et al., 2005). This is where CRM has a role to play-both, as a strategy, as well as an automated system.

CRM is a widely implemented strategy for managing a company's interactions with customers (Anton, 2002), clients, and sales prospects. It involves using technology to organize, automate, and synchronize business processes—principally sales activities, but also those for marketing, customer service, and technical support. CRM applications are customer relationship management solutions for businesses. These software programs are used to store data and organize tasks to make a business run more smoothly and increase sales and profitability. CRM applications may stand alone or run in conjunction with other business software used by a company for contact and task management. With CRM applications, companies can create the positive, personal, and efficient experience that customers will repeatedly return. CRM applications can meet the needs of a small business and allow it to provide the quality service of a large corporation. Salespeople can boost their individual productivity and exceed their sales goals with the information held in the CRM applications database. Using CRM applications, salespeople are able to do regular follow-ups with their clients, assuring customer satisfaction and top notch service.

KEY CRM APPLICATIONS

Sales Force Automation (SFA):

Functionalities of SFA solutions (Wright et al., 2008) allow interface with campaign management software so sales people can receive a comprehensive view of the ongoing and completed marketing campaigns. Some SFA solutions guide the sales representatives through conversations with the customers during first contact. At the higher levels of the sales departments, sales managers must be able to identify their expenses, deploy sales representatives to the proper territories, forecast revenues, and proactively address trends in the markets and address shortfalls through proper reassignment. While the Contact Management functionality stores critical information about each customer contact, Account Management functionality aids in building a deep understanding of target accounts by documenting complete account history, key contacts, customer communications, and internal account discussions from lead capture to close. The Territory Management functionality helps manage and execute sales activities territory wise. Coverage areas usually include Order processing, Contact Management, Information Sharing, Inventory monitoring and control, Order tracking Customer Management, Sales forecast analysis and Employee performance evaluation.

Campaign Management

Campaign management solutions help segment customers and develop targeting and positioning strategies for each segment, define products which match customer requirements, price and select appropriate distribution channels for those products, and implement communication strategies to build brand awareness, generate interest and motivate purchase (Shainesh & Sheth, 2005).

Often, due to lack of data regarding the consumer sentiment for the organization and its products, organizations resort to blanket promotions for their consumers, thereby not matching true consumer expectations. Campaign Management software applications allow marketers to segment groups of customers (and prospective customers) into smaller groups by identifying and understanding unique customer patterns, and then specify the interaction that should take place with those individuals, by creation of customized offers for small groups of customers that correspond to those patterns, (Boulding et al., 2005). This involves the process of response modelling–evaluating consumer interactions with the organization and modelling organizational responses accordingly. Through campaign management, all areas of the company participate in the development of programs targeted to customers. Campaign management involves monitoring and leveraging customer interactions to sell a company's products. Campaigns are based directly on data obtained from consumers through a series of interactions. Hence, marketing managers need to plan, design, coordinate, execute, and assess all campaigns (Mithas, 2005). Simultaneously, metrics are required to calculate the effectiveness of each campaign. Monitoring the success of respective campaigns is important information for altering unsuccessful campaigns and for response modelling.

Key Account Management (KAM)

Key accounts or strategic accounts are the most valuable customers for a company. Simply stated, a company cannot afford to lose these customers without experiencing serious difficulties. KAM can be defined as the systematic selection, analysis, and management of the most important current and potential customers of a company. Additionally, it also includes the systematic set up and maintenance of the necessary infrastructure. Without a systematic approach (Dirk, 2008), KAM becomes a process of trial and error which may miss some necessary elements, creates additional costs, and offer no opportunity for corporate learning. KAM is typically associated with the business to business context, and most KAM literature deals with industrial relationships (Pardo et al., 2006). However, Services also include business-to-business. KAM clearly has potential in any kind of business relationship. After all, most business relationships include both tangible and service elements (Gronroos, 2004). This can also be called Systems Selling (Millman, 1996) which involves offering and delivering a comprehensive package or bundle of product/service attributes and benefits to selected customers. KAM plays an important role in this context. Thus, successful KAM often requires an understanding of the logic of both product and service management. Moreover, excellent operational level capabilities are useless if strategic level management is inferior, and vice versa, the KAM approach combines strategic and operational level marketing management.

A successful KAM consists of four basic elements (Ojasalo, J., 2001):

1. Identifying the key accounts
2. Analyzing the key accounts
3. Selecting suitable strategies for the key accounts
4. Developing operational level capabilities to build grow and maintain profitable and long-lasting relationships with them

Table 1. CRM tools and functionalities offered by Salesforce.com

Sales Cloud	Sales Application -Accounts and Contacts -Marketing and Leads -Opportunities and Quotes -Approvals and Workflow -Content Library
Service Cloud	Service Applications comprising Customer Portals, Social Media and Analytics
Chatter	A company's own private social network which serves as a collaboration enabler
Radian6	Social media monitoring and engagement platform
Force.com	The Cloud Service offered by SalesForce.com allows its clients to- • build and run social, mobile and real-time employee apps. • Apps that automate and extend business processes. • Apps with workflow and analytics. • Apps that are mobile and social. • All built using visual tools, library of components, and open APIs.
Heroku	Built on open standards. • Heroku supports multiple open frameworks, languages, and databases. • Developers love Heroku because they can leverage their existing skillsets, work on the tools they choose and keep their focus on building amazing apps.
Chatter	Aids in sales force automation. Chatter provides a fast and easy way to share important information through business profiles to help increase productivity.
Database.com	Helps creation of databases with millions of high-quality business contacts and in-depth company profiles, all unified and delivered right inside the Sales Cloud to reach decision makers fast, easily plan territories, and build highly targeted prospecting lists.

Table 2. CRM tools and functionalities offered by mySAPCRM

CRM for Small and Medium Enterprises	Generate qualified leads, close more deals faster and keep customers happy with CRM for small and midsize companies Benefit from an integrated business solutions and focus on business while saving time and system costs Effectively manage all aspects of the customer relationships across channels
On-Demand CRM for Small and Medium Enterprises	Support the entire customer relationship management process, maximize revenue and deliver superior service with SAP Business By Design. Complete, fully integrated business management solution delivered on demand Large-scale solution functionality designed for small and midsize businesses Managed, monitored and maintained by SAP experts, so organizations can focus on their business and not on IT
CRM Marketing	Plan, execute and analyze marketing programs for organisations– with support for everything from campaign management to loyalty marketing and analytics. Drive demand with timely, targeted marketing messages across all channels Identify and target high-value customers while building loyalty Get the most value from marketing spend and resources
CRM Sales	Drive profitable revenue growth through focused sales execution – with support for everything from sales planning to sales analytics. Achieve sales goals with accurate customer and product targeting Streamline sales processes across channels for greater efficiency Manage accounts more easily with effective contact management
CRM Service	Boost customer satisfaction and reduce service costs – with support for everything from warranty and claim management to field service. Resolve issues quickly with on-the-spot customer support Equip employees with the information and tools they need to retain profitable customers Provide a consistent, positive user experience across all service channels
Interaction Centre	Use the interaction centre as a strategic delivery channel for marketing, sales and service – for lower costs and higher revenue. Get quick access to information to support customer interactions via phone, e-mail or chat Seamlessly handle inbound and outbound calls, thanks to integration with telephone systems Enhance collaboration with built-in communication-enabled business processes
Business Communications Management	Deliver a great customer experience across contact channels using the SAP IP platform Improve service with back-office experts and work-at-home agents Deliver stellar customer communications across all channels Replace outdated, proprietary hardware with an open IP contact centre solution
E-marketing **Web Channel:**	Support demand generation and customer loyalty processes via the Internet. Personalize customers' Web experiences with the most relevant and convenient online interactions and information. Generate additional revenue through a Web-based channel via comprehensive support for catalog management, content management, campaign execution, customer segmentation, personalization, and a store locator.
E-commerce	Run business-to-consumer (B2C) or business-to-business (B2B) selling processes on the Internet. Enable a full range of online selling processes, including quote and order management, pricing and contracts, interactive selling and configuration, web auctions, and selling via partners. Streamline sales and fulfillment operations with an end-to-end order-to-cash process.
E-Service	Offers customers an intuitive channel to perform service tasks, from requesting a service visit to logging a complaint or registering a product. Enable customers to perform service-related tasks such as checking order status, obtaining order tracking information, managing accounts and payments, and researching and resolving product problems. Service complex products that require sophisticated maintenance
Web channel analytics	Gain insight into, analyze, and act on e-business trends. Measure and optimize the success of online transactions and online content. Perform analysis across the breadth of marketing, sales, and service from a Web perspective, and track and use Web behavior to target customers and drive future marketing activities.

Table 3. CRM tools and Functionalities offered by SiebelCRM (Source:www.siebelcrm.com)

Marketing Resource Management	• Automate and streamline key marketing processes and improve quality • Align global spending with corporate objectives and priorities. • Gain visibility into marketing performance. • Manage activities more effectively with a common platform across brands.
Campaign Management	• Permission-Based Marketing which aims to create personalized campaigns across channels • Improve outbound telemarketing and inbound call handling • Targeted E-Mail Campaigns by leveraging the internet to acquire new customers. • Joint Marketing i.e. leverage business partners to maximize sales and marketing opportunities. • Field Conversion Rates which ensures the effectiveness of field sales campaigns.
Loyalty Management	• Improve customer profitability by rewarding the "right" customer through loyalty programs. • Reduce costs by automating loyalty management business process • Maximize the effectiveness of customer interactions • Reduce expenses by having members update information online
Marketing Analytics	• Targets market planning and allocate resources more effectively by identifying what drives campaign results. • Measure campaign performance, understand factors that drive campaign results and lead conversion rates, target metrics. • Customer Insight to understand product affinity for targeted promotions, profile customers' buying behavior for more effective promotions,
Event Management	• Increase ROI for event-based marketing programs • Maintain the quality of marketing events, while reducing costs • Expertly manage the entire process, from planning to results analysis • Quickly route sales leads to the right channels • sReduce event support cost with online registration and payment
Sales Forecasting	• Comprehensive matrix organization for forecasting • Real time analysis as well as close dates, dynamic forecasting and rollups. • Manage recurring revenues in multiple currencies with automatic currency conversion • Manage revenues by account, opportunity, product line, project, partner, division, organization or employee.
Territory management	• Define territories using direct name rules indirect name rules • Analyze territory evolution • Define territory hierarchy allowing administrators to model different sales force structure.
E-Commerce and E-Billing	• Provides customers with personalized bills online with multiple payment options. • Online Service-Eliminate costly phone calls by providing electronic access to statement reprints and account information. Empower customers to contact service representatives from within a bill. • Paperless Accounts-Reduce carbon footprint, eliminate lockbox fees, exception processing, printing and mailing costs. • Online Dispute Adjudication-Accelerate processing, speed up cash receipts and reduce cash float. • Targeted Promotion-Increase revenue by cross-selling products and services. • Updated user interface design-Increase adoption rates with easy-to-customize UI to meet the most demanding corporate identity look-and-feel and design.
Partner Relationship Management	• Partner Ecosystem—facilitate a collaborative relationship between partners and brand managers • Program Management-plan and execute collaborative sales, marketing, and service initiatives improved • Business Intelligence-enhance forecasting accuracy and pipeline visibility • Worldwide Oversight-orchestrate channel operations around the globe • Increase lead closure rate with closed loop lead management that provides sophisticated lead matching and routing for distributing high-quality leads to the right partner at the right time • Gain actionable insight into all aspects of the channel activities and performance with channel and partner analytics • Predict and manage channel revenue by leveraging channel pipeline and forecast management

Table 4. Comparison between functionalities of Salesforce.com, MySAPCRM and SiebelCRM.

S.No.	Salesforce.com	MySAPCRM	SiebelCRM
1.	SalesForce has its sales and service models offering different functionalities to solve different purposes, but these models are same for all types of clients. It offers same set of functionalities for companies like Microsoft having a very large client database, and for a small firm whose client database spans only few cities.	This problem is addressed by MySAPCRM. It offers different business solutions for companies of different business levels.	Siebel CRM has the upper hand in the depth and breadth of their CRM applications. Siebel has a large install base of customers compared to the other two tools. In addition, Siebel industry-specific applications are stronger.
2.	The interactive **user interface** is very easy to use. It does not require any training for usage. By using the user interface, individuals can access all the functionalities in one single **window,** which too is neatly managed using tabs. As a result, company employees using it save a lot of time and effort wasted on locating information in different opened windows and are able to concentrate better on the task at hand. The integrated content library in the Sales Cloud eliminates the need to search through mazes of folders and mountains of email. With popular consumer Web features like tagging, search, and popularity rankings, everyone finds what they need in a flash. Individuals can share presentations with customers and colleagues entirely in the cloud—no downloading required.	The User interface of SAP is not very intuitive and may require training prior to usage. However, it provides out of the box integration and functionality to its consumers.	Provides Web Services support as well as pre-built integration to Oracle business applications and other applications to fully integrate the enterprise with the power of CRM. The real-time integration capabilities go beyond simple data sharing and enable organisations to deploy end-to-end business processes across applications. Availability of a comprehensive set of flexible Web Services aids enterprises in working faster and in being more agile to improve customer experience, increase revenue and lower operating costs.
3.	Offers functions/modules only, solving the purposes for keeping track of sales and service. Its analytical tools provide only basic information. For e.g. Individual team's performance in sales and service departments is specified, but the system does not provide information on customer satisfaction levels and prospective consumers.	It offers functionalities/ modules that serve as complete business solutions. Along with providing functionalities of sales and services, it offers solutions for- *Financial management* *Human capital management* *Product lifecycle management* *Supplier Relationship management*	Offers detailed functionalities across all aspects of Marketing Resource Management, Analytics, Sales Forecasting, Activity and Opportunity Management.
4.	The cloud service allows companies to use its server space to build applications according to their need and put in whatever functionalities they want. For instance, an organization using Microsoft Outlook or Gmail, does not have to change the way they work. The Sales Cloud and the concerned applications are joined together to enable organizations to simply work smarter.	Although it provides large no. of modules that may solve individual business needs, no server space is offered if any company wants to model any module according to their need.	
5.	Its intercompany social networking tool **CHATTER** is very useful to instantly get in touch with teams and other employees in the organization which might help individuals to perform tasks better. Using chatter, individual employee profiles can be accessed.	It also provides tools like Chatter having almost the same functionalities but due to its not so intuitive UI, it becomes difficult to use it efficiently.	Provides complete multi-channel footprint which consistently extend sales reach across all customer interactions with ecommerce solutions. Provides customer interactions and transition from self-service, to assisted care, into the call center, and back out to the self-service channel while giving customers transparent access to the real time information they need to do business. Manage multi-channel interactions with consistency and agility.

continued on following page

Table 4. Continued

S.No.	Salesforce.com	MySAPCRM	SiebelCRM
6.	Force.com appexchange provides numerous pre-built solutions	Enable customers to **troubleshoot their product issues**, create service requests, register products and warranties, and track orders. Ensure alignment between IT operations and business priorities through native **integration between SAP CRM and SAP ERP.** Support **demand generation** and customer loyalty processes via the Internet. Run **business-to-consumer (B2C) or business-to-business (B2B)** selling processes on the Internet.	Multi-site/Multi-tenancy to deploy **centralized contact center technologies** on a "single system" infrastructure shared by all locations.
7.	Well defined functionalities for consumer segmentation present.	Well defined functionalities for consumer segmentation and list management, trade promotion lead management and quotation management.	No such well defined functionalities available. Users have to make do with marketing resource management and other sales functionalities.
8.	Well defined cloud apps for better collaboration, integration, automatic updates and easy access benefits.	EMarketing and Channel Marketing functionalities available, EBilling and Event management functions are absent.	EBilling and Event Management functionalities are present. EMarketing and Channel Marketing Functionalities are absent.

An account manager who works in this role will engage in a variety of tasks including project management, coordination, strategic planning, relationship management, negotiation, leadership and innovative development of opportunities.

Customer Value Management (CVM):

Companies can boost profits by increasing annual customer retention as selling a product or service to an existing customer has a higher probability of success than selling a product or service to an entirely new prospect. As it costs much more to acquire new customers, the firm should retain customers, once acquired, and realize their CVM to the maximum possible extent. CVM is the present value of the future cash flows attributed to the customer relationship. Firms should invest in an appropriate consumer segmentation process once a new consumer is acquired, to target them appropriately. Organisations should manage each customer relationship with the goal of achieving maximum lifetime profit from the entire customer base. Not every individual customer will be profitable, but each must be managed to maximize overall profit, even when the management consists of identifying which customers have little value to the business, and focusing development and retention efforts elsewhere.

Customer Service and Support (CSS)

CSS functionalities usually include Multiple Channel Access, Solutions Knowledge Base, Managing requests, Contract and Warranty Status, Field Service and Support, and Billing.

The following tables provide descriptions of tools offered by Salesforce.com, mySAPCRM and SiebelCRM. Organisations can choose a tool on the basis of their current organizational objectives, functionality requirements, and business challenges. Identification of relevant customer focused processes which need to be supported with technology and finally defining the products that support that functionality are crucial aspects which aid organizations in the final CRM product procurement process.

Table 1 shows a brief description of the CRM tools and functionalities offered by Salesforce.com *(Source:www.salesforce.com)*

Table 2 offers a brief description of the CRM tools offered by mySAPCRM *(Source:www.mysapcrm.com).*

IMPLEMENTATION ISSUES

Organisations typically consider the following criteria while evaluating a CRM solution: functionalities supported by the package, multiplicity of interaction channels, compatibility with existing infrastructure, scalability, integration, flexibility in incorporating changes, and upgradability and pricing issues.

CONCLUSION

Small organizations with few employees should invest in Salesforce.com as this tool should solve their requirements from a sales and service perspective, in addition to intercompany employee interactions regarding the details of their projects. Large companies having many departments ranging from production, supplies, sales and services, and having adequate budget to train their employees on SAP should invest in mySAP CRM as it is a complete business solution which, once adopted, will provide long-term gains for the organization (Table 3 and Table 4).

Siebel CRM provides greater depth and breadth in its CRM applications. Siebel has a large install base of customers compared to the other two tools. In addition, Siebel industry-specific applications are stronger. However, Siebel does not have a traditional Enterprise Resource Planning (ERP) product. The integration costs with so-called "back-end" ERP systems are very high. However, this may no longer be a factor if Siebel demonstrates seamless integration with Oracle back-end applications. A so-called "front-office system," mySAP CRM is stronger than Siebel in terms of tighter integration with its back-end ERP systems. Tighter integration of sales, service, and logistics is also an inherent strength of SAP CRM. SAP has a deep knowledge of manufacturing and engineer industry verticals. SAP has not made significant progress into the non-SAP ERP customer base. SAP CRM customers are mostly clients who have the SAP ERP installed base.

REFERENCES

Anton, J., & Hoeck, M. (2002). *E-business Customer Service*. Santa Monica, CA: The Anton Press.

Berry, L. L., Wall, E., & Lewis, C. (2006). Service Clues and Customer assessment of the Service Experience. *The Academy of Management Perspectives*. doi:10.5465/AMP.2006.20591004.

Boulding, W., Richard, S., Michael Ehret, M., & Johnston, W. J. (2005). A Customer Relationship Management Roadmap: What Is Known, Potential pitfalls and where to go. *Journal of Marketing*, *69*, 155–166. doi:10.1509/jmkg.2005.69.4.155.

Buttle, F. (2001). The CRM Value Chain. *Marketing Business*(February), 52–55.

Dirk, Z. (2008). International Key Account Management in Manufacturing Companies: An Exploratory Approach of Situative Differentiation. *Journal of Business-To-Business Marketing*, *15*(4), 455–475. doi:10.1080/15470620802325807.

Glazer, R. (2002). Measuring the value of information: The information-intensive organization. *IBM Systems Journal*, *32*(1), 99–110. doi:10.1147/sj.321.0099.

Gordon, I. (2002). Best Practices Customer Relationship Management. *Ivey Business Journal*.

Grönroos. (2004). The relationship marketing process: Communication, interaction, dialogue, value. *Journal of Business and Industrial Marketing*, *19*(2), 99–113. doi:10.1108/08858620410523981.

Hobby, J. (1999). Looking After the One Who Matters. *Accountancy Age*, (October 28), 28–30.

Jayachandran, S., Sharma, S., Kaufman, P., & Raman, P. (2005). The Role of Relational Information Processes and Technology Use in Customer Relationship Management. *Journal of Marketing*, *69*, 177–192. doi:10.1509/jmkg.2005.69.4.177.

Joseph, P. B., Peppers, D., & Rogers, M. (1995). Do you want to keep your customers forever? *Harvard Business Review*, *73*(2), 103–104.

Marketing Association. ISSN: 0022-2429 (print), 1547-7185 (electronic) 168 / *Journal of Marketing*.

Millman, T. F. (1996). Global account management and systems selling. *International Business Review*, *5*(6), 631–645. doi:10.1016/S0969-5931(96)00031-5.

Mithas, S., Krishnan, M. S., & Fornell, C. (2005). Why do customer relationship management applications affect customer satisfaction. *Journal of Marketing*, *69*(4), 20209. doi:10.1509/jmkg.2005.69.4.201.

Mukerjee, K. (2007). *Customer Relationship Management – A Strategic approach to marketing*. Prentice Hall of India.

Ojasalo, J. (2001). Key account management at company and individual levels in business-to-business relationships. *Journal of Business and Industrial Marketing*, *16*(3), 199–220. doi:10.1108/08858620110389803.

Pardo, C., Stephan, C., Henneberg, S. M., & Naudè, P. (2006). Unpicking the meaning of value in key account management. *European Journal of Marketing*, *40*(11/12), 1360–1374. doi:10.1108/03090560610702858.

Parvatiyar, A., & Sheth, J. (2002). *Handbook of Relationship Marketing*. Response Book.

Payne, A., & Frow, P. (2005). A Strategic Framework for Customer Relationship Management. *Journal of Marketing*, *69*(October), 167–176. doi:10.1509/jmkg.2005.69.4.167.

Peppers, D., Rogers, M., & Dorf, B. (1999). Is Your Company Ready for One-to-One Marketing? *Harvard Business Review*, *77*, 151–160. PMID:10345390.

Ryals, L., & Payne, A. F. T. (2001). Customer Relationship Management in financial services: Towards information-enabled relationship marketing. *Journal of Strategic Marketing*, *9*(March), 1–25.

Shainesh, G., & Sheth, J. (2006). *Components of eCRM Solutions. Customer Relationship Management: A Strategic Initiative*. New York: Macmillan.

Shainesh, G., & Sheth, J. (2006). *Conceptual Foundations of CRM, Customer Relationship Management: A Strategic Initiative*. New York: Macmillan.

Sheth, J. N., & Parvatiyar, A. (2000). *The Evolution of Relationship Marketing, Handbook of Relationship Marketing*. New York: Sage Publications.

Singh, D., & Agrawal, D. P. (2003). CRM Practices in Indian Industries. *International Journal of Customer Relationship Management*, *5*(December–January), 241–257.

Wright, G., Fletcher, K., Donaldson, B., & Lee, J.-H. (2008). Sales force automation systems: An analysis of factors underpinning the sophistication of deployed systems in the UK financial services industry. *Industrial Marketing Management*, *37*(8), 992–104. doi:10.1016/j.indmarman.2007.08.005.

Compilation of References

Aaker, D. A. (1991). *Managing Brand Equity: Capitalizing on the Value of a Brand Name*. New York: The Free Press.

Aaker, D. A., Stayman, D. M., & Hagerty, M. R. (1986). Warmth in advertising: Measurement, impact, and sequence effects. *The Journal of Consumer Research*, *12*(4), 365–381. doi:10.1086/208524.

Abbe, A., Gulick, L. M. V., & Herman, J. L. (2007). *Cross-cultural competence in Army leaders: A conceptual and empirical foundation*. Washington, DC: U.S. Army Research Institute. doi:10.1037/e551892009-001.

Abdel-Kader, M., & Luther, R. (2008). The impact of firm characteristics on management accounting practices: A UK-based empirical analysis. *The British Accounting Review*, *40*(1), 2–27. doi:10.1016/j.bar.2007.11.003.

Abdel-Maksoud, A. (2007). Shop-floor non-financial performance measures and the contingent variables. In Abdel-Maksoud, A., & Abdel-Kader, M. (Eds.), *Non-financial performance measurement and management practices in manufacturing firms: A comparative international analysis* (pp. 35–70). Oxford, UK: Elsevier.

Abdel-Maksoud, A., Dugdale, D., & Luther, R. (2005). Non–financial performance measurement in manufacturing companies. *The British Accounting Review*, *37*(3), 261–297. doi:10.1016/j.bar.2005.03.003.

Abdul-Aziz, Z., Chan, J. F. L., & Metcalfe, A. V. (2000). Quality Practices in the Manufacturing Industry in the UK and Malaysia. *Total Quality Management*, *11*(8), 1053–1064. doi:10.1080/095441200440322.

Abdullah, F. (2005). HEdPERF versus SERVPERF: The quest for ideal measuring instrument of service quality in higher education sector. *Quality Assurance in Education*, *13*(4), 305–328. doi:10.1108/09684880510626584.

Abdullah, F. (2006a). Measuring service quality in higher education: HEdPERF versus SERVPERF. *Marketing Intelligence & Planning*, *24*(1), 31–47. doi:10.1108/02634500610641543.

Abdullah, F. (2006b). Measuring service quality in higher education: Three instruments compared. *International Journal of Research & Method in Education*, *29*(1), 71–89. doi:10.1080/01406720500537445.

Abdullah, F. (2006c). The development of HEdPERF: A new measuring instrument of service quality for the higher education sector. *International Journal of Consumer Studies*, *30*(6), 569–581. doi:10.1111/j.1470-6431.2005.00480.x.

Abegglen, J., & Stalk, G. (1985). *Kaisha: The Japanese Corporation*. New York: Basic Books.

Abel, A. B., & Eberly, J. C. (1994). A Unified Model of Investment Under Uncertainty. *The American Economic Review*, *84*(5), 1369–1384.

Abrahamsson, P., Salo, O., Ronkainen, J., & Warsta, J. (2002). *Agile Software Development Methods: Review and Analysis*. Espoo, Finland: VTT Publications.

Abreu, M., Mendes, V., & Santos, J. A. C. (2011). Home country bias: Does domestic experience help investors enter foreign markets? *Journal of Banking & Finance*, *35*(9), 2330–2340. doi:10.1016/j.jbankfin.2011.01.032.

Abudayyeh, O., Temel, B., Al-Tabtabai, H., & Hurley, B. (2001). An Intranet-Based Cost Control System. *Advances in Engineering Software*, *32*, 87–94. doi:10.1016/S0965-9978(00)00094-6.

Acker, J. (1990). Hierarchies, jobs, bodies: A theory of gendered organizations. *Gender & Society*, *4*(2), 139–158. doi:10.1177/089124390004002002.

Acker, J. (2006). Inequality regimes: Gender, class, and race in organizations. *Gender & Society*, *20*(4), 441–464. doi:10.1177/0891243206289499.

Adams, D. A., & Nelson, R. R. (1992). Perceived usefulness, ease of use, and usage of Information Technology: A replication. *Management Information Systems Quarterly*, *16*(2). doi:10.2307/249577.

Adams, J. D. (2001). Managing dispersed work effectively. *OD Practitioner*, *33*(1), 381–391.

ADB. (2003). Vietnam Development Report 2004: Poverty (Joint Donor Report to the Vietnam Consultative Group Meeting). Hanoi, Vietnam: Vietnam Development Information Centre.

Adler, N. (1997). *International dimensions of organizational behavior*. Cincinnati, OH: South Western.

Adler, N. J., & Gunderson, A. (2007). *International dimensions of organizational behavior*. Boston, MA: PWS-Kent.

Advisory Panel for the Dictionary of Occupational Titles. (1993). *The new dot: A database of occupational titles for the twenty-first century*. Washington, DC: U.S. Department of Labor, Employment and Training Administration.

Aerts, W. (2005). Picking up the pieces: Impression management in the retrospective attributional framing of accounting outcomes. *Accounting, Organizations and Society*, *30*, 493–517. doi:10.1016/j.aos.2004.07.001.

Agarwal, R. (1999). *Individual acceptance of information technologies*. Retrieved from http://www.pinnaflex.com/pdf/framing/CH06.pdf

Agarwal, S., & Ramaswami, S. (1992). Choice of foreign market entry mode: Impact of ownership, location and internationalization factors. *Journal of International Business Studies*, *23*(3), 1–27. doi:10.1057/palgrave.jibs.8490257.

Aguinis, H., & Pierce, C. A. (2008). Enhancing the relevance of organizational behavior by embracing performance management research. *Journal of Organizational Behavior*, *29*, 139–145. doi:10.1002/job.493.

Ahmad, I., Azhar, S., & Ahmed, S. (2002). *Web-Based Construction Project Management: Scope*. Potential And Trends.

Ahmed, S., & Schroeder, R. G. (2011). Knowledge management through technology Strategy: Implications for Competitiveness. *Journal of Manufacturing Technology Management*, *22*(1), 6–24. doi:10.1108/17410381111099789.

Ahn, H., Kwon, M. W., & Sung, Y. (2010). Online Brand Community across Cultures. *International Journal of e-Business Management*, *4*(1), 34-52.

Ajzen, I. (2001). Nature and operation of attitudes. *Annual Review of Psychology*, *52*, 27–58. doi:10.1146/annurev.psych.52.1.27 PMID:11148298.

Ajzen, I., & Fishbein, M. (1980). *Understanding attitudes and predicting social behavior*. Englewood Cliffs, NJ: Prentice-Hall.

Alavi, M. & Leidner, D. E. (2001). Review: Knowledge Management and Knowledge

Alden, D. L., Steenkamp, J.-B. E., & Batra, R. (1999). Brand Positioning Through Advertising in Asia, North America, and Europe: The Role of Global Consumer Culture. *Journal of Marketing*, *63*(1), 75–87. doi:10.2307/1252002.

Algesheimer, R., Dholakia, U. M., & Gurău, C. (2011). Virtual Team Performance In A Highly Competitive Environment. *Group & Organization Management*, *36*, 161–190. doi:10.1177/1059601110391251.

Ali, M. (2011). *Chartis Launches ReputationGuard®, Reputational Risk Insurance*. Press Release. New York: ChartisChartis. Retrieved from http://www.chartisinsurance.com/searchresults/search_295_195443.html

Alierta, C. (2011). The Promise of Technology. In W. E. Forum, *The Global Information Technology Report 2010-2011* (p. 435). Geneva, Switzerland: World Economic Forum Editors.

Allee, V. (1997). Twelve Principles of Knowledge Management. *Journal of Training and Development*, *51*(11), 4–71.

Allen, J. (2011). *$16 muffins, $8 coffee served in Justice Audit*. Retrieved on September 21, 2011, from http://www.reuters.com/article/2011/09/21/us-usa-justice-muffins-idUSTRE78J7B020110921

Alnoukari, M. (2009). Using business intelligence solutions for achieving organization's strategy: Arab International University case study. *Internetworking Indonesia Journal*, *1*(2), 11–15.

Al-Omiri, M., & Drury, C. (2007). A survey of factors influencing the choice of product costing systems in UK organizations. *Management Accounting Research*, *18*, 399–424. doi:10.1016/j.mar.2007.02.002.

Alon, I., Jaffe, E. D., & Vianelli, D. (2012). *Global Marketing: Contemporary Theory, Practice, and Cases*. London: McGraw Hill Higher Education.

Alvadbi, A., Keramati, A., & Razmi, J. (2007). Assessing the impact of information technology on firm performance considering the role of intervening variables: Organizational infrastructures and business processes reengineering. *International Journal of Production Research*, *45*(12), 2697–2734. doi:10.1080/00207540600767780.

Anawati, D., & Craig, A. (2006). Behavioral Adaptation Within Cross-Cultural Virtual Teams. *Professional Communication. Ieee Transactions On*, *49*, 44–56.

Andersen, J. P., & Meyer, T. P. (1988). *Mediated Communication. A Social Action Perspective*. Newbury Park, CA: Sage.

Andersen, O. (1993). On the internationalization process of firms: A critical analysis. *Journal of International Business Studies*, *24*(2), 209–231. doi:10.1057/palgrave.jibs.8490230.

Anderson, A., Mcewan, R., Bal, J., & Carletta, J. (2007). Virtual Team Meetings: An Analysis Of Communication And Context. *Computers in Human Behavior*, *23*, 2558–2580. doi:10.1016/j.chb.2007.01.001.

Anderson, E. W., & Fornell, C. (1994). A customer satisfaction research prospectus. In Rust, R. T., & Oliver, R. L. (Eds.), *Service Quality: New Directions in Theory and Practice* (pp. 241–268). Thousand Oaks, CA: Sage. doi:10.4135/9781452229102.n11.

Anderson, E., & Gatignon, H. (1986). Modes of entry: A transaction cost analysis and propositions. *Journal of International Business Studies*, *17*(3), 1–26. doi:10.1057/palgrave.jibs.8490432.

Anderson, J. C., & Gerbing, D. W. (1988). Structural equation modeling in practice: A review and recommended two-step approach. *Psychological Bulletin*, *103*(3), 411–423. doi:10.1037/0033-2909.103.3.411.

Anderson, N., Ones, D. S., Sinangil, H. K., & Viswesvaran, C. (2001). *Handbook of industrial, work and organizational psychology*. London: Sage.

Anderson, S. W., & Young, S. M. (1999). The impact of contextual and process factors on the evaluation of activity based costing systems. *Accounting, Organizations and Society*, *24*, 525–559. doi:10.1016/S0361-3682(99)00018-5.

Anderson, V., & Boocock, G. (2002). Small firms and internationalization: Learning to manage and managing to learn. *Human Resource Management Journal*, *12*(3), 5–24. doi:10.1111/j.1748-8583.2002.tb00068.x.

Angell, R. J., Heffernan, T. W., & Megicks, P. (2008). Service quality in postgraduate education. *Quality Assurance in Education*, *16*(3), 236–254. doi:10.1108/09684880810886259.

Ang, Z., & Massingham, P. (2007). National Culture and the Standardization versus Adaptation of Knowledge Management. *Journal of Knowledge Management*, *11*(2), 5–21. doi:10.1108/13673270710738889.

ANIF. (2012). *Informe de Resultados Gran Encuesta PYME 2012-1*. Bogotá: ANIF.

Anker, R. (1997). Theories of occupational sex segregation: An overview. *International Labour Review*, *136*(3), 315–339.

Anton, J., & Hoeck, M. (2002). *E-business Customer Service*. Santa Monica, CA: The Anton Press.

Anwar, S. A., & Jabnoun, N. (2006). The development of a contingency model relating national culture to total quality management. *International Journal of Management*, *23*(2), 272–280.

Aoki, M. (1991). *Information, Incentives and Bargaining in the Japanese Economy*. New York: Cambridge University Press.

Apostolou, G., & Economides, A. A. (2008). *Airlines websites evaluation around the world. The Open Knowledge Society. A Computer Science and Information Systems Manifesto, First World Summit*. Athens, Greece: WSKS.

Appadurai, A. (1990). Disjuncture and Difference in the Global Cultural Economy. *Theory, Culture & Society*, *7*, 295–310. doi:10.1177/026327690007002017.

Appiah-Adu, K., & Singh, S. (1998). Customer orientation and performance: A study of SMEs. *Management Decision*, *36*(6), 385–395. doi:10.1108/00251749810223592.

Applbaum, K., & Jordt, I. (1996). Notes toward an application of McCraken's 'cultural categories' for cross-cultural consumer research. *The Journal of Consumer Research*, *23*(3), 204–218. doi:10.1086/209478.

Arasaratnam, L. A., & Doerfel, M. L. (2005). Intercultural communication competence: Identifying key components from multicultural perspectives. *International Journal of Intercultural Relations*, *29*, 137–163. doi:10.1016/j.ijintrel.2004.04.001.

Araujo, A. L., & Chidambaram, L. (2008). A Dynamic Perspective of Trust in Virtual Teams: The Role of Task, Technology, and Time. *International Journal of Networking and Virtual Organizations*, *5*(1), 4–16. doi:10.1504/IJNVO.2008.015995.

Arbuckle, J. L., & Wothke, W. (1995). *AMOS 4.0 User's Guide*. Chicago, IL: Smallwaters Corporation.

Arena, M., & Azzone, G. (2005). ABC, Balanced Scorecard, EVA: An empirical study on the adoption of innovative management accounting techniques. *International Journal of Accounting. Auditing and Performance Evaluation*, *2*(3), 206–225. doi:10.1504/IJAAPE.2005.007673.

Arena, M., Azzone, G., & Caimi, N. (2004). I sistemi di controllo di gestione nelle imprese italiane: diffusione e determinant. *Budget*, *58*, 47–57.

Argyris, C., & Schon, D. (1978). *Organizational Learning: A Theory of Action Perspective*. Reading, MA: Addison-Wesley.

Armario, J. M., Ruiz, D. M., & Armario, E. M. (2008). Market Orientation and Internationalization in Small and Medium-Sized Enterprises. *Journal of Small Business Management*, *46*(4), 485–511. doi:10.1111/j.1540-627X.2008.00253.x.

Armenakis, A., & Harris, S. (2002). Crafting a change message to create transformational readiness. *Journal of Organizational Change Management*, *1*(2), 169–183. doi:10.1108/09534810210423080.

Armstrong, S. J., & Overton, T. S. (1977). Estimating nonresponse bias in mail surveys. *JMR, Journal of Marketing Research*, *14*(3), 396–402. doi:10.2307/3150783.

Arnold, P. (2005). Disciplining domestic regulation: The World Trade Organization and the market for professional services. *Accounting, Organizations and Society*, *30*, 299–330. doi:10.1016/j.aos.2004.04.001.

Ashforth, B. E., & Mael, F. (1989). Social Identity Theory and the Organization. *Academy of Management Review*, *14*(1), 20–39.

Asiedu, E., & Esfahani, H. S. (2001). Ownership Structure in Foreign Direct Investment Projects. *The Review of Economics and Statistics*, *83*(4), 647–662. doi:10.1162/003465301753237731.

Aspers, P. (2009). Empirical phenomenology: A qualitative research approach - The Cologne seminars. *Indo-Pacific Journal of Phenomenology*, *9*(2), 1–12.

Astley, W. G., & Zammuto, R. F. (1992). Organization science, managers and language games. *Organization Science*, *3*(4), 443–460. doi:10.1287/orsc.3.4.443.

Atkins, A. S., Sharp, B., & Atkins, L. (2010b). Decision Support System for Strategic Outsourcing Risk Reduction. In *Proceedings of the 4th International Conference on Software, Knowledge, Information Management and Applications*. Paro, Bhutan.

Atkins, A. S., Sharp, B., Hickey, D. S., & Ho, L. (2010a). HABIO Management of Outsourcing: Systems, Capabilities and Cybernetics. *Technia-International Journal of Computing Science & Communication Technologies*, 2(2), 407–413.

Atrostic, B. K., & Nguyen, S. V. (2005). It And Productivity In Us Manufacturing: Do Computer Networks Matter? *Economic Inquiry*, *43*, 493–506. doi:10.1093/ei/cbi033.

Atsmon, Y. & Magni, M. (2010). China's Internet obsession. *McKinsey Quarterly*, March.

Atsmon, Y., Dixit, V., Magni, M., & St-Maurice, I. (2010). China's new pragmatic consumers. *McKinsey Quarterly*, October.

Auffret, P. & World Bank. (2003). *Trade Reform in Vietnam: Opportunities with Emerging Challenges* (World Bank Policy Research Working Paper No. 3076). Hanoi, Vietnam: World Bank.

Avery, A., Baradwaj, B., & Siner, D. (2008). An examination of Hofstede's cultural factors in explanation of differences in Citibank international retail banking web sites. *Journal of Business and Economics Studies*, *14*(2), 73–90.

Baack, D. W., & Singh, N. (2007). Culture and web communications. *Journal of Business Research*, *60*, 181–188. doi:10.1016/j.jbusres.2006.11.002.

Babbie, E. (2007). *The Practice of Social Research*. Belmont, CA: Wadsworth.

Bacchus, M. K. (2004). Reducing international conflicts by improving economic conditions of the poor through education. *SangSaeng*, *9*, 10–15.

Bacheldo, B. (2000). Worldwide e-Commerce: It's more than a Web Site. *Informationweek*, *785*, 47–48.

Badenhausen, K. (1996). Blind faith. *Financial World*, *165*(July 8), 50-65.

Bagozzi, R. P. (2007). The Legacy of the Technology Acceptance Model and a Proposal for a Paradigm Shift. *Journal of the Association for Information Systems*, *8*(4).

Baird, I., Lyles, M., & Orris, J. (1994). The choice of international strategies by small business. *Journal of Small Business Management*, *48*(1), 48–59.

Baker, M. (1991). *Research in Marketing*. London: MacMillan.

Baker, S. M., & Kennedy, P. F. (1994). Death by nostalgia: A diagnosis of context-specific cases. *Advances in Consumer Research. Association for Consumer Research (U. S.)*, *21*, 169–174.

Bakry, S. H., & Bakry, F. H. (2001). A strategic view for the development of E-Business. *International Journal of Network Management*, *11*(2), 103–112. doi:10.1002/nem.395.

Bal, Y., Bal, M., Demirhan, A., & Bozkurt, S. (2011). A new paradigm in decision making process in business: Using soft computing methods. In *Proceedings of 2nd World Conference on Information Technology*. Antalya, Turkey.

Balabanis, G. (1998). Antecedents of cooperation, conflict, and relationship longevity in an international trade intermediary's supply chain. *Journal of Global Marketing*, *12*(2), 25–46. doi:10.1300/J042v12n02_03.

Baldwin, J. R. (1997). *The Importance of Research and Development for Innovation in Small and Large Canadian Manufacturing Firms, 11F0019MIE, No. 107*. Ottawa: Statistics Canada.

Baliga, G. & Baker, J. C. (1985). Multinational corporation policies for expatriate managers: Selection, training, and evaluation. *Advanced Management Journal*, 31-38.

Bali, R., Wickramsinghe, N., & Lehaney, B. (2009). *Knowledge Management Primer*. London: Routledge.

Bal, J., & Teo, P. (2000). Implementing Virtual Teamworking. Part 1: A Literature Review Of Best Practice. *Logistics Information Management*, *13*, 346–352. doi:10.1108/09576050010355644.

Bal, J., & Teo, P. K. (2001). Implementing Virtual Teamworking: Part 2--A Literature Review. *Logistics Information Management*, *14*, 208–222. doi:10.1108/09576050110390248.

Bal, M., Bal, Y., & Demirhan, A. (2011). Creating competitive advantage by using data mining technique as an innovative method for decision making process in business. *International Journal of Online Marketing*, *1*(3), 38–45. doi:10.4018/ijom.2011070104.

Bandura, A. (1995). Exercise of personal and collective efficacy in changing societies. In Bandura, A. (Ed.), *Self-efficacy in changing societies*. New York: Cambridge University Press. doi:10.1017/CBO9780511527692.003.

Banker, Rajiv D., Potter, G., & Schoreder, R. G. (1993). Reporting manufacturing performance measures to workers: An empirical study. *Journal of Management Accounting Research*, Fall, 33-53.

Bannister, D., & Mair, J. M. M. (1968). *The Evaluation of Personal Constructs*. New York: Academic Press, Inc..

Barczak, G. J., & Wilemon, D. (1992). Successful New Product Team Leaders. *Industrial Marketing Management*, *21*(February), 61–68. doi:10.1016/0019-8501(92)90034-Q.

Barham, K., & Devine, M. (1991). *The quest for the international manager: A survey of global human resource Strategies*. London: Ashridge Management Guide/Economist Intelligence Unit.

Barkema, H. G., & Vermeulen, F. (1997). What Differences in the Cultural Backgrounds of Partners Are Detrimental for International Joint Ventures? *Journal of International Business Studies*, *28*(4), 845–864. doi:10.1057/palgrave.jibs.8490122.

Barro, R. J. (1998). Notes on Growth Accounting. *National Bureau of Economic Research*. Working Paper 6654. Retrieved on December 6, 2011, from http://www.nber.org/papers/w6654

Barry, D., & Elmes, M. (1997). Strategy Retold: Towards a Narrative View of Strategic Discourse. *Academy of Management Review*, *22*(2), 429–452.

Bartlett, C. A., & Ghoshal, S. (1998). *Managing across borders: The transnational solution* (2nd ed.). Boston, MA: Harvard Business School Press.

Barton, S. M., Corbitt, B., & Nguyen, L. (2009). Academic social networks affecting the adoption of e-learning in Turkey. *International Journal on E-Learning*, *8*(4), 561–575.

Bashiekh, A., & Abdel-Maksoud, A. (2008). Operational performance measures used and contemporary management practices deployed in manufacturing firms: The case of Kingdom of Saudi Arabia. *Arab Journal of Administrative Sciences*, *15*(1), 151–183.

Baskerville-Morley, R. (2005). A research note: The unfinished business of culture. *Accounting, Organizations and Society*, *30*, 389–391. doi:10.1016/j.aos.2004.08.002.

Baskerville, R. (2003). Hofstede never studied culture. *Accounting, Organizations and Society*, *28*, 1–14. doi:10.1016/S0361-3682(01)00048-4.

Bass, B. M. (1974). The substance and the shadow. *The American Psychologist*, *29*, 870–886. doi:10.1037/h0037515.

Bass, B. M. (1990). *Bass and stogdill's handbook of leadership: Theory research, and managerial applications*. New York: Free Press.

Bass, B. M. (1995). Theory of transformational leadership redux. *The Leadership Quarterly*, 6.

Bass, B. M. (1997). Does the Transactional and Transformational Leadership paradigm transcend Organizational and National Boundaries? *The American Psychologist*, *52*(2), 130–139. doi:10.1037/0003-066X.52.2.130.

Bass, B. M. (2000). The Future of Leadership in Learning Organizations. *Journal of Leadership & Organizational Studies*, *7*, 18–40. doi:10.1177/107179190000700302.

Batra, R., & Homer, P. M. (2004). The situational impact of brand image beliefs. *Journal of Consumer Psychology*, *14*(3), 318–330. doi:10.1207/s15327663jcp1403_12.

Batra, R., & Ray, M. L. (1986). Affective responses mediating acceptance of advertising. *The Journal of Consumer Research*, *13*(2), 234–249. doi:10.1086/209063.

Battin, R. D., Crocker, R., Kreidler, J., & Subramanian, K. (2001). Leveraging resources in global software development. *IEEE Software*, *18*(2), 70–77. doi:10.1109/52.914750.

Bauer, T., & E. Berrin (2009). Organizational Behavior. *Flat World Knowledge*. 2009.

Baum, J. A. C., & Ingram, P. (1998). Survival-Enhancing Learning in the Manhattan Hotel Industry, 1898-1980. *Management Science*, *44*(7), 996–1016. doi:10.1287/mnsc.44.7.996.

Bayes, A., von Braun, J., & Akhter, R. (1999). Village Pay Phones and Poverty Reduction: Insights from a Grameen Bank Initiative in Bangladesh. In *Discussion Papers on Development Policy*. Bonn, Germany: University of Bonn.

Bazerman, M., & Neale, M. (1992). *Negotiating Rationally*. New York: The Free Press.

BBC NEWS. (2010a). *New high-speed rail plan unveiled*. Retrieved on October 26, 2012, from http://news.bbc.co.uk/1/hi/8221540.stm

Beamish, P. W. (1988). *Multinational joint ventures in developing countries*. London, UK: Routledge.

Beamish, P. W., & Banks, J. C. (1987). Equity Joint Ventures and the Theory of the Multinational Enterprise. *Journal of International Business Studies*, *18*(2), 1–16. doi:10.1057/palgrave.jibs.8490403.

Beamish, P. W., & Killing, J. P. (Eds.). (1997). *Cooperative Strategies: Asian Pacific Perspectives*. San Francisco, CA: New Lexington Press.

Beaumont, N., & Sohal, A. (2004). Outsourcing in Australia. *International Journal of Operations & Production Management*, *24*(7), 688–700. doi:10.1108/01443570410541993.

Belch, G. E., & Belch, M. A. (2009). *Advertising and Promotion – An Integrated Marketing Communications Perspective* (8th ed.). McGraw-Hill.

Belderbos, R., & Sleuwaegen, L. (1996). Japanese Firms and the Decision to Invest Abroad: Business Groups and Regional Core Networks. *The Review of Economics and Statistics*, *78*(2), 214–220. doi:10.2307/2109923.

Bellamy, T., Williams, A., Sher, W., Sherratt, S., & Gameson, R. (2005). Preliminary Examination Of Ict Collaborative Design And Management. In *The Construction Industry*. Newcastle, UK: The University Of Newcastle's Digital Repository.

Bell, B. S., & Kozlowski, S. W. J. (2002). A Typology Of Virtual Teams. *Group & Organization Management*, *27*, 14–49. doi:10.1177/1059601102027001003.

Bell, B. S., & Kozlowski, S. W. J. (2002). A typology of virtual teams: Implications for effective leadership. *Group & Organization Management*, *27*, 12–49. doi:10.1177/1059601102027001003.

Bello, C. D., & Gilliland, D. I. (1997). The effect of output controls, process controls, and flexibility on export channel performance. *Journal of Marketing*, *61*(1), 22–38. doi:10.2307/1252187.

Benbasat, I., & Zmud, R. W. (1999). Empirical Research in Information Systems: The Practice of Relevance. *Management Information Systems Quarterly*, *23*(1), 3–16. doi:10.2307/249403.

Benito, G. R. G., & Gripsrud, G. (1992). The expansion of foreign direct investments: Discrete rational location choices or a cultural learning process? *Journal of International Business Studies*, *23*(3), 461–476. doi:10.1057/palgrave.jibs.8490275.

Bennett, E. E. (2009). Virtual HRD: The Intersection of Knowledge Management, Culture, and Intranets. *Advances in Developing Human Resources*, *11*(3), 362–374. doi:10.1177/1523422309339724.

Bentler, P. M., & Bonett, D. G. (1980). Significance tests and goodness of fit in the analysis of covariance structures. *Psychological Bulletin*, *88*, 588–606. doi:10.1037/0033-2909.88.3.588.

Beresford, M., & Tran, A. N. (2004). Reaching for the dream: Challenges of sustainable development in Vietnam. Copenhagen, Denmark: Nordic Institute of Asian Studies (NIAS).

Beresford, M. (1988). *Vietnam: Politics, economics, and society*. London, New York: Pinter.

Beresford, M. (1989). *National unification and economic development in Vietnam*. London, UK: Macmillan.

Berry, J. W. (1979). In Berkowitz, L. (Ed.). Advances in experimental social psychology: *Vol. 12. A cultural ecology of social behavior*. Orlando, FL: Academic Press.

Berry, J. W. (1980). Introduction to Methodology. In Triandis, H. C., & Berry, J. W. (Eds.), *Handbook of Cross Cultural Psychology* (*Vol. 2*). Boston, MA: Allyn and Bacon.

Berry, L. L., Wall, E., & Lewis, C. (2006). Service Clues and Customer assessment of the Service Experience. *The Academy of Management Perspectives*. doi:10.5465/AMP.2006.20591004.

Bethlehem, J. (2010). Selection Bias in Web Surveys. *International Statistical Review*, *78*(2), 161–188. doi:10.1111/j.1751-5823.2010.00112.x.

Bhagat, R., Kedia, B. L., Harveston, P. D., & Triandis, H. C. (2002). Cultural Variations in the Cross-Border Transfer of Organizational Knowledge: An Integrative Framework. *Academy of Management Review*, *27*(2), 204–221.

Bhatt, D. (2001). Knowledge Management in Organizations: Examining the Interaction between Technologies, Techniques and People. *Journal of Knowledge Management*, *5*(1), 68–75. doi:10.1108/13673270110384419.

Bhimani, A. (1994). Monitoring performance measures in UK manufacturing companies. *Management Accounting*, January, 34-36.

Biasutti, M., & Heba, E. D. (2012). Using Wiki in Teacher Education: Impact on Knowledge Management Processes and Student Satisfaction. *Computers & Education*, *59*(3), 861–872. doi:10.1016/j.compedu.2012.04.009.

Biere, M. (2003). *Business Intelligence for the Enterprise*. New York: Pearson Education.

Bilkey, W. J., & Tesar, G. (1977). The export behavior of smaller Wisconsin manufacturing firms. *Journal of International Business Studies*, *9*(Spring/Summer), 93–98. doi:10.1057/palgrave.jibs.8490783.

Birkinshaw, J., Bessant, J., & Delbridge, R. (2007). Finding, Forming, and Performing: Creating Networks for Discontinuous Innovation. *California Management Review*, *49*(3), 67–84. doi:10.2307/41166395.

Bjerke, V. A. (2006). *Assessing the relationship between market orientation and organizational culture in Midwestern hospitals: An empirical study*. Doctoral dissertation, Capella University, Ann Arbor, MI: ProQuest Information and Learning Company.

Bjorkman, I., & Schaaps, A. (1994). Outsiders in the Middle Kingdom. *European Management Journal*, *12*(2), 147–153. doi:10.1016/0263-2373(94)90005-1.

Bjornenak, T. (1997). Diffusion and accounting: The case of ABC in Norway. *Management Accounting Research*, *8*, 3–17. doi:10.1006/mare.1996.0031.

Bjørn, P., & Ngwenyama, O. (2009). Virtual Team Collaboration: Building Shared Meaning, Resolving Breakdowns And Creating Translucence. *Information Systems Journal*, *19*, 227–253. doi:10.1111/j.1365-2575.2007.00281.x.

Bjørn, P., & Ngwenyama, O. (2010). Technology Alignment: A New Area In Virtual Team Research. *Professional Communication. Ieee Transactions On*, *53*, 382–400.

Blacker, F. (1995). Knowledge, Knowledge Work and Organizations: An Overview and Interpretation. *Organization Studies*, *15*(6), 1021–1046. doi:10.1177/017084069501600605.

Blacker, F., Reed, M., & Whitaker, A. (1993). Editorial: Knowledge Workers and Contemporary Organization. *Journal of Management Studies*, *30*(6), 851–862. doi:10.1111/j.1467-6486.1993.tb00469.x.

Black, J. S. (1988). Work Role Transitions - A Study of American Expatriate Managers in Japan. *Journal of International Business Studies*, *19*(2), 277–294. doi:10.1057/palgrave.jibs.8490383.

Black, J. S. (1988). Work role transitions: A study of American expatriate managers in Japan. *Journal of International Business Studies*, *19*, 277–294. doi:10.1057/palgrave.jibs.8490383.

Black, J. S. (1990). The relationship of personal characteristics with the adjustment of Japanese expatriate managers. *Management International Review*, *30*(2), 119–134.

Black, J. S., & Gregersen, H. B. (1991). The other half of the picture: Antecedents of spouse cross-cultural adjustment. *Journal of International Business Studies*, *22*(3), 3, 461–477. doi:10.1057/palgrave.jibs.8490311.

Black, J. S., & Gregersen, H. B. (1999). The right way to manage expats. *Harvard Business Review*, (March-April): 52–62.

Black, J. S., Gregersen, H. B., & Mendenhall, M. (1992). *Global assignments: Successfully expatriating and repatriating international managers*. San Francisco, CA: Jossey-Bass.

Black, J. S., Gregersen, H. B., & Stroh, L. K. (1999). *Globalizing people through international assignment*. Reading, MA: Addison-Wesley.

Black, J. S., & Mendenhall, M. E. (1990). Cross-cultural training effectiveness: A review and a theoretical framework for future research. *Academy of Management Review*, *15*(1), 113–136.

Black, J. S., Mendenhall, M., & Oddou, G. (1991). Towards a comprehensive model of international adjustment: An Integration of multiple theoretical perspectives. *Academy of Management Review*, *16*, 291–317.

Black, J. S., & Stevens, G. K. (1989). The influence of the spouse on American expatriate adjustment and intent to stay in pacific rim overseas assignments. *Journal of Management*, *15*, 529–544. doi:10.1177/014920638901500403.

Blomstermo, A., & Sharma, D. D. (2006). Choice of foreign market entry mode in service firms. *International Marketing Review*, *23*(2), 211–229. doi:10.1108/02651330610660092.

Blomstrom, M., & Sjoholm, F. (1999). Technology transfer and spillovers: Does local participation with multinationals matter? *European Economic Review*, *43*(4-6), 915–923. doi:10.1016/S0014-2921(98)00104-4.

Bloodgood, J. M., & Chilton, M. A. (2012). *Performance Implications of Matching Adaptation and Innovation Cognitive Style with Business Environment, Knowledge Management and Knowledge Management Technology*. Chandice Publishing Ltd..

Bloom, N., Kretschmer, T., & Van Reenen, J. (2006). *Work-life balance, management practices and productivity*. Retrieved on June 13, 2012, from http://www.stanford.edu/~nbloom/WorkLifeBalance.pdf

Boland, R. J. Jr, & Day, W. F. (1989). The Experience of Systems Design: A Hermeneutic of Organization Action. *Scandinavian Journal of Management*, *5*(2), 87–104. doi:10.1016/0956-5221(89)90017-1.

Bolino, M. C. (2007). Expatriate assignments and intra-organizational career success: Implications for individuals and organizations. *Journal of International Business Studies*, *38*, 819–835. doi:10.1057/palgrave.jibs.8400290.

Bolino, M. C., & Feldman, D. C. (2000). Increasing the skill utilization of expatriates. *Human Resource Management*, *39*(4), 367–379. doi:10.1002/1099-050X(200024)39:4<367::AID-HRM7>3.0.CO;2-7.

Bollen, K. A., & Stine, R. A. (1992). Bootstrapping goodness-of-fit measures in structural equation models. *Sociological Methods & Research*, *21*, 205–229. doi:10.1177/0049124192021002004.

Bonn, M. A., Furr, H. L., & Susskind, A. M. (1998). Using the Internet as a pleasure travel planning tool: An examination of the sociodemographic and behavioral characteristics among Internet users and non-users. *Journal of Hospitality & Tourism Research (Washington, D.C.)*, *22*(3), 303–317. doi:10.1177/109634809802200307.

Boone, L. E., & Kurtz, D. L. (2003). *Contemporary Business*. New York: Thomson Western Publishing.

Booth, B. (2011). Examining The Critical Factors Of Success. In *Virtual Team Performance. Ph.D. 3442987*. Prescott Valley, AZ: Northcentral University.

Booth, S. (1997). On phenomenography, learning and teaching. *Higher Education Research & Development*, *16*(2), 135–159. doi:10.1080/0729436970160203.

Borgerson, J. L., & Schroeder, J. E. (2002). Ethical issues of global marketing: Avoiding bad faith in visual representation. *European Journal of Marketing*, *36*(5/6), 570–594. doi:10.1108/03090560210422399.

Borman, W. C., Klimoski, R. L., & Ilgen, D. R. (2003). Stability and change in industrial and organizational psychology. In W. C. Borman, D. R. Ilgen, & R. J. Klimoski (Eds.), Handbook of psychology, Vol. 12: Industrial and organizational psychology. New York: John Wiley and Sons.

Borman, W. C., Ilgen, D. R., & Klimoski, R. L. (2003). Handbook of psychology: *Vol. 12. Industrial and organizational psychology*. New York: Wiley.

Borstorff, P. C., Harris, S. G., Field, H. S., & Giles, W. F. (1997). Who'll go? A Review of factors associated with employee willingness to work overseas. *Human Resources Planning*, *20*(3), 29–40.

Bose, I. (2008). Lessons learned from distributed agile software projects: A case-based analysis. *Communications of the Association for Information Systems*, *23*(34), 619–632.

Botten, N., Kusiak, A., & Raz, T. (1989). Knowledge Bases: Integration, Verification, and Partitioning. *European Journal of Operational Research*, *42*(2), 1. doi:10.1016/0377-2217(89)90315-9.

Boulanger, C. (1996). Ethnicity and practice in Malaysian unions. *Ethnic and Racial Studies*, *19*(3), 660–679. doi:10.1080/01419870.1996.9993929.

Boulding, W., Richard, S., Michael Ehret, M., & Johnston, W. J. (2005). A Customer Relationship Management Roadmap: What Is Known, Potential pitfalls and where to go. *Journal of Marketing*, *69*, 155–166. doi:10.1509/jmkg.2005.69.4.155.

Bouquet, C., Hebert, L., & Delios, A. (2004). Foreign expansion in service industries separability and human capital intensity. *Journal of Business Research*, *57*, 35–46. doi:10.1016/S0148-2963(02)00282-5.

Bouwens, J., & Abernethy, M. (2000). The consequences of customization on management accounting system design. *Accounting, Organizations and Society*, *25*, 221–241. doi:10.1016/S0361-3682(99)00043-4.

Bowden, J. (2005). Reflections on the phenomenographic research process. In Bowden, J., & Green, P. (Eds.), *Doing Developmental Phenomenography*. Melbourne, Australia: RMIT University Press.

Bower, J. L., & Christensen, C. M. (1995). Disruptive Technologies: Catching the Wave. *Harvard Business Review*, *73*(1), 43–53.

Bradley, D., Noonan, P., Nugent, H., & Scales, B. (2008). *Review of Australian Higher Education (E. a. W. R. Department of Education, Trans.)*. Canberra, Australia: Department of Education, Employment and Workplace Relations.

Bradshaw, R., Maycock, C. & Öztel, H. (2008). Exploring SME market orientation: An organizational learning perspective. *Education + Training, 50*(8), 764-777.

Brancato, C. K. (1995). New corporate performance measures, Research Report No. 1118-95-RR. New York: The Conference Board.

Bransford, J., Vye, N., Stevens, R., Kuhl, P., Schwartz, D., & Bell, P. ... Sabelli, N. (2005). Learning theories and education: Toward a decade of synergy. In P. Alexander & P. Winne (2nd ed.), Handbook of educational psychology. Mahwah, NJ: Erlbaum.

Brewster, C. (1991). *The management of expatriates*. London: Kogan Page.

Briscoe, D. R., Schuler, R. S., & Claus, L. (2009). *International human resource management: Policies and practices for multinational enterprises* (3rd ed.). New York: Routledge.

Britannica. (2012). *Fernando Ortiz*. Retrieved June 27, 2012, from http://www.britannica.com/EBchecked/topic/848801/Fernando-Ortiz

Brodbeck, F. (2001). Leadership In Organizations, Psychology Of. In Neil, J. S., & Paul, B. B. (Eds.), *International Encyclopedia Of The Social &Amp; Behavioral Sciences*. Oxford, UK: Pergamon. doi:10.1016/B0-08-043076-7/01404-2.

Brogden, H. E. (1949). When testing pays off. *Personnel Psychology*, *2*, 171–183. doi:10.1111/j.1744-6570.1949.tb01397.x.

Bromwich, M., & Bhimani, A. (1994). *Management accounting: Pathways to progress*. London: The Chartered Institute of Management Accountants.

Brooker, G., & Wheatley, J. J. (1994). Music and radio advertising: Effects of tempo and placement. *Advances in Consumer Research. Association for Consumer Research (U. S.)*, *21*, 286–290.

Brouthers, K. D. (2002). Institutional, Cultural and Transaction Cost Influences on Entry Mode Choice and Performance. *Journal of International Business Studies*, *33*(2), 203–221. doi:10.1057/palgrave.jibs.8491013.

Brown, C., Varley, P., & Pal, J. (2009). University course selection and services marketing. *Marketing Intelligence & Planning*, *27*(3), 310–325. doi:10.1108/02634500910955227.

Brown, D., & Porter, R. (1996). *Management Issues in China* (*Vol. 1*). London, UK: Routledge.

Brownell, J. (2003). Applied Research in Managerial Communication. *The Cornell Hotel and Restaurant Administration Quarterly*, *44*(2), 39–49. doi:10.1016/S0010-8804(03)90017-6.

Brown, J. S., & Duguid, P. (1991). Organizational Learning and Communities of Practice –Towards a Unified View of Working. *Organization Science*, *2*(1). doi:10.1287/orsc.2.1.40.

Bruner, J. (1990). *Acts of Meaning*. Cambridge, MA: Harvard University Press.

Bruning, N. S., Sonpar, K., & Wang, X. (2012). Host-country national networks and expatriate effectiveness: A mixed-methods study. *Journal of International Business Studies*, *43*(4), 444–450. doi:10.1057/jibs.2012.5.

Bryan, W. L., & Harter, N. (1897). Studies in the physiology and psychology of the telegraphic language. *Psychological Review*, *4*, 27–53. doi:10.1037/h0073806.

Bryman, A. (2006). Integrating quantitative and qualitative research: How is it done? *Qualitative Research*, *6*(1), 97–113. doi:10.1177/1468794106058877.

Bryman, A., & Bell, E. (2007). *Business Research Methods*. Oxford, UK: Oxford University Press.

Bryman, A., & Cramer, D. (2001). *Quantitaive Data Analysis*. London: Routledge.

Bucci, A., Codeluppi, V., & Ferraresi, M. (2011). *Il made in Italy*. Rome, Italy: Carrocci Editore.

Buckley, P. J. (1988). The Limits of Explanation: Testing the Internalization Theory of the Multinational Enterprise. *Journal of International Business Studies*, *19*(2), 181–193. doi:10.1057/palgrave.jibs.8490382.

Buckley, P. J., & Casson, M. (1976). *The future of the multinational enterprise*. London, UK: Macmillan.

Buckley, P. J., & Casson, M. C. (1985). *The economic theory of the multinational enterprise*. London: Macmillan.

Buckley, P. J., & Casson, M. C. (1998). Analyzing Foreign Market Entry Strategies: Extending the Internalization Approach. *Journal of International Business Studies*, *29*(3), 539–562. doi:10.1057/palgrave.jibs.8490006.

Buhalis, D. (2003). eTourism: Information technology for strategic tourism management. London: Prentice Hall.

Buhalis, D., & Law, R. (2008). Progress in information technology and tourism management: 20 years on and 10 years after the Internet—The state of eTourism research. *Tourism Management*, *29*(4), 609–623. doi:10.1016/j.tourman.2008.01.005.

Burbules, N. C., & Torres, C. A. (2000). Globalisation and education: An introduction. In Burbules, N. C., & Torres, C. A. (Eds.), *Globalisation and Education: Critical Perspectives* (pp. 1–26). New York: Routledge.

Burgel, O., & Murray, G. C. (2000). The International Market Entry Choices of Start-Up Companies in High-Technology Industries. *Journal of International Marketing*, *8*(2), 33–62. doi:10.1509/jimk.8.2.33.19624.

Burgmann, I., Kitchen, P. J., & Williams, R. (2006). Does culture matter on the web? *Marketing Intelligence & Planning*, *24*(1), 62–76. doi:10.1108/02634500610641561.

Burke, M. C., & Edell, J. A. (1989). The impact of feelings on ad-based affect and cognition. *JMR, Journal of Marketing Research*, *26*(1), 69–83. doi:10.2307/3172670.

Burt, R. S. (1997). A note on social capital and network content. *Social Networks*, *19*, 355–373. doi:10.1016/S0378-8733(97)00003-8.

Burtt, H. E. (1929). *Psychology and industrial efficiency*. New York: Appleton.

Bustamante, L., Arboleda, A., & Gutiérrez, J. (2010). Cultura, política industrial y competitividad internacional de PyMEs en Colombia. *Revista Ad-Minister*, (16), 83-98.

Bustamante, L., & Aguilar, S. (2012). *Retos de gestión intercultural en las actividades de internacionalización de microempresas de Medellín*. Medellín, Colombia: Universidad de Medellín.

Butler, P., & Peppard, J. (1998). Consumer purchasing on the Internet: Processes and prospects. *European Management Journal*, *16*(5), 600–610. doi:10.1016/S0263-2373(98)00036-X.

Buttle, F. (2001). The CRM Value Chain. *Marketing Business*(February), 52–55.

Buttle, F. (1991). What do people do WITH advertising! *International Journal of Advertising*, *10*(April-June), 95–110.

Buttle, F. (1996). SERVQUAL: Review, critique, research agenda. *European Journal of Marketing*, *30*(1), 8–32. doi:10.1108/03090569610105762.

Byham, W. C. (1997). *The Outsourcing Question*. Pittsburgh, PA: Development Dimensions International.

Calhoun, C. (2011). Communication as Social Science (and More). *International Journal of Communication*, *5*, 1479–1496.

Caligiuri, P. M. (2000). The Big Five Personality Characteristics as Predictors of Expatriate's Desire to Terminate the Assignment and Supervisor-Rated Performance. *Personnel Psychology*, *53*(1), 67–88. doi:10.1111/j.1744-6570.2000.tb00194.x.

Calle, A., & Tamayo, V. (2005). Estrategia e internacionalización en las pymes: Caso Antioquia. *Cuadernos de Administración*, *18*(30), 137–164.

Camarinha-Matos, L. M., & Afsarmanesh, H. (2003). Elements Of A Base Ve Infrastructure. *Computers in Industry*, *51*, 139–163. doi:10.1016/S0166-3615(03)00033-2.

Camarinha-Matos, L., Afsarmanesh, H., & Ollus, M. (2005). *Virtual Organizations: Systems And Practices*. New York: Springer Verlag. doi:10.1007/b102339.

Camillo, A. A., & Di Pietro, L. (2011). The Importance of Managerial Communication for Hospitality Organizational Settings in the Era of High-Tech Evolution. *Hosteur*, *20*(2), 19–27.

Campbell, D. P., & Level Dale, A. (1985). A Black Box Model of Communication. *Journal of Business Communication*, *22*(3), 37–47. doi:10.1177/002194368502200304.

Campion, M., Gowing, M., Lancaster, A., & Pearlman, K. (1994). *United states department of labor database of occupational titles reinvention project: DOT transition team final report*. Washington, DC: U.S. Department of Personnel Management.

Cannon-Bowers, J. A., Tannenbaum, S. I., Salas, E., & Volpe, C. E. (1995). Defining Competencies And Establishing Team Training Requirements. *Team Effectiveness And Decision Making In Organizations*, *333*, 380.

Cantwell, J. A., & Piscitello, L. (2000). Accumulating Technological Competence: Its Changing Impact on Corporate Diversification and Internationalisation. *Industrial and Corporate Change*, *9*(1), 21–51. doi:10.1093/icc/9.1.21.

Cao, Q., & Dowlatshahi, S. (2005). The Impact Of Alignment Between Virtual Enterprise And Information Technology On Business Performance In An Agile Manufacturing Environment. *Journal of Operations Management*, *23*, 531–550. doi:10.1016/j.jom.2004.10.010.

Cap Gemini. (2004). *The Outsourcing Report: Making Choices – Insights into Successful Outsourcing*.

Cari, M., Tuba, M., & Moisil, I. (N. Y.). *Web-based testing and self-assessment system implemented with open technologies*. Retrieved on August 18, 2012, from http://www.wseas.us/e-library/conferences/2010/Corfu/EDUCATION/EDUCATION-50.pdf

Carlson, S. (1951). *Executive Behavior*. Stockholm, Sweden: Strombergs.

Carmel, E. (1999). *Global software teams: Collaborating across borders and time zones*. Upper Saddle River, NJ: Prentice-Hall.

Carmel, E., & Agarwal, R. (2001). Tactical approaches for alleviating distance in global software development. *IEEE Software*, *18*(2), 22–29. doi:10.1109/52.914734.

Caro, R. A. (2002). *Master of the senate: The years of Lyndon Johnson*. New York: Knopf.

Caru, A., & Cova, B. (2007). Consuming experiences: An introduction. In Caru, A., & Cova, B. (Eds.), *Consuming Experience*. London: Routledge.

Cascio, W. F. (2007). Evidence-based management and the marketplace for idea. *Academy of Management Journal*, *50*, 1009–1012. doi:10.5465/AMJ.2007.27151942.

Cascio, W. F. (2008). To prosper, organizational psychology should bridge application and scholarship. *Journal of Organizational Behavior*, *29*, 455–468. doi:10.1002/job.528.

Cascio, W. F., & Aguinis, H. (2008). Research in industrial and organizational psychology from 1963 to 2007: Changes, choices, and trends. *The Journal of Applied Psychology*, *93*(5), 5, 1062–1081. doi:10.1037/0021-9010.93.5.1062 PMID:18808226.

Cascio, W. F., & Shurygailo, S. (2003). E-Leadership And Virtual Teams. *Organizational Dynamics*, *31*, 362–376. doi:10.1016/S0090-2616(02)00130-4.

Castells, M. (2007). Communication, power and counter-power in the network society. *International Journal of Communication*, *1*(1), 238–266.

Cauldron, S. (1998). Diversity watch. *Black Enterprise*, *29*, 91.

Caves, R. E. (1982). *Multinational enterprises and economic analysis*. New York: St. Martin's Press.

Cavusgil, S. T., Knight, G., & Riesenberger, J. R. (2008). *International Business: Strategy, Management and the New Realities*. Upper Saddle River, NJ: Prentice Hall.

Cavusgil, S. T., & Nevin, J. R. (1981). State-of-the-art in international marketing: An assessment. In Enis, B. M., & Roering, K. J. (Eds.), *Review of Marketing* (pp. 195–216). Chicago, IL: American Marketing Association.

Cavusgil, T. (1980). On the Internationalization Process of Firms. *European Research*, *8*(6), 273–281.

Cavusgil, T., & Das, A. (1997). Methodological issues in empirical cross-cultural research: A survey of the management literature and a framework. *Management International Review*, *37*(1), 71–96.

Central Intelligence Agency. (2011). *The World Factbook - East & Southeast Asia: Vietnam*. Retrieved January 2, 2012, from https://www.cia.gov/library/publications/the-world-factbook/geos/vm.html

Chandy, R. K., & Tellis, G. J. (1998). Organizing for Radical Product Innovation: The Overlooked Role of Willingness to Cannibalize. *JMR, Journal of Marketing Research*, *35*(4), 474–487. doi:10.2307/3152166.

Chaney, I., & Gamble, J. (2008). Retail store ownership influences on Chinese consumers. *International Business Review*, *17*, 170–183. doi:10.1016/j.ibusrev.2008.02.008.

Chang, C. M. (2011). New Organizational Designs For Promoting Creativity: A Case Study Of Virtual Teams With Anonymity And Structured Interactions. *Journal of Engineering and Technology Management*, *28*, 268–282. doi:10.1016/j.jengtecman.2011.06.004.

Chang, J. (2007). International Expansion Path, Speed, Product Diversification and Performance Among Emerging-Market MNEs: Evidence from Asia-Pacific Multinational Companies. *Asian Business & Management*, *6*(4), 331–354. doi:10.1057/palgrave.abm.9200228.

Chang, M. L. (2000). The evolution of sex segregation regimes. *American Journal of Sociology*, *105*(6), 1658–1701. doi:10.1086/210469.

Chang, S. C., & Lee, M. S. (2007). A Study on Relationship among Leadership, Organizational Culture, the Operation of Learning Organization and Employees' Job Satisfaction. *The Learning Organization*, *14*, 155–185. doi:10.1108/09696470710727014.

Chang, S. J. (1995). International expansion strategy of Japanese firms: Capability building through sequential entry. *Academy of Management Journal*, *38*(2), 383–407. doi:10.2307/256685.

Chang, S. J. (1995). International Expansion Strategy of Japanese Firms: Capability Building through Sequential Entry. *Academy of Management Journal*, *38*(2), 383–407. doi:10.2307/256685.

Chang, S. J., & Rosenzweig, P. M. (2001). The Choice of Entry Mode in Sequential Foreign Direct Investment. *Strategic Management Journal*, *22*(8), 747–776. doi:10.1002/smj.168.

Chapman, C. (1997). Reflections on a contingent view of accounting. *Accounting, Organizations and Society*, *22*, 189–205. doi:10.1016/S0361-3682(97)00001-9.

Chatman, S. (1978). *Story and Discourse: Narrative Structure in Fiction and Film*. Ithaca, NY: Cornell University Press.

Chen, C. (2008). Entry mode selection for international construction markets: The influence of host country related factors. *Construction Management and Economics*, *26*, 303–314. doi:10.1080/01446190701882382.

Chen, C., & Huang, J. (2007). How Organizational Climate and Structure Affect Knowledge Management – the Social Interaction Perspective. *International Journal of Information Management*, *27*(2), 104–118. doi:10.1016/j.ijinfomgt.2006.11.001.

Chen, C., & Messner, J. I. (2010). A Recommended Practices System For A Global Virtual Engineering Team. *Architectural Engineering And Design Management*, *6*, 207–221. doi:10.3763/aedm.2010.0121.

Chen, G. M., & Starosta, W. J. (1998). *Foundations of Intercultural Communication*. Boston, MA: Allyn and Bacon.

Chen, H. C., & Shih, H. T. (2005). *High-Tech Industries in China*. Cheltenham, UK: Edward Elgar Publishing.

Chenhall, R. (2003). Management control systems design within its organizational context: Findings from contingency-based research and directions for the future. *Accounting, Organizations and Society*, *28*, 127–188. doi:10.1016/S0361-3682(01)00027-7.

Chenhall, R. H. (1997). Reliance on manufacturing performance measures, total quality management and organisational performance. *Management Accounting Research*, *8*, 187–206. doi:10.1006/mare.1996.0038.

Chenhall, R. H., & Langfield-Smith, K. (1998). Factors influencing the role of management accounting in the development of performance measures within organisational change programs. *Management Accounting Research*, *9*, 361–386. doi:10.1006/mare.1998.0080.

Chetty, S., & Campbell-Hunt, C. (2004). Internationalisation strategy and its impact on learning during the process. *Journal of Asia-Pacific Marketing*, *3*(2), 38–52.

Chieochan, O., Lindley, D., & Dunn, T. (2000). Factors affecting the use of information technology in Thai agricultural cooperatives: A work in progress. *Electronic Journal on Information Systems in Developing Countries*, *2*(1), 1–15.

Child, J., & Kieser, A. (1979). Organisational and Management Roles in British and German Companies: An Examination of the Culture-Free Thesis. In C.J. Lammus & D.J. Hickson (Eds.), *Organisations Alike and Unlike*. London: Routledge.

Child, J. (1996). *Management in China during the age of reform*. Cambridge, MA: Cambridge University Press.

Childs, J. T. Jr. (2005). Managing workforce diversity at IBM: A global HR topic that has arrived. *Human Resource Management*, *44*(1), 73–77. doi:10.1002/hrm.20042.

China Statistical Yearbook. 1988-2006. Beijing, China: China Statistical Information and Consultancy Service Centre.

Chin, K. S., Sun, H., Xu, Y., & Hua, H. (2002). A Comparative Study of Quality Management Practices in Hong Kong and Shanghai Manufacturing Industries. *International Journal of Management*, *19*(4), 576–581.

Chinowsky, P. S., & Rojas, E.M., (2003). *Virtual Teams: Guide To Successful Implementation; Journal of management in engineering, 19, 98-106.*

Chmiel, N. (2000). History and context for work and organizational psychology. In Chmiel, N. (Ed.), *Introduction to work and organizational psychology: A european perspective*. Malden, MA: Blackwell.

Cho, C.-H., & Cheon, H. J. (2005). Cross-Cultural Comparisons of Interactivity on Corporate Web Sites. *Journal of Advertising*, *34*(2), 99–115. doi:10.1080/00913367.2005.10639195.

Chong, A. Y., Ooi, K., Lin, B., & Tan, B. (2010). Online banking adoption: An empirical analysis. *International Journal of Bank Marketing*, *28*(4), 267–287. doi:10.1108/02652321011054963.

Chow, C., Harrison, P., Lindiquist, T., & Wu, A. (1997). Escalating commitment to unprofitable projects: Replication and cross – cultural extension. *Management Accounting Research*, *8*(3), 347–361. doi:10.1006/mare.1996.0046.

Choy, K. W. (2007). Globalization and workforce diversity: HRM implications for multinational corporations in Singapore. *Singapore Management Review.*, *29*(2), 1–19.

Christensen, C. M. (1997). *The Innovator's Dilemma*. New York: HarperCollins Publishing, Inc..

Christensen, C. M. (2006). The Ongoing Process of Building a Theory or Disruption. *Journal of Product Innovation Management*, *23*(1), 39–55. doi:10.1111/j.1540-5885.2005.00180.x.

Christensen, C. M., Johnson, M. W., & Rigby, D. K. (2002). Foundations for Growth: How to Identify and Build Disruptive New Businesses. *Sloan Management Review*, *43*(3), 22–31.

Christensen, C. M., & Raynor, M. E. (2003). *The Innovator's Solution*. Boston, MA: Harvard Business School.

Chua, W. F. (2007). Accounting, measuring, reporting and strategizing –Re-using verbs: A review essay. *Accounting, Organizations and Society*, *32*, 487–494. doi:10.1016/j.aos.2006.03.010.

Church, A. (1982). Sojourner adjustment. *Psychological Bulletin*, *91*, 540–572. doi:10.1037/0033-2909.91.3.540.

Churchill, G. A. (1979). A paradigm for developing better measures of marketing constructs. *Journal of Marketing*, *16*(2), 64–73.

CIA. (2012). The *World Factbook – China*. Retrieved from https://www.cia.gov/library/publications/the-world-factbook/geos/ch.html

Ciganek, A. P., Mao, E., & Srite, M. (2008). Organizational Culture for Knowledge Management Systems: A Study of Corporate Users. *Journal of Knowledge Management*, *4*(1), 1–15. doi:10.4018/jkm.2008010101.

CIMA. (1993). *Performance measurement in the manufacturing sector*. London: Charted Institute of Management Accountants.

CIMA. (1996). *Management accounting official terminology*. London: Charted Institute of Management Accountants.

Clampitt, P. (2005). *Communicating for Managerial Effectiveness*. New York: Sage Publications.

Clark, R. Y. A., & Anker, R. (2003). Cross-national analysis of women in the labour market. In Garcia, B. A., & Pinelli, A. (Eds.), *Women in the Labour Market on Changing Economies: Demographic issues*. Oxford, UK: Oxford University Press.

Claver-Cortes, E., Zaragoza-Saez, P., & Pertusa-Ortega, E. (2007). Organizational Structure Features Supporting Knowledge Management Processes. *International Journal of Knowledge Management*, *11*(4), 45–57. doi:10.1108/13673270710762701.

CNN. (2011). *Money, Annual Ranking of America's Largest Corporations. Fortune 500 companies*. Retrieved from http://money.cnn.com/magazines/fortune/fortune500/2011/full_list/)

Coakes, E. (2006). Storing and Sharing Knowledge – Supporting the Management of Knowledge Made Explicit in Transnational Organizations. *The Learning Organization*, *13*(6), 579–593. doi:10.1108/09696470610705460.

Coakes, E., Amar, A. D., & Grandos, M. L. (2010). Knowledge Management, Strategy, and Technology: A Global Snapshot. *Journal of Enterprise Information Management*, *23*(3), 282–304. doi:10.1108/17410391011036076.

Coelli, T., Rao, D. S. P., O'Donnell, C. J., & Battese, G. E. (1998). *An introduction to efficiency and productivity analysis* (1st ed.). New York: Springer. doi:10.1007/978-1-4615-5493-6.

Cohen, D., Lindvall, M., & Costa, P. (2004). An introduction to agile methods. *Advances in Computers*, *62*, 1–66. doi:10.1016/S0065-2458(03)62001-2.

Coleman, J. C. (1988). Social capital in the creation of human capital. *American Journal of Sociology*, *94*, S95–S120. doi:10.1086/228943.

Coleman, T. (1994). Managing diversity: Keeping it in focus. *Public Management*, *76*, 10–16.

Collins, J. D., Holcomb, T. R., Certo, S. T., Hitt, M. A., & Lester, R. H. (2009). Learning by doing: Cross-border mergers and acquisitions. *Journal of Business Research*, *62*(12), 1329–1334. doi:10.1016/j.jbusres.2008.11.005.

Colombian Ministry of Commerce. (2012). *Acuerdos suscritos, vigentes y en negociación*. Retrieved October 29, 2012, from http://www.tlc.gov.co/

Colombian Ministry of Education. (2012). *Estadísticas del Sector Educativo en Colombia*. Retrieved October 29, 2012, from http://menweb.mineducacion.gov.co/seguimiento/estadisticas/

Colombian Ministry of Education. (2012, September). *Resumen de indicadores de Educación Superior*. Retrieved October 29, 2012, from http://www.mineducacion.gov.co/sistemasdeinformacion/1735/w3-article-212350.html

Commins, S., Gevers, C., Randa, J., & World Bank. (2001). *Adjustment from Within: Lessons from the Structural Adjustment Participatory Review Initiative* (World Bank Report).

Comscore. (2011). *ComScore Releases Overview of European Internet Usage in September 2011*. Retrieved from http://www.comscore.com/Press_Events/Press_Releases/2011/11/comScore_Releases_Overview_of_European_Internet_Usage_in_September_2011

Conboy, K. (2009). Agility from first principles: Reconstructing the concept of agility in information systems development. *Information Systems Research*, *20*(3), 329–354. doi:10.1287/isre.1090.0236.

Conboy, K., Coyle, S., Wang, X., & Pikkarainen, M. (2011). People over process: Key challenges in Agile development. *IEEE Software*, *28*(4), 48–57. doi:10.1109/MS.2010.132.

Condit, C. M. (1989). The rhetorical limits of polysemy. *Critical Studies in Mass Communication*, *6*(2), 103–122. doi:10.1080/15295038909366739.

Conger, J., & Kanungo, R. N. (1994). Charismatic leadership in organizations: Perceived behavioral attributes and their management. *Journal of Organizational Behavior*, *15*, 439–452. doi:10.1002/job.4030150508.

Connaughton, S. L., & Shuffler, M. (2007). Multinational And Multicultural Distributed Teams. *Small Group Research*, *38*, 387–412. doi:10.1177/1046496407301970.

Conti, T. (1993). *Building Quality: A Guide to Management*. London: Chapman and Hall. doi:10.1007/978-94-011-1546-9.

Cooke, F. L., & Saini, D. S. (2010). Diversity management in India: A study of organizations in different ownership forms and industrial sectors. *Human Resource Management*, *49*(3), 477–500. doi:10.1002/hrm.20360.

Copeland, L., & Briggs, L. (1985). *Going international*. New York: Random House.

Copley, P. (2004). *Marketing Communications Management. Concepts and Theories, Cases and Practices*. Oxford, UK: Elsevier.

Corbett, L. M., Adam, E. E., Harrison, N. J., Lee, T. S., Rho, B. H., & Samson, D. (1998). A Study of Quality Management Practices and Performance in Asia and the South Pacific. *International Journal of Production Research*, *36*(9), 2597–2607. doi:10.1080/002075498192724.

Cormier, D., Magnan, M., & Van Velthoven, B. (2005). Environmental disclosure quality in large German companies: Economic incentives, public pressures or institutional conditions? *European Accounting Review*, *14*(1), 3–39. doi:10.1080/0963818042000339617.

Cornelissen, J. (2004). *Corporate communications. Theory and Practice*. London: Sage Publications Cornell University (2011). *Managerial Communication. An introduction to key library resources for Hotel Administration*. Retrieved from http://guides.library.cornell.edu/HADM3365)

Corsini, R., & Marsella, A. J. (1983). *Personality Theories, Research and Assessment*. Itasca, IL: Peacock Publishers, Inc..

Corson, D. (2000). Emancipatory leadership. *International Journal of Leadership in Education*, *3*(2), 93–120. doi:10.1080/136031200292768.

Coulson, J. S. (1989). An investigation of mood commercials. In Cafferata, P., & Tybout, A. M. (Eds.), *Cognitive and Affective Responses to Advertising*. Lexington, MA: Lexington Books.

Covaleski, M., Dirsmith, M., & Samuel, S. (1996). Managerial accounting research: The contribution of organizational and sociological theories. *Journal of Management Accounting Research*, *8*, 1–35.

Covin, T., Sightler, K., Kolenko, T., & Tudor, R. (1996). An investigation of post-acquisition satisfaction with the merger. *The Journal of Applied Behavioral Science*, *32*(2), 125–141. doi:10.1177/0021886396322001.

Cox, A. (1996). Relational competence and strategic procurement management. *European Journal of Purchasing and Supply Management*, *2*(1), 57–70. doi:10.1016/0969-7012(95)00019-4.

Cox, T. (2001). *Creating the Multicultural Organization*. San Francisco, CA: Jossey-Bass.

Cramer, D., & Howitt, D. (2004). *The sage dictionary of statistics, a guide for social scientists*. East Sussex, UK: Routledge.

Crawford, C. B. (2005). Effects of Transformational Leadership and Organizational Position on Knowledge Management. *International Journal of Knowledge Management*, *9*, 6–16. doi:10.1108/13673270510629927.

Crawford, K. M., Blackstone, J. H. Jr, & Cox, J. F. (1988). A study of JIT implementation and operating problems. *International Journal of Production Research*, *26*(9), 1561–1568. doi:10.1080/00207548808947966.

Creswell, J. W. (2003). *Research Design: Qualitative, Quantitative, and Mixed Methods Approaches* (2nd ed.). Thousand Oaks, CA: Sage.

Cronin, J., Brady, M., & Hult, G. (2000). Assessing the effect of quality, value, and customer satisfaction on consumer behavioral intentions in service environments. *Journal of Retailing*, *76*(2), 193–218. doi:10.1016/S0022-4359(00)00028-2.

Cronin, J., & Taylor, S. (1992). Measuring service quality: A re-examination and extension. *Journal of Marketing*, *56*(3), 55–68. doi:10.2307/1252296.

Cronin, J., & Taylor, S. (1994). SERVPERF versus SERVQUAL: Reconciling performance-based and perceptions-minus-expectations measurement of service quality. *Journal of Marketing*, *58*(1), 125–131. doi:10.2307/1252256.

Cross, R., & Cummings, J. N. (2004). Tie and network correlates of individual performance in knowledge-intensive work. *Academy of Management Journal*, *47*(6), 928–937. doi:10.2307/20159632.

Crotts, J. C., & Erdmann, R. (2000). Does national culture influence consumers' evaluation of travel services? A test of Hofstede's model of cross-cultural differences. *Managing Service Quality*, *10*(6), 410–419. doi:10.1108/09604520010351167.

Cruz, N. M., Perez, V. M., & Cantero, C. T. (2009). The Influence of Employee Motivation on Knowledge Transfer. *International Journal of Knowledge Management*, *13*(6), 478–490. doi:10.1108/13673270910997132.

Cua, K. O., McKone, K. E., & Schroeder, R. G. (2001). Relationships between implementation of TQM, JIT, and TPM and manufacturing performance. *Journal of Operations Management*, *19*(1), 675–694. doi:10.1016/S0272-6963(01)00066-3.

Cukur, C. S., De Guzman, M., & Gustavo, C. (2004). Religiosity, Values, and Horizontal and Vertical Individualism/Collectivism: A Study of Turkey, the United States and the Philippines. *The Journal of Social Psychology*, *144*(6), 613–635. doi:10.3200/SOCP.144.6.613-634 PMID:15565828.

Cupach, W. R., & Canary, D. J. (1997). *Competence in Interpersonal Conflict*. Long Grove, IL: Waveland Press.

Curseu, P. L., Schalk, R., & Wessel, I. (2008). How Do Virtual Teams Process Information? A Literature Review And Implications For Management. *Journal of Managerial Psychology*, *23*, 628–652. doi:10.1108/02683940810894729.

Curtis, G., & Cobham, D. (2002). *Business Information Systems: Analysis, Design and Practice* (4th ed.). Upper Saddle River, NJ: Prentice Hall.

Cushner, K., & Brislin, R. W. (1996). *Intercultural interactions: A practical guide*. Thousand Oaks, CA: Sage.

Cusick, J., & Prasad, A. (2006). A practical management and engineering approach to offshore collaboration. *IEEE Software*, *23*(5), 20–29. doi:10.1109/MS.2006.118.

Cusumano, M. A., MacCormack, A., Kemerer, C. F., & Crandall, W. (2009). Critical decisions in software development: Updating the state of the practice. *IEEE Software*, *26*(5), 84–87. doi:10.1109/MS.2009.124.

Cuz, I., Scapens, R., & Major, M. (2011). The localisation of a global management control systems. *Accounting, Organizations and Society*, *36*, 412–427. doi:10.1016/j.aos.2011.08.001.

Cyr, D. (2008). Modeling Web Site Design Across Cultures: Relationships to Trust, Satisfaction, and E-Loyalty. *Journal of Management Information Systems*, *24*(4), 47–72. doi:10.2753/MIS0742-1222240402.

Cyr, D., Bonanni, C., Bowes, J., & Ilsever, J. (2005). Beyond Trust: Web Site Design Preferences Across Cultures. *Journal of Global Information Management*, *13*(4), 25–54. doi:10.4018/jgim.2005100102.

Cyr, D., Head, M., & Larios, H. (2010). Colour appeal in website design within and across cultures: A multi-method evaluation. *International Journal of Human-Computer Studies*, *68*, 1–21. doi:10.1016/j.ijhcs.2009.08.005.

Cyr, D., Kindra, G. S., & Dash, S. (2008). Web site design, trust, satisfaction and e-loyalty: The Indian experience. *Online Information Review*, *32*(6), 773–790. doi:10.1108/14684520810923935.

Cyr, D., & Trevor-Smith, H. (2004). Localization of Web Design: An Empirical Comparison of German, Japanese, and U.S. Website Characteristics. *Journal of the American Society for Information Science and Technology*, *55*(13), 1199–1208. doi:10.1002/asi.20075.

Czarniawska-Joerges, B. (1995). Narration or Science? Collapsing the Division in Organization Studies. *Organization*, *2*(1), 11–33. doi:10.1177/135050849521002.

D'souza, G. C., & Colarelli, S. M. (2010). Team Member Selection Decisions For Virtual Versus Face-To-Face Teams. *Computers in Human Behavior*, *26*, 630–635. doi:10.1016/j.chb.2009.12.016.

Dafoulas, G. & Macaulay, L. 2002. Investigating Cultural Differences In Virtual Software Teams. *The Electronic Journal Of Information Systems In Developing Countries, 7*.

Daft, R. L. (2001). *Organization theory and design* (7th ed.). South-Western College Publishing.

Daft, R. L. (2008). *New Era of Management* (2nd ed.). New York: Thomson South Western Publishing.

Dagher, J., D'Netto, B., & Sohal, A. S. (1998). Managing workforce diversity in the Australian manufacturing industry. *Human Factors and Ergonomics in Manufacturing*, *8*(2), 177–192. doi:10.1002/(SICI)1520-6564(199821)8:2<177::AID-HFM6>3.0.CO;2-0.

Dahlman, C. (2008). Technology, Globalisation, and International Competitiveness: Challenges for Developing Countries. In O'Connor, D., & Kjöllerström, M. (Eds.), *Industrial Development for the 21st Century* (pp. 29–84). Hyderabad, India: Orient Longman Zed Books and United Nations.

Dahlstrom, R., Nygaard, A., & Crosno, J. (2008). Strategic, metric and methodological trends in marketing research and their implications for future theory and practice. *Journal of Marketing Theory and Practice*, *16*(2), 139–152. doi:10.2753/MTP1069-6679160204.

Dalkir, K. (2011). *Knowledge management in theory and practice*. Cambridge, MA: MIT Press.

Dance, F. (1970). The concept of communication. *The Journal of Communication*, *20*, 201–210. doi:10.1111/j.1460-2466.1970.tb00877.x.

Danciu, V. (2010). The Impact of the Culture on the International Negotiations: An Analysis Based on Contextual Comparisons. *Theoretical and Applied Economics*, *17*(8), 87–102.

Dang, P., & Beresford, M. (1998). *Authority relations and economic decision-making in Vietnam: An historical perspective*. Copenhagen, Denmark: NIAS.

Davenport, T. H. (2005). *Thinking for a Living: How to Get Better Performance and Results from Knowledge Workers*. Boston, MA: Harvard Business School Press.

Davenport, T. H., & Prusak, L. (2000). *Working Knowledge: How Organizations Manage What They Know*. Boston, MA: Harvard Business School Press. doi:10.1145/347634.348775.

David, G. C., Newell, S., & Resende-Santos, J. O. (2008). Integrated collaboration across distributed sites: The perils of process and the promise of practice. *Journal of Information Technology*, *23*(1), 44–54. doi:10.1057/palgrave.jit.2000126.

Davidson, W. H. (1980). The mode choice and change decision process and its impact on international performance. *International Business Review*, *2*(1), 97–120.

Davis, F. D. (1989). Perceived usefulness, perceived ease of use and user acceptance of information technology. *Management Information Systems Quarterly*, *13*(3). doi:10.2307/249008.

Davis, J. E., Subrahmanian, E., & Westerberg, W. (2005). The "Global" and the "Local" in Knowledge Management. *International Journal of Knowledge Management*, *9*(1), 101–112. doi:10.1108/13673270510582992.

Davison, L., & Al-Shaghana, K. (2007). The link between Six-Sigma and quality culture – An empirical study. *Total Quality Management Journal*, *18*(3), 249–265. doi:10.1080/14783360601152269.

Day, G. S. (1994). The capabilities of market-driven organizations. *Journal of Marketing*, *58*(4), 37–52. doi:10.2307/1251915.

De Long, D. W., & Fahey, L. (2000). Diagnosing Cultural Barriers to Knowledge Management. *The Academy of Management Executive*, *14*(4), 113–127.

de Luca, P., Vianelli, D., & Marzano, F. C. (2011). L'internazionalizzazione delle imprese italiane nel mercato cinese: Fattori propulsivi e difficoltà percepite. *Micro & Macro Marketing*, *3*, 33–51.

De Mooij, M. (1998). *Global Marketing and Advertising: Understanding Cultural Paradoxes*. Thousand Oaks, CA: Sage Publications.

de Mooij, M. (2010). *Global Marketing and Advertising: Understanding Cultural Paradoxes* (3rd ed.). Thousand Oaks, CA: Sage Publications.

Deal, T. E., & Kennedy, A. A. (1982). *Corporate cultures: The rites and rituals of corporate life*. New York: Basic Books.

Debowski, S. (2006). *Knowledge Management*. Hoboken, NJ: John Wiley & Sons.

Dedic, G., & Pavlovic, D. K. (2011). A tale of two nations empirical examination of influence of national culture on perceived service quality. *International Journal of Management Cases*, *13*(3), 92–104.

Dekker, D. M., Rutte, C. G., & Van Den Berg, P. T. (2008). Cultural Differences In The Perception Of Critical Interaction Behaviors In Global Virtual Teams. *International Journal of Intercultural Relations*, *32*, 441–452. doi:10.1016/j.ijintrel.2008.06.003.

Delios, A., & Beamish, P. W. (1999). Geographic Scope, Product Diversification, and the Corporate Performance of Japanese Firms. *Strategic Management Journal*, *20*(8), 711–727. doi:10.1002/(SICI)1097-0266(199908)20:8<711::AID-SMJ41>3.0.CO;2-8.

Delios, A., & Henisz, W. (2003). Political Hazards, Experience, and Sequential Entry Strategies: The International Expansion of Japanese Firms, 1980-1998. *Strategic Management Journal*, *24*(11), 1153–1164. doi:10.1002/smj.355.

DeLuca, D., & Valacich, J. S. (2006). Virtual teams in and out of synchronicity. *Information Technology & People*, *19*(4), 323–344. doi:10.1108/09593840610718027.

Denison, D. (1996). What is the difference between organizational culture and organizational climate? In Cartwright, S., & Cooper, C. (Eds.), *The handbook of organizational culture*. London: John Wiley & Sons.

Denzin, N. K., & Lincoln, Y. S. (2005). *The Sage Handbook of Qualitative Research*. Thousand Oaks, CA: Sage Publications.

Deresky, H. (2005). *International Management. Managing across Borders and Cultures*. Upper Saddle River, NJ: Prentice Hall.

Deshpande, R. (1983). Paradigms Lost: On Theory and Method in Research in Marketing. *Journal of Marketing*, *47*(Fall), 101–110. doi:10.2307/1251403.

Deshpandé, R., Farley, J. U., & Webster, F. E. Jr. (1993). Corporate culture, customer orientation, and innovativeness in Japanese firms: A quadrad analysis. *Journal of Marketing*, *57*(1), 23–37. doi:10.2307/1252055.

Desouza, K., & Evaristo, R. (2003). Global Knowledge Management Strategies. *European Management Journal*, *21*(1), 62–67. doi:10.1016/S0263-2373(02)00152-4.

Dessler, G. (2012). *Human resource management* (13th ed.). England: Pearson Education.

Devanna, M., Fombrum, N., & Tichy, N. (1981). Human resources management: A strategic perspective. *Organizational Dynamics*, *10*, 51–67. doi:10.1016/0090-2616(81)90038-3.

Dewey, P. (2004). From arts management to cultural administration. *International Journal of Arts Management*, *6*(3), 13–22.

Dex, S. (1991). *Life and Work History Analyses*. London: Routledge.

Dhanaraj, C., & Beamish, P. W. (2003). Effect of equity ownership on the survival of international joint ventures. *Strategic Management Journal*, *25*(3), 295–305. doi:10.1002/smj.372.

Diani, M. (2000). Social movement networks virtual and real. *Information Communication and Society*, *3*(3), 386–401. doi:10.1080/13691180051033333.

Dillman, D. A., Smyth, J. D., & Christian, L. M. (2009). *Internet, Mail and Mixed-mode Surveys: The Tailored Design Method*. Hoboken, NJ: John Wiley & Sons.

Dipboye, R. L. (2007). Eight outrageous statements about HR science. *Human Resource Management Review*, *76*, 96–106. doi:10.1016/j.hrmr.2007.04.001.

Dirk, Z. (2008). International Key Account Management in Manufacturing Companies: An Exploratory Approach of Situative Differentiation. *Journal of Business-To-Business Marketing*, *15*(4), 455–475. doi:10.1080/15470620802325807.

Do, T., Quilty, M., Milner, A., & Longstaff, S. (2007). Business culture issues in Vietnam: Case studies market, working paper series, Volume 2: No.2. Retrieved July 2, 2012, from http://dspace.anu.edu.au/handle/1885/44441

Dollar, D. (2001). *Reform, Growth, and Poverty in Vietnam*. Paper presented at the Conference on Economic Growth and Household Welfare: Policy Lessons for Vietnam. Hanoi, Vietnam.

Donaldson, T., & Dunfee, T. W. (2001). When ethics travel: The promise and peril of global business ethics. In J. S. Osland, D. A. Kolb, & I. M. Rubin (7th ed.), The organizational behavior reader. Upper Saddle River, NJ: Prentice Hall.

Donate, M. J., & Guadamillas, F. (2010). The Effect of Organizational Culture on Knowledge Management Practices and Innovation. *Knowledge and Process Management*, *17*(2), 82. doi:10.1002/kpm.344.

Dong, B., Zou, S., & Taylor, C. R. (2008). Factors that influence multinational corporations' control of their operations in foreign markets: An empirical investigation. *Journal of International Marketing*, *16*(1), 98–119. doi:10.1509/jimk.16.1.98.

Dong, M. C., Tse, D. K., & Cavusgil, S. T. (2008). Efficiency of governance mechanisms in China's distribution channels. *International Business Review*, *17*, 509–519. doi:10.1016/j.ibusrev.2008.07.001.

Donthu, N., & Boonghee, Y. (1998). Cultural influences on servcie quality expectations. *Journal of Service Research*, *1*(2), 178–186. doi:10.1177/109467059800100207.

Dougherty, S. M., & McGuckin, R. H. (2004). *The Effects of Federalism and Privatization on Productivity in Chinese Firms*. National School of Development Working Paper 2036. Peking University. Retrieved on December 6, 2011, from http://www.ccer.pku.edu.cn/download/2036-1.pdf

Dougherty, D. (1990). Understanding new markets for new products. *Strategic Management Journal*, *11*, 59–78.

Dowling, P., Welch, D., & Schuler, R. (1999). *International human resource management. Managing people in a multinational context*. Cincinnati, OH: South-Western.

Downey, H. K., Hellriegel, D., & Slocum, J. W. (1977). Individual Characteristics as Sources of Perceived Uncertainty Variability. *Human Relations*, *30*(2), 161–174. doi:10.1177/001872677703000205.

Draghici, A. (2008). Influence Of Multi-Culturality. In *Virtual Teams*. Berlin, Heidelberg: Springer Berlin Heidelberg.

Drezner, D., & Farrell, H. (2004). *The power and politics of blogs*. Paper presented at the American Political Science Association Conference. Chicago, IL.

Driscoll, A., & Paliwoda, S. J. (1997). Dimensionalizing international market entry mode choice. *Journal of Marketing Management*, *13*(1-3), 57–87. doi:10.1080/0267257X.1997.9964459.

Druce, L. (2009). *Knowledge process outsourcing offers significant growth opportunities*. Retrieved on October 26, 2012, from http://searchcio.techtarget.com/sDefinition/0,sid182_gci212731,00.html

Drucker, P. (1977). *People and Performance*. New York: Harper`s College Press.

Drucker, P. (1993). *Inovatia si sistemul antreprenorial*. Bucharest: Editura Enciclopedica.

Drucker, P. E. (1990). *The emerging theory of manufacturing* (pp. 94–102). Boston, MA: Harvard Business Review.

Drucker, P. F. (1959). *Landmarks of Tomorrow*. New York: Harper.

Drucker, P. F. (1974). *Management: Tasks, responsibilities, practices*. New York: Harper & Row Publishers, Inc..

Drucker, P. F. (1991). The New Productivity Challenge. *Harvard Business Review*, *69*(6), 69–76. PMID:10114929.

Drucker, P. F. (1993). *Post-Capitalist Society*. Oxford, UK: Butterworth/Heinemann.

Drucker, P. F. (1999). *Management Challenges fir the 21st Century*. New York: Harper Collins.

Drury, C. (1996). *Management Accounting Handbook*. Oxford, UK: Butterworth-Heinemann.

Duarte, D. L., & Snyder, N. T. (2006). *Mastering Virtual Teams: Strategies, Tools, And Techniques That Succeed*. Jossey-Bass.

Duggal, S. M. (2002). Global ınformation technology management. *Informing Science*, 397–406.

Dul, J., Bruder, R., Buckle, P., Carayon, P., & Falzon, P., Marras, …van der Doelen, B. (2012). A strategy for human factors/ergonomics: Developing the discipline and profession. *Ergonomics*, *55*(4), 377–395. doi:10.1080/00140139.2012.661087 PMID:22332611.

Dunnette, M. D. (1990). Blending the science and practice of industrial and organizational psychology: Where are we and where are we going? In Dunnette, M. D., & Hough, L. M. (Eds.), *Handbook of industrial and organizational psychology* (2nd ed., *Vol. 1*). Palo Alto, CA: Consulting Psychologists Press.

Dunnette, M. D., & Hough, L. M. (1990). *Handbook of industrial and organizational psychology* (2nd ed., *Vol. 1*). Palo Alto, CA: Consulting Psychologists Press.

Dunnette, M. D., & Hough, L. M. (1991). *Handbook of industrial and organizational psychology* (2nd ed., *Vol. 2*). Palo Alto, CA: Consulting Psychologists Press.

Dunnette, M. D., & Hough, L. M. (1992). *Handbook of industrial and organizational psychology* (2nd ed., *Vol. 3*). Palo Alto, CA: Consulting Psychologists Press.

Dunning, J. H. (1976). Trade, location of economic activity and the MNE: A search for an eclectic approach. P.O. Ohlin, P.M. Hesselborn, Wijkman (Eds.), *Proceedings of Nobel Symposium - The International*

Dunning, J. H. (1977). Trade location of economic activity and the MNE: A search for an eclectic approach. In Ohlin, B. (Ed.), *The International Allocation of Economic Activity*. London: Macmillan.

Dunning, J. H. (1981). *International production and the multinational enterprise*. London: Allen and Unwin.

Dunning, J. H. (1988). Explaining the international direct investment position of countries: Toward a dynamic or development approach. *Weltwirtschaftliches Archiv*, *117*(1), 30–64. doi:10.1007/BF02696577.

Dunning, J. H. (1993). *Multinational enterprise and the global economy*. Boston, MA: Addison Wesley.

Dunning, J. H. (1995). Reappraising the eclectic paradigm in an age of alliance capitalism. *Journal of International Business Studies*, *26*(3), 461–491. doi:10.1057/palgrave.jibs.8490183.

Dunning, J. H. (1998). Location and the Multinational Enterprise: A Neglected Factor? *Journal of International Business Studies*, *29*(1), 45–66. doi:10.1057/palgrave.jibs.8490024.

Dunning, J. H. (2001). The eclectic (OLI) paradigm of international production: Past, present and future. *International Journal of the Economics of Business*, *8*(2), 173–190. doi:10.1080/13571510110051441.

Dunning, J. H. (2009). Location and the Multinational Enterprise: A Neglected Factor? *Journal of International Business Studies*, *40*(1), 5–19. doi:10.1057/jibs.2008.74.

Duranti, A. (1997). Linguistic Anthropology. Cambridge, MA: Cambridge University Press.

Duyshart, B., Walker, D., Mohamed, S., & Hampson, K. (2003). An Example Of Developing A Business Model For Information And Communication Technologies (Ict) Adoption On Construction Projects–The National Museum Of Australia Project. *Engineering, Construction, and Architectural Management*, *10*, 179–192. doi:10.1108/09699980310478430.

Dwyer, S., Mesak, H., & Maxwell, H. (2005). An Exploratory Examination on the Influence of National Culture on Cross-National Product Diffusion. *Journal of International Marketing*, *13*(2), 1–27. doi:10.1509/jimk.13.2.1.64859.

Dyba, T., & Sharp, H. (2011). A whisper of evidence in global software engineering. *IEEE Software*, *28*(4), 15–18. doi:10.1109/MS.2011.70.

Eagly, A. H., & Chaiken, S. (1998). Attitude Structure and Function. In D. T. Gilbert, S. T. Fiske, & G. Lindzey (Eds.), The Handbook of Social Psychology (4th ed.), 54. New York: McGraw-Hill.

Earley, C., Murnieks, C., & Mosakowski, E. (2007). Cultural Intelligence and the Global Mindset. In M. Javidan, R. Steers, & M. Hitt (Eds.), The Global Mindset (Advances in International Management, vol. 19, pp. 75-103). Oxford, UK: JAI Press.

Earley, C., Ang, S., & Tan, J. (2006). *CQ: Developing Cultural Intelligence at Work*. Palo Alto, CA: Stanford University Press.

Earley, P. (2002). Redefining Interactions across Cultures and Organizations: Moving Forward with Cultural Intelligence. *Research in Organizational Behavior*, *24*(1), 271–299. doi:10.1016/S0191-3085(02)24008-3.

Earley, P. C., & Ang, S. (2003). *Cultural intelligence: Individual interactions across cultures*. Stanford, CA: Stanford University Press.

Earley, P. C., & Mosakowski, E. (1995). A Framework for Understanding Experimental Research in an International and Intercultural Contextd. In Punnett, B. J., & Shenkar, O. (Eds.), *Handbook of International Management Research*. Hoboken, NJ: Blackwell Publishers, Inc..

Earley, P., & Mosakowski, E. (2004). Toward culture intelligence: Turning cultural differences into a workplace advantage. *The Academy of Management Executive*, *18*(3), 151–157. doi:10.5465/AME.2004.28561784.

Earley, P., & Peterson, R. (2004). The Elusive Cultural Chameleon: Cultural Intelligence as a New Approach to Intercultural Training for the Global Manager. *Academy of Management Learning & Education*, *3*(1), 100–115. doi:10.5465/AMLE.2004.12436826.

Ebbinghaus, H. (1973). *Psychology: An elementary textbook*. New York: Arno Press. (Original work published 1908).

Ebrahim, N. A., Ahmed, S., & Taha, Z. (2009). Virtual Teams: A Literature Review. *Australian Journal Of Basic And Applied Sciences*, *3*, 2653–2669.

Eby, L. T., Casper, W. J., Lockwood, A., Bordeaux, C., & Brinley, A. (2005). Work and family research in io/obl: Content analysis and review of the literature (1980-2002). *Journal of Vocational Behavior*, *66*(1), 124–197. doi:10.1016/j.jvb.2003.11.003.

Edell, J. A., & Burke, M. C. (1987). The power of feelings in understanding advertising effects. *The Journal of Consumer Research*, *14*(3), 421–433. doi:10.1086/209124.

Eden, C., & Wheaton, G. (1980). *In Favour of Structure, Centre for the Study of Organisational Change and Development*. Working paper. University of Bath, Bath, UK.

Eden, C., & Jones, S. (1984). Using Repertory Grids for Problem Construction. *Journal of Operations Research*, *35*(9), 779–798.

Edvinson, L., & Malone, M. S. (1997). *Intellectual Capital: Realizing Your Company's True Value by Finding its Hidden Brainpower*. New York: Harper Business.

Ellis, N., & Hopkinson, G. (2010). The construction of managerial knowledge in business networks: Managers' theories about communication. *Industrial Marketing Management*, *39*, 413–424. doi:10.1016/j.indmarman.2007.08.011.

Elo, S., Elo, K., & Kyngas, H. (2008). The qualitative content analysis process. *Journal of Advanced Nursing*, *62*(1), 107–115. doi:10.1111/j.1365-2648.2007.04569.x PMID:18352969.

Ely, R., & Thomas, D. (2001). Cultural diversity at work: The effects of diversity perspectives on work group processes and outcomes. *Administrative Science Quarterly*, *46*(2), 229–273. doi:10.2307/2667087.

Emery, F. (1990). The nine-step model. In Trist, E. L., & Murray, H. (Eds.), *The Social Engagement of Social Science, A Tavistock Anthology: The Socio-Technical Perspective* (*Vol. 2*). Philadelphia, PA: University of Pennsylvania Press.

Engardio, P., Bernstein, A., & Kripalani, M. (2003). The New Global Job Shift. *Business Week*.

Epstein, M. (1995). *After the Future: The paradoxes of postmodernism and contemporary Russian culture*. Retrieved from http://www.emory.edu/INTELNET/af.culturology.html

Erdem, T., & Swait, J. (1998). Brand equity as a signaling phenomenon. *Journal of Consumer Psychology*, *7*(April), 131–157. doi:10.1207/s15327663jcp0702_02.

Erdem, T., & Swait, J. (2004). Brand credibility, brand consideration, and choice. *The Journal of Consumer Research*, *31*(1), 191–198. doi:10.1086/383434.

Erez, M. (1997). A culture-based model of work motivation. In Earley, P. C., & Erez, M. (Eds.), *New perspective on international industrial/organizational psychology*. San Francisco, CA: The New Lexington Press.

Erez, M., & Early, P. C. (1993). *Culture, self-identity, and work*. New York: Oxford University Press. doi:10.1093/acprof:oso/9780195075809.001.0001.

Erramilli, M. K. (1991). The experience factor in foreign market entry behaviour of service firms. *Journal of International Business Studies*, *22*(3), 479–501. doi:10.1057/palgrave.jibs.8490312.

Erramilli, M. K. (1996). Nationality and subsidiary ownership patterns in multinational corporations. *Journal of International Business Studies*, *27*(2), 225–248. doi:10.1057/palgrave.jibs.8490133.

Erramilli, M. K., & Rao, C. P. (1990). Choice of foreign market entry modes by service firms: Role of market knowledge. *Management International Review*, *30*(2), 135–150.

Erramilli, M. K., & Rao, C. P. (1993). Service firms' international entry mode choice: A modified transaction-cost analysis approach. *Journal of Marketing*, *57*(3), 19–38. doi:10.2307/1251852.

Etemadih, H., Dilami, Z., Baza, M., & Parameswaran, R. (2009). Culture, management accounting and managerial performance: Focus Iran. *Advances in Accounting, incorporating*. *Advances in International Accounting*.

Euromonitor International (2011). *Internet Retailing in China*. December.

Eurostat (2012). Internet use in households and by individuals in 2011. Retrieved on August 4, 2012, from http://epp.eurostat.ec.europa.eu/cache/ITY_OFFPUB/KS-SF-11-066/EN/KS-SF-11-066-EN.PDF

Evans, J., Mavondo, F. T., & Bridson, K. (2008). Psychic distance: Antecedents, retail strategy implications, and performance outcomes. *Journal of International Marketing*, *16*(2), 32–63. doi:10.1509/jimk.16.2.32.

Evaristo, R. (2003). The management of distributed projects across cultures. *Journal of Global Information Management*, *11*(4), 58–70. doi:10.4018/jgim.2003100104.

Faiola, A., & Matei, S. A. (2006). Cultural Cognitive Style and Web Design: Beyond a Behavioral Inquiry into Computer-Mediated Communication. *Journal of Computer-Mediated Communication*, *11*, 375–394. doi:10.1111/j.1083-6101.2006.tb00318.x.

Falk, M., & Wolfmayr, Y. (2005). *The Impact of International Outsourcing on Employment: Empirical Evidence from EU Countries*. Vienna, Austria: Austrian Institute of Economic Research WIFO.

Fang, X., & Rau, P.-L. P. (2003). Culture differences in design of portal sites. *Ergonomics*, *46*(1-3), 242–254. doi:10.1080/00140130303535 PMID:12554409.

Fardoust, S., Kim, Y., & Sepulveda, C. P. (2010). *Postcrisis Growth and Development: A Development Agenda for the G-20*. Washington, DC: World Bank.

Farrell, M. A. (2000). Developing a market-oriented learning organization. *Australian Journal of Management*, *25*(2), 201–222. doi:10.1177/031289620002500205.

Fayerweather, J., & Kapoor, A. (1976). *Strategy and Negotiation for the International Corporation*. Cambridge, MA: Ballinger. doi:10.1002/tie.5060180210.

Fayol, H. (1974). *Administración Industrial y General*. México: Herrero Hnos. Svcs. S.A..

Fayyad, U. M., Piatetsky-Shapiro, G., Smyth, P., & Uthurasamy, R. (1996). *Advances in Knowledge Discovery and Data Mining*. Palo Alto, CA: AAAI Press.

Feldman, R., & Dagan, I. (1995). Kdt-knowledge discovery in texts. In U.M. Fayyad & R. Uthurusamy (Eds.), *Proceedings of the 1st International Conference on Knowledge Discovery* (pp.112-117). Palo Alto, CA: AAAI Press.

Felipe, J. (1997). *Total Factor Productivity in East Asia: A Critical Survey*. Asian Development Bank. Economic Development and Resource Center Report Series No. 65. Retrieved on December 6, 2011, from http://www.adb.org/Documents/EDRC/Reports/ER065.pdf

Fenna, A. (2004). *Australian Public Policy* (2nd ed.). Frenchs Forest, Australia: Pearson Education Australia.

Ferraro, G. P. (1994). *The cultural dimension of international business* (2nd ed.). Upper Saddle River, NJ: Prentice Hall.

Ferreira, G. (2007). Consumer perceptions of global branding and iconization. *Dissertation of Doctor of Management in Organizational Leadership in University of Phoenix*. Phoenix, AZ: ProQuest Information and Learning Company.

Fetscherin, M., Voss, H., & Gugler, P. (2010). 30 Years of foreign direct investment to China: An interdisciplinary literature review. *International Business Review*, *19*, 235–246. doi:10.1016/j.ibusrev.2009.12.002.

Fina, E., & Rugman, A. (1996). A test of internalization theory and internationalization theory: The Upjohn company. *Management International Review*, *36*(3), 199–213.

Fishbein, M., & Ajzen, I. (1975). Introduction. In Fishbein, M., & Ajzen, I. (Eds.), *Belief, attitude, intention, and behavior: An introduction to theory and research 18*. Boston, MA: Addison-Wesley.

Fisher, J. (1995). Contingency-based research on management control systems: Categorization by level of complexity. *Journal of Accounting Literature*, *14*, 24–53.

Fisher, R., Ury, W., & Patton, B. (1991). *Getting to yes: Negotiating agreement without giving in*. New York: Penguin.

Fish, S. (1980). Literature in the reader: Affective stylistics. In Tompkins, J. (Ed.), *Reader-Response Criticism. From Formalism to Post-structuralism*. Baltimore, MD: The John Hopkins University Press.

Fiske, J. (1990). *Introduction to Communication Studies* (2nd ed.). London: Routledge.

Fleenor, P., & Raven, P. (2002). Barriers to Effective E-Business in Developing Countries. *International Business & Economics Research Journal*, *1*(4), 39–47.

Fleischman, G., & Herz, P. (2005). An empirical investigation of trends in barter activity in the Russian federation. *The International Journal of Accounting*, *40*, 39–63. doi:10.1016/j.intacc.2004.11.001.

Fletcher, D. (2000). Learning to think global and act local: Experiences from the small business Sector. *Education + Training*, *42*(4), 211–219. doi:10.1108/00400910010373651.

Fletcher, R. (2006). The impact of culture on web site content, design, and structure: An international and a multicultural perspective. *Journal of Communication Management*, *10*(3), 259–273. doi:10.1108/13632540610681158.

Fleury, M. T. L. (1999). The management of culture diversity: Lessons from Brazilian companies. *Industrial Management & Data Systems*, *99*(3), 109–114. doi:10.1108/02635579910252635.

Flores, L. G., Zheng, W., Rau, D., & Thomas, C. H. (2012). *Organizational Learning: Sub Process Identification, Construct Validation, and an Empirical Test of Cultural antecedents, 38*(2), 640-667.

Flynn, B. B., & Saladin, B. (2006). Relevance of Baldridge constructs in an international context: A study of national culture. *Journal of Operations Management*, *24*(5), 583–603. doi:10.1016/j.jom.2005.09.002.

Flynn, B. B., Schroeder, R. G., & Sakakibara, S. (1994). The Impact of Quality Management Practices on Performance and Competitive Advantage. *Decision Sciences*, *16*(5), 659–691.

Fogel, G., & Zapalska, A. (2001). A comparison of small and medium-size enterprise development in Central and Eastern Europe. *Comparative Economic Studies*, *43*(3), 35–68. doi:10.1057/ces.2001.13.

Fon Sim, O. (1993). Chinese ethnicity: Its relationship to some selected aspect of consumer behaviour. *Malaysian Management Review*, *28*(2), 29–43.

Fontaine, R. (2007). Cross-cultural management: Six perspectives. *Cross-Cultural Management. International Journal (Toronto, Ont.)*, *14*(2), 125–135.

Fontaine, R., & Richardson, S. (2005). On cultural values in Malaysia: Malays, Chinese and Indians compared. *Journal of Cross Cultural Management*, *12*(4), 63–77. doi:10.1108/13527600510798141.

Forbes. (2011, December). *Starbucks CEO: Lesson in Communication Skills*. Retrieved from http://www.forbes.com/sites/carminegallo/2011/03/25/starbucks-ceo-lesson-in-communication-skills/)

Form, W. (1979). Comparative industrial Sociology and the convergence hypothesis. *Annual Review of Sociology*, *5*, 1–25. doi:10.1146/annurev.so.05.080179.000245.

Fornell, C., & Larcker, D. F. (1981). Evaluating structural equation models with unobservable variables and measurement error. *JMR, Journal of Marketing Research*, *18*(1), 39–50. doi:10.2307/3151312.

Forsgren, M. (2004). The Use of Network Theory in MNC Research. In Mahnke, V., & Pedersen, T. (Eds.), *Knowledge Flows, Governance and the Multinational Enterprise*. New York: Palgrave Macmillan.

Forsgren, M., Holm, U., & Johanson, J. (2005). *Managing the Embedded Multinational: A Business Network View*. Northampton, MA: Edward Elgar Publishing, Inc..

Forster, N., & Johnsen, M. (1996). Expatriate management policies in UK companies new to the international scene. *International Journal of Human Resource Management*, *7*(1), 177–205. doi:10.1080/09585199600000124.

Fortis, M. (2005). *Il Made in Italy nel nuovo mondo: Protagonisti, sfide, azioni*. Bologna, Italy: Il Mulino.

Francis, G. (2001). *Introduction to SPSS for Windows* (3rd ed.). Sydney, Australia: Pearson Education Australia.

Francis, G. (2007). *Introduction to SPSS for Windows* (5th ed.). Sydney, Australia: Pearson Prentice Hall.

Fransella, F. (Ed.). (1981). *Personality - Theory, Measurement and Research*. New York: Methuen and Co..

Freling, T. H., & Forbes, L. (2005). An examination of brand personality through methodological triangulation. *Journal of Brand Management*, *13*(2), 148–162. doi:10.1057/palgrave.bm.2540254.

Fritz, C., & Sonnentag, S. (2005). Recovery, health, and job performance: Effects of weekend experiences. *Journal of Occupational Health Psychology*, *10*(3), 187–199. doi:10.1037/1076-8998.10.3.187 PMID:16060723.

Frohlich, M., & Robb Dixon, J. (2001). A taxonomy of manufacturing strategies revisited. *Journal of Operations Management*, *19*(5), 541–558. doi:10.1016/S0272-6963(01)00063-8.

Frohlich, M., & Westbrook, R. (2001). Arcs of integration: An international study of supply chain strategies. *Journal of Operations Management*, *19*(5), 185–200. doi:10.1016/S0272-6963(00)00055-3.

Fu, C.-S., & Wu, W.-Y. (2010). The means-end cognitions of web advertising: A cross-cultural comparison. *Online Information Review*, *34*(5), 686–703. doi:10.1108/14684521011084573.

Fuller, C. M., Marett, K., & Twitchell, D. P. (2012). An Examination Of Deception In Virtual Teams: Effects Of Deception On Task Performance, Mutuality, And Trust. *Professional Communication. Ieee Transactions On*, *55*, 20–35.

Fuller, M. A., Hardin, A. M., & Davison, R. M. (2007). Efficacy In Technology-Mediated Distributed Teams. *Journal of Management Information Systems*, *23*, 209–235. doi:10.2753/MIS0742-1222230308.

Fuller, M., Hardin, A., & Davison, R. (2006). Efficacy. *Journal of Management Information Systems*, *23*(3), 209–235. doi:10.2753/MIS0742-1222230308.

Fullerton, R., & McWatters, C. (2002). The role of performance measures in relation to the degree of JIT implementation. *Accounting, Organizations and Society*, *27*, 711–735. doi:10.1016/S0361-3682(02)00012-0.

Furnham, A. (1997). *The psychology of behavior at work*. East Sussex, UK: Taylor and Francis.

Furrer, O., & Liu, B. S. C., & shudharshan, D. (2000). The relationships between culture and service quality perceptions: Basis for cross-cultural market segmentation and resource allocation. *Journal of Service Research*, *2*(4), 355–371. doi:10.1177/109467050024004.

Furst, S. A., Reeves, M., Rosen, B., & Blackburn, R. S. (2004). Managing the life cycle of virtual teams. *The Academy of Management Executive*, *18*(2), 6–20. doi:10.5465/AME.2004.13837468.

Fynes, B. (1998). Quality Management Practices: A Review of the Literature. *Irish Business and Administrative Research*, *19/20*(2), 113–138.

Gabrielsson, M., & Kirpalani, V. H. M. (2004). Born globals: How to reach new business space rapidly. *International Business Review*, *13*(5), 555–571. doi:10.1016/j.ibusrev.2004.03.005.

Gallear, D., & Ghobadian, A. (2004). An empirical investigation of the channels that facilitate a Total Quality culture. *Quality Management Journal*, *15*(8), 1043–1067.

Gallo, C. (2011). *The communications coach for the world's most admired brands*. Retrieved from http://gallocommunications.com/

Galván, I. (2003). *La formación de la estrategia de selección de mercados exteriores en el proceso de internacionalización de las empresas*. Retrieved August 25, 2009, from http://www.eumed.net/tesis/igs/

Gamble, P. R., & Blackwell, J. (2001). *Knowledge Management: A State of the Art Guide*. Kogan Page Ltd..

Gankema, H., Snuif, H., & Zwart, P. (2000). The internationalization process of small and medium-sized enterprises: An evaluation of stage theory. *Journal of Small Business Management*, *38*(4), 15–27.

Gao, L., Chang, E., & Han, S. (2005). Powerful tool to expand business intelligence: Text mining. *Transactions on Enformatika. Systems Sciences and Engineering-ESSE*, *8*, 110–115.

Garcia, M. F., Posthuma, R. A., & Colella, A. (2008). Fit perceptions in the employment interview: The role of similarity, liking, and expectations. *Journal of Occupational and Organizational Psychology*, *81*(2), 173–189. doi:10.1348/096317907X238708.

Garg, R., & Ma, J. (2005). Benchmarking culture ad performance in Chinese organisations. *Benchmarking: An International Journal*, *12*(3), 260–274. doi:10.1108/14635770510600375.

Garvin, D. (1993). Building a Learning Organization. *Harvard Business Review*, *71*(4), 78–91. PMID:10127041.

Gaski, J. F., & Etzel, M. J. (1986). The index of consumer sentiment toward marketing. *Journal of Marketing*, *50*(4), 71–81. doi:10.2307/1251586.

Gassmann, O., & Von Zedtwitz, M. (2003). Trends and Determinants of Managing Virtual R&D teams. *R & D Management*, *33*(3), 243–262. doi:10.1111/1467-9310.00296.

Gatfield, T., Barker, M., & Graham, P. (1999). Measuring Student Quality Variables and the Implications for Management Practices in Higher Education Institutions: An Australian and international student perspective. *Journal of Higher Education Policy and Management*, *21*(2), 239–252. doi:10.1080/1360080990210210.

Gatignon, H., & Anderson, E. (1988). The multinational corporation's degree of control over foreign subsidiaries: An empirical test of a transaction cost explanation. *Journal of Law Economics and Organization*, *4*(Fall), 305–335.

Geertz, C. (1973). *The interpretation of cultures*. New York: Basic.

Gelade, G. A. (2006). But what does it mean in practice? *Journal of Occupational and Organizational Psychology*, *79*, 153–160. doi:10.1348/096317905X85638.

George, J. M. (2000). Emotions and leadership: The role of emotional intelligence. *Human Relations*, *53*, 1027–1055. doi:10.1177/0018726700538001.

George, J. M., & Jones, G. R. (2006). *Contemporary Management* (4th ed.). New York: McGraw Hill.

Gerdin, J. (2005). Managing accounting system design in manufacturing departments: An empirical investigation using a multiple contingencies approach. *Accounting, Organizations and Society*, *30*, 99–126. doi:10.1016/j.aos.2003.11.003.

Geroski, P. A., & Gregg, P. (1997). *Coping with recession: UK Company Performance in Adversity*. Cambridge, MA: NIESR.

Geuens, M., & De Pelsmacker, P. (1998). Product category involvement and the reaction of Belgian and Polish consumers to different advertising appeals. *European Advances in Consumer Research*, *3*, 33–41.

Gevorgyan, G., & Manucharova, N. (2009). Does Culturally Adapted Online Communication Work? A Study of American and Chinese Internet Users' Attitudes and Preferences Toward Culturally Customized Web Design Elements. *Journal of Computer-Mediated Communication*, *14*, 393–413. doi:10.1111/j.1083-6101.2009.01446.x.

Gevorgyan, G., & Porter, L. V. (2008). One Size Does Not Fit All: Culture and Perceived Importance of Web Design Features. *Journal of Website Promotion*, *3*(1), 25–38. doi:10.1080/15533610802052589.

Ghauri, P., & Usunier, J. (2003). *International Business Negotiations*. New York: Pergamon.

Ghazanfari, M., Jafari, M., & Rouhani, S. (2011). A tool to evaluate the business intelligence of enterprise systems. *Scientia Iranica*, *18*(6), 1579–1590. doi:10.1016/j.scient.2011.11.011.

Gheorghe, P., Gardan, D., & Geangu, P. (2009). *The Importance of Managerial Communication in Establishing the Company Marketing Communication*. Paper presented at the International Conference on Administration and Business, ICEA – FAA. Bucharest, Romania.

Ghoshal, S., & Bartlett, C. A. (1990). The Multinational Corporation as an Interorganizational Network. *Academy of Management Review*, *15*(4), 603–625.

Ghoshal, S., Korine, H., & Szulanski, G. (1994). Interunit Communication in Multinational Corporations. *Management Science*, *40*(1), 96–110. doi:10.1287/mnsc.40.1.96.

Gibson, C. B., & Cohen, S. G. (2003). *Virtual teams that work: Creating conditions for virtual team effectiveness*. San Francisco, CA: Jossey-Bass.

Gibson, C. B., & Gibbs, J. L. (2006). Unpacking The Concept Of Virtuality: The Effects Of Geographic Dispersion, Electronic Dependence, Dynamic Structure, And National Diversity On Team Innovation. *Administrative Science Quarterly*, *51*, 451–495.

Gignac, F. (2005). *Building Successful Virtual Teams*. Boston, MA: Artech House.

Gillam, C., & Oppenheim, C. (2006). Reviewing the Impact of Virtual Teams in the Information Age. *Journal of Information Science*, *32*(2), 160–175. doi:10.1177/0165551506062328.

Gilmour, B., & Gale, F. (2002). Transportation and Distribution: Will Bottlenecks be Eliminated? In Gale, F. (Ed.), *China's Food and Agriculture: Issue for the 21st Century*.

Girard, K. (2011). *It's Not Nagging-Why Persistent, Redundant Communication Works*. Paper presented at the Research and Ideas, Working Knowledge Conference. Boston, MA.

Girden, E. R. (2001). *Evaluating Research Articles – From Start to Finish* (2nd ed.). Thousand Oaks, CA: Sage Publications.

Glaser, B. G., & Strauss, A. L. (1976). *The Discovery of Grounded Theory: Strategies for Qualitative Research*. New York: Aldine De Gruyter.

Glazer, R. (2002). Measuring the value of information: The information-intensive organization. *IBM Systems Journal*, *32*(1), 99–110. doi:10.1147/sj.321.0099.

Glick, B. (2004). *Does your Outsourcing agreement measure up*? Retrieved on February 16, 2010, from http://www.computing.co.uk/computing/features/2072394/does-outsourcing-agreement- measure?vnu_lt=ctg_art_related_articles

Godar, S. H., & Ferris, S. P. (2004). *Virtual And Collaborative Teams*. Hershey, PA: IGI Global.

Goffman, E. (1976). *Replies and responses*. LIS.

Goh, S. H. (2010). Leader-Member Relationships. In *Virtual World Teams. Ph.D. 3462304*. Tallahassee, FL: The Florida State University.

Goldberg, M. E., & Gorn, G. J. (1987). Happy and sad TV programs: How they affect reactions to commercials. *The Journal of Consumer Research*, *14*, 387–403. doi:10.1086/209122.

Goldman, A. (2001). The transfer of retail formats into developing economies: The example of China. *Journal of Retailing*, *77*, 221–242. doi:10.1016/S0022-4359(01)00044-6.

Gomes-Casseres, B. (1992). *International trade, competition, and alliances in the computer industry*. Working Paper 92-044. Boston, MA: Harvard Business School Press.

Goodbody, J. (2005). Critical Success Factors For Global Virtual Teams. *Strategic Communication Management*, *9*, 18–21.

Gooderham, P., & Nordhaug, O. (2004). *International management: Cross-boundary challenges*. Malden, MA: Wiley-Blackwell.

Goodman, J., Fields, D., & Blum, T. (2003). Cracks in the glass ceiling: In what kind of organizations do women make it to the top? *Group & Organization Management*, *28*(4), 475–501. doi:10.1177/1059601103251232.

Goodman, J., & Truss, C. (2004). The medium and the message: Communicating effectively during a major change initiative. *Journal of Change Management*, *4*(3), 217–229. doi:10.1080/1469701042000255392.

Gordon, I. (2002). Best Practices Customer Relationship Management. *Ivey Business Journal*.

Grandon, E. E., & Pearson, J. M. (2004). Electronic commerce adoption: An empirical study of small and medium US businesses. *Information & Management*, *42*, 197–216. doi:10.1016/j.im.2003.12.010.

Granovetter, M. (1985). Economic Action And Social Structure: The Problem of Embeddedness. *American Journal of Sociology*, *91*(3), 481–510. doi:10.1086/228311.

Greene, J. C., Caracelli, V. J., & Graham, W. F. (1989). Toward a Conceptual Framework for Mixed-method Evaluation Designs. *Educational Evaluation and Policy Analysis*, *11*(3), 255–274.

Greenfield, P. M. (2000). Three approaches to the psychology of culture: Where do they come from? Where can they go? *Asian Journal of Social Psychology*, *3*, 223–240. doi:10.1111/1467-839X.00066.

Grier, S. A., & Brumbaugh, A. M. (1999). Noticing cultural differences: Ad meanings created by target and non-target markets. *Journal of Advertising*, *28*(1), 79–93.

Griffith, D., Cavusgil, T., & Xu, S. (2008). Emerging themes in international business research. *Journal of International Business Studies*, *39*(7), 1220–1235. doi:10.1057/palgrave.jibs.8400412.

Griffith, T. L., & Neale, M. A. (2001). Information processing in traditional, hybrid, and virtual teams: From nascent knowledge to transactive memory. In Staw, B., & Sutton, R. (Eds.), *Research in organizational behavior* (pp. 379–421). Stamford, CT: JAI Press. doi:10.1016/S0191-3085(01)23009-3.

Groeschel, S., & Doherty, L. (2000). Conceptualising culture. *Cross Cultural Management -. International Journal (Toronto, Ont.)*, *7*(4), 12–17.

Grönroos. (2004). The relationship marketing process: Communication, interaction, dialogue, value. *Journal of Business and Industrial Marketing*, *19*(2), 99–113. doi:10.1108/08858620410523981.

Gröschl, S., & Doherty, L. (1999). Diversity management in practice. *International Journal of Contemporary Hospitality Management.*, *11*(6), 262–268. doi:10.1108/09596119910281757.

Grosse, C. U. (2002). Managing Communication Within Virtual Intercultural Teams. *Business Communication Quarterly*, *65*, 22–38. doi:10.1177/108056990206500404.

Grosse, C. U. (2007). Web-Based Communication of Global Companies: Do Languages and Culture Matter? *Global Business Languages*, *12*(7), 67–83.

Gross, L. (2011). Communication as the Discipline of the 21st Century. *International Journal of Communication*, *5*, 1497–1498.

Grossler, A., & Grubner, A. (2006). An empirical model of the relationships between manufacturing capabilities. *International Journal of Operations & Production Management*, *26*(5), 458–485. doi:10.1108/01443570610659865.

Grossman, G. M., & Helpman, E. (1994). Endogenous Innovation in the Theory of Growth. *The Journal of Economic Perspectives*, *8*(1), 23–44. doi:10.1257/jep.8.1.23.

Grossman, S. J., & Hart, O. D. (1986). The Costs and Benefits of Ownership: A Theory of Vertical and Lateral Integration. *The Journal of Political Economy*, *94*(4), 691–719. doi:10.1086/261404.

Groves, R. (1989). *Survey errors and survey results*. New York: Wiley. doi:10.1002/0471725277.

Guadamillas-Gomez, F., & Donate-Manzanares, M. J. (2011). Ethics and Corporate Social Responsibility Integrated into Knowledge Management and Innovation Technology. *Journal of Management Development*, *30*(6), 569–581. doi:10.1108/02621711111135170.

Gudykundst, W., Matsumoto, Y., Ting-Tconey, T., Nishida, T., Kirn, K., & Seyman, S. (1996). The Influence of Cultural Individualism-Collectivism, Self Construal, and Individual Values on Communication Styles across Cultures. *Human Communication Research*, *22*(June), 510–543. doi:10.1111/j.1468-2958.1996.tb00377.x.

Gudykunst, W. B., Ting-Toomey, S., & Chua, E. (1988). *Culture And Interpersonal Communication*. New York: Sage Publications, Inc..

Gudykunst, W. B., Ting-Toomey, S., & Nishida, T. (1996). *Communication in Personal Relationships Across Cultures*. Thousand Oaks, CA: Sage Publications.

Guilford, J. (1954). *Psychometric methods* (2nd ed.). London: McGraw-Hill.

Guillen, M. F. (2002). Business groups and economic development: A resource-based view. M. Kotabe, P.S. Aulakh (Eds.) Emerging issues in international business research. Cheltenham, UK: Edward Elgar Publishing.

Gupta, A. K., & Govindarajan, V. (1991). Knowledge Flows and the Structure of Control within Multinational Corporations. *Academy of Management Review*, *16*(4), 768–792.

Gupta, A. K., & Govindarajan, V. (2000). Knowledge Flows Within Multinational Corporations. *Strategic Management Journal*, *21*, 473–496. doi:10.1002/(SICI)1097-0266(200004)21:4<473::AID-SMJ84>3.0.CO;2-I.

Gupta, B., Iyer, L. S., & Aronson, J. E. (2000). Knowledge Management: Practices and Challenges. *Industrial Management & Data Systems*, *100*(1), 17–21. doi:10.1108/02635570010273018.

Gursoy, D., & Umreit, T. (2004). Tourist information search behavior: Cross-cultural comparison of European Union member states. *Hospital Management*, *23*(1), 55–70. doi:10.1016/j.ijhm.2003.07.004.

Guzzo, R. A., & Dickson, M. W. (1996). Teams in organizations: Recent research on performance and effectiveness. *Annual Review of Psychology*, *47*, 307–338. doi:10.1146/annurev.psych.47.1.307 PMID:15012484.

Haag, S., Cummings, M., McCubbrey, D., Pinsonneault, A., & Donovan, R. (2006). *Management Information Systems For the Information Age* (3rd ed.). Whitby, Canada: McGraw Hill Ryerson.

Haag, S., & Cunnings, M. (2008). *Management Information Systems for the Information Age*. New York: McGraw Hill.

Hackman, J. R. (2002). *Leading teams: Setting the stage for great performances*. Boston, MA: Harvard Business School Press.

Hair, J. F. Anderson, R. E., Tatham, R.L., & Black, W.C. (1998). Multivariate Data Analysis. New York: MacMillan.

Hair, J. F. J., Anderson, R. E., Tatham, R. L., & Black, W. C. (1998). *Multivariate data analysis* (5th ed.). Upper Saddle River, NJ: Prentice Hall.

Hair, J. F., Black, W. C., Babin, B. J., & Anderson, R. E. (2010). *Multivariate Data Analysis: A Global Perspective*. New York: Pearson Prentice Hall.

Hall Edward, T. (1959). *The Silent Language*. New York: Doubleday.

Hall, E. T. (1976). *Beyond Culture*. New York: Doubleday.

Hall, E. T., & Hall, R. M. (1987). *Hidden Differences. Doing Business with the Japanese*. New York: Anchor Press Doubleday.

Hall, R. W., Johnson, H. T., & Turley, P. B. (1991). *Measuring Up: Changing Pathways to Manufacturing Excellence, 111*. Homewood: Business One Irwin.

Hamel, G. (2000). *Leading the Revolution*. Boston, MA: Harvard Business School Press.

Hamel, G., & Prahalad, C. K. (2005). Strategic Intent. *Harvard Business Review*, , 148–161. PMID:10303477.

Hancock, P. A. (1997). *Essays on the future of human-machine systems*. Minneapolis, MN: Author.

Hanisch, J., Thanasankit, T., & Corbitt, B. (2001). Exploring the cultural and social impacts on the requirements engineering process - Highlighting some problems challenging virtual team relationships with clients. *Journal of Systems and Information Technology*, *5*(2), 1–19. doi:10.1108/13287260180000763.

Han, J., & Kamber, M. (2001). *Data Mining: Concepts and Techniques*. San Francisco, CA: Morgan Kaufmann Publishers.

Hannerz, U. (1990). Cosmopolitans and Locals in World Culture. In Featherstone, M. (Ed.), *Global Culture: Nationalism, Globalization and Modernity* (pp. 237–252). Thousand Oaks, CA: Sage Publications.

Hannerz, U. (1996). *Transnational connections. Culture, people, places*. LondonRoutledge.

Han, S., & Shavitt, S. (1994). Persuasion and Culture: Advertising Appeals in Individualistic and Collectivistic Societies. *Journal of Experimental Social Psychology*, *30*(4), 326–350. doi:10.1006/jesp.1994.1016.

Hansen, M. T. (1999). The Search-Transfer Problem: The Role of Weak Ties in Sharing Knowledge across Organization Subunits. *Administrative Science Quarterly*, *44*(1), 82–111. doi:10.2307/2667032.

Hanser, L. M., & Muchinsky, P. M. (1978). Work as an information environment. *Organizational Behavior and Human Performance*, *21*, 47–60. doi:10.1016/0030-5073(78)90038-7 PMID:10306432.

Hardie, N., & Walsh, P. (1994). Towards a Better Understanding of Quality. *International Journal of Quality & Reliability Management*, *11*(4), 54–60. doi:10.1108/02656719410057953.

Harland, C., Knight, L., Lamming, R., & Walker, H. (2005). Outsourcing: Assessing the risks and benefits for organisations, sectors and nations. *International Journal of Operations & Production Management*, *25*(9), 831–850. doi:10.1108/01443570510613929.

Harman, G. S., Hayden, M., & Pham, T. N. (2010). Higher education in Vietnam: Reforms, challenges and priorities. In Harman, G. S., Hayden, M., & Pham, T. N. (Eds.), *Reforming Higher Education in Vietnam: Challenges and Priorities* (1st ed., pp. 1–14). Dordrecht, The Netherlands: Springer. doi:10.1007/978-90-481-3694-0_1.

Harrigan, K. R. (1985a). Exit barriers and vertical integration. *Academy of Management Journal*, *28*(3), 686–697. doi:10.2307/256124.

Harrigan, K. R. (1985b). Vertical integration and corporate strategy. *Academy of Management Journal*, *28*(2), 397–425. doi:10.2307/256208.

Harris, G. (1994). International Advertising Standardization: What Do the Multinationals Actually Standardize? *Journal of International Marketing*, *2*(4), 13–30.

Harris, H., & Brewster, C. (1999). The coffee-machine system: How international selection really works. *International Journal of Human Resource Management*, *10*(3), 488–500. doi:10.1080/095851999340440.

Hartenian, L. S. (2003). Team Member Acquisition Of Team Knowledge, Skills, And Abilities. *Team Performance Management*, *9*, 23–30. doi:10.1108/13527590310468033.

Hartmann, F. G. (2000). The appropriateness of RAPM: Towards the further development of theory. *Accounting, Organizations and Society*, *25*, 451–482. doi:10.1016/S0361-3682(98)00036-1.

Hart, S. (1987). The use of the survey in industrial market research. *Journal of Marketing Management*, *3*(1), 25–38. doi:10.1080/0267257X.1987.9964025.

Hart, S. L. (2005). Innovation, Creative Destruction and Sustainability. *Research Technology Management*, *48*(5), 21–27.

Harvey, C., & Allard, J. (2002). *Understanding and Managing Diversity*. Upper Saddle River, NJ: Prentice Hall.

Harvey, M., Novicevic, M. M., & Garrison, G. (2004). Challenges To Staffing Global Virtual Teams. *Human Resource Management Review*, *14*, 275–294. doi:10.1016/j.hrmr.2004.06.005.

HassabElnaby, H. & Mosebach, M. (2005). Culture's consequences in controlling agency costs: Egyptian evidence. *Journal of International Accounting, Auditing & Taxation*, *14*, 19–32. doi:10.1016/j.intaccaudtax.2005.01.003.

Hasselgren, B., & Beach, D. (1997). Phenomenography: A good-for-nothing brother of phenomenology? Outline of an analysis. *Higher Education Research & Development*, *16*(2), 191–202. doi:10.1080/0729436970160206.

Hays-Thomas, R. (2004). Why now? A contemporary focus on managing diversity. In Stockdale, M. S., & Crosby, F. J. (Eds.), *The Psychology and Management of Workplace Diversity* (pp. 3–30). Malden, MA: Blackwell Publishing.

Haywood, M. (1998). *Managing Virtual Teams: Practical Techniques For High-Technology Project Managers*. Boston, MA: Artech House.

HBS. (2004). *Face-to-Face Communications for Clarity and Impact by the Results-Driven Manager*. Boston, MA: Harvard Business School Press.

Headland, T. N., Pike, K. L., & Harris, M. (1990). *Emics and etics: The insider/outsider debate*. Newbury Park, CA: Sage Publications.

Heine, S. J. (2008). *Cultural psychology*. New York: W. W. Norton.

Hejazi, W., & Safarian, A. E. (1999). Trade, Foreign Direct Investment, and R&D Spillovers. *Journal of International Business Studies*, *30*(3), 491–511. doi:10.1057/palgrave.jibs.8490080.

Helander, M. (1997). The human factors professions. In Salvendy, G. (Ed.), *Handbook of human factors and ergonomics* (2nd ed.). New York: John Wiley.

Held, D., McGrew, A., Goldblatt, D., & Perraton, J. (1999). *Global Transformations: Politics, Economics and Culture*. Oxford, UK: Polity Press.

Helgesen, S. (1990). *The female advantage: Women's ways of leadership*. New York: Doubleday.

Henderson, L. S. (1986). Unraveling the Meaning of Managerial Communication: A Conceptual Explication and Model for Guiding Future Research. *Academy Of Management Best Papers Proceedings*, 219-223.

Henderson, R. M., & Clark, K. B. (1990). Architectural Innovation: The Reconfiguration of Existing Systems and the Failure of Established Firms. *Administrative Science Quarterly*, *35*(1), 9–30. doi:10.2307/2393549.

Hennart, J. F., & Park, Y. R. (1994). Location, Governance, and Strategic Determinants of Japanese Manufacturing Investment in the United States. *Strategic Management Journal*, *15*(6), 419–436. doi:10.1002/smj.4250150602.

Henttonen, K., & Blomqvist, K. (2005). Managing Distance In A Global Virtual Team: The Evolution Of Trust Through Technology-Mediated Relational Communication. *Strategic Change*, *14*, 107–119. doi:10.1002/jsc.714.

Hermeking, M. (2006). Culture and Internet Consumption: Contributions from Cross-Cultural Marketing and Advertising Research. *Journal of Computer-Mediated Communication*, *11*, 192–216. doi:10.1111/j.1083-6101.2006.tb00310.x.

Hernes, H. (1987). *Welfare State and Women Power – Essays in State Feminism*. Oslo, Norway: Norwegian University Press.

Hertel, G., Geister, S., & Konradt, U. (2005). Managing Virtual Teams: A Review Of Current Empirical Research. *Human Resource Management Review*, *15*, 69–95. doi:10.1016/j.hrmr.2005.01.002.

Hertel, G., Konradt, U., & Voss, K. (2006). Competencies For Virtual Teamwork: Development and Validation Of A Web-Based Selection Tool For Members Of Distributed Teams. *European Journal of Work and Organizational Psychology*, *15*, 477–504. doi:10.1080/13594320600908187.

Herzberg, F. (1966). *Work and the nature of man*. Cleveland, OH: World Publishing.

Hewstone, M. (2003). Intergroup contact: Panacea for prejudice? *The Psychologist*, *16*(7), 352–355.

Highhouse, S. (2007). Applications of organizational psychology: Learning though failure or failure to learn? In Koppes, L. L. (Ed.), *Historical perspectives in industrial and organizational psychology*. Mahwah, NJ: Erlbaum.

Highsmith, J. (2001). *History: The Agile manifesto*. Retrieved February 1, 2012 from http://agilemanifesto.org/history.html

Highsmith, J., & Cockburn, A. (2001). Agile software development: The business of innovation. *IEEE Computer*, *34*(9), 120–122. doi:10.1109/2.947100.

Hill, C. W. L., Hwang, P., & Kim, W. C. (1990). An eclectic theory of the choice of international entry mode. *Strategic Management Journal*, *11*(2), 117–128. doi:10.1002/smj.4250110204.

Hill, C., & Jones, G. (2000). *Administración estratégica: Un enfoque integrado*. México: McGraw-Hill.

Hill, G. M. (2007). *The Complete Project Management Office Handbook*. Boca Raton, FL: Auerbach. doi:10.1201/9781420046823.

Hill, J. S. (2009). *International Business*. Thousand Oaks, CA: Sage Publications.

Hirschheim, R., & Newman, M. (1991). Symbolism and Information Systems Development: Myth, Metaphor and Magic. *Information Systems Research*, *2*(1), 29–62. doi:10.1287/isre.2.1.29.

Hirschman, E., & Thompson, C. (1997). Why media matter: Toward a richer understanding of consumers, relationships with advertising and mass media. *Journal of Advertising*, *26*(1), 44–59.

Hislop, D. (2003). Linking Human Resource Management and Knowledge Management via Commitment. *Employee Relations*, *25*(2), 182–202. doi:10.1108/01425450310456479.

Hislop, D., Newell, S., Scarbrough, H., & Swan, J. (2000). Networks, Knowledge and Power: Decision Making, Politics and the Process of Innovation. *Technology Analysis and Strategic Management*, *12*(3), 399–411. doi:10.1080/713698478.

Hitson, M. C. (2008). *An Analysis Of Leadership Methodology And Job Satisfaction Among Virtual Team Members. D.M. 3324077*. University Of Phoenix.

Ho, L., Atkins, A. S., Prince, I., & Sharp, B. (2006b). Alignment of a Strategic Outsourcing Framework to Practitioner Case Studies. In *Proceedings of European and Mediterranean Conference on Information Systems (EMCIS)*. Alicante, Spain.

Hobby, J. (1999). Looking After the One Who Matters. *Accountancy Age*, (October 28), 28–30.

Ho, C.-I., Lin, M.-H., & Chen, H.-M. (2012). Web users' behavioural patterns of tourism information search: From online to offline. *Tourism Management*, *33*(6), 1468–1482. doi:10.1016/j.tourman.2012.01.016.

Hodgetts, R. M., & Luthans, F. (1993). U.S. Multinational's Expatriate Compensation Strategies. *Compensation and Benefits Review*, *25*(1), 57–62. doi:10.1177/088636879302500111.

Hodgkinson, G. P. (2006). The role of joop (and other scientific journals) in bridging the practitioner-researcher divide in industrial, work, and organizational (i/o) psychology. *Journal of Occupational and Organizational Psychology*, *79*, 173–178. doi:10.1348/096317906X104013.

Hodson, R. (1991). The Active Worker: Compliance and Autonomy at the Workplace. *Journal of Contemporary Ethnography*, *20*(1), 47–78. doi:10.1177/089124191020001003.

Hofstede, G. (2012). National Culture. Retrieved June 10 2012, from http://geert-hofstede.com/countries.html

Hofstede, G. (1979). Value Systems in Forty Countries: Interpretation, Validation and Consequences for Theory. In Eckensberger, L., Looner, W., & Poortinga, Y. (Eds.), *Cross Cultural Contribution to Psychology*. Lisse, The Netherlands: Swets & Zeitlingerd.

Hofstede, G. (1980). *Culture's Consequences: International Differences in Work-Related Values*. Beverly Hills, CA: Sage Publications.

Hofstede, G. (1980). *Culture's consequence: International differences in work-related values*. Beverly Hills, CA: Sage.

Hofstede, G. (1980). *Culture's Consequences*. Beverly Hills, CA: Sage Publications.

Hofstede, G. (1983). Dimensions of National Culture in Fifty Countries and Three Regions. In Deregowski, J., Dzieurawiec, S., & Annios, R. (Eds.), *Explications in Cross Cultural Psychology*. Lisse, The Netherlands: Swets & Zeitlinger.

Hofstede, G. (1983). The Cultural Relativity of Organizational Practices and Theories. *Journal of International Business Studies*, (Fall): 75–89.

Hofstede, G. (1984). The Cultural Relativity of the Quality of Life Concept. *Academy of Management Review*, *9*(3), 389–398.

Hofstede, G. (1991). *Culture and organizations: Software of the mind*. London: McGraw-Hill.

Hofstede, G. (1993). Cultural Constraints in Management Theories. *The Academy of Management Executive*, *7*(1), 81–94.

Hofstede, G. (1997). *Cultures and organizations: Software of the mind*. London: McGraw Hill.

Hofstede, G. (2001). *Culture's Consequences: Comparing Values, Behaviors, Institutions and Organizations across Nations*. Thousand Oaks, CA: Sage Publications.

Hofstede, G. (2002). Dimensions do not exist: A reply to Brendan McSweeney. *Human Relations*, *55*(11), 1355–1361.

Hofstede, G. (2002). The pitfalls of cross-national survey research: A reply to the article by spector et al. on the psychometric properties of the hofstede values survey module 1994. *Applied Psychology*, *51*, 170–173. doi:10.1111/1464-0597.084_2.

Hofstede, G. (2003). What is culture? A reply to Baskerville. *Accounting, Organizations and Society*, *28*(7–8), 811–813. doi:10.1016/S0361-3682(03)00018-7.

Hofstede, G. (2006). What did GLOBE really measure? Researchers' minds versus respondents' minds. *Journal of International Business Studies*, *37*(1), 882–896. doi:10.1057/palgrave.jibs.8400233.

Hofstede, G., & Bond, M. (1984). Hofstede culture dimensions- An independent validation using rokeach value survey. *Journal of Cross-Cultural Psychology*, *15*, 411–437. doi:10.1177/0022002184015004003.

Hofstede, G., & Bond, M. H. (1988). The Confucius Connection: From Cultural Roots to Economic Growth. *Organizational Dynamics*, *16*(4), 4–21. doi:10.1016/0090-2616(88)90009-5.

Hofstede, G., Hofstede, G. J., & Minkov, M. (2010). *Cultures and Organizations: Software of the Mind* (2nd ed.). New York: McGraw-Hill.

Hofstede, G., & Minkov, M. (2010). Long- versus Short-term Orientation: New Perspectives. *Asia Pacific Business Review*, *16*(4), 493–504. doi:10.1080/13602381003637609.

Hofstede, G., Neuijen, B., Ohayv, D. D., & Sanders, G. (1990). Measuring Organizational Cultures: A Qualitative and Quantitative study Across Twenty Cases. *Administrative Science Quarterly*, *35*, 286–316. doi:10.2307/2393392.

Hogan, R., & Kaiser, R. B. (2005). What we know about leadership. *Review of General Psychology*, *9*(2), 169–180. doi:10.1037/1089-2680.9.2.169.

Ho, L., & Atkins, A. S. (2006a). IT Outsourcing: Impacts and Challenges. In Walters, B., & Tang, Z. (Eds.), *IT Enabled Strategic Management – Increasing Returns for the Organization* (pp. 244–274). Hershey, PA: Idea Group Inc. doi:10.4018/978-1-59140-908-3.ch012.

Ho, L., & Atkins, A. S. (2006c). Outsourcing Decision-Making: A Review of Strategic Frameworks and Proposal of a Multi-Perspective Approach. In Kehal, H. S., & Singh, V. (Eds.), *Outsourcing and Offshoring in the 21st Century: A Socio-Economic Perspective* (pp. 165–196). Hershey, PA: Idea Group Inc. doi:10.4018/978-1-59140-875-8.ch008.

Ho, L., & Atkins, A. S. (2009). IT Portfolio Management: A Holistic Approach to Outsourcing Decisions. In Tan, A. (Ed.), *Handbook on Strategic Information Technology and Portfolio Management* (pp. 100–112). Hershey, PA: IGI Global. doi:10.4018/978-1-59904-687-7.ch005.

Holbrook, M. B., & Batra, R. (1987). Assessing the role of emotions as mediators of consumer responses to advertising. *The Journal of Consumer Research*, *14*(3), 404–420. doi:10.1086/209123.

Holden, N. (2002). *Cross Cultural Management: A Knowledge Management Perspective*. Harlow, UK: Pearson.

Holland, N. (1980). Unity identity text self. In Tompkins, J. (Ed.), *Reader-Response Criticism. From Formalism to Post-structuralism* (pp. 118–133). Baltimore, MD: The John Hopkins University Press.

Holliday, A. R. (2007). *Doing and Writing Qualitative Research*. London: Sage Publications.

Hollway, W. (2000). *Work psychology and organizational behaviour: Managing the individual at work*. Thousand Oaks, CA: Sage.

Holmstrom, H., Fitzgerald, B., Agerfalk, P. J., & Conchuir, E. O. (2006). Agile practices reduce distance in global software development. *Information Systems Management*, *23*(3), 7–18. doi:10.1201/1078.10580530/46108.23.3.20060601/93703.2.

Homer, P. M. (1990). The mediating role of attitude towards the ad: Some additional evidence. *JMR, Journal of Marketing Research*, *27*, 78–86. doi:10.2307/3172553.

Hopwood, A. (2005). Editorial: After 30 years. *Accounting, Organizations and Society*, *30*, 585–586. doi:10.1016/j.aos.2005.06.002.

Hoque, Z., Mia, L., & Alam, M. (2001). Market competition, computer-aided manufacturing and use of multiple performance measures: An empirical study. *The British Accounting Review*, *33*(1), 23–45. doi:10.1006/bare.2000.0149.

Horne, J., & Lupton, T. (1965). The work activities of middle managers: An exploratory study. *Journal of Management Studies*, *1*(21), 14–33. doi:10.1111/j.1467-6486.1965.tb00563.x.

Horwitch, M., & Armacost, R. (2002). Helping Knowledge Management be All it can be. *International Journal of Business Strategy*, *23*(3), 26–32. doi:10.1108/eb040247.

Hossain, E., Babar, M. A., & Paik, H. (2009). Using scrum in global software development: A systematic literature review. *4th IEEE International Conference on Global Software Engineering*. Limerick, Ireland.

Hosseini, M. R., & Chileshe, N. (2013). Global Virtual Engineering Teams (Gvets): A Fertile Ground For Research In Australian Construction Projects Context. *International Journal Of Project Management*. Retrieved from Http://Dx.Doi.Org/10.1016/J.Ijproman.2013.01.001

Hosseini, M. R., Chileshe, N., Zuo, J., & Baroudi, B. (2012). Approaches For Implementing Ict Technologies Within Construction Industry. *Australasian Journal Of Construction Economics And Building The Conference Series, 1*(2), 1–12.

Hotho, A., Nürnberger, A., & Paass, G. A. (2005). Brief survey of text mining. *GCDV Journal of Computational Linguistics and Language Technology, 20*(1), 19–62.

House, R. J., Hanges, P. J., Javidan, M., & Dorfman, P. W. (2002). Understanding cultures and implicit leadership theories across the globe: An introduction to project GLOBE. *Journal of World Business, 37*(1), 3–10. doi:10.1016/S1090-9516(01)00069-4.

House, R. J., Hanges, P. J., Javidan, M., Dorfman, P. W., & Gupta, V. (2004). *Culture, Leadership and Organizations: The GLOBE Study of 62 Societies*. Thousand Oaks, CA: Sage.

House, R., Hanges, P., Ruiz-Quintanilla, S., Dorfman, P., Javidan, M., & Dickson, M. (1999). Cultural influences on leadership and organizations: Project GLOBE. In Mobley, W., Gessner, M., & Arnold, V. (Eds.), *Advances in global leadership* (pp. 171–233). Stamford, CT: JAI.

Hovland, C. I., Janis, I. L., & Kelley, H. H. (1953). *Communication. and persuasion: Psychological studies of opinion change*. New-Haven, CT: Vale University Press.

Howald, F. (2001). *Obstáculos al desarrollo de la pyme causados por el estado en Colombia: el caso del sistema tributario*. Santiago, Chile: McGraw-Hill.

Hsieh, H. F., & Shannon, S. E. (2005). Three Approaches to Qualitative Content Analysis. *Qualitative Health Research, 15*(9), 1277–1288. doi:10.1177/1049732305276687 PMID:16204405.

Huang, J.-H. (2001). Consumer Evaluations of Unethical Behaviors of Web Sites: A Cross-Cultural Comparison. *Journal of International Consumer Marketing, 13*(4), 51–71. doi:10.1300/J046v13n04_04.

Hubbard, E. (2004). *The Diversity Scorecard: Evaluating the Impact of Diversity on Organisational Performance*. San Francisco, CA: Elsevier.

Hughes, R. L., Ginnett, R. C., & Curphy, C. G. (1996). *Leadership: Enhancing the lessons of experience*. Chicago, IL: Irwin.

Hunsaker, P. L., & Hunsaker, J. S. (2008). Virtual Teams: A Leader's Guide. *Team Performance Management, 14*, 86–101. doi:10.1108/13527590810860221.

Hunter, M. G. (1994). "Excellent" Systems Analysts: Key Audience Perceptions. *Computer Personnel*, April, 15-31.

Hunter, M. G., & Tan, F. (2001). Information Systems Professionals in New Zealand: Reflective Career Biographies. In *Proceedings of International Conference of the Information Resources Management Association* (pp. 132-133). Toronto, CA.

Hunter, M. G. (1993). A Strategy for Identifying "Excellent" Systems Analysts. *The Journal of Strategic Information Systems, 2*(1), 15–26. doi:10.1016/0963-8687(93)90019-7.

Hunter, M. G. (1997). The Use of RepGrids to Gather Interview Data about Information Systems Analysts. *Information Systems Journal, 7*(1), 67–81. doi:10.1046/j.1365-2575.1997.00005.x.

Hunter, M. G., & Beck, J. E. (1996). A Cross-Cultural Comparison of "Excellent" Systems Analysts. *Information Systems Journal, 6*(4), 261–281. doi:10.1111/j.1365-2575.1996.tb00018.x.

Hunter, M. G., & Beck, J. E. (2000). Using Repertory Grids to Conduct Cross-Cultural Information Systems Research. *Information Systems Research, 11*(1), 93–101. doi:10.1287/isre.11.1.93.11786.

Huysman, M., Steinfield, C., Jang, C. Y., David, K., In't Veld, M. H., Poot, J., & Mulder, I. (2003). Virtual Teams And The Appropriation Of Communication Technology: Exploring The Concept Of Media Stickiness. *Computer Supported Cooperative Work (Cscw), 12*, 411–436. doi:10.1023/A:1026145017609.

Hwang, A., & Francesco, A. M. (2010). The influence of individualism-collectivism and power distance on use of feedback channels and consequences for learning. *Academy of Management Learning & Education, 9*(2), 243–357. doi:10.5465/AMLE.2010.51428546.

Hyde, K. F. (2008). Information processing and touring planning theory. *Annals of Tourism Research*, *35*(3), 712–731. doi:10.1016/j.annals.2008.05.001.

Hymer, S. H. (1976). *The International Operations of National Firms: A Study of Direct Foreign Investment*. Cambridge, MA: MIT Press.

ICE. (2011). *L'interscambio commerciale tra l'Italia e il resto del mondo nel 2010*. Retrieved March 30, 2011, from http://www.ice.gov.it/statistiche/interscambio_def.pdf

Ichijo, K., & Nonaka, I. (Eds.). (2007). *Knowledge Creation and Management: New Challenges for Managers*. New York: Oxford University Press.

Im, I., Hong, S., & Kang, M. S. (2011). An International Comparison Of Technology Adoption: Testing The Utaut Model. *Information & Management*, *48*, 1–8. doi:10.1016/j.im.2010.09.001.

Im, I., Kim, Y., & Han, H.-J. (2008). The Effects Of Perceived Risk And Technology Type On Users' Acceptance Of Technologies. *Information & Management*, *45*, 1–9. doi:10.1016/j.im.2007.03.005.

Imrie, B. C., Cadogan, J. W., & McNaughton, R. (2002). The service quality construct on a global stage. *Managing Service Quality*, *12*(1), 10–18. doi:10.1108/09604520210415353.

Indart, B. (2006). Operationalizing business ıntelligence - Turning ınsight into action. *Business Intelligence Journal*, *11*(2), 35–38.

Inkpen, A. C., & Beamish, P. W. (1997). Knowledge, Bargaining Power, and the Instability of International Joint Ventures. *Academy of Management Review*, *22*(1), 177–202.

Inkpen, A. C., & Dinur, A. (1998). Knowledge Management Processes and International Joint Ventures. *Organization Science*, *9*(4), 454–468. doi:10.1287/orsc.9.4.454.

Institute of Labour, Science and Social affairs (ILSSA). (2004). *Determining the Impact of Information and Communication Technology on Decent Work in the Asian and Pacific Region: Viet Nam Report*. Hanoi, Vietnam: ILO/JIL Networking of National Institute for Labour Studies.

International Federation of Accountants (IFAC). (1998). *International Management Accounting Practice Statement*. Management.

International Monetary Fund (2003). *World Economic Outlook. World Economic and Financial Surveys*. Retrieved on December 6, 2011, from http://www.imf.org/external/pubs/ft/weo/2003/01/pdf/chapter1.pdf

Internet World Stats (2011). Retrieved from http://www.internetworldstats.com/stats.htm

Internet World Stats. (2009). Internet usage statistics: World internet users and population stats. Retrieved on August 8, 2012, from http://www.internetworldstats.com/stats.htm

Internet World Stats. (2012, July 29). *Internet Usage Statistics*. Retrieved August 3, 2012, from http://www.internetworldstats.com/stats.htm

Ismail, S., & Ebrahimpour, M. (2003). Examination and Comparison of the Critical Factors of Total Quality Management (TQM) Across Countries. *International Journal of Production Research*, *41*(2), 235–268. doi:10.1080/0020754021000022212.

ISTAT. (2008). *Internazionalizzazione delle medie e grandi imprese*. Anni 2001-2006 e previsioni 2007-2009. Retrieved October 7, 2011 from http://www.3.istat.it/salstampa/ comunicati/nob_calendario/20080318_00/testointegrale20080318.pdf

Ivens, B. S. (2006). Identifying differences in foreign customers' relational behavior: An exploratory study using multidimensional scaling. In Solberg, C. A. (Ed.), *Advances in international marketing. Relationship between exporters and their foreign sales and marketing intermediaries* (*Vol. 16*, pp. 245–266). Oxford, UK: Elsevier. doi:10.1016/S1474-7979(05)16010-4.

Jabbour, C. J., Gordono, F. S., De-Oliveira, J. H. C., Martinez, J. C., & Battistelle, R. A. G. (2011). Diversity management: Challenges, benefits, and the role of Human Resource Management in Brazilian organizations. *Equality, Diversity and Inclusion. International Journal (Toronto, Ont.)*, *30*(1), 58–74.

Jaffe, E. D., & Yi, L. (2007). What are the drivers of channel length? Distribution reform in the People's Republic of China. *International Business Review*, *16*, 474–493. doi:10.1016/j.ibusrev.2007.04.001.

Jagne, J., & Smith-Atakan, A. (2006). Cross-cultural interface design strategy. *Universal Access in the Information Society*, *5*, 299–305. doi:10.1007/s10209-006-0048-6.

Jalinek, M., & Schoonhoven, C. B. (1993). *The Innovation Marathon*. San Francisco, CA: Jossey-Bass.

James, L. R., & Brett, J. M. (1984). Mediators, moderators, and tests for mediation. *The Journal of Applied Psychology*, *69*(2), 307–321. doi:10.1037/0021-9010.69.2.307.

James, P., & Thorpe, N. (1994). *Ancient inventions*. New York, NY: Ballentine.

Jarvenpaa, S. L., Shaw, T. R., & Staples, D. S. (2004). Toward Contextualized Theories Of Trust: The Role Of Trust In Global Virtual Teams. *Information Systems Research*, *15*, 250–267. doi:10.1287/isre.1040.0028.

Jarvenpaa, S. L., & Tanriverdi, H. (2003). Leading Virtual Knowledge Networks. *Organizational Dynamics*, *31*, 403–412. doi:10.1016/S0090-2616(02)00127-4.

Jassawalla, A. R., & Sashittal, H. C. (2009). Thinking strategically about integrating repatriated managers in MNCs. *Human Resource Management*, *48*(5), 769–792. doi:10.1002/hrm.20313.

Javenpaa, S. L., & Leidner, D. E. (1998). Communication and trust in global virtual teams. *Organization Science*, *10*(6), 791–815. doi:10.1287/orsc.10.6.791.

Jaworski, B. J., Kohli, A. K., & Sahay, A. (2000). Market-driven versus driving markets. *Journal of the Academy of Marketing Science*, *28*(1), 45–54. doi:10.1177/0092070300281005.

Jayachandran, S., Sharma, S., Kaufman, P., & Raman, P. (2005). The Role of Relational Information Processes and Technology Use in Customer Relationship Management. *Journal of Marketing*, *69*, 177–192. doi:10.1509/jmkg.2005.69.4.177.

Jazayeri, M., & Hopper, T. (1999). Management accounting within world class manufacturing: A case study. *Management Accounting Research*, *10*, 263–301. doi:10.1006/mare.1999.0106.

Jiang, B., & Prater, E. (2002). Distribution and logistics development in China. The revolution has begun. *International Journal of Physical Distribution & Logistics Management*, *32*(9), 783–798. doi:10.1108/09600030210452459.

Johanson, J., & Vahlne, J. (2009). The Uppsala internationalization process model revisited: From liability of foreignness to liability of outsidership. *Journal of International Business Studies*, 1411–1431. doi:10.1057/jibs.2009.24.

Johanson, J., & Vahlne, J. E. (1977). The internationalization process of the firm: A model of knowledge development and increasing foreign market commitment. *Journal of International Business Studies*, *8*(1), 23–32. doi:10.1057/palgrave.jibs.8490676.

Johanson, J., & Vahlne, J. E. (2006). Commitment and opportunity development in the internationalization process: A note on the Uppsala internationalization process model. *Management International Review*, *46*(2), 165–177. doi:10.1007/s11575-006-0043-4.

Johanson, J., & Vahlne, J.-E. (1990). The mechanism of internationalization. *International Marketing Review*, *7*(4), 11–24. doi:10.1108/02651339010137414.

Johanson, J., & Vahlne, J.-E. (1990). The mechanism of internationalization. *International Marketing Review*, *7*(4), 11–24. doi:10.1108/02651339010137414.

Johansson, C., & Heide, M. (2008). Speaking of change: Three communication approaches in studies of organizational change. *Corporate Communications: An International Journal*, *13*(3), 288–305. doi:10.1108/13563280810893661.

Johne, F. A. (1984). How Experienced Product Innovators Organize. *Journal of Product Innovation Management*, *4*(12), 210–223. doi:10.1016/S0737-6782(84)80002-8.

Johnson & Johnson. (2011). *Director, Corporate Communications Job, Health Care Systems Inc*. Retrieved from http://www.careers.jnj.com/region

Johnson, C. (2011). *Case Against Wiki Leaks Part Of Broader Campaign*. Retrieved from http://www.npr.org/2011/05/11/136173262/case-against-wikileaks-part-of-broader-campaign

Johnson, J., & Tellis, G. J. (2008). Drivers of Success for Market Entry into China and India. *Journal of Marketing*, *72*(May), 1–13. doi:10.1509/jmkg.72.3.1.

Johnson, M. (1997). *Outsourcing in brief*. Oxford, UK: Elsevier Butterworth-Heinemann.

Johnson, R., & Winchell, W. (1988). Educating for quality. *Quality Progress*, *2*(1), 48–50.

Johnston, W. B., & Packer, A. E. (1987). *Workforce 2000*. Indianapolis, IN: Hudson Institute.

Jones, C. (2006). *Positive and Negative Innovation in Software Engineering*. Retrieved February 10, 2012 from www.compaid.com/caiinternet/ezine/capers-posneg.pdf

Jones, M. L. (2007). *Hofstede - Culturally questionable?* Paper presented at the Oxford Business & Economics Conference. Oxford, UK.

Jones, R., Stevens, M., & Fischer, D. (2000). Selection In Team Contexts. *Managing Selection In Changing Organizations: Human Resource Strategies*, 210-241.

Jones, G. K., & Davis, H. J. (2000). National Culture and Innovation: Implications for Locating Global R&D Operation. *Management International Review*, *40*(1), 11–39.

Jones, G. R. (2004). *Organizational theory, design, and change: Text and cases* (4th ed.). Upper Saddle River, NJ: Pearson Prentice Hall.

Jones, S., & Fox, S. (2009). *Generations Online in 2009*. Washington, DC: Pew Internet & American Life Project.

Jongeward, C. (1999). Shifting the ground of the familiar: Using autobiography and intercultural learning in a time of transition. *CJSAE*, *13*(1), 21–40.

Jonsen, K., & Ozbilgin, M. F. (in press). *Models of Global Diversity Management, Diversity at Work: The Practice of Inclusion* (Ferdman, B. M., & Deane, B., Eds.). Hoboken, NJ: Jossey-Bass.

Jöreskog, K. G., & Sörbom, D. (1999). *LISREL 8: User's Reference Guide*. Lincolnwood, IL: Scientific Software International.

Jöreskog, K. G., Sörbom, D., Du Toit, S., & Du Toit, M. (2003). *LISREL 8: New Statistical Features*. Lincolnwood, IL: Scientific Software International.

Jo, S., & Jung, J. (2005). A cross-cultural study of the World Wide Web and public relations. *Corporate Communications: An International Journal*, *10*(1), 24–40. doi:10.1108/13563280510578187.

Joseph, G. (2005). Global Virtual Engineering Team Utilization. In *The Engineering, Procurement, And Construction (Epc) Industry. State College*. PA: Pennsylvania State University.

Joseph, P. B., Peppers, D., & Rogers, M. (1995). Do you want to keep your customers forever? *Harvard Business Review*, *73*(2), 103–104.

Judge, T. A., & Simon, L. S. (2007). The globalization of industrial-organizational psychology: A comparative analysis. *Psychology of Human Resources*, *5*, 6–13.

Julian, C. C. (2003). Export marketing performance: A study of Thailand firms. *Journal of Small Business Management*, *41*(2), 213–221. doi:10.1111/1540-627X.00077.

Jun, S. H., Vogt, C. A., & MacKay, K. J. (2007). 'Relationships between travel information search and travel product purchase in pretrip contexts'. *Journal of Travel Research*, *45*, 266–274. doi:10.1177/0047287506295945.

Juran, J. M., & Gryna, F. M. (1980). *Quality Planning and Analysis*. New York: McGraw Hill.

Kagitcibasi, C., & Berry, J. W. (1989). Cross-cultural psychology: Current research and trends. *Annual Review of Psychology*, *40*, 493–531. doi:10.1146/annurev.ps.40.020189.002425.

Kaiser, R., & Prange, H. (2004). Managing diversity in a system of multi-level governance: The open method of co-ordination in innovation policy. *Journal of European Public Policy*, *11*(2), 249–266. doi:10.1080/1350176042000194421.

Kakabadse, N. K., Kakabadse, A., & Kouzmin, A. (2003). Reviewing the Knowledge Management Literature: Towards a Taxonomy. *International Journal of Knowledge Management*, *7*(4), 75–91. doi:10.1108/13673270310492967.

Kalkan, V. D. (2008). An Overall View of Knowledge Management Challenges for Global Business. *Business Process Management Journal*, *14*(3), 390–400. doi:10.1108/14637150810876689.

Kampf, C. (2007). Corporate social responsibility: WalMart, Maersk and the cultural bounds of representation in corporate web sites. *Corporate Communications: An International Journal*, *12*(1), 41–57. doi:10.1108/13563280710723741.

Kanawattanachai, P., & Yoo, Y. (2002). Dynamic Nature Of Trust In Virtual Teams. *The Journal of Strategic Information Systems*, *11*, 187–213. doi:10.1016/S0963-8687(02)00019-7.

Kanter, R. M. (1977). *Men and Women of the Corporation*. New York: Basic Books.

Kaplan, R. S. (1983). Measuring performance: A new challenge for managerial accounting research. *Accounting Review*, *18*(4), 686–705.

Kaplan, R., & Norton, D. (2001). Using the balanced scorecard as a strategic management system: Building a scorecard can help managers links today's actions with tomorrow's goals. In Young, S. M. (Ed.), *Readings in management accounting* (pp. 190–198). Upper Saddle River, NJ: Prentice Hall.

Karabacakoğlu, F., & Özbilgin, M. (2010). Global diversity management at Ericsson: The business case. In Costanzo, L. (Ed.), *Cases in Strategic Management*. London: McGraw-Hill.

Karoui, M., Gürkan, A., & Dudezert, A. (2010). Virtual Team Collaboration: A Review Of Literature. *And Perspectives*.

Karwowski, W. (1991). Complexity, fuzziness and ergonomic and incompatibility issues: The control of dynamic work environments. *Ergonomics*, *34*(6), 676–686. doi:10.1080/00140139108967345.

Karwowski, W. (2001). *International encyclopedia of ergonomics and human factors*. London: Taylor and Francis.

Kassim, N., & Abdullah, N. A. (2010). The effect of perceived service quality dimensions on customer satisfaction, trust, and loyalty in e-commerce settings: A cross cultural analysis. *Asia Pacific Journal of Marketing and Logistics*, *22*(3), 351–371. doi:10.1108/13555851011062269.

Katz, D., & Kahn, R. L. (1978). *The social psychology of organizing* (2nd ed.). New York: Wiley.

Katz, J. P., & Seifer, D. M. (1996). It's a Different World Out There: Planning for Expatriate Success Through Selection, Pre-departure Training and On-site Socialization. *HR. Human Resource Planning*, *19*(2), 32–54.

Kautish, P. (2012). Paradigm of workforce cultural diversity and Human Resource Management. *The Indian Journal of Management.*, *5*(1), 37–40.

Kayworth, T. R., & Leidner, D. E. (2002). Leadership Effectiveness In Global Virtual Teams. *Journal of Management Information Systems*, *18*, 7–40.

Kayworth, T., & Leidner, D. (2000). The Global Virtual Manager: A Prescription For Success. *European Management Journal*, *18*, 183–194. doi:10.1016/S0263-2373(99)00090-0.

Keck, G. L., & Mueller, B. (1994). Intended vs. unintended messages: Viewer perceptions of United States Army television commercials. *Journal of Advertising Research*, *34*(2), 70–78.

Keith, K. D. (2010). Introduction to cross-cultural psychology. In K. D. Keith (Ed.), Cross-cultural psychology: Contemporary themes and perspectives. Wiley-Blackwell.

Keller, K. L. (1993). Conceptualizing, measuring, and managing brand equity. *Journal of Marketing*, *57*(January), 1–22. doi:10.2307/1252054.

Kellough, E. J. (2006). *Understanding Affirmative Action: Politics, Discrimination, and the Search for Justice*. Washington, DC: Georgetown University Press.

Kelly, G. A. (1955). *The Psychology of Personal Constructs*. New York: Norton.

Kelly, G. A. (1963). *A Theory of Personality*. New York: Norton.

Kelly, J. (1964). The study of executive behavior by activity sampling. *Human Relations*, *17*, 277–287. doi:10.1177/001872676401700310.

Kelly, K. (1999). *New Rules for the New Economy: 10 Radical Strategies for a Connected World*. New York: Penguin Books.

Kennard, R. B. (1991). From Experience: Japanese Product Development Process. *Journal of Product Innovation Management*, *8*(September), 184–188. doi:10.1016/0737-6782(91)90025-T.

Kenyon, S. (2010). The impacts of Internet use upon activity participation and travel: Results from a longitudinal diary-based panel study. *Transportation Research Part C, Emerging Technologies*, *18*(1), 21–35. doi:10.1016/j.trc.2009.04.014.

Kerlinger, F. N. (1986). *Foundations of behavioural research* (3rd ed.). New York: Holt.

Keskin, H. (2006). Market orientation, learning orientation, and innovation capabilities in SMEs. *European Journal of Innovation Management*, *9*(4), 396–417. doi:10.1108/14601060610707849.

Khan, M. S. (2012). Role Of Trust And Relationships In Geographically Distributed Teams: Exploratory Study On Development Sector. *International Journal Of Networking And Virtual Organisations*, *10*, 40–58. doi:10.1504/IJNVO.2012.045210.

Khoury, S. J. (1979). International banking: A special look at foreign banks. *Journal of International Business Studies*, *10*(3), 36–52. doi:10.1057/palgrave.jibs.8490642.

Kim, H., & Marcus, H. R. (1999). Deviance or Uniqueness, Harmony or Conformity? A Cultural Analysis. *Journal of Personality and Social Psychology*, *77*(4), 785–800. doi:10.1037/0022-3514.77.4.785.

Kim, I., & Kuljis, J. (2010). Manifestations of Culture in Website Design. *Journal of Computing and Information Technology*, *18*(2), 125–132.

Kim, S., & Lee, Y. (2006). Global online marketplace: A cross-cultural comparison of website quality. *International Journal of Consumer Studies*, *30*(6), 533–543. doi:10.1111/j.1470-6431.2006.00522.x.

Kim, W. C., & Hwang, P. (1992). Global strategy and multinationals' entry mode choice. *Journal of International Business Studies*, *23*(1), 29–53. doi:10.1057/palgrave.jibs.8490258.

Kim, W. G., Lee, C., & Hiemstra, S. (2004). Effects of an online virtual community on customer loyalty and travel product purchases. *Tourism Management*, *25*, 343–355. doi:10.1016/S0261-5177(03)00142-0.

King, W. R. (2008). Questioning the Conventional Wisdom: Culture-Knowledge Management Relationships. *International Journal of Knowledge Management*, *12*(3), 35–47. doi:10.1108/13673270810875840.

Kirby, E. L., & Harter, L. M. (1992). Speaking the language of the bottom-line: The metaphor of "managing diversity". *Journal of Business Communication*, *40*(1), 28–49. doi:10.1177/002194360304000103.

Kirca, A. H., Jayachandran, S., & Bearden, W. O. (2005). Market orientation: A meta-analytic review and assessment of its antecedents and impact on performance. *Journal of Marketing*, *69*(2), 24–41. doi:10.1509/jmkg.69.2.24.60761.

Kirkman, B. L., Rosen, B., Gibson, C. B., Tesluk, P. E., & Mcpherson, S. O. (2002). Five Challenges To Virtual Team Success: Lessons From Sabre, Inc. *The Academy Of Management Executive (1993-2005)*, 67-79.

Kirkman, B. L., & Mathieu, J. E. (2005). The Dimensions And Antecedents Of Team Virtuality. *Journal of Management*, *31*, 700–718. doi:10.1177/0149206305279113.

Kirkman, B. L., Rosen, B., Tesluk, P. E., & Gibson, C. B. (2004). The Impact Of Team Empowerment On Virtual Team Performance: The Moderating Role Of Face-To-Face Interaction. *Academy of Management Journal*, , 175–192. doi:10.2307/20159571.

Kirkman, B., Lowe, K., & Gibson, C. (2006). A Quarter Century of Culture's Consequences: A Review of Empirical Research Incorporating Hofstede's Cultural Values Framework. *Journal of International Business Studies*, *37*(3), 285–320. doi:10.1057/palgrave.jibs.8400202.

Kirmani, A. (1997). Advertising repetition as a signal of quality: If it's advertised so much, something must be wrong. *Journal of Advertising*, *26*(3), 77–86.

Kittler, M. G., Rygl, D., & Mackinnon, A. (2011). Beyond culture or beyond control? Reviewing the use of Hall's high-/low-context concept. *International Journal of Cross Cultural Management*, *11*(1), 63–82. doi:10.1177/1470595811398797.

Kivel, T. (2002). *Uprooting racism: How white people can work for racial justice*. Gabriola Islands, CA: New Society Publishers.

Klein, K., & Kozlowski, S. (2000). *Multilevel Theory, Research and Methods in Organizations: Foundations, Extensions and New Directions*. San Francisco, CA: Jossey-Bass.

Klein, S., Frazier, G. L., & Roth, V. J. (1990). A transaction cost analysis model of channel integration in international markets. *JMR, Journal of Marketing Research*, *27*(2), 196–208. doi:10.2307/3172846.

Klimenko, M., & Saggi, K. (2007). Technical Compatibility and the Mode of Foreign Entry with Network Externalities. *The Canadian Journal of Economics. Revue Canadienne d'Economique*, *40*(1), 176–206. doi:10.1111/j.1365-2966.2007.00404.x.

Kluckhohn, C. (1954). *Culture and behavior*. New York: Free Press.

Kluckhohn, F. R., & Strodtbeck, F. Z. (1961). *Variations in Value Orientations*. West Port, CT: Greenwood Press.

Knight, G. A., & Cavusgil, S. T. (2004). Innovation, organizational capabilities, and the born global firm. *Journal of International Business Studies*, *35*(2), 124–141. doi:10.1057/palgrave.jibs.8400071.

Knight, G., Madsen, T. K., & Servais, P. (2004). An inquiry into born-global firms in Europe and the USA. *International Marketing Review*, *21*(6), 645–665. doi:10.1108/02651330410568060.

Kobrin, S. J. (1988). Expatriate reduction and strategic control in American multicultural corporations. *Human Resource Management*, *27*, 63–75. doi:10.1002/hrm.3930270104.

Kocbek, A., & Juric, M. B. (2010). Using advanced business intelligence methods in business process management. Retrieved June 12, 2012, from http://ailab.ijs.si/dunja/SiKDD2010/Papers/Kocbek_Final.pdf

Kochan, T., Bezurlova, K., Ely, R., Jackson, S., Aparna, J., & Jehn, K. et al. (2003). The effects of diversity on business performance: Report of the diversity research network. *Human Resource Management*, *42*(1), 3–22. doi:10.1002/hrm.10061.

Kogut, B., & Zander, U. (1992a). *Knowledge of the Firm, Technology Transfer, and the Theory of the Multinational Corporation*. Working Paper, Institute of International Business, Stockholm School of Economics, Stockholm, Sweden.

Kogut, B., & Singh, H. (1988). The effect of national culture on the choice of entry mode. *Journal of International Business Studies*, *19*(3), 411–432. doi:10.1057/palgrave.jibs.8490394.

Kogut, B., & Zander, U. (1992b). Knowledge of the Firm, Combinative Capabilities and the Replication of Technology. *Organization Science*, *3*(3), 383–397. doi:10.1287/orsc.3.3.383.

Kogut, B., & Zander, U. (1993). Knowledge of The Firm and The Evolutionary Theory of The Multinational Corporation. *Journal of International Business Studies*, *24*(4), 625–645. doi:10.1057/palgrave.jibs.8490248.

Kohli, A. K., & Jaworski, B. J. (1990). Market orientation: The construct, research propositions, and managerial implications. *Journal of Marketing*, *54*(2), 1–18. doi:10.2307/1251866.

Kondratova, I., & Goldfarb, I. (2007). Color Your Website: Use of Colors on the Web. In N. Aykin (Ed.), *Proceedings of the 12th HCI International Conference* (pp. 123–132). Beijing, China: Heidelberg Springer.

Kondratova, I., & Goldfarb, I. (2006). Cultural Interface Design: Global Colors Study. In Meersman, Z. T. R. (Ed.), *OTM Workshops* (pp. 926–934). Montpellier, VT: Heidelberg Springer.

Kornhauser, A. W. (1929). Industrial psychology in England, Germany and the United States. *The Personnel Journal*, *8*, 421–434.

Kossek, E. E., & Lobel, S. A. (1996). Introduction: Transforming human resource systems to manage diversity: An introduction and orienting framework. In Kossek, E. E., & Lobel, S. A. (Eds.), *Managing Diversity: Human Resource Strategies for Transforming the Workplace*. Cambridge, MA: Blackwell.

Kossek, E. E., Lobel, S., & Brown, J. (2006). Human resource strategies to manage work force diversity: Examining "the business case". In Konrad, A. M., Prasad, P., & Pringle, J. K. (Eds.), *Handbook of Workplace Diversity* (pp. 53–74). Thousand Oaks, CA: Sage. doi:10.4135/9781848608092.n3.

Kostova, T. (1999). Transnational Transfer of Strategic Organizational Practices: A Contextual Perspective. *Academy of Management Review*, *24*(2), 308–324.

Kostova, T., & Roth, K. (2003). Social Capital in Multinational Corporations and a Micro-Macro Model of its Formation. *Academy of Management Review*, *28*(2), 297–317.

Kozlowski, S. W. J., & Ilgen, D. R. (2006). Enhancing The Effectiveness Of Work Groups And Teams. *Psychological Science in the Public Interest*, *7*, 77–124.

Kraut, R. E., Egido, C., & Galegher, J. (2002). Patterns of contact and communication in scientific research collaboration. In Galegher, J., & Kraut, R. (Eds.), *Intellectual Teamwork: Social and technological foundations of group work*. New York: Lawrence Earlbaum Associates.

Kraut, R. E., Lewis, S. H., & Swezey, L. W. (1982). Listener responsiveness and the coordination of conversation. *Journal of Personality and Social Psychology*, *43*, 718–731. doi:10.1037/0022-3514.43.4.718.

Kremenyuk, V. (2002). *International Negotiation. Analysis, Approaches, Issues*. San Francisco, CA: Jossey-Bass.

Krippendorff, K. (2004). *Content analysis: An introduction to its methodology*. London: Sage.

Kroeber, A. L., & Kluckhohn, F. (1991). Culture: A critical review of concepts and definitions, peabody museum papers, (Vol. 47, no. 1). In N. J. Adler (Ed.), International dimensions of organizational behavior. Boston, MA: PWS-Kent.

Kropp, F., Lindsay, N. J., & Shoham, A. (2006). Entrepreneurial, market, and learning orientations and international entrepreneurial business venture performance in South African firms. *International Marketing Review*, *23*(5), 504–523. doi:10.1108/02651330610703427.

Krosolid, D. (1999). *In Search of Quality Management – Rethinking and Reinterpreting*. Linkoping, Sweden: Linkoping University.

Krueger, R. A. A., & Casey, M. A. A. (2000). *Focus Groups: A Practical Guide for Applied Research*. London: Sage.

Kruse, G. & Berry, C. (2004). Outsourcing: The How-to Guide. *IEE Manufacturing*, August/September, 36-39.

Kuo, T. S., Chi, H., & Dorjgotov, B. (2011). Mediation Effect of Knowledge Management in the Relationship Between Technology and Organizational Effectiveness – An Empirical Study of Mongolian Academy of Sciences. *Journal of Human Resource and Adult Learning*, *7*(1), 1–10.

Kwan, P. Y. K., & Ng, P. W. K. (1999). Quality indicators in higher education: Comparing Hong Kong and China's students. *Managerial Auditing Journal*, *14*, 20–27. doi:10.1108/02686909910245964.

Kyle, M. (2004). Does Locale Affect R and D Productivity? The Case of Pharmaceuticals. In FRBSF Economic Letter 32.

Kyoon Yoo, D., Subba Rao, S., & Hong, P. (2005). A comparative study on cultural differences and quality practices – Korea, USA, Mexico and Taiwan. *International Journal of Quality & Reliability Management*, *23*(6), 607–624.

Ladhari, R., Pons, F., Bressolles, G., & Zins, M. (2011). Culture and personal values: How they influence perceived service quality. *Journal of Business Research*, *64*, 951–957. doi:10.1016/j.jbusres.2010.11.017.

Lafferty, B. A., & Hult, G. T. M. (2001). A synthesis of contemporary market orientation perspectives. *European Journal of Marketing*, *35*(1/2), 92–109. doi:10.1108/03090560110363364.

Lagrosen, S. (2002). Quality management in Europe: A cultural perspective. *The TQM Magazine*, *14*(5), 275–283. doi:10.1108/09544780210439707.

Lagrosen, S. (2003). Exploring the impact of culture on quality management. *International Journal of Quality & Reliability Management*, *20*(4/5), 473–482. doi:10.1108/02656710310468632.

Lai, V. S., & Li, H. (2005). Technology Acceptance Model For Internet Banking: An Invariance Analysis. *Information & Management*, *42*, 373–386. doi:10.1016/j.im.2004.01.007.

Lai, Y. L., & Lin, F. J. (2012). The Effects of Knowledge Management and Technology Innovation on New Product Development Performance – An Empirical Study of Taiwanese Machine Tool Industry. *Proceed. –. Social and Behavioral Sciences*, *40*, 157–164.

Lalonde, K. (2011). Communication Among Virtual Teams.[The College Of St. Scholastica.]. *Ms*, , 1493595.

Lambe, P. (2011). The Three Tribes: Knowledge Management, Learning and Intellectual Capital – Towards a Common Agenda. *Keynote Presentation, 8th International Conference on Intellectual Capital, Knowledge Management & Organizational Learning – ICICKM 2011*. Bangkok, Thailand: IKI SEA

Lam, Y. L. J. (2002). Defining the Effect of Transformational Leadership on Organizational Learning: A Cross-Cultural Comparison. *School Leadership & Management*, *22*, 439–452. doi:10.1080/1363243022000053448.

Landsberger, H. (1961). Horizontal Dimension in Bureaucracy. *Administrative Science Quarterly*, *6*, 299–322. doi:10.2307/2390705.

Landy, F. J., & Conte, J. M. (2004). *Work in the 21st century: An introduction to industrial and organizational psychology*. Boston, MA: McGraw-Hill.

Lang, T. (2000). The effect of the Internet on travel consumer purchasing behavior and implications for travel agencies. *Journal of Vacation Marketing*, *6*(4), 368–385. doi:10.1177/135676670000600407.

Lapointe, J. B. (1990). Industrial/organizational psychology: A view from the field. In Murphy, K. R., & Saal, F. E. (Eds.), *Psychology in organizations: Integrating science and practice*. Hillsdale, NJ: Erlbaum.

Laroche, M., Ueltschy, L. C., Abe, S., Cleveland, M., & Yannopoulos, P. P. (2004). Service quality perceptions and customer satisfaction: Evaluating the role of culture. *Journal of International Marketing*, *12*(3), 58–85. doi:10.1509/jimk.12.3.58.38100.

Latta, G. F., & Swigger, K. (1992). Validation of the Repertory Grid for Use in Modelling Knowledge. *Journal of the American Society for Information Science American Society for Information Science*, *42*(2), 115–129. doi:10.1002/(SICI)1097-4571(199203)43:2<115::AID-ASI2>3.0.CO;2-I.

Laudon, K. C., & Laudon, J. P. (2009). *Essentials of Management Information Systems* (8th ed.). New York: Prentice Hall.

Laudon, K. C., & Traver, C. G. (2010). *E-Commerce 2010 – Business, Technology, Society*. New York: Pearson.

Laungani, P. (2002). Cross-cultural psychology: A handmaiden to mainstream western psychology. *Counselling Psychology Quarterly*, *15*, 385–397. doi:10.1080/09515 07031000069392.

Lawlor, B.R. (2007). *The Age of Globalization: Impact of Information Technology on Global Business Strategies*. Senior captone project.

Lawrence, P. R., & Lorsch, J. W. (1967). *Organization and Environment: Managing Differentiation and Integration*. Cambridge, MA: Harvard University Press.

Le, V. H., & Filiatrault, P. (2006). *The Adoption of E-commerce in SMEs in Vietnam: A Study of Users and Prospectors*. Paper presented at the PACIS 2006 Proceedings. Kuala Lumpur, Malaysia.

Leavy, P. (2011). *Essentials of Transdisciplinary Research*. Walnut Creek, CA: Left Coast Press.

LeBlanc, G., & Nguyen, N. (1997). Searching for excellence in business education: An exploratory study of customer impressions of service quality. *International Journal of Educational Management*, *11*(2), 72–79. doi:10.1108/09513549710163961.

Lee, A. S. (1999). Rigor and Relevance in MIS Research: Beyond the Approach of Positivism Alone. *Management Information Systems Quarterly*, *23*(1), 29–33. doi:10.2307/249407.

Lee, C., & Chen, W. J. (2005). The Effects of Internal Marketing and Organizational Culture on Knowledge Management in the Information Technology Industry. *International Journal of Management*, *22*(4), 661–672.

Leeds-Hurwitz, W. (1990). Notes in the History of Intercultural Communication: The Foreign Service Institute and the Mandate for Intercultural Training. *The Quarterly Journal of Speech*, *76*(3), 262–281. doi:10.1080/00335639009383919.

Lee, K., Joshi, K., & Bae, M. (2009). A Cross-National Comparison of the Determinants of Customer Satisfaction with Online Stores. *Journal of Global Information Technology Management*, *12*(4), 25–51.

Lee, K., & Mirchandani, D. (2010). Dynamics of the importance of IS/IT skills. *Journal of Computer Information Systems*, *50*(4), 67–78.

Le, H. (2004). Changes in Arts Organisations under the Open Market Economy in Vietnam. *International Journal of Knowledge. Culture and Change Management*, *4*, 1539–1547.

Le, H. (2005). *Performing Arts Management in a Climate of Adjustment: Case Studies from Vietnam and Australia. Unpublished PhD*. Sydney, Australia: University of Sydney.

Le, H. (2008). Economic Reforms, Cultural Policy: Opportunities and Challenges to the Arts and Culture in Vietnam in the Age of Globalization. *Journal of Arts Management. Law & Society*, *38*(1), 5–18.

Le, H. (2009). Performing arts management in a climate of adjustment: Case studies from Vietnam and Australia. *Asia Pacific Journal of Arts and Cultural Management*, *6*(2), 488–503.

Le, H., Rentschler, R., & Frederick, H. (2010). Breaking through the 'glass ceiling': Gender and arts leaders in Vietnam. *International Journal of the Arts in Society*, *5*(2), 1–14.

Le, H., & Sargent, J. (2010). The use of the web as a marketing tool by selected arts organisations in Vietnam: A preliminary investigation. *TMC Academic Journal*, *4*(2), 50–63.

Lehaney, B., Clark, S., & Coakes, E. (2003). *Beyond Knowledge Management*. Hershey, PA: IGI Global. doi:10.4018/978-1-59140-180-3.

Lehman, C. (2005). Accounting and the public interest: All the world's a stage. *Accounting, Auditing & Accountability Journal*, *18*(5), 675–689. doi:10.1108/09513570510620501.

Lei, D., & Hitt, M. (1995). Strategic restructuring and outsourcing: The effect of mergers and acquisitions and LBO's on building firm skills and capabilities. *Journal of Management*, *21*(5), 835–859. doi:10.1177/014920639502100502.

Leidel, S. (2008).*German Companies Eye Moving Production Back Home*. Retrieved on October 26, 2012, from http://www.dw-world.de/dw/article/0,2144,3462948,00.html

Leidner, D., & Kayworth, T. (2006). A review of culture in information systems research: Toward a theory of information technology culture conflict. *Management Information Systems Quarterly*, *30*(2), 357–399.

Leigh, T. W., Rethans, A. J., & Whitney, T. R. (1987). Role portrayals of women in advertising: Cognitive responses and advertising effectiveness. *Journal of Advertising Research*, *27*(October-November), 54–62.

Lengnick-Hall, C. A., & Lengnick-Hall, M. (1988). Strategic human resource management: A review of the literature and a proposed typology. *Academy of Management Review*, *13*(3), 454–470.

Lenhart, A., & Fox, S. (2006). *Bloggers: A portrait of the Internet's new story tellers*. Washington, DC: Pew Internet & American Life Project.

Leonard-Barton, D. (1992). Core Capabilities and Core Rigidities: A Paradox in Managing New Product Development. *Strategic Management Journal*, *13*(Summer), 111–125. doi:10.1002/smj.4250131009.

Leonardi, P. M., & Treem, J. W. (2012). Knowledge Management Technology as a Stage for Strategic Self-Presentation: Implications for Knowledge Sharing in. *Information and Organization*, *22*, 37–59. doi:10.1016/j.infoandorg.2011.10.003.

Leonidas, L., & Katsikeas, C. (1996). The export development process: An integrative review of empirical models. *Journal of International Business Studies*, *27*(3), 517–551. doi:10.1057/palgrave.jibs.8490846.

Leung, K., Bhagat, R., Buchan, N., Erez, M., & Gibson, C. (2005). Culture and international business: Recent advances and their implications for the future. *Journal of International Business Studies*, *36*(4), 357–378. doi:10.1057/palgrave.jibs.8400150.

Le, V. H., Rowe, F., Truex, D., & Huynh, M. Q. (2012). An Empirical Study of Determinants of E-Commerce Adoption in SMEs in Vietnam: An Economy in Transition. *Journal of Global Information Management*, *20*(3), 23–54. doi:10.4018/jgim.2012070102.

Levitt, T. (1983). The globalization of markets. *Harvard Business Review, 5*(6), 92–102.

Lewis, P. & Simpson, R. (2010). Meritocracy, difference and choice: Women's experiences of advantage and disadvantage at work. *Gender in Management: An International Journal, 25*(3).

Lewis, B. R. (1989). Quality in the service sector-a review. *International Journal of Bank Marketing, 7*(5), 4–12. doi:10.1108/02652328910134590.

Liao, H., Proctor, R. W., & Salvendy, G. (2007). Content preparation for cross-cultural e-commerce: A review and a model. *Behaviour & Information Technology, 27*(1), 43–61. doi:10.1080/01449290601088424.

Li, L., Li, D., & Dalgic, T. (2004). Internationalization process of small and medium-sized enterprises: Toward a hybrid model of experiential learning and planning. *Management International Review, 44*(1), 93–117.

Lin, C., Standing, C., & Liu, Y.-C. (2008). A Model To Develop Effective Virtual Teams. *Decision Support Systems, 45*, 1031–1045. doi:10.1016/j.dss.2008.04.002.

Lindberg, P., Voss, C., & Blackmon, K. (1998). *International Manufacturing Strategies: Context, Content, and Change*. London: Kluver Academic.

Linder, J. C. (2004). *Outsourcing for radical change*. New York: American Management Association.

Lin, E.-Y. (2012). A Cross-Cultural Study of Luxury e-Branding: Standardization vs. Adaptation, Product Category, and Country-of-Origin. *Marketing Review, 9*(1), 91–120.

Linehan, M., & Scullion, H. (2002). Repatriation of female executives: Empirical evidence from Europe. *Women in Management Review, 17*(2), 80–88. doi:10.1108/09649420210421781.

Ling, C. Y. (2001). *Model of factors influences on electronic commerce adoption and diffusion in small and medium sized enterprises*. Paper presented at the European Conference on Information Systems (ECIS).

Ling, Y., & Jaffe, E. D. (2007). Economic development and channel evolution in The People's Republic of China. *Asia Pacific Journal of Marketing and Logistics, 19*(1), 22–39. doi:10.1108/13555850710720885.

Lin, H. (2000). Choice of market entry mode in emerging markets: Influences on entry strategy in China. *Journal of Global Marketing, 14*(1/2), 83–109. doi:10.1300/J042v14n01_05.

Li, T., & Calantone, R. J. (1998). The impact of market knowledge competence on new product advantage: Conceptualization and empirical examination. *Journal of Marketing, 62*(4), 13–29. doi:10.2307/1252284.

Lituchy, T. R., & Barra, R. A. (2008). International issues of the design and usage of websites for e-commerce: Hotel and airline examples. *Journal of Engineering and Technology Management, 25*, 93–111. doi:10.1016/j.jengtecman.2008.01.004.

Liu, C., Marchewka, J. T., & Ku, C. (2004). Americana dn Taiwanese Perceptions Concerning Privacy, Trust, and Behavioral Intentions in Electronic Commerce. *Journal of Global Information Management, 12*(1), 18–40. doi:10.4018/jgim.2004010102.

Liu, H., & Wang, Y. P. (1999). Co-ordination of international channel relationships: Four case studies in the food industry in China. *Journal of Business and Industrial Marketing, 14*(2), 130–150. doi:10.1108/08858629910259008.

Liu, R., & Hart, S. (2011). Does experience matter? - A study of knowledge processes and uncertainty reduction in solution innovation. *Industrial Marketing Management, 40*, 691–698. doi:10.1016/j.indmarman.2011.05.004.

Li, X., Hess, T. J., McNab, A. L., & Yu, Y. (2009). A Cross-Country Study of the Effects of National Cultural Values on Acceptance of a Personal Web Portal. *ACM SIGMIS Database, 40*(4), 62–87. doi:10.1145/1644953.1644959.

Li, X., Pan, B., Zhang, L., & Smith, W. W. (2009). The effect of online information search on image development: Insights from a mixed-methods study. *Journal of Travel Research, 48*(1), 45–57. doi:10.1177/0047287508328659.

Locke, E. A. (1968). Toward a theory of task motivation and incentives. *Organizational Behavior and Human Performance, 3*, 157–189. doi:10.1016/0030-5073(68)90004-4.

Locke, E. A. (1970). Job satisfaction and job performance. *Organizational Behavior and Human Performance, 5*, 484–500. doi:10.1016/0030-5073(70)90036-X.

Lockwood, N. R. (2003). Work/life balance: Challenges and solutions. *HRMagazine*, *48*(6), 2–11.

London, T., & Hart, S. L. (2004). Reinventing Strategies for Emerging Markets: Beyond the Transnational Model. *Journal of International Business Studies*, *35*(5), 350–370. doi:10.1057/palgrave.jibs.8400099.

Lonsdale, C. (1999). Effectively managing vertical supply relationships: a risk management model for outsourcing. *Supply Chain Management: An International Journal*, *4*(4), 176–183. doi:10.1108/13598549910284499.

Lopez-Nicolas, C., & Merono-Cerdan, A. L. (2009). The Impact of Organizational Culture on the Use of ICT for Knowledge Management. *Electronic Markets*, *19*, 211–219. doi:10.1007/s12525-009-0020-4.

Lord, M. D., & Ranft, A. L. (2000). Organizational learning about new international markets: Exploring the internal transfer of local market knowledge. *Journal of International Business Studies*, *31*(4), 573–589. doi:10.1057/palgrave.jibs.8490923.

Loseke, D. R., & Cahil, S. E. (2007). Publishing qualitative manuscripts: Lessons learned. In Seale, C., Gobo, G., Gubrium, J. F., & Silverman, D. (Eds.), *Qualitative Research Practice: Concise Paperback Edition* (pp. 491–506). London: Sage.

Louis, M. R. (1980). Surprise and sense making: What newcomers experience in entering unfamiliar organizational settings. *Administrative Science Quarterly*, *25*, 226–251. doi:10.2307/2392453 PMID:10247029.

Luckham, D. (2002). *The Power of Events: An Introduction to Complex Event Processing in Distributed Systems*. Berlin, Germany: Springer Verlag.

Luft, J., & Shields, M. (2003). Mapping management accounting: graphics and guidelines for theory-consistent empirical research. *Accounting, Auditing & Accountability Journal*, *8*, 71–90.

Lu, J. W., & Beamish, P. W. (2006). Partnering strategies and performance of SMEs' international joint ventures. *Journal of Business Venturing*, *21*(4), 461–486. doi:10.1016/j.jbusvent.2005.02.002.

Luk, S. (1998). Structural changes in China's distribution system. *International Journal of Physical Distribution & Logistics Management*, *28*(1), 44–67. doi:10.1108/09600039810205953.

Lumsden, G., Lumsden, D., & Wiethoff, C. (2009). Communicating. In *Groups And Teams: Sharing Leadership*. Wadsworth.

Luna, D., Peracchio, L. A., & Juan, M. D. (2002). Cross-Cultural and Cognitive Aspects of Web Site Navigation. *Journal of the Academy of Marketing Science*, *30*(4), 397–410. doi:10.1177/009207002236913.

Luo, Y. (2001). *Strategy, Structure, and Performance of MNCs in China*. Westport, CT: Quorum Books.

Luo, Y. (2002). *Multinational Enterprises in Emerging Markets*. Copenhagen, Denmark: Copenhagen Business School Press.

Luo, Y., & Tung, R. L. (2007). International Expansion of Emerging Market Enterprises: A Springboard Perspective. *Journal of International Business Studies*, *38*(4), 481–498. doi:10.1057/palgrave.jibs.8400275.

Luthans, F. (2010). *Organizational behavior: An evidence-based approach* (12th ed.). New York: McGraw-Hill.

Maclure, S., & Davies, P. (1991). Learning to think: Thinking to learn (Eds.). Oxford, UK: Pergamon Press.

Madsen, T. K., & Servais, P. (1997). The internationalisation of born globals: An evolutionary process? *International Business Review*, *6*(6), 561–583. doi:10.1016/S0969-5931(97)00032-2.

Madu, C. N., Kuei, C., & Lin, C. (1995). A Comparative Analysis of Quality Practice in Manufacturing Firms in the U.S. and Taiwan. *Decision Sciences*, *26*(5), 621–635. doi:10.1111/j.1540-5915.1995.tb01443.x.

Magnier-Watanabe, R., & Senoo, D. (2008). Organizational Characteristics as Prescriptive Factors of Knowledge Management Initiatives. *International Journal of Knowledge Management*, *12*(1), 21–36. doi:10.1108/13673270810852368.

Magnier-Watanabe, R., & Senoo, D. (2010). Shaping Knowledge Management: Organization and National Culture. *Journal of Knowledge Management*, *14*(2), 214–227. doi:10.1108/13673271011032364.

Maitland, E., Rose, E. L., & Nicholas, S. (2005). How Firms Grow: Clustering as a Dynamic Model of Internationalization. *Journal of International Business Studies*, *36*(4), 435–451. doi:10.1057/palgrave.jibs.8400140.

Makino, S., & Delios, A. (1996). Local Knowledge Transfer and Performance: Implications for Alliance Formation in Asia. *Journal of International Business Studies*, *27*(5), 905–927. doi:10.1057/palgrave.jibs.8490156.

Malami, T. (1999). Activity-based costing diffusion across organizations: As exploratory empirical analysis of Finnish firms. *Accounting, Organizations and Society*, *24*, 649–672. doi:10.1016/S0361-3682(99)00011-2.

Malhotra, A., & Majchrzak, A. (2012). How Virtual Teams Use Their Virtual Workspace To Coordinate Knowledge. *Acm Trans. Manage. Inf. Syst.*, *3*, 1–14.

Malhotra, A., Majchrzak, A., & Rosen, B. (2007). Leading Virtual Teams. *The Academy Of Management Perspectives Archive*, *21*, 60–69. doi:10.5465/AMP.2007.24286164.

Malhotra, N. K., Ulgado, F. M., Agarwal, J., & Baalbaki, I. B. (1994). International Services Marketing: A Comparative Evaluation of the Dimensions of Service Quality between Developed and Developing Countries. *International Marketing Review*, *11*(2), 5–15. doi:10.1108/02651339410061937.

Malmi, T., & Granlund, M. (2009). In search of management accounting theory. *European Accounting Review*, *18*(3), 597–620. doi:10.1080/09638180902863779.

Mangan, K. (2004). This political hot potato is a course in demand. *The Chronicle of Higher Education*, A12-A13. May 14.

Marchesi, M., Succi, G., Wells, D., Williams, L., & Wells, J. D. (Eds.). (2003). *Extreme Programming Perspectives*. Reading, MA: Addison-Wesley.

Marcotte, C., & Niosi, J. (2005). Small and Medium-sized Enterprises Involved in Technology Transfer to China: What do their Partners Learn? *International Small Business Journal*, *23*(1), 27–47. doi:10.1177/0266242605048871.

Marcussen (2003). Trends in European Internet Distribution. *Travel and Tourism Services Centre for Regional and Tourism Research*. Retrieved on August 9, 2012, from http://www.crt.dk/uk/staff/chm/trends.htm

Marketing Association. ISSN: 0022-2429 (print), 1547-7185 (electronic) 168 / *Journal of Marketing*.

Markides, C. (2007). In search of ambidextrous professors. *Academy of Management Journal*, *50*, 762–768. doi:10.5465/AMJ.2007.26279168.

Martínez-López, F. J., Sousa, C. M., & Gázquez-Abad, J. C. (2011). A Cultural Constructivist Analysis of the Internet's Role in the International Approximation of Markets. *Journal of Marketing Theory and Practice*, *19*(1), 57–79. doi:10.2753/MTP1069-6679190104.

Martínez, P. (2009). Proceso del desarrollo exportador de la PYME Colombiana. *Cuadernos de Gestión*, *9*(1), 47–66.

Martin, J. (1992). *Cultures in organizations: Three perspectives*. Oxford, UK: Oxford University Press.

Martins, L. L. & Schilpzand, M. C. (2011). Global Virtual Teams: Key Developments, Research Gaps, And Future Directions. *Research In Personnel And Human Resources Management, 30*.

Martin, S. S., Camarero, C., & Jose, R. S. (2011). Dual effect of perceived risk on cross-national e-commerce. *Internet Research*, *21*(1), 46–66. doi:10.1108/10662241111104875.

Martins, L. L., Gilson, L. L., & Maynard, M. T. (2004). Virtual Teams: What Do We Know And Where Do We Go From Here? *Journal of Management*, *30*, 805–835. doi:10.1016/j.jm.2004.05.002.

Marton, F. (1986). Phenomenography. A research approach to investigating different understandings of reality. *Journal of Thought*, *21*(3), 28–49.

Marulanda, E. (2004). *La Competitividad de las Pymes, Como ingresar exitosamente en el mercado globalizado. El Empresariado Colombiano y el TLC*. Bogotá, Colombia: CONFECAMARAS.

Maskell, B. H. (1992). Performance measurement for world class manufacturing. *Corporate Controller*, January/February, 44-48.

Mathews, A. (1998). Diversity: A principle of Human Resource Management. *Public Personnel Management*, *27*(2), 175–185.

Mathews, B. P., Ueno, A., Kekale, T., Repka, M., Lopes Pereira, Z., & Silva Graca, S. (2001). European quality management practices, the impact of national culture. *International Journal of Quality & Reliability Management*, *18*(7), 692–707. doi:10.1108/EUM0000000005776.

Matsumoto, D. (2009). Teaching about culture. In Gurung, R. A. R., & Prieto, L. R. (Eds.), *Getting culture: Incorporating diversity across the curriculum*. New York: Stylus.

Mattila, A. S. (1999). The role of culture in the service evaluation processes. *Journal of Service Research*, *1*(3), 250–261. doi:10.1177/109467059913006.

Mawanda, H. J. (2012). *Beyond Technology, An Analysis Of The Perceived Impact Of Transformational Leadership And Contingent Rewards As Extrinsic Motivation On Virtual Team Member Satisfaction And Leadership Effectiveness: A Quantitative Study. Ph.D. 3503075.* Minneapolis, MN: Capella University.

Maxwell, J. C. (2002). *Cele 21 de legi supreme ale liderului*. Bucharest, Romania: Editura Amaltea.

Maynard, M. T., Mathieu, J. E., Rapp, T. L., & Gilson, L. L. (2012). Something(S) Old And Something(S) New: Modeling Drivers Of Global Virtual Team Effectiveness. *Journal of Organizational Behavior*, *33*, 342–365. doi:10.1002/job.1772.

Maynard, M., & Tian, Y. (2004). Between global and glocal: Content analysis of the Chinese Web Sites of the 100 top global brands. *Public Relations Review*, *30*, 285–291. doi:10.1016/j.pubrev.2004.04.003.

Mayrhofer, U. (2004). International market entry: Does the home country a ffect entry-mode decisions? *Journal of International Marketing*, *12*(4), 71–96. doi:10.1509/jimk.12.4.71.53211.

Maznevski, M. L., & Chudoba, K. M. (2000). Bridging space over time: Global virtual team dynamics and effectiveness. *Organization Science*, *11*(5), 473–492. doi:10.1287/orsc.11.5.473.15200.

Mc Sweeney, B. (2002). Hofstede's model of national cultural differences and their consequences: A Triumph of faith - A failure of analysis. *Human Relations*, *55*(1), 89–118.

McCarty, J., & Hattwick, P. (1992). Cultural Value Orientations: A Comparison of Magazine Advertisements from the United States and Mexico. *Advances in Consumer Research. Association for Consumer Research (U. S.)*, *19*, 34–38.

McCracken, G. (1986). Culture and consumption: A theoretical account of the structure and movement of the cultural meaning of consumer godos. *The Journal of Consumer Research*, *13*(1), 71–84. doi:10.1086/209048.

McCracken, G. (1988). *The Long Interview*. New York: Sage Publications.

McCracken, G. (1989). Who is the celebrity endorser? Cultural foundations of the endorsement process. *The Journal of Consumer Research*, *16*(3), 310–321. doi:10.1086/209217.

McCracken, G. (1993). The Value of the Brand: An Anthropological Perspective. In Bowl, D. A. (Ed.), *Brand Equity and Advertising: Advertising's Role in Building Strong Brands* (pp. 125–139). Hillsdale, NJ: Lawrence Erlbaum Associates.

McDonald, G. M. (1993). Et go home? The successful management of expatiate transfer. *Journal of Managerial Psychology*, *8*(2), 18–29. doi:10.1108/02683949310032758.

McDougall, P., & Oviatt, B. (2000). International entrepreneurship: The intersection of two research paths. *Academy of Management Journal*, *43*(5), 902–906. doi:10.2307/1556418.

McEwen, W., Fang, X., Zhang, C., & Burkholder, R. (2006). Inside the Mind of the Chinese Consumer. *Harvard Business Review*, *84*(3), 68–76. PMID:16846190.

McHenry, J. (2007). *We are the very model*. Presidential address delivered at the annual meeting of the Society for Industrial and Organizational Psychology. New York.

McKay, J., & Marshall, P. (2004). *Strategic management of e-business*. Milton, Australia: John Wiley & Sons.

Mckinney, E. H. Jr, Barker, J. R., Davis, K. J., & Smith, D. (2005). How Swift Starting Action Teams Get off the Ground: What United Flight 232 and Airline Flight Crews Can Tell Us About Team Communication. *Management Communication Quarterly*, *19*(2), 198–237. doi:10.1177/0893318905278539.

McQuarrie, E., & Mick, D. G. (1999). Visual rhetoric in advertising: Text-interpretive, experimental, and reader-response analyses. *The Journal of Consumer Research*, *26*(1), 37–54. doi:10.1086/209549.

McSweeney, B. (2002). Hofstede's Model of national cultural differences and their consequences: A triumph of faith – A failure of analysis. *Human Relations*, *55*(1), 89–118.

Mead, R. (2005). *International management: Cross-cultural dimensions*. London: Blackwell.

Meister, D. (1999). *The history of human factors and ergonomics*. Mahwah, NJ: Lawrence Erlbaum Associates.

Mendenhall, M. E., Dunbar, E., & Oddou, G. R. (1987). Expatriate selection, training, and career-pathing: A review and critique. *Human Resource Management*, *26*, 331–345. doi:10.1002/hrm.3930260303.

Mendenhall, M. E., & Oddou, G. R. (1985). The dimensions of expatriate acculturation: A review. *Academy of Management Review*, *10*(1), 39–47.

Meskaran, F., Abdullah, R., & Ghazali, M. (2010). A Conceptual Framework of Iranian Consumer Trust in B2C Electronic Commerce. *Computer and Information Science*, *3*(2), 126–139.

Meyer, K. E., Tran, Y. T. T., & Nguyen, H. V. (2006). Doing business in...Vietnam. *Thunderbird International Business Review*, *48*(2), 263–290. doi:10.1002/tie.20095.

Meziou, F. (1991). Areas of strength and weakness in the adoption of the marketing concept by small manufacturing firms. *Journal of Small Business Management*, *29*(4), 72–78.

Mick, D. G., & Buhl, C. (1992). A meaning-based model of advertising experiences. *The Journal of Consumer Research*, *19*(3), 317–338. doi:10.1086/209305.

Miles, M., & Huberman, M. (1994). *Qualitative data analysis: An expanded source book*. Thousand Oaks, CA: Sage Publications.

Miller, V., Johnson, J., & Grau, J. (1994). Antecedents to willingness to participate in a planned organizational change. *Journal of Applied Communication Research*, *22*, 59–80. doi:10.1080/00909889409365387.

Millman, T. F. (1996). Global account management and systems selling. *International Business Review*, *5*(6), 631–645. doi:10.1016/S0969-5931(96)00031-5.

Ministerio de Comercio. Industria y Turismo. (2008). *Reporte de Mipymes No. 03*. Retrieved July 22, 2009, from http://www.mincomercio.gov.co/econtent/Documentos/mipymes/2008/ReporteMipymes03.pdf

Ministero dello Sviluppo Economico & Interprofessionalnetwork (Ed.). (2010). *Dossier Cina. L'impresa verso i mercati internazionali*. Rome, Italy. Retrieved September 30, 2011, from http://www.sviluppoeconomico.gov.it/pdf_upload/documenti/Dossier_Cina.pdf

Ministry of Commerce. Industry and Tourism of Colombia. (2008). *Reporte de Mipymes No. 03*. Retrieved July 22, 2009, from http://www.mincomercio.gov.co/econtent/Documentos/mipymes/2008/ReporteMipymes03.pdf

Miniwatts Marketing Group. (2012). *Internet World Stats: Usage and Population Statistics; Top 20 Internet countries – 2012 Q1 with highest number of users*. Retrieved July 9, 2012, from http://www.internetworldstats.com/top20.htm

Mintzberg, H. (1992). *Structure in fives: Designing effective organizations*. Upper Saddle River, NJ: Prentice Hall.

Mintzberg, H. T. (1979). *The structuring of organizations*. Englewood Cliffs, NJ: Prentice-Hall.

MIT Massachusetts Institute of Technology. (2009). Advanced Managerial Communication. Retrieved from http://ocw.mit.edu/courses/sloan-school-of-management/

Mitchell, A. A. (1986). The effect of verbal and visual components of advertisements on brand attitudes and attitude towards the advertisement. *The Journal of Consumer Research*, *13*(June), 12–23. doi:10.1086/209044.

Mitchell, A. A., & Olson, J. C. (1981). Are product attribute beliefs the only mediator of advertising effects on brand attitude? *JMR, Journal of Marketing Research*, *18*(3), 318–332. doi:10.2307/3150973.

Mitchell, A., & Zigurs, I. (2009). Trust in virtual teams: Solved or still a mystery? *The Data Base for Advances in Information Systems*, *40*(3), 61–83. doi:10.1145/1592401.1592407.

Mitchell, D. J., Kahn, B. E., & Knasko, S. (1995). There's something in the Air: Effects of congruent or incongruent ambient odor on consumer decision making. *The Journal of Consumer Research*, *22*(September), 229–238. doi:10.1086/209447.

Mithas, S., Krishnan, M. S., & Fornell, C. (2005). Why do customer relationship management applications affect customer satisfaction. *Journal of Marketing*, *69*(4), 20209. doi:10.1509/jmkg.2005.69.4.201.

Mittleman, D. D., Briggs, R. O., & Nunamaker Jr., J. F. (2000). Best Practices In Facilitating Virtual Meetings: Some Notes From Initial Experience. *Group Facilitation: A Research And Applications Journal, 2*, 5-14.

Moe, N. B., Dingsoyr, T., & Dyba, T. (2009). Overcoming barriers to self-management in software teams. *IEEE Software*, *26*(6), 20–26. doi:10.1109/MS.2009.182.

Moen, Ø. (2002). The born globals: A new generation of small European exporters. *International Marketing Review*, *19*(2), 156–175. doi:10.1108/02651330210425015.

Moen, Ø., & Servais, P. (2002). Born global or gradual global? Examining the export behavior of small and medium-sized enterprises. *Journal of International Marketing*, *10*(3), 49–72. doi:10.1509/jimk.10.3.49.19540.

Mohd Yusof, S. A., & Zakaria, N. (2012). Exploring the State of Discipline on the Formation of Swift Trust within Global Virtual Teams. In *Proceedings of 45th Hawaii International Conference on System Sciences.* Hawaii: IEEE.

Mok, K.-H., & Welch, A. R. (2003a). Globalisation, structural adjustment and educational reform. In Mok, K.-H., & Welch, A. R. (Eds.), *Globalisation and Educational Restructuring in the Asia Pacific Region* (pp. 1–31). Basingstoke, UK: Palgrave Macmillan. doi:10.1057/9781403990488.

Mok, K.-H., & Welch, A. R. (Eds.). (2003b). *Globalisation and Educational Restructuring in the Asia Pacific Region*. Basingstoke, UK: Palgrave Macmillan. doi:10.1057/9781403990488.

Möller, J., & Eisend, M. (2010). A Global Investigation into the Cultural and Individual Antecedents of Banner Advertising Effectiveness. *Journal of International Marketing*, *18*(2), 80–98. doi:10.1509/jimk.18.2.80.

Monash University. (2010). *Managerial Communication*. Retrieved on November 20, 2011, from http://www.monash.edu.au/Munter, M. (2011). *Guide to Managerial Communication* (8th ed.). Upper Saddle River, NJ: Prentice Hall.

Monteiro, L. F., Arvidsson, N., & Birkinshaw, J. (2008). Knowledge Flows Within Multinational Corporations: Explaining Subsidiary Isolation and Its Performance Implications. *Organization Science*, *19*(1), 90–107. doi:10.1287/orsc.1070.0264.

Montoya, M., Massey, A. P., & Lockwood, N. S. (2011). 3D Collaborative Virtual Environments: Exploring the Link between Collaborative Behaviors and Team Performance. *Decision Sciences*, *42*(2), 451–476. doi:10.1111/j.1540-5915.2011.00318.x.

Montoya-Weiss, M. M., Massey, A. P., & Song, M. (2001). Getting It Together: Temporal Coordination And Conflict Management In Global Virtual Teams. *Academy of Management Journal*, , 1251–1262. doi:10.2307/3069399.

Moore, C. D. (1987). Outclass the competition with service distinction. *Mortgage Banking*, *47*(11), 24–32.

Moorthy, S., & Zhao, H. (2000). Advertising spending and perceived quality. *Marketing Letters*, *11*(3), 221–233. doi:10.1023/A:1008135126025.

Morcillo, P. & Garces, I. (N. Y.). *The cultural organization model: A review of the organizational culture literature.* Retrieved on June 14, 2012 fromhttp://patriciomorcillo.com/publicacion4.pdf

Morgan, D. L. (1988). *Focus groups as qualitative research*. London: Sage.

Morgan, G. (1997). *Images of organization* (2nd ed.). Sage Publications, Inc..

Morozov, E. (2009). Texting toward utopia: Does the Internet spread democracy? *Boston Review*, March/April. Retrieved from http://bostonreview.net/BR34.2/morozov.php

Morris, M. H., Davis, D. L., & Allen, J. W. (1994). Fostering Corporate Entrepreneurship: Cross-Cultural Comparisons of the Importance of Individualism Versus Collectivism. *Journal of International Business Studies*, *25*(1), 65–89. doi:10.1057/palgrave.jibs.8490849.

Morris, S. S., Snell, S. A., & Wright, P. M. (2005). A resource-based view of international human resources: Towards a framework of integrative and creative capabilities. In Bjorkman, I., & Stahl, G. (Eds.), *Handbook of Research into International HRM*. London, UK: Edward Elgar.

Mueller, B. (1987). Reflections of Culture: An Analysis of Japanese and American Advertising Appeals. *Journal of Advertising Research*, *27*(June/July), 51–59.

Mueller, J. (2012). The Interactive Relationship of Corporate Culture and Knowledge Management: A Review. *Review of Managerial Science*, *6*(2), 183–201. doi:10.1007/s11846-010-0060-3.

Mukerjee, K. (2007). *Customer Relationship Management –A Strategic approach to marketing*. Prentice Hall of India.

Mukherjee, D., Lahiri, S., & Billing, T. K. (2012). Leading Virtual Teams: How Do Social, Cognitive, And Behavioral Capabilities Matter? *Management Decision*, *50*, 6–6. doi:10.1108/00251741211203560.

Mumford, E., Hickey, S., & Matthies, H. (2006). *Designing Human Systems – An agile approach to ETHICS*. Morrisville, NC: Lulu Press.

Murphy, J., & Scharl, A. (2007). An investigation of global versus local online branding. *International Marketing Review*, *24*(3), 297–312. doi:10.1108/02651330710755302.

Murphy, K. R., & Saal, F. E. (1990). What should we expect from scientist-practitioners? In Murphy, K. R., & Saal, F. E. (Eds.), *Psychology in organizations: Integrating science and practice*. Hillsdale, NJ: Erlbaum.

Murray, P. (2000). Designing Business Benefits from Knowledge Management. In Despres, C., & Chauvel, D. (Eds.), *The Present and the Promise of Knowledge Management*. Boston, MA: Butterworth-Heinemann.

Murray, P., & Meyers, A. (1997). The Facts about Knowledge. *Information Strategy*, *2*(7), 29–33.

Murugesan, S. (2010). *Intelligence and value*. Retrieved on October 21, 2012, from http://alinement.net/component /content/ article/6-governance/62-intelligence-a-value

Musso, F. (2008). *La Cina come mercato: prospettive, vincoli, illusioni*. Paper presented at the Conference Cina e oltre. Piccola e media impresa fra innovazione e internazionalizzazione. Lodi, Italy.

Myers, M. D. (2009). *Qualitative Research in Business and Management*. Los Angeles, CA: Sage Publications.

Myers, M. D., & Tan, F. (2002). Beyond models of national culture in information systems research. *Journal of Global Information Management*, *10*(1), 24–32. doi:10.4018/jgim.2002010103.

Nacar, R., & Burnaz, S. (2011). A cultural content analysis of multinational companies' web sites. *Qualitative Market Research: An International Journal*, *14*(3), 274–288. doi:10.1108/13522751111137505.

Nahapiet, J., & Ghoshal, S. (1998). Social Capital, Intellectual Capital, and The Organizational Advantage. *Academy of Management Review*, *23*(2), 242–266.

Nakata, C., & Sivakumar, K. (1996). National Culture and New Product Development: An Integrative Review. *Journal of Marketing*, *60*(1), 61–72. doi:10.2307/1251888.

Nakata, C., & Sivakumar, K. (2001). Instituting the Marketing Concept in a Multinational Setting: The Role of National Culture. *Journal of the Academy of Marketing Science*, *29*(3), 255–275. doi:10.1177/03079459994623.

Narver, J. C., & Slater, S. F. (1990). The effect of a market orientation on business profitability. *Journal of Marketing*, *54*(4), 20–35. doi:10.2307/1251757.

National Italian Institute of Statistics. (2011). The resident foreign population in Italy. *Istat.it*. Retrieved from http://www.istat.it/it/archivio/39726

NCSSH. (2001). National Human Development Report 2001: Doi Moi and Human Development in Vietnam. Hanoi, Vietnam: The Political Publishing House.

Neely, A., Gregory, M., & Platts, K. (1995). Performance measurement systems design: A literature review and research agenda. *International Journal of Operations & Production Management*, *15*(4), 80–116. doi:10.1108/01443579510083622.

Nelson, R. R., & Phelps, E. S. (1966). Investment in humans, technological diffusion, and economic growth. *The American Economic Review*, *56*(1), 69–75.

Nesbit, P. L. (2002). Opportunities And Developments Of Hrm Within The E-Business Environment. *Employment Relations Record*, *2*, 41–52.

Netemeyer, R. G., Bearden, W. O., & Sharma, S. (2003). *Scaling Procedures: Issues and Applications*. Thousand Oaks, CA: Sage.

Neuendorf, K. A. (2001). *The Content Analysis Guidebook*. Thousand Oaks, CA: Sage Publications.

Neuendorf, K. A. (2005). *The Content Analysis Guidebook*. London: Sage.

Neupert, K., Baughn, C., & Dao, T. (2005). International management skills for success in Asia: A needs-based determination of skills for foreign managers and local managers. *Journal of European Industrial Training*, *29*(2), 165–180. doi:10.1108/03090590510585118.

New Zealand Trade & Enterprise. (2007). *Market Profile for Food and Beverage Retail in China*. Retrieved from www.ntze.govt.nz

Newburry, W., Belkin, L. Y., & Ansari, P. (2008). Perceived career opportunities from globalization: Globalization capabilities and attitudes towards women in Iran and the US. *Journal of International Business Studies*, *39*(5), 814–832. doi:10.1057/palgrave.jibs.8400335.

Newman, K. L., & Nollen, S. D. (1996). Culture and congruence: The fit between management practices and national culture. *Journal of International Business Studies*, *27*(4), 753–779. doi:10.1057/palgrave.jibs.8490152.

Newman, K., & Nollen, S. D. (1996). Culture and Congruence: The Fit between Management Practices and National Culture. *Journal of International Business Studies*, *27*(4), 753–779. doi:10.1057/palgrave.jibs.8490152.

News, B. B. C. (2009). *Firms move production back to UK*. Retrieved on October 26, 2012, from http://news.bbc.co.uk/go/pr/fr/-/2/hi/business/8434458.stm

News, B. B. C. (2010b), *London-to-Birmingham high speed train route announced*. Retrieved on October 26, 2012, from http://www.bbc.co.uk/news/uk-politics-12035524

Ngok, K.-l., & Kwong, J. (2003). Globalisation and educational restructuring in China. In Mok, K.-H., & Welch, A. R. (Eds.), *Globalisation and Educational Restructuring in the Asia Pacific Region* (pp. 160–188). Basingstoke, UK: Palgrave Macmillan.

Nguyen, H. N., & Mohamed, S. (2011). Leadership Behaviors. *Organizational Culture and Knowledge Management Practices*, *30*(2), 206–221.

Nguyen, N. T. D., Takanashi, C., & Aoyama, A. (2012). Can Efficient Technology Transfer Be Achieved through a Hybrid Corporate Culture? A Study on Japanese Manufacturing Subsidiaries in Vietnam. *International Journal of Business and Management*, *7*(7), 24–39.

Nickels, W. G., McHugh, J. M., & McHugh, S. M. (2010). *Understanding Business* (9th ed.). New York: McGraw Hill.

Nielsen, J. F., Høst, V., Jaensson, J.-E., Kock, S., & Selnes, F. (2003). Market orientation in Nordic banks: Does nationality matter? *European Journal of Marketing*, *37*(11/12), 1818–1841. doi:10.1108/03090560310495474.

Niemi, T., Nummenmaa, J., & Thanisch, P. (2003). Normalising OLAP cubes for controlling sparsity. *Data & Knowledge Engineering*, *46*, 317–343. doi:10.1016/S0169-023X(03)00035-1.

Nitsch, D., Beamish, P. W., & Makino, S. (1996). Entry mode and performance of Japanese FDI in Western Europe. *Management International Review*, *36*(1), 27–34.

Nohria, N., & Ghoshal, S. (1997). *The differentiated Network: Organizing multinational corporations for value creation*. San Francisco, CA: Jossey-Bass Publishers.

Nohria, N., Prichard, C., Hull, R., Chumer, M., & Willmostt, H. (Eds.), *ManagingKnwowledge: Critical Investigations of Work and Learning*. Macmillan Business.

Nonaka, I. (1991). The Knowledge Creating Company. *Harvard Business Review*, 96–104.

Nonaka, I. (1994). A Dynamic Theory of Organizational Knowledge Creation. *Organization Science*, *5*(1), 14–37. doi:10.1287/orsc.5.1.14.

Nonaka, I., & Konno, N. (1998). The Concept of 'Ba': Building a Foundation for Knowledge Creation. *California Management Review*, *40*(3), 40–54. doi:10.2307/41165942.

Nonaka, I., & Takeuchi, H. (1995). *The Knowledge Creating Company*. New York: Oxford University Press.

Nonaka, I., & Takeuchi, H. (1996). Theory of organizational knowledge creation. *International Journal of Technology Management*, *11*(7-8), 833.

Nonaka, I., & Takeuchi, H. (2011). The Wise Leader. *Harvard Business Review*, *89*(5), 58–67. PMID:21548419.

Nonaka, I., Toyama, R., & Konno, N. (2000). SECI, "Ba" and Leadership: A Unified Model of Dynamic Knowledge Creation. *Long Range Planning*, *33*, 5–34. doi:10.1016/S0024-6301(99)00115-6.

Noon, M. (2010). The shackled runner: Time to rethink positive discrimination? *Work, Employment and Society*, *24*(4), 728–739. doi:10.1177/0950017010380648.

Nordhaug, I., & Nordhaug, O. (2004). Omstillingtil et mangfoldingarbeidsliv. *Magma (New York, N.Y.)*, 4.

Nordström, K. (1991). *The internationalization process of the firm - Searching for new patterns and explanations*. Doctoral dissertation. Stockholm School of Economic, Stockholm, Sweden.

North Staffordshire Regeneration Partnership Business Plan 2009-12. (2009). *"Stoke-on-Trent City Centre Partnership Business Plan 2009-2012*. Retrieved on October 26, 2012, from http://www.atcm.org/uploads/DOCS/553-Stoke_CCP_Bcapital_Plan_09_-_12_low_resolution.pdf

Nummela, N., Saarenketo, S., & Puumalainen, K. (2004). A global mindset – A prerequisite for successful internationalization? *Canadian Journal of Administrative Sciences*, *21*(1), 51–64. doi:10.1111/j.1936-4490.2004.tb00322.x.

Nunnally, J. C., & Bernstein, I. H. (1994). *Psychometric Theory* (3rd ed.). New York: McGraw Hill.

Nurluoz, O., & Birol, C. (2011). The Impact of Knowledge Management and Technology: An Analysis of Administrative Behaviors. *The Turkish Online Journal of Educational Technology*, *10*(1), 202–208.

Nyambegera, S. M. (2009). The ethnic factor in IHRM: A research agenda. In Sparrow, P. (Ed.), *Handbook of International Human Resource Management: Integrating people, process and context*. London, UK: John Wiley & Sons.

O'Keefe, D. J. (2003). Message properties, mediating states, and manipulation checks: Claims, evidence, and data analysis in experimental persuasive message effects research. *Communication Theory*, *13*(3), 251–274. doi:10.1111/j.1468-2885.2003.tb00292.x.

O'Leary-Kelly, S. W., & Vokurka, R. J. (1998). The empirical assessment of construct validity. *Journal of Operations Management*, *16*(4), 387–405. doi:10.1016/S0272-6963(98)00020-5.

O'Leary, M. B., & Cummings, J. N. (2007). The spatial, temporal and configurational characteristics of geographic dispersion of teams. *Management Information Systems Quarterly*, *31*(3), 433–452.

Oddou, G., & Mendenhall, G. (1991). Succession planning for the 21st century: How well are we grooming our future business leaders? *Business Horizons*, *34*, 26–34. doi:10.1016/0007-6813(91)90078-A.

O'Donnell, S. W. (2000). Managing Foreign Subsidiaries: Agents of Headquarters, or An Interdependent Network? *Strategic Management Journal*, *21*, 525–548. doi:10.1002/(SICI)1097-0266(200005)21:5<525::AID-SMJ104>3.0.CO;2-Q.

Ojasalo, J. (2001). Key account management at company and individual levels in business-to-business relationships. *Journal of Business and Industrial Marketing*, *16*(3), 199–220. doi:10.1108/08858620110389803.

Okazaki, S. (2004). Do multinationals standardise or localise? The cross-cultural dimensionality of product-based Web sites. *Internet Research*, *14*(1), 81–94. doi:10.1108/10662240410516336.

Okazaki, S. (2005). Searching the web for global brands: how American brands standardise their web sites in Europe. *European Journal of Marketing*, *39*(1/2), 87–109. doi:10.1108/03090560510572034.

Okazaki, S., & Rivas, J. A. (2002). A content analysis of multinationals' Web communication strategies: Cross-cultural research framework and pre-testing. *Internet Research*, *12*(5), 380–390. doi:10.1108/10662240210447137.

Okazaki, S., & Skapa, R. (2008). Global web site standardization in the new EU member states: Initial observations from Poland and the Czech Republic. *European Journal of Marketing*, *42*(11/12), 1224–1245. doi:10.1108/03090560810903655.

Oldfield, B., & Baron, S. (2000). Student perceptions of service quality in a UK university business and management faculty. *Quality Assurance in Education*, *8*(2), 85–95. doi:10.1108/09684880010325600.

O'leary, M., & Mortensen, M. (2011). *Go (Con) Figure: Subgroups*. Imbalance, And Isolates In Geographically Dispersed Teams.

Oner, H., Surgevil, O., Kaya, E., & Özbilgin, M. (2012). Leveraging global diversity through management strategies at Ceva Logistics. In Scott, C. L., & Byrd, M. Y. (Eds.), *Handbook of Research on Workforce Diversity in a Global Society: Technologies and Concepts*. doi:10.4018/978-1-4666-1812-1.ch018.

Oracle. (2011, August). *Oracle open world*. Retrieved from http://blogs.oracle.com/oracleopenworld/. (2011, September 12).

Osservatorio Italia Cina. (2011). *La Cina nel 2011*. Milano, Italy: Fondazione Italia Cina.

Otley, D. (1997). Better performance management. *Management Accounting, 44*.

Otley, D. (1980). The contingency theory of management accounting: Achievement and progress. *Accounting, Organizations and Society*, *5*(4), 413–428. doi:10.1016/0361-3682(80)90040-9.

Otley, D. (1999). Performance management: A framework for management control systems research. *Management Accounting Research*, *10*, 363–382. doi:10.1006/mare.1999.0115.

Ouchi, W. (1981). *Theory Z: How American business can meet the Japanese challenge*. Boston, MA: Addison-Wesley. doi:10.1016/0007-6813(81)90031-8.

Ouintas, P., Lefrere, P., & Jones, G. (1997). Knowledge Management: A Strategic Agenda. *Long Range Planning*, *30*(3), 91–385.

Oviatt, B. M., & McDougall, P. P. (1995). Global start-ups: Entrepreneurs on a worldwide stage. *The Academy of Management Executive*, *9*(2), 30–44.

Oviatt, B., & McDougall, P. (1994). Toward a theory of international new ventures. *Journal of International Business Studies*, *25*(1), 45–64. doi:10.1057/palgrave.jibs.8490193.

Oviatt, B., & McDougall, P. (1997). Challenges for internationalization process theory: The case of international new ventures. *Management International Review*, *37*, 23–40.

Özbilgin, M., Jonsen, K., Tatli, A., Surgevil, O., & Vassilopoulou, J. (in press). Global diversity management. In Roberson, Q. (Ed.), *Oxford Handbook of Research on Diversity in the Workplace*. Oxford, UK: Oxford University Press. doi:10.4135/9781412982764.n23.

Ozbilgin, M., & Tatli, A. (2008). *Global Diversity Management: An Evidence-Based Approach*. London: Palgrave Macmillan.

Oz, E. (2009). *Management Information Systems* (6th ed.). Boston, MA: Thomson Publishing.

Paap, J., & Katz, R. (2004). Anticipating Disruptive Innovation. *Research Technology Management*, *47*(5), 13–22.

Pagell, M., Katz, J. P., & Sheu, C. (2005). The importance of national culture in operations management research. *International Journal of Operations & Production Management*, *25*(4), 371–394. doi:10.1108/01443570510585552.

Palanisamy, R. (2008). Organizational Culture and Knowledge Management in ERP Implementation: An Empirical Study. *Journal of Computer Information Systems*, *48*(2), 100–119.

Panaccio, A.-J., & Waxin, M.-F. (2010). HRM case study: Diversity management: Facilitating diversity through the recruitment, selection and integration of diverse employees in a Quebec bank. *Journal of the International Academy for Case Studies.*, *16*(4), 53–66.

Pan, Y., & Chi, P. S. K. (1999). Financial performance and survival of multinational corporations in China. *Strategic Management Journal*, *20*(4), 359–374. doi:10.1002/(SICI)1097-0266(199904)20:4<359::AID-SMJ31>3.0.CO;2-9.

Pan, Y., & Tse, D. K. (2000). The hierarchical model of market entry modes. *Journal of International Business Studies*, *31*(4), 535–554. doi:10.1057/palgrave.jibs.8490921.

Papadopoulos, N. (1987). Approaches to international market selection for small and medium sized enterprises. In Rosson, P., & Reid, S. (Eds.), *Managing Export Entry and Expansion* (pp. 128–158). New York: Praeger Publishers.

Pappu, R., Quester, P. G., & Cooksey, R. W. (2006). Consumer-based brand equity and country-of-origin relationships: Some empirical evidence. *European Journal of Marketing*, *40*(5/6), 696–717. doi:10.1108/03090560610657903.

Parasuraman, A., Zeithaml, V. A., & Berry, L. L. (1985). A conceptual model of service quality and its implications for future research. *Journal of Marketing*, *49*(4), 41–50. doi:10.2307/1251430.

Parasuraman, A., Zeithaml, V. A., & Berry, L. L. (1988). SERVQUAL: A multiple-item scale for measuring consumer perceptions of service quality. *Journal of Retailing*, *64*(1), 12–40.

Parasuraman, A., Zeithaml, V. A., & Berry, L. L. (1994). Reassessment of expectations as a comparison standard in measuring service quality - Implications for further research. *Journal of Marketing*, *58*(1), 111–124. doi:10.2307/1252255.

Pardillo, J., Mazon, J. N., & Trujillo, J. (2010). Extending OCL for OLAP querying on conceptual multidimensional models of data warehouses. *Information Sciences*, *180*, 584–601. doi:10.1016/j.ins.2009.11.006.

Pardo, C., Stephan, C., Henneberg, S. M., & Naudè, P. (2006). Unpicking the meaning of value in key account management. *European Journal of Marketing*, *40*(11/12), 1360–1374. doi:10.1108/03090560610702858.

Park, C. L., & Jun, J.-K. (2003). A cross-cultural comparison of Internet buying behavior: Effects of Internet usage, perceived risks, and innovativeness. *International Marketing Review*, *20*(5), 534–553. doi:10.1108/02651330310498771.

Parker, B. (1998). Exploring life themes and myths in alcohol advertisements through a meaning-based model of advertising experiences. *Journal of Advertising*, *27*(1), 97–112.

Park, H., Ribiere, V., & Schulte, W. D. Jr. (2004). Critical Attributes of Organizational Culture that Promote Knowledge Management Technology Implementation Success. *Journal of Knowledge Management*, *8*(3), 106–117. doi:10.1108/13673270410541079.

Parvatiyar, A., & Sheth, J. (2002). *Handbook of Relationship Marketing*. Response Book.

Pascale, R. T., & Athos, A. G. (1982). *The art of Japanese management: Applications for american executives*. Warner Books.

Pauleen, D. (2004). *Virtual Teams: Projects, Protocols And Processes*. Hershey, PA: IGI Global.

Pauleen, D. J. (2003). Lessons Learned Crossing Boundaries In An Ict-Supported Distributed Team. *Journal of Global Information Management*, *11*, 1–19. doi:10.4018/jgim.2003100101.

Pauwels, L. (2012). A Multimodal Framework for Analyzing Websites as Cultural Expressions. *Journal of Computer-Mediated Communication*, *17*, 247–265. doi:10.1111/j.1083-6101.2012.01572.x.

Payne, A., & Frow, P. (2005). A Strategic Framework for Customer Relationship Management. *Journal of Marketing*, *69*(October), 167–176. doi:10.1509/jmkg.2005.69.4.167.

Peansupap, V. (2004). An Exploratory Approach To The Diffusion Of Ict In A Project Environment.

Pearlson, K. E. (2001). *Managing and using Information Systems: A Strategic Approach*. New York: John Wiley & Sons.

Pearlson, K. E., & Saunders, C. S. (2010). *Managing and Using Information Systems* (4th ed.). Hoboken, NJ: John Wiley & Sons, Inc..

Pegan, G. (2011). Il made in Italy in Cina: Un quadro di sintesi. In Vescovi, T. (Ed.), *Libellule sul drago. Modelli di business e strategie di marketing per le imprese italiane in Cina*. Padova, Italy: Cedam.

Pelham, A., & Wilson, D. T. (1996). A longitudinal study of the impact of market structure, firm structure, strategy and market orientation culture on dimensions of performance. *Journal of the Academy of Marketing Science*, *24*(1), 27–43. doi:10.1007/BF02893935.

Peñarroja, V., Orengo, V., Zornoza, A., & Hernández, A. (2013). The Effects Of Virtuality Level On Task-Related Collaborative Behaviors: The Mediating Role Of Team Trust. *Computers in Human Behavior*, *29*, 967–974. doi:10.1016/j.chb.2012.12.020.

People's Daily. (2006). Few firms in Vietnam keen on e-commerce: Survey. Retrieved July 3, 2012, from http://english.peopledaily.com.cn/200602/09/eng20060209_241189.html

Peppers, D., Rogers, M., & Dorf, B. (1999). Is Your Company Ready for One-to-One Marketing? *Harvard Business Review*, *77*, 151–160. PMID:10345390.

Perea, A., & Slater, M. (1999). Power Distance and Collectivist/Individualist Strategies in Alcohol Warnings: Effects by Gender and Ethnicity. *Journal of Health Communication*, *4*, 295–310. doi:10.1080/108107399126832 PMID:10790786.

Pervin, L. A. (1986). *Personality – Theory and Research* (5th ed.). New York: John Wiley and Sons.

Peters, L. M., & Manz, C. C. (2007). Identifying Antecedents Of Virtual Team Collaboration. *Team Performance Management*, *13*, 117–129. doi:10.1108/13527590710759865.

Peterson, N. G., Mumford, M. D., Borman, W. C., Jeanneret, P. R., & Fleishman, E. A. (1999). *The occupation information network*. Washington, DC: American Psychological Association.

Peterson, N. G., Mumford, M. D., Borman, W. C., Jeanneret, P. R., Fleishman, E. A., & Levin, K. Y. et al. (2001). Understanding work using the occupational information network: Implications for practice and research. *Personnel Psychology*, *54*, 451–492. doi:10.1111/j.1744-6570.2001.tb00100.x.

Peters, T., & Waterman, R. H. Jr. (1982). *In search of excellence: Lessons from America best-run companies*. New York: HarperCollins.

Phillips, N. (1992). *Managing international teams*. London: Pitman.

Phythian, G. J., & King, M. (1992). Developing an Expert System for Tender Enquiry Evaluation: A Case Study. *European Journal of Operational Research*, *56*(1), 15–29. doi:10.1016/0377-2217(92)90289-L.

Piccoli, G., Powell, A., & Ives, B. (2004). Virtual Teams: Team Control Structure, Work Processes, And Team Effectiveness. *Information Technology & People*, *17*, 359–379. doi:10.1108/09593840410570258.

Pickle, L., & Dinh, T. T. V. (2009). A comparative study of Vietnamese and American customers' behaviour in negotiation style. *Global Journal of International Business Research*, *2*(2), 37–50.

Piekkari, R. M., Welch, D., & Welch, L. (1999). Adapting a common corporate language: IHRM implications. *The International Journal of International Human Resource Management.*, *10*(3), 377–390. doi:10.1080/095851999340387.

Pike, R. (1954). *Language in relation to a united theory of the structure of human behaviour*. Glendale, AZ: Summer Institute of Linguistics.

Pinto, A. & P. (2011). Leveraging the power of differences workforce diversity. *SCMS Journal of Indian Management*, 27-39.

Pitariu, H. D. (1992). I/O psychology in Romania: Past, present and intentions. *The Industrial-Organizational Psychologist*, *29*(4), 29–33.

Pizam, A., & Reichel, A. (1997). Nationality versus industry cultures: Which has greater effect on managerial behaviour? *International Journal of Hospitality Management*, *16*(2), 127–145. doi:10.1016/S0278-4319(97)00001-7.

Plummer, J. T. (1985). Brand personality: A strategic concept for multinational advertising. In *Marketing Educators' Conference* (pp. 1–31). New York: Young and Rubicam.

Podsakoff, P. M., & Organ, D. W. (1986). Self-reports in organizational research: Problems and prospects. *Journal of Management*, *12*(4), 531–544. doi:10.1177/014920638601200408.

Poe, A. C. (2002). Selection savvy. *HRMagazine*, *47*(4), 77–83.

Poell, R. F., Chivers, G. E., Van Der Krogt, F. J., & Wildemeersch, D. A. (2000). Learning-Network Theory: Organizing the Dynamic Relationships between Learning and Work. *Management Learning*, *31*(1), 25–49. doi:10.1177/1350507600311004.

Poister, T., & Streib, G. (1999). Performance measurement in municipal government: Assessing the state of the practice. *Public Administration Review*, *59*(4), 325–335. doi:10.2307/3110115.

Polanyi, M. (1958). *Personal knowledge; Towards a post-critical philosophy*. Chicago, IL: University of Chicago Press.

Politis, J. D. (2001). The Relationship of Various Leadership Styles to Knowledge Management. *Leadership and Organization Development Journal*, *22*, 355–364. doi:10.1108/01437730110410071.

Politis, J. D. (2002). Transformational and Transactional Leadership Enabling (Disabling) Knowledge Acquisition of Self-Managed Teams: the Consequence for Performance. *Leadership and Organization Development Journal*, 23.

Politis, J. D. (2004). Transformational and Transactional Leadership Predictors of the 'Stimulant' Determinants to Creativity in Organizational Work Environments. *Electronic Journal of Knowledge Management*, *2*, 23–34.

Pollach, I. (2011). The Readership of Corporate Websites. *Journal of Business Communication*, *48*(1), 27–53. doi:10.1177/0021943610385657.

Pollaned, R., & Abdel-Makoud, A. (2010). (Forthcoming). Deployment of contemporary management accounting practices in Canadian firms: A contingency approach. *International Journal of Managerial and Financial Management*.

Pollanen, R., & Maheshwari, B. (2007). Performance measurement and organizational change management. In Abdel-Maksoud, A., & Abdel-Kader, M. (Eds.), *Non-Financial Performance Measurement and Management Practices in Manufacturing Firms: A Comparative International Analysis* (pp. 273–303). Oxford, UK: Elsevier.

Porter, L. W., & Lawler, E. E. (1968). *Managerial attitudes and performance*. Homewood, IL: Dorsey Press.

Porter, M. (1985). *Competitive Advantage: Creating and Sustaining Superior Performance*. New York: Free Press.

Posada, M. (2012, June 13). *Colombia's FDI Profile*. Retrieved October 29, 2012, from http://www.vcc.columbia.edu/files/vale/documents/Colombia_IFDI_-_FINAL_-_13_June_2012.pdf

Posada, M. (2012, June 13). *Inward FDI in Colombia and its policy context, 2012*. Retrieved August 7, 2012, from http://www.vcc.columbia.edu/files/vale/documents/Colombia_IFDI_-_FINAL_-_13_June_2012.pdf

Powell, A., Piccoli, G., & Ives, B. (2004). Virtual teams: A review of current literature and directions for future research. *The Data Base for Advances in Information Systems*, *35*(1), 6–36. doi:10.1145/968464.968467.

Prahalad, C. K., & Hamel, G. (1990). The Core Competence of the Corporation. *Harvard Business Review*, *68*(3), 79–91.

Prahalad, C. K., & Hammond, A. (2002). Serving the World's Poor, Profitably. *Harvard Business Review*, *80*(9), 48–57. PMID:12227146.

Prahalad, C. K., & Ramaswamy, V. (2003). The New Frontier of Experience Innovation. *MIT Sloan School of Management*, *44*(4), 12–18.

Prahalad, C., & Krishnah, H. (2008). *The New Age of Innovation*. New York: McGraw Hill.

Prasad, K., & Akhilesh, K. (2002). Global Virtual Teams: What Impacts Their Design And Performance? *Team Performance Management*, *8*, 102–112. doi:10.1108/13527590210442212.

Prasad, K., & Akhilesh, K. B. (2002). Global virtual teams: What impacts their design and Performance? *Team Performance Management*, *8*(5/6), 102–112. doi:10.1108/13527590210442212.

Prikladnicki, R., Audy, J. L. N., & Shull, F. (2010). Patterns in effective distributed software development. *IEEE Software*, *27*(2), 12–15. doi:10.1109/MS.2010.48.

Prior, J. B., & Whalen, N. J. (1997). A Typology of Sexual Harassment: Characteristics of Harassers and the Social Circumstances under Which Sexual Harassment Occurs.W. O'Donohue (Ed.), In Sexual Harassment: Theory, Research, and Treatment. Boston, MA: Allyn & Bacon.

Proexport Colombia (2010). Foreign Direct Investment Report in Colombia. Retrieved on July 26, 2012, from http://www.bnamericas.com/cgi-bin/getresearch?report=157029.pdf&documento=1120796&idioma=I&login

Pucik, V. (2007). Reframing global mindset: From thinking to acting. In Schuler, R. S., & Jackson, S. E. (Eds.), *Strategic human resource management* (2nd ed., pp. 200–213). Hoboken, NJ: Blackwell Publishing.

Punch, K. F. (2005). *Introduction to Social Research: Quantitative and Qualitative Approaches*. London: Sage.

Puntoni, S., Schroeder, J. E., & Ritson, M. (2010). Meaning Matters Polysemy in Advertising. *Journal of Advertising*, *39*(2), 51–64. doi:10.2753/JOA0091-3367390204.

Qiang, C. Z., Clarke, G. R., & Halewood, N. (2006). *The Role of ICT in Doing Business*. Washington, DC: World Bank.

Qiu, Y. (2005). Problems of Managing Joint Ventures in China's Interior: Evidence from Shaanxi. *SAM Advanced Management Journal*, (Summer), 46-57.

Raghunathan, T. S., Subba Rao, S., & Solis, L. E. (1997). A Comparative Study of Quality Practices: USA, China and India. *Industrial Management & Data Systems*, *97*(5), 192–202. doi:10.1108/02635579710367270.

Rai, R. K. (2011). *Knowledge Management and Organizational Culture: A Theoretical Integrative Framework.*, *15*(5), 779-801.

Ralston, D. A., Holt, D. H., Terpstra, R. H., & Kai-Cheng, Y. (1997). The impact of national culture and economic ideology on managerial work values: A study of the United States, Russia, Japan, and China. *Journal of International Business Studies*, *28*(1), 177–207. doi:10.1057/palgrave.jibs.8490097.

Ralston, D. A., Nguyen, V. T., & Napier, N. K. (1999). A Comparative Study of the Work Values of North and South Vietnamese Managers. *Journal of International Business Studies*, *30*(4), 655–672. doi:10.1057/palgrave.jibs.8490889.

Ramesh, V., & Dennis, A. R. (2002). The Object-Oriented Team: Lessons For Virtual Teams From Global Software Development (pp. 212-221).

Ranjan, J. (2009). Business intelligence: Concepts, components, techniques and benefits. *Journal of Theoretical and Applied Information Technology*, *9*(1), 60–70.

Rappaport, J. (1993). Narrative Studies, Personal Stories and Identity Transformation in the Mutual Help Context. *The Journal of Applied Behavioral Science*, *29*(2), 239–256. doi:10.1177/0021886393292007.

Rastogi, P. N. (2000). Knowledge Management and Intellectual Capital – The New Virtuous Realty of Competitiveness. *Hum Systems Manage*, *19*(1), 39–49.

Ravichandram, T. (2000). Quality management and systems development: An organizational system perspecitive. *Management Information Systems Quarterly*, *24*(3), 381–415. doi:10.2307/3250967.

Rayport, J., & Jaworski, B. (2001). *E-Commerce*. New York: McGraw-Hill.

Reason, P., & Rowan, J. (Eds.). (1981). *Human Inquiry – A Sourcebook of New Paradigm Research*. Chichester, UK: John Wiley and Sons.

Reed, A. H., & Knight, L. V. (2010). Effect Of A Virtual Project Team Environment On Communication-Related Project Risk. *International Journal of Project Management*, *28*, 422–427. doi:10.1016/j.ijproman.2009.08.002.

Reeves, C. A., & Bednar, D. A. (1994). Defining Quality: Alternatives and Implications. *Academy of Management Review*, *19*(3), 419–445.

Rehder, R. R. (1989). Japanese transplants: In search of a balanced and broader perspective. *The Columbia Journal of World Business*, *24*(4), 17–28.

Reich, B. H., Gemino, A., & Sauer, C. (2012). Knowledge Management and Project-based Knowledge in IT Projects: A Model and Preliminary Empirical Results. *International Journal of Project Management*, *30*, 663–674. doi:10.1016/j.ijproman.2011.12.003.

Reiche, B. S. (2011). Knowledge transfer in multinationals: The role of inpatriates' boundary spanning. *Human Resource Management*, *50*(3), 365–389. doi:10.1002/hrm.20423.

Reiche, B. S. (2012). Knowledge benefits of social capital upon repatriation: A longitudinal study of international assignees. *Journal of Management Studies*, *49*(6), 1052–1077. doi:10.1111/j.1467-6486.2012.01050.x.

Reinhardt, W., Schmidt, B., Sloep, P., & Drachsler, H. (2011). Knowledge Worker Roles and Actions – Results of Two Empirical Studies. *Knowledge and Process Management*, *18*(3), 150–174. doi:10.1002/kpm.378.

Rezgui, Y. (2001). Review Of Information And The State Of The Art Of Knowledge Management Practices In The Construction Industry. *The Knowledge Engineering Review*, *16*, 241–254. doi:10.1017/S026988890100008X.

Rezgui, Y., & Zarli, A. (2006). Paving The Way To The Vision Of Digital Construction: A Strategic Roadmap. *Journal of Construction Engineering and Management*, *132*, 767. doi:10.1061/(ASCE)0733-9364(2006)132:7(767).

Rialp, A. (1999). *Los Enfoques Micro-organizativos de la Internacionalización de la Empresa: Una Revisión y Síntesis de la Literatura. Información Comercial Española* (ICE), *October*(781), 17-128.

RIAP. (2003). *BICA Report 2003 (Building Institutional Capacity in Asia - Project commissioned by the Ministry of Finance, Japan): Re-defining the Border between Public and Private in Southeast Asia: Malaysia, Philippines, Vietnam, Thailand and Indonesia*. Sydney, Australia: Research Institute for Asia and the Pacific, The University of Sydney.

Ribeiro, G. L. (1998). Cybercultural politics. In Alvarez, S. E., Dagnino, E., & Escobar, A. (Eds.), *Cultures of politics, politics of cultures: Revisioning Latin American social movements*. Boulder, CO: Westview Press.

Richard, O., & Kirby, S. (1999). Organizational justice and the justification of work force diversity programs. *Journal of Business and Psychology*, *14*, 109–118. doi:10.1023/A:1022962618674.

Ringberg, T., & Reihlen, M. (2008). Communication assumptions in consumer research: An alternative socio-cognitive approach. *Consumption. Markets and Culture*, *11*(September), 173–189. doi:10.1080/10253860802190512.

Ritson, M., & Elliott, R. (1995). Advertising literacy and the social signification of cultural meaning. In F. Hansen (Ed.), European Advances in Consumer Research, 2, 113-117. Provo, UT: Association for Consumer Research.

Robbins, S. S., & Stylianou, A. C. (2003). Global corporate web sites: An empirical investigation of content and design. *Information & Management*, 205–212. doi:10.1016/S0378-7206(02)00002-2.

Robbins, S., & Stylianou, A. (2002). A Study of Cultural Differences in Global Corporate Web Sites. *Journal of Computer Information Systems*, *42*(2), 3–9.

Robertson, R. (1992). *Glocalization: Social theory and global culture*. London: Sage Publications.

Robertson, R. (1995). Glocalization: Time-space and homogeneity–heterogeneity. In Featherstone, M., Lash, S., & Robertson, R. (Eds.), *Global modernities* (pp. 25–44). London: Sage Publications. doi:10.4135/9781446250563.n2.

Robey, D., & Markus, M. L. (1998). Beyond Rigor and Relevance: Producing Consumable Research about Information Systems. *Information Resources Management Journal*, *11*(1), 7–15.

Robinson, J. P., Shaver, P. R., & Wrightsman, L. S. (1991). Criteria for scale selection and evaluation. In Robinson, J. P., Shaver, P. R., & Wrightsman, L. S. (Eds.), *Measures of Personality and Social Psychological Attitudes*. San Diego, CA: Academic Press.

Rodríguez, A. (2003). *La realidad de la pyme colombiana: desafío para el desarrollo*. Bogotá, Colombia: FUNDES.

Roethlisberger, F. J., & Dickson, W. J. (1939). *Management and the worker*. Cambridge, MA: Harvard University Press.

Rogelberg, S. G. (2007). Introduction. In Rogelberg, S. G. (Ed.), *Encyclopedia of industrial and organizational psychology* (*Vol. 1*). Thousand Oaks, CA: Sage.

Rogers Everett, M., & Steinfatt Thomas, M. (1999). *Intercultural Communication*. Prospect Heights, IL: Waveland Press.

Rogers, E. M., Hart, W. B., & Miike, Y. (2002). Edward T. Hall and the History of Intercultural Communication: The United States and Japan. *Keio Communication Review, 24*, 1–5.

Romero, M., & Ramírez, J. (2012, July 5). *Conozca los próximos tratados de libre comercio de Colombia*. Retrieved October 29, 2012, from http://www.portafolio.co/negocios/conozca-los-proximos-tratados-libre-comercio-colombia

Ronen, S. (1986). *Comparative and Multinational Management*. New York: John Wiley.

Ronen, S., & Shenkar, O. (1985). Clustering countries on attitudinal dimensions: A review and synthesis. *Academy of Management Review, 10*(3), 435–454.

Root, F. R. (1994). *Entry strategies for international markets*. Lexington, VA: Lexington Books.

Rosca, A., & Voicu, C. (1982). *A concise history of psychology in roamnia*. Bucharest: Editura Stiintifica Psychologica si Enciclopedia.

Rose, G. M., Evaristo, R., & Straub, D. (2003). Culture and Consumer Responses to Web Download Time: A Four-Continent Study of Mono and Polychronism. *IEEE Transactions on Engineering Management, 50*(1), 31 44. doi:10.1109/TEM.2002.808262.

Rose, G., & Straub, D. (1998). Predicting general IT use: Applying TAM to the Arabic World. *Journal of Global Information Management, 6*(3).

Rosen, B., Furst, S., & Blackburn, R. (2006). Training For Virtual Teams: An Investigation Of Current Practices And Future Needs. *Human Resource Management, 45*, 229–247. doi:10.1002/hrm.20106.

Rosen, B., Furst, S., & Blackburn, R. (2007). Overcoming Barriers To Knowledge Sharing In Virtual Teams. *Organizational Dynamics, 36*, 259–273. doi:10.1016/j.orgdyn.2007.04.007.

Roth, H., Schiefer, J., Obweger, H., & Rozsnyai, S. (2010). Event data warehousing for complex event processing. In P. Loucopoulos & J.L. Cavavero (Eds.), *Proceedings of the 4th IEEE International Conference on Research Challenges in Information Science* (pp.203-212). IEEE.

Rottman, J. W., & Lacity, M. C. (2006). Proven practices for effectively offshoring IT work. *MIT Sloan Management Review, 47*(3), 56–63.

Rozinat, A., Alves de Medeiros, A. K., Günther, C. W., Weijters, A. J. M. M., & Van der Alst, W. M. P. (2007). Towards on evaluation framework for process mining algorithm. *BPM Center Report, BPM-07-06, Eindhoven University of Technology*. Retrieved June 10, 2012, from http://www.processmining.org/_media/publications/bpm-07-06.pdf

Rubery, J., Earnshaw, J., Marchington, M., Cooke, F., & Vincent, S. (2002). Changing Organisational Forms and the Employment Relationship. *Journal of Management Studies, 39*(5), 645–672. doi:10.1111/1467-6486.00306.

Rugman, A., Oh, C., & Lim, D. (2012). The regional and global competitiveness of multinational firms. *Journal of the Academy of Marketing Science, 40*(2), 218–235. doi:10.1007/s11747-011-0270-5.

Ruiz-Mafe, C. et al. (2009). Drivers and barriers to online airline ticket purchasing. *Journal of Air Transport Management, 15*(6), 294–298. doi:10.1016/j.jairtraman.2009.02.001.

Rungtusanatham, M., Forza, C., Koka, B. R., Salvadora, F., & Nie, W. (2005). TQM across multiple countries: Convergence hypothesis versus national specificity arguments. *Journal of Operations Management, 23*(1), 43–63. doi:10.1016/j.jom.2004.10.002.

Ruokonen, M., & Saarenketo, S. (2009). The strategic orientations of rapidly internationalizing software companies. *European Business Review, 21*(1), 17–41. doi:10.1108/09555340910925166.

Rupp, D. E., & Beal, D. (2007). Checking in with the scientist-practitioner model: How are we doing? *The Industrial-Organizational Psychologist, 45*, 35–40.

Russo, F. K., Shah, R. H., & Park, C. W. (1994). The impact of emotional valence and intensity on ad evaluation and memory. *Advances in Consumer Research. Association for Consumer Research (U. S.), 21*, 583–588.

Ruzzier, M., Hisrich, R. D., & Antoncic, B. (2006). SME internationalization research: Past, present, and future. *Journal of Small Business and Enterprise Development, 13*(4), 476–497. doi:10.1108/14626000610705705.

Ryals, L., & Payne, A. F. T. (2001). Customer Relationship Management in financial services: Towards information-enabled relationship marketing. *Journal of Strategic Marketing*, *9*(March), 1–25.

Ryckewaert, L. (2011). *PM Harper takes communications strategy to new level*. Retrieved on November 30, 2011, from http://www.hilltimes.com/news/2011/11/21/pm-harper-takes-communications-strategy-to-new-level/28868

Rynes, S. L., Bartunek, J. M., & Daft, R. L. (2001). Across the great divide: Knowledge creation and transfer between practitioners and academics. *Academy of Management Journal*, *44*, 340–355. doi:10.2307/3069460.

Rynes, S. L., Colbert, A. E., & Brown, K. G. (2002). HR professionals' beliefs about effective human resource practices: Correspondence between research and practice. *Human Resource Management*, *41*, 149–174. doi:10.1002/hrm.10029.

Sabherwal, R., & Fernandez, I. B. (2010). *Business Intelligence: Practices, Technologies and Management*. Hoboken, NJ: John Wiley and Sons.

Sabiote, C. M., Frias, D. M., & Castaneda, J. A. (2012). E-service quality as antecedent to e-satisfaction: The moderating effect of culture. *Online Information Review*, *36*(2), 157–174. doi:10.1108/14684521211229011.

Safayeni, F., Purdy, L., van Engelen, R., & Pal, S. (1991). Difficulties of Just-in-Time implementation: A classification scheme. *International Journal of Operations & Production Management*, *11*(7), 27–36. doi:10.1108/EUM0000000001272.

Salacuse, J. W. (2010). Teaching International Business Negotiation: Reflections on Three Decades of Experience. *International Negotiation*, *15*, 187–228. doi:10.1163/157180610X506956.

Salas, E., Burke, C. S., & Cannon-Bowers, J. A. (2000). Teamwork: Emerging Principles. *International Journal of Management Reviews*, *2*, 339–356. doi:10.1111/1468-2370.00046.

Sallenave, J. (2002). *La Gerencia Integral*. Bogotá, Colombia: Editorial Norma.

Salmaninezhad, R. A., & Daneshwar, M. (2012). Relationship Between Intellectual Capital and Knowledge Management – Case Study: Tehran Science & Technology Park. *Interdisciplinary Journal of Contemporary Research in Business*, *3*(10), 135–143.

Salvendy, G. (2012). *Handbook of human factors and ergonomics* (4th ed.). Wisley. doi:10.1002/9781118131350.

Sanchez, J. I., Spector, P. E., & Cooper, C. L. (2000). Adapting to a boundaryless world: A developmental expatriate model. *The Academy of Management Executive*, *14*(2), 96–106.

Sandberg, B., & Hansen, S.-O. (2004). Creating and International Market for Disruptive Innovations. *European Journal of Innovation Management*, *7*(1), 23–32. doi:10.1108/14601060410515619.

Sanglin-Grant, S., & Schneider, R. (2000). *Moving on Up? Racial equality and the corporate agenda*. London, UK: Runnymede Trust.

Sarantakos, S. (1997). *Social Research*. Melbourne, Australia: Macmillan Education Australia Pty Ltd..

Sarin, S., & McDermott, C. (2003). The Effect of Team Leader characteristics on learning, knowledge application and performance of cross-functional new product development teams. *Decision Sciences*, *34*, 707–739. doi:10.1111/j.1540-5414.2003.02350.x.

Sarker, S., & Sarker, S. (2009). Exploring agility in distributed information systems development teams: An interpretive study in an offshoring context. *Information Systems Research*, *20*(3), 440–461. doi:10.1287/isre.1090.0241.

Saville & Holdsworth Limited. (2001). *The work profiling system (WPS) technical manual*. Boulder, CO: Author.

Sax, L. J., Gilmartin, S. K., & Bryant, A. N. (2003). Assessing response rates and nonresponse bias in web and paper surveys. *Research in Higher Education*, *44*(4), 409–432. doi:10.1023/A:1024232915870.

Schein, E. (1996). *Organizational culture and leadership* (2nd ed.). Jossey-Bass.

Schein, E. (1998). *Process consultation revisited: Building the helping relationship*. Boston, MA: Addison Wesley Longman.

Schmalleger, D., & Carson, D. (2008). Blogs in tourism: Changing approaches to information exchange. *Journal of Vacation Marketing*, *14*(2), 99–110. doi:10.1177/1356766707087519.

Schneider, B. D., Smith, B., & Paul, M. C. (2001). P-E fit and the Attraction-Selection-Attrition Model of Organisational Functioning: Introduction and overview. In Erez, M., Kleinbeck, U., & Thierry, H. (Eds.), *Work Motivation in the Context of a Globalising Economy*. Mahwah, NJ: Lawrence Erlbaum.

Schneider, B., & Schmitt, N. (1986). *Staffing organizations* (2nd ed.). New York: HarperCollins Publishers, Inc..

Schneider, S. C. (1988). National Vs. Corporate Culture: Implications for Human Resource Management. *Human Resource Management*, *27*(2), 231–246. doi:10.1002/hrm.3930270207.

Schneider, S., & Barsoux, J. (1997). *Managing across cultures*. London: Prentice-Hall.

Scholes, R. (1981). Language, Narrative, and Anti-Narrative. In Mitchell, W. (Ed.), *On Narrativity* (pp. 200–208). Chicago: University of Chicago Press.

Schonberger, R. J. (1996). *World class manufacturing: The next decade*. New York: The Free Press.

Schraeder, M. (2001). Identifying employee resistance during the threat of a merger: An analysis of employee perceptions and commitment to an organization in a premerger context. *The Mid-Atlantic Journal of Business*, *37*(4), 191–204.

Schramm, W. (1955). *The Process and Effects of Mass Communication*. Urbana, IL: University of Illinois Press.

Schuler, R. S., Budhwar, P. S., & Florkowski, G. W. (2002). International Human Resource Management: Review and critique. *International Journal of Management Reviews*, *4*(1), 41–70. doi:10.1111/1468-2370.00076.

Schuler, R., Dowling, S. P., & Cieri, H. D. (1993). An integrative framework of strategic international Human Resource Management. *Journal of Management*, *19*(2), 419–459.

Schulz, M. (2003). Pathways of Relevance: Exploring Inflows of Knowledge into Subunits of Multinational Corporations. *Organization Science*, *14*(4), 440–459. doi:10.1287/orsc.14.4.440.17483.

Schumann, J. H., Wangenheim, F., Stringfellow, A., Yang, Z., Blazevic, V., & Praxmarer, S. et al. (2010). Cross-cultural differences in the effect of received word-of-mouth referral in relational service exchange. *Journal of International Marketing*, *18*(3), 62–80. doi:10.1509/jimk.18.3.62.

Schumpeter, J. (1942). *Capitalism, Socialism, and Democracy*. New York: Harper.

Schwartz, S. H., & Bilsky, W. (1990). Toward a Theory of the Universal Content and Structure of Values: Extensions and Cross-Cultural Replications. *Journal of Personality and Social Psychology*, *58*(5). doi:10.1037/0022-3514.58.5.878.

Schweitzer, L., & Duxbury, L. (2010). Conceptualizing And Measuring The Virtuality Of Teams. *Information Systems Journal*, *20*, 267–295. doi:10.1111/j.1365-2575.2009.00326.x.

Scott, L. M. (1994). The bridge from text to mind: Adapting reader-response theory to consumer research. *The Journal of Consumer Research*, *21*(3), 461–480. doi:10.1086/209411.

Scott, W. K., & Howell, D. (2008). Clarifying analysis and interpretation in grounded theory: Using a conditional relationship guide and reflective coding matrix. *International Journal of Qualitative Methods*, *7*(2), 1–15.

Searle, W., & Wards, C. (1990). The predication of psychological and sociocultural adjustment during cross-cultural transitions. *International Journal of Intercultural Relations*, *14*, 449–464. doi:10.1016/0147-1767(90)90030-Z.

Seierstad, C. (2011). *Exploring the Norwegian paradox of vertical sex segregation: Strategies and experiences in politics, academia and company boards*. PhD Thesis, University of London, London, U.K.

Seierstad, C., & Healy, G. (2012). Women's equality in the Scandinavian academy – A distant dream? *Work, Employment and Society*, *26*, 296–313. doi:10.1177/0950017011432918.

Seierstad, C., & Opsahl, T. (2011). For the few not the many? The effects of affirmative action on presence, prominence, and social capital of female directors in Norway. *Scandinavian Journal of Management*, *27*(1). doi:10.1016/j.scaman.2010.10.002.

Seitz, J. L. (2002). *Global Issues: An Introduction* (2nd ed.). Oxford, UK: Blackwell Publishers.

Selmer, J. (1995). *Expatriate Management*. Westport, CT: Westport Greenwood Publishing Group.

Senge, P. (2004). *La quinta disciplina: El arte y la práctica de la organización abierta al aprendizaje*. Barcelona, Spain: Granica.

Senge, P. M. (1990). The Leader's New Work: Building Learning Organizations. *Sloan Management Review*, 7–23.

Serenko, A. & Bontis. (2004). Meta Review of Knowledge Management and Intellectual Capital Literature: Citation Impact and Research Productivity Rankings. *Knowledge and Process Management*, *11*(3), 185–198. doi:10.1002/kpm.203.

Sever, H., & Oğuz, B. (2003). *Veri Tabanlarında Bilgi Keşfine Formel Bir Yaklaşım: Kısım II- Eşleştirme Sorgularının Biçimsel Kavram Analizi ile Modellenmesi* (pp. 15–44). Bilgi Dünyası.

Shachaf, P. (2008). Cultural diversity and information and communication technology impacts on global virtual teams: An exploratory study. *Information & Management*, *45*(2), 131–142. doi:10.1016/j.im.2007.12.003.

Shafei, R., Ghaderzadeh, H., Salavati, A., & Lavei, S. (2011). *Survey of Relationship between Knowledge Management and Organizational Culture Dimensions in Public Organizations - A Case of Iranian Public Organizations*, *2*(11), 355-370.

Shafritz, J. M. Ott, J. S., & Jang, Y. S. (2005). Classics of organization theory (6th ed.). Belmont, CA: Thomson-Wadsworth.

Shah, D. V., Cho, J., Eveland, W. P., & Kwak, N. (2005). Information and expression in a digital age: Modelling Internet effects on civic participation. *Communication Research*, *32*(5), 531–565. doi:10.1177/0093650205279209.

Shainesh, G., & Sheth, J. (2006). *Components of eCRM Solutions. Customer Relationship Management: A Strategic Initiative*. New York: Macmillan.

Shainesh, G., & Sheth, J. (2006). *Conceptual Foundations of CRM, Customer Relationship Management: A Strategic Initiative*. New York: Macmillan.

Shane, S. (1992). Why Do Some Societies Invent More Than Others? *Journal of Business Venturing*, *7*(January), 29–46. doi:10.1016/0883-9026(92)90033-N.

Shane, S. (1993). Cultural Influences on National Rates of Innovation. *Journal of Business Venturing*, *8*(January), 59–73. doi:10.1016/0883-9026(93)90011-S.

Shanghai, I. C. E. (2009). Il *mercato cinese dei prodotti agroalimentari e del vino*. Retrieved from www.ccio.it

Shapiro, D. L., Furst, S. A., Spreitzer, G. M., & Von Glinow, M. A. (2002). Transnational Teams In The Electronic Age: Are Team Identity And High Performance At Risk? *Journal of Organizational Behavior*, *23*, 455–467. doi:10.1002/job.149.

Sharma, D. D., & Johanson, J. (1987). Technical consultancy in internationalization. *International Marketing Review*, *4*(4), 20–29. doi:10.1108/eb008339.

Sharp, J. H., & Ryan, S. D. (2011). Global Agile team configuration. *Journal of Strategic Innovation and Sustainability*, *7*(1), 120–134.

Shaw, M. L. G. (1980). *On Becoming a Personal Scientist - Interactive Computer Elicitation of Personal Models of the World*. London: Academic Press.

Shay, J., & Tracey, J. B. (1997). Expatriate managers: Reasons for failure and implications for training. *The Cornell Hotel and Restaurant Administration Quarterly*, *38*, 30–35. doi:10.1177/001088049703800116.

Shen, S.-T., Prior, S. D., Chen, K.-M., & You, M.-L. (2007). Chinese Web Browser Design Utilising Cultural Icons. In N. Aykin (Ed.), *Proceedings of the 12th HCI International*

Shen, J., Chanda, A., D'Netto, B., & Monga, M. (2009). Managing diversity through Human Resource Management: An international perspective and conceptual framework. *International Journal of Human Resource Management*, *20*(2), 235–251. doi:10.1080/09585190802670516.

Shen, J., D'Netto, B., & Tang, J. (2010). Effects of human resource diversity management on organizational citizen behaviour in the Chinese context. *International Journal of Human Resource Management*, *21*(12), 2156–2172. doi:10.1080/09585192.2010.509622.

Shenkar, O. (2001). Cultural Distance Revisited: Towards a More Rigorous Conceptualization and Measurement of Cultural Differences. *Journal of International Business Studies*, *32*(3), 519–536. doi:10.1057/palgrave.jibs.8490982.

Sheth, J. N., & Parvatiyar, A. (2000). *The Evolution of Relationship Marketing, Handbook of Relationship Marketing*. New York: Sage Publications.

Shimmin, S., & van Strien, P. J. (1998). History of the psychology of work and organization. In Drenth, P. J. D., Thierry, H., & de Wolff, C. J. (Eds.), *Handbook of work and organizational psychology*. Hove, UK: Psychology Press.

Shimmin, S., & Wallis, D. (1994). *Fifty years on occupational psychology*. Leicester, UK: British Psychological Society.

Shimp, T. A. (1981). Attitude towards the ad as a mediator of consumer brand choice. *Journal of Advertising*, *10*(Summer), 9–15.

Shin, Y. (2005). Conflict Resolution In Virtual Teams. *Organizational Dynamics*, *34*, 331–345. doi:10.1016/j.orgdyn.2005.08.002.

Shiraev, E. B., & Levy, D. A. (2010). *Cross-cultural psychology: Critical thinking and contemporary applications* (4th ed.). Boston, MA: Allyn and Bacon.

Shoham, A., Rose, G. M., & Kropp, F. (1997). Conflict in international channels of distribution. *Journal of Global Marketing*, *11*(2), 5–22. doi:10.1300/J042v11n02_02.

Shon, Z. Y., Chen, F. Y., & Chang, Y. H. (2003). Airline e-commerce: The revolution in ticketing channels. *Journal of Air Transport Management*, *9*, 325–331. doi:10.1016/S0969-6997(03)00040-1.

Shweder, R. A., & LeVine, R. A. (1984). *Culture theory: Essays on mind, self and emotion*. New York: Cambridge University Press.

Sieck, W. R., Rasmussen, L. J., & Smart, P. R. (2010). Cultural Network Analysis: A Cognitive Approach to Cultural Modeling. In Verma, D. (Ed.), *Network Science for Military Coalition Operations: Information Extraction and Interaction*. Hershey, PA: IGI Global. doi:10.4018/978-1-61520-855-5.ch011.

Sigman, S. (1987). A Perspective on Social Communication. Lexington, VA: Lexington.

Simmonds, P. G. (1990). The combined diversification breadth and mode dimensions and the performance of large diversified firms. *Strategic Management Journal*, *11*(5), 399–410. doi:10.1002/smj.4250110506.

Singer P., Ferri M-A., Aiello L., & Cacia C. (2010). Internet as a "point of synergy" between communication and distribution: Hypothesis of model applied to tourism. *International Journal of Digital Content Technology and its Applications, 4*(7), 23-37.

Singh, D., & Agrawal, D. P. (2003). CRM Practices in Indian Industries. *International Journal of Customer Relationship Management*, *5*(December–January), 241–257.

Singh, N., Baack, D. W., Kundu, S. K., & Hurtado, C. (2008). U.S. Hispanic Consumer E-Commerce Preferences: Expections and Attitudes toward Web Content. *Journal of Electronic Commerce Research*, *9*(2), 162–175.

Singh, N., Fassott, G., Zhao, H., & Boughton, P. D. (2006). A Cross-cultural analysis of German, Chinese and Indian consumers' perception of web site adaptation. *Journal of Consumer Behaviour*, *5*, 56–68. doi:10.1002/cb.43.

Singh, N., & Matsuo, H. (2004). Measuring cultural adaptation on the Web: A content analytic study of U.S. and Japanese Web sites. *Journal of Business Research*, *57*, 864–872. doi:10.1016/S0148-2963(02)00482-4.

Singh, N., Zhao, H., & Hu, X. (2003). Cultural adaptation on the Web: A study of American companies' domestic and Chinese websites. *Journal of Global Information Management*, *11*(3), 63–80. doi:10.4018/jgim.2003070104.

Singh, N., Zhao, H., & Hu, X. (2005). Analyzing the cultural content of web sites: A cross-national comparision of China, India, Japan, and US. *International Marketing Review*, *22*(2), 129–146. doi:10.1108/02651330510593241.

Singh, S. K. (2008). Role of Leadership in Knowledge Management. *International Journal of Knowledge Management*, *12*(4), 3–15. doi:10.1108/13673270810884219.

Singh, T., Jayashankar, J. V., & Singh, J. (2001). E-Commerce in the U.S. and Europe - Is Europe Ready to Compete? *Business Horizons*, *44*(22), 6–16. doi:10.1016/S0007-6813(01)80017-3.

Sinha, D. (2002). Culture and psychology: Perspective of cross-cultural psychology. *Psychology and Developing Societies*, *14*, 11–25. doi:10.1177/097133360201400102.

Sinkovics, R. R., Yamin, M., & Hossinger, M. (2007). Cultural Adaptation in Cross Border e-Commerce: A Study of German Companies. *Journal of Electronic Commerce Research*, *8*(4), 221–235.

Skibniewski, M. & Abduh, M. Web-Based Project Management For Construction: Search For Utility Assessment Tools. 2000. 56-77.

Skinner, B. F. (1969). *Contingencies of reinforcement*. New York: Appleton Century Crofts.

Sklair, L. (1999a). Competing conceptions of globalisation. *Journal of World-systems Research*, *5*(2), 143–163.

Sklair, L. (1999b). Globalisation. In Taylor, S. (Ed.), *Sociology: Issues and Debates* (pp. 321–345). Basingstoke, UK: Macmillan Press.

Slak Valek, N., & Podovšovnik Axelsson, E. (2012). Understanding Internet use among passive and active tourists. Is there a need for a different web approach? *Innovative Issues and Approaches in Social Science*, *5*(1), 88–106.

Slater, S. F., & Narver, J. C. (1995). Market orientation and the learning organization. *Journal of Marketing*, *59*(3), 63–74. doi:10.2307/1252120.

Slater, S. F., & Narver, J. C. (2000). The positive effect of a market orientation on business profitability: A balanced replication. *Journal of Business Research*, *48*(1), 69–73. doi:10.1016/S0148-2963(98)00077-0.

Smedley, J. (2010). Modeling the Impact of Knowledge Management Using Technology. *OR Insight*, *23*, 233–250. doi:10.1057/ori.2010.11.

Smith, M. (1997). Putting NFIs to work in a balanced scorecard environment. *Management Accounting*, 32-35.

Smit, H. (2009). *The depth facilitator's handbook: Transforming group dynamics*. Cape Town, South Africa: Moonshine Media.

Smith, C., & Jenner, P. (1998). Tourism and the Internet. *Travel & Tourism Analyst*, *1*, 62–81.

Smith, E. D. J., & Pham, C. (1996). Doing business in Vietnam: A cultural guide. *Business Horizons*, *39*(3), 47–51. doi:10.1016/S0007-6813(96)90007-5.

Smith, P. B., & Bond, M. H. (1999). *Social psychology across cultures*. Boston, MA: Allyn and Bacon.

Smith, P. B., Dugan, S., Peterson, M. F., & Leung, K. (1998). Individualism: Collectivism and the handling of disagreement - A 23 country study. *International Journal of Intercultural Relations*, *22*(3), 351–367. doi:10.1016/S0147-1767(98)00012-1.

Snell, R. S., & Hui, S. K. K. (2000). Towards the Hong Kong learning organization: An exploratory case study. *Journal of Applied Management Studies*, *9*(2), 150–175. doi:10.1080/713674364.

Society for Industrial and Organizational Psychology. (2007). *Mission statement*. Retrieved June 15, 2012, from http://www.siop.org

Søderberg, A., & Holden, N. (2002). Rethinking Cross Cultural Management in a Globalizing Business World. *International Journal of Cross Cultural Management*, *2*(103), 103–121.

Sodergaard, M. (1994). Hofstede's consequences: A study of reviews, citations and replications. *Organization Studies*, *15*(3), 447–456. doi:10.1177/017084069401500307.

Sohail, A., & Rehman, K.U., Shams-ul-Haq, I., JaaM, J., Razaq, A., & Sabir, M. S. (2011). The impact of diversity training on commitment, career satisfaction and innovation. *Journal of Economics and Behavioral Studies*, *3*(4), 257–263.

Solberg, C. A. (2008). Product complexity and cultural distance effects on managing international distributor relationships: A contingency approach. *Journal of International Marketing*, *16*(3), 57–83. doi:10.1509/jimk.16.3.57.

Solberg, C. A. (Ed.). (2006). *Advances in international marketingRelationship between exporters and their foreign sales and marketing intermediaries* (*Vol. 16*). Oxford, UK: Elsevier.

Solow, R.M. (1956). A Contribution to the Theory of Economic Growth. *The Quarterly Journal of Economics, 70*(1)\, 65-94.

Solow, R. M. (1957). Technical Change and the Aggregate Production Function. *The Review of Economics and Statistics, 39*(3), 312–320. doi:10.2307/1926047.

Solow, R. M. (2000). *Growth theory: An exposition.* New York: Oxford University Press.

Soltani, E. (2010). The overlooked variable in managing human resources of Iranian organizations: Workforce diversity-some evidence. *International Journal of Human Resource Management, 21*(1), 84–108. doi:10.1080/09585190903466871.

Sondergaard, M. (1994). Research Note: Hofstede's Consequences: A Study of Reviews, Citations and Replications. *Organization Studies, 15*(3), 447–456. doi:10.1177/017084069401500307.

South Africa business forecast report 2011, 3.

Souza-Poza, A., Nystrom, H., & Wiebe, H. (2000). A cross-cultural study of the differing effects of corporate culture on TQM in three countries. *International Journal of Quality & Reliability Management, 18*(7), 744–761. doi:10.1108/EUM0000000005778.

Sparks, B. A., & Browning, V. (2011). The impact of online reviews on hotel booking intentions and perception of trust. *Tourism Management, 32*(6), 1310–1323. doi:10.1016/j.tourman.2010.12.011.

Sparrow, P. R., & Braun, W. (2007). Human resource strategy in international context. In Schuler, R. S., & Jackson, S. E. (Eds.), *Strategic human resource management* (2nd ed., pp. 162–199). Hoboken, NJ: Blackwell Publishing.

Spector, P. E., Cooper, C. L., & Sparks, K. (2001). An international study of the psychometric properties of the hofstede values survey module 1994: A comparison of individual and country/province level results. *Applied Psychology, 50*, 269–281. doi:10.1111/1464-0597.00058.

Spry, A., Pappu, R., & Cornwell, T. B. (2011). Celebrity endorsement, brand credibility and brand equity. *European Journal of Marketing, 45*(6), 882–909. doi:10.1108/03090561111119958.

Sriprasert, E., & Dawood, N. (2002). *Next Generation Of Construction Planning And Control System: The Lewis Approach*. Taylor & Francis.

Srite, M., & Karahanna, E. (2006). The Role of Espoused National Cultural Values in Technology Acceptanc. *Management Information Systems Quarterly, 30*(3), 679–704.

Srull, T. K. (1983). Affect and memory: The impact of affective reactions in advertising on the representation of product information in memory. *Advances in Consumer Research. Association for Consumer Research (U. S.), 10*, 520–525.

SRV. (2002). *The Comprehensive Poverty Reduction and Growth Strategy (CPRGS) (No. 2685/VPCP-QHQT).* Hanoi: Vietnam.

Stackowiak, R., Rayman, J., & Greenwald, R. (2007). *Oracle Data Warehousing and Business Intelligence Solutions*. Indianapolis, IN: Wiley Publishing.

Stahl, G. K., & Bjorkman, I. (2006). *Handbook of Research in International Human Resource Management.* Northampton, MA: Edward Elgar Publishing.

Starbucks, (2011). Starbucks *to Present at Morgan Stanley Global Consumer Conference*. Retrieved on December 3, 2011, from http://investor.starbucks.com/phoenix.zhtml?c=99518&p=irol-irhome

Stavros, C., & Westberg, K. (2009). Using triangulation and multiple case studies to advance relationship marketing theory. *Qualitative market research. International Journal (Toronto, Ont.), 12*(3), 307–320.

Stawarski, C., & Phillips, P. (2008). *Data Collection: Planning for and Collecting All Types of Data*. San Francisco, CA: John Wiley & Sons.

Stayman, D. M., & Aaker, D. A. (1988). Are all the effects of ad-induced feelings mediated by Aad? *The Journal of Consumer Research, 15*(December), 368–373. doi:10.1086/209173.

Steenkamp, J. E. M. (2001). The role of national culture in international marketing research. *International Marketing Review*, *18*(1), 30–44. doi:10.1108/02651330110381970.

Steenkamp, J.-B. E. M., Hofstede, F. T., & Michel, W. (1999). A Cross-National Investigation into the Individual and National Culture Antecedents of Consumer Innovativeness. *Journal of Marketing*, *63*(April), 55–69. doi:10.2307/1251945.

Steenkamp, J.-B. E., & Geyskens, I. (2006). How Country Characteristics Affect the Perceived Value of Web Sites. *Journal of Marketing*, *70*, 136–150. doi:10.1509/jmkg.70.3.136.

Stefanescu, C., & Popa, L. (2008). *Managerial Communication*. Paper No. 7172. Retrieved on October 19, 2011, from http://mpra.ub.uni-muenchen.de/7172/

Steiger, J. H., & Lind, J. C. (1980). *Statistically-based tests for the number of common factors*. Paper presented at the Annual Meeting of the Psychometric Society. Iowa City, IA.

Sterman, J. (2000). *Business Dynamics: System Thinking and Modeling for a Complex World*. New York: McGraw-Hill.

Stern, B. (1989). Literary criticism and consumer research: Overview and illustrative analysis. *The Journal of Consumer Research*, *16*(3), 322–334. doi:10.1086/209218.

Stevens, B. (2005). What communication skills do employers want? Silicon Valley recruiters respond. *Journal of Employment Counseling*, *42*(1), 2–9. doi:10.1002/j.2161-1920.2005.tb00893.x.

Stewart, D. W., Shamdasani, P. N., & Rook, D. W. (2007). *Focus groups: Theory and practice*. London: Sage.

Stewart, S., & Vogt, C. (1999). A Case-Based Approach to Understanding Vacation Planning. *Leisure Sciences*, *21*, 79–95. doi:10.1080/014904099273165.

Stewart, V., & Stewart, A. (1981). *Business Applications of Repertory Grid*. London: McGraw-Hill.

Steyn, M., & Foster, D. (2008). Repertoires for talking white: Resistant whiteness in post-Apartheid South Africa. *Ethnic and Racial Studies*, *31*(1), 25–51. doi:10.1080/01419870701538851.

Stinchcombe, A. L. (1974). *Creating Efficient Industrial Administration*. New York: Academic Press.

Stopford, J. M., & Wells, L. T. (1972). *Managing the multinational enterprise: Organiztion of the firm and ownership of the subsidiaries*. New York: Basic Books.

Strauss, A., & Corbin, J. (1990). *Basics of Qualitative Research: Grounded Theory Procedures and Techniques*. Newbury Park, CA: Sage Publications.

Stroh, L. K., Black, J. S., Mendenhall, M. E., & Gregersen, H. B. (2005). *International Assignments: An Integration of Strategy, Research, and Practice*. Mahwah, NJ: Lawrence Erlbaum Associates.

Stroh, L. K., Gregersen, H. B., & Black, J. S. (1998). Closing the gap: Expectations versus reality among repatrates. *Journal of World Business*, *33*(2), 111–124. doi:10.1016/S1090-9516(98)90001-3.

Struwig, M., & Meru, A. (2011). The Relationship between Business Environment and Business Incubation. *China-USA Business Review*, *10*(9), 880–892.

Stuart, E. W., Shimp, T. A., & Engle, R. W. (1987). Classical conditioning of consumer attitudes: Four experiments in an advertising context. *The Journal of Consumer Research*, *14*(3), 334–349. doi:10.1086/209117.

Study, G. A. O. (2004). *International Trade*. Retrieved on October 26, 2012, from www.gao.gov/new.items/d04932.pdf

Subba Rao, S., Raghunathan, T. S., & Solis, L. E. (1997). A Comparative Study of Quality Practices and Results in India, China and Mexico. *Journal of Quality Management*, *2*(2), 235–250. doi:10.1016/S1084-8568(97)90005-5.

Succi, G., & Marchesi, M. (Eds.). (2001). *Extreme Programming Examined*. Reading, MA: Addison-Wesley.

Suddaby, R., Elsbach, K., Greenwood, R., Meyer, J. W., & Tilber, J. B. (2012). Organizations and their institutional environments-bringing meaning, values, and culture back in: Introduction to the special research forum. *Academy of Management Journal*, *53*(6), 1234–1240. doi:10.5465/AMJ.2010.57317486.

Sultan, P., & Wong, H. Y. (2010a). Performance-based service quality model: An empirical study on Japanese universities. *Quality Assurance in Education*, *18*(2), 126–143. doi:10.1108/09684881011035349.

Sultan, P., & Wong, H. Y. (2011). Service quality in a higher education context: Antecedents and dimensions. *International Review of Business Research Papers*, *7*(2), 11–20.

Surborg, B. (2009). Is it the 'Development of Underdevelopment' all over again? Internet Development in Vietnam. *Globalizations*, *6*(2), 225–247. doi:10.1080/14747730902854182.

Swan, J., & Newell, S. (2000). Linking Knowledge Management and Innovation. In H.R. Hansen, M. Bichler, & H. Mahrer, (Eds), Proceedings *of the 8th European Conference on Information Systems* (pp. 591-598)., Vienna, Austria: Vienna University of Economics and Business Administration.

Swap, W., Schields, M., & Abrams, L. (2001). Using Mentoring and Storytelling to Transfer Knowledge in the Workplace. *Journal of Management Information Systems*, *18*(1), 95–114.

Synott, J. (2004). *Global and International Studies: Transdisciplinary Perspectives*. Southbank, Australia: Social Science Press.

Systems, M. Conceptual Foundations and Research Issues. *Management Information Systems Quarterly*, *25*(1), 36–107.

Takeuchi, R., Tesluk, P. E., & Yun, S. H. (2005). An integrative view of international experience. *Academy of Management Journal*, *48*(1), 85–100. doi:10.5465/AMJ.2005.15993143.

Talbott, S. P. (1996). Building a global workforce starts with recruitment. *The Personnel Journal*, *3*, 9–12.

Tata, J., Prasad, S., & Motwani, J. (2000). Benchmarking Quality Management Practices: U.S. Versus Costa Rica. *Multinational Business Review*, *8*(2), 37–42.

Tatli, A. (2011). Multi-layered exploration of the diversity management field: Diversity discourses, practices and practitioners in the UK. *British Journal of Management*, *22*, 238–253. doi:10.1111/j.1467-8551.2010.00730.x.

Tatli, A., Vassilopoulou, J., Ariss, A., & Ozbilgin, M. (in press). The role of regulatory and temporal context in the construction of diversity discourses: The case of the UK, France and Germany. *European Journal of Industrial Relations*.

Taylor, C. R., Zou, S., & Osland, G. E. (2000). Foreign market entry strategies of Japanese MNCs. *International Marketing Review*, *17*(2), 146–163. doi:10.1108/02651330010322624.

Taylor, E. B. (1871a). *Origins of culture*. New York: Harper & Row.

Taylor, E. B. (1871b). *Primitive culture*. New York: J. P. Putman's Sons.

Taylor, P. (Ed.). (2004). *Social Inequality in Vietnam and the Challenges to Reform*. Singapore: Institute of Southeast Asian Studies.

Teece, D. J. (2007). Explicating Dynamic Capabilities: The Nature and Microfoundations of (Sustainable) Enterprise Performance. *Strategic Management Journal*, *28*(8), 1319–1350. doi:10.1002/smj.640.

Teece, D. J., Pisano, G., & Shuen, A. (1997). Dynamic Capabilities and Strategic Management. *Strategic Management Journal*, *18*(7), 509–534. doi:10.1002/(SICI)1097-0266(199708)18:7<509::AID-SMJ882>3.0.CO;2-Z.

Teigen, M. (2003). *Kvoteringogkontrovers: Omlikestillingsompolitikk*. Oslo, Norway: Universiteteti Oslo.

Tellis, G. J., & Ambler, T. (2007). Handbook of Advertising. In Tellis, G. J., & Ambler, T. (Eds.), *The Sage Handbook of Advertising* (pp. 3–16). London: Sage. doi:10.4135/9781848607897.n1.

Tellis, G. J., & Golder, P. N. (2003). First to Market, First to Fail? Real Causes of Enduring Market Leadership. In Katz, R. (Ed.), *The Human Side of Managing Technological Innovation*. New York: Oxford University Press.

Tenev, S., Calier, A., Chaudry, O., & Nguyen, Q. T. (2003). *Informality and the playing field in Vietnam's business sector*. Washington, DC: IFC, World Bank, and MPDF.

Terpstra, V., & Yu, C. (1988). Determinants of foreign investment of US advertising agencies. *Journal of International Business Studies*, *19*(1), 33–46. doi:10.1057/palgrave.jibs.8490373.

Terracciano, A., Abdel-Khalek, A. M., Adam, N., Adamovova, L., Ahn, C. K., & Ahn, H. N. et al. (2005). National character does not reflect mean personality trait levels in 49 cultures. *Science*, *310*, 96–100. doi:10.1126/science.1117199 PMID:16210536.

Thanasankit, T., & Corbitt, B. (1999). Cultural context and its impact on requirements elicitation in Thailand. *Electronic Journal on Information Systems in Developing Countries*, *1*(1), 15–32.

Tharp, B. M. (2009). *Defining culture and organizational culture: From anthropology to the office*. Retrieved on June 14, 2012, from http://www.haworth.com/en-us/Knowledge/Workplace-Library/Documents/Defining-Culture-and-Organizationa-Culture_5.pdf

Thashakkori, A., & Teddlie, C. (1998). *Mixed Methodology: Combining Qualitative and Quantitative Approaches*. Thousand Oaks, CA: Sage.

Thashakkori, A., & Teddlie, C. (2003). *Handbook of Mixed Methods in Social and Behavioral Research*. Thousand Oaks, CA: Sage.

Thatam, S. A. (2008). *Strategic Communication: A Primer*. UK: Advanced Research and Assessment Group.

The China Post. (2008). Foreign direct investment in Vietnam triples in 2008. *The China Post*. Retrieved from http://www.chinapost.com.tw/business/asia/vietnam/2008/12/27/189529/Foreign-direct.htm

The Conference Board. (1992). *Recruiting and Selecting International Managers (report no. 998)*. New York: The Conference Board.

The Economist. (2008). *Core Competence*. Retrieved on October 16, 2012, from http://www.economist.com/node/12231124

Theodoratos, D., & Tsois, A. (2003). Processing OLAP queries in hierarchically clustered databases. *Data & Knowledge Engineering*, *45*, 205–224. doi:10.1016/S0169-023X(02)00180-5.

Thierauf, R. J. (2001). *Effective Business Intelligence Systems*. New York: Greenwood Publishing.

Thomas, D. (2004). Diversity as a strategy. *Harvard Business Review*, *82*(9), 98–108. PMID:15449859.

Thomas, D. (2006). Domain and development of cultural intelligence: The importance of mindfulness. *Group & Organization Management*, *31*(1), 78–99. doi:10.1177/1059601105275266.

Thomas, D. (2008). *Cross-Cultural Management: Essential Concepts*. Los Angeles: Sage Publications.

Thomas, D., & Inkson, K. (2003). *Cultural Intelligence. People Skills for the Global Business*. San Francisco, CA: Berrett-Koehler Publishers.

Thomas, D., & Inkson, K. (2004). Cultivating your cultural intelligence. *Security Management*, *48*(8), 30–33.

Thomas, D., Stahl, G., Ravlin, E., Poelmans, S., Pekerti, A., & Maznevski, M. et al. (2008). Cultural Intelligence: Domain and Assessment. *International Journal of Cross Cultural Management*, *8*(2), 123–143. doi:10.1177/1470595808091787.

Thomas, R. R. (1996). A diversity framework. In Chemers, M. M., Oskampand, S., & Costanzo, M. A. (Eds.), *Diversity in Organisations: New Perspectives for a Changing Workplace* (pp. 245–263). Thousand Oaks, CA: Sage Publications.

Thomas, R. R. (2005). *Building on the Promise of Diversity: How Can We Move to the Next Level in Our Workplaces, Our Communities, and Our Society*. New York: AMACOM.

Thompson, C. J. (1997). Interpreting Consumers: A Hermeneutical Framework for Deriving Marketing Insights from the Texts of Consumers' Consumption Stories. *JMR, Journal of Marketing Research*, *34*, 438–455. doi:10.2307/3151963.

Thurlow, C., Lengel, L., & Tomic, A. (2004). *Computer Mediated Communication: Social Interaction and the Internet*. London: Sage.

Thurlow, C., & Mroczek, K. (Eds.). (2011). *Digital Discourse: Language in the New Media*. New York: Oxford University Press. doi:10.1093/acprof:oso/9780199795437.001.0001.

Thwaites, D. (1992). Organizational Influences on the New Product Development Process in Financial Services. *Journal of Product Innovation Management*, *9*(June), 303–313. doi:10.1111/1540-5885.940303.

Tillema, S. (2005). Towards an integrated contingency framework for MAS sophistication: Case studies on the scope of accounting instruments in Dutch power and gas companies. *Management Accounting Research*, *16*, 101–129. doi:10.1016/j.mar.2004.12.001.

Ting-Toomey, S. (1999). *Communicating across cultures*. New York: Guilford.

Tissen, R., Andreiessen, D., & Depres, F. L. (2000). *The Knowledge Dividend*. London: Prentice Hall.

Tixier, M. (2005). Globalization and Localization of Contents: Evolution of Major Internet Sites Across Sectors of Industry. *Thunderbird International Business Review*, *47*(1), 15–48. doi:10.1002/tie.20039.

Toh, S. M., & DeNisi, A. (2005). A local perspective on expatriate success. *The Academy of Management Executive*, *19*(1), 132–145.

Toh, S. M., & DeNisi, A. S. (2005). A local perspective to expatriate success. *The Academy of Management Executive*, *19*(1), 132–146.

Tong, M. C., & Robertson, K. (2008). Political and Cultural Representation in Malaysian Websites. *International Journal of Design*, *2*(2), 67–79.

Toor, S. R., & Ofori, G. (2008). Leadership For Future Construction Industry: Agende For Authentic Leadership. *International Journal of Project Management*, *26*, 620–630. doi:10.1016/j.ijproman.2007.09.010.

Torbiorn, I. (1982). *Living abroad: Personal adjustment and personnel policy in the overseas setting*. New York: Wiley.

Torres, G. (2007). The New "Export-Culture" in Latin America. *Global Business Languages, 12*(Article 12), 149-165.

Townsend, A. M., DeMarie, S. M., & Hendrickson, A. R. (1998). Virtual teams: Technology and the workplace of the future. *The Academy of Management Executive*, *12*, 17–29.

Traavik, L. E. M. (2006). Ledelseavmangfold. *Magma (New York, N.Y.)*, 2.

Traindis, H. (2004). The Many Dimensions of Culture. *The Academy of Management Executive*, *19*(1), 88–95. doi:10.5465/AME.2004.12689599.

Tran, B. (2008). *Expatriate selection and retention*. Doctoral dissertation, Alliant International University, San Francisco, CA.

Tran, N. C. (2002). *Learning Technological Capability for Vietnam's Industrial Upgrading: Challenges of Globalisation*. Hanoi, Vietnam: National Institute for Science and Technology Policy and Strategy Studies (NISTPASS).

Tran, B. (2012). Gendered technology-based organizations: A view of the glass cliff through the window of the glass ceiling. In Jemielniak, D., & Marks, A. (Eds.), *Managing dynamic technology-oriented businesses: High-tech organizations and workplaces*. Hershey, PA: IGI Global. doi:10.4018/978-1-4666-1836-7.ch015.

Trandis, H., Bontempo, R., & Villareal, M. (1988). Individualism and collectivism: Cross-cultural perspectives on self-group relationships. *Journal of Personality and Social Psychology*, *54*(2), 323–338. doi:10.1037/0022-3514.54.2.323.

Trent, R. J. (2003). Planning To Use Work Teams Effectively. *Team Performance Management*, *9*, 50–58. doi:10.1108/13527590310482235.

Triandia, H. C., Dunnette, M. D., & Hough, L. M. (1994). *Handbook of industrial and organizational psychology* (2nd ed., *Vol. 4*). Palo Alto, CA: Consulting Psychologists Press.

Triandis, H. C. (1972). *Analysis of subjective culture*. New York: Wiley Interscience.

Triandis, H. C. (1996). The psychological measurement of cultural syndromes. *The American Psychologist*, *51*, 407–415. doi:10.1037/0003-066X.51.4.407.

Triandis, H. C. (2000). Dialectics between cultural and cross-cultural psychology. *Asian Journal of Social Psychology*, *3*, 185–195. doi:10.1111/1467-839X.00063.

Triandis, H. C., Kurowski, L., Tecktiel, A., & Chan, D. (1993). Extracting the emics of cultural diversity. *International Journal of Intercultural Relations*, *17*, 217–234. doi:10.1016/0147-1767(93)90026-5.

Trompenaars, F. (1994). *Riding the Waves of Culture*. New York: Irwin.

Trompenaars, F., & Hampden-Turner, C. (1997). *Riding the Waves of Culture: Understanding Diversity in Global Business*. Boston, MA: Nicholas Brealey Publishing.

Truong, Q. Heijden, B. I. v. d., & Rowley, C. (2010). Globalisation, competitiveness, and human resource management in a transitional economy: The case of Vietnam. *International Journal of Business Studies*, *18*(1), 75–100.

Truong, Q., & Nguyen, T. V. (2002). Management Styles and Organisational Effectiveness in Vietnam. *Research and Practice in Human Resource Management*, *10*(2), 36–55.

Tsai, W. (2002). Social Structure of "Coopetition" Within a Multiunit Organization: Coordination, Competition, Intraorganizational Knowledge Sharing. *Organization Science*, *13*(2), 179–191. doi:10.1287/orsc.13.2.179.536.

Tsai, W., & Ghoshal, S. (1998). Social Capital and Value Creation: The Role of Intrafirm Networks. *Academy of Management Journal*, *41*(4), 464–476. doi:10.2307/257085.

Tsui, J. (2001). The implication of culture on relationship between budgetary participation, management accounting systems, and managerial performance: An analysis of Chinese and Western managers. *The International Journal of Accounting*, *36*, 125–146. doi:10.1016/S0020-7063(01)00101-7.

Tulving, E. (1972). Episodic and Semantic Memory. In Tulving, E., & Donaldson, W. (Eds.), *Organization of Memory* (pp. 381–404). New York: Academic Press.

Tung, R. L. (1981). Selection and training of personnel for overseas assignments. *The Columbia Journal of World Business*, *16*, 21–25.

Tung, R. L. (1982). Selection and training procedures of United States, European, and Japanese multinationals. *California Management Review*, *25*, 57–71. doi:10.2307/41164993.

Tung, R. L. (1988). Career issues in international assignments. *The Academy of Management Executive*, *11*, 241–244. doi:10.5465/AME.1988.4277265.

Turban, E., Sharda, R., & Delen, D. (2011). *Decision Support and Business Intelligence Systems*. Upper Saddle River, NJ: Pearson.

Turnbull, P. (1987). A challenge to the stages theory of internationalization process. In Rosson, P. S., & Ford, S. D. (Eds.), *Managing export entry and expansion* (pp. 21–40). New York: Praeger Publishers.

Turner, J. H. (1991). Structuration Theory. In The Structure of Sociological Theory.

Tushman, M. L., & Anderson, P. (1986). Technological Discontinuities and Organizational Environments. *Administrative Science Quarterly*, *31*(3), 439–465. doi:10.2307/2392832.

Tushman, M. L., & O'Reilly, C. A. (1997). *Winning through Innovation: A Practical Guide to Leading Organizational Change and Renewal*. Cambridge, MA: Harvard Business School Press.

Uma, S. (2011). Workforce diversity and HR challenges. *Advances in Management.*, *4*(10), 33–36.

Uncles, M. D. (2010). Retail change in China: Retrospect and prospects. *International Review of Retail, Distribution and Consumer Research*, *20*(1), 69–84. doi:10.1080/09593961003594501.

UNCTAD. (1996). *Trade and Development Report: Responding to the New Global Environment*. Retrieved on December 6, 2011, from http://vi.unctad.org/resources-mainmenu-64/digital-library?act=show&doc_name=tdr96-ch3

UNDP. (2002). *Briefing Report for Vietnam* (No. UNDP/POST/VIE/Rev12). Hanoi, Vietnam: Office of the United Nations Resident Coordinator, Vietnam.

UNESCO. (2010). Transcultural Communication in the Digital Age. Retrieved on October 9, 2012, from http://www.unesco.org/en/university-twinning-and-networking/access-by-region/europe-and-north-america/austria/unesco-chair-in-multilingual-transcultural-communication-in-the-digital-age-902/

Usunier, J. C. (1996). *Marketing across Cultures*. London: Prentice Hall.

Usunier, J.-C., & Roulin, N. (2010). The Influence of High- and Low-Context Communication Styles on the Design, Content, and Language of Busines-to-Business Web Sites. *Journal of Business Communication*, *47*(2), 189–227. doi:10.1177/0021943610364526.

Usunier, J.-C., Roulin, N., & Ivens, B. S. (2010). Cultural, National, and Industry-Level Differences in B2B Web Site Design and Content. *International Journal of Electronic Commerce*, *14*(2), 41–87. doi:10.2753/JEC1086-4415140202.

Uzzi, B. (1997). Social structure and competition in interfirm networks: The paradox of embeddedness. *Administrative Science Quarterly*, *42*(1), 35–67. doi:10.2307/2393808.

Valkokari, K., Paasi, J., & Rantala, T. (2012)... *Knowledge Management and Practice*, *10*(1), 27–40. doi:10.1057/kmrp.2011.39.

Van Arkadie, B., & Mallon, R. (2003). *Viet Nam: A Transition Tiger?* Canberra, Australia: Asia Pacific Press at the Australian National University.

Van de Donk, W., Loader, B. D., Nixon, P. G., & Rucht, D. (2004). *Cyberprotest: New Media, Citizens and Social movements*. London: Routledge.

Van der Alst, W. M. P., Rubin, V., Van Dongen, B. F., Kindler, E., & Günther, C. W. (2006). Process mining: A two-step approach using transition systems and regions. *BPM Center Report, BPM-06-30, Eindhoven University of Technology*. Retrieved June 10, 2012, from http://wwwis.win.tue.nl/~wvdaalst/BPMcenter/reports/2006/BPM-06-30.pdf

Van der Stede, W., Young, S., & Chen, C. (2005). Assessing the quality of evidence in empirical management accounting research: The case of survey studies. *Accounting, Organizations and Society*, *30*, 655–684. doi:10.1016/j.aos.2005.01.003.

Van der Vegt, G. S., Van der Vliert, E. V. D., & Huang, X. (2005). Location-Level Links Between Diversity and Innovative Climate Depend on National Power Distance. *Academy of Management Journal*, *48*(6), 1171–1182. doi:10.5465/AMJ.2005.19573116.

van Drunen, P., & van Strien, P. J. (1999). Psychology in the Netherlands: Recent trends and current situation. *European Psychologist*, *4*, 263–271. doi:10.1027//1016-9040.4.4.263.

Van Pelt, S. (2010). *The Complexities Of Leading Virtual Teams: A Phenomenological Study*. University Of Phoenix.

van Strien, P. J. (1998). Psychotechnics in the Netherlands. *Revista de Historia de la Psicología*, *19*, 121–141.

Van Vianen, A. E. M., & Kristof-Brown, A. L. (2004). Fitting in: Surface- And Deep- Level Cultural Differences and Expatriates Adjustment. *Academy of Management Journal*, *47*(5), 697–709. doi:10.2307/20159612.

Vance, C. M., McClaine, S. R., Boje, D. M., & Stage, D. (1992). An examination of the transferability of traditional performance appraisal principles across cultural boundaries. *Management International Review*, *32*, 313–326.

Vanhonacker, W. (1997). Entering China: An Unconventional Approach. *Harvard Business Review*, *75*(2), 130–140. PMID:10165447.

Vecchi, A., & Brennan, L. (2009). Quality management: A cross-cultural perspective. *Cross-Cultural Management: An International Journal*, *16*(2), 149–164. doi:10.1108/13527600910953900.

Vecchi, A., & Brennan, L. (2011). Quality management: A cross-cultural perspective based on GLOBE. *International Journal of Production and Operations Management*, *3*(5), 527–553. doi:10.1108/01443571111126319.

Velásquez, F. (2004). La estrategia, la estructura y las formas de asociación: Fuentes de ventaja competitiva para las pymes colombianas. *Estudios Gerenciales*, *93*, 73–97.

Vendola, M. T. (1998). Narrating Corporate Reputation: Becoming Legitimate Through Storytelling. *International Journal of Management and Organization*, *28*(3), 120–137.

Venkatesh, V., Morris, M. G., Davis, G. B., & Davis, F. D. (2003). User Acceptance of Information Technology: Towards a Unified View. *Management Information Systems Quarterly*, *27*(3), 425–478.

Venkatesh, V., Thong, J., & Xu, X. (2012). Consumer Acceptance And Use Of Information Technology: Extending The Unified Theory Of Acceptance And Use. *Technology (Elmsford, N.Y.)*.

Vera, D., & Crossan, M. (2004). Strategic Leadership and Organizational Learning. *Academy of Management Review*, *29*, 222–240.

Vercellis, C. (2009). *Business intelligence: Data mining and optimization for decision making*. London, UK: John Wiley and Sons.

Vereecke, A., & Muylle, S. (2006). Performance improvement through supply chain collaboration in Europe. *International Journal of Operations & Production Management*, *26*(11), 1176–1198. doi:10.1108/01443570610705818.

Verhees, F. J. H. M., & Meulenberg, M. T. G. (2004). Market orientation, innovativeness, product innovation, and performance in small firms. *Journal of Small Business Management*, *42*(2), 134–154. doi:10.1111/j.1540-627X.2004.00102.x.

Vermeulen, I. E., & Seegers, D. (2009). Tried and tested: The impact of online hotel reviews on consumer consideration. *Tourism Management*, *30*(1), 123–127. doi:10.1016/j.tourman.2008.04.008.

Veryzer, R. W. (1998). Discontinuous Innovation and the New Product Development Process. *Journal of Product Innovation Management*, *15*(4), 304–321. doi:10.1016/S0737-6782(97)00105-7.

Veryzer, R. W. (2005). The Roles of Marketing and Industrial Design in Discontinuous New Product Development. *Journal of Product Innovation Management*, *22*(1), 22–41. doi:10.1111/j.0737-6782.2005.00101.x.

Viaene, S., & Van den Bunder, A. (2011). The secrets to managing business analytics projects. *MIT Sloan Management Review*, *53*(1), 64–70.

Vianelli, D., de Luca, P., & Pegan, G. (2012). *Modalità d'entrata e scelte distributive del made in Italy in Cina*. Milano, Italy: Franco Angeli.

Vicini, J. (2011). *Government did not pay $16 for muffins after all*. Retrieved on November 18, 2011, from http://www.reuters.com/article/2011/09/30/us-usa-justice-muffins-idUSTRE78T54220110930

Vikøren, B. M. (1990). Market orientation: A sustainable small scale advantage? *Entrepreneurship & Regional Development*, *2*(4), 335–343. doi:10.1080/08985629000000021.

Vinekar, V.T., & James, T.C., & Chennamaneni. (2009). The ınteraction of business ıntelliegence and knowledge management in organizational decision making. *Journal of International Technology and Information Management*, *18*(2), 143–159.

Viteles, M. S. (1926). Psychology in industry. *Psychological Bulletin*, *23*, 631–680. doi:10.1037/h0070328.

Viteles, M. S. (1928). Psychology in industry. *Psychological Bulletin*, *25*, 309–340. doi:10.1037/h0072719.

Viteles, M. S. (1930). Psychology in industry. *Psychological Bulletin*, *27*, 567–635. doi:10.1037/h0073024.

Viteles, M. S. (1932). *Industrial psychology*. New York: W. W. Norton.

Volitich, D. (2008). *IBM Cognos 8: Business Intelligence The Official Guide*. New York: Mc Graw Hill.

Vollman, T. (1989). *Changing manufacturing performance measurements, Service Organizations*. Sarasota, FL: American Accounting Association.

Volpel, S. C., & Han, Z. (2005). Managing Knowledge Sharing in China: The Case of Siemens ShareNet. *International Journal of Knowledge Management*, *9*(3), 51–63. doi:10.1108/13673270510602764.

Vora, D. & Kostova, T. (2007). A model of dual organizational identification in the context of the multinational enterprise. *Jounral of organizational Behavior, 28*, 327-350.

Voss, C. (2005). Alternative paradigms for manufacturing strategies. *International Journal of Operations & Production Management*, *25*(12), 1211–1222. doi:10.1108/01443570510633611.

Voss, C., & Blackmon, K. (1998). Differences in manufacturing strategy decisions between Japanese and Western manufacturing plants: The role of strategic time orientation. *Journal of Operations Management*, *16*(2), 147–158. doi:10.1016/S0272-6963(97)00034-X.

Vroom, V. H. (1964). *Work and Motivation*. New York: Wiley.

Vroom, V. H., & Yetton, P. W. (1973). *Leadership and decision making*. Pittsburgh, PA: University of Pittsburgh Press.

Wacker, J. F., & Sprague, L. G. (1998). Forecasting accuracy: Comparing the relative effectiveness of practices between seven developing countries. *Journal of Operations Management*, *16*(2), 271–290. doi:10.1016/S0272-6963(97)00042-9.

Waldman, D. A., Luque, M. S. d., Washburn, N., & House, R. J. (2006). Cultural and Leadership Predictors of Corporate Social Responsibility Values of Top Management: A Globe Study of 15 Countries. *Journal of International Business Studies*, *37*(6), 823–837. doi:10.1057/palgrave.jibs.8400230.

Walker, D., & Dubitsky, T. M. (1991). *Do they like it? Does it matter? An ASI perspective*. Paper presented at the 36th Annual Conference of the Advertising Research Foundation. New York.

Wallerstein, I. M. (1974). *The modern world-system*. New York: Academic Press.

Wallerstein, I. M. (2011). *The Modern World-system: The Second Era of Great Expansion of the Capitalist World-economy, 1730's-1840's*. University of California Press.

Walsham, G. (2001). *Making a World of Difference: IT in a Global Context*. Chichester, UK: Wiley.

Walsham, G. (2002). Cross-Cultural Software Production And Use: A Structurational Analysis. *Management Information Systems Quarterly*, , 359–380. doi:10.2307/4132313.

Walsh, J. P., & Ungson, G. R. (1991). Organizational Memory. *Academy of Management Review*, *16*(1), 57–91.

Walter, M. (2007). Just how good is globalization? *Wall Street Journal*.

Walvoord, A. A. G., Redden, E. R., Elliott, L. R., & Coovert, M. D. (2008). Empowering Followers In Virtual Teams: Guiding Principles From Theory And Practice. *Computers in Human Behavior*, *24*, 1884–1906. doi:10.1016/j.chb.2008.02.006.

Wanberg, C. R., & Banas, J. T. (2000). Predictors and outcomes of openness to changes in a reorganizing workplace. *The Journal of Applied Psychology*, *85*(1), 132–142. doi:10.1037/0021-9010.85.1.132 PMID:10740964.

Wang, F., Head, M., & Arthur, N. (2002). E-tailing: An analysis of web impacts on the retail market. *The Journal of Business Strategy*, *19*(1), 73–93.

Wang, Y. (2007). Understanding Contractual Joint Ventures in China. *Journal of Chinese Economic and Business Studies*, *5*(1), 75–90. doi:10.1080/14765280601109394.

Warner, B. (2001). *Vietnam: Economic and Financial Management* (Working paper 1). Canberra, Australia: The Australian Government's Overseas Aid Program. The Australia Agency for International Development (AusAID).

Watanabe, S., Takahashi, K., & Minami, T. (1997). The emerging role of diversity and work-family values in a global context. In Earley, P. C., & Erez, M. (Eds.), *New perspective on international industrial/organizational psychology*. San Francisco, CA: The New Lexington Press.

Watts, R. (2005). *Subcontinental drift*. Retrieved on October 26, 2012, from http://www.telegraph.co.uk/finance/2903629/Subocontinental-drift.ttml

Webber, M. J., Wang, M., & Zhu, Y. (2002). Knocking on WTO's door. In Webber, M. J., Wang, M., & Zhu, Y. (Eds.), *China's Transition to a Global Economy* (pp. 1–13). New York: Palgrave Macmillan. doi:10.1057/9781403918604.

Webber, R. H. (1969). Convergence and Divergence. *The Columbia Journal of World Business*, *4*(3), 75–83.

Weber, R. P. (1990). Basic Content Analysis (Quantitative Applications in the Social Sciences) (2nd. ed.). Thousand Oaks, CA: Sage Publications.

Weber, K., & Roehl, W. S. (1999). Profiling people searching for purchasing travel products on the World Wide Web. *Journal of Travel Research*, *37*(3), 291–298. doi:10.1177/004728759903700311.

Wederspahn, G. (1992). Costing failures in expatriate human resource management. *Human Resource Planning*, *15*, 27–35.

Weetman, P. (2006). Discovering the international in Accounting and Finance. *The British Accounting Review*, *38*(4), 351–370. doi:10.1016/j.bar.2006.09.001.

Weick, K. (1995). *Sensemaking in organizations*. London: Sage Publications.

Weick, K., Sutcliffe, K. M., & Obstfeld, D. (2005). Organizing and the process of sensemaking. *Organization Science*, *16*(4), 409–421. doi:10.1287/orsc.1050.0133.

Weimann, P., Hinz, C., Scott, E., & Pollock, M. (2010). Changing the Communication Culture of Distributed Teams in a World Where Communication is Neither Perfect nor Complete. *The Electronic Journal Information Systems Evaluation*, *13*(2), 187–196.

Weinstein, A. K. (1977). Foreign investment by service firms: The case of multinational advertising agencies. *Journal of International Business Studies*, *8*(1), 83–91. doi:10.1057/palgrave.jibs.8490681.

Wei, T. T., Marthandan, G., Chong, A. Y. L., Ooi, K. B., & Arumugam, S. (2009). What drives Malaysian m-commerce adoption? An empirical analysis. *Industrial Management & Data Systems*, *109*(3), 370–388. doi:10.1108/02635570910939399.

Wei, Y., Liu, B., & Liu, X. (2004). Entry modes of foreign direct investment in China: A multinomial logit approach. *Journal of Business Research*, *58*(11), 1495–1505. doi:10.1016/j.jbusres.2004.10.002.

Welch, A. R. (2003). Globalisation, structural adjustment and contemporary educational reforms in Australia: The politics of reform, or the reform of politics? In Mok, K.-H., & Welch, A. R. (Eds.), *Globalisation and Educational Restructuring in the Asia Pacific Region* (pp. 262–301). Basingstoke, UK: Palgrave Macmillan.

Welch, L., & Luostarinen, R. (1988). Internationalisation: Evolution of a Concept. *Journal of General Management*, *14*(2), 34–55.

Wellman, J. L. (2009). *Organizational Learning*. Basingstoke, UK: Palgrave Macmillan. doi:10.1057/9780230621541.

Werthner, H., & Klein, S. (1999). *Information technology and tourism: A challenging relationship*. Vienna, Austria: Springer. doi:10.1007/978-3-7091-6363-4.

Wertsch, J. (1985). *Culture, communication, and cognition*. New York: Cambridge University Press.

Wertz, F. J. (2005). Phenomenological research methods for counselling psychology. *Journal of Counseling Psychology*, *52*(2), 167–177. doi:10.1037/0022-0167.52.2.167.

Whiting, J. W. M. (1986). George Peter Murdock (1897–1985). *American Anthropologist*, *88*(3), 682–686. doi:10.1525/aa.1986.88.3.02a00120.

Whittler, T. E., & Spira, J. S. (2002). Model's race: A peripheral cue in advertising messages? *Journal of Consumer Psychology*, *12*(4), 291–301. doi:10.1207/15327660260382333.

Wholefoods. (2011). *John Mackey's Blog*. Retrieved from http://www2.wholefoodsmarket.com/blogs/jmackey/. (2011, October 9).

Wild, J., Wild, K., & Han, J. (2001). *International Business: An Integrated Approach*. Upper Saddle River, NJ: Prentice Hall.

Williamson, J. (1990). What Washington means by policy reform? In Williamson, J. (Ed.), *Latin American Adjustment: How Much Has Happened?* Washington, DC: Institute for International Economics.

Wilson, I. (2001). U.K. SMEs in China - Performance and market entry strategies. *Journal of International Marketing and marketing research, 26*(3), 151-164.

Winsted, K. F. (1997). The service experience in two cultures: A behavioral perspective. *Journal of Retailing*, *73*(3), 337–360. doi:10.1016/S0022-4359(97)90022-1.

Wong, H. Y., & Merrilees, B. (2006). Determinants of SME brand adaptation in global marketing. *International Journal of Entrepreneurship and Small Business*, *3*(3/4), 477–497.

Wong, H. Y., & Merrilees, B. (2007). Multiple roles for branding in international marketing. *International Marketing Review*, *24*(4), 384–408. doi:10.1108/02651330710760982.

Wong, H. Y., & Merrilees, B. (2009). Service versus product brands: Understanding international adaptation. *Journal of International Business and Entrepreneurship Development*, *4*(3), 231–242. doi:10.1504/JIBED.2009.029014.

Wong, H. Y., & Merrilees, B. (2009a). Foreign market entry mode choice of Australian firms. *International Journal of Trade and Global Markets*, *2*(3/4), 250–266. doi:10.1504/IJTGM.2009.028992.

Wong, H. Y., & Merrilees, B. (2009b). Service versus product brands: Understanding international adaptation. *Journal of International Business and Entrepreneurship Development*, *4*(3), 231–242. doi:10.1504/JIBED.2009.029014.

Woodcock, C. P., Beamish, P. W., & Makino, S. (1994). Ownership-based entry mode strategies and international performance. *Journal of International Business Studies*, *25*(2), 253–273. doi:10.1057/palgrave.jibs.8490200.

World Bank. (2011). *Vietnam development report 2012: Market economy for a middle-income Vietnam (Joint Donor Report to the Vietnam Consultative Group Meeting No. 65980)*. Hanoi: Vietnam.

World Bank. (2012). *Doing business in a more transparent world 2012 - economic profile: Vietnam - comparing regulation for domestic firms in 183 economies* (Working paper). Washington, DC: World Bank.

World Bank. (2012). GDP growth. Retrieved on July 26, 2012, from http://data.worldbank.org/indicator/NY.GDP.MKTP.KD.ZG/countries

World Bank. (2012). *World Bank data*. Retrieved from http://www.worldbank.org, retrieved 11th September 2012

World Economic Forum. (2012). The Global Competitiveness Report 2011-2012. Retrieved on July 26, 2012, from http://www3.weforum.org/docs/WEF_GCR_Report_2011-12.pdf

Wortzel, H. V. (1985). The logistics of distribution in China. *International Journal of Physical Distribution & Materials Management*, *15*(5), 51–60. doi:10.1108/eb014618.

Wright, G., Fletcher, K., Donaldson, B., & Lee, J.-H. (2008). Sales force automation systems: An analysis of factors underpinning the sophistication of deployed systems in the UK financial services industry. *Industrial Marketing Management*, *37*(8), 992–104. doi:10.1016/j.indmarman.2007.08.005.

Wright, P. M. (1998). Introduction: Strategic human resource management research in the 21st century. *Human Resource Management Review*, *8*(3), 187–191. doi:10.1016/S1053-4822(98)90001-8.

Würtz, E. (2006). Intercultural Communication on Web sites: A Cross-Cultural Analysis of Web sites from High-Context Cultures and Low-Context Cultures. *Journal of Computer-Mediated Communication*, *11*, 274–299. doi:10.1111/j.1083-6101.2006.tb00313.x.

Wyszomirski, M. J. (2000). *Negotiating the Global Maze Artfully*. Paper presented at the 2000 Barnett Arts and Public Policy Symposium. Columbus, OH: Ohio Arts Council and Ohio State University College of the Arts.

Xiang, Z., & Gretzel, U. (2010). Role of social media in online travel information search. *Tourism Management*, *31*(2), 179–188. doi:10.1016/j.tourman.2009.02.016.

Yacine, R. (2007). Exploring Virtual Team-Working Effectiveness In The Construction Sector. *Interacting with Computers*, *19*, 96–112. doi:10.1016/j.intcom.2006.07.002.

Yaghoubi, N. M., Yazdani, B. O., Ahoorani, N., & Banihashemi, S. A. (2011). Information Technology Infrastructures and Knowledge Management: Towards Organizational Excellence. *Computer and Information Science*, *4*(5), 20–27. doi:10.5539/cis.v4n5p20.

Yamazaki, Y., & Kayes, D. C. (2004). An Experiential Approach to Cross-Cultural Learning: A Review and Integration of Competencies for Successful Expatriate Adaptation. *Academy of Management Learning & Education*, *3*(4), 18. doi:10.5465/AMLE.2004.15112543.

Yang, K. S. (1986). Will Societal Modernization Eventually Eliminate Cross-Cultural Psychological Differences. In Bond, M. H. (Ed.), *The Cross-Cultural Challenge to Social Psychology*. Newbury Park, CA: Sage Publications.

Yang, K. S. (2000). Monocultural and cross-cultural indigenous approaches: The royal road to the development of a balanced global psychology. *Asian Journal of Social Psychology*, *3*, 241–263. doi:10.1111/1467-839X.00067.

Yan, Y. (1999). *International Joint Ventures in China: Ownership, Control, and Performance*. New York: St. Martin's Press. doi:10.1057/9780333983898.

Yao, W., Chu, C. H., & Li, Z. (2011). Leveraging complex event processing for smart hospitals Using RFID. *Journal of Network and Computer Applications*, *34*, 799–810. doi:10.1016/j.jnca.2010.04.020.

Yates, K. (2006). Internal communication effectiveness enhances bottom-line results. *Journal of Organizational Excellence*, *25*, 71–79. doi:10.1002/joe.20102.

Yeh, A., & Bounds, A. (2006). Ferrero Rocher dispute calls for diplomacy. Retrieved October 3, 2011, from http://www.ft.com/cms/s/0/766d0fe4-8c8c-11db-9684-0000779e2340.html#axzz1a MkwSkWO

Yeniyurt, S., & Townsend, J. D. (2003). Does Culture Explain Acceptance of New Products in a Country?: An Empirical Investigation. *International Marketing Review*, *20*(4), 377–396. doi:10.1108/02651330310485153.

Yerkes, R. M. (1921). *Memories of the national academy of sciences: Psychological examining in the United States army* (*Vol. 15*). Washington, DC: U.S. Government Printing Office. doi:10.1037/10619-000.

Yin, R. (2009). *Case Study Research: Design and Methods* (4th ed.). Thousand Oaks: Sage Publications.

Yli-Renko, H., Autio, E., & Sapienza, H. (2001). Social capital, knowledge acquisition, and knowledge exploitation in young technology-based firms. *Strategic Management Journal*, *22*, 587–613. doi:10.1002/smj.183.

Yoo, B., & Donthu, N. (2001). Developing and validating a multidimensional consumer-based brand equity scale. *Journal of Business Research*, *52*(1), 1–14. doi:10.1016/S0148-2963(99)00098-3.

Yoo, D. K., Rao, S. S., & Hong, P. (2006). A comparative study on cultural differences and quality practices – Korea, USA, Mexico and Taiwan. *International Journal of Reliability and Quality Management*, *23*(6), 607–624. doi:10.1108/02656710610672452.

Yoshii, T., & Saski, K. (2010). Information/Communication Technologies and Travel Behaviour. *Transportation Research Part C, Emerging Technologies*, *18*(1), 1–2. doi:10.1016/j.trc.2009.04.021.

Young, J. (2000). *The Career Paths of Computer Science and Information Systems Major Graduates*. Unpublished doctoral thesis. University of Tasmania, Tasmania, Australia.

Young, M. (1997). Principles for lasting change. *Journal of Cost Management*, *1*, 16–20.

Yu, H. J., Paek, H.-J., & Bae, B. (2008). Cross-cultural comparison of interactivity and advertising appeals on antismoking web sites in the United States and South Korea. *Internet Research*, *18*(5), 454–476. doi:10.1108/10662240810912738.

Yu, J., & Meyer-Ohle, H. (2008). Working for Japanese Corporations in China: A Qualitative Study. *Asian Business & Management*, *7*(1), 33–51. doi:10.1057/palgrave.abm.9200250.

Yun, G. W., Park, S.-Y., & Ha, L. (2008). Influence of Cultural Dimensions on Online Interactive Review Feature Implementations: A Comparison of Korean and U.S. Retail Web Sites. *Journal of Interactive Marketing*, *22*(3), 40–50. doi:10.1002/dir.20116.

Yusof, S. A. M., & Zakaria, N. (2012). *Exploring The State Of Discipline On The Formation Of Swift Trust Within Global Virtual Teams* (pp. 475–482). IEEE. doi:10.1109/HICSS.2012.272.

Yusuf, S., & Weiping, W. (1997). *The dynamics of urban growth in three Chinese cities*. New York: Oxford University Press.

Zacharakis, A. L. (1997). Entrepreneurial Entry into Foreign Markets: A Transaction Cost Perspective. *Entrepreneurship Theory and Practice*, *21*(3), 23–40.

Zack, M. H. (1999). Developing a Knowledge Strategy. *California Management Review*, *41*(3), 125–145. doi:10.2307/41166000.

Zahedi, F. M., & Bansal, G. (2011). Cultural Signifiers of Web Site Images. *Journal of Management Information Systems*, *28*(1), 147–200. doi:10.2753/MIS0742-1222280106.

Zahra, S. A. (2005). A theory of international new ventures: A decade of research. *Journal of International Business Studies*, *36*(1), 20–28. doi:10.1057/palgrave.jibs.8400118.

Zahra, S. A., Hayton, J., Marcel, J., & O'Neill, H. (2001). Fostering entrepreneurship during international expansion: Managing key challenges. *European Management Journal*, *19*(4), 359–369. doi:10.1016/S0263-2373(01)00037-8.

Zahra, S., & George, G. (2002). International Entrepreneurship: The Current Status of the Field and Future Research Agenda. In Hitt, M., Ireland, D., Sexton, D., & Camp, M. (Eds.), *Strategic Entrepreneurship: Creating an Integrated Mindset* (pp. 255–288). Oxford, UK: Blackwell Publishers.

Zakaria, N., & Abdul Talib, A. N. (2011). What Did You Say? Cross-Cultural Analysis of the Distributive Communicative Behaviors of Global Virtual Teams. In *Proceedings of International Conference on Computational Aspects of Social Networks*. Salamanca, Spain: IEEE.

Zbaracky, M. (1998). The rhetoric and reality of Total quality Management. *Administrative Science Quarterly*, *43*(3), 602–636. doi:10.2307/2393677.

Zedeck, S. (1997). Commentary on diversity and work-family values. In Earley, P. C., & Erez, M. (Eds.), *New perspective on international industrial/organizational psychology*. San Francisco, CA: The New Lexington Press.

Zeira, Y., & Banai, M. (1985). Selection of expatriate-managers in multinational corporations: The host environment point of view. *International Studies of Management and Organization*, *15*, 33–51.

Zeithaml, V. A. (1988). Consumer perceptions of price, quality, and value: A means-end model and synthesis of evidence. *Journal of Marketing*, *52*(3), 2–22. doi:10.2307/1251446.

Zeithaml, V. A., Berry, L. L., & Parasuraman, A. (1996). The behavioral consequences of service quality. *Journal of Marketing*, *60*(2), 31–46. doi:10.2307/1251929.

Zeithaml, V. A., Parasuraman, A., & Berry, L. L. (1985). Problems and strategies in service marketing. *Journal of Marketing*, *49*(2), 33–46. doi:10.2307/1251563.

Zeng, L., Xu, L., Shi, Z., & Wang, M. (2006). Techniques, process and enterprise solutions of business ıntelligence. In *Proceedings of the IEEE International Conference on Systems, Man and Cybernetics* (pp.4722-4726). IEEE.

Zenun, M., Loureiro, G., & Araujo, C. (2007). The Effects Of Teams' Co-Location On Project Performance. *Complex Systems Concurrent Engineering*, 717-726.

Zhang, D., & Lowry, P. J. (2008). Issues, Limitations and Opportunities in Cross-Cultural Research on Collaborative Software in Information Systems. *Journal of Global Information Management*, *16*(1), 61–92. doi:10.4018/jgim.2008010103.

Zhang, D., Lowry, P. J., Zhou, L., & Fu, X. (2007). The Impact of Individualism-Collectivism, Social Presence and Group Diversity on Group Decision making under Majority Influence. *Journal of Management Information Systems*, *23*(4), 53–80. doi:10.2753/MIS0742-1222230404.

Zhang, Y., Gregory, M., & Shi, Y. (2008). Global Engineering Networks (Gen): Drivers, Evolution, Configuration, Performance And Key Patterns. *Journal Of Manufacturing Technology Management*, *19*, 299–314. doi:10.1108/17410380810853740.

Zhang, Z. (2012). A Social Software Strategy for Knowledge Management and Organization Culture. *OR Insight*, *25*(2), 60–79. doi:10.1057/ori.2011.14.

Zhao, W., Massey, B. L., Murphy, J., & Fang, L. (2003). Cultural Dimensions of Website Design and Content. *Prometheus*, *21*(1), 75–84. doi:10.1080/08109020320 00051027.

Zhao, X., Maheshwari, S. K., & Zhang, J. (1995). Benchmarking Quality practices in India, China and Mexico. *Benchmarking for Quality Management & Technology*, *2*(3), 20–32. doi:10.1108/14635779510099220.

Zheng, W., & Yang, B., McLean, & G. N. (2010). Linking Organizational Culture, Structure, Strategy, and Organizational Effectiveness: Mediating Role of Knowledge Management. *Journal of Business Research*, *63*, 763–771. doi:10.1016/j.jbusres.2009.06.005.

Zhou, J., & George, J. M. (2003). Awakening employee creativity: The role of leader emotional intelligence. *The Leadership Quarterly*, *14*, 545–568. doi:10.1016/S1048-9843(03)00051-1.

Zhou, N., & Belk, R. (2004). Chinese consumer readings of global and local advertising appeals. *Journal of Advertising*, *33*(3), 63–76. doi:10.1080/00913367.2004.10639169.

Zhu, K., & Kraemer, K. L. (2005). Post-adoption variations in usage and value of e-business by organizations: Cross-country evidence from the retail industry. *Information Systems Research*, *16*(1), 16–24. doi:10.1287/isre.1050.0045.

Zimmermann, A. (2011). Interpersonal Relationships In Transnational, Virtual Teams: Towards A Configurational Perspective. *International Journal of Management Reviews*, *13*, 59–78. doi:10.1111/j.1468-2370.2010.00284.x.

Zorn, T., Page, D., & Cheney, G. (2000). Nuts about change: Multiple perspectives on change-oriented communication in a public sector organization. *Management Communication Quarterly*, *13*(4), 515–566. doi:10.1177/0893318900134001.

Zou, S., & Cavusgil, S. T. (2002). The GMS: A broad conceptualization of global marketing strategy and its effect on firm performance. *Journal of Marketing*, *66*(October), 40–56. doi:10.1509/jmkg.66.4.40.18519.

Zukin, S., & Dimaggio, P. (1990). *Structures of Capital: The social organizaion of the economy*. New York: Cambridge University Press.

About the Contributors

Bryan Christiansen has been the Chairman of PryMarke, LLC since 2004, a Business Analytics and Management Consultancy in Michigan, USA. He has also been an Adjunct Business Professor since 2003 at Capella University and Ellis University (formerly Ellis College of New York Institute of Technology) in the USA and Gumushane University in Turkey. Born in Washington, DC and raised in Asia, Bryan is fluent in Chinese, Japanese, Spanish, and Turkish and has traveled to 38 countries during his 27-year business career with Global 500 firms and smaller. Bryan is an avid writer on business and education subjects and is currently based in Istanbul, Turkey, where he is doing research for future books on these topics. Bryan holds a Bachelor's degree in Marketing from the University of the State of New York and an MBA degree from Capella University. He will complete his Doctor of Business Administration (DBA) degree in International Business at Walden University in 2013.

Ekaterina Turkina has been with HEC Montreal in Canada since 2010. Her main research areas are state business relationship, inter-firm networks, and socio-cultural and politico-economic factors in international business. She teaches various courses in the domain of international affairs, such as international management, multinational firms, culture and human resources, global governance, and she is actively involved in research groups in international affairs (GRAI). Dr. Turkina also has extensive experience working in international organizations including International Marketing Solutions, American Councils, and Council of Europe. She holds a Master of Arts and a PhD from the Graduate School of Public and International Affairs at the University of Pittsburgh.

Nigel L. Williams (nwilliams@bournemouth.ac.uk) is a Senior Lecturer in Project Management at the School of Tourism at the Bournemouth University. Nigel completed a PhD in 2010 at the Institute for Manufacturing at Cambridge University in the UK, where he examined the international evolution of company production systems using data from Trinidad and Tobago firms. His current research interests include Production Systems, Organizational Project Management and Festival Internationalization. Before joining the University, Nigel worked for 15 years as an engineer, project manager, and business consultant for organizations in the Caribbean region. A member of the Project Management Institute, he holds the Project Management Professional (PMP) certification along with the Prince 2 qualification.

* * *

Ahmed Abdel-Maksoud is an Associate Professor of Management Accounting and Chair of the Accounting Department (AACSB-Accounting Accredited) at the College of Business and Economics atUnited Arab Emirates University. He has worked for several international universities. His research interests are in the fields of performance measurement systems, strategic performance measurement systems, eco-control systems, and environmental management accounting. Over the past few years, he has been involved in funded research projects totaling around $2M received from international research centres. Ahmed authored an Elsevier book on non-financial performance measurement and management practices in international manufacturing firms in 2007. His work was published in several reputable international journals. One of his papers was published in *The British Accounting Review Journal* (BAR) in 2005 and was ranked by Scopus, amongst the top 10 cited BAR papers. Two of his BAR papers (2005 and 2010) were ranked amongst the hottest 25 BAR articles to date. Ahmed compiled a postgraduate teaching textbook, "Accounting for Strategic Decisions" with McGrawHill in 2011. He contributed with a chapter case in Horngren et al.'s, "Cost Accounting: A Managerial Emphasis" (2012). Ahmed is on the editorial board and an *ad hoc* reviewer for many international journals and conferences in the accounting field. He is a Director for the Asia-Pacific Management Accounting Association (APMAA) 2013.

Vandana Ahuja is an Assistant Professor at the Jaypee Business School,, the business arm of the Jaypee Institute of Information Technology,, India. She teaches E-Marketing, Advanced Services Marketing and Customer Relationship Management. She worked previously with JILIT--The IT arm of the Jaypee Group, where she was involved in Business Development and Marketing Communication activities for Teaching Solution Bhartiyavidya, with special focus on International Marketing activities for the UK, USA, and South Asia. Prior to this, she had worked as a Business Manager with NIIT in India, where she was responsible for corporate training, business development, and marketing. She has research interests in diverse areas of marketing, especially customer-centric branding, CRM, and digital marketing. She has been actively researching the domain of the collaborative Web with focus on its contributions to the field of marketing and CRM. She has several publications published across international and national journals/conferences and actively serves on the editorial review board of several journals. She was associated with *Customerthink Corp.*, U.S.A (formerly crmguru.com)--The Global Thought Leader in Customer Centric Business Strategy, as a member of their Advisory Council (2008).

Ghadeer Al-Safi completed her undergraduate degree in Accountancy at the University of Wollongong in Dubai. During that time, she was a teaching assistant as well as a research assistant under a Cross-Cultural Project. This research project examines the impact of culture on global virtual teams' performance. She also had the experience of participating in a global-scale student virtual collaboration team project as part of one of her course assessment tasks which complemented her research project.

Kurt April is a Sainsbury Fellow and Professor of Leadership, Diversity & Inclusion at the Graduate School of Business of the University of Cape Town in South Africa; Programme Director and Faculty Member of DukeCE (Duke University, USA); an Associate Fellow of Said Business School (University of Oxford, UK); Research Fellow of Ashridge (UK); and Visiting Professor at Rotterdam School of Management (Erasmus University, Netherlands). Outside of academia, Kurt also currently plays executive roles in business: Managing Partner of LICM Consulting (Management Consulting, Global), Owner-Director of Helderview BMW *(*Automobile Industry, South Africa*),* Non-Executive Board Director of Achievement Awards Group (Strategic Consulting & Performance Management, South Africa), Non-Executive Holdings Board Director of the Power Group (Construction & Property Development, Africa), Chairman of the International Advisory Council to Novartis International (Pharmaceutical & Health Care, Switzerland), and Member of the Special Agenda Council on Talent & Diversity of the World Economic Forum (International Affairs, Switzerland). He holds a a PhD in Economics & Technology, a Certificate in Japanese Production, an MBA in Business Administration, an M.S. in Electronic Engineering, an HDE in Education, a B.S. in Electrical Engineering, a National Diploma in Electronics, and a National Diploma in Logic Systems; completed at the University of Cape Town (South Africa), University of Oxford (UK), Wingfield College (South Africa), and AOTS (Nagoya, Japan).

Amit Arora is a PhD candidate in Logistics and Supply Chain Management at Georgia Southern University in Statesboro, Georgia, USA. He holds a M.S. degree in Energy and Environmental Management from Indian Institute of Technology (Delhi, India) and a B.S. in Mechanical Engineering from Aligarh University (India). Amit has won the best PhD Student Research Paper Awards in 2011 for research papers presented at the annual meetings of the Southeastern Institute for Operations Research and the Management Sciences (SEINFORMS) and Southeast Decision Sciences Institute (SEDSI). His current research interests are sustainability strategies in supply chain management, supply chain collaboration and experiential innovative gaming exercises for teaching. Amit has a decade-long automobile industry experience in India, having worked with Honda Motors and Hyundai Motors, where he was responsible for providing technical and warranty support to dealers at domestic and international levels. He plans to join academia after completion of his PhD.

Anshu Arora is the Assistant Professor of Marketing and Director of Global Logistics and International Business Education and Research (G-LIBER) Center of Excellence at the College of Business Administration at Savannah State University inSavannah, Georgia, USA. She is a certified Project Management Professional (PMP) from Project Management Institute (PMI) in Pennsylvania, USA. Dr. Arora has more than a decade of corporate and academic experience. She has been on the Editorial Review Boards of the *International Journal of Online Pedagogy and Course Design* since 2010 and the *International Journal of Web-Based Learning and Teaching Technologies* since 2008. Her research interests include consumer behavior, advertising polysemy, ambient advertising, stereotypes in advertising, social media strategy mix, and supply chain strategy relationships.

Anthony Atkins is a Reader in Applied Computing in the Faculty of Computing, Engineering and Science at Staffordshire University, and is a Chartered Engineer in both computing and engineering. He is also a Churchill Fellow in bioengineering and environmental engineering and has several industrial patents in bioengineering and waste recycling covering the UK, EU, Canada, Australia, and the USA. His main interests include knowledge management, outsourcing and sensor technology in e-health, and waste recycling in the construction and mining industries. He has over 160 refereed publications consisting of journals, chapters in books, and conferences with his colleagues and research students.

Lyn Atkins holds a B.S. in Economics and a Masters degree in Computing Science (IT for Strategic Management). After a career of over 25 years in management services, including roles of a Management Services Officer and Principal Research Analyst in the UK public sector organisations, she spent some time as a Researcher at Staffordshire University, contributing from both her academic and professional experience.

Eva Podovšovnik Axelsson is an Assistant Professor of the Research Methodology in Tourism at the Faculty of Tourism Studies Portorož – Turistica at theUniversity of Primorska in Slovenia. In her undergraduate and postgraduate studies at the University of Ljubljana's (Slovenia) Faculty of Social Sciences, she has always shown strong interest for the methodology of (social) research and for the impact of the new technologies in society, especially in education. Her main research areas are quantitative research methodology, the diffusion of new technologies in society, e-tourism, and social network analysis. She is also organising seminars of statistics and research methodology for students and teachers. She is the author or co-author of one scientific monography and many scientific articles. She has also presented the results of her research work at different international scientific conferences, such as An Enterprise Odyssey: Economics and Business in the New Millennium 2002, and the International Conference on Methodology and Statistics.

Mert Bal is a research assistant at the Mathematical Engineering Department of Yildiz Technical University. He received his B.S.c, M.S., and PhD from the Mathematical Engineering Department of Yildiz Technical University (1999, 2001, and 2008, respectively). His areas of interest include machine learning, uncertainty reasoning, artificial intelligence, soft computing, rough set theory, formal concept analysis, and decision support systems.

Yasemin Bal started her academic career as a research assistant at Yildiz Technical University in 2005. She completed her PhD in the Human Resources Management Department at Istanbul University Business Administration Faculty. She currently continues her academic career as Assistant Professor at Yildiz Technical University Business Administration Department in Istanbul, Turkey. Her areas of interest include management, human resources management, and strategic management.

Dr. Serdar Bozkurt started his academic career as a Research Assistant at Yildiz Technical University. He completed his PhD in the field of Human Resources Management at Istanbul University Business Administration Faculty. He currently continues his academic career as Assistant Professor at Yildiz Technical University Business Administration Department in Istanbul, Turkey. His areas of interest include organizational behavior and human resources management.

Louis Brennan is Director of the Institute for International Integration Studies at Trinity College, a Fellow of Trinity College, and Professor within the School of Business. He holds Bachelor's and Master's Degrees in Industrial Engineering, a PhD from the Department of Mechanical Engineering at the University of Manchester (Institute of Science and Technology) for his work on the modelling of manufacturing systems, and an MBA degree with a concentration in International and Cross-Cultural Management. Dr. Brennan has served as a faculty member and researcher in Engineering and Business schools in the USA, Europe, and Asia. His fields of interest include Global Strategy and International Business, Global Supply Chain Management, Operations Strategy, and Technology Management. He has published extensively in these areas in internationally refereed journals, conference proceedings, and edited books. His most recent books have been *The Emergence of Southern Multinationals: Their Impact on Europe* and *the Business of Space – The Next Frontier of International Competition,* co-authored with Alessandra Vecchi.

Ulysses J. Brown, III is an Associate Professor of Management in the College of Business Administration at Savannah State University, joining the SSU faculty in the fall of 2004. Before assuming his academic duties, Dr. Brown served ten years in the United States Navy as an enlisted man, including three years onboard the USS Dahlgren (DDG-43), which was home ported in Norfolk, Virginia. He earned a Master's in Industrial-Organizational Psychology from Valdosta State University and a PhD in Business Administration from Jackson State University. In his leisure time, he enjoys jazz, bowling, and traveling. Dr. Brown's teaching interests include business statistics, business research, operations management, and supply chain management at both the undergraduate and graduate levels. His research interests are in the areas of ethics, propensity for military service, organizational climate and performance in military units, and management education.

Sebnem Burnaz is a Professor of Marketing at Istanbul Technical University, Faculty of Management. She holds a PhD in Management with a major in Marketing from Bogazici University. Her research interests are in the fields of marketing, retailing, decision making, and business ethics. She has published articles which have appeared in *Advances in International Marketing*, *Journal of Business Ethics*, *Sex Roles: A Journal of Research*, and *Journal of Multi-Criteria Decision Analysis.*

Angelo A. Camillo is an Associate Professor of Strategic Management at Woodbury University in Los Angeles, California, USA. He has over 35 years of international management experience and has worked and lived in ten countries and four continents. He holds an undergraduate degree from Heidelberg (Germany) School of Hotel Management, an MBA from San Francisco State University, and a PhD from Oklahoma State University. He teaches courses in Strategy, Global Enterprise Management, Business Ethics, Organizational Behavior, and special topics in Hospitality Entrepreneurship and Business Development. He is a Visiting Professor at China Normal University in Guangzhou, China. He is also a Woodbury University faculty member of the Carl Benz Academy in Beijing, China, in collaboration with the Guanghua School of Management and Freie University (Berlin, Germany). He was Visiting Professor at the Cassa Marca Ca' Tron Institute in Venice, Italy. His research encompasses three streams of interest that reflect his specializations and courses he teaches: strategic management (mainstream), industry specific (Hospitality), and cross-disciplinary. Research topics include strategic and international management, food and wine business, marketing best practice, social responsibility, and ethics.

Harish C. Chandan is Professor of Business at Argosy University in Atlanta, Georgia, USA. He was Interim Chair of the Business Program in 2011. He received the President's Award for Excellence in Teaching in 2007, 2008, and 2009. His teaching philosophy is grounded in the learner engagement and life-long learning. His research interests include research methods, leadership, marketing, and organizational behavior. He has published 15 peer-reviewed articles in business and management journals. Dr. Chandan presented caucus discussion on green innovation and distance learning at the Academy of Management. Dr Chandan presented a professional development workshop on leading organizational change through action research and solutions focused learning at the Academy of Management. In addition, Dr. Chandan has presented papers at the International Academy of Management and Business and Southeast Association of Information Systems Conferences. Prior to joining Argosy, Dr. Chandan managed optical fiber and cable product qualification laboratories for Lucent Technologies, Bell Laboratories. During his career with Lucent, he had 40 technical publications, a chapter in a book, and five patents.

Edward T. Chen is a Professor of Management Information Systems (MIS) in the Operations and Information Systems Department at the University of Massachusetts Lowell. Dr. Chen has published over 60 refereed research articles in scholarly journals such as *Information & Management*, *Journal of Computer Information Systems*, *Project Management*, *Comparative Technology Transfer and Society*, *Journal of International Technology and Information Management*, and *International Journal of Innovation and Learning*. Dr. Chen has served as vice-president, board director, track chair, and session chair of many professional associations and conferences. Professor Chen has also served as journal editor, editorial reviewer, and ad hoc reviewer for various academic journals. Dr. Chen has received the Irwin Distinguished Paper Award at the Southwestern Federation of Administrative Disciplines conference and the Best Paper Award at the International Conference on Accounting and Information Technology. His main research interests are in the areas of project management, knowledge management, and Green IT.

Nicholas Chileshe is a Senior Lecturer in Construction & Project Management in the School of Natural and Built Environments at the University of South Australia. He is also the Research Education and Portfolio Leader. Dr Chileshe obtained his PhD in Construction Management from the Sheffield Hallam University. Prior to his appointment in July 2009, he worked in the UK for ten years at Sheffield Hallam University. Nicholas is also a Fellow of the Chartered Institute of Building (FCIOB), Fellow of the Australian Institute of Building (FAIB), Fellow of the Association of Building Engineers (FEBng), Fellow of the Higher Education Academy (FHEA), Member of the Chartered Institute of Management (MICM), and Member of the Australian Institute of Project Management (MAIPM). His current research interests relate to the built environment, including total quality management, sustainability, construction management, risk management, project management, and project success.

Mary L. Connerley is a professor and head of the Management Department at the University of Northern Iowa. Connerley received her PhD in Human Resource Management from the University of Iowa. Before joining UNI, Dr. Connerley taught in the Pamplin College of Business at Virginia Tech. Dr. Connerley has published articles in many respected journals, including *Personnel Psychology, Academy of Management Learning and Education, Journal of Management, Human Relations, Journal of Occupational and Organizational Psychology, and Journal of Management Education* in addition to others. In addition to over 20 articles on human resource and diversity-related issues, she is co-author of the book titled, "Leading in a Diverse and Multicultural Environment: Developing Awareness, Knowledge, and Skills." Her current research and teaching interests center on diversity in the workplace, issues of multiculturalism, and recruiting.

Birton J. Cowden is an International Business doctoral candidate at the Boeing Institute of International Business at Saint Louis University. His research and publication focus is in international strategy, entrepreneurship, and innovation. His current research looks at the types of new ventures in emerging economies. Mr. Cowden has published in the *Multinational Business Review* and has proceedings from the Academy of Management, the Academy of International Business, the Southern Management Association, and the United States Association for Small Business and Entrepreneurship. Birton can be reached at 3674 Lindell Blvd., John Cook School of Business, Saint Louis University, St. Louis, Mo 63108, via e-mail at bcowden@slu.edu or by phone at 618-340-3019.

Pascal da Rocha is a professor, trainer, and mediator. His expertise is in conflict mediation, cultural analysis, and transnational leadership. He has over 16 years of experience in violent conflict zones and he has expanded his work into strategic and change management, innovation management and sustainability for the corporate world. He has worked for the UN, the OSCE, NATO, the World Bank, and he has consulted clients, such as DaimlerChrysler, Volkswagen, Unilever, and PAREXEL, among many others. When not practicing, he teaches on conflict resolution, leadership and equality, human rights, and peace and conflict studies at Columbia University, the University of Uppsala, Philips-Marburg University, Southern Russian Federal University, and other centers of excellence. He lives and travels with his wife and son in the United States and South Africa.

Patrizia de Luca, PhD, is Professor at the University of Trieste, Italy, where she teaches Marketing and Research Methodology for Management Decisions. She is Deputy Director of the Department of Economics, Business, Mathematics and Statistics and member of some academic committees. She has authored five books and 36 refereed publications in national and international books and journals. She has recently participated in a large research program on distribution and sales of Italian products in the Chinese market and in other research projects on international marketing. Her research focus is on distribution channels, retail marketing, and cross-cultural consumer behavior.

Loredana Di Pietro is an Assistant Professor of Organizational Studies in the Department of Business and in the Department of Human and Social Sciences at the University of Molise, Italy. She teaches course in Event Management, Business Organization, and Organizational Behavior. She is a post-doc researcher in organizational behavior, group conflict, and team dynamics. Her research applies qualitative and quantitative research methodologies and statistical analysis. She is Editor of the International Journal of Digital Content Technology and its Applications and of the Journal of Next Generation Information Technology. She is an ad hoc reviewer for the *International Journal of the Digital Human*, *Journal of Computer - Mediated Communication*, *Electronic Commerce Research and Applications*, and the *International Journal of Digital Content Technology and its Application*. She has presented research papers at the International Workshop at the University of Groningen Research School in Holland, at the EIASM (European Institute for Advanced Study in Management) in Belgium, and at the University of Madrid Institute of Research in Spain. She has been a tutor for the Master in European Planning organized by the University of Molise, in collaboration with EIPA (European Institute of Public Administration) at Bruxelles and Maastricht. She is the recipient of the prestigious Roberto Marrana Award "Alla ricerca di Talenti-Research Section" (In search of Research Talent).

Francesca Di Virgilio is an Assistant Professor of Organizational Studies in the Department of Human and Social Sciences at the University of Molise, Italy. She teaches courses in organizational studies, event management, organizational behavior, and group processes. She received her PhD in Organization, Technology and Development of Human Resources from the University of Molise, Italy. She was a Visiting Researcher at the Research Center of Industrial Relations & Organizational Behavior (IROB) at the Warwick Business School in Warwick, UK. She has been teaching courses at the undergraduate and graduate levels, including international master programs in several universities in Italy on topics such as organization design, organizational behavior, knowledge management, and human resources management. She has taught in some of the territorial Public Administration involved in tailored training program on topics such as job design and organizational analysis, leadership, team building and organizational change. She is Editor for the *International Journal of Digital Content Technology,* and its Applications. Research topics include human knowledge, transfer knowledge, consumer's group knowledge, and social network, groups' dynamic.

Massimo Franco is a Professor of Organization Behavior and Human Resources Management at the University of Molise and at the University of Naples Federico II. I.T.P.; International Teachers Program, and at the International School of Business Management. He is the Director of the University of Molise Organization and Team Management Laboratory, and teaches undergraduate, graduate, and PhD courses in organizational behavior, teambuilding, team management, and human resource development. He is a member of the Evaluation Board of the University of Sannio in Benevento, and founding member of Arethuse:Association des Rencontres Economiques Thematiques des Universites du Sud de Europe IERSO Universitè Bordeaux, France. Massimo Franco has been a Visiting Professor at several universities and is member of many domestic and international editorial boards, organizations, and academic associations. He has published several books and numerous papers as author and co-author. His current research interests and publications focus on team based organizations, teamwork and teambuilding, leadership, employee motivation, knowledge management and competences, and well-being and distress in organizations.

M. Reza Hosseini is currently a lecturer and PhD Candidate in Construction Management at the University of South Australia. He has been the CEO of a construction company with practical experience in the construction industry for over 11 years in the Middle East. In addition, he has conducted many research projects for the Building Code Office of the Iranian Ministry of Housing for five years, and has been co-author for many published works including books, journals, and conference papers. M. Reza has a Master of Science (M.S.) in Construction Management, and his main research fields are virtual teams, productivity, benchmarking, and project performance within construction. He is a member of the Board of Directors for the Project Management Institute (PMI) Adelaide chapter, and a member of the Australian Institute of Building (AIB) and Australian Institute of Project Management (AIPM).

M. Gordon Hunter is Professor of Information Systems in the Faculty of Management at The University of Lethbridge in Alberta, Canada. He has also been appointed Visiting Professor of the Faculty of Business, Computing and Information Management at London South Bank University. Dr. Hunter has previously held academic positions at universities in Canada, Hong Kong, and Singapore, and visiting positions at universities in Australia, England, Germany, Monaco, New Zealand, Poland, Turkey, and the USA. In 2012, he received the Lloyd Houlden Research Fellowship from the Canadian Insolvency Foundation. From April to July of 2009, Dr. Hunter was a Fellow at the University of Applied Sciences in Munich, Germany, and during July and August of 2005, he was an Erskine Fellow at the University of Canterbury in Christchurch, New Zealand. He has a Bachelor of Commerce Degree from the University of Saskatchewan in Saskatoon in Saskatchewan, Canada, and a PhD from the Strathclyde Business School at the University of Strathclyde in Glasgow, Scotland. Dr. Hunter has also obtained a Certified Management Accountant (CMA) designation from the Society of Management Accountants of Canada and was appointed a Fellow of the Society in 2010. In 2011, he was appointed CMA Distinguished Scholar by CMA Alberta. At the University of Lethbridge, Dr. Hunter is the Director of the Small Business Institute.

Fiona Ji is a full time Visiting Assistant professor at Ohio University. Her current research focuses on how firms effectively balance exploitation and exploration in the situation of organizational learning and innovation. She is specifically interested in researching international firms and technology new ventures. She has presented articles in major conferences in both international management and entrepreneurship fields. In addition, she has interests in methodology issues in organization studies and has published work in the field of organization research methods. She is also active at providing services to the academic field, participating as reviewer and discussant for several academic journals. Fiona Ji had her PhD studies in Strategy at Virginia Tech and received her Master's Degree in Management from Grenoble Ecole de Management (France), and her Bachelor's Degree from Foreign Affairs University (China). She has work experiences with several multinational corporations, which were based in France, China and the United States. This interdisciplinary educational background and diverse industrial experience in different countries informs both her teaching and research.

Morris Kalliny is currently an Assistant Professor of Marketing at Saint Louis University. Dr. Kalliny earned a PhD in International Business and Marketing from The University of Texas-Pan American. Prior to joining Saint Louis University, he served as the Business Program Director at Missouri University of Science and Technology. Professor Kalliny has written extensively about culture and marketing with a particular focus on advertising and media. Dr. Kalliny's research has appeared in many scholarly journals, such as the *Journal of Advertising Research*, the *Journal of Global Marketing*, *The Multinational Business Review*, *The Journal of Marketing Communications*, *The Journal of Current Issues and Research in Advertising*, *Journal of Promotion Management*, and the *International Journal of Cross Cultural Management*. Dr. Kalliny can be reached at 3674 Lindell Blvd. John Cook School of Business, Saint Louis University, St. Louis, Mo 63108 or via e-mail at kalliny@slu.edu or by phone at 314-977-2590.

Oxana Karnaukhova is an Associate Professor at the Department of Philosophy and Cultural Studies, Southern Federal University (Russia), co-director of the Master's Program in Intercultural Communications, and Executive Director of the Centre of European Union in the South West Russia (Southern Federal University, Russia). Her research within the Intercultural Communications concerns exploitation of the cultural approach to socio-economic development of multicultural agglomerations and investigation of communicative strategies within cooperation accounts. Her publication list includes articles on intercultural communications in transnational corporations, communicative strategies and informal entrepreneurship, multicultural policy and practices in the EU states, among others.

Fung Kuen (Tebbin) Koo (PhD, University of Sydney) is a Lecturer at the Sydney Nursing School at the University of Sydney. Dr. Koo has strong research background in cultural and health beliefs. Her research interests include cultural studies, migrant issues, health promotion and education. Dr. Koo can be contacted at fung.koo@sydney.edu.au.

Satu Lautamäki is a Principal Lecturer in the Department of Business Economics and Tourism at Vaasa University of Applied Sciences, Finland, where she has been a faculty member since 2008. She is developing the international business curriculum as well as teaching and supervising bachelor's and master's degree students. She also is a co-founder of a company focused on design activities and business consultation. She completed her PhD at the University of Vaasa in 2000. In her prior position, she acted as a director for a design center (between the years 2000 to 2008), being responsible for general management, research and training activities, and company services. She has led several international research and company development projects as well as acting as a member or chairperson of the executive group in these projects. Her research interests lie in the area of international business, corporate identity and design management, distribution channel management, and user research, ranging from theory to design and implementation. She has published several articles in scientific conference proceedings and journals as well as co-authored some books and reports based on the prior research and company projects. In recent years, she has focused on SME internationalization, analyzing how small and medium-sized companies internationalize and how to support the internationalization activities and processes.

Huong Le (PhD, University of Sydney) is a Lecturer in Management in the School of Management and Marketing at Deakin University in Australia. Her research has been published widely in refereed journals and in chapters in edited books. Her research interests include cross-cultural research in management and marketing, international education, and tourism research. Dr. Le can be contacted at huong.le@deakin.edu.au.

Fabio Marzano has a research contract at the University of Trieste, Italy. He holds a B.S. and a M.S.in Business. His research focus is on country of origin, modes of entry, and retailing.

Ramazan Nacar is currently a PhD candidate at the Management Engineering Program in the Institute of Science and Technology at Istanbul Technical University, Turkey, and a Research Assistant in the Division of Marketing of the Department of Management at Yalova University, Turkey. He is interested in marketing and his focused research areas are cross-cultural marketing, international marketing, and information technologies. Nacar can be reached at ramazannacar@gmail.com, or by telephone at +90 226 814 22 23 (5740).

Rosmeriany Nahan-Suomela has been a Senior Lecturer in the Department of Business Economics and Tourism at Vaasa University of Applied Sciences, Finland, since 2002. She has been working actively in developing a curriculum for an international business degree program as well as teaching and supervising bachelor's and master's degree students. Working intensively with different universities, institutes and corporations, both Small- and Medium-sized Enterprises (SMEs) and Multinational Enterprises (MNEs), she has also been acting as a guest lecturer in both Asia and Europe in cross-cultural business management. Born in Indonesia and having studied in Australia and Finland, she is fluent in several languages. She holds her Master's Degree in Marketing from Hanken School of Economics and is a part time researcher (PhD graduate) at the same university. Her research interests focus on internationalization, business networks, and cross-cultural business management.

Mustafa F. Özbilgin is a Turkish-born British academic and social scientist. He is a Professor of Human Resource Management at Brunel Business School at Brunel University in the UK. Since 2010, he has been the Editor-in-Chief of the *British Journal of Management*. He is also co-chair of Management and Diversity at University Paris-Dauphne in France. Between 2006 and 2010, he served as the Editor-in-Chief of *Equal Opportunities International*. He holds visiting professorships at Cornell University, Pantheon-Assas University, St. Gallen University, Istanbul Bilgi University, CEPS-INSTEAD, and the

Japan Institute of Labour Policy. His papers are published in top journals, including the *Academy of Management Review*, *Academy of Management Learning & Education*, and the *Journal of Vocational Behavior.* He obtained a B.A. in Business Administration from Boğaziçi University in Turkey in 1993, an M.A. in Human Resource Management and Development at Marmara University in Turkey in 1995, and a PhD in Social Sciences at the University of Bristol in 1998. His research focuses on equality, diversity, and fairness at work from relational, comparative, and international perspectives.

Jason Sargent (PhD, University of Sydney) is a Lecturer in Information Systems in the Faculty of Information and Communication Technologies at Swinburne University of Technology in Melbourne, Australia. Dr Sargent has investigated information systems' adoption and implementation in areas as diverse as regional tourism organisations, ambulatory care, and humanitarian disaster relief. Dr. Sargent can be contacted at jpsargent@swin.edu.au.

Cathrine Seierstad is a Lecturer in HRM at Brunel Business School at Brunel University in London. Her research and publications focus upon aspects of gender, equality, leadership, corporate governance, and the use of affirmative action strategies. Her research spans both public and private sectors.

Bernadette Sharp is a Professor of Applied Artificial Intelligence in the School of Computing at Staffordshire University, UK. She is a Chartered IT Professional Fellow of the British Computer Society. She has published over 90 referred publications in the areas of natural language processing (NLP), text mining, agent systems, and applied artificial intelligent systems. She is Chair and Editor of the International Workshop for Natural Language Processing and Cognitive Science (NLPCS).

Parves Sultan is a Senior Lecturer in Marketing at the Central Queensland University, Australia. Prior to this, he was an assistant professor at the University of Canberra in Australia. His research interests include: marketing approach to higher education, services marketing, social/sustainable marketing, tourism marketing, consumer behavior, branding, marketing promotions, internationalization of firms, international trade, and qualitative and quantitative research methods. His research articles appeared in a number of scholarly journals. Among these, *Asia Pacific Journal of Marketing and Logistics*, *Quality Assurance in Education*, *International Journal of Quality and Service Sciences*, *International Review of Business Research Papers*, *Journal for Global Business Advancement*, *Journal of Business Administration*, *Journal of Business Studies*, *Indian Journal of Open Learning*, *Malaysian Journal of Distance Education*, *Ritsumeikan Journal of Asia Pacific Studies*, The *Global Journal of Finance and Economics*, and *Journal of Economic Cooperation* are worth mentioning.

Ben Tran received his Doctor of Psychology (Psy.D) in Organizational Consulting/Organizational Psychology from the California School of Professional Psychology (formerly known as the Marshall Goldsmith School of Management) at Alliant International University in San Francisco, California, USA. Dr. Tran's research interests include domestic and expatriate recruitment, selection, retention, evaluation, & training, corporate social responsibility, business and organizational ethics, organizational and international organizational behavior, and minorities in multinational corporations. Dr. Tran has presented articles on topics of business and management ethics, expatriate, knowledge management, and gender and minorities in multinational corporations at the Academy of Management, Society for the Advancement of Management, and International Standing Conference on Organizational Symbolism. Dr. Tran has also published articles and book chapters with the *Social Responsibility Journal*, *Journal of International Trade Law and Policy*, *Journal of Economics*, *Finance and Administrative Science*, *Financial Management Institute of Canada*, and IGI Global. Dr. Tran can be reached at tranconsulting@gmail.com.

Nimet Uray is a Professor of Marketing in Faculty of Management of Istanbul Technical University, Turkey. She obtained her B.S. and M.S. in Management Engineering from Istanbul Technical University. She received her PhD in Management with a concentration in Marketing (1992) from Bogazici University in Turkey. Her research interests include consumer behavior and attitude, marketing and technology interaction, advertising content and culture, and international marketing strategy. Her studies have appeared in international journals such as *International Journal of Physical Distribution and Logistic Management*, *Service Industries Journal*, *Journal of International Consumer Marketing*, *Journal of Euro-Marketing*, and *Sex Roles: A Journal of Research*. In addition, she has also published numerous articles in the proceedings of major national and international conferences.

Nataša Slak Valek has a PhD in Business and Administration and a Bachelor's Degree in Sport, both gained at the University of Ljubljana, Slovenia. At the same time of preparing her PhD, she started to work as a researcher at the national tourist office in Slovenia. She merged all three topics (business, sport and tourism) to sport tourism, which was the main topic of her PhD. Her career as a professor started in the Faculty of Tourism at the University of Maribor. She has always shown a deep interest in foreign countries and cultures and this is why she accepted an invitation from I-Shou University from Taiwan R.O.C. where she teaches Sport Tourism and Management Studies. She published several papers in domestic and international scientific journals recently. She can be reached at natasa.slak@gmail.com.

Joana Vassilopoulou is a Lecturer in Organisational Behaviour and Human Resource Management at the School of Business, Management and Economics at the University of Sussex. She received her PhD from Norwich Business School at the University of East Anglia on the Organisational Habitus of Managing Ethnic Diversity in Germany. Previous to her PhD studies, she worked at the University of Duisburg-Essen as a research associate and lecturer. Her recent research includes a project funded by the Chartered Institute of Personnel and Development (CIPD) on "Global Talent Management in Emerging Economies" and another project on "Movers and Shakers of Talent Management in the UAE for 21st Century," funded by the Federal Demographic Council, United Arab Emirates (FDC). She has published in edited collections and journals such as the *European Journal of Industrial Relations*, *International Business Review,* and the *International Journal of Human Resource Management*. Her research interests include the management of ethnic diversity, discrimination at work, race and racism, immigration and integration in Europe, gender and race inequalities at work, talent management, global diversity management, and social and organisational change.

Alessandra Vecchi is the Course Director for the Graduate Diploma in Fashion Management and Senior Research Fellow at London College of Fashion. She was formerly based in the School of Business and in the Institute for International Integration Studies (IIIS) at Trinity College in Dublin, where she still holds the position of IIIS Research Associate. She has been recently nominated Assistant Professor in the Department of Management at the University of Bologna. Besides teaching several subjects, mostly in the field of international business and operations management at the postgraduate level, she supervises

M.A. and PhD students in a wide array of fashion management related subjects. She has a significant track record of high-profile publications and her research interests tend to be of a multidisciplinary nature and rather eclectic. They span from value creation and strategic upgrading of industrial clusters, governance of family business groups, luxury firms' strategic use of social media to quality management, and the adoption of new technologies, both from a marketing and supply chain management perspective. She is author of two books, the latest of which on the space industry (Brennan, L., and Vecchi, A., 2011): *The Business of Space – The Next Frontier of International Competition.*

Donata Vianelli, PhD, is a professor at the University of Trieste, Italy, where she teaches International Marketing and International Business; and is the Head Coordinator of the Bachelor Degree in Management. During her 20 years of teaching experience, she collaborated with numerous universities and business schools in France, China, Austria, Slovenia, and the United States. Vianelli has authored four books and 63 refereed publications that have appeared in national and international books and journals. Her research focus is on global distribution and cross-cultural consumer behavior, with a regional focus on Europe and Asia, where she has recently coordinated a large research program on distribution and sales of Italian products in the Chinese market.

Alexander Wollenberg has been an Assistant Professor of International Business at the Univesidad EAFIT in Medellin, Colombia (Department of International Business) since July of 2011. His research focus is on the generation of innovative capabilities of local companies and their potential to transfer these regionally and abroad eventually, and a generation of outward investment from these emerging markets (Latin America). He received a PhD in 2011 from the National University of Singapore, specializing in entry modes of high-tech companies from Japan in emerging markets (e.g., China). He received a M.A. in 2003 in International Relations from Waseda University in Tokyo, Japan specializing in Japanese industrial structures and technology transfer to China. He received a B.S. in 2000 in Business Administration from Hawaii Pacific University in Honolulu, HI, USA, with major in International Business and Asian Studies. Alexander enjoys the dynamic environments of emerging economies and enjoys learning languages. He speaks Mandarin, Thai, Russian, Japanese, and Spanish fluently.

Ho Yin Wong is a senior lecturer at the Deakin Graduate School of Business in the Faculty of Business & Law at Deakin University (Burwood Campus), Australia. He has published in *International Marketing Review*, *Journal of Strategic Marketing*, *Journal of Product and Brand Management*, and *Journal of Global Marketing*, among others. Dr Wong co-authored an article for the Journal of Islamic Marketing, which was chosen as a Highly Commended Award Winner at the Emerald Literati Network Awards for Excellence 2011. He is also a co-author of a book, *Building a Marketing Plan: A Complete Guide*. His main research interests are international marketing, branding, and Small- and Medium Enterprises (SMEs).

Norhayati Zakaria is an Associate Professor at the Faculty of Business and Management of the University of Wollongong in Dubai, and a Research and Teaching Associate at the Center of Collaboratory on Technology Enhanced Learning Communities Lab (COTELCO) at American University and Syracuse University, USA, in which she leads a global virtual team for a globally distributed collaboration research project. Dr. Zakaria can be contacted at yatizakaria11@gmail.com.

Luis Fernando Bustamante Zapata is a Colombian business professional with expertise in high level management, project management, organizational development, international business, and corporate finances. He received an MBA from EAFIT University and is currently enrolled in the PhD in Humanities programme at the same university. He holds over five years' experience in research and education at the postgraduate level.

Index

M

N

O

P

Q

R

S

T

U

V

W

CPSIA information can be obtained at www.ICGtesting.com
Printed in the USA
BVOW041648180413

318454BV00007B/65/P